S0-ABC-132

Overnight
Loan

THE ENCYCLOPEDIA OF MAMMALS

THE ENCYCLOPEDIA OF
MAMMALS

VOLUME III

Marsupials, Insect Eaters,
and Small Herbivores

EDITED BY
PROFESSOR DAVID MACDONALD
ASSISTANT EDITOR SASHA NORRIS

Facts On File, Inc.

Published in North America by:
Facts On File, Inc.
132 West 31st Street,
New York NY 10001

AN ANDROMEDA BOOK
Planned and produced by
Andromeda Oxford Limited,
11–13 The Vineyard, Abingdon,
Oxfordshire, OX14 3PX, United Kingdom.
www.andromeda.co.uk

Publishing Director Graham Bateman
Project Manager Peter Lewis
Editors Tony Allan, Mark Salad
Art Director Chris Munday
Designers Frankie Wood, Mark Regardsoe
Cartographic Editor Tim Williams
Picture Manager Claire Turner
Picture Researcher Vickie Walters
Production Director Clive Sparling
Editorial and Administrative Assistants
Rita Demetriou, Marian Dreier, Moira Elliott
Proofreader Lynne Wycherley
Indexer Ann Barrett

Library of Congress Cataloging in Publication Data

Encyclopedia of mammals / edited by David Macdonald.
p. cm.
Rev. ed. of: Encyclopedia of mammals. 1984.
Includes bibliographical references (p.).
ISBN 0-8160-4267-5 (set)
ISBN 0-8160-4270-5 (vol. 3)
1. Mammals. I. Macdonald, David W. (David Whyte) II. Encyclopedia of mammals.

QL703 .E53 2001
599'.03—dc21

2001033615

Facts On File books are available at special discounts when purchased in bulk quantities for businesses, associations, institutions or sales promotions. Please call our Special Sales Department in New York at (212) 967-8800 or (800) 322-8755.

You can find Facts On File on the World Wide Web at http://www.factsonfile.com

Cover design by Cathy Rincon

Originated in Malaysia by Global Colour Ltd.
Printed in Italy by Milanostampa SpA, Milan

10 9 8 7 6 5 4 3 2 1

This book is printed on acid-free paper.

Advisory Editors

Dr. Richard Connor,
University of Massachusetts at Dartmouth, North Dartmouth, Massachusetts

Dr. Guy Cowlishaw,
Institute of Zoology, London, England

Dr. Christopher R. Dickman,
University of Sydney, Australia

Professor Johan du Toit,
Mammal Research Institute, University of Pretoria, South Africa

Professor John Harwood,
Gatty Marine Laboratory, University of St. Andrews, Scotland

Dr. Gareth Jones,
University of Bristol, England

Professor Hans Kruuk,
Centre for Ecology and Hydrology, Banchory, Scotland

Professor Jerry O. Wolff,
University of Memphis, Memphis, Tennessee

Artwork Panels

Priscilla Barrett
Denys Ovenden
Malcolm McGregor
Michael R. Long
Graham Allen

Cuscuses
see page 828

Photo page ii: *Antelope ground squirrels* Stephen J. Krasemann/Bruce Coleman Collection.

Contributors

SMALL HERBIVORES pp. 578–721

GA Greta Ågren, Univ. of Stockholm, Sweden
KBA Kenneth B. Armitage, Univ. of Kansas, Lawrence, Kansas
CB Claude Baudoin, Univ. of Franche Comté, France
DB Diana Bell, Univ. of East Anglia, England
RB Robin Boughton, Univ. of Florida, Gainesville, Florida
PB Peter Busher, Boston Univ., Boston, Massachusetts
TMB Thomas M. Butynski, Kibale Forest Project, Uganda
MC Marcelo Cassini, Univ. of Lujan, Argentina
GBC Gordon B. Corbet, Leven, Scotland
DPC David P. Cowan, Central Science Laboratory, York, England
MJD Michael J. Delany, Univ. of Bradford, England
CRD Christopher R. Dickman, Univ. of Sydney, Australia
JFE John F. Eisenberg, Univ. of Florida, Gainesville, Florida
JE James Evans, US Fish and Wildlife Service, Olympia, Washington
JF Julie Feaver, Univ. of Cambridge, England
THF Theodore H. Fleming, Univ. of Miami, Coral Gables, Florida
WG Wilma George, Univ. of Oxford, England
GH Göran Hartman, Univ. of Agricultural Sciences, Sweden
EH Emilio Herrera, Simon Bolivar Univ., Venezuela
TH Tony Holley, Brent Knoll, Somerset, England
UWH U. William Huck, Princeton Univ., Princeton, New Jersey
JH Jane Hurst, Univ. of Liverpool, England
JUMJ Jenny U. M. Jarvis, Univ. of Cape Town, South Africa
PJ Paula Jenkins, Natural History Museum, London, England
TK Takeo Kawamichi, Univ. of Osaka, Japan
CJK Charles J. Krebs, Univ. of British Columbia, Canada
TEL Thomas E. Lacher, Texas A&M Univ., College Station, Texas
KMacK Kathy MacKinnon, World Bank, Washington, D.C.
DWM David W. Macdonald, WildCRU, Univ. of Oxford, England
JP James Patton, Univ. of California, Berkeley, California
GBR Galen B. Rathbun, California Academy of Sciences, Cambria, California
DAS Duane A. Schlitter, Texas A&M Univ., College Station, Texas
ES Eberhard Schneider, Univ. of Göttingen, Germany
GIS Georgy I. Shenbrot, Ramon Science Center, Mizpe Ramon, Israel
PWS Paul W. Sherman, Cornell Univ., Ithaca, New York
GS Grant Singleton, CSIRO Wildlife and Ecology, Australia
ATS Andrew T. Smith, Arizona State Univ., Tempe, Arizona
DMS D. Michael Stoddart, Hobart Univ., Tasmania, Australia
RS Robert Strachan, WildCRU, Univ. of Oxford, England
AT Andrew Taber, Wildlife Conservation Society, New York, New York
RJvA Rudi J. van Aarde, Univ. of Pretoria, South Africa
LW Luc Wauters, Univ. of Insubria, Varese, Italy
JW John O. Whitaker, Indiana State Univ., Terre Haute, Indiana
JOW Jerry O. Wolff, Univ. of Memphis, Memphis, Tennessee
CAW Charles A. Woods, Florida State Museum, Gainesville, Florida
HY Hannu Ylonen, Univ. of Jyvaskyla, Finland
ZZ Zhang Zhibin, Chinese Academy of Sciences, Beijing, China

INSECTIVORES AND MARSUPIALS pp. 722–865

MLA Mike L. Augee, Univ. of New South Wales, Australia
CJB Christopher J. Barnard, Univ. of Nottingham, England
JWB Jack W. Bradbury, Cornell Univ., Ithaca, New York
GB Gary Bronner, Univ. of Cape Town, South Africa
LB Linda S. Broome, New South Wales National Parks and Wildlife Service, Australia
AC Andrew Cockburn, Australian National Univ., Canberra, Australia
CRD Christopher R. Dickman, Univ. of Sydney, Australia
BF Brock Fenton, York Univ., Ontario, Canada
THF Theodore H. Fleming, Univ. of Miami, Coral Gables, Florida
GG Greg Gordon, Queensland National Parks and Wildlife Service, Australia
MLG Martyn L. Gorman, Univ. of Aberdeen, Scotland
TG Tom Grant, Univ. of New South Wales, Australia
PJ Peter Jarman, Univ. of New England, Australia
CJ Christopher Johnson, James Cook Univ., Australia
GJ Gareth Jones, Univ. of Bristol, England
MJ Menna Jones, Australian National Univ., Canberra, Australia
AKL A.K. Lee, Monash Univ., Australia
DL David Lindenmayer, Australian National Univ., Canberra, Australia
WJL W. Jim Loughry, Valdosta State Univ., Valdosta, Georgia
CMM Colleen M. McDonough, Valdosta State Univ., Valdosta, Georgia
RM Roger Martin, James Cook Univ., Australia
VN Virginia Naples, Northern Illinois Univ., De Kalb, Illinois
MEN Martin E. Nicholl, Smithsonian Institution, Washington, D.C.
MAO'C Margaret A. O'Connell, Eastern Washington Univ., Cheney, Washington
MP Mike Perrin, Univ. of Pretoria, S. Africa
RAR Renee Ann Richer, Harvard Univ., Cambridge, Massachusetts
CR Carlo Rondinini, Institute of Applied Ecology, Rome, Italy
EMR Eleanor M. Russell, CSIRO Wildlife and Rangelands Research Division, Australia
JR Jens Rydell, Gothenburg Univ., Sweden
JBS Jeremy B. Searle, Univ. of York, England
JHS John H. Seebeck, Department of Natural Resources and Environment, Victoria, Australia
ES Erik Seiffert, Duke Univ., Durham, North Carolina
PS Paula Stockley, Univ. of Liverpool, England
JW Jerry Wilkinson, Univ. of Maryland, College Park, Maryland
RDW Ron D. Wooller, Murdoch Univ., Perth, Australia
AW Andrew Wroot, Royal Holloway College, London, England

CONTENTS

Ryukyu flying fox
see page 775

PREFACE

This book is dedicated to my wife, Jenny, and Ewan, Fiona, and Isobel

THIS THIRD VOLUME OF THE *ENCYCLOPEDIA* encompasses a huge variety of animals, beginning with rodents (order Rodentia), rabbits and hares (Lagomorpha), and elephant shrews (Macroscelidea). The diminutive size of these creatures makes them difficult to study, but their lifestyles are nevertheless intriguing. Inconspicuous scuttlings of mice and the pestilential image of rats that characterize these small mammals in the public's mind belie the extraordinary interest of the rodents. This order embraces some 2,000 species, nearly half of all mammals. Rodents are captivating for at least two reasons. First, they are outstandingly successful. Not only does one form or another occupy almost every habitable cranny of the earth's terrestrial environments, but many do so with conspicuous success while every man's hand is turned against them. Their adaptability, and particularly their ability to breed with haste and profligacy, is stunning. Second, rodents are fascinating because so many of them do not conform to our stereotypes. Some burrow like moles, others climb, while yet others hunt fish in streams; in South America some rodents (capybaras) are the size of sheep, while others (maras) are, at a glance, indistinguishable from small antelopes. As these pages illustrate, their societies are no less varied than their bodies, giving us an insight into a community in microcosm beneath our feet that reverberates with life.

The lagomorphs share many of the characteristics of rodents: global distribution, small size, incredible breeding capacity, and pestilential propensities. They mostly conform to the "bunny" stereotype, but one group – the pikas – look more like hamsters, and are to be found mostly living on rocky outcrops in North America and Asia. The elephant shrews possess characteristics displayed by several other groups – snouts like elephants, the diet of shrews, and the body form of a small antelope with a rat-like tail. However, their precise relationship with other mammalian orders is still far from clear.

Finally, the *Encyclopedia* describes a diverse series of orders (insectivores, bats, xenarthrans, pholidotes, marsupials, and monotremes). Here, the reader will find accounts of mammals that fly, burrow, run and swim, that can navigate, hunt, and communicate with ultrasounds and echoes quite beyond human perception. Some are nearly naked, some blind, some are poisonous, and some even lay eggs. That most of these species may be unfamiliar makes them all the more intriguing.

The insectivores include small predatory creatures that not only bear "primitive" resemblance to the very earliest mammals, but which, with their tiny size and racing metabolisms, push modern mammalian body processes to the very limit. The bats (order Chiroptera) alone comprise about one-quarter of all mammal species, making them the second-largest order after the rodents. Bats have filled the aerial niche so successfully that within this vast assemblage are to be found plant and fruit eaters, insectivores, carnivores, fish eaters, and even blood eaters. For a group so large, knowledge of their lifestyles is slim, but within these pages will be found insights into how they are adapted to life on the wing and how their societies work. A taste for ants and termites, lack of teeth, and possession of a long, sticky tongue are the hallmarks of two other orders – the Xenarthra (represented by the anteaters, sloths, and armadillos) and Pholidota (pangolins), treated here under the rubric Edentates.

Many people wrongly regard marsupials as a small, exclusively Australasian group of mammals, typified by kangaroos and the koala. In fact, this group comprises some 300 species, in all manner of shapes and sizes, and represents one of the major surviving mammalian subdivisions, occurring throughout the Australian region as well as parts of South and North America. Among the marsupials there are species inhabiting almost all of the niches that placental mammals occupy elsewhere. The two types of mammals, placentals and marsupials, represent a worldwide evolutionary experiment in the making of mammals: the fact that the results are often strikingly similar animals with quite distinct origins but adapted in the same way to cope with the same niche is compelling evidence for the processes of evolution. Today, it seems that the third such "experiment" in mammalhood, which produced the egg-laying monotremes (platypus, echidnas), is imperiled, since only three species survive.

David W. Macdonald

DAVID W. MACDONALD
DEPARTMENT OF ZOOLOGY AND LADY MARGARET HALL
UNIVERSITY OF OXFORD

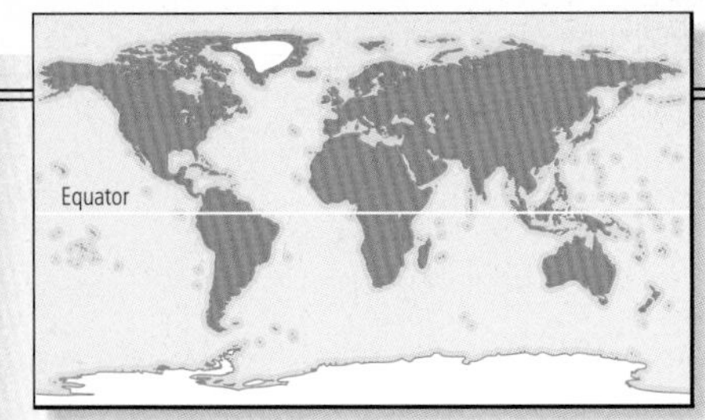

RODENTS

RODENTS HAVE INFLUENCED HISTORY AND human endeavor more than any other group of mammals. Over 42 percent of all mammal species belong to this one order, whose members live in almost every habitat, often in close association with humans. Frequently this association is to people's disadvantage, since rodents consume prodigious quantities of carefully stored food and spread fatal diseases. It is said that rat-borne typhus has had a greater influence upon human destiny than has any single person, and in the last millennium rat-borne diseases have taken more lives than all wars and revolutions put together.

It is nevertheless testimony to the entrepreneurial spirit of rodents that they have thrived in human-dominated environments from which so many other animal groups have been extinguished. Furthermore, many rodent species have an important function in ecosystems, and are therefore highly beneficial to man. Rodents play key roles in maintaining the relationship between plants and fungi. Many fungi form mycorrhizal (mutually beneficial) associations with the roots of plants that increase the ability of the plants to extract nutrients and water from the soil by many thousands of times. So important is this relationship that many plants simply cannot survive without the fungi, and vice versa. One of the most important groups of mycorrhizal fungi are the truffles, which are related to mushrooms but form their fruiting bodies underground. Truffles and truffle-like fungi rely on animals to dig up the fruiting bodies and to disperse the spores, either in the wind or in the animal's feces after eating the fungus. When gaps form in forests, for example, small mammals deposit fungal spores in their feces in the gaps, thereby bringing the fungi to the places where plant seeds are germinating. In the forests of North America and Australia, it is believed that this three-sided relationship between plants, fungi, and small mammals – including rodents – is vital for ecosystem

Right *A giant among rodents, the capybara can weigh up to 66kg (146lb) – fully 10,000 times the weight of the smallest mice. The animals share the close-knit social life and herbivorous diet of many other rodent species, but are unusual in their semi-aquatic lifestyle.*

Left *On the alert for food, a Eurasian harvest mouse* (Micromys minutus) *investigates a wheat crop in summer. Rodents are supreme opportunists; their rapid rate of reproduction and wide-ranging diets have made them among the most successful mammals.*

function. The role of rodents in other ecosystems, like grasslands, is not so well studied but is probably just as important.

In South America, Africa, and Asia, some larger species are also an important source of protein, being trapped or deliberately bred for food. Species in the latter category are the guinea pigs in South America, and the grasscutter rats and the edible dormouse (*Myoxus glis*) in Africa. Among other rodents, hamsters and gerbils are popular pets in the western world, with the prairie dog becoming increasingly common in the United States. Moreover, rats, mice, and guinea pigs today play an indispensable role in the testing of drugs and in biological research. Rodents are also keystone species in many ecosystems, providing an important food source for many species of medium-sized carnivores and birds of prey. For example, in agricultural ecosystems it is not unusual to have 50–100kg (110–220lb) of rodents per ha distributed over tens of thousands of hectares. This provides a huge variety of food for predators living in agricultural systems or in neighboring forest habitats. The Black-footed ferret (*Mustela nigripes*), which is the subject of much human nurturing through a reintroduction program after having become Extinct in the Wild, relies on a diet of prairie dogs for its survival.

Equipped for Gnawing

FORM AND FUNCTION

Rodents occur in virtually every habitat, from the high arctic tundra, where they live and breed under the snow (for example, lemmings), to the hottest and driest of deserts (gerbils). Others glide from tree to tree (flying squirrels), seldom coming down to the ground, or else spend their entire lives in underground networks of burrows (mole-rats). Some have webbed feet and are semi-aquatic (muskrats), often undertaking complex engineering programs to regulate water levels (beavers), while others never touch a drop of water throughout their entire lives (gundis). Such species can derive their water requirements from fat reserves.

Most rodents are small, weighing 100g (3.5oz) or less. There are only a few large species; the biggest of them, the capybara, may weigh up to 66kg (146lb).

The term "rodent" derives from the Latin verb *rodere*, which means "to gnaw." All rodents have characteristic teeth, including a single pair of razor-sharp incisors. With these teeth, the rodent can gnaw through the toughest of husks, pods, and shells to reach the nutritious food contained within. Gnawing is facilitated by a sizable gap, known as the diastema, immediately behind the incisors, into which the lips can be drawn, so sealing off the mouth from inedible fragments dislodged by the incisors. Rodents have no canine teeth, but they do possess a substantial battery of molar teeth by which all food is finely ground. Convoluted layers of enamel traverse these often massive and intricately structured teeth. The pattern made by these layers is often of taxonomic significance. Most rodents have no more than 22 teeth, although one exception is the Silvery mole-rat from Central and East Africa, which has 28. The Australian water rat has just 12. Since rodents feed on hard materials, the incisors have open roots and grow continuously throughout life. They are constantly worn down by the action of their opposite number on the other jaw. If the teeth of rodents become misaligned so that they are not automatically worn down during feeding, they will continue to grow and may eventually end up piercing the skull.

Most rodents are squat, compact creatures with short limbs and a tail. In South America, where there are no antelopes, several species have evolved long legs for a life on the grassy plains (e.g., maras, pacas, and agoutis), and show some convergence with the antelope body form. A very variable anatomical feature is the tail (see panel overleaf and Squirrel-like Rodents).

Modern taxonomists divide rodents into two suborders. For convenience, we present these in three sections, the squirrel-like and the mouse-like forms – both part of the suborder Sciurognathi – and the porcupine and cavy-like forms, the suborder Hystricognathi. Rodents were formerly split into three suborders on the basis of jaw musculature. The main jaw muscle is the masseter, which not only closes the lower jaw on the upper, but also pulls the lower jaw forward, so creating the unique gnawing action. In the extinct Paleocene

ORDER: RODENTIA
28 families: 431 genera: 1,999 species

SCIUROGNATHS Suborder Sciurognathi

SQUIRREL-LIKE RODENTS p588

284 species in 56 genera in 5 families
Includes **beavers** (Family Castoridae); **squirrels** (Family Sciuridae); **springhare** (Family Pedetidae).

MOUSE-LIKE RODENTS p616

1,477 species in 312 genera in 5 families
Includes **rats, mice, voles, gerbils, hamsters,** and **lemmings** (Family Muridae); **jumping mice, birch-mice,** and **jerboas** (Family Dipodidae).

HYSTRICOGNATHS Suborder Hystricognathi

CAVY-LIKE RODENTS
Suborder Hystricognathi p668

238 species in 63 genera in 18 families
Includes **New World porcupines** (Family Erethizontidae); **cavies** (Family Caviidae); **capybara** (Family Hydrochaeridae); **agoutis and acouchis** (Family Dasyproctidae); **chinchillas** and **viscachas** (Family Chinchillidae); **octodonts** (Family Octodontidae); **tuco-tucos** (Family Ctenomyidae); **cane rats** (Family Thryonomyidae); **Dassie rat** (Family Petromuridae); **coypu** (Family Myocastoridae); **Old World porcupines** (Family Hystricidae); **gundis** (Family Ctenodactylidae); **African mole-rats** (Family Bathyergidae).

Note There is some divergence in the numbers of species and genera between the following accounts and the established 1993 list of mammalian species. The interested reader is referred to the Appendix, which contains a comprehensive list of rodent species based on the 1993 taxonomy.

rodents, the masseter was small and did not spread far onto the front of the skull. In the squirrel-like rodents the lateral masseter extends in front of the eye onto the snout; the deep masseter is short and used only in closing the jaw. In the cavy-like rodents it is the deep masseter that extends forward onto the snout to give the gnawing action. Both the lateral and deep branches of the masseter are thrust forward in the mouse-like rodents, providing the most effective gnawing action of all, with the result that they are the most successful in terms of distribution and number of species.

Most rodents eat a range of plant products, from leaves to fruits, along with small invertebrates, such as spiders and grasshoppers. Many northern rodents such as the Field vole (*Microtus agrestis*) eat the bark of woody trees in times of food scarcity due to high populations. In Field voles the toxic effects of bark seem to be neutralized by specially secreted enzymes in the stomach, which allow dietary flexibility in times of famine. A few species are specialized carnivores; for example, the Australian water rat (*Hydromys chrysogaster*) feeds on small fish, frogs, and mollusks.

To facilitate bacterial digestion of cellulose rodents have a relatively large cecum (appendix) that houses a dense bacterial flora. After the food they have eaten has been softened in the stomach, it passes down the large intestine and into the cecum. There the cellulose is split by bacteria into its digestible carbohydrate constituents, but absorption can only take place higher up the gut, in the stomach. Therefore rodents practice refection – reingesting the bacterially-treated food taken directly from the anus. On its second visit to the stomach the carbohydrates are absorbed and the fecal pellet that eventually emerges is hard and dry. It is not known how rodents know which type of feces is being produced. The rodent's digestive system is very efficient, assimilating as much as 80 percent of the ingested energy.

EVOLUTION OF RODENTS

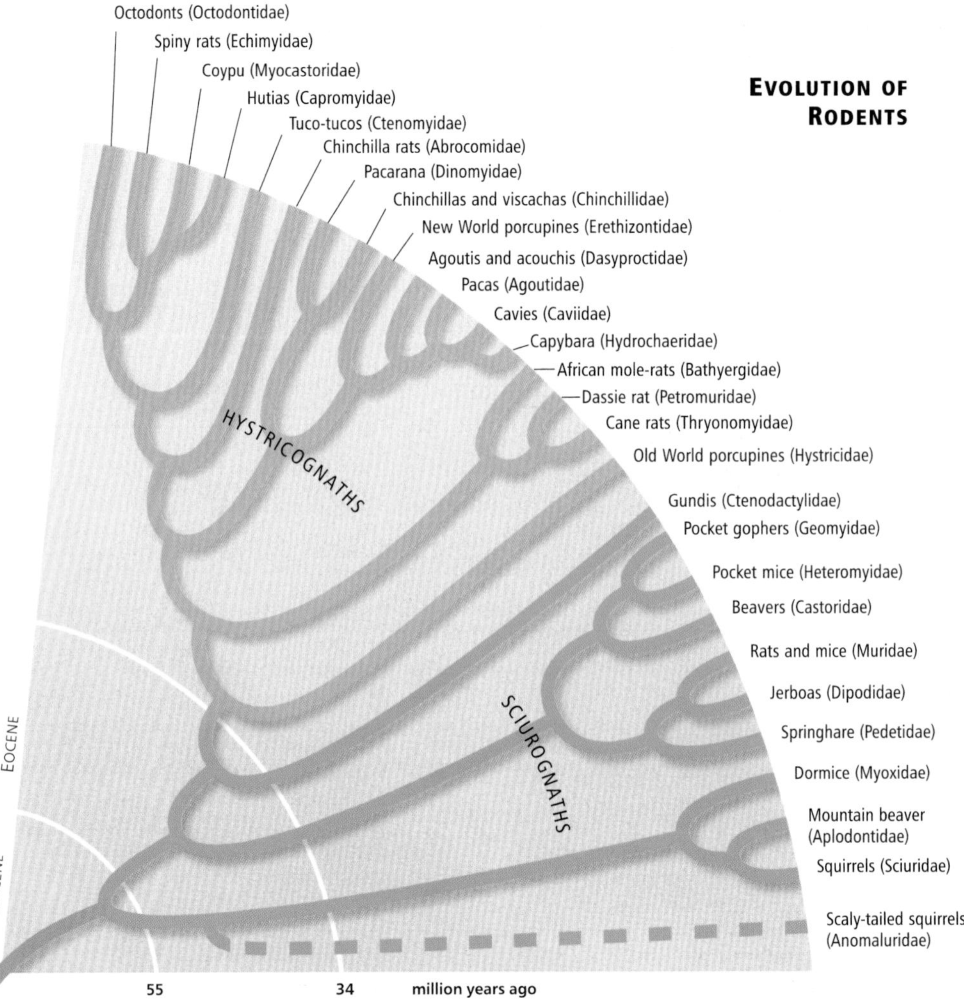

All members of at least three families (hamsters, pocket gophers, pocket mice) have cheek pouches. Fur-lined folds of skin projecting inwards from the corner of the mouth, these may reach back to the shoulders, and can be everted for cleaning. They are used for carrying provisions, and rodents equipped with them often build up large stores – up to 90kg (198lb) in Common hamsters.

Rodents are intelligent and can master simple tasks for obtaining food. They can be readily conditioned, and easily learn to avoid fast-acting poisoned baits – a factor that makes them difficult pests to eradicate. Their sense of smell and their hearing are keenly developed. Nocturnal species have large eyes; in addition, all rodents have long, touch-sensitive whiskers (vibrissae).

Above *In evolutionary terms, rodents are quite young and so retain large, untapped stocks of genetic variability. This evolutionary tree, compiled by biologist Rodney Honeycutt, is based on relationships revealed by molecular techniques. Thus the lengths of the branches are proportional to genetic similarity, and not necessarily to time of separation, which is largely unknown thanks to limited fossil evidence.*

Left *A South African ground squirrel nibbles on a melon. Manual dexterity is particularly well developed in squirrels, though other rodents also make good use of their front paws for digging, grooming, and gathering food and nesting materials.*

RODENT BODY PLAN

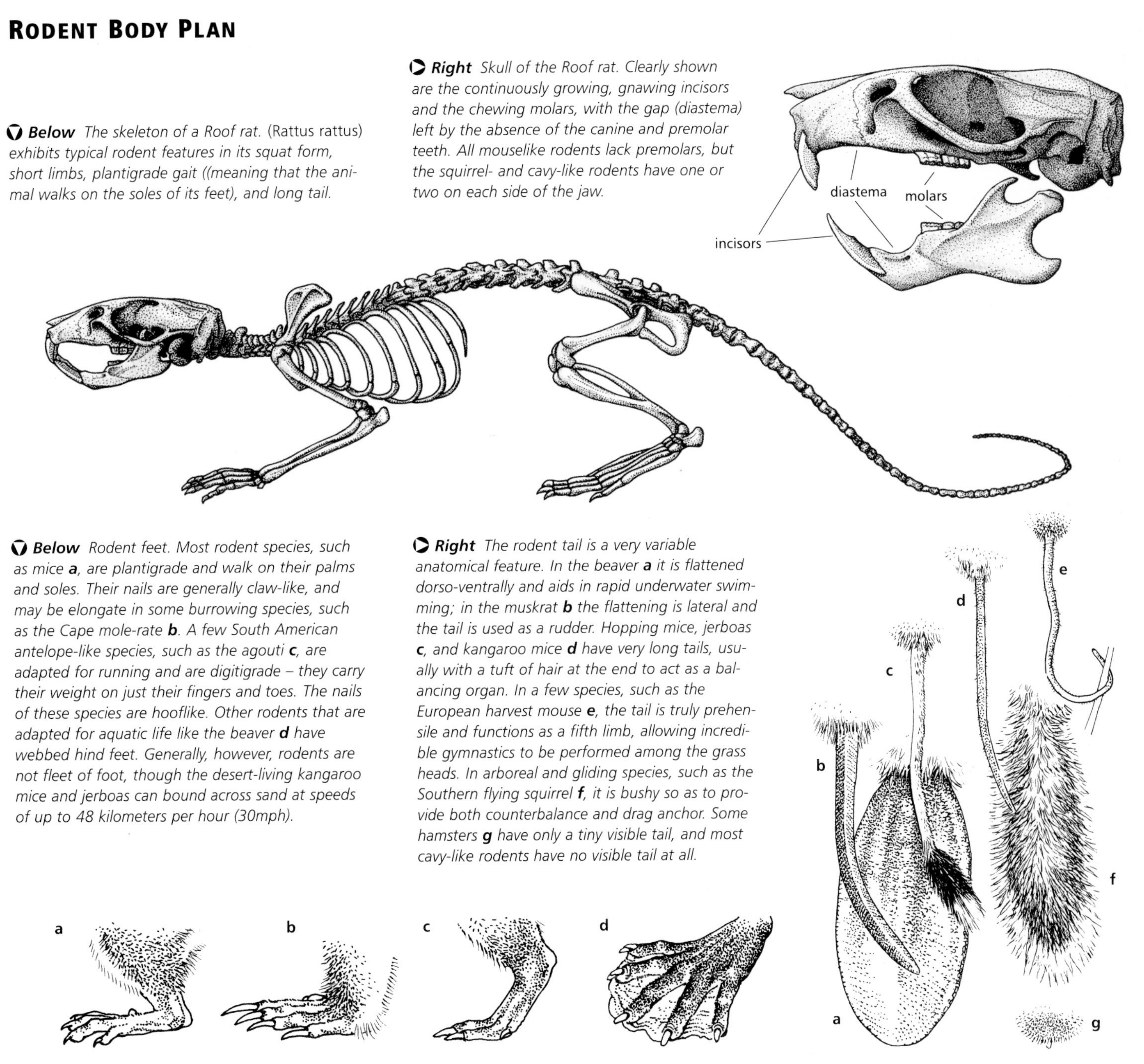

Below *The skeleton of a Roof rat. (Rattus rattus) exhibits typical rodent features in its squat form, short limbs, plantigrade gait ((meaning that the animal walks on the soles of its feet), and long tail.*

Right *Skull of the Roof rat. Clearly shown are the continuously growing, gnawing incisors and the chewing molars, with the gap (diastema) left by the absence of the canine and premolar teeth. All mouselike rodents lack premolars, but the squirrel- and cavy-like rodents have one or two on each side of the jaw.*

Below *Rodent feet. Most rodent species, such as mice* ***a****, are plantigrade and walk on their palms and soles. Their nails are generally claw-like, and may be elongate in some burrowing species, such as the Cape mole-rate* ***b****. A few South American antelope-like species, such as the agouti* ***c****, are adapted for running and are digitigrade – they carry their weight on just their fingers and toes. The nails of these species are hooflike. Other rodents that are adapted for aquatic life like the beaver* ***d*** *have webbed hind feet. Generally, however, rodents are not fleet of foot, though the desert-living kangaroo mice and jerboas can bound across sand at speeds of up to 48 kilometers per hour (30mph).*

Right *The rodent tail is a very variable anatomical feature. In the beaver* ***a*** *it is flattened dorso-ventrally and aids in rapid underwater swimming; in the muskrat* ***b*** *the flattening is lateral and the tail is used as a rudder. Hopping mice, jerboas* ***c****, and kangaroo mice* ***d*** *have very long tails, usually with a tuft of hair at the end to act as a balancing organ. In a few species, such as the European harvest mouse* ***e****, the tail is truly prehensile and functions as a fifth limb, allowing incredible gymnastics to be performed among the grass heads. In arboreal and gliding species, such as the Southern flying squirrel* ***f****, it is bushy so as to provide both counterbalance and drag anchor. Some hamsters* ***g*** *have only a tiny visible tail, and most cavy-like rodents have no visible tail at all.*

The Prehistory of Rodents

EVOLUTION AND RADIATION

Almost two-thirds of all rodent species belong to just one family, the Muridae, with 1,303 species at present, although numbers change constantly as new species are identified. Its members are distributed worldwide, including Australia and New Guinea, where it is the only terrestrial placental mammal family found (excluding dingoes, introduced approximately 4,000 years ago, and modern introductions such as the rabbit). The second most numerous family is that of the squirrels (Sciuridae), with 273 species distributed throughout Eurasia, Africa, and North and South America.

The fossil record of the rodents is pitifully sparse, partly because finding small bones requires very careful looking. Rodent remains are known from as far back as the late Paleocene era (57 million years ago), by which time all the main characteristics of the order had already developed. The earliest rodents apparently belonged to an extinct sciuromorph family, the Paramyidae.

During the Eocene era (55–34 million years ago) there was a rapid diversification of the rodents, and by the end of that epoch it seems that leaping, burrowing, and running forms had evolved. By the Eocene/Oligocene boundary (34 million years ago) many families recognizable today were already occurring in North America, Europe, and Asia, and during the Miocene (about 20 million years ago) the majority of present-day families had arisen. Subsequently the most important evolutionary event was the appearance of the Muridae from Europe in the Pliocene epoch (5–1.8 million years ago). At the start of the Pleistocene, they entered Australia, probably via Timor, and then underwent a rapid evolution. At the same time murids invaded South America from the north once it was united to North America by a land bridge, with the result that there was an explosive radiation of New World rats and mice across South America.

How Rodents Interact

SOCIAL BEHAVIOR

Rodents are often highly social, frequently living in huge aggregations. Prairie dog townships may contain more than 5,000 individuals. The solitary way of life appears to be restricted to those species that can defend food resources against intruders. These include some that live in arid grasslands and deserts – hamsters and some desert mice – and also species such as the North American red squirrel (*Tamiasciurus hudsonicus*), which lives in northern coniferous forests and stores cones in large central caches called middens.

The Norway or Brown rat (*Rattus norvegicus*) is a miscreant species that originated in Southeast Asia but has spread right around the globe in company with humans. Its social structure is central to the species' ecology and hence to the effectiveness of control measures. Socially dominant rats gain feeding priority and greater reproductive access and success. Social pressures force subordinate male rats to migrate into less favorable areas, resulting in a strongly unbalanced sex ratio (with more females than males) in breeding areas. Larger male rats tend to win dominance contests with smaller rats but, strangely, retain their higher social status long after subsequently losing body weight to levels at or below younger rats in the group. This means that dominance tends to be age-related, with the dominant alpha male often being smaller than many of his subordinates. Rats, it seems, respect their elders. Larger rats tend to accept the status quo because the costs of aggression are too great relative to the value of the contested resource. Moreover, dominant males cannot strictly control access to receptive estrous females. Sometimes, lower-ranking males actually achieve more matings.

Indications are that male Norway rats undergo scramble competition for mates. In naturalistic enclosures, a string of up to seven males may pursue a receptive female whenever she leaves her burrow. To test if female rats actually selected mates in this mad scramble or whether they mated promiscuously by choice, female rats were placed in a central arena surrounded by cubicles in which males were housed (a "rodent invertabrothel"). A circular passage gave the female access to the males but was too narrow for the males to pass. In such conditions, females formed enduring bonds with a single male, but also mated promiscuously. Even solitary rats seem to be profoundly affected by the knowledge that others of their species are in the vicinity. When female captive Heerman's kangaroo rats were entirely separated from males by wooden barriers rather than by clear plastic barriers, their estrous cycles were immediately doubled in length.

Rodent behavior is as adaptable as every other aspect of rodent biology. Having alert and active senses, rodents communicate by sight, sound, and smell. House mice have a sophisticated system of scent communication (See "A Scent-based Information Superhighway"). Kangaroo rats, however, tap-dance to talk. Three species living in the same area in California were each found to have a different rhythm when drumming on the desert floor. The Desert kangaroo rat thumped every 0.2–0.3 seconds, while the Giant kangaroo drummed long footrolls that could last for 100 drums at 18 drums per second; the Banner-tailed thumped footrolls at 3–38 drums per second. Even more intriguing is that individual Bannertails seemed to have their own signature rhythms. The sounds travel seismically through the ground to the ears of listening kangaroo rats hidden in burrows. Rats in burrows respond with carefully-timed drumming which does not overlap with those of the above-ground drummer. Drumming provides useful information about spacing and serves to reinforce territorial ownership. Female rats drumming at males tend to be saying "go away." Mother bannertails drum vigorously at snakes. Bannertails moving into a new neighborhood were found to alter their drums to be different from their neighbors.

While the social systems of some rodents have been well studied (See African Mole Rats), the habits of most of the 2,000 or so species are still a mystery awaiting investigation. Some insights have been achieved. Female Gunnison's prairie dogs mate with several males whereas they should be able to gain all the sperm necessary to fertilize their eggs from a single male. However, the probability of getting pregnant increases from 92 percent to 100 percent if they mate with three males instead of one, and females who mate with more males tend to have larger litters.

Some of the best-known visual displays are seen in the arboreal and the day-active terrestrial species. Courtship display in tree squirrels may be readily observed in city parks in early spring. The male pursues the female through the trees, flicking his bushy tail forward over his body and head when he is stationary. The female goads him by running slightly ahead, but he responds by uttering plaintive sounds similar to those that infants make to keep their mothers close. These sounds stop the female, allowing the male to catch up. Threat displays are dramatic in some species.

Rodents make considerable use of vocalizations in their communication. North American red squirrels and ground squirrels use a wide range of calls to advertise their presence to neighbors, to defend territories, and to sound the alarm when predators are detected. In other rodents, the sounds are far above the range of human hearing (at about 45kHz).

Rodents communicate extensively through odors produced by a variety of scent glands. Males tend to produce more and stronger odors than females, and young males are afforded a measure of protection from paternal attack by smelling like their mothers until they are sexually mature.

ODOR AND RODENT REPRODUCTION

Every phase of rodent reproduction, from initial sexual attraction to mating and the successful rearing of young, is influenced, if not actually controlled, by odor signals. Male rats are attracted to the urine of sexually receptive females, and sexually experienced males are more strongly attracted than naive males. Furthermore, if an experienced male is presented with the odor of a novel mature female alongside that of his mate, he prefers the novel odor. Females, on the other hand, prefer the odor of their mate to that of a stranger. The male's reproductive fitness is, it seems, best suited by seeking out and impregnating as many females as possible. The female, however, needs to produce many healthy young, so her fitness is maximized by mating with the best-quality male – one who has already proved himself. In gregarious species like the House mouse, a dominant male can mate with 20 females in 6 hours if their cycles are synchronized.

In young females, the odor of male urine accelerates not only the peak of sexual receptivity but also the onset of sexual maturity; it also brings sexually quiescent females into breeding condition. The effect is particularly strong from the urine of dominant males, while urine from castrated males has no such effect. It would appear, then, that the active ingredient – a pheromone – is made from, or is dependent upon the presence of, the male sex hormone testosterone. Male urine has such a powerful effect that if a newly-pregnant female is exposed to the urine odor of an unfamiliar male, she will resorb her litter and come rapidly into heat. In contrast, the odor of female urine has either no effect on the onset of sexual maturity or else slightly retards it. DMS

Above *Disturbed by an intruder, a North American porcupine displays its quills. The species is found in forests across most of the USA, northern Mexico, and Canada. Porcupines have quite poor eyesight, move slowly, and cannot jump, but nonetheless frequently climb trees to enormous heights in search of food.*

Left *Threat displays are very dramatic in some rodent species.* ***1*** *When slightly angry the Cape porcupine raises its quills and rattles the specialized hollow quills on its tail. If this fails to have the desired effect the hind feet are thumped on the ground in a war dance accompaniment to the rattling. Only if the threat persists will the porcupine turn its back on its opponent and charge backwards with its lethal spines at the ready.* ***2*** *Slightly less dramatic is the threat display of the Kenyan crested rat. This slow and solidly built rodent responds to danger by elevating a contrastingly colored crest of long hairs along its back, and in so doing exposes a glandular strip along the body. Special wick-like hairs lining the gland facilitate the rapid dissemination of a strong, unpleasant odor.* ***3*** *Finally, the little Norway lemming stands its ground in the face of danger and lifts its chin to expose the pale neck and cheek fur, which contrast strongly with the dark upper fur.*

Controlling Spiraling Populations

RODENTS AND HUMANKIND

With their high powers of reproduction and ability to invade all habitats, rodents are of great economic and ecological importance. Most rodent species are pregnant for just 19–21 days, mate again within 2 days of giving birth, and the young begin breeding at 6 weeks of age; theoretically, a single breeding pair of mice can generate 500 mice in 21 weeks. In good conditions, rodent numbers can soar, up to 1,000–2,000 per hectare (400–800 per acre). Aperiodic outbreaks occur repeatedly in the House mouse on farmland in Australia, in rat species in the uplands of Laos, and among grassland species such as the Common vole.

Of approximately 2,000 rodent species, about 200–300 are economically important, and some of these occur worldwide. A telling example of their economic impact comes from Southeast Asia, where rodents are economically the most important pre-harvest pest. In Indonesia, rodents cause annual losses of around 17 percent of rice production; if these could be halved, there would be enough rice to provide 70 percent of the energy requirements of an extra 17.5 million people. In Vietnam, rodent damage to rice affected 63,000ha (155,000 acres) in 1995, rising to more than 700,000ha (1.7 million acres) in 1999. In 1998, an estimated 82 million rats were killed under bounty schemes. Over 5 million rat tails were returned from January to September in the province of Vinh Phuc alone, where the authorities estimate that there are more than 10 million rats and only 1.1 million people.

For farmers in mountainous regions of Laos, rodents are the pest problem they currently have least control over. It is not unusual for a family to lose more than 70 percent of its crop to rodents; if this occurs to one crop it is a major cause for concern, but if it happens to two crops in a row, the situation becomes catastrophic. And the impact of rodents does not stop once the crop is harvested; they also consume and contaminate significant amounts of stored grain. It is estimated that post-harvest losses are of a similar magnitude to those that occur pre-harvest.

Other than rice, tropical crops damaged by rodents include coconuts, maize, coffee, field beans, oil palm, citrus, melons, cocoa, and dates. Every year rodents consume food equivalent to the world's entire cereal and potato harvest; it has been estimated that a train 5,000km (3,000mi) long – as long as the Great Wall of China – would be needed to haul the take.

The challenge of managing the rodent impact in Southeast Asia is complicated because there are at least 15 major pest species, each with its own peculiarities. The variables include their level of tolerance to a commensal life with humans; their breeding ecology; use of habitat; social behavior; feeding behavior; climbing, swimming, or burrowing abilities; physiological tolerances to climatic conditions (including periods when water is scarce or only present at high levels of salinity); and responses to major disturbances such as fire, new cultivation practices, or floods. Although the use of rodenticides offers short-term respite from the depredations of most species, more environmentally benign and sustainable approaches to pest management demand good knowledge of the ecology of the particular species to be controlled.

The most universal pests are the Norway rat, the Roof rat, and the House mouse. House mouse populations undergo spectacular eruptions in Australian cereal-growing areas, with devastating economic, environmental, and social consequences. Squirrel-like pests include the European Red and Gray squirrels, but in terms of the damage they cause, these are relatively minor. Other problem species include the gerbils, the multi-mammate rats, and the Nile rat, all of which devastate agricultural crops in Africa. In North America as well as eastern and western Europe, voles are prominent pests: they strip bark from trees, often killing them, and consume seedlings in forest plantations or fields. When vole populations peak (once every 3–4 years) there may be 2,000 voles per hectare (almost 5,000 per acre). Other major pests include the Cotton or Cane rat and Web-footed marsh rat (*Holochilus brasiliensis*) from, principally, Latin America; the Polynesian rat (*Rattus exulans*) of the Pacific Islands and Southeast Asia; the Bandicota rats of the Indian subcontinent and Malaysian Peninsula; the Ricefield rat (*Rattus argentiventer*), Lesser ricefield rat (*Rattus losea*), and Philippines ricefield rat (*Rattus tanezumi*) in Southeast Asia; and the prairie dogs, marmots, pikas, Brandt's vole (*Microtus brandti*), Chinese zokor (*Myospalax fontanierii*), and ground squirrels of the Mongolian and Californian grasslands.

The characteristics that enable these animals to become such a problem are a simple body plan adapted to a variety of habitats and climates; opportunistic feeding behavior; gnawing and burrowing habits; and high reproductive potential. Many rodents of the arctic tundra and taiga undergo population explosions every 3-4 years (for instance, the Norway lemming in Europe and the Brown and Collared lemmings in North America). The population density builds up to a high level and then dramatically declines. Several theses have been advanced to explain the decline, none of them wholly satisfactory; for example, it was long held that disease (tularemia or lemming fever, found in many rodent populations) was the root cause of the decline, but it now seems more likely that it simply hastens it. Other suggestions are that the rodents become more aggressive at high density, leading to a failure of courtship and reproduction, or that the decline is due to the action of predators or the impoverishment of the forage. Objective observation of lemming behavior at high density shows it to be adaptive, providing the lemmings with the best chances for survival (see Voles and Lemmings).

In Britain, Norway rats may live in fields during the warm summer months when food is plentiful, and they seldom reach economically important numbers; but after harvest, with the onset of cold weather, they move into buildings. Also in Britain, and some other western European countries, the Long-tailed field mouse (*Apodemus sylvaticus*), normally only a pest in the winter when it may for example nibble stored apples, has learned to locate, probably by smell, pelleted sugar-beet seed. The damage it causes, which possibly went unnoticed before the advent of precision drilling, can lead to large barren patches in fields of sugar beet and sometimes necessitates complete re-sowing.

Although rodents usually consume about 15 percent of their body weight in food per day, much of the damage they do is not due to direct consumption. Three hundred rats in a grain store can eat 3 tonnes of grain in a year; but every 24 hours they also contaminate the grain with 15,000 droppings, 3.5 liters (6 pints) of urine, and countless hairs and greasy skin secretions. In sugar cane, rats may chew at the cane directly, consuming only a part of it; the damage, however, may cause the cane to fall over, so the impact of the sun's rays is reduced and harvesting impeded. In addition, the gnawed stem allows microorganisms to enter, reducing the sugar content. Apart from the value of the lost crop itself, a 6 percent drop in sugar content represents an equivalent reduction in the return on investment on land preparation, fertilizers, pesticides, irrigation water, management, harvesting, and processing.

Structural damage attributable to rodents results, for example, from the animals burrowing

◐ ***Left*** *A Brown rat* (Rattus norvegicus) *cares for a helpless infant. Although the young are born naked and blind, they are quick developers; within 15 days they are fully furred, and after another week are weaned and ready to leave the nest. Newborns will themselves be ready to start breeding within 90 days.*

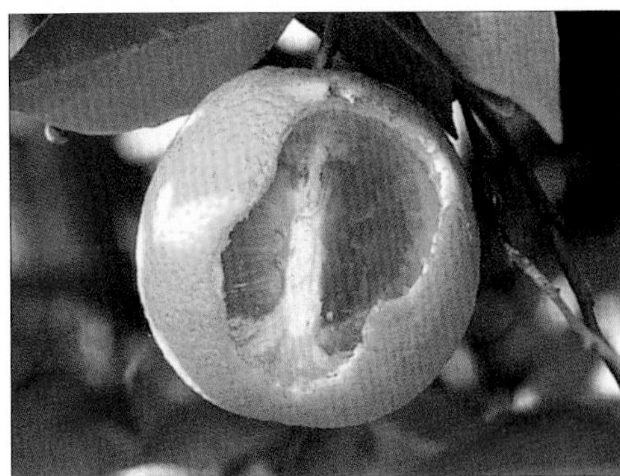

◐◐ ***Above and below*** *Competition for food is a major cause of conflict between rodents and humans. Species like the Roof rat* (Rattus rattus; below) *are famed marauders of stored vegetables and grains; and rats will also attack fruit on the tree, as a damaged Egyptian orange* (above) *testifies. In Asia, rodents routinely consume 5–30 percent of the rice crop, sometimes devastating areas of 10,000 hectares (25,000 acres) or more; they have also been held responsible for destroying annually 5–10 percent of China's stored grain – enough to feed up to 100 million people.*

THE IMPACT OF RODENT-BORNE DISEASES

Rodent pests are involved in the transmission of more than 20 pathogens, including bubonic plague (transmitted to man by the bite of the rat flea), which was responsible for the death of 25 million Europeans from the 14th to the 17th century. Rats also transmit debilitating chronic diseases. In the late 1970s, 80 percent of the inhabitants of the capital of one developing Asian country were seropositive for murine typhus. Forty percent of those admitted to hospital were diagnosed as having fever of unknown origin; at least some of these, and maybe most, were probably suffering from murine typhus. The impact of the disease on the economy of the country is impossible to determine – and the same country also suffered frequent outbreaks of plague.

Apart from plague, which persists in many African and Asian countries as well as in the USA (where wild mammals transmit the disease, killing fewer than 10 people a year), murine typhus, salmonella food poisoning, leptospirosis, and the West African disease Lassa fever, to mention just a few, are all potentially fatal diseases transmitted by rats.

In the late 1990s, however, attention has tended to focus on rodent-borne hemorrhagic fever viruses. From 1995–2000, at least 25 "new" hantaviruses and arenaviruses were identified, all of them associated with rodents from the family Muridae. The hantaviruses cause pulmonary ailments in the New World (50 percent of infected humans die) and fever with renal ailments in the Old World (approximately 200,000 human cases each year in Asia, with 1–15 percent mortality). The arenaviruses cause South American hemorrhagic fever in the New World (mortality in humans is 10–33 percent) and Lassa fever in the Old World (100,000–300,000 human infections each year in West Africa, causing 5,000 deaths annually). Each virus is normally associated with a specific rodent host. Infection is passed on to humans via rodent urine, feces, or saliva.

After a period in which much work was done on describing and understanding the degree of rodent viral diversity that can generate human infections, the focus for the control or prevention of rodent-borne hemorrhagic disease is now switching to understanding the biology and ecology of the host–disease association.

◑ ***Right*** *A German engraving shows the bizarre protective clothing worn by a doctor to treat victims of bubonic plague in Nuremberg in 1656.*

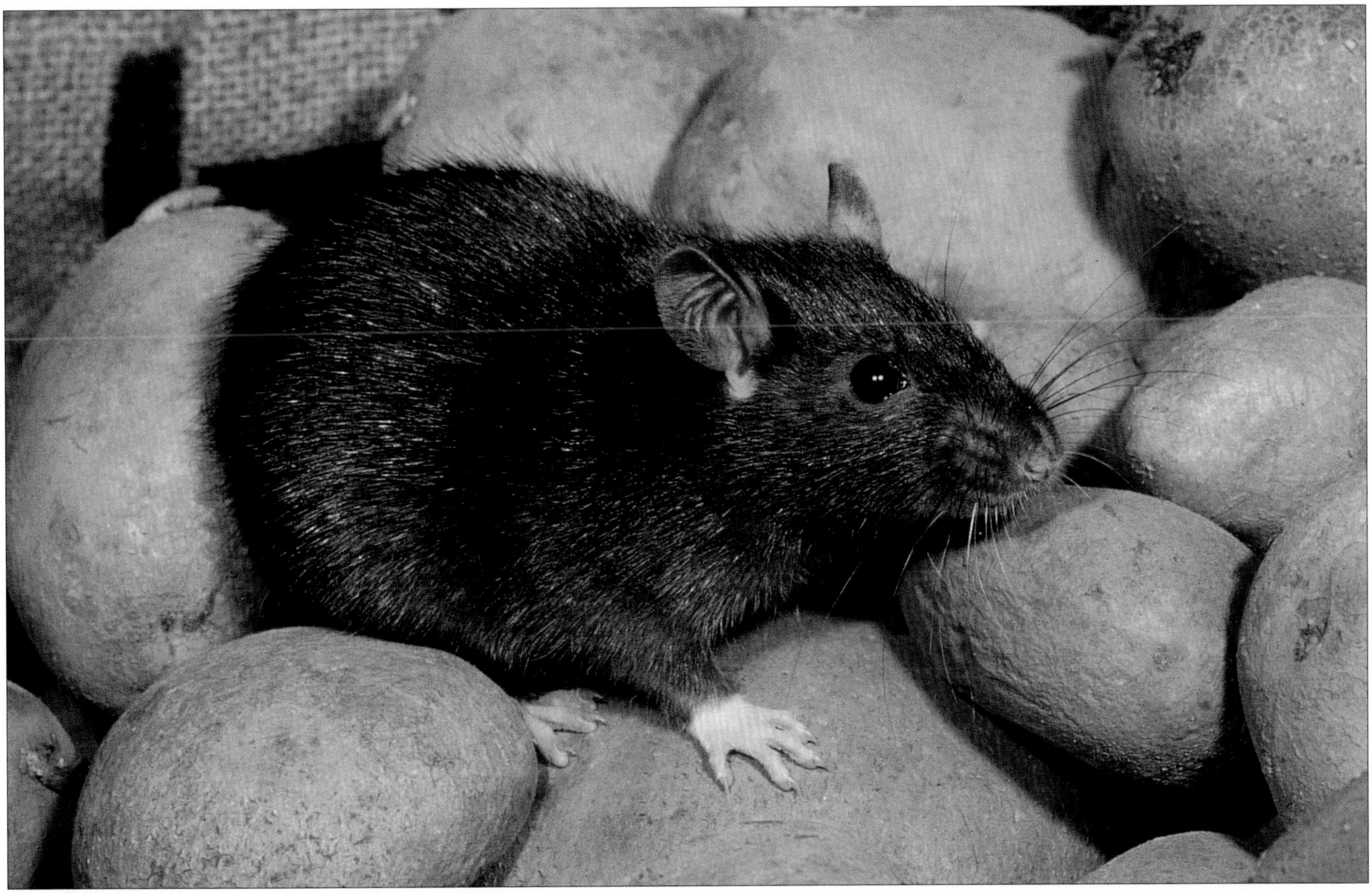

into banks or sewers, or under roads. The effects include subsidence, flooding, and even soil erosion in many areas of the world. Gnawed electrical cables can cause fires, leading to enormous economic impact. Rodents also gnaw through electric wires in the insulated walls of modern poultry and pork units, causing malfunctions of air-conditioning units and subsequent severe economic losses.

Apart from the immediate economic costs that the hordes may bring to farmers, high densities can have a profound effect upon the ecological balance of an entire region. Firstly, considerable damage is often inflicted on vegetation, from which it may take several years to recover. Secondly, predators increase in numbers in response to the abundance of rodents, and when the rodents have gone they turn their attention to other prey. Eruptions of Long-haired rat (*Rattus villosissimus*) populations over hundreds of thousands of square kilometers in northwestern Queensland and the Northern Territory of Australia lead to a feeding bonanza for Letter-winged kites, dingoes, foxes, and cats, and these predators in turn increase dramatically in numbers. In the mid-1990s there were so many cats living in the area that after the rat populations rapidly declined there was grave concern for other native fauna – in some areas many trees were literally a ball of cat fur. The situation was so desperate that the army was called in to help eradicate the feral cat population.

The simplest method of controlling the impact of rodents is to reduce harborage and available food and water. This, however, is often impossible. At best such "good housekeeping" can prevent rodent numbers building up, but it is seldom an effective method for reducing existing populations. One imperative is to develop management techniques based on an understanding of the ecology and behavior of the pest species concerned. The same principles of management apply in controlling the impact of rodents in fields, stores, or domestic premises.

To reduce existing populations of rodents, predators – wild (for example, birds of prey) or domestic (cats or dogs) – have relatively little effect. Their role may lie in limiting population growth. It is a widely accepted principle that predators do not control, in absolute terms, their prey, although the abundance of prey may affect the numbers of predators. Mongooses were introduced to the West Indies and Hawaiian Islands and cobras to Malaysian oil palm estates, both to control rats. The rats remain, however, and the mongooses and cobra are themselves now considered pests, the one a reservoir for rabies, the other a direct risk to people. Even the farm cat will not usually have a significant effect on rodent numbers: the reproductive rate of rodents keeps them ahead of the consumption rate of cats!

One of the simplest methods for combating small numbers of rodents is trapping. Few traps, however, are efficient: most simply maim their

Above *Indian villagers dig out rats' nests in their fields. For farmers, the battle against rodent damage is worldwide and never-ending. Over the centuries poison has been a favorite weapon, but the use of powerful pesticides can come at a cost, as the toxins may also harm non-targeted species, and there is also a risk of contaminating human food supplies. In the fight against rodent-borne maladies, an alternative approach is to dust nests with insecticides to kill disease-bearing parasites, like the exterminator dusting a ground squirrel's den in California (inset).*

Left *A Barn owl heads for the nest with a Field mouse clasped firmly in its beak. Many terrestrial predators as well as birds of prey rely on a plentiful supply of fast-breeding rodents for a large part of their diet. Programs aimed at the local eradication of pest species can have unintended knock-on effects higher up the food chain by depriving these species of their prey.*

victims. One promising method of physical control is the use of multiple capture traps placed at the base of fences (25 x 25m) that enclose early-planted crops (lure crops). These "trap-barrier" systems, which remain in place for the duration of the crop, have significantly reduced the impact of the Ricefield rat in lowland irrigated rice crops in Indonesia, Malaysia, and Vietnam. In Malaysia, 6,872 rats were caught in one night and over 44,000 rats in a 9-week period. In Indonesia and Vietnam, yield increases from surrounding crops have ranged from 0.3 to 1.0 tonne per ha (0.1–0.4 tonnes an acre), representing a 10–25 percent increase in production. The disadvantage of this approach is that it is labor-intensive and requires a coordinated community approach.

The oldest kind of rodenticide – fast-acting, non-selective poison – appears in the earliest written record of chemical pest control; the Greek philosopher Aristotle described the use of strychnine as early as 350 BC. However, fast-acting poisons such as strychnine, thallium sulfate, sodium monofluoroacetate (Compound 1080), and zinc phosphide have various technical and ecological disadvantages, including causing long-lasting poison shyness in sub-lethally poisoned rodents. They also represent a hazard to other animals.

Since 1945, when warfarin was first synthesized, several anticoagulant rodenticides have been developed. These compounds decrease the blood's ability to clot, and consequently bring about death by internal or external bleeding. The first generation of anticoagulants required multiple feeds of the poison, and were initially effective at controlling susceptible species such as the Norway rat. However some Norway rats have since acquired genetic resistance to the substances, while other species, such as the Roof rat, had a natural resistance from the start. These inadequacies have led to the development of more potent "second generation" anticoagulants, with active ingredients such as brodifacoum and bromadiolone, that only require single feeds and generally have a high kill rate for most rodent species. However, there are concerns about the risk to non-target species from these more potent chemicals, which are more persistent in the environment and which accumulate in predators as they eat more and more poisoned rodents until the predators themselves succumb to the poison.

Apart from the choice of toxicant, the timing of rodent control and the coordinated execution of a planned campaign are important in serious control programs. The most effective time to control agricultural rodents, for example, is when little food is available to them and when populations are low (probably just before breeding). "Avant-garde" methods of rodent control involving such relatively novel means as chemosterilants, ultrasonic sound, or electromagnetism are sometimes suggested, but none can yet claim to be as effective as anticoagulant rodenticides.

Species at Risk

CONSERVATION AND ENVIRONMENT

Not all rodents have thrived with the spread of humans. At least 54 species have become extinct in the last two centuries, and another 380 currently face a similar fate. At greatest risk are 78 critically endangered species that have small, isolated populations (often less than 250 individuals) that are continuing to decline. For some of these, such as Margaret's kangaroo rat and the Brazilian arboreal mouse, habitat protection offers hope that extinction will be averted. For others, such as the Bramble Cay mosaic-tailed rat, the future is bleak. This stocky rodent occurs on only one sparsely vegetated coral cay, 340m (1,100ft) long and 150m (500ft) wide, at the northern tip of Australia's Great Barrier Reef. Although its population numbers several hundred individuals, the rat is declining inexorably as the tides erode the coral and threaten to inundate the land.

At slightly less risk are the 100 or so endangered species. These may have total populations of up to 2,500, often scattered among several locations that are at risk of disturbance. Two species of Central American agoutis fall within this category, as do six species of Mexican woodrats.

Active management is assisting the survival of some endangered species. For example, Greater stick-nest rats numbered less than 1,500 individuals in 1990 and were restricted to Franklin Island off the southern coast of Australia. Successful translocations of captive-bred animals to three new islands and also to three large enclosed areas on the Australian mainland allowed the total population to double within nine years. Programs of captive breeding and habitat management currently benefit over 20 endangered species, including Vancouver marmots, Stephens' kangaroo rats, and Shark Bay mice.

While still threatened, almost 200 species classed as Vulnerable face less risk of imminent extinction than their endangered relatives, and may achieve populations up to 10,000 individuals. Examples include the Plains rat and Dusky hopping mouse of central Australia, the Utah prairie dog, and Menzbier's marmot of Tien Shan.

Some rodents are elusive, making it difficult to confidently identify their status. Arboreal species such as the Prehensile-tailed rat and the South American climbing rats do not readily enter traps, while others, such as the southern Australian Heath rat, so resemble other common species that they are easily overlooked. In many instances a lack of recent survey work makes status assessment impossible. The New Britain water rat and the Orange and Mansuela mosaic-tailed rats of Ceram are known only from one or two specimens collected in the early 20th century. Whether abundant or extinct, these rodents will remain known only from museum specimens until intrepid biologists foray back to the sites where they were originally collected. GS/CRD/DMS

DISTRIBUTION Worldwide except for Australia region, Polynesia, Madagascar, southern S America and some desert regions.

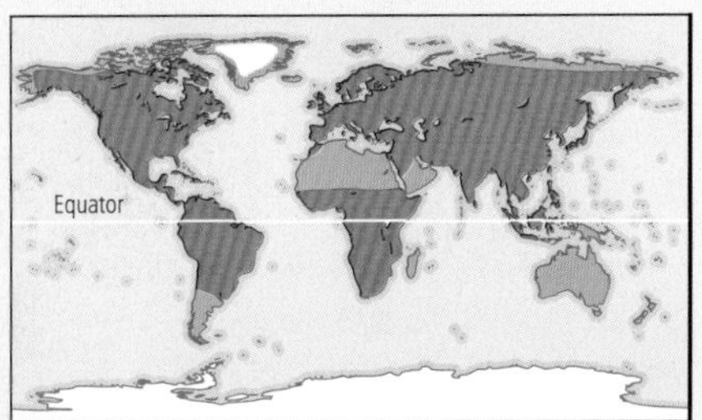

SCIUROGNATHS (part only) Suborder Sciurognathi
284 species in 56 genera and 5 families

BEAVERS Family Castoridae p590
2 species in the genus *Castor*

MOUNTAIN BEAVER Family Aplodontidae p596
1 species *Aplodontia rufa*

SQUIRRELS Family Sciuridae p598
273 species in 50 genera

SCALY-TAILED SQUIRRELS
Family Anomaluridae p608
7 species in 3 genera *Anomalurus, Idiurus, Zenkerella*

SPRINGHARE
Family Pedetidae p614
1 species *Pedetes capensis*

Squirrel-like Rodents

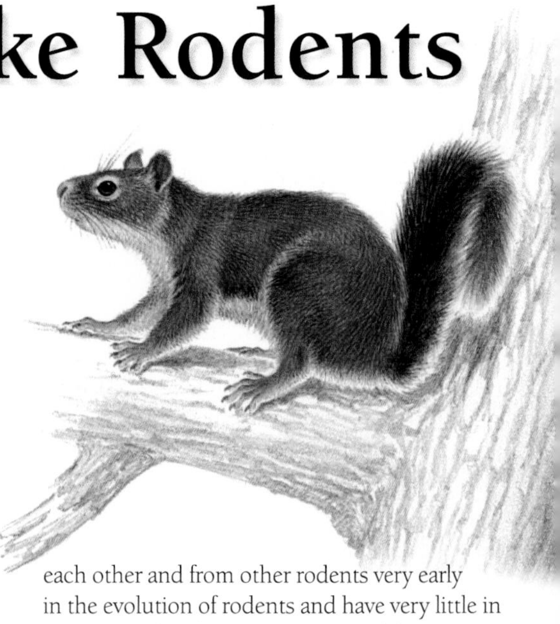

SQUIRRELS ARE PREDOMINANTLY SEEDEATERS and are the dominant arboreal rodents in many parts of the world. However, in the same family there are almost as many terrestrial species, including the ground squirrels of the open grasslands – also mostly seedeaters – as well as the more specialized and herbivorous marmots.

Although they may be highly specialized in other respects, members of the squirrel family have a relatively primitive, unspecialized arrangement of the jaw muscles and therefore of the associated parts of the skull, in contrast to the mouse-like ("myomorph") and cavy-like ("hystricognath") rodents, which have these areas specialized in ways not encountered in any other mammals. In squirrels the deep masseter muscle is short and direct, extending up from the mandible to terminate on the zygomatic arch. Because this particular feature is shared by some smaller groups of rodents, notably the Mountain beaver and the true beavers, these families have been grouped together with the squirrels in the suborder Sciuromorpha.

These families appear to have diverged from each other and from other rodents very early in the evolution of rodents and have very little in common other than the retention of the "sciuromorph" condition of the chewing apparatus.

A further primitive feature retained by these rodents is the presence of one or two premolar teeth in each row, giving four or five cheekteeth in each row instead of three as in the murids.

The superficially similar scaly-tailed squirrels of the African rain forests are only distantly related and are now placed within a separate suborder, Anomaluromorpha, which also includes the aberrant springhare of the African plains. GBC

DIFFERENT STROKES...

There is a great deal of variation in the shape and function of the tail among the families of squirrel-like rodents. One highly specialized adaptation is found in the various species of flying squirrel (RIGHT), in which the tail is used in conjunction with the gliding membrane to control the precise angle of descent. In another group of "flying" squirrel-like rodents – the scaly-tailed squirrels of the tropical African rain forests – the tail aids not only gliding but also climbing; overlapping scales on its underside give the squirrel purchase as it lands and grips onto the bark of trees. The semi-aquatic beaver employs its broad, flat tail both as a means of propulsion and as a rudder. When slowly patrolling on the lake's surface, its tail moves from side to side. However, when swimming fast underwater (INSET) the beaver propels itself with powerful up-and-down thrusts of the tail. The long, bushy tail of the kangaroo-like springhare acts as a counterbalance, helping it maintain equilibrium while hopping along at speed. When the springhare is at rest, and standing on its hind feet, it braces itself with its tail. The familiar, bushy tails of squirrels perform different roles depending on the habitat of the individual species – serving as warm cloaks for the denizens of northern forests, and as parasols to shade Cape ground squirrels from the fierce heat of the sun in the Kalahari desert.

SHAPING THE ENVIRONMENT

Among squirrel-like rodents, the beaver is renowned for its skill in altering the landscape of its habitat. It cuts down trees with its strong incisors, uses the felled material to build dams and lodges, and excavates canals with its forepaws.

Somewhat less spectacular is the way that smaller sciuromorphs such as squirrels shape their environment, and yet this devastation is far more significant, thanks to the prolific and widespread nature of the squirrel family. Red squirrels, which live predominantly in conifer plantations, cause much damage by feeding on young shoots. Their cousins the Gray squirrels specialize in peeling the bark from relatively young trees, up to 30–40 years old. The reasons for doing this are twofold: some bark is taken as a soft lining for nests; but the majority is stripped to gain access to the sweet, tasty sap beneath – a valuable dietary supplement when other food is in short supply (for example, in mid-summer). This destructive activity is especially prevalent where squirrel populations are dense and low-status males are forced to search widely for food during lean times. Bark-stripping presents the forestry industry with a serious problem; though trees are remarkably resilient, if their bark is stripped off entirely around the trunk and the soft tissue gnawed away, the vascular bundles that transport water, sugar, and nutrients through the tree are severed and it dies.

Crop-raiding is also a cause of conflict between humans and squirrel-like rodents. Ground squirrel species feed principally on low-growing vegetation.

Left and above *A Red squirrel, from Europe and Asia, and (above) a Douglas squirrel from western North America both display the classic squirrel profile – a long body and bushy tail.*

SKULLS AND DENTITION

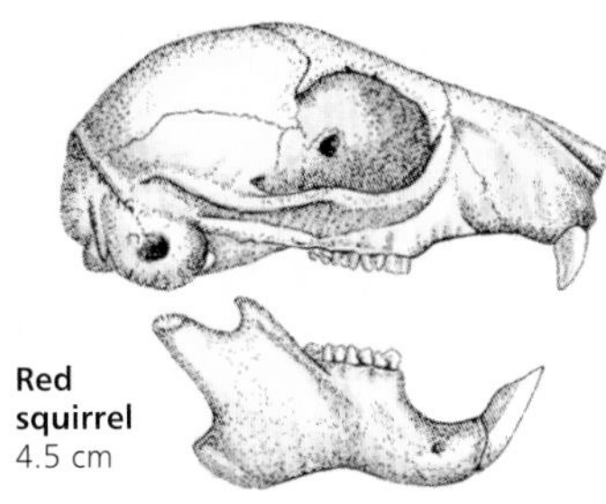

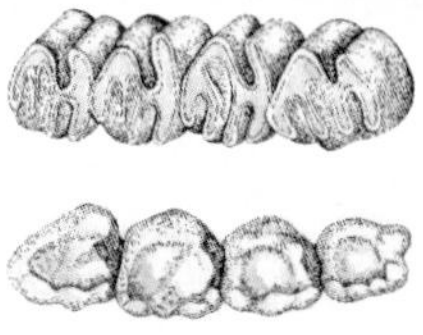

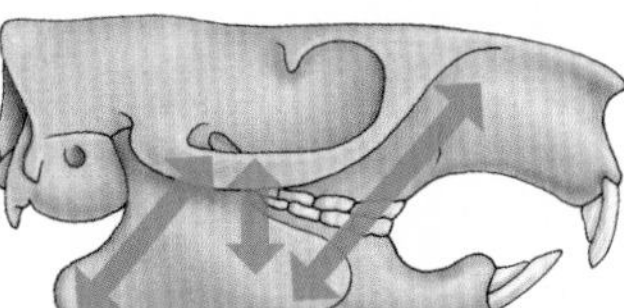

Skulls of squirrels show few extreme adaptations, although those of the larger ground squirrels, such as the marmots, are more angular than those of the tree squirrels. Most members of the squirrel family have rather simple teeth, lacking either the strongly projecting cusps or the sharp enamel ridges found in many other rodents. In the beavers, however, there is a pattern of ridges, adapted to their diet of bark and other fibrous and abrasive vegetation and convergent with that found in some unrelated but ecologically similar rodents like the coypu.

The primitive jaw musculature is characteristic of squirrel-like rodents. The lateral masseter muscle (blue) extends in front of the eye onto the snout, moving the lower jaw forward during gnawing. The deep masseter muscle (red) is short and used only in closing the jaw. Shown above is the skull of a marmot.

Beavers

Few wild animals have had as great an influence on the world's history and economics as the beaver. Exploration of the North American interior by Europeans was stimulated in large part by the demand for beaver pelts, used for hats and clothing. Records of the Hudson's Bay Company show an annual catch of 100,000 animals. So lucrative was this fur trade that conflicts erupted over access to trapping areas – notably the series of French and Indian Wars in the 18th century, which culminated in British control over the whole of northern North America.

The former importance of beavers may be judged from the fact that they are portrayed on the coats of arms of cities as distant as Härnösand in Sweden and Irkutsk in Siberia. In North America, many indigenous peoples valued the beaver both as a resource and as a spiritual totem. Central to the religion of the Montagnais of Quebec was a benevolent Beaver guardian spirit, while the tribe west of Lake Athabasca in Alberta were named for the main river of their homeland: *Tsades*, or "River of Beavers" (now called the Peace River).

Heavyweights of the Rodent World

FORM AND FUNCTION

Biologically, the beaver's large incisor teeth, flat, scaly, almost hairless tail, and webbed hind feet with a split grooming claw on the second digit are all distinctive, as is the internal anatomy of the throat and digestive tract. Beavers display a rich variety of construction, communication, and social behaviors that set them apart from other mammals. Like humans, beavers live in family groups, have complex communication systems, build homes (lodges and burrows), store food, and develop transportation networks (ponds linked by canals). Furthermore, they too change their environment to suit their needs; the dams they build promote ecological diversity, increase wetlands, affect water quality and yields, and help shape landscape evolution.

After the capybaras of South America, beavers are the heaviest rodents in the world; adults average 20–30kg (44–66lb), up to a maximum recorded weight of 45.5kg (100lb). Beavers always live near water. The animals scull slowly along the surface of lakes, using side-to-side movements of the tail for steering and propulsion. By contrast, when swimming fast or diving, beavers moves their tails up and down in synchrony with powerful thrusts of the hind feet.

Beavers may appear slow and awkward on land, waddling on large, pigeon-toed rear feet, short front legs, and trim forefeet. Yet they can put on a turn of speed if alarmed, outpacing both predators and researchers as they gallop for the water.

A History of Comings and Goings

DISTRIBUTION PATTERNS

The North American beaver ranges over most of the continent from the Mackenzie River delta in Canada south to northern Mexico. By the late 1800s, beavers had effectively been extirpated locally over much of this range, especially in the eastern United States, but state and federal wildlife agencies have reestablished many populations through translocations and reintroductions. The animals have also been introduced into Finland, Russia (to the Karelian Isthmus, the Amur basin, and the Kamchatka peninsula), and in many central European countries, including Germany, Austria, and Poland. The largest population of North American beavers in Europe is today in southeastern Finland, numbering an estimated 10,500. North American beavers were also introduced in

FACTFILE

BEAVERS

Order: Rodentia

Family: Castoridae

2 species of the genus *Castor*

DISTRIBUTION N America, Scandinavia, W and E Europe, C Asia, NW China, Far E Russia, S America.

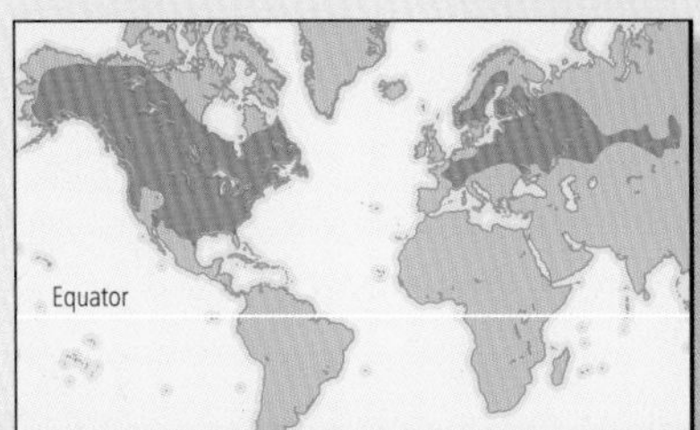

Habitat Riparian, semiaquatic wetlands associated with ponds, lakes, rivers, and streams.
Diet Wood (especially aspen), grasses, roots.

NORTH AMERICAN BEAVER *Castor canadensis*
North American or Canadian beaver
N America from Alaska E to Labrador, S to N Florida and Tamaulipas (Mexico); introduced to S America (Tierra del Fuego, Argentina), Europe, and Asia. HBL 80–120cm (32–47in); TL 25–50cm 10–20in); SH 30–60cm (12–23in); WT 11–30kg (24–66lb); no difference between sexes. Coat: yellowish brown to almost black; reddish brown is most common. Underfur is dense and dark gray. Breeding: gestation about 105–107 days. Longevity: 10–15 years. 24 subspecies are recognized.

EURASIAN BEAVER *Castor fiber*
Eurasian or European beaver
NW and C Eurasia, in isolated, but increasing, populations from France E to Lake Baikal and Mongolia; also in far-eastern Russia (Khabarovsk). Other details as for *C. canadensis*. 8 subspecies are recognized.

Abbreviations HBL = head–body length TL = tail length SH = shoulder height WT = weight

Above *Though somewhat ungainly when out of water, the semiaquatic beaver* (Castor canadensis) *is perfectly adapted to a wetland environment. Its dense, luxuriant pelage made the beaver vulnerable to hunting by fur trappers, and it was exterminated in many countries. However, aided by reintroduction programs, it is now making a comeback.*

Left *Battling against the current, a beaver feeds on the bark of a silver birch branch. When a beaver dives, it shuts its nose and ears tight, while a translucent membrane covers its eyes and the back of the tongue prevents water from entering its throat. This effective, watertight adaptation allows beavers to gnaw and carry sticks underwater without choking; but the comic aspect of closing the lips behind the front teeth is much beloved of cartoonists when depicting the animals.*

South America (to Tierra del Fuego) in 1946. While 24 subspecies are recognized, local exterminations, translocations, and reintroductions have altered the purity of many of these.

The Eurasian beaver was once found throughout Europe and Asia, but only isolated populations have survived the long association with humans. By the early 1900s, only eight relic populations totaling an estimated 1,200 individuals remained, in France, Germany, Norway, Belarus, Russia, Ukraine, Mongolia, and China respectively. Reintroduction and translocation programs began in most European countries in the early to mid 1900s, and many continue at the present time. The Eurasian beaver population is growing (the current estimate is 500,000–600,000 animals) and its range is expanding throughout Europe and Asia. Eight subspecies are recognized, but translocations and reintroductions have altered their historic distributions.

The earliest direct ancestor of the Eurasian beaver was probably *Steneofiber* from the Oligocene, about 32 million years ago. The genus *Castor*, which originated in Europe during the Pliocene (5–1.8 m.y.a.), entered North America while the continents were still connected; thus the present-day North American beaver is thought to be evolutionarily younger than the Eurasian beaver. During the Pleistocene, 10,000 years ago, the two species coexisted with giant forms that weighed 270–320kg (600–700lb), for example *Castoroides* in North America and *Trogontherium* in Eurasia. The two present species are externally similar in size and coloration and are indistinguishable in appearance, but they differ in cranial morphology and chromosome number (*C. fiber* has 48 chromosomes, *C. canadensis* 40). The North American beaver is believed to be derived from the Eurasian beaver because it has fewer chromosomes. It is thought that the reduced

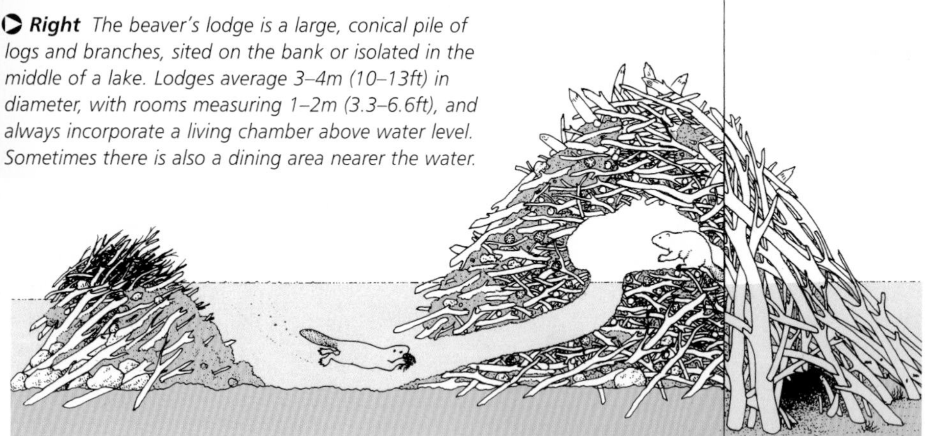

Right *The beaver's lodge is a large, conical pile of logs and branches, sited on the bank or isolated in the middle of a lake. Lodges average 3–4m (10–13ft) in diameter, with rooms measuring 1–2m (3.3–6.6ft), and always incorporate a living chamber above water level. Sometimes there is also a dining area nearer the water.*

number of chromosomes in *C. canadensis* resulted from the fusion of 8 chromosome pairs in the ancestral *C. fiber*, and that this difference prevents the two species from interbreeding.

Choosy Generalists

DIET

Beavers are generalist herbivores whose diet varies seasonally. In spring and summer they feed on relatively non-woody plants (leaves, roots, herbs, ferns, grasses, and algae), but they turn to trees and shrubs, especially in the fall. Aspen is the preferred tree species, but birch, maple, oak, dogwood, and fruit trees are also taken. In many regions, shrubs such as willow and alder form the bulk of the diet. Wood is not easy to digest; to cope with it, beavers have special microbial fermentation in the cecum, and digestion occurs twice to extract the maximum nutritive advantage.

Beavers are only able to survive the harsh winters of northern latitudes by caching food. Woody stems are stored underwater, where they are safe from other browsers. The beavers can then swim under the ice to fetch the food without having to leave the safety of the pond.

Many European beavers do not cache food (in some populations, only 50 percent of families do so). Instead, they venture onto land to find food in winter. Another strategy that beavers use to survive at this time is to live off the fat stored in their tails.

How Colonies Work

SOCIAL BEHAVIOR

Beavers live in small, closed family units, which are often referred to as "colonies." An established colony contains an adult pair, young of the current year (called "kits"), yearlings born the previous year, and possibly one or more subadults from previous breeding seasons. There are typically four to eight beavers in a family. The inclusion of offspring older than 24 months usually occurs in high-density populations, and these young adults generally do not breed. Under high-density conditions, the normal family structure has been reported to change, with more than one reproductively active adult female present.

Above *Beaver kits are extremely precious – females produce only one small litter each year. At birth, they have a full coat of fur and open eyes, and are able to move around inside the lodge. All family members share in bringing the kits solid food, with the adult male most actively supplying provisions.*

The main beaver predator, beside humans, is the wolf, for which beavers are an important prey item. Other large carnivores, such as lynx, coyotes, wolverines, bears, and foxes, may also kill them.

Beavers are unusual among mammals in that they exhibit long-term monogamy. The mated pair occupies a discrete, individual territory, and the relationship usually lasts until one adult dies. The family unit is exceptionally stable, thanks to a low birth rate (one litter annually of 1–5 young in the Eurasian and up to 8 in the North American beaver), a high survival rate for all age–sex classes, and long-term parental care, with the young usually staying in the colony for 2 years. Both Eurasian and North American beavers have an average litter size of 2–3 kits, and the dominance hierarchy within the family is by age class, with adults dominant to yearlings and yearlings to kits. A sex-based hierarchy, with the adult female dominant to all other family members, has occasionally been reported. Physical aggression is rare, although beavers in dense populations are reported to have more tail scars – a sign of fighting, usually with outsiders over territory boundaries.

Mating occurs in winter, usually in the water but also in the lodge or burrow. Kits are born in

THE BEAVER'S 29-HOUR DAY

For most of the year, beavers are active at night, rising at sunset and retiring to their lodges at sunrise. This regular daily cycle is termed a circadian rhythm. During winter at northern latitudes, however, when ponds freeze over, beavers stay in their lodges or under the ice, because temperatures there remain near 0°C (32°F), while air temperatures are generally much lower. Activity above ice would require a very high use of energy.

In the dimly lit world of the lodge and the water surrounding it, light levels remain constant and low throughout the 24-hour day, so that sunrise and sunset are not apparent. In the absence of solar "cues," activity, recorded as noise and movement, is not synchronized with the solar day. The circadian rhythm breaks down, and "beaver days" become longer, varying in length from 26 to 29 hours. This type of cycle is termed a "free-running circadian rhythm."

late spring, which may coincide with the dispersal of 2-year-olds away from the family territory. Though they can swim within a few hours, the kits' small size and dense fur make them too buoyant to submerge easily, so they are unable to dive down the passage out of the lodge. Kits nurse for between 6–8 weeks, although they may begin eating solid food before they are weaned.

While the kits are very young, the adult male may spend more time in territorial defense (patrolling and scent marking the family territory) while the female is more involved in care and nursing. The kits grow rapidly, but require many months of practice to perfect their ability to construct dams and lodges. As yearlings, they participate in all family activities, including construction. Dispersal of the young adults usually occurs in the spring of their second year, when they are approximately 24 months old; they head off to set up territories of their own, usually within 20km (12mi), although they may travel as far as 250km (155mi).

One of the ways in which beavers communicate is by depositing scent, usually at the borders of the family territory. Both species of beaver scentmark on small waterside mounds made of mud and vegetation dredged up from underwater. Eurasian beavers also mark tufts of grass, rocks, and logs, as well as directly onto the ground. The scent, produced by the substance known as castoreum (from the castor sacs) and secretions from the anal glands, is pungent and musty. All members of a beaver family participate, but the adult male marks most frequently. Scentmarking is most intense in the spring, and probably serves to convey information about the resident family to passing strangers and to neighbors. Another mode of communication is to slap the tail against the water. Adults do this more often than younger animals, to let an approaching interloper know they have been spotted. The slap often elicits a response from the stranger, which enables the beaver to gauge what level of threat is posed. Beavers also communicate through vocalizations (hissing and grunting), tooth sharpening, and posture.

Of the various construction activities in which beavers engage, canal-building is the least complex and was probably the first that the animals developed. They use their forepaws to loosen mud and sediment from the bottom of shallow streams and marshy trails, pushing it out of the way to the sides. The resulting channels enable the beavers to stay in the water while moving between ponds or to feeding areas. This behavior occurs most often in summer when water levels are low.

Beavers are efficient excavators and usually dig multiple burrows in the family area. A burrow may be a single tunnel or a whole maze, hollowed into the bank from a stream or pond and ending in one or more chambers. In many habitats, beaver families use burrows as the primary residence. Alternative riverside accommodation is provided by the beaver equivalent of a log cabin – the lodge.

Above *Of all rodents, the beaver is one of the best-adapted for movement in water. Its torpedo-shaped body is hydrodynamically efficient and its fur is waterproof. It uses its broad tail for propulsion and steering, and also gains thrust from its webbed feet.*

Meat, Fur, and Medicines

CONSERVATION AND ENVIRONMENT

Historically, beavers have provided humans with meat, fur, and medicinal products, and they continue to supply the first two to this day. From 200,000–600,000 pelts are collected in Canada each year, while the harvest in the United States is 100,000–200,000. Scandinavian countries take around 13,000 pelts, and Russia some 30,000. However, the global fur market is depressed, and there is little economic incentive for trappers.

Another beaver product of value to humans – especially in the past – was castoreum, a complex substance consisting of hundreds of compounds, including alcohols, phenols, salicylaldehyde, and castoramine. This substance is produced in the animal's castor sacs. As far back as 500–400 BC Hippocrates and Herodotus note its efficacy in treating diseases of the womb. Later writers, such as Pliny the Elder and Galen, mention it as a remedy for cramps and intestinal spasms. Down the ages, castoreum has also variously been suggested as a treatment for sores, ulcers, earache, constipation, and even as an antidote to snake venom. Modern studies have remarked on its similarity to the synthetic drug aspirin, which is derived from salicylic acid; castoreum also contains salicin, which the beavers obtain by eating the bark of willow and aspen. Although it no longer appears in the conventional pharmacopoeia, it is still used by homeopathic practitioners, and also serves as a base for perfume.

Beavers are today established once more in Belgium and the Netherlands, and a reintroduction program is planned in Britain. As with most such initiatives, there is controversy over the potential effect on land used by humans. North American beavers in Europe add to an already charged situation. Currently, large populations exist in Finland and northwestern Russia and there is no consensus on how the two species are competing for the limited wetland resource. New techniques make it possible to distinguish the two species in the field, either by using genetic analysis of hair root cells or else by comparing anal-gland secretions.

Beavers and humans conflict when beavers make wetlands out of agricultural fields. In the midwestern and eastern United States, where beavers were once nearly extirpated, they have made a tremendous comeback, and beaver–human conflict is growing, a trend that is likely to continue. Beavers are keystone species in wetland habitats, and it remains for humans to acknowledge their environmental contributions and develop strategies that allow both humans and beavers to share the landscape. PB/GH

THE CONSTRUCTION WORKER RODENT

❸ *Although many beaver barrages are built across streams under 6m (20ft) wide and in water less than 1m (3.3ft) deep, the animals keep adding material until some dams end up over 100m (330ft) long and 3m (10ft) high. Dam-building is at its most intense in the spring and fall, although construction may go on throughout the year.*

❶ *Just as a lumberjack's ax is hardened with iron, so the front enamel of beaver teeth is reinforced. The softer inner surface wears down more rapidly, creating a sharp, chisel-like edge that makes cutting down trees for food and building easier. In common with all rodents, beavers have large incisors that grow as fast as they are worn down.*

❷ *Trees felled by beavers; although the damage caused by gnawing may appear terminal, the trees that beavers favor (aspens, poplars, cottonwoods, and willows) are characterized by rapid growth, and beaver "pruning" often stimulates reinvigorated growth the next spring.*

4

④ *In areas where beavers and humans coexist, beavers' dam-building activity (especially their propensity to block culverts and cause road flooding) is seen as a hazard. But the ecological advantages are often overlooked; by slowing the flow of rivers and streams, dams boost sediment deposition – a natural filtration system that removes potentially harmful impurities from the water. In addition, the large areas of wetland that dams create bring other benefits, such as reduced erosion damage and greater biodiversity.*

5

⑤ *The mud, stones, sticks, and branches that beavers use to construct their dams make for a very robust structure, behind which a substantial pond will form. By impounding a large body of water, they effectively surround their home with a wide moat, which increases their security from predators. Moreover, the bigger the lake, the more access the beavers have by water to distant food items. Several lakes and lodges may be the work of a single colony (so, simply counting these in any one area is not a reliable way of estimating the local beaver population). Colonies are forced to move on when the accumulation of sediment in a pond becomes too great. Abandoned, silted-up beaver ponds form the basis of rich new ecosystems; they develop into wetland meadows whose soil, rich in decaying plant matter, supports reeds and sedges, and eventually even large trees.*

Mountain Beaver

THE MOST PRIMITIVE OF ALL PRESENT-DAY rodents, Mountain beavers live only in southwestern Canada and along the west coast of the USA, where they inhabit some of the most productive coniferous forest lands in North America.

Not to be confused with the flat-tailed stream beaver (genus *Castor*), Mountain beavers are strictly terrestrial animals. They are secretive and nocturnal, spending much of their time in burrows, where they sleep, eat, defecate, fight, and reproduce; they even do most of their traveling underground. Consequently, they are seldom seen outside zoos.

FACTFILE

MOUNTAIN BEAVER

Aplodontia rufa

Mountain beaver, boomer, or sewellel

Order: Rodentia

Sole member of family Aplodontidae

DISTRIBUTION USA and Canada along Pacific coast

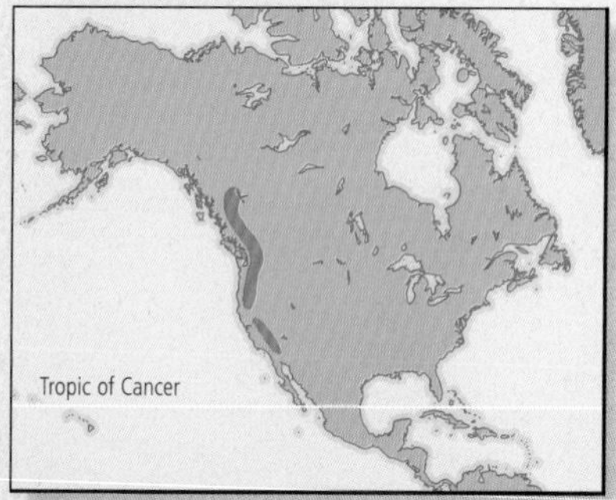

HABITAT Coniferous forest

SIZE Head–body length 30–41cm (12-16in); tail length 2.5–3.8cm (1–1.5in); shoulder height 11.5–14cm (4.5–5.5in); weight 1–1.5kg (2.2–3.3lb). Sexes are similar in size and shape, but males weigh slightly more than females.

COAT Young in their year of birth have grayish fur, adults blackish to reddish brown, tawny underneath.

DIET Leafy materials, grasses, roots.

BREEDING Gestation 28–30 days

LONGEVITY 5–10 years

CONSERVATION STATUS Lower Risk: Near Threatened; two subspecies – the Point Arena and Point Reyes Mountain beavers – are listed as Vulnerable.

Built for Burrowing

FORM AND FUNCTION

Mountain beavers are medium-sized, bull-necked rodents with a round, robust body and a moderately flat and broad head that is equipped with small, black, beady eyes and long, stiff, whitish whiskers (vibrissae). Their incisor teeth are rootless and continuously growing, as are their premolars and molars. Their ears are relatively small, and covered with short, soft, light-colored hair. Their short legs give them a squat appearance; the tail is short and vestigial. The fur on their back presents a sheen, whereas white-to-translucent-tipped long guard hairs impart their flanks with a grizzled effect. A distinctive feature is a soft, furry white spot under each ear.

Mountain beavers can be found at all elevations from sea level to the treeline, and in areas with rainfall of 50–350cm (20–138in) per year and where winters are wet, mild, and snow-free, summers moist, mild, and cloudy. Their home burrows are generally in areas with deep, well-drained soils and abundant fleshy and woody plants. In drier areas Mountain beavers are restricted to habitats on banks and to ditches that are seasonally wet or have some free-running water available for most of the year.

The distribution of Mountain beavers is in part explained by the fact that they cannot adequately regulate the temperature of their bodies and must therefore live in stable, cool, moist environments. Nor can they effectively conserve body moisture or fat, which prevents them from either hibernating or spending the summer in torpor. Mountain beavers require considerable amounts of both food and water, and they must line their nests well for insulation. They satisfy most of their requirements with items obtained from within 30m (100ft) of their nest. Water is obtained mainly from succulent plants, dew, or rain.

Unlike any other rodent or rabbit, Mountain beavers extract fecal pellets individually with their incisors when defecating and toss them on piles in underground toilet chambers. However, they also share with other rodents and rabbits the habit of reingesting some of the pellets.

Mountain beavers are strictly vegetarians. They harvest leafy materials such as fronds of Sword fern, new branches of salal and huckleberry, stems of Douglas fir and Vine maple, and clumps of grass or sedge, and also seek out succulent, fleshy foods, such as fiddle heads of Bracken fern and roots of False dandelion and Bleeding heart. If these foods are not eaten immediately they will be stored underground for subsequent consumption.

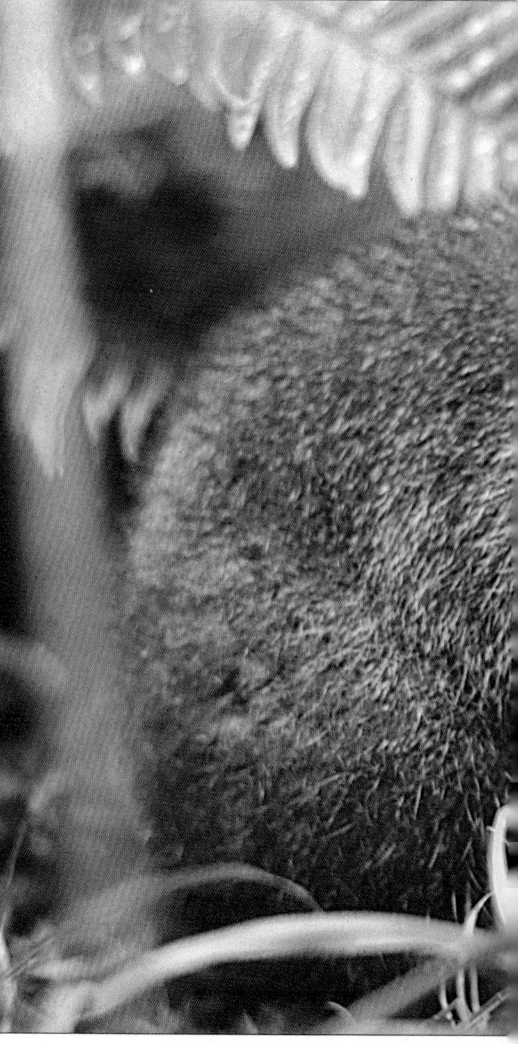

Most food and nest items are gathered above ground between dusk and dawn and consumed underground. Decaying, uneaten food is abandoned or buried in blind chambers; dry, uneaten food is added to the nest.

Life below the Forest Floor

SOCIAL BEHAVIOR

It used to be thought that all Mountain beavers were solitary except during the breeding and rearing season, but recent studies using radio tracking have demonstrated that this view is inadequate. Some Mountain beavers spend short periods together in all seasons. Neighbors, for example, will share nests and food caches, or a wandering beaver will stay a day or two in another beaver's burrow system. Sometimes a beaver's burrow will also be occupied, in part if not in its entirety, by any of a range of other animals, such as salamanders, frogs, or deer mice.

Unlike many rodents, Mountain beavers have a low rate of reproduction. Most do not mate until they are at least 2 years old, and females conceive only once a year, even if they lose a litter. Breeding is to some extent synchronized. Males are sexually active from about late December to early March, with aggressive older males doing most of the breeding. Conception normally occurs in January or February. Litters of between 2–4 young are born in February, March, or early April. The young

Left *Mountain beavers seldom appear above ground during daylight hours. This rare image shows well the squat, thickset appearance of this most elusive of North American mammals.*

are born blind, hairless, and helpless in the nest. They are weaned when they reach about 6–8 weeks old and continue to occupy the nest and burrow system with their mother until late summer or early fall. Juveniles disperse and leave their natal site to find a territory and burrow system of their own.

Once on its own, a young beaver may establish a new burrow system or, more commonly, restore an abandoned one. New burrows may be within 100m (330ft) of the mother's burrow, or up to 2km (1.2mi) away, the distance depending on population densities and on the quality of the land. Both sexes disperse in the same manner. Dispersing young travel mainly above ground: they become very vulnerable to predators, for example owls, hawks, and ravens, coyotes, bobcats, and man. Those living near roads are liable to be killed by vehicles.

The Forester's Foe

CONSERVATION AND ENVIRONMENT

Mountain beavers are classed as non-game mammals, and so are not managed in the same way as game animals like deer and elk or furbearing animals such as beavers and muskrats. They can pose a huge threat to young conifers planted for timber; the damage they cause affects about 111,000ha (275,000 acres). Almost all damage occurs while they are gathering food and nest materials.

Although some of the Mountain beavers' forest habitat has given way to urban development and agriculture, they range over about as extensive an area now as they did 200–300 years ago. They are probably more abundant now than they were in the early 20th century, thanks to forest logging practices. Mountain beavers do not appear to be in any immediate danger of extermination from man or natural causes. JE

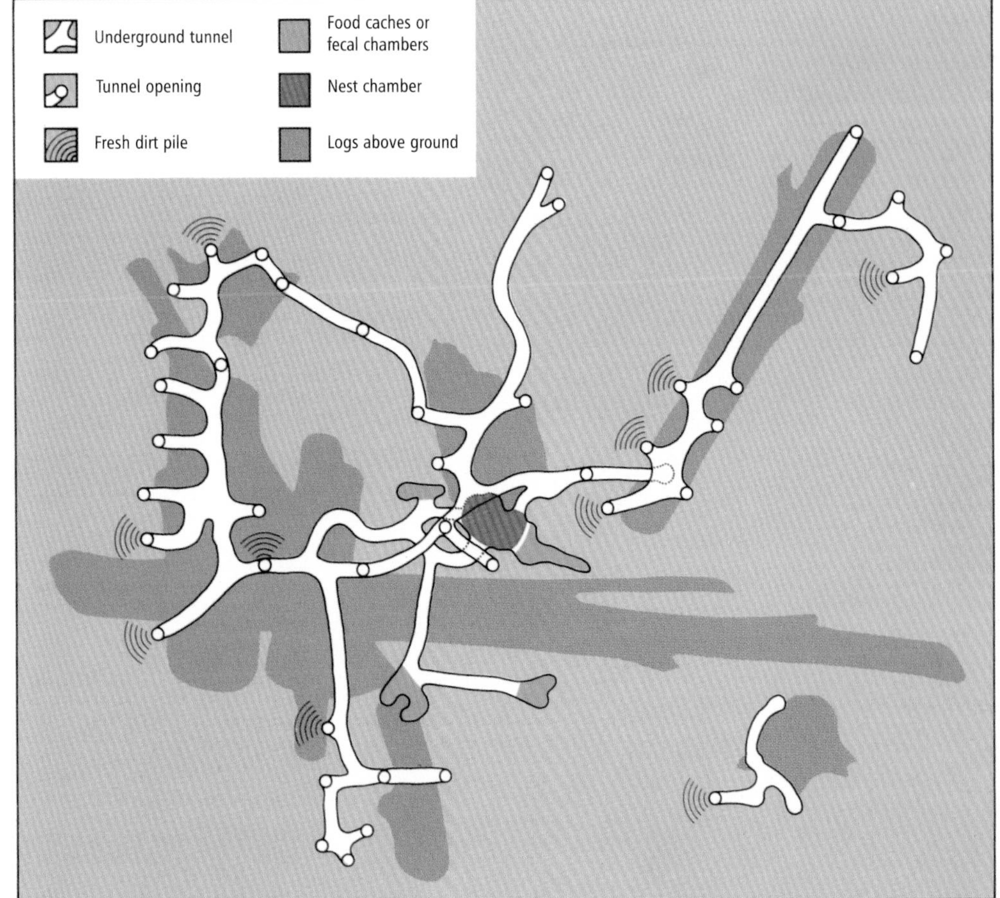

Right *The burrow system of a Mountain beaver. Each burrow system consists of a single nest chamber and underground food caches and fecal chambers which are generally close to the nest. Most nests are about 1m (3.3ft) below ground in a well-drained, dome-shaped chamber, although some may occur 2m (6.6ft) or more below ground. Tunnels are generally 15–20cm (6–8in) in diameter and occur at various levels; those closest to the surface are used for travel; deep ones lead to the nest and food caches. Burrow openings occur every 4–6m (13–20ft) or more, depending on vegetative cover and number of animals occupying a particular area. Densities vary from 1 or 2 Mountain beavers per hectare (2.5 acres) in poor habitat to 20 or more per hectare in good habitat. Up to 75 per hectare have been kill-trapped in reforested clear-out areas, but such densities are rare. Individual burrow systems often interconnect.*

Squirrels

TEMPERATE-ZONE SQUIRRELS ARE A LITTLE like daffodils: they appear suddenly in early spring, add life to the habitat for a few months, and then disappear again. For the ground-dwellers, disappearance signals the start of hibernation, for many of these mammals spend at least half their lives in dormancy: they are active above ground for only 4–6 months and hibernate for the rest of the year in grass-lined nests deep underground.

Because they are relatively unspecialized, squirrels have been able to evolve different body forms and habits that fit them for life in a broad range of habitats, from lush tropical rain forests to semi-arid deserts, and from open prairies to town gardens. This successful family includes such diverse forms as the ground-dwelling and burrowing marmots, ground squirrels, prairie dogs, and chipmunks; the arboreal and day-active tree squirrels; and the nocturnal flying squirrels. The scaly-tailed squirrels (Anomaluridae) are also treated here, though they are taxonomically distinct from true squirrels.

Squirrel Groups and Genera

Pygmy squirrels: *Exilisciurus, Glyphotes, Myosciurus, Nannosciurus, Sciurillus*
Dwarf squirrels: *Microsciurus, Prosciurillus*
Giant squirrels: *Ratufa, Rubrisciurus*
Flying squirrels: *Aeretes, Aeromys, Belomys, Biswamoyopterus, Eupetaurus, Glaucomys, Hylopetes, Iomys, Petaurillus, Petinomys, Pteromys, Pteromyscus, Trogopterus*
Giant flying squirrels: *Petaurista*
Beautiful squirrels: *Callosciurus*
Sun squirrels: *Heliosciurus*
Groove-toothed squirrels: *Rheithrosciurus, Syntheosciurus,*
Palm squirrels: *Epixerus, Funambulus, Menetes, Protoxerus*
Long-nosed squirrels: *Hyosciurus, Rhinosciurus*
Rock squirrels: *Sciurotamias*
Red-cheeked squirrels: *Dremomys*
American red squirrels: *Tamiasciurus*
Tree squirrels: *Sciurus, Sundasciurus*
Striped squirrels: *Funisciurus, Lariscus, Tamiops*
African bush squirrels: *Paraxerus*
Chipmunks: *Tamias*
Ground squirrels: *Ammospermophilus, Atlantoxerus, Xerus (Geosciurus), Spermophilus, Spermophilopsis*
Prairie dogs: *Cynomys*
Marmots: *Marmota*

For full species list see Appendix ▷

Diggers, Climbers, and Gliders

FUNCTION AND FORM

Squirrels are instantly recognizable, with their cylindrical bodies, bushy tails, and prehensile limbs. They have short forelegs, with a small thumb and four toes on the front feet, and longer hind legs with either four (woodchucks, *Marmota monax*) or five toes (ground squirrels and tree squirrels) on the hind feet. Most are diurnal, conspicuous, active, and – often – amusingly clever. They exhibit a wide array of body sizes and behaviors, from ground-dwelling, fossorial species (marmots, ground squirrels, prairie dogs) to arboreal tree squirrels and nocturnal flying squirrels. Their abilities to live in contrasting habitats and to forage opportunistically are the bases for their widespread distribution and numerical abundance, both in species and populations.

Squirrels have large eyes, surrounded by light-colored rings, that are placed on the sides of their heads, affording them a broad field of vision. Keen eyesight enables them to recognize dangerous predators from nondangerous conspecifics at

FACTFILE

SQUIRRELS

Order: Rodentia

Family: Sciuridae

273 species in 50 genera

DISTRIBUTION Among the most widespread of mammals, found worldwide except for in Australia, Polynesia, Madagascar, S South America, and the Sahara desert (Africa and Arabia).

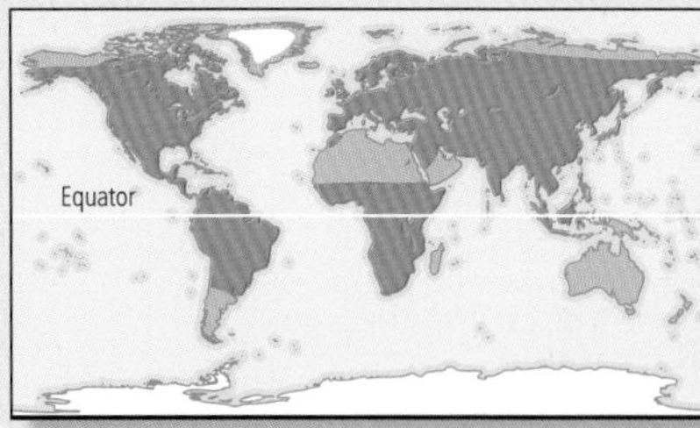

HABITAT Various, from tropical rain forests to temperate and boreal coniferous forests, tundra and alpine meadows to semiarid deserts, and cultivated fields to city parks. Some species are arboreal and nest in tree branches or cavities; others are terrestrial and excavate subterranean burrows.

SIZE **Head–body length** ranges from 6.6–10cm (2.6–3.9in) in the diminutive African pygmy squirrel, *Myosciurus pumilio* to 53–73cm (20.8–28.7in) in the Alpine marmot, *Marmota marmota*; **tail length** from 5–8cm (2–3in) to 13–16cm (5.1–6.3in); **weight** from 10g (0.35oz) to 4–8kg (8.8–17.6lb), in the same two species.

COAT Squirrels come in many colors. Most squirrels molt twice per year. In northern areas a soft, fine summer coat alternates with a stiff, thick winter coat. There are no sexual dimorphisms or age variations in coat texture or colors.

DIET Tree and flying squirrels eat nuts, seeds, fruits, buds, flowers, sap, and occasionally fungi; ground-dwelling squirrels eat grasses, forbs, flowers, bulbs, and especially seeds (*Spermophilus* means "seed loving"). Most species will also eat insects, birds' eggs and nestlings, and small vertebrates if they are available.

BREEDING In most species, females mature sexually before males, usually reproducing by age 1 year. Males are polygynous and, in some species, females also mate with multiple partners, resulting in litters of mixed paternity. Most ground-dwelling squirrels, flying squirrels, and northern populations of tree squirrels bear one litter in late spring; temperate-zone tree squirrels and chipmunks often have another summer litter. Litters typically contain 1–6 (up to 11) pups; larger species have smaller litters.

LONGEVITY Ground and tree squirrels live 2–3 years on average and 6–7 years maximum; larger species, such as Yellow-bellied marmots (*Marmota flaviventris*), live 4–5 years on average and 13–14 years maximum. Females usually live longer than males.

CONSERVATION STATUS Many species are threatened or endangered due to loss of habitat, introduction of exotic species, and harassment. Red squirrels are listed as Near Endangered in the UK and N Italy due to exclusion by the introduced Gray squirrel.

Above *The Harris' antelope squirrel inhabits burrows that it has excavated. Within its range it may have several burrows, one of which will have a nest. The species is diurnal and quite conspicuous.*

Left *The Red squirrel, which lives in woodland across Europe and Central Asia, has distinctive tufting on its ears. It is hunted in Russia for its dark brown winter pelage.*

great distances. Tree and flying squirrels and chipmunks also have large ears; some, like Red squirrels and Tassel-eared squirrels (*Sciurus aberti*), have conspicuous ear-tufts. All squirrels have touch-sensitive whiskers (vibrissae) on the head, feet, and the outsides of the legs.

Squirrels have the usual arrangement of teeth in rodents: a single pair of chisel-shaped incisors in each jaw, a large gap in front of the premolars, and no canine teeth. Their incisors grow continuously and are worn back by use; the cheek teeth are rooted and have abrasive chewing surfaces. The lower jaw is movable, and the lower incisors can operate independently. Some chipmunks and ground squirrels have internal cheek pouches for carrying food.

Ground-dwelling squirrels are heavy-bodied, with powerful forelimbs and large scraping claws for digging, whereas arboreal squirrels have lighter, longer bodies, less muscular forelimbs, and sharp claws on all toes. Tree squirrels descend tree trunks head first, turning their hind feet backward and sticking the claws into the bark to act as anchors. Their bushy tails are multifunctional: they serve as a balance when the squirrel runs and climbs, as a rudder when it jumps, as a flag to communicate social signals, and as a wrap-around blanket when the animal sleeps. All squirrels have soft pads on the soles of their feet, affording them a better grip of the substrate and food items. When feeding, squirrels squat on their haunches and hold the morsel in their forepaws. Footpads of desert-living Long-clawed ground squirrels (*Spermophilopsis leptodactylus*) are furry, which insulates them as they scurry over hot sand; in addition, fringes of stiff hairs on the outside of the hind feet serve to push away sand during burrowing.

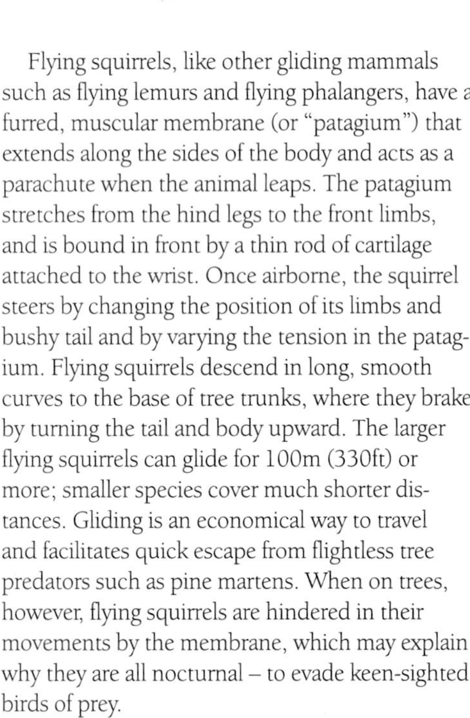

Flying squirrels, like other gliding mammals such as flying lemurs and flying phalangers, have a furred, muscular membrane (or "patagium") that extends along the sides of the body and acts as a parachute when the animal leaps. The patagium stretches from the hind legs to the front limbs, and is bound in front by a thin rod of cartilage attached to the wrist. Once airborne, the squirrel steers by changing the position of its limbs and bushy tail and by varying the tension in the patagium. Flying squirrels descend in long, smooth curves to the base of tree trunks, where they brake by turning the tail and body upward. The larger flying squirrels can glide for 100m (330ft) or more; smaller species cover much shorter distances. Gliding is an economical way to travel and facilitates quick escape from flightless tree predators such as pine martens. When on trees, however, flying squirrels are hindered in their movements by the membrane, which may explain why they are all nocturnal – to evade keen-sighted birds of prey.

The Winter Larder

DIET

Squirrels are primarily vegetarians. Tree squirrels favor nuts and seeds, but will also eat leafy greenery. Gray squirrels in the United Kingdom and the Malabar giant squirrels (*Ratufa indica*) of Indian rain forests will also debark branches and feed on the underlying growing tissue; Horsetail squirrels in Malayan rain forests specialize on bark and sap from the boles of trees. In addition, insects are an important dietary component for some species. Gray and Red squirrels in broadleaf woodlands feed on caterpillars in the spring and early summer when other nutritious foods are scarce. Several tropical squirrels only eat insects; indeed, the Long-nosed squirrel (*Rhinosciurus laticaudatus*) has incisors modified into forceps-like vices perfect for grabbing such small prey. Most tree and flying squirrels will also eat birds' eggs and nestlings.

Ground-dwelling squirrels are similarly omnivorous. Although they feed primarily on plant parts, they will in addition eat insects, birds' eggs, carrion, and, occasionally, each other's young. Typically, no one plant makes up more than 10 percent of a species' diet. Early in the growing season, ground squirrels seek out new grass shoots, which they pull up and eat blade by blade, starting at the base. As the season progresses, flowers and unfurling leaves of forbs are their mainstays. In late summer, species that hibernate concentrate on energy-rich bulbs and seeds of grasses and

Left *Representative species of squirrels:* ***1*** *Southern flying squirrel* (Glaucomys volans) *gliding from a nest hole in a tree trunk;* ***2*** *Prevost's squirrel* (Callosciurus prevostii)*;* ***3*** *African pygmy squirrel* (Myosciurus pumilio) *descending a tree head-first;* ***4*** *Abert or Tassel-eared squirrel* (Sciurus aberti)*;* ***5*** *American red squirrel* (Tamiasciurus hudsonicus) *hanging by its hind legs;* ***6*** *Indian giant or Malabar squirrel* (Ratufa indica)*;* ***7*** *Asiatic or Siberian chipmunk* (Tamias sibiricus) *with filled cheek pouches;* ***8*** *Alpine marmot* (Marmota marmota) *in vigilant upright posture giving alarm whistle;* ***9*** *Shrew-faced ground or Long-nosed squirrel* (Rhinosciurus laticaudatus) *foraging for termites;* ***10*** *Geoffroy's or Western ground squirrel* (Xerus erythropus) *with its tail arched and fluffed, an indication of anxiety.*

legumes, and on nuts. Sometimes foraging activities affect the local vegetational structure: prairie dogs bite off and discard tall plants around their burrows to enhance their field of view, and this constant cropping discourages all but the fastest-growing plants. Most squirrels get all the water they require from ingested plant materials; however, tree squirrels regularly visit sources of drinking water, especially during hot, dry summers.

Because of the seasonal nature of flowering and fruiting in temperate forests, the squirrels that live there depend on different foods at different times of year. Another way of ensuring a constant food supply is to cache seeds and nuts, which can be unearthed and eaten during the winter. From July, when the first fruits mature, until the following April, Gray and Red squirrels in broadleaf woodlands depend on fresh and buried nuts. A poor mast crop can have disastrous consequences in terms of high overwinter mortality (particularly of subadults), and may even prevent breeding the following spring. Adult Red squirrels that recover many cached pine cones and beechnuts are more likely to survive the next spring and summer than those that must rely only on buds, shoots, and flowers; and females are more likely to produce a spring litter if they feed heavily on cached seeds than if they feed mainly on other vegetation.

Tree squirrels within forests may act as foresters; by burying seeds and nuts safely in the soil they promote regeneration of the trees. Squirrels of all ages hoard nuts and seeds; even juveniles exhibit characteristic burying behaviors. As poaching of squirrels' larders is not uncommon, some scatter their stores widely to avoid theft by neighbors. Individual Red and Gray squirrels may bury hundreds of nuts in a season, some close to the tree that bore them but others as much as 30–60m (100–200ft) away. And, although individuals can smell nuts buried as deep as 30cm (12in) below the surface, many are never retrieved. Burying behavior and failed retrieval result, inadvertently, in tree-seed dispersal. There has been a long co-evolution of tree squirrels with many coniferous and mast-producing trees, such as pine, oak, and beech. This may seem odd, as squirrels' teeth can gnaw through hard shells and destroy the embryo of any nut they discover; but trees in fact benefit, by producing crops so abundant that many buried nuts are never recovered, enabling them to germinate.

Douglas squirrels (*Tamiasciurus douglasii*) and American red squirrels (*T. hudsonicus*) do not scatter-hoard. Instead they cut unopened pine and spruce cones off trees and cache them in a single larder, often located in a hollow stump or under a log. Larders may contain up to 4,000 cones in Jack pine forests, and as many as 18,000 in White spruce forests. The food contained in these so-called "middens" is essential for surviving the long winters in the boreal forest, so each squirrel defends a territory surrounding 1–3 middens. Males and females defend similar-sized territories: 0.4–0.5ha (about 1 acre) in spruce forests, and 0.6–0.7ha (1.5 acres) in Jack pine forests. Territories are defended year round: females rarely leave home, and males depart only for a few days in the spring when neighboring females are sexually receptive. The squirrels warn away potential rivals by screeching and rattling calls; if an intruder persists, they will resort to chases and physical combat. Territorial defense is most intensive close to the midden, where the stakes are highest, and most evident in the autumn, when new cones are ready to harvest and dispersing juveniles are attempting to establish territories of their own.

The area defended around "primary" middens varies in size between years. When cone crops are good, juvenile recruitment is high, because territories of adults shrink and there is plenty to eat. Young, transient animals can temporarily reside between territories centered on primary middens. When cone crops fail, however, juvenile recruitment drops due to starvation and lack of living space. Interestingly, female American red squirrels may in very good years leave their territory and its middens to one or two sons or daughters. Being

Above *A White-tailed prairie dog eating a flower. Prairie dogs live in colonies or "towns." Populations of these animals fell during the 20th century, mostly as a result of poisoning programs; indeed, some prairie dog species have been reduced by several hundred million.*

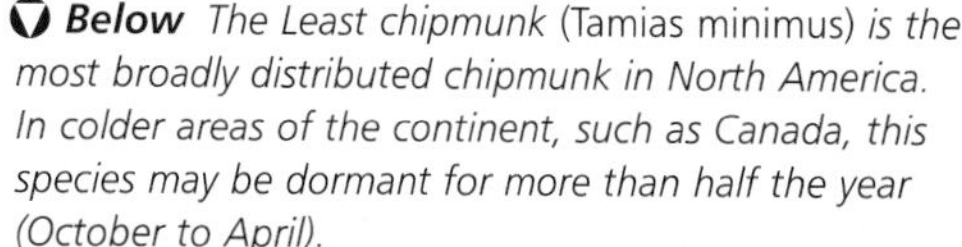

Below *The Least chipmunk* (Tamias minimus) *is the most broadly distributed chipmunk in North America. In colder areas of the continent, such as Canada, this species may be dormant for more than half the year (October to April).*

larger, older, and more experienced, the mother is more likely to compete successfully for a new territory than her young would be, so leaving her territory to her offspring increases their likelihood of survival and reproduction.

North American flying squirrels also hoard food and guard their larders throughout the year. These larders are hidden in tree cavities or underground, and are marked by sweat and sebaceous gland secretions. Larders of Southern flying squirrels (*Glaucomys volans*), primarily containing acorns, may be defended by a single individual or, in winter, by aggregations of up to 15 squirrels. Huddling together reduces daily energy expenditure by about 30 percent, and squirrels in a group are less likely to be taken by predators than an individual living on its own.

In coniferous forests, Northern flying squirrels (*G. sabrinus*) do not have access to acorns, so lichens and hypogeal (subterranean) fungi are the predominant winter food. Nests are constructed in tree cavities or attached to branches, and are composed almost entirely of certain special arboreal lichens that lack acids and other secondary compounds. The lichen-covered walls then serve not only as insulation but also as winter food caches. By spring, the squirrels have almost literally eaten themselves out of house and home!

Above *The Arizona gray squirrel is a tree squirrel found in forested areas of Arizona, New Mexico, and Mexico. Tree squirrels are not hibernators, but in very cold weather they will take to their nests, only leaving when it becomes necessary to find food. The diet is mainly nuts, seeds, fruit, young shoots, and buds.*

Photos and documentary film of tree squirrels curling up in their winter nests have led to the popular misconception that all squirrels hibernate. Tropical and desert-dwelling species may remain active all year round, and even holarctic tree squirrels stay alert, putting on limited fat reserves in the autumn and relying on the constant availability of high-energy nuts and seeds to get them through the winter. Their winter activity pattern represents a balance between short, frenetic feeding bouts (of about 3–4 hours per day) to meet their energy demands – about 400–700 kJ/24–42kcal per day for a Red squirrel weighing 300–350g (10–12oz) – and long resting periods in the nest.

Slightly flattened and spherical in shape, the drey is made of small branches, twigs, and grasses (or a tree cavity may be used), and is thickly lined with dry grass, moss, and fur. It is so well insulated that, in freezing conditions when the owner is inside, the internal temperature is about 20°C higher than the air temperature outside. During a squirrel's extended resting periods, its body temperature decreases from about 41°C to 39°C, which further reduces energy expenditure. Nonetheless, the animal cannot afford to spend more than two days inside its cozy drey without foraging outside, even in bad weather.

Ground-dwelling squirrels living in temperate and northern climates spend the winter in subterranean burrows. They prepare for this period of forced inactivity either by storing food in their dens or by accumulating fat on their bodies; some will undertake both activities. Food-storing species typically undergo long bouts of torpor that are interspersed with brief periods of activity. Siberian chipmunks (*Tamias sibiricus*) store seeds, acorns, buds, and mushrooms, each in a different burrow compartment. They can carry up to 9g (0.3oz) of grain in their cheek pouches for distances in excess of 1km (0.6mi), and an individual animal may store as much as 2.6kg (5.7lb) of winter food.

Most fat-storing ground squirrels and marmots spend the winter months in hibernation, sometimes in groups of close relatives. The last animal into the den (among Alpine marmots, *Marmota marmota*, this is usually an adult male) plugs the entrance hole with hay, earth, and rocks, for insulation and safety from predators.

Physiologically, hibernation is a state of suspended animation during which a squirrel's metabolism slows down to one-third of its normal rate, and its heartbeat, body temperature, and respiratory rate plummet. When the temperature outside is below freezing, a hibernating Alpine marmot's body temperature will drop to 4.5–7.5°C (40–45.5°F), and the animal may breathe only once or twice per minute. Every 2–4 weeks, hibernators awaken to defecate and urinate; by the time they emerge properly from hibernation in the spring, they will have lost more than half their pre-hibernation body weight. At that point they may feed on the bulbs and seeds that they stored away the previous fall. Such stores are essential when late spring storms keep the animals below ground.

Some ground-dwelling hibernators also become torpid during the summer (estivation) if the vegetation withers away due to heat and drought. In such circumstances it is much better to be safely out of sight doing nothing rather than busily scurrying around on the hot surface, especially when there is no food to be found there. When entering estivation, the animals conceal and insulate the mouth of their den with plugs of grass and sand.

Right *A Eurasian red squirrel* (Sciurus vulgaris) *– a species that occurs throughout Europe and northern Asia – drinking from a pond. Most species of squirrel get most of the water they require from their food; however, tree squirrels will visit watering spots quite frequently, especially during hot periods.*

Scaly-tailed Squirrels

The tropical and subtropical forests of the Old World are inhabited by an interesting array of gliding mammals. In tropical Africa this niche is filled by the scaly-tailed squirrels, members of the Anomaluridae family (7 species in 3 genera – see Appendix for full list), which apparently share only a distant evolutionary relationship with true squirrels.

With the exception of the Cameroon scaly-tail, which does not fly, the anomalures' most distinctive feature is a capelike membrane, stretched between their four limbs, that lets them glide from branch to branch in the depths of the African rain forest. The membrane is supported at the front by a rod of cartilage extending from the elbow or the wrist; at the rear it attaches to the ankles. Spread out in flight, it forms a rough square that permits the squirrels to soar over distances that can exceed 100m (330ft). Although this adaptation resembles the patagia of the flying squirrels and the Australian flying possums, these species too are evidently not closely related; instead, they have developed along convergent lines to fill similar ecological niches in different parts of the world.

The anomalures are squirrel-like in form, with a relatively thin, short-furred tail. They take their name from an area of rough, overlapping scales near its base. The scales help the squirrels get a purchase on trees when they land from a glide, and also provide grip for climbing trunks.

The ecology and behavior of scaly-tailed squirrels are poorly known, because they live in areas that are rarely visited by outsiders and are nocturnal in their habits. Even so, such species as the Lord Derby's Zenker's squirrels are relatively common, and do sometimes come into contact with humans.

The scant information available about anomalure reproduction indicates that females may have two litters of 1–3 young per year. At birth babies are large, well-furred, and active, and their eyes are open. Female pygmy scaly-tail squirrels apparently leave the colonies to bear their single young alone.

Except for Lord Derby's scaly-tailed flying squirrel, these interesting but poorly-known rodents depend entirely on primary tropical forest for their existence. To the extent that African primary forests are being destroyed, they are endangered, for they require for their survival a mature forest habitat with hollow trees in which they can nest. For want of more detailed information on their condition, the IUCN currently lists most species as Near Threatened. THF

Above *A White-tailed antelope squirrel on a Joshua tree. This species, which is found in Baja California and New Mexico, has stable dominance hierarchies. The breeding season for this species is from February to June.*

Below *Cape ground squirrels sunning themselves in the Kalahari Gemsbok Park. The species lives in social groups in burrows that may have anything up to 100 openings. Colonies average about 5–10 members, but can number as many as 25–30 individuals.*

Living in Clusters

SOCIAL BEHAVIOR

All squirrels raise young. Ground-dwelling hibernators reproduce very early in the spring, presumably to maximize the time their young have to grow and fatten before winter returns. Males typically emerge first and wait for the females, who mate soon after emergence. The exact timing of emergence and mating depends on the severity of the preceding winter, and it differs greatly between species, among populations of the same species at different altitudes and latitudes, and within the same population under different weather conditions. For example, Belding's ground squirrels (*Spermophilus beldingi*) living at 2,200m (7,200ft) emerge and mate 5–8 weeks before conspecifics living just 800m (2,600ft) higher and 15km (9mi) away; however, the timing of emergence at 3,000m (9,800ft) may itself vary by 5–6 weeks, depending on snow depth and spring weather.

Squirrels' mating systems are diverse. In some species, such as Belding's ground squirrels, males defend small mating territories which females visit when they are receptive. The males of other species such as Thirteen-lined ground squirrels (*S. tridecemlineatus*) search for widely scattered females, and wait in line to mate with them. At the opposite extreme, some marmots mate while still submerged in their winter burrows. Sometimes, as in the case of Idaho ground squirrels (*S. brunneus*), males guard females closely before and after mating. And, in most marmots, many ground squirrels, and Black-tailed prairie dogs, males vigorously defend territories surrounding the burrows of several females, who mate exclusively with the territory-holder.

In tree squirrels and chipmunks, receptive females attract males using chemical signals and vocalizations, then lead the males on long, spectacular mating chases that may last from 4 to 10 hours. Often numerous males simultaneously chase the same female (3–5 in Red squirrels, up to 10 in Gray squirrels, and 9–17 in Beautiful squirrels). By running away but remaining conspicuous (rather than hiding), receptive females force males to compete, enabling the females to compare their suitors' stamina and fighting abilities. In general, the dominant male stays closest to the female and accounts for 80–90 percent of copulations. After mating, he guards the female for up to an hour. In some species males also hinder further mating with physical barriers of coagulated sperm and seminal fluids. However, females occasionally solicit matings with males other than the alpha (up to 4 or more in Beautiful squirrels), and females often remove copulatory plugs to facilitate

Above *Idaho ground squirrels. The male is on guard against rivals and stays close to the female with whom he has just mated. Since females of this species are widely dispersed and locating them is a time-consuming activity, to ensure he fathers some young each season, the male adopts the strategy of keeping competitors away rather than looking for more females. The females are only sexually receptive for a few hours, just after they emerge from hibernation.*

remating, as in the case of Gray and Fox squirrels (*Sciurus niger*). Multiple mating may enable females to hedge their bets against the possibility of the dominant male being infertile. Ground squirrel females also mate with multiple males after removing copulatory plugs. Genetic analyses of Arctic (*S. parryii*), Belding's, and Thirteen-lined ground squirrel litters indicate that mixed paternity is frequent, though the first male to mate with a female (usually the dominant male) sires the majority of each litter.

The young are gestated for 3–6 weeks and then suckled for slightly longer again, especially in tree and flying squirrels. Litter sizes range from 1 in the Giant squirrel (*Ratufa macroura*) and Giant flying squirrel (*Petaurista elegans*) to 2 in beautiful squirrels, 2–5 in most tree squirrels and marmots, 4–6 in prairie dogs and chipmunks, and 5–11 in ground squirrels. In many species, middle-aged females in good condition produce larger litters and heavier pups than younger or older females and than females in poor condition. Across species, litter sizes vary inversely with female body size and degrees of sociality: bigger, more social species have smaller litters.

Young squirrels are born naked, toothless, and helpless, with skin over their eyes. They develop rapidly. Young Red squirrels begin to sprout hair at 10–13 days, and are fully furred by 3 weeks; lower incisors appear at 22 days, upper ones at 35 days; eyes open at 30 days; self-cleaning begins around 35 days. Juveniles take their first solid food and begin venturing from the nest at about 40 days. At 8–10 weeks juveniles are independent, although they remain near their mother

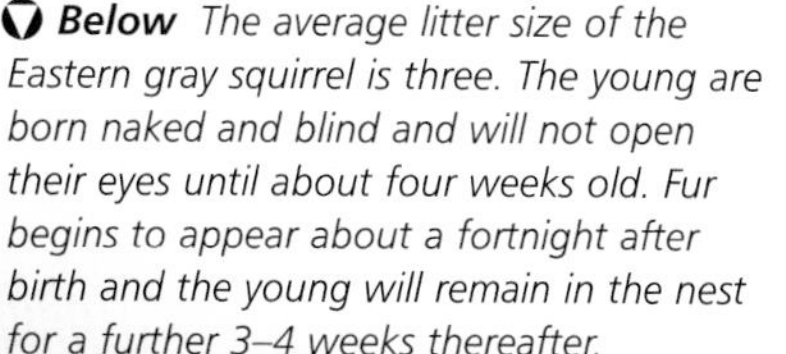

Below *The average litter size of the Eastern gray squirrel is three. The young are born naked and blind and will not open their eyes until about four weeks old. Fur begins to appear about a fortnight after birth and the young will remain in the nest for a further 3–4 weeks thereafter.*

and may still share her nest. The ontogeny of young flying squirrels is similar.

Interestingly, young ground-dwelling squirrels develop much more rapidly: chipmunk and ground squirrel pups are independent by 3–4 weeks, and marmot pups by 6 weeks. These differences probably relate to each species' ecology. So, for ground-dwellers it is dangerous to remain in the maternal nest too long because pups can be trapped by digging predators, whereas for young tree and flying squirrels it is risky to leave the nest too soon because climbing about in trees requires considerable balance and coordination.

In most tree squirrels, ground squirrels, and chipmunks, parental care is provided solely by the mother, but marmots, prairie dogs, and certain other ground squirrels live in family groups. The basic social unit is a cluster of female kin, with daughters spending their lives in the group they were born into (natal philopatry). Females display nepotism (kin-assisting behavior) by sharing and jointly defending territories, and giving warning calls when predators approach (see the Role of Kinship special feature page).

In some species, one or more males append themselves to these female clusters; they sire the next generation and, sometimes, help care for the young. Alpine marmots live in just such mixed-sex colonies, ranging in size from 2 or 3 to over 50 animals. One large colony may occupy an immense burrow system. Colony members scent-mark their territory with substances secreted from cheek glands, and chase unrelated intruders, accompanied by tooth gnashing and calling. While the young marmots play, other members of the family stand guard. Juveniles hibernate and live together in the parents' burrow for the summer or two after they are born. Black-tailed prairie dogs also live in mixed-sex family groups, and these too are aggregated into immense colonies. Each female has her own burrow, but families cooperate to defend their shared territory, to nurse hungry pups, and to warn each other of danger.

Among tree squirrels, social behavior often varies between populations of the same species according to seasonal and spatial variation in seed and nut crops. Among Red squirrels, when food availability is stable in time and space, site-fidelity is high and home-range size is small (about 2–4ha/5–10 acres in females and 6–8ha/15–20 acres in males). Females defend territories (especially the core area around the nest) against other females, and dominant individuals will not move unless a territory with greater food abundance becomes available nearby. Males do not defend territories, but neighboring males that share foraging areas differ in social status: heavy, old males dominate the rest. Both sexes exclude dispersing juveniles and subadults from territories, and these young become "floaters," searching over large areas for a vacant home range. In high-quality woodlands in central Europe, Red squirrel

Niche Separation in Tropical Tree Squirrels

For two or more species to live in the same habitat, their use of resources must be sufficiently different to avoid the competitive exclusion of one species by another. Such lifestyle differences as ground living or tree dwelling, daytime or nocturnal activity, and insectivory or frugivory are obvious types of ecological separation. Sometimes, however, squirrel species occurring naturally in the same habitat appear to utilize the same food resources. Do they actually occupy different niches?

This situation is illustrated by squirrels found in the lowland forests of West Malaysia. Of the 25 species found there, 11 are nocturnal and 14 diurnal. The latter can be divided into terrestrial, arboreal, and climbing categories, with different species making different use of the various forest strata. For example, the Three-striped ground squirrel and Long-nosed squirrel feed on the ground or around fallen trees, whereas the Slender squirrel is most active on tree trunks at lower forest levels. Plantain and Horse-tailed squirrels travel and feed mainly in the lower and middle forest levels, but nest in the upper canopy. The three largest species live highest in the canopy.

Malaysian squirrels show considerable divergence in food choices when food is abundant, but considerable overlap when it is scarce; then, all species rely heavily on bark and sap. Unlike African or temperate forest species of comparable size, none of the smaller species, except *Sundasciurus hippurus*, are seed specialists. The Three-striped ground squirrel feeds on plant and insect material, and the Long-nosed squirrel is an insectivore; diets of these species overlap with those of tree shrews more than with other arboreal squirrels. Horse-tailed squirrels feed mainly on bark and sap, and most beautiful squirrels feed opportunistically on a variety of plant materials and insects. The larger flying squirrels eat a higher proportion of leaves than the smaller species, which eat mainly fruit.

The three largest species of diurnal squirrels diverge less than the smaller species in the lower forest levels. All three are fruiteaters, but the Pale giant squirrel (*Ratufa affinis*) primarily uses the middle canopy levels and prefers leaves. The Black giant squirrel (*Ratufa bicolor*) and Prevost's squirrel (*Callosciurus prevostii*) are often seen feeding together at the same fruit trees, but the latter eats a smaller range of fruit, and the two species also have different foraging patterns. The giant squirrel is larger, giving it a competitive advantage, but it cannot move as far or as fast as the smaller Prevost's squirrel; the latter can afford to spend less time feeding each day and is able to travel farther to scattered food sources, consuming them before the giant squirrels arrive. KMacK

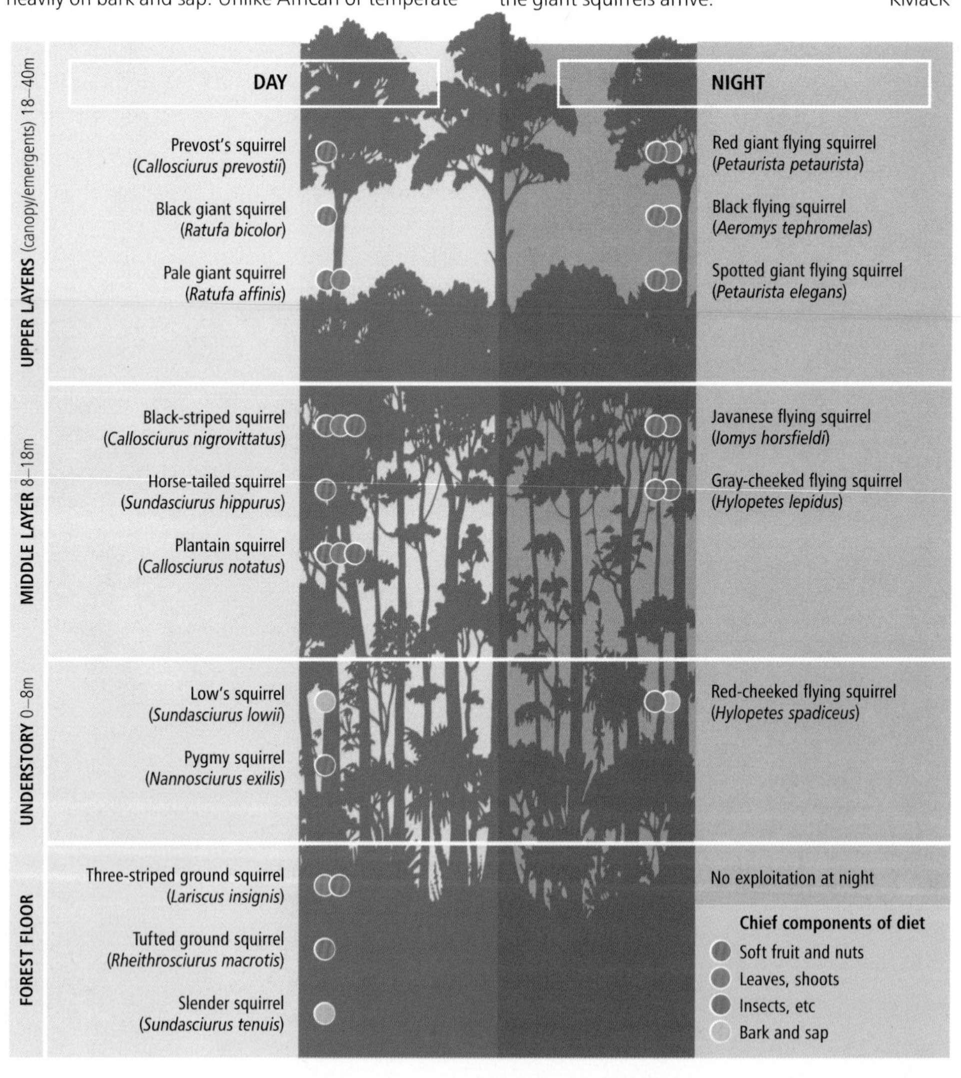

numbers vary little between years (numbering 0.7–2.2 squirrels per hectare, or 0.3–0.9 an acre). By contrast, in boreal coniferous forests in which pine and spruce seed abundance varies over time and between areas, both males and females frequently abandon territories when food becomes scarce. When the spruce cone crop fails, adult males disperse after mating, and adult females after they wean their litter. Since reproductive rates and adult and juvenile survival are directly related to the food supply, Red squirrel numbers within an area can vary between years by an order of magnitude of 0.03 –0.3 squirrels per hectare (0.01–0.1 squirrels an acre).

Gray squirrel populations also fluctuate annually in size, and density varies with habitat (e.g., 2–10 squirrels a hectare, or 1–4 per acre). These differences can be traced to variations in acorn and hickory-nut production, through their effects on the animals' reproductive rates, litter sizes, and, ultimately, survival. Population density is determined largely by the recruitment or otherwise of locally-born young, but interactions between resident squirrels and juveniles drive dispersal behavior. Adult males aggressively chase juveniles of both sexes (but especially males), whereas females allow daughters to remain on their home range. For females, living together with relatives leads to communal nesting and other forms of amicable behavior.

Squirrels, Predators, and Man

CONSERVATION AND ENVIRONMENT

Squirrels are prey for many carnivores, including badgers, weasels, foxes, coyotes, bobcats, and (feral) cats on the ground, and hawks, eagles, falcons, and owls from the air. Sometimes squirrel populations are decimated by infectious diseases, particularly bubonic plague and tularemia.

Yet the greatest threat to squirrel populations worldwide is undoubtedly human population expansion, and the associated habitat fragmentation and loss due to the growth of cities, changes of land use practices in rural areas (e.g., from rangeland to intensive agriculture), tree harvesting, fire suppression, and the introduction of non-native plants. Squirrels are hunted for pelts and meat and for sport, and both hunting and poisoning is still largely unregulated – if not actually encouraged – by governmental agencies that consider squirrels primarily as pests and carriers of disease. Little notice has been taken of the ecological and aesthetic losses associated with the dwindling size of many squirrel species, or of the benefits their activities bring. For example, the burrowing activities of ground-dwelling squirrels aerate the soil and bring nutrients to the surface, promoting plant growth, while the health of many forest ecosystems depends critically on tree squirrels' role as seed dispersers and controllers of insect outbreaks. PWS/LW

Above *The Northern striped palm squirrel is quite social and several may be observed in the same tree. Found in parts of Iran, India, Nepal, and Pakistan. Females can produce several litters per year.*

Below *In its woodland domain, the Malabar or Indian giant squirrel is very agile, rarely descending to the ground. However, along with all other species in the genus* Ratufa *, it is listed as Vulnerable, largely as a result of extensive recent habitat loss.*

SPECIAL FEATURE

THE ROLE OF KINSHIP

The annual round in Belding's ground squirrels

BELDING'S GROUND SQUIRRELS ARE SOCIAL rodents inhabiting grasslands in the cold deserts of the far western United States (California, Nevada, Oregon, and Idaho). They are active above ground most of the day, going to subterranean burrows for refuge from predators and inclement weather and to spend the night. Primarily vegetarians, they forage on forbs and grasses, and are particularly fond of flower heads and seeds; but they will also eat birds' eggs, carrion, and, occasionally, each other's young.

A population of Belding's ground squirrels at Tioga Pass, high in the central Sierra Nevada of California (3,040m/9,945ft), has been studied for more than two decades. The animals are active only from May to October, hibernating for the rest of the year. Adult males emerge first each spring, often tunneling through several meters of accumulated snow to do so. Once the snow melts the females emerge, and the annual cycle of social and reproductive behavior starts – a complex and intriguing mix of competition and cooperation.

Females mate about a week after emergence. Although they are only receptive for a single afternoon, they take full advantage of this opportunity, typically mating with at least three (and sometimes up to eight) different males. Genetic analyses have revealed that about two-thirds of litters are fathered by more than one male, so that pups develop *in utero* among full- and half-brothers and sisters. Although a female's first mate is the predominant sire of her offspring, some litters are sired by as many as four different males.

In order to mate successfully, males defend small, exclusive territories. In the presence of receptive females, they threaten, chase, and fight with each other. Virtually every male sustains physical injuries during the mating period, some of them serious. The heaviest and most experienced males usually win such conflicts, and receptive females remain near those males. Dominant males copulate with multiple females (up to 13 in a season), but more than half of all males mate only once or not at all in any given year.

After mating, each female digs her own nest burrow in which she will rear her young. Females produce only one litter per season. Gestation lasts about 24 days, lactation 27 days, and the mean litter size is five pups. Females shoulder the entire parental role; indeed, some males do not even interact with the young, because by the time weaned juveniles begin to emerge above ground in July, they have already gone back into hibernation. Adult females hibernate early in the fall; and finally, when it starts snowing, the year's young begin their first long, risky winter underground.

The hibernation period, lasting 7–8 months, is a time of heavy mortality in which two-thirds of the juveniles and one-third of the adults perish. Most die because they deplete their stores of body fat and freeze to death; others are eaten by digging predators such as badgers and coyotes. Males live 2–3 years on average, whereas females typically live 3–4 years; the males apparently die younger due to infection from wounds incurred during fights over females or from the increased exposure to predators resulting from their higher levels of mobility, leading to more rapid aging (senescence). The sexes also differ markedly in their respective tendencies to leave the area where

Above *Eager to explore a new world, Belding's ground squirrel pups emerge for the first time from the burrow in which they were born 27 days previously. As shown in the diagram, which charts the Tioga Pass squirrels' annual cycle, juveniles usually venture above ground in July or early August.*

Left *A female ground squirrel gathers grass to line a nest. Typically, burrows are 5–8m (16–26ft) long, 30–60cm (12–24in) below ground, and have multiple surface openings. It can take more than 50 loads of dry grass to line a single nest.*

Above *Keeping watch for the benefit of the kin community in which she lives, a female squirrel notices the approach of a predator. She gives a repeated alarm cry, even at the risk of drawing the intruder's attention to herself.*

they were born. Juvenile males begin dispersing soon after they are weaned and never return home, whereas females seldom disperse, staying close to the natal burrow and interacting with maternal kin throughout their lives.

The ground squirrels' matrilocal population structure has set the stage for the evolution of nepotism (the giving of favors to family members) among females. This manifests itself in four main ways. First, close relatives (mothers and offspring and sisters) seldom attack or fight each other when establishing nests; females with living kin thus obtain residences with less expenditure of time and energy, and lower danger of injury, than those without kin. Second, close relatives share portions of their nesting territory and permit each other access to food and hiding places on these defended areas. Third, close kin help each other to evict distantly related and unrelated squirrels from each other's territories. Fourth, females give warning cries when predatory mammals approach.

At the sight of a badger, coyote, or weasel, some females stand erect and utter staccato alarm trills. A greater proportion of callers than non-callers are attacked and killed, so giving such calls is dangerous. However, not all individuals take the same risks. The most frequent callers are old, lactating, resident females with living offspring or sisters nearby, whereas males and immigrant females with no relatives in the area call infrequently. Callers thus apparently behave altruistically – as if they were trading the risks of exposure to predators for the safety and survival of dependent kin.

The squirrels also vocalize when predatory hawks swoop at them, but these calls sound quite different: they are high-pitched whistles, each containing only a single note. Interestingly, these calls also apparently have a different function. Upon hearing a whistle, all the other squirrels scamper for cover, and their rapid flight inadvertently benefits the caller, both by creating pandemonium, which can confuse the predator's focus, and a scurrying group, in which there is numerical safety. So where the staccato alarm trill promotes the survival of offspring and other relatives, the single-note whistle call promotes self-preservation. The implication is that Belding's ground squirrels have different sounds for different degrees of danger.

Another important manifestation of nepotism is cooperative territory defense by related females. During gestation and lactation, such females will exclude others from the area surrounding their nest burrow. Territoriality functions to protect the helpless pups from predation by other squirrels, for when territories are left unattended, even briefly, unrelated females or yearling males sometimes attempt to kill the young.

In the males' case, infanticide is motivated by hunger, since they typically eat their victims. Females seldom do so; in their case, the killing is triggered by the loss of their own litters to predators. After such a loss, they often leave the burrow that proved unsafe and move to a more secure site – and if there are young already present there, they will try to kill them, thereby reducing future competition for themselves and their daughters.

Females with close relatives as neighbors lose fewer offspring in this way than do females without neighboring kin, because groups detect marauders more quickly and expel them more rapidly; also, pups are defended by their mother's relatives even when she is temporarily away from home foraging. In sum, living in extended families is a strategy for survival and reproduction among female Belding's ground squirrels. PWS

THE ROOTS OF MARMOT SOCIALITY

The advantages of living in extended family groups

MARMOT SOCIALITY BEGINS WITH HIBERNATION. All 14 species of marmots live in the northern hemisphere, mainly in mountainous areas where food is unavailable during the winter. When the weather is fine, they lay down fat to keep them alive during a hibernation that may last 9 months. Some species, including the Black-capped, Long-tailed, and Steppe marmots, live in environments so harsh that they mate, initiate gestation, and even give birth before emerging above ground.

When active, marmots use energy at a rate 8–15 times greater than during hibernation. To meet this heavy energy demand, they store copious amounts of body fat – comprising about 30 percent of body mass in the case of *Marmota bobak*, rising to 53 percent in *M. olympus*. Larger animals can store more fat and, relative to smaller animals, burn it more slowly. Marmots are the largest true hibernators, and the average adult body mass at the time of immergence ranges from 3.4kg (7.5lb) for *M. flaviventris*, the smallest species, to 7.1kg (15.7lb) for *M. olympus*, the largest. Even with the advantage of large body size, the demands on energy for reproduction, growth, activity, and hibernation are so great that individual females of at least 10 species, including *M. camtschatica*, *M. caudata*, and *M. menzbieri*, cannot accumulate sufficient resources for annual reproduction, which they skip, sometimes for two or more years.

To reach full size, marmots need to grow for a long time. Only one species, the woodchuck (*M. monax*), has an active season sufficiently long (at 5 months or more) to allow youngsters to mature and reproduce when 1 year old. Young woodchucks disperse and hibernate singly. The woodchuck is the only non-social species of marmot. Adult female woodchucks live alone, and males defend a home range that includes one or more females. Widespread forest–meadow-edge habitat enables the young to establish independence.

Marmots of most species live with their parents until they are 2 years old. The Yellow-bellied marmot (*M. flaviventris*) requires one additional year. While male Yellow-bellies disappear from the natal area to make their own way in the world, half of the females remain. Thus mother–daughter–sister assemblages of up to five are formed into matrilines. One male will enter an area containing more than one matriline and defend it.

Male Olympic (*M. olympus*) and Hoary (*M. caligata*) marmots typically live with two females and their young. The females look after the young until they are 2 years old, and do not produce another litter during this time. Adolescent young disperse at age 2 and breed one year later. All members of the group hibernate together in a burrow.

The social lives of other marmot species involve living in extended family groups in which a dominant pair shares the home range with young of various ages that may stay at home beyond the age when they could be reproducing for themselves. This apparently paradoxical behavior would be explicable if the youngsters stood a chance of inheriting the parents' territory. In fact, however, if a member of the dominant pair were to die and a son or daughter inherited the territory, the new owner could end up mating with its own mother or father. To avoid this inbreeding, which could lead to physical inadequacies in the young, yearling Yellow-bellied marmot males always disperse away from home, while half of the yearling females remain. The young females do not normally end up mating with their father, as he does not usually hold ownership of the territory long enough – for only 2.2 years on average. A female is in her third year of residency before she can breed, and her breeding career lasts an additional 2.95 years. Only about 17 percent of the males reach an age that makes reproduction likely. Male mortality is higher than that of females; at age 2, when many males are still in the dispersal stage, about 50 percent die, as opposed to only about 30 percent of the two-year-old females. Some level of inbreeding does occur in family groups, but there is no evidence of deleterious effects. In addition, relatedness, and hence inbreeding, is reduced when a male or female from some other family replaces the territorial dominant.

For Yellow-bellied marmots, family living seems to bring all kinds of benefits. Animals in larger groups survive better and have more offspring. Group defense of resources ensures that they never go hungry, while the many extra pairs of eyes increase the chances of spotting a predator before it gets within striking distance. The rate of survival increases from about 0.6 for a single female to about 0.8 in groups of three or more. Net reproductive rate increases from 0.5 for a single female to 1.15 in groups of three.

Setting out to find a new home as a young marmot is a treacherous business, and waiting until 2 years or older increases the chances of success. Survival rates are significantly greater in *M. caudata* and *M. vancouverensis*, which disperse at age 3 or older, than in *M. flaviventris*, which disperses at 1 year old. However, staying at home with their parents results in reproductive suppression. In Gray marmots (*M. baibacina*), most breeding is carried out by older females, and young females only get an opportunity when the population has been reduced. Reproductive suppression may be so pervasive that even when a dominant female Alpine

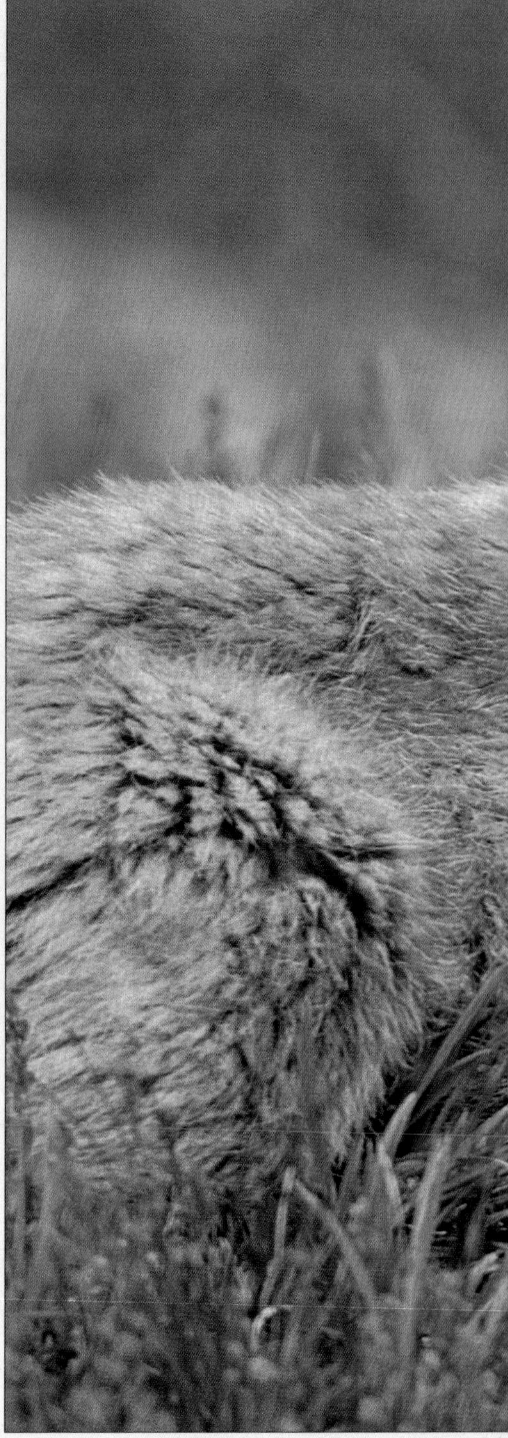

Above *A juvenile Olympic marmot approaches an adult marmot in grassland, Olympic National Park, Washington. Olympic marmots, the largest marmot species, are very tolerant and sociable and such face-to-face encounters are very common. The dispersal of young is a relatively slow process and appears to be determined by the young themselves rather than as a result of adult aggression driving them out.*

marmot does not produce any young, as in the case of *M. marmota*, the subordinate females will still fail to reproduce.

Any animal that spends its entire life caring for others without having offspring of its own will die without passing its genes on to the next generation, and the genes responsible for causing such caring behavior will die with the childless carer. Thus such indiscriminate "caring genes" cannot evolve. Relatives, however, share genes, so those that cause individual animals to care for close kin and thus increase their likelihood of successfully rearing more young with more of those "relative-caring" genes can flourish. In biology, this principle is known as "kin selection." Individuals can afford to adopt an altruistic attitude toward family members because they share sufficient genes for their efforts not to be wasted. This is especially the case if having a family of one's own involves potentially dangerous activities, such as searching for a new home alone.

One reason why young marmots stay at home may be to help raise their siblings. Alpine marmots cuddle up to the young, preventing heat loss that would otherwise burn up fat reserves and hence cause weight loss, which in turn would reduce their chances of survival. When subordinate full siblings are present, juvenile mortality is about 5 percent, but this figure increases to about 22 percent when they are not present.

Even so, the benefits of kin selection hardly compensate fully for failing to produce young of one's own. A further reason why marmots stay at home when they could be establishing their own territories may be that there is simply nowhere for them to go. Habitats may become saturated, so that there are no territories available for a young family. In such circumstances they will stay at home, gaining experience by helping to raise their siblings and waiting for an opportunity to finally strike out on their own, richer in experience and still alive thanks to their parents' tolerance. KBA

Springhare

SCATTERED THROUGH THE ARID LANDS OF East and South Africa are numerous flood plains and fossil lake beds. After the rainy season grass is superabundant here, but for much of the year it is too short and sparse for large grazers to forage efficiently. The result is an unused food supply or, to use the ecological term, an empty niche. To fill it requires an animal small enough to use the grass efficiently, yet large and mobile enough to travel to it from areas that can provide shelter from the weather and from predators. These are attributes of the springhare.

In spite of its adaptiveness, the springhare still faces formidable problems. In terms of its size it is small enough to be killed by snakes, owls, and mongooses, and yet big enough to be attractive to large predators, including lions, wild dogs, and man. Many of the animal's specialized physical and behavioral features are adaptations, not just for an arid environment, but also for the efficient avoidance of predators.

Squirrel, Hare, or Kangaroo?

FORM AND FUNCTION

There is little evidence of the springhare's origins. Some people believe that its closest living relatives are the scaly-tailed flying squirrels of the genus *Anomalurus*. The springhare, except for the bushy tail, actually resembles a miniature kangaroo; its hind legs are very long, and each foot pad has four toes, each equipped with a hoof-like nail. Its most frequent and rapid type of movement is hopping on both feet. Its tail – slightly longer than its body – helps to maintain balance while hopping. The tail has a thick brush at the end that is of a darker coloration. The front legs, which are only about a quarter of the length of the hind legs, have long, sharp claws that are curved for use in digging burrows. The head is rabbit-like, with large ears and eyes and a protruding nose; sight, hearing, and smell are well-developed. When pursued by a predator, a springhare can leap 3–4m (10–13ft). If captured, it will try to bite the predator with its large incisors and to rake it with the sharp nails of its hind feet.

Though springhares are herbivorous, they occasionally eat mineral-rich soils and accidentally ingest insects, such as locusts and beetles. They are very selective grazers, preferring green grasses high in protein and water. However, they also eat bulbs and roots. If necessary, a springhare can go for at least 7 days without drinking by reducing food intake and producing concentrated urine and very dry feces.

Keeping Out of the Way of Predators

SOCIAL BEHAVIOR

Springhares are nocturnal; shunning the midday sun means they avoid losing water in the arid regions they inhabit. Normally they forage within a maximum of 250m (820ft) of their burrows but occasionally they have been observed to travel much farther away. While foraging, they are highly vulnerable to predators because they are completely exposed to detection. On nights with a full moon they appear to be particularly at risk, and venture only an average of 4m (13ft) to the feeding area; in contrast, on moonless nights they travel some 58m (190ft). When they are above ground springhares spend about 40 percent of their time in groups of 2–6 animals, presumably because a group is more efficient at detecting danger.

Springhares spend the hours of daylight in burrows located in well-drained, sandy soils. Burrows lie about 80cm (31in) deep, have 2–11 entrances, and vary in length from 10–46m (33–151ft). Each burrow is occupied either by a single springhare or by a mother and an infant. Burrows provide considerable protection against the arid environment and also against predators. Some predators, such as snakes and mongooses, can enter burrows, however, so springhares often block entrances and passageways with soil after entering. When predators do enter, the tunnels and openings in the burrow system provide many escape routes. The absence of chambers and nests within the burrow suggests that springhares do not rest consistently in any one location – probably another precaution against predators.

In springhare populations the number of males equals the number of females. There is no breeding season, and about 76 percent of the adult females may be pregnant at any one time. Adult females undergo about three pregnancies per year, usually resulting in the birth of a single, large, well-developed infant; twins are born, but this is a rare occurrence.

Newborn springhares are well furred and are able to see and move about almost immediately. However, they are confined to the burrow and are totally dependent on milk until they are half-grown, at which time they can become completely active above ground. Immature springhares

usually account for about 28 percent of all the individuals that are active above ground.

Although the reproductive rate of springhares is surprisingly low, there are two distinctive advantages to the animals' reproductive strategy. First, the time and energy available to the female for reproduction is funneled into a single infant, resulting apparently in low infant and juvenile mortality. When the juvenile springhare first emerges from its burrow, its feet are 97 percent, and its ears 93 percent, of their adult size: it is almost as capable of coping with predators and other environmental hazards as a fully-grown adult. Second, in having to provide care and nutrition for only one infant, the mother is subject to minimal strain.

A Tale of Declining Numbers

CONSERVATION AND ENVIRONMENT

Springhares are generally common where they occur, despite the fact that they are frequently hunted by man. In the best habitats there may be more than 10 springhares per hectare (4 per acre), and this can include areas where domestic stock have grazed the forage to a suitable height. However, when arid, ecologically sensitive areas are overgrazed by domestic stock, as occurs in the Kalahari Desert, springhare densities are lower.

Springhares are of considerable importance to man as a source of food and skins. In Botswana they are the most prominent wild animal in the human diet, and a single band of bushmen may kill more than 200 annually. They can be a significant pest to agriculture, feeding on a wide variety of crops including corn, sweet potatoes, and wheat. Partly as a result, there has been an upsurge in hunting activity that, together with habitat loss, is reckoned to have reduced springhare numbers by at least 20 percent in the 1990s alone. The animals are now classed as Vulnerable by the IUCN. TMB

FACTFILE

SPRINGHARE

Pedetes capensis

Springhare or springhass

Order: Rodentia

Family: Pedetidae (sole member of family)

DISTRIBUTION Kenya, Tanzania, Angola, Zimbabwe, Botswana, Namibia, South Africa.

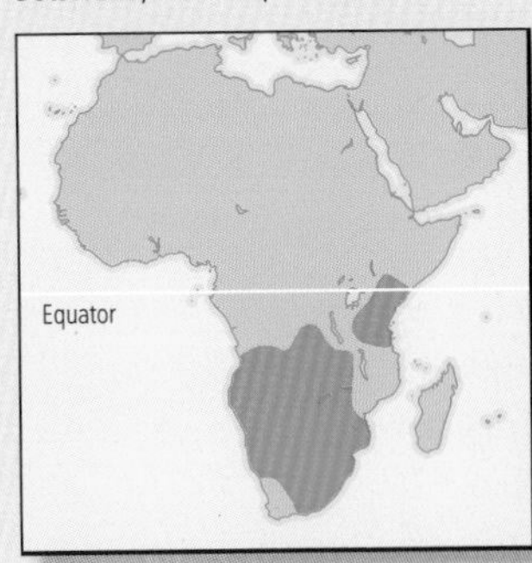

HABITAT Flood plains, fossil lake beds, savanna, other sparsely vegetated arid and semi-arid habitats on or near sandy soils.

SIZE Head-body length 36–43cm (14–17in); tail length 40–48cm (16–19in); ear length 7cm (3in); hind foot length 115cm (6in); weight 3–4kg (6–9lb). (Dimensions are similar for both female and male.)

COAT Upper parts, lower half of ears, basal half of tail yellow-brown, cinnamon, or rufous brown; upper half of ears, distal half of tail, and whiskers black; underparts and insides of legs vary from white to light orange.

DIET Herbivorous, with a preference for protein-rich green grasses.

BREEDING Gestation about 77 days.

LONGEVITY Unknown in wild; more than 14 years in captivity.

CONSERVATION STATUS Vulnerable

Above *With its short front paws and hopping motion, the springhare resembles a miniature kangaroo. It is a vital resource for the indigenous Bushmen of southwest Africa, who eat its meat, make its skin into garments, use its long tail sinew as thread, and even smoke its fecal pellets.*

Left *Some typical postures of the springhare:* ***1*** *sitting down to groom;* ***2*** *hopping – when the springhare is in motion, it holds its tail (thought to be an aid to balance) either horizontally or curled up;* ***3*** *foraging on all fours;* ***4*** *standing on its hind legs.*

DISTRIBUTION Worldwide except for Antarctica.

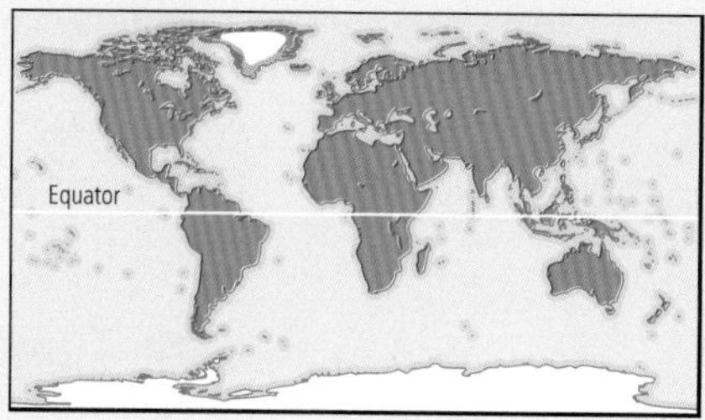

SCIUROGNATHS (part only) Suborder Sciurognathi
1,477 species in 312 genera and 5 families

Mouse-like Rodents

MORE THAN A QUARTER OF ALL SPECIES OF mammals can loosely be described as mouse-like rodents. Although today they join the squirrels in the suborder Sciurognathi, they once occupied their own order, the Myomorpha. They are very diverse – so much so that they are difficult to describe in terms of a typical member. However, the Brown rat and House mouse are fairly representative, both in size and overall appearance. The great majority are small, terrestrial, prolific, nocturnal seedeaters. The justification for believing them to comprise a natural group derived from a single ancestor is debatable but lies mainly in two features: the structure of the chewing muscles of the jaw and the structure of the molar teeth.

Most mouse-like rodent species belong to the mouse family. The minority groups are the dormice, the jerboas and jumping mice,the pocket mice, and the pocket gophers. These represent early offshoots that have remained limited in species numbers and also somewhat specialized, the dormice being arboreal and (in temperate regions) hibernating, the jerboas adapted for the desert. The murids have undergone more recent and much more extensive changes (adaptive radiation) beginning in the Miocene epoch, i.e. within the last 24 million years. Some of the resultant groups are specialists, for example the voles and lemmings, which are adapted to feeding on grass and other tough but abundant vegetation. Yet many species have remained versatile generalists, feeding on seeds, buds, and sometimes insects, all more nutritious but less abundant than grass.

In ecological terms, most mouse-like rodents may be classified as "r-strategists," that is, they are adapted for early and prolific reproduction rather than for long individual life spans ("k-strategists"). Although this applies in some degree to most rodents, the rats and mice show it more strongly and generally than, for example, their nearest relatives, the dormice and the jerboas. GBC

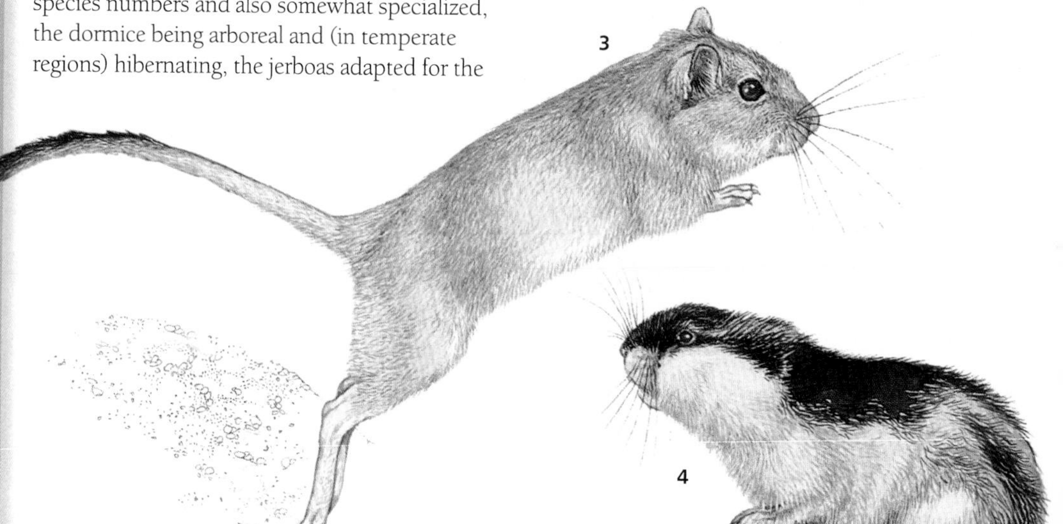

3

4

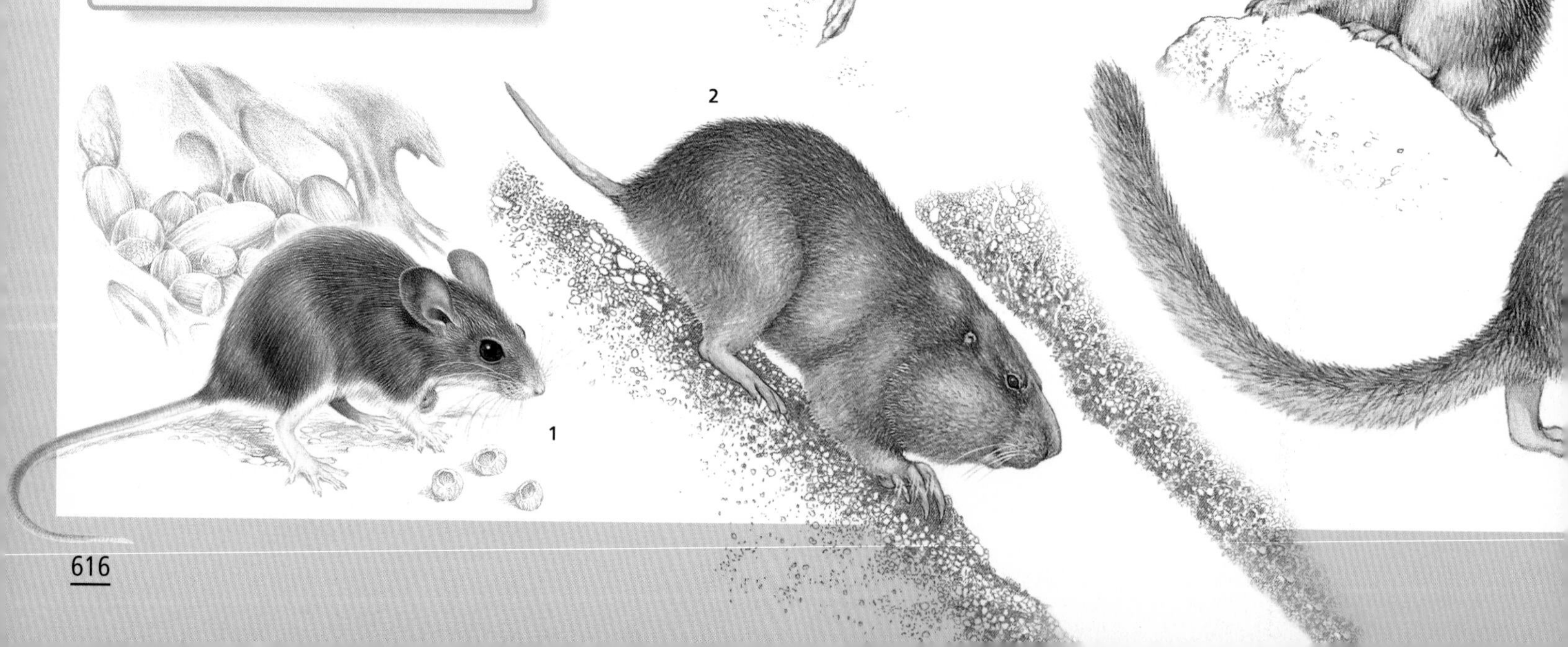

2

1

GREAT PROLIFERATORS

The greatest diversification of species in the entire evolution of mammals has occurred in the mouse family, which has over 1,000 living species. Its members are found around the world in almost every terrestrial habitat. Those that most closely resemble the common ancestor of the group are probably the common mice and rats found in forest habitats world-wide. These are versatile animals, predominantly seedeaters but capable of using their seedeating teeth to exploit many other foods, such as buds and insects.

From such an ancestor many more specialized groups have arisen, capable of exploiting more difficult habitats. Most gerbils (subfamily Gerbillinae) have remained seedeaters but have adapted to hot arid conditions in Africa and Central Asia. The hamsters (subfamily Cricetinae) have adapted to colder arid conditions by perfecting the arts of food storage and hibernation; the voles and lemmings (subfamily Arvicolinae) and the superficially similar African swamp rats (subfamily Murinae) have cracked the problem of feeding on tough herbage, opening up fresh possibilities for expansion.

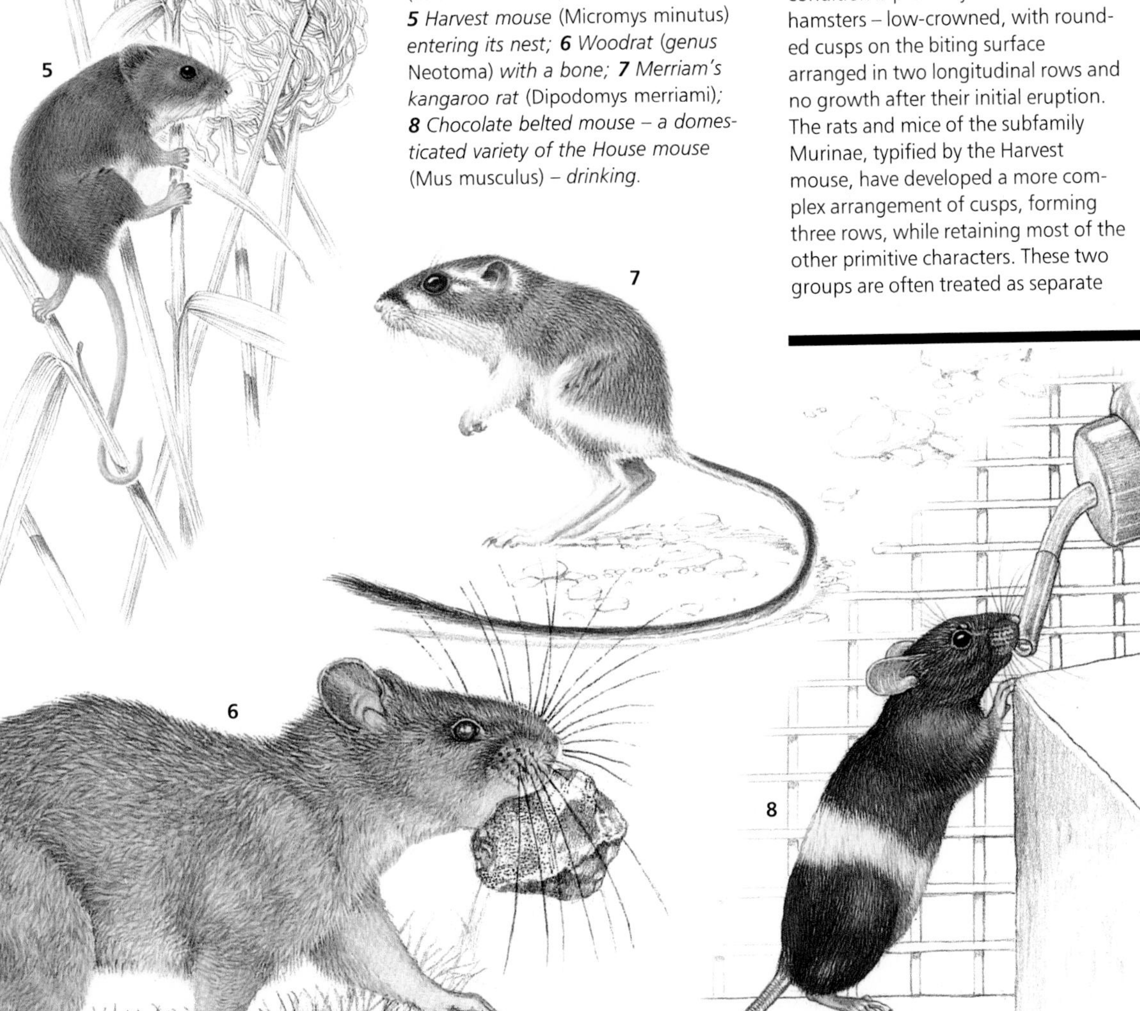

Below *Representative species of mouse-like rodents (not to scale):* **1** *Wood mouse* (Apodemus sylvaticus) *with a store of nuts;* **2** *Plains pocket gopher* (Geomys bursarius) *descending its burrow;* **3** *Libyan jird* (Meriones libycus) *leaping;* **4** *Norway lemming* (Lemmus lemmus) *on the lookout;* **5** *Harvest mouse* (Micromys minutus) *entering its nest;* **6** *Woodrat* (genus Neotoma) *with a bone;* **7** *Merriam's kangaroo rat* (Dipodomys merriami)*;* **8** *Chocolate belted mouse – a domesticated variety of the House mouse* (Mus musculus) *– drinking.*

SKULLS AND DENTITION

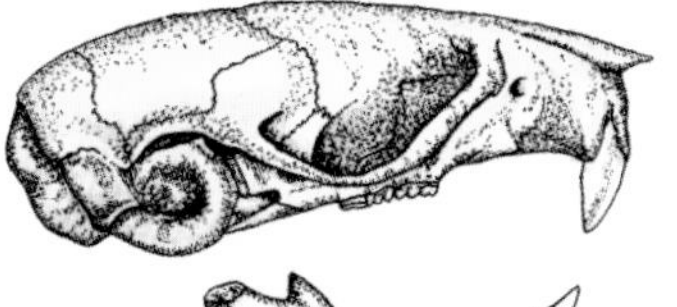

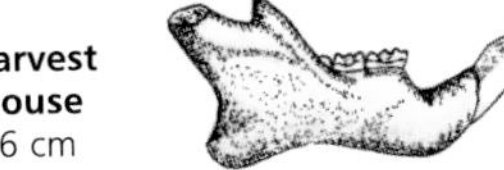

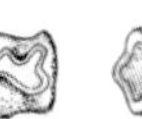

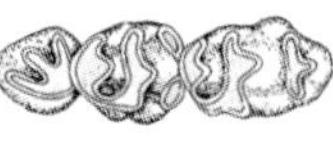

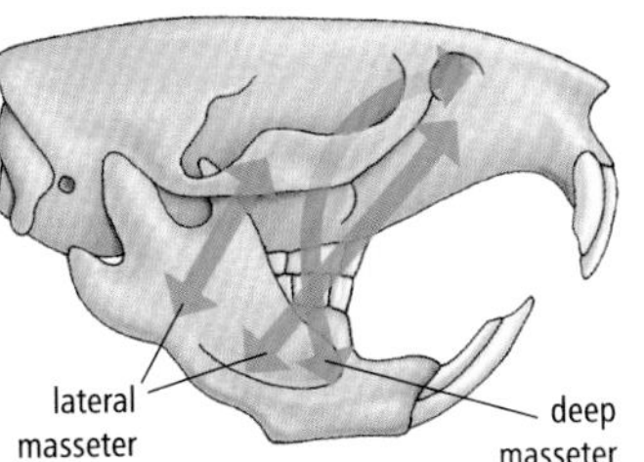

Most mouse-like rodents have only three cheekteeth in each row, but they vary greatly in both their capacity for growth and the complexity of the wearing surfaces. The most primitive condition is probably that found in the hamsters – low-crowned, with rounded cusps on the biting surface arranged in two longitudinal rows and no growth after their initial eruption. The rats and mice of the subfamily Murinae, typified by the Harvest mouse, have developed a more complex arrangement of cusps, forming three rows, while retaining most of the other primitive characters. These two groups are often treated as separate families, the Cricetidae (so-called cricetine rodents) and Muridae (so-called murine rodents) respectively.

The gerbils have high-crowned but mostly rooted teeth, in which the original pattern of cusps is soon transformed by wear into a series of transverse ridges. The voles and lemmings take this adaptation to a tough, abrasive diet – in this case mainly grass-even further by having teeth with high crowns and complex shearing ridges of hard enamel that continue to grow and develop roots only late in life or, more commonly, not at all.

The other feature that principally distinguishes the mouse-like rodents from other rodent groups is the structure of the jaw muscles. In the mouse-like rodents, both the lateral (blue in the diagram LEFT) and deep (red) masseter muscles are thrust forward, providing a very effective gnawing action, with the deep masseter passing from the lower jaw through the orbit (eye socket) to the muzzle. Shown here is the skull of a muskrat.

RATS AND MICE AS PETS

Keeping mice as pets began in the Orient, probably first in China but also in Japan. Early records indicate that mouse breeding was flourishing in the 18th century; in 1787 a Japanese writer published a work on how to breed colored varieties, and domestication must have begun much earlier for such a pamphlet to have been produced. Sailors returning from the Far East probably took pet animals home with them, providing the stimulus for mouse breeding in the west.

Tame mice differ from wild ones in several respects. Apart from their docility, they are larger and have more prominent eyes, larger ears, and longer tails. All are bred to the same body conformation, implying that there are no breeds as such, only varieties.

Keeping rats as pets is a relatively recent activity. It probably began about 1850, possibly in England. The number of varieties is less than for mice, probably because of the shorter period of domesticity and smaller numbers.

New World Rats and Mice

THE INNOCENT PHRASE "NEW WORLD RATS and mice" hides a plethora of 434 species in 86 genera, found in habitats ranging from the northern forests of Canada to the Americas' southernmost tip. Their adaptations and habits are so diverse that an entire volume could scarcely do them justice.

FACTFILE

NEW WORLD RATS AND MICE

Order: Rodentia

Family: Muridae

Subfamily: Sigmodontinae (Hesperomyinae)

434 species in 86 genera and 15 tribes, combined into 6 groups

HABITAT All terrestrial habitats (including northern forests, tropical forest, and savanna) excluding permanently snow-covered mountain peaks and extreme high Arctic.

SIZE **Head–body length** ranges from 5–8.1cm (2–3.2in) in the Pygmy mouse to 16–28.7cm (6.3–11.3in) in the South American giant water rat; **tail length** from 3.5–5.5cm (1.4–2.2in) to 7.6–16cm (3–6.3in), and **weight** from 7g (0.25oz) to 700g (1.5lb), both in the same two species.

COAT Most New World rat and mouse species have a brown back and white belly, but some exhibit very attractive coat colors; the Chinchilla mouse, for instance, has a strongly contrasting combination of buff-to-gray back and white belly. The color of the back often matches the surrounding soil to provide camouflage against owls and other airborne predators.

DISTRIBUTION N and S America and adjacent offshore islands

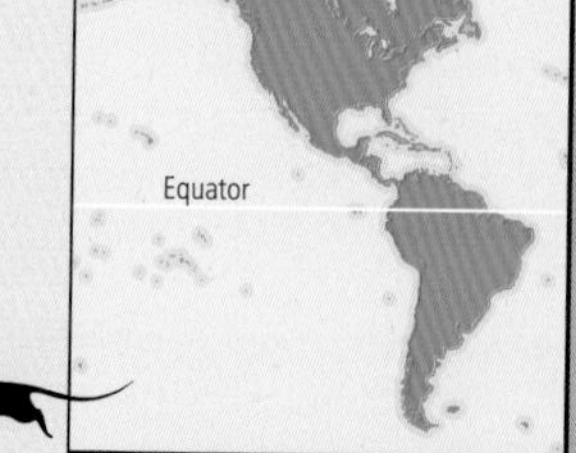

DIET Mostly plant material and invertebrates, though some take small vertebrates including fish.

BREEDING Gestation 20–50 days

LONGEVITY Maximum 2 years in the wild; some species live up to 6 years in captivity.

CONSERVATION STATUS 8 species are currently listed as Critically Endangered, and a further 24 as Endangered, including 6 species of woodrats (genus *Neotoma*) and 4 of the 5 species of fish-eating rats (*Neusticomys*).

See tribes table ▷

New World rats and mice are uniformly small: in head–body length, even the largest living species measure less than 30cm (c.12in). The length depends on how much tree-climbing their lifestyle demands; the greater the need to balance in high places, the longer the tail. Tails are usually almost hairless but, as is to be expected in such a large and diverse group, some species such as the aptly named Bushy-tailed woodrat buck the trend. There are, however, very few exceptions to the basic arrangement of teeth common to all highly-evolved rodents, with three molars on each side of the jaw separated by a distinct gap from a pair of incisors, which grow continuously and have enamel on their anterior surfaces, enabling a sharp cutting edge to be maintained.

Natural selection has shaped the New World rats and mice to a multitude of forms for different habitats. Burrowing species have short necks, short ears, short tails, and long claws, while those living in water, such as the marsh rats, often have webbed feet or, like the fish-eaters, a fringe of hair on the hind feet that increases the surface area to form a paddle. In forms even more developed for aquatic life, the external ear is reduced in size or even absent, as is the case with the Ecuadorian fish-eating rat (*Anotomys leander*).

Above the generic level, the classification of New World rats and mice is controversial. The genera can be grouped into 15 tribes, and these in turn can be thought of as belonging to six groups (see table), though these groupings are of varying validity; currently only one of the tribes has been shown convincingly to be monophyletic.

*▽ **Below** Restricted to salt marshes in the San Francisco Bay area of California, the Salt-marsh harvest mouse is among the rarer New World rodents; it was officially declared endangered by the US government in 1970. As an adaptation to its salty habitat, it has become one of the few mammals able to drink sea water.*

North American Rats and Mice

NEOTOMINE–PEROMYSCINE GROUP

The **white-footed mice and their allies** (tribe *Peromyscini*) are among the most extensively studied murides. In particular, the White-footed mouse itself (*Peromyscus leucopus*) has been used as a model to investigate how males and females compete with members of their own sex to maximize individual reproductive opportunities.

The mating systems of White-footed mice range from polygyny to promiscuity. Males typically occupy home ranges of approximately 500–1,000sq m (600–1,200 sq yds), about twice the size of those occupied by females. During the breeding season, a male may spend most of his time with one primary female, but his home range often overlaps that of two or three others. Males with larger home ranges have access to more potential mates, thereby increasing mating opportunities. Males that mate with the most females pass on the most genes, so males benefit by moving over large areas. At low densities, a male may develop a wandering strategy; he may associate with one primary female until she is pregnant, then wander off to reside with neighboring, or secondary, females while they are in estrus, before returning eventually to his primary female.

Females usually mate with one male, but may mate promiscuously with several, such that a given litter may be sired by as many as three males; however, the actual number of males a

Above *Constantly on the look-out for potential threats, a Deer mouse* (Peromyscus *sp.) nurses her two-day-old young in her nest. Like most mouse species, Deer mice are prolific breeders: in the wild they average 3 or 4 litters of up to 9 young a year.*

female mates with could be more. Mating with several males may increase the genetic diversity of the offspring or help ensure fertility, but it also functions to confuse the question of paternity. One reproductive strategy adopted by male White-footed mice, as by many other species of mammals, is to kill offspring that they have not sired. Infanticide both removes the offspring of competitor males and provides a reproductive opportunity for the perpetrator. In White-footed mice, a female that loses her litter stops lactating and is ready to breed again within a few days, so by committing infanticide a male may be able to mate sooner than if the young were permitted to suckle until weaning.

Males do not recognize their own offspring, but they do associate copulation with a given place and time, and will not kill pups within the area where they mated. Hence, a female who confuses paternity by mating with neighboring males also reduces the chances that these males will commit infanticide. Multi-male mating appears to be a behavioral mechanism used by females as a counter-strategy to infanticide by males.

Female White-footed mice also commit infanticide, but as a mechanism to compete for breeding space. Dispersing females that do not have a territory of their own may attempt to kill the offspring of other females as a way of competing to take over their territories. At low densities when space is available for colonization, females space themselves out and are relatively non-aggressive, but when breeding space becomes limited, they aggressively defend their turf to insure the survival of their offspring. At high densities, females defend breeding territories of approximately 300–500sq m (400–600sq yds).

Females provide most of the parental care in White-footed mice, but males do make some contributions. Males often nest with litters, retrieve wandering youngsters, provide warmth for the pups, and deter infanticide by intruding males. Pups are nursed for a period of 21–24 days and are then ready to leave the nest. Leaving involves risks, but if all the offspring were to remain at the natal site, unsustainable competition would ensue for resources and for mates.

An even greater cost to not dispersing is

inbreeding, which is avoided in White-footed mice by sex-biased dispersal. At the time of weaning, young males will leave the natal site if their mothers are present in the territory, while young females depart if their fathers are present. In practice, mothers are almost always present, whereas fathers seldom are, so males disperse much more often than females. If for some reason offspring cannot disperse because all of the neighboring breeding sites are occupied, juveniles remain in their maternal site and form extended families for one to two generations. In these situations inbreeding is avoided by delaying the sexual maturation of older juveniles.

Sometimes mothers will share part of the natal site with their daughters. Mothers and daughters usually raise their young in separate nests, but at very high densities when breeding space is limited, the two will occasionally raise them in the same nest, nursing each others' offspring indiscriminately. In such circumstances the same male may well be the father of both litters, although other males may also have mated with either or both of the females.

During the winter non-breeding season, white-footed mice often aggregate, with 5–8 individuals nesting communally and thereby sharing body heat. In some cases, these communal groups are relatives from the last litters of the breeding season, but occasionally they are unrelated. Food is typically stored during these inclement times. During food shortages, White-footed mice commonly enter daily torpor to conserve energy. Torpor periods vary in length, but typically last less than 12 hours.

White-footed mice are at risk from a variety of aerial and terrestrial predators. Their nocturnal lifestyle protects them from some of these, and they further increase their chances by being less active during full moons and by trying to avoid running on dry fall leaves that crunch underfoot, choosing instead to move over logs or else to forage among branches or shrubs. When active on a noisy substrate such as dry leaves, White-footed mice adjust their gait by placing their hind feet in the path of their forefeet, thus halving the number of foot contacts with the ground. Unsurprisingly, they are most active on cloudy or rainy nights or when the ground is damp.

To have the option of selectively foraging or remaining inactive, the mice must have supplies of food readily on hand. Mice are seasonal hoarders and store non-perishable seeds for consumption in hot summer and cold winter periods. Acorns are a favorite crop that is harvested and stored in underground caches and hollow logs and trees. In fact, the abundance of the acorn crop determines to a large part survival rates and population size among White-footed mice. Following autumns of high mast production, which occur episodically once every 4–5 years, White-footed mice have high winter survival and may even breed all winter. Consequently, the following

Above *Representative species from six tribes of New World rats and mice:* ***1*** *South American climbing rat (genus* Rhipidomys*; tribe Thomasomyini).* ***2*** *Central American vesper rat (genus* Nyctomys*; tribe Nyctomyini).* ***3*** *Central American climbing rat (genus* Tylomys*; tribe Tylomyini).* ***4*** *pygmy mouse (genus* Baiomys*; tribe Baiomyini).* ***5*** *white-footed or deer mouse (genus* Peromyscus*; tribe Peromyscini).* ***6*** *woodrat or pack rat, carrying a bone (genus* Neotoma*; tribe Neotomini).*

Colonizing the Continents

Rats and mice originated in North America from the same kind of primitive rodents as the hamsters of Europe and Asia and the pouched rats of Africa, their nearest Old World relatives today. These ancestors, the so-called "cricetine" rodents, first appeared in the Old World in the Oligocene era about 34 million years ago, and were found in North America by the mid-Oligocene some 5 million years later. They were adapted to living among the treetops in forest environments, but as land dried during the succeeding Miocene era (24–5 million years ago) some became more ground-dwelling and developed into forms recognizable as those of modern New World rats and mice, the Sigmondontinae. In the course of their evolution they adapted to many habitats similar to those also occupied by Old World counterparts; for example, harvest mice of the genus *Reithrodontomys* reflect the Old World *Micromys*, while *Peromyscus* wood mice have counterparts in the Murinae genus *Apodemus*.

The rats and mice of South America developed in a similar way. A land bridge formed between North and South America during the Pliocene era 5–1.8 million years ago, and several stocks of primitive North American rodents moved across it. Equipped for climbing and forest life, they underwent an extensive radiation in the new continent's spacious grasslands. Subsequently they adapted to many other habitats, some of which are not occupied by rodents in any other part of the world. The absence of insectivores and lagomorphs (rabbits and hares) from much of the continent allowed them room for maneuver, and some evolved to resemble shrews, moles, or even rabbits: today's South American species include mole mice, the Shrew mouse, and the Bunny rat.

Above *Like a wolf howling, a Northern grasshopper mouse* (Onychomys leucogaster) *raises its head to utter the shrill cry for which the species is famous. Humans can hear the calls, which can last for a second or more, from as much as 100m (330ft) away. The cries probably serve to warn approaching mice that a patch of land is already tenanted.*

summers, mice are at their highest densities. When mice are abundant, they may selectively prey on larvae such as those of gypsy moths, reducing the numbers that defoliate oak and other deciduous trees in eastern North America. Less beneficially for humans, the mice can host a number of illnesses including Lyme disease and the deadly hantavirus that causes Hantaviral Pulmonary Syndrome.

Closely related to the white-footed mice is the Volcano mouse of Mexico, a burrow-user that is quite terrestrial in its habits. It occurs at elevations of 2,600–4,300m (8,530–14,100ft), and there is a birth peak in July and August

The size of harvest mice varies considerably, from 6–14cm (2–5.7in) in head–body length and from 6.5–9.5cm (2.5–3.7in) in tail length. The North American species tend to be smaller than the Central American species, rarely weighing more than 15g (0.5oz). The Western harvest mouse is typical of the species inhabiting the grassland areas of western North America, emerging at night to eat seeds or grain and living in a globular nest approximately 24cm (9in) off the ground in tall grass.

Grasshopper mice, which are about 10cm (4in) long with short tails, live in arid and semi-arid areas, feeding on insects and small vertebrates. A pair will live together in a burrow during the breeding season, after which the weaned young disperse; it is not known whether the parents then stay together to raise further litters. These rodents are well-known for their high-pitched squeak (usually above 20kHz), which may be used to indicate tenancy of a patch as burrows are widely spaced.

The Golden mouse (*Ochrotomys nuttalli*) is confined to the moderately wet, wooded habitats of the southeastern USA. The distinctive golden-brown color of its back contrasts sharply with its white belly. This is an extremely arboreal form that builds a complex leafy nest in tangles of vines.

The **woodrats and their allies** (tribe Neotomini) are rat-sized rodents, varying in color from dark buff on the back to paler shades on the belly. In general they eat a wide range of foods, but some species are highly adapted for feeding on the green parts of plants; indeed, *Neotoma stephensi* feeds almost entirely on the foliage of juniper trees. Some of the rats take refuge in crevices or cracks in rocky outcrops, while others construct burrows. All like to collect a mound of sticks and other detritus around the nest hole or crack.

The pads of spiny cacti may prove perfect tools for desert species; indeed, the name "pack rats" comes from this habit of transporting materials around their range. Each stick nest tends to be inhabited by a single adult individual, but they do make calls on neighboring nests; in particular, males visit receptive females.

The Magdalena rat occurs in an extremely restricted area of tropical deciduous forest in the states of Jalisco and Colima in western Mexico, where it may have an extended season of reproduction. This small, nocturnal woodrat is an excellent climber.

The Diminutive woodrat (*Nelsonia neotomodon*) is found in the mountainous areas of central and western Mexico, where it is known to shelter in crevices of rock outcroppings at elevations exceeding 2,000m (6,500ft).

The home-range sizes of New World mice vary hugely. **Pygmy mice** and **brown mice** (tribe Baiomyini) are the smallest New World rodents, and they possess correspondingly small home ranges that are often less than 900sq m (9,700sq ft) in extent; in comparison, a larger seed-eating rodent such as *Peromyscus leucopus* has a home range of 1.2–2.8ha (2.9–6.9 acres). Pygmy mice are seed-eaters that inhabit a grass nest, usually under a stone or log. They may be monogamous while pairing and rearing their young. Brown mice are small, subtropical mice with a high-pitched call, probably used to demarcate territory. Males produce this call more frequently than females.

The **Central American climbing rats** (tribe Tylomyini) live in the forest canopy never far from water. They rarely descend from the trees or emerge before sundown, and eat mainly fruits, seeds, and nuts. The Big-eared climbing rat, the smallest of these species, forages both in the trees and on the ground, and is unique among the New World rats in another crucial way: its young are born fully-furred, are few in number, and are very well-developed (precocial), opening their eyes after just 6 days. In contrast, most New World rats and mice produce hairless young whose eyes open only after 10–12 days. Furthermore, the Big-eared climbing rat mother gestates her growing young for 6.5 weeks, while most New World rats and mice gestate for only 3 weeks.

Vesper Rats

NYCTOMYINE GROUP

The tribe Nyctomyini contains just two species of vesper rat. The Central American vesper rat is a specialized, nocturnal, arboreal fruiteater that builds nests in trees and has a long tail and large eyes. Its young are born furred with open eyes.

The Yucatan vesper rat, also highly arboreal, is a relict species in the Yucatan peninsula. It probably was once more broadly distributed under different climatic conditions, but became isolated during one of the drying cycles in the Pleistocene era 1.8 million–10,000 years ago.

Paramo and Rice Rats

THOMASOMYINE–ORYZOMYINE GROUP

The **Paramo rats** and their allies of the tribe Thomasomyini are distributed throughout South America. In the mountains of the Andes, many species are adapted for life at elevations exceeding 4,000m (13,000ft). Otherwise they are almost always confined to forests, or else live along rivers. All that is known about them is that they confine most of their activity to the hours of darkness, and that they eat fruit. Litters of two to four young have been recorded, but in general their reproductive potential is considered to be quite low.

The South American climbing mice are likewise adapted for life in trees. They are also nocturnal, and feed upon fruits, seeds, fungi, and insects. Their litter size is small: for the Long-tailed climbing mouse (*Rhipidomys mastacalis*), two or three young per litter have been recorded.

Right *The Vesper rat* (Nyctomys sumichrasti) *is a tree-dweller in the rain forests of central America, where it builds nests rather like those of Red squirrels. Individuals sometimes inadvertently find their way to the USA, concealed in bunches of imported bananas.*

Below *The Cotton mouse owes its name to its distribution in the cotton-growing states of the American south, where it can be found in woodland, swamps, and rocky areas. A nocturnal omnivore, it feeds on insects and other invertebrates as much as on plants.*

Rice rats and their allies (tribe Oryzomini) are an assemblage with three tendencies: they may live in the trees, on the ground, or next to water. The species often replace each other up an altitudinal gradient. In northern Venezuela *Oryzomys albigularis* occurs above elevations of 1,000m (3,300ft), but at lower elevations it is replaced by *O. capito*. Alternatively, when two species occur in the same habitat, one may be more adapted to life in the trees than the other. *O. capito*, a terrestrial species, can happily share territory with *Oecomys bicolor*, a species adapted for climbing.

The South American water rat (one of the three species of *Nectomys*) is semiaquatic and the dominant aquatic rice rat over much of South America. *Oryzomys palustris*, found from northern Mexico up to southern Maryland, is also semiaquatic. This rat has catholic taste in food, though at certain times of year over 40 percent of its diet may consist of snails and crustaceans. It has an extended breeding season (from February to November) across much of its range, and so is able to produce four young every 30 days. As a consequence, it can become a serious agricultural pest.

The small bristly mice, which have a distinctive spiny coat, are nocturnal and eat seeds. *Neacomys tenuipes*, in northern South America, exhibits wide variations in population density.

Over evolutionary time rice rats have excelled at colonizing islands in the Caribbean and the Galapagos group, but many of the genus *Oryzomys* are currently threatened with extinction. The introduction of the Domestic cat and murine rats and mice by humans has had a severe impact on the Galapagos population in particular.

South American Field and Burrowing Mice

AKODONTINE–OXYMYCTERINE GROUP

South American field mice (tribe Akodontini) are adapted for foraging on the ground, and many are also excellent burrowers.

The grass mice of the genus *Akodon* are another group that have excelled at occupying all the available vacancies in the ecosystems they inhabit. In general they are omnivorous, eating green vegetation, fruits, insects, and seeds, and most are adapted to moderate and high elevations. The Northern grass mouse (*A. urichi*) typifies the adaptability of the genus; besides being active both by day and night, it is terrestrial and eats an array of different foods.

Members of the genus *Bolomys* are closely allied to *Akodon* but are more specialized for terrestrial existence. The tail, neck, and ears are shortened for burrowing, and the eyes are also reduced. Members of the genus *Microxus* are similar to *Bolomys* in appearance, but their eyes show yet further reduction in size.

Cane mice (tribe Zygodontomini) are widely distributed in South America, taking the place of *Akodon* at low elevations in grasslands and bushlands. The runways they construct can be visible to a human observer. Cane mice eat a considerable quantity of seeds and do not seem to be specialized for processing green plant food. In grassland habitats subject to seasonal fluctuations in rainfall, the cane mice may show vast oscillations in population density. In the llanos of Venezuela when the grass crop is exceptionally good, enabling them to harvest seeds and increase their production of young, they show population explosions. Densities can vary from a high of 15 per ha (6 per acre) to a low of less than 1 per ha (0.4 per acre), depending on the weather.

The **burrowing mice and their relatives** (tribe Oxymycterini) are closely allied to the South American field mice. These mice, like other rodents that feed on insects, have relatively small molar teeth and an elongated snout used for getting insects out of holes. Long claws help in digging for soil arthropods, larvae, and termites.

Feeding on insects and termites has its downside, however, which may be reflected in the limited number of offspring these groups are capable of producing. Termites are wrapped in protective armor in the form of an exoskeleton made of the protein chitin. The nutritional content of this substance is relatively low compared to other sources of protein or carbohydrate. Consequently, mammals relying on chitin for their daily supper tend to have low metabolic rates to compensate for the low energy return from their food. The relatively small litters of 2–3 young born to *Oxymycterus* species may be a constraint of their poor diet.

The Shrew mouse, with its tiny eyes and ears hidden in its fur, represents an extreme adaptation for a tunneling way of life. It constructs a deep burrow under the litter of the forest floor. Its molar teeth are very reduced in size, a characteristic that indicates adaptation for a diet of insects.

Mole mice of the genera *Chelemys*, *Notiomys*, and *Geoxus* are widely distributed in Argentina and Chile and exhibit an extensive array of adaptations for exploiting both semi-arid steppes and wet forests. Some species are adapted to higher-elevation forests, others to moderate elevations in central Argentina. They have extremely powerful claws, which may exceed 0.7cm (0.3in) in length. The name "mole mice" derives from their habit of spending most of their life underground.

Fish-eating Rats and Mice

ICHTHYOMYINE GROUP

The **fish-eating** or **crab-eating rats and mice** (tribe Ichthyomyini) live the aquatic lives their name suggests, on or near higher-elevation freshwater streams, where they exploit small crustaceans, aquatic arthropods, and fish as their primary food sources. The rest of their biology remains a mystery.

Fish-eating rats of the genus *Ichthyomys* are among the most specialized of the genera. Their fur is short and thick, their eyes and ears are reduced in size, and their whiskers are stout. A fringe of hairs on the toes of the hind feet aids in swimming, and the toes are partially webbed to propel a body about 33cm (9in) in length. They resemble large water shrews, or some of the fish-eating insectivores of West Africa and Madagascar.

Fish-eating rats of the genus *Neusticomys* are similar to *Ichthyomys*, and are distributed disjunctly in the mountain regions of Venezuela, Columbia, and Peru.

Water mice are smaller than the *Ichthyomys* species, rarely exceeding 19cm (7in) in head–body length. They occur in central American mountain streams, and are known to feed on snails, aquatic insects, and possibly fish.

Cotton and Marsh Rats and Allied Species

SIGMODONTINE–PHYLLOTINE–SCAPTEROMYINE GROUP

Cotton rats and marsh rats (tribe Sigmodontini) are united by a common feature, namely folded patterns of enamel on the molars that tend to approximate to an "S" shape when viewed from above. They exhibit a range of adaptations; the species referred to as marsh rats are adapted for a semi-aquatic life, whereas the cotton rats are terrestrial. Both groups, however, feed predominantly on herbaceous vegetation.

The marsh rats, which are web-footed, form the genus *Holochilus*. Two species are broadly distributed in South America, while another is limited to the chaco of Paraguay and northeastern Argentina. The underside of the tail has a fringe of hair that functions as a rudder when swimming. These rats build a grass nest that may exceed 40cm (15.7in) in diameter, locating it near water, sufficiently high up to avoid flooding. In the more southerly parts of their range in temperate South America, breeding tends to be confined to the spring and summer (September–December).

Cotton rats are broadly distributed from the southern USA to northern South America. In line with their adaptations for terrestrial life, tail length is always considerably shorter than head–body length. Cotton rats are active both by day and night; they are omnivores, taking advantage of the fresh growth in herbs and grasses that follows after the onset of rains.

A striking feature of the Hispid cotton rat is that its young are born fully furred; their eyes open within 36 hours of birth. This species has a very high reproductive capacity, and although it produces precocial young, the gestation period is only 27 days. Litter sizes are quite high, ranging from five to eight, with 7.6 as an average. The female is receptive after giving birth and only lactates for 10–15 days. Thus the turn-around time between litters is very brief; a female can produce a litter every month during the breeding season. In agricultural regions this prolific rat can quickly become a serious pest.

Leaf-eared mice and their allies (tribe Phyllotini) are typified by the genera *Phyllotis* and *Calomys*. *Calomys* (vesper mice) includes a variety of species distributed over most of South America. They feed primarily on plant material; arthropods form an insignificant portion of their diet. Most of the species making up the genus *Phyllotis* (the leaf-eared mice) occur at high altitudes. They are often active by day, and may bask in the sun. They feed primarily on seeds and herbaceous plant material.

Above *Large ears have given South America's leaf-eared mice their common name. This Darwin's leaf-eared mouse* (Phyllotis darwini) *is foraging 4,300m (14,000ft) up on the Andean* altiplano.

Below *Representative New World rats and mice:* ***1*** *South American grass mouse (genus* Akodon*; tribe Akodontini) grooming its tail;* ***2*** *cotton rat (genus* Sigmodon*; tribe Sigmodontini) attempting to move an egg;* ***3*** *mole mouse (genus* Chelemys*; tribe Akodontini) in an underground burrow;* ***4*** *South American water rat (genus* Nectomys*; tribe Oryzomini) at the water's edge;* ***5*** *fish-eating rat (genus* Ichthyomys*; tribe Ichthyomyini);* ***6*** *Swamp rat (*Scapteromys tumidus*; tribe Scapteromyini);* ***7*** *leaf-eared mouse (genus* Phyllotis*; tribe Phyllotini).*

The variations in form, and the way in which several species of different size occur in the same habitat, are reminiscent of the white-footed mice of the tribe Peromyscini.

The vegetarian, cathemeral Bunny rat (*Reithrodon physodes*) is of moderate size and has thick fur adapted to the open-country plains of temperate Chile, Argentina, and Uruguay.

The Highland gerbil mouse (*Eligmodontia puerulus*) is one of the few South American rodents specialized for semi-arid habitats. Its hind feet are long and slender, resulting in a peculiar, galloping gait in which the forelimbs simultaneously strike the ground, and then are driven upward by a powerful thrust from the hind legs. The kidneys of this species are very efficient at recovering water; it can exist for considerable periods of time without drinking, being able to derive its water as a by-product of its own metabolism.

Patagonian chinchilla mice are distributed in wooded areas from central Argentina south to Cape Horn. The Puna mouse is found only in the *altiplano* of Peru. This rodent is the most vole-like in bodyform of any South American rodent. It is active both by day and night, and its diet is apparently confined to herbaceous vegetation. The Chilean rat is an inhabitant of humid temperate forests; this extremely arboreal species may be a link between the phyllotines and the oryzomyine rodents or rice rats. The Andean marsh rat occurs at high elevations near streams and appears to occupy a niche appropriate for a vole.

The **southern water rats and their allies** (tribe Scapteromyini) are adapted for burrowing in habitats by or near rivers. The Swamp rat (*Scapteromys tumidus*), also known as the Argentinian water rat, is found near rivers, streams, and marshes. It has extremely long claws and can construct extensive burrow systems.

The giant South American water rats prefer moist habitats and have considerable burrowing ability. The Woolly giant rat (*Kunsia tomentosus*) is one of the largest living New World rats, with a head–body length that may reach 28cm (11in) and a tail length of up to 16cm (6.3in).

Red-nosed rats are small burrowing forms allied to the larger genera. As with so many of the animals in this section, their biology and habits are poorly known. JFE/RB/JOW

New World Rat and Mouse Tribes

THE SHEER NUMBER OF NEW WORLD RAT and mouse species makes it convenient to have some grouping system through which to make sense of their diversity. Yet attempts to combine them at anything between subfamily and genus level (and, in some cases, even at that) have proved taxonomically controversial. The arrangement of groups and tribes suggested here is only provisional; readers should be aware that only one tribe has been convincingly shown to be monophyletic (arising from a single ancestor).

North American Neotomine–Peromyscine Group

White-footed Mice and their Allies
Tribe Peromyscini

10 genera: **White-footed** or **deer mice** (*Peromyscus*, 54 species), from N Canada (except high Arctic) S through Mexico to Panama. **Harvest mice** (*Reithrodontomys*, 19 species), from W Canada and USA S through Mexico to W Panama. **Crested-tailed deer mice** (*Habromys*, 4 species) from C Mexico S to El Salvador. **Florida mouse** (*Podomys floridanus*), Florida peninsula. **Volcano mouse** (*Neotomodon alstoni*), montane areas of C Mexico. **Grasshopper mice** (*Onychomys*, 3 species), SW Canada, NW USA S to north-central Mexico. **Michoacan deer mouse** (*Osgoodomys bandaranus*), W C Mexico. **Isthmus rats** (*Isthmomys*, 2 species), Panama. **Thomas's giant deer mouse** (*Megadontomys thomasi*), C Mexico. **Golden mouse** (*Ochrotomys nuttalli*), SW USA.

Woodrats and their Allies
Tribe Neotomini

4 genera: **Woodrats** (*Neotoma*, 19 species), USA to C Mexico. **Allen's woodrat** (*Hodomys alleni*), W C Mexico. **Magdalena rat** (*Xenomys nelsoni*), W C Mexico. **Diminutive woodrat** (*Nelsonia neotomodon*), C Mexico.

Pygmy Mice and Brown Mice
Tribe Baiomyini

2 genera: **Pygmy mice** (*Baiomys*, 2 species), SW USA S to Nicaragua. **Brown mice** (*Scotinomys*, 2 species), Brazil, Bolivia, Argentina.

Central American Climbing Rats
Tribe Tylomyini

2 genera: **Central American climbing rats** (*Tylomys*, 7 species), S Mexico to W Columbia. **Big-eared climbing rat** (*Ototylomys phyllotis*), Yucatan peninsula of Mexico S to Costa Rica.

Nyctomyine Group

Vesper Rats Tribe Nyctomyini

2 genera: **Central American vesper rat** (*Nyctomys sumichrasti*), S Mexico S to C Panama. **Yucatan vesper rat** (*Otonyctomys hatti*), Yucatan peninsula of Mexico and adjoining areas of Mexico and Guatemala.

Thomasomyine–Oryzomyine Group

Paramo Rats and their Relatives
Tribe Thomasomyini

8 genera: **Paramo rats** (*Thomasomys*, 25 species), Andean areas of high altitude from Colombia S to Bolivia. **Atlantic forest rats** (*Delomys*, 2 species), SE Brazil to adjacent areas of Argentina. **Wilfred's mice** (*Wilfredomys*, 2 species), SE Brazil to NW Argentina and Uruguay. **Brazilian spiny rat** (*Abrawayaomys ruschii*), SE Brazil. **South American climbing rats** (*Rhipidomys*, 14 species), low elevations from extreme E Panama S across northern S America to C Brazil. **Colombian forest mouse** (*Chilomys instans*), high elevations in Andes in W Venezuela S to Colombia and Ecuador. **Montane mice** (*Aepomys*, 2 species), high elevations in Andes in Venezuela, Colombia, Ecuador. **Rio de Janeiro rice rat** (*Phaenomys ferrugineus*), vicinity of Rio de Janeiro.
Note: *Chilomys, Delomys, Wilfredomys, Phaenomys* have uncertain affinities.

Rice Rats and their Allies
Tribe Oryzomini

13 Genera: **Dusky rice rats** (*Melanomys*, 3 species), Central America S to Peru. **Montane dwarf rice rats** (*Microryzomys*, 2 species), mountains of Venezuela S to Bolivia. **Arboreal rice rats** (*Oecomys*, 12 species), lowland tropical forest of C. America to Brazil. **Pygmy rice rats** (*Oligoryzomys*, 15 species), S Mexico to S Brazil. **Rice water rats** (*Sigmodontomys*, 2 species), forests of Costa Rica to Ecuador. **Rice rats** (*Oryzomys*, 36 species), SE USA S through C America and N S America to Bolivia and C Brazil. **Galapagos rice rats** (*Nesoryzomys*, 5 species), Galapagos archipelago of Ecuador. **Spiny mouse** (*Scolomys*, 3 species), Ecuador, Peru. **False rice rats** (*Pseudoryzomys*, 2 species), Bolivia, E Brazil, N Argentina. **Bristly mice** (*Neacomys*, 3 species), E Panama across lowland S America to N Brazil. **South American water rats** (*Nectomys*, 3 species), lowland S America to NE Argentina. (*Amphinectomys savamis*), E Peru. **Brazilian arboreal mouse** (*Rhagomys rufescens*), SE Brazil.

Right *Some desert-dwelling woodrats like this White-throated individual* (Neotoma albigula) *make elaborate dens that may be passed down through successive generations. The spiny materials used in their construction makes it difficult for enemies to enter them, though the rats themselves apparently come and go unscathed.*

Wied's Red-nosed Mouse
Tribe Wiedomyini

Wied's red-nosed mouse (*Wiedomys pyrrhorhinos*), E Brazil. Relationships uncertain.

Akodontine–Oxymycterine Group

South American Field Mice
Tribe Akodontini

11 genera: **South American field mice** (*Akodon*, 45 species), found in most of S America from W Colombia to Argentina. **Bolo mice** (*Bolomys*, 6 species), montane areas of SE Peru S to Paraguay and C Argentina. ***Microxus*** (3 species), montane areas of Colombia, Venezuela, Ecuador, Peru. **Altiplano mice** (*Chroeomys*, 2 species), Andes from Peru to N Argentina. **Mole mice** (*Chelemys*, 2 species), Andes on the Chile–Argentina boundary. **Long-clawed mole mouse** (*Geoxus valdivianus*), S Chile and adjacent Argentina. ***Pearsonomys annectens***, montane-central Chile. **Cerrado mice** (*Thalpomys*, 2 species), cerrado of S Brazil. **Andean rat** (*Lenoxus apicalis*), SE Peru and W Bolivia. **Edwards's long-clawed mouse** (*Notiomys edwardsii*), Argentina and Chile. **Mount Roraima mouse** (*Podoxymys roraimae*), at junction of Brazil, Venezuela, Guyana.

Cane Mice
Tribe Zygodontomini

Cane mice (*Zygodontomys*, 3 species), Costa Rica and N S America. Relationships uncertain.

Burrowing Mice and their Relatives
Tribe Oxymycterini

4 genera: **Burrowing mice** (*Oxymycterus*, 12 species), SE Peru, W Bolivia E over much of Brazil and S to N Argentina. **Brazilian shrew mouse** (*Blarinomys breviceps*), E C Brazil. **Juscelin's mouse** (*Juscelinomys candango*), vicinity of Brasilia. ***Brucepattersonius*** (7 species), S C Brazil and adjacent northeastern Argentina and Uruguay.

Ichthyomyine Group

Fish-eating Rats and Mice
Tribe Ichthyomyini

5 genera: **Fish-eating** or **crab-eating rats** (*Ichthyomys*, 4 species), premontane habitats of Venezuela, Columbia, Ecuador, Peru. **Chibchan water mice** (*Chibchanomys*, 2 species), W Venezuela S in the Andes to Peru. **Ecuador fish-eating rat** (*Anotomys leander*), montane Ecuador. **Fish-eating rats** (*Neusticomys*, 4 species), Andes region of S Colombia and N Ecuador, N Venezuela, W Peru, and French Guyana. **Water mice** (*Rheomys*, 5 species), C Mexico S to Panama.

Sigmodontine–Phyllotine–Scapteromyine Group

Cotton Rats and Marsh Rats

Tribe Sigmodontini

3 genera: **Marsh rats** (*Holochilus*, 4 species), most of lowland S America. **Cotton rats** (*Sigmodon*, 10 species), S USA, Mexico, C America, NE S America as far S as NE Brazil. **Giant water rat** (*Lundomys molitor*), extreme S Brazil and adjacent areas of Uruguay.

Leaf-eared Mice and their Allies

Tribe Phyllotini

17 genera: **Leaf-eared mice** (*Graomys*, 3 species), Andes of Bolivia S to N Argentina and Paraguay. **Chaco mice** (*Andalgalomys*, 3 species), Paraguay and NE Argentina. **Garlepp's mouse** (*Galenomys garleppi*), high altitudes in S Peru, W Bolivia, N Chile. **Big-eared mice** (*Auliscomys*, 3 species), mountains of Bolivia, Peru, Chile, and Argentina. **Puna mouse** (*Punomys lemminus*), montane areas of S Peru. **Bunny rat** (*Reithrodon physodes*), steppe and grasslands of Chile, Argentina, Uruguay. **Vesper mice** (*Calomys*, 9 species), most of lowland S America. **Chinchilla mouse** (*Chinchillula sahamae*), high elevations S Peru, W Bolivia, N Chile, Argentina. **Chilean rat** (*Irenomys tarsalis*), N Argentina, N Chile. **Andean mouse** (*Andinomys edax*), S Peru, N Chile. **Gerbil mice** (*Eligmodontia*, 4 species), S Peru, N Chile, Argentina. **Leaf-eared mice** (*Phyllotis*, 12 species), from NW Peru S to N Argentina and C Chile. **Patagonian chinchilla mice** (*Euneomys*, 4 species), temperate Chile and Argentina. **Andean swamp rat** (*Neotomys ebriosus*), Peru S to NW Argentina. **Bolivian big-eared mouse** (*Maresomys boliviensis*), N Argentina and adjacent Bolivia. **Southern big-eared mouse** (*Loxodontomys micropus*), W Argentina. ***Salinomys delicatus***, known from just 9 specimens found in NW Argentina.

Southern Water Rats and their Allies

Tribe Scapteromyini

3 genera: **Red-nosed rats** (*Bibimys*, 3 species), SE Brazil W to NW Argentina. **Argentinean water rat** (*Scapteromys tumidus*), SE Brazil, Paraguay, E Argentina. **Giant South American water rats** (*Kunsia*, 2 species), N Argentina, Bolivia, SE Brazil.

For full species list see Appendix ▷

Voles and Lemmings

POPULAR LEGEND TELLS OF LEGIONS OF *lemmings periodically flinging themselves into rivers or the sea to drown en masse. However, there is no factual evidence of suicidal tendencies either in lemmings or in voles, their partners in the subfamily Microtinae, although it is true that lemmings embark from time to time on mass migrations, in the course of which thousands of individual animals may die.*

Lemmings and voles have two features of particular interest. First, their populations expand and contract considerably, in line with cyclical patterns. This has made them the most studied subfamily of rodents (and the basis of much of our understanding about the population dynamics of small mammals). Secondly, though they neither hibernate like such larger mammals as ground squirrels nor can rely on a thick layer of fat like bears, many voles and lemmings live in habitats covered by snow for much of the year. They are able to survive thanks to their ability to tunnel beneath the snow, where they are insulated from extreme cold.

Thickset Bodies and Rounded Muzzles

FORM AND FUNCTION

Voles and lemmings are small, thickset rodents with bluntly rounded muzzles, and tails that are usually less than half the length of their bodies. Only small sections of their limbs are visible. Their eyes and ears tend to be small, and in lemmings the tail is usually very short. Coat colors vary not only between species but often within them. Lemmings' coats are especially adapted for cold temperatures: they are long, thick, and waterproof. The Collared lemming is the only rodent that molts to a completely white coat in winter.

Some species display special anatomical features. The claws of the first digit of the Norway

Above left *A Field vole eating. Although males are quite territorial, the females tend to be less so, with considerable overlapping of territories. Young males will be forced to disperse by older resident males.*

FACTFILE

VOLES AND LEMMINGS

Order: Rodentia

Family: Muridae

Subfamily: Arvicolinae (Microtinae)

143 species in 26 genera. Species include: Collared lemming (*Dicrostonyx torquatus*); Norway lemming (*Lemmus lemmus*); Northern mole-vole (*Ellobius talpinus*); Bank vole (*Clethrionomys glareolus*); and muskrat (*Ondatra zibethicus*).

DISTRIBUTION N and C America, Eurasia from Arctic S to Himalayas; small relict population in N Africa.

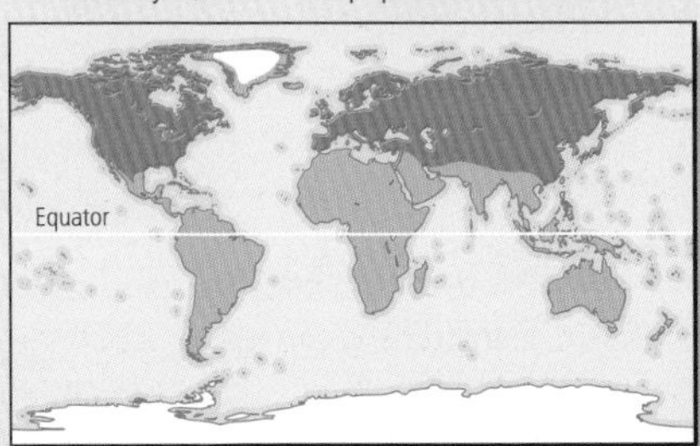

HABITAT Burrowing species are common in tundra, temperate grasslands, steppe, scrub, open forest, rocks; 5 species are aquatic or arboreal.

SIZE In most species, head–body length 10–11cm (4–4.5in), tail length 3–4cm (1.2–1.6in), weight 17–20g (0.6–0.7oz).

COAT Thickly furred in various shades of gray and brown.

DIET Herbivorous; mostly the green parts of plants, though some species eat bulbs, roots, and mosses. Muskrats occasionally eat mussels and snails.

BREEDING Gestation 16–28 days. Litter size varies between species from 1–12; at least 2 litters, and sometimes 4 or more, are produced each year.

LONGEVITY 0.5–2 years

CONSERVATION STATUS 3 species are listed as Critically Endangered and 3 more as Endangered. The Bavarian vole (*Microtus bavaricus*) is now considered Extinct.

See tribes table ▷

Left *Muskrats are well adapted to life around water. They have partial webbing on their back feet and can use their tail, which is slightly flattened, as a rudder. Consequently, muskrats occur in a wide variety of aquatic environments.*

Right *Bank voles such as this* (Clethrionomys glareolus) *live in Europe and Central Asia in woods and scrubs, in banks and swamps, usually within a home range of about 0.8ha (2 acres).*

lemming are flattened and enlarged for digging in the snow, while each fall the Collared lemming grows an extra big claw on the third and fourth digits of its forelegs, shedding them in spring. Muskrats have long tails and small webbing between toes that assist in swimming. The mole lemmings, adapted for digging, have a more cylindrical shape than other species, and their incisors, used for excavating, protrude extremely.

Adult males and females are usually the same color and approximately the same size, though the shade of juveniles' coats may differ from the adults'. Although most adult voles weigh less than 100g (3.5oz), the muskrat grows to over 1,400g (50oz). The size of the brain, in relation to body size, is lower than average for mammals.

Smell and hearing are important, well-developed senses, able to respond, respectively, to the secretions that are used to mark territory boundaries, to indicate social status, and perhaps to aid species recognition, and to vocalizations (each species has a characteristic range of calls). Calls can be used to give the alarm, to threaten, or as part of courtship and mating. Brandt's voles, which live in large colonies, sit up on the surface and whistle like prairie dogs.

Tundra, Grassland, Forest

DISTRIBUTION PATTERNS

Microtines, especially lemmings, are widely distributed in the tundra regions of the northern hemisphere, where they are the dominant small mammal species. Their presence there is the result of recolonization since the retreat of the last glaciers. Voles are also found in temperate grasslands and in the forests of North America and Eurasia.

Because the Pleistocene era (1.8 million–10,000 years ago) has yielded a rich fossil record of microtine skulls, much of the taxonomy of this subfamily is based on the structure and kind of teeth, which are also used to distinguish the microtines from other rodents. All microtine teeth have flattened crowns, and prisms of dentine surrounded by enamel. There are twelve molars (three on each side of the upper and lower jaws) and four incisors. Species are differentiated by the particular pattern of the enamel of the molars. Dentition has not proved sufficient for solving all taxonomic questions, and some difficulties remain both in delimiting species and defining genera. It is often possible to distinguish the species of live animals from the general body size, coat color, and length of tail. The subdivision of species into many subspecies (not listed here) reflects geographic variation in coat color and size in widely distributed species. *Microtus*, the largest genus (accounting for nearly 50 percent of the subfamily), is a heterogeneous collection of species.

Many species have widely overlapping ranges. For example, there are six species – two lemmings and four voles – in the southern tundra and forest of the Yamal Peninsula in Russia. Each can be differentiated by its habitat preference or diet. The ranges of Siberian lemmings and Collared lemmings overlap extensively, but Collared lemmings prefer upland heaths and higher and drier tundra, whereas Siberian lemmings are found in the wetter grass-sedge lowlands. Competition between closely related microtines has been suggested but rarely demonstrated by field experiments.

Busy Grazers and Diggers

DIET

Voles and lemmings are herbivores that usually eat the green parts of plants, though some species prefer bulbs, roots, mosses, or even pine needles. The muskrat occasionally eats mussels and snails. Diet usually changes with the seasons and varies according to location, reflecting local abundances of plants. Species living in moist habitats, such as lemmings and the Tundra vole, prefer grasses and sedges, while those inhabiting drier habitats, such as Collared lemmings, prefer herbs. But animals select their food to some extent; diets do not just simply mimic vegetation composition.

Voles and lemmings can be found foraging both by day and night, although dawn and dusk might be preferred. They obtain food by grazing or digging for roots; grass is often clipped and placed in piles in their runways. Some cache food in summer and fall, but in winter, when the snow cover insulates the animals that nest underneath the surface, food is obtained by burrowing; animals also feed on plants at ground surface. The Northern red-backed vole feeds on (among other items) berries, and in summer has to compete for them with birds; in winter, when the bushes are covered with snow, this vole can burrow to reach the berries, so only during the spring thaw is the animal critically short of food. In winter the Sagebrush vole utilizes the height of snow packs to forage on shrubs it normally cannot reach.

Most microtines – for example the Florida water rat, the Steppe lemming, and all species of *Microtus* – have continuously growing molars, and can chew more (and more abrasive) grasses than species with rooted molars. In tundra and grasslands, voles and lemmings help the recycling of nutrients by eliminating waste products and clipping and then storing food below ground.

A Short, Hectic Life

SOCIAL BEHAVIOR

The life span of microtines is short. They reach sexual maturity at an early age and are very fertile. Mortality rates, however, are high: during the breeding season, only 70 percent of the animals alive one month will still be alive the next. The age of sexual maturity can vary considerably. The females of some species may become mature only 2–3 weeks after birth. Males take longer, usually 6–8 weeks. The Common vole has an extraordinarily fast development. Females have been observed coming into heat while still suckling, and may be only 5 weeks old at the birth of their first litter. In species that breed only during the summer, young born early will probably breed that summer, while later litters may not become sexually mature until the following spring.

The length of the breeding season is highly variable, but lemmings can breed in both summer and winter. Winter breeding is less common in voles, which tend to breed from late spring to fall. Voles in Mediterranean climates, on the other hand, breed in winter and spring, during the wet season, but not in summer. Within a species, the breeding season often varies widely in different years or in different parts of the range. The muskrat breeds all year in the southern part of its range but only in summer elsewhere. Some meadow vole species breed in winter during the phase of population increase, but not when numbers are falling.

In many species, such as the Montane, Field, and Mexican voles, the presence of a male will induce ovulation in a female. (Physical contact is unnecessary; ovulation is probably induced by social odors produced by the male.) The normal gestation time is 21 days, but it may be less if conditions are good, falling to just 17 days in a Bank vole with optimal nutrition. The gestation period may also lengthen – up to 24 days in the Bank vole's case – if a female has mated within a few hours of giving birth and is therefore pregnant while lactating.

The reproductive cycle is liable to be disrupted. A mated female can sometimes fail to become pregnant, or will abort spontaneously if exposed to a strange male (both phenomena have been observed in Field, Meadow, and Prairie voles in the laboratory; however, attempts to show it in the field have so far failed). Males are under pressure to sire as many litters as possible in the short breeding season. Collared lemming females have

WATER VOLES IN BRITAIN

The changing fortunes of British water vole populations through the 20th century have only recently come to light following the pioneering national surveys carried out by the Vincent Wildlife Trust in 1989–90 and 1996–98. These surveys confirmed that the species had been getting scarcer along waterways since the 1930s due to habitat loss and land use change associated with the intensification of agriculture. In recent years this decline has accelerated due to predation by feral American mink (established as escapees from fur farms).

The decline has now developed into a serious population crash with a further loss of the remaining population by 88 percent in only seven years. The 1996–98 survey reports that the population loss has been most severe in the north and southwest of England, reaching 97 percent of the population in Yorkshire! This makes the water vole Britain's most rapidly declining mammal, and as such it has been given legal protection under the Wildlife and Countryside Act 1981.

The threats to water voles are complex but involve habitat loss and degradation (due to river engineering or agricultural practice), population isolation and fragmentation, fluctuations in water levels, pollution, predation (especially by mink), or indirect persecution through rat control operations.

Saving the water vole is going to take some complex habitat manipulation, and cooperation between many sectors of British society. Habitat restoration creates dispersal corridors for isolated populations to reach each other between restored backwaters, ponds, wet grassland, marshes, reedbeds, and a network of ditches. Riverbanks are central to water vole activity and the possibility of a coordinated scheme to connect whole lengths of river along their banks by the withdrawal of farming would be invaluable. When banks are left free from cultivation, wild plants perfect for water vole food and cover often soon colonize, their seeds carried along the river by water or wind. Where this doesn't happen, planting can speed things considerably. Highly layered bankside vegetation with tall grasses and stands of flowers such as willowherb, loosestrife, and meadowsweet, fringed with thick stands of rushes, sedges, or reed are the best habitat. In winter, the roots and bark of woody species such as willows and sallows are an important part of the water vole's diet, together with rhizomes, bulbs, and roots of herbaceous species. Already underway are projects on the River Cole at Coleshill, Wiltshire, in which 2km of degraded river has been restored to meanders, and on the River Skerne at Darlington, County Durham, where backwater pools are creating small-scale water vole havens. RS

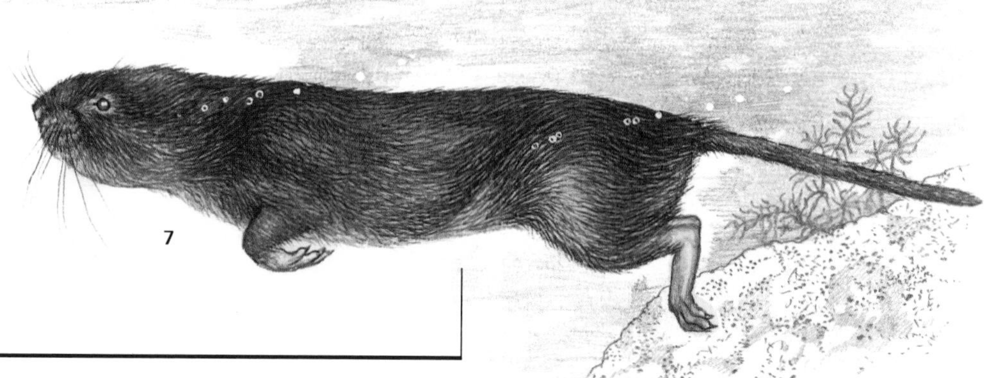

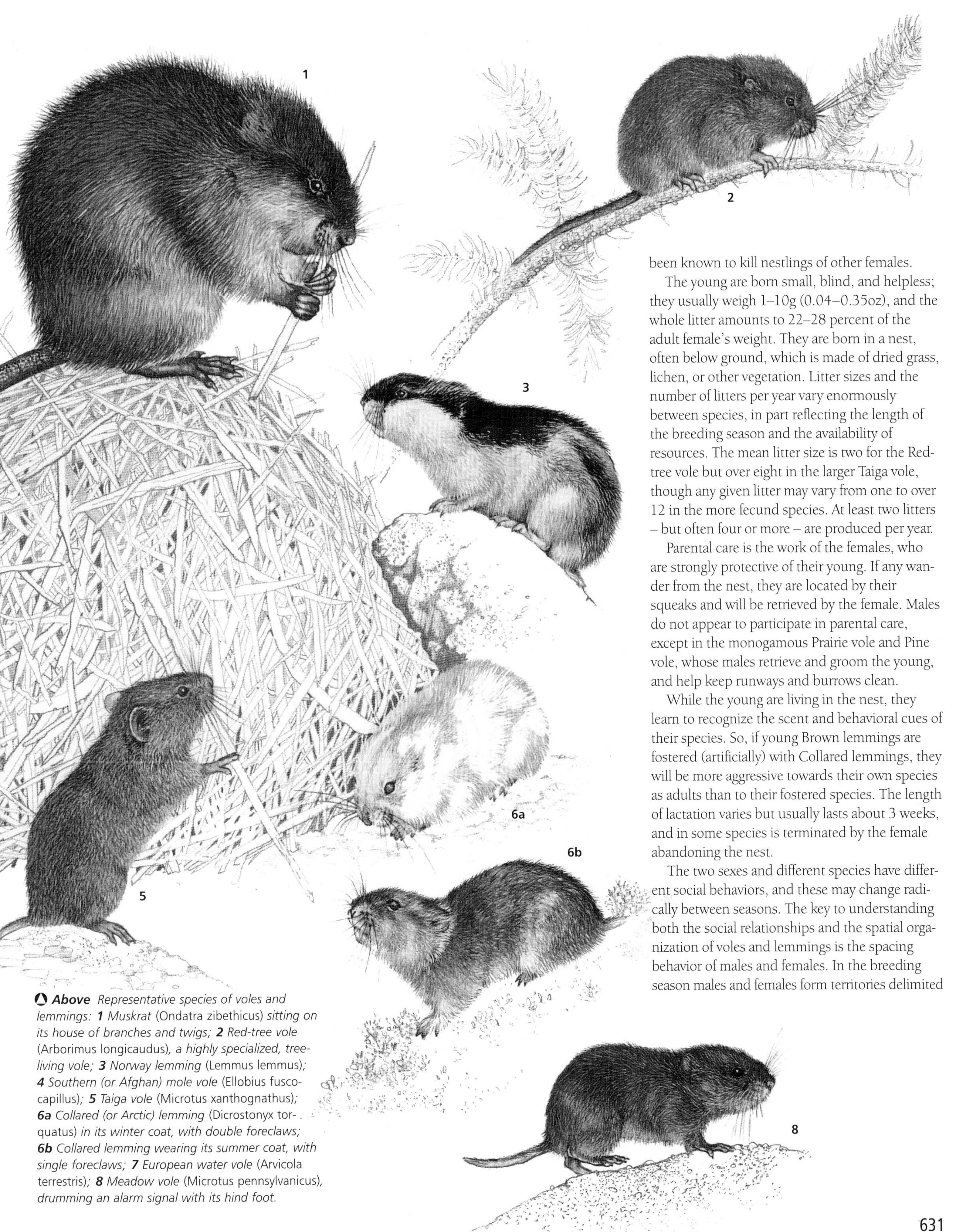

been known to kill nestlings of other females.

The young are born small, blind, and helpless; they usually weigh 1–10g (0.04–0.35oz), and the whole litter amounts to 22–28 percent of the adult female's weight. They are born in a nest, often below ground, which is made of dried grass, lichen, or other vegetation. Litter sizes and the number of litters per year vary enormously between species, in part reflecting the length of the breeding season and the availability of resources. The mean litter size is two for the Red-tree vole but over eight in the larger Taiga vole, though any given litter may vary from one to over 12 in the more fecund species. At least two litters – but often four or more – are produced per year.

Parental care is the work of the females, who are strongly protective of their young. If any wander from the nest, they are located by their squeaks and will be retrieved by the female. Males do not appear to participate in parental care, except in the monogamous Prairie vole and Pine vole, whose males retrieve and groom the young, and help keep runways and burrows clean.

While the young are living in the nest, they learn to recognize the scent and behavioral cues of their species. So, if young Brown lemmings are fostered (artificially) with Collared lemmings, they will be more aggressive towards their own species as adults than to their fostered species. The length of lactation varies but usually lasts about 3 weeks, and in some species is terminated by the female abandoning the nest.

The two sexes and different species have different social behaviors, and these may change radically between seasons. The key to understanding both the social relationships and the spatial organization of voles and lemmings is the spacing behavior of males and females. In the breeding season males and females form territories delimited

Above *Representative species of voles and lemmings:* **1** *Muskrat* (Ondatra zibethicus) *sitting on its house of branches and twigs;* **2** *Red-tree vole* (Arborimus longicaudus), *a highly specialized, tree-living vole;* **3** *Norway lemming* (Lemmus lemmus)*;* **4** *Southern (or Afghan) mole vole* (Ellobius fuscocapillus)*;* **5** *Taiga vole* (Microtus xanthognathus)*;* **6a** *Collared (or Arctic) lemming* (Dicrostonyx torquatus) *in its winter coat, with double foreclaws;* **6b** *Collared lemming wearing its summer coat, with single foreclaws;* **7** *European water vole* (Arvicola terrestris)*;* **8** *Meadow vole* (Microtus pennsylvanicus), *drumming an alarm signal with its hind foot.*

by scent marks. Males compete for access to receptive females, while females compete for space that contains high-quality food and serves to protect their litters from infanticide. Male and female territories may be separate (as in the Montane vole and the Collared lemming) or else overlap (as in the European water and Meadow voles); alternatively, several females may live in overlapping ranges within a single male territory (for example, in Taiga and Field voles). Males form hierarchies of dominance – subordinates may be excluded from breeding – and may act to exclude strange males from an area. The Common, Sagebrush, and Brandt's voles live in colonies. The animals build complicated burrows.

Although in most species males are promiscuous, a few are monogamous. In the Prairie vole the males and females form pair bonds, while the Montane vole appears to be monogamous at low density as a result of the spacing of males and females, but with no pair bond. At high density this species is polygynous (males mate with several females). Monogamy is favored when both adults are needed to defend the breeding territory from intruders bent on infanticide.

The social system may vary seasonally. In the Taiga vole, the young animals disperse and their territories break down late in summer. Groups of five to ten unrelated animals then build a communal nest, which is occupied throughout the winter by both sexes. Communal nesting or local aggregations of individuals are also observed in the Meadow, Gray, and Northern red-backed voles. Huddling together reduces energy requirements.

Dispersal (the movement from place of birth to place of breeding) is an important aspect of microtine behavior, and has been the subject of considerable research. It plays an important role in regulating population size, and allows the animals

Vole and Lemming Tribes

Lemmings Tribe Lemmini

17 species in 4 genera. N America and Eurasia, inhabiting tundra, taiga, and spruce woods. Skull broad and massive, tail very short, hair long; 8 mammae.
Collared lemmings (*Dicrostonyx*, 11 species).
Brown lemmings (*Lemmus*, 3 species). Includes Norway lemming (*L. lemmus*).
Bog lemmings (*Synaptomys*, 2 species).
Wood lemming (1 species) *Myopus schisticolor*.

Mole voles Tribe Ellobiini

5 species in 1 genus. C Asia, inhabiting steppe. Form is modified for a subterranean life; coat color varies from ocher sand to browns and blacks; tail short; no ears; incisors protrude forward. Species include Northern mole vole (*Ellobius talpinus*), Southern mole vole (*E. fuscocapillus*).

Voles Tribe Microtini

121 species in 21 genera. N America, Europe, Asia, the Arctic.
Meadow voles (*Microtus*, 61 species). N America, Eurasia, N Africa. Coat and size highly variable, molars rootless, skull weak; 4–8 mammae; burrows on surface and underground. Includes Common vole (*M. arvalis*), Field vole (*M. agrestis*), American pine vole (*M. pinetorum*).
Mountain voles (*Alticola*, 12 species). C Asia. Includes Large-eared vole (*A. macrotis*).
South Asian voles (*Eothenomys*, 9 species) E Asia, includes Père David's vole (*E. melanogaster*).
Red-backed voles (*Clethrionomys*, 7 species). Japan, N Eurasia, N America, inhabiting forest, scrub, and tundra. Back usually red, cheek teeth rooted in adults, skull weak; 8 mammae. Includes Bank vole (*C. glareolus*).
Musser's voles (*Volemys*, 4 species). China.
Tree voles (*Arborimus*, 3 species). W USA.
Brandt's voles (*Lasiopodomys*, 3 species). C Asia.
Snow voles (*Chionmys*, 3 species). S Europe, SW Asia, Turkey.
Japanese voles (*Phaulomys*, 2 species). Japan.
Kashmir voles (*Hyperacrius*, 2 species) Kashmir and the Punjab. Includes True's vole (*H. fertilis*).
Water voles (*Arvicola*, 2 species). N America, N Eurasia. Includes European water vole (*A. terrestris*).
Heather voles (*Phenacomys*, 2 species) W USA and Canada. Includes Red-tree vole (*P. longicaudus*).
Afghan voles (*Blanfordimys*, 2 species). C Asia.
Martino's snow vole (1 species), *Dinaromys bogdanovi*. Yugoslavia.
Duke of Bedford's vole (1 species), *Proedromys bedfordi*. China.
Sagebrush vole (1 species), *Lemmiscus curtatus*. W USA.
Muskrat (1 species), *Ondatra zibethicus*. N America.
Round-tailed muskrat (1 species), *Neofiber alleni*. Florida.
Long-clawed mole vole (1 species), *Prometheomys schaposchnikowi*. Caucasus, Russia.
Steppe lemming (1 species), *Lagurus lagurus*. C Asia .
Yellow steppe lemmings (*Eolagurus*, 2 species). E C Asia.

For full species list see Appendix ▷

enable voles to rapidly colonize vacant habitats.

The numbers of juvenile males and females are equal, except in the Wood lemming, which has an unusual feature for mammals: some females are genetically programmed to have only daughters, which is advantageous in an increasing population. In most species, however, there are usually more female adults than males, probably as a consequence of dispersal by males, which are then more susceptible to predators. In the European water vole it is the females who usually disperse, and there is a slight excess of males. In Townsend's vole, the survival and growth of juveniles are higher when the density of adult females is low and adjacent females are relatives.

Territory size varies, but males usually have larger territories than females. In the Bank vole, home ranges were found in one study to be 0.7ha (1.7 acres) for females and 0.8ha (2 acres) for males. Territory size decreases as population density rises. In the Prairie vole, home range length drops from 25m (82ft) at low density to 10m (33ft) at high density.

LEMMING MIGRATIONS

According to Scandinavian legend, every few years regimented masses of lemmings descend from birch woods and invade upland pastures, where they destroy crops, foul wells, and infect the air with their decomposing bodies. Driven by an irresistible compulsion they press on, not pausing at obstacles, until they end their suicidal march in the sea.

The truth is in fact very different. The life cycle of Norway lemmings is not exceptional. The animals are active throughout the year. During the winter, they tunnel and build nests under the snow, where they can breed in safety from predators except for an occasional attack by a weasel or ermine. With the coming of the spring thaw, the burrows risk collapse, so the animals are forced to move to higher ground, or lower to parts of the birch–willow forest, where they spend the summer months in the safety of cavities in the ground or in burrows dug through shallow layers of soil and vegetation. In the fall, with the freezing of the ground and withering of the sedges, there is a seasonal movement back to sheltered places in the alpine zone. Lemmings are particularly vulnerable at this time: should freezing rain and frost blanket the vegetation with ice before the establishment of snow cover, the difficulties in gathering food can prove fatal.

The mass migrations that have made the Norway lemming famous usually begin in the summer or fall following a period of rapid population growth. The migrations start as a gradual movement from densely-populated areas in mountain heaths down into the willow, birch, and conifer forests. At first the lemmings seem to wander at random, but as a migration continues, groups of animals may be forced to coalesce by local topography, for instance if caught in a funnel between two rivers. In such situations the continuous accumulation of animals becomes so great that a mass panic ensues and the animals take to reckless flight – upward, over rivers, lakes, and glaciers, and occasionally into the sea.

Although the causes of mass migrations are far from certain, it is widely thought that they are triggered by overcrowding. Females can breed in their third week and males as early as their first month; reproduction continues year-round. Litters consist of five to eight young, and may be produced every 3–4 weeks, so in a short period lemmings can produce several generations. Short winters without sudden thaws or freezes, followed by an early spring and late fall, provide favorable conditions for continuous breeding and a rapid increase in population density.

Lemmings are generally intolerant of one another and, apart from brief encounters for mating, lead solitary lives. It is possible that in peak years the number of aggressive interactions increases drastically, and that this triggers the migrations. Supporting evidence comes from reports that up to 80 percent of migrating lemmings are young animals (and thus are likely to have been defeated by larger individuals). Food shortages do not seem to be an important factor, since enough food seems to be available even in areas where the animals are most numerous.

The essential feature of long-distance migrations would therefore seem to be a desire for survival. Lemming species in Alaska and northern Canada also engage in similar, if less spectacular, expeditions. Although countless thousands of Norway lemmings may perish on their long journeys, the idea that such ventures always end in mass suicide is a myth. UWH

Left In normal years, the distribution of the Norway lemming covers the tundra region of Scandinavia and northwestern Russia. However, during "lemming years," when there is a vast increase in the size of the population, the distribution expands considerably.

Below Norway lemmings are individualistic, intolerant creatures. When their numbers rise so does aggressive behavior, which is well developed. In the conflict shown here, two males box **1**; engage in wrestling **2**; and adopt a threatening posture toward one another **3**.

to exploit efficiently the highly seasonal, patchy nature of their habitat: strategies change according to population density. Norway lemmings move in summer onto wet, grassy meadows but in the fall move into deep mossy hillsides to overwinter.

Dispersers differ from nondispersing animals in several ways. There is some evidence that, in the Meadow and Prairie voles, animals that disperse are on average genetically different from permanent residents. Juvenile males disperse from their natal site to seek unrelated mating partners and to avoid inbreeding. Additionally, in Field, Prairie, Meadow, Tundra, and European water voles, many young pregnant females will disperse. This is quite unusual for mammals, but it does

Potential for Harm

CONSERVATION AND ENVIRONMENT

Many microtines live in areas of little or no agricultural value, or in areas little changed by human habitation. These species are neither persecuted nor endangered. However, species living in temperate areas can be agricultural pests. The American pine vole burrows in winter around the base of apple trees and chews on the roots or girdles the stems, resulting in a loss in apple production. The extensive underground burrows of Brandt's vole can become a danger to grazing stock.

In addition to their status as pests, many species harbor vectors of diseases such as plague (mole voles) and sylvatic plague (Sagebrush vole). In parts of eastern Europe and central Asia, *Microtus* species and water voles carry tularemia, an infectious disease that causes fever, chills, and inflammation of the lymph glands. The clearing of forest has increased both *Microtus* habitat and the incidence of tularemia. In the 1990s, hantavirus disease, which is carried by several species of voles and lemmings, emerged as an important viral ailment that can be fatal in more than 50 percent of cases. As a result, considerable research effort is now being directed to the epidemiology of the rodent-borne hemorrhagic fevers. CJK

THE SCENT OF DEATH

The effect of weasel odor on vole reproduction

FOR MANY DESERT RODENTS, IT IS BETTER BY FAR to stay hungry but safe for a night or so than to risk death by seeking a meal outside of the burrow during the full moon. In open deserts and other arid areas, birds of prey are a serious threat. They have keen vision, which in many birds extends to seeing UV reflectance. Hunting raptors can even see the scent trails of voles reflecting UV light better than they can the average surroundings.

Things are different in holarctic and boreal areas with a dense cover, whether in forest, meadow, or agricultural areas. Preferred rodent habitats in these areas are characterized by an undercover of grasses, herbs, scrubs, ferns, and bushes. Protection provided by this low canopy of vegetation considerably reduces the risk of airborne predation, and the same applies where there is permanent snow cover that forms a canopy during the winter. However, under the snow's protective canopy, the rodents face the threat of Europe's smallest carnivore, the Least weasel (*Mustela nivalis*). Along with its slightly larger cousin, the stoat (*M. erminea*), it is the only predator of boreal areas that can follow prey into their own world: the burrows and crevices they occupy in old fields and forests, and the subnivean space under the snow.

Small mustelids are specialized vole hunters, and their population fluctuations closely follow those of the boreal voles on which they depend. The Least weasel is committed to a lifestyle based on eating rodents; some specialists reckon that weasel predation is among the forces causing the three-yearly round known as the Northern European vole cycle. During vole population peaks, the Least weasel and stoat can be responsible for 90 percent of total Field and Bank vole mortality.

Any strategy that helps the voles to avoid being killed will be favored in this harsh natural-selection regime. One way of assessing danger is to tap into the communicatory systems of the enemy themselves, and to use the information gained to predict areas of highest risk. Both weasels and stoats secrete a strong odor from their anal glands that is used in territory marking and sexual behavior. So alarming is the scent of weasels to voles that it has been used as a repellent to protect forestry and orchards from browsing. When the presence of scents indicates a lot of predator activity, voles stay in their burrows, becoming less active and avoiding going to distant foraging sites. If they do go out, they are more likely to forage in trees, keeping above the ground and out of the weasels' way.

These behaviors might well decrease the number and intensity of signs left to orient a weasel or stoat lurking somewhere inside the grass thicket or behind stones. Yet there is a price to pay for the enhanced security, in that the voles go hungry. This is especially a problem for females. Breeding is energetically costly, and, during pregnancy and lactation, reproductively active females need two or three times the amount of food required by nonbreeding females.

However, the most intricate tangle of adaptation and counteradaptation concerns the impact of weasel odors on the vole's sex life. Like weasels, voles also communicate by scent, so just as voles can spy on weasel activity by reading their scent messages, so too can weasels use vole scent marks to track them down. More chillingly still, weasels may even be able to distinguish the scents left by voles of different ages and reproductive condition to ensure that, when they do hunt, they are led to the best possible prizes. Female voles that have just given birth make for large, slow, and profitable prey, and the weasel may also benefit from an additional meal – the pups.

Thus if the risk of mortality from weasels is already high, and if it is particularly directed toward breeding females, what can the voles do? Laboratory experiments on the Bank vole and the Field vole have revealed that, in both species, the impact of mustelid odor on breeding was the same: in risky environments over 80 percent of females suppressed breeding, while in safe conditions the same percentage of control-group females bred successfully. Females exposed to mustelid treatment also lost weight, indicating decreased foraging success. Young females were more responsive to predator odor, while older females, closer to death anyway, were more likely to risk breeding.

Field experiments also showed that additional weasel smells suppressed Field vole activity, while removing predators from some areas caused an upturn in reproduction. Yet some parts of this puzzle are still missing. Further experiments are needed in the field to compare rich habitats with dense and thriving rodent populations with the pattern among more marginal, less successful populations. Such studies would clarify the picture by showing what happens when rodents occupying marginal habitats face a strong risk of predation in addition to hunger and cold. Nonetheless, the exciting finding that vole breeding is influenced by the scent of the animals' predators is in itself a clear illustration of the pervasive importance of odor in most mammalian lives. HY

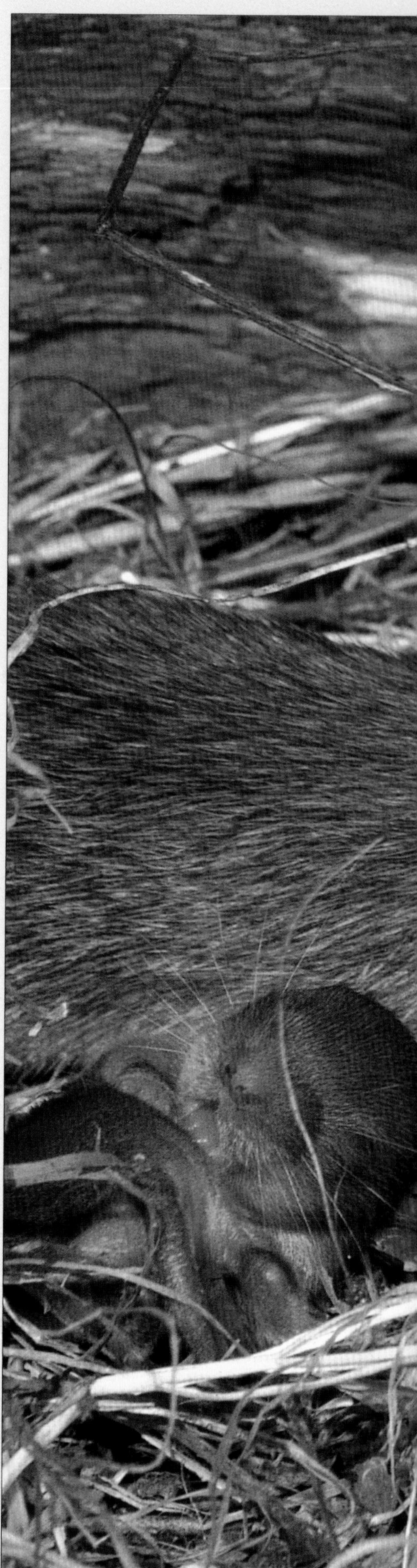

Right *A female Bank vole with young that are just over a week old. Female voles, especially younger ones, will suppress breeding if they detect a powerful presence of weasel odor.*

Old World Rats and Mice

THE OLD WORLD RATS AND MICE, OR MURINAE, include at least 542 species distributed over the major Old World land masses, from immediately south of the Arctic Circle to the tips of the southern continents. If exuberant radiation of species and the ability to survive, multiply, and adapt quickly are criteria of success, then the Old World rats and mice must be regarded as the most successful of all mammals.

The Murinae probably originated in Southeast Asia in the late Oligocene or early Miocene about 25–20 million years ago from a primitive (cricetine) stock. The earliest fossils (*Progonomys*), in a generally poor fossil representation, are known from the late Miocene of Spain, about 8–6 million years ago. Slightly younger fossils (*Leggadina*, *Pseudomys*, and *Zyzomys*) have been discovered recently from the early Pliocene of Australia (5 m.y.a.). Old World rats and mice are primarily a tropical group that have sent a few hardy migrant species into temperate Eurasia.

An Evolutionary Success Story

FORM AND FUNCTION

The murines' success lies in a combination of features probably inherited and adapted from a primitive, mouselike archimurine This is a hypothetical form, but many features of existing species point to such an ancestor, from which they are little modified. The archimurine would have been small, perhaps about 10cm (4in) long in head and body, with a scaly tail of similar length. The appendages would have been of moderate length, thereby facilitating the subsequent development of elongated hind legs in jumping forms and short, robust forelimbs in burrowers. It would have had a full complement of five fingers and five toes. The sensory structures (ears, eyes, whiskers, and olfactory organs) would have been well-developed. Its teeth would have consisted of continuously growing, self-sharpening incisors and three elaborately rasped molar teeth on each side of each upper and lower jaw, with powerful jaw muscles for chewing a wide range of foods and preparing material for nests. The archimurine would have had a short gestation period, would have produced several young per litter, and therefore

Right *Although the tiny Wood mouse* (Apodemus sylvaticus) *is often held responsible for the destruction of young plants, it also plays a role in the dispersal of seeds, which it buries underground. The Wood mouse does not move far from its burrow and may never travel more than 200m (660ft) from its home.*

would have multiplied quickly. With its small size, it could have occupied many different microhabitats. Evolution has produced a wide range of adaptations, but only a few, if highly significant, lines of structural change.

Modifications to the tail have produced organs with a wide range of different capabilities. It has become a long balancing organ, sometimes with a pencil of hairs at its tip (as in the Australian hopping mice) and sometimes without (as in the Wood mouse). In the Harvest mouse it has developed into a grasping organ to help in climbing. In some species including the Greater tree mouse it serves as a sensory organ, with numerous tactile hairs at the end furthest from the animal; in others like the Bushy-tailed cloud rat, it is now thickly furred. In some genera, for example rock rats and spiny mice, as in some lizards, the tail is readily broken, either in its entirety or in part, though unlike lizards' tails it does not regenerate. In species where the proximal part of the tail is dark and the distal part white (for example the Smooth-tailed giant rat), the tail may even serve as an organ of communication

Hands and feet show a similar range of adaptation. In climbing forms, big toes are often opposable, though sometimes relatively small, as in the Palm mouse. The hands and/or feet can be broadened to produce a firmer grip, for instance in the Pencil-tailed tree mouse or Peter's arboreal forest rat. In jumping forms, the hind legs and feet may be much elongated (as in Australian hopping mice), while in species living in wet, marshy conditions (for instance, African swamp rats), the hind feet can be long and slightly splayed, somewhat reminiscent of the webbed feet of ducks. This type of adaptation is at its most pronounced in the Australian and New Guinea water rats and the shrew rats of the Philippines, which possess broadly webbed hind feet.

The claws are also often modified. They may be short and recurved for attaching to bark and other rough surfaces, as in Peter's arboreal forest rat, or large and strong in burrowing forms like those of the Lesser bandicoot rat. In some of the species with a small, opposable digit, the claw of this digit becomes small, flattened, and nail-like (for instance in the Pencil-tailed tree mouse).

Fur is important for insulation. In some species such as spiny mice, some hairs of the back are modified into short, stiff spines, while in others the fur can be bristly (harsh-furred rats), shaggy (African marsh rat), or soft and woolly (African forest rat). The function of spines is not known, although it is speculated that they deter predators.

FACTFILE

OLD WORLD RATS AND MICE

Order: Rodentia

Family: Muridae

Subfamily: Murinae

542 species in 118 genera

DISTRIBUTION Europe, Asia, Africa (excluding Madagascar), Australasia; also found on many offshore islands.

HABITAT Very varied; mostly terrestrial, but some are arboreal, fossorial, or semi-aquatic.

SIZE **Head–body length** ranges from 4.5–8.2cm (1.7–3.2in) in the Pygmy mouse to 48cm (19in) in Cuming's slender-tailed cloud rat; **tail length** from 2.8–6.5cm (1.1–2.5in) to 20–32cm (8–13in); **weight** from about 6g (0.2oz) to 1.5–2kg (3.3–4.4lb), both in the same two species.

COAT Typically medium to dark brown on the back and flanks, sometimes with a lighter-colored belly. Some species are striped for camouflage.

DIET Mostly plant material and invertebrates, though some take small vertebrates.

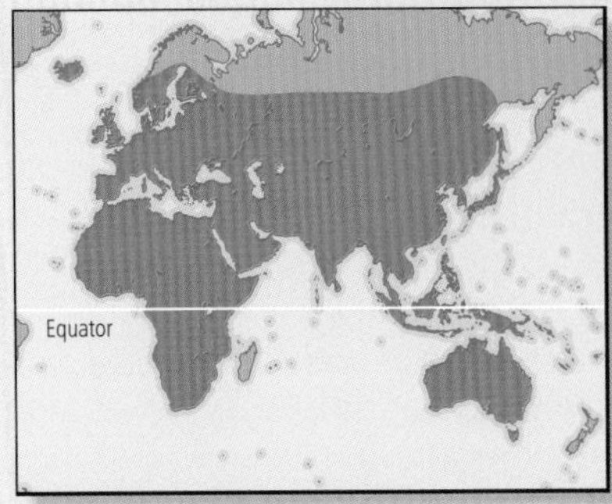

BREEDING In most small species, gestation lasts 20–30 days, though longer in species that give birth to precocious young (e.g. 36–40 days in spiny mice), and also in "old endemic" Australian rodents (e.g. 32–50 days in Australian hopping mice). Duration not known for large species.

LONGEVITY Small species live little over 1 year; larger species like the giant naked-tailed rats over 4 years.

CONSERVATION STATUS Although many Murinae species are flourishing, 15 are currently listed as Critically Endangered, including 2 species each of the genera *Zyzomys* (rock rats) and *Pseudomys* (Australian pseudo-mice); 36 are Endangered.

For full species list see Appendix ▷

Ears can range from the large, mobile, and prominent (as in the Rabbit-eared tree-rat) to the small and inconspicuous, well covered by surrounding hair (the African marsh rat). As its common name indicates, the Earless water rat of Papua New Guinea lacks any external ears, an adaptation that helps streamline its body for a life spent in water. In addition, this highly specialized species has a longitudinal fringe of long white hairs on its tail, remarkably similar to that found in the completely unrelated Elegant water shrew (*Nectogale elegans*) of the Himalayas. The tail fringe is thought to act as an effective rudder.

In teeth, there is considerable adaptation among murines in the row of molars. In what is presumed to be the primitive condition, there are three rows of three cusps on each upper molar tooth, but the number of cusps is often much smaller, particularly in the third molar, which is often small. The cusps may also coalesce to form transverse ridges. But the typical rounded cusps, although they wear with age, make excellent structures for chewing a wide variety of foods.

The molars of Australian water rats and their allies, however, show great simplification, lacking as they do the strong cusps or ridges found in most of the murine rodents. In some species the molars are also reduced in number, the extreme being seen in the One-toothed shrew-mouse which has only one small, simple molar in each row. This adaptation is most likely to be related to a diet of fruit or soft-bodied invertebrates.

The shrew rats of the Philippines have slender, protruding incisor teeth like delicate forceps, presumably adapted, as in the true shrews, for capturing insects and other invertebrates. However, the remaining teeth are small and flat-crowned, quite unlike the sharp-cusped batteries of the true shrews. The two species of the genus *Rhynchomys* offer pronounced examples of this adaptation.

These adaptations of teeth have, at the extremes, resulted in the development of robust

Right *The Norway rat – also called the Brown or Common rat – is practically omnivorous (even eating soap) and found mainly in urban areas, where it causes a good deal of damage. The species' particular preference is for animal matter; it has been known to attack poultry and even young lambs.*

a
b
c
d
1
2
3
4
5
6
e
f
g
h

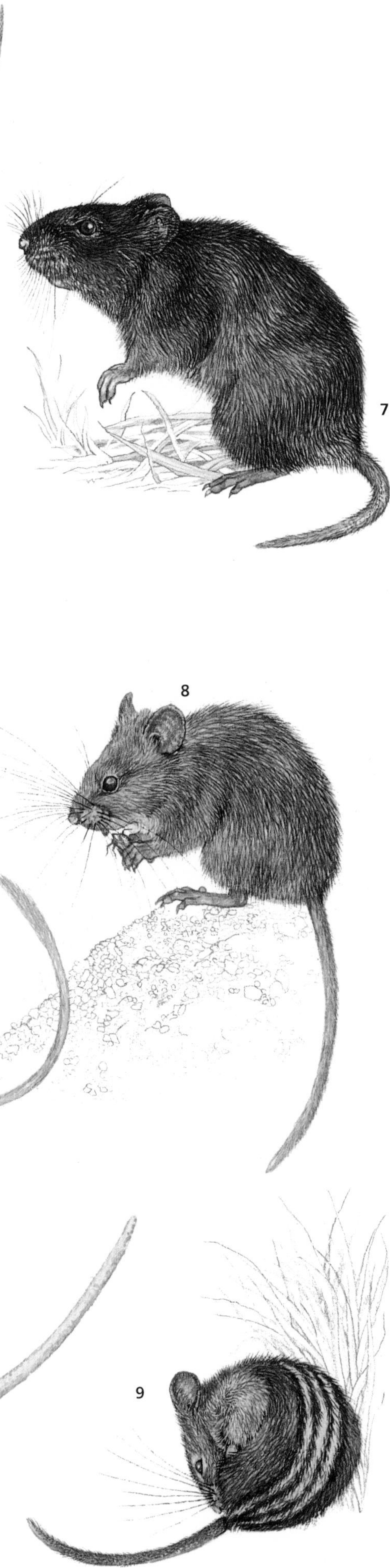

Left *Old World rats and mice:* ***1*** *Smooth-tailed giant rat* (Mallomys rothschildi)*;* ***2*** *Pencil-tailed tree mouse* (Chiropodomys gliroides)*;* ***3*** *African marsh rat* (Dasymys incomtus)*;* ***4*** *a spiny mouse (genus* Acomys)*;* ***5*** *Natal multimammate rat* (Mastomys natalensis)*;* ***6*** *Fawn-colored hopping mouse* (Notomys cervinus)*;* ***7*** *a Vlei rat* (Otomys irroratus) *sitting in a grass runway;* ***8*** *Brush-furred rat* (Lophuromys sikapusi) *eating an insect;* ***9*** *Four-striped grass mouse* (Rhabdomys pumilio)*;* ***10*** *Australian water rat* (Hydromys chrysogaster) *diving;* ***a*** *tail of a field mouse (genus* Apodemus)*;* ***b*** *tail of the Harvest mouse* (Micromys minutus)*;* ***c*** *tail of the Greater tree mouse* (Chiruromys forbesi)*;* ***d*** *tail of the Bushy-tailed cloud rat* (Crateromys schadenbergi)*;* ***e*** *hind foot of the Asiatic long-tailed climbing mouse* (Vandeleuria oleracea)*; first and fifth digits opposable to provide grip for living in trees;* ***f*** *hind foot of the Shining thicket rat* (Grammomys rutilans)*; has broad, short digits for providing grip;* ***g*** *paw of the Lesser bandicoot rat* (Bandicota bengalensis) *showing long, stout claws;* ***h*** *hind foot of an African swamp rat (genus* Malacomys) *showing long, splayed foot with digits adapted for walking in swampy terrain.*

and relatively large teeth (in Rufous-nosed and Nile rats) and in the reduction of the whole tooth row to a relatively small size, as in the Lesser small-toothed rat of New Guinea. The food of this rat probably requires little chewing, possibly consisting of soft fruit or small insects.

Teeming and Ubiquitous

DISTRIBUTION PATTERNS

Murines are found throughout the Old World. There are considerable variations in the numbers of species in different parts of their range, though in examining their natural distribution the House mouse, Roof rat, Norway rat, and Polynesian rat must be discounted, as they have been inadvertently introduced in many parts of the world.

The north temperate region is poor in species. In Europe, countries such as Norway, Great Britain, and Poland have respectively as few as 2, 3, and 4 species each. In Africa, the density of species is low from the north across the Sahara until the savanna is reached, where the richness of species is considerable. Highest densities occur in the tropical rain forest and adjacent regions of the Congo basin. This fact can be shown by reference to selected sites. The desert around Khartoum, the arid savanna at Bandia, Senegal, the moist savanna in Ruwenzori Park, Uganda, and the rain forests of Makokou, Gabon, support 0, 6, 9, and 13 species respectively. The Democratic Republic of Congo boasts 45 species, and Uganda 37.

Moving to the Orient, species are most numerous south of the Himalayas. India and Sri Lanka have about 35 species, Malaysia 22. In the East Indies some islands are remarkably rich: there are about 60 species in New Guinea, 38 in Sulawesi (Celebes), and 35 in the Philippines. Within the Philippines there has been a considerable development of native species, with 10 of the 12 genera and a total of 30 species found only there (in other words, they are endemic); only two species of *Rattus* are found elsewhere. A notable feature is the presence of 10 large species having head–body lengths of about 20cm (8in) or more.

Left *Cane rats are mostly nocturnal creatures but sometimes engage in diurnal activity. As the name suggests, they often inhabit sugar-cane plantations, in which they are capable of wreaking so much damage that large, rodent-eating snakes are occasionally protected, as the lesser of two evils.*

Below *The Plains, or Desert mouse, of Australia inhabits quite shallow burrows. Like many other species native to Australia, its prevalence has been affected by the influx of predators and other animals competing for the same resources that resulted from European colonization and subsequent expansion.*

Right *A Golden-backed tree rat, found in northern parts of Western Australia and the far north of Northern Territory. It is reputed to have a fierce temper and the more annoyed it becomes the louder the noises it makes are. It is known to nest in the Pandanus tree, from which matting is made.*

The largest known murine, Cuming's slender-tailed cloud rat, is found in the Philippines; it grows to over 40cm (16in) in head–body length, and the Pallid slender-tailed rat and the Bushy-tailed cloud rat are only slightly shorter. This high degree of endemism and the tendency to evolve large species is also found in the other island groups. In New Guinea there are 8 species with head–body lengths of more than 30cm (12in), including the Smooth-tailed giant rat, the Rough-tailed eastern white-eared giant rat, the giant naked-tailed rats and the Rock-dwelling giant rat. The most gigantic of all New Guinea's rodents, the Sub-alpine woolly rat, which exceeds 40cm in length and weighs up to 2kg (4.4lb), was discovered only in 1989. There are only two small species, the New Guinea jumping mouse, about the size of the House mouse, and the diminutive Delicate mouse, about half its size again. In Australia there are around 72 species, with the eastern half of the continent having a far greater diversity of species than elsewhere.

Niche Specialists

ECOLOGICAL ADAPTATION

It has proved difficult to give an adequate and comprehensive explanation of the evolution and species richness of the murines. There are some pointers to the course evolution may have followed, based on structural affinities and ecological considerations. The murines are a structurally similar group, and many of their minor modifications are clearly adaptive, so there are few characters that can be used to distinguish between, in terms of evolution, primitive and advanced conditions. In fact only the row of molar teeth has been used in this way: primitive dentition can be recognized in the presence of a large number of well-formed cusps. Divergences from this condition may represent specialization or advancement, while ecological considerations account for a species' abundance and for the types of habitat preference it may show.

From this analysis, two groups of genera have been recognized. The first contains the dominant genera (African soft-furred rats, Oriental spiny rats, Old World rats, giant naked-tailed rats, the *Mus* species, African grass rats and African marsh rats) which have been particularly successful, living in dense populations in the best habitats. These are believed to have evolved slowly, because they display relatively few changes from the primitive dental condition. The second group contains many of the remaining genera which are less successful, living in marginal habitats and often showing a combination of aberrant, primitive, and specialized dental features.

The dominant genera (with the exception of the African marsh rat) contain more species than the peripheral genera and are constantly attempting to extend their range. Considerable numbers of new species have apparently arisen within what is now the range center of a dominant genus (for example, soft-furred rats in central Africa and Old World rats in Southeast Asia). The reasons for this await explanation.

It is quite common for two or more species of murine to occur in the same habitat, particularly in the tropics. One of the more interesting and

important aspects of studies of the animals is to explain the ecological roles assumed by each species in a particular habitat, and then to deduce the patterns of niche occupation and the limits of ecological adaptations by animals with a remarkably uniform basic structure. A particularly favorable habitat, and one amenable to this type of study, is regenerating tropical forest.

In Mayanja Forest, Uganda, 13 species have been found in a small area of about 4sq km (1.5sq mi). Certain species – the Rusty-bellied rat and the Punctated grass mouse – are of savanna origin and are restricted to grassy rides. Of the remaining 11 species, all have forest and scrub as their typical habitat with the exception of the two smallest species, the Pygmy mouse and the Larger pygmy mouse, which are also found in grasslands and cultivated areas. Three species, the Tree rat, the Climbing wood mouse, and Peter's arboreal forest rat, seldom, if ever, come to the ground. The small Climbing wood mouse – often found within the first 60cm (24in) off the ground – prefers a bushy type of habitat. The two other arboreal species are strong branch-runners and are able to exploit the upper and lower levels of trees and bushes. All three species are found alongside a variety of plant species (in the case of the Wood mouse, 37 were captured beside 19 different plants, with *Solanum* among the most favored). All species are herbivorous and nocturnal, and the two larger species construct elaborately woven nests of vegetation.

Two species are found on both the ground and in the vegetation up to 2m (6.5ft) above ground level. Of these, the African forest rat is abundant and the Rufous-nosed rat is much less common. The African forest rat lives and builds its nests in burrows whose entrances are often situated at the bases of trees; it is nocturnal, feeding on a wide range of both insect and plant foods. The Rufous-nosed rat is both nocturnal and diurnal, and constructs nests with downwardly-projecting entrances in the shrub layer, made out of grass, on which this species is known to feed.

Of the 11 forest species, Peter's striped mouse, the Speckled harsh-furred rat, the Long-footed rat, the Pygmy mouse, the Larger pygmy mouse, and Hind's bush rat are all ground-dwellers. Of these, the striped mouse is a vegetarian, preferring the moister parts of the forest. The harsh-furred rat is an abundant species, predominantly predatory, favoring insects but also prepared to eat other types of flesh. The Long-footed rat is found in the vicinity of streams and swamps; it is nocturnal, and includes in its diet insects, slugs, and even toads (a specimen in the laboratory constantly attempted to immerse itself in a bowl of water). The two small mice are omnivores, while Hind's bush rat is a vegetarian species that inhabits scrub.

A further important feature, which could well account for the dietary differences in these species, is their respective sizes. The three mice are in the 5–25g (0.2–0.9oz) range, with the

Above *The blind, hairless litter of the House mouse. This species is found almost worldwide, except in locations where it is excluded by either climate or competition from other small mammals.*

Right *A female Brants' whistling rat* (Parotomys brantsii) *with her young clinging to one of her nipples. Rodents of this species seldom venture far from their burrows, to which they return at the slightest provocation after emitting a loud alarm whistle.*

Below *A male Harvest mouse with a non-receptive female. Harvest mice construct nests for the young, usually about 1m (3.3ft) above ground. Litter size is about 4–7; sexual maturity is reached at five weeks.*

Pygmy mouse rather smaller than the other two. The Rufous-nosed rat is in the 70–90g (2.5–3.2oz) range, and the Long-footed rat and Hind's bush rat above this. The remaining species – the Tree rat, Peter's arboreal forest rat, the African forest rat, the Speckled harsh-furred rat, and Peter's striped mouse – have weights between 35g and 60g (1.2–2.1oz).

Within the tropical forests there is a high precipitation, with rain falling in all months of the year. This results in continuous flowering, fruiting, and herbaceous growth, which is reflected in the breeding activity of the rats and mice found there. In Mayanja Forest, the African forest rat and the Speckled harsh-furred rat were the only species obtained in sufficient numbers to permit the monthly examination of reproductive activity. The African forest rat bred throughout the year, while in the Speckled harsh-furred rat the highest frequency of conception coincided with the wetter periods of the year, from March to May and October to December.

Of Mice and Men

Conservation and Environment

Some Old World rats and mice have a close, detrimental association with humans through consuming or spoiling their food and crops, damaging their property, and carrying disease.

The most important species commensal with humans are the Norway or Brown or Common rat, the Roof rat, and the House mouse; now found worldwide, they originated from around the Caspian Sea, India, and Turkestan respectively. In addition to these cosmopolitan commensals, there are the more localized Multimammate rat in Africa, the Polynesian rat in Asia, and the Lesser bandicoot rat in India.

While the Roof rat and the House mouse have been extending their ranges for centuries, the Norway rat's progress has been much slower; it was unknown in the West before the 11th century, though now it is established in urban and rural situations in temperate regions, and is the rodent most commonly found in sewers; in the tropics, it is mainly found in large cities and ports. The Roof rat is more successful in the tropics, where towns and villages are often infested, though it cannot compete with the indigenous species in the field. In many Pacific, Atlantic, and Caribbean islands, Roof rats are common in agricultural and natural habitats in the absence of competitors.

With even the solitary House mouse capable of causing considerable damage, the scale of mass outbreak damage is difficult to envisage. An Australian farmer recorded 28,000 dead mice on his veranda after one night's poisoning, and 70,000 were killed in a wheat yard in an afternoon.

There are many rodent-borne diseases, transmitted either directly or through an intermediate host. The Roof rat, along with other species, hosts the plague bacterium, which is transmitted through the flea *Xenopsylla cheopis*. The lassa fever virus of West Africa is transmitted through urine and feces of the Multimammate rat. Other diseases in which murines are involved include murine typhus, rat-bite fever, and leptospirosis.

In the past, some Old World rats and mice were persecuted for reasons other than pest control. Notably, the sheer size of the beaver rat of Australia – which weighs 650–1,250g (23–44oz) – once told against it, when it was hunted for its luxurious pelt from the 1930s onward. As a result of hunting restrictions, this species is now on the increase. Most murine species now regarded as threatened are in danger from habitat destruction.

The Old World rats and mice are a remarkably rich and adaptable group of mammals. In spite of their abundance and ubiquity in the Old World, particularly the tropics, the murines remain a poorly studied group. Exceptions include a few species of economic importance and the Wood mouse. Many species are known only from small numbers in museums, supported by the briefest information on their biology. The Bisa rat, for example, is known only from a single skull retrieved from Bisa Island in 1990. There are undoubtedly endless opportunities for future research on this fascinating and accessible group of mammals. GS/CRD/MJD

Old World Rat and Mouse Species

Species include: African forest rat (*Praomys jacksoni*), **African grass rats** (genus *Arvicanthis*), **African marsh rat** (*Dasymys incomtus*), **African soft-furred rats** (genus *Praomys*), **African swamp rats** (genus *Malacomys*), **Asiatic long-tailed climbing mouse** (*Vandeleuria oleracea*), **Australian hopping mice** (genus *Notomys*), **Australian pseudo-mice** (genus *Pseudomys*), **beaver rats** (genus *Hydromys*), **Bisa rat** (as yet undescribed), **Bushy-tailed cloud rat** (*Crateromys schadenbergi*), **Cuming's slender-tailed cloud rat** (*Phloeomys cumingi*), **Delicate mouse** (*Pseudomys delicatulus*), **giant naked-tailed rats** (genus *Uromys*), **Greater tree mouse** (*Chiruromys forbesi*), **Harvest mouse** (*Micromys minutus*), **Hind's bush rat** (*Aethomys hindei*), **House mouse** (*Mus musculus*), **Larger pygmy mouse** (*Mus triton*), **Lesser bandicoot rat** (*Bandicota bengalensis*), **Lesser ranee mouse** (*Haeromys pusillus*), **Lesser small-toothed rat** (*Macruromys elegans*), **Long-footed rat** (*Malacomys longipes*), **Multimammate mouse** (*Mastomys natalensis*), **New Guinea jumping mouse** (*Lorentzimys nouhuysi*), **Nile rat** (*Arvicanthis niloticus*), **Norway, Brown, or Common rat** (*Rattus norvegicus*), **Old World rats** (genus *Rattus*), **Oriental spiny rats** (genus *Maxomys*), **Pallid slender-tailed rat** (*Phloeomys pallidus*), **Pencil-tailed tree mouse** (*Chiropodomys gliroides*), **Peter's striped mouse** (*Hybomys univittatus*), **Polynesian rat** (*Rattus exulans*), **Punctated grass mouse** (*Lemniscomys striatus*), **Pygmy mouse** (*Mus minutoides*), **Rabbit-eared tree rat** (*Conilurus penicillatus*), **Rock-dwelling giant rat** (*Xenuromys barbatus*), **rock rats** (genus *Zyzomys*), **Roof rat** (*Rattus rattus*), **Rough-tailed eastern white-eared giant rat** (*Hyomys goliath*), **Rufous-nosed rat** (*Oenomys hypoxanthus*), **Rusty-bellied brush-furred rat** (*Lophuromys sikapusi*), **shrew rats** (genus *Rhynchomys*), **Smooth-tailed giant rat** (*Mallomys rothschildi*), **Yellow-spotted brush-furred rat** (*Lophuromys flavopunctatus*), **spiny mice** (genus *Acomys*), **Subalpine woolly rat** (*Mallomys istapantap*), **thicket rats** (genus *Thamnomys*), **vlei rats** (genus *Otomys*), **whistling rats** (genus *Parotomys*), **Wood mouse** (*Apodemus sylvaticus*).

For full species list see Appendix ▷

A Scent-Based Information Superhighway

Communication patterns among House mice

In the darkness behind our kitchen cupboards or in the house footings, mice live, feeding on the superabundant food that is a by-product of our wasteful lives. As many as 50 may live together in family groups, with several adult females, their offspring, subdominant males, and a dominant male defending the territory. They may be quiet, but be sure that they are communicating, relaying complex and subtle messages of life, death, property rights, sex, and family matters through the medium of their own urine.

Urine – a substance we think of as disposable if not disgusting – is the essence of the mouse information superhighway. In addition to urea and other waste products, their urine contains a complex mixture of chemicals: small-molecular-weight volatile odorants and much higher-weight non-volatile proteins. Together these are the mouse equivalent of visiting cards, providing information on identity, species, sex, social and reproductive status, and state of health. Many genetic differences between individual mice contribute to each individual's unique scent signature, including the highly variable (polymorphic) genes of the major histocompatibility complex (MHC). Because scents used for individual recognition are inherited, mice can recognize relatives they have not met before from the similarity of their scents to that of known family members. The system is much more sophisticated than that used by humans to recognize their long-lost aunts or uncles.

Mice are also capable of producing their scent marks in slow-release capsules to ensure maximum effect. Mouse urine contains a high concentration of small (18–20kDa) lipocalin proteins, termed Major Urinary Proteins (MUPs), that are manufactured in the liver and filtered through the kidneys into the urine. Adult males excrete around 30mg of protein per ml (.004oz per fluidram) of urine per day, while adult females excrete about 40 percent as much. These urinary proteins bind the signalling chemicals inside a central cavity to cause their slow release from scent marks.

Each individual mouse within a group deposits urine in small streaks and spots as they move around their home area, particularly when they encounter an unmarked surface, so that all surfaces become covered with a thin smear. Communication "posts" of dried urine mixed with dust build up like small stalagmites in frequently-used locations, around feeding sites, at entrances to nest areas, or along trails.

Since mice are always surrounded by a familiar mixture of urine marks, they rapidly detect any new objects in their environment – or precipitous edges in the dark – by the absence of the strong, accustomed smell. Scent marks deposited around the territory also help to maintain familiarity and recognition between group members. Intruders can be recognized immediately because their scent contrasts with the background odors, stimulating investigation and attack by resident mice, and especially by the dominant male. In addition, adult males excrete signaling volatiles that are highly attractive to females and induce caution or stimulate aggression from other males.

Dominant males advertise their territory ownership and competitive ability by scentmarking at a much higher rate than other mice. They deposit hundreds of urine marks per hour, compared to only tens of marks by females or subordinates, using hairs on the end of their prepuce as a "wick." Since only a male successfully dominating an area can ensure that it is suffused with his own odor, this is a reliable signal that a territory is owned – by the male. Dominant territory owners seek out and attack any other males that deposit competing scent marks in their territory, and immediately countermark a competitor's scent by depositing their own urine nearby, ensuring that their own scent is always the freshest. Other

	URINE DONOR		
	Unfamiliar adult male	**Non-breeding grouped female**	**Pregnant or lactating female**
Juvenile female	Accelerates puberty	Delays puberty	Accelerates puberty
Adult female	Induces estrus and shortens cycle	Prolongs anestrus or induces pseudopregnancy	Prolongs estrus
Pregnant female	Terminates early pregnancy and induces estrus		

Right *As the table shows, the scent of urine has different priming effects on female House mice depending both on the reproductive state of the female and the identity of the donor. The strength of the inhibition caused by urine from non-breeding females increases with the size of the group and length of exposure.*

males will usually flee if they meet the owner of the scent marks within his scentmarked area, or will avoid entering it, considerably reducing the need for aggressive defence by the owner. However, if a male is not defending his territory very successfully and other males are able to deposit competing scents, the owner may be challenged.

Females take advantage of these urinary competitions to select the best father for their young. While they will nest in one male's territory, they may well wander off to mate with other males, particularly if their patch is exclusively and freshly marked. They also prefer to mate with animals whose scents are dissimilar to their parents', thus avoiding inbreeding problems. If there is no choice, however, they will mate anyway. Males do not distinguish their own young from those fathered by another male.

If there is no territory available, some males will live within those of dominant males, spreading urine with low concentrations of signaling chemicals in fewer deposits. This allows the dominant male to recognize that they are not a threat, but it also means they are not attractive to females.

Mouse urine can also alter the reproductive state of females according to their opportunities, as spelled out in the table above. A young female exposed to the scent of a new male will come into puberty, and therefore become ready to breed, up to 6 days earlier than normal for first estrus, which typically falls at 36–40 days of age (the familiar odor of a father has no such effects). The urine of an unfamiliar male can also prevent a pregnancy from proceeding in a newly-conceived female who encounters the scent before the embryo has implanted into the wall of her uterus, so that the new male may stand a chance of becoming the father of the next litter. Unfamiliar male urine also induces estrus and shortens the cycle of adult females, thereby synchronizing their estruses.

As female mice live in communes sharing the chores of motherhood, it is unsurprising that a final, major role of mice scents is that of girl talk. Preferring to share their nest sites with other familiar females (usually close relatives), females will come into breeding condition earlier if they are receiving signs that other female kin are already breeding. Overcrowding, however, is a problem, and may inhibit further reproduction. If three or more females live together and are waiting for an opportunity to breed, they produce a scent that can inhibit puberty in other young females by more than 20 days, and that inhibits estrous cycling among other adult females. This behavior delays reproduction in overcrowded conditions. These ingenious responses allow females to reproduce rapidly under favorable conditions, but to delay their reproduction at times of high population density when their offspring would stand little chance of survival. JH

Below *At least since the start of cereal-growing around 10,000 years ago, House mice have lived in wary co-existence with humans, using their sensitive noses to sniff out information about their environment and each other.*

Other Old World Rats and Mice

1

THROUGHOUT THE OLD WORLD THERE ARE groups of rats and mice that cannot be included in the three major Muridae subfamilies. Here they are grouped in eight subfamilies, placed for convenience in a west–east geographical sequence. Some of these rodents are superficially similar to members of the major groups; for example, the zokors can be considered as specialized voles. Two groups, the blind mole rats and the bamboo rats, are more distinctive and are sometimes treated as separate families.

Blind Mole Rats

SUBFAMILY SPALACINAE

Of all the subterranean rodents, the blind mole rats show the most extreme adaptations to life underground. Their eyes are completely and permanently hidden under their skin, and there are no detectable external ears or tail. The incisors protrude so far that they are permanently outside the mouth and can be used for digging without the mouth having to be opened. A unique feature is the horizontal line of short, stiff, presumably touch-sensitive hairs on each side of the head. Most blind mole rats are about 13–25cm (5–9in) long, but in one species, the Giant mole rat of southern Russia, they can reach 35cm (14in).

Blind mole rats are found in dry but not desert habitats from the Balkans and southern Russia around the eastern Mediterranean to Libya. Apart from being entirely vegetarian they live very much like the true moles (which are predators belonging to the order Insectivora). Each animal makes its own system of tunnels, which may reach as much as 350m (1,150ft) in length, throwing up heaps of soil. They feed especially on fleshy roots, bulbs, and tubers, but also on whole plants. Although originally animals of the steppes, they have adapted well to cultivation and are a considerable pest in crops of roots, grain, and fruit.

Blind mole rats breed in spring. There are usually two or three in a litter, and they disperse away from the mother's tunnel system as soon as they are weaned, at about 3 weeks. There is sometimes a second litter later in the year.

As in many other burrowing mammals, the blind mole rats' limited movement has led to the evolution of many local forms, making the individual species very difficult to define but providing a bonanza for the study of genetics and the processes of evolution and species formation. The number of species that should be recognized, and how they should best be classified, are still very uncertain. Eight species are recognized here, but these have been reduced to three elsewhere.

African Pouched Rats

SUBFAMILY CRICETOMYINAE

The five species of African pouched rats resemble hamsters in having a storage pouch opening from the inside of each cheek. The two short-tailed pouched rats are hamster-like in general appearance also, but the other three species are ratlike, with a long tail and large ears.

The giant pouched rats are among the largest of the murid rodents, reaching 40cm (16in) in head–body length. They are common throughout Africa south of the Sahara, and in some areas are hunted for food. They feed on a wide variety of items, including insects and snails as well as seeds and fruit. In addition to serving to carry food to underground storage chambers, the cheek pouches can be inflated with air as a threat display. The gestation period is about 6 weeks, and litter size usually two or four.

The three large species are associated with peculiar, blind, wingless earwigs of the genus *Hemimerus*, which occur in their fur and in their nests, where they probably share the rats' food.

2

3

4

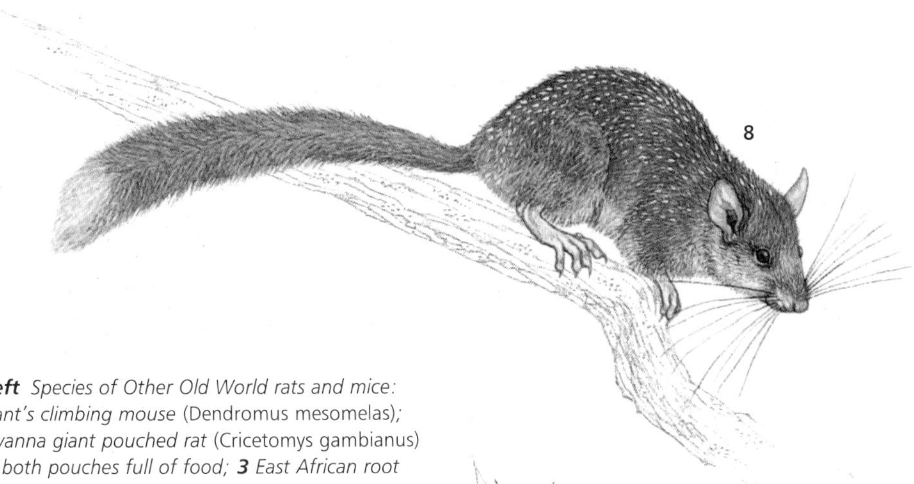

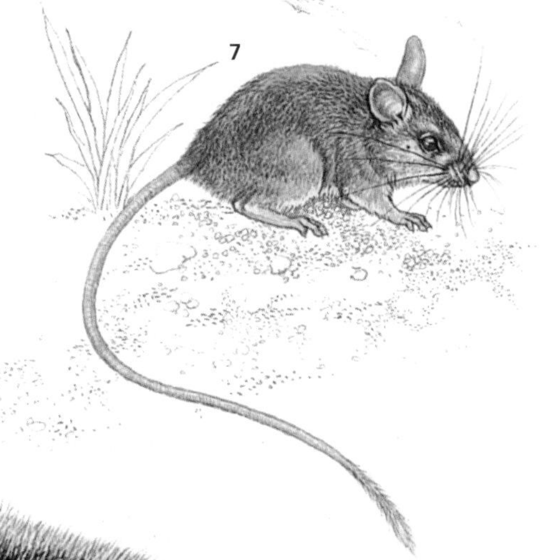

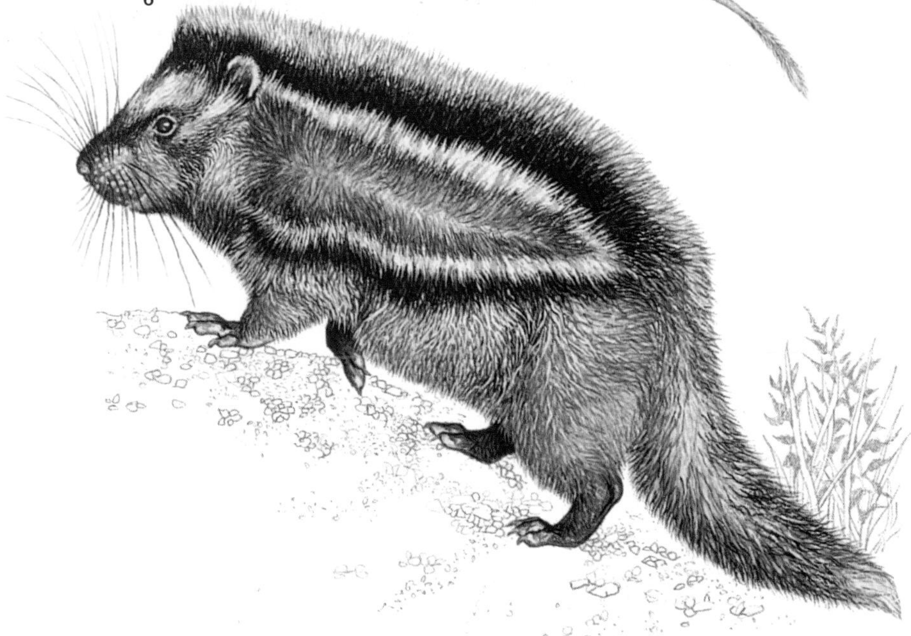

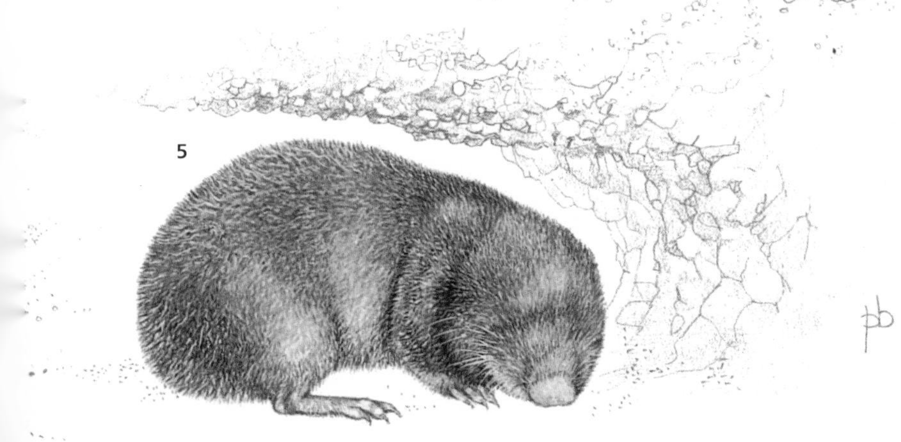

Left *Species of Other Old World rats and mice:* **1** *Brant's climbing mouse* (Dendromus mesomelas)*;* **2** *Savanna giant pouched rat* (Cricetomys gambianus) *with both pouches full of food;* **3** *East African root rat* (Tachyoryctes splendens) *burrowing with its incisors;* **4** *East Siberian zokor* (Myospalax aspalax)*, kicking back excavated soil with its hind feet;* **5** *Ehrenberg's mole rat* (Nannospalax ehrenbergi)*, showing the broad nose used for ramming soil and tactile hairs on the face – note the absence of external eyes;* **6** *Crested rat* (Lophiomys imhausi) *with mane erect, showing a glandular patch;* **7** Macrotarsomys ingens *(one of the Madagascan rats);* **8** *Spiny dormouse* (Platacanthomys lasiurus).

FACTFILE

OTHER OLD WORLD RATS & MICE

65 species in 30 genera and 8 subfamilies

DISTRIBUTION Balkans, S Russia, Africa, Madagascar, S India, China

See subfamilies table ▷

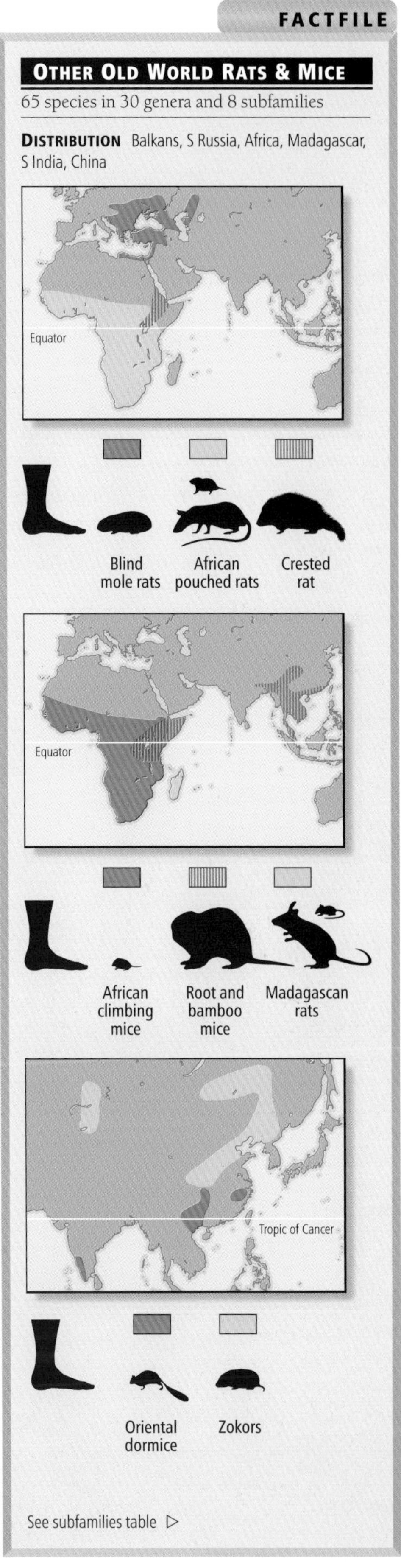

Crested Rat

SUBFAMILY LOPHIOMYINAE

The Crested rat has so many peculiarities that it is placed in a subfamily of its own, and it is not at all clear what its nearest relatives are. It is a large, dumpy, shaggy rodent with a bushy tail and tracts of long hair along each side of the back that can be erected. These are associated with specialized scent glands in the skin, and the individual hairs of the crests have a unique, lattice-like structure that probably serves to hold and disseminate the scent. These hair tracts can be suddenly parted to expose the bold, striped pattern beneath, as well as the scent glands themselves.

The skull is also unique in possessing a peculiar granular texture and in having the cavities occupied by the principal, temporal chewing muscles roofed over by bone – a feature not found in any other rodent.

Crested rats are nocturnal and little is known of their way of life. They spend the day in burrows, rock crevices, or hollow trees. They are competent climbers and feed on a variety of vegetable materials. The stomach is unique among rodents in being divided into a number of complex chambers similar to those found in ruminant ungulates such as cattle and deer.

African Climbing Mice

SUBFAMILY DENDROMURINAE

The majority of African climbing mice are small, agile mice with long tails and slender feet, adapted to climbing among trees, shrubs, and long grass. Although they are confined to Africa south of the Sahara, some of them closely resemble mice in other regions that show similar adaptations, such as the Eurasian harvest mouse (subfamily Murinae) and the North American harvest mice (subfamily Sigmodontinae). They are separated from these mainly by a unique pattern of cusps on the molar teeth, and it is on the basis of this feature that some superficially very different rodents have been associated with them in the subfamily Dendromurinae.

Typical dendromurines, for instance those of the genus *Dendromus*, are nocturnal and feed on grass seeds, but are also considerable predators on small insects such as beetles and even on young birds and lizards. Some species in other genera are suspected of being more completely insectivorous. In the genus *Dendromus*, some species make compact, globular nests of grass above ground, for instance in bushes; others nest underground. Breeding is seasonal, with usually three to six naked, blind nestlings in a litter.

Of the other genera, the most unusual are the fat mice. They make extensive burrows and spend long periods underground in a state of torpor during the dry season, after developing thick deposits of fat. Even during their active season fat mice become torpid, with reduced body temperature during the day.

Many species of this subfamily are poorly known. Several distinctive new species have been discovered in the course of the past 40 years, and it is likely that others remain to be found, especially arboreal forest species.

The genera *Petromyscus* and *Delanymys* have sometimes been separated from the others in a subfamily of their own, Petromyscinae.

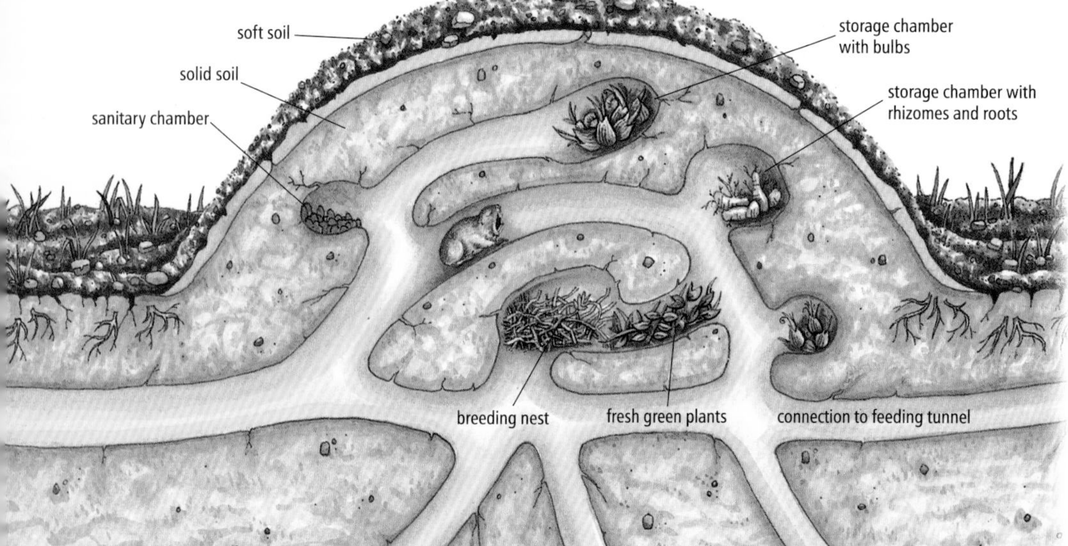

Above *Despite its common name, the Island mouse* (Nesomys rufus) *is ratlike in appearance. It is one of a group of 14 rodents found only on the island of Madagascar, where it lives in complex burrows often located under fallen treetrunks.*

Left *Breeding mound of a blind mole rat, Ehrenberg's mole rat* (Nannospalax ehrenbergi). *Each animal makes its own system of tunnels which may be as much as 350m (1,150ft) long, throwing up heaps of soil. The rats feed especially on fleshy roots, bulbs, and tubers, but also on whole plants, which they pull down into their tunnels by the roots. Their underground food storage chambers have been known to hold as much as 14kg (31lb) of assorted vegetables.*

Root and Bamboo Rats

SUBFAMILY RHIZOMYINAE

Root rats are large rats adapted for burrowing, and they show many of the characteristics found in other burrowing rodents – short extremities, small eyes, large, protruding incisor teeth, and powerful neck muscles, reflected in a broad, angular skull. The bamboo rats, found in southeast Asian forests, show all these features in less extreme form than the East African root rats. They make extensive burrows in which they spend the day, emerging at night to do at least some feeding above ground. The principal diet consists of the roots of bamboos and other plants, but above-ground shoots are also eaten. In spite of their size, breeding is similar to the normal murid pattern.

The African root rats are more subterranean than the bamboo rats, but less so than African mole rats or the blind mole rats. They make prominent "mole hills" in open country. Roots and tubers are stored underground. As in most molelike animals, each individual occupies its own tunnel system. The gestation period is unusually long – between 6 and 7 weeks.

Madagascan Rats

SUBFAMILY NESOMYINAE

It has long been debated whether the 14 indigenous rodents of the island of Madagascar form a single interrelated group (implying they have evolved from a single colonizing species), or whether there have been multiple colonizations, meaning that some of the present species may be more closely related to mainland African rodents than to their fellows on Madagascar. The balance of evidence seems to favor the first hypothesis – hence their inclusion here in a single subfamily.

The South African white-tailed rat has also been included – the implication being that it is the sole survivor on the African mainland of the stock that colonized Madagascar – although it actually might be best placed in a separate subfamily, Mystromyinae. The problem arises from the diversity of the Madagascan species, coupled with the fact that none of them match very closely any of the non-Madagascan groups of murid rodents.

The group includes small, agile mice with long tails, long, slender hind feet, and large eyes and ears (e.g. *Macrotarsomys bastardi* and *Eliurus minor*). *Nesomys rufus* is typically ratlike in its proportions, while *Hypogeomys antimena* is rabbit-sized and makes deep burrows, although it forages for food on the surface. The two *Brachyuromys* species are remarkably vole-like in form, dentition, and ecology. They live in wet grassland or marshes, and are apparently adapted to feeding on grass. Externally, they can only be distinguished with difficulty from Eurasian water voles.

Oriental Dormice

SUBFAMILY PLATACANTHOMYINAE

The three species of Oriental dormice have been considered to be closely related to the true dormice (family Gliridae), which they resemble externally and in the similar pattern of transverse ridges on the molar teeth, although there are only three molars on each row, not preceded by a premolar as in the true dormice. More recently, opinion has swung toward treating them as aberrant members of the family Muridae (in its widest sense, as used here). Whatever their affinities, they are distinctive arboreal mice with no close relatives, and little is known of their way of life. The Spiny dormouse, a seedeater, is a pest of pepper crops in numerous parts of southern India.

Zokors

SUBFAMILY MYOSPALACINAE

Zokors are burrowing, vole-like rodents found in steppes and open woodlands in much of China. Although they live almost entirely underground, they are less extremely adapted than the blind mole rats. Both eyes and external ears are clearly visible, although tiny, and the tail is also distinct. Digging is done mainly with the very large claws of the front feet rather than the teeth.

Like the blind mole rats, zokors feed on roots, rhizomes, and bulbs, but they also occasionally collect food such as seeds from the surface. Massive underground stores of food are accumulated, enabling the animals to remain active all winter.

Breeding takes place in spring, when one litter of up to six young is produced. Their social organization is little known, but the young appear to stay with the mother for a considerable time. GBC

Other Old World Rat and Mouse Subfamilies

Blind mole rats Subfamily Spalacinae

8 species in 2 genera: greater blind mole rats (*Spalax*, 5 species); lesser blind mole rats (*Nannospalax*, 3 species). Balkans, S Russia, E Mediterranean, N Africa. 5 species are Vulnerable.

African pouched rats Subfamily Cricetomyinae

5 species in 3 genera: giant pouched rats (*Cricetomys*, 2 species); Lesser pouched rat (*Beamys hindei*); short-tailed pouched rats (*Saccostomus*, 2 species). Africa S of the Sahara. 1 species is Vulnerable.

Crested rat Subfamily Lophiomyinae

1 species, *Lophiomys imhausi*. Kenya, Somalia, Ethiopia, E Sudan, in mountain forests from 1,200m (4,000ft).

African climbing mice Subfamily Dendromurinae

21 species in 10 genera: climbing mice (*Dendromus*, 6 species); Nikolaus's mouse (*Megadendromus nikolausi*); Dollman's tree mouse (*Prionomys batesi*); Link rat (*Deomys ferrugineus*); Velvet climbing mouse (*Dendroprionomys rousseloti*); Groove-toothed forest mouse (*Leimacomys buettneri*); Gerbil mouse (*Malacothrix typica*); fat mice (*Steatomys*, 6 species); rock mice (*Petromyscus*, 2 species); Delany's swamp mouse (*Delanymys brooksi*). Subsaharan Africa. 2 species are Critically Endangered; 1 is Endangered, and 3, including Nikolaus's mouse, are Vulnerable.

Root and bamboo rats Subfamily Rhizomyinae

6 species in 3 genera: bamboo rats (*Rhizomys*, 3 species); Lesser bamboo rat (*Cannomys badius*); root rats (*Tachyoryctes*, 2 species). E Africa and SE Asia.

Madagascan rats Subfamily Nesomyinae

15 species in 8 genera: big-footed mice (*Macrotarsomys*, 2 species); Island mouse (*Nesomys rufus*); White-tailed rat (*Brachytarsomys albicauda*); tufted-tailed rats (*Eliurus*, 6 species); voalavoanala (*Gymnuromys roberti*); Malagasy giant rat (*Hypogeomys antimena*); short-tailed rats (*Brachyuromys*, 2 species); White-tailed mouse (*Mystromys albicaudatus*). Madagascar (1 species in S Africa). 2 species are Critically Endangered, 2 Endangered, and 2 Vulnerable.

Oriental dormice Subfamily Platacanthomyinae

3 species in 2 genera: Spiny dormouse (*Platacanthomys lasiurus*); Chinese pygmy dormice (*Typhlomys*, 2 species). S India (Spiny dormouse); S China and N Vietnam (Chinese dormice). 1 *Typhlomys* species is Critically Endangered.

Zokors Subfamily Myospalacinae

6 species in 1 genus (*Myospalax*). China and Altai Mountains. Underground. 1 species is Vulnerable.

For full species list see Appendix ▷

Hamsters

FAMILIAR IN THE WEST AS CHILDREN'S PETS, hamsters in their natural setting are solitary animals that react with aggression when they encounter other members of their own species. One breed that currently flourishes in captivity virtually all around the world was on the brink of extinction less than a century ago.

FACTFILE

HAMSTERS

Order: Rodentia

Family: Muridae

Subfamily: Cricetinae

24 species in 5 genera: **Mouse-like hamsters** (Genus *Calomyscus*, 5 species; Iran, Pakistan Afghanistan, S Russia,). **Rat-like hamsters** (Genus *Cricetulus*, 11 species; SE Europe, Asia Minor, N Asia). **Common hamster** or **Black-bellied hamster** (*Cricetus cricetus*; C Europe, Russia). **Golden hamsters** (Genus *Mesocricetus*, 4 species; E Europe, Middle East.). **Dwarf hamsters** (Genus *Phodopus*, 3 species; Siberia, Mongolia, N China).

DISTRIBUTION Europe, Middle East, Russia, China.

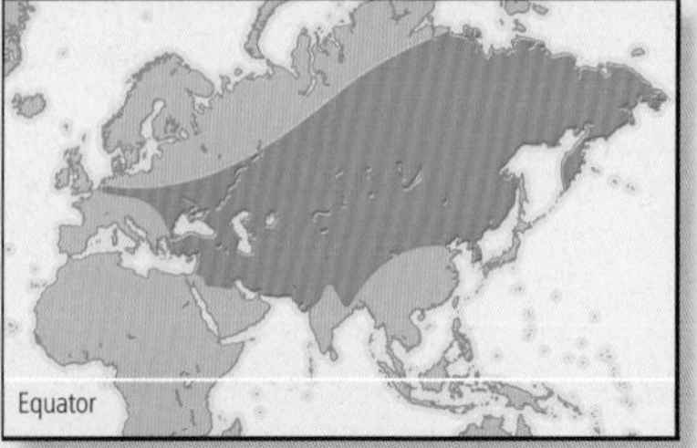

HABITAT Arid or semiarid areas, varying from rocky mountain slopes and steppe to cultivated fields.

SIZE Ranges from **head–body length** 5.3–10.2cm (2–4in) to 20–28cm (7.9–11in), **tail length** 0.7–1.1cm (0.3–0.4in), **weight** 50g (1.8oz) to 900g (32oz)

COAT Soft, thickly-furred in shades of gray and brown

DIET Mostly herbivorous – seeds, shoots, root vegetables – though occasionally hamsters will take insects, lizards, small mammals, and young birds.

BREEDING Gestation ranges from 15 days in the Golden hamster to 37 days in the White-tailed rat.

LONGEVITY 2–3 years

CONSERVATION STATUS *Calomyscus hotsoni* and *Mesocricetus auratus* are listed as Endangered; *Mesocricetus newtoni* is listed as Vulnerable; others not threatened.

For full species list see Appendix ▷

Until the 1930s the Golden hamster was known only from a single specimen found in 1839. However, in 1930 a female with 12 young was collected in Syria and taken to Israel. There the littermates bred, and some descendants were taken to England in 1931 and to the USA in 1938, where they proliferated. Today the Golden hamster is one of the most familiar pets and laboratory animals in the West. The other hamster species are less well-known, though the Common hamster has been familiar for many years.

Pouches for Foraging

FORM AND FUNCTION

Most hamsters have small, compact, rounded bodies with short legs, thick fur, large ears, prominent dark eyes, long whiskers, and sharp claws. Most have cheek pouches that consist of loose folds of skin, starting from between the prominent incisors and premolars and extending along the outside of the lower jaw. When hamsters forage they can push food into the pouches, which then expand, enabling them to carry large quantities of provisions to their underground storage chambers – a useful adaptation for animals that live in habitats where food may occur irregularly but in great abundance. The paws of the front legs are modified hands, giving the animals great dexterity when they manipulate food. Hamsters also use a characteristic forward squeezing movement of the paws as a means of emptying their cheek pouches of food. Common hamsters are reputed to inflate their cheek pouches with air when crossing streams, presumably to create extra buoyancy.

Hamsters are mainly herbivorous. The Common hamster may hunt insects, lizards, frogs, mice, young birds, and even snakes, but such prey contribute only a small amount to its diet. Normally hamsters eat seeds, shoots, and root vegetables, including wheat, barley, millet, soybeans, peas, potatoes, carrots, and beets, as well as leaves and flowers. Small items such as millet seeds are carried to the hamster's burrow in its pouches, larger items like potatoes in its incisors. Food is either stored for the winter, eaten on returning to underground quarters, or, in undisturbed conditions, eaten above ground. One Korean gray rat managed to carry 42 soybeans in its pouches. The record for storage in a burrow probably goes to the Common hamster: chambers of this species have been found to contain as much as 90kg (198lb) of plant material collected by a single hamster. Hamsters spend the winter in hibernation in their burrows, only waking on warmer days to eat food from their stores.

Baby Machines

SOCIAL BEHAVIOR

Though considered docile pets, hamsters in the wild are solitary and exceptionally aggressive toward members of their own species. These characteristics may result from intense competition for patchy but locally abundant food resources, but may also serve to disperse population throughout a particular area. Large species, such as the Korean gray rat, also behave aggressively toward other species, and have been known to attack dogs or even people when threatened. To defend itself from attack, the Korean gray rat may throw itself on its back and utter piercing screams.

Species studied in the laboratory have been shown to have acute hearing. They communicate with ultrasound as well as with squeaks audible to the human ear. Ultrasound appears to be most important between males and females during mating. The sense of smell is also acute; the Golden hamster can recognize individuals, probably from flank gland secretions, and males can detect stages of a female's estrous cycle and recognize a receptive female by odor.

Most hamsters become sexually mature soon after weaning (or even during it). Female Common hamsters become receptive to males at 43 days and can give birth at 59 days. Golden

Above *The Striped dwarf hamster* (Cricetulus barabensis) *has capacious cheek pouches, enabling it to transport large quantities of food quickly to its burrow. This species of ratlike hamster is reported to be very aggressive, especially toward conspecifics.*

hamsters have slightly slower development and become sexually mature between 56 and 70 days. In the wild they probably breed only once – occasionally twice – per year, during spring and summer, but in captivity they can breed year round.

Courtship is simple and brief, as befits animals that generally meet only to copulate. Odors and restrained movement indicate that the partners are ready and willing to mate. Immature animals or females not in heat will either attack or be attacked by other individuals. After copulation a pair separate and may never meet again. The female builds a nest for the young in her burrow from grass, wool, and feathers, and gives birth after 16–20 days (in the Common hamster). The young – born hairless and blind – are cared for by the female alone. During this time she may live off her food store in another section of the burrow. The young are weaned at about 3 weeks in the Golden hamster. In the slowest-developing species, the Mouse-like hamster, adult coloration and size may not be reached until 6 months old.

Above *The Golden hamster* (Mesocricetus auratus) *has been familiar worldwide for several decades as a pet. However, in the wild it is found only in a small area of northwestern Syria and is classified as Endangered by the IUCN.*

One species, *Cricetulus (Tscherskia) triton*, has been extensively studied in the North China Plain. It begins to breed in March and ends by August. While older females can manage 3 litters in a year, hamsters born that year produce only 1–2 litters. Litter size may be between 2 and 22, but the average is 9–10, after a gestation of about 20 days. It takes 2 months for a new-born female hamster to produce a first litter. The interval between two litters for an adult female is also about 2 months. The population oscillates greatly from year to year. Weasels and hawks are the major predators.

Male Dzhungarian hamsters are extraordinary fathers, and even act as midwife to their partner. They help pull the young from the birth canal, and then clean up the newborns, consuming the placenta and licking out the nostrils to allow the little ones to breath. The male then stays close to the mother and young to keep them warm. These behaviors may be mediated by hormonal changes, as just before a birth the male's levels of estrogen and cortisol – the female and stress hormones – rise, to be replaced by testosterone thereafter. Later on, the male babysits while the female goes out to feed.

Pets or Pests?

CONSERVATION AND ENVIRONMENT

Hamsters are considered serious pests to agriculture in some areas – in some countries dogs are trained to kill them. Chinese peasants sometimes catch large hamsters to feed to cats or other pets, and may dig the burrows in autumn to recover stored grain; in addition, the Common hamster is trapped for its skin. Despite these pressures, most hamster species are not endangered, perhaps because most live in inhospitable regions and have high reproduction rates. JF/ZZ

Gerbils

To most people, gerbils are attractive pets with large, dark eyes, white bellies and feet, and furry tails. The animal they have in mind, however, is the Mongolian jird, just one of the many species of gerbils, jirds, and sand rats that together make up the world's largest group of rodents adapted to arid environments.

Gerbils are distinctive among rodents, mostly resembling the familiar Mongolian jird in overall appearance but varying in dimensions from the mouse-sized slender gerbils to robust-bodied jirds and sand rats. Within genera, however, the visible differences between species are subtle, often only expressed by small changes in fur and nail color, tail length, and the presence or absence of a tail tuft. Given such complexities, it is impossible to know for sure how many species exist; sometimes it is even hard to identify the genus to which a species belongs without using chromosomal, protein, and molecular comparisons.

Adaptations for Arid Climes

FORM AND FUNCTION

Most gerbils live in arid habitats and harsh climates, having adapted to both in interesting ways. To survive in such inhospitable conditions, an animal must not lose more water than it normally takes in. Water loss usually occurs by evaporation from the skin, in air exhaled from the lungs, and via urination and defecation. The gerbil's predicament is that it has a large body surface compared with its volume, and so has to find ways of minimizing water loss.

As a consequence, gerbils cannot afford to sweat, and indeed cannot survive temperatures of 45°C (113°F) or higher for more than about two hours. Most species are nocturnal; during the day they live underground, often with the burrow entrance blocked, at a depth of about 50cm (20in) where the temperature remains a constant 20–25°C (68–77°F). Only some northern species – for example, Great gerbils and Mongolian jirds – live on the surface in daytime, though some jirds that live farther south also emerge during the day in winter.

In the arid world of the gerbil, the only foods that are often available are dry seeds or leaves. The animal's nocturnal activity enables it to make the most of this poor sustenance. By the time it comes out of its burrow, such foods are permeated with dew, and it can improve the burrow's humidity, already high in relative terms, by taking them back there to eat. The gerbil's digestive system extracts water efficiently from the food, minimizing the water lost in feces, and the kidneys produce only a few drops of concentrated urine.

Other gerbil adaptations reduce the risk of capture by predators. Gerbils take on the color of the ground on which they live; this ability extends even to local populations of a single species living in different habitats, so animals found on dark lava soils are dark brown whereas conspecifics living on red sand are red. The effectiveness of the camouflage is only compromised by the tail, which ends in a tuft of a contrasting color. Even so, the tail is a vital survival aid; it helps with balance during movement; it can be used to twirl sand over a burrow entrance, effectively concealing it; and it may act as a decoy too, distracting predators from the animal's body and coming away either whole or in part if a predator happens to catch hold of it.

Another distinctive feature of gerbil anatomy is a particularly large middle ear, which is at its biggest in species living in open desert habitats; this enables the animals to hear low-frequency sounds such as the beating of an owl's wings. Gerbils also have large eyes, positioned high on the head so that they give the animals a wide field of vision.

The Three Gerbil Zones

DISTRIBUTION PATTERNS

The geographical range of gerbils can be divided into three major regions. The first includes not just the extensive savannas of Africa but also the Namib and Kalahari deserts, where the temperature rarely falls below freezing in winter. The second takes in the "hot" deserts and semidesert regions along the Tropic of Cancer in north Africa and southwest Asia, plus the arid Horn of Africa. The third covers the deserts, semideserts, and steppes of Central Asia, where winter temperatures fall well below freezing. The different gerbil genera fall broadly into groups linked to one or other of these regions. So, with the exception of the Indian gerbil, gerbils of the *Gerbillurus* and *Taterillus* groups occur in the first region, *Ammodillus*, *Gerbillus*, and *Pachyuromys* gerbils live in the second, while only species belonging to the *Rhombomys* group live in the third (though some of these also occur in the second region).

FACTFILE

GERBILS

Order: Rodentia

Family: Muridae

Subfamily: Gerbillinae

95 species in 14 genera

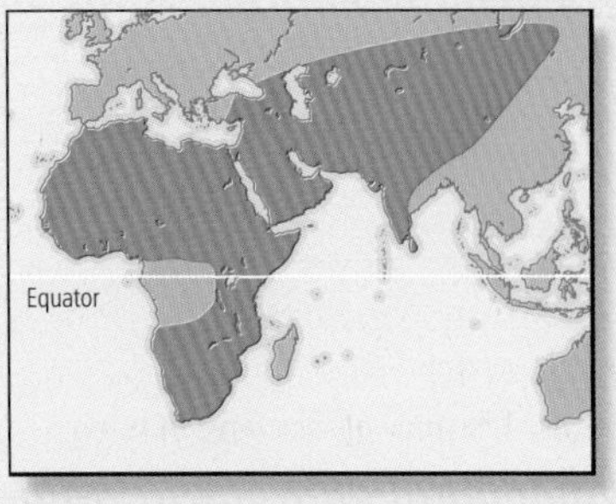

DISTRIBUTION African deserts and savannas; Asian deserts and steppes, from Turkey and Transcaucasia to NE China.

HABITAT Desert, savanna, steppe, rocks, cultivated land.

SIZE **Head–body length** ranges from 6.2–7.5cm (2.4–2.9in) in the Pygmy gerbil to 15–20cm (5.9–7.9in) in the Indian gerbil; **tail length** from 7.2–9.5cm (2.8–3.7in) to 16–22cm (6.2–8.7in) and **weight** from 8–11g (0.3–0.4oz) to 115–190g (4–6.7oz), both in the same two species.

COAT Mouselike in appearance, with soft pale yellow, light brown, or grayish fur. The underparts are customarily white or cream-colored.

DIET Primarily seeds, roots, and other plant matter, although some species also eat insects, snails, and (occasionally) small mammals and reptiles.

BREEDING Gestation 21–28 days

LONGEVITY Usually 1–2 years

CONSERVATION STATUS Of the 95 species, 13 in the genus *Gerbillus* and 1 in the genus *Meriones* (jirds) are listed as Critically Endangered. In addition, 4 *Meriones* species are Endangered, while 3 *Gerbillus* and the sole *Ammodillus* species, *Ammodillus imbellis*, are Vulnerable.

See genera table ▷

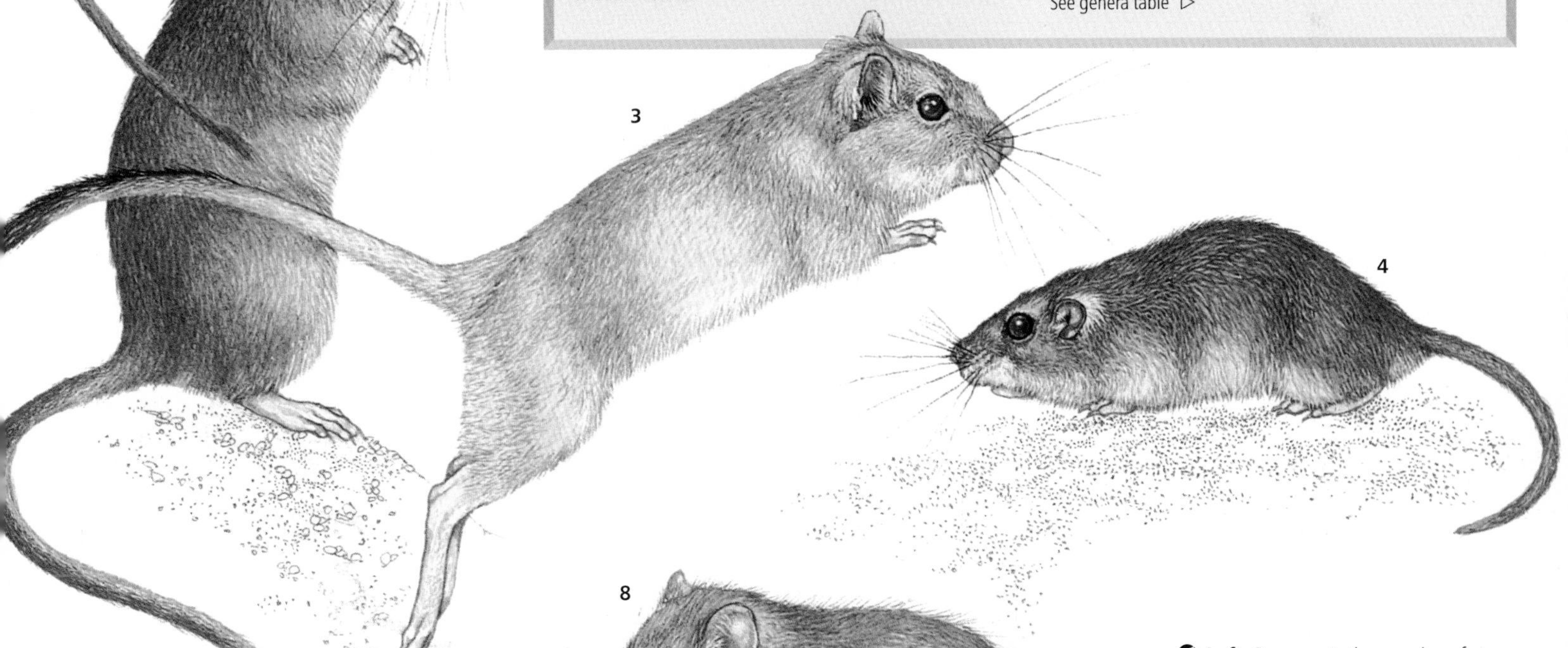

◐ **Left** *Representative species of gerbils:* ***1*** *Common brush-tailed gerbil* (Gerbillurus paeba) *grooming its muzzle and spreading secretions;* ***2*** *Tamarisk jird* (Meriones tamariscinus) *exposing its ventral gland;* ***3*** *Libyan jird* (Meriones libycus) *making an attack;* ***4*** *Short-eared gerbil* (Desmodillus auricularis) *making a submissive crouch;* ***5*** *Great gerbil* (Rhombomys opimus) *with a heap of sand and feces or urine;* ***6*** *Lesser Egyptian gerbil* (Gerbillus gerbillus), *one of the smaller gerbils, marking sand with secretions from its ventral gland;* ***7*** *female Mongolian jird* (Meriones unguiculatus) *with hair raised darting away from a male (part of the mating sequence);* ***8*** *Fat sand rat* (Psammomys obesus) *holding and sniffing a ball of sand and urine.*

Gerbil Groups

Ammodillus

1 genus: *Ammodillus*

Somali gerbil or walo (*Ammodillus imbellis*) Somalia, E Ethiopia, inhabiting savanna and desert.

Gerbillus

3 genera: *Desmodilliscus, Gerbillus, Microdillus*

Pouched pygmy gerbil (*Desmodilliscus braueri*) Senegal and Mauritania E to C Sudan, inhabiting savanna.

Northern pygmy gerbils (*Gerbillus*, 45 species) N Africa, Middle East, Iran, Afghanistan, to NW India, inhabiting desert, semidesert, and coastal plains. Species include Pygmy gerbil (*G. henleyi*), Lesser Egyptian gerbil (*G. gerbillus*), Greater rock gerbil (*G. campestris*), Wagner's gerbil (*G. dasyurus*).

Somali pygmy gerbil (*Microdillus peeli*) Somalia inhabiting dry savanna.

Gerbillurus

2 genera: *Desmodillus, Gerbillurus*

Short-eared gerbil (*Desmodillus auricularis*) S Africa, inhabiting desert, savanna.

Southern pygmy gerbils (*Gerbillurus* 4 species) S Africa, inhabiting savanna and desert. Species include Namib brush-tailed gerbil (*G. setzeri*).

Pachyuromys

1 genus: *Pachyuromys*

Fat-tailed jird (*Pachyuromys duprasi*) Morocco to Egypt inhabiting desert and semidesert.

Rhombomys

5 genera: *Brachiones, Meriones, Psammomys, Rhombomys, Sekeetamys*

Przewalski's gerbil (*Brachiones przewalskii*) N China, inhabiting desert.

Jirds (*Meriones*, 16 species) N Africa, Turkey, SW Asia, Kazakhstan, to Mongolia, N China and NW India inhabiting desert and semidesert. Species include Silky jird (*M. crassus*), Mongolian jird (*M. unguiculatus*).

Sand rats (*Psammomys*, 2 species) N African to Syria and Arabian peninsula inhabiting desert and semidesert. Species include Fat sand rat (*P. obesus*) and Lesser sand rat (*P. vexillaris*).

Great gerbil (*Rhombomys opimus*) Kazakhstan, Iran, Afghanistan, Pakistan to N China and Mongolia inhabiting steppe and desert.

Bushy-tailed jird (*Sekeetamys calurus*) E Egypt, S Israel, Jordan, to C Saudi Arabia inhabiting desert.

Taterillus

2 genera: *Tatera, Taterillus*

Large naked-soled gerbils (*Tatera*, 12 species) S, E, and W Africa, Syria to India, Nepal and Sri Lanka inhabiting savanna and steppe. Species include Indian gerbil (*T. indica*), Black-tailed gerbil (*T. nigricauda*).

Small naked-soled gerbils (*Taterillus*, 8 species) Senegal, Mauritania to S Sudan and S to N Tanzania inhabiting semi-desert, savanna and wooded grassland. Species include: Emin's gerbil (*T. emini*), Harrington's gerbil (*T. harringtoni*).

For full species list see Appendix ▷

Omnivorous Vegetarians

DIET

Gerbils are basically vegetarians, eating various parts of plants – seeds, fruits, leaves, stems, roots, and bulbs; many species, however, will eat anything they encounter, including insects, snails, reptiles, and even other small rodents. The nocturnal *Gerbillus* species often search for wind-blown seeds in deserts. Gerbils living in the very dry desert regions of southern Africa are primarily insectivorous.

Some species are very specialized, living on a single type of food. The Fat sand rat, Great gerbil, and Indian gerbil, for example, are all basically herbivorous. Of these, the Fat sand rat only occurs where it can find salty, succulent plants, while the Indian gerbil depends on fresh food all year round, so it tends to occur near irrigated crops. Wagner's gerbil has such a liking for snails that it threatens the existence of local snail populations; big piles of empty shells are found outside this gerbil's burrows.

Most gerbils take the precaution of carrying their food back to their burrows before they consume it. Species that live in areas with cold winters must hoard in order to survive. One Mongolian jird was found to have hidden away 20kg (44lb) of seeds in its burrow. Great gerbils not only hoard plants but also construct stacks outside the burrow that can be 1m (3.3ft) high and 3m (9.8ft) long.

A Link with Climate and Food

SOCIAL BEHAVIOR

The social organization of gerbils is only beginning to be studied. Species that live in authentic deserts, whatever genus or group they belong to, tend to lead solitary lives, sometimes in extensive burrow systems, though the burrows are often close enough not to preclude the existence of colonies. Perhaps because the supply of food cannot be guaranteed in such an environment, each animal fends for itself. In contrast, species from savannas, where food is more abundant, are more social. There have been reports of stable pairs forming, and even of family structures emerging.

The most complex social arrangements of all have been observed in species in the Rhombomys group that live in regions with cold winters. Groups larger than families gather in single, extensive burrows, perhaps to huddle together for warmth but also maybe to guard food supplies. The best-known example is the Great gerbil of the Central Asian steppes, which lives in large colonies composed of numerous subgroups that themselves have developed from male–female pairs. A similar social structure is found among Mongolian jirds, although other jird species in North Africa and Asia are reported to be solitary in hot climates but social in cooler regions.

Above *The characteristically slender form of a northern pygmy gerbil, in this case a Cheesman's gerbil embroiled in clearing sand from the entrance to its burrow in the Wahiba Sands, Oman. Many species of this genus are Endangered.*

In savanna species, reproduction too seems to be linked to climate and food. These gerbils give birth after the rainy season. Species living in areas where fresh food is available may reproduce all the year round, with females giving birth to two or three litters a year. Some desert species, however, reproduce only in the cooler months, although those found in southern African deserts may give birth at any time.

Litter size can vary between 1 and 12, with a mean of 3–5, depending on species. The young are born helpless and hairless with their eyes closed, and are unable to regulate their body

Right *The Bushveld gerbil has a ratlike appearance. These gerbils inhabit sandy plains, savannas, and woodlands. Despite their small stature they can leap vast heights and distances when frightened, fleeing from predators in a series of running bounds. Burrows for this genus may be up to 1m (3ft) underground.*

The Communal Life of the Mongolian Jird

Mongolian jirds live in sizable social groups that, at their largest in summer, consist of 1–3 adult males and 2–7 adult females, plus numerous subadults and juveniles, all dwelling in a single burrow system. Detailed studies have demonstrated that the animals engage in various group activities, for example collectively hoarding food for the winter and spending the cold months huddled together in the burrow. The integrity of the community seems, under normal circumstances, to be jealously guarded. Strange jirds and other animals are chased off.

Who, then, among the adults in the group are the parents of the subadults and juveniles? Parenthood is not evident from the behavior of the males and females within the community, even though they have been observed to form pairs.

The young might conceivably be the offspring of young adults that have migrated from another burrow, but for many reasons this has never seemed likely to be the case. If animals were to leave their own group late in the summer to establish another burrow community elsewhere, they would be vulnerable to predators and the effects of bad weather, and would also have to contend with other jirds into whose territories they might wander. (When population densities are high, there may be as many as 50 burrows per hectare, or 20 per acre). In addition, they would not have access to the food collected for the winter. The most serious objection, however, is that if the animals traveled in groups, such behavior would perpetuate inbreeding and so produce genetic problems.

The unexpected answer to this conundrum has come from observation of animals in captivity. Such studies have shown that communal groups do remain stable and territorial, but when females are in heat they leave their own territories and visit neighboring communities to mate. The females then return to their own burrows, where their offspring will eventually grow up under the protection and care not of their mother and father but rather of their mother and uncles.

Right *This Mongolian jird is probably two to three weeks old. Litter size is usually 4–6; infants, which open their eyes at 2–3 weeks, are weaned after about 3–4 weeks.*

temperature. For about two weeks they depend entirely on their mother's care, and are nursed constantly. Where there is a breeding season, only those born early within it become sexually mature in time to themselves breed in the same season (when aged about 2 months). Those born later become sexually mature after about 6 months, and breed during the following season.

Contradictory Relations with Humans

CONSERVATION AND ENVIRONMENT

Most gerbils live in largely uninhabited areas of the world. When they do come into contact with humans, especially in the African savannas, the Asian steppes, and India, their activities bring them into conflict with people. When collecting food, especially to hoard for winter, they pilfer from crops. When burrowing, they can cause great damage to pastures, irrigation channels, road and railway embankments, and even to the foundations of buildings. They also carry the fleas that transmit deadly disease, including plague, and are reservoirs of the skin disease leishmaniasis.

Though they serve humankind in medical research and as pets, they become pests when they interfere with peoples' lives. Many gerbils are destroyed by gassing; alternatively, burrow systems may be plowed up, even though they may have been used by generations of gerbils for hundreds of years. In some regions too, the sweet, lightly-colored meat is considered a delicacy and is readily eaten. DAS/GA

Dormice

Right *Worldwide, many dormouse species are at risk; the Japanese dormouse is classified by the IUCN as Endangered.*

Above *Despite its name, the Garden (or Orchard) dormouse* (Eliomys quercinus) *is mostly found in forests across central Europe, though some inhabit shrubs and crevices in rocks.*

THE DORMICE OR MYOXIDAE ORIGINATED AT least as early as the Eocene era, 55–34 million years ago. In the Pleistocene (1.8 million–10,000 years ago), giant forms lived on some Mediterranean islands. Today dormice are the intermediates, in form and behavior, between mice and squirrels.

Key features of dormice are their accumulations of fat and their long hibernation period (about seven months in most European species). The Romans fattened dormice for eating in a special enclosure, the *glirarium*, while the French have a phrase "To sleep like a dormouse," equivalent to the English "To sleep like a log."

Equipped for Scurrying

FORM AND FUNCTION

Dormice are extremely agile. Most species are adapted to climbing, but some – for example Garden and Forest dormice – also live on the ground; however, the Masked mouse-tailed dormouse is the only species that does so exclusively. The four digits of the forefeet and the five digits of the hind feet have short, curved claws. The underside of each foot is bare with a cushion-like covering. The tail is usually bushy and often long, and in some species such as the Fat, Hazel, Garden, Forest, and African dormice it can detach from the body when it is seized upon by predators – or even other dormice. The sense of hearing is particularly well-developed, as is the ability to vocalize. Fat, Hazel, Garden, and African dormice make use of clicks, whistles, and growling sounds across a broad range of behavior: antagonistic, sexual, explorative, playful.

The Desert dormouse, which is placed in a genus of its own, occurs in deserts to the west and north of Lake Balkhash in eastern Kazakhstan, Central Asia. It has very dense, soft fur, a naked tail, small ears, and sheds the upper layers of skin when it molts. It eats invertebrates such as insects and spiders, and is mostly active at twilight and in the night. It probably hibernates in cold weather.

Feeding Up for Winter

DIET

Dormice are the only rodents that do not have a cecum, which indicates that their diet contains little cellulose. Analysis of the contents of their stomachs has shown that they are omnivores whose diet varies according to season and that there is dietary variation between species according to region. The Fat and Hazel dormice are the most vegetarian, eating quantities of fruits, nuts, seeds, and buds. Garden, Forest, and African dormice are the most carnivorous – their diets include insects, spiders, earthworms, and small vertebrates, but also eggs and fruit.

In France, 40–80 percent of the diet of the Garden dormouse is comprised of insects, according to region and season. However, there is also another factor to be considered. In summer the Garden dormouse eats mainly insects and fruit while in the fall it eats little except fruit, even though the supply of insects is plentiful at this time of year. This change in the content of the diet is part of the preparation for entering hibernation; the intake of protein is reduced, and consequently sleep is induced.

A Long Time Sleeping

SOCIAL BEHAVIOR

In Europe, dormice hibernate from October to April with the precise length of time varying between species and according to region. During the second half of the hibernation period they sometimes wake intermittently – a sign of the onset of the hormone activity that stimulates sexual activity.

Dormice begin to mate as soon as they emerge from hibernation, females giving birth from May onward through to October according to age. (Not all dormice that have recently become sexually mature participate in mating.) The Fat and Garden dormice produce one litter each per year, but Hazel and Forest dormice can produce up to three. Vocalizations play an important part in mating. In the Fat dormouse, the male emits calls as he follows the female; in the Garden dormouse, the female uses whistles to attract the male. The female goes into hiding just before she is due to give birth, and builds a nest, usually globular in shape and located off the ground, for example in a hole in a tree or in the crook of a branch. Materials used include leaves, grass, and moss. The Garden and Fat dormice use hairs and feathers as lining materials. The female Garden dormouse scent-marks the area around the nest and defends it.

Female dormice give birth to between two and nine young, with four being the average litter size in almost all species. The young are born naked and blind. In the first week after birth they become able to discriminate between smells, although an exchange of saliva between mother and young appears to be the means whereby mother and offspring learn to recognize each other. This behavior may also aid the transition from a milk diet to a solid food one. At about 18 days the young become able to hear, and at about the same time their eyes open. They become independent after about 4–6 weeks. Young dormice then grow rapidly until

FACTFILE

DORMICE

Order: Rodentia

Families: Myoxidae

26 species in 8 genera and 3 subfamilies

DISTRIBUTION Europe, Africa, Turkey, Asia, Japan.

HABITAT Wooded and rocky areas, steppe, gardens.

SIZE Head–body length 6.1–19cm (2.4–7.5in); tail length 4–16.5cm (1.6–6.5in); weight 15–200g (0.5–7oz).

COAT Soft-furred and squirrel-like, with bushy tails (except in *Myomimus*).

DIET Omnivorous, including insects, worms, spiders, fruit, seeds, nuts, and eggs.

BREEDING Gestation 21–32 days

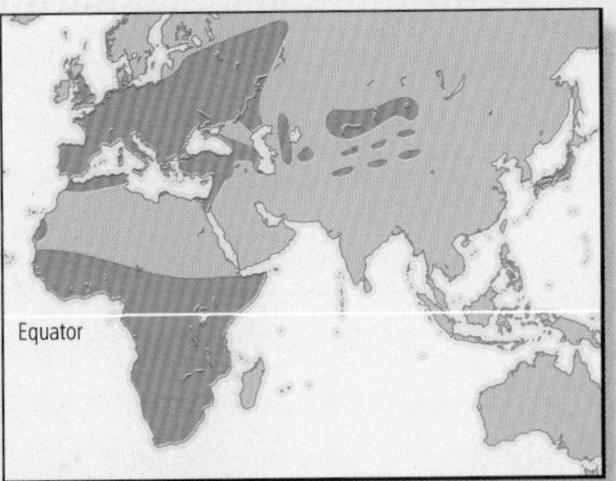

LONGEVITY 3–6 years in wild

CONSERVATION STATUS Half of all dormouse species are listed by the IUCN: 4 as Endangered, 4 as Vulnerable, and 5 as Lower Risk – Near Threatened.

See subfamilies table ▷

Above *The richly colored Hazel dormouse lives in thickets and areas of secondary growth in forests; it has a particular fondness for nut trees and is very well-adapted to climbing in them.*

Left *Curled up tightly, this Hazel dormouse is in hibernation. For its long winter sleep this dormouse resorts to a nest, either in a tree stump, amid debris on the ground, or in a burrow. The length of hibernation is related to climate and can last nine months.*

Dormouse Subfamilies

Subfamily Graphiurinae

African Dormice (*Graphiurus*, 14 species). 1 species Vulnerable.

Subfamily Leithiinae

Forest Dormice (*Dryomys*, 3 species). 1 species Endangered.
Garden dormice (*Eliomys*, 2 species). 1 species Vulnerable.
Mouse-tailed dormice (*Myomimus*, 3 species). 1 species Endangered, 2 species Vulnerable.
Desert dormouse (*Selvinia betpakdalaensis*). Endangered.

Subfamily Myoxinae

Japanese dormouse (*Glirulus japonicus*). Endangered.
Hazel dormouse (*Muscardinus avellanarius*).
Fat dormouse (*Myoxus glis*).

For full species list see Appendix ▷

the time for hibernation approaches, when their development slows. Sexual maturity is reached about one year after birth, towards the end of or after the first hibernation.

Dormice populations are usually less dense than those of most other rodents. There are normally between 0.1 and 10 dormice per ha (0.04–4 per acre). They live in small groups, half of which normally consist of juveniles, and each group occupies a home range, the main axis of which can vary from 100m (330ft) in the Garden dormouse to 200m (660ft) in the Fat dormouse. In urban areas the radio-tracking of Garden dormice has indicated that their home range describes an elliptical shape and is related to the availability of food. In the fall the home range is about 1,000sq m (10,800sq ft).

One study of the social organization of the Garden dormouse revealed significant changes in behavior in the active period between hibernations. In the spring, when Garden dormice are emerging from hibernation, males form themselves into groups in which there is a clearcut division between dominant and subordinate animals. As the groups form, some males are forced to disperse. Once this has happened, although groups remain cohesive, behavior within them becomes somewhat more relaxed, so that by the end of the summer the groups have a family character. In the fall social structure includes all categories of age and sex. Despite the high rate of renewal among its members, a colony can continue to exist for many years. CB

Right *Fat dormice have a predilection for fruit and are one of the most vegetarian species. This made them highly suitable for human consumption, hence their alternative name of Edible dormice.*

Jumping Mice, Birchmice, and Jerboas

TO A GREATER OR LESSER EXTENT, ALL THE members of the Dipodidae family have evolved to move in leaps and bounds. As their names suggest, jumping mice and birchmice are small and mouse-like; the jerboas are mostly rather larger, and are remarkable for their kangaroo-like hind legs.

These small and relatively defenseless rodents seem to have adapted to jumping as an anti-predator strategy. Mostly nocturnal, they are shy and are seldom seen in the wild, not least because some species hibernate for up to 9 months of the year.

Left *A Meadow jumping mouse drinks from a puddle. Like all jumping mice, it will spend more than half the year in hibernation, entering torpor in October and only re-emerging in late April.*

Hop, Crawl, and Jump

FORM AND FUNCTION

All jumping mice are equipped for jumping, with long back feet and long tails to help them keep their balance in the air; even so, the most common species, those of the genus *Zapus*, are more likely to crawl under vegetation or make a series of short hops rather than long leaps. And yet the Woodland jumping mouse will often move by bounding 1.5–3m (5–10ft) at a time. Along with the feet and tail, the outstanding characteristics of jumping mice are their colorful fur and grooved upper incisors. The function of the groove is unknown: it may improve the teeth's cutting efficiency, or simply strengthen them.

Jumping mice are not burrowers. They live on the surface, although their nests may be underground or in a hollow log or other protected place, and the hibernating nest is often at the end of a burrow in a bank or other raised area. For the most part, though, they hide by day in vegetation. They also usually travel about in thick herbaceous cover, although they will use runways or sometimes other species' burrows when present.

Birchmice differ from jumping mice in having scarcely enlarged hind feet and upper incisors without grooves. Their legs and tail are shorter, yet they too travel by jumping, and climb into bushes using their outer toes to hold on to vegetation and their tails for partial support. Birchmice also dig shallow burrows and make nests of herbaceous vegetation underground.

Jerboas are nocturnal and have large eyes. Their hind limbs are elongated to at least four times the length of their front legs, and in most species the three main foot bones are fused into a single "cannon bone" for greater strength. Jerboas living in sandy areas have tufts of hair on the undersides of the feet that serve as "snowshoes" on soft sand and help them to maintain traction and kick sand backwards when burrowing. These jerboas also have hair tufts to help keep sand out of their ears.

The well-developed jumping ability of jerboas enables them to escape from predators as well as to move about. Only the hind legs are used in moving; the front feet then can be used for gathering food. Jerboas use their long tails as props when standing upright and as balancing organs when jumping. Jumps of 1.5–3m (5–10ft) are used when the animal moves rapidly.

Subfamilies of Jumping Mice, Birchmice, and Jerboas

Jumping mice Subfamily Zapodinae

3 genera: *Zapus, Eozapus, Napaeozapus*

Jumping mice (*Zapus*, 2 species): Meadow jumping mouse (*Zapus hudsonius*) and *Z. princeps*. (The animal sometimes classified separately as *Z. trinotatus* is here considered synonymous with *Z. princeps*). N America, in wooded areas, grassy fields, and alpine meadows.

Woodland jumping mouse (*Napaeozapus insignis*) N America, in forests.

Chinese jumping mouse (*Eozapus setchuanus*) China.

Birchmice Subfamily Sicistinae

1 genus: *Sicista*

Birchmice (*Sicista*, 13 species). Species include *S. betulina* (N Eurasia), *S. caucasica* (W Caucasus and Armenia), *S. subtilis* (Russia and E Europe).

Jerboas 5 subfamilies

Subfamily Cardiocraniinae

2 genera: *Cardiocranius, Salpingotus*

Five-toed pygmy jerboa (*Cardiocranius paradoxus*), W China, Mongolia.

Three-toed pygmy jerboas (*Salpingotus*, 6 species) Asian deserts.

Subfamily Dipodinae

4 genera: *Dipus, Jaculus, Stylodipus, Eremodipus*

Northern three-toed jerboa (*Dipus sagitta*) Russia, Kazakhstan, Turkestan (sandy deserts), C Asia (sandy and sandy-gravel deserts).

Desert jerboas (*Jaculus*, 4 species) N Africa, Iran, Afghanistan, Pakistan, Turkestan, in various desert habitats.

Three-toed jerboas (*Stylodipus*, 3 species) S European Russia, in sandy semidesert; Kazakhstan, Mongolia, China, in clay and gravel deserts.

Lichtenstein's jerboa (*Eremodipus lichtensteini*) Sandy deserts of Turkestan.

Subfamily Paradipodinae

1 genus: *Paradipus*

Comb-toed jerboa (*Paradipus ctenodactylus*) Turkestan, in sandy deserts.

Subfamily Allactaginae

3 genera: *Allactaga, Allactodipus, Pygeretmus*

Four- and five-toed jerboas (*Allactaga*, 11 species) NE Africa (Libyan desert), Middle East, Russia, Kazakhstan, Turkestan, C Asia.

Fat-tailed jerboas (*Pygeretmus*, 3 species) S European Russia, Kazakhstan, Mongolia, China, in salt and clay deserts.

Bobrinski's jerboa (*Allactodipus bobrinskii*) Gravel deserts of Turkestan.

Subfamily Euchoreutinae

1 genus: *Euchoreutes*

Long-eared jerboa (*Euchoreutes naso*) China and Mongolia, in gravel deserts.

For full species list see Appendix ▷

Living off Plants and Insects

DIET

The major animal foods eaten by jumping mice are moth larvae (primarily cutworms) and ground and snout beetles. Also important is the subterranean fungus *Endogone*, which make up about 12 percent of the diet (by volume) in the Meadow jumping mouse and about 35 percent in the Woodland jumping mouse. Meadow jumping mice eat many things, but seeds, especially those from grasses, are the most important food. The seeds eaten change with availability.

Birchmice can eat extremely large amounts of food at one time and can also spend long periods without eating. Their main foods are seeds, berries, and insects.

Jerboas have a wide spectrum of diets. Some species are specialized feeders and use only seeds (*Cardiocranius*), insects (*Euchoreutes*), or fresh leaves and stems of succulent plants (*Pygeretmus*

◐ **Left** *A desert jerboa (*Jaculus jaculus*) crouches in Saharan sand. The* Jaculus *species are extraordinarily powerful jumpers, able to leap from a standing position to a height of almost 1m (3ft).*

and *Paradipus*). Other species have mixed diets of seeds and insects (*Salpingotus*), seeds and green plants (*Dipus*, *Stylodipus*, *Eremodipus*, *Jaculus* and *Allactodipus*) or equal proportions of seeds, insects, and green and underground plant parts (*Allactaga*). In *Dipus* all individuals in a population emerge for their nightly forays at about the same time, and move by long leaps to their feeding grounds, which may be some distance away. There they feed on plants, especially those with milky juices, but they also smell out underground sprouts and insect larvae in underground galls. Like pocket mice, jerboas do not drink water, but instead manufacture "metabolic water" from food.

The Big Sleep

SOCIAL BEHAVIOR

Jumping mice are profound hibernators, hibernating for 6–9 months of the year according to species, locality, and elevation. The Meadow jumping mouse in the eastern USA usually hibernates from about October to late April. Individuals that hibernate successfully put on 6–10g (0.21–0.35oz) of fat in the two weeks prior to entering hibernation. They do this by sleeping for increasingly longer periods until they attain deep hibernation with their body temperature just a little above freezing. Their heart rate, breathing rate, and all bodily functions drop to low levels. However, the animals wake about every two weeks, perhaps to urinate, then go back to sleep. In the spring the males appear above ground about two weeks before the females. Of the animals active in the fall, only about a third – the larger ones – are apparently able to survive hibernation. The rest – young individuals or those unable to put on adequate fat – perish during the winter retreat.

Jumping mice give birth to their young in a nest of grass or leaves either underground or in some other protected place. Gestation takes 17–18 days, or up to 24 if the female is lactating. Each litter contains 4–7 young. Litters may be produced at any time between May and September, but most enter the world in June and August. Most females probably produce one litter per year.

Like jumping mice, birchmice are active primarily by night. Birchmice hibernate in their underground nests for about half of the year. Gestation probably lasts 18–24 days, and parental care for another four weeks. Studies of *Sicista betulina* in Poland have shown that one litter a year is produced and that any female produces only two litters during her lifetime.

Some jerboas hibernate during the winter, surviving off body fat, and in addition some species enter torpor during hot or dry periods. They are generally quiet, but when handled will sometimes shriek or grunt. Some species have been known to tap with a hind foot when inside their burrows.

In northern species mating first occurs shortly after the emergence from hibernation, but most female jerboas probably breed at least twice in a season, producing litters of 2–6 young.

There are four kinds of burrows used by various jerboas, depending on their habits and habitats: temporary summer day burrows for hiding during the day, temporary summer night burrows for hiding during nightly forays, permanent summer burrows used as living quarters and for producing young, and permanent winter burrows for hibernation. The two temporary burrows are simple tubes, in length respectively 20–50cm (8–20in) and 10–20cm (4–8in).

The permanent summer burrows have one nest chamber and no secondary chamber for food storage, while the permanent winter burrows have the main hibernation chamber 1.5–2.5m (5–8ft) below the surface, and also have secondary chambers 40–70cm (15–28in) down. Permanent burrows have one to three accessory exits. Temporary summer-night burrows have widely open exits with a ground gutter near the entrance, but all other burrow exits are always closed with ground plugs and camouflaged. GIS/JW

FACTFILE

JUMPING MICE, BIRCHMICE, & JERBOAS

Order: Rodentia

Family: Dipodidae

50 species in 15 genera and 7 subfamilies

DISTRIBUTION **Jumping mice:** N America; 1 species (*Eozapus setchuanus*) in China. **Birchmice:** Eurasia. **Jerboas:** N Africa and Asia.

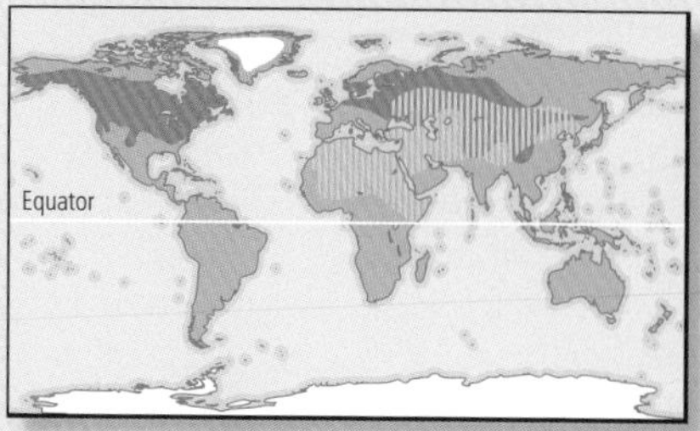

Jumping mice and Birchmice

Jerboas

HABITAT **Jumping mice:** meadows, moors, steppe, thickets, woods. **Birchmice:** forests, meadows, steppe. **Jerboas:** desert, semidesert, steppe, including patches of bare ground.

SIZE **Jumping mice:** head–body length 7.6–11cm (3–4.3in), tail length 15–16.5cm (5.9–6.5in), weight up to 29g (1oz). **Birchmice:** head–body length 5–9cm (1.9–3.5in), tail length 6.5–10cm (2.6–3.9in), weight up to 28g (1oz). **Jerboas:** head–body length 4–23cm (1.6–9in), tail length 7–30cm (2.7–11in). hind foot length 2–10cm (0.8–4in).

COAT Coarse in the jumping mice and birchmice, silky in the jerboas. Coloration usually matches the habitat in which the different species live.

DIET **Jumping mice:** moth larvae, beetles, fungi, and (in Meadow jumping mice) seeds. **Birchmice:** seeds, berries, insects. **Jerboas:** seeds, insects and insect larvae, fresh leaves and stems of succulent plants.

BREEDING Gestation times range from 17–21 days in jumping mice (*Zapus* and *Napaeozapus* species) to 18–24 days in birchmice (*Sicista betulina*) and 25–35 days in jerboas.

LONGEVITY Probably 1–2 years in jumping mice, at least 1.5 years in birchmice, and 2–3 years in jerboas.

CONSERVATION STATUS Among the 4 jumping mouse species, the Chinese jumping mouse (*Eozapus setchuanus*) is listed as Vulnerable. Of 16 birchmouse species, one (*Sicista armenica*) is Critically Endangered and another (*S. caudata*) Endangered. In the jerboas, one *Allactaga* species (*A. firouzi*) is Critically Endangered and another (*A. tetradactyla*) Endangered, as is the Long-eared jerboa (*Euchoreutes naso*). The Five-toed dwarf jerboa (*Cardiocranius paradoxus*) and one of the six Three-toed dwarf jerboa species (*Salpingotus crassicauda*) are Vulnerable.

Pocket Gophers

POCKET GOPHERS ARE ONE OF SEVEN OR EIGHT rodent groups around the world that spend most of their lives below ground in self-dug burrow systems. Native to North and Central America and to northwestern Colombia in South America, they present a paradox: they are extraordinarily diverse, even though all species share a common body plan and a similar life cycle, adapted for a life of digging.

Pocket gophers take their name from the fur-lined cheek pouches that serve as built-in carrier bags both for food items and nesting materials. Unlike those of hamsters and squirrels, the gophers' pouches are external, located on either side of the mouth. They share this feature among mammals only with their close relatives in the family Heteromyidae – the pocket mice, kangaroo mice, and kangaroo rats.

Designed to Dig

FORM AND FUNCTION

Designed for digging, pocket gophers have thickset, tubular bodies, with no apparent neck. Fore and hind limbs are short, powerful, and of approximately equal size. The small, nearly naked tail is particularly sensitive to touch.

The front teeth project through furred lips, an adaptation that allows the gophers to use them for digging or cutting roots without getting dirt in their mouths. Even so, they generally excavate soil with the enlarged claws on their forefeet, and are thus categorized as "claw" or "scratch" diggers, though the incisors are used as helpful adjuncts in some genera. In *Thomomys* species, for example, populations living in harder soils tend to have more forward-pointing incisors that they use as chisels for digging. All pocket gophers push soil from their burrows with rapid movements of their forefeet, chest, and chin, and use an earthen plug to block the entrance. As a result, fresh gopher mounds can be distinguished by their characteristic triangular, or deltaic, shape, with an obvious round plug of soil located at the apex.

Gopher skin fits loosely. It is usually clothed in short, thick fur, interspersed with hairs sensitive to touch. The fur of more tropical species is coarser and less dense, perhaps as an adaptation for warmer climates. The loose skin enables individuals to make tight turns in their constricted burrows. Gophers are very agile and surprisingly fast, capable of rapid movement back or forward on their squat, muscular legs.

The gopher's skull is massive and strongly ridged, with heavy zygomatic arches and a broad temporal region holding powerful jaw muscles. The upper incisors may be either smooth or grooved on their anterior surface, depending on the genus. The four cheek teeth in each quarter of the jaw form a battery for grinding tough and abrasive foodstuffs. Strong and effective, these teeth grow continuously from birth to death, so that the grinding surface is present in all from the youngest to the oldest individuals. In the Valley pocket gopher, both teeth and foreclaws can grow at a rate of 0.5–1mm (0.02-0.04in) per day.

Male pocket gophers are larger than females, though the extent of this dimorphism varies greatly geographically. In the Valley pocket gopher, it seems to depend on habitat quality, and therefore on the density of animals in the population. In high-quality habitat such as agricultural fields, males can have twice the body mass of females, and may be 25 percent larger in skull dimensions, but in poorer habitat such as deserts, the differences shrink to about 15 percent and 6 percent respectively. These variations are a result of both the nutritional quality of the food available to the animals – individuals of both sexes get larger if they eat well, particularly as juveniles – and the cessation of growth in females as they reach reproductive maturity and shift energy from growth to producing young.

Pocket gophers have the oldest fossil record of, and are taxonomically more diverse than, any other group of subterranean rodents. They originated in the late Eocene (36 million years ago) and underwent two pulses of diversification; the latest, beginning in the Pliocene (5 million years ago) led to the living genera. Fossils of both *Geomys* and *Thomomys* species date from Pliocene deposits; the other genera are known either from the early Pleistocene (*Pappogeomys*) or only from the modern record (*Orthogeomys* and *Zygogeomys*). Throughout the history of the family, there has been a relatively stable number of genera and constant extinction and origination rates.

The evolutionary history of the family is characterized by successive attempts to invade the fossorial (digging) niche. Each successive group exhibits better-developed adaptations for subterranean existence, with some modern pocket gophers exhibiting the best adaptations of all. The entire fossil history of the family is contained within North America.

In order to distinguish the genera, biologists examine overall size, details of the skull bones and the cheek teeth, and the presence and number of grooves found on the front surface of the upper incisors. The differences between populations of

Above *In common with many other mammals that lead a subterranean existence, pocket gophers have certain adaptations, such as relatively small eyes and ears, that make it easier to excavate burrows. The Northern pocket gopher* (Thomomys talpoides) *inhabits a wider range of soil types than any other species in the family.*

Below *A Northern pocket gopher feeding with filled pouches. When suitable vegetation is found, the gopher will cut this down into smaller pieces, which can be pushed into the cheek pouches using the fore feet, thus enabling the gopher to transport a relatively large quantity of food back to its burrow.*

FACTFILE

POCKET GOPHERS

Order Rodentia

Family Geomyidae

39 species in 5 genera, divided into 2 tribes

DISTRIBUTION N and C America, from C and SW Canada through the W and SE USA and Mexico to extreme NW Colombia.

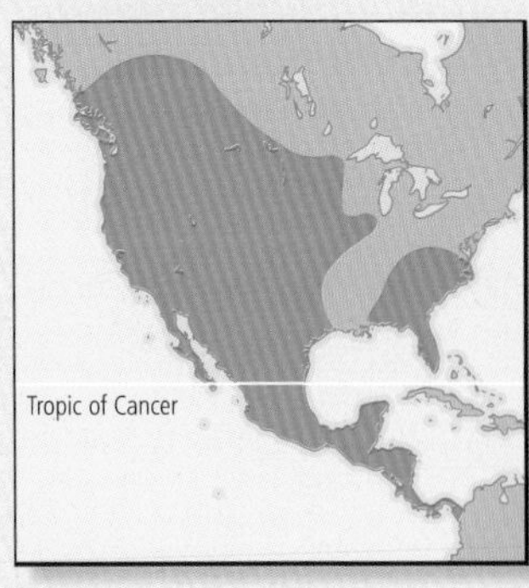

HABITAT Friable soils in desert, scrub, grasslands, montane meadows, and arid tropical lowlands.

SIZE Head–body length ranges from 12–22.5cm (4.7–8.9in) in genus *Thomomys* to 18–30cm (7–11.8in) in genus *Orthogeomys*; **weight** from 45–400g (1.6–14oz) to 300–900g (11–32oz) in the same genera. Males are always larger than females, and up to twice the weight.

COAT Short and thick, in shades of brown and gray.

DIET Plant matter, particularly forbs, grasses, roots, and tubers.

BREEDING Gestation 17–21 days in *Thomomys* and *Geomys* genera.

LONGEVITY Maximum 5 years (6 years recorded in captivity).

CONSERVATION STATUS 2 species are listed as Critically Endangered, one as Endangered, and 3 as Vulnerable. 2 US subspecies are now classed as Extinct.

See tribes table ▷

the same species that live apart can be more striking than the differences that exist between separate species; so the Valley pocket gopher exhibits size, color, and habitat variations that span the entire range exhibited by all the other species in the genus *Thomomys*. As a consequence of this, species limits are, for the most part, poorly known, and a multitude of subspecies have been described – no fewer than 185 in the case of Valley pocket gophers. Some species, including Wyoming, Idaho, and Northern pocket gophers, are distinguished by hidden characteristics, such as chromosome number, rather than by any external features.

Species by Species

DISTRIBUTION PATTERNS

All genera and species are distributed contiguously; except in very narrow zones of overlap, only a single kind of pocket gopher can be found in any particular area, as different species are apparently unable to share the space they occupy underground (the fossorial niche). In areas where several species and/or genera do meet, the pattern of species distribution is mosaic-like. In the mountains of the western USA and Mexico, for example, pocket gopher species replace each other in succession according to altitude.

Within the range of their distribution, pocket gophers are ubiquitous in virtually all habitats that have extensive patches of friable soil. The range of habitats in which they are found can be extreme: for instance, the Valley pocket gopher ranges from desert soils below sea level to alpine meadows that are – at 3,500m (11,500 ft) – well above the timberline. In tropical latitudes populations of the same species may be found in mountain forest meadows and in arid tropical scrub, although few species penetrate true tropical savannas.

Plants are the pocket gophers' dietary mainstay. Above ground, they take leafy vegetation from the vicinity of burrow openings; underground, they devour succulent roots and tubers. They often prefer forbs and grasses, but their diet shifts seasonally according to both availability and the gophers' requirements for nutrition and water. In deserts during the summer, water-laden cactus plants are consumed.

To transport food to caches in the burrow, gophers use their forepaws dextrously to fill their external cheek pouches. Food storage areas are usually sealed off from the main tunnel system.

A Lonely Life Underground

SOCIAL BEHAVIOR

Pocket gophers are solitary creatures. Individuals live in self-excavated burrows that abut those of other gophers. Male burrows tend to be longer and more dendritic than those of females, so that each male burrow might contact those of several females. In the Valley pocket gopher, the maximum territory size is about 250sq m (2,700sq ft), while in the Yellow-faced pocket gopher individual burrow length may exceed 80m (260ft) of actual tunnel. Where habitat is good, the gophers become more crowded and space out evenly across the land; in low-quality habitat, groups of gophers concentrate in the best regions, while other areas remain gopher-free. During breeding, this strict organization relaxes somewhat as males and females briefly cohabit in the same burrow, and females share burrows with their young until they are weaned. Each individual gopher still maintains a tunnel system for their own exclusive use, but adjacent males and females may have both common burrows and deep, shared nesting chambers. Results from genetic studies would seem to suggest that females selected their mate from among the males whose territories are adjacent to their own.

Densities in small species such as the Valley pocket gopher rarely exceed 40 adults per ha (16 per acre), and they sink as low as 7 per ha (3 per acre) in the case of the large-bodied Yellow-faced pocket gopher. In high-quality habitat, individual territories are stable in both size and position, with most individuals living their entire adult lives

Above *Members of the five pocket gopher genera:* ***1*** *male Valley pocket gopher* (Thomomys bottae) *making a mound;* ***2*** *Valley pocket gopher of a different color showing the pouch cheeks in detail;* ***3*** *Plains pocket gopher* (Geomys bursarius) *returning from foraging;* ***4*** *second color variant of Valley pocket gopher, a female;* ***5*** *Large pocket gopher* (Orthogeomys grandis) *in an underground food store making threats;* ***6*** *Michoacan pocket gopher* (Zygogeomys trichopus) *digging with its claws;* ***7*** *Buller's pocket gopher* (Pappogeomys bulleri) *using its incisors for digging.*

in very limited areas; in low-quality environments, they shift throughout the year as animals search for food and mates.

Male and female young disperse from the mother's underground domicile at the same time, still wearing their juvenile coats. In the Valley pocket gopher, female young of the year initially move the farthest to establish territories, although most still seem to settle within 40–50m (130–165ft) of their natal area. If conditions are favorable, they may even breed in the same season as their birth, at just 70 days old. Male young tend to live in shallow systems in marginal and peripheral habitat, until they disperse to establish territories just prior to the next breeding season. As a consequence, their mortality is typically higher than that of females, which results in a prevalence of females in pocket gopher populations. Despite their adaptations for digging, pocket gophers can,

and do, move considerable distances; most dispersal takes place above ground on dark nights, although movements over distances of just a few meters may take advantage of long tunnels just beneath the surface.

Individuals of both sexes are pugnacious and aggressive, and will fight for parcels of land. Males in particular exhibit heavy scarring around the mouth and on the rump, most of which will have been acquired during the breeding season.

As in most animals, reproduction is strongly affected by the changing seasons. In montane regions, breeding follows the melting snow in the late spring and early summer, but in coastal and desert valleys and in temperate grasslands, it coincides with winter rainfall.

Most Valley gopher females have only one litter each season; however, some will have as many as three or four, depending on the quality of habitat – and therefore the nutrition – that is available to the mother. Animals that inhabit irrigated fields may breed nearly year-round while neighboring populations living amid natural vegetation have sharply delimited seasonal breeding. Females of Yellow-faced and Plains pocket gophers typically produce only one or two litters each year. Litter size varies between the species; *Pappogeomys* gophers usually give birth to twins, while *Thomomys* mothers typically produce five young, but may have to deal with as many as 10 per pregnancy. The onset of breeding, the length of the season, and the number of litters are largely controlled by local environmental conditions – primarily temperature, moisture, and the quality of the vegetation.

Pocket gophers are born with both their eyes and cheek pouches closed. The pouches open at 24 days and eyes and ears at 26 days. Additionally, Northern and Valley pocket gophers have a juvenile coat that molts within 100 days of birth.

After a helpless early life spent in the shelter of the mother's burrow, infants are weaned at around 40 days. Within a couple of weeks of weaning the young head off alone, when still less than 2 months old. Unsurprisingly, most of the young that are produced each year do not survive long enough to be able to reproduce. In the Valley pocket gopher, only 6–12 percent of newborns are recruited into the breeding population the following year. The maximum longevity in nature can be as great as 4–5 years, but the average life span of an adult is usually only just over a year. No more than half of the population survive from one year to the next and some years only 15 percent will survive to the next year.

Females live nearly twice as long as males. Among Yellow-faced pocket gophers, they survive on average for 56 weeks, as compared to the average 31-week lifespan of the male; in Valley pocket gophers, females may live for as long as 4.5 years, compared to the maximum expectation of 2.5 years for the male. One possible explanation for this huge difference in longevity is the extreme inter-male aggression that occurs during the breeding season. In addition, males appear to grow continuously throughout their life, while females cease growth when they reach reproductive maturity.

The sex ratio among adults varies geographically in all pocket gophers, a variation that in Valley, Northern, Plains, and Yellow-faced populations has been shown to be related to habitat quality. There are roughly equal numbers of both sexes in poor-quality habitats, such as desert areas, but in agricultural land there is a preponderance of females, with three to four for every adult male. As the population size increases males become less common, which is at least in part due to male mortality during or after fights over territories and access to mates. While almost all the adult females in a population breed each season, many males are not so lucky; some may never breed, while others will monopolize the females and father all the young.

Soil Engineers

CONSERVATION AND ENVIRONMENT

Pocket gophers play a major role in soil dynamics, and in so doing become agriculturalists to suit their own needs. Cattle and other grazers compact soil, but underground, gophers counter this with their constant digging. They cycle soil vertically, which increases porosity, slows the rate of water run-off, and provides increased aeration. Gophers can thus have a profound effect on plant communities, often, through continual soil disturbance, creating conditions that favor growth of the herbaceous plants that they prefer eating.

Voracious eaters, pocket gophers can become agricultural pests; in the western deserts of North America, the annual productivity of irrigated alfalfa fields can be reduced by as much as 50 percent in the year following an invasion by the animals. They also disturb irrigation channels. As a result, millions of dollars have been spent in the USA on programs to control gopher populations, but even so it has proved hard to curb their spread, so perfectly does agriculture suit their expansion.

Even so, some local US populations and subspecies are now considered threatened as a result of habitat loss, while in Mexico the Michoacan pocket gopher is at risk primarily because of its localized geographic distribution. Mostly, though, pocket gophers are among the few animals to have benefited from human development – particularly the replacement of native grass- and shrubland by agriculture. JP

The Two Tribes of Pocket Gophers

Tribe Geomyini

4 genera: *Geomys, Orthogeomys, Pappogeomys, Zygogeomys.*

Eastern pocket gophers (*Geomys*, 9 species), including: Desert pocket gopher (*G. arenarius*); Plains pocket gopher (*G. bursarius*); Texas pocket gopher (*G. personatus*); Southeastern pocket gopher (*G. pinetis*); Tropical pocket gopher (*G. tropicalis*).

Taltuzas (*Orthogeomys*, 11 species) including: Chiriqui pocket gopher (*O. cavator*); Darien pocket gopher (*O. dariensis*); Variable pocket gopher (*O. heterodus*); Big pocket gopher (*O. lanius*).

Yellow and Cinnamon pocket gophers (*Pappogeomys*, 9 species) including: Buller's pocket gopher (*P. bulleri*); Smoky pocket gopher (*P. fumosus*); Queretaro pocket gopher (*P. neglectus*); Zinser's pocket gopher (*P. zinseri*).

Michoacan or Tuza pocket gopher (*Zygogeomys trichopus*, single species).

Tribe Thomomyini

1 genus, *Thomomys*.

Western pocket gophers (Genus *Thomomys*, 9 species) including: Valley pocket gopher (*T. bottae*); Wyoming pocket gopher (*T. clusius*); Northern pocket gopher (*T. talpoides*); Mexican pocket gopher (*T. umbrinus*).

For full species list see Appendix ▷

Pocket Mice and Kangaroo Rats

POCKET MICE AND KANGAROO RATS ARE nocturnal burrow-dwellers that inhabit many different American environments from arid deserts to humid forests. On returning from their nightly forays in search of food, they sometimes plug the burrow entrance with soil for added protection from predators and the weather.

The Heteromyidae family brings together the pocket mice, which take their name from the deep, fur-lined cheek pouches in which they store food, and the kangaroo rats and mice, which as their name suggests are adapted to travel by hopping. They too have cheek pouches, the heteromyids' most distinctive feature; these can be turned inside out for cleaning, then pulled back into place with the help of a special muscle.

Built-in Carrying Pouches

FORM AND FUNCTION

Unusually for burrowers, the heteromyids are thin-skulled, and do most of their digging with their front paws. The most distinctive feature of the head are the two cheek-pouches, opening externally on either side of the mouth and extending back to the shoulders. The mice use their paws to fill the pouches with food and nest material for carrying back to the safety of the burrow.

While the pocket mice travel on all fours, the kangaroo rats and mice, in contrast, have long hind limbs and shrunken forelimbs that are used mainly for feeding; these animals normally move in hops, only lowering themselves onto their front legs to scramble over short distances. The leg muscles are powerful enough to launch kangaroo rats 2m (6.6ft) or more with each leap when hurrying to escape from predators. All heteromyids have long tails; the jumping species rely on them to help keep their balance when traveling and as props to rest on when standing still.

In Search of Seeds

DISTRIBUTION PATTERNS

By day, summer conditions in the deserts of the southwestern USA are formidable. Surface temperatures soar to over 50°C (122°F), sparsely distributed plants are parched and dry, and signs of mammalian life are minimal. As the sun sets, however, the sandy or gravelly desert floor comes alive with rodents. The greatest diversity occurs among the pocket mice, of which five or six species can coexist in the same barren habitat.

Contrast these hot, dry (or in winter, cold and apparently lifeless) conditions with the tropical rain forests of central and northern South America. Rich in vegetation, the rain forest is nearly bare of heteromyid species: only one species, Desmarest's spiny pocket mouse, occurs at most sites.

The most likely explanation for this difference in species richness lies in the diversity and availability of seeds. In North American deserts, seeds of annual species can accumulate in the soil to a depth of 2cm (0.8in) in densities of up to 91,000 seeds per sq m (8,450 per sq ft). Patchily distributed by wind and water currents, small seeds weighing about 1mg tend to accumulate in great numbers under bushes and on the leeward sides of rocks, whereas larger seeds occur in clumps in open areas between vegetation, providing plentiful opportunities for the nocturnal seed-gathering activities of the heteromyid rodents.

Tropical forests are also rich in seeds, but many of those produced by tropical shrubs and trees are protected chemically against predation. This is especially true of large seeds weighing several grams, which considerably reduces the variety of seeds available to rodents. In effect, then, the tropical rain forest is a desert in the eyes of a seed-eating rodent, whereas the actual desert is a "jungle," as far as seed availability is concerned. Most of the 15–20 species of rodents inhabiting New World tropical forests are either omnivorous or exclusively fruiteating.

Above *An Ord's kangaroo rat sets out to forage. Kangaroo rats compete with smaller pocket mice for food where their ranges overlap; experiments in Arizona have shown that pocket mice numbers more than tripled over an 8-month period when kangaroo rats were excluded from their territory.*

Left *The Desert pocket mouse lives in arid areas of the American southwest and northwest Mexico. Like many heteromyids, it emerges from of its burrow at night to exploit the wealth of seeds blown across the desert floor.*

Right *Long tails are a feature of Dipodomys species, like this Merriam's kangaroo rat; they serve as counterweights when the rats are traveling and as supports when they are resting.*

FACTFILE

POCKET MICE & KANGAROO RATS

Order: Rodentia

Family: Heteromyidae

59 species in 5 genera

DISTRIBUTION
N, C, and northern S America

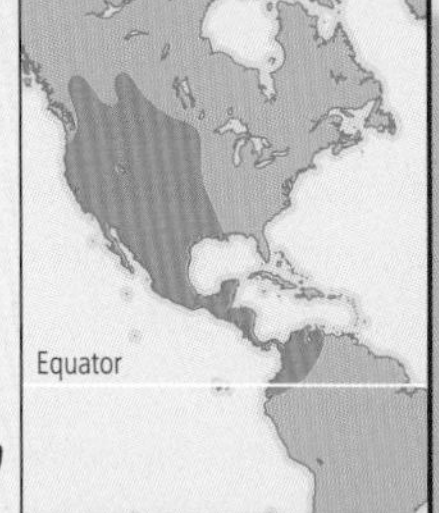

POCKET MICE Genus *Perognathus*
SE Canada, W USA south to C Mexico. Quadrupedal. 24 species, sometimes separated into 2 genera: the silky pocket mice (Genus *Perognathus*) and the coarse-haired pocket mice (genus *Chaetodipus*). HBL from 6–12.5cm (2.4–5in); TL from 4.5–14.5cm (1.8–5.7in); WT from 7–47g (0.25–1.7oz). Longevity: 2 years in the wild; up to 8 in captivity.

SPINY POCKET MICE Genus *Liomys*
Mexico and C America S to C Panama. Mostly in semi-arid country. Quadrupedal. 5 species.

FOREST SPINY POCKET MICE Genus *Heteromys*
Mexico, C America, northern S America. Forests, up to 2,500m (8,200ft). Quadrupedal. 7 species including Desmarest's spiny pocket mouse (*H. desmarestianus*). Conservation status: *H. nelsoni* is Critically Endangered.

KANGAROO RATS Genus *Dipodomys*
SW Canada and USA W of Missouri River to south C Mexico. Arid and semiarid country with some brush or grass. Bipedal (hind legs long, front legs reduced). 21 species. HBL from 10–20cm (4–8in); TL from 10–21.5cm (4–8.5in); WT from 35–180g (1.2–6.3oz). Longevity: up to 9 years in captivity. Conservation status: 3 species – *D. ingens*, *D. insularis*, and *D. margaritae* – are Critically Endangered; 1 more, the San Quintin kangaroo rat (*D. gravipes*) is Endangered, and the Texas kangaroo rat (*D. elator*) is Vulnerable.

KANGAROO MICE Genus *Microdipodops*
USA in S Oregon, Nevada, parts of California and Utah. Near shrubs in gravelly soil or sand dunes. Bipedal (hind legs long, front legs reduced). 2 species.

Abbreviations HBL = head–body length TL = tail length WT = weight

For full species list see Appendix ▷

With large cheek pouches and a keen sense of smell, heteromyid rodents are admirably adapted for gathering seeds. Most of the time that they are active outside their burrow systems is spent collecting seeds within their home ranges. Members of the two tropical genera (*Liomys* and *Heteromys*) search through the soil litter for seeds, some of which will be buried in shallow pits scattered around the home range; others are stored underground in special burrow chambers.

Boom or Bust

SOCIAL BEHAVIOR

Breeding in desert heteromyids is strongly influenced by the flowering activities of winter plants, which germinate only after at least 2.5cm (1in) of rain has fallen between late September and mid-December. In dry years, seeds of these plants fail to germinate, and a new crop of seeds and leaves is not produced by the following April and May. In the face of a reduced food supply heteromyids do not breed, and their populations decline in size. In years following good winter rains most females produce two or more litters of up to five young, and populations increase rapidly.

This "boom or bust" pattern of resource availability also influences heteromyid social structure and levels of competition between species. When seed availability is low, seeds stored in burrow or surface caches become valuable, defended resources. Behavior becomes asocial in most arid-land species (including species of *Liomys*): adults occupy separate burrow systems (except for mothers and their young), and when two members of a species meet away from their burrows they engage in boxing and sand-kicking. In the forest, in contrast, *Heteromys* species are socially more tolerant; individuals have widely overlapping home ranges, share burrow systems, and are less likely to fight .

The diversity and availability of edible seeds is the key to the evolutionary success of heteromyid rodents. Seed availability affects foraging patterns, population dynamics, and social behavior. In North American deserts, because seed production influences levels of competition not just between heteromyids themselves but also with ants and other seedeaters, there is a clear link between resources and the structure of an animal community. Thus the abundance and diversity of seedeaters is directly related to plant productivity. THF

DISTRIBUTION America, Africa, Asia.

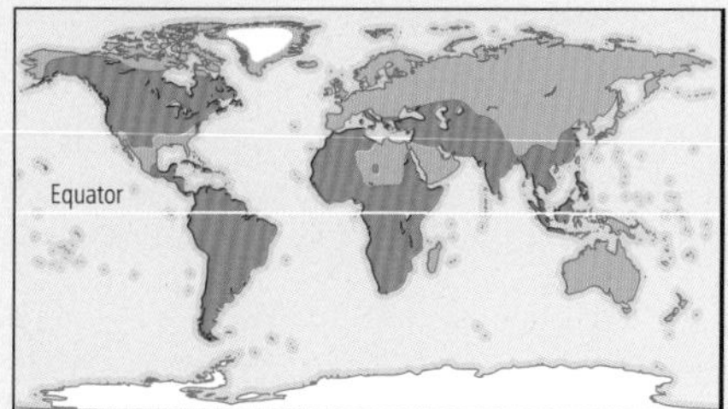

HYSTRICOGNATHS Suborder Hystricognathi
238 species in 63 genera and 18 families

NEW WORLD PORCUPINES
Family Erethizontidae p670
12 species in 4 genera

CAVIES Family Caviidae p672
14 species in 5 genera

CAPYBARA Family Hydrochaeridae p678
1 species: *Hydrochaeris hydrochaeris*

COYPU Family Myocastoridae p685
1 species *Myocastor coypus*

HUTIAS Family Capromyidae p685
15 species in 6 genera

PACARANA Family Dinomyidae p683
1 species *Dinomys branickii*

PACAS Family Agoutidae p684
2 species in the genus *Agouti*

AGOUTIS AND ACOUCHIS
Family Dasyproctidae p684
13 species in 2 genera

CHINCHILLA RATS Family Abrocomidae p685
3 species in the genus *Abrocoma*

SPINY RATS Family Echimyidae p685
70 species in 16 genera

CHINCHILLAS AND VISCACHAS
Family Chinchillidae p683
6 species in 3 genera

OCTODONTS
Family Octodontidae p684
10 species in 6 genera

TUCO-TUCOS Family Ctenomyidae p684
56 species in the genus *Ctenomys*

CANE RATS Family Thryonomyidae p682
2 species in the genus *Thryonomys*

DASSIE RAT Family Petromuridae p682
1 species *Petromus typicus*

OLD WORLD PORCUPINES
Family Hystricidae p686
11 species in 4 genera

GUNDIS Family Ctenodactylidae p688
5 species in 4 genera

AFRICAN MOLE-RATS Family Bathyergidae p690
15 species in 5 genera

Cavy-like Rodents

THE FAMILIAR GUINEA PIG IS A REPRESENTATIVE of a large group of rodents classified as the suborder Hystricognathi (formerly Caviomorpha). Most are large rodents confined to South and Central America. Although they are extremely diverse in external appearance and are generally classified in separate families, the hystricognaths share sufficient characteristics to make it likely that they constitute a natural, interrelated group.

Externally, many of these rodents have large heads, plump bodies, slender legs, and short tails – as in the guinea pigs, the agoutis, and the giant capybara, the largest of all rodents at over one meter (39in) in length. Others, however – for example, some spiny rats of the family Echimyidae – come very close in general appearance to the common rats and mice.

Internally, the most distinctive character uniting these rodents is the form of the masseter jaw muscles, one branch of which extends forwards through a massive opening in the anterior root of the bony zygomatic arch to attach on the side of the rostrum. At its other end it is attached to a characteristic outward-projecting flange of the lower jaw. Hystricognaths are also characterized by producing small litters after a long gestation period, resulting in well-developed young. Guinea pigs, for instance, usually have two or three young after a gestation of 50–75 days, compared with seven or eight young after only 21–24 days in the Brown (murid) rat.

The modern suborder name Hystricognathi serves to emphasize the close relationship of the Old World porcupines – family Hystricidae – with the South American "caviomorphs." However, despite the fact that both groups share the features described above, there has been considerable debate as to whether such features signify a common ancestry or are merely indicative of convergent evolution. This controversy over systematics is intrinsically linked to the question of whether the caviomorphs reached South America from North America or from Africa (rafting across in the late Eocene, when the continents were far closer together). The African cane rats (family Thryonomyidae) are closely related to the Hystricidae but some other families, namely the gundis (Ctenodactylidae) and the Dassie rat (Petromuridae) are much more doubtfully related, exhibiting only some of the "caviomorph" characters.

Most of the American caviomorphs are terrestrial and herbivorous but a minority, the porcupines (Erethizontidae) are arboreal, and one group, the tuco-tucos (Ctenomyidae) are burrowers. GBC

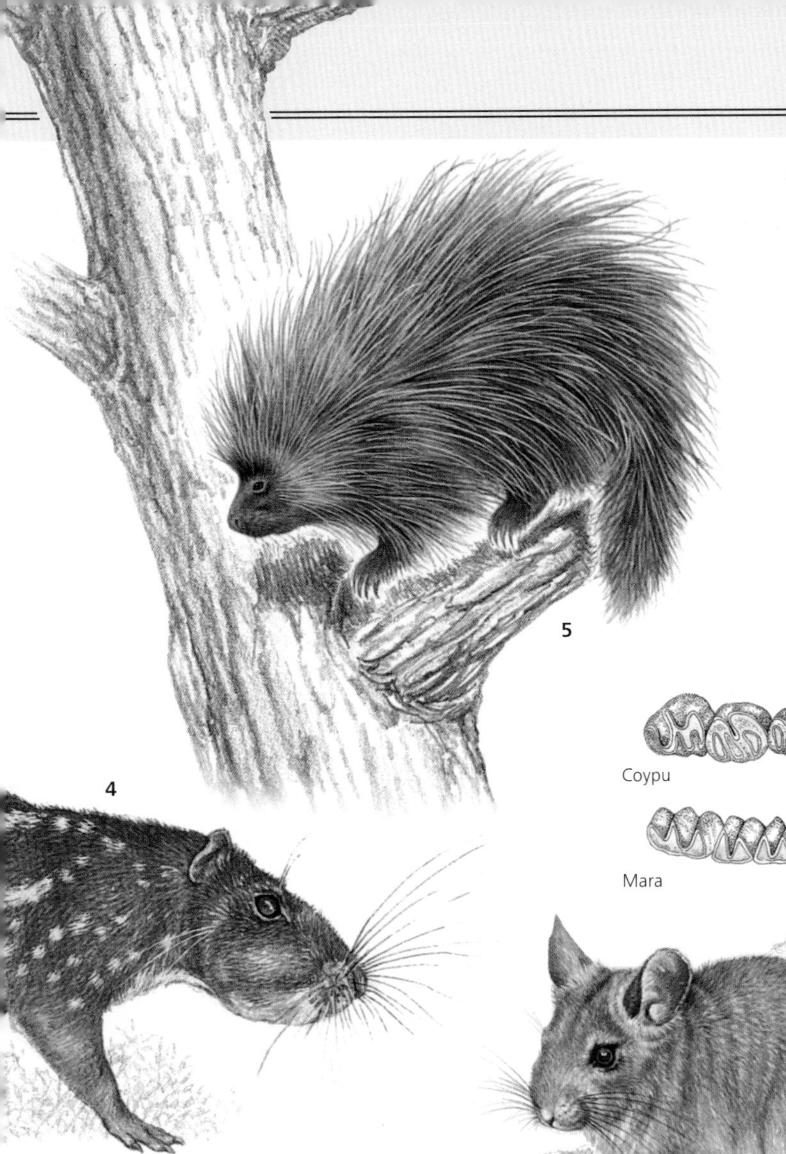

5

4

SKULLS AND DENTITION

Most cavy-like rodents have rather angular skulls and very strongly developed incisor teeth. The wearing surfaces of the four cheekteeth show enormous variation in pattern and complexity amongst the different species. Those of the coypu are typical of a large group of herbivorous species, including the agoutis and the American porcupines, and are closely paralleled in the Old World porcupines and cane rats. The teeth of the mara and of the capybara. although superficially very different in degree of complexity, resemble each other in being evergrowing as in the unrelated but also grass-eating voles and rabbits. At the other extreme, the tuco-tucos have surprisingly simple cheekteeth considering that they feed mainly on roots and tubers.

One distinguishing feature of cavy-like rodents is the deep masseter muscle in their jaws (see diagram BELOW). This extends forward through an opening in the zygomatic arch to attach to the muzzle and provides the powerful gnawing action characteristic of this suborder. The lateral masseter is only used in closing the jaw.

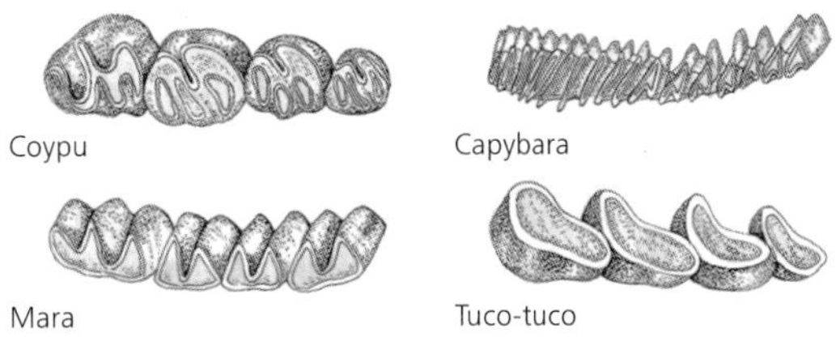

Coypu

Capybara

Mara

Tuco-tuco

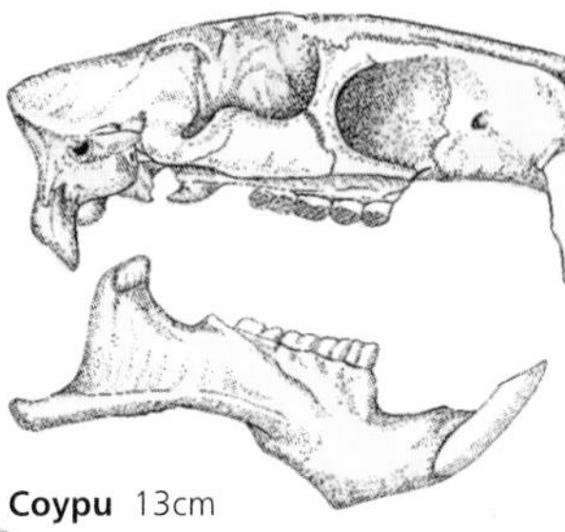

Coypu 13cm

6

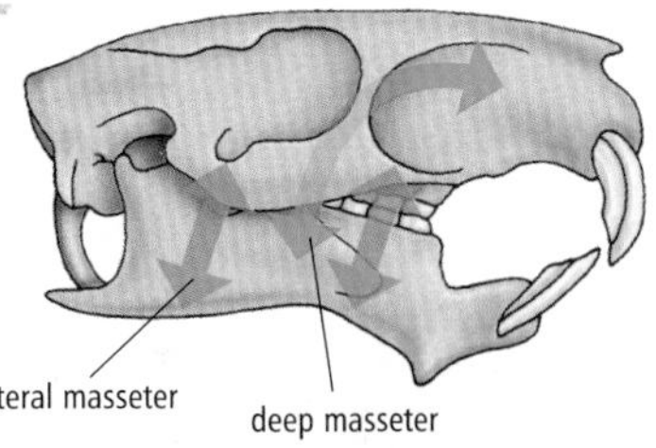

lateral masseter

deep masseter

Above Representative species of cavy-like rodents (not shown to scale): **1** North African gundi (Ctenodactylus gundi); **2** a domesticated form of the cavy, or "guinea pig" (Cavia porcellus); **3** the distinctively deep, blunt muzzle of the capybara (Hydrochaeris hydrochaeris); **4** Paca (Agouti paca) – this sizable species is particularly prized as a game animal by indigenous peoples of Amazonia; **5** North American porcupine (Erethizon dorsatum); **6** Short-tailed chinchilla (Chinchilla brevicaudata) – hunted for its soft, valuable fur, this species is now listed as Critically Endangered.

Below Perhaps the most bizarre of the cavy-like rodents are the Naked mole-rats of East Africa – virtually hairless creatures that spend almost all their time underground in extensive colonies. This is a breeding female.

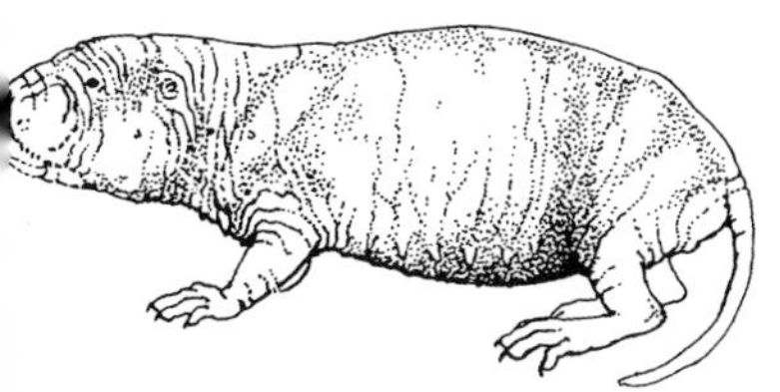

CAVIES AS A FOOD RESOURCE

The true cavy, or "guinea pig," has been highly regarded in South America since ancient times as an important source of meat for human consumption. There is clear evidence that many of the cultures that flourished along the Pacific coast of what is now Peru domesticated the cavy, adding variety to a diet based on fish and cultivated staple crops such as maize and manioc. Cavy bones dating from before 1800BC were discovered in a midden at the coastal site of Culebras. Even the later cultures that arose on the High Andean *altiplano* and farmed llamas and alpacas continued to value the cavy; chroniclers of the 16th century reported that the animal was among sacrificial offerings made by the Inca. Cavies are still widely kept and traded in the region (RIGHT); they make ideal livestock for the smallholder, since they can be kept with little attention in compounds and thrive on greenfoods unpalatable to humans such as brassicas.

New World Porcupines

New World porcupines bear a strong resemblance to Old World porcupines in both their adaptations and lifestyle. However, while the former are arboreal and have singly embedded quills, the latter are decidedly terrestrial and have quills that are grouped in clusters.

For heavy-bodied animals that can weigh as much as 18kg (40lb), the New World porcupines are excellent climbers, with well-developed claws and unfurred soles on their large feet. The soles consist of pads and creases that increase the gripping power of the feet.

Equipped for Climbing

FORM AND FUNCTION

Individual genera have further modifications to improve their climbing abilities. The prehensile-tailed porcupines and the hairy dwarf porcupines – the most arboreal genera – have smaller first digits on their hind feet than those in the other genera, but they are incorporated in the footpads, which increases the width and the gripping power of the pads.

The same genera also have long, spineless tails for grasping. Their tips form upward-directed curls and have a hard skin or callus on the upper surface. In the prehensile-tailed porcupines the tail contributes 9 percent of the total body weight; nearly half of the weight of the tail is composed of muscle fibers.

New World porcupines are very near-sighted, but have keen senses of touch, hearing, and smell. They produce a variety of sounds – moans, whines, grunts, coughs, sniffs, shrieks, barks, and wails. All porcupines have large brains and appear to have good memories.

In winter North American porcupines feed on conifer needles and on the bark of a variety of trees, excepting Red maple, White cedar, and hemlock. During the summer these porcupines feed more frequently on the ground and select roots, stems, leaves, berries, seeds, nuts, and flowers. In the spring they frequently come out from forested areas into meadows to feed on grasses in the evening hours. They will eat bark at all times of the year, however, and can be destructive to forest plantations.

Prehensile-tailed and hairy dwarf porcupines feed more on leaves and both have many characteristics of arboreal leaf-eaters. However, they are also reported to feed on tender stems, fruits, seeds, roots, tubers, and insects, and will even consume small reptiles.

FACTFILE

NEW WORLD PORCUPINES

Order: Rodentia

Family: Erethizontidae

12 species in 4 genera

DISTRIBUTION N America (except SE USA), S Mexico, C America, northern S America

Habitat Forest areas, open grasslands, desert, canyon.
Coat Sharp, barbed quills interspersed with long guard hairs cover the upper part of the body. Each quill protrudes individually from the skin, unlike in Old World porcupines in which they are clustered in groups of 4–6.
Diet Bark, leaves, and conifer needles; also roots, stems, berries, fruits, seeds, nuts, grasses, flowers, and, in some species, insects and small reptiles.

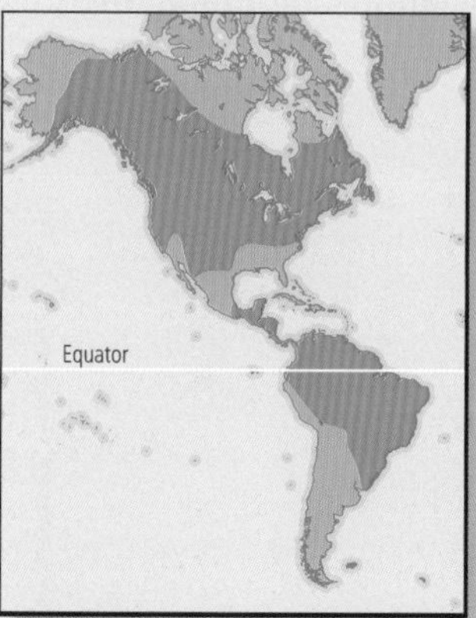

PREHENSILE-TAILED PORCUPINES Genus *Coendou*
S Panama, Andes from NW Colombia to N Argentina, NW Brazil. Forest areas. 4 species: Brazilian porcupine (*C. prehensilis*), Bicolor-spined porcupine (*C. bicolor*), Koopman's porcupine (*C. koopmani*), and Rothschild's porcupine (*C. rothschildi*). HBL 30cm (12in); WT 900g (32oz).

HAIRY DWARF PORCUPINES Genus *Sphiggurus*
S Mexico, C America, S America as far S as N Argentina. Forest areas. 6 species, including: Mexican tree porcupine (*S. mexicanus*), South American tree porcupine (*S. spinosus*). Conservation status: one species, *S. vestitus* from Colombia and W Venezuela, is listed as Vulnerable.

NORTH AMERICAN PORCUPINE *Erethizon dorsatum*
Alaska, Canada, USA (except extreme SW, SE, and Gulf coast states), N Mexico. Forest areas. HBL 86cm (34in); WT 18kg (40lb). Breeding: gestation 210 days. Longevity: up to 17 years.

STUMP-TAILED PORCUPINE *Echinoprocta rufescens*
C Colombia. Forest areas.

Abbreviations HBL = head–body length WT = weight
For full species list see Appendix ▷

On the Move

SOCIAL BEHAVIOR

In habits porcupines range from the North American porcupine, which is semiarboreal, to prehensile-tailed and hairy dwarf porcupines, which are specialized arboreal feeders. All forms spend much of their time in trees, but even tree porcupines are known to come to the ground to feed and to move from one tree to another.

In the North American porcupine, the female reaches sexual maturity when about 18 months old. The estrous cycle is 29 days, and these animals may have more than one period of estrus in a year. They have a vaginal closure membrane, so females form a copulatory plug. The gestation period averages 210 days, and in both North American and prehensile-tailed porcupines usually one young is produced (rarely twins). The weight of the precocial newborn is about 400g

Right *The prehensile-tailed porcupines* (Coendou sp.) *live mainly in the middle and upper layers of forests in Central and South America, only descending to the ground to eat. The tail, which can be coiled around branches, has a callus pad which provides grip.*

Left *Despite its poor eyesight, inability to jump, general clumsiness, and size – large males can weigh in excess of 15kg (33lb) – the North American porcupine frequently climbs to great heights in search of food, such as berries, nuts, and shoots.*

(14oz) in prehensile-tailed porcupines and 600g (21oz) in the North American porcupine. Lactation continues for 56 days, but the animals also feed on their own after the first few days. Porcupine young are born with their eyes open and are able to walk. They exhibit typical defensive reactions, and within a few days are able to climb trees. These characteristics probably explain why infant mortality is very low. Porcupines grow for 3–4 years before they reach adult body size.

The home range of the North American porcupine in summer averages 14.6ha (36 acres). In winter, however, they do not range great distances, instead staying close to their preferred trees and shelters. Prehensile-tailed porcupines can have larger ranges, though these vary from 8 to 38ha (20–94 acres). They are reported to move to a new tree each night, usually 200–400m (660–1,300ft) away, but occasionally up to 700m (2,300ft). Prehensile-tailed porcupines in South Guyana are known to reach densities of 50–100 individuals per sq km (130–260 per sq mi). They have daily rest sites in trees, usually on a horizontal branch 6–10m (20–33ft) above the ground. These porcupines are nocturnal, changing locations each night and occasionally moving on the ground during the day. Male prehensile-tailed porcupines are reported to have ranges up to four times as large as those of females.

Sharing their Fate with the Forests

CONSERVATION AND ENVIRONMENT

Porcupines, in general, are not endangered, and the North American porcupine can in fact be a pest. The fisher (a species of marten) has been reintroduced to some areas of North America to help control porcupines, one of its preferred prey. The fisher is adept at flipping the North American porcupine over so that its soft and generally unquilled chest and belly are exposed. The fisher attacks this area. A study found that porcupines declined by 76 percent in an area of northern Michigan following the introduction of the fisher.

Prehensile-tailed porcupines are often used for biomedical research, which contributes to the problem of conservation, but the main threat is habitat destruction. In Brazil prehensile-tailed porcupines have been affected by the loss of the Atlantic forest, and the Paraguayan hairy dwarf porcupine is on the endangered species list published by the Brazilian Academy of Sciences. One species of porcupine may have become extinct in historic times: *Sphiggurus pallidus*, reported in the mid-19th century in the West Indies, where no porcupines now occur. CAW

Cavies

FACTFILE

CAVIES

Order: Rodentia

Suborder: Hystricognathi

Family: Caviidae

14 species in 5 genera

DISTRIBUTION
S America (mara in C and S Argentina only)

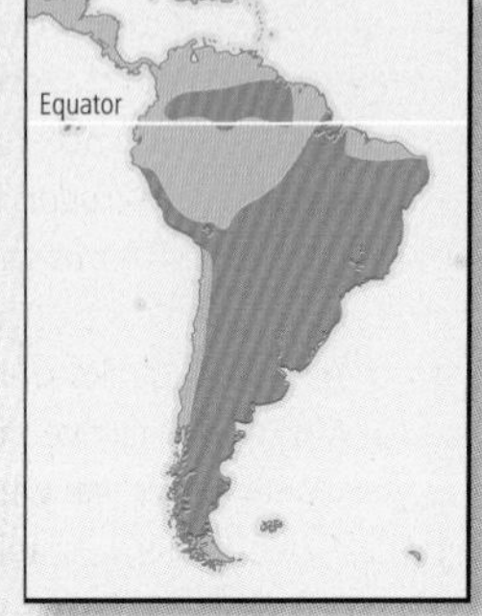

GUINEA PIGS AND CAVIES Genus *Cavia*
S America, in the full range of habitats. Coat: grayish or brownish agouti; domesticated forms vary. 5 species: *C. aperea, C. fulgida, C. magna, C. porcellus* (Domestic guinea pig), *C. tschudii.*

MARA Genus *Dolichotis*
Mara or Patagonian hare or cavy
S America (C and S Argentina), occurring in open scrub desert and grasslands. HBL 50–75cm (19.7–30in), TL 4.5cm (1.8in), WT 8–9kg (17.6–19.8lb). Coat: head and body brown, rump dark (almost black) with prominent white fringe round the base; belly white. Gestation: 90 days. Longevity: up to 15 years. 2 species: *D. patagonum* and *D. salinicola*. Conservation status: Lower Risk – Near Threatened.

YELLOW-TOOTHED CAVIES Genus *Galea*
Yellow-toothed cavies or cuis
S America, in the full range of habitats. Coat: medium to light brown agouti, with grayish-white underparts. Gestation: 50 days. 3 species: *G. flavidens, G. musteloides, G. spixii.*

ROCK CAVY *Kerodon rupestris*
NE Brazil, occurring in rocky outcrops in thorn-scrub. HBL 38cm (15in), WT 1kg (2.2lb). Coat: gray, grizzled with white and black; throat white, belly yellow-white, rump and backs of thighs reddish. Gestation: 75 days.

DESERT CAVIES Genus *Microcavia*
Argentina and Bolivia, in arid regions. HBL 22cm (8.7in), weight 300g (10.7oz). Coat: a coarse dark agouti, brown to grayish. Gestation: 50 days. Longevity: 3–4 years (up to 8 in captivity). 3 species: *M. australis, M. niata, M. shiptoni.*

Abbreviations HBL = head–body length TL = tail length WT = weight

MOST PEOPLE ARE FAMILIAR WITH CAVIES, but under a different and somewhat misleading name: guinea pigs. "Guinea" refers to Guyana, a country where cavies occur in the wild, while "pig" derives from the short, squat body of this rodent (the pork-like quality of the flesh doubtless also played a part in its naming). The Domestic guinea pig was being raised for food by the Incas when the conquistadors arrived in Peru in the 1530s, and is now found the world over, with one exception: it no longer occurs in the wild.

Cavies are among the most abundant and widespread of all South American rodents. They live in a variety of habitats ranging from tropical floodplains through open grasslands and forest edges to rocky meadows 4,000m (13,000ft) up. For a long time, they – or at least their domesticated cousins – were considered very stupid animals; psychologists found it difficult to set up tests in which guinea pigs showed any sign of learning or intelligence. However, it now appears that the tasks set for them may have been inappropriate.

To remedy this and to give cavies a fair chance to display their brainpower, experiments have recently been designed to play to their strengths. The basic prerequisites are a satisfactory laboratory and experiment habituation period; providing the animal with its daily requirements of vitamin C; a choice of task adapted to the animal's natural habits; and, finally, a controlled environment with as little extraneous noise as possible, to prevent the guinea pig from "freezing." In these conditions, guinea pigs have shown that they can learn at a similar rate to other mammalian species, particularly rats. Furthermore, when they were trained to forage under different experimental conditions (which included manipulations of travel time between food sources, food gain rates, and food availability), guinea pigs proved adept at optimizing their foraging efficiency.

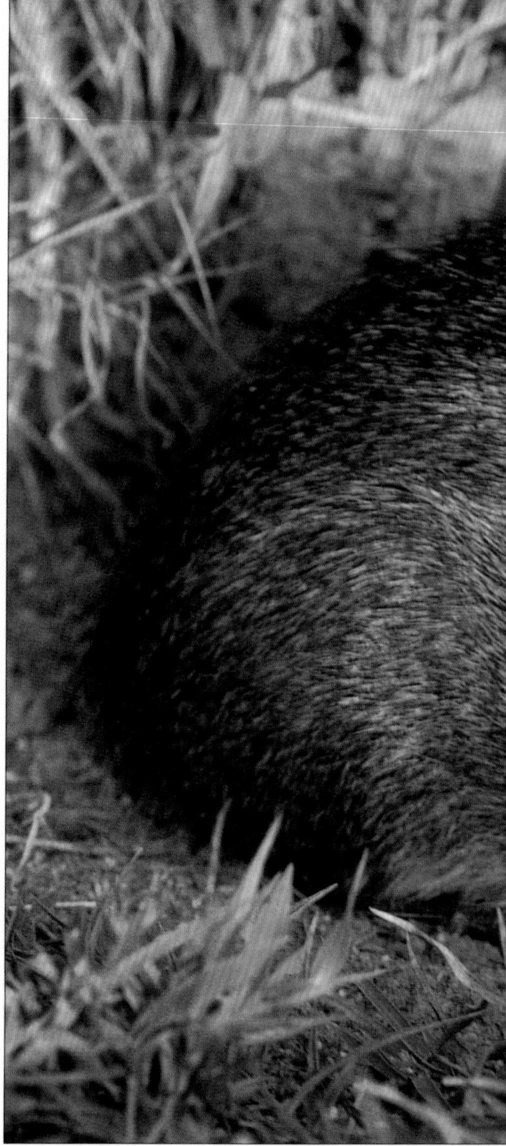

Above *The Brazilian guinea pig (*Cavia aperea*) is one of three wild species from which the familiar Domestic guinea pig may have derived. The coats of the wild species are relatively long and coarse.*

Below *Rock cavies' unusual mating behavior entails defending isolated rock piles to which females are drawn in search of shelter; in this way, the males accumulate harems. When approaching a female in estrus, the male circles around her to block her path* ***1****, then passes under her chin* ***2*** *before attempting to mount* ***3****.*

Small, Alert, and Nervous

FORM AND FUNCTION

Cavies are among the most abundant and widespread of all South American rodents. All except the mara share a basic form and structure. The body is short and robust and the head large, contributing about one-third of the total head–body length. The eyes are fairly large and alert, the ears big but close to the head. The fur is coarse and easily shed when the animal is handled. There is no tail. The forefeet are strong and flat, usually with four digits, each equipped with sharp claws; the hind feet, with three clawed digits, are elongated. Cavies walk on their soles, with the heels touching the ground. The incisors are short, and the cheek teeth, which are arranged in rows that converge towards the front of the mouth, have the shape of prisms and are constantly growing. Both sexes are alike, apart from each possessing certain specialized glands.

Cavies are very vocal, making a variety of chirps, squeaks, churrs, and squeals. One genus, *Kerodon*, emits a piercing whistle when frightened. *Galea* species rapidly drum their hind feet on the ground when anxious.

Cavies first appeared in the mid-Miocene era in South America. Since their appearance some 20 million years ago, the family has undergone an extensive adaptive radiation, reaching peak diversity between 5 and 2 million years ago. From a peak of 11 genera during the Pliocene, they fell to their current 5 genera during the Pleistocene, about 1 million years ago.

The Cautious Life of Prey Species

SOCIAL BEHAVIOR

The 12 remaining species of the subfamily Caviinae, which comprises all the cavies except the *Dolichotis* species, are widely distributed throughout South America. All 12 are to a degree specialized for exploiting open habitats. Cavies are found in grasslands and scrub forests from Venezuela to the Straits of Magellan, but each genus has evolved to exist in a slightly different habitat.

Cavia is the genus most restricted to grasslands. In Argentina, *Cavia aperea* is limited to the humid pampas in the northeastern provinces. *Microcavia australis* is the desert specialist, and is found throughout the arid Monte and Patagonian deserts of Argentina. Other *Microcavia* species, *M. niata* and *M. shiptoni*, occur in the arid, high-altitude *puña* (subalpine zone) of Bolivia and Argentina. The specialized genus *Kerodon* is found only in rocky outcrops called *laleiros* that dot the countryside in the thorn-scrub of northeastern Brazil. *Galea* seem to be the "jacks-of-all-trades" of the cavies, found in all the above habitats; it is also the only genus that coexists with other genera.

Regardless of habitat, all cavies are herbivorous. *Galea* and *Cavia* feed on herbs and grasses. *Microcavia* and *Kerodon* seem to prefer leaves; both genera are active climbers, which in the case of the *Kerodon* species is surprising because they lack claws and a tail, two adaptations usually associated with life in trees. The sight of an 800g (28oz) guinea pig hurrying along a pencil-thin branch high in a tree is quite striking.

All cavies become sexually mature early, at 1–3 months. The gestation period is fairly long for rodents, varying from 50–75 days. Litter sizes are small, averaging about 3 for *Galea* and *Microcavia*, 2 for *Cavia*, and 1.5 for *Kerodon*. The young are born highly precocial. Males contribute little obvious parental care, and generally ignore the female and her young once the litter is born.

Three species of cavies have been studied in northeastern Argentina: *Microcavia australis*, *Galea musteloides*, and *Cavia aperea*. *Cavia* and *Microcavia* never occur in the same area, *Cavia* preferring moist grasslands and *Microcavia* more arid habitats. *Galea* occurs with both genera. Competition between *Galea* and *Microcavia* seems to be minimized by the use of different foraging tactics: *Microcavia* is more of a browser, and arboreal. The degree to which *Cavia* and *Galea* interact within the same areas is unknown. Home-range sizes are, on average, 3,200sq m (34,500sq ft) for *Microcavia*, and 1,300sq m (14,000sq ft) for *Galea* and *Cavia*. They are diurnal, and are active mainly during early morning and evening hours.

The genus *Cavia* is the most widely distributed of all cavies, ranging over almost all South America from Colombia to Argentina. *Cavia* species breed year-round, but are less active in the winter. In the Pampas region they can occur in high densities, especially in late autumn, typically inhabiting linear habitats such as field margins and roadsides which have a zone of tall and dense vegetation. They feed in open areas of short vegetation, but return to the borders for protection.

The amount of time cavies spend watching for danger while feeding varies with the chances of being attacked by predators. In the open delta of the Paraná river, Argentina, those feeding in short grass away from cover were found by researchers to look up for danger three times more often than those close to shelter. Almost 50 percent of feeding occurred within 1m (3.3ft) of shelter, and the animals never strayed more than 4m (13ft) from cover. They recognized safety in numbers, staying in the open more than twice as long when in groups than when they were alone.

Cavies have several important predators. The grison – a South American weasel – has been known to almost wipe out a population of cavies over a period of five months. High-density populations also attract several species of raptor, which seem to kill more prey than they can consume, as evidenced by the presence of uneaten cavy carcasses where raptors have been.

Little is known of cavy reproductive behavior in the wild. Captive males are very aggressive, making it almost impossible to keep them together in the presence of females. As a result, only one male is present whenever a female comes into estrus. Females organize themselves in linear dominance hierarchies that are strictly age-dependent.

Cavies are considered a major pest of tree crops in many regions of Argentina. For example, in the Paraná Delta, cavies and Red rats (*Holochilus brasiliensis*) destroyed more than 50 percent of the cultivated salicaceous trees by gnawing a fringe of bark 40cm (16in) up above ground level. Several methods of reducing their impact on forestry have been experimentally introduced, including chemical repellents and covering the stalks of seedlings with polyethylene tubes.

Below *Two Rock cavies* (Kerodon rupestris) *huddle on a branch in northeast Brazil. The animals take their name from the rock piles in which they live and breed, leaving them each evening to forage. Agile climbers, they spend much of their feeding time in trees, where they go in search of their chief staple, tender leaves.*

Galea musteloides can live both at sea level and at altitudes up to 5,000m (16,400ft). Males living in large, mixed-sex groups form hierarchies in which higher-ranking animals sire more young than do subordinates – between 70 and 90 percent of all offspring, according to one observation of captive animals that employed DNA fingerprinting techniques. Aggression directed towards subordinates in the colony by higher-ranking individuals may have the effect of suppressing the losers' sex hormones. Equally intriguing is the fact that females appear to be tolerant of unfamiliar pups while they are breeding, probably as an adaptation to living in reproductive groups of related females with synchronized births and communal suckling.

In *Microcavia* species, aggression between males defines a linear dominance hierarchy within colonies. The stability of the social groups seems to vary between habitats: in deserts they keep strict fidelity to a burrow system to which their

Above *A Southern mountain cavy* (Microcavia australis) *keeps watch over her growing brood on the Valdés Peninsula in Argentina. Three is a typical litter size for this short-lived species; mothers become receptive again immediately after giving birth, and can have up to five litters a year.*

group territoriality is restricted, but in less arid habitats they show a lax social organization without permanent groups. *Microcavia* sites its colonial burrows beneath bushes with broad canopies that are low to the ground, presumably as protection from predators. Grazing by *Microcavia* can damage an important number of plants; a study conducted in the Nacuñán Reserve, western Argentina, showed that herbivory by Highland tuco-tucos (*Ctenomys opimus*) and *Microcavia* species affected 35 percent of the total plants of a creosote bush community dominated by *Larrea cuneifolia*.

Two species of cavies coexist in northeastern Brazil: *Kerodon rupestris* and *Galea spixii*. *Galea spixii* is similar to the Argentine *Galea* in ecology, morphology, color, and behavior. The animals inhabit thorn forests, are grazers, and have a noncohesive social organization.

The Rock cavy (*Kerodon rupestris*) is markedly different from all the other small cavy species. It is larger and leaner, and has a face that is almost doglike. All small cavies except *Kerodon* have sharply clawed digits; *Kerodon* has nails growing from under the skin, with a single grooming claw on the inside hind-toes and extensively padded feet. The modifications of the feet facilitate movement on slick rock surfaces. Rock cavies are strikingly agile as they leap from boulder to boulder, executing graceful mid-air twists and turns. They are also exceptional climbers, and forage almost exclusively on leaves in trees. There is little competition for resources with *Galea*.

Perhaps the most interesting difference between *Kerodon* and *Galea* is behavioral. *Galea* species, like the Argentine cavies, live in thorn-scrub forest and have a promiscuous mating system. Rock cavies inhabit isolated patches of boulders, many of which can be defended by a single male, and single males seem to have exclusive access to two or more females. The boulder piles attract females, so by defending these sites males monopolize the female tenants. This system parallels that of the unrelated hyraxes of eastern Africa (see Subungulates: Hyraxes).

Natural Adaptors in Need of Help

CONSERVATION AND ENVIRONMENT

Most cavy species can adapt to altered and disturbed habitat, and some do well among human settlements. But one species, *Kerodon*, is in trouble. Hunted extensively, these Rock cavies are declining in numbers and are in desperate need of protection. Because they are patchily dispersed throughout their range, large areas will have to be set aside; indeed, two such research reserves have already been established in Brazil. TEL/MC

LIFELONG PARTNERS

Colonial breeding in the monogamous mara

AS DAWN BROKE ACROSS THE PATAGONIAN thorn-scrub a large female rodent, with the long ears of a hare and the body and legs of a small antelope, cautiously approached a den, followed by her mate. They were the first pair to arrive, and so walked directly to the mouth of the den. At the burrow's entrance the female made a shrill, whistling call, and almost immediately eight pups burst out. The youngsters were hungry and all thronged around the female, trying to suckle. Under this onslaught she jumped and twirled to dislodge the melee of unwelcome mouths which sought her nipples. The female sniffed each carefully, chasing off all but her own. Finally, she managed to select her own two offspring from the hoard and led them 10m (33ft) to a site where they would be nursed.

In the meantime her mate sat alert nearby. If another adult pair had approached the den while his female was there, coming to tend their own pups, he would have made a vigorous display directly in front of his mate. If the newcomers had not moved away he would have dashed towards them, with his head held low and neck outstretched, and chased them off. The second pair would then have waited, alert or grazing, at a distance of 20-30m (65-100ft). When the original pair had left the area the new pair would then approach the den, to collect their own pups.

The animal being observed was the mara or Patagonian cavy, an 8kg (17.6lb) hare-like day-active cavy, *Dolichotis patagonum*. (The behavior of the only other member of the subfamily Dolichotinae, the Salt desert cavy, *Dolichotis salinicola*, is unknown in the wild.) A fundamental aspect of the mara's social system is the monogamous pair bond, which in captivity, and probably in the wild, lasts for life. The drive that impels males to bond with females is so strong that it can lead to "cradle snatching" – adult bachelor males attaching themselves to females while the latter are still infants. Contact between paired animals is maintained primarily by the male, who closely follows the female wherever she goes, discouraging approaches from other maras by policing a moving area around her about 30m (100ft) in diameter. In contrast, females appear less concerned about the whereabouts of their mates. While foraging, members of a pair maintain contact by means of a low grumble.

Monogamy is not common in mammals and in the mara several factors probably combine to favor this system. It typically occurs in species where there are opportunities for both parents to care for the young, yet in maras virtually all direct care of the offspring is undertaken by the mother. However, the male does make a considerable indirect investment. Due to the high amount of energy a female uses in bearing and nursing her young, she has to spend a far greater part of the day feeding than the male: time during which her head is lowered and her vigilance for predators impaired. On the other hand, the male spends a larger proportion of each day scanning and is thus able to warn the female and offspring of danger. Also, by defending the female against the approaches of other maras, he ensures uninterrupted time for her to feed and care for his young. Furthermore, female maras are sexually receptive only for a few hours twice a year; in Patagonia females mate in June or July and then come into heat again in September or October, about 5 hours after giving birth, so a male must stay with his female to ensure he is with her when she is receptive.

Mara pairs generally avoid each other and outside the breeding season it is rare to see pairs within 30m (about 100ft) of each other. Then their home ranges are about 40ha (96 acres). Perhaps the avoidance between pairs is an adaptation to the species' eating habits. Maras feed primarily on short grasses and herbs which are sparsely, but quite evenly, distributed in dry scrub desert. So far, detail of their spatial organization is unknown, but there is at least some overlap in the movements of neighboring pairs. Furthermore, there are some circumstances when, if there is an abundance of food, maras will aggregate. In the Patagonian desert there are shallow lakes, 100m to several kilometers in diameter, which contain water for only a few months of the year. When dry, they are sometimes carpeted with short grasses that maras relish. At these times, toward the end of the breeding season, up to about 100

Above *A mother and pups. A female mara will normally give birth at one time to a maximum of three well-developed young. She will nurse them for an hour or more once or twice a day for up to four months.*

Left *Foraging and feeding can be a dangerous time for maras, since it leaves them more vulnerable to attacks from predators. It is therefore essential that one of a pair remains alert.*

maras will congregate. However, individual pairs remain loyal to one another after the congregations have dispersed.

The strikingly cohesive monogamy of maras is noteworthy in its contrast with, and persistence throughout, the breeding season when up to 15 pairs become at least superficially colonial by depositing their young at a communal den. The dens are dug by the females and not subsequently entered by adults. The same den sites are often used for three or more years in a row. Each female gives birth to one to three young at the mouth of the den; the pups soon crawl inside to safety. Although newborn pups are moving about and grazing within 24 hours of birth, they remain in the vicinity of the den for up to four months, and are nursed by their mother once or twice a day during this period. Around the den an uneasy truce prevails amongst the pairs whose visits coincide. The number of pairs of maras breeding at a den varies from 1 to at least 15 and may depend on habitat. Pairs come and go around the den all day and in general at the larger dens at least one pair is always in attendance there. Even when 20 or more young are kept in a crèche, cohabiting amicably, the monogamous bond remains the salient feature of the social system. Each female sniffs the infants seeking to suckle and they respond by proffering their anal regions to the female's nose. Infants clambering to reach one female may differ by at least one month in age. A female's rejection of a usurper can involve a bite and violent shaking. However, interlopers occasionally secure an illicit drink. Although females may thus be engaging in communal nursing they rarely seem to do so willingly.

Above *In the open grasslands of Patagonia, where cover is scarce, maras spend a large part of the day grazing or basking, but keep their keen sense of hearing attuned to any potential danger.*

The reasons why normally unsociable pairs of maras keep their young in a communal crèche are unknown, but it may be that it lowers the likelihood of them falling victim to a predator; indeed, the more individuals at a den (both adults and young) the more pairs of eyes there are to detect danger. Furthermore, some pairs travel as much as 2km (1.2mi) from their home range to the den, so the opportunities for shared surveillance of the young may diminish the demands on each pair for protracted attendance at the den. The unusual breeding system of the monogamous mara may thus be a compromise, conferring on the pups the benefits of coloniality, in an environment wherein association between pairs is otherwise apparently disadvantageous. AT/DWM

Capybara

SAVANNA-DWELLING SOCIAL GRAZERS averaging a hefty 50kg (110lb), capybaras are unusual animals. They are found only in South America, where they live in groups near water. Members of the suborder known as caviomorphs, which also includes cavies and chinchillas, they are in fact the largest of all the rodents.

The first European naturalists to visit South America called capybaras "water pigs" or "Orinoco hogs," and the first of those names has carried over into their present scientific designation as hydrochaerids. Yet in truth, they are neither pigs nor totally aquatic; their nearest relatives are actually the cavies. The other hydrochaerids, now all extinct, were larger than present-day capybaras; the biggest were twice as long and probably weighed eight times as much, making them heavier than the largest North American Grizzly.

The Biggest Rodents

FORM AND FUNCTION

Capybaras are ponderous, barrel-shaped animals. They have no tail, and their front legs are shorter than their back legs. Their slightly webbed toes, four on the front feet and three on the back, make them very strong swimmers, able to stay under water for up to 5 minutes. Their skin is extremely tough and covered by long, sparse, bristle-like hairs. The nostrils, eyes, and ears are situated near the top of the large, blunt head, and hence protrude out of the water when the animal swims. Two pairs of large, typically rodent incisors enable capybaras to eat very short grasses, which they grind up with their molar teeth. There are four molars on each side of each lower jaw. The fourth molar is characteristic of the subfamily in being as long as the other three.

Two kinds of scent glands are present in the capybara. One gland, highly developed in males but almost nonexistent in females, is located on top of the snout and is known as the *morrillo* (literally, "hillock" in Spanish). This is a dark, oval-shaped, naked protrusion that secretes a copious, white, sticky fluid. Both sexes also produce odors from two glandular pockets located on either side of the anus. Male anal glands are filled with easily detachable hairs abundantly coated with layers of hard, crystalline calcium salts. Female anal pockets also have hairs, but theirs are not detachable and are coated in a greasy secretion rather than with crystalline layers. The proportions of each chemical present in the secretions of individual capybaras are different, providing a potential for individual recognition via personal "olfactory fingerprints." The snout scent gland also plays a role in signaling dominance status, while the anal gland appears to be important in group membership recognition and perhaps in territoriality.

FACTFILE

CAPYBARA

Hydrochaeris hydrochaeris

Order: Rodentia

Family: Hydrochaeridae

Sole member of genus and of family. 2 populations, one E of the Andes from Venezuela to N Argentina, the other from NW Venezuela through N Colombia up to the Panama Canal. Some authorities regard the two as separate species, named respectively *Hydrochaeris hydrochaeris* and *H. isthmius*.

DISTRIBUTION South America

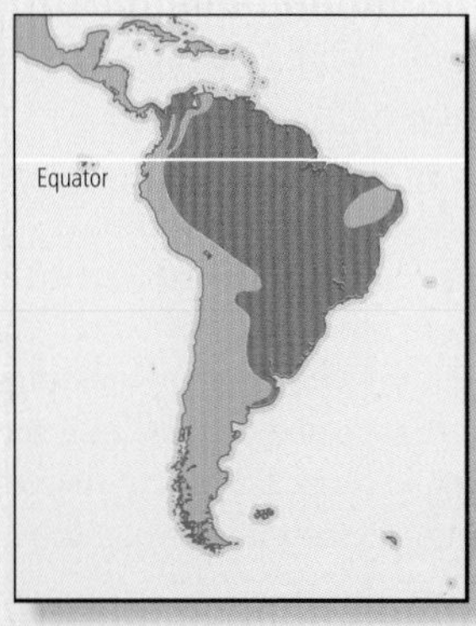

HABITAT Flooded savanna or grassland next to water holes; also, along ponds and rivers in tropical forest.

SIZE Head–body length 106–134cm (42–53in); **shoulder height** 50–62cm (20–24in); **weight** male 35–64kg (77–141lb), female 37–66kg (81.6–146lb).

COAT Light brown, consisting of short, abundant hairs in young; adults have long, sparse, bristle-like hairs of variable color, usually brown to reddish.

DIET Mostly grasses, especially aquatic; occasionally water hyacinths and other dicotyledons.

BREEDING Females are sexually mature at 12 months, males at 18 months. Gestation 150 days. 1–8 (average 4) young, born mostly at the end of the wet season, after 150–day gestation. Very precocial: young graze within hours of birth.

LONGEVITY About 6 years (12 in captivity).

CONSERVATION STATUS Lower Risk – Conservation Dependent.

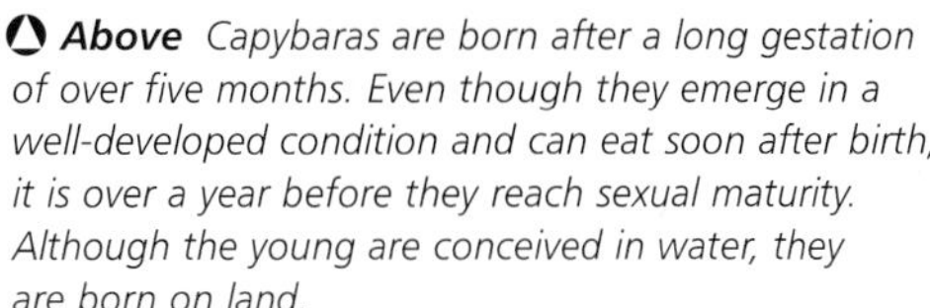

Above Capybaras are born after a long gestation of over five months. Even though they emerge in a well-developed condition and can eat soon after birth, it is over a year before they reach sexual maturity. Although the young are conceived in water, they are born on land.

Left Water is a place of refuge for capybaras. Capybaras live either in groups averaging 10 in number or in temporary larger aggregations, which may contain up to 100 individuals and will be composed of the smaller groups. The situation varies according to the season.

Capybaras have several distinct vocalizations. Infants and the young constantly emit a guttural purr, probably to maintain contact with their mothers or other group members. This sound is also made by losers in altercations, perhaps to appease their adversary. Another vocalization, the alarm bark, is given when a predator is detected. This coughing sound is often repeated several times, and the reaction of nearby animals may be to stand alert or to rush into the water.

Recycling Cellulose

DIET

Capybaras are exclusively herbivorous, feeding mainly on grasses that grow in or near water. They are very efficient grazers, and can crop the short, dry grasses left at the end of the tropical dry season. Because a large proportion of the grasses they eat consists of cellulose, which is indigestible by any mammal's digestive enzymes, capybaras possess a huge fermentation chamber called the cecum, equivalent to our tiny appendix. However, since the cecum is located between the small and large intestine, the animal cannot absorb the products of the fermentation carried out by microbial symbionts. To solve this problem, capybaras resort to coprophagy – reingestion of feces – in order to be able to take advantage of the work of their symbionts. Thus, for a few hours every morning during their resting period, capybaras recycle what they ate the previous evening and night. Usually they spend the morning resting, then bathe during the hot midday hours; in the late afternoon and early evening they graze. At night they alternate rest periods with feeding bouts. They never sleep for long, instead dozing in short bouts throughout the day.

Gregarious Grazers

SOCIAL BEHAVIOR

Capybaras live in groups of 10–30 animals, apparently depending on the habitat: greener and more homogeneous pastures promote larger groups. Pairs are rarely seen, but a proportion of adult males are solitary or loosely associated to one or more groups. In the dry season groups coalesce around the dwindling pools, forming temporary aggregations of 100 or more animals. When the wet season returns, these large aggregations split up into the original groups that formed them. Thus, capybara social units may last three years, and probably more.

Groups of capybaras are closed social units, in which little variation in core membership is observed. A typical group is composed of a dominant male (often distinguishable by his large *morrillo*), one or more females, several infants and young, and one or more subordinate males. Among the males there is a dominance hierarchy, maintained by aggressive interactions that usually take the form of simple chases. Dominant males repeatedly shepherd their subordinates to the periphery of the group, but fights are rarely seen. Females are much more tolerant of each other, although the precise details of their social relationships, hierarchical or otherwise, are unknown. Each home range is used almost exclusively by one group, and can therefore be regarded as a territory. Territories are defended by all adult members of the group against conspecific intruders. Any animal of either sex may chase an interloper away, irrespective of its sex, as long as the chaser is within its own territory.

Capybaras are found in a wide variety of habitats, ranging from open grasslands to tropical rain forest. Groups may occupy an area varying in size from 2–200ha (4–494 acres), with 10–20ha (24.7–49.4 acres) being most common. Each home range is used mainly, but not exclusively, by one group and can therefore be considered a territory. Territories are defended against conspecific intruders by all adult members of the group. Particularly in the dry season, but at other times as well, two or more groups may be seen grazing side by side. In some areas density may reach 2 individuals per hectare (5 per acre), but lower densities of less than 1 per hectare are more frequent.

Capybaras reach sexual maturity at 18 months. In Venezuela and Colombia they appear to breed year round, with a marked peak at the beginning of the wet season in May. In Brazil, in more temperate areas, they probably breed just once a year. When a female becomes sexually receptive, a male will start a pursuit that may last for an hour or more. The female will walk in and out of the water, repeatedly pausing while the male follows close behind. The mating takes place in the water; the female stops, and the male clambers on her back, sometimes thrusting her under water with his weight. As is usual in rodents, copulation lasts only a few seconds, but each sexual pursuit typically involves several mountings.

150 days later, up to seven babies are born; four is the average litter size. To give birth the female leaves her group and walks to nearby cover. Her young are born a few hours later, and are precocial, able to eat grass within their first week. A few hours after the birth the mother rejoins her group, the young following as soon as they become mobile, which should occur when the babies are still very young. Females seem to share the burden of nursing by allowing infants other than their own to suckle. The young in a group spend most of their time within a tight-knit crèche, moving between nursing females. When active, they constantly emit a churring purr.

Capybara infants tire quickly, and are therefore vulnerable to predators. They have most to fear from vultures and feral or semiferal dogs, which prey on them. Caymans and foxes may also take young capybaras. Jaguar and smaller cats were certainly important predators in the past, though today they are nearly extinct in most of Venezuela and Colombia. In some areas of Brazil, however, jaguars seize capybaras in substantial numbers.

When a predator approaches a group the first animal to detect it will emit an alarm bark. The normal reaction of other group members is to stand alert, but if the danger is very close, or the caller keeps barking, they will all rush into the water, where they form a close aggregation with young in the center and adults facing outward.

Putting a Cap on Hunting

CONSERVATION AND ENVIRONMENT

Capybara populations have dropped so substantially in Colombia that, from 1980 onward, the government prohibited capybara hunting. In Venezuela they have been killed since colonial times in areas that are devoted to cattle ranching. In 1953 hunting became subject to legal regulation and controlled, but to little effect until 1968 when, after a 5-year moratorium, a management plan was devised, based on a study of the species' biology and ecology. Since then, 30–35 percent of the annually censused population in licensed ranches with populations of over 400 animals have been harvested every year. This has apparently resulted in local stabilization of capybara populations. Capybaras are now listed as Lower Risk: Conservation Dependent by the IUCN, in recognition of the fact that control on hunting and harvesting must remain if population levels are to be maintained. DWM/EH

Left A capybara marking its territory. It is instantly recognizable as a male from the prominent, bare lump on top of its snout – the morrillo *sebaceous gland, which contains the animal's highly individual scent.*

Below A South American waterbird – the jacana – searches a capybara's coat for parasitic insects. The capybara spends much of its time in water and can travel long distances submerged; its small eyes and ears are thought to be an adaptation for living in water.

FARMING CAPYBARA

In Venezuela there has been a demand for capybara meat at least since the early 16th century, when Roman Catholic missionary monks classified it, along with terrapin, as legitimate Lenten fare; the amphibious habits of the two species presumably misled the monks into thinking they had an affinity with fish. Today, because of their size and high reproductive rate as well as the tasty meat and valuable leather they can provide, capybaras are candidates for both ranching and intensive husbandry.

It has been calculated that, where the savannas are irrigated to mollify the effects of the dry season, the optimal capybara population for farming is 1.5–3 animals per hectare (or about 1 per acre), yielding 27kg of meat per ha (24lb per acre) per annum. Ranches licensed to harvest the population can sustain yields of about 1 animal per 2 ha in good habitat. An annual cull takes place in February, when reproduction is at a minimum and the animals congregate around waterholes. Horsemen herd them together, and they are then surrounded by a cordon of cowboys on foot. An experienced slaughterman selects adults weighing over 35kg (77lb), excluding pregnant females, and kills them with a blow from a heavy club. The average animal weighs 44.2kg (97.4lb), of which 39 percent (17.3kg; 38lb) is dressed meat. These otherwise unmanaged wild populations thus yield over 8kg of meat per hectare (7lb per acre) annually.

In spite of this yield, farmers have traditionally feared that large populations of capybaras would compete with domestic stock. In fact, however, capybaras selectively graze on short vegetation near water and so do not compete significantly with cattle, which take taller, drier forage, except in wet, low-lying habitats. In these regions, capybaras are actually much more efficient at digesting the plant material than are cattle and horses. So, ranching capybara in their natural habitat appears to be, both biologically and economically, a viable adjunct to cattle ranching.

Other Cavy-like Rodents

1

THE FAMILIES ASSEMBLED HERE ARE PART OF a disparate group of predominantly South American mammals known as the Caviomorpha. The diversity they show is in marked contrast to the relative homogeneity of other rodent groups, such as the squirrels or the rats and mice.

The group includes small, medium, and very large rodents; some are covered with barbed spines, others have soft, silky fur; nearly all are herbivorous, although a few are not averse to including insects or larger prey in their diet. Many are terrestrial but others live as burrowers or tree-dwellers, or else spend much of their time swimming and feeding in water. They inhabit forests and grasslands, water and rocky deserts, coastal plains and high mountains; some are solitary, others colonial. Some species are common and widespread, others known only from a few specimens in museums; yet others have become extinct, some of them within historical times, often as a result of human activities. Many species are eaten by humans, others are prized for their fur; some are pests, while others carry the diseases of humankind and domestic animals.

The larger species of South American rodents, such as agoutis, pacas, pacaranas, and viscachas, are prey for the large and medium-sized carnivores (jaguars, ocelots, Pampas cats, Maned wolves, Bush dogs, foxes, and others). They are herbivorous, and may be considered the South American equivalents of the vast array of ungulate herbivores that are so important in the African ecosystems. It is thought that these rodents radiated into this role as the primitive native herbivores became extinct, and before the arrival of the new fauna from the north.

Despite their obvious diversity, the cavy-like rodents have many anatomical and other features in common. Particularly striking are the similarities in reproduction, such as the long gestation period exhibited by many species, the small number of young in each litter, and the advanced state of development many show at birth. Especially in many of the medium to large species, the young are born fully furred and with their eyes open; some are able to run within a few hours of birth, and many become independent of their mothers relatively soon afterwards.

Dassie Rat

FAMILY PETROMYIDAE

The Dassie rat is superbly adapted to the dry, rocky hillside country of southern Africa in which it lives. The soft pelage is gray, buff, or tawny in color, making the animal difficult to spot when lying on rocks, and it has a flattened skull and very flexible ribs, enabling it to squeeze into narrow crevices. It forages on the ground or in bushes for leaves, berries, and seeds, and is particularly active at dawn and dusk, resting and sunning itself below projecting rocks so as to avoid predatory birds. Dassie rats are solitary or else found in pairs, yet utter a warning whistling call if alarmed. One or two well-developed young are born once per year, at the start of the rainy season, so the species has a relatively slow reproduction rate for a small tropical mammal.

Cane Rats

FAMILY THRYONOMYIDAE

Cane rats or grasscutters are robust African rodents with a coarse, bristly pelage, the bristles being flattened and grooved along their length. The pelage is brown speckled with yellow or gray above, buff-white below, allowing them to blend well with the grasses and reeds in which they feed and live. The preferred semi-aquatic habitat for *Thryonomys swinderianus* is reed beds, marshes,

2

4

6

3

5

and the margins of lakes and rivers, while *T. gregorianus* occurs in dryer areas of moist savanna grasslands. Cane rats live in small groups, communicating by calls and stamping their hind feet. They shelter among tall grasses or in rock crevices, or in the abandoned burrows of other animals; they also sometimes excavate their own shallow burrows. As their common name suggests, they feed mainly on grass and cane, but also a variety of other vegetation including bark, nuts, and fruits, and they may be pests of plantations and cultivated land, especially where population densities are high. Cane rats are prey for leopards, mongooses, snakes, birds of prey, and humans. In some parts of their range, they breed all year round, but most have two litters each year with an average of four young per litter. The young are well-developed at birth.

Chinchillas and Viscachas

FAMILY CHINCHILLIDAE

Chinchillids live in relatively barren regions, and all have thick, soft fur, although chinchillas and mountain viscachas, occurring at higher elevations, have denser fur than that of the pampas-dwelling Plains viscacha. They are slender-bodied animals with large ears and tails up to one-third the length of the body, and their long, strong hind legs enable them to run and jump agilely.

All the family are colonial. Chinchillas live in holes and crevices among rocks, and emerge at dusk to forage during the night for any available vegetation. In contrast, mountain viscachas forage for grasses, mosses, and lichens, and sun themselves on rocks during the day; they generally live in family groups that coexist with others to form small to very large colonies. Colonies of Plains viscachas live in extensive and complex burrows, consisting of a central chamber from which radiating tunnels lead to various entrances; they feed mainly on grass and seeds at dawn and dusk.

All species are subject to pressure from human hunting. Chinchillas have been pursued for their valuable fur to near-extinction; mountain and Plains viscachas are prized for both food and fur, and the Plains viscacha competes for grazing with domestic animals. In addition, they destroy pasture with their acidic urine, and so undermine the pampas that men, horses, and cattle are often injured by falling into their concealed tunnels.

Pacarana

FAMILY DINOMYIDAE

The pacarana is solitary or lives in pairs. It has a broad head with short, rounded ears, a robust body, and broad, heavily clawed feet. The pelage is coarse, black or brown with two more or less continuous white stripes on each side. A forest-dwelling species, seldom encountered and little known, this slow-moving, inoffensive herbivore is prey for jaguars, ocelots, and other medium-sized carnivores, and is hunted for food by humans.

Left *Representatives of 10 of the 12 families of other cavy-like rodents:* ***1*** *chinchilla, with soft fur and bushy tail;* ***2*** *cane rat from sub-Saharan Africa;* ***3*** *Chinchilla rat* (Abrocoma bennettii)*;* ***4*** *American spiny rat climbing a mound.* ***5*** *paca* (Agouti paca) *– the species has internal and external cheek pouches;* ***6*** *Dassie rat* (Petromus typicus)*;* ***7*** *pacarana* (Dinomys branickii) *feeding on vegetation;* ***8*** *tuco-tuco* (Ctenomys opimus) *digging with its incisors;* ***9*** *hutia sunning itself on a branch;* ***10*** *degu* (Octodon degus).

7

9

8

10

FACTFILE

OTHER CAVY-LIKE RODENTS

180 species in 12 families and 40 genera

DISTRIBUTION S America; West Indies; Africa S of the Sahara.

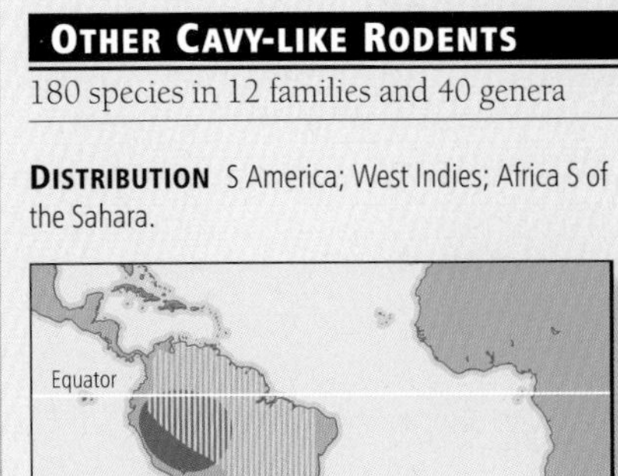

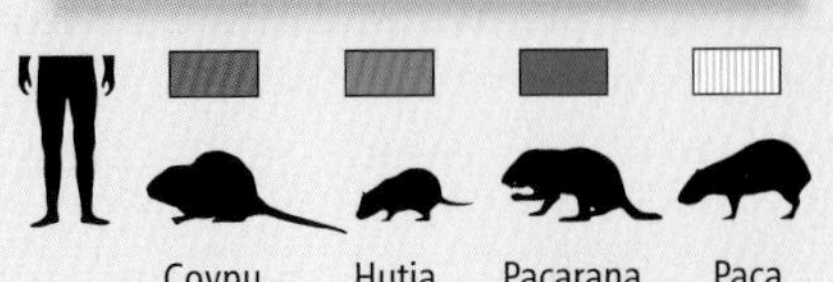

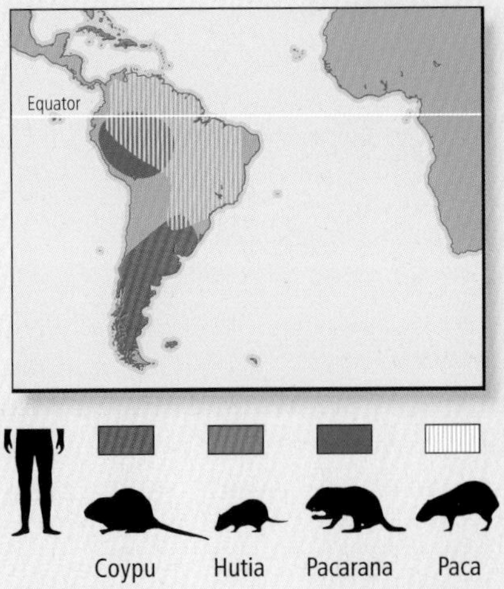

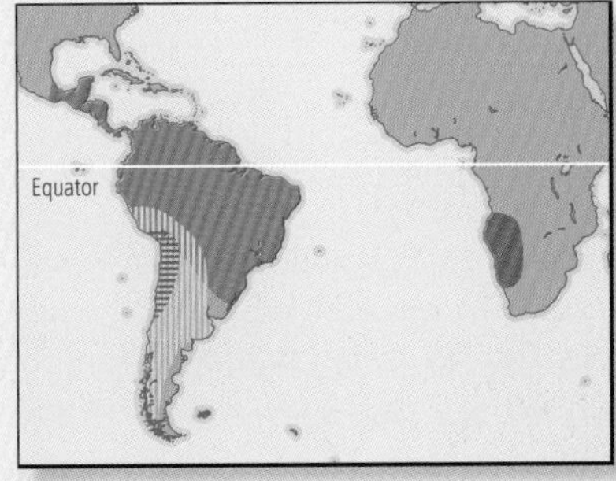

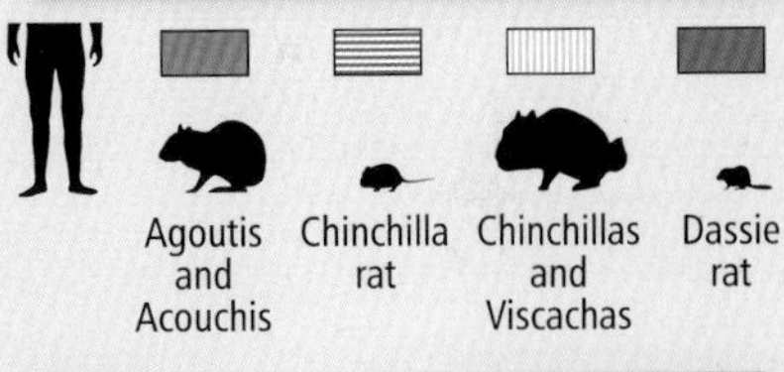

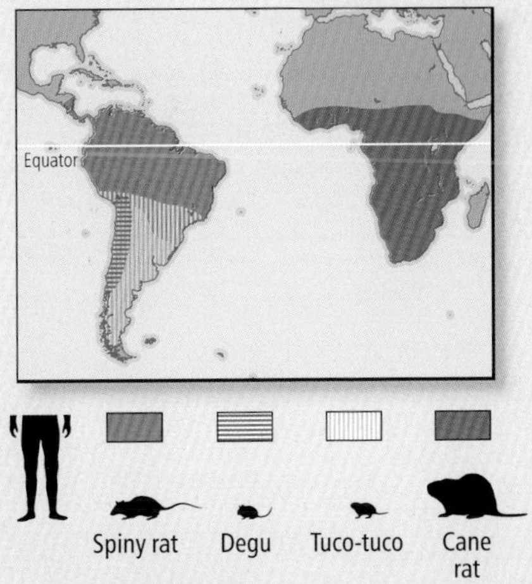

Equator

Spiny rat
Degu
Tuco-tuco
Cane rat

See families table ▷

Agoutis and Acouchis

FAMILY DASYPROCTIDAE

Agoutis and acouchis are relatively large rodents with very short tails and a coarse, usually unpatterned pelage. The long limbs are modifications for running, as is the reduction in the number of toes on the hind feet to three. The animals occur in a variety of habitats including forest, thick brush, and savanna; agoutis in particular are usually found close to water. All species are diurnal but secretive, and in areas of disturbance wait until dusk before emerging to forage for a wide variety of vegetation, especially fruit, nuts, and succulent parts of plants. When food is abundant, agoutis bury some for use in time of dearth, which is an important, if inadvertent, means of dispersing the seeds of many forest trees. In some areas, agoutis are known to breed throughout the year, litters normally consisting of one or two well-developed young that are able to run within an hour of birth. Agoutis and acouchis usually occur in small social groups of an adult male and female with several juveniles. They are preyed upon by a variety of carnivores including humans.

Pacas

FAMILY AGOUTIDAE

Pacas have often been included with the agoutis and acouchis as a separate subfamily of the Dasyproctidae; they are not dissimilar in appearance, but have relatively shorter legs, less reduced digits on the hind feet, and a spotted pelage. To add to the confusion, the scientific name of the paca is *Agouti*, which in common parlance is applied to the *Dasyprocta* species. Pacas usually occur in forested areas near water, often spending the day in burrows excavated by themselves or abandoned by other animals. They emerge at night to feed on leaves, stems, roots, nuts, seeds, and fruit, and may be a major pest of cultivated land. They are hunted by humans in addition to other large carnivores, and have become rare in some areas due to overhunting and habitat loss.

Tuco-tucos

FAMILY CTENOMYIDAE

The body form of tuco-tucos is robust and compact and shows many features associated with their burrowing lifestyle. The head is large, with small eyes and ears. The strong incisors, very prominent with their bright orange enamel, are used to cut through roots when tunneling. The limbs are short and muscular, and the claws on the forefeet in particular are long and strong, serving to dig the extensive burrow systems in which the animals live. The hind feet bear strong bristle fringes, which are used for grooming; the animals' scientific name, meaning "comb-toothed," is derived from the comblike nature of these bristles. The numerous species comprising this genus generally prefer the dry, sandy soils typical of coastal areas, grassy plains, and the *altiplano*, but also of forests. Some species are solitary, others colonial; most individuals occupy single burrows. Both sexes are territorial, with the more aggressive males holding larger territories than the females. Their shallow burrows may have several entrances. Although active mainly during the day, tuco-tucos rarely emerge to forage until after dark. They feed mainly on roots, stems, and grasses. Tuco-tucos are considered pests of cultivated and grazing land in some areas, and their burrows occasionally collapse, injuring people and livestock. As a consequence, some species have been hunted intensively and their numbers greatly reduced.

Degus or Octodonts

FAMILY OCTODONTIDAE

Octodontids occur in southern South America from sea level to about 3,500m (11,500ft). The family name of Octodontidae refers to the worn enamel surface of their teeth, which forms a pattern in the shape of a figure of eight. Most are adapted to digging, particularly rock rats and the coruro, and dig their own burrows, take over burrows abandoned by other animals, or live in rock piles and crevices. The pelage is usually long, thick, and silky. Degus and chozchoris are gray to brown above, creamy yellow or white below. Degus are active during the day; they are colonial and construct extensive burrow systems, with a central section connected to feeding sites by a complex maze of tunnels and surface paths. In contrast, the chozchoz is nocturnal and lives in burrows, rock crevices, and caves, feeding on acacia pods and cactus fruits. Coruros are brown or black, and rock rats dark brown all over; both are adapted to a burrowing lifestyle, with compact bodies, small eyes and ears, muscular forelimbs, and strong incisors, although these are less prominent in rock rats than in coruros. Little is known about the viscacha rats, which are buff above and

Cavy-like Rodent Families

Dassie rat or African rock rat
Family: Petromuridae

1 species (*Petromus typicus*), S Angola, Namibia and NW South Africa

Cane rats or grasscutters
Family: Thryonomyidae

2 species in 1 genus (*Thryonomys*)
Africa S of the Sahara

Chinchillas and viscachas
Family: Chinchillidae

6 species in 3 genera: chinchillas (*Chinchilla*), 2 species; mountain viscachas (*Lagidium*), 3 species; Plains viscacha (*Lagostomus maximus*).
W and S South America. 1 species – the Short-tailed chinchilla – is listed by the IUCN as Critically Endangered, 1 other is Vulnerable.

Pacarana Family: Dinomyidae

1 species (*Dinomys branickii*)
Venezuela, Colombia, Ecuador, Peru, Brazil, and Bolivia. Endangered.

Agoutis and Acouchis
Family: Dasyproctidae

13 species in 2 genera: agoutis (*Dasyprocta*), 11 species; acouchis (*Myoprocta*), 2 species.
S Mexico to S Brazil and Lesser Antilles. 2 agouti species are Endangered, 1 Vulnerable.

Pacas Family: Agoutidae

2 species in 1 genus (*Agouti*)
S Mexico to S Brazil

Tuco-tucos Family: Ctenomyidae

56 species in 1 genus (*Ctenomys*)
Peru S to Tierra del Fuego. 1 species Vulnerable.

Octodonts Family: Octodontidae

10 species in 6 genera:
rock rats (*Aconaemys*), 2 species; degus (*Octodon*), 4 species; Mountain degu or chozchoz (*Octodontomys gliroides*); Viscacha rat (*Octomys mimax*); coruro (*Spalacopus cyanus*); Plains viscacha rat (*Tympanoctomys barrerae*).
Peru, Bolivia, Argentina, Chile. 2 species Vulnerable.

Chinchilla rats or chinchillones
Family: Abrocomidae

3 species in 1 genus (*Abrocoma*), plus 1 other species known only from skeletal remains
Peru, Bolivia, Chile, Argentina. 1 species Vulnerable.

Spiny rats Family: Echimyidae

70 species in 16 genera:
Bristle-spined rat (*Chaetomys subspinosus*); coro-coros (*Dactylomys*), 3 species; Atlantic bamboo rat (*Kannabateomys amblyonyx*); olalla rats (*Olallamys*), 2 species; Arboreal soft-furred spiny rats (*Diplomys*), 3 species; arboreal spiny rats (*Echimys*), 14 species; toros (*Isothrix*), 2 species; Armored spiny rat (*Makalata armata*); Owl's spiny rat (*Carterodon sulcidens*); Lund's spiny rats (*Clyomys*), 2 species; guiara (*Euryzygomatomys spinosus*); Armored rat (*Hoplomys gymnurus*); Tuft-tailed spiny tree rat (*Lonchothrix emiliae*); spiny tree rats (*Mesomys*), 5 species; terrestrial spiny rats (*Proechimys*), 32 species; punare (*Thrichomys apereoides*)
S and C America and West Indies. 5 species are currently listed as Vulnerable; in addition, 4 others have recently been declared Extinct.

Hutias Family: Capromyidae

15 species in 6 genera:
Desmarest's hutia (*Capromys pilorides*); Bahaman and Jamaican hutias (*Geocapromys*), 2 species; small Cuban or sticknest hutias (*Mesocapromys*), 4 species; long-tailed Cuban hutias (*Mysateles*), 5 species; laminar-toothed hutias (*Isolobodon*), 2 species; Hispaniolan hutia (*Plagiodontia aedium*).
W Indies. 6 species are Critically Endangered, and 4 more are Vulnerable; in addition, 6 species have recently been declared Extinct.

Coypu or Nutria
Family: Myocastoridae

1 species, *Myocastor coypus*
S Brazil, Paraguay, Uruguay, Bolivia, Argentina, Chile; introduced into N America, N Asia, E Africa, Europe.

For full species list see Appendix ▷

from less than 200g (7oz) to 8.5kg (19lb), while the body mass of some extinct species is thought to have exceeded 20kg (44lb). The fur is harsh but with a soft underfur, and is generally brownish or grayish in coloration. Most of the living genera are partially, and the long-tailed Cuban hutias highly, arboreal. They live in forests, plantations, and rocky areas; in addition, small Cuban hutias occur in coastal swamps. Most are nocturnal, although Desmarest's hutia is diurnal in some areas. The diet includes a variety of vegetation but also small animals such as lizards. Hutias are and were preyed on by birds, snakes, introduced domestic dogs, cats, and mongooses, and they have been intensively hunted by humans for food; remains of several of the extinct species have been found in caves and kitchen middens.

whitish below with a particularly bushy tail, except that they are nocturnal, burrowing herbivores inhabiting desert scrub. *Tympanoctomys* is similarly poorly known; it is apparently restricted to plains with salt-rich vegetation.

Chinchilla Rats

FAMILY ABROCOMIDAE

As their name suggests, chinchilla rats are soft-furred, rat-like rodents that live in burrows or rock crevices. They are mainly nocturnal and may be colonial. Little information is available about these animals. Their diet includes a wide variety of plant material, although *Abrocoma vaccarum* may be specialized to feed on creosote bush. The pelage is silver gray or brown above, white or brown below, and consists of soft, dense underfur overlain with long, fine guardhairs. The pelts are occasionally sold, but are of much poorer quality than those of true chinchillas.

Spiny Rats

FAMILY ECHIMYIDAE

Spiny rats comprise a diverse group of medium-sized, ratlike, herbivorous rodents, most of which have a spiny or bristly coat, although some are soft-furred. Some are very common and widespread, while others are extremely rare; three genera known only from skeletal remains are probably, and a fourth certainly, extinct. The taxonomy of some genera is poorly understood, and the number of species is only tentative. The body form in this family is correlated with lifestyle. Robust, short-tailed forms (*Clyomys*, *Carterodon*, and *Euryzygomatomys*) are burrowing savanna species; relatively slender, long-tailed forms (*Olallamys*, *Dactylomys*, *Kannabateomys*) are arboreal. Of the intermediate forms, *Proechimys*, *Isothrix*, and *Hoplomys* are more or less terrestrial, and *Mesomys*, *Lonchothrix*, *Echimys*, and *Diplomys* are mostly arboreal. Spiny rats are mainly herbivores: the diet of *Proechimys* and *Echimys* is mainly fruit, *Kannabateomys* and *Dactylomys* eat bamboo and vines, while *Mesomys* eats fruit and other plant material but also insects.

Hutias

FAMILY CAPROMYIDAE

Found only in the West Indies, hutias were once a very diverse group, with different genera grouped into several subfamilies. Approximately half of these genera are now extinct, most within historical times, and a further two include rare and endangered species. The living genera have a robust body, a broad head with relatively small eyes and ears, and short limbs. In size they range

Coypu

FAMILY MYOCASTORIDAE

The coypu is a large, robust rodent, well adapted to its semi-aquatic life in marshes, lakes, and streams. The eyes and ears are small, the mouth closes behind the incisors while swimming, the whiskers are long, the limbs relatively short, and the hind feet webbed. The pelage is yellowish or reddish brown; the outer hair is long and coarse and overlays the thick, soft underfur. Coypus live in burrows in river banks and are expert swimmers, able to remain underwater for up to five minutes. Their diet includes a wide range of vegetation, mussels, and snails. They are pests of cane fields and plantations. Coypus are nocturnal and live in pairs or small family groups. Females may have two or three litters a year, with an average of five young to a litter. The young are born fully furred and with their eyes open. Coypus are preyed on by alligators, fish, snakes, and birds of prey, and they are also hunted by humans for their meat. In addition, they are both hunted and farmed for their valuable pelt, known in the fur trade as nutria – a corruption of the Spanish for "otter." They have been introduced for fur farming to many parts of the world, where escaped individuals have formed feral populations (for example, in East Anglia, England), causing extensive damage to watercourses and cultivated land. PJ

Above In Brazil's Amazonas province a Black agouti confronts the problem of opening a large brazil nut. Agoutis often squat on their haunches to consume smaller food items, holding them in their hands squirrel-style to eat.

Right A swimming coypu reveals the bright orange incisors that are unexpected features of this semi-aquatic species. Coypus spend most of their waking hours in water; they live in riverside burrows, and have webbed hind feet.

Old World Porcupines

TO THE HUMAN EYE, PORCUPINES, WITH THEIR array of quills, are among nature's strangest creations, though in terms of bodily protection for the porcupines themselves, the spikes make perfect sense. The two Old World subfamilies are mostly terrestrial, unlike the New World porcupines.

Many people mistakenly believe that porcupines are related to hedgehogs or pigs, but in fact guinea pigs, chinchillas, capybaras, agoutis, viscachas, and cane rats are their closest relatives. Many of these animals have in common an extraordinary appearance, and are well known for their unusual ways of solving the problems of reproduction.

An Armor of Sharp Spines

FUNCTION AND FORM

Old World porcupines belong to two distinct subfamilies, Atherurinae and Hystricinae. The brush-tailed porcupines of the former branch have long, slender tails that end in tufts of stiff, white hairs containing hollow sections that rustle when the tail is shaken. The animals' elongated bodies and short legs are covered with short, chocolate-colored bristles, with a few long quills on the back.

The crested porcupines of the Hystricinae subfamily have short tails surrounded by stout, sharp, cylindrical quills. The tip of the tail is armed with a cluster of hollow, open-ended quills. When the tail is shaken, these produce a rattle that acts as a warning signal that the animal is annoyed. The back of the upper parts and flanks is covered with black and white spines; as a modified form of hair, these are made of keratin.

When threatened, porcupines erect and rattle their quills, stamp their hind feet, and make a grunting noise. If threatened further, they turn their rump to the intruder and run sideways or backwards toward it. If the quills penetrate the skin, they become stuck and detach.

The rest of the body is covered with flat, black bristles. Most species have a crest of erectile hair extending from the top of the head to the shoulders. The head is blunt and exceptionally broad across the nostrils, with small, piglike eyes set far back on either side of the face. The two sexes look alike, though the females have mammary glands that are situated on the side of the body, enabling mothers to suckle lying on their stomachs.

The majority of Old World porcupines are vegetarians, feeding on the roots, bulbs, fruits, and berries of a wide variety of plants. Porcupines play a role in shaping local plant diversity and productivity; for example, the digging sites of Indian porcupines serve as important germination locations for seedlings. In cultivated areas, they will eat such crops as groundnuts, potatoes, and pumpkins. African porcupines are able to feed on plant species that are poisonous to domestic stock. Brush-tailed porcupines are tree-climbers and feed on a variety of fruits.

Porcupines manipulate food with their front feet, pinning it to the ground and gnawing at it. Usually they feed alone, though they will eat in groups of two or three. Bones also appear occasionally in the porcupines' diets, littering their shelters. They are carried there for gnawing, either to sharpen teeth or as a source of phosphates.

Above *The Indonesian porcupine* ***1*** *has a dense coat of flat, flexible spines. There are three species – in Borneo, Sumatra, and the Philippines. The African porcupine* ***2*** *is one of five crested species. It is very adaptable, inhabiting forest, grassland, and desert.*

Communities on the Cape

SOCIAL BEHAVIOR

Among Cape porcupines sexual behavior is normally initiated by the female. Approaching a male, she will take up the sexual posture – rump and tail raised and quills pointed away from her partner – who mounts her from behind with his forepaws resting on her back. Intromission only occurs when the female is in heat (every 28–36 days) and the vaginal closure membrane becomes perforated. Sexual behavior without intromission is exhibited during all stages of the sexual cycle.

The young are born in grass-lined chambers that form part of an underground burrow system. At birth they are unusually precocial: fully-furred, they have their eyes open and are covered in

Left *Although lions have been known to eat African porcupines, even they find it very difficult to penetrate the armory of quills. Contrary to folklore, the barbs cannot be projected; they can, however, become embedded and can cause septic, sometimes fatal, wounds.*

bristles that will become quills, although, fortunately for the mother, these only harden after birth. Newborn babies weigh 300–330g (10.6–11.6oz), and start to nibble on solids at 9–14 days. At 4–6 weeks they begin to feed, though they continue to be nursed for 13–19 weeks, by which time they weigh 3.5–4.7kg (7.7–10.4lb). Litter sizes are small; 60 percent of births produce one young and 30 percent produce twins. In the wild porcupines produce only one litter each summer.

Despite foraging alone, Cape porcupines are sociable, living in burrows with as many as 6–8 animals – usually an adult pair and their consecutive litters. Both sexes are aggressive towards strangers, and all colony members protect the young. Only one female in a group reproduces; should a litter be lost, she can conceive again within days. Sexual maturity is attained at 2 years.

Both parents may accompany the young when foraging for up to 6–7 months, although adult males are more frequently encountered with young then adult females. The occurrence of family groups is probably related to the opportunities available for mature offspring to disperse; when a population dips, young individuals are able to take advantage of newly-available territories to reproduce. Thus disturbance can reduce the age of first reproduction from 24 to 12 months.

Porcupines live in groups in order to huddle together for warmth. Newborn offspring do not leave the burrow for the first 9 weeks of their lives, and, when warmed by the bodies of other group members, may be able to allocate more energy to growth. Sharing burrows also reduces porcupines' vulnerability to predation and encourages cooperative rearing.

Population density in the semi-arid regions of South Africa varies from 1–29 individuals per sq km (up to 75 per sq mi). Forty percent of the population are less than 1 year old.

Territories are maintained by scentmarking, using anal glands. Males mark more frequently in preferred feeding patches. Porcupines seem to forage up to 16km (10mi) from their burrows, moving along well-defined tracks, almost exclusively by night. They are catholic in their habitat requirements, provided they have shelter to lie in during the day.

On the Defensive

CONSERVATION AND ENVIRONMENT

Porcupines are often viewed as a threat to crops. In addition, African porcupines carry fleas, which are responsible for the spread of bubonic plague, and ticks, which spread babesiasis, rickettsiasis, and theilerioses. Brush-tailed porcupines are also known to be hosts of the disease organism of malaria, *Plasmodium atheruri*. As a result, they are often persecuted and killed as pests. Indigenous peoples eat their flesh and kill porcupines for recreation.

Nevertheless, the animals occur in great numbers, thanks to the near absence of natural predators over much of their range, and also because of the increase in crop cultivation. At the time of writing, there is no reason to believe that porcupines as a whole are endangered, though certain species and subspecies are now considered at risk. For example, one subspecies of the Asiatic brush-tailed porcupine is currently listed as Endangered by the IUCN, while the Malayan porcupine is classified as Vulnerable. RJvA

FACTFILE

OLD WORLD PORCUPINES

Order: Rodentia

Family: Hystricidae

11 species in 4 genera and 2 subfamilies

DISTRIBUTION Africa, Asia; some in S Europe.

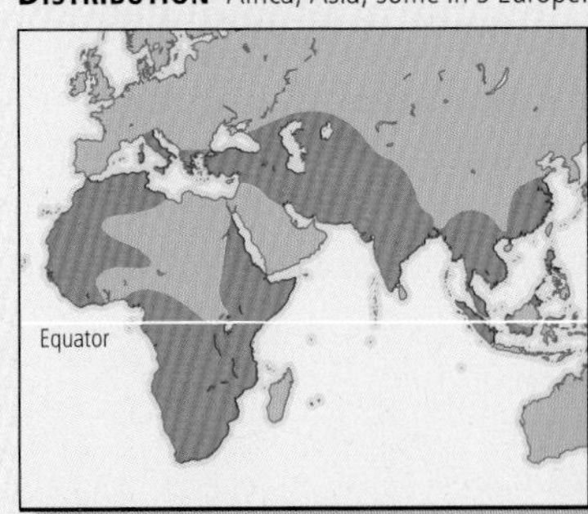

Habitat Varies from dense forest to semi-desert.

Size Ranges from **head–body length** 37–47cm (14.6–18.5in) and **weight** 1.5–3.5kg (3.3–7.7lb) in the brush-tailed porcupines to **head–body length** 60–83cm (23.6–32.7in) and **weight** 13–27kg (28.6–59.4lb) in the crested porcupines.

Coat Head, body, and sometimes the tail, are covered in long, sharp quills – hardened hairs – that are brown or blackish in color, sometimes with white bands.

Diet Roots, tubers, bulbs, fruit, bark, carrion.

Breeding Gestation 90 days for the Indian porcupine, 93–94 days for the Cape porcupine, 100–110 days for the African brush-tailed porcupine, 105 days for the Himalayan porcupine, 112 days for the African porcupine.

Longevity Approximately 21 years recorded for crested porcupines in captivity.

BRUSH-TAILED PORCUPINES Genus *Atherurus*
C Africa and Asia. Forests. Brown to dark brown bristles cover most of the body; some single-color quills on the back. 2 species: **African brush-tailed porcupine** (*A. africanus*), **Asiatic brush-tailed porcupine** (*A. macrourus*).

CRESTED PORCUPINES Genus *Hystrix*
Africa, India, SE Asia, Sumatra, Java and neighboring islands, S Europe; recently introduced to Great Britain. Varied habitats. Hair on back consists of long, stout, cylindrical black and white erectile spines and quills; body covered with black bristles; grayish crest well developed. 5 species: **African porcupine** (*H. cristata*); **Cape porcupine** (*H. africaeaustralis*); **Himalayan porcupine** (*H. hodgsoni*); **Indian porcupine** (*H. indica*); **Malayan porcupine** (*H. brachyura*).

INDONESIAN PORCUPINES Genus *Thecurus*
Indonesia, Philippines. Coat dark brown in front, black on posterior; body densely covered with flattened, flexible spines; quills have a white base and tip, with central parts black; rattling quills on tail are hollow. 3 species: **Bornean porcupine** (*T. crassispinis*); **Philippine porcupine** (*T. pumilis*); **Sumatran porcupine** (*T. sumatrae*).

LONG-TAILED PORCUPINE *Trichys fasciculata*
Malay peninsula, Sumatra, Borneo. Forests. Body covered with brownish, flexible bristles; head and underparts hairy.

Gundis

Right *An extraordinary feature of the Mzab gundi is that its ears are flat and immovable.*

GUNDIS ARE SMALL, HERBIVOROUS RODENTS of North Africa's mountains and deserts. When the animals first came to the attention of Western naturalists, in Tripoli in 1774, they were given the name of "gundi-mice" (gundi is the local word). The family name, Ctenodactylidae, means "comb-toes."

In the mid-19th century, the British explorer John Speke shot gundis in the coastal hills of Somalia, and later French naturalists found three more species; skins and skulls began to arrive in museums. But no attempt was made to study the ecology of the animal. Some authors said gundis were nocturnal, others diurnal; some claimed they dug burrows, others that they made nests; there were reports of the animals whistling, while other sources had them chirping like birds; and there were fantastic tales about them combing themselves with their hind feet in the moonlight. In 1908 two French doctors isolated a protozoan parasite, now known to occur in almost every mammal, from the spleen of a North African gundi and called it *Toxoplasma gondii*.

Powder Puffs in the Desert Sun

FORM AND FUNCTION

Gundis have short legs, short tails, flat ears, big eyes, and long whiskers. Crouched on a rock in the sun with the wind blowing through their soft fur, they look like powder puffs.

The North African and the Desert gundi have tiny, wispy tails, but the other three have fans that they use as balancers. Speke's gundi has the largest and most elaborate fan, which it uses in social displays. Gundis also have rows of stiff bristles – their "combs" – on the two inner toes of each hind foot, and these stand out white against the dark claws. They use the combs for scratching. Sharp claws adapted to gripping rocks would destroy the soft fur coat that insulates them from extremes of heat and cold. The rapid circular scratch of the rump with the combed instep is characteristic of gundis.

The gundi's big eyes convinced some earlier authors that the animal was nocturnal. In fact the gundi is adapted to popping out of sunlight into dark rock shelters. Equally, the gundi can flatten its ribs to squeeze into a crack in the rocks.

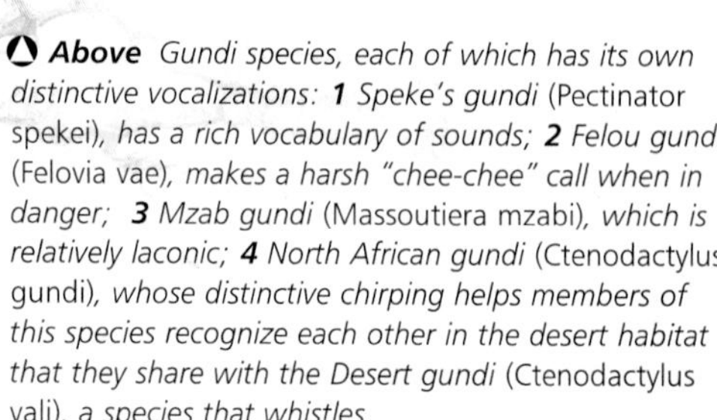

Above *Gundi species, each of which has its own distinctive vocalizations:* **1** *Speke's gundi* (Pectinator spekei), *has a rich vocabulary of sounds;* **2** *Felou gundi* (Felovia vae), *makes a harsh "chee-chee" call when in danger;* **3** *Mzab gundi* (Massoutiera mzabi), *which is relatively laconic;* **4** *North African gundi* (Ctenodactylus gundi), *whose distinctive chirping helps members of this species recognize each other in the desert habitat that they share with the Desert gundi* (Ctenodactylus vali), *a species that whistles.*

FACTFILE

GUNDIS

Order: Rodentia

Family: Ctenodactylidae

5 species in 4 genera

DISTRIBUTION N Africa

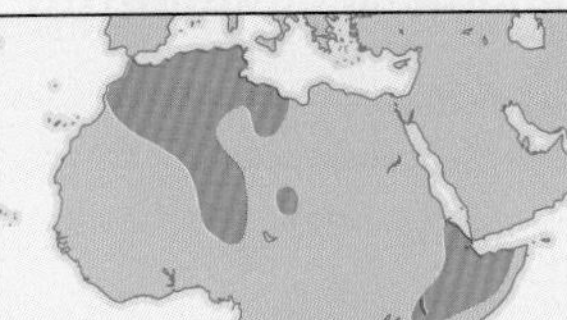

SPEKE'S GUNDI *Pectinator spekei*
Speke's or East African gundi
Ethiopia, Somalia, N Kenya. Arid and semi-arid rock outcrops. HBL 17.2–17.8cm (6.9–7.1in); TL 5.2–5.6cm (2–2.2in); WT 175–180g (6.2–6.3oz). Longevity: Unknown in wild; 10 years recorded in captivity.

FELOU GUNDI *Felovia vae*
SW Mali, Mauritania. Arid and semi-arid rock outcrops. HBL 17–18cm (6.8–7.2in); TL 2.8–3.2cm (1.1–1.3in); WT 178–195g (6.3–6.9oz).

DESERT GUNDI *Ctenodactylus vali*
Desert or Sahara gundi
SE Morocco, NW Algeria, Libya. Desert rock outcrops. Breeding: gestation 56 days.

NORTH AFRICAN GUNDI *Ctenodactylus gundi*
SE Morocco, N Algeria, Tunisia, Libya. Arid rock outcrops. Longevity: 3–4 years.

MZAB GUNDI *Massoutiera mzabi*
Mzab or Lataste's gundi
Algeria, Niger, Chad. Desert and mountain rock outcrops.

Abbreviations HBL = head–body length TL = tail length WT = weight

Foraging in the Cool of the Day

DIET

Gundis are herbivores: they eat the leaves, stalks, flowers, and seeds of almost any desert plant. Their incisors lack the hard orange enamel that is typical of most rodents. Gundis are not, therefore, great gnawers. Food is scarce in the desert, and gundis must forage over long distances – sometimes as much as 1km (0.6mi) a morning. Regular foraging is essential as they do not store food. Home range size varies from a few square meters to 3sq km (1.9sq mi).

Foraging over long distances generates body heat, which can be dangerous on a hot desert day. It is unusual for small desert mammals to be active in daytime, but gundis behave rather like lizards. In the early morning they sunbathe until the temperature rises above 20°C (68°F), and then they forage for food. After a quick feed they flatten themselves again on the warm rocks. Thus they make use of the sun to keep their bodies warm and to speed digestion – an economical way of making the most of scarce food. By the time the temperature has reached 32°C (90°F), the gundis have taken shelter from the sun under the rocks, and they do not come out again until the temperature drops in the afternoon. When long foraging expeditions are necessary, gundis alternate feeding in the sun and cooling off in the shade.

In extreme drought, gundis eat at dawn when plants contain most moisture. They obtain all the water they need from plants; their kidneys have long tubules for absorbing water. Their urine can be concentrated if plants dry out completely, but this emergency response can only be sustained for a limited period.

Family Life in the Colonies

SOCIAL BEHAVIOR

Gundis are gregarious, living in colonies that vary in density from the Mzab gundi's 0.3 per ha (0.12 per acre) to over 100 per ha (40 per acre) for Speke's gundi. Density is related to the food supply and the terrain. Within colonies there are family territories occupied by a male, female, and juveniles or by several females and offspring. Gundis do not make nests, and the "home shelter" is often temporary. Usually a shelter retains the day's heat through a cold night and provides cool draughts on a hot day. In winter, gundis pile on top of one another for warmth, with juveniles shielded from the crush by their mother or draped in the soft fur at the back of her neck.

Each species of gundi has its own repertoire of sounds, varying from the infrequent chirp of the Mzab gundi to the complex chirps, chuckles, and whistles of Speke's gundi. In the dry desert air their low-pitched alert calls carry well. Short, sharp calls warn of predatory birds; gundis within range will hide under the rocks. Longer calls signify ground predators and inform the predator it has been spotted. The Felou gundi's harsh "chee-chee" will last as long as the predator is around.

Long complex chirps and whistles can be a form of greeting or recognition. The *Ctenodactylus* species – whose ranges overlap – produce the most different sounds: the North African gundi chirps, the Desert gundi whistles. Thus members can recognize their own species.

All gundis thump with their hind feet when alarmed. Their flat ears give good all-round hearing and a smooth outline for maneuvering among rocks. The bony ear capsules of the skull are huge, like those of many other desert rodents. The acute hearing is important for picking up the weak, low-frequency sounds of predators – sliding snake or flapping hawk – and for finding parked young. Right from the start, the young are left in rock shelters while the mother forages. They are born fully furred and open-eyed. The noise they set up – a continuous chirruping – helps the mother to home in on the temporary shelter.

The young have few opportunities to suckle: from the mother's first foraging expedition onward they are weaned on chewed leaves. (They are fully weaned after a period of about 4 weeks.) The mother has four nipples – two on her flanks and two on her chest – and the average litter size is two. But a gundi has little milk to spare in the dry heat of the desert.

WG

African Mole-Rats

While African mole-rats may not be the most aesthetically pleasing creatures in the animal kingdom, they nonetheless rank among the more interesting members. Discoveries made regarding the habits and behavior of the social species have rocked the scientific community.

The African mole-rat is a ratlike rodent that has assumed a molelike existence and become totally adapted to life underground. It excavates an extensive system of semi-permanent burrows, complete with sleeping and food storage areas; and it pushes the soil it digs out to the surface as "molehills." Whereas most rodents of comparable size grow rapidly and live for only a couple of years, mole-rats take over a year to reach their full adult size and can live for several years. Indeed, the lifespan of captive Naked mole-rats may even exceed 25 years.

Teeth for Tunneling

FORM AND FUNCTION

Mole-rats have cylindrical bodies with short limbs so as to fit as compactly as possible within the diameter of a burrow. Their loose skin helps them to turn within a confined space: a mole-rat can almost somersault within its skin as it turns. Mole-rats can also move rapidly backward with ease, and so they often shunt to and fro without turning round when moving along a burrow.

All genera except the dune mole-rats use chisel-like incisors protruding out of the mouth cavity for digging. To prevent soil from entering the mouth, there are well-haired lip-folds behind the incisors, so that the mouth is closed, so to speak, behind the gnawing teeth. Dune mole-rats dig with the long claws on their forefeet and are less efficient at mining very hard soils; moreover, their body size is larger. These features restrict them to areas with easily dug sandy soil. This difference in digging method is reflected in the animals' teeth: the incisors of tooth-diggers protrude more than those of the dune mole-rats, and the roots extend back behind the row of cheek teeth for strength.

When a mole-rat is tunnelling, it pushes the soil under its body with its forefeet. Then, with the body weight supported by the forefeet, both hind feet are brought forward to collect the soil and kick it behind the animal. Once a pile has accumulated, the mole-rat reverses along the burrow, pushing the soil behind it. Most mole-rats force solid cores of soil out onto the surface, but Naked mole-rats kick a fine spray out of an open hole – an "active" hole looks like an erupting volcano. A number of Naked mole-rats cooperate in digging, one animal excavating, a number transporting soil, and another kicking it out of the hole – this unfortunate individual is particularly vulnerable to predation by snakes. All mole-rats have hind feet that are fringed by stiff hairs, as is the tail in all but Naked mole-rats; both adaptations help hold the soil during digging.

Because mole-rats live in complete darkness for most of their lives, their eyes are small and can only detect light and dark. (Interestingly, the Cape mole-rat, which occasionally travels on the surface, has eyes that are larger than those of other species.) It has been suggested that the surface of the eye may be used to detect air currents that would indicate damage to the burrow system; certainly, if damage occurs, the mole-rats rapidly repair it. Touch is important in finding the way

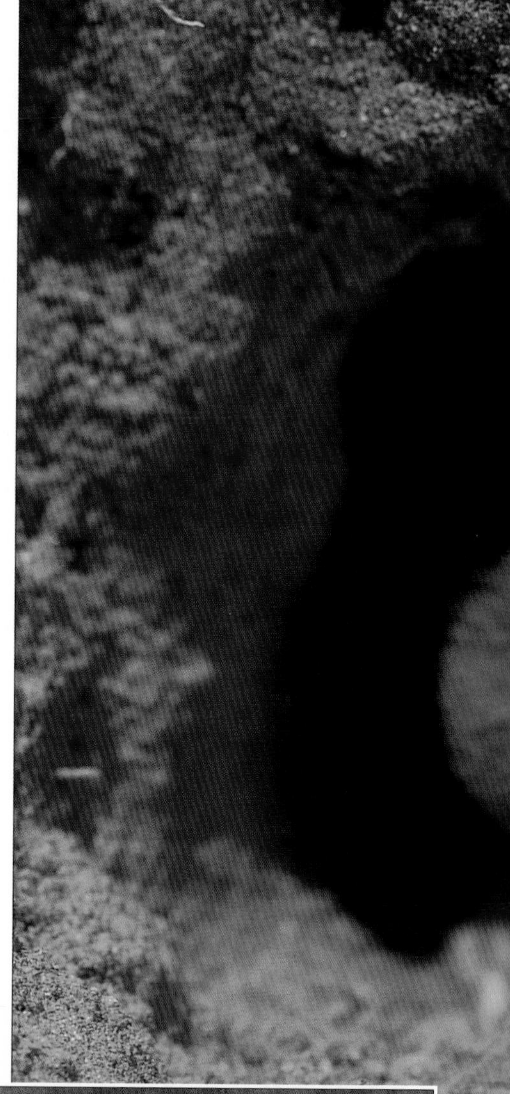

Right *A Damara mole-rat emerging from its tunnel. A tunnel system's depth usually depends on local soil conditions. In areas of loose soil, they lie deeper underground than in areas of hard soil.*

Below *The powerful incisors of Mechow's mole-rat are used for excavation. Clearly, keeping soil out of various orifices is important and its head is well adapted for this: the lips fold behind the incisors, the nostrils can be closed, and the ears and eyes are small.*

AFRICAN MOLE-RATS

Order: Rodentia

Family: Bathyergidae

At least 15 species in 5 genera: **Dune mole-rats** (genus *Bathyergus*, 2 species), the largest mole-rats,inhabiting sandy coastal soils of S Africa; **common mole-rats** (genus *Cryptomys*, at least 9 species), widespread in W, C, and S Africa; **silvery mole-rats** (genus *Heliophobius*, 2 species), C and E Africa; **Cape mole-rat** (*Georychus capensis*), Cape Province of the Republic of S Africa, along the coast from the SW to the E; and **Naked mole-rat** (*Heterocephalus glaber*), in arid regions of Ethiopia, Somalia, and Kenya.

DISTRIBUTION Africa S of the Sahara

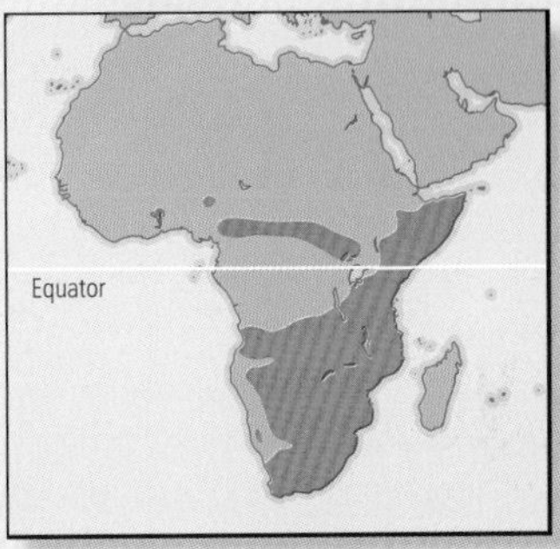

HABITAT Underground in different types of soil and sand.

SIZE Head–body length ranges from 9–12cm (3.5–4.7in) in the Naked mole-rat to 30cm (11.8in) in the genus *Bathyergus*; **weight** from 30–60g (1–2.1oz) to 350–1,800g (26–63oz) in the same species.

COAT Thick, soft, and woolly or velvety in all but the Naked mole-rat, which is almost hairless.

DIET Roots, tubers, geophytes, herbs, and grasses.

BREEDING Gestation 44–111 days (44–48 days in the Cape mole-rat; 66–74 days in the Naked mole-rat; 97–111 days in the Giant Zambian mole-rat).

LONGEVITY Unknown (captive Naked mole-rats have lived for over 25 years and several species of *Cryptomys* for more than 8 years).

CONSERVATION STATUS Four species – *Bathyergus janetta, Cryptomys foxi, C. zechi,* and *Heliophobius argenteocinereus* – are currently listed as Lower Risk: Near Threatened. The other species are not considered threatened.

For full species list see Appendix ▷

around the burrow system; many genera have long, touch-sensitive hairs scattered over their bodies (in the Naked mole-rat, these are the only remaining hairs). The animals' sense of smell and their hearing of low-frequency sounds are good, and their noses and ears are modified on the outside so as to cope with the problems of living in a sandy environment: the nostrils can be closed during digging, while the protruding parts of the ears (pinnae) have been lost.

Subterranean Farmers

DIET

Mole-rats are vegetarians, and obtain their food by digging foraging tunnels. These enable them to find and collect roots, storage organs (geophytes), and even the aboveground portions of plants without having to come to the surface. They appear to blunder into food rather than to detect it – tests failed to reveal any evidence that they could locate food items even half a meter (1.6ft) from the foraging burrow. The large dune mole-rats are not specialist feeders and live on grass, herbs, and geophytes, but Common and Naked mole-rats live entirely on geophytes and roots.

Foraging burrows can be very extensive: one system containing 10 adults and 3 young Common mole-rats was 1km (0.6mi) long, and burrows of Naked mole-rats may exceed 3km (1.9mi) in length. Burrow length depends on the number and ages of mole-rats in a system and on the abundance and distribution of food items.

Apart from providing nest, food storage, and toilet areas, the rest of the burrow system is dug in search of food. Excavating is easiest when the soil is soft and moist. After rain, there is a flurry of digging – indeed, in the first month after rain, colonies of Naked and Damaraland mole-rats can dig 1km (0.6mi) of burrows and throw up more than 2 tonnes of soil as molehills. In the arid regions where the two species live, many months may elapse before it next rains, so it is vitally important to find enough food in these brief periods of optimal digging to see the colony through the drought. Small food items are eaten or stored (by Damaraland, Common, and Cape mole-rats, for example), while larger items are left growing in situ and are gradually hollowed out, thus ensuring a constantly fresh and growing food supply. At a later stage, the hollow is plugged with soil so the tuber will regenerate. This "farming" of geophytes enables colonies to remain resident in the same area for many years.

In some areas where Naked mole-rats occur, tubers may weigh as much as 50kg (110lb). When feeding, the mole-rat holds small items with its forefeet, shakes them free of soil, cuts them into pieces with its incisors, and then chews these with its cheek teeth. In southwestern Cape Province, South Africa, differences in diet, burrow diameter and depth, and perhaps also of social organization enable three genera – *Bathyergus*, *Georychus*, and *Cryptomys* – to occupy different niches within the same area, and sometimes even the same field. This sympatry is unusual for burrowing mammals, where the normal pattern is for one species to occupy an area exclusively.

Life Below Ground

Social Behavior

The social behavior of three genera (*Bathyergus*, *Georychus*, and *Heliophobius*) follows the normal pattern for subterranean mammals: they are solitary, and aggressively defend their burrows against conspecifics. They signal to neighboring animals by drumming with their hind feet; at the onset of breeding, *Georychus* males and females drum with a different tempo to attract a mate. Mating is brief, and the male then leaves the female to rear her pups. When about 2 months old, the pups begin to fight, and this is the prelude to dispersing; if forcibly kept together in captivity, siblings will eventually kill each other. In *Georychus*, the dispersing young often burrow away from the parent system and block up the linking burrows; this probably also occurs in the other solitary genera and would ensure that the young are protected from predators during this otherwise very vulnerable phase in their life history.

In the social mole-rats (see box), only a single female breeds in each colony. In all the *Cryptomys* studied there is a strong inhibition against incest, and colonies are founded by a pair of animals originating from different colonies. The rest of the colony is composed of their offspring which, unlike the solitary mole-rats, remain in the natal colony, helping to locate food and rear their siblings until conditions are favorable for dispersing. In fact many never get the chance to breed.

Colony sizes of the Common mole-rat rarely exceed 14 animals, whereas 41 Damaraland mole-rats may occur together (although 14–25 is more common). Naked mole-rat colonies may contain over 300 individuals (the mean is about 80), but here there is no inhibition to incest and the breeders may come from within the colony. The breeding female is the dominant individual in the colony, which she controls through stress-related behaviors such as violent shoving. She has a distinctively elongated body (her vertebrae lengthen during her first few pregnancies), and this serves to better accommodate the large litters typical of this species. Up to three males may mate with her, and multiple paternity of litters can occur. Except for the dispersers, Naked mole-rats are very xenophobic and will kill foreign animals. They recognize colony members by scent, probably through a cocktail of odors that they spread on their bodies in the communal toilet area.

Because they live in a well-protected, relatively safe environment, mole-rats are less exposed to predators than are surface-dwelling rodents. This better life assurance may be why they produce smaller litters, usually of between two and five pups. There are exceptions: the Cape mole-rat produces up to 10 pups, and the Naked mole-rat has as many as 28, although the average litter size is 12. Pups weigh about 1g (0.04oz), while breeding females weigh 65–80g (2.3–2.8oz).

Snakes may occasionally pursue the solitary mole-rats underground, but more often lie in wait for them. Field evidence suggests that the Mole snake (*Pseudaspis cana*) is attracted to the smell of freshly turned soil and will penetrate the burrow system via a new molehill. It usually pushes its head into the burrow and waits for the mole-rat as it reverses with its next load of soil. This may also be true of the Eastern beaked snake (*Rhamphiophis oxythunchus rostrutus*), which has been seen preying on Naked mole-rats as they kick soil out of the burrow. Other predators also take mole-rats: their skulls are not uncommon in the pellets of birds of prey and small carnivores such as jackals, caracals, and zorillas.

In addition to protecting the mole-rat against many predators, the underground environment provides a uniformly humid microclimate. This,

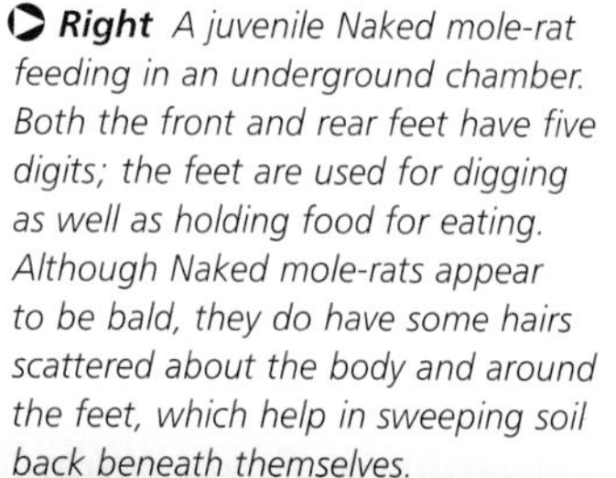

Right A juvenile Naked mole-rat feeding in an underground chamber. Both the front and rear feet have five digits; the feet are used for digging as well as holding food for eating. Although Naked mole-rats appear to be bald, they do have some hairs scattered about the body and around the feet, which help in sweeping soil back beneath themselves.

Left A Naked mole-rat queen suckling several youngsters. The queen is effectively the leader of the colony and is a nonworker, weighing significantly more than the others. Although only a small number of animals are actively involved in the breeding process, the others are not incapable of breeding, merely suppressed; research has shown that if non-breeding females are removed from a colony and paired with a male, they become capable of breeding very quickly.

THE INSECT-LIKE RODENT

At least two species of mole-rat, the Naked and Damaraland, have a colony structure similar to that of social insects. Within each colony, a single female and 1–3 males breed; the remaining males and females, while not infertile, remain nonreproductive while members of their natal colony. In Naked mole-rat colonies, the more numerous, small-sized, worker mole-rats dig and maintain the foraging burrows and carry food and nesting material to the communal nest. Large-sized individuals spend much of the time in the nest with the breeding female. When the workers give an alarm call, however, they are mobilized to defend the colony.

The young born to the colony are cared for by all the mole-rats but suckled only by the breeding female. Once weaned, they join the worker force, but whereas some individuals apparently remain workers throughout their lives, others eventually grow larger than the rest and become colony defenders. It is from these big, and usually older, individuals that new reproductive Naked mole-rats emerge when a breeder dies.

In Naked as in all the social mole-rats, therefore, a colony is composed of the progeny of a number of closely related litters. As with social insects, this relatedness is probably an important factor in the evolution and maintenance of a social structure in which some individuals in the colony never breed. By caring for closely-related mole-rats that share their genetic make-up, the nonbreeding individuals nonetheless ensure the passing on of their own genetic characteristics.

This system seems to prevail among social mole-rats living in arid regions where for many months conditions are unsuitable for extensive burrowing. When it does rain, a workforce must be mobilized rapidly to find sufficient food to see the colony through the dry months. By joining forces and channeling the energies of colony members along specific avenues (some finding food, some acting as soldiers, and a select few bearing young), these mole-rats can survive in areas where single mole-rats or pairs cannot.

Experiments have shown that nonbreeding mole-rats are not sterile. Suppression is more severe in females than in males, which show some sperm production. Nonbreeders can rapidly become sexually active (within 7–10 days) and can found new colonies or, in the case of Naked mole-rats, can replace the breeding animals if they die. In this latter case, several of the older females initially show signs of sexual activity, and there is often a time of severe (sometimes fatal) fighting, before one female becomes sexually dominant, increases in size, and becomes the new breeder. Occasionally succession occurs without fighting.

Unlike in social insects, pheromones do not seem to be the prime means of control. Yet in many captive colonies, the whole colony is affected by the reproductive state of the breeding female. For example, just before a litter is born all colony members (male and female) develop teats, and some females come close to breeding condition. This strongly suggests that the colony is responding to chemical stimuli produced by the breeding female: in this case, the stimuli seem to prime the colony to receive and care for young that are not their own.

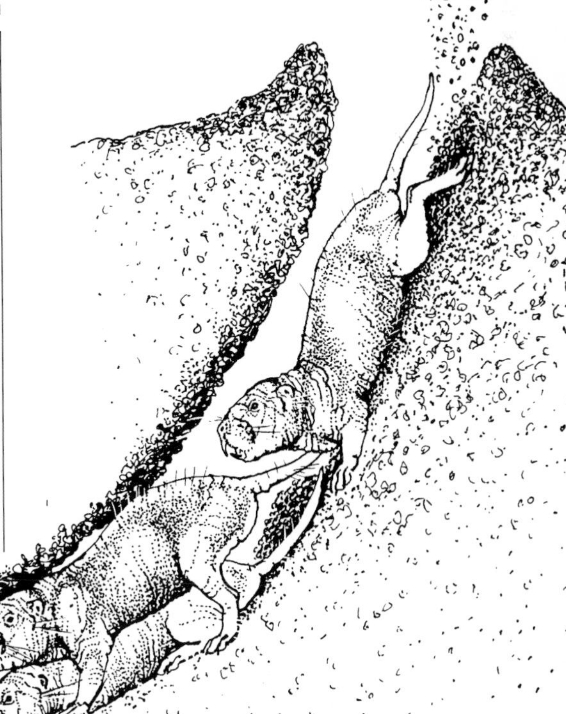

Above *Cross-section of a burrow system. On the left* **a** *Naked mole-rats hollow out a growing tuber; in the center* **b** *is the main chamber, which is occupied by the breeding female, subsidiary adults and young; on the right* **c** *a digging chain is at work.*

Top *A mole-rat digging chain. The lead animal digs with its teeth and pushes the soil backward. The one behind drags the load backward, keeping close to the tunnel floor, and passes it to the animal responsible for dispersal. It then returns to the front, straddling other mole-rats pushing soil away.*

plus the high moisture content of the mole-rat's food, precludes the necessity of having to drink free water. The burrow temperature remains relatively stable throughout the day, often in stark contrast to the surface temperature. In Naked mole-rat country, for example, surface temperatures of over 60°C (140°F) have been recorded while burrows 20cm (8in) below ground registered a steady 28–30°C (82–86°F). In response, Naked mole-rats have almost lost the ability to regulate body temperature, which consequently remains close to that of the burrow. If they need to alter it, they huddle together when cold or bask in surface burrows for warmth; they also take refuge in cooler areas within the system if they overheat, for example after digging near the surface

Helping and Harming

CONSERVATION AND ENVIRONMENT

Though inconspicuous, mole-rats can cause considerable damage to property. Dune mole-rats chew through underground cables, undermine roadways, and sometimes devour root and cereal crops. The molehills they create can damage the blades of harvesting machines, not to mention garden lawns and golf courses. The human response has been to attempt to exterminate all those causing the problems.

Yet mole-rats also have beneficial effects on their environment. They are important agents in soil drainage and soil turnover (a Cape dune mole-rat may throw up as much as 500kg/1,100lb of soil each month). They may play a role in dispersing geophytes (plants with underground storage organs) and they also eat geophytes that are poisonous to livestock. JUMJ

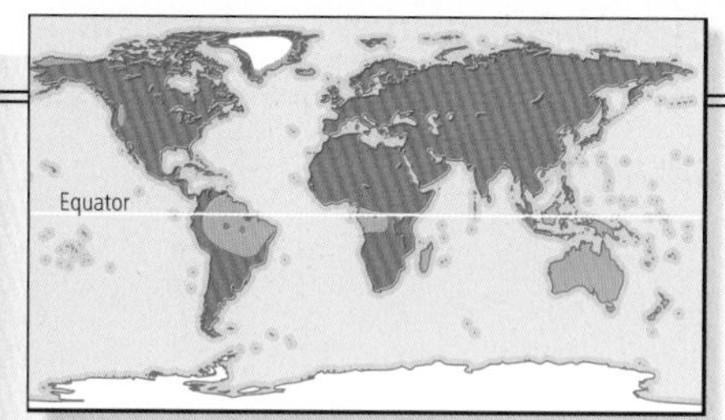

LAGOMORPHS

EITHER AS NATIVE SPECIES OR AS A RESULT OF human introductions, lagomorphs – meaning literally "hare-shaped" – are found all around the globe. The order contains two families: the small, rodent-like pikas, weighing under 0.5kg (1.1lb); and the rabbits and hares, weighing up to 5kg (11lb).

The pikas are thought to have separated from the rabbits and hares in the late Eocene, around 38–35 million years ago. Recent DNA sequence analysis suggests that most rabbit and hare genera arose from a single rapid diversification event approximately 12–16 m.y.a. The first pikas appeared in Asia in the middle Oligocene and spread to North America and Europe in the Pliocene (5–1.8 m.y.a.). Pikas seem to have peaked in distribution and diversity during the Miocene (24–5 m.y.a.) and since declined, while the rabbits and hares have maintained a widespread distribution since the Pliocene.

Rabbits and hares have elongated hind limbs adapted for running at speed over open ground. Their ears are long, the nasal region elongated, and their tail typically has a conspicuous white under-surface. By contrast, pikas are small with short legs, and are well adapted for living in rocky steppe and alpine habitats; the tail is virtually absent, and the ears short and rounded. They are far more vocal than rabbits and hares, but all three groups use scent products from special glands. Other features shared by all lagomorphs include coats of long, soft fur that fully covers the feet, ears that are large relative to body size, and eyes positioned for good broad-field vision.

What Makes a Lagomorph?

DIGESTION, DENTITION, AND DISTRIBUTION

Rabbits, hares, and pikas are all herbivores that feed predominantly on grasses but consume a range of other plant species in different habitats. Their digestive system is adapted for processing large volumes of vegetation, and they re-ingest some of their fecal matter, a behavior known as coprophagy. As herbivores with gnawing incisors, rabbits, hares, and pikas were initially classed by taxonomists within the order Rodentia, but in 1912 J. W. Cridley brought them together within the new order Lagomorpha. Significant among the several distinctive features that set them apart from rodents is the possession of a second pair of small incisors, known as "peg teeth," behind the long, constantly-growing pair in the upper jaw. This gives rabbits and hares a total of 28 teeth and a dental formula of 2/1 incisors, 0/0 canines, 3/2 pre-molars, and 3/3 molars; while pikas have 26 teeth (one fewer upper molar on each side).

Only 2 pika species occur in North America; the rest are distributed across Asia. Rabbits and hares, on the other hand, have diversified to produce species occupying a wide range of habitats, from tropical forest (the Forest rabbit) through swamps, desert, and montane grassland (the North American Marsh rabbit, Black-tailed jackrabbits, and Mexico's Volcano rabbit) to the snow-covered arctic (Snowshoe and Arctic hares).

Phenomenal Numbers

BREEDING PATTERNS

Within their home ecosystems, lagomorphs are often key fodder for a range of mammalian and avian predators. To counter high mortality rates, they breed prodigiously. Most species reach sexual maturity relatively early (after just 3 months in

Right The European rabbit is a prodigious breeder, capable of producing 10–30 young each year. And yet, in this species, over half of all pregnancies are aborted, with the embryos being resorbed into the female's body.

female European rabbits). The gestation period is short – 40 days in *Lepus* species, and around 30 days in all other genera – and litter sizes are often large. Other features of lagomorph reproduction that minimize inter-birth intervals for females include the phenomenon of induced ovulation, by which eggs are shed in response to copulation rather than on a cyclic basis; and post-partum estrus, permitting a female to conceive immediately after giving birth. Female lagomorphs are also capable of resorbing embryos under adverse conditions, for example in times of climatic or social stress. There is further evidence that species such as the European hare are capable of conceiving a second litter before the birth of the last young, an amazing feat called "superfetation."

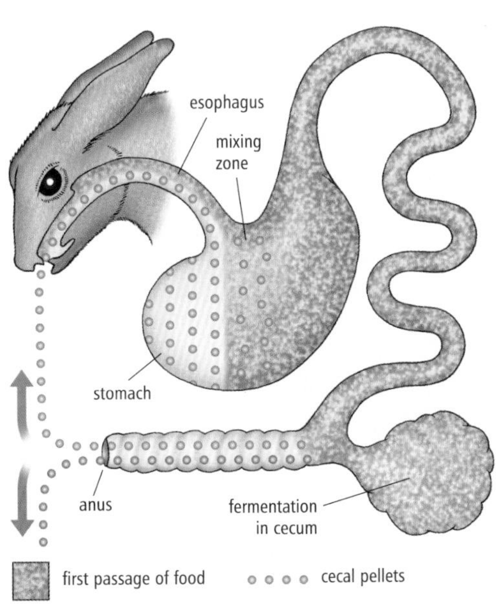

Losses and Gains

CONSERVATION ISSUES

Over 20 percent of lagomorph species are currently listed as threatened. Some are island endemics, like the Mexican Tres Marías cottontail; others, such as Koslov's pika (China), the Riverine rabbit (South Africa), and the Volcano rabbit (Mexico), have a distribution that has been severely reduced by destruction of their highly specialized habitats.

More encouragingly, the Sumatran rabbit (*Nesolagus netscheri*) – representing a unique genus of striped rabbit until recently feared extinct – has been caught on auto-trap camera in its tropical forest habitat. Furthermore, a possible second species of striped rabbit, the Annamite, has also come to light in remote montane forests between Laos and Vietnam. Three freshly-killed specimens were found in a meat market in 1995–96, and live animals have subsequently been photographed. The species' phylogenetic position has yet to be resolved. DB/ATS

Left *The digestive system of lagomorphs is highly modified for coping with large quantities of vegetation. The gut has a large, blind-ending sac (the cecum) between the large and small intestines, which contains bacterial flora to aid the digestion of cellulose. Many products of the digestion in the cecum can pass directly into the blood stream, but others such as the important B vitamins would be lost if lagomorphs did not eat some of the feces (refection) and so pass them through their gut twice. As a result, lagomorphs have two kinds of feces. First, soft black viscous cecal pellets which are produced during the day in nocturnal species and during the night in species active in the daytime. These are usually eaten directly from the anus and stored in the stomach, to be mixed later with further food taken from the alimentary mass. Second, round hard feces which are passed normally.*

Left *Alpine pikas have a fondness for sunning themselves and often bask on rocks, choosing for camouflage those with a similar color to their coat. Although many pikas live in regions with very severe winters, they do not appear to hibernate.*

ORDER: LAGOMORPHA

87 species in 12 genera and 2 families

Distribution Worldwide, except for S South America, the West Indies, Madagascar, and some Southeast Asian islands.

RABBITS AND HARES Family Leporidae p696

58 species in 11 genera

Includes **Riverine rabbit** (*Bunolagus monticularis*); **Hispid hare** (*Caprolagus hispidus*); **European rabbit** (*Oryctolagus cuniculus*); **Amami rabbit** (*Pentalagus furnessi*); **Volcano rabbit** (*Romerolagus diazi*); **Bunyoro rabbit** (*Poelagus marjorita*); **Pygmy rabbit** (*Brachylagus idahoensis*); **Sumatran rabbit** (*Nesolagus netscheri*); **Redrock hare** (*Pronolagus spp*); **Forest rabbit** (*Sylvilagus brasiliensis*); **Eastern cottontail** (*S. floridanus*); **Antelope jackrabbit** (*Lepus alleni*); **Black-tailed jackrabbit** (*L. californicus*); **Snowshoe hare** (*L. americanus*); **European hare** (*L. europaeus*); **Arctic hare** (*L. arcticus*).

PIKAS Family Ochotonidae p710

29 species in the genus *Ochotona*

Includes **Alpine pika** (*O. alpina*); **American pika** (*O. princeps*); **Northern pika** (*O. hyperborea*); **Royle's pika** (*O. roylei*); **Daurian pika** (*O. daurica*); **Gansu pika** (*O. cansus*); **Moupin pika** (*O. thibetana*); **Koslov's pika** (*O. koslowi*); **Plateau pika** (*O. curzoniae*); **Steppe pika** (*O. pusilla*).

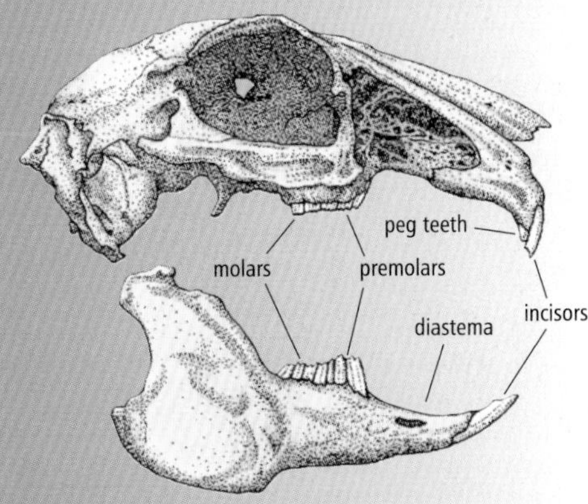

Above *The skull of a rabbit. Lagomorphs have long, constantly growing incisors, as do rodents, but lagomorphs differ in having two pairs of upper incisors, the back non-functional ones being known as peg teeth. There is a gap (diastema) between the incisors and premolars. The dental formula of rabbits and hares (family Leporidae) is I2/1, C0/0, P3/2, M3/3, with the pikas (family Ochotonidae) having one fewer upper molar in each jaw.*

Rabbits and Hares

THERE ARE FEW MAMMALS WHOSE FATE HAS been so intimately intertwined over the centuries with humans' as the European rabbit. Its domestication probably began in North Africa or Italy in Roman times; today there are well over a hundred varieties of domestic rabbit, all selectively bred from this single species. In addition, wild or domesticated offspring of the original stock have, through invasion or deliberate introduction, spread worldwide, with many populations reaching pest proportions. Yet the European rabbit is just one of a family of more than 50 leporid species, some of which lead a far more precarious existence, numbering in the hundreds rather than the tens of millions.

The family Leporidae splits broadly into two groups: the jackrabbits and hares of the genus *Lepus*, and the rabbits in the remaining 10 genera. Just to confuse matters, several species – for example, the African Red rockhare and the endangered Hispid hare – are commonly known as hares, even though behaviorally they are quite clearly rabbits!

Telling Rabbits from Hares

FORM AND FUNCTION

The major differences between the *Lepus* hares and the rabbits relate to differences in the strategies the two groups employ in evading predators and in reproduction. Basically, the longer-legged hares try to outrun their pursuers – some reputedly reaching speeds of 72 km/h (45 mph) in full flight – while the shorter-limbed rabbits run to seek refuge in dense cover or underground burrows. In addition, young hares (leverets) are better developed (precocial) at birth compared to altricial newborn rabbits (kittens). In the non-burrowing hares, the leverets are born after longer gestation periods (37–50 days) with a full covering of fur, their eyes open, and capable of coordinated movement. In contrast, rabbit kittens are born naked or with sparse fur covering after shorter gestation periods (27–30 days), their eyes opening after 4–10 days. Long ears are a conspicuous feature of all leporids, but typically these are at their most magnificent in the jackrabbits, where

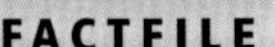

Above *Like several other northern species, Snowshoe hares may molt twice a year, donning a white coat for camouflage each winter only to lose it again in the spring. Individuals of the species that live outside areas of continuous snow cover generally do not make the change.*

Left *With its large ears pricked for unfamiliar sounds and its eyes wide open to catch sudden movements, a Savanna hare in Tanzania's Serengeti National Park freezes briefly, alert for danger. In general, hares rely on their exceptional speed to outrun predators, while rabbits make rapidly for the nearest cover.*

they can grow to over 17cm (7in). The eyes of both rabbits and hares are large and adapted to their crepuscular and nocturnal activity patterns. All leporids are herbivorous, but some, like the Mountain and Snowshoe hares, may be more selective in their choice of feeding material than others, including the European rabbit.

Open Terrain or Dense Cover

DISTRIBUTION PATTERNS

Apart from a few forest-dwelling species such as the Snowshoe hare, most hares prefer open habitats with some cover offered by terrain or vegetation. They therefore have a widespread distribution, occurring in habitats ranging from desert to grasslands and tundra. Rabbits, on the other hand, are rarely found far from dense cover or underground tunnels. They occupy a variety of disturbed, successional, and climax habitats, often characterized by grass communities associated with dense cover; in the American cottontails this cover is often provided by plants such as sage brush and bramble. Other species are highly specialized in their habitat requirement, the two striped Sumatran and Annamite rabbits and the Japanese Amami rabbit living in tropical forest cover while the Riverine rabbit and Hispid hare (actually a rabbit!) are restricted respectively to pockets of riverine scrub in the central karoo of South Africa and to tall grassland in the Indian subcontinent. In marked contrast to rabbits, hares tend to use cover for daytime shelter, but will run into the open when confronted with a predator.

Warrens and Absentee Parents

SOCIAL BEHAVIOR

The burrowing lifestyle familiar in the warren-digging European rabbit is actually rather unusual, even among leporid genera. Apart from the European rabbit, only the Pygmy, Amami, and Bunyoro rabbits are reported to dig underground refuges themselves, while a few opportunists (for instance, the Eastern, Desert, and Mountain cottontails) will use burrows dug by other species. A small number of hares are reported to dig burrows to avoid extreme temperatures: the Black-tailed jackrabbit and Cape hare, for example, do so to escape high desert temperatures, while Snowshoe and Arctic hares may burrow into snow. Forms – surface depressions in the ground or vegetation – are more commonly used as resting-up sites by

FACTFILE

RABBITS AND HARES

Order: Lagomorpha

Family: Leporidae

58 species in 11 genera, 7 of them monotypic (containing only a single species): the Riverine rabbit (*Bunolagus monticularis*), Hispid hare (*Caprolagus hispidus*), European rabbit (*Oryctolagus cuniculus*), Amami rabbit (*Pentalagus furnessi*), Volcano rabbit (*Romerolagus diazi*), Bunyoro rabbit (*Poelagus marjorita*), and Pygmy rabbit (*Brachylagus idahoensis*). In addition, there are 2 species of striped rabbit (*Nesolagus*); 3 species of red rockhare (*Pronolagus*); 14 species of cottontail rabbit (*Sylvilagus*), including the Forest rabbit (*S. brasiliensis*) and Eastern cottontail (*S. floridanus*); and 32 species of hare (*Lepus*), including the Antelope jackrabbit (*Lepus alleni*), Black-tailed jackrabbit (*L. californicus*), Snowshoe hare (*L. americanus*), and European hare (*L. europaeus*).

DISTRIBUTION Americas, Europe, Asia, Africa; introduced to Australia, New Zealand, and other islands.

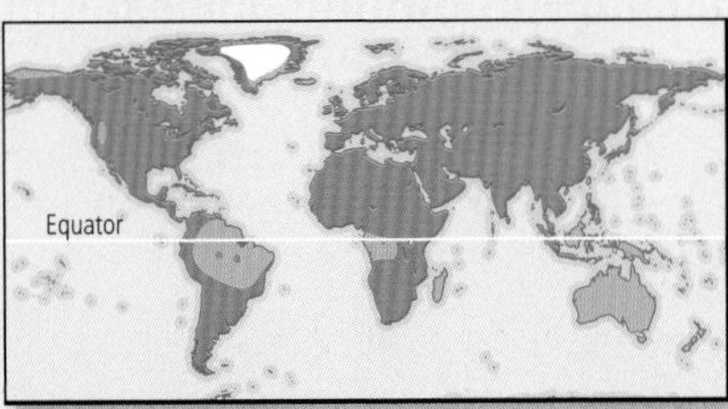

HABITAT Wide-ranging; includes desert, montane forest, tropical rain forest, Arctic tundra, swamp, tall grassland, agricultural landscapes.

SIZE **Head–body length** ranges from 25cm (10in) in the Pygmy rabbit to 75cm (30in) in the European hare; **tail length** from 1.5cm (0.6in) to 12cm (4.7in), and **weight** from around 400g (14oz) to 6kg (13.2lb), both in the same two species. **Ear length** reaches 17cm (7in) in the Antelope jackrabbit. Leporid hind limbs are regularly longer than the forelimbs.

COAT Usually thick and soft, but coarse or woolly in some species (Hispid hare and Woolly hare); hair shorter/sparser on the ears; tail well furred or even bushy (Riverine rabbit and Red rockhares); feet hairy on both surfaces; coloration ranges through reddish brown, brown, buff, and gray, to white; the belly is often covered with lighter or pure white hair. Two species (*Nesolagus*) are striped, and arctic/northern species change into white for winter (Snowshoe, Arctic, Mountain, Japanese hares).

DIET Herbivorous

BREEDING Gestation typically longer in hares (up to 55 days in the Mountain hare) than in rabbits (30 days in the European rabbit). The young are precocial at birth in hares, but altricial in rabbits.

LONGEVITY Average less than 1 year in the wild; maximum of 12 years recorded in European hare and European rabbit.

CONSERVATION STATUS 12 species are listed as threatened (i.e. Critically Endangered, Endangered, or Vulnerable), and another 6 as Near Threatened.

See species table ▷

hares. These may be well-established sites used by successive generations or, alternatively, temporary refuges occupied for only a few hours.

The underground warrens dug by European rabbits form the focus of stable, territorial breeding groups – a social system unknown amongst other leporid species. Most hares and rabbits are non-territorial, moving over individual home ranges of up to 300ha (740 acres) in some hares, with ranges overlapping in favored feeding areas. Temporary feeding aggregations have been seen in a number of leporids, including the Yarkand and Mountain hares, the Black-tailed jackrabbit, and the Brush rabbit. In the European hare these aggregations may be structured, with dominant individuals maintaining priority of access to food patches. Large flocks of Snowshoe hares may be sighted in the winter months, when these animals are in their white camouflage coat. Individual animals are thought to gather together to reduce their chance of being preyed upon.

Apart from "policing," in which males intervene to protect young under attack from adult females, no form of male paternal care has been reported in the leporids, and even maternal care is pretty thin on the ground – a reproductive strategy known as "absentee parentism." In hares, the precocial, fur-covered, fully mobile leverets are born into surface-depression forms, while the poorly developed rabbit kittens are delivered into carefully constructed fur-lined nests built in underground chambers or dense cover (thick clumps of montane bunch-grass in the case of the Volcano rabbit). After birth, a consistent and unusual feature of leporid maternal care is the nursing or suckling of litters for just one brief period, typically less than 5 minutes, once every 24 hours. In fact, the milk is highly nutritious, with a very high fat and protein content, and can be pumped into the youngsters at great speed during the brief lactation period, which lasts for 17–23 days. In the European rabbit, for example, this will be the only contact between mother and young until the kittens are weaned at around 21 days, after which the mother will start preparing for the birth of the litter conceived as she emerged from giving birth to the last one!

As a strategy, this lack of social contact between the mother and her offspring may be designed to reduce the chances of drawing a predator's attention to the highly vulnerable nestlings. In the case of those rabbit species that breed in purpose-dug breeding tunnels, or "stops," the soil entrance will be carefully re-sealed after each short suckling bout. In the surface-breeding hares, the leverets disperse to separate hiding locations about 3 days after birth, but regroup with litter-mates at a specific location at precisely defined intervals (often around sunset) for a frenzied, similarly brief, bout of suckling from mother.

Relationships between climate and reproduction are clearly demonstrated in both the hares and the New World cottontail rabbits. In the cottontails there is a direct correlation between latitude and litter size; species and subspecies in the north produce the largest litters during the shortest breeding season. The Eastern cottontail appears to be the most fecund of the genus, producing up to 35 young a year, whilst the Forest rabbit produces the least, at around 10 per annum. Amongst the *Lepus* hares and jackrabbits, productivity varies from a single litter of 6–8 in the far north to eight litters of 1–2 young at the equator, giving a fairly standard production statistic of about 10 young a year per female. Reproductive output is more variable in the Snowshoe hare (5–18 young per female), a species well-known for its population cycles, which are synchronous over a wide geographical range.

Compared to the more vocal pikas, communicating rabbits and hares appear to rely more heavily on scent than sound for communication. However, some species appear to be more vocal than others, and exceptions like the Volcano rabbit do exist. Most leporids make high-pitched distress squeals when captured by a predator, and five species of rabbit, all comparatively gregarious, give specific alarm calls. The European, Brush, and Desert rabbits are known to thump their hind feet on the ground in response to danger, possibly as a warning to underground nestlings. In addition, many leporids possess a conspicuous white underside to their tail which could serve as a visual warning signal during flight from a predator. Interestingly, those species with tail flags tend to be found in more open habitats than those like the Forest and Volcano rabbits and Hispid hare that have a dark underside to their tails.

All rabbits and hares have scent-secreting glands in the groin and under the chins. These appear to be important in sexual communication; in the gregarious European rabbit, where the activity of the glands is known to be related to testes size and levels of male hormones, they may also signal social status. Dominant male European rabbits are essentially the smelliest, scentmarking at higher frequency with scent-gland secretions and carefully-aimed squirts of pungent urine.

Left *Representative species of rabbits and hares:* ***1*** *Antelope jackrabbit* (Lepus alleni); ***2*** *Amami rabbit* (Pentalagus furnessi) *digging a burrow;* ***3*** *Riverine rabbit* (Bunolagus monticularis) *in an alert posture;* ***4*** *Bunyoro rabbit* (Poelagus marjorita), *hopping;* ***5*** *dominant male European rabbit* (Oryctolagus cuniculus) *scentmarking with its chin;* ***6*** *Sumatran rabbit* (Nesolagus netscheri), *grooming its muzzle and spreading scent;* ***7*** *male Eastern cottontail* (Sylvilagus floridanus) *in an alert posture;* ***8*** *European hare* (Lepus europaeus), *boxing;* ***9*** *Greater red rockhare* (Pronolagus crassicaudatus) *in an alert scanning posture;* ***10*** *Hispid hare* (Caprolagus hispidus), *sitting among cuttings and pellets;* ***11*** *Volcano rabbit* (Romerolagus diazi), *reingesting pellets amid a vegetation of zacatón grasses.*

Above *Desert cottontail kittens crowd a shallow nest in California. The mother will not live in the nest with them, but will crouch over it to feed her young. This litter will be only one of several that she will raise in the course of the year, while the kittens themselves will be ready to start breeding within 3 months.*

Left *Built to make quick getaways, a European hare shows a clean pair of heels to a pursuer. Hares are the champion sprinters among the smaller mammals; their long hind legs can drive them forward at speeds of over 70 km/h (45mph).*

UNWELCOME INTRODUCTIONS

Although many rabbit species are now at risk, the European rabbit (*Oryctolagus cuniculus*) is so successful that it has sometimes acquired the status of a major pest. Problems have arisen particularly following the introduction of the species to areas where it was previously unknown – for example Australia and New Zealand in the early 19th century. The result was a population explosion that proved highly costly for the nations' arable and livestock farmers and that was only finally controlled by the deliberate introduction of the rabbit disease myxomatosis in the 1950s

The reasons for the rabbit's dramatic capacity to increase its numbers are built into its biology. Unlike many of its cousins, the European rabbit is not a fussy eater; it can feed off the same plants at many different stages in their growth. It is also almost unique in its habit of living communally in large burrows, a lifestyle that encourages high population densities. Above all, it is hugely prolific. Adult females can bear five litters a year, each containing an average of five or six young. Female offspring will themselves start breeding after just 5–6 months – an unfailing recipe for spiraling demographics.

Relict Species at Risk

CONSERVATION AND ENVIRONMENT

Sadly, the image of rabbits and hares has been somewhat tainted by a few species like the European rabbit and hare that are notorious for the damage they inflict on agricultural crops or forestry plantations. A preoccupation with rabbits' and hares' potential as pests has caused us to neglect the significant positive roles the leporid species play in ecosystems worldwide, both as prey items for small- to medium-sized vertebrate predators and through their grazing activities. Their pestilential reputation can also draw attention away from the larger number of rabbits and hares now listed as highly threatened in international registers.

Typically, those leporids threatened with extinction are primitive relict species, often the only members of their genus and usually the victims of habitat destruction by man. Most are highly specialized in their habitat requirements. The very handsome Riverine rabbit currently clings on in remnants of riverine scrub habitat associated with two seasonal rivers in the central karoo in South Africa: its habitat has been destroyed to promote the irrigation of encroaching agricultural crops. Similarly, the distribution of the primitive Hispid hare is now restricted to isolated fragments of tall thatch grassland habitat located in a few protected areas across the northern Indian subcontinent, while the tiny Mexican Volcano rabbit, or zacatuche, is isolated in pockets of endemic bunch-grass habitat on the slopes of just a few volcanoes around Mexico City, one of the world's largest conurbations. It is time that this group of attractive, long-eared mammals received more attention – and a far more positive press. ATS/DB

Rabbit and Hare Species

GENUS *BRACHYLAGUS*

Pygmy rabbit LR
Brachylagus idahoensis

SW Oregon to EC California, SW Utah, N to SE Montana; isolated populations in WC Washington State. Prefers habitat comprising clumps of dense sagebrush; extensive runways may cross the thickets. Lives in burrows of its own construction.
HBL 21–27cm; TL 1.5–2cm; WT 50–470g. The smallest rabbit.
COAT: reddish, similar to red rockhares with bushy tail.
CONSERVATION STATUS: LR – Near Threatened.

GENUS *BUNOLAGUS*

Riverine rabbit En
Bunolagus monticularis
Riverine rabbit or Bushman hare

Central Cape Province (South Africa). Dense riverine scrub (not the mountainous situations often attributed). Nocturnal, resting by day in hollows on the shady side of of bushes. Now extremely rare.
HBL 34–48cm; TL 7–11cm; WT 1–1.5kg
FORM: coat reddish, similar to red rockhares with bushy tail.

GENUS *CAPROLAGUS*

Hispid hare En
Caprolagus hispidus
Hispid hare, Assam or Bristly rabbit

Uttar Pradesh to Assam; Tripura (India). Mymensingh and Dacca on the W bank of River Brahmaputra (Bangladesh). Sub-Himalayan *sal* forest where grasses grow up to 3.5m in height during the monsoon months; occasionally also in cultivated areas. Inhabits burrows that are not of its own making. Seldom leaves forest shelter.
HBL 48cm; TL 5.3cm; EL 7cm; HFL 10cm; WT 2.5kg.
FORM: coat coarse and bristly; upperside appears brown from intermingling of black and brownish-white hair; underside brownish-white, with chest slightly darker; tail brown throughout, paler below. Claws straight and strong.

GENUS *LEPUS*

Most inhabit open grassy areas, but: Snowshoe hare occurs in boreal forests; European hare occasionally forests; Arctic hare prefers forested areas to open country; Cape hare prefers open areas, occasionally evergreen forests. Instead of seeking cover, hares rely on their well-developed running ability to escape from danger: also on camouflage, by flattening on vegetation. Vocalizations include a deep grumbling, and shrill calls are given when in pain. Usually solitary, but the European hare is more social. Habitat type has a marked effect on home-range size within each species, but differences also occur between species, e.g. from 4–20ha (10–50 acres) in Arctic hares to over 300ha (745 acres) in European hares. Individuals may defend the area within 1–2m of forms, but home ranges generally overlap and feeding areas are often communal. Most live on the surface, but some species, e.g. Snowshoe and Arctic hares, dig burrows, while others may hide in holes or tunnels not of their making.
HBL 40–76cm; TL 3.5–12cm; WT 1.2–5kg.
FORM: coat usually reddish-brown, yellowish-brown or grayish-brown above, lighter or pure white below; ear tips black-edged, with a significant black area on the exterior in most species; in some species the upperside of the tail is black. The Indian hare has a black nape. Species inhabiting snowy winter climes often molt into a white winter coat, while others change from a brownish summer coat into a grayish winter coat.
DIET: usually grasses and herbs, but cultivated plants, twigs, bark of woody plants are the staple food if other alternatives are not available.
BREEDING: breed throughout the year in southern species; northern species produce 2–4 litters during spring and summer. Gestation up to 50 days in Arctic hare, other species shorter. Litter size 1–9.
LONGEVITY: Only a minority of hares survive their first year in the wild, though survivors can reach 5 years; in captivity, hares can live to 6 or 7 years.

Antelope jackrabbit
Lepus alleni

S New Mexico, S Arizona to N Nayarit (Mexico), Tiburon Island. Locally common. Avoids dehydration in hot desert by feeding on cactus and yucca.

Snowshoe hare
Lepus americanus

Alaska, coast of Hudson Bay, Newfoundland, S Appalachians, S Michigan, N Dakota, N New Mexico, Utah, E California. Locally common.

Arctic hare
Lepus arcticus

Greenland and Canadian Arctic Islands south to WC shore of Hudson Bay. Quebec and W maritime provinces of Canada.

Japanese hare
Lepus brachyurus

Honshu, Shikoku, Kyushu (Japan). Locally common.

Black-tailed jackrabbit
Lepus californicus

N Mexico (Baja California), Oregon, Washington, S Idaho, E Colorado, S Dakota, W Missouri, NW Arkansas, Arizona, N Mexico. Locally common.

White-sided jackrabbit LR
Lepus callotis

SE Arizona, SW New Mexico, and Oaxaca (Mexico). Locally common, but declining.
CONSERVATION STATUS: LR – Near Threatened.

Cape hare
Lepus capensis

Sub-Saharan Africa, N Africa through Sinai desert to Arabia, Mongolia, Middle East W of River Euphrates. Locally common.

Broom hare Vu
Lepus castroviejoi

Cantabrian Mountains (N Spain).

Yunnan hare
Lepus comus

Yunnan and W Guizhou (China).

Korean hare
Lepus coreanus

Korean peninsula, S Jilin, S Liaoning, E Heilongjiang (China).

Corsican hare
Lepus corsicanus

Italy (including Sicily); introduced to Corsica (France).

Savanna hare
Lepus crawshayi

S Africa, Kenya, S Sudan; relict populations in NE Sahara. Locally common.

European hare
Lepus europaeus
European or Brown hare

S Scandinavia, S Finland, Great Britain (introduced in Ireland), Europe south to N Iraq and Iran, W Siberia. Locally common but declining.

Ethiopian hare
Lepus fagani

N and W Ethiopia and neighboring SE Sudan south to NW Kenya.

Tehuantepec jackrabbit En
Lepus flavigularis

Restricted to sand-dune forest on shores of saltwater lagoons on N rim of Gulf of Tehuantepec (S Mexico). Nocturnal.

Granada hare
Lepus granatensis
Granada or Iberian hare

Iberian peninsula, Mallorca.

Hainan hare Vu
Lepus hainanus

Hainan (China).

Black jackrabbit LR
Lepus insularis

Espiritu Santo Island (Mexico).
CONSERVATION STATUS: LR – Near Threatened.

Manchurian hare
Lepus mandshuricus

Jilin, Liaoning, Heilongjiang (NE China), far NE Korea, Ussuri region (E Siberia, Russia). Range decreasing.

Indian hare
Lepus nigricollis
Indian or Black-naped hare

Pakistan, India, Sri Lanka (introduced into Java and Mauritius).

Woolly hare
Lepus oiostolus

Tibetan (Xizang) plateau and adjoining areas.

ABBREVIATIONS

HBL = head–body length TL = tail length EL = ear length
HFL = hind-foot length WT = weight
Approximate nonmetric equivalents: 10cm = 4in 30g = 1oz 1kg = 2.2lb

Ex Extinct
EW Extinct in the Wild
Cr Critically Endangered
En Endangered
Vu Vulnerable
LR Lower Risk

Above *The Black-tailed jackrabbit lives in dry, sunny regions, where its huge ears help control heat intake. Even so, it is mostly active at night.*

Alaskan hare
Lepus othus

W and SW Alaska (USA), E Chukotsk (Russia).

Burmese hare
Lepus peguensis

Burma to Indochina and Hainan (China).

Scrub hare
Lepus saxatilis

S Africa, Namibia.

Chinese hare
Lepus sinensis

SE China, Taiwan, S Korea.

Ethiopian highland hare
Lepus starcki

C Ethiopian mountains.

Mountain hare
Lepus timidus
Mountain or Blue hare

Alaska, Labrador, Greenland, Scandinavia, N Russia to Siberia and Sakhalin, Hokkaido (Japan), Sikhoto Alin Mts, Altai, N Tien Shan, N Ukraine, Baltic states. Locally common. Isolated populations in the Alps, Scotland, Wales, and Ireland.

Tolai hare
Lepus tolai

N Caspian Sea S along E shore of Caspian to N Iran, E through Afghanistan, Kazakhstan to Mongolia and W, C, and NE China.

White-tailed jackrabbit
Lepus townsendii

S British Columbia, S Alberta, SW Ontario, SW Wisconsin, Kansas, N New Mexico, Nevada, E California. Locally common.

African savanna hare
Lepus victoriae

Atlantic coast of NW Africa, E across Sahel to Sudan and Ethiopia, S through E Africa to NE Namibia, Botswana, and S Africa.

Malawi hare
Lepus whytei

Malawi. Locally common.

Yarkand hare LR
Lepus yarkandensis

SW Xinjiang (China), margins of Takla Makan desert.
CONSERVATION STATUS: LR – Near Threatened

GENUS *NESOLAGUS*

Sumatran rabbit Cr
Nesolagus netscheri
Sumatran rabbit or Sumatran short-eared hare

W Sumatra (1°–4°S) between 600–1,400m (2,000–4,600ft) in Barisan range. Primary mountain forest. Strictly nocturnal; spends the day in burrows or in holes not of its own making.
HBL 37–39cm; TL 1.7cm; EL 4.3–4.5cm.
FORM: variable; body from buff to gray, the rump bright rusty with broad dark stripes from the muzzle to the tail, from the ear to the chin, curving from the shoulder to the rump, across the upper part of the hind legs, and around the base of the hind foot.
DIET: juicy stalks and leaves.

Annamite rabbit
Nesolagus timminsi

Annamite Mts. between Laos and Vietnam.

GENUS *ORYCTOLAGUS*

European rabbit
Oryctolagus cuniculus
European or Old World Rabbit

Endemic on the Iberian peninsula and in NW Africa; introduced in rest of W Europe 2,000 years ago, and to Australia, New Zealand, S America, and some islands. Opportunistic, having colonized habitats from stony deserts to subalpine valleys; also found in fields, parks, and gardens, rarely reaching altitudes of over 600m (2,000ft). Very common. All strains of domesticated rabbit derived from this

species. Colonial organization associated with warren systems. Utters shrill calls in pain or fear.
HBL 38–50cm; TL 4.5–7.5cm; EL 6.5–8.5cm; HFL 8.5–11cm; WT 1.5–3kg.
FORM: coat grayish with a fine mixture of black and light brown tips of the hair above; nape reddish-yellowish brown; tail white below; underside light gray; inner surface of the legs buff-gray; total black is not rare.
DIET: grass and herbs; roots and the bark of trees and shrubs, cultivated plants.
BREEDING: breeds from February to August/September in N Europe; 3–5 litters with 5–6 young, occasionally up to 12; gestation period 28–33 days; young naked at birth; weight about 40–45g, eyes open when about 10 days old.
LONGEVITY: about 10 years in wild.

GENUS *PENTALAGUS*

Amami rabbit En
Pentalagus furnessi
Amami or Ryukyu rabbit

Two of the Amami Islands (Japan). Dense forests. Nocturnal. Digs burrows.
HBL 43–51cm; EL 4.5cm.
FORM: coat thick and woolly, dark brown above, more reddish below. Claws are unusually long for rabbits at 1–2cm. Eyes small.
BREEDING: 1–3 young are born naked in a short tunnel; two breeding seasons.

GENUS *POELAGUS*

Bunyoro rabbit
Poelagus marjorita
Bunyoro or Central African rabbit, or Uganda grass hare

S Sudan and Chad, NW Uganda, NE Zaire, Central African Republic, Angola. Savanna and forest. Locally common. Nocturnal. While resting, hides in vegetation. Reported to grind teeth when disturbed.
HBL 44–50cm; TL 4.5–5cm; EL 6–6.5cm; WT 2–3kg.
FORM: coat stiffer than that of any other African leporid; grizzled brown and yellowish above, becoming more yellow on the sides and white on the underparts; nape reddish-yellow; tail brownish-yellow above and white below. Ears small; hind legs short.
BREEDING: Young reared in burrows; less precocious than those of true hares.

GENUS *PRONOLAGUS*

Nocturnal, feeding on grass and herbs. Inhabits rocky grassland, shelters in crevices. Utters shrill vocal calls even when not in pain.
HBL 35–50cm; TL 5–10cm; HFL 7.5–10cm; EL 6–10cm; WT 2–2.5kg.
FORM: coat thick and woolly, including that on the feet, reddish.

Greater red rockhare
Pronolagus crassicaudatus
Greater red rockhare or Natal red rock rabbit

SE South Africa, S Mozambique.

Jameson's red rockhare
Pronolagus randensis

NE South Africa, E Botswana, Zimbabwe, W Mozambique, W Namibia.

Smith's red rockhare
Pronolagus rupestris

South Africa to SW Kenya.

GENUS *ROMEROLAGUS*

Volcano rabbit En
Romerolagus diazi
Volcano rabbit, teporingo, or zacatuche

Restricted to two volcanic sierras (Ajusco and Ixtaccihuatl–Popocatepetl ranges) close to Mexico City. Habitat unique "zacatón" (principally *Epicampes*, *Festuca*, and *Muhlenbergia*) grass layer of open pine forest at 2,800–4,000m. Lives in warren-based groups of 2–5 animals. Vocalizations resemble those of picas.
HBL 27–36cm; EL 4–4.4cm; WT 400–500g.
FORM: coat dark brown above, dark brownish-gray below. Smallest leporid; features include short ears, legs, and feet, articulation between collar and breast bones, and no visible tail.
BREEDING: breeding season December to July; gestation 39–40 days; average litter 2. Mainly active in daytime, sometimes at night.

GENUS *SYLVILAGUS*

Most species common. Range extends from S Canada to Argentina and Paraguay, and a great diversity of habitats is occupied. Distributions of some species overlap. Most preferred habitat open or brushy land or scrubby clearings in forest areas, but also cultivated areas or even parks. Various species frequent forests, marshes, swamps, sand beaches, or deserts. All species occupy burrows made by other animals or inhabit available shelter or hide in vegetation. Not colonial, but some species form social hierarchies in breeding groups. Active in daytime or at night. Not territorial; overlapping stable home ranges of a few hectares. Vocalizations rare. Most species are locally common.
HBL 25–45cm; TL 2.5–6cm; WT 0.4–2.3kg.
FORM: coat mostly speckled grayish-brown to reddish-brown above; undersides white or buff-white; tail brown above and white below ("cottontail"); Forest rabbit and Marsh rabbit have dark tails. Molts once a year, except Forest and Marsh rabbits. Ears medium-sized (about 5.5cm) and same color as the upper side; nape often reddish, but may be black.
DIET: mainly herbaceous plants, but in winter also bark and twigs.
LONGEVITY: 10 years (in captivity).

Swamp rabbit
Sylvilagus aquaticus

E Texas, E Oklahoma, Alabama, NW to S Carolina, S Illinois. A strong swimmer.
BREEDING: Gestation period 39–40 days; eyes open at 2–3 days.

Desert cottontail
Sylvilagus audubonii
Desert or Audubon's cottontail

C Montana, SW to N Dakota, NC Utah, C Nevada, and N and C California (USA), and Baja California and C Sinaloa, NE Puebla, W Veracruz (Mexico).

Brush rabbit
Sylvilagus bachmani

W Oregon to Baja California, Cascades to Sierra Nevada ranges.
BREEDING: Average 5 litters per year; gestation 24–30 days; young are covered in hair at birth.

Forest rabbit
Sylvilagus brasiliensis
Forest rabbit or tapiti

S Tamaulipas (Mexico) to Peru, Bolivia, N Argentina, S Brazil, Venezuela.
BREEDING: Average litter size 2; gestation about 42 days.

Mexican cottontail LR
Sylvilagus cunicularius

Sinaloa to Oaxaca and Veracruz (Mexico).
CONSERVATION STATUS: LR – Near Threatened.

Dice's cottontail En
Sylvilagus dicei

C American isthmus: SE Costa Rica to NW Panama.

Eastern cottontail
Sylvilagus floridanus

Venezuela through disjunct parts of C America to NW Arizona, S Saskatchewan, SC Quebec, Michigan, Massachusetts, Florida. Very common.
BREEDING: Gestation period 26–28 days; young naked at birth.

Tres Marías cottontail En
Sylvilagus graysoni

Maria Madre and Maria Magdalena Islands (Tres Marías Islands, Navarit, Mexico).

Omilteme cottontail Cr
Sylvilagus insonus

Sierra Madre del Sur, C Guerrero (Mexico).

Brush rabbit LR
Sylvilagus mansuetus
Brush rabbit or San José brush rabbit

Known only from San José Island, Gulf of California. Often regarded as subspecies of *S. bachmani*.
CONSERVATION STATUS: LR – Near Threatened.

Mountain cottontail
Sylvilagus nuttallii
Mountain or Nuttall's cottontail

Intermountain area of N America from S British Columbia to S Saskatchewan, S to E California, NW Nevada, C Arizona, NW New Mexico.

Appalachian cottontail
Sylvilagus obscurus

New York State (W of Hudson River) to N Alabama along Appalachian Mountain chain.

Marsh rabbit
Sylvilagus palustris

Marsh rabbit or Lower Keys marsh rabbit Florida Keys to S Virginia on the coastal plain. Strong swimmer.

New England cottontail Vu
Sylvilagus transitionalis

S Maine to N Alabama. Distinguished from overlapping Eastern cottontail by presence of gray mottled cheeks, black spot between eyes and absence of black saddle and white forehead. ES

Right As its name suggests, the Marsh rabbit is a habitat specialist, found only in swampy areas of the southern USA. A subspecies from the lower Florida Keys, *S. p. hefneri*, is considered Endangered.

ABBREVIATIONS
HBL = head–body length TL = tail length EL = ear length
HFL = hind-foot length WT = weight
Approximate nonmetric equivalents: 10cm = 4in 30g = 1oz 1kg = 2.2lb

Ex Extinct
EW Extinct in the Wild
Cr Critically Endangered
En Endangered
Vu Vulnerable
LR Lower Risk

THE SOCIAL LIFE OF RABBITS

How burrows shape interactions between group members

THE EUROPEAN RABBIT IS UNUSUAL AMONG rabbits and hares in constructing its own burrows. These can vary from single-entrance breeding "stops" through to extensive burrow systems, each containing a myriad of interconnected underground tunnels, accessed from as many as 60 entrances and containing a number of potential nest sites. Multiple-entrance burrow systems are generally referred to as "warrens."

The burrowing habit has a number of implications for rabbit ecology and behavior. First, it allows rabbits to live in relatively open habitats, as the burrow affords shelter from predators. Rabbits can also raise large numbers of young by giving birth in the safe confines of the warren.

Female rabbits usually nurse their young in underground nesting chambers situated within pre-existing burrow systems. Alternatively, young are raised in purpose-built stops with only one entrance. The mother animal visits the young only once a day for suckling, which may last as little as 5 minutes. When she leaves, she carefully covers the entrance. Despite these efforts, such stops are prone to being dug out by predators. Hence, nest sites deep in the main warrens are at a premium.

Where space underground is in short supply, natural selection should favor females that successfully defend nest sites. Good evidence of this was obtained from a long-term study of a population in southern England. There, the burrows were clustered together in tight groups in the form of warrens, which were themselves randomly distributed over the down.

Distinct social groups were established, the members of each having exclusive access to one or more burrow systems in their territory. Adult females, which do most of the burrow excavation, rarely attempted more than the expansion of an existing burrow system in the hard chalky soil. Completely new warrens hardly ever appeared, although breeding stops were constructed occasionally, and were at the core of the few new warrens that did appear during the study. Of the disputes between adult females, over 70 percent took place within 5m (16.5ft) of a burrow entrance. These were the most aggressive interactions seen during the course of the study, with the fur sometimes literally flying.

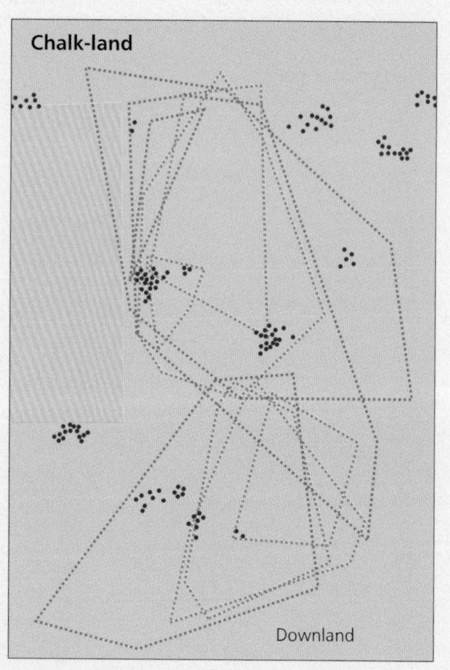

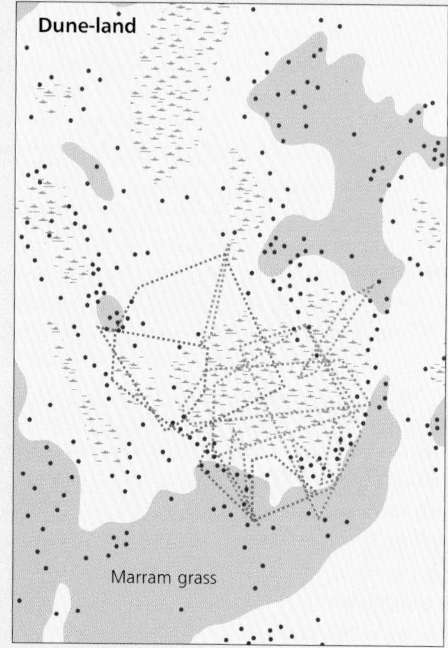

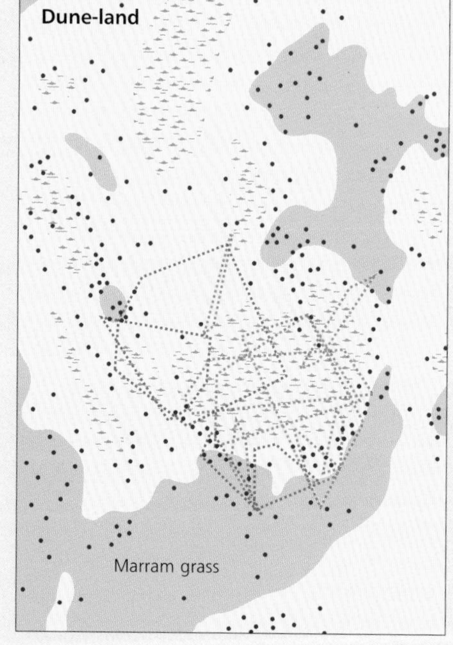

Above. *Maps comparing group-living and social behavior in European rabbits on chalk- and dune-land respectively. On chalk-land rabbits have clustered burrows with females living as reluctant partners around each cluster. Fights often break out between females and their home ranges overlap considerably within each group but not with those of adjacent groups.*

On dune-land rabbit burrows are not clustered and are randomly distributed, although they do not occur in the slacks, which are prone to flooding. Females move freely between burrows and there is little fighting between individuals. Home ranges overlap less than on chalk-land. In both habitats males have larger territories which overlap those of several females.

There was also a direct relationship between the size of a warren and the number of adult females taking refuge in it: the larger the warren, the more females that lived there. Thus a group of females sharing one or more warrens and feeding in extensively overlapping ranges around them are best regarded as reluctant partners in an uneasy alliance. This reluctance reflects the fact that only costs seem to accrue to group-living females, especially in terms of the survival of their offspring, which can be impaired by increases in both disease and predation. Solitary females, with exclusive access to a warren and attendant nest sites, do best in terms of reproductive success.

The pattern of dispersal also gave some insight into the importance of burrow availability. Overall, both adult males and females were rather sedentary, with only 20 percent and 5 percent respectively moving breeding groups between years. Dispersal was much more common among juvenile males, two-thirds of which bred in a different group from that into which they had been born, as compared with only one-third of juvenile

relatedness of females in breeding groups is at least twice the average relatedness of males. This pattern is reinforced by very infrequent movement of individual rabbits between breeding groups once they reach adulthood.

Between 1987 and 1990, the number of adults in the population more than doubled, from 22 to 45. This resulted in an increase in the number of adults per social group rather than in the formation of new groups. Groups did seem to split when the number of female kin members expanded above six individuals; one or two females would restrict their activities to peripheral burrows within the group territory, and new males would start defending these does to form a new breeding group.

We can now recognize that the burrow shapes both the ecology and behavior of the wild rabbit. It is at the heart of its success as an invasive species throughout the world, so perhaps it is not surprising that it is also at the core of much conflict in rabbit societies. DPC/DB

Above *Post-coital grooming between a mating pair. Females enter estrus again shortly after giving birth. With a gestation period of only about 30 days, females can produce perhaps 4–5 litters per year.*

females. Interestingly, however, those juvenile females that did disperse entered breeding groups that were significantly less crowded in terms of burrow availability.

What of the males? Male rabbits do not contribute directly to parental care. Consequently, their reproductive success will reflect how many matings they have achieved. Females come into heat for 12–24 hours about every seventh day, or soon after giving birth. Males apparently monitor female condition closely: adult does were "escorted" by single males for about a quarter of their time above ground in the breeding season. Male home ranges were on average about twice the size of those of neighboring females, with which they had an extensive overlap. Consequently, these bucks could have been acquiring information, perhaps largely on the basis of scent rather than direct encounters, about the reproductive state of numerous females. The frequent aggressive interactions observed between males, whether or not they were escorting does, may be best interpreted as attempts to curtail each other's use of space and access to females. The behavior of bucks following females around can be regarded as "mate-guarding." Each female is usually accompanied by only one male.

Despite bucks' efforts to monopolize matings with does, the females are promiscuous. An Australian study involved the genetic typing (using blood proteins) of all potential parents in a population, together with their weaned young. The resulting analysis showed that at least 16 percent of the young were not fathered by the male known to be the usual escort of their mother.

Long-term studies of a natural population of European wild rabbits living in eastern England have provided insights into relationships between social organization and the genetic structure of populations. Here, the rabbits live in highly territorial breeding groups that defend areas around the warrens. These breeding groups typically comprise 1–4 males and 1–9 females. Analyses of genetic relatedness between colony members confirmed predictions made from patterns of juvenile dispersal where sons disperse while daughters stay on to breed. As a consequence, females within breeding groups tend to be very closely related, with several generations living together. Indeed, the genetic

Above *A European rabbit at a burrow entrance in southern England. Differences in soil type play a major role in social systems. Locations in which warrens can be dug quickly and easily cause rabbit populations to spread out, whereas in hard-soil areas populations center on long-established warren systems.*

SPECIAL FEATURE

THE TEN-YEAR CYCLE

Population fluctuations in the Snowshoe hare

ANIMAL POPULATIONS RARELY, IF EVER, REMAIN constant from year to year. Populations of the great majority of species fluctuate irregularly or unpredictably. An exception is the Snowshoe hare, whose populations in the boreal forest of North America undergo remarkably regular fluctuations that peak every 8–11 years.

These cycles were first analyzed quantitatively when wildlife biologists began to plot the fur-trading records of the Hudson's Bay Company during the early 1900s. Established in 1671, the company kept meticulous account of the numbers of furs traded from different posts across Canada. The most famous time series drawn from the records was that of the Canadian lynx published by Charles Elton and Mary Nicholson in 1942. The lynx is a specialist predator of Snowshoe hares, and the 9–10 year rise and fall in lynx numbers turned out to mirror, with a slight time lag, the rise and fall of Snowshoe hare populations (see graph).

The spectacular cycles of Snowshoe hares and their predators seem to violate the implicit assumption of many ecologists that there is a balance in nature; anyone living in the boreal forest would be hard pressed to recognize any equilibrium in the boom-and-bust pattern of nature's economy. The challenge to biologists has been to understand the mechanisms behind these cycles. Over the last 40 years ecologists working in Alberta, the Yukon Territory, and Alaska have put together an array of studies that have resolved most, but not all, of the enigmas underlying them.

The demographic pattern of the hare cycle is remarkably clear and consistent. The key finding is that both reproduction and survival begin to decay in the increase phase of the cycle, two years before peak densities are reached. Maximal reproduction and highest survival rates occur early in this phase; as it progresses, reproduction slows and survival rates of both adults and juveniles fall. Both reproduction and survival rates continue to decline for 2–3 years after the cycle has peaked, then start to recover over the low phase. This time lag in changes in reproduction and mortality is the proximate cause of the variation in density that makes up the hare cycle, which can see populations rise or fall 30- or even 100-fold.

What causes the changes? The three main factors involved seem to be food, predation, and social interactions. There are two variants of the food hypothesis: first, that the hares may simply run out of food in winter and starve, or that the quality of the food available to them may decline. Yet feeding experiments have failed to change the pattern of the cycle or prevent the cyclic decline, so this hypothesis has now been rejected. Food by itself does not seem to be the primary limitation on hare numbers.

Predation is the next most obvious explanation. Studies with radio-collared hares have in fact shown that the immediate cause of death of 95 percent of adult hares is predation by a variety of animals, the main ones in Canada being lynx, coyotes, goshawks, and Great horned owls. For leverets the figure is 81 percent, most of these being killed by various small raptors or else by Red or Arctic ground squirrels. Few animals die of malnutrition. Obviously such huge losses must play an important role in the cycle.

As for the predators themselves, the evidence indicates that all show strong numerical changes that lag behind the hare cycle by 1–2 years. In addition, both lynx and coyotes kill more hares per day in the peak and decline phases than during the increase. These kill rates have turned out to be well above previous estimates, and are also in excess of energetic demands. Surplus killing seems to be a characteristic of these predators.

By constructing electric fences around 1sq km (0.39sq mi) blocks of boreal forest, researchers

Left *A Snowshoe hare in its summer coat. Female hares show remarkable variations in litter size at different stages of the population cycle, bearing more than twice as many young when numbers are low.*

Right *A lynx carries off its prey. When hare numbers decline, the shortage of alternative food sources leads to a rise in mortality among lynx kittens as well as to a drop in the number of young that are born.*

have been able to test the impact of excluding mammalian predators from hares. The main effects were to increase survival rates and to temporarily stop the cycle inside the fence, indicating that predation is indeed the immediate cause of the mortality changes over the cycle.

Yet if predation causes the changes in mortality, what about the varying rates of reproduction that accompany the cycle? Two possible explanations for these have been suggested. Lower-quality food in the time of high density may reduce reproductive output; alternatively, predators may cause the decline by stressing hares through repeated, unsuccessful attacks. Chronic stress has many direct detrimental effects on mammals, one of which is reduction in reproductive rate. Stress effects may also be indirect and long-term, affecting offspring viability.

Ecologists are now close to understanding the Snowshoe hare cycle. They believe that it results from the interaction between predation and food; but of these two factors, predation is clearly the main one. The impact of food shortages is felt largely in winter and is indirect; hares do not die directly of starvation or malnutrition. But food quality and quantity may nonetheless play a part by affecting the hares' body condition, and so predisposing them to increased parasite loads and higher levels of chronic stress, which in turn probably cause reduced reproductive output.

Hares in peak and declining populations must trade off safety for food. The result is a time lag in both the direct and indirect effects of predation that causes the cyclical pattern. CJK

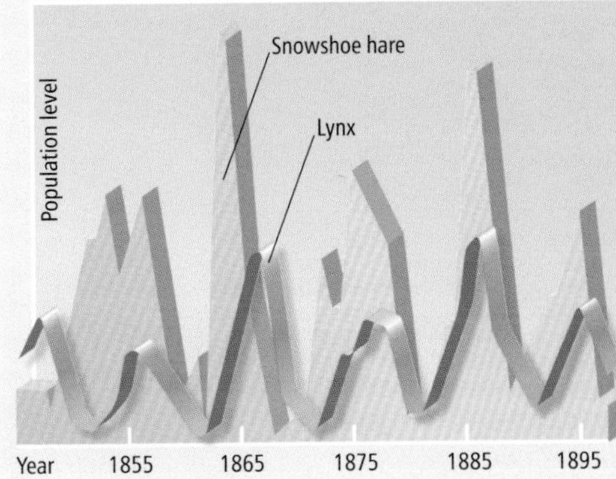

__Above__ The Snowshoe hare makes up 80–90 percent of the Canadian lynx's diet. Populations of the two mammals closely mirror each other; when food shortages and predation bring about a decline in hare numbers, the lynx population drops sharply soon after; conversely, the recovery of hare populations presages an upturn in lynx numbers. This parallel fluctuation in the animals' fortunes is plotted on the graph, which derives from the records of the Hudson's Bay Company.

PHOTO STORY

MAD WORLD OF THE EUROPEAN HARE

1 With no underground sanctuary to provide refuge, the hare relies on its superb senses – and its long legs – for survival. Its sensory equipment includes eyes on the side of the head for allround vision, huge ears, and a sensitive nose.

2 3 "Mad as a March hare," people say, recalling the seemingly wild behavior of hares in the mating season (January–August). At this time does are receptive for just a few hours on one day in each of their six-weekly cycles, perhaps six well-spaced days in all. Local bucks then compete for their favors; the dominant male strives to keep all others at bay, while the doe herself will fight off any that approach before she is ready. "Mad" behavior becomes visible in March only because the nights, which hares prefer for their activities, become shorter, forcing them to enter the daylight arena.

4 Females do not pull their punches when beating off over-eager suitors, as the scarred ears of many bucks testify. When she is ready, the doe will start a wild chase over the countryside, shaking off the following bucks until only one, probably the fittest, remains. Then at last she will stop and allow him to mate.

5 *A young hare shelters in its form, or daytime resting place; unlike their rabbit cousins, leverets enter the world fully coated, sighted, and mobile. Around sunset it will move cautiously to the spot where it was born a few days previously, where it will be joined by its littermates to await the mother. She will arrive about 45 minutes after sunset to suckle them for perhaps 5 minutes, and will then depart again, not to return for another 24 hours. By 4–5 weeks of age the leverets will be consuming vegetation and the doe's visits will cease.* TH

Pikas

PIKAS ARE SMALL, EGG-SHAPED LAGOMORPHS with relatively large, rounded ears, short limbs, and a barely visible tail. They are lively and agile, but often sit hunched up on a rock or in an alpine meadow, their long, silky fur making them resemble balls of fluff.

Pikas' generic name, *Ochotona*, is derived from the Mongolian term for the animals (*ogdoi*), while the word "pika" itself evolved from a vernacular term used by the Tungus of Siberia in attempting to mimic the call ("peeka...") of the Northern species. To this day, most pikas are denizens of high, remote mountains and wild country, serving as symbols of untamed nature.

Miniature Haymakers

FORM AND FUNCTION

Pikas are primarily active by day; only the Steppe pika is predominantly nocturnal. They do not hibernate, and are well-adapted to the cold alpine environments that they inhabit. They have a high body temperature, yet can perish in even moderately warm environmental conditions (American pikas have been known to die following a 30-minute exposure to 25°C/77°F). Thus they have little margin for error in their exposure to heat, and most species are active only during cool times of the day. High-altitude American pikas can be active all day, whereas populations at low altitudes (where it is hotter) emerge from their shelters only at dawn and dusk. Himalayan species demonstrate the same trend; Royle's pika is active in the morning and evening, while the Large-eared pika, which lives at cooler elevations above 4,000m (13,000ft), basks in the midday sun.

Pikas either live among rocks or else dig burrows in open meadow–steppe environments. Afghan and Pallas's pikas are intermediate in their use of habitat (they sometimes live in rocks, but also burrow), but their life-history closely parallels those of the burrowing pikas. Almost every facet of the biology of pikas is sharply divided between rock-dwelling and burrowing forms. Rock-dwelling pikas have very low reproductive rates due to the combination of small litter size and few litters per year; for example, most American pikas successfully wean only two young from one litter annually. In contrast, female burrowing pikas are baby machines; some species have as many as five litters containing up to 13 young.

Pikas can utilize whatever plants are available near their burrows or at the edge of their rocky scree territories, although they prefer those plants highest in protein or other important chemicals. They cannot grasp plants with their forepaws, so they eat grasses, leaves, and flowering stalks with a side-to-side motion of their jaws. During summer and fall, most species devote considerable time to harvesting mouthfuls of vegetation that they carry back to their dens to store for winter consumption in caches that resemble large piles of hay. American pikas may devote over 30 percent of their active time to haying, dashing back and forth with mouthfuls of vegetation. Haypiles rarely run out – pikas tend to overharvest, and there are often midden-like remains from the previous year.

In winter pikas also make tunnels in the snow to harvest nearby vegetation. Some species, such as Royle's, Large-eared, and Plateau pikas, live where winter snows are uncommon, and consequently do not construct haypiles – instead they continue to forage throughout the winter.

Pikas, like other lagomorphs, produce two different types of feces: small, spherical pellets resembling pepper seeds, and a soft, dark-green viscous excrement. The soft feces have high energy value (particularly in B vitamins) and are re-ingested either directly from the anus or after being dropped.

Gregarious or Reclusive?

SOCIAL BEHAVIOR

The dramatic differences between rock-dwelling and burrowing pikas are most apparent in their social behavior. Rock-dwelling pikas defend large territories, either as individuals (in North American species) or in pairs (Asian species). The resulting population density is low (about 2–10/ha, or 5–25/acre) and fairly stable over time. Rock-dwelling pikas rarely interact, and when they do it is usually to repel an intruding neighbor. Even the Asian forms that contribute to a shared haypile spend most of the day living solitary lives. The apparent lack of social activity can be somewhat misleading, however, as these animals are clearly aware of all the goings-on across the talus (see special feature: Securing a Vacancy).

In sharp contrast, burrowing pikas are among the most social of mammals. Family groups occupy communal dens, and local densities can exceed 300 animals per hectare (750 per acre) at the end of the breeding season, though the figures can fluctuate wildly, both seasonally and annually. During the breeding season family groups are composed of many siblings of different ages, and social interactions may occur as frequently as once

◐ **Left** *The collared pika is found mainly on rocky outcrops in Alaska and northwestern Canada. Its name derives from the grayish patches below its cheek and around its neck. It spends roughly half its time above ground, sitting on prominent rocks*

◐ **Above** *A characteristic activity of pikas in late summer is the gathering of vegetation to store in haypiles, in part to serve as food during the winter. Most of these stores of food are kept under overhanging rocks.*

FACTFILE

PIKAS

Order: Lagomorpha

Family: Ochotonidae

29 species of the genus *Ochotona*. Rock-dwelling species include: Alpine pika (*O. alpina*); North American pika (*O. princeps*); Northern pika (*O. hyperborea*); Collared pika (*O. collaris*). Burrowing pikas comprise: Daurian pika (*O. dauurica*); Gansu pika (*O. cansus*); Koslov's pika (*O. koslowi*); Moupin pika (*O. thibetana*); Plateau pika (*O. curzoniae*); Steppe pika (*O. pusilla*).

DISTRIBUTION Mountains of W North America; across much of Asia N of the Himalayas, from the Middle East and the Ural Mountains E to the N Pacific Rim; from sea level to 6,130 m (20,100 ft).

Equator

HABITAT Rock-dwellers: talus (rocky scree) on mountains or occasional piles of fallen logs. Burrowing forms: alpine meadow, steppe, or semi-desert.

SIZE Head–body length 120–285mm (4.7–11.2in); **weight** 50–350g (1.8–12.3oz); **tail length** barely visible at about 5mm (0.2in); **ear length** 12–36mm (0.5–1.4in).

COAT Dense and soft; grayish-brown in most species (though one is reddish), usually darker above than below.

DIET Generalized herbivorous

BREEDING Rock-dwellers: litter size 1–5; 2 litters a year, but generally only 1 successfully weaned; gestation approximately 1 month. Burrowing forms: litter size 1–13; up to 5 litters a year; gestation approximately 3 weeks.

LONGEVITY Rock-dwellers: up to 7 years. Burrowing forms: up to 3 years, but most live only 1 year.

CONSERVATION STATUS 6 species and 13 subspecies are listed as threatened in some measure. The Helan Shan pika (*O. helanshanensis*) is Critically Endangered.

For full species list see Appendix ▷

a minute. Pikas sit in contact, rub noses, socially groom, and play-box together. Young line up behind an adult – generally their father – and follow him like a miniature train. Nearly all these friendly social interactions occur within family groups, while interactions involving animals from different groups are normally aggressive – most notably the long chases of adult males.

Communication styles also differ between rock-dwelling and burrowing pikas. Most rock-dwellers have only two characteristic vocalizations: a short call used to announce their presence on the talus or to warn others of approaching predators, and a long call (or song) uttered by adult males during the breeding season. Some rock-dwelling species (Large-eared and Royle's pikas, for instance) rarely utter even weak sounds. Burrowing pikas, on the other hand, have a vast repertoire: predator alarm calls (short, soft, and rapidly repeated); long calls (given by adult males); and also whines, trills, muffle calls, and transition calls, these last two usually uttered by young pikas and serving to promote cohesion among siblings.

Burrowing pikas also have an unusually flexible mating system. In adjoining Plateau pika burrows, one can observe monogamous, polygynous, polyandrous, and complex (multiple male and female) adult associations side-by-side. Polyandry is extremely rare in mammals, yet two males from the same burrow may be seen alternately mating with the resident female and then sitting side by side or grooming one another, even while the female is in estrus – apparently an adaptation to maximize reproductive rates in face of harsh environmental conditions.

Not Just a Pest

CONSERVATION AND ENVIRONMENT

Several species and subspecies of pika are globally listed as threatened. In general, these are forms confined to restricted rocky habitats or found in isolated locations of central Asia. In reality, the status of many pika species is difficult to determine because they inhabit such remote areas.

On the other hand, some of the burrowing pikas are treated as pests because they reach such high densities and are believed to cause rangeland degradation. For example, the Plateau pika has been poisoned across 200,000sq km (77,000sq mi) in Qinghai province of China alone – an area half the size of California.

However, others consider the Plateau pika a keystone species for biodiversity on the Tibetan plateau because its burrows contribute to increased plant diversity and are the primary homes for a wide variety of birds and lizards. In addition, it serves as the principal prey for many predator species; and it contributes positively to ecosystem-level dynamics by recycling nutrients and minimizing erosion. TK/ATS

◑ **Right** *A pika at its burrow entrance in Ladakh, northeastern India. Only some pika species live in burrows and even these are not especially well adapted for digging. One of the main distinctions between burrowing and rock-dwelling pikas is that the former tend to be far less social than the latter.*

SECURING A VACANCY

The social organization of the North American pika

TWO NORTH AMERICAN PIKAS DARTED INTO AND out of sight on a rock-strewn slope (known as a talus). The second, a resident male, was in aggressive pursuit of the first, an immigrant male. The chase continued onto an adjoining meadow, before turning into the dense cover of a nearby spruce forest. When next seen, dashing back toward the talus, the pair were being chased by a weasel. The pursuing pika was caught, and death followed swiftly less than 1m (3.3ft) from the safety of the talus. Immediately, all the pikas in the vicinity, with one exception, broke into a chorus of consecutive short calls, the sounds that pikas utter when they are alarmed by the presence of predators. The dead pika had initiated the chase, but the object of his aggression had managed to escape the weasel. Perched in silence on a prominent rock, he now surveyed his new domain.

Most accounts of the natural history of pikas have emphasized their individual territoriality;

Above *A pika sits amid its pile of winter provisions. Many pikas have a tendency to overprovision and collect far more leaves and grass than they will consume over the cold season.*

Left *Pikas have two characteristic vocalizations: the short call and the long call (or song). Long calls (a series of squeaks lasting up to 30 seconds) are given by males primarily during the breeding season. Short calls normally contain one-to-two note squeaks and may be given from promontories either before or after movement, in response to calls from another pika, while chasing or being chased, or when predators are active.*

however, studies conducted in the Rocky Mountains of Colorado have helped add detail to this basic insight. For example, adjacent territories are normally occupied by pikas of opposite sexes. Male and female neighbors overlap each other's home ranges more, and have centers of activity that are closer to one another's, than the ranges or activity centers of same-sex neighbors. The possession and juxtapositions of territories tend to be stable from year to year, consequently – as North American pikas can live for up to 6 years – the appearance and whereabouts of vacant territories on the talus are unpredictable. For a pika, therefore, trying to secure a vacancy on the talus is like entering a lottery in which an animal's sex in part determines whether or not it will have a winning ticket, for territories are almost always claimed by a member of the same sex as the previous occupant.

The behaviors that sustain this pattern of occupancy are apparently a compromise between the contrasting aggressive and affiliative tendencies of the pika. Although all pikas are pugnacious when they are involved in defending territories, females are less aggressive toward neighboring males, and conversely more aggressive to proximate females. Male residents rarely exhibit aggression toward each other because they do not come into contact with each other very frequently, apparently avoiding one another by the use of both scentmarking and vocalizations. Resident males will, however, vigorously attack unfamiliar (immigrant) males. The pika described in the account above had forayed from his home territory to chase an unfamiliar, immigrant adult male.

Affiliative behavior is seen in pairs of neighboring males and females, who are not only frequently tolerant of each other but also engage in duets of short calls. Such behavior is rarely seen between neighbors of the same sex or between non-neighbor heterosexual pairs.

Adults treat their offspring in the same way as neighbors of the opposite sex. Some aggression is directed toward juveniles, but there are also frequent expressions of social tolerance. Most juveniles will remain on the home ranges of their parents throughout their first summer before subsequently dispersing.

Ecological constraints have apparently led to a monogamous mating system in rock-dwelling pikas. Although males do not contribute directly to the raising of their offspring, they still primarily associate with a single neighboring female. Polygyny evolves when males can either monopolize sufficient resources to attract several females, or when they can directly defend several females. But in pikas the essentially linear reach of vegetation at the base of the talus precludes resource-defense polygyny, while males cannot defend groups of females because the females are dispersed and kept apart by their mutual antagonism, which thus precludes female-defense polygyny.

Juveniles of both sexes are likely to be repelled should they disperse and attempt to colonize an occupied talus. As a result, they normally settle close to their place of birth ("philopatry"). This pattern of settlement may lead to incestuous matings, which contributes to the low genetic variability that is found in pika populations.

The close association among male–female pairs and the near relatedness of neighbors may actually underlie the evolution of cooperative behavior patterns in pikas. First, attacks on intruders by residents may be an expression of indirect parental care: if the adults can successfully repel immigrants, they may increase the probability of their own offspring obtaining a territory should a local site subsequently become available for colonization. Second – to return to the opening account – the alarm calls given by both sexes when the weasel struck the resident pika served as a warning to the close kin – note that the unrelated immigrant was the only pika that did not call out. Uncontested, the newcomer immediately moved across the talus to claim the slain pika's territory, a half-completed haypile, and access to a neighboring female. ATS

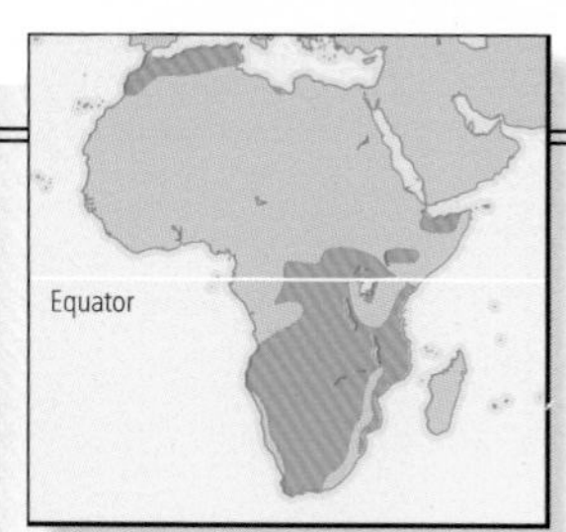

ELEPHANT SHREWS

APPEARING MUCH LIKE GIANT VERSIONS OF true shrews, elephant shrews were not described in the scientific literature until the mid-19th century, partly because they are cryptic, difficult to trap, and confined to Africa. Almost another century passed before a few short notes on their natural history appeared in print. Knowledge of them has expanded greatly over the last 50 years, revealing for the first time just how unique these animals really are.

In the past, the animals were sometimes referred to as "jumping shrews," but this is something of a misnomer since only the smaller species make pronounced leaps when alarmed; the normal method of locomotion is to walk on all fours. The name "elephant shrew," bestowed by field naturalists in Africa, alludes to their long snouts. With large eyes, a trunklike nose, high-crowned cheek teeth, and a large cecum similar to that found in herbivores, long legs like those of small antelopes, and a long, ratlike tail, elephant shrews sometimes seem like walking anthologies of other animals.

Anteaters on Stilts

FORM AND FUNCTION

The elephant shrews found in Africa today give little insight into the family's long and diverse evolutionary history. Fossil sengis first appeared in the early Eocene 50 million years ago, but they reached their maximum diversity by the Miocene (24 million years ago), when they comprised six subfamilies. One included a small, herbivorous form (*Mylomygale*) weighing about 50g (1.8oz) that resembled a grass-eating rodent; another a large planteater (*Myohyrax*) ten times that weight that was so ungulate-like it was initially thought to be a hyrax. Today, all that remains from these ancient forms are representatives of two well-defined, insectivorous subfamilies, the giant elephant shrews (Rhynchocyoninae) and the soft-furred elephant shrews (Macroscelidinae). The other four subfamilies mysteriously died out by the Pleistocene, 1.5 million years ago.

Taxonomically, elephant shrews have long been a source of controversy. At first, biologists included them with other insect-eaters in the Insectivora. Then they were briefly thought to be distantly related to ungulates. Next there was a scheme to include them with the tree shrews in a new grouping, the Menotyphla. More recently, they have been associated with rabbits and hares. Most biologists now agree that elephant shrews belong in their own order, the Macroscelidea. Perhaps to avoid the old association with true shrews, it has been recently suggested that elephant shrews should also be known as sengis, a name derived from several African Bantu languages.

So what is their exact phylogenetic relationship with other mammals? With the advent of molecular techniques to unravel evolutionary relationships, there is a growing consensus that the Macroscelidea belong to an ancient radiation of African mammals that today share few obvious morphological similarities. The latest proposal includes the elephant shrews in the superorder Afrotheria, which also includes elephants, hyraxes, sea cows (the Paenungulata), aardvarks, golden moles, and tenrecs.

Widespread, but Not Common

DISTRIBUTION PATTERNS

Elephant shrews are widespread in Africa, occupying very diverse habitats. For example, the distribution of the Short-eared elephant shrew (*Macroscelides proboscideus*) includes the Namib Desert in southwestern Africa as well as gravelly thornbush plains in South Africa's Cape Province, while the two rock elephant shrew species (*Elephantulus myurus* and *E. rupestris*) are largely restricted to rocky outcrops and boulder fields in southern Africa. Most other species of *Elephantulus* live in the vast steppes and savannas of southern and eastern Africa. The three giant elephant shrews of the *Rhynchocyon* genus and the Four-toed elephant shrew (*Petrodromus tetradactylus*) are restricted to lowland and mountain forests and associated thickets in central and eastern Africa. *Elephantulus rozeti* is found in semi-arid, mountain habitats in extreme northwestern Africa, isolated from all other species by the Sahara. The absence of sengis from western Africa has never been adequately explained. Nowhere are elephant shrews particularly common, and despite being highly terrestrial and mostly active above ground during the day and in the evening, they often escape detection because of their swift locomotion and secretive habits.

Golden-rumped elephant shrews spend up to 80 percent of their active hours searching for invertebrates, which they track down in the leaf litter on the forest floor by using their long, flexible noses as probes, in the manner of coatis or pigs. *Rhynchocyon* species also use their forefeet, which have three long claws, to excavate small, conical holes in the soil. Important prey include beetles, centipedes, termites, spiders, and earthworms. The soft-furred species spend only half as much time foraging. They normally glean small invertebrates, especially termites and ants, from leaves, twigs, and the soil's surface, but they also eat plant matter, especially small, fleshy fruits and seeds. All elephant shrews have long tongues that extend well beyond the tips of their noses and are used to flick small food items into their mouths.

Monogamy and Trail-Clearing

SOCIAL BEHAVIOR

While elephant-shrew species look diverse and live in vastly differing habitats, they all have similar sex lives. Individuals of the Golden-rumped, Four-toed, Short-eared, Rufous, and Western rock species live as monogamous pairs, but there appears to be little affection between partners.

Rufous elephant shrews that inhabit Kenya's densely wooded savannas are distributed as male–female pairs on territories that vary in size from 1,600 to 4,500sq m (0.4–1.1 acres). The same pattern is found in Golden-rumped elephant shrews in coastal forests of Kenya, although the territory sizes are larger, averaging 1.7ha (4.2 acres). Although monogamous, individuals of both species spend

Right *Representative species of elephant shrews:* ***1*** *Checkered elephant shrew* (Rhynchocyon cirnei) *scentmarking with its anal glands;* ***2*** *Rufous elephant shrew* (Elephantulus rufescens) *foraging for insects;* ***3*** *Short-eared elephant shrew* (Macroscelides proboscideus) *clearing a trail;* ***4*** *North African elephant shrew* (Elephantulus rozeti) *washing its face at a burrow entrance;* ***5*** *Four-toed elephant shrew* (Petrodromus tetradactylus) *extruding its tongue after insects;* ***6*** *Black and rufous elephant shrew* (Rhynchocyon petersi) *tearing at prey with its teeth and claws;* ***7*** *Golden-rumped elephant shrew* (R. chrysopygus) *stalking before a chase.*

ORDER: MACROSCELIDEA

Elephant shrews or Sengis
Family: Macroscelididae
2 subfamilies; 4 genera; 15 species

Distribution N Africa, E, C and S Africa, absent from W Africa and Sahara

Habitat Varied, including montane and lowland forest, savanna, steppe, desert.

Size Ranges from Short-eared elephant shrew, with **head-body length** 10.4–11.5cm (4.1–4.5in), **tail length** 11.5–13cm (4.5–5in), **weight** about 45g (1.6oz), to the Golden-rumped elephant shrew with a **head-body length** of 27–29.4cm (11–12in), **tail length** 23–25.5cm (9.5–10.5in), **weight** about 540g (19 oz).

Coat Soft, in various shades of gray and brown.

Diet Beetles, spiders, centipedes, earthworms, ants, termites and other small invertebrates; also fruits and seeds.

Breeding Gestation 57–65 days in the Rufous elephant shrew, about 42 days in the Golden-rumped elephant shrew.

Longevity $2\frac{1}{2}$ years in the Rufous elephant shrew ($5\frac{1}{2}$ in captivity), 4 years in the Golden-rumped elephant shrew.

Conservation status *R. chrysopygus, R. petersi,* and *E. revoili* are classed as Endangered; *R. cirnei, M. proboscideus, E. edwardii,* and *E. rupestris* as Vulnerable.

GENUS *RHYNCHOCYON*

Golden-rumped elephant shrew (*Rhynchocyon chrysopygus*), Black and rufous elephant shrew (*R. petersi*), Checkered elephant shrew (*R. cirnei*).

GENUS *PETRODROMUS*

Four-toed elephant shrew (*Petrodromus tetradactylus*)

GENUS *MACROSCELIDES*

Short-eared elephant shrew (*Macroscelides proboscideus*)

GENUS *ELEPHANTULUS*

Short-nosed elephant shrew (*Elephantulus brachyrhynchus*), Cape elephant shrew (*E. edwardii*), Dusky-footed elephant shrew (*E. fuscipes*), Dusky elephant shrew (*E. fuscus*), Bushveld elephant shrew (*E. intufi*), Eastern rock elephant shrew (*E. myurus*), Somali elephant shrew (*E. revoili*), North African elephant shrew (*E. rozeti*), Rufous elephant shrew (*E. rufescens*), Western rock elephant shrew (*E. rupestris*).

Note: Elephant shrews may shortly be reassigned, with other endemic African placentals (e.g. golden moles, tenrecs, and elephants), to a new grouping, the "Afrotheria" – see p.723.

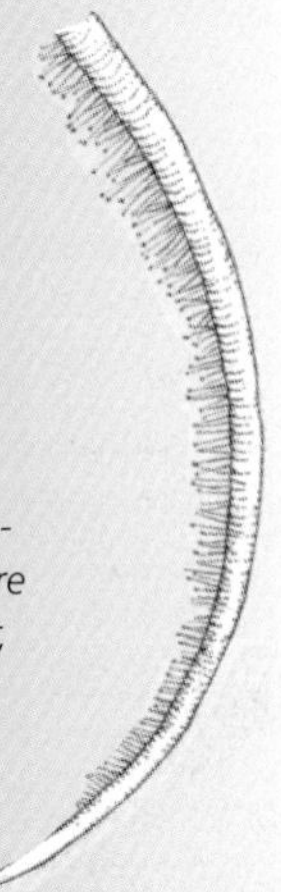

Right *Elephant shrew tails – the one shown is from the Four-toed elephant shrew – are lined with knobbed bristles. Their exact function is controversial, but it has been noted that, during aggressive and sexual encounters, individuals lash their tails across the ground, dragging the bristles across the substrate. It may be that the animals are scentmarking through this behavior, with the knobs acting as swabs to spread scent-bearing sebum from large glands on the tail's undersurface.*

Right *Rufous elephant shrews visibly mark their territories by creating small piles of dung in areas where the paths of two adjoining pairs meet. Occasionally aggressive encounters occur in these territorial arenas. In these situations, two animals of the same sex face one another and, while slowly walking in opposite directions, stand high on their long legs and accentuate their white feet, much like small mechanical toys. If neither of the animals then retreats, a fight usually develops and the loser is routed from the area.*

Below *A perfect ball of fur but for the protruding nose, a Short-eared elephant shrew basks in the sun. The species – the only representative of the* Macroscelides *genus – is limited to a region of about 20,000sq km (7,700sq mi) of southern African plain and desert, and is listed as Vulnerable by the IUCN.*

little time together. The male and female share precisely the same territory, but defend this area individually, with females seeing off other females and males evicting intruding males. This system of monogamy, characterized by limited cooperation between the sexes, is also found in several small antelopes, such as the dikdik and klipspringer. As in most monogamous mammals, the sexes are similar in size and appearance, but male giant elephant shrews have larger canine teeth.

In territorial encounters, visual signals are important, but elephant shrews also bring to bear their scent glands to mark out their land. These are located on the bottom of the tail in several *Elephantulus* species, on the soles of the feet in the Rufous elephant shrew, on the chest of the Dusky-footed, Rufous, and Somali elephant shrews, and just behind the anus in the giant elephant shrews of the *Rhynchocyon* genus. Vocal communication is unimportant, although the Four-toed elephant shrew and some species of *Elephantulus* create sounds by drumming their rear feet on the ground, while *Rhynchocyon* species slap their tails on the leaf litter. When captured, several elephant-shrew species emit sharp, high-pitched screams, although all are surprisingly gentle when handled and rarely attempt to bite despite their well-developed teeth.

In several respects elephant shrews are similar to small ungulates, especially in their avoidance of predators. Initially they rely on camouflage to elude detection, but if this fails they use their long legs to swiftly outdistance pursuing snakes and carnivores. This is no mean feat for a creature standing only 6cm (2.4in) high at the shoulder and weighing 58g (2oz); the trick is achieved by utilizing a system of trails to rival the road network of a city like London.

Even so, this explanation begs a question about the purpose of monogamy in the case of the Golden-rumped elephant shrew, which does not clear trails, apparently leaving the male of the pair jobless. The answer in its case lies in the forest habitat it inhabits. The tropical climate allows these particular sengis to breed continuously throughout the year, and their food resources are relatively evenly and widely distributed. Under these circumstances, the most productive strategy for a male may be to remain with one female, ensuring that he fathers her young, rather than to wander over huge expanses of forest trying to keep track of the reproductive condition of several females, and thereby running the very real risk of missing opportunities to mate. This resource-based explanation for monogamy is also thought to explain the paired sex lives of several small antelopes, such as the dikdik and some duikers.

In contrast to the path-using Four-toed and Rufous elephant shrews, several other sengis, including the Short-eared, Western rock, and Bushveld species, dig short, shallow burrows in sandy substrates for shelter. Where the ground is too hard, these species will use abandoned rodent burrows. But even the burrow-using sengis do not incorporate nesting material in their shelters, as do most rodents. The giant elephant shrews are more typical of small mammals, in that they spend each night in a leaf nest on the forest floor. To deny predators the reward of a meal in each nest that they find and tear open, the elephant shrews build several nests and then sleep alone in a different nest every few nights.

ON THE TRAIL OF THE RUFOUS ELEPHANT SHREW

Near Tsavo National Park in Kenya, the Rufous elephant shrew lives in dense thickets in which each pair builds, maintains, and defends a complex network of criss-crossing trails. To enable the sengis to run at full speed along these paths, the trails must be kept immaculately clean. Just a single twig could break an elephant shrew's flight from a fast-moving predator with disastrous consequences, so the sengis regularly go road-sweeping. Every day, individuals of a pair spend 20–40 percent of the daylight hours separately traversing much of their trail network, removing accumulated leaves and twigs with swift sidestrokes of their fore feet. Little-used paths consist merely of a series of small, bare, oval patches on the sandy soil on which the sengi lands as it bounds along the trail; those that are heavily used form continuous bare channels through the litter.

The trails of Rufous elephant shrews, and also those of *Petrodromus*, are exceptionally important because neither species nests or lives in burrows or shelters. They spend their entire lives relatively exposed, as would small antelopes. Their distinct black-and-white facial pattern probably serves to disrupt the contour of their large black eyes, thus camouflaging them from predators while they are exposed on the trails.

The Rufous elephant shrew produces only 1 or 2 highly precocial and independent young per litter. Since the female alone can nurse her young, the male of the pair can do little to assist. This begs the question of why the animals should be monogamous in the first place.

In the Rufous elephant shrew, part of the answer apparently relates to the system of paths. Males spend nearly twice as much time trail-cleaning as females do – a rather similar arrangement to that of mara couples, which are also monogamous and in which the males put their effort into vigilance, freeing the female to graze. Although this sort of indirect help is not as obvious as the direct cooperation of wolf and marmoset pairs in raising their altricial young, it is just as vital to the elephant shrew's reproductive success, for without paths, its ungulate-like habits would be completely ineffective.

Sengis in the tropics produce several litters throughout the year, but at higher latitudes reproduction becomes seasonal, usually in association with the wet season. Litters normally contain one or two young, but the North African elephant shrew and Checkered elephant shrew may produce three young per litter. Although all elephant shrews are born in a well-developed state with a coat pattern similar to that of adults, the young of giant elephant shrews are not as precocial as those of the soft-furred species, and thus they are confined to the nest for several days before they accompany their mother.

Giant elephant shrews are exceedingly difficult to keep in captivity, and they have never been bred. In contrast, the Rufous and Short-eared elephant shrews have been successfully exhibited and bred in several zoos, which has resulted in numerous laboratory studies of their biology. For example, physiological studies of Short-eared elephant shrews have shown that they can go into torpor, with body temperatures dropping from about 37°C (98.6°F) to as low as 9.5°C (49°F) for short periods when food resources are limited. This is thought to be an adaptation to conserve energy. Research on captive Rufous elephant shrews has shown that they can recognize the identities of family members and neighbors from scentmarks alone, so individuals can presumably closely monitor the use of their large territories by smell as well as by sight.

Above *Looking somewhat like a miniature anteater, a melanistic variant of the Checkered elephant shrew* (Rhynchocyon cirnei) *combs the forest floor for insects.*

Disappearing Forests

CONSERVATION AND ENVIRONMENT

Generally, sengis are of little economic importance to man, although Golden-rumped and Four-toed elephant shrews are snared and eaten along the Kenya coast. This subsistence trapping is illegal, but is so far thought to be sustainable. A bigger problem for these forest-dwellers is severe habitat depletion, especially for those species occupying small, isolated patches of woodland in eastern Africa that are being degraded by tree-cutting for the woodcarving trade, or else being destroyed outright to make way for subsistence farming, exotic tree plantations, or urban developments. It would be a dreadful loss if these unique, colorful mammals were to disappear after more than 50 million years just because their dwindling patches of forest could not be adequately protected. GBR

Escape and Protection

The tactics and adaptations of the Golden-rumped elephant shrew

THE AFRICAN SUN WAS JUST STARTING TO SET when a Golden-rumped elephant shrew made its way up to an indistinct pile of leaves about 1m (3ft) wide on the forest floor. The animal paused at the edge of the low mound for 15 seconds, sniffing, listening, and watching for the least irregularity. Sensing nothing unusual, it quietly slipped under the leaves. The leaf nest shuddered for a few seconds as the elephant shrew arranged itself for the night, then everything was still.

At about the same time the animal's mate was retreating for the night into a similar nest located on the other side of the pair's home range. As this elephant shrew prepared to enter its nest, a twig snapped somewhere. The animal froze, and then quietly left the area for a third nest, which it eventually entered, but not before dusk had fallen.

Every evening, within a few minutes of sunset, pairs of elephant shrews like this one separately approach and cautiously enter any one of a dozen or more nests they have constructed throughout their home range. They use a different nest each evening to discourage forest predators such as leopards and eagle-owls from ascertaining exactly where they can be found.

Changing nests is just one of several stratagems Golden-rumped elephant shrews regularly use to avoid predators. The problem they face is considerable. During the day they spend over 75 percent of their time exposed while foraging in leaf litter on the forest floor, where they fall prey to Black mambas, Forest cobras, and harrier eagles. To prevent capture by such enemies the animals have developed tactics that involve not only the ability to run fast but also a distinctive coat pattern that is notable for its flashy coloration.

Extraordinarily, Golden-rumped elephant shrews can bound across open forest floor at speeds above 25km/h (16mph)—about as fast as an average person can run. Because they are relatively small, they can also pass easily through patches of undergrowth, leaving larger terrestrial and aerial predators behind as they do so. Despite their speed and agility, however, they still remain vulnerable to ambush by sit-and-wait predators, such as the Southern banded harrier eagle. Most small terrestrial mammals have cryptic coloration on their coats or skins to serve as camouflage. However, the forest floor along the coast of Kenya where the Golden-rumped elephant shrew lives is relatively open, so any defense against predation that relied on camouflage would be ineffective.

Instead, the elephant shrew's tactic is to actively invite predators to take notice of it. It has a rump patch that is so visible that a waiting predator will discover a foraging shrew while it is too far away to make a successful ambush. The predator's initial reaction to the sight, such as rapidly turning its head or shifting its weight from one leg to another, may be enough to reveal its presence. By inducing the predator to disclose prematurely its intent to attack, a surprise ambush can be averted.

An elephant shrew that discovers a predator while still outside its flight distance does not bound away; instead it pauses and then repeatedly slaps the leaf litter with its tail at intervals of a few seconds. The sharp sound produced probably conveys a message to the predator: "I know you are there, but you are outside my flight distance, and I can probably outrun you if you attack." Through experience, the predator learns that when it hears this signal it is generally futile to attempt a pursuit,

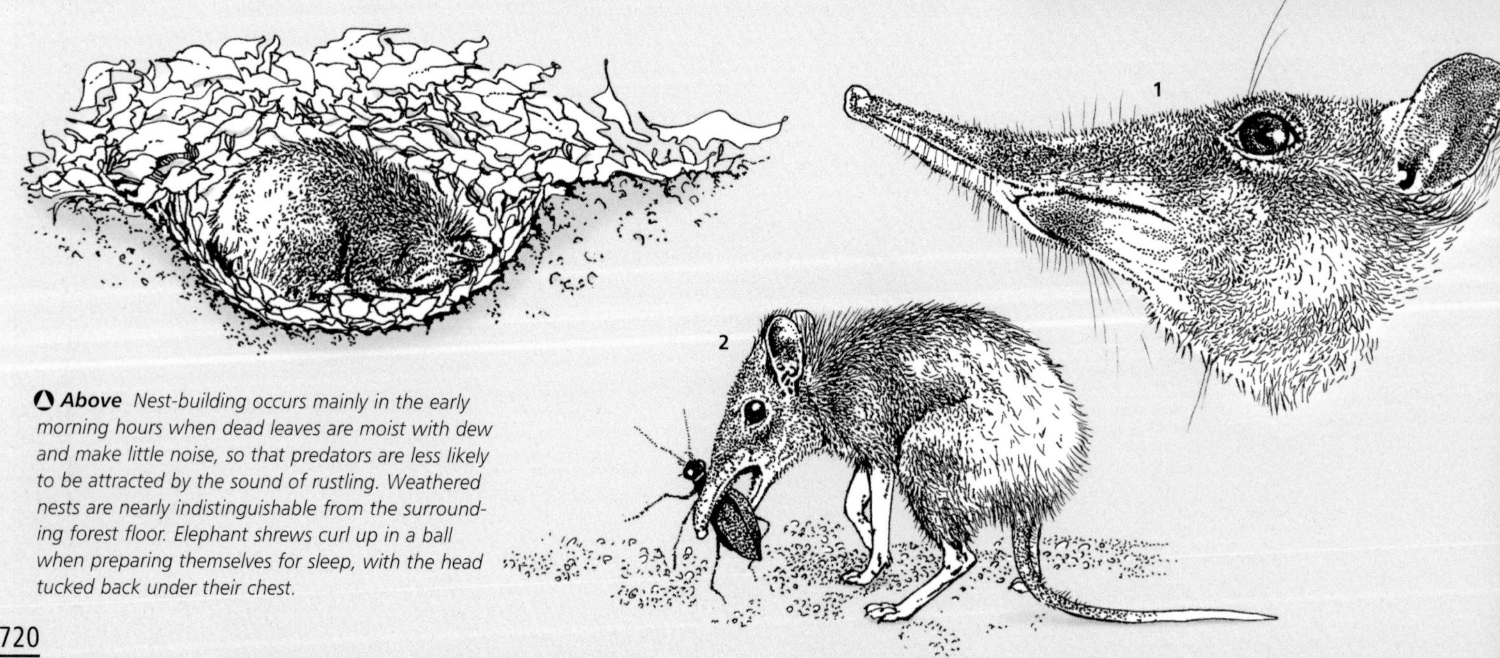

Above *Nest-building occurs mainly in the early morning hours when dead leaves are moist with dew and make little noise, so that predators are less likely to be attracted by the sound of rustling. Weathered nests are nearly indistinguishable from the surrounding forest floor. Elephant shrews curl up in a ball when preparing themselves for sleep, with the head tucked back under their chest.*

*◀ ▲ **Above and Left** Foraging in the leaf litter on the forest floor. The Golden-rumped elephant shrew has a small mouth **1** located far behind the top of its snout, which makes it difficult to ingest large prey items. Small invertebrates are eaten by flicking them into the mouth with a long, extensible tongue. **2** In the Arabuko-Sokoke forest of coastal Kenya, elephant shrews feed mainly on beetles, centipedes, termites, cockroaches, ants, spiders, and earthworms, in decreasing order of importance.*

because the animal is on guard and can easily make its escape back to a place of refuge.

The situation is very different when an elephant shrew becomes aware of a predator – say, for example, an eagle – so close that a safe escape cannot be guaranteed. In those circumstances, the animal will take flight across the forest floor towards the nearest cover as the bird swoops to make its kill, noisily pounding the leaf litter with its rear legs as it bounds away. Only speed and agility can save it in such a situation.

The Golden-rumped elephant shrew is monogamous, but pairs spend only about 20 percent of their time in visual contact with each other; the remainder is spent resting or foraging alone. So for most of the time they must communicate via scent or sound. The distinct sound of an elephant shrew tail-slapping or bounding across the forest floor can be heard over a large part of a pair's 1.5ha (3.7 acre) territory. These sounds not only signal to the predator that it has been discovered, but also communicate to the elephant shrew's mate and young that an intruder has been detected.

Each pair of elephant shrews defends its territorial boundaries against neighbors and wandering subadults in search of their own territories. During an aggressive encounter a resident will pursue an intruder on a high-speed chase through the forest. If the intruder is not fast enough, it will be gashed by the long canines of the resident.

These conflicts between elephant shrews can be thought of as a special type of predator–prey interaction, revealing yet another way in which the animal's coloration may serve to avoid successful predation. The skin under the animal's rump patch is up to three times thicker than that on the middle of its back. The golden color of the rump probably serves as a target, diverting attacks on such vital parts of the body as the head and flanks to an area of the body that is better suited to take assaults.

Deflective marks are common in invertebrates, and have been shown to be effective in foiling predators; for example, the distinctive eye spots on the wings of some butterflies attract the predatory attacks of birds, allowing the insects to escape relatively unscathed. The yellow rump and the white tip on the black tail of the elephant shrew may serve a similar function by attracting the talons of an eagle or the fangs of a striking snake, thus improving the animal's chances of making a successful escape. GBR

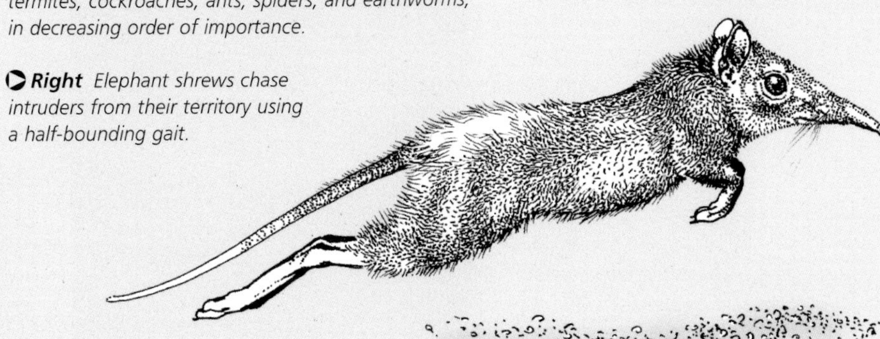

*▶ **Right** Elephant shrews chase intruders from their territory using a half-bounding gait.*

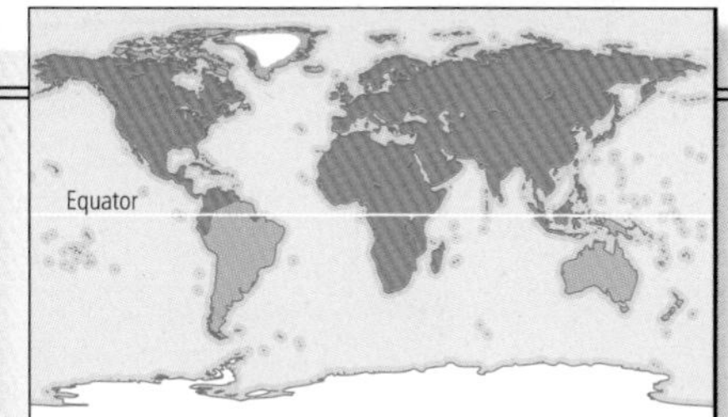

INSECTIVORES

ALTHOUGH AMONG THE LARGEST ORDERS OF mammals, the Insectivora (or Lipotyphla) is still one of the least well-studied. All insectivores are small animals (none larger than rabbits) with long, narrow snouts that are usually very mobile. Most move by walking or running, although some swim and/or burrow. Body shapes vary widely, from the streamlined form of the otter shrews to the short, fat body of hedgehogs and moles. All walk with their soles and heels on the ground (plantigrade gait) and most have short limbs, with five digits on each foot. Eyes and ears are sometimes so small as not to be visible.

The insectivores are often divided into three suborders to emphasize the relationships between the families. The Tenrecomorpha comprises tenrecs and golden moles; the hedgehogs and moonrats (the latter considered the most primitive of the living insectivores) are placed in the Erinaceomorpha; and the Soricomorpha consists of shrews, moles, and solenodons.

However, recent DNA analysis suggests that the golden moles and tenrecs should be assigned to a new order – the Afrosoricida – which is part of the supraordinal assemblage that make up the Afrotheria (see panel opposite and the introductory essay What is a Mammal?). Correspondingly in this new scheme, the shrews, moles, and hedgehogs become a new order, the Eulipotyphla. While anticipating these changes, this section retains traditional insectivore systematics until a consensus is confirmed.

While the order as a whole is very widely distributed, only three families can be said to be widespread. These are the Erinaceidae (hedgehogs and moonrats), Talpidae (moles and desmans), and Soricidae (shrews), which between them account for almost all of the worldwide distribution. The other three families have very limited distributions indeed! The Solenodontidae (solenodons) are found only on the Caribbean islands of Hispaniola and Cuba. The Tenrecidae (tenrecs) are also found mainly on islands – Madagascar and the Comoros in the Indian Ocean – with some members of the family (the otter shrews) occurring only in the wet regions of Central Africa. Because of the differences in their distribution, lifestyle, and habitat, the otter shrews were at various times considered to be in a separate family, the Potamogalidae, although their teeth indicate that they are true tenrecs; they are treated in the following pages as a subfamily of the tenrecs. The golden moles occur only in the drier parts of southern Africa.

Above *An Alpine shrew* (Sorex alpinus) *in a Bavarian forest. Shrews are by far the most speciose family of the order Insectivora.*

Primitive Placentals

INSECTIVORE SYSTEMATICS

As a group, the insectivores are generally considered to be the most primitive of living placental mammals and therefore representative of the ancestral mammals from which modern mammals are derived. This was not the original purpose of the grouping. The term "insectivore" was first used in a system of classification produced in 1816 to describe hedgehogs, shrews, and Old-World moles (all primarily insect-eaters). The order soon became a "rag bag" into which any animal was placed that could not be neatly assigned elsewhere. In 1817, the naturalist Georges Cuvier added the American moles, tenrecs, golden moles, and desmans. Forty years later, tree shrews, elephant shrews, and colugos were included. All were new discoveries in need of classification but none looked much like any other members of the group.

Confronted in 1866 by an order Insectivora containing a number of very different animals, the taxonomist Ernst Haeckel subdivided it into two distinct groups that he called Menotyphla and Lipotyphla. Menotyphlans (tree shrews, elephant shrews, and colugos) were distinguished by the presence of a cecum (the human appendix) at the beginning of the large intestine; lipotyphlans (moles, golden moles, tenrecs, and shrews) by its absence. Menotyphlans also differ greatly from

Below *In contrast to shrews and moles, hedgehogs are not generally territorial and appear to wander at random on their foraging expeditions.*

lipotyphlans in external appearance: large eyes and long legs are only two of the more obvious characters. The colugos are so different that the new order Dermoptera was created for them as early as 1872. In 1926 the anatomist Le Gros Clarke suggested that the tree shrews are more similar to lemur-like primates than to insectivores, but the most modern view is that tree shrews comprise a separate order, the Scandentia. The elephant shrews also cannot be readily assigned to any existing order, so they have become the sole family in the new order Macroscelidea. Modern phylogenetic analyses also present conflicting results concerning the origins of remaining families in the Insectivora. Morphological analyses suggest that lipotyphlan members of the group are probably descended from a common ancestor, but molecular evidence indicates that this is unlikely. Multiple origins may also be assumed for the fossil members of the Insectivora, which includes a vast assortment of early mammals and remains very much a "waste-basket" group. Many of these early forms are known only from fossil fragments and teeth; they are assigned to the Insectivora largely as a matter of convenience, having insectivore affinities and no clear links with anything else.

Interestingly, the phylogenetic placement of afrotherians (and edentates – the armadillos) – see below – at the base of the placental mammal evolutionary tree suggests that the earliest placental mammals were habitually terrestrial, not arboreal, as has been argued in the past.

Primitive and Derived Characters

EVOLUTIONARY BIOLOGY

Not all of the insectivores are primitive mammals. Most living species have evolved specializations of form and behavior that mask some of their truly primitive characters (namely, those features that probably would have been found in their ancestors). These are contrasted with "derived" (or advanced) characters, found in animals that have developed structures and habits not found in their ancestors. The cecum is a primitive character, and its lack is therefore a derived character, a feature of the Insectivora as it now stands. There are, however, a number of characters considered to be primitive which are more commonly found in the

ORDER: INSECTIVORA (LIPOTYPHLA)
6 families; 67 genera; 424 species

TENRECS Family Tenrecidae p728

24 species in 10 genera
Includes **Aquatic tenrec** (*Limnogale mergulus*), **Common tenrec** (*Tenrec ecaudatus*), **Giant otter shrew** (*Potamogale velox*).

SOLENODONS Family Solenodontidae p732

2 species in a single genus
Hispaniola solenodon (*Solenodon paradoxus*), **Cuban solenodon** (*Solenodon cubanus*).

HEDGEHOGS Family Erinaceidae p734

23 species in 7 genera
Includes **Western European hedgehog** (*Erinaceus europaeus*), **Greater moonrat** (*Echinosorex gymnura*), **Lesser gymnure** (*Hylomys suillus*).

SHREWS Family Soricidae p742

312 species in 23 genera
Includes **Eurasian water shrew** (*Neomys fodiens*), **European common shrew** (*Sorex araneus*), **Vagrant shrew** (*Sorex vagrans*).

GOLDEN MOLES Family Chrysochloridae p748

21 species in 9 genera
Includes **Giant golden mole** (*Chrysospalax trevelyani*).

MOLES AND DESMANS Family Talpidae p750

42 species in 17 genera
Includes **European mole** (*Talpa europaea*), **Pyrenean desman** (*Galemys pyrenaicus*), **Russian desman** (*Desmana moschata*), **Star-nosed mole** (*Condylura cristata*).

THE AFROTHERIA – A NEW GROUPING

The Insectivora or Lipotyphla may be totally re-aligned as a result of molecular findings that point to an ecologically diverse assemblage of endemic African placentals – the "Afrotheria."

Placental mammals began to diversify in the later Cretaceous, after continental drift had isolated the Afro-Arabian landmass. Because primitive placentals were present in northern continents (Laurasia) at this time, many paleontologists discounted Afro-Arabia as a major center for early placental diversification. Yet it now appears that the southern continents (Gondwana) in fact played a seminal role, with Afrotheria possibly as the very first branch on the placental family tree. Certain characters, such as a very basic male reproductive system and a poorly-developed, almost "reptilian" thermoregulatory system, show the afrotherians to be more primitive than other placentals.

The recognition of Afrotheria as a distinct clade reveals a remarkable pattern of parallel adaptation in the independent evolutionary histories of Gondwanan and Laurasian placentals. Similar selection pressures acting on a similar skeletal body plan produced ricochetal herbivorous forms (e.g., Gondwanan elephant shrews vs. Laurasian rabbits), burrowing forms (golden moles vs. true moles), habitually aquatic forms (manatees vs. whales), and dedicated herbivores (hyraxes vs. perissodactyls). ES

Insectivora than in other mammalian orders. These include relatively small brains, with few wrinkles to increase the surface area, primitive teeth, with incisors, canines, and molars easily distinguishable, and primitive features of the auditory bones and collar bones. Other primitive characteristics shared by some or all insectivores are intra-abdominal testes (i.e. no scrotal sac), a plantigrade gait, and possession of a cloaca, a common chamber into which the genital, urinary and fecal passages empty. Some of these primitive features, such as the cloaca and abdominal testes, are also characteristic of the marsupials, but insectivores, like all Eutherian (placental) mammals, are distinguished by the possession of the chorio-allantoic placenta, which permits the young to develop fully within the womb.

Many insectivores have acquired extremely specialized features, such as the spines of the hedgehogs and tenrecs, the poisonous saliva of the solenodons and some shrews, and the adaptations for burrowing found in many insectivore families. A number of shrew and tenrec species are thought to have developed a system of echolocation similar to that used by bats.

Below *Hedgehogs will feed on birds' eggs and young when the opportunity arises. Their extremely varied diet also includes all manner of invertebrates, such as earthworms, beetles, and slugs.*

If all these derived characters are disregarded, it is possible to sketch a very general impression of early mammals. They would have been shy animals, running along the ground in the leaf litter but capable of climbing trees or shrubs. Small and active, about the size of a modern mouse or shrew (the largest known fossil is about the size of a Eurasian badger), they probably fed mainly on insects; some may have been scavengers. They would have looked much like modern shrews, with small eyes and a long, pointed snout with perhaps a few long sensory hairs or true whiskers. A dense coat of short fur would have covered all of the body except the ears and soles of the paws. It is speculated that they may have had a dun-colored coat, with a stripe of darker color running through the eye and along the side of the body – a common pattern, found even on reptiles and amphibians. The development of the ability to regulate body temperature, combined with the warm mammalian coat, meant that the early mammals could be active at night when the dinosaurs (their competitors and predators) were largely inactive due to lower air temperatures.

From this basic stock, two slightly different forms are believed to have developed, known today only from teeth and fragments of bone dating from the late Cretaceous (80 million years ago). These two groups are characterized mainly by very different teeth. It appears that one group, the Paleaoryctoidea, eventually gave rise to the creodonts, a type of early carnivore, while the Leptictoidea were once thought to have produced the modern insectivores. Recent research on leptictoid fossils suggests instead that most of them were less closely related to the Insectivora, and were perhaps "dead-end" offshoots from the main branch of insectivore evolution.

INSECTIVORE BODY PLAN

Right *Skeleton of the Vagrant shrew, a typical insectivore. The skull is elongate and flattened. Typical characteristics of insectivores include a small brain case, and the absence of a zygomatic arch (cheek bone), in all except hedgehogs and moles, or auditory bullae (bony) prominences around the ear opening. The teeth of shrews are well differentiated into molars, premolars, and canines, with pincer-like front incisors. The dental formula of the Vagrant shrew is I3/1, C1/1, P3/1, M3/3 = 32. The teeth are partially colored by a brownish-red pigment.*

Below *Skulls of insectivores. Unlike shrews, the cheek bone of hedgehogs is fully formed. The front incisors are enlarged and the molars are adapted to an omnivorous rather than an insectivorous diet. The dental formula is I2–3/3, C1/1, P3–4/2–4, M3/3 = 36–44. The Common tenrec has a long, tapered snout and, in the adult male, long canines, the tips of the bottom pair fitting into pits in front of the upper ones. The dental formula is I2/3, C1/1, P2/3, M3/3 = 36. Solenodons have an unusual cartilaginous snout which articulates with the skull via a "ball-and-socket" joint. Solenodons produce a toxic saliva which is released from a gland at the base of the second lower incisor. The dental formula is I3/3, C1/1, P3/3, M3/3 = 40.*

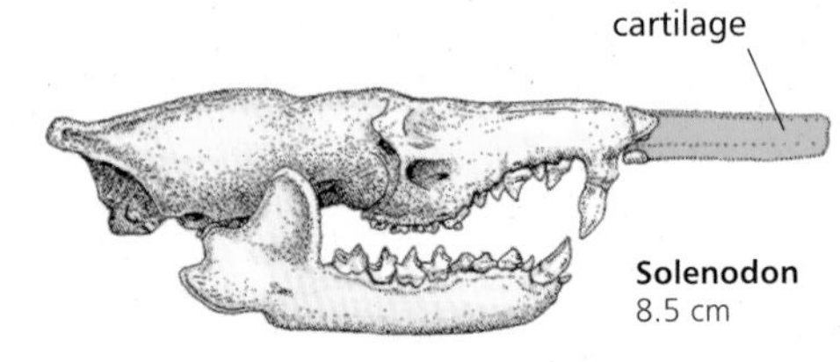

Diversify and Survive

ADAPTIVE SUCCESS

Despite the evolutionary relationships between the families, insectivores have little in common other than their apparent primitiveness. It is perhaps this diversity that is responsible for the success of the three larger families. The family Talpidae contains both the true moles, which live mainly in subterranean burrows, and the desmans, which spend much of their time in the water and construct burrows in stream banks only

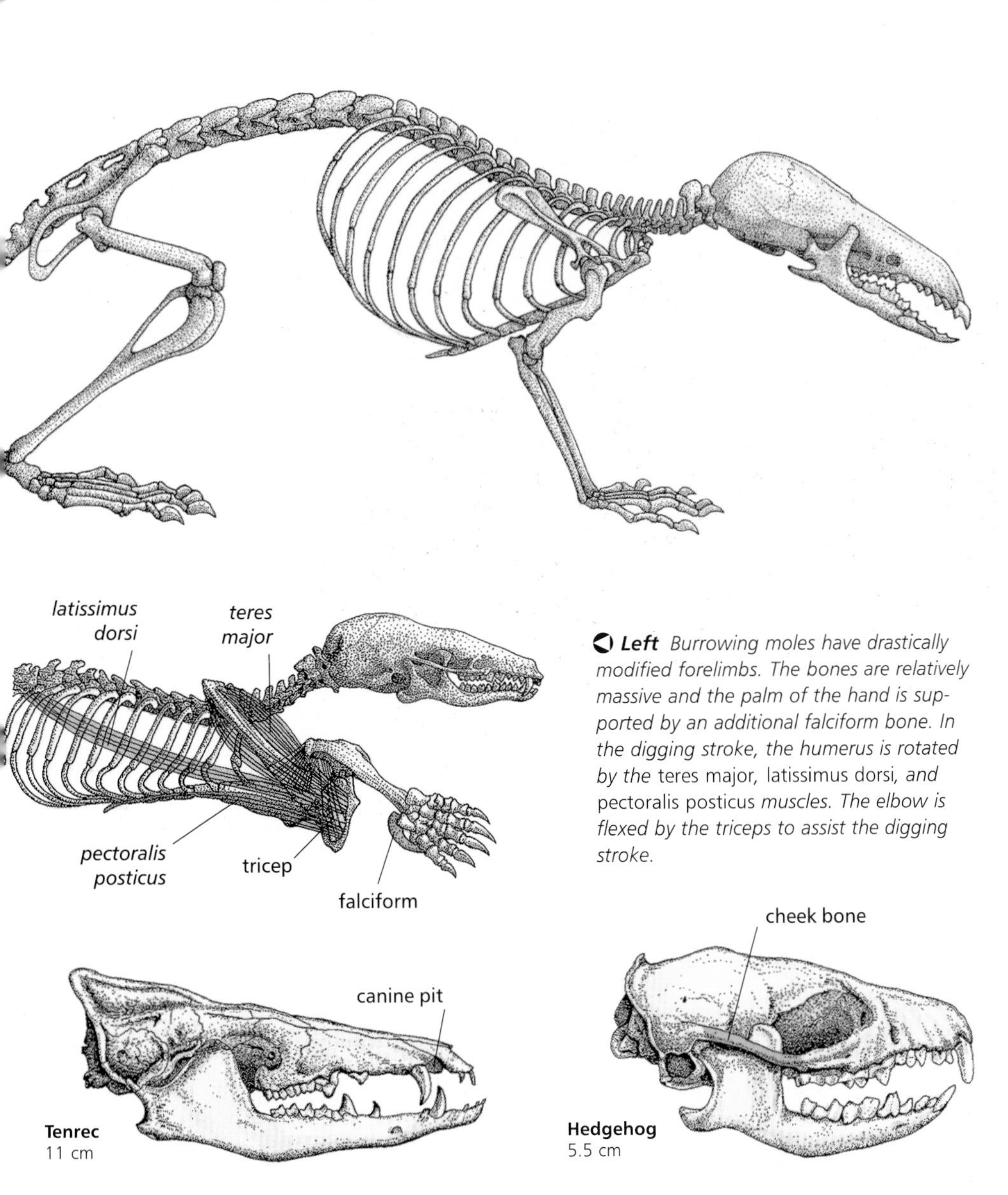

Left *Burrowing moles have drastically modified forelimbs. The bones are relatively massive and the palm of the hand is supported by an additional falciform bone. In the digging stroke, the humerus is rotated by the* teres major, latissimus dorsi, *and* pectoralis posticus *muscles. The elbow is flexed by the triceps to assist the digging stroke.*

for shelter. Similarly, the mainly terrestrial family Tenrecidae also includes the rice tenrecs, which burrow in the banks of rice paddies, while the Aquatic tenrec leads a semi-aquatic life. The Soricidae show adaptations to every type of habitat – as well as the "standard" shrew, running along the ground, there are also species, such as the American short-tailed shrew, that burrow like miniature moles, and those like the European water shrew that swim like the tenrecid otter shrews.

The order Insectivora is rich in examples of convergent evolution. Moles and golden moles, for example, are not closely related within the order yet both have adopted similar burrowing lifestyles and even look much alike. According to the fossil record, moles developed from an animal resembling a shrew, whereas golden moles appear to be more closely related to the tenrecs. The similarity between golden moles and the marsupial moles of Australia is even more remarkable. In this case, the lineages have been separate for 70 million years; one is placental, the other pouched – yet the golden mole is more similar in appearance to the marsupial moles (even in the texture of its fur) than to the true mole. The eyes of both marsupial and golden moles are covered by skin – the eyelids have fused, whereas the minute eyes of the true moles are still functional.

The ability to curl up, combined with a dense coat of spines (as in hedgehogs and some species of tenrecs), is an obvious deterrent to predators. Some non-spiny species, moles and shrews for example, have strongly distasteful secretions from skin glands which may have a similar effect. Many of the other specializations are more likely to be the result of competition for food. If two or more species compete for food or some other resource, then either the worst competitor will become (at least locally) extinct, or all will evolve to specialize on different aspects of the resource and reduce the competition. Moles, for example, may have developed their burrowing lifestyle to avoid both predation and competition with surface-dwelling insectivores. Some species of both shrews and moles have become semi-aquatic, probably to exploit a different source of invertebrate food.

The tenrecs are thought to have been one of the first mammalian groups to arrive on Madagascar. Like the Australian marsupials, they provide a fascinating example of adaptive radiation, having evolved, in the absence of competition with an established fauna, a variety of forms which use most of the available habitats.

Insectivores rely heavily on their sense of smell to locate their prey, as would be expected from the relatively large center of smell in the brain. Invertebrates are the main food – most insectivores are thought to feed on insects and earthworms, although some of those associated with water also eat mollusks and possibly fish. Where food habits have been closely studied, the animals appear to eat almost anything organic they find or can catch, and many will attempt to kill prey which are substantially larger than themselves: hedgehogs, for example, can kill chickens; water shrews can kill frogs. The poisonous saliva of solenodons and some shrews may have evolved to enable these animals to catch larger prey than their body size would normally permit. The poison acts mainly on the nervous system, paralyzing the victim.

Shrews, in particular, have a reputation for gluttony, consuming more than their own bodyweight daily, but recent studies indicate that their food is less nutritious than the dry seeds eaten by rodents of a similar size, so they need to consume a correspondingly greater bulk. High food requirements also result from the high metabolic rates of the shrews, which in the case of some northern shrews may be an adaptation to a highly seasonal climate. The respiration rate of a shrew can be more than 5,000cu cm (305cu in) of air per kilogram of body weight per hour, compared with 200cu cm (12cu in) for humans.

Reported litter sizes vary widely in those species that have been studied. Females of the genus *Tenrec* have been found to have up to 32 developing embryos, of which probably only 12–16 survive to birth. Other tenrec species, along with moles, hedgehogs, and shrews, have litters of 2–10; solenodons have only one or two young per litter. Young are typically altricial or underdeveloped at birth; newborn shrews of the genus *Sorex* may weigh as little as 0.25g. The offspring develop rapidly, and, in large litters, mortality can result from high levels of competition. The timing of the breeding season is governed mainly by food availability and thus the young of animals living in arid areas are usually born in the rainy season (winter), while temperate species breed in the spring and summer. Some tropical species (the moonrats, for example) are thought to breed throughout the year.

Solitary but Promiscuous

SOCIAL BIOLOGY

Because most insectivores are shy, nocturnal, secretive creatures, they do not lend themselves to field study. Thus, relatively little is known about their social biology. Those few species that have been the subject of research (mainly shrews, plus some hedgehogs and tenrecs) are solitary, with little communication between adults except at breeding times. Studies of European hedgehogs indicate that individuals do not defend territories, although shrews do.

Shrews are territorial in that their home ranges – about 500sq m (5,400sq ft) in the European common shrew – are mutually exclusive. When shrews meet they generally act aggressively. Home ranges are often maintained by juveniles. Reproductive females may extend their ranges when breeding, which can result in some overlap of their movements. Mating systems have been studied for several species of shrews. Promiscuity is probably the most common mating pattern and multiple paternity is known in some species. In the European common shrew, litters may be sired by up to six different males, and there is considerable overlap of male movements during the breeding season. Monogamy is also known to occur in at least one shrew – the European house shrew. Unlike the European common shrew, males of this species defend exclusive access to females and may invest in care of their offspring. Moles are even less sociable and, once the juveniles have been expelled from a female's burrow system, she will not normally tolerate another mole in her home burrow except for a few hours in the spring when she is ready to mate. It is likely that scent plays an important role in keeping moles apart, and they are probably circumspect about entering unfamiliar places smelling of other moles. This pattern of mutual avoidance is probably common among some other insectivore groups too. Mole home ranges are essentially linear, being constrained by tunnel walls. The burrow system acts as a pitfall trap which collects soil invertebrates as prey and in poor soils, longer burrow systems are needed to supply sufficient food. Thus, a mole's linear home range may vary from 30–120m (100–400ft) or more, depending on soil type and food density. Surface activity, especially among dispersing juveniles may extend this home range considerably. Hedgehogs, such as the European hedgehog, which forage over an area from 1–5ha (2.5–12.5 acres) in a night, may use a home range of up to 30ha (74 acres) in a season; males travel further and have larger ranges than females. Unlike some small rodents, insectivores do not normally seem to make use of a three-dimensional home range by climbing into bushes and trees. In desmans, the home range is linear, along a stream edge; in tenrecs it is an area around the burrow or den; but for many species there is no detailed ecological information at all.

Friends and Enemies

CONSERVATION ISSUES

A large proportion of insectivore species is found only in tropical countries, where the primary emphasis is on development and exploitation of resources rather than wildlife conservation. Being in the main unprepossessing animals, threats to the survival of insectivores do not usually receive wide publicity.

Habitat destruction is undoubtedly the single most significant threat. In Western Europe, increasingly intensive farming methods and the drainage of wetlands are having a major impact on insectivore numbers and distribution. Worldwide, many species are in great peril. Thirteen Eurasian species are currently classified as Critically Endangered. Alarmingly, the lack of field data may conceal an even more desperate situation. Human introduction of new competitors and predators also poses a serious threat, particularly to the tenrecs and solenodons. These competitors, which are effective generalists and can thrive almost anywhere, also have high rates of reproduction, and so are able to overwhelm native species before they have a chance to adapt to the changed situation. For example, solenodons were the principal small carnivores in the Antilles until the 17th century, when the Spaniards brought with them dogs, cats, and rats. Mongooses were introduced in the late 19th century to combat a proliferation of Black rats. The latter two proved highly effective as competitors for food and all apparently added solenodons to their diet. Predation and forest clearance continue to put intense pressure on the remaining solenodon species, which are heavily dependent on conservation programs for their survival.

Left and Below Moles are solitary animals and usually do not trespass into each others' tunnel systems. However, they will quickly take over a territory if its occupant is removed. The extensive damage that moles can cause to pasture is evident from the line of spoil heaps in this English field.

The remnant Russian desman population is now protected by law, though numbers continue to decline. This species was once a staple of the fur trade, with tens of thousands of skins exported annually to western Europe, but hunting, combined with pollution of its aquatic habitat and competition from introduced coypus and muskrats, saw numbers fall drastically. The small population of Pyrenean desmans in the Pyrenees is threatened by water pollution and escaped mink. Several species of golden mole are also threatened by various changes in their habitat.

Few attempts have been made to domesticate insectivores, although hedgehogs are growing in popularity as pets, particularly in the United States. Hedgehogs have generally had a favorable relationship with humans. The folklore of both Europe and Asia abounds in tales of hedgehogs and although they are regarded as pests by some – notably gamekeepers and the greenkeepers on golf courses – householders in the urban areas of western Europe regularly provide them with bowls of food. The Asian musk shrew has apparently adapted well to use as a laboratory animal; in contrast, many other insectivores are difficult to breed in captivity. Elsewhere in the world, the larger insectivores are occasionally eaten (especially in Madagascar and the West Indies) and the smaller ones are probably rarely noticed. Most insectivores are too small and too scarce to be any use for food, and equally are unlikely to be serious economic pests. Yet some are extremely abundant, and it has been suggested that if all shrews were to disappear suddenly, the number of insect pests in fields and gardens would increase noticeably. Other insectivores are more likely to become accidental victims of human activities than to be persecuted as pests or fostered as allies.

Some species have been exploited as an economic resource. The Russian desmans have a dense lustrous coat and, in the past, considerable numbers of these animals were caught in nets and traps. They were also chased from their burrows and shot or clubbed. A century ago, a fortunate hunter might obtain 40 desman skins during the month-long hunting season at the time of the spring thaw. Despite their value, desman pelts were never a major commodity and the "industry" seems to have been opportunistic.

Moleskins were used extensively for garments and accessories from Roman times up to the 20th century. So heavy was the demand in Germany from the 17th century onward that fears were raised for the mole's survival there; however, changing fashions saw the market slump by 1914. However, just as demand was falling in Europe, a new market opened up in North America; even as late as the 1950s, a million moles a year were being trapped in Britain alone for skinning and export. Moleskins have now largely been supplanted by cheaper, more durable synthetic substitutes. AW/PS

Tenrecs

TENRECS AND OTTER SHREWS ARE REMARKABLE in having a greater diversity of shape and form than any other living family of insectivores. Yet this has been achieved in virtual isolation, since tenrecs themselves are confined to Madagascar, which they were one of the first mammals to colonize, and the otter shrews (Potamogalinae; sometimes regarded as a separate family) to West and central Africa.

Tenrecs retain characters that were perhaps more widespread among early placental mammals. These conservative features include a low and variable body temperature, retention of a common opening for the urogenital and anal tracts (the cloaca), and undescended testes in the male. Some of the family comprise a more conspicuous part of the native fauna than temperate zone insectivores, being either an important source of food, relatively large and bold, or conspicuously colored. Even though detailed studies of the family are few and restricted to a handful of species they provide an excellent basis for the elucidation of mammalian evolution. The earliest fossils date from Kenyan Miocene deposits (about 24 million years ago), but by then the Tenrecidae were well differentiated, and had probably long been part of the African fauna.

Diversity in Isolation

FORM AND FUNCTION

Among the largely nocturnal tenrecs and otter shrews, eyesight is generally poor, but the whiskers are sensitive, and smell and hearing are well developed. Vocalizations range from hissing and grunting to twittering and echolocation clicks. The brain is relatively small and the number of teeth ranges from 32–42.

The aquatic Tenrecidae are active creatures of streams, rivers, lakes, and swamps. The Giant otter shrew and Mount Nimba least otter shrew are confined to forest, but the Ruwenzori least otter shrew and the Aquatic tenrec are

Above *Species of tenrecs:* ***1*** *Aquatic tenrec* (Limnogale mergulus); ***2*** *Giant otter shrew* (Potamogale velox); ***3*** *Ruwenzori least otter shrew* (Micropotamogale ruwenzorii); ***4*** *Streaked tenrec* (Hemicentetes semispinosus nigriceps); ***5*** *Common tenrec* (Tenrec ecaudatus); ***6*** *Lesser hedgehog tenrec* (Echinops telfairi); ***7*** *Long-tailed tenrec* (Microgale melanorrachis); ***8*** *Greater hedgehog tenrec* (Setifer setosus); ***9*** *Four-toed rice tenrec* (Oryzorictes tetradactylus).

less restricted. All four species have a sleek, elegant body form with a distinctive, flattened head that allows the ears, eyes, and nostrils to project above the surface while most of the body remains submerged. Stout whiskers radiate from around the muzzle, providing a means of locating prey. The fur is dense and soft; frequent grooming ensures that it is waterproof and traps insulating air during dives. Grooming is accomplished by means of the two fused toes on each hind foot, which act as combs. All otter shrews and the Aquatic tenrec have a chocolate-brown back; the Aquatic tenrec has a gray belly and otter shrews have white bellies. The Madagascan Aquatic tenrec shows strong convergence with the least otter shrews, with a rat-size body and a tail approximately the same length. The Ruwenzori least otter shrew and the Aquatic tenrec have webbed feet, which probably provide most of the propulsion in the water, and their tails are slightly compressed laterally, providing each with an effective rudder and additional propulsion.

The Mount Nimba least otter shrew is probably the least aquatic, having no webbing and a rounded tail. However, all are probably agile both in water and on land. The Giant otter shrew, which is among the most specialized of the aquatic insectivores, often figures as part fish and part mammal in African folklore, giving rise to such names as "transformed fish." The unmistakable deep, laterally flattened tail that tapers to a point is the main source of such beliefs, even though it is covered by fine, short hair, but the animal's proficiency in water no doubt also plays a part. Sinuous thrusts of the powerful tail extending up the lower part of the body provide the propulsion for swimming, allowing a startling turn of speed and great agility. Although most of the active hours are spent in the water the agility also extends to foraging on dry land. The Boulou of southern Cameroon call the Giant otter shrew the *jes*: a person is said to be like a *jes* if he flares up in anger but calms down again just as rapidly.

The long-tailed and Large-eared tenrecs are shrew-like, and the former have the least modified body plan within the Tenrecidae. Evergreen forest and wetter areas of the central plateau of Madagascar are the primary habitats for long-tailed tenrecs, with only one species extending into the deciduous forests of the drier western region. These tenrecs have filled semi-arboreal and terrestrial niches. The longest-tailed species, with relatively long hind legs, can climb and probably spring among branches; jumpers and runners live on the ground, together with short-legged semi-burrowing species. The Large-eared tenrec is also semi-burrowing in its western woodland habitat and is apparently closely related to one of the oldest fossil species.

The rice tenrecs, with their mole-like velvet fur, reduced ears and eyes, and relatively large forefeet, fill Madagascar's burrowing insectivore niche. In undisturbed areas of northern and western Madagascar, these tenrecs burrow through the humus layers in a manner similar to the North American shrew mole, but the extensive cultivation of rice provides new habitats for them.

The subfamily Tenrecinae contains some of the most fascinating and bizarre insectivores. The tail has been lost or greatly reduced and varying degrees of spininess are linked with elaborate and striking defensive strategies. Both the Greater hedgehog tenrec and its smaller semi-arboreal counterpart, the Lesser hedgehog tenrec, can form a nearly impregnable spiny ball when threatened, closely resembling the Old World hedgehogs. Continued provocation may also lead to them advancing, gaping, hissing, and head-bucking, the latter being common to all Tenrecinae. The brown adult Common tenrec, which is among the largest living insectivores, is the least spiny species, but it

FACTFILE

TENRECS

Order: Insectivora

Family: Tenrecidae

24 species in 10 genera and 4 subfamilies

DISTRIBUTION Madagascar, with one species introduced to the Comoros, Réunion, and the Seychelles; W and C Africa.

HABITAT Wide-ranging, from semi-arid to rain forest, including mountains, rivers, and human settlements.

SIZE **Head–body length** ranges from 4.3cm (1.7in) in the Pygmy shrew tenrec to 25–39cm (10–15in) in the Common tenrec; **tail length** from 5–10mm (0.2–0.4in) to 4.5cm (1.8in), and **weight** from 5g (0.18oz) to 500–1,500g (18–53oz), both in the same two species.

COAT Soft-furred to spiny; coloration ranges from brown or gray to contrasted streaks.

DIET Tenrecs and otter shrews are opportunistic feeders, taking a wide variety of invertebrates as well as some vertebrates and vegetable matter. Rice tenrecs mostly live off invertebrate prey, but also consume vegetable matter. Fruit supplements the invertebrate diet of the more omnivorous species such as the Common and hedgehog tenrecs.

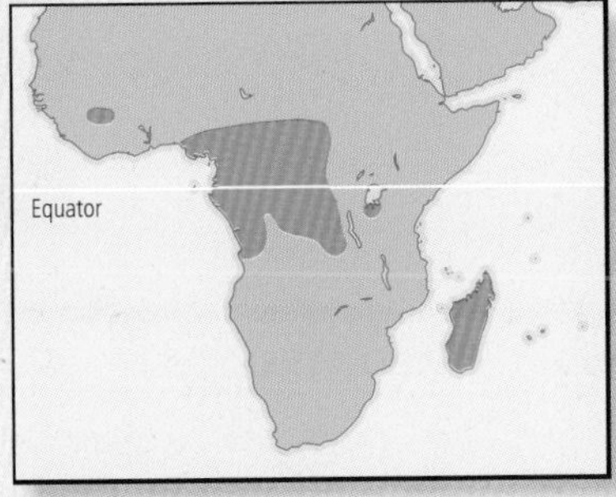

Common tenrecs are also large enough to take reptiles, amphibians, and even small mammals. The Streaked tenrec feeds on earthworms.

BREEDING Gestation relatively aseasonal within the Oryzorictinae, Geogalinae, and Tenrecinae where known (50–64 days); unknown in Potamogalinae.

LONGEVITY Up to 6 years.

CONSERVATION STATUS Nine species are considered Vulnerable or Endangered by the IUCN (6 Oryzorictinae, 3 Potamogalinae), while one – the Tree shrew tenrec (*Microgale dryas*) – is Critically Endangered.

See subfamilies table ▷

combines a lateral, open-mouthed slashing bite with head-bucking that can drive spines concentrated on the neck into an assailant. A fully-grown male with a gape of 10cm (4in) has canines that can measure up to 1.5cm (0.6in), and the bite is powered by the massively developed masseter (jaw) muscles. A pad of thickened skin on the male's mid-back provides some additional protection. The black-and-white striped offspring relies less on biting but uses numerous barbed, detachable spines to great effect in head-bucking. Common tenrecs have better eyesight than most other species in the family but may also detect disturbances through long, sensitive hairs on the back. When disturbed, the young can communicate their alarm through stridulation, which involves rubbing together stiff quills on the mid-back to produce an audible signal. Streaked tenrecs are remarkably similar to juvenile Common tenrecs in coloration, size, and possession of a stridulating organ. Like juvenile Common tenrecs, they forage in groups, and their principal defense involves scattering and hiding under cover. If they are cornered, they advance, bucking violently, with their spines bristling.

Seeking Prey by Land and Water

DIET

Tenrecs and otter shrews are opportunistic feeders, taking a wide variety of invertebrates as well as some vertebrates and vegetable matter. Otter shrews scour the water, stream bed, and banks with their sensitive whiskers, snapping up prey and carrying it up to the bank if caught in the water. Crustaceans are the main prey, including crabs of up to 5–7cm (2–3in) across the carapace. Rice tenrecs probably encounter most of their invertebrate prey in underground burrows or surface runs, but also consume vegetable matter. Fruit supplements the invertebrate diet of the more omnivorous species such as the Common and hedgehog tenrecs. Common tenrecs are also large enough to take reptiles, amphibians, and even small mammals. Prey are detected by sweeping whiskers from side to side, and by smell and sound. Similarly, semi-arboreal Lesser hedgehog tenrecs and long-tailed tenrecs perhaps encounter and eat lizards and nestling birds. The Streaked tenrec, which is active during daytime, has delicate teeth and an elongated, fine snout for feeding on earthworms.

Complex Multigenerational Groupings

SOCIAL BEHAVIOR

Tenrec reproduction is diverse and includes several features peculiar to the family. Where known, ovarian processes differ from those in other mammals in that no fluid-filled cavity, or antrum, develops in the maturing ovarian follicle. Spermatozoa also penetrate developing follicles and fertilize the egg before ovulation; this is known in only one other mammal, the Short-tailed shrew.

Tenrec and Otter Shrew Subfamilies

Tenrecs

Subfamily Oryzorictinae

Sixteen species in 3 Madagascan genera, including **Aquatic tenrec** (*Limnogale mergulus*); **rice tenrecs** (*Oryzorictes*, 3 species), **long-tailed tenrecs** (*Microgale*, 12 species). The Tree shrew tenrec (*Microgale dryas*) is Critically Endangered; the Pygmy shrew tenrec (*M. parvula*), Greater Long-tailed shrew tenrec (*M. principula*), and Aquatic tenrec are Endangered; while the Gracile shrew tenrec (*M. gracilis*), the Dark pygmy shrew tenrec (*M. pulla*), and Thomas's shrew tenrec (*M. thomasi*) are Vulnerable.

Subfamily Geogalinae

One species in one Madagascan genus: **Large-eared tenrec** (*Geogale aurita*).

Subfamily Tenrecinae

Four species in 4 Madagascan genera: **Greater hedgehog tenrec** (*Setifer setosus*); **Lesser hedgehog tenrec** (*Echinops telfairi*); **Common tenrec** (*Tenrec ecaudatus*), introduced to Réunion, Seychelles, and Mauritius; **Streaked tenrec** (*Hemicentetes semispinosus*).

Otter shrews

Subfamily Potamogalinae

Three species in 2 African genera: **Giant otter shrew** (*Potamogale velox*), Nigeria to W Kenya and Angola; **Ruwenzori least otter shrew** (*Micropotamogale ruwenzorii*), Uganda, DRC; Mount Nimba; **Least otter shrew** (*M. lamottei*), Guinea, Liberia, and Côte d'Ivoire. All species are Endangered.

For full species list see Appendix ▷

TENREC BODY TEMPERATURE

Body temperature is relatively low among tenrecs, with a range of 30–35°C (86–95°F) during activity. The Large-eared tenrec and members of the Tenrecinae enter seasonal hypothermia, or torpor, during dry or cool periods of the year, which ranges from irregular spells of a few days to continuous periods lasting six months; then it is integral to the animal's physiological and behavioral cycles. So finely arranged are the cycles of hypothermia, activity, and reproduction that the Common tenrec must complete such physiological changes as activation of the testis or ovary while still torpid, since breeding begins within days of commencing activity.

The Giant otter shrew, some Oryzorictinae, and the Tenrecinae save energy at any time of year because body temperature falls close to air temperature during daily rest. Interactions between these fluctuations in body temperature and reproduction in the Tenrecidae are unique. During comparable periods of activity in the Common tenrec, body temperatures of breeding males are on average 0.6°C (1.1°F) lower than those of nonbreeding males. This is because sperm production or storage can only occur below normal body temperature. Other mammals either have a mechanism for cooling reproductive organs or, rarely, tolerate high temperatures. Normally, thermoregulation improves during pregnancy, but female Common tenrecs continue with their regular fluctuations in temperature dependent on activity or rest, regardless of pregnancy. This probably accounts for variations in gestation lengths, as the fetuses could not develop at a constant rate if so cooled during maternal rest. Although torpor during pregnancy occurs among bats, it is well regulated, and the type found in tenrecs is not known elsewhere.

Left The Streaked tenrec (Hemicentetes semispinosum semispinosum) *has brown markings and a stripe that runs from the nose to the back of the head; stripes also run lengthwise on the body. The hairs on the underbelly are spiny, in contrast to the softer ones of* Hemicentetes semispinosum nigriceps.

Most births occur in the wet season, coinciding with maximum invertebrate numbers, and the offspring are born in a relatively undeveloped state. Litter size varies from two in the Giant otter shrew and some Oryzorictinae to an extraordinary maximum of 32 in the Common tenrec. This seems to be related to survival rates, which in turn are conditioned by the stability of the environment. For example, oryzorictines in the comparatively stable high rainforest regions seem to be long-lived and bear small litters. Average litter size of Common tenrecs in relatively seasonal woodland/savanna regions with fluctuating climatic conditions is 20, compared to 15 in rainforest regions, and 10 in Seychelles rain forests within 5° of the Equator. Weight variation within the litter can reach 200–275 percent in Common and hedgehog tenrecs.

A recent study of Large-eared tenrecs revealed that four out of ten breeding females exhibited postpartum estrus, the first time this phenomenon has been recorded within the Tenrecidae. Gestation length is around 57 days, confirming that all tenrecs have a uniformly slow fetal development rate. Pregnant females may enter torpor, which contributes to variety in length of gestation. Litter size ranged from 2–5 neonates.

The Common tenrec feeds her offspring from up to 29 nipples, the most recorded among mammals. Nutritional demands of lactation are so great in this species that the mother and offspring must extend foraging beyond their normal nocturnal regime into the relatively dangerous daylight hours. This accounts for the striped camouflage coloration of juveniles, which only become more strictly nocturnal at the approach of the molt to the adult coat. Moreover, adult females have a darker brown coat than adult males, presumably because it affords better protection for daylight feeding throughout their brief spell of lactation. The striking similarity between juvenile Common tenrecs and adult Streaked tenrecs suggests that a striped coat associated with daylight foraging has been an important factor in the evolution toward modern Streaked tenrecs.

Rainforest Streaked tenrecs form multigenerational family groups comprising the most complex social groupings among insectivores. Young mature rapidly and can breed at 35 days after birth, so that each group may produce several litters in a season. The group, of up to 18 animals, probably consists of three related generations. They forage together, in subgroups or alone, but when together they stridulate almost continuously. Stridulation seems to be primarily a device to keep mother and young together as they search for prey.

The primary means of communication among the Tenrecidae is through scent. Otter shrews regularly deposit feces either in or near their burrows and under sheltered banks. Marking by tenrecs includes cloacal dragging, rubbing secretions from eye glands, and manual depositing of neck-gland secretions. Common tenrecs cover 0.5ha (1.2–5 acres) per night, although receptive females reduce this to about 200sq m (2,150sq ft) in order to facilitate location by males. Giant otter shrews may range along 800m (0.5mi) of their streams in a night.

Mixed Fortunes

CONSERVATION AND ENVIRONMENT

Common tenrecs have been a source of food since ancient times, but are not endangered by this traditional hunting. Undoubtedly, some rainforest tenrecs are under threat as Madagascar is rapidly being deforested, but some species thrive around human settlements. Tourism may be a threat to other species. At the mid-altitude rainforest reserve of Analamazaotra, Madagascar, which is used for tourism, seven endemic tenrec species, and three endemic rodent species were recently found. Of the sites surveyed, most biological diversity was demonstrated at the most undisturbed site, though individual species abundance was reduced. Forest subjected to infrequent logging by local people exhibited an intermediate level of species richness, and it seems apt to conclude that core areas of the reserve should be left undisturbed in order to preserve small mammal species diversity. Forest destruction is also reducing the range of the Giant otter shrew and perhaps also of the Mount Nimba least otter shrew and the Ruwenzori least otter shrew. MEN

Solenodons

Left *When hunting, solenodons use their long sharp claws to upturn stones and tear off bark from fallen branches in search of prey. Although able to climb, solenodons spend most of their time foraging on the forest floor.*

THE EXTRAORDINARY SOLENODONS OF CUBA and Hispaniola face a real and immediate threat to their survival. They are so rare and restricted that the key to their conservation lies in prompt government action to set aside suitable, well-managed forest reserves in remote mountainous regions. Without such efforts, these distinctive, ancient, Antillean insectivores are likely to follow their relatives, the West Indian shrews (Nesophontidae), into extinction.

In addition to the living genus, solenodons are known from North American middle and late Oligocene deposits (about 32–26 million years ago). Their affinities are difficult to ascertain owing to their long isolation, but their closest allies are probably the true shrews (Soricidae), or the Afro-Madagascan tenrecs and otter shrews. Some mammalogists have also considered the extinct West Indian nesophontid shrews to be within the Solenodontidae. Solenodons were among the dominant carnivores on Cuba and Hispaniola before Europeans arrived with their alien predators, and were probably only occasionally eaten themselves by boas and birds of prey.

Poisoning Prey

FORM AND FUNCTION

The solenodons are among the largest living insectivores, resembling, to some extent, large, well-built shrews. Their most distinctive feature is the elongated snout, extending well beyond the length of the jaw. In the Hispaniola solenodon, the remarkable flexibility and mobility of the snout results from a unique ball-and-socket joint attaching it to the skull. The snout of the Cuban solenodon is also highly flexible but lacks the round articulating bone. Solenodons have 40 teeth, and the front upper incisors project below the upper lip. The Hispaniola solenodon secretes toxic saliva, and this probably occurs also in the Cuban species. Each limb has five toes, and the forelimbs are particularly well developed, bearing long, stout, sharp claws. Only the hind feet are employed in self-cleaning; they can reach most of the body surface, thanks to flexible hip joints. Only the rump and the base of the tail cannot be reached, but because these areas are hairless they require little attention. The tail is stiff and muscular and may play a role in balancing.

As in most nocturnal terrestrial insectivores, brain size is relatively small, and the sense of touch is highly developed, while smell and hearing are also important. Vocalizations include puffs, twitters, chirps, squeaks, and clicks; the clicks comprise pure high-frequency tones similar to those found among shrews, and probably provide a crude means of echolocation. Scentmarking is probably important, as evidenced by the presence of anal scent glands, while contact is thought to play a role in some situations.

Soil- and litter-dwelling invertebrates make up a large part of the solenodons' diet, including beetles, crickets, and various insect larvae, together with millipedes, earthworms, and termites. Vertebrate remains that have appeared in feces may be the result of scavenging carrion, but solenodons are large enough to take small vertebrates such as amphibians, reptiles, and perhaps small birds. Solenodons are capable of climbing near-vertical surfaces, but spend most time foraging on the ground. The snout is used to investigate cracks and crevices, while the massive claws are used to expose the prey under rocks, bark, and soil. A solenodon may lunge at prey and pin it to the ground with the claws and toes of the forefeet, while simultaneously scooping up the prey with the lower jaw. Occasionally the prey is pinned to the ground only by the nose, and must be held there as the solenodon advances. These advances take the form of rapid bursts to prevent the prey's escape, and a maneuvering of the lower jaw into a scoop position. Once it is caught, the prey is presumably immobilized by the toxic saliva.

Slow Breeders

SOCIAL BEHAVIOR

The natural history of solenodons is characterized by a long life span and low reproductive rate, features resulting from its position as one of the dominant predators in pre-Columbian times. The frequency and timing of reproduction in the wild is not known, but receptivity lasts less than one day and recurs at approximately 10-day intervals. Events leading up to mating involve scentmarking by both sexes, soft calling, and frequent body contacts. In captivity, the scentmarking involves marking projections in the female's cage with anal drags and also defecating and urinating in locations previously used by the female. The young (one, rarely two) are born in a nesting burrow, and they remain with the mother for an extended

FACTFILE

SOLENODONS

Order: Insectivora

Family: Solenodontidae

2 species in a single genus

DISTRIBUTION

Cuba and Hispaniola

HISPANIOLA SOLENODON *Solenodon paradoxus*

Hispaniola or Haitian solenodon

Hispaniola, now restricted to remote regions. Forest-dwelling, nocturnal. HBL 28.4–32.8cm (11–13in); TL 22.2–25.5cm (8.5–10in); WT 700–1,000g (25–35oz). Coat: forehead black, back grizzled gray-brown, white spot on the nape, yellowish flanks; tail gray except for white at base and tip. Breeding: single young (rarely two), weighing 40–55g (1.4–1.9oz). Longevity: 11 years in captivity; unknown in wild. Conservation status: Endangered.

CUBAN SOLENODON *Solenodon cubanus*

Cuba. Forest-dwelling; nocturnal. HBL 28.4–32.8cm (11–13in); TL 17.5–25.5cm (7–10in); WT 700–1,000g (25–35oz). Coat: finer and longer than in the Hispaniola solenodon, dark gray except for pale yellow head and mid-belly. Breeding: as for Hispaniola solenodon. Longevity: 6.5 years in captivity; unknown in wild. Conservation status: Endangered.

Abbreviations HBL = head–body length TL = tail length HT = height WT = weight

*▲ **Above** The solenodon's snout is a unique feature, in that it is a cartilaginous (not osseous) appendage that extends well beyond the jaw. In the Hispaniola solenodon the snout is connected to the skull via a ball-and-socket joint, making it very flexible.*

period of several months, which is exceptionally long among insectivores. During the first two months, each young solenodon may accompany the mother on foraging excursions by hanging onto her greatly elongated teats by the mouth. Solenodons are the only insectivores that practice teat transport, and carrying the offspring in the mouth is more widespread within this order. Initially, the offspring are simply dragged along, but as they grow they are able to walk with the mother, pausing when she stops. Teat transport would undoubtedly be useful if nursing solenodons change burrow sites regularly. More advanced offspring continue to follow the mother, learning food preferences from her by licking her mouth as she feeds, and getting to know routes around the nest burrow. The mother–offspring tie is the only enduring social grouping among solenodons; adults are otherwise solitary.

Threatened by Progress

CONSERVATION AND ENVIRONMENT

Skeletal remains discovered on Hispaniola and Cuba indicate that there were formerly two further species of solenodon – *S. arredondoi* (on Cuba) and *S. marcanoi* (on Hispaniola); the former is thought to have been half the size again of extant species and twice as heavy, while the latter was slightly smaller than living solenodons. They may have gone extinct after European encroachment on the islands.

There are no accurate estimates of solenodon numbers on Cuba or Hispaniola. The Cuban species appears to be the rarer, though small, formerly unknown populations were found in the east of the island in the 1990s. The low reproductive rate is one factor in the decline in solenodon abundance, but more significant reasons for their rarity are habitat destruction and predation by introduced carnivores, against which solenodons have no defense. Mongooses and feral cats are the main predators on Cuba, whereas dogs decimate solenodon populations in the vicinity of settlements on Hispaniola. There is little hope for the Hispaniola solenodon in Haiti, the nation comprising the western half of Hispaniola, but protected areas of dense forest now exist in remote regions of the neighboring Dominican Republic, and on Cuba. These require prompt, efficient management to ensure the solenodon's survival. Such is the pressure for new land accompanying the human population explosion on these islands that the solenodons' survival may ultimately depend upon the efforts of zoos. MEN

Hedgehogs and Moonrats

THE HEDGEHOG IS ONE OF THE MOST familiar wild mammals seen in the European landscape and also among the most thoroughly studied in the field. One reason for this familiarity is the hedgehog's intriguing defensive adaptation against predators. Having spines reduces the requirement for hedgehogs to run for cover, which means that they are relatively easy to spot in gardens, prime habitat in which to amble about on lawns looking for tasty beetles, worms, and other invertebrate prey. However, the habit of not running has ill-served them in the age of the motor vehicle and nowadays they are as common a sight – dead or dying – by the roadside as they are in the garden.

Not all hedgehogs, though, live in close proximity to humans in densely-populated Europe. Some species range the dry steppes and deserts of Africa and the Middle East. The rather poorly known moonrats and gymnures, hedgehog relatives that are lacking spines, inhabit the humid forests of south Asia and exhibit behavior more akin to that of the elusive shrews.

Spiny and Spineless

FORM AND FUNCTION

Hedgehogs, moonrats, and gymnures are plantigrade animals, which means that at each step the entire sole of the foot makes contact with the ground. They have an elongated head and snout, a small braincase, and well-developed eyes and ears. Males and females generally look alike, but the distance between the anus and genitals is larger in the males. Hedgehogs have 2–3 incisors, 1 canine, 2–4 premolars, and 3 molar teeth on each half dental arch, and the first incisor is usually larger than the others.

The spiny coat covering the back and the crown of the head makes hedgehogs unmistakable (see box). The spines have sharp tips, and incorporate many small internal cavities to reduce weight. The basal portion is flexible and works as a shock absorber if the hedgehog is hit hard. Spines normally lie flat along the back: each is erected by a single muscle (as is true of hairs in all mammals), and when lifted they crisscross and support each other. Hedgehogs' underparts are furry rather than spiny, which prevents the animals from spiking themselves when they roll up!

Below *Hedgehogs eat a wide variety of foods and will consume almost any invertebrate prey. Here, a Western European hedgehog feasts on snails.*

Hedgehogs have other features that distinguish them from moonrats and gymnures, including a larger number of mammae (4–5 as opposed to 2–4); they also lack the well-developed anal glands that, in moonrats and gymnures, produce an unpleasant odor that presumably assists in deterring predators. Hedgehogs have powerful front limbs and strong claws that they can use to dig when they are searching for food or constructing nest burrows; they cannot run very quickly – the maximum speed reported is around 10km/h (6mph) – but they can easily climb over such obstacles as wire-netting fences. Moonrats and gymnures move much more speedily, in the manner of large shrews; however, they are also much less efficient at digging.

While spines may protect the hedgehog from larger animals that seek to prey on their flesh, they positively encourage the presence of small bloodsuckers, since their impenetrability makes it difficult for hedgehogs to groom themselves. Fleas, ticks, mites, and fungal infections of the skin can reach a very high density on hedgehogs; some individuals may carry in excess of 1,000 fleas.

Left A Greater moonrat foraging. This species is generally black with a whitish head and shoulders, but some animals, like this individual, are white all over.

Right A Western European hedgehog curls up on a pile of dead leaves, revealing its relatively vulnerable underside. The tighter the ball that a hedgehog curls itself up into, the spinier it becomes.

FACTFILE

Hedgehogs and Moonrats

Order: Insectivora

Family: Erinaceidae

23 species in 7 genera

DISTRIBUTION Africa, Europe, and Asia N to the limits of deciduous forest; SE Asian islands. Absent from Madagascar, Sri Lanka, and Japan. European hedgehog introduced to New Zealand.

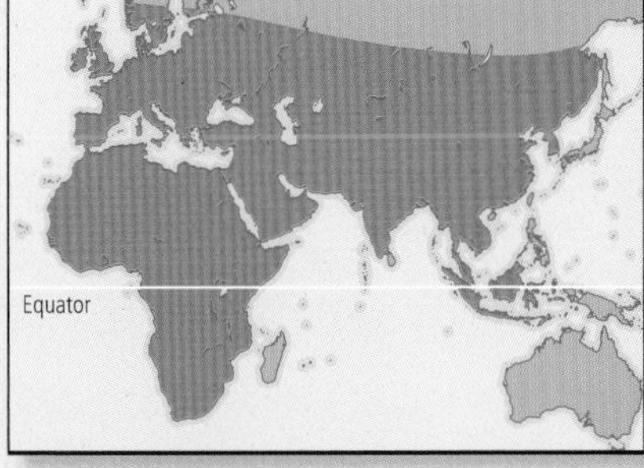

HABITAT Woodland, grassland, urban areas, dry steppe, desert, lowland forest, mangroves, tropical forest, montane areas.

SIZE Head–body length ranges from 10–15cm (4–6in) in the Lesser and Dwarf gymnures to 27–45cm (11–18in) in the Greater moonrat; **tail length** from 1–3cm (0.4–1.2in) to approximately 20cm (8in), and **weight** from 15–80g (0.5–3oz) to 1–2kg (35–70oz), both in the same species.

COAT Hedgehogs are distinctively covered in sharp spines – modified hairs that are typically 2–3cm (0.8–1.2in) long. Moonrats and gymnures have fur in place of spines.

DIET Typically invertebrates including beetles, earthworms, caterpillars, earwigs, slugs, grasshoppers, plus some carrion. African and Asian hedgehogs eat more vertebrates than their European counterparts – up to 40 percent of total food intake in the case of the Collared hedgehog.

BREEDING Gestation period ranges from 30–32 days in the Long-eared hedgehog to 40–48 days in the Algerian hedgehog.

LONGEVITY Up to 7 years, both in the wild and in captivity.

CONSERVATION STATUS 5 of the 7 species of moonrats and gymnures are listed by the IUCN, along with 1 of 16 species of hedgehogs. The Dwarf gymnure is Critically Endangered, and the Hainan gymnure and Dinagat and Mindanao moonrats are both Endangered due to the rapid habitat destruction and fragmentation occurring in their already narrow range; the Chinese Hugh's hedgehog is Vulnerable for the same reason.

See subfamilies box ▷

They also play host to a variety of internal parasites as well as bacterial diseases, including leptospirosis, which they can transmit to humans through their urine.

Reports of rabid hedgehogs foaming at the mouth, however, probably stem from the animals' unique habit of self-anointing, which involves spreading a huge amount of foamy saliva from the mouth all over their own back. This practice, which requires a surprising amount of agility on the hedgehog's part, may be exhibited in response to either strong-smelling or novel food, or the presence of other hedgehogs, foxes, or glue. Only tentative explanations exist for self-anointing: it may serve to clean the spines and act as an insecticide, however, it may also prove to have a part to play in courtship.

Hedgehogs are primarily nocturnal creatures. Their eyes are good enough to enable them to distinguish objects, but they probably only have monochromatic vision. Like many other nocturnal animals they rely mainly on their senses of smell and hearing to relate to the external world. The olfactory lobes of the brain are accordingly well-developed, and are augmented by a Jacobson's organ in the palate, which also serves an olfactory function. This supplementary sensory organ is found in a number of vertebrate species, in which it is associated with functions as different as prey detection and mating: the functions with which it is associated in hedgehogs still need to be thoroughly investigated.

A variety of hedgehog glands produce potentially odorous secretions. There are sexual scent-marking glands present in males, lubricating glands in the vagina of females, and sebaceous glands in the corners of the mouth. The sense of hearing has only been well studied in the Long-eared hedgehog, a species in which hearing is thought to be especially sensitive. Long-eared hedgehogs seem to perceive high-frequency sounds up to 45KHz, in comparison with a human range of only up to about 18–20KHz; this sense probably helps hedgehogs to locate underground invertebrate prey making high-pitched noises as they move in the soil and leaf litter. In contrast, low-frequency sound perception is relatively weak. Little is known about the aural senses of moonrats and gymnures, but the general considerations outlined for hedgehogs should also apply to them.

The genetic relationships of hedgehog species are controversial, although recent studies of mitochondrial DNA and karyotype are shedding some light on the situation; the DNA research helps to determine the genetic relatedness between populations on the basis of differences in the DNA sequence, while karyology studies account for differences in the number of chromosomes – 48 in all hedgehog species analysed so far – and their appearance. Western and Eastern European hedgehogs are capable of interbreeding, which would normally link them within a single species; however, mitochondrial DNA analyses have suggested that they are in fact sufficiently different to qualify as two separate species. Individuals from islands, such as Great Britain and Crete, are smaller than their Eastern counterparts; in addition, Western individuals are paler on the back and darker on the underparts. Karyotypes of African and European hedgehogs have confirmed that species that are assigned to the same genus on the basis of similar appearance are indeed genetically more closely related than those assigned to different genera.

Prey and Predator

DIET

Although hedgehogs, moonrats, and gymnures live in diverse habitats and pursue different lifestyles, most include beetles and earthworms in their diet, and also show a penchant for other invertebrate prey including caterpillars, earwigs, slugs, crickets, and grasshoppers. European hedgehog populations foraging in house gardens and on playing fields feed mainly on earthworms and slugs (but not on large snails, since they seem to be incapable of breaking their thick shells), while those foraging in bushes and maquis (a dense shrub vegetation found in wild, dry Mediterranean areas) rely on other invertebrates. The stomachs and droppings of European hedgehogs also commonly contain the remains of vertebrate prey; frogs, bird chicks, mice, shrews, moles, voles, lizards, and snakes have all been detected there. With the exception of chicks, which some hedgehogs might occasionally kill, these are probably not the results of predatory behavior but were more likely consumed as carrion. Generally, meat does not make up a significant proportion of the hedgehogs' diet. Dietary changes with age have been investigated, showing that European hedgehogs apparently learn to forage more efficiently as they grow older. Young hedgehogs eat prey of a wide variety of size, while older ones focus on the biggest insects; this may reduce competition between different age classes.

African, Long-eared, Collared, and Asian hedgehogs feed on a higher proportion and variety of vertebrates than the European hedgehog, including frogs, toads, sand and spiny lizards, snakes, and small rodents. A study of the Collared hedgehog found that vertebrates (amphibians and mammals in particular) made up 40 percent by dry weight of the stomach contents. The very few studies that have been conducted on the diets of moonrats and gymnures living in montane or tropical forests indicate that they forage on invertebrates, and possibly also on some vegetable matter. The only exception is the Greater moonrat, which also inhabits mangroves and lowland plantations and has been reported to enter the water to prey on crabs, mollusks, and fish.

A Solitary Life behind the Prickles

SOCIAL BEHAVIOR

Thanks to their spiny coats, hedgehogs have few natural enemies. Dogs and foxes can only occasionally overcome their defenses, and even lions have sometimes been observed abandoning a rolled-up African hedgehog after painful attempts to bite it. The only specialized hedgehog predators are large owls, which are able to "shell" the hedgehog with their claws, and badgers. These last can sneak their muzzles into the tightly-clenched opening of a rolled-up hedgehog, and eat it, leaving behind an empty, spiny coat. Badgers as hedgehog predators are, in fact, an interesting ecological case study, since both species feed on

Right *Some representative species of hedgehogs and moonrats:* **1** *Desert hedgehog* (Hemiechinus aethiopicus) *eating a beetle;* **2** *North African hedgehog* (Atelerix algirus)*;* **3** *Shrew gymnure* (Hylomys sinensis)*;* **4** *Long-eared hedgehog* (Hemiechinus auritus)*;* **5** *Short-tailed gymnure* (Hylomys suillus)*;* **6** *Greater moonrat* (Echinosorex gymnura)*;* **7** *Mindanao moonrat* (Podogymnura truei)*;* **8** *Hainan gymnure* (Hylomys hainanensis).

the same prey (earthworms) and badgers feed opportunistically on hedgehogs whenever they encounter them. This can affect the distribution pattern of hedgehogs, since they can be excluded from areas rich in food and cover that would otherwise be suitable habitat for them solely because of predation by badgers. Experiments conducted over the last 10 years suggest that hedgehog densities can be ten times higher in badger-free areas than where badgers are present (less than 0.5 as opposed to 2–3 hedgehogs per hectare). Captive and free-ranging hedgehogs both tend to avoid foraging areas tainted by badger odor. Moreover, the presence of badgers can increase mortality rates and the dispersal of hedgehog populations.

When it gets cold hedgehogs enter hibernation,

Hedgehog Subfamilies

Hedgehogs
Subfamily Erinaceinae

16 species in 4 genera, including **Western European hedgehog** (*Erinaceus europaeus*), W Europe and British Isles; **Eastern European hedgehog** (*E. concolor*), E Europe; **North African hedgehog** (*Atelerix algirus*), SW Europe and N Africa; **Four-toed hedgehog** (*A. albiventris*), N and C Africa; and **Indian hedgehog** (*Hemiechinus micropus*), Pakistan and NW India. The **Bare-bellied hedgehog** (*H. nudiventris*) and **Hugh's hedgehog** (*Mesechinus hughi*) are both Vulnerable.

Moonrats and Gymnures
Subfamily Hylomyinae

7 species in 3 genera, including **Greater moonrat** (*Echinosorex gymnura*), SE Asia; **Short-tailed gymnure** (*Hylomys suillus*), SE Asia; **Hainan gymnure** (*H. hainanensis*), SE Asia; **Dinagat moonrat** (*Podogymnura aureospinula*), Philippines; and **Mindanao moonrat** (*P. truei*), Philippines. The **Dwarf gymnure** (*Hylomys parvus*) is Critically Endangered, the Hainan, Dinagat, and Mindanao gymnures all Endangered.

For full species list see Appendix ▷

drastically reducing the energy they normally expend on remaining active and maintaining body temperature. While hibernation does increase survival rates, approximately half of the individuals that enter it nonetheless die before the next spring. Hedgehogs hibernate when and where they need to in response to adverse climatic conditions, rather than rigidly every season. In North Africa, for example, the African hedgehog is active throughout the year; those living in southern Europe have a short, 0–4 month hibernation period during winter, while the populations inhabiting the coldest South African regions go into hibernation from June to August. On average European hedgehogs hibernate from October to April in the northern parts of the continent, while those living in temperate climes undergo dormancy only during the coldest winters. Hedgehogs in captivity never hibernate, provided that they are kept warm and are given sufficient food.

Hibernating requires accumulating resources to survive long periods without eating. This is accomplished by depositing subcutaneous and abdominal white fat, and axillary, thorax, neck, and spinal brown fat, in late summer. White fat (the commonest type) acts as an insulating layer and is used for ordinary metabolic activity. Brown fat is characteristic of hibernators and is used to kickstart the heating needed to arouse individuals from hibernation.

Even with large fat deposits hedgehogs need to stop hibernation for 1–2 days every week or two in order to forage, urinate, and defecate, thereby avoiding accumulating catabolites, the organic and inorganic by-products of the organism's biochemical cycles, which could otherwise poison the hedgehog as they concentrate. During hibernation hedgehog body temperature falls from around 35°C to 15–20°C, and the heart rate decreases from about 250 beats/min to around 10 beats/min. The respiration rate similarly decreases, and can even cease entirely for up to 2 hours. Depending on external conditions, the metabolic rate of a hedgehog can slow down a hundredfold during hibernation.

Besides external cues, hormonal circannual cycles play a key role in the onset of dormancy in male hedgehogs. Melatonin (secreted by the pineal gland) and testosterone (secreted by gonads) have opposite effects on the animals' hibernation and sexual activity. The lengthening of the hours of darkness in winter causes melatonin

Spines and Curling in Hedgehogs

The most distinctive features of hedgehogs are their spines. An average adult carries around 5,000, each about 2-3cm (1in) long, with a needle-sharp point. Each creamy white spine usually has a subterminal band of black or brown. Spines are actually modified hair, and along the animal's sides where spines give way to true hair, thin spines or thick, stiff hairs can often be found, which may show the transition from one to the other. To minimize weight without losing strength, each spine is filled with many small, air-filled chambers, separated by thin plates. Towards its base, each spine narrows to a thin, angled, flexible neck, and then widens again into a small ball that is embedded in the skin. This arrangement transforms any pressure exerted along the spine (from a blow or a fall, for example) into a bending of the thin, flexible part rather than driving the base of the spine into the hedgehog's body. Connected to the base of each spine is a small muscle that is used to pull it erect. Normally, the muscles are relaxed and the spines laid flat along the back. If threatened, a hedgehog will often not immediately roll up but will first simply erect the spines and wait for the danger to pass. When erected, the spines stick out at a variety of different angles, criss-crossing over one another and supporting each other to create a virtually impenetrable barrier.

Hedgehogs are additionally protected by their ability to curl up into a ball. This is achieved by the presence of rather more skin than is necessary to cover the body, beneath which lies a powerful muscle (the *panniculus carnosus*) covering the back. The skin musculature is more strongly developed around its edges than at the center (where it forms a circular band, the *orbicularis* muscle) and is only very loosely connected to the body beneath. When the orbicularis contracts, it acts like the drawstring around the opening of a bag, forcing the contents deeper into the bag as the string is drawn tighter.

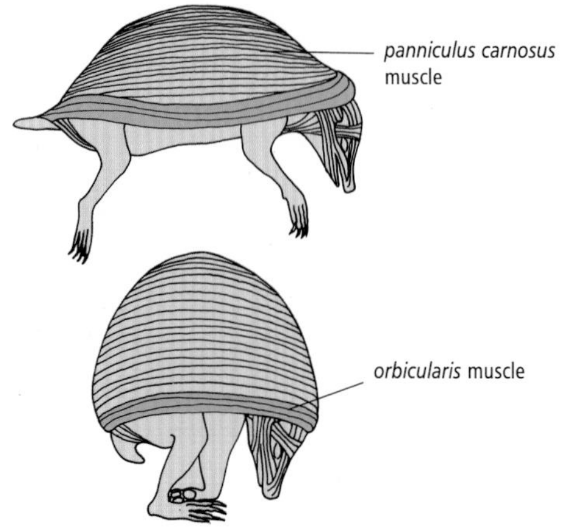

When a hedgehog starts to curl up, two small muscles first pull the skin and underlying circular muscle forward over the head and down over the rump. Then the circular *orbicularis* muscle contracts, the head and hindquarters are forced together, and the spine-covered skin of the back and sides is drawn tightly over the unprotected underparts. So effective is this stratagem that, on a fully-curled hedgehog, the spines that formerly covered its flanks and the top of the head are brought together to block the small hole (smaller than the width of a finger) corresponding to the opening of the bag. As the skin is pulled tightly over the body, the muscles that erect the spines are automatically stretched and the spines erected, so that the tighter the hedgehog curls, the spinier it becomes. AW

Above *Hedgehogs are born with the spines present, however, they are located just beneath the skin in order to avoid damaging the mother's birth canal. These spines, which are white, emerge from beneath the skin in a matter of hours. Within a couple of days of birth several additional, darker pigmented spines will also have sprouted. As well as being born naked, hedgehogs also leave the womb deaf and blind; yet within a few weeks, the young are generally quite functional and are fully weaned at about 6 weeks.*

levels to rise, reducing the activity of the sexual organs and the level of blood testosterone and inducing dormancy. Conversely, testosterone promotes gonadal activity and inhibits hibernation. Experiments involving the administration of hormones to female hedgehogs have demonstrated that hibernation in females is, in contrast, more environment-driven

During the daytime, hedgehogs rest in hidden nests lined with leaves, grass, and twigs. If the climate is warm enough, they may sleep under wood piles, thick bushes, pine needles, or simply foliage. A hedgehog uses many day nests in a season, and each nest is usually frequented by many individuals. Although hedgehogs in captivity often sleep together, no report exists of the simultaneous sharing of a nest in the wild. Breeding nests, where females give birth to their litter, have the same structure as day nests, but wintering nests are normally more robust since they have to last for months of continuous use. Long-eared, Collared, and Desert hedgehogs, all of which live in relatively arid regions, use burrows more frequently than the European hedgehog.

Every night a hedgehog moves around its home range at an average speed of 100–200m (110–220yds) per hour. Unlike many other mammals, European hedgehogs do not own and defend an exclusive territory: the area they use for foraging, resting, and breeding is normally shared with others of both sexes. This type of spatial organization is likely to arise when resources are so dispersed, or so unpredictably distributed in space and/or time, that a territory would be too large to be defended efficiently. This may be the case for hedgehogs, as earthworms and other invertebrates are patchily distributed and their availability fluctuates over time. Hedgehogs can forage in close contact with others if the feeding patch is rich enough to allow it: otherwise they stay apart, but no aggressive interaction seems to occur in order to achieve a more even spacing.

A European hedgehog's yearly home range is generally less than 40ha (100 acres) in area, and often much smaller if resources are abundant: suburban areas with gardens allow hedgehogs to reach very high densities (many individuals per hectare), each occupying an area of just 5–10ha (12–25 acres). On average males have larger home ranges than females – up to twice the size – and accordingly move longer distances in one activity cycle. Little is known about the home ranges of other hedgehogs, moonrats, and gymnures, although desert hedgehogs probably have larger yearly home ranges than European ones. The Greater moonrat is solitary and territorial.

Male hedgehogs emerge from hibernation before females, and start foraging to gain weight. When females also emerge, 3–4 weeks later, the males widen their ranging area looking for mates. Mating lasts from May to the end of August, with limited differences between species. Courtship is a conspicuous behavior and occurs frequently, but only in a few cases (less than 10 percent according to the data available hitherto) does it end in mating. When approached, the female reacts aggressively, lowering her spiny forehead and snorting loudly. The male circles her (generally silently, although the male African hedgehog makes a characteristically high-pitched courtship vocalization), and from time to time tries to mount. The male often gives up during this phase, in which case the pair will separate.

Mating starts if the female accepts the male. Contrary to Aristotle's opinion, hedgehogs do not mate face to face, but from the rear like most other mammals. To facilitate male penetration, the female will press her belly to the ground, exposing the vagina, which is located very close to the anus. The male penis lies forward under the belly, which assists him in copulating without being pricked. While mounting, the male grips the female's shoulder spines with his teeth to hold her in position.

At the end of mating the pair separates: the male does not guard the female to protect her from other males, nor does he help her build a nest or to rear the offspring. Rather than try to invest in the survival of his progeny by any one female, the male practices a lottery policy, gambling that the more females he can impregnate the greater his chances of leaving surviving young. Females too can mate more than once before starting gestation, but it is unknown if they can in some way select a preferred male's sperm, or if a

Above *A hedgehog in aggressive posture. Because they rely on their spines for protection, hedgehogs often wander in areas with little or no cover. If disturbed they usually freeze and erect their spines.*

Right *Although they are primarily terrestrial, hedgehogs are quite adept at swimming. Here, a Western European hedgehog is seen crossing a pond.*

Hedgehogs and Adders

For centuries folktales passed on knowledge of an adaptation peculiar to hedgehogs that was long neglected by the scientific community: the animals' resistance to adder venom. This resistance, probably incomplete and individually variable, is conferred by an anti-hemorrhagic factor called erinacin, a protein obtained from hedgehog muscle extracts that inhibits the venom's hemorrhagic and proteolytic activity. In combination with the defensive spines, erinacin actually allows hedgehogs to attack (BELOW) and eat snakes, although this does not happen frequently.

Venom resistance is not restricted to hedgehogs – other animals as unrelated as opossums and mongooses also exhibit this quality. Among European insectivores, extracts from shrew and mole muscles also have an anti-hemorrhagic effect, although this is less marked; those of such other mammals as mice, rats, and rabbits do not.

single litter is fathered by more than one male. In mild climates females try to maximize reproductive success by raising a second litter later in the season, even though few individuals from it will grow large enough to survive hibernation.

After 35 days of gestation, four or five baby hedgehogs are born, each 7cm (3in) in length and weighing 10–25g (0.3–0.9oz). At birth the spines are hidden underneath the skin in a space filled with fluid, to avoid hurting the mother during parturition. The fluid is absorbed within 24 hours and the spines emerge, to be supplemented and then replaced by pigmented adult spines within 2–3 weeks. Baby hedgehogs are capable of erecting spines at the age of 2–3 days and can roll up into a ball after 2–3 weeks. As their milk teeth erupt, around the third week, they start to venture out of the nest with their mother. Weaning occurs around 6 weeks of age, after which the young forage intensively to accumulate fat reserves and search for a suitable wintering nest of their own. They will be sexually mature by the next spring. Living in tropical climates, the Greater and Lesser moonrat and the Dwarf gymnure breed throughout the year (the latter probably has no more than two litters annually, while nothing is known about the former), generating 1–3 offspring per litter.

Coexisting with Humans

CONSERVATION AND ENVIRONMENT

Concern has been raised about a possible decline in the numbers of European hedgehogs in the last 20 years. This decline can mainly be attributed to the huge number of hedgehogs killed on roads, where the roll-up defensive strategy that has proved so effective against animal predators often dooms them to be crushed by vehicles.

One suspected effect of roads on hedgehog decline is habitat fragmentation as a result of human activity, a key issue in conservation biology that has been the main cause of animal extinctions in the last two centuries. Habitat fragmentation divides large populations into many smaller subpopulations, which are no longer connected to each other. As individuals cannot disperse from one subpopulation to another, genetic mixing is prevented, and the probability of subpopulation survival in the long term is reduced. One study has demonstrated that hedgehog populations living as close as 15km (10mi) to each other have a different genetic composition, meaning that dispersal between populations rarely occurs. Since no correlation between geographic and genetic distance was found, it is possible that roads could act as barriers to hedgehog dispersal. However, a viability analysis on another group of hedgehog populations has concluded that fencing roads to avoid hedgehog roadkills would make them impenetrable, definitely isolating each one.

Roads are a major cause of hedgehog mortality, accounting for around half of all deaths except those occurring during hibernation. Yet roads can sometimes be successfully crossed, and their verges serve as corridors for dispersal. Hedgehogs following road verges often end up in urban areas, where they tend to prefer foraging in fields and gardens. Since urban areas support higher hedgehog densities than the surrounding woods and arable land, the abundance of food probably overcompensates for the added risk of roadkill.

Above *The head of the Desert hedgehog. Increasing desertification is leading to the fragmentation of populations of this species.*

Different lifestyles and geographic distribution will most likely ensure different destinies for the members of the Erinaceidae family. The animals' wide distribution and tolerance of people will probably see them survive in densely-populated areas of Europe and Asia, while African hedgehogs seem secure in the unpopulated desert and steppes. By contrast, the survival of moonrats and gymnures, like that of many other poorly known tropical forest species, is by no means assured, being intrinsically linked to the fate of the remnant forest itself. CR

Shrews

IN 1607 THE ENGLISH NATURALIST EDWARD Topsell wrote one of the first known descriptions of the Eurasian common shrew, and it was not flattering. "It is a ravening beast," he stated, "feigning itself gentle and tame, but being touched it biteth deep, and poisoneth deadly. It beareth a cruel mind, desiring to hurt anything, neither is there any creature it loveth."

This negative attitude toward the shrew has even established itself in the English language; the words "shrewd," "shrewish," and "shrew" were all coined to describe cunning, ill-tempered, or villainous people, although the meaning of "shrewd" at least has become less pejorative over time. Elsewhere, shrews have been more appreciated; the ancient Egyptians, for example, mummified – and are thought to have deified – the African giant and Egyptian pygmy shrews.

The Red and the White

FORM AND FUNCTION

Shrews are small, secretive mammals, superficially rather mouse-like but with characteristically long, pointed noses. They are typically terrestrial, foraging in and under the litter in woods and in the vegetation mat beneath herbage. Some are able to climb trees, others live underground, while a number of species are aquatic. A highly successful group of small insectivores, shrews comprise the third most speciose family of mammals, occurring over much of the globe except Australasia and the major part of South America.

The eyes of shrews are small, sometimes hidden in the fur, and vision seems to be poor. Hearing and smell, however, are acute. Even so, the external ears are reduced and difficult to discern in some species. The species that shows the greatest reduction in eye and ear size is the burrowing Mole shrew, which closely resembles a mole in external appearance, except that the forelimbs are barely modified from the typical shrew condition. There is a more dramatic change to the feet in the Tibetan water shrew, which has webbing between the digits. Other "aquatic" species, like the American water shrew, have their feet, digits, and tail all fringed with stiff hairs, which increase the surface area, thereby aiding propulsion underwater. The hairs also trap air, allowing the shrews to "run" on the surface of the water. Fringing of hair on the feet is additionally found in the Piebald shrew, in its case to aid running on sand.

The first set of teeth is shed or resorbed during embryonic development, so that shrews are born with their final set. The teeth are very important taxonomically. Some species can only easily be distinguished from close relatives by differences in tooth shape. At a higher taxonomic level, shrews are divided into two subfamilies on the basis of whether they have red tips to their teeth (the so-called "red-toothed shrews," or Soricinae) or not (the "white-toothed shrews," or Crocidurinae). The redness reflects the presence of a deposition of iron in the enamel.

A skeletal feature found in the Armored shrew – and in no other mammal – is the possession of interlocking lateral, dorsal, and ventral spines on the vertebrae. Along with the large number of facets for articulation, the spines create an exceptionally sturdy vertebral column. There are reliable reports of the Armored shrew surviving the pressure of a full-grown man standing on it.

The most conspicuous vocalizations of shrews are the high-pitched screams and twitterings used in disputes with members of their own species. One species, the House shrew, makes a sound like jangling coins as it moves around buildings and is consequently known as the "money shrew." Some species, at least of the genera *Sorex* and *Blarina*, may use ultrasound; this seems to be generated in the larynx and may be used to provide a crude form of echolocation.

Shrews are often viewed as "primitive" forms, and the earliest mammals are often portrayed as shrew-like. In fact, shrews are a clearly modern family of eutherians with origins within the Tertiary. The earliest shrew fossils have been found in North America in the middle Eocene (45 million years ago). Eurasian fossils date back to the early Oligocene (34 million years ago), and African shrews are known from the middle Miocene (14 million years ago). Those features that shrews probably do have in common with the earliest mammals, for example their plantigrade gait, put them at no disadvantage for their way of life as small terrestrial mammals. Shrews are in fact highly successful forms, supremely adapted to survive as miniature insectivores.

One of the most striking features of shrews is their extraordinary chromosomal variation. Species of shrew often differ from close relatives in the number and morphology of their chromosomes. Indeed the chromosomal differences may, in some cases, have contributed to the reproductive isolation necessary for speciation. In this context, the within-species variation of chromosomes

Left *The smallest terrestrial mammal is the Pygmy white-toothed shrew which, at 2g (0.07oz), is similar in size to the tiniest bats and hummingbirds.*

Far right *Plastered with air bubbles, a Eurasian water shrew plunges vertically downward to forage underwater. These shrews feed on aquatic invertebrates, small fish, and amphibians.*

Below *The white-toothed shrews are by far the most numerous of the various shrew groups. This is the Lesser white-toothed shrew* (Crocidura suaveolens).

FACTFILE

Shrews

Order: Insectivora

Family: Soricidae

312 species in 23 genera and 2 subfamilies

DISTRIBUTION Eurasia, Africa, N America, northern S America.

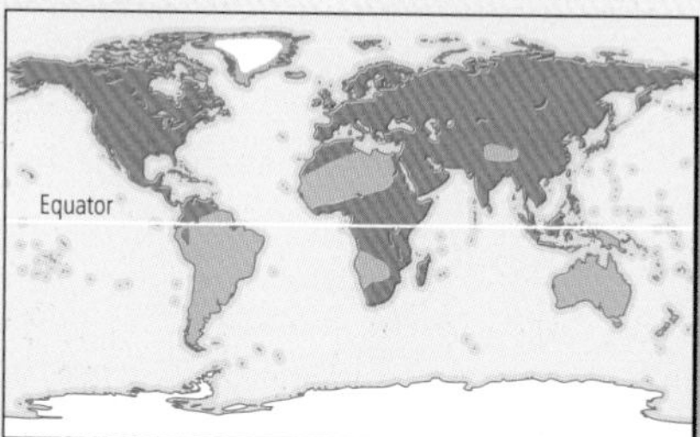

HABITAT Forest, woodland, grassland, desert, terrestrial; but some species partially aquatic.

SIZE Head–body length from 3.5cm (1.4in) in the Pygmy white-toothed shrew, the smallest living terrestrial mammal, to 15cm (5.9in) in the House shrew; **weight** from 2g (0.07oz) to 106g (3.7oz), in the same two species.

COAT Small, mouse-like bodies are covered in short, thick fur, mostly in shades of gray or brown.

DIET Depending on size, seeds, nuts, and other plant matter; invertebrate and vertebrate prey, including earthworms, lizards, newts, frogs, and fish.

BREEDING Gestation period 17–32 days

LONGEVITY 12–30 months

CONSERVATION STATUS 29 species of shrew are classed as Critically Endangered, 30 as Endangered, and 56 as Vulnerable.

See subfamilies box ▷

Above *A Greater white-toothed shrew dines on a grasshopper. Shrews have voracious appetites – some species need to eat every couple of hours to survive.*

of some species of shrews is of particular interest. Some of the "races" within species that have distinctive chromosomes may themselves be progenitors of new species. The Eurasian common shrew is particularly impressive as regards its chromosomal variation; altogether, over 60 different chromosome races with chromosome numbers ranging from 20 to 33 have been described. Eurasian common shrews are also unusual among mammals in that males and females of a particular race have different chromosome numbers. Females have two sex chromosomes (XX) while males have three (XY1Y2).

Tenacious Survivors

DIET

Shrews are very active and consume large amounts of food for their size. Some species cannot survive more than an hour or two without food. Their high metabolic rate is associated with other extraordinary features; for example, heartbeats of over a thousand beats per minute have been recorded (for an adult human, the resting rate is closer to 70 beats per minute). In several northern species, including the Eurasian common shrew, the skull, skeleton, and certain internal organs shrink during the winter in order to reduce energy demands.

Shrews cope with their high requirement for food and water primarily by living in habitats where these are abundant. However, their generally small size enables them to utilize thermally-protected microhabitats. At least one species of red-toothed shrew, the Desert shrew, has mastered the physiological problems of living in a hot, arid climate by lowering its metabolic rate in a similar way to other desert-dwelling mammals. Several species, mainly among the white-toothed shrews but also including the Desert shrew, are capable of going into torpor at times of day when they are not able to obtain food. Hibernation, however, has not been demonstrated for any shrew.

Interestingly, the red-toothed shrews have higher metabolic rates than the white-toothed. This difference may be related to their different origins, northern and tropical respectively. The iron-rich red tips to the teeth may increase resistance to wear, of importance given the substantial throughput of hard and gritty invertebrate food required by these animals. Despite this, the teeth may wear down substantially, rendering them ineffective. Adult specimens of the Eurasian common shrew are often found dead in the open during the fall. These are old individuals that have bred the previous summer and whose teeth are worn. The apparent cause of death is starvation, and the carcasses remain uneaten owing to the presence of scent glands on the flanks, whose secretions make shrews unpalatable to most carnivores.

Many shrews are opportunists in their feeding habits, showing little specialization. The Eurasian common shrew, for instance, will eat almost every invertebrate that it comes across. It spends its time scurrying along rodent runs or through vegetation, coming across prey in a haphazard way.

Other species are more adventurous in their feeding habits. The aquatic species will make dives of over 30 seconds to find small fish or other prey. The Piebald shrew feeds on lizards.

The bite of some shrews is venomous. The salivary glands of the American short-tailed shrew, for instance, produce enough poison to kill about 200 mice by intravenous injection. The poison acts to kill or paralyze before ingestion, and may be important in helping to subdue large vertebrate prey. The poison may also immobilize insects for eating at a later time. Food-caching is an activity known in several species of shrews, including the American short-tailed, and seems to be a means of securing short-term food supplies when competition is fierce or food is temporarily very abundant.

A number of shrew species – very possibly all – practice refection (the reingestion of excreted food). In the Eurasian common shrew, the animal curls up and begins to lick its anus, sometimes gripping the hind limbs with the forefeet to maintain position. After a few seconds, abdominal contractions cause the rectum to extrude and the end is then nibbled and licked for some minutes before being withdrawn. It appears that refection does not start until the intestine is free of feces. If the shrew is killed, the stomach and first few

Right *A young Eurasian water shrew swallows a worm. The animals' small size belies their status as fierce predators with omnivorous eating habits.*

Shrew Subfamilies

White-toothed shrews
Subfamily Crocidurinae

White-toothed shrews Genus *Crocidura*
151 species in Africa and S Eurasia, including African giant shrew (*C. olivieri*), Egyptian pygmy shrew (*C. religiosa*), Greater white-toothed shrew (*C. russula*), Lesser white-toothed shrew (*C. suaveolens*); forest to semidesert. Seventeen species are classified as Critically Endangered.

Mouse shrews Genus *Myosorex*
12 species in central and southern Africa, including Dark-footed forest shrew (*M. cafer*); forest. The Rumpi mouse shrew (*M. rumpii*) and Schaller's mouse shrew (*M. schalleri*) are Critically Endangered.

African shrews Genus *Paracrocidura*
3 species in central Africa, including Lesser large-headed shrew (*P. schoutedeni*); forest. Grauer's shrew (*P. graueri*) is Critically Endangered.

Pygmy and Dwarf shrews Genus *Suncus*
16 species in Africa and southern Eurasia, including Pygmy white-toothed shrew (*S. etruscus*), House shrew (*S. murinus*), Lesser dwarf shrew (*S. varilla*); forest, scrub, savanna; commensal. The Black shrew (*S. ater*), Flores shrew (*S. mertensi*), and Gabon dwarf shrew (*S. remyi*) are Critically Endangered.

Kenyan shrews Genus *Surdisorex*
2 species in Kenya: Mount Kenya mole shrew (*S. polulus*); montane; Aberdare shrew (*S. norae*); Aberdare range. Both species are Vulnerable.

Forest musk shrews Genus *Sylvisorex*
10 species in C Africa, including Climbing shrew (*S. megalura*); forest, grassland. The Arrogant shrew (*S. morio*) is Endangered.

Congolese shrew (*Congosorex polli*)
S Democratic Republic of Congo (DRC); forest. Critically Endangered.

Piebald shrew (*Diplomesodon pulchellum*)
W C Asia; desert.

Kelaart's long-clawed shrew (*Feroculus feroculus*). India and Sri Lanka; montane forest. Endangered.

Ruwenzori shrew (*Ruwenzorisorex suncoides*). C Africa; montane forest. Vulnerable.

Armored shrew (*Scutisorex somereni*)
C Africa; forest.

Pearson's long-clawed shrew (*Solisorex pearsoni*). C Sri Lanka; montane. Endangered.

Red-toothed shrews
Subfamily Soricinae

American short-tailed shrews Genus *Blarina*. 3 species in E North America, including Northern short-tailed shrew (*B. brevicauda*); forest grassland.

Asiatic short-tailed shrews Genus *Blarinella*. 2 species in China and Burma: Chinese short-tailed shrew (*B. quadraticauda*), montane forest; Ward's short-tailed shrew (*B. wardi*), Burma, Yunnan.

Oriental water shrews Genus *Chimarrogale*. 6 species in S and E Asia, including Himalayan water shrew (*C. himalayica*); montane streams. The Malayan (*C. hantu*) and Sumatra water shrews (*C. sumatrana*) are Critically Endangered.

Small-eared shrews Genus *Cryptotis*
14 species in E North America, C America, N South America, including American least shrew (*C. parva*); forest, grassland. Enders's small-eared shrew (*C. endersi*) is Endangered.

Old World water shrews Genus *Neomys*
3 species in N Eurasia, including Eurasian water shrew (*N. fodiens*); woodland, grassland, streams, wetlands.

Holarctic shrews Genus *Sorex*
70 species in N and C Eurasia and N America, including Eurasian common shrew (*S. araneus*), Masked shrew (*S. cinereus*), Smoky shrew (*S. fumeus*), Eurasian pygmy shrew (*S. minutus*), American water shrew (*S. palustris*), Trowbridge's shrew (*S. trowbridgii*); tundra, grassland, woodland. Kozlov's shrew (*S. kozlovi*) and the Gansu shrew (*S. cansulus*) are Critically Endangered.

Genus *Soriculus*. 10 species in S Central Asia from Pakistan to China and Vietnam, including Long-tailed mountain shrew (*S. macrurus*); montane forest. Salenski's shrew (*S. salenskii*) is Critically Endangered.

Mole shrew (*Anourosorex squamipes*)
S Asia; montane forest.

Mexican giant shrew (*Megasorex gigas*)
SW Mexico; forest, semi-arid areas.

Tibetan water shrew (*Nectogale elegans*)
Sikkim to Shenshi; montane streams.

Desert shrew (*Notiosorex crawfordi*)
S USA and Mexico; semidesert scrub, montane.

For full species list see Appendix ▷

centimeters of the intestine can be seen to be filled with a milky fluid containing fat globules and partially digested food. It is thought that shrews may obtain trace elements and vitamins B and K in this way.

Caravans and Tunnels

SOCIAL BEHAVIOR

In species occupying temperate and arctic zones, breeding is seasonal, while tropical species may breed continuously. An example of a northern temperate species is the Eurasian common shrew. Individuals of this species generally do not breed until the year following birth. The breeding season starts in April, and females can potentially produce up to 4 or 5 litters of as many as 11 young. Usually, however, adult females produce one or two litters of 4–8 young, and then die. Likewise, there is mortality of adult males, so by late summer the population is dominated by immature individuals. The gestation period is 20 days in this species and lactation lasts for about 23 days. The first estrus of the breeding season is synchronized within a population, with the result that almost all females are mated within a few days. These must be frantic periods, for the estrus of each female lasts no more than a few hours. It has been demonstrated by DNA fingerprinting of offspring, their mothers, and potential fathers, that a single female may mate with as many as six different males during one estrus. Mating itself has been observed in captivity. The male grips the female on the nape and it is possible to identify mated females by the bite mark , which develops into a patch of white hair.

Among the tropical species, the best studied is the House shrew. Like the Eurasian common shrew, it is promiscuous and has been observed to accept as many as eight males and to copulate 278 times within a period of 2 hours. House shrews have a gestation period of 30 days and a litter size of usually 2–4 young. As with other shrews, the young are born naked and blind, but develop fast.

The House shrew is one of a number of species of *Suncus* and *Crocidura* whose young exhibit "caravanning" behaviour. When mature enough to leave the nest the young form a line. Each animal grips the rump of the one in front and the foremost grips that of the mother. The grip is quite tenacious and the whole caravan can be lifted off the ground intact by picking up the mother.

Most shrews are solitary and it is likely that the promiscuous mating system found in the Eurasian common shrew and the House shrew is frequent. Because of high food requirements, individuals of some species defend territories for all or part of their lives. This is seen particularly clearly in the Eurasian common shrew during the winter months. The only time many shrews come into close contact is during fighting, mating, and at the nestling stage. However, at least one species, the Lesser dwarf shrew, has been shown to form very long-lasting pair bonds. Other species are even more social. The American least shrew is believed to be more or less permanently colonial, and individuals of the Greater white-toothed shrew huddle together in groups during the winter, presumably to help maintain body temperature.

Several species dig tunnel systems and these may be the focal point of defended territories. The American short-tailed shrew, the American least shrew, the Eurasian common shrew, and the Eurasian water shrew have all been observed digging. Observations in captivity of the Smoky shrew, the Masked shrew, Trowbridge's shrew, and the Eurasian pygmy shrew suggest that they do not burrow. In the Eurasian water shrew, the tunnel system is important in squeezing water from the fur, and it also seems to be significant in maintaining fur condition in the Eurasian common shrew. In captivity, Eurasian common shrews often cache food in their tunnels. Tunnel systems may also be important in avoiding predators and usually have more than one entrance. Nests of grass and other plant material are usually built in a chamber off the tunnel system, and shrews spend most of their sleeping and resting time there.

Endemics in Danger

CONSERVATION AND ENVIRONMENT

It might be thought that shrews, as a highly successful group of small, fast-breeding mammals with great reproductive potential, would be rather resistant to human-induced extinction. Sadly, nothing could be further from the truth. Many tropical species are extremely restricted in their distribution and occur at low densities. At current rates of destruction of the tropical forest, it is certain that many of these species will go extinct.

Above *Caravanning: young shrews find their way around their terrain by forming chains, led by their mother. They continue to hang on even if the mother is picked up off the ground.*

Right *Two Northern short-tailed shrews* (Blarina brevicauda) *confront one another. This species, like several others, digs tunnel systems that form the basis of defended territories.*

Left *Refection: some species, like this Eurasian pygmy shrew* (Sorex minutus), *obtain vital nutrients by licking the rectum, which is extruded from the anus to facilitate access.*

Below *A Common Eurasian shrew* (Sorex araneus) *suckling her infants. Males make no contribution to raising the young.*

In contrast, some shrews appear to have flourished alongside humans. The House shrew is an extreme example: it is a tropical, commensal species that feeds on insects found around people's houses. House shrews have been unwittingly transported with humans to many parts of the tropics. Unfortunately, such passive transport of human-tolerant shrews can be very dangerous to endemic species of shrews on islands. Thus, it is thought that the genus *Nesiotites*, known from Mediterranean islands such as Corsica, Sardinia, and the Balearics, became extinct following the accidental introduction of Greater, Lesser, and Pygmy white-toothed shrews by humans. This is an instance of competitively superior shrews leading to the demise of other species.

It is not just very local species of shrews that are vulnerable to extinction. Recent evidence from Britain suggests that the Eurasian common shrew is declining there. This is particularly alarming, since this species would otherwise have appeared to be the ultimate survivor. It can utilize marginal habitats such as roadside verges, and appears to have unusual resistance to some pollutants such as heavy metals. Shrews, as much as tigers and rhinos, need to be monitored and cared for during the coming years of threat to the world's mammalian fauna. JBS/CJB

Golden Moles

GOLDEN MOLES ARE SO CALLED FROM THEIR *family name, Chrysochloridae, deriving from the Greek terms for "gold" and "pale green." The appellation refers to the iridescent sheen of coppery green, blue, purple, or bronze on the animals' fur rather than to the color of the fur itself, which is usually a shade of brown.*

Golden moles are known from as far back as the late Eocene, about 40 million years ago. Climatic modifications may be responsible for their present discontinuous distribution, but they have special adaptations for a burrowing mode of life in a wide geographic range of subterrestrial habitats.

FACTFILE

GOLDEN MOLES

Order: Insectivora

Family: Chrysochloridae

21 species in 9 genera

DISTRIBUTION Sub-Saharan Africa, including Somalia.

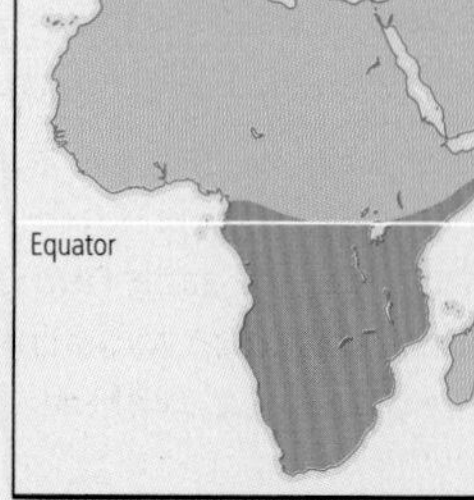

Habitat Almost exclusively burrowing.

Size **Head–body length** ranges from 7–8.5cm (2.7–3.3in) in Grant's desert golden mole to 19.8–23.5cm (7.8–9in) in the Giant golden mole.

LARGE GOLDEN MOLES Genus *Chrysospalax*
The 2 largest species: **Giant golden mole** (*C. trevelyani*), forests in E Cape Province, Endangered; and **Rough-haired golden mole** (*C. villosus*), grasslands and swamp in E South Africa, Vulnerable.

SECRETIVE GOLDEN MOLES Genus *Cryptochloris*
2 species, both found in arid regions of Little Namaqualand, W Cape: **De Winton's golden mole** (*C. wintoni*), Vulnerable; and **Van Zyl's golden mole** (*C. zyli*), Critically Endangered.

CAPE GOLDEN MOLES Genus *Chrysochloris*
3 species: **Stuhlmann's golden mole** (*C. stuhlmanni*), mountains in C and E Africa; **Cape golden mole** (*C. asiatica*), W Cape to Little Namaqualand; and **Visagie's golden mole** (*C. visagiei*), succulent karoo of W Cape, Critically Endangered.

AFRICAN GOLDEN MOLES Genus *Chlorotalpa*
2 species: **Sclater's golden mole** (*C. sclateri*), high-altitude grasslands and scrub in W Cape, Lesotho, E Free State, and Mpumalanga, Vulnerable; and **Duthie's golden mole** (*C. duthieae*), coastal forests in W and E Cape, Vulnerable.

SOUTH AFRICAN GOLDEN MOLES Genus *Amblysomus*
5 species, including the **Hottentot golden mole** (*A. hottentotus*), all found in grasslands and forests in W and E Cape, KwaZulu–Natal, NE Free State, Mpumalanga, Swaziland.

GENUS *NEAMBLYSOMUS*
2 species: **Gunning's golden mole** (*N. gunningi*), forests in Northern Province, Vulnerable; and **Juliana's golden mole** (*N. julianae*), sandy soils in savannas of Gauteng and Mpumalanga, Critically Endangered.

GENUS *CALCOCHLORIS*
3 species: **Yellow golden mole** (*C. obtusirostris*), Zululand to Mozambique and SE Zimbabwe; **Congo golden mole** (*C. leucorhinus*), forests of W and C Africa; **Somali golden mole** (*C. tytonis*), NE Somalia.

GRANT'S GOLDEN MOLE *Eremitalpa granti*
Sandy desert and semidesert of W Cape, Little Namaqualand, Namib Desert. Vulnerable.

AREND'S GOLDEN MOLE *Carpitalpa arendsi*
Forests and adjacent grasslands in E Zimbabwe and NE Mozambique.

For full species list see Appendix ▷

Equipped for Extremes

FORM AND FUNCTION

Golden moles are solitary, burrowing insectivores with compact, streamlined bodies, short limbs, and no visible tail. The backward-set fur is moisture-repellent, remaining sleek and dry in muddy situations; a dense, woolly undercoat provides insulation. The skin is thick and tough, particularly on the head. The eyes are vestigial and covered with hairy skin, and the optic nerve is degenerate. The ear openings are covered by fur, and the nostrils are protected by a leathery pad that assists in soil excavations; in some species such as the Yellow golden mole, the nostrils also have foliaceous projections that prevent sand from entering the nose during burrowing. The wedge-shaped head and extremely muscular shoulders push and pack the soil, whereas the strong forelimbs are equipped with curved, picklike digging claws.Of the four claws, the third is extremely powerful, while the first and fourth are usually rudimentary. The hind feet are webbed with five digits, each bearing a small claw, and are used to shovel loose soil backward along tunnels.

The key to the evolutionary success of golden moles lies in their unique physiology. Despite a high thermal conductance, they have a low basal metabolic rate and do not thermoregulate when at rest, thereby considerably reducing their energy requirements. All species enter torpor, either daily or in response to cold. Body temperature in the thermal neutral zone is lower than in other similarly-sized mammals. Lowered metabolism and efficient renal function effectively reduce water requirements to the extent that most species do not need drinking water. Far from being "primitive" characteristics, such physiological specializations allow the moles to survive in habitats where temperatures are extreme and food is scarce.

The chief senses in golden moles are hearing, touch, and smell. The ear ossicles of some species are disproportionately large, giving great sensitivity to vibrations, which trigger rapid locomotion either toward prey or unerringly toward an open burrow entrance (on the surface) or a bolthole (when underground). Those species without enlarged ear ossicles have a well-developed hyoid apparatus that may transmit low-frequency sounds to the inner ear. Golden moles also have an extraordinary ability to orientate themselves underground; when parts of burrow systems are damaged, the new tunnels that repair them always link up precisely with the existing tunnels.

Golden moles forage in subsurface tunnels, visible from above as soil ridges. Desert-dwelling species "swim" through the sand just below the surface, leaving U-shaped ridges. Most species also excavate deeper burrows connecting grass-lined nests, defecation chambers, and spiraling boltholes, depositing excess soil in small mounds on the surface. Average sustained burrowing lasts for about 44 minutes, separated by inactive periods of about 2.6 hours. Non-random surface locomotion minimizes foraging costs.

The Underground Larder

DIET

Golden moles are opportunistic foragers, preying predominantly on earthworms and insect larvae. Grant's golden moles feed mainly on soft-bodied termites, a sedentary prey occurring in patches of high concentration. De Winton's golden moles also prey on legless lizards, using their long, slender claws to hold these reptiles. Giant golden moles feed mainly on oniscomorph millipedes, which abound in leaf litter, but also take giant earthworms (*Microchaetus* spp.); they probably also consume any small vertebrates they may stumble across. Captive moles take a wide spectrum of terrestrial invertebrates except for mollusks, and can be trained to eat ground beef.

Contacts between the Burrows

SOCIAL BEHAVIOR

Territorial behavior is influenced by the availability of food. Hottentot golden mole burrow systems are more numerous in the summer when food is more abundant, and a certain amount of home range overlap is tolerated. The systems are larger and more aggressively defended in less fertile areas; a neighboring burrow may be taken over by an individual as an extension of its home range. Occupancy is detected by scrutiny of tunnel walls by smell. Fighting occurs between individuals of the same sex, and sometimes between male and female. Hottentot golden moles tolerate herbivorous mole rats in the same burrow systems, and in the Drakensberg range golden mole burrows open into those of Sloggett's vlei rats (*Otomys sloggetti*).

Courtship in Hottentot golden moles involves much chirruping vocalization, head-bobbing, and foot stamping in the male, and grasshopper-like rasping and prolonged squeals with the mouth wide open in the female. Both sexes have a single external urogenital opening. Females display aseasonal polyestry. Litters comprise 1–3 (usually 2) naked young with a head–body length of 4.7cm (1.9in) and a weight of 4.5g (0.16oz). Birth and lactation take place in grass-lined nests, and eviction from the maternal burrow system occurs once the young weigh 35–45g (1.2–1.6oz).

Sadly, eleven species of golden moles are now threatened with extinction owing to habitat degradation induced by human activities. These threats include urbanization, the mining of alluvial sands for diamonds and building materials, poor agricultural practices, and predation by domestic dogs and cats. GB/MP

Right *A telltale ridge of earth indicates the location of a golden mole foraging tunnel. Most species also dig deeper nesting burrows.*

Below *In the Namib Desert in southern Africa, a Grant's golden mole feeds on a locust – a change from its usual diet of soft-bodied termites.*

Moles and Desmans

THE FAMILY TALPIDAE CONTAINS AS QUEER A set of bedfellows as one could hope to meet; on the one hand the moles and shrew-moles, which are more or less fossorial (diggers), and, on the other, the desmans, which are semi-aquatic (swimmers). Today there are 40 species of moles placed in 15 genera and just two species of desmans, each in its own genus.

Most people in Europe and North America have seen molehills, but very few have seen moles. Their subterranean way of life makes these animals difficult to study, and it is only in the last three decades that detailed information has been gathered. The other major group within the family, the desmans, are also little-known, due to their inaccessibility in the mountain streams of the Pyrenees and in the vastness of Russia.

Adaptations for Digging and Swimming

FORM AND FUNCTION

Moles and desmans have elongated, cylindrical bodies. The muzzle is long, tubular, and naked, apart from sensory whiskers. It is highly mobile and extends beyond the lower lip. In the Star-nosed mole the nose divides at the end into a naked fringe of 22 mobile and touch-sensitive fleshy tentacles, used to detect prey. The penis is directed to the rear and there is no scrotum.

The eyes – structurally complete but minute – are largely hidden within the fur, or, in the case of the Mediterranean mole, covered by protective skin. The eyes are sensitive to changes in light level but have little visual acuity. Moles have no external ears except in the Asiatic shrew moles. Both moles and desmans rely to a great extent on touch. The muzzle is richly endowed with projections called Eimer's organs, which are probably touch-sensitive. In addition, various parts of the body including the muzzle, tail, and also the legs of desmans, have sensory whiskers.

Desmans are adapted for swimming: they have a long, flat tail like a rudder, broadened by a fringe of stiff hairs. The legs and feet are proportionally long and powerful, ending in webbed toes and half-webbed fingers, both also fringed with stiff hairs. The nostrils and ears are opened and closed by valves. When swimming, the hind legs provide the main propulsive force.

In moles, the forelimbs are adapted for digging. The hands are turned permanently outward, rather like a pair of oars. The hands are large, almost circular, and equipped with five large and strong claws. The teeth are unspecialized and typical of the Insectivora.

The moles and desmans originated in Europe, where their fossil record extends back some 45 million years into the mid-Eocene. Today, moles are spread throughout Europe, Asia, and North America, but are absent from Africa, where their niche as underground hunters of invertebrates is occupied by the golden moles (family Chrysochloridae). Recent analyses suggest that the ancestors of *Condylura*, *Neurotrichus*, and

Below *The Star-nosed mole has a unique nose that is divided into a number of fleshy tentacles – almost coral-like in appearance – which are used for detecting prey.*

2

3

5

◐ **Left** *Representative species of moles and desmans:* **1** *European mole* (Talpa europaea)*;* **2** *American shrew-mole* (Neurotrichus gibbsi)*;* **3** *Lesser Japanese shrew-mole* (Urotrichus pilirostris)*;* **4** *Star-nosed mole* (Condylura cristata)*;* **5** *Pyrenean desman* (Galemys pyrenaicus).

Parascalops dispersed to Europe and North America separately from the common ancestor of *Scalopus* and *Scapanus*.

During the Pleistocene, the Russian desman, *Desmana moschata*, was found across Europe in a broad band from southern Britain to the Caspian Sea. Since then it has become progressively restricted in distribution, and today is confined to the southern part of European Russia, in the basins of the rivers Dnieper, Don, Kama, Ural, and Volga. Fossils of *Galemys pyrenaicus*, the Pyrenean desman, are known only from the Pyrenees and their foothills, and today the species is restricted to the northern half of the Iberian Peninsula and to the French side of the Pyrenees.

Diets of Worms

DIET

Moles dig permanent tunnels and obtain most of their food from soil invertebrates that fall into them. When digging new tunnels, they brace themselves with their hind feet and dig with the fore feet, which are thrust alternately into the soil and moved sideways and backward. Periodically, they dig a vertical shaft to the surface and push up the soil to make a molehill. Tunnels range in depth from a few centimeters to 1m (3.3ft). Probably 90 percent of the diet is foraged from the permanent tunnels; moles eat whatever is locally available but favor earthworms, beetle and fly larvae, and slugs. The European mole stores worms with their heads bitten off near its nest in October and November.

Desmans obtain nearly all their food from water, especially aquatic insects such as stonefly and caddis-fly larvae, freshwater shrimps, and snails. The Russian desman also takes larger prey such as fish and amphibians.

FACTFILE

MOLES AND DESMANS

Order: Insectivora

Family: Talpidae

42 species in 17 genera and 3 subfamilies. Subfamily Desmaninae contains 2 monotypic genera of desmans; subfamily Talpinae 14 genera of moles, including the Old World moles (*Talpa* spp.); subfamily Uropsilinae 1 genus of shrew mole (*Uropsilus* spp.)

DISTRIBUTION Europe, Asia, and N America

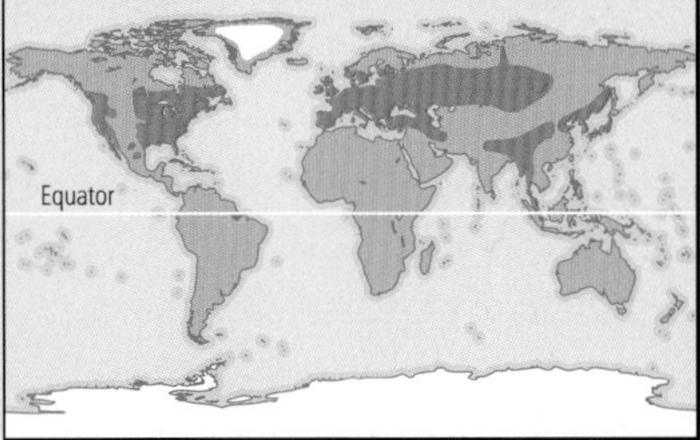

HABITAT Moles are largely subterranean, usually living under forests and grasslands but also under heaths. Desmans are aquatic in lakes and rivers. Shrew moles construct tunnels, but forage in the litter layer.

SIZE **Head–body length** ranges from 2.4–7.5cm (1–3in) in the shrew moles to 18–21.5cm (7–8.5in) in the Russian desman; **tail length** from 2.4–7.5cm (1–3in) to 17–21.5cm (6.5–8.5in), and **weight** from under 12g (0.4oz) to about 550g (19.5oz), both in the same species.

COAT Desman fur is double-layered, with a short, dense waterproof underfur and oily guard hairs; stiff hairs enlarge the paws and tail for swimming. Moles have short fur of uniform length, which lies in any direction during tunneling. Shrew moles have guard hairs and underfur directed backward. Moles are usually uniformly brownish black or gray, desmans brown or reddish on the back, merging to gray below.

DIET Moles live mainly on earthworms, beetle and fly larvae, and slugs; desmans on larvae, freshwater shrimps, snails, small fish, and amphibians.

BREEDING Gestation unknown (but greater than 15 days) in shrew moles and desmans; 30 days in the European and 42 days in the Eastern American mole.

LONGEVITY Up to 4 years in the European and Eastern American mole, 4–5 years in the Hairy-tailed mole.

CONSERVATION STATUS Two species – the Small-toothed and Persian moles – are Critically Endangered, and a further 5 species Endangered. The Japanese mountain mole and both species of desman are listed as Vulnerable.

For full species list see Appendix ▷

From Tunnel to Tunnel

SOCIAL BEHAVIOR

Little is known about the population density and social organization of desmans beyond the following sparse details: Pyrenean desmans appear to be solitary and inhabit small permanent home ranges, which they scentmark with latrines. There is some evidence that Russian desmans are at times nomadic as a result of unpredictable water levels. They may be social, since as many as eight adults have been found together in one burrow.

There is much more information on the moles, although it relates in the main to the European mole. There are equal numbers of males and females in populations of European moles, and populations appear to be relatively stable, unlike those of small rodents. Most mole species are solitary and territorial, with individuals defending all or the greater part of their home range. The Star-nosed mole is exceptional in that, for reasons that are poorly understood, a male and female may live together during the winter. In other species, males and females meet only briefly, to mate.

Population densities vary from species to species and from habitat to habitat. Between 5–25 European moles may be found per hectare; the equivalent figures for Eastern American moles are 5–12, for Star-nosed moles 5–25, and for Hairy-tailed moles 5–28.

Radio-tracking studies have shown that territory sizes in the European mole vary between the sexes, from habitat to habitat, and from season to season. The habitat and sex differences reflect differences in food supply and the greater energy demands of the larger male. Males increase territory size dramatically in the spring, as they seek out receptive partners. Normally, moles remain within their territories for their whole lives. However, radio-tracking has revealed that during hot, dry weather some moles leave their range and travel as far as 1km (0.6mi) to drink at streams. This entails crossing the territories of up to 10 other moles!

Moles' social organization is better understood than their ranges. European moles are territorial and spend almost their whole lives underground. Radio-tracking studies have shown that although neighboring moles each inhabit their own tunnel systems, territories do overlap to a small extent. Whether tunnels in overlapping areas are shared or separate, running between each other in the soil column, is not known. There is evidence, however, that moles are aware of the presence and activities of their neighbors. For example, during any particular activity period, neighbors forage in non-adjacent parts of their territories, avoiding contact. It is a testimony to the efficiency of this system of avoidance that conflict between established neighbors has not been recorded.

When a mole dies, or is trapped and removed, neighbors quickly detect its absence and invade the vacated area. For example, after several weeks of observation one radio-tagged animal was trapped and removed: within 12 hours a neighboring mole was spending its morning activity period foraging in the vacated territory, and his afternoon shift in his own territory.

In other cases, a vacated territory may be shared among neighbors. Such was the case with a group of four moles that occupied neighboring territories until one was removed. Within a matter of hours, the others had enlarged their territories to incorporate the vacated area. The enlarged territories were retained for at least several weeks.

Moles probably advertise their presence and their tenure of an area by scentmarking. Both sexes possess preputial glands that produce a highly odorous secretion that accumulates on the fur of the abdomen; this is deposited on the floor of tunnels, as well as at latrines. The scent is highly volatile and must be renewed regularly if the mole is to maintain its claim to ownership of the territory. In the absence of such a scent, the territory is quickly invaded.

Desmans are primarily nocturnal, but they often also have a short active period during the day. In contrast, most of the moles are active both by day and night. Until recently it was thought

that European moles always had three active periods per day, alternating with rest periods. Recent studies of moles fitted with radio transmitters reveal a more complex picture. In the winter, males and females do show three activity periods, each of about four hours, separated by a rest of four hours in the nest. At this time they almost always leave the nest at sunrise. Females maintain this pattern for the rest of the year, except for a period in summer when they are lactating. Then they return to the nest more often in order to feed their young.

Males are less predictable. In spring they start to seek out receptive females and remain away from the nest for days at a time, snatching catnaps in their tunnels. In the summer they return to their winter routine, but in September they display just two activity periods per day.

Life-cycle details are known only for a few species, again the European mole in particular; little is known about the desmans and shrew moles. In general, moles have a short breeding season, and produce a single litter of 2–7 young each year. Lactation lasts for about a month. The males take no part in the care of the young, and the young normally breed in the year following their birth.

In a number of species including the European mole, it is difficult to tell the two sexes apart. This is because the external sexual features are similar, a problem exacerbated by the fact that the testes do not descend into an external scrotum. Females of these species are exceptional among mammals in that they possess ovotestes. The ovotestis contains a morphologically normal ovarian component that develops during the spring and that produces eggs, but also a testicular region that enlarges during the autumn and produces high levels of testosterone. This may be the reason why the sexes are externally similar, and also why female moles are just as aggressive to other moles as males. Whether this physiological system conveys real advantages to the mole, or is just an evolutionary quirk, is unknown, and for the moment remains an unresolved mystery.

Above right The fate of many moles is to be killed by farmers. For centuries moles have been trapped, to reduce damage to fields and for their skins. Eradication campaigns are waged when they become serious pests, but moles' pelts no longer have any real commercial value.

Left Breaking cover, a European mole emerges from the middle of a molehill. The relatively huge, powerful, outward-facing forelimbs are clearly visible. Molehills– the most obvious sign of the presence of these animals – are often all that most people see of this elusive animal.

In Britain, European moles mate in March to May, and the young are born in May or June. The time of breeding varies with latitude: the same species is pregnant in mid-February in northern Italy, but not until May or June in northeast Scotland. This variation suggests that the length of daylight controls breeding, which may seem strange for a subterranean animal. However, moles do come to the surface to collect grass and other materials for their nests – one nest, located close to a licensed hotel, was constructed entirely of discarded potato-chip bags!

The average litter size in Britain is 3.7, but it can be higher in continental Europe; an average of 5.7 has been reported for Russia. One litter per year is the norm, but there are records of animals that were pregnant twice in one year (the second pregnancy coming in the fall). Sperm production lasts for only two months, but sufficient spermatozoa may be stored to allow the insemination of females coming into this late or second period of heat.

The young are born in the nest. They are naked at birth, have fur at 14 days, and open their eyes at 22 days. Lactation lasts for 4–5 weeks, and the young leave the nest weighing 60g (2.1oz) or more, some 35 days after birth.

After leaving the nest, the young leave their mother's territory and move overground to seek an unoccupied area. At this time many are killed by predators and by cars. With an average litter size of about four, the numbers of animals present in May must be reduced by 66 percent by death or emigration if the population is to remain stable.

Martyrs to Moleskin

CONSERVATION AND ENVIRONMENT

The Russian desman is widely trapped for its lustrous fur, and most of the skins in Western museums have come from the fur trade. To increase production the species was introduced to the River Dnieper.

All moles, particularly North American and European, are regarded as pests by farmers, gardeners, and greenkeepers. Moles disturb the roots of young plants, causing them to wilt and die; in addition, soil from molehills contaminates silage, and the stones they bring to the surface cause damage to cutting machinery. On the positive side, they have on occasion brought worked flints and Roman tesserae to the surface.

Nowadays, moles are usually controlled by poison. In Britain the most widely used agent is strychnine, which has the disadvantage of being unacceptably cruel and also endangers other animals: although available only by government permit, a disturbing amount is diverted to killing other forms of "vermin," including birds of prey.

In the past, professional trappers and agricultural workers trapped European moles on a massive scale and sold the skins to be made into breeches, waistcoats, and ladies' coats. There was a similar trade in moleskins in North America, particularly from the Townsend mole. This trade largely collapsed after the First World War.

The two extant species of desmans are both endangered: the Russian because of over-hunting for its fur, and the Pyrenean from overzealous scientific collecting and from habitat destruction, such as the damming of mountain streams. The formulation of management plans is hampered by a lack of knowledge of the basic biology of both of these species. MLG

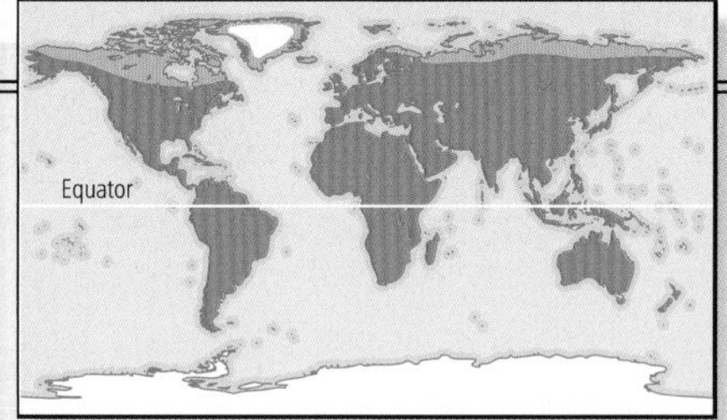

BATS

BATS ARE EXTRAORDINARY CREATURES. THEY are exemplary mothers, and some also care for each other's young; they can fly at speeds of up to 50km/h (30mph) through complete darkness, thanks to sophisticated orientation systems; and one of the few convincing examples of altruistic behavior in the animal kingdom is exhibited by bats. Bats can show specialized reproductive adaptations, including sperm storage, delayed fertilization, and delayed implantation. They are heterothermic; their body temperature may vary from up to 41°C (106°F) in flight to under 2°C (36°F) during hibernation. They can form aggregations of 20 million animals – the largest known in vertebrates. Their wonderful diversity and specializations have inspired important programs for their conservation worldwide.

Even so, bats rarely appear on people's top-ten lists of favorite animals. Perhaps their lack of public charisma stems from the same characteristics that make them so fascinating and unique. About one quarter of all living mammal species are bats. Houses, caves, mines, and trees in leaf all provide them with roosting sites, while some species make their own tents from plant parts. Most are largely nocturnal – small bats fly at night to avoid predators, while it is thought large megachiropterans do so to avoid overheating during the day. They are found everywhere except on the highest mountains and isolated oceanic islands, and have even been discovered breeding north of the Arctic Circle; on some islands such as the Azores, Hawaii, and New Zealand, they are the only native land mammals. Flight and echolocation have especially contributed to their diversity and cosmopolitan nature, permitting them to effectively exploit a food resource for which they have no animal competitors – insects that fly at night.

Mega and Micro Species

CLASSIFICATION AND EVOLUTION

Bats (order Chiroptera) are classified in two suborders, the Megachiroptera and Microchiroptera. Megachiropterans comprise a single family, the flying foxes (Pteropodidae), and are restricted to the tropics and subtropics of the Old World, where they feed mainly on fruit and nectar. The smallest megachiropterans weigh only 15g (0.5oz), while the heaviest weigh over 1.3kg (2.9lb). Flying foxes usually have a claw on their second fingers as well as on their thumbs, and their simple ears lack the tragus – a lobe in the ear – seen in many microchiropterans. Megachiropterans have well-developed vision and make little use of echolocation; the bats of only one Megachiroptera genus – the rousettes – use an echolocatory system, a relatively crude one employing tongue movements to produce largely ultrasonic double clicks of a few milliseconds' duration to aid orientation in dark caves. In addition, the Dawn bat slaps its wings in flight, perhaps to create echoes for similar reasons.

Above *An epauletted fruit bat (*Epomophorus *genus) rests at a roost in the Okavango Delta, Botswana. Its folded wings reveal not only the clawlike thumb possessed by nearly all bat species but also a longer claw on the second finger; this feature, found in most Megachiroptera genera, is never found in the Microchiroptera, the other division of the bat order.*

Right *The huge ears of this Bechstein's bat* (Myotis bechsteinii) *help in the hunt for insects. The 84* Myotis *species are found everywhere except the polar regions and some oceanic islands, and are reckoned to have the widest natural distribution of any group of terrestrial mammals other than the human race.*

Extraordinarily, some scientists have proposed that the Megachiroptera may in fact be more closely related to primates than to the Microchiroptera. As well as having no vocal echolocation, megachiropterans share advanced features of their vision with primates, and also have similar ratios between the lengths of their finger bones. This "flying-primate" hypothesis, which would require wings to have evolved independently in each of the two suborders, has, however, received little support from molecular studies, which instead emphasize the similarity between the bat groups, in that both have high levels of adenine and thymine bases in their genes. Biologists who support the flying-primate theory argue against this that the genetic resemblance may simply be a consequence of both suborders needing to consume high levels of energy in flight; in their view, the genomes of the two groups are similar because evolution has shaped them separately in similar ways rather than because they shared a recent common ancestor. The debate continues, but it remains true to say that most molecular studies now support a monophyletic origin for bats, by which flying foxes and microchiropterans would share a common ancestor.

The molecular evidence also suggests that horseshoe bats, along with such near relatives as the Old World false vampires, are more closely related to the Megachiroptera than they are to other Microchiroptera. Confusingly, however, horseshoe bats have some of the most sophisticated echolocation systems seen in the animal kingdom, while the Megachiroptera species have almost none. This hypothesis would therefore suggest either that horseshoe bats evolved echolocation independently of the other microchiropteran species, or alternatively that the various Megachiroptera species once had similar sensory capacities that they subsequently lost. Neither of these propositions seems very likely, and a third possibility is that the molecular evidence placing horseshoe bats close to the Megachiroptera may simply be misleading.

The earliest known fossil bat is the 50-million-year-old *Icaronycteris index*, which was found in Wyoming, USA. Superb fossil bats also dating from the Eocene have been found in the Messel beds in Germany, their stomachs containing identifiable fossils insects. Many of these early bats resemble living Microchiroptera, so earlier stages in their evolution are difficult to reconstruct, though the structure of the cochlea (inner ear) suggests that they almost certainly echolocated. The earliest fossils resembling megachiropteran

ORDER: CHIROPTERA

18 families, 174 genera, more than 900 species; figures change constantly as new species are described and taxonomic revisions are made.

Distribution Worldwide except for the highest mountains, some isolated islands, and extreme Polar regions (though some bats breed N of the Arctic Circle).

Size The smallest species is the Hog-nosed bat, with a body mass of 1.9g (0.07oz) and a wingspan of 16 cm (6.3in). Some flying foxes (*Pteropus* spp.) may exceed 1.3kg (2.9lb) in weight and have wingspans of 1.7m (5.6ft).

Diet In 70 percent of bat species, primarily insects and other small arthropods; the rest mainly subsist on fruit, nectar, and pollen. Some tropical species are carnivorous, and three species of vampire bats feed on blood.

Coat Variable; mostly browns, grays, and blacks.

Gestation Variable; can range from 3–10 months in a single species with delayed implantation.

Longevity Maximum 33 years; probably averages 4–5 years in many species.

SUBORDER MEGACHIROPTERA

FLYING FOXES Family Pteropodidae

41 genera and 164 species in the Old World, including: **Straw-colored flying fox** (*Eidolon helvum*); **rousettes** (*Rousettus* spp.); **Rodriguez flying fox** (*Pteropus rodricensis*); **Mariana flying fox** (*Pteropus mariannus*); **Large flying fox** (*P. vampyrus*); **Hammer-headed bat** (*Hypsignathus monstrosus*); **Dawn bat** (*Eonycteris spelaea*); **Short-nosed fruit bat** (*Cyanopterus sphinx*); **Long-tongued fruit bats** (*Macroglossus* spp.).

SUBORDER MICROCHIROPTERA

MOUSE-TAILED BATS Family Rhinopomatidae

1 genus and 3 species in the Old World, including: **Greater mouse-tailed bat** (*Rhinopoma microphyllum*).

HOG-NOSED BAT Family Craseonycteridae

1 species in the Old World: **Hog-nosed bat** (*Craseonycteris thonglongyai*).

SHEATH-TAILED BATS Family Emballonuridae

12 genera and 47 species in Old and New Worlds, including: **Greater white-lined bat** (*Saccopteryx bilineata*).

SLIT-FACED BATS Family Nycteridae

1 genus and 13 species in the Old World, including: **Large slit-faced bat** (*Nycteris grandis*).

OLD WORLD FALSE VAMPIRE BATS Family Megadermatidae

4 genera and 5 species in the Old World, including: **Greater false vampire bat** (*Megaderma lyra*); **Yellow-winged bat** (*Lavia frons*).

HORSESHOE AND OLD WORLD LEAF-NOSED BATS Family Rhinolophidae

10 genera and 129 species in the Old World, including: **Greater horseshoe bat** (*Rhinolophus ferrumequinum*); **Diadem leaf-nosed bat** (*Hipposideros diadema*); **Short-eared trident bat** (*Cloeotis percivali*).

NEW ZEALAND SHORT-TAILED BATS Family Mystacinidae

1 species in the Old World: **New Zealand lesser short-tailed bat** (*Mystacina tuberculata*).

BULLDOG BATS Family Noctilionidae

1 genus and 2 species in the New World: **Greater bulldog bat** (*Noctilio leporinus*); **Lesser bulldog bat** (*N. albiventris*).

SPECTACLED BATS Family Mormoopidae

2 genera and 8 species in the New World, including: **Parnell's moustached bat** (*Pteronotus parnellii*).

NEW WORLD LEAF-NOSED BATS Family Phyllostomidae

48 genera and 139 species in the New World, including: **California leaf-nosed bat** (*Macrotus californicus*); **Greater spear-nosed bat** (*Phyllostomus hastatus*); **Fringe-lipped bat** (*Trachops cirrhosus*); **Seba's short-tailed bat** (*Carollia perspicillata*); **Tent-building bat** (*Uroderma bilobatum*); **Common vampire bat** (*Desmodus rotundus*).

FUNNEL-EARED BATS Family Natalidae

1 genus (*Natalus*) and 5 species in the New World.

THUMBLESS BATS Family Furipteridae

2 genera and 2 species in New World: **Smoky bat** (*Amorphichilus schnablii*) and **Thumbless bat** (*Furipterus horrens*).

DISK-WINGED BATS Family Thyropteridae

1 genus and 2 species in the New World: **Peter's disk-winged bat** (*Thyroptera discifera*) and **Spix's disk-winged bat** (*T. tricolor*).

OLD WORLD SUCKER-FOOTED BAT Family Myzopodidae

1 species in the Old World: **Sucker-footed bat** (*Myzopoda aurita*)

VESPERTILIONID BATS Family Vespertilionidae

34 genera and 308 species in the Old and New Worlds, including: **Large mouse-eared bat** (*Myotis myotis*); **Daubenton's bat** (*M. daubentonii*); **Little brown bat** (*M. lucifugus*); **Common pipistrelle** (*Pipistrellus pipistrellus*); **noctule** (*Nyctalus noctula*); **Big brown bat** (*Eptesicus fuscus*); **Silver-haired bat** (*Lasionycteris noctivagans*); **Bamboo bat** (*Tylonycteris pachypus*).

PALLID BAT Family Antrozoidae

1 species in the New World: *Antrozous pallidus*

FREE-TAILED BATS Family Molossidae

12 genera and 77 species in the Old and New Worlds, including: **Brazilian free-tailed bat** (*Tadarida brasiliensis*); **European free-tailed bat** (*T. teniotis*); **Black mastiff bat** (*Molossus ater*); **Hairless bat** (*Cheiromeles torquatus*).

See family table ▷

species date to about 35 million years ago.

There are three main hypotheses to explain the evolution of flight and echolocation in bats. The first suggests that flying and finding food by biosonar are inextricably linked. Echolocation calls can contain considerable acoustic power, and are often energetically expensive to produce when a bat is at rest. When flying, however, many bats use the same muscular processes both for powering their wings and for emitting echolocation calls, which are thus produced at no extra cost. The link between flying and calling explains why many bats produce one intense call per wingbeat when searching for prey.

Other researchers have, however, suggested that flapping flight evolved before echolocation, or vice versa. Under either of these hypotheses, the initial function of echolocation was orientation, and it only later became refined for the more demanding tasks involved in the detection and localization of prey.

Comprising 17 families, the microchiropterans are ecologically diverse, particularly in the tropics. They include the smallest bat species, the Hog-nosed bat, which at about 1.9g (0.07oz) is the tiniest of all mammals.

The largest microchiropteran species are the New World false vampire bat (a phyllostomid, unrelated to the Old World false vampires), and the Hairless bat of Indo-Malaysia, which weigh in at 175g (6oz). All microchiropterans echolocate, some just to find their way about. The microchiropterans' small size may help them to produce the high-pitched frequencies needed for finding small insects; because ultrasonic echolocation is a short-range process, large bats may be unable to maneuver quickly enough to respond to echoes that can only be detected at close range. Moreover, large bats flap their wings slowly and so, because echolocation and wingbeat are coupled, produce calls at a rate that may be too drawn-out for efficient prey detection.

As biologists try to establish the exact relationships between the various types of bats, the number of ascribed species changes constantly. Molecular techniques have revealed several "cryptic" species that look very similar to other species but show large genetic differences. In Europe, the common and easily observed pipistrelle bat has recently been found to comprise two cryptic species that emit echolocation calls at different frequencies (see feature on Hidden Biodiversity).

Wings Fitted for the Job

FUNCTIONAL MORPHOLOGY AND FLIGHT

Like other mammals, bats have heterodont (complex) dentition, including incisors, canines, premolars, and molars. Small insectivorous bats may have 38 teeth, while vampire bats have only 20 since they have no need to chew. Among insectivorous bats, species that feed on hard-bodied prey

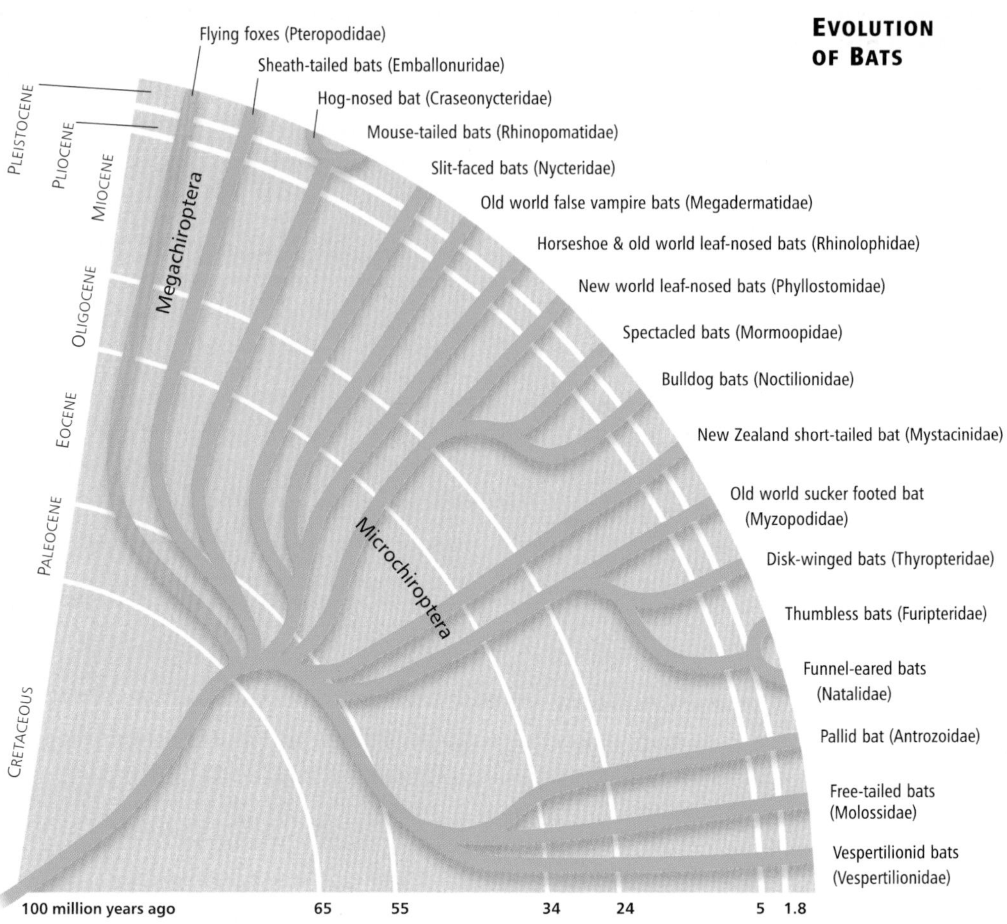

Above *The evolutionary relationships between bat families are controversial as the fossil record is poor. In particular, there are no known early flying foxes (Megachiroptera), so it is not known when the two suborders split, although most taxonomists now accept that they did once share a common ancestor.*

Below *The Australian false vampire* (Macroderma gigas) *is an oddity among bats in that it is carnivorous. After sunset it flies from its roost, usually in a cave or abandoned mine shaft, to a feeding site on a branch. There it hangs vertically, waiting to drop on mice and other small animals that pass underneath.*

BAT BODY PLAN

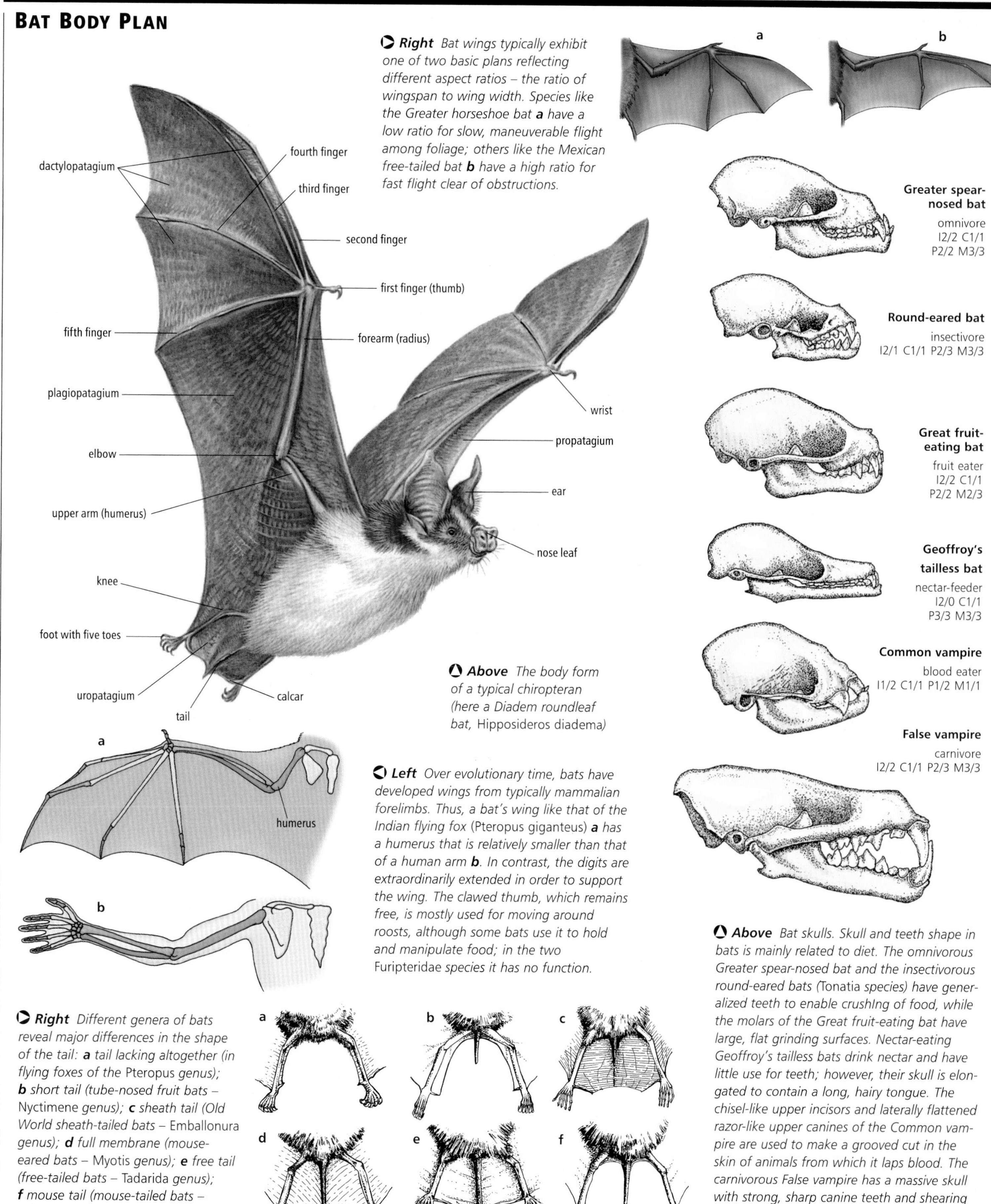

Right *Bat wings typically exhibit one of two basic plans reflecting different aspect ratios – the ratio of wingspan to wing width. Species like the Greater horseshoe bat* ***a*** *have a low ratio for slow, maneuverable flight among foliage; others like the Mexican free-tailed bat* ***b*** *have a high ratio for fast flight clear of obstructions.*

Above *The body form of a typical chiropteran (here a Diadem roundleaf bat,* Hipposideros diadema*)*

Left *Over evolutionary time, bats have developed wings from typically mammalian forelimbs. Thus, a bat's wing like that of the Indian flying fox (*Pteropus giganteus*)* ***a*** *has a humerus that is relatively smaller than that of a human arm* ***b****. In contrast, the digits are extraordinarily extended in order to support the wing. The clawed thumb, which remains free, is mostly used for moving around roosts, although some bats use it to hold and manipulate food; in the two* Furipteridae *species it has no function.*

Above *Bat skulls. Skull and teeth shape in bats is mainly related to diet. The omnivorous Greater spear-nosed bat and the insectivorous round-eared bats (*Tonatia *species) have generalized teeth to enable crushing of food, while the molars of the Great fruit-eating bat have large, flat grinding surfaces. Nectar-eating Geoffroy's tailless bats drink nectar and have little use for teeth; however, their skull is elongated to contain a long, hairy tongue. The chisel-like upper incisors and laterally flattened razor-like upper canines of the Common vampire are used to make a grooved cut in the skin of animals from which it laps blood. The carnivorous False vampire has a massive skull with strong, sharp canine teeth and shearing molars for crushing bones and cutting flesh.*

Right *Different genera of bats reveal major differences in the shape of the tail:* ***a*** *tail lacking altogether (in flying foxes of the* Pteropus *genus);* ***b*** *short tail (tube-nosed fruit bats –* Nyctimene *genus);* ***c*** *sheath tail (Old World sheath-tailed bats –* Emballonura *genus);* ***d*** *full membrane (mouse-eared bats –* Myotis *genus);* ***e*** *free tail (free-tailed bats –* Tadarida *genus);* ***f*** *mouse tail (mouse-tailed bats –* Rhinopoma *genus).*

tend to have larger and fewer teeth, with more robust mandibles and longer canines, than those that feed on soft-bodied insects. Nectar-eating microchiropterans have long snouts, large canines, and small cheek teeth, while frugivorous microchiropterans have modified cusps on their cheek teeth that operate like mortars and pestles to crush fruit.

Bats are the only mammals capable of powered flight. Although flight is energetically expensive in terms of units of time, the energy expenditure per unit of distance covered is low. Bats can therefore fly considerable distances and exploit food over a wide range, allowing them to migrate and exploit farflung parts of the globe.

The finger and arm bones in mammals have evolved into many different types of tools, but none is perhaps so unusual as the bat's wing. The thumb is free, while the fifth digit spans the entire width of the wing. The other three digits support the area of the wing between the thumb and fifth digit, which is known as the dactylopatagium, or "hand wing." The upper arm bone (the humerus) is shorter than the major forearm bone (the radius), and the wing area supported by these bones is called the plagiopatagium, or "arm wing." During flight, inertial forces are greatest on the arm wing.

Many species of microchiropteran also have a tail membrane. This feature, which is absent in *Pteropus* species and reduced in the mouse-tailed bats, is most developed in species such as the slit-faced bats (Nycteridae) that use it to scoop prey from surfaces. The tail membrane is also supported by the legs. Fishing bats and species such as Daubenton's bat that trawl insects from the water's surface often capture prey with the claws on their feet.

Bats' legs project sideways and backward, and the knee bends back rather than forward as in other mammals. The legs are adapted for pulling rather than pushing; the lower leg is formed of a single bone, the tibia. Resting bats hang with their weight suspended on the toes and their well-developed claws. Most bats have a tendon-locking mechanism that keeps the claws bent without the need for muscular contraction. Hanging upside down allows bats to take flight rapidly from a resting position.

Some species such as Common vampires and the New Zealand short-tailed bat crawl on all fours, a feat of which horseshoe bats and others are incapable of accomplishing. Common vampires often approach prey when on the ground, while the New Zealand short-tailed bat evolved in the absence of small terrestrial mammals and with few predators, and so may fill a more terrestrial niche than other species.

The wingbeat of bats is configured primarily to generate thrust, most of it from the hand-wing. Visualizations of the airflow behind flying bats shows that the downstroke generates lift at all speeds, while the upstroke becomes active only at high speed when the bat changes gait.

Wing-shape profoundly influences bats' flying performance. Two aerodynamic properties are especially significant – wing loading and aspect ratio. Wing loading describes the ratio of weight to wing area; a high loading – in other words, small wings for a given weight – means fast flight but limited maneuverability. Aspect ratio is a measure of the wing's relative width, and is calculated as wingspan squared divided by wing area; a high aspect ratio wing is long and narrow and experiences little drag. High aspect ratio wings are therefore efficient, and are often associated with high wing loading and fast flight.

The shape of the wings helps determine where different species can survive. Those that fly in obstacle-rich habitats such as woodlands need to be maneuverable, and therefore have low wing loadings. Species like the noctules and Hoary bats that operate in open areas, however, need to fly

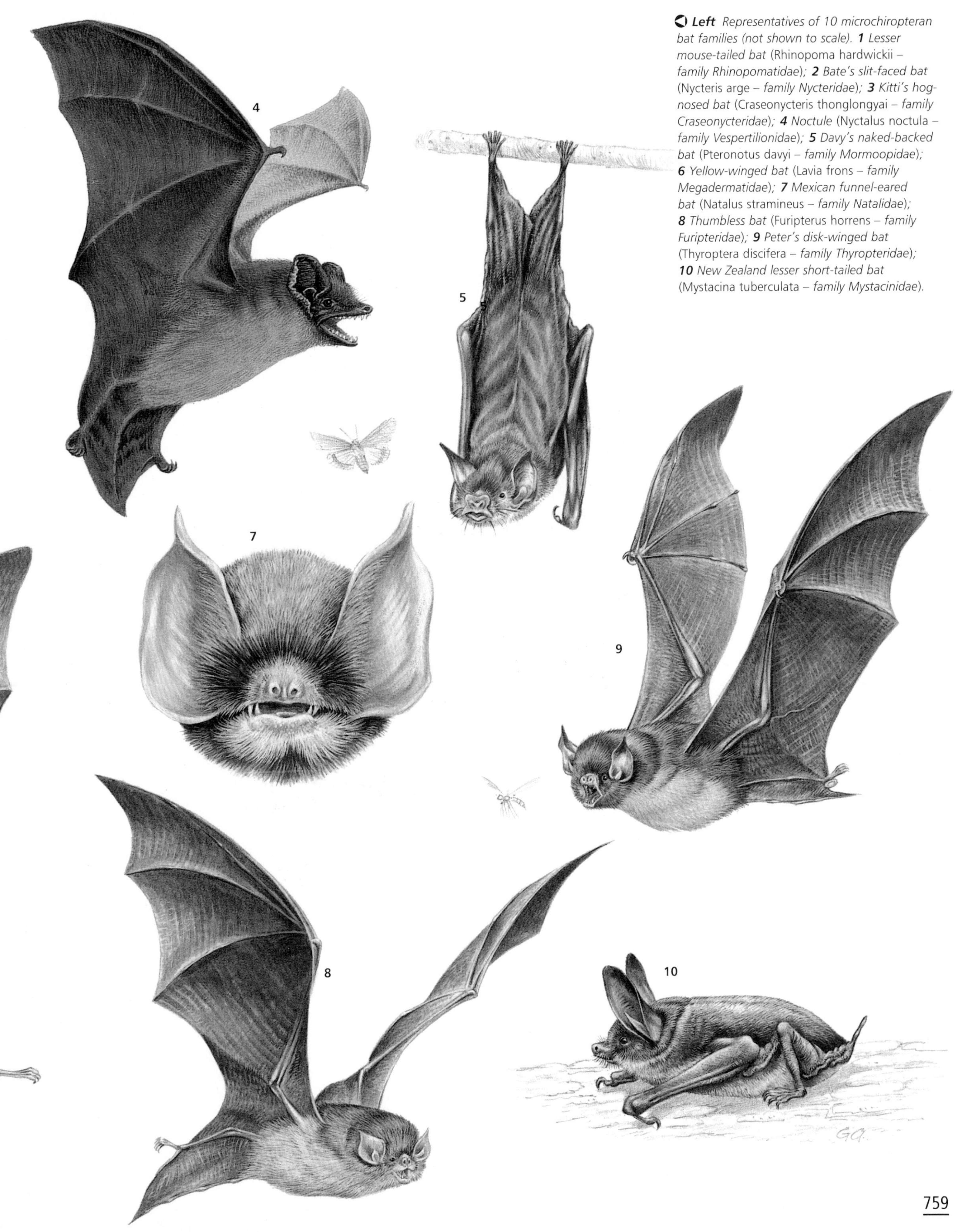

Left *Representatives of 10 microchiropteran bat families (not shown to scale).* ***1*** *Lesser mouse-tailed bat* (Rhinopoma hardwickii – *family Rhinopomatidae);* ***2*** *Bate's slit-faced bat* (Nycteris arge – *family Nycteridae);* ***3*** *Kitti's hog-nosed bat* (Craseonycteris thonglongyai – *family Craseonycteridae);* ***4*** *Noctule* (Nyctalus noctula – *family Vespertilionidae);* ***5*** *Davy's naked-backed bat* (Pteronotus davyi – *family Mormoopidae);* ***6*** *Yellow-winged bat* (Lavia frons – *family Megadermatidae);* ***7*** *Mexican funnel-eared bat* (Natalus stramineus – *family Natalidae);* ***8*** *Thumbless bat* (Furipterus horrens – *family Furipteridae);* ***9*** *Peter's disk-winged bat* (Thyroptera discifera – *family Thyropteridae);* ***10*** *New Zealand lesser short-tailed bat* (Mystacina tuberculata – *family Mystacinidae).*

Right *Sonograms show the search and capture phases of hunting activity in two bat species that use echolocation to track down insect prey. The North American Big brown bat* **a** *produces broadband calls (see text) that sweep steeply from 65–20kHz at a rate of 5–6 per second while the bat is foraging. When an insect is located, the rate accelerates rapidly, up to a peak of about 200 pulses a second.* *In contrast, horseshoe bats* **b** *produce higher-frequency narrowband calls – well suited for detecting prey but not so accurate when homing in on a target – at a rate of about 10 per second during the search phase. Their calls also speed up on approach, although less dramatically; in addition, they rise slightly in frequency.*

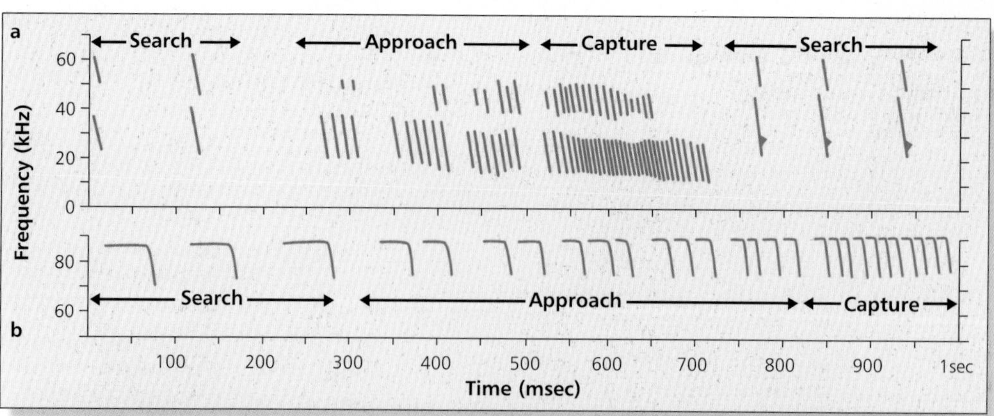

fast and efficiently, and so have high aspect ratio wings that confer high wing loadings. The flight speed of small- to medium-sized bats searching for prey varies between 3–15m (10–50ft) per second, and species with the highest wing loadings fly the fastest. Migratory species also have high aspect ratios; Brazilian free-tailed bats may migrate over more than 1,000km (620mi) from the southeastern United States to overwinter in Mexico. In contrast, some nectar-feeding bats have such low loading that they can hover.

Steering by Sound

SENSES

Bats are not blind. Megachiropterans use their large eyes to locate food and to orientate themselves; in low light, flying foxes can see better than humans. A few microchiropteran species also see well; for example, the Californian leaf-nosed bat flexibly switches off echolocation in adequate light and instead uses vision to locate prey. Most microchiropterans, however, do not see well, and their echolocation range is usually more limited than small mammals' vision; a medium-sized bat may detect a beetle at about 5m (16.5ft). Large landmarks may be detected at greater range – perhaps 20m (65ft). Bats are thus susceptible to predation in the daytime, a risk that may explain why most echolocating bats are nocturnal.

Bat have also not lost the sense of smell that is so vital to most mammals. New World leaf-nosed bats locate ripe pepper-plant fruits first by using olfaction, relying on echolocation only at close range. Large mouse-eared bats and New Zealand short-tailed bats may sniff out prey buried in leaf litter. Olfaction is also used in communication; for example, Soprano pipistrelles use smell to distinguish other bats in their maternity roosts from strangers, and female Brazilian free-tailed bats sometimes use olfactory cues to identify their offspring in crèches. Male Greater white-lined bats store secretions from their genital region and gular (throat) glands, together with urine and saliva, in glands in the wing. When courting, they hover in front of females, seducing them with the odor, and females gather about the males that perform the greatest number of these dances. What exactly attracts the females to the smell is unknown.

Above and right *Bats rely on their echolocating abilities to succeed as nocturnal insect-hunters. Many have large ears, such as those that give the Brown big-eared bat (above) its name, and curiously shaped noses, as on this Eastern horseshoe bat (right), which are used to focus the ultrasonic squeak generated in the larynx.*

Below *By analyzing the ultrasound waves bouncing back off a flying insect, the bat can pinpoint it in total darkness, and detect its direction and size.*

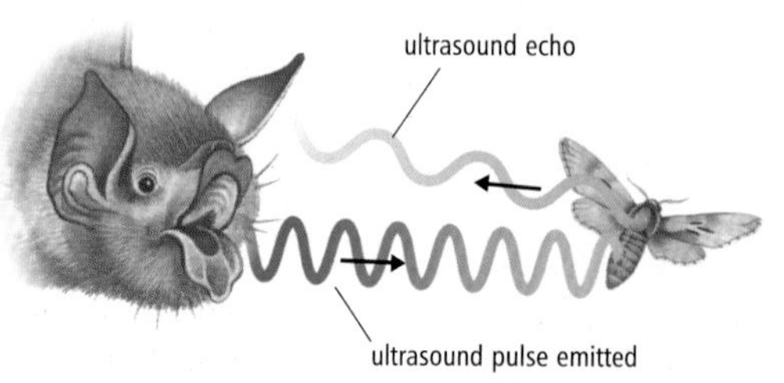

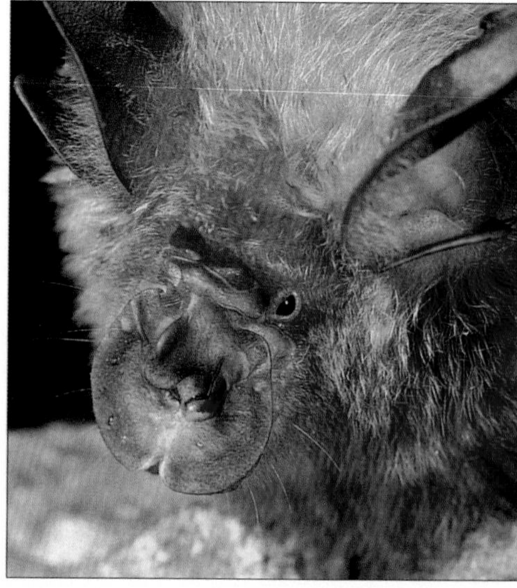

Bats' auditory powers are exceptional; some are capable of hearing an insect walking on a leaf. Old World false vampire bats have the most sensitive hearing yet discovered in mammals, particularly in the frequencies between 10 and 20kHz produced by prey rustling through vegetation. In cluttered environments such as forests in leaf, listening for prey-generated sounds is a more effective tool than echolocation, so many gleaning bats rely on their ears to find food.

Bats also converse. Social calls may serve to attract mates, defend feeding patches, attract conspecifics, perhaps aid in repelling predators. These calls are often pitched at low frequencies (many are audible to humans) so they can travel over considerable distances, and they may be individually distinctive; for example, infant bats utter "isolation calls" when separated from their mothers,

Above *Like many microchiropterans, Natterer's bat* (Myotis nattereri) *hunts at night and rests by day. Such bats rely chiefly on their sophisticated sense of hearing to navigate, using the ultrasonic echoes bounced back from high-frequency calls to draw a mental map of their continually changing surroundings.*

which can apparently identify their own infants from their vocalizations. Unsurprisingly, many microchiropterans are most sensitive to the sound frequencies they use in echolocation.

In 1793 an Italian, Lazzaro Spallanzani, discovered that bats lost their sense of direction when deafened, but could still find their way about when blinded. Spallanzani never discovered how bats oriented themselves, but he did propose that they used their ears to hunt insects. Details of how microchiropterans orientate and detect prey remained unresolved until 1938, when Donald Griffin of Harvard University listened to bats with a microphone that could detect ultrasound.

Bats emit sounds from their larynxes, like humans, and these bounce back off their surroundings; the echoes are then used to create a mental map of the area through which the bat is traveling. Bat echolocation calls are usually ultrasonic – in other words, above the human range of hearing. Among other feats, bats can determine the location of an object to within 2–5° in the horizontal and vertical planes, and can detect objects as small as 1mm (0.04in) in dimension, as well as distinguishing between two identical objects 12mm (0.5in) apart. In addition, Greater horseshoe bats can determine the wingbeat rate of flying insects with a high degree of accuracy.

The ornate faces of bats reflect the importance of sound in their lives. Many bats have a lobe in

the ear (the tragus) that helps them to pinpoint echoes in the vertical plane. Although most bat species emit calls through their mouths, some, like the horseshoe bats, the Old World false vampires, and the Old and New World leaf-nosed bats, transmit sound through their nostrils, in effect calling through their noses. These bats have elaborate ornamentation around their nostrils to direct and focus sound.

From a bat's perspective human responses would seem sluggish, for bats process information at a phenomenal rate, varying the structure of their calls according to the tasks required of them. Search calls are intense, and are often emitted at a rate of one call per wingbeat, which equates to 5–15 calls a second for many species. Once a target insect has been located, the calling gets faster; homing in, the bat passes from the approach phase of echolocation to the terminal phase, in which the shortest calls of all are produced, at rates of up to 200 per second. After the moment of capture there is a pause as the prey is handled, although bats can if necessary continue echolocating while chewing food.

Bats have a "duty cycle" when echolocating that represents the proportion of time actually spent generating sound. Some bats spend only 20 percent of their time echolocating, because they cannot process outgoing pulses and returning echoes at the same time; to do so, they would run the risk of deafening themselves, for echolocation calls can have a volume equivalent in bat terms to that exerted by a pneumatic drill on human ears. To counter the danger, the middle-ear muscles contract, acting as an effective earplug when calls are being made. These bats must leave long gaps between the sounds they emit, during which they process the returning echoes; they also shorten the length of the pulse as they approach targets, so that outgoing pulses do not overlap with echoes that come back all the sooner as objects are approached. To separate the outgoing pulse and the returning echo in time to avoid overlap, their calls are usually shorter than 30 milliseconds in duration. Thus bats shout and listen, then shout and listen again, at a rate faster than humans can well imagine – a fact that explains

Above *A foraging Greater horsehoe bat homes in on a moth – a staple item of its diet. Studies using radio-tracking devices have revealed much about the behavior and roost selection of this species. For example, two of its key habitats are woodland and adjacent old pasture, both of which are rich in insect life, yet which are in decline.*

KEEPING AN EAR OPEN FOR BATS

How hearing helps moths evade echolocating predators

OBSERVED UNDER AN ISOLATED STREET-LIGHT, a flying moth spirals toward the light. Suddenly the moth changes its flight behavior and dives for the ground, just before a bat zooms through the air along the moth's original flight path. The simple explanation is that the moth heard the bat coming and took evasive action; more specifically, it responded to the echolocation or biosonar calls emitted by the bat. The change in the moth's flight behavior in response to the bat´s imminent attack is a revelation in the remarkable world of the ongoing war between predators and prey.

Prey species from a variety of groups including many moths, some lacewings, and a selection of crickets, katydids, mantids, and beetles can detect echolocation calls, indicating that bat-detecting ears have evolved independently many times in insects. In most cases, bat sounds appear to be the only ones that many of these insects heed. Calling insects, however, such as crickets, katydids, and some moths, not only listen to their enemies' echolocation calls but also to the communication signals of their own kinds.

Bat-detecting ears derive from pre-existing sense organs – the so-called chordotonal organs – and occur in different parts of the insects' bodies, from the head, thorax, and abdomen to the wings and legs. Most insect ears are elaborate enough to allow the hearer to distinguish strong from weak signals, and insects use the strength of impulses on the auditory nerve to assess the proximity of the bat and the threat it poses. Moths can hear bats from about 20–40m (65–130ft) away, although bats can normally only detect moths within about 5m (16.5ft). Moths that simply change their flight direction in response to a distant bat will launch themselves into an unpredictable repertoire of spirals, loops, and dives that usually terminate on the ground when the bat is in close range. The ultrasonic echolocation calls used by bats attenuate rapidly in air, and since the sounds detected by the bats are echoes that have traveled two ways instead of one, the insect will nearly always be at an advantage. Insects with pairs of ears show a very general left/right directional response to a bat's echolocation calls; mantids, however, have only a single ear, and so cannot determine the direction of the sound.

Advances in the study of bat echolocation and moth hearing indicate that there is more to the bat–insect story than first meets the ear. On the bat side, echolocators can use very strong or very weak calls, and different species use calls dominated by different acoustic frequencies. Bats using strong calls are aerial feeders hunting flying insects, which they detect, track, and evaluate through the use of echolocation. The intensity of the calls is impressive, ranging up to 125dB measured 10cm (4in) from the bat´s mouth. Bats that employ such strident calls include noctules, serotines, pipistrelles, Big and Little brown bats, the Red and Hoary bat, and many others. On the other hand, some insect-eating bats that feed near and within vegetation use low-intensity (60–80dB) calls. These "whispering" bats – which include slit-faced bats, false-vampire bats, many mouse-eared bats, long-eared bats, and New World leaf-nosed bats – detect and track their prey by the sounds of fluttering wings or insect footfalls rather than by echolocation.

On the insect side, moths do not hear all sounds equally well. For example, the quiet echolocation calls of whispering bats are not picked up until the bat is within 1m (3.3ft) or so – too late for the moth to take evasive action. Most moths hear best at frequencies of 20–60kHz, the frequency band used by most bats. But some aerial-feeding species, including many horseshoe bats, Old World leaf-nosed bats, and a few free-tailed bats, use echolocation calls dominated by frequencies either above 60kHz or below 20kHz. Although these calls may be intense, they are not conspicuous to moths because they contain frequencies that the moths cannot detect easily.

One study showed that moths with ears were 40 percent less likely to be caught by bats than moths that had been experimentally deafened. Within the diets of aerial-feeding bats, moths are more commonly food for those species whose calls are not conspicuous. This generalization requires qualification, however, for some bats with conspicuous echolocation calls eat a lot of moths. Red and Hoary bats, for example, often hunt around street-lights, which not only attract insects but also make them easy to catch by interfering with their defensive responses when they are looking into the light. Likewise, the barbastelle seems to specialize on deaf species of moths.

Below *Moths evade bats in several ways. Some zig-zag **1** to escape attack; others drop to the ground, either passively **2** or in a powered dive **3**, where they may be difficult to detect among plants and stones. Certain unpleasant-tasting tiger moths emit clicks **4** that apparently warn attackers that they are not prey species, causing the bats to veer away.*

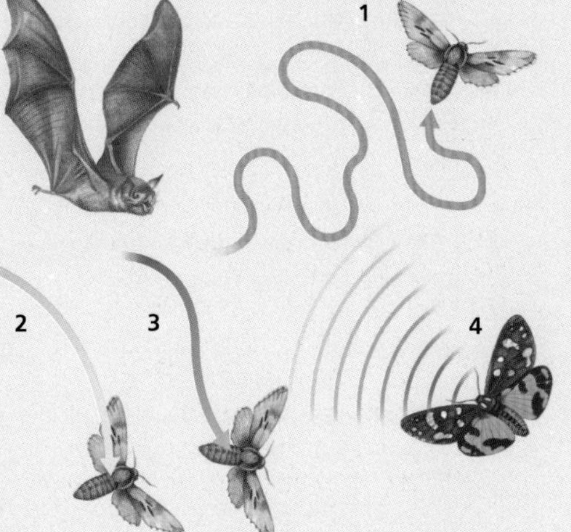

Some moths have escalated the sound-based arms race with bats. Many species of tiger moths have an unpleasant taste, because their caterpillars eat plants containing secondary compounds serving to protect them from herbivores. These moths are often brightly colored and conspicuous, defensive signals apparently directed at predators like birds, which learn to associate the bright colors with an unappetizing taste. Some of these moths also have noisemakers, and the clicks they produce are often directed at bats. Hunting Red and Hoary bats will normally approach, but then veer away from, flying Painted lichen moths; if the moths' noisemakers are damaged, however, the bats will seize them, only to quickly release them unharmed, presumably because they recognize the smell or taste immediately. So the clicks emitted by the moths apparently serve as warnings to the bats that the moths are inedible. In time and frequency parameters, the clicks of tiger moths match the intensity, frequency pattern, and duration of echo of the bats' calls, and are therefore well designed to get an echolocating bat's attention. It has also been suggested that the clicks work by startling the bat or else interfere with its information-processing by disturbing the echoes.

Some insects use ears for listening to sounds other than bat echolocation calls, and there are also many nocturnal insects that lack bat-detectors. However, these too have various means of evasion. Some deaf moths practice "acoustic concealment" by hiding among the massive echoes from the vegetation on which they feed. Others are particularly fast and swift flyers, and use an elevated body temperature to achieve the same end. Many dipterans and mayflies hide in dense swarms of conspecifics.

The most efficient of all means to avoid bats is, of course, to fly by day, when bats do not hunt. This may in fact explain why some moths long ago turned into butterflies. Moths apparently did indeed evolve many new traits during the Eocene and Oligocene eras 30–50 million years ago, the period when the first echolocating bats evolved.

Meanwhile, male moths flying toward a female releasing a plume of pheromones will disappear rapidly when presented with bat-like sounds. Bats are clearly enemies to taken seriously if, for some moths at least, avoiding them even takes precedence over sex! JR/BF

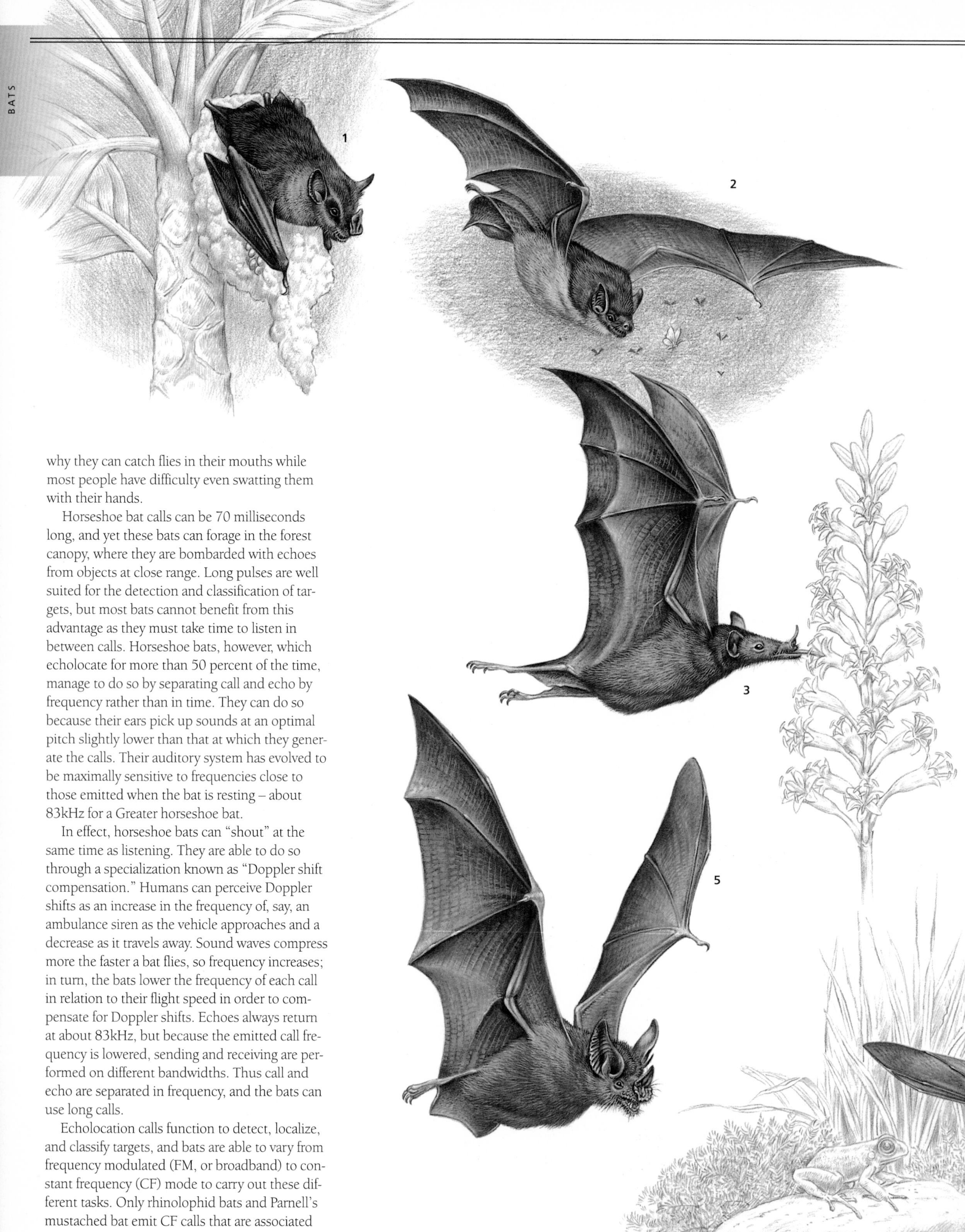

why they can catch flies in their mouths while most people have difficulty even swatting them with their hands.

Horseshoe bat calls can be 70 milliseconds long, and yet these bats can forage in the forest canopy, where they are bombarded with echoes from objects at close range. Long pulses are well suited for the detection and classification of targets, but most bats cannot benefit from this advantage as they must take time to listen in between calls. Horseshoe bats, however, which echolocate for more than 50 percent of the time, manage to do so by separating call and echo by frequency rather than in time. They can do so because their ears pick up sounds at an optimal pitch slightly lower than that at which they generate the calls. Their auditory system has evolved to be maximally sensitive to frequencies close to those emitted when the bat is resting – about 83kHz for a Greater horseshoe bat.

In effect, horseshoe bats can "shout" at the same time as listening. They are able to do so through a specialization known as "Doppler shift compensation." Humans can perceive Doppler shifts as an increase in the frequency of, say, an ambulance siren as the vehicle approaches and a decrease as it travels away. Sound waves compress more the faster a bat flies, so frequency increases; in turn, the bats lower the frequency of each call in relation to their flight speed in order to compensate for Doppler shifts. Echoes always return at about 83kHz, but because the emitted call frequency is lowered, sending and receiving are performed on different bandwidths. Thus call and echo are separated in frequency, and the bats can use long calls.

Echolocation calls function to detect, localize, and classify targets, and bats are able to vary from frequency modulated (FM, or broadband) to constant frequency (CF) mode to carry out these different tasks. Only rhinolophid bats and Parnell's mustached bat emit CF calls that are associated with Doppler shift compensation. Calls that are almost constant in frequency are termed "narrowband." Broadband calls sweep through a wide range of frequencies in a short time (almost 100–20kHz in under 2.5 milliseconds in a Natterer's bat), and are well suited for the localization of targets but are not so good at target detection (finding prey in the wider landscape). Narrowband and constant frequency calls, in contrast, are ideal for the detection of targets but are poorly suited for localization. Hence some bat species such as the pipistrelles use narrowband calls to detect insects but switch to broadband calls to locate them. Horseshoe bats add broadband components to their CF calls and extend the bandwidth of the terminal broadband component during localization.

Long CF calls are also used to classify targets. Insect wingbeats produce small modulations in the frequency and amplitude of echoes (glints). Because small insects flap their wings more rapidly than large ones, glint frequency relates to insect size. Horseshoe bats can distinguish profitable prey items from unprofitable ones by glint characteristics, and eat unprofitable items such as small dung flies only when profitable prey such as moths and large beetles are scarce.

Most bat species call by using frequencies in the 20–60kHz range. Frequencies lower than 20kHz have wavelengths larger than most insects, and so travel round them rather than bouncing back to the bat. Frequencies higher than 60kHz attenuate rapidly in air, which restricts their useful range, although for slow-flying bats that can react more easily at close range they are ideal. The Short-eared trident bat emits the highest-frequency call of all, at 212kHz, whereas some free-tailed species, such as the Spotted bat, echolocate at frequencies as low as 11kHz. Another advantage of using exceptionally high or low frequencies is that these are poorly detected by insect prey, allowing bats that call at these frequencies to catch large numbers of insects that are otherwise equipped to hear ultrasound.

An insect's life depends on whether or not it survives a predation event, so it is hardly surprising that insects have evolved defenses against echolocating bats. Some of these are behavioral; for example, male Ghost swift moths, which display at leks, do so early in the evening, when predation risks from both bats and diurnal birds are minimized. The moths display by flying close to the ground, where their acoustic profiles are masked by ground echoes; if they fly above the highest grass panicles, they lose their acoustic crypsis and are readily caught by bats.

Ghost swifts are primitive moths that lack hearing organs, but sensitivity to ultrasound has evolved in orthopterans, lacewings, beetles, flies,

Left *The forests of Panama are rich in bats: more than 30 species live there. Such abundance is made possible by niche diversification: different species have different food preferences.* ***1*** *Jamaican fruit bat* (Artibeus jamaicensis), *a frugivore.* ***2*** *Big brown bat* (Eptesicus fuscus) *pursuing insects.* ***3*** *Mexican long-nosed bat* (Leptonycteris nivalis), *a nectar eater.* ***4*** *Spectral bat* (Vampyrum spectrum), *a carnivore.* ***5*** *Fringe-lipped bat* (Trachops cirrhosus), *which takes larger prey such as frogs.* ***6*** *Mustached bat* (Pteronotus parnellii), *also insectivorous.* ***7*** *Greater bulldog bat* (Noctilio leporinus), *fishing.*

BAT BLOOD DONORS

Feeding and sharing in vampire bat colonies

NO SPECIES HAVE CONTRIBUTED MORE TO THE misunderstanding and fear of bats than the vampires. Three species of vampire bats occur in Central and South America, where, as their name implies, they feed exclusively on blood. Hairy-legged (*Diphylla ecaudata*) and White-winged vampire bats (*Diaemus youngi*) favor bird blood, and are adept at climbing tree branches to feed on roosting chicks. Common vampires (*Desmodus rotundus*) prefer mammal blood, and are usually found where cattle, horses, and other livestock are common. If livestock are absent, they feed instead on tapirs, deer, peccaries, agoutis, and sea lions.

People have some reason to fear vampire bats. Attacks on humans do sometimes occur, often following the removal of livestock from an area. Vampire bites are not painful, but they can be dangerous, for they are known to transmit paralytic rabies. Because the bats themselves are also susceptible to the virus, their populations undergo periodic crashes in response to rabies epidemics. The remarkable blood-sharing behavior of the bats – by which well-fed bats regurgitate blood to hungry companions – almost certainly facilitates the transmission of saliva-borne viruses, including the one responsible for rabies.

Vampire blood-sharing is a rare example among animals of reciprocity (the "You scratch my back, I'll scratch yours" principle). Understanding why bats would share food even at the risk of infection requires an appreciation of the social organization and life history of these extraordinary creatures.

Common vampire bats often use caves, tunnels, or hollow trees as day roosts. While some roosts may contain more than 2,000 individuals, colonies most often contain 20–100 bats. Within a colony, groups of 10–20 females often roost together for years. Some of these females are related, because female offspring remain with their mothers after reaching sexual maturity in their second year. However, female groups also contain unrelated animals, as a consequence of adult females occasionally switching day roosts. Groups of up to ten males also occur, but they are not related and do not remain together for extended periods. Young males from 12–18 months of age disperse independently, often after fighting with an adult male in their natal group. Typically one adult male roosts with females and their young, while others hang nearby and periodically fight viciously to gain access to the females. On average, a male in a preferred spot fathers half of the pups born to females in that group, retaining control of his position for about 2 years. A roosting group of Common vampire bats typically consists, therefore, of a few unrelated adult males and of sets of females with young related through different matrilines.

For their size, vampires expend more time caring for their young than any other bat. Females give birth to single pups weighing nearly 20 percent of their body weight (30–35g/1–1.2oz). Although the pups are active at birth, they grow slowly and continue to receive milk from their mothers for over 6 months. Females supplement their diet with regurgitated blood shortly after birth, and also periodically during the first year. Pups begin to fly after 6 months, but do not reach adult weight until they are 1 year old.

Common vampires use smell and sound to find prey. Females from a roosting group hunt in adjacent areas, and will defend bite sites by chasing other bats away. Even when prey are abundant, successfully obtaining a blood meal can be difficult. To make a bite, a bat must first locate a warm spot where blood vessels are near the surface of the skin, using heat receptors located on its nose pad. It then uses its razor-sharp incisors to remove a small piece of skin, rather like a golf divot. Anticoagulants in the bat's saliva ensure that the blood flows freely as the vampire laps up the blood with its tongue. Bats' feeding skills improve with age: those aged 1–2 fail to feed one night out of three on average, but those over 2 years old are unsuccessful only one time in ten. Failure results from the wariness of the animals under attack, which will sometimes try to brush off the feeding bats. Not surprisingly, young bats sometimes feed simultaneously or sequentially from the same wound site as their mothers, and individuals may return to the same wound site on consecutive nights.

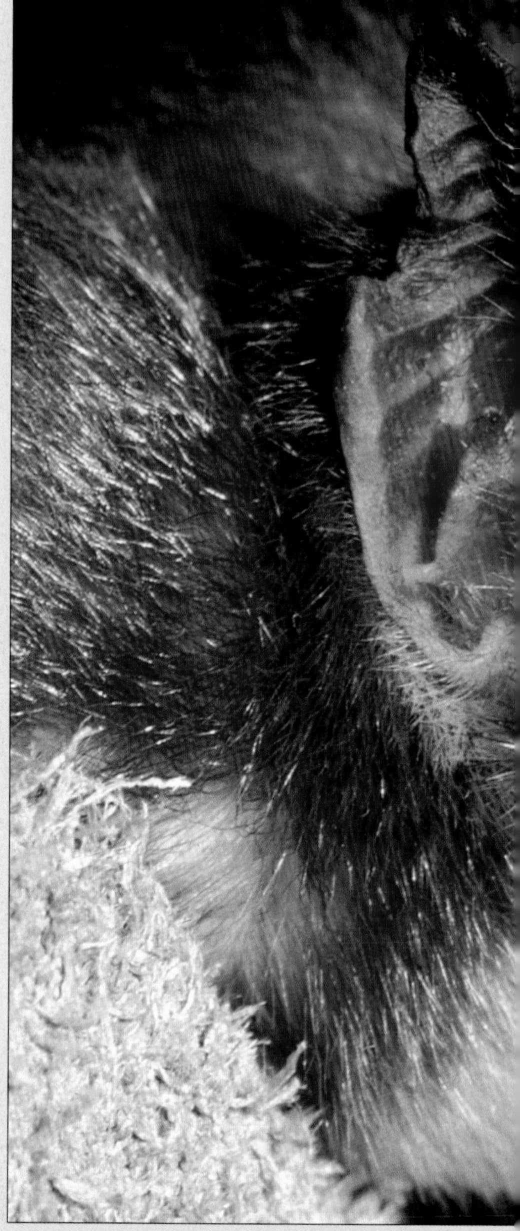

If a bat fails to obtain a meal, it will return to the roost and beg blood from a roost mate by licking its lips. The likelihood that a bat will regurgitate and share blood depends on its association and kinship with the hungry bat. Bats do not share blood unless they have roosted together for more than 60 percent of the time. Some, but not all, blood-sharing events involve related bats.

Failing to feed is risky, as bats that go hungry starve to death within 3 days. Because starving bats lose weight more slowly than recently-fed bats, the transfer of blood buys the recipient more survival time than the donor loses. Reciprocal blood-sharing therefore results in a net benefit to participating bats. In the absence of reciprocity, annual mortality should exceed 80 percent, yet female vampire bats are known sometimes to survive for more than 15 years in the wild.

One problem for the donor is knowing how to ensure that the recipient is a genuine reciprocator and not a cheat who will receive blood without giving it in return. One way bats can at least assess each other's hunger levels is during episodes of mutual grooming. Bats that have successfully fed typically ingest over half their body weight in blood in a 30-minute period, which causes their stomach to bulge. This gut distention is likely to be noticed by another bat in the course of grooming, which frequently occurs just prior to blood regurgitation. Since both mutual grooming and blood sharing only occur between individuals that have reliably roosted together, partner fidelity appears to be essential for the persistence of this amazing reciprocal-exchange system. JW

Above *A Common vampire bat* (Desmodus rotundus) *reveals the razor-sharp incisors that make the puncture marks through which the bat laps its prey's blood. The truncated muzzle allows the bat to press its mouth close up against the flesh of the animal on which it is feeding.*

Left *In Trinidad, a vampire bat takes blood from a resting donkey. To feed, the bat first of all chooses a site on an animal's skin where a blood vessel is close to the surface. It then licks the spot with its tongue before using its teeth to shear away protective hairs or feathers. Finally it removes an almost circular patch of skin to access the blood beneath.*

Right *Bats cluster in a roost within a crevice. Although vampires sometimes gather in colonies up to 2,000 strong, these large agglomerations subdivide into smaller units, typically composed of groups of 10–20 females and their young. Blood-sharing is normally limited to these close-knit groupings.*

and mantids, as well as several times in other moth species. Many insects show startle responses on hearing ultrasound pulses, flying away from those exhibiting low sound intensities (probably corresponding to distant predators), but sometimes making dives or spiral flights when alerted by intense sounds. Some arctiid moths and tiger beetles click in response to ultrasound pulses, perhaps in order to startle the predator, to interfere with echo processing, or else to warn the bat that they are distasteful prey.

Many insects clearly evolved ears as bat detectors. Whether bats have in turn responded by changing their calls to increase their chances of catching these insects remains controversial. Some bats, such as those that use very high- or low-frequency echolocation calls, catch many prey that can hear ultrasound. Exploitation of these insects could simply be a by-product of other advantages associated with these calls, however, rather than reflecting specific adaptations to facilitate predation on hearing insects.

Helping Out with the Young

BREEDING AND REPRODUCTION

Many tropical bats are polyestrous, undergoing several reproductive cycles in a year. Female Common vampire bats, for instance, may experience four reproductive cycles in a year, giving them four opportunities for breeding. Most temperate bat species are monestrous, however, with only one reproductive cycle annually. Hibernation constrains the timing of reproduction, and spermatogenesis in males and estrus in females typically occur in late summer or autumn. Females may store sperm overwinter for as long as 7 months in their uterus and oviduct, and ovulation and fertilization are delayed until a few days after their arousal from hibernation. Male bats can also store sperm in their epididymes (tubules at the back of the testes) or in the vas deferens (the sperm duct) for long periods. Bats in three families – Pteropodidae, Rhinolophidae, and Vespertilionidae – have also shown delayed implantation, and several species including the Jamaican fruit-eating bat show diapause (delays) during embryonic development. Lactation is energetically costly, and parturition is synchronized to coincide with times of high food abundance.

Most bats produce one offspring, but some species produce twins (which may have different fathers, as in noctules) and occasionally triplets or quadruplets (as in Red bats). Infants are relatively large at birth, weighing as much as 40 percent of the mother's body mass, and grow rapidly. Lactation lasts about 45 days in Greater horseshoe bats. During their first foraging trips (at between 28 and 30 days old), young Greater horseshoe bats forage close to the roost independently of their mothers, which may travel as far as 2–3km (1.2–1.9mi) from the roost. When the young are past their first winter, however, they may share foraging grounds with their mothers and other close relatives. Some species including the Lesser bulldog bat may provide maternal tuition by guiding the young to suitable foraging areas.

Above *Newborn Brazilian free-tailed bats* (Tadarida brasiliensis) *crowd a nursery colony in Texas. No other bat or mammal species comes together in larger numbers than this one: an estimated 25–50 million individuals – mainly mothers and young – are recorded to have inhabited a single cave.*

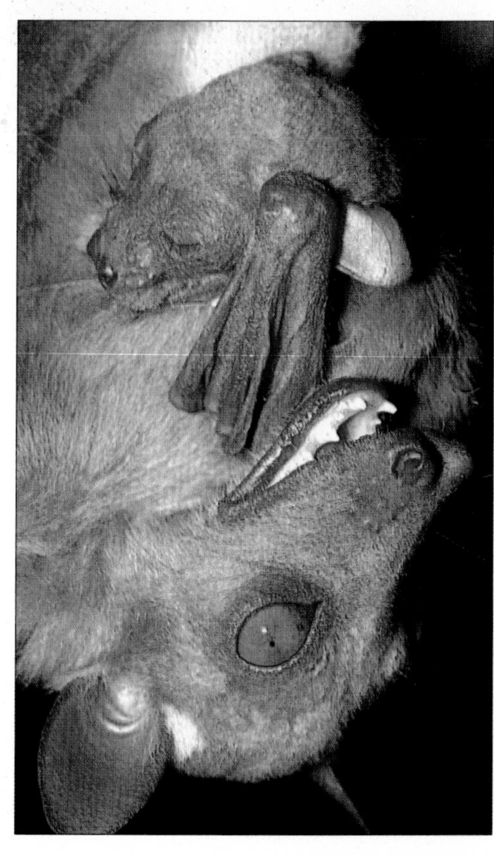

Right *A female flying fox nurses her offspring. Mothers normally bear one baby at a time, typically carrying their young with them for anything from 1 to 6 months. In the nursery colonies they may receive help with their maternal duties; other females have been seen to assist in grooming baby bats and also in maneuverng them into a suckling position.*

Parental care is usually given exclusively by mothers, although fathers of the monogamous Yellow-winged bat may provide assistance by defending foraging territories where the young are learning to feed. In some bat species, individuals other than the parents help raise the babies. For example, Evening bats undertake allosuckling, by which females (31 percent in one study) suckle infants (24 percent, and mostly female) to which

Above *A highly unusual roosting technique is employed by the tent-making bats* (Uroderma bilobatum) *of Central and South America. They chew through structural parts of the leaves of palms and other plants, causing them to collapse into tent-like shelters.*

they are not related. Because females are usually philopatric, returning to their natal colony to breed, allosuckling may have evolved in this species to increase future colony size and to improve the potential for transferring information about feeding sites.

Mating Habits and Mutual Aid

SOCIAL ORGANIZATION

Bats show considerable variety in social organization. A few species, such as the Yellow-winged bat, are monogamous. Promiscuity (with both males and females mating with several individuals) may occur in certain species, especially when males mate with torpid females during hibernation, although in some of these – the Little brown bat for one – molecular analysis of parentage now suggests that mating is biased towards particular males rather than being purely promiscuous as originally believed. Most bats are polygynous, with some males mating with more than one female and many failing to mate at all. However, females may also mate polyandrously – with several males – in one breeding cycle, as has been shown by DNA fingerprinting of twins

Many bats including pipistrelles and noctules show "resource defense polygyny," by which a male defends a resource (for example a roost site) that is important to females. The reproductive success of Greater white-lined bats that defend roost sites is three times higher than that of peripheral males that linger around the edges of the roosts. Males are unable to monopolize access to females, however, and on average 29 percent of the young born to females in a male's mating group are fathered by other males. Greater horseshoe bats defend roost sites and/or groups of females during the autumn, while pipistrelle males perform songflights to attract females.

Some female Greater horseshoe bats rear young sired by the same male in consecutive years. Their reasons for doing so can only be speculated upon – it may simply be that the males concerned are of high quality – but it is possible that the aim is to increase the co-ancestry of the offspring; if they are closely related, their behavior toward each other is more likely to be altruistic, which may bring benefits. After copulating, some of the male's ejaculate produces a "vaginal plug" that probably functions to safeguard paternity.

Certain species of bats even congregate to mate in the strange system known as lekking, by which males gather at recognized locations where they defend a small territory that has no benefit to the females other than as a place to come for sex. Hammerheaded bat males aggregate in groups and display vigorously at these mating arenas, producing ritualized calls that sound like glass being rapped hard on a porcelain sink. A tiny number of males (6 percent) are responsible for 79 percent of the copulations, since females seem to have

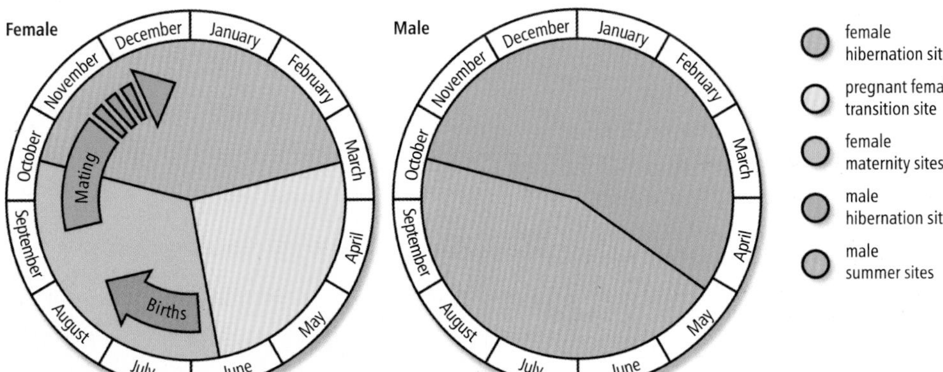

Left *A year in the life of the Greater horseshoe bat. Adult males and females generally lead separate lives except during the mating season, when females will usually go in search of a partner at a traditional male roost, although males occasionally visit females at the maternity roost instead. Juveniles are seen more with mature females than males. The female cycle shows that, on leaving hibernation sites (at which the oldest females tend to be solitary), pregnant females gather at transition roosts before moving on to the maternity sites where birth and mating occurs. Most juveniles remain in the maternity roost during the summer. In contrast, males tend to occupy the same traditional sites both during winter hibernation and in the summer.*

strong preferences for particular sites at the lek.

In temperate regions, female bats gang together during the summer in maternity colonies in which they give birth and rear offspring. Aggregation keeps the growing young warm and allows mothers to indicate the best foraging sites to one another. Maternity roosts may be large – one colony of Brazilian free-tailed bats holds the record as the largest aggregation of vertebrates ever known, containing over 20 million individuals. Males are usually more dispersed in the summer.

Common vampire bats show some of the best evidence of reciprocal altruism – when an individual chooses to act altruistically to another that acted thus in the past – in the animal kingdom. Reciprocity can evolve when the recipient gains more than the donor loses, and when at some future time the two are likely to swap roles.

Another essential element for the evolution of such behavior is that the animals involved should be able to recognize individuals who cheat the system by failing to provide help in their turn, in order to prevent them from benefiting from the system at no expense. These criteria appear to be fulfilled in the regurgitation of blood between individuals within colonies of Common vampire bats. Bats that go hungry will beg blood from other bats in the colony and are often rewarded, but only if they have a family connection or have proved themselves good friends in the past (see Bat Blood Donors).

Natural Energy-saving

TORPOR AND HIBERNATION

In order to get through the many rainy and cold and lean days of winter, many temperate bat species shut down body systems, lower their body temperature close to ambient levels, and enter torpor. During hibernation, a bat's heart rate may drop from 400 beats a minute to just 11–25 beats. Bat hibernacula can vary in temperature from –10° to 21°C (14°–70°F), with a mode of 6°C (43°F) for vespertilionids and 11°C (52°F) for horseshoe bats. A Brown long-eared bat in a torpid state at 5°C (41°F) expends only 0.7 percent as much energy as when fully active at the same temperature. Insectivorous bats may become torpid even during lactation, when both the young and their mothers may enter the state in periods of severe food shortage. Torpor has been studied in bats from the Vespertilionidae, Rhinolophidae, Molossidae, and Mystacinidae families. Some small megachiropterans may also enter shallow torpor for short periods.

In southwest England, Greater horseshoe bats enter torpor for periods of up to 12 days, waking up at dusk on mild winter nights to forage. The energy to wake up comes initially from brown adipose tissue, fat specialized for heat production; later in arousal, bats shiver in order to generate more heat. On arousing from 3.5°C (38°F), a Brown long-eared bat takes about 40 minutes to reach a body temperature suitable for flight. Arousals must be crucial to survival, since they are costly, accounting for 85 percent of overwinter fat depletion in Little brown bats, even though the bat is fully homeothermic for only 2–4 percent of the time. Arousal may allow bats to drink, to restore metabolic imbalances, to resist disease, and even to make up for sleep deprivation, because the low brain temperatures during torpor inhibit the normal restorative functions of sleep.

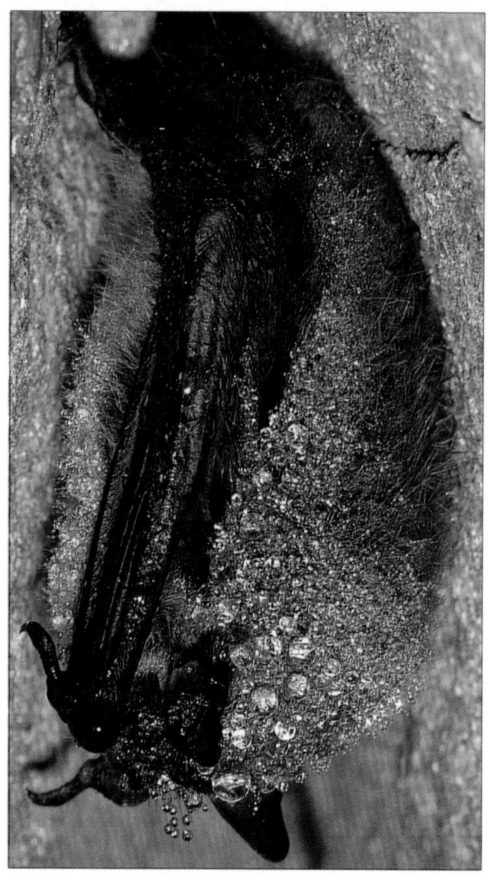

Above *Dew droplets caught in the fur of a hibernating Daubenton's bat* (Myotis daubentonii) *indicate that its body temperature has fallen to that of its very humid surroundings in a cold cave. Other hibernation sites favored by this species include cellars, mines, and disused military bunkers.*

Fruit Bats and Insect-eaters

FEEDING BEHAVIOR

About 70 percent of bat species eat mainly insects and other small arthropods, usually on the wing. Millimeter-long midges and beetles measuring 2.5cm (1in) are at opposite ends of the bat insect intake spectrum. Flies, beetles, moths, orthopterans, bugs, termites, hymenopterans, mayflies, and caddis flies are among the preferred insect prey.

The movements of millions of Brazilian free-tailed bats from caves in Texas have been studied by radar. Aggregations of bats can be detected moving from the caves and heading towards concentrations of billions of Corn earworm moths over croplands. Corn earworm moths are the major agricultural pest in the USA, and free-tailed bats from the largest roosts in Texas may eat 1,000 tonnes of insects in a night. The bats can detect insects by echolocation at altitudes as high as 750m (2,500ft) or more, and they may fly as high as 3,000m (10,000ft).

Some slow-flying species such as the Brown long-eared bat glean insects from vegetation. Others, including many horseshoe bats, hunt from perches. Some species including Daubenton's bat and the Lesser bulldog bat trawl prey from the water's surface. The Greater bulldog bat catches fish, which it finds by detecting irregularities or movements on the water's surface by means of echolocation, or by raking randomly in areas where it has previously captured prey. Some tropical bats are carnivorous, and three species of vampire bats feed on blood.

One third of the world's bat species eat fruit, nectar, and pollen. In the Old World tropics the bats in the family Pteropodidae (Megachiroptera) occupy these dietary niches, which are filled in the New World tropics by the Phyllostomidae (Microchiroptera). Plant-visiting bats pollinate or disperse many economically important plants including balsa, mango, durian, and wild-banana trees. Phyllostomids feed on nectar from the maguey plants that are used to produce tequila. At least 443 products used by humans derive from 163 different plant species that rely to some extent on pollination or dispersal by bats.

Sixty-two percent of pteropodids live on islands, where they can be keystone species for fruit dispersal; on many they are the only seed dispersers and pollinators, filling niches occupied by sunbirds, hummingbirds, primates, and other organisms elsewhere in the tropics. In the Philippines, large pteropodids tend to eat fruit in the tree of origin, while smaller bats carry fruits to other trees. Many Australian eucalyptus species may largely depend on flying foxes for their pollination. In West Africa, Straw-colored flying foxes are the only known dispersers of the iroko tree, whose timber has great commercial value.

Some plants have evolved flowers and fruits that increase their conspicuousness to bats. Flowers of bat-pollinated plants are often large, strong, inconspicuously colored, and heavily scented; they are also often exposed and open at night. They produce copious nectar, and their pollen is high in protein. Plant-visiting bats may feed singly on plants with few fruits, but forage in groups at superabundant food sources such as trees with many fruits. Female Greater spear-nosed bats emit low-frequency "screech calls" to attract members

Right *One of the smallest of all Megachiroptera species, the tiny Southern blossom bat* (Syconycteris australis) *is a nectar-eater averaging just 6cm (2.5in) in head–body length. Its exceptionally long tongue is equipped with brushlike projections that pick up nectar and pollen from the flowers on which it feeds.*

Left *Nearly three-quarters of all bat species rely mainly on insects for their food. Here a Striped hairy-nosed bat* (Mimon crenulatum) *makes a meal of a grasshopper in Ecuador's Yasuni National Park.*

Below *Another principal source of food for bats is fruit, as demonstrated by this Hairy big-eyed bat* (Chiroderma villosum) *carrying a fig. Bats of this genus, which is part of the family Phyllostomidae, inhabit Central and South America and the Caribbean.*

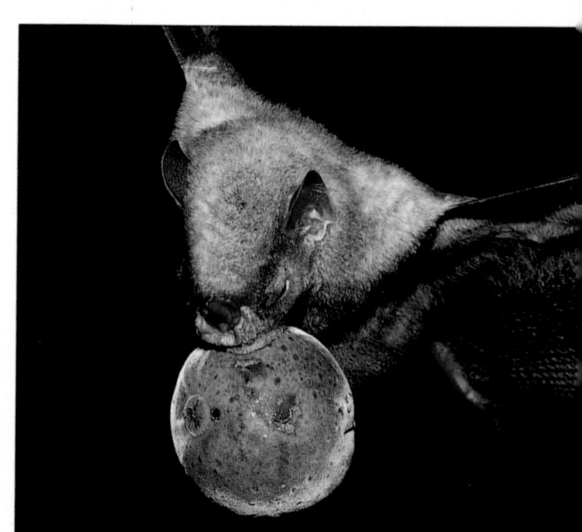

HIDDEN BIODIVERSITY

Pipistrelles are the most abundant bat species in Britain, with perhaps 2 million bats feeding in a range of habitats from urban areas to rivers and lakes. Until 1993 they were considered as a single species, *Pipistrellus pipistrellus*. Research on their echolocation calls, however, showed that some echolocated close to 45kHz while others did so nearer 55kHz. Bats from any one maternity colony consisted of only one phonic type, and differences in the surroundings could not explain the differences in call frequency. Subsequently it was found that the two phonic types also differ in habitat use (the 55kHz bats are more dependent on riparian habitats) and in diet, with the 55kHz bat eating more biting and nonbiting midges while the 45kHz bats prefer owl- and window-midges and dung flies. In addition, the maternity roosts of 55kHz pipistrelles usually contain more bats than those of the 45kHz bats, sometimes attracting 1,000 individuals. it has also been discovered that the two phonic types emit subtly different "social calls" to warn off conspecifics at feeding sites when food is scarce, and males utter different mate-attraction calls during songflights – perhaps a mechanism to facilitate reproductive isolation, as males only associate with females of the same phonic type as themselves at mating roosts.

Overwhelming evidence that the two phonic types are indeed different species also came from molecular studies. The cytochrome-b gene of mitochondrial DNA evolves rapidly, and is often used by evolutionary biologists interested in determining genetic differences between species. A portion of this gene was found to differ in its sequence by 11 percent between the two phonic types – a larger gap than that separating other bat species that appear quite different to the naked eye.

The two phonic types are in fact what biologists call "cryptic species": ones whose distinct identity is camouflaged by similar appearance. Although no one morphological character has yet been found to distinguish them, the 55kHz bats are usually lighter in color, and the 45kHz bats often have a black face mask. Presumably there has been stronger selection for the species to differ in their acoustic characteristics than in looks.

The two species are sympatric over much of Europe. As the first known representation of *Pipistrellus pipistrellus* is found in a book published in 1774 that clearly shows a bat with a black face mask, that name has been retained for the 45kHz phonic type, while the 55kHz species has been proposed as *P. pygmaeus*. Because the existence of *P. pygmaeus* was first inferred from its high-pitched call, the title "Soprano pipistrelle" has been proposed as its vernacular name.

Left *Caves make favorite roosting sites for many species of bats, providing shelter from the elements and usually also from human interference. Here a mixed flock of funnel-eared, spear-nosed, and mustached bats takes to flight in Tamana Cave, Trinidad.*

of their social group to rich foraging sites, often flowering or fruiting trees. Flying foxes find fruit by a mixture of vision and olfaction. Phyllostomids detect fruit at a distance by olfaction, then used echolocation for localization. One bat-pollinated vine in the Neotropics – *Mucuna holtonii* – directs bats to its nectar with a specialized petal that reflects most of an echolocation call's energy directly back at the bat; if this acoustic guide is removed, the visitation rate of bats to the flowers decreases dramatically.

Gathering-places on a Grand Scale

ROOSTS

Bats may spend over half their lives in roosts, where they cluster together for warmth and improved protection from predators. Sometimes over a million flying foxes will roost together, exposed in forest "camps." Roost sites include crevices in rocks and trees, tree cavities and foliage, mines, and caves (which are also sometimes used for breeding). Vespertilionid bats in British Columbia are very particular, preferring tall trees that are close to others but with little surrounding foliage. Silver-haired bats in Oregon roost in trees that protrude above the forest canopy, which perhaps act as signposts to guide in bats that fly past. Roosting in the canopy can be dangerous, however, and many foliage-roosting species have coloring that breaks up their outline, such as the two white lines on the back of the Greater white-lined bat. The Golden-tipped bat roosts in the abandoned, dome-shaped nests of birds, while in West Africa woolly bats of the *Kerivoula* genus have been found roosting in the large webs of colonial spiders.

Bats in three families (Thyropteridae, Myzopodidae, and Vespertilionidae) have cling-on pads: modified thumb and foot pads or disks to facilitate attachment on moist surfaces such as leaves or the insides of bamboo stems. At least one megachiropteran (the Short-nosed fruit bat) and 16 species of phyllostomids make tents from leaves and other plant parts. A single male and several females usually occupy the tents, sometimes with their young. Many bat species now roost in manmade structures such as mines and buildings; where their natural roosts have been removed with the harvesting of mature trees, they can be encouraged into artificial boxes.

Many bats change roost sites frequently. Most (70 percent) of the roosts used by the New Zealand long-tailed bat are used for only a single night, and females of this species often carry their young between roosts, perhaps in order to reduce predation or else to move them to more favorable microclimates. Pallid bats that move roost frequently have fewer ectoparasites than more sedentary individuals, so roost-switching may function to reduce parasite load.

Threats and Promises

CONSERVATION AND ENVIRONMENT

Throughout the world the populations of many bat species are declining. In Britain, the numbers of pipistrelles emerging from maternity colonies declined by 62 percent between 1978 and 1986. Lesser horseshoe bats are now almost extinct over much of northwest Europe.

Flying foxes are threatened mainly by habitat destruction, by conflict with fruit growers, and by hunting. A looming threat to flying foxes on oceanic islands comes from global warming, bringing with it the risk of higher sea levels and changing weather patterns. On the island of Anjouan in the Comoros group, which holds the world's largest population of Livingston's flying foxes, forest cover has decreased by 70 percent in the last 20 years; educational programs and a captive-breeding project have been set up to protect the bats. In Israel, cave roosts of rousettes have been fumigated in an attempt to restrict damage to fruit crops, resulting in the deaths not just of many rousettes but also of other, nontargeted

insectivorous bats; because the caves were sprayed with the persistent organochlorine lindane, they will remain toxic for years to come.

The native people of Guam have hunted flying foxes in small numbers for food for at least a millennium. After World War I the introduction of guns resulted in the Mariana flying fox becoming endangered. By 1975 native flying foxes were becoming difficult to find, so about 230,000 bats of at least 10 species were imported onto the island for food between 1975 and 1990. Since 1989 all pteropodids, and also related species in the genus *Acerodon*, have been protected under the Convention on International Trade in Endangered Species (CITES). Yet enforcing CITES regulations to protect flying foxes has proved difficult; perhaps the greatest hope for Guam's flying foxes comes from changing dietary habits on the island: a recent study suggested that most of the people who eat flying foxes are more than 55 years old.

Other problems face insectivorous bats in temperate regions. Roost sites such as old barns have been renovated or destroyed, and disturbances at hibernacula have probably contributed to population declines. The loss of natural and seminatural habitats has sometimes occurred at alarming rates. Hedgerows provide commuting routes and feeding sites for many bat species, and the drastic reduction in their numbers has probably affected bats significantly in western Europe. The intensification of farming practices, with increased emphasis on the application of pesticides, has probably reduced the availability of quality foraging areas for bats. Antiparasitic drugs that cure livestock of worms also kill dung beetles and other invertebrates that live in cowpats, thereby reducing the availability of an important prey species for Greater horseshoe bats.

Many bats have been killed as a result of coming into contact with the chlorinated hydrocarbon insecticides and fungicides that were formerly used to protect roof timbers against wood-boring beetles and timber-rotting fungi. In many countries bats have also accumulated toxic residues from agricultural pesticides such as DDT; fortunately, the dangers associated with these substances are now recognized, and their use is often restricted. Water pollution, with its associated effects on aquatic insects, and the accumulation of metals such as cadmium and methyl mercury may also have contributed to population declines among pipistrelles in industrialized areas.

Above *Thousands of Mexican free-tailed bats emerge from their cave. Such impressive sights may become increasingly rare, as bat species around the world suffer habitat loss and poisoning by agricultural chemicals.*

Bats' reputations have not been helped by the negative mythological connotations associated with their name. They are frequently linked to witchcraft and magic; for instance, "wool of bat" features in the potion prepared by the three witches in Shakespeare's play *Macbeth*. There is also, of course, an extensive folklore about vampires – the transformed bodies or souls of the dead, who suck the blood of humans at night. The first time that vampires took the form of bats, however, was in Bram Stoker's novel *Dracula*, which appeared in 1897, although it is not clear whether Stoker knew of the existence of genuine vampire bats at the time. Interestingly, bats are viewed more positively in Chinese culture, where they are symbols of joy; stylized bats appear in many Chinese decorations and artforms. Bats also suffer from stories of their getting tangled in people's hair, although the sophistication of their echolocation equipment make such an occurrence unlikely.

Bats are also often identified as vectors of disease. A small number of bat species do indeed carry rabies, although this disease now accounts for only one or two human deaths per year in the USA (in comparison, about 20 people are killed in dog attacks annually). Flying foxes in Australasia may be the natural host of the *Hendra* virus that is thought to cause death in humans and horses. Public reaction to rabies and *Hendra* viruses in bats has been hysterical at times, although humans can easily avoid infection not just through vaccination but also by taking standard hygiene precautions and avoiding the handling of bats.

Given the bad publicity that often attaches to bats, it is encouraging to note that highly successful programs exist for their conservation. Many important hibernacula have been fitted with grilles at their entrances to restrict human access, a measure that can increase population numbers dramatically. Bat boxes may encourage bats to roost in habitats that otherwise would be unsuitable, and artificial hibernacula have also been constructed with some success.

Recently a major campaign undertaken to protect the single most important hibernation site in Europe ended in success. Thirty thousand bats of 12 different species annually hibernate in underground fortifications that were built in western Poland to combat the German invasion during World War II. The Polish government initially planned to store radioactive waste at the site, but extensive campaigning by bat conservationists has resulted in its protection as a bat reserve.

In Britain, the public's attitude to bats has warmed dramatically over the past 20 years. The International Convention on Biological Diversity, established in Rio de Janeiro in 1992, has triggered the formulation of action plans to conserve five species of British bats, and a network of about 90 groups now works to promote bat conservation. Research on the foraging ecology of Greater horseshoe bats has led to recommendations for the protection of their maternity roosts, and landowners can now obtain government grants to enhance this species' favored habitats.

National and regional policies to protect bats have now been developed in many countries, including Australia, Brazil, and the United States. Migratory bats are protected in the European Union, and European law also confers some protection on foraging sites. Bat Conservation International exists to promote the conservation cause. In addition, many researchers working on these fascinating creatures have become so impressed by their amazing adaptations that they have also become committed to their preservation. It is not hard to see why. GJ

Above *Three representative endangered species suggest the range of problems now facing bats around the world. The Ryukyu flying fox* ***1*** *is only found on the Ryukyu Islands at Japan's southern tip; long hunted for its meat, it is now also threatened by the felling of the trees on which it feeds and roosts. The Gray bat* ***2*** *from the southeastern USA is at risk because the caves where it hibernates are increasingly disturbed by tourists and quarryers. The Sucker-footed bat* ***3*** *is restricted to Madagascar, and like many of the island's mammalian species is threatened as the growing human population encroaches on the forests where it lives.*

Bat Families

NEW BAT SPECIES ARE BEING IDENTIFIED continuously, often as a consequence of molecular studies, and various authorities recognize differing numbers of families, genera, and species. This categorization lists diagnostic features of the families as recognized by the most recent, phylogeny-based approach to bat relationships, based on molecular and morphological (i.e. "total-evidence") research.

SUBORDER MEGACHIROPTERA

Flying foxes
Family Pteropodidae
Flying foxes or Old World fruit bats

164 species in 41 genera. Old World tropics and subtropics from Africa to E Asia and Australia, including many islands in the Indian and Pacific Oceans. A few species reach warmer temperate regions N to Turkey and Syria and to the extreme S of Africa and SE Australia. Species include: **Indian flying fox** (*P. giganteus*); **Leschenault's rousette** (*Rousettus leschenaulti*); **Blanford's fruit bat** (*Sphaerias blanfordi*); **Southern blossom bat** (*Syconycteris australis*); **Sulawesi fruit bat** (*Acerodon celebensis*); **Lesser naked-backed fruit bat** (*Dobsonia minor*); **Common tube-nosed fruit bat** (*Nyctimene albiventer*).
SIZE: Ranges from fairly small to the largest of all bats, with wing spans of 1.7m; HBL 50–400 mm; tail short or absent except in one species where it is half head–body length; FL 37–220mm; WT 15–1,500g. Male Hammer-headed bats (*Hypsignathus monstrosus*) show the most extreme sexual dimorphism in bats; males are almost twice the mass of females, and have swollen muzzles with flaring lip flaps. A huge larynx fills more than half of the body cavity, and is used to produce calls at lek sites. Males of other species have tufts of hair or glandular patches on their shoulders that are used in display.
COAT: Usually brown, but a few species are brightly colored, e.g. the Rodriguez flying fox (*Pteropus rodricensis*) varies from black to silver, yellow, orange, and red. Tube-nosed bats (genus *Nyctimene*) can be brightly colored, with speckled membranes and a dorsal stripe; cryptic coloration may camouflage bats roosting in foliage.
FORM: Most species have doglike faces, large eyes, and conspicuous, widely separated simple ears that lack a tragus. The second finger retains independence and, like the thumb, usually bears a claw. Most species orientate visually, except bats in the genus *Rousettus*, which echolocate by clicking the tongue to detect obstacles in caves. Dawn bats (*Eonycteris spelaea*) clap their wings when flying in caves, and this might function as a rudimentary form of echolocation.
DIET: Mainly plant material, largely ripe fruit but also flowers, nectar, and leaves. Some species may supplement their diet with a small numbers of insects. Nectar-feeding species (e.g. blossom bats in genus *Macroglossus*) have long tongues with bristle-like papillae. Many species are essential for pollination and dispersal of economically important plants.
BEHAVIOR: Some of the larger species may form "camps" in forest patches, sometimes containing over a million bats. The largest colonies of all are formed in caves by rousettes (*Rousettus* spp); they may contain several million bats, which may make round trips of 40–50km in a night to forage. Straw-colored fruit bats (*Eidolon helvum*) are migratory, and may make round trips in E Africa of up to 2,500km.
CONSERVATION STATUS: 8 species are now considered Extinct by the IUCN; in addition, 14 species (including all 4 *Pteralopex* spp) are Critically Endangered, 7 are Endangered, and 39 Vulnerable.

SUBORDER MICROCHIROPTERA

Mouse-tailed bats
Family Rhinopomatidae
Mouse-tailed, rat-tailed, or long-tailed bats

3 species in 1 genus (*Rhinopoma*). N Africa to the S Sudan, Middle East, India, and SE Asia; Sumatra. Arid or semi-arid areas, also agricultural and disturbed habitats. Species are: **Lesser mouse-tailed bat** (*Rhinopoma hardwickii*); **Greater mouse-tailed bat** (*R. microphyllum*); **Small mouse-tailed bat** (*R. muscatellum*).
SIZE: Generally small. HBL 50–90mm; TL 40–80mm; FL 45–75mm; WT 6–14g.
FORM: Tail exceptional, being almost as long as head–body length and entirely free of membrane. Ears joined by inner margins, tragus well developed; snout bears a small, simple noseleaf like a pig's muzzle. Least derived of Microchiroptera.
BEHAVIOR: Fast-flying aerial insectivores that emit long, narrowband, multiharmonic echolocation calls. Roost in caves and buildings, including Egyptian pyramids where they have occurred for 3,000 years or more. May enter torpor when insects are scarce, and then utilize fat stored in the abdominal region. Roosts may comprise thousands of bats.
CONSERVATION STATUS: 1 species (*Rhinopoma hardwickii*) is Vulnerable.

Hog-nosed bat
Family Craseonycteridae
Craseonycteris thonglongyai
Bumblebee or Butterfly bat

1 species, first described in 1974. W. Thailand. Bamboo forests and teak plantations (much of the natural vegetation in area removed). SIZE: The world's smallest bat (and mammal). HBL 29–33mm; tail absent; FL 22–26mm; WT 2g.
COAT: Upperparts brown to reddish gray, underside paler, wings darker.
FORM: Muzzle piglike in appearance. Glandular swelling on underside of throat in males.
BEHAVIOR: Aerial insectivore, feeding on small beetles and other insects. Hunts in open areas for 30–45 mins after sunset and for a short period before dawn. Echolocation calls narrowband and multiharmonic. Forms small colonies in caves.
CONSERVATION STATUS: Endangered.

Sheath-tailed bats
Family Emballonuridae
Sheath-tailed or sac-winged bats

47 species in 12 genera. Africa, S and SE Asia, Australia, tropical America, many islands in the Indian and Pacific Oceans. Species include: **Shaggy bat** (*Centronycteris maximiliani*); **Greater ghost bat** (*Diclidurus ingens*); **Peter's sheath-tailed bat** (*Emballonura atrata*); **Lesser doglike bat** (*Peropterxy macrotis*); **Proboscis bat** (*Rhynchonycteris naso*); **Egyptian tomb bat** (*Taphozous perforatus*).
SIZE: Varies from small to relatively large. HBL 37–157mm; TL 6–36mm; FL 37–97mm; WT 5–105g.
COAT: Mostly drab or brown, although some species have cryptic patterns and tufts of hair. Bats in one genus, *Diclidurus* (ghost bats), are largely white.
FORM: Ears often joined, tragus present. Short tail pierces the tail membrane, so its tip appears exposed on membrane's dorsal surface. Many species have glandular wing sacs (larger in males) that open on the upper surface of the wing; in the Greater white-lined bat (*Saccopteryx bilineata*), these are used for odor storage. Some species have throat glands that secrete odorous compounds.
BEHAVIOR: Many are fast-flying aerial insectivores that emit long, narrowband, multiharmonic echolocation calls. Roost in a wide range of sites from hollow trees to buildings and caves. Some species highly colonial (e.g. the tomb bats, *Taphozous* spp). Most are tropical, but some species in cooler regions use torpor and may hibernate.
CONSERVATION STATUS: 2 species are Critically Endangered, 2 Endangered, and 10 Vulnerable.

Right *A Pallas's tube-nosed fruit bat* (Nyctimene cephalotes) *rests with its wings folded at a roost in northern Sulawesi, Indonesia. The* Nyctimene *species makes up one of the 41 genera of the Pteropodidae – the flying-fox family of Old World fruit bats.*

Slit-faced bats
Family Nycteridae
Slit-faced, hollow-faced, or hispid bats

13 species in 1 genus. Africa, SW and SE Asia. Arid areas as well as rain forests. Species include: **Large slit-faced bat** (*Nycteris grandis*); **Hairy slit-faced bat** (*N. hispida*); **Dwarf slit-faced bat** (*N.nana*).
SIZE: Medium-sized. HBL 40–93mm; TL 43–75mm, FL 32–60mm, WT 10–30g.
COAT: Usually long, rich brown to gray.
FORM: Furrow in muzzle from nostrils to pit between eyes; noseleaves and fur sometimes conceal furrow externally. Ears large, tragus small. Broad wings. Tail T-shaped at tip, uniquely among mammals.
DIET: Orthopterans, spiders, caterpillars, scorpions. The Large slit-faced bat (*Nycteris grandis*) eats fish, frogs, birds, and other bats.
BEHAVIOR: The bats often carry prey to a perch for eating. Echolocation calls faint, broadband, and multiharmonic. Roost often in small groups in a variety of sites including hollow trees, culverts, and even aardvark burrows.
CONSERVATION STATUS: 2 species are Vulnerable.

Old World false vampire bats
Family Megadermatidae
Old World false vampire bats, false vampire bats, yellow-winged bats

5 species in 4 genera. Old World tropics and subtropics of Africa, SC and SE Asia, and Australasia. Species include: **Heart-nosed bat** (*Cardioderma cor*); **Greater false vampire bat** (*Megaderma lyra*).
SIZE: Among the largest microchiropterans, with the Australian false vampire bat (*Macroderma gigas*) the largest. HBL 65–140mm; FL 50–115mm; WT 37–123g.
COAT: Drab but variable, from gray to brown, even whitish. Yellow-winged bat (*Lavia frons*) very colorful, with ears and wings yellow-orange and fur gray to olive.

ABBREVIATIONS HBL = head–body length TL = tail length FL = forearm length WT = weight
Approximate nonmetric equivalents: 25mm = 1in 10cm = 4in; 100g =3.5oz

Dusky roundleaf bat (*Hipposideros ater*).

FORM: Long, erect, simple noseleaves. Ears very large and fused at base, each with large tragus. Broad tail membrane, but tail itself vestigial or absent. Eyes large.
DIET: Some of the most carnivorous bats, eating small vertebrates, other bats, reptiles, amphibians, fish, and arthropods. Often hunt from and eat prey at perches.
BEHAVIOR: Broad wings confer slow, maneuverable flight and strong take-off from ground. The Yellow-winged bat is often active by day and lives in territorial, monogamous pairs, which remain with young for about 30 days after weaning. Hearing very sensitive to rustling sounds made by prey moving in vegetation. These bats often hunt by listening for prey-generated sounds, although they also detect prey by echolocation in non-cluttered environments. Echolocation calls faint, broadband, and multiharmonic. Roost in caves, buildings, and hollow trees, often in small groups. The African false vampire bat (*Cardioderma cor*) "sings" to establish defended foraging areas.
CONSERVATION STATUS: The Australian false vampire bat (*Macroderma gigas*) is Vulnerable, and exists in isolated populations that show strong genetic divergence.

Horseshoe and Old World leaf-nosed bats

Family Rhinolophidae

129 species in 10 genera. Many authors treat the horseshoe bats and Old World leaf-nosed bats as separate families (Rhinolophidae and Hipposideridae respectively), although modern classifications consider both as belonging to one family. Africa, S Eurasia, SE Asia, Australia, especially in tropical regions. Species include: **Thomas's horseshoe bat** (*Rhinolophus thomasi*); **Trident leaf-nosed bat** (*Asellia tridens*); **Flower-faced bat** (*Anthops ornatus*);
SIZE: Mostly relatively small. HBL 35–110mm; TL 15–70mm; FL 30–105mm; WT 4–180g.
COAT: Variable, including yellows, browns, grays, blacks; some species have whitish fur patches. Some species occur in two color phases.
FORM: Prominent noseleaves; in horseshoe bats the front part of the noseleaf is horseshoe-shaped, and a sella projects forward with a generally pointed lancet running lengthways. Old World leaf-nosed bats have a noseleaf lacking a well-defined horseshoe, and the lancet is a transverse leaf often with three points; there is no sella in the center of the noseleaf. Ears generally large and pointed, and always lack a tragus. Heads face downward. Hind legs poorly developed; the bats are unable to walk quadrupedally. Dummy teats on female abdomens for attachment of young.
BEHAVIOR: Broad wings confer slow, maneuverable flight, often within dense vegetation. The bats catch prey (usually insects) by aerial hawking and gleaning, and large species often hunt from and eat prey at perches. Sophisticated echolocation involves nasal emission of relatively long constant-frequency pulses, usually as second harmonic of call. Horseshoe bats echolocate by compensating for Doppler shifts induced by their flight speed; Old World leaf-nosed bats compensate partially. All roost in caves, mines, trees, buildings. Some species may be monogamous, others polygynous. At roosts, fold their wings around themselves. Can hibernate.
CONSERVATION STATUS: 2 of the 64 horseshoe bats are Endangered, and 8 are Vulnerable. Of the 65 Old World leaf-nosed bats, 2 are Critically Endangered, 1 Endangered, and 15 Vulnerable.

New Zealand short-tailed bat

Family Mystacinidae

Mystacina tuberculata

New Zealand short-tailed or Lesser short-tailed bat

1 species. New Zealand and adjacent islands. Another putative species, *M. robusta*, is now almost certainly extinct.
SIZE: Small. HBL 60mm; TL 18mm; FL 40–46mm; WT 13–22g.
COAT: Fur brown-gray, short and velvety.
FORM: Thumb and toe claws have extra projection or talon, uniquely among bats; wings can be rolled tightly against body; tail perforates upperside of tail membrane, as in the Emballonuridae; ears simple, separate, and large, with long tragus; tongue with papillae at tip.
DIET: Broad diet includes aerial insects, terrestrial arthropods, nectar, pollen, fruit.

BEHAVIOR: Agile on the ground; evolved in the absence of terrestrial mammals and perhaps with few predators, facilitating terrestrial habits. Molecular studies suggest affinities to Mormoopidae, Noctilionidae, and Phyllostomidae families, suggesting Gondwanaland ancestry. Echolocation calls broadband and multiharmonic. The bat catches aerial prey by echolocation; listens for prey-generated sounds and uses olfaction to locate prey in leaf litter; roosts in tree holes, often in large numbers. Males "sing" at aggregations of tree roosts, probably to attract females. Large foraging range. Often hosts a wingless fly that feeds on fungi that grow in its guano. Can use torpor and probably hibernates. This and a vespertilionid bat are the only indigenous nonmarine mammals in New Zealand.
CONSERVATION STATUS: Vulnerable

Bulldog bats
Family Noctilionidae
Bulldog or fisherman bats

2 species in 1 genus (*Noctilio*). Tropical C and S America, Caribbean islands.
SIZE: **Greater bulldog bat**, or **Fisherman bat** (*Noctilio leporinus*): HBL 98–132mm; FL 70–92mm; WT 54–90g. **Lesser bulldog bat** (*N. albiventris*): HBL 57–85mm; FL 54–70mm; WT 18–44g.
COAT: Fisherman bat has short yellow or orange fur that sheds water easily.
BEHAVIOR: The fisherman bat is the only bat to specialize in eating fish; also eats insects and crabs. Fish up to 8cm (3in) long are detected by echolocation when they protrude or form ripples on the water's surface; huge feet with long, sharp claws are used to catch fish from just under the surface. Catches are stored in cheek pouches. Roosts often in sea caves, where colonies can be located by their musky odor. Insectivorous Lesser bulldog bat captures insects in midair or from water's surface, and may be preadapted for piscivory. Echolocation calls include narrowband and broadband components to detect fish and insects that often break the water's surface.
CONSERVATION STATUS: Not threatened.

Spectacled bats
Family Mormoopidae
Spectacled bats, naked-backed bats, leaf-chinned bats, mustached bats

8 species in 2 genera. Extreme SW USA, through C America and Caribbean S to central S Brazil. Species include: **Ghost-faced bat** (*Mormoops megalophylla*); **Sooty mustached bat** (*Pteronotus quadridens*).
SIZE: Small to medium-sized. HBL 40–77 mm; TL 15–30 mm; FL 35–65 mm; WT 3.5–20g.
COAT: Fur short and dense, reddish through brown and gray.
FORM: Lack a noseleaf but can funnel lips to create a dish shape. Several species have naked backs because wing membranes join on dorsal midline of body. Ears small with tragus. Tail projects slightly beyond tail membrane.
BEHAVIOR: Insectivorous. Can form large colonies in caves. Echolocation calls include narrowband and broadband components. Parnell's mustached bat (*Pteronotus parnellii*) evolved echolocation with Doppler shift compensation independently of the Rhinolophidae.
CONSERVATION STATUS: 1 species (*Pteronotus macleayii*) is Vulnerable.

New World leaf-nosed bats
Family Phyllostomidae
New World leaf-nosed bats or spear-nosed bats

About 140 species in 48 genera. New World from extreme SW USA throughout C America and Caribbean south to N Argentina. Species include: **California leaf-nosed bat** (*Macrotus californicus*); **Golden bat** (*Mimon bennettii*); **Pale-faced bat** (*Phylloderma stenops*); **Greater spear-nosed bat** (*Phyllostomus hastatus*); **Greater round-eared bat** (*Tonatia bidens*); **Western nectar bat** (*Lonchophylla hesperia*); **Lesser long-tailed bat** (*Choeroniscus minor*); **Tent-making bat** (*Uroderma bilobatum*); **Large fruit-eating bat** (*Artibeus amplus*); **Jamaican flower bat** (*Phyllonycteris aphylla*); **Hairy-legged vampire bat** (*Diphylla ecaudata*).
SIZE: Variable. HBL 40–135mm; TL absent or 4–55mm; FL 31–105mm, WT 7–200g. Includes the microchiropteran with the longest forearm length, the carnivorous Spectral bat (*Vampyrum spectrum*).
COAT: Apart from one almost white bat, the Honduran white bat (*Ectophylla alba*), others are brown, gray, or black, occasionally with red or white hair tufts. Several species have whitish lines on the face and/or body.
FORM: Most species have a spear–shaped noseleaf, but 5 have none, or a more complex shape. Ears usually simple, can be large; tragus present. Vampire bats' muzzles are swollen and glandular, resembling a noseleaf, and they have specialized teeth, with a reduction in tooth number and sharp incisors and canines.
DIET: Show virtually every type of food habit known for bats. Many species feed on fruit, pollen, or nectar; others are insectivorous, and a few are omnivorous or even carnivorous. Three species of vampire bats in C and S America feed on blood, whose flow is increased by anti-coagulants in the saliva. The Common vampire bat (*Desmodus rotundus*) feeds mainly on mammalian blood, the other two principally on bird blood.
BEHAVIOR: Phyllostomids detect food by echolocation, olfaction, and probably vision. Echolocation calls usually faint, broadband, and multiharmonic. One species, the Fringe-lipped bat (*Trachops cirrhosus*), hunts frogs, which it locates by listening for their calls. The bats roost in a variety of sites including caves, culverts, hollow trees, and among foliage. Some species make "tents" by biting through leaf ribs. None hibernate. Vampire bats are agile on the ground.
CONSERVATION STATUS: The Puerto Rican flower bat (*Phyllonycteris major*) is now thought to be extinct; 4 other species are Endangered, and 25 are Vulnerable.

Funnel-eared bats
Family Natalidae
Funnel-eared or long-legged bats

5 species in 1 genus (*Natalus*). N Mexico through C America to Brazil, also Caribbean islands. Species include **Mexican funnel-eared bat** (*N. stramineus*).
SIZE: Small and delicate. HBL 35–55mm; TL 50–60mm; FL 27–41mm; WT 4–10g.
COAT: Often reddish or brown.
FORM: Second digit of wing reduced to metacarpal, phalanx lost. Lightly built with long, slender wings and legs; tails longer than head and body. Ears funnel-shaped and large, with a short, triangular tragus; nose simple.
BEHAVIOR: Poorly studied. Often roost in caves, also in tree hollows. Slow-flying and maneuverable. Insectivorous. Adult males have a "natalid organ" on face or muzzle, of unknown function.
CONSERVATION STATUS: 1 species – *N. tumidifrons* – is Vulnerable.

Thumbless bats
Family Furipteridae
Thumbless or smoky bats

2 species in 2 genera: **Thumbless bat** (*Furipterus horrens*) and **Smoky bat** (*Amorphochilus schnablii*). Costa Rica to N Chile and SE Brazil; Trinidad.
SIZE: Small bats. HBL 33–58mm; TL 24–36mm; FL 30–40mm; WT 3–5g.
COAT: Brown to gray.
FORM: Small, functionless thumbs; ears funnel-shaped with small tragus. Wings relatively long; crown elevated above face. Truncated snout ends in disklike structure. Females have one pair of abdominal mammae.
BEHAVIOR: Little is known about these bats, except that they are insectivorous and roost in caves, buildings, tunnels, among boulders, or in tree hollows.
CONSERVATION STATUS: The Smoky bat is Vulnerable.

Disk-winged bats
Family Thyropteridae
Disk-winged bats or New World sucker-footed bats

2 species in 1 genus: **Peter's disk-winged bat** (*Thyroptera discifera*) and **Spix's disk-winged bat** (*T. tricolor*). S Mexico to N Bolivia and SE Brazil; Trinidad.
SIZE: Small bats. HBL 34–52mm; TL 25–33mm; FL 27–38mm; WT 4–5g.
COAT: Red-brown or blackish, white below.
FORM: Wrists, ankles, and functional thumbs have disk suckers borne on small stalks. One sucker can support the bat's weight as it roosts in smooth, furled leaves, such as bananas or those of *Heliconia*. Ears funnel-shaped, tragus present. As in Smoky bats, third and fourth toes are joined.
BEHAVIOR: Insectivorous, roost in small groups in moist, evergreen forest. Echolocation calls low in intensity, variable, including both broadband, multiharmonic, and narrowband calls.

Old World sucker-footed bat
Family Myzopodidae
Myzopoda aurita

1 species. Restricted to Madagascar.
SIZE: Small to medium-sized. HBL 57mm; TL 48mm; FL 46–50mm.
FORM: Suction disks present on wrists and ankles differ in structure from those in *Thyroptera*, and probably evolved independently. Large ear, with tragus and mushroom-shaped structure at base. Long tail projects beyond tail membrane.
BEHAVIOR: Rare and little studied. Roosts in palm leaves; one captured bat had fed on microlepidoptera. Emits unusual echolocation calls that are long, multiharmonic, and consist of several elements. Similar bats found in E Africa in Pleistocene.
CONSERVATION STATUS: Vulnerable.

Vespertilionid bats
Family Vespertilionidae

At least 308 species in 34 genera. The second largest mammalian family after the Muridae (Old World rats and mice). Worldwide except for extreme Polar regions and remote islands. Species include: **Smith's woolly bat** (*Kerivoula smithii*); Pied bat (*Chalinolobus superbus*); **Cape serotine** (*Eptesicus capensis*); **Large myotis** (*Myotis chinensis*); **noctule** (*Nyctalus noctula*); **Mouselike pipistrelle** (*Pipistrellus musciculus*); Robust yellow bat (*Scotophilus robustus*); **Brown tube-nosed bat** (*Murina suilla*); **Greater bamboo bat** (*Tylonycteris robustula*); Peter's tube-nosed bat (*Murina grisea*).
SIZE: Mostly small, but a few are medium to large. HBL 32–105mm; TL 25–75mm; FL 22–75mm; WT 4–50g.
COAT: Usually browns and grays, undersides often paler. Some species yellow, red, or orange. Painted bat (*Kerivoula picta*) has scarlet or orange fur, black membranes with orange finger bones. The cryptic coloration may provide camouflage in flowers and foliage; small clusters resemble the

hanging mud nests of wasps. Butterfly bats (*Glauconycteris* spp.) usually have white spots and stripes on their pelage. These bats often roost in foliage, and may show cryptic or disruptive color patterns.
FORM: Most have simple muzzles, though bats in 2 genera have a slight noseleaf, and tubular nostrils are also present in 2 genera. Ears normally separate, with tragus, and vary from small to enormous, especially in the long-eared bats (*Plecotus* spp.) where they approach head–body length. Bats in 5 genera have wing and/or foot discs to aid gripping smooth leaves or bamboo.
BEHAVIOR: Mainly insectivorous, with insects captured by aerial hawking, gleaning, or even trawling from water's surface (e.g. *Myotis daubentonii*). At least one species, the Fish-eating bat (*Myotis vivesi*) sometimes eats fish. Echolocation calls vary from broadband in species that feed in obstacle-rich environments to narrowband in more open habitats. Species that feed in clutter often locate prey by listening for prey-generated sounds rather than by echolocation. Roost sites include tree hollows, under bark, rock crevices, birds' nests, in foliage, and in buildings and caves. Bamboo bats (*Tylonycteris* spp.) have flat heads and suckers on their thumbs and feet, and roost in bamboo stems. Roost sizes vary from a few individuals to over 1 million. Some species migrate, though temperate species generally hibernate.
CONSERVATION STATUS: Of the 308 species, 6 are considered Critically Endangered, 19 Endangered, and 50 Vulnerable. 1 pipistrelle – *Pipistrellus sturdeei* – is listed as Extinct.

Pallid bat
Family Antrozoidae
Antrozous pallidus

1 species. Recent phylogenetic studies based on morphology place the Pallid bat closer to free-tailed bats than to vespertilionids, and suggest that it should be placed in a family of its own, as here. N America to C Mexico; Cuba.
SIZE: Medium-sized. HBL 60–85mm; TL 35–57mm; FL 45–60mm; WT 17–28g.
COAT: Cream , yellowish, or light brown, paler ventrally.
FORM: large ears with tragus; small, horseshoe-shaped ridge on square muzzle, with nostrils underneath. Broad wings confer maneuverable flight.
DIET: Eats beetles, orthopterans, moths, spiders, scorpions, centipedes, and even small vertebrates, which are often captured on the ground.
BEHAVIOR: Often inhabits desert areas, though also occurs in forests. Locates prey on the ground by listening for rustling sounds. Highly social, with a rich repertoire of communication calls.

Right *Proboscis bats* (Rhynchonycteris naso) *form a line on a tree stump. These bats may roost on branches during the day. Pale lines on their backs disrupt their shape; this, plus their habit of tilting their heads backward, makes the roosting bats resemble the curved edges of lichen.*

Free-tailed bats
Family Molossidae

At least 77 species in 12 genera. Warm or tropical areas from central USA south to C Argentina; S Europe, Africa, E to Korea, the Solomons, and Australasia. Species include: **Spotted free-tailed bat** (*Chaerephon bivittata*); **Hairless bat** (*Cheiromeles torquatus*); **Malayan free-tailed bat** (*Mops mops*); **Cinnamon dog-faced bat** (*Molossops abrasus*).
SIZE: Most are small- to medium-sized, though the Hairless bat (*Cheiromeles torquatus*) is the heaviest microchiropteran. HBL 40–130mm; TL 14–80mm; FL 27–85mm; WT 8–180g.
COAT: Fur usually short and sleek, brown, gray, or black, but some are reddish with whitish patches, e.g. in *Mops spurrelli*.
FORM: Robust bats with a large proportion of the thick tail projecting beyond the tail membrane. Membranes leathery, wings long and narrow, conferring fast, unmaneuverable flight. Ears small to relatively long, usually joined across forehead and directed forward in small-eared species. Tragus present. Several species in the genus *Chaerephon* have tufts of glandular hairs on crown. The large Hairless bats have very thick skin, with wings joining at the midline of the back, and large skin pouches laterally into which the wing tips are tucked when at rest. They are largely naked, with a few hairs around a throat sac. They emit a pungent odor.
BEHAVIOR: Molossids are usually aerial hawkers that emit long-duration, narrowband calls. They feed mainly on moths and beetles captured in open habitats. Roost sites include caves, rock crevices, hollow trees, and buildings. Nursery colonies of the Brazilian free-tailed bat (*Tadarida brasiliensis*) in SW USA form the largest aggregations of vertebrates known, with up to 20 million bats in a colony. Sodium nitrate extracted from guano at these large roosts was used to produce gunpowder. Some species (e.g. *T. brasiliensis*) may migrate, others (e.g. the European free-tailed bat, *Tadarida teniotis*) can hibernate in rock crevices, emerging to feed on mild winter nights.
CONSERVATION STATUS: 3 species are Critically Endangered, 1 Endangered, and 16 Vulnerable. Brazilian free-tailed bat declines are partly attributable to poisoning by breakdown products of DDT. GJ

For full species list see Appendix ▷

SPECIAL FEATURE

BATS AND COLUMNAR CACTI

A symbiotic relationship between pollinator and pollinated

FLOWERS AND BATS MAY NOT SEEM THE MOST likely bedfellows, but they have formed mutually beneficial partnerships throughout the tropics worldwide. In the Old World, six genera and 14 species of pteropodid bats – the flying foxes and their allies – feed from flowers; they apparently evolved to do so independently from the 15 genera and 38 species of New World Phyllostomidae (leaf-nosed bats) that do the same. Together, these bats are the major, if not exclusive, pollinators of hundreds of species of tropical and subtropical trees, shrubs, lianas, and epiphytes, including such commercially important species as kapok, balsa, wild bananas, and durian.

While a majority of bat-pollinated plants occur within the wet tropics, one ecologically conspicuous group of neotropical plants, the columnar cacti, live in semi-arid to very arid habitats and depend on a specialized group of phyllostomid bats for their pollination (and, often, for seed dispersal). Containing about 100 genera and 1,500 species classified in three or four subfamilies, the Cactaceae form one of the New World's most distinctive plant families. Whereas most species are relatively small in stature and are pollinated by insects, the giants of this family, especially those of the Pachycereeae and Leptocereeae tribes, are often pollinated by bats.

Columnar cacti such as saguaros, cardóns, organ pipes, and their relatives attain the dizzy heights of 10–15m (33–50ft), and tend to be the dominant species in the deserts of the southwestern United States, Mexico, northern South America, and the Andes. Located high above the desert floor at or near the tips of long branches or stems, their robust, cream-colored flowers open up at night to produce substantial amounts of energy-rich nectar (up to 2ml and 8.8kJ) and pollen (up to 0.5g). Unlike insect-pollinated flowers, which typically remain open for several days at a time, most bat-pollinated cactus flowers close within 12 hours of opening.

Although a variety of phyllostomid bats opportunistically visit the flowers of columnar cacti, most of the pollination is accomplished by just four species, all specialized members of the subfamily Glossophaginae. Three of these – *Leptonycteris curasoae*, *L. nivalis*, and *Choeronycteris mexicana* – occur in Mexico and the southwestern United States; one (*Platalina genovensium*) is exclusive to South America, where *L. curasoae* is also found. In this group of bats, certain adaptations – a greatly elongated rostrum and tongue, long, relatively narrow wings, and large size (for the subfamily) – have evolved independently three times to aid their floral way of life. Nectar and pollen can be rapidly

extracted from large cactus flowers, and the bats can fly long distances quickly and efficiently. Physiologically, they can extract all of the nutrients contained within the pollen grains in their stomachs and use the amino acids for protein synthesis, which means that they have to eat fewer insects to make up their diet, which in some seasons and locations consists almost entirely of nectar and pollen. Finally, these bats are migratory and often move seasonally among habitats in search of rich patches of flowering plants.

Each spring, pregnant female Lesser long-nosed bats (*L. curasoae*) migrate nearly 1,200km (750mi) from the tropical dry forests of south-central Mexico to the Sonoran Desert of northwestern Mexico and Arizona, where they form large maternity colonies containing tens of thousands of individuals. Although details of its migration routes, or "nectar corridors," are unknown, *P. genovensium* also probably migrates over long distances among cactus-rich habitats in the Peruvian Andes, especially in years affected by the El Niño weather phenomenon, when heavy rains disrupt the normal flowering schedules of Andean columnar cacti.

When the bats were experimentally kept away from night-blooming columnar cacti, the results revealed an interesting geographic pattern. In the arid regions of central Mexico and northern Venezuela, including the island of Curaçao, nectar-feeding bats were found to be the only pollinators of these cacti, and flowers from which bats were excluded invariably aborted. North and south of these areas, however, diurnal flower visitors such as birds and bees become important pollinators. In the Sonoran Desert, for example, fruit set is strongly dependent on Lesser long-nosed bats only in cardón (*Pachycereus pringlei*); white-winged doves are the major vertebrate pollinators of saguaro (*Carnegiea gigantea*), and hummingbirds of organ pipe (*Stenocereus thurberi*). In the Andes of southern Peru, the cactus *Weberbauerocereus weberbaueri* is effectively pollinated by the bat *P. genovensium* at night and by the Andean giant hummingbird (*Patagona gigas*) during the day. In the Sonoran Desert, changes in the time of flower closing and the duration of stigma receptivity, rather than changes in flower morphology, have permitted diurnal flower visitors to become effective pollinators. In the Peruvian Andes, *W. weberbaueri* opens its blooms in the later afternoon, and considerable variation in the size, shape, and color

Above *Lesser long-nosed bats queue up to feed from a cactus flower. Because the bats cannot hover, they spend only a fraction of a second feeding at each pass. They extract the nectar with their extraordinary tongues, which extend for almost the length of their bodies and are tipped with fleshy bristles.*

of its flowers indicates that selection for both bat and hummingbird pollination has been strong in this species. Thus the scarcity of migratory bats has led to the evolution of more generalized pollination systems in bat-pollinated columnar cacti at both the northern and southern limits of their geographical distribution.

In both the the Sonoran Desert and in Venezuela, the blooming seasons of bat-pollinated cacti tend to be seasonally displaced in order to avoid competition for nocturnal pollinators. In Sonora, for example, flowering peaks of cardón and saguaro occur in late April, whereas that of organ pipe occurs in mid-June; saguaro avoids competing for pollinators with cardón by staying open longer during the day. In central Mexico, however, co-occurring columnar cacti tend to bloom at the same time of year (in April–June); how these species avoid competing for bat pollinators is currently unknown.

In another example of bat–cactus coevolution, the form of cardón's breeding system in the Sonoran Desert varies geographically, in part as a result of geographic variation in the abundance of Lesser long-nosed bats. In areas near maternity roosts, cardón populations contain separate male, female, and hermaphrodite individuals (a breeding system technically known as "trioecy"). Away from these roosts, populations contain only females and hermaphrodites, which produce both pollen and ovules in their flowers (this system is known as "gynodioecy"). Males are present in cardón populations only in areas where the nocturnal pollinators are abundant.

Finally, as an unusual method of reducing the impact of competition for bat pollinators, some organ pipe cacti flower early, and in the absence of their own pollen use cardón or saguaro pollen to stimulate the asexual production of fruits bearing mature seeds. In this way, organ pipe flowers that receive the "wrong" pollen, which in the Sonoran Desert happens frequently in April and early May, are not wasted via abortion. Thus, bats serve as the bees of the desert. THF

SHOWING OFF TO THE FEMALES

How lek mating works among Hammerheaded bats

THE HAMMERHEADED FRUIT BAT IS ONE OF A small number of mammalian species that practice lek mating. A lek is an aggregation of displaying males to which females come solely for the purpose of mating. Females usually visit a lek, examine a number of males, and then select one with which to mate. Females are remarkably consistent in their choice, so that only a few males do all the mating. Females undertake all the parental care in lek species. Other forms exhibiting lek behavior include the Uganda kob, the topi, and the Fallow deer among mammals, as well as some birds, frogs, fishes, and insects.

The bat (*Hypsignathus monstrosus*) occurs in tropical forests from Senegal through the Congo basin to western Uganda. In the core of the range in Gabon, the bats form leks at traditional locations and mate during the two annual dry seasons, from January to early March and from June to August respectively. Populations in more peripheral parts of the range may show more dispersed and less stable distributions of displaying males.

A Gabon Hammerheaded bat lek nearly always borders a waterway, and varies from 0.7–1.5km (0.4–0.9mi) in length. Males are spaced about 10–15m (33–49ft) apart along the site, and the array is usually about two males deep, the full range being 1–4. There are calling males on the sites for about 15 weeks each dry season. Early and late in the season, only a few males call. The number increases rapidly to a peak in February and July, and then declines more slowly as the season draws to an end.

Each night at sunset during the mating period, males leave their day roosts and fly directly to the traditional lek sites. At the lek they hang in the foliage at the canopy's edge and emit a loud, metallic call while flapping their wings at twice the call rate. Early in the mating season, there is usually some fighting between males for calling territories. By the time females begin visiting the lek – and they start to do so before they are ready to mate – males are settled in their territories and there is little subsequent interference between them. This is in marked contrast to most ungulate leks, in which male turnover is very high even during the season and males frequently interfere with each others' courtship efforts.

Typical Hammerheaded bat leks contain 30–150 displaying males, each one calling 1–4 times a second and flapping its wings furiously. Females fly along the ranks and periodically hover before a chosen male. This causes the male to perform a staccato variation of its call and to tuck its wings close against its body. Females will make repeated visits on the same night to a decreasing number of males, each time eliciting a "staccato buzz." Finally, selection is complete, the female lands by the male of her choice, and mating is accomplished in 20–30 seconds. Females usually terminate mating with several squeals, and then fly off.

The importance of display in enabling a male to breed has obviously favored a heavy investment in the equipment the bats uses to advertise themselves. Males are twice as large as females, weighing 425g (15oz) compared to 250g (8.8oz); they have an enormous bony larynx that fills their chest cavity, and a bizarre head with enlarged cheek pouches, inflated nasal cavities, and a funnel-like mouth. The larynx and associated head structures are all specializations for producing the loud call.

Females can mate at 6 months, and reach adult size at about 9 months. They can thus produce their first offspring (only one young is born at a time) as yearlings. Females come into heat immediately after birth (post-partum estrus), and thus can produce two successive young each year. In fact, many of the females mating during any dry season are carrying newborn young conceived at the last mating or lek period. As with many lek species, males mature later than females.

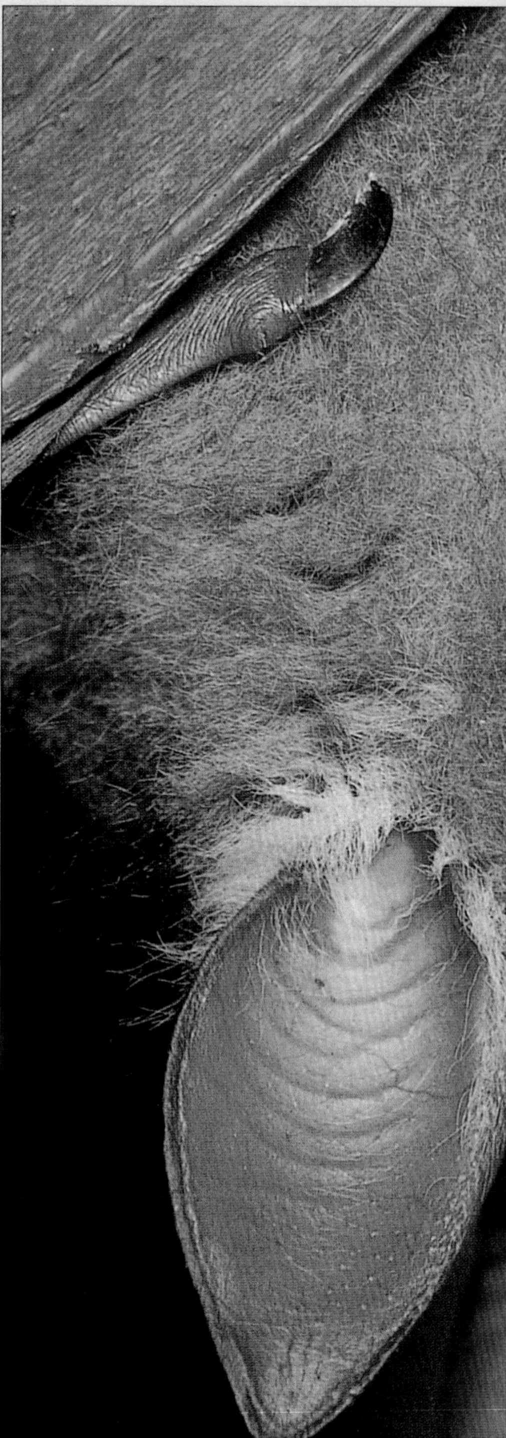

Above *Male Hammerheaded bats owe their bizarre head shape to the competitive demands of lek mating. The broad muzzle encloses inflatable air sacs and a hugely enlarged larynx that extends back to fill much of the chest cavity. The continuous croaking produced with its aid apparently serves to attract potential mates. One naturalist has compared the noise of a lek in full throat to that of "a pondful of noisy American wood-frogs, greatly magnified and transported to the tree-tops."*

Left *Female Hammerheads are more conventional in their appearance, and are also much smaller, with a body length little more than half that of the males.*

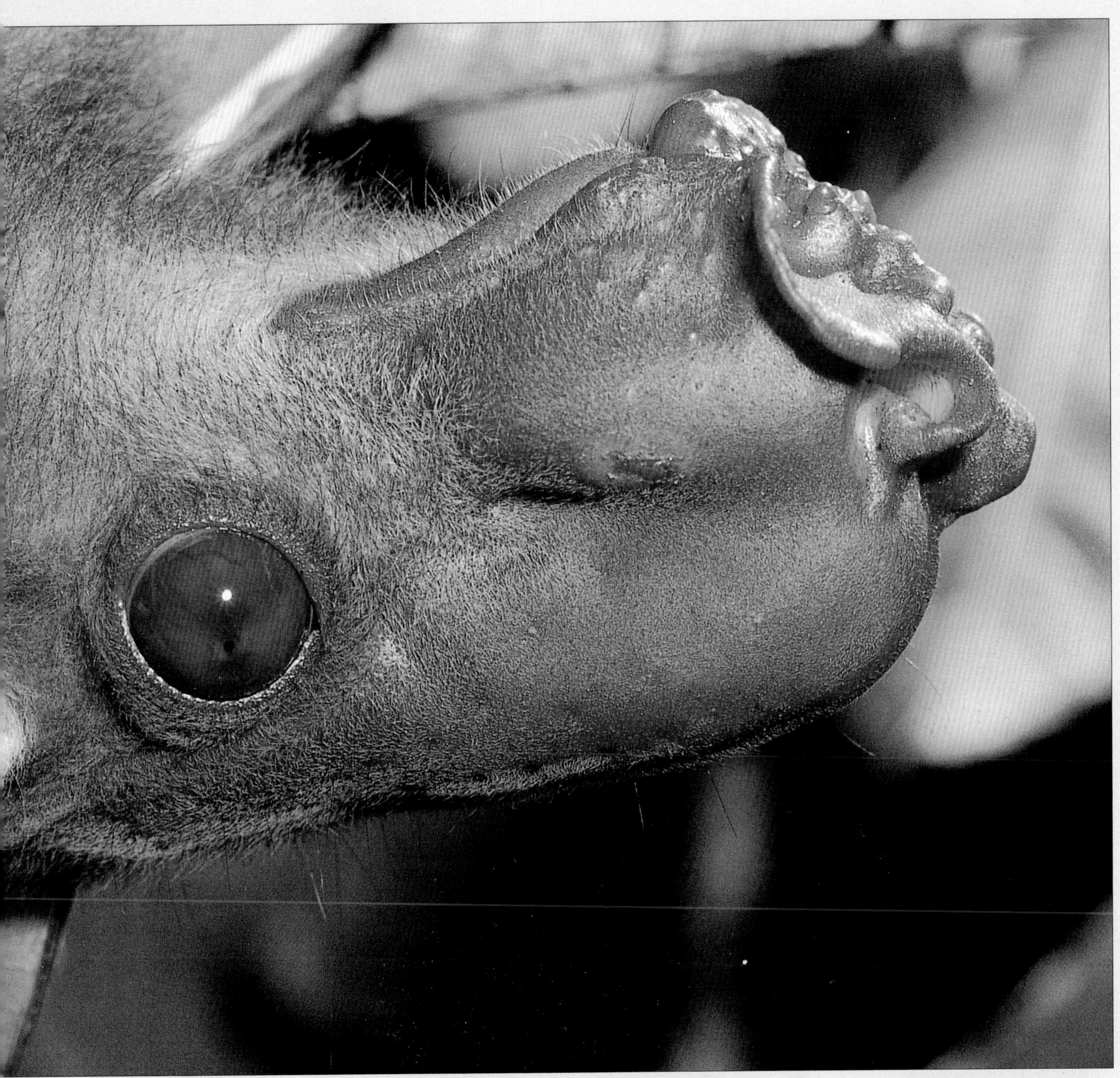

Despite early reports to the contrary. these bats are exclusively frugivorous. Figs and the fruit of several species of *Anthocleista* form the major part of their diets in Gabon. Females and juvenile males appear to feed more on the easily located *Anthocleista*, which is generally found closer to the roost (within 1–4km/0.6–2.5mi) but is also less profitable, for its fruits ripen slowly and a few at a time. By contrast, adult males fly 10km (6.2mi) or more to find the less predictable but more profitable patches of ripe figs, where large numbers of fruits are available on a single trip, but only for a short while. This extra effort by the males presumably pays off by providing more energy for vigorous mating displays. It has the cost, however, that the males may risk starvation if they are unsuccessful. The effects of variable food levels and the high energetic outlays during display may explain the higher parasitic loads (primarily hemosporidians in the blood cells) found in adult males, and also their higher mortality rates. They are also reflected in the abandonment of display by all males following days of colder than average weather, even though females may be visiting for mating.

Lek mating is often considered a "default" mating system, adopted when males cannot provide parental care, protect resources that females require, or defend groups of females. It is easy to understand that the expensive and chancy business of self-advertisement in competition with other males might be undesirable for males if not absolutely necessary. But Hammerheaded bats do not appear to fit these generalizations: there is little males could do to assist itinerant females with young, females rarely form groups (and those formed are at best transient aggregations), and neither roosts nor food sources are defensible, the latter because fig trees are widely dispersed and come randomly and unpredictably into fruit. The costs of display are certainly significant, yet even so males are committed both physically and behaviorally to the system.

JWB

A Second to Live

1

2

3

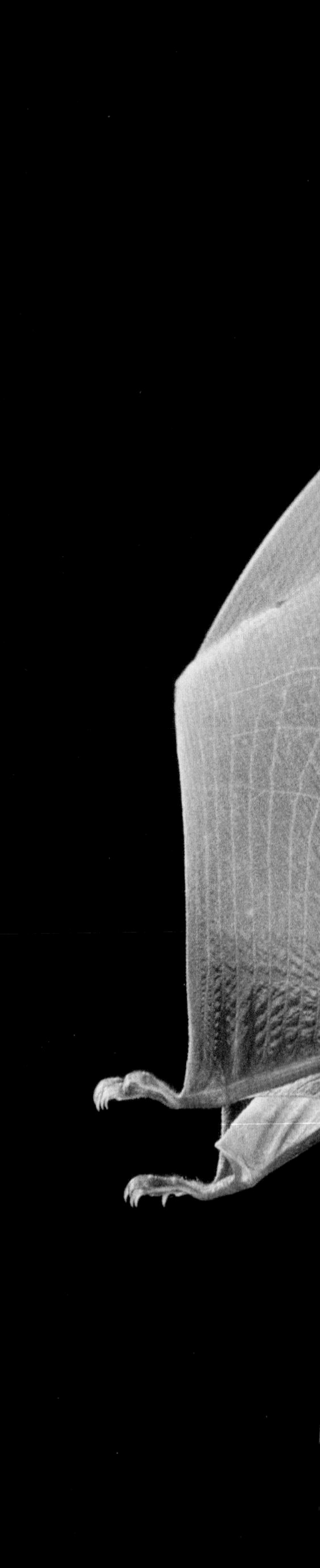

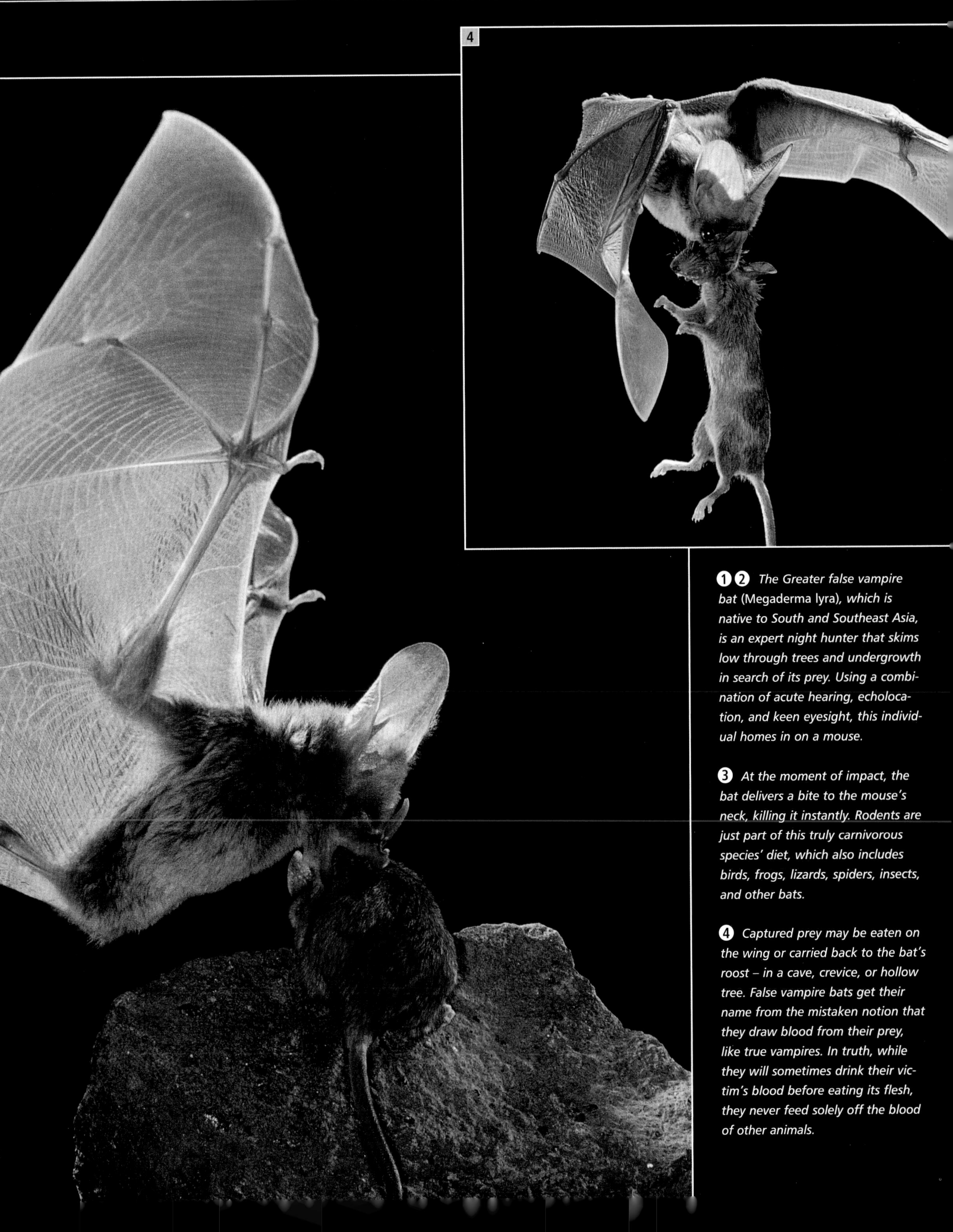

❶❷ *The Greater false vampire bat* (Megaderma lyra), *which is native to South and Southeast Asia, is an expert night hunter that skims low through trees and undergrowth in search of its prey. Using a combination of acute hearing, echolocation, and keen eyesight, this individual homes in on a mouse.*

❸ *At the moment of impact, the bat delivers a bite to the mouse's neck, killing it instantly. Rodents are just part of this truly carnivorous species' diet, which also includes birds, frogs, lizards, spiders, insects, and other bats.*

❹ *Captured prey may be eaten on the wing or carried back to the bat's roost – in a cave, crevice, or hollow tree. False vampire bats get their name from the mistaken notion that they draw blood from their prey, like true vampires. In truth, while they will sometimes drink their victim's blood before eating its flesh, they never feed solely off the blood of other animals.*

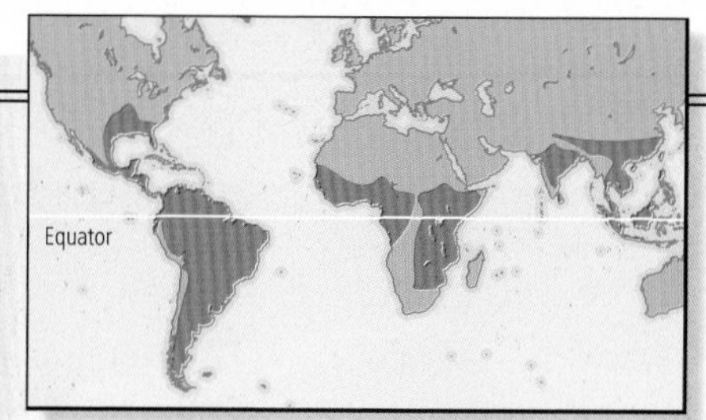

EDENTATES

The designation "Edentates" is a misnomer. Firstly, it contradicts the fact that most species treated here are not toothless, but have at least vestigial teeth. Secondly, it has no taxonomic validity; the order Edentata, which once embraced anteaters, sloths, armadillos, pangolins (and even the aardvark), is now defunct. The perceived similarities that occasioned such a grouping are now thought to be the result of convergent evolution, and not of any phylogenetic connection. "Edentate" is thus retained only as a convenient umbrella term for this most diverse group of mammals.

By the early Tertiary 60 million years ago (the beginning of the "Age of Mammals"), the ancestral edentates had already diverged into two quite distinct lines. The first, comprising small, armorless animals of the suborder Palaeanodonta, rapidly became extinct (there is now a broad consensus that this suborder was ancestral to the Pholidota only, and not to the Xenarthra). The other line, comprising the xenarthrans, was on the brink of a spectacular radiation that was later to produce some of the most distinctive and bizarre of all the New World mammals.

Sluggish Specialists

ANATOMY AND EVOLUTION

The living and recently extinct members of the order Xenarthra are distinguished from all other mammals – including pangolins – by additional articulations between the lumbar vertebrae, which are called xenarthrales (or xenarthrous vertebrae). These bony elements provide lumbar reinforcement for digging, and are especially important for the armadillos. The living xenarthrans also differ from most mammals in having a double posterior vena cava vein (single in other mammals), which returns blood to the heart from the hindquarters of the body. Females have a primitive, divided womb only a step removed from the double womb of marsupials, and a common urinary and genital duct, while males have internal testes, and a small penis with no glans.

Despite these unifying characteristics, the extinct xenarthrans differed greatly in size and appearance from their modern relatives and, in terms of numbers of genera, were more than ten times as diverse. The rise and fall of these early forms is closely linked to the fact that throughout the Tertiary South America was a huge, isolated island. At the beginning of this epoch, ancestral xenarthrans shared the continent only with early marsupials and other primitive mammals, and flourished in the virtual absence of competition. By the late Eocene (38 million years ago), three families of giant ground sloths had emerged, with some species growing to the size of modern elephants. In their heyday during the late Miocene, 30 million years later, ground sloths appeared in the West Indies and southern North America, apparently having rafted across the sea barriers as waif immigrants. Four families of armored, armadillo-like xenarthrans were contemporary with the ground sloths for much of the Oligocene. The largest species, *Glyptodon*, achieved a length of 5m (16.5ft) and carried a rigid 3m (10ft) shell on its back, while the related *Doedicurus* had a massive tail with the tip armored like a medieval mace. Although *Glyptodon* and the giant ground sloths survived until historical times – and are spoken of in the legends of the Tehuelche and Araucan Indians of

1

2

Right Prehistoric edentates. The edentates produced three major groups: "shelled" forms (Loricata), including the extinct glyptodonts and living armadillos; "hairy" forms (Pilosa), including the extinct Giant ground sloth and living tree sloths; and the anteaters (Vermilingua). **1** The Giant ground sloth (Megatherium), from the Pleistocene of South America, was up to 6m (20ft) long. **2** Eomanis waldi, a small armored pangolin from the Eocene of Germany. **3** Glyptodon panochthus, a giant shelled form from the Pleistocene of South America. **4** Giant anteater (Scelidotherium), from the Pleistocene of South America.

Patagonia – only the smaller tree sloths, anteaters, and armadillos persisted to the present day.

The extinct xenarthrans are believed to have been ponderous, unspecialized herbivores that inhabited scrubby savannas. They were probably out-competed and preyed upon by the new and sophisticated northern invaders. In contrast, the success of the living xenarthrans was due to their occupation of relatively narrow niches, which allowed little space for the less specialized newcomers. The anteaters and leaf-eating sloths, for example, have very specialized diets. To cope with the low energy contents of their foods, both groups evolved metabolic rates that are only 33–60 percent of those expected for their bodyweights, and variable but low (32.7–35°C/91–95°F) body temperatures that burn fewer kilojoules. Armadillos eat a wide range of foods, but are specialized for a partly subterranean way of life; they also have low metabolic rates and body temperatures (33–35.5°C/91.5–96°F) to avoid overheating in their closed burrows. Lacking similarly sluggish metabolisms, the invading mammals were not able fully to exploit these habitats, so competition was probably minimal.

Living in Niches

SOCIAL BEHAVIOR

As consequences of specializing and slowing their metabolisms, the sloths and anteaters use energy frugally, and generally move slowly over small home ranges. Females attain sexual maturity at 2–3 years of age and breed only once a year thereafter. They produce small, precocious litters (usually one young), and invest much time and energy in weaning and post-weaning care. Defense against predators is passive and primarily dependent on cryptic camouflage. While anteaters, and occasionally sloths, may try to flee from an assailant, they more often stand their ground and strike out with their claws. Sloths are reputedly able to survive the most severe injuries; bite wounds and deep scars rarely become infected, and heal completely within weeks. Armadillos show similar trends toward economizing their use of energy, but these are not as marked as in their ant- and plant-eating relatives. The armadillos are less constrained because of their more varied and energy-rich diets, and the ability (at least of some species) to store fat and enter torpor.

The social lives of xenarthrans and pangolins are probably dominated by the sense of smell. All species produce odoriferous secretions from anal glands, which are used to mark paths, trees, or conspicuous objects; these probably advertise the presence, status, and possibly the sexual condition of the marking individual. Scentmarks may also serve as territorial markers, and allow individuals priority of access to scarce resources, such as food. Pangolins can employ their anal secretions as a form of defense, squirting a jet of foul-smelling fluid at an aggressor.

With their lack of teeth, long, sticky tongues, and taste for ants, the pangolins exploit a niche equivalent to that occupied by the South American anteaters. These similarities suggest that selection for the anteating habit has acted in parallel in both the Old and New World. CRD

ORDERS: XENARTHRA AND PHOLIDOTA

36 species in 14 genera and 5 families

ORDER XENARTHRA

ANTEATERS Family Myrmecophagidae p788

4 species in 3 genera. **Silky anteater** (*Cyclopes didactylus*), **Giant anteater** (*Myrmecophaga tridactyla*), **Northern tamandua** (*Tamandua mexicana*), and **Southern tamandua** (*T. tetradactyla*).

SLOTHS

Families Megalonychidae and Bradypodidae p792

5 species in 2 genera. **Brown-throated three-toed sloth** (*Bradypus variegatus*), **Pale-throated three-toed sloth** (*B. tridactylus*), **Maned three-toed sloth** (*B. torquatus*), **Hoffmann's two-toed sloth** (*Choloepus hoffmanni*), and **Southern two-toed sloth** (*C. didactylus*).

ARMADILLOS Family Dasypodidae p796

20 or 21 species in 8 genera. Includes **Nine-banded** or **Common armadillo** (*Dasypus novemcinctus*), **Southern naked-tailed armadillo** (*Cabassous unicinctus*), **Larger hairy armadillo** (*Chaetophractus villosus*), **Brazilian three-banded armadillo** (*Tolypeutes tricinctus*), **Greater fairy armadillo** (*Chlamyphorus retusus*), **Yellow armadillo** (*Euphractus sexcinctus*), **Pichi** (*Zaedyus pichiy*), and the **Giant armadillo** (*Priodontes maximus*).

ORDER PHOLIDOTA

PANGOLINS Family Manidae p800

7 species in 1 genus. **Indian pangolin** (*Manis crassicaudata*), **Giant pangolin** (*M. gigantea*), **Malayan pangolin** (*M. javanica*), **Chinese pangolin** (*M. pentadactyla*), **Ground pangolin** (*M. temminckii*), **Long-tailed pangolin** (*M. tetradactyla*), and **Tree pangolin** (*M. tricuspis*).

SKULLS AND DENTITION

Edentates have the least complex skulls of all mammals; for example, pangolins have smooth, conical skulls with a simple, bladelike structure for their lower jaw. Although the name Edentata means "without teeth," it is in fact only the pangolins, and among the xenarthrans only the anteaters (such as the Southern tamandua) that are completely toothless. Both sloths and armadillos are equipped with a series of uniform, peg-shaped cheek or grinding teeth (premolars and molars). These lack an enamel covering and have a single so-called "open root" that allows continuous growth of the teeth throughout life. True incisor and canine teeth are absent in all edentates, but sloths have enlarged, canine-like premolars.

The diet of edentates ranges from an almost total reliance on ants and termites in the anteaters and pangolins, through a wide range of insects, tubers, and carrion in the armadillos, to plants in the sloths.

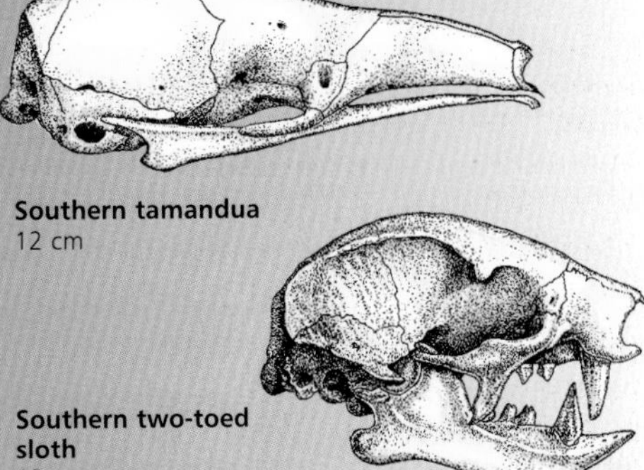

Southern tamandua
12 cm

Southern two-toed sloth
12 cm

Anteaters

ANTEATERS FEED EXCLUSIVELY ON SOCIAL *insects, primarily ants and termites. Their adaptations to this diet affect not only masticatory and digestive structures but behavior, metabolic rate, and locomotion. Anteaters are solitary, except that a mother may carry her young on her back for up to a year, until it is nearly adult in size.*

While the different anteater species do not overlap greatly in distribution, they nonetheless operate at different times and in different strata: the Giant anteater feeds mostly by day (although it becomes nocturnal when it is disturbed by people), whereas tamanduas are variably active both by day and by night and the Silky anteater is strictly nocturnal. Similarly, Giant anteaters are terrestrial, tamanduas partially arboreal, and Silky anteaters almost exclusively arboreal. All anteaters can both dig and climb, as well as walk on the ground. However, the Giant anteater rarely climbs and the Silky anteater descends to the ground only infrequently. There is further niche separation in diet, with Giant anteaters eating the largest-bodied ants and termites, tamanduas the medium-sized insects and Silky anteaters the smallest.

Right *The Southern tamandua has strong claws and a powerful tail, which is used to gain additional purchase when climbing in trees. The tail can also act as a prop, enabling the animal to rear up on its back legs.*

Toothless Insect-eaters

FORM AND FUNCTION

The anteaters share membership in the Order Xenarthra with the sloths, the armadillos, and the extinct glyptodonts, but are the only toothless (edentulous) members of the Order. Mouths in all species are small and only open to a small oval. Anteater snouts are disproportionately long, the Giant anteater's head appearing to be almost tubular and over 30cm (12in) in length. Their narrow, rounded tongues are even longer than their heads; the tongues of tamanduas protrude some 40cm (16in), while that of the Giant anteater can extend up to 61cm (24in). In all anteaters, the tongues are covered in minute, posteriorly directed spines and coated with a thick, sticky saliva secreted from salivary glands relatively larger than those of any other animals. Anteater stomachs are unusual in not secreting hydrochloric acid, but depend instead on the formic acid content of the ants they eat to assist with digestion.

The only natural predators of Giant anteaters are pumas and jaguars – if threatened they rear up on their hind legs, slashing with claws that can be up to 10cm (4in) in length. They have even been known to embrace and crush an attacker. The largest claws are on fingers two and three in Giant and Silky anteaters, but digits two, three, and four in tamanduas. All have five fingers and four or five toes, although some fingers are reduced in size and enclosed within the skin of the hand. The fifth finger of the Giant anteater and the first, fourth and fifth fingers of the Silky anteater are the reduced digits. Anteaters move with the fingers of the forefeet flexed and turned inward to keep the sharp claw tips from contacting the ground. Sometimes they walk on the sides of their hind feet, turning the claws inward, much as did some of the extinct ground sloths to which they are related. Climbing in trees the tamanduas and Silky anteaters use their prehensile tails, and claws that may be up to 400mm (16in) in length to grip branches. When threatened, a tamandua on the ground balances on hind feet and tail, swiping ferociously with the foreclaws. The defensive posture of Silky anteaters also uses the prehensile tail and hind feet to grasp a supporting branch, but initially the forefeet are raised to the level of the shoulders with the claws aimed forward and inward. Amazingly, Silky anteaters can stretch out horizontally from the supporting branch, an unusual feat (shared with tree sloths) made possible by additional (xenarthrous) articulations between vertebrae. Furthermore, an additional (and unique) joint in the sole of the foot allows the claws to be turned back under the foot to enhance the grasp. The most common predators of arboreal anteaters include Harpy eagles, hawk eagles and the Spectacled owl. These hunters fly above the canopy and search visually for prey; thus, the coat of the Silky anteater, which closely resembles the massive balls of silvery fluff that make up the seed pods of the silk-cotton Ceiba tree, may serve as protective coloration. Silky anteaters are frequently found in these trees. None of the anteaters is particularly vocal, but Giant anteaters bellow when threatened. If separated from the mother, young animals produce short, high-pitched whistles.

Digging for Dinner

DIET

Anteaters detect prey mainly by smell, but their vision is probably poor. Giant anteaters feed on large-bodied colonial ants and termites. Anteaters feed rapidly. Typically they dig a small hole in the nest, and lick up worker ants as they emerge, and with tongue movements as rapid as 150 times a minute take larvae and cocoons as well. Insects trapped on the sticky saliva-coated tongue are crushed against the hard palate prior to swallowing. Anteaters avoid large-jawed ant and termite

FACTFILE

ANTEATERS

Order: Xenarthra

Family: Myrmecophagidae

4 species in 3 genera

DISTRIBUTION
S Mexico, C & S America S to Paraguay and N Argentina; Trinidad.

GIANT ANTEATER *Myrmecophaga tridactyla*
C America; S America E of the Andes to Uruguay and NW Argentina. Grassland, swamp, lowland tropical forest. HBL 1–1.3m (3.3–4.2ft); TL 65–90cm (25.5–35.5in); WT 22–39kg (48–86lb); male anteaters are 10–20 percent heavier than females. Coat: coarse, stiff, dense; coloration gray with black-and-white shoulder stripe. Breeding: 1 young born in spring after a gestation of 190 days. Longevity: unknown in the wild, but up to 26 years in captivity. Conservation status: Vulnerable.

NORTHERN TAMANDUA *Tamandua mexicana*
Northern tamandua, Northern collared or lesser anteater
S Mexico to NW Venezuela and NW Peru. Savanna, thorn scrub, wet and dry forest. HBL 52.5–57cm (21–22in); TL 52.5–55cm (21–21.5in); WT 3.2–5.4kg (7–12lb). Coat: light fawn to dark brown with variable patches of black or reddish-brown from shoulders to rump. Breeding: Gestation 130–150 days. Longevity: unknown in the wild but to at least 9 years in captivity.

SOUTHERN TAMANDUA *Tamandua tetradactyla*
Southern tamandua, Southern collared or lesser anteater
S America E of the Andes from Venezuela to N Argentina; Trinidad. HBL 58–61cm (23–24in); TL 50–52.5cm (19.5–21.5in); WT 3.4–7kg (7.5–15.5lb). Coat: as for Northern tamandua, but black "vest" is only present in specimens from SE portion of range.

SILKY ANTEATER *Cyclopes didactylus*
C and S America, from S Mexico to the Amazon basin and N Peru. Tropical forest. HBL 18–20cm (7–8in); TL 18–26cm (7–10in); WT 375–410g (13.2–14.4oz). Coat: soft, silky gray to yellowish-orange, with darker mid-dorsal stripe.

Abbreviations HBL = head–body length TL = tail length WT = weight

Left A Giant anteater with offspring in Brazil. The young Giant anteater may continue to ride around on its mother's back for up to a year, well past the weaning stage, which occurs at about six months.

soldiers. Even though the skin on their muzzles is thick it is evidently not impervious to the bites of insect soldiers. Because they utilize each nest for only a short period, and take as few as 140 insects (only about 0.5 percent of their daily food requirement) per feeding bout, anteaters cause little permanent damage to nests. Their density appears to depend on the number of nests that are available in a given area; many must be visited daily to get sufficient nutrition (which may amount to 35,000 ants a day). Beetle larvae are also taken. Water requirements are generally met by their food.

The way anteaters eat is unique among mammals. They contract their chewing (temporal and masseter) muscles to roll the two halves of the lower jaw towards the middle, thereby separating the anterior tips to open the mouth. The mouth is closed by the pterygoid muscles that pull the lower rear (posteroventral) edges of the two lower jaw bones inward (medially), raising the anterior tips to close the mouth. The result is simplified and minimal jaw movement which, when coupled with movements in and out of the tongue and nearly continuous swallowing, maximize the rate of food intake. The extraordinary movements of the tongue are controlled by a sternoglossus muscle that attaches to the base of the sternum.

Tamanduas specialize in smaller-bodied termites and ants than do the Giant anteater, and also avoid the soldier castes. They also refrain from eating ant and termite species that have chemical defenses, and will eat bees and honey. A tamandua will typically consume 9,000 ants in a day. The average length of arboreal ants and termites eaten by Silky anteaters is 4mm (0.15in) as opposed to the 8mm (0.3in) or larger prey of Giant anteaters.

Precocious Young

SOCIAL BEHAVIOR

All species of anteater are usually solitary. Home ranges in Giant anteaters may be as small as 0.5sq km in areas of high food availability, such as the tropical forests of Barro Colorado Island, Panama, or the southeastern highlands of Brazil. In habitats that support fewer ant and termite colonies such as the mixed deciduous forests and semi-arid

▲▼ ***Above and below*** *Silky anteaters taking a break: above, curled in defensive posture with the claws in front of the face; below, suspended from a branch. An adaptation in the foot of Silky anteaters allows the claws to be turned back under the foot to improve grip.*

llanos of Venezuela one individual Giant anteater may require as much as 2,480ha (6,200 acres). The ranges of female Giant anteaters may overlap by as much as 30 percent, while those of males typically overlap by less than 5 percent. Tamanduas are less than half the size of the Giant anteater and in favorable habitats such as Barro Colorado, occupy home ranges of 50–140ha (124–346 acres). In the open llanos one animal may require as much as 340–400ha (840–988 acres). Silky anteater females on Barro Colorado have a home range that averages 2.8ha (7 acres) while that of a single male is approximately 11ha (27 acres). The home range of this male overlapped those of two females, but not the range of an adjacent male. Although the geographic distribution of the four anteater species differ, when they occur in the same habitat, home ranges of one do not appear to be affected by the presence of another.

Giant anteaters and tamanduas mate in the fall, and the single young is born in the spring. The Giant anteater gives birth standing, using her tail as a third support. The young are precocious and have sharp claws that allow them to crawl to the mother's back shortly after being born. Twins occur rarely and the young are suckled for approximately six months but may remain with the mother up to the age of two years, by which time they will have reached sexual maturity. Young Giant anteaters can gallop by about a month after birth, but generally either move slowly or are carried on the mother's back. Tamanduas may place the young one on a branch near a preferred feeding location, or leave them for a short period of time alone in a leaf nest, a practice that is shared with Silky anteaters. The young of the Silky anteater is fed semidigested ants that are regurgitated by both parents, and the infant may be carried by either parent. Giant anteater young are miniatures copies of their parents; however, tamandua infants do not resemble the parents and range in color from white to black.

Giant anteaters do not actually burrow, but instead scoop out shallow depressions in which they rest for up to 15 hours a day. They remain cryptic by covering their bodies with the great fanlike tail. Tamanduas generally rest in hollows in trees while Silky anteaters sleep during the day curled up on a branch with the tail wrapped around the feet. They generally do not spend more than one day in a single tree.

Giant anteaters and tamanduas can produce strong-smelling secretions from their anal glands. Silky anteaters have a facial gland; however, its purpose is unknown. Giant anteaters can also distinguish the scent of their own saliva, although it is not known whether they use salivary secretions to communicate.

All anteaters have low metabolic rates: Giant anteaters have the lowest recorded body temperature for a placental mammal, 32.7°C (90.9°F), and the tamanduas' and Silky anteater's body temperatures are not especially higher. Daily activity periods generally do not average more than eight hours for the Giant anteater and tamandua and about four hours for the Silky anteater.

Primarily resulting from slight color pattern differences, Giant anteaters have been divided into three subspecies, and *T. mexicana* into five. Color variation in *T. mexicana* depends on the size and darkness of the black vest, although all individuals of this species show some degree of this marking. In contrast, *T. tetradactyla* shows great variation in this trait. In animals in the northern part of the range the coat is a uniform light color, while those in the southern part may have striking vest development. The species differences are most striking where the geographic ranges abut, and may be an excellent example of character displacement. This coat color variation probably explains why this species has been divided into thirteen subspecies. Differences in coat color probably also explain the naming of seven subspecies of Silky anteater. In the northern regions the animal is a uniformly golden color, or has a darker dorsal stripe, but it becomes progressively grayer, and the mid-dorsal stripe darker, in the south.

Above *Inserting its long snout into a hollow log, a Giant anteater feeds on the insects inside. Anteaters are choosy about the type of ants they consume, taking care to avoid the aggressive soldiers.*

Prey for Trophy Hunters

CONSERVATION AND ENVIRONMENT

With the exception of small-scale use of tamandua skin in local leather industries, anteaters have little commercial value and are seldom hunted for food. However, the Giant anteater has disappeared from most of its historic range in Central America as a result of habitat loss and human encroachment. In South America, it is frequently hunted as a trophy or captured by animal dealers. It has been extirpated in some parts of Peru and Brazil. Tamanduas also suffer when they occur near human habitations. They put on spectacular defenses and may be hunted with dogs for sport, or are often killed on the roads around areas of human settlement. In the Venezuelan llanos, young individuals may be tamed and prove to be popular as pets. However, the most serious threat to these creatures is the loss of habitat and the destruction of the limited number of prey species upon which they feed.

VN

Sloths

ALTHOUGH SLOTHS ARE RENOWNED FOR their almost glacial slowness of movement, they are the most spectacularly successful large mammals in Central and tropical South America. On Barro Colorado Island, Panama, two species – the Brown-throated three-toed sloth and Hoffmann's two-toed sloth – account for two-thirds of the biomass and half of the energy consumption of all terrestrial mammals, while in Surinam they comprise at least a quarter of the total mammalian biomass. Success has come from specializing in an arboreal, leaf-eating way of life to such a remarkable extent that the effects of competitors and predators are scarcely perceptible.

Oviedo y Valdes, one of the first Spanish chroniclers of the Central American region in the 16th century, wrote that he had never seen an uglier or more useless creature than the sloth. Fortunately, little commercial value has since been attached to these animals, although large numbers, especially of two-toed sloths, are hunted locally for their meat in many parts of South America. Beauty, however, is in the eye of the beholder, and modern-day tourists will pay to have their photograph taken with sloths stolen from the forests and touted on the streets of South American cities. The Maned three-toed sloth of southeastern Brazil is considered Endangered due to the destruction of its coastal rainforest habitat, and the fortunes of all five species are inextricably bound up with the future of the tropical forests.

A Walking Ecosystem

FORM AND FUNCTION

Sloths have rounded heads and flattened faces, with small ears hidden in the fur; they are distinguished from other tree-dwelling mammals by their simple teeth (five upper molars, four lower), and their highly modified hands and feet which terminate in curved claws 8–10cm (3–4in) long.

Below *At home in the trees, a Brown-throated three-toed sloth takes its ease in Bolivia's Gran Chaco National Park. The three-toed sloths spend almost all their lives in the branches, only descending to the ground once or twice a week to defecate.*

Their general appearance is extraordinary, but most remarkable of all is the fact that sloths are green; they possess a short, fine underfur and an overcoat of longer and coarser hairs which, in moist conditions, turn green, owing to the presence of two species of blue-green algae that grow in longitudinal grooves in the hairs. This helps to camouflage animals in the tree canopy. The ecology of sloth fur does not end there, for it also harbors animals, including moths (*Cryptoses* spp), ticks (*Amblyomma varium*, *Boophilus* spp), and beetles (*Trichilium* spp). All species have extremely large, multi-compartmented stomachs, which contain cellulose-digesting bacteria. A full stomach may account for almost a third of the body weight of a sloth, and meals may be digested there for more than a month before passing completely into the relatively short intestine. Feces and urine are passed only once a week, at habitual sites at the bases of trees.

The sloths are grouped into two distinct genera and families, which can be distinguished most easily by the numbers of fingers: those of genus *Choloepus* have two fingers and those of genus *Bradypus* have three. Misleadingly, despite the fact that both genera have three toes, the two-fingered forms are known as two-toed and the three-fingered forms as three-toed sloths.

Both two- and three-toed sloths maintain low but variable body temperatures, from 30–34°C (86–93°F), which fall during the cooler hours of the night, during wet weather, and whenever the animals are inactive. Such labile body temperatures help to conserve energy: sloths have metabolic rates that are only 40–45 percent of those expected for their body weights as well as reduced muscles (about half the relative weight for most terrestrial mammals), and so cannot afford to keep warm by shivering. Both species frequent trees with exposed crowns and regulate their body temperatures by moving in and out of the sun.

Left A Southern two-toed sloth rests on the fork of a branch. Two-toed sloths spend much of their lives hanging upside down, supported by their hooked claws; they even sleep and give birth in that position.

Below This Brown-throated three-toed sloth clinging to a tree in Panama owes its green coloration to an algal growth. The algae provide camouflage and possibly also a source of nutrition, either absorbed through the skin or licked directly from the hair.

Sharing the Forest

DISTRIBUTION PATTERNS

While representatives of both sloth families occur together in tropical forests through much of Central and South America, sloths within the same genus occupy more or less exclusive geographical ranges. These closely related species differ little in body weight (staying within a 10 percent range), and have such similar habits that they are apparently unable to coexist.

Where two- and three-toed sloths occur together, the two-toed form is 25 percent heavier than its relative and it uses the forest in different ways. In lowland tropical forest on Barro Colorado Island in Panama's Canal Zone, the Brown-throated three-toed sloth achieves a density of 8.5 animals per ha (3.5 per acre), over three times that of the larger Hoffmann's two-toed sloth. The smaller species is sporadically active for over 10 hours out of 24, compared with just 7.6 hours for the two-toed sloth and, unlike its nocturnal relative, it is active both by day and by night. Three-toed sloths maintain overlapping home ranges averaging 6.6ha (16.3 acres), three times those of the larger species. Despite their apparent alacrity, however, only 11 percent of three-toed sloths travel further than 38m (125ft) in a day, and some 40 percent remain in the same tree

FACTFILE

SLOTHS

Order: Xenarthra

Families: Megalonychidae (two-toed sloths) and Bradypodidae (three-toed sloths)

5 species in 2 genera

DISTRIBUTION C and S America

Habitat Lowland and upland tropical forest; montane forest to 2,100m/7,000ft (Hoffmann's two-toed sloth only).

Coat Stiff, coarse, grayish-brown to beige, with a greenish cast provided by the growth of blue-green algae on the hairs; dark hair on face and neck, lighter fur on shoulders; hair grows to 6cm (2.4in) on three-toed sloths and to 15cm (6in) on two-toed sloths.

Breeding Gestation period 6 months (Southern two-toed sloth, three-toed sloths); 11.5 months (Hoffmann's two-toed sloth).

Longevity 12 years (up to at least 31 in captivity).

TWO-TOED SLOTHS Genus *Choloepus*
From Nicaragua S through C American isthmus to Colombia, Venezuela, Surinam, Guyana, French Guiana, NC Brazil, and N Peru. 2 species: **Hoffmann's two-toed sloth** (*C. hoffmanni*); **Southern** or **Linné's two-toed sloth** (*C. didactylus*). HBL 58–70cm (23–28in), WT 4–8kg (8.8–17.6lb), tail absent.

THREE-TOED SLOTHS Genus *Bradypus*
From Honduras S through C American isthmus to Colombia, Venezuela, Surinam, Guyana, and French Guiana; coastal Ecuador, Bolivia, Paraguay, and N Argentina. 3 species: **Brown-throated three-toed sloth** (*B. variegatus*), **Pale-throated three-toed sloth** (*B. tridactylus*), **Maned three-toed sloth** (*B. torquatus*). HBL 56–60cm (22–24in), TL 6–7cm (2.4–2.8in), WT 3.5–4.5kg (7.7–9.4lb). The Maned three-toed sloth is classed as Endangered.

Abbreviations HBL = head–body length TL = tail length WT = weight

on two consecutive nights; the three-toed sloths, by contrast, change trees four times as often.

Three Maned three-toed sloths in an Atlantic forest reserve of south-eastern Brazil were observed to eat 99 percent leaves, with tree leaves (83 percent) preferred to liana leaves (16 percent). Moreover, young leaves (68 percent) were favored over mature ones (7 percent) throughout the year. Their diet included a total of 21 plant species (16 tree and 5 liana), but each individual made up its diet from an even smaller number of plant species (7–12). The sloths consumed only a tiny fraction of the species available to them, and those they ate were not particularly abundant. It seems likely that sloths have evolved resistance to the defensive poisons produced by certain plants and so eat predominantly those. Their metabolism is extremely slow, which may allow their gut to neutralize the plant toxins as they pass through, contributing to the sloth's success as the ultimate plant-eater.

Inheriting the Mother's Domain

SOCIAL BEHAVIOR

Sloths are believed to breed throughout the year, but in Guyana births of the Pale-throated three-toed sloth occur only after the rainy season, between July and September. Reproduction in the Maned three-toed sloth is aseasonal. The single young, weighing 300–400g (10.5–14oz), is born above ground and is helped to a teat by the mother. The young of all species cease nursing at about 1 month, but may begin to take leaves even earlier. They are carried by the mother alone for 6–9 months and feed on leaves they can reach from this position; they utter bleats or pure-toned whistles if separated. After weaning, the young inherit a portion of the home range left vacant by the mother, as well as her taste for leaves. A consequence of inheriting preferences for different tree species is that several sloths can occupy a similar home range without competing for food or space; this will tend to maximize their numbers at the expense of howler monkeys and other leaf-eating rivals in the forest canopy. Two-toed sloths may not reach sexual maturity until the age of 3 years (females) or 4–5 years (males).

Adult sloths are usually solitary, and patterns of communication are poorly known. However, males are thought to advertise their presence by wiping secretions from an anal gland onto branches, and the pungent-smelling dung middens conceivably act as trysting places. Three-toed sloths produce shrill "ai-ai" whistles through the nostrils, while two-toed sloths hiss if disturbed. CRD

Left *A large adolescent Pale-throated three-toed sloth clings protectively to its mother in the rain forest of Brazil's Manaus province. Even though they are weaned at 4 weeks, the young usually stay with their mothers for at least another 5 months, relying on them for transport through the trees.*

Armadillos

ARMADILLOS ARE ONE OF THE OLDEST, AND oddest, groups of mammals. Because of the tough protective carapace they all possess, early zoologists often linked them with shelled vertebrates like turtles. Modern taxonomists put them in the order Xenarthra with the anteaters and sloths.

Fossil evidence suggests that the armadillo lineage forms one of the earlier branches in the evolution of placental mammals, arising about 65–80 million years ago. However, recent molecular genetic studies have indicated armadillos may be closely related to such later-evolving groups as the ferroungulates, which include the carnivores, cetaceans, and artiodactyls.

Presently classified in the order Xenarthra, armadillos were long included in the now-obsolete order Edentata, which means "without teeth." This was always spurious, as they all possess rudimentary, peglike teeth that are undifferentiated (in other words, not divided into incisors, canines, or molars) and that serve to mash up their food. Most species have 14–18 teeth in each jaw, but the Giant armadillo, with 80–100, has more than almost any other mammal. In the long-nosed species of the genus *Dasypus*, the jaws do not open very wide, so, as with the anteaters, they capture prey with their long tongues.

Though hardly lightweights, modern armadillos are puny compared to their ancestors. The largest extant species, the Giant armadillo (*Priodontes maximus*), weighs 30–60kg (66–132lb), but the extinct glyptodonts were far more massive, with weights estimated at 100kg (220lb) or more. Some of these fossil forms were so large that their carapaces (up to 3m/10ft long) were used as roofs or tombs by early South American Indians.

Our knowledge of living armadillos is extremely sparse. Many species have not been studied extensively in the wild, and attempts to breed armadillos for study in captivity have been largely unsuccessful. The only well-known species currently is the Nine-banded armadillo, which has been the subject of a few long-term field studies.

Insect-eaters in Armor

FORM AND FUNCTION

All armadillos possess a number of distinctive features, most notably a tough carapace that covers some portion of the upper surface of their bodies. This shell probably provides some protection from predators and minimizes damage from the thorny vegetation that armadillos frequently pass through. The carapace develops from the skin, and is composed of strong bony plates, or scutes, overlaid by horny skin. There are usually broad and rigid shields over the shoulders and hips, and a variable number of bands (from 3–13) over the middle of the back that are connected to the flexible skin beneath. The tail, the top of the head, and the outer surfaces of the limbs are also usually armored (although the tail is not covered in the genus *Cabassous*), but the undersurface is just soft, hairy skin. To protect this vulnerable area, most species are able to withdraw the limbs under the hip and shoulder shields and sit tight on the ground, while some, such as the three-banded armadillos of the genus *Tolypeutes*, can roll up into a ball. While this strategy may prove effective against most predators, it has unfortunately made these species easy prey for human hunters, possibly contributing to their current listing as Endangered species.

While apparently well-protected, armadillos are not invulnerable to predation. Juvenile mortality can be twice that of adults, much of it due to coyotes, bobcats, mountain lions, some raptors, and even domestic dogs. Juveniles may be more vulnerable to predators because of their small size

Above *A Three-banded armadillo rolling itself up into a defensive ball. When fully curled, it has the appearance of a puzzle ball, leaving no chinks for natural predators to attempt to prize it open. Yet this defense has afforded little help against predation by humans, who have exploited armadillos as a source of food for centuries.*

ARMADILLOS AND LEPROSY

In the 1960s, Eleanor Storrs made the remarkable discovery that armadillos inoculated with the leprosy bacillus can develop the disfiguring human disease, and in the 1970s the condition was found in wild populations. In wild Nine-banded armadillos, its occurrence varies regionally: Floridian armadillos lack leprosy, while as many as 20 percent of the animals from populations in Texas and Louisiana may be infected.

Unlike humans, armadillos exhibit no external symptoms until the disease has progressed sufficiently to fatally damage the internal organs. It is not yet known whether people can contract leprosy from armadillos, but the risk may depend on where they are from: unlike individuals from more tropical regions, people of northern European descent are relatively immune to the malady.

and softer carapace, but adult carcasses have also been found in the guts of large predators like jaguars, alligators, and black bears.

Most armadillos find prey by digging in the soil. In addition, many species excavate burrows that are used as refuges, resting-places, and nest sites for rearing young. Consequently, most armadillos have muscular fore and hind limbs, ending in large, sharp claws that facilitate digging. While the hind limbs always bear five-clawed digits, the fore limbs may have from three to five digits with curved claws, depending on the species. In some species such as the Naked-tailed armadillos and the Giant armadillo the front claws are greatly enlarged, perhaps to facilitate opening ant and termite mounds for foraging. As a result, however, these species are unable to run quickly when danger appears.

Because they are usually active at night, most armadillos have poor eyesight. They seem, however, to have well-developed senses of hearing and smell, which may be used in the detection of both predators and prey. Olfaction may also be employed to determine the identity (and, during the breeding season, the reproductive condition) of other armadillos. The Yellow armadillo and species in the genus *Chaetophractus* have 3–4 gland pits located on the back carapace. The long-nosed armadillos of the genus *Dasypus* have glands on the ears, eyelids, and soles of the feet, as well as a bean-shaped pair of anal glands that produce a yellowish secretion. These glands may be important in chemical communication, as armadillos are frequently observed sniffing this area when they encounter one another; they may also rub the glands on the ground in spots along the periphery of their home range. Although their hearing seems fairly acute, most armadillos are silent. What sounds they do produce are usually just low grunts or squeals, so most communication is probably chemical.

While there are reports of modest differences in body size between the sexes, the males being larger than the females, most armadillos exhibit no obvious sexual dimorphism. One interesting anatomical feature is the male penis, one of the longest among mammals, extending two-thirds of the body length in some species. Armadillos were at one time thought to be the only mammals other than humans to copulate face to face, though this is now no longer believed to be the case; it seems instead that the males mount females from behind, as in most other mammals. If so, then the long penis may be necessary to permit intromission, given the necessity to extend beyond the

Above *The Nine-banded armadillo, unlike the other species, is able to traverse water by inflating its stomach and intestine with air for buoyancy. Since it can hold its breath for several minutes, it can cross smaller streams underwater.*

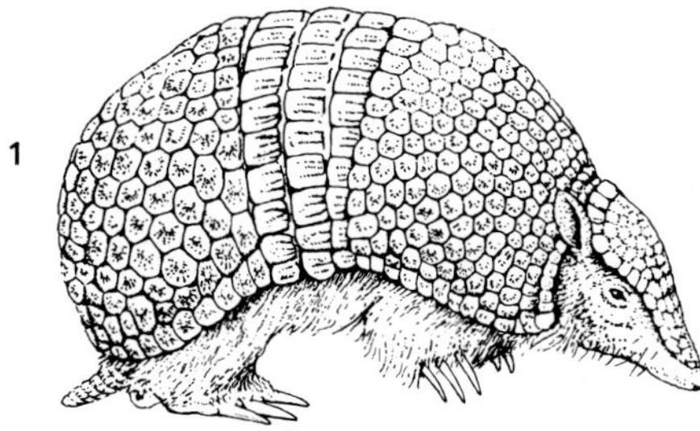

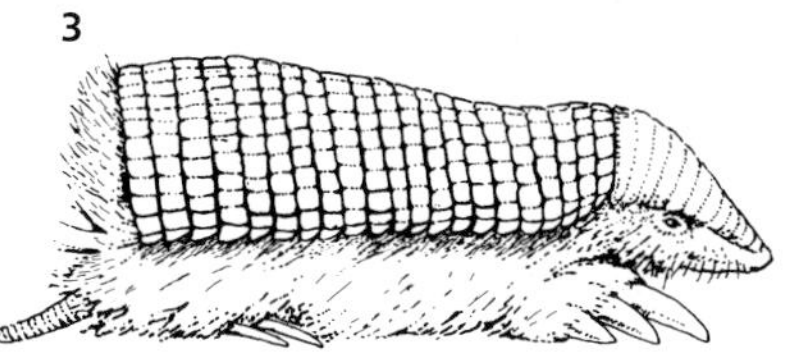

Below *The configuration of the armored shell varies markedly between species of armadillo:* ***1*** *the Southern three-banded armadillo* (Tolypeutes matacus)*;* ***2*** *the pichi* (Zaedyus pichiy)*;* ***3*** *the Lesser fairy armadillo* (Chlamyphorus truncatus).

FACTFILE

ARMADILLOS

Order: Xenarthra

Family: Dasypodidae

20 or 21 species in 8 genera

DISTRIBUTION Florida (except Everglades), Georgia, and South Carolina W to Kansas; E Mexico, C and S America to Straits of Magellan; Trinidad and Tobago, Grenada, Margarita.

HABITAT Savanna, pampas, arid desert, thorn scrub, and deciduous, cloud, and rain forest.

SIZE **Head–body length** ranges from 12.5–15cm (5–6in) in the Lesser fairy armadillo to 75–100cm (30–39in) in the Giant armadillo; **tail length** ranges from 2.5–3cm (1–1.2in) to 45–50cm (18–20in) and **weight** from 80–100g (2.8–3.5oz) to 30–60kg (66–132lb), both in the same two species.

COAT Broad shield of pale pink or yellowish dark brown armor (scute plates) over shoulders and pelvis, with varying numbers of flexible half-rings over middle of back; some species have white to dark brown hairs between the scute plates.

DIET Soil invertebrates, especially ants and termites. Will also feed on some plant matter, and are occasionally observed scavenging vertebrate carcasses.

BREEDING Both sexes are sexually mature at about 1 year. Breeding can occur year-round, but is most frequent during summer. Gestation varies from 60–65 days (in the Yellow and hairy armadillos) to 120 days (prolonged by delayed implantation) in the Nine-banded armadillo. Litter size usually 1–4, but reaching 8–12 in some species.

LONGEVITY Unknown in the wild, but may be about 8–12 years (up to 20 in captivity).

CONSERVATION STATUS At present, 6 species are considered Vulnerable or Endangered by the IUCN, and 2 more are listed as Lower Risk: Near Threatened. Four species are classed as Data Deficient.

See genera box ▷

armored carapace to reach the vaginal opening. The musculature of the penis consists of a series of longitudinal and circumferential supporting fibers, an arrangement that is thought to be common to all mammals.

New World Burrowers

Distribution Patterns

Armadillos are strictly New World species; the majority of fossil forms come from South America, suggesting that this was where the group originally evolved. They subsequently colonized North America, where glyptodont fossils are found as far north as Nebraska, during periods when a land bridge connected the two continents. These fossil forms eventually went extinct, leaving no armadillos in North America until recent times, when, from the late 1800s onward, the Nine-banded armadillo (*Dasypus novemcinctus*) rapidly expanded its range from northern Mexico to include much of the southern USA, with current sightings as far north as Nebraska, southern Missouri, and southwestern Tennessee. In Florida, several armadillos escaped from zoos or private owners in the 1920s, and these also established wild populations, which have slowly spread northward and westward. Florida-derived and Texas-derived populations of armadillos have probably made contact by now, possibly in Alabama or Mississippi.

Although normally associated with moist, tropical habitats, armadillos can be found almost anywhere in the New World. For example, the pichi is found in the Patagonian region of Argentina all the way south to the Straits of Magellan; the Hairy long-nosed armadillo is known only from high-altitude regions of Peru from 2,400–3,200m (7,900–10,500ft); while the Greater long-nosed armadillo occurs only in the rain forests of the Orinoco and Amazon basins.

Species of armadillo vary dramatically in their abundance. The Nine-banded armadillo, also aptly known as the Common long-nosed armadillo, can reach population densities of 50 per sq km (130 per sq mi) in the coastal prairies of Texas and elsewhere. However, the maximum density estimated for the Southern naked-tailed armadillo in the Venezuelan llanos is only 1.2 per sq km (3.1 per sq mi), and the Giant armadillo, even in optimum lowland forest habitat in Surinam, was only found to reach half that figure. Yellow armadillos have been found in Brazilian savanna and forest at densities of up to 2.9 animals per sq km (7.5 per sq mi), while Southern three-banded armadillos in southern Brazil may reach densities of 7 animals per sq km (18 per sq mi).

Even if no live animals are observed, a good sign of the presence of armadillos in a habitat is a burrow. Armadillos dig between 1 and 20 burrows, each 1.5–3m (5–10ft) long, in their home ranges, occupying a given burrow for anything from 1–29 consecutive days. Because armadillos use multiple burrows, counting burrows in a habitat may not provide a reliable estimate of actual population density. Burrows are generally not very long and tend to run horizontally under the surface rather than to extend vertically down into the ground. Most burrows usually have just one or two entrances.

Above *The Southern naked-tailed armadillo has five curved claws on its forefeet, the middle one of which is especially powerful. Its gait is unusual – it walks on the soles of its hind feet (plantigrade), but on the tips of the claws on its fore feet (digitigrade).*

Snuffling through the Leaf Litter

Diet

Perhaps because of their armor, armadillos are often fairly conspicuous, making a considerable racket as they snuffle along searching for food in dry vegetation. For armadillos, foraging consists of moving slowly along with the nose in the soil and leaf litter, then digging up material with the foreclaws. The animals may also use their claws to rip open rotting logs.

With their large front claws, Giant and naked-tailed armadillos seem specialized for ripping open ant and termite mounds. Other species have a more catholic diet; analyses of gut contents have revealed a mix of invertebrates, mostly beetles and ants. The Nine-banded armadillo is one of the few species to have been observed bravely feeding on fire ants (*Solenopsis geminata*), enduring their painful stings to dig open the nest and eat the larvae within. In addition to invertebrates, armadillos are also known to feed on some vegetable matter, including persimmons and other fruits, and, rarely, on certain vertebrates, such as snakes and small lizards; they may also scavenge carrion and the eggs of ground-nesting birds.

Nature's Clones

Armadillos in the genus *Dasypus* are the only vertebrates known to exhibit obligate polyembryony, in which a female produces one fertilized egg that divides into multiple embryos. Because of this, all the offspring produced are genetically identical to one another. Genetic uniformity of siblings in the Nine-banded armadillo (BELOW) has been confirmed using modern molecular techniques.

One proposed reason for such a strange system may be to encourage offspring to help each other out. Altruistic behavior reaps more evolutionary dividends when directed towards relatives, as they share a higher proportion of genes. Because of polyembryony, armadillo littermates are clones, and thus might be predicted to be particularly helpful to each other. As it turns out, however, armadillos get very little opportunity to mix with their sibs as adults, and it seems more likely that polyembryony represents an ingenious way of countering a physical restriction on reproduction, helping to overcome a constraint in the female's reproductive system that leaves space for only one egg prior to implantation.

Armadillo Genera

Long-nosed armadillos
Genus *Dasypus*

S USA, Mexico, C America, Colombia, Venezuela, Guiana, Surinam, Brazil, Paraguay, Argentina, Ecuador, Peru; also Grenada and Trinidad and Tobago. 6 or 7 species: the **Nine-banded** or **Common long-nosed** (*D. novemcinctus*), **Seven-banded** or **Brazilian lesser** (*D. septemcinctus*), **Greater** (*D. kappleri*), **Southern lesser** (*D. hybridus*), **Hairy** (*D. pilosus*), and **Northern** (*D. sabanicola*) **long-nosed armadillos**; and, possibly, *D. yepesi* (from northeastern Argentina). The Hairy long-nosed armadillo is classed as Vulnerable.

Naked-tailed armadillos
Genus *Cabassous*

C and S America E of the Andes from S Mexico and Colombia to Paraguay, Uruguay, and N Argentina. 4 species: the **Southern** (*C. unicinctus*), **Northern** (*C. centralis*), **Chacoan** (*C. chacoensis*), and **Greater** (*C. tatouay*) **naked-tailed armadillos**. The Greater naked-tailed armadillo is classed as Lower Risk: Near Threatened.

Yellow armadillo
Euphractus sexcinctus

Yellow or **Six-banded armadillo**. S Surinam and adjacent areas of Brazil; also E Brazil to Bolivia, Paraguay, N Argentina, Uruguay.

Giant armadillo *Priodontes maximus*

S America E of the Andes, from N Venezuela and the Guianas to Paraguay and N Argentina. Endangered.

Hairy armadillos
Genus *Chaetophractus*

Bolivia, Paraguay, Argentina, Chile. 3 species: the **Andean** (*C. nationi*), **Screaming** (*C. vellerosus*), and **Larger** (*C. villosus*) **hairy armadillos**. The Andean hairy armadillo is classed as Vulnerable.

Three-banded armadillos
Genus *Tolypeutes*

Brazil and E Bolivia S through the Gran Chaco of Paraguay to Buenos Aires (Argentina). 2 species: the **Southern** (*T. matacus*) and **Brazilian** (*T. tricinctus*) **three-banded armadillos**. The Brazilian three-banded armadillo is classed as Vulnerable, while the Southern three-banded armadillo is Lower Risk: Near Threatened.

Fairy armadillos
Genus *Chlamyphorus*

Argentina, Paraguay, Bolivia. 2 species: the **Greater** or **Chacoan** (*C. retusus*) and **Lesser** or **Pink** (*C. truncatus*) **fairy armadillos**. The Lesser fairy armadillo is classed as Endangered, while the Greater fairy armadillo is Vulnerable.

Pichi *Zaedyus pichiy*

C and S Argentina, and E Chile S to the Straits of Magellan.

Life beneath the Carapace

SOCIAL BEHAVIOR

Most armadillos are relatively solitary, and with a few exceptions most species are active at night, although this can vary with age – juveniles are often active in the late morning or early afternoon – and with the time of year: there is more diurnal activity when the weather is colder.

Among adults, most social interactions usually occur during breeding. For most species, breeding is seasonal, with matings occurring primarily during the summer months, although captive animals may breed year-round. Prior to mating, males and females may engage in extended bouts of courtship in which the males avidly follow the females. After mating, most species initiate embryonic development right away, but in northern populations of the Nine-banded armadillo (*Dasypus novemcinctus*), possibly as an adaptation to the different timing of the seasons, implantation of the fertilized egg may be delayed by 3–4 months or more; one captive female of this species reportedly gave birth at least three years after the last date at which she could possibly have been inseminated. *D. novemcinctus* may be polygynous, with males mating with 2–3 females per breeding season, while females typically mate with just a single male. Yet not all individuals are reproductively successful: as many as one third of the females in a population may not reproduce in a given year, and, in a 4-year study, only about a third of all adults were identified as parents of at least one litter. Litter sizes are usually small, varying from 1–4 young per litter for most species, with a maximum of 8–12 reported for captive *D. hybridus*. The majority of species only reproduce once per year.

In *D. novemcinctus*, males occasionally chase, kick, and scratch each other with their claws either in defence of their home ranges or when competing for access to females. Although female home ranges may overlap quite extensively, pregnant or lactating adult females can also be quite aggressive, primarily targeting other females and younger individuals of both sexes.

D. novemcinctus home ranges vary from about 1.5ha (4 acres) for a population in Oklahoma to over 10ha (25 acres) for a population in Florida. Home range sizes for other species are largely unknown, but the low population densities of most species suggest they may range widely.

Conserving the Hoover Hog

CONSERVATION AND ENVIRONMENT

For centuries, armadillos have been exploited by humans for their meat, and they continue to be a favored food item in many areas of Latin America. In North America people partake of armadillo meat less frequently; however, during the Great Depression of the 1930s, destitute southern sharecroppers came to rely on armadillos for food, and the animals were nicknamed "Hoover hogs," a wry allusion to US President Herbert Hoover.

Habitat loss from deforestation, agriculture, and other sources is another significant cause of declining populations, as is the eradication of digging armadillos from both agricultural areas and the well-manicured lawns of suburban communities. On the bright side, the Brazilian three-banded armadillo, which was formerly classed as Extinct in the Wild, has been rediscovered recently in several areas of Brazil. CMM/WJL

Right The Larger hairy armadillo has been known to burrow under animal carcasses in order to feed on the maggots and other insects that accumulate there. This species relies on insects, rodents, and lizards in summer, but half of its winter diet is vegetation.

Pangolins

APPEARING LIKE TILES ON A HOUSE ROOF, the overlapping, horny scales on pangolins' backs distinguish these animals from all other Old World mammals. The scales, which grow from the thick underlying skin, protect every part of the body except the underside and inner surfaces of the limbs, and are shed and replaced periodically.

In Africa, large numbers of pangolins are caught up in the bushmeat trade and are killed for their flesh, while the scales are used in traditional medicine. As a result, the Cape pangolin is threatened. In Asia, powdered scales are believed to have medicinal and aphrodisiacal qualities, and the animals are hunted indiscriminately. Unless controlled, the population densities and ranges of the three Asian pangolins will continue to dwindle.

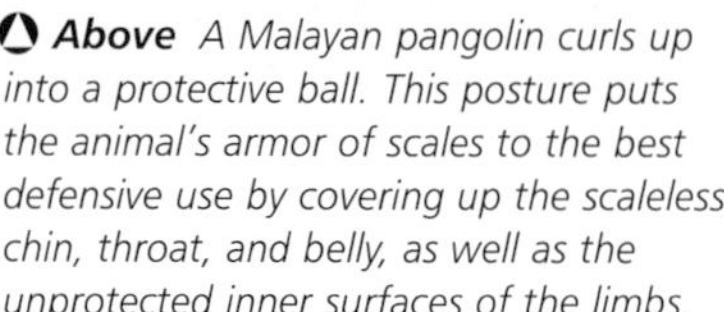

Above *A Malayan pangolin curls up into a protective ball. This posture puts the animal's armor of scales to the best defensive use by covering up the scaleless chin, throat, and belly, as well as the unprotected inner surfaces of the limbs.*

Left *A Tree pangolin* (Manis tricuspis) *hangs from a branch with the aid of its long, prehensile tail. The tail has a bare patch at its tip, equipped with a sensory pad that makes it easier for the animal to find and secure a good grip.*

A Suit of Armor

FORM AND FUNCTION

Pangolins specialize in eating ants and termites and, like South American anteaters, they probe the nests of their prey with long, narrow tongues. In the largest species, the Giant pangolin, the strap-like tongue can be extended for 40cm (16in), in total it is 70cm (27.5in) long, and is housed in a sheath that extends to an attachment point on the pelvis. Viscous saliva is secreted onto the tongue by an enormous salivary gland, 360-400cu cm (22–24.5cu in) in capacity, which sits in a recess in the chest. The simple skull lacks teeth and chewing muscles; captured ants are ground up in the specialized, horny stomach. Pangolins have a small, conical head with a reduced or absent outer ear, and an elongate body that tapers to a stout tail. Thick lids protect their eyes from the bites of ants, and special muscles close the nostrils during feeding. The limbs are short but powerful and terminate in five clawed digits; the three middle claws on the forefoot are 55–75mm (2.2–2.9in) long and curved.

In Africa, two of the four pangolin species are principally arboreal, inhabiting the rain-forest belt from Senegal to the Great Rift Valley. While the common Small-scaled tree pangolin occupies home ranges of 20–30ha (49–74 acres) in the lower strata of the forest, the smaller Long-tailed pangolin is more restricted to the forest canopy. Here, moving often by day to avoid its larger relative, it seeks the soft, hanging nests of ants and termites (preferring arboreal species), or attacks the columns that move among the leaves. Both species have a slender but strongly prehensile tail (the 46 or 47 tail vertebrae of the Long-tailed pangolin are a mammalian record), with a bare patch at the tip containing a sensory pad. They scale vertical tree trunks by gaining a purchase with the foreclaws and then drawing up the hindfeet just behind them; the jagged edges of the tail-scales provide additional support. These arboreal pangolins sleep aloft, curled up among epiphytes (plants growing on trees) or in forked branches.

The terrestrial African pangolins are larger than their tree-dwelling relatives, and occur in a spectrum of habitats from forest to open savanna. They sleep in the burrows of other digging animals. As protection against predators pangolins

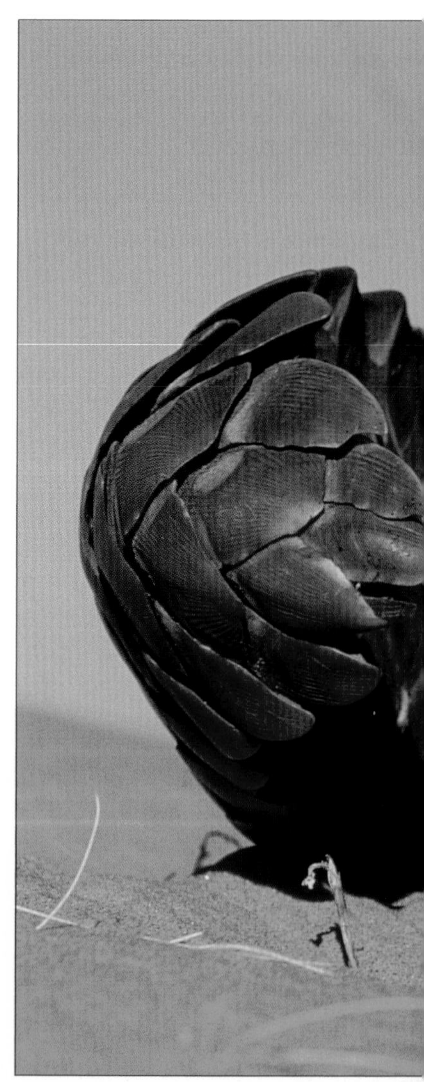

curl tightly into a ball, their scales forming a shield that is impregnable to all but the larger cats and hyenas. They use their powerful claws to demolish the nests of ground termites and ants. The Giant pangolin may take 200,000 ants a night, weighing over 700g (25oz). Because of their huge digging claws, the terrestrial pangolins must walk slowly on the outer edges of their forefeet with the claws tucked up underneath; the sight of this plated animal with its curious, shuffling gait has been likened to that of a perambulating artichoke! However, all species can move more swiftly up to 5km/h (3mph) by rearing up and running on their hind legs, using the tail as a brace.

The three Asian pangolins are less well known than their African counterparts, and are distinguished from them by the presence of hair at the bases of the body-scales. Intermediate in size between the African species, the Asian pangolins are nocturnal and usually terrestrial, but can climb with great agility. They inhabit grasslands, subtropical thorn forest, rain forest, and barren hilly areas almost devoid of vegetation, but are nowhere abundant. The geographical range of the Chinese pangolin is said to approximate that of its preferred prey species, the subterranean termites.

Socializing by Smell

SOCIAL BEHAVIOR

Although pangolins are usually solitary, their social life is dominated by the sense of smell. Individuals advertise their presence by scattering feces along the tracks of their home ranges, and by marking trees with urine and a pungent secretion from an anal gland. These odors may communicate dominance and sexual status, and possibly facilitate individual recognition. The vocal expressions of pangolins are limited to puffs and hisses; however, these are not known to serve any particular social function.

Pangolins usually bear one young weighing 200–500g (7–18oz), although two and even three young have been reported in the Asian species. In the arboreal species, the young clings to the mother's tail soon after birth, and may be carried in this fashion until weaned at the age of 3 months. When alarmed, mothers protect the infants by curling up around them. Young of the terrestrial species are born underground with small, soft scales, and are first carried outside on the mother's tail at 2–4 weeks. In all species, births usually occur between November and March; sexual maturity is reached at 2 years. CRD/RAR

PANGOLINS

Order: Pholidota

Family: Manidae

7 species of the genus *Manis*. Four African species: Giant pangolin (*M. gigantea*), Cape or Ground pangolin (*M. temminckii*), Tree or Small-scaled tree pangolin (*M. tricuspis*), Long-tailed pangolin (*M. tetradactyla*); three Asian species: Indian or Thick-tailed pangolin (*M. crassicaudata*), Chinese pangolin (*M. pentadactyla*), Malayan pangolin (*M. javanica*).

DISTRIBUTION Senegal to Uganda, Angola, W Kenya, S to Zambia and N Mozambique; Sudan, Chad, Ethiopia to Namibia and South Africa; India, Sri Lanka, Nepal, and S China to Taiwan and Hainan; S through Thailand, Myanmar (Burma), Laos, Malaysia, Java, Sumatra, Kalimantan, and offshore islands.

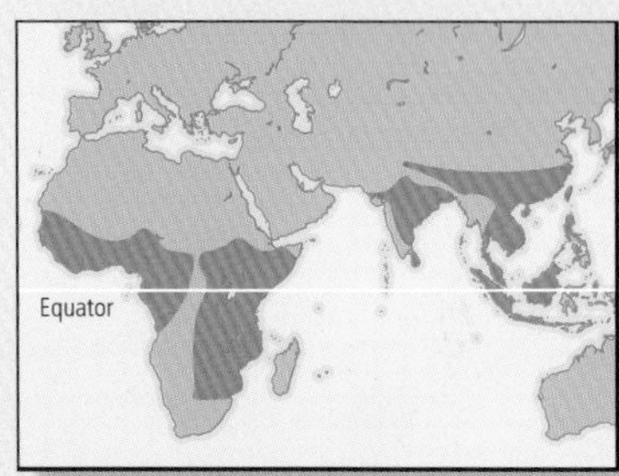

HABITAT Forest to open savanna

SIZE **Head–body length** ranges from 30–35cm (12–14in) in the Long-tailed pangolin to 75–85cm (30–33in) in the Giant pangolin, **tail length** from 55–65cm (22–26in) to 65–80cm (26–31in), and **weight** from 1.2–2.0kg (2.6–4.4lb) to 25–33kg (55–73lb), both in the same two species. In most species, males are 10–50 percent heavier than females, but up to 90 percent heavier in the Indian pangolin.

COAT Horny, overlapping scales on head, body, outer surfaces of limbs, and tail, varying in color from light yellowish-brown through olive to dark brown. The scales of young Chinese pangolin are purplish-brown. Undersurface hairs are white to dark brown.

DIET Termites and ants

BREEDING Gestation period from 65–70 days (Indian pangolin) to 139 days (Cape and Tree pangolins); litter size one, rarely two.

LONGEVITY At least 13 years in captivity (Indian pangolin); unknown in wild.

CONSERVATION STATUS The Cape, Indian, Chinese, and Malayan pangolins are all classed as Lower Risk: Near Threatened.

*◐ **Left** Its scales the shape of artichoke leaves, a Ground pangolin advances across sand in southern Africa. As the name suggests, this species is terrestrial, living in burrows that may be several meters deep and that terminate in circular chambers that are sometimes big enough for a man to stand up in.*

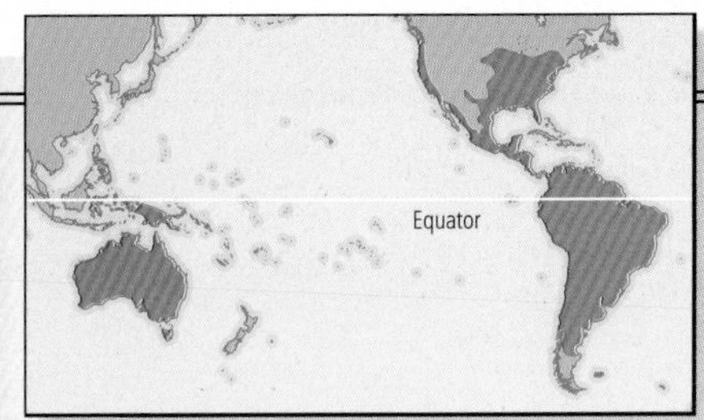

MARSUPIALS

Although marsupials had long been familiar to the indigenous peoples of the Americas and Australasia, they remained unknown to the rest of the world until the 16th century. The first marsupial seen in Europe was a Brazilian opossum that was brought back in 1500 as a gift to Queen Isabella and King Ferdinand of Spain by the explorer Vicente Yáñez Pinzón. Yet it was three centuries before zoologists ascertained that marsupials were not aberrant rodents but a distinctive natural group of mammals united by a unique mode of reproduction.

Above *In spite of its distinctive appearance, the Long-footed potoroo of Australia was only identified as a separate species as recently as 1980.*

Right *At birth a koala weighs only one-fiftieth of an ounce. Weaning begins after five months when the mother provides partly digested leaves for the infant.*

From North to South

EARLY BEGINNINGS

The most ancient marsupial-like fossil, *Kokopellia juddi*, hails from early Cretaceous deposits in Utah aged at least 100 million years, but its position as a true marsupial is contentious. The earliest undisputed marsupial, from the now-extinct family Stagodontidae, has been dated at about 80 million years from other fossil deposits in Utah. At least 20 other genera of slightly younger Cretaceous marsupials are known from other North American sites, suggesting that the group originated in that region. Despite their early ascendancy in the north, marsupials soon dwindled there as placental mammals increased in diversity, and they became extinct in North America by 15–20 million years ago. The one presently extant marsupial in North America, the Virginia opossum, recolonized less than 1 million years ago from the south.

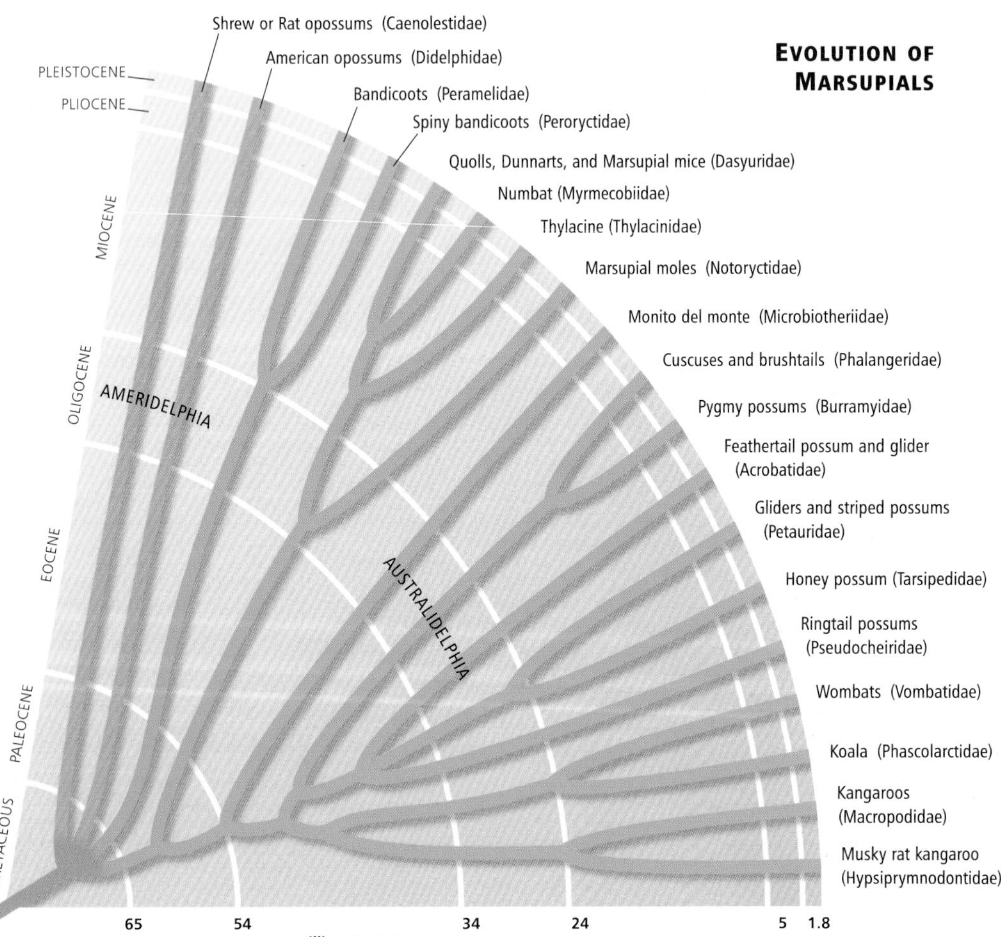

Shortly after their appearance and radiation in North America, ancestral marsupials dispersed across land bridges to South America and also to Europe. Marsupial diversity in South America remained high from the middle Paleocene (60 million years ago) until the Pliocene (5–1.8 million years ago) during a period of "splendid isolation." In the Pliocene, a land bridge to North America reformed, allowing invasion of the southern continent by placental mammals including raccoons, bears, cats, and other carnivores. In the face of this onslaught, all South America's large (i.e. over 5kg/11lb) carnivorous marsupials disappeared. Its present marsupial fauna is dominated by omnivores

weighing less than 1kg (2.2lb), with a minority of species specializing on insects or small vertebrates. The marsupial emigrants to Europe arrived by the early Eocene (52 m.y.a.) and stayed for perhaps 35 million years. Although this radiation was not spectacular, comprising only six described fossil genera in the family Didelphidae, it extended to many parts of Europe, North Africa, and east to Thailand and eastern China.

The origin of Australasian marsupials is unclear, but the most likely scenario is an invasion of taxa with South American affinities sometime in the early Paleocene, some 65–60 million years ago. The earliest Australian marsupial fossils date to the early Eocene 55 million years ago and, intriguingly, two genera appear similar to marsupials of the same age from Argentina. During the Paleocene Australia, Antarctica, and South America were united as the last surviving remnants of the old supercontinent Gondwana. Australia severed its geological umbilical cord between 46 and 35 million years ago, while Antarctica and South America parted company 5 million years later. The climate of the early Eocene was warm and humid, with beech forest covering much of the Antarctic. That it was conducive to dispersal is suggested by the discovery of two genera of polydolopid marsupials from the middle Eocene of Antarctica.

Following its separation from Antarctica, the Australian ark drifted northward towards the equator, allowing its marsupial cargo to incubate in isolation. There is, frustratingly, a 30-million year "dark age" lasting until the Miocene 24 million years ago that has yielded no fossils. However, by the early Miocene a spectacularly rich forest fauna had appeared, with many arboreal and browsing terrestrial marsupials represented. Climatic oscillations in the middle Miocene 15

SUPERCOHORT: MARSUPIALIA
289 species in 83 genera, 18 families, and 7 orders.

COHORT AMERIDELPHIA

ORDER DIDELPHIMORPHIA

ORDER PAUCITUBERCULATA

COHORT AUSTRALIDELPHIA

ORDER MICROBIOTHERIA

ORDER DASYUROMORPHIA

ORDER NOTORYCTEMORPHIA

ORDER PERAMELEMORPHIA

ORDER DIPROTODONTIA

million years ago were associated with losses of entire marsupial families, including the enigmatic miralinids, pilkipildrids, and wynyardiids. With the end of greenhouse conditions, forest contracted to coastal areas and savanna woodland and grassland dominated the interior. These shifts favored grazing marsupials, and set the scene for an explosive radiation of grazing kangaroos.

At the same time that the Miocene climate deteriorated, the Australian and Southeast Asian crustal plates collided, creating the highlands of New Guinea. These new mountainous areas, and parts of northeastern Queensland, allowed the continuation of lush conditions that had prevailed earlier in the Miocene, and provided opportunities for colonization for forest taxa. Many of the marsupials in New Guinea's rain forests now bear a striking resemblance to extinct taxa known only from fossils from the Miocene of central Australia. In contrast to the Australian marsupial fauna, in which only 30 of the 155 species are arboreal, at least 50 of New Guinea's 83 present marsupial species are restricted to the tree top environment.

Modern Radiation

Distribution Patterns

Although today's marsupials comprise only some 7 percent of the world's mammals, they occur widely in the Americas and predominate in Australasia. There is no evidence that marsupials ever dispersed naturally to New Zealand (the Common brushtail possum was introduced to establish a fur trade in 1858, and a further six species of wallabies were introduced shortly after), but two species of cuscus occur on Sulawesi, one occurs throughout the Solomons, and others are scattered as island endemics in the Banda, Timor, Arafura, Coral, and Solomon seas. Australasian marsupials are ecologically more diverse than their American counterparts, and often occupy similar niches to placental mammals elsewhere. Thus, there are insectivores, carnivores, herbivores, and omnivores, and a honey possum that is unusual in specializing on nectar and pollen. All terrestrial habitats are exploited, from deserts to rain forests and high alpine areas. The smallest species, the Long-tailed planigale, weighs no more than 4.5g, some 20,000 times less than male Red kangaroos.

There is much that is still to be learned about the marsupials. Since the 1980s there has been a steady stream of discoveries of new species, for example the distinctive Long-footed potoroo in Australia in 1980, and two spectacular species of tree kangaroos in New Guinea in the early 1990s, the Dingiso and Tenkile.

The Amazing Journey

Reproductive Strategies

Despite their ecological and morphological diversity, it is the mode of reproduction that unites marsupials and sets them apart from other mammals. In its form and early development in the

Marsupial Body Plan

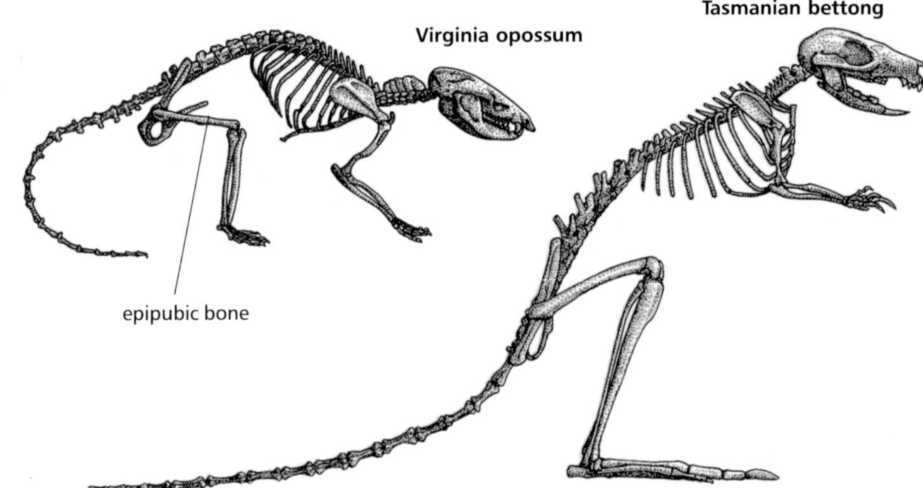

Above *Skeletons of the Virginia opossum and Tasmanian bettong. The Virginia opossum is medium-sized, with unspecialized features shared with its marsupial ancestors. These include the presence of all digits in an unreduced state, all with claws. The skull and teeth are those of a "generalist," the long tail is prehensile, acting as a "fifth hand," and there are epipubic or "marsupial bones" that project forward from the pelvis and help support the pouch. The hindlimbs in this quadruped are only slightly longer than the forelimbs. The larger rat-kangaroo has small forelimbs, and larger hindlimbs for leaping. The hindfoot is narrowed and lengthened (hence macro-podoid, "large-footed"), and the digits are unequal. Stance is more, or completely, upright, and the tail is long, not prehensile but used as an extra prop or foot.*

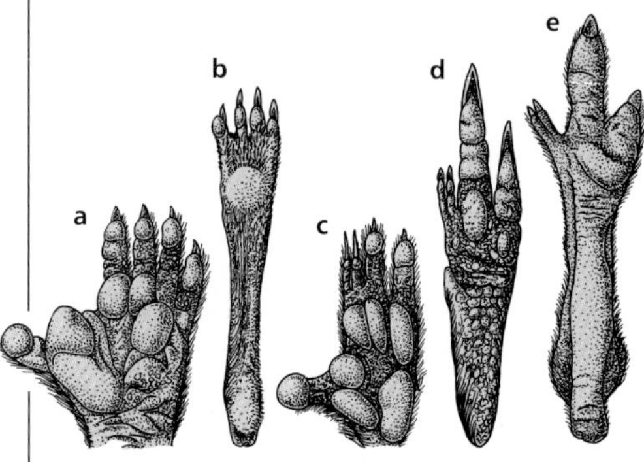

Above *Feet of marsupials:* ***a*** *opposable first digit in foot of the tree-dwelling Virginia opossum;* ***b*** *long narrow foot, lacking a first digit, of the kultarr, a species of inland Australia with a bounding gait: both these species have the second and third digits separate (didactylous); in many marsupials (eg kangaroos and bandicoot) these digits are fused (syndactylous), forming a grooming "comb";* ***c*** *opposable first digit and sharp claws for landing on trees in Feathertail glider;* ***d*** *first digit much reduced In long foot of terrestrial Short-nosed bandicoot – fourth digit forms axis of foot;* ***e*** *first digit entirely absent in foot of kangaroo.*

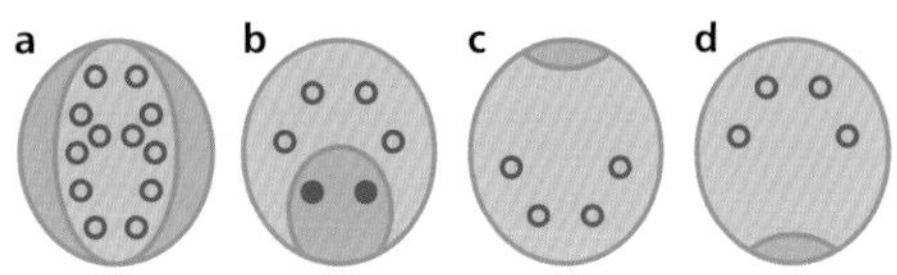

Above *Pouches (marsupia) occur in females of most marsupials. Some small terrestrial species have no pouch. Sometimes a rudimentary pouch* ***a*** *is formed by a fold of skin on either side of the nipple area that helps protect the attached young (eg mouse opossums, antechinuses, quolls). In* ***b*** *the arrangement is more of a pouch (e.g., Virginia and Southern opossums, Tasmanian devil, dunnarts). Many of the deepest pouches, completely enclosing the teats, belong to the more active climbers, leapers or diggers. Some, opening forward* ***c****, are typical of species with smaller litters of 1–4 (e.g., possums, kangaroos). Others* ***d*** *open backward and are typical of digging and burrowing species (e.g., bandicoots, wombats).*

Below *Anatomy of reproduction, and its physiology, set marsupials apart. In the female, eggs are shed into a separate (lateral) uterus, to be fertilized. The two lateral vaginae are often matched in the male by a two-lobed penis. Implantation of the egg may be delayed, and the true placenta of other mammals is absent. The young are typically born through a third, central, canal; this is formed before each birth in most marsupials, such as American opossums: in the Honey possum and kangaroos the birth canal is permanent after the first birth.*

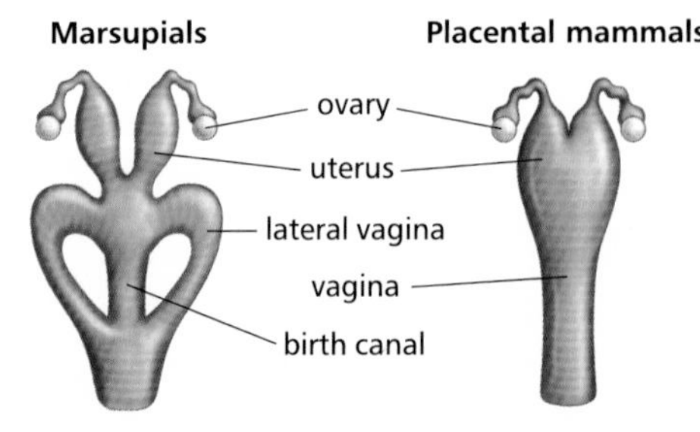

Below *Marsupial skulls generally have a large face area and a small brain-case. There is often a sagittal crest for the attachment of the temporal muscles that close the jaws, and the eye socket and opening for the temporal muscles run together, as in most primitive mammals. There are usually holes in the palate, between the upper molars. The rear part of the lower jaw is usually turned inward, unlike placental mammals.*

Many marsupials have more teeth than placental mammals. American opossums for instance have 50. There are usually three premolars and four molars on each side in both upper and lower jaws.

Marsupials with four or more lower incisors are termed polyprotodont. The Eastern quoll (Dasyurus viverrinus) *has six. Its chiefly insectivorous and partly carnivorous diet is reflected in the relatively small cheek teeth, each with two or more sharp cusps, and the large canines with a cutting edge. Its dental formula is I4/3, C1/1, P2/2, M4/4 = 42. The largely insectivorous bandicoot* (Perameles) *has small teeth of even size with sharp cusps for crushing the insects which it seeks out with its long pointed snout (I4–5/3, C1/1, P3/3, M4/4 = 46–48).*

Diprotodont marsupials have only two lower incisors, which are usually large and forward-pointing. The broad, flattened skull of the leaf-eating Brush-tailed possum contains reduced incisors, canines, and premolars, with simple low-crowned molars (I3/2, C1/0, P2/l, M4/4 = 34). The large wombat has rodent-like teeth and only 24 of them (I1/1, C0/0, P1/1, M4/4), all rootless and ever-growing to compensate for wear in chewing tough, fibrous grasses.

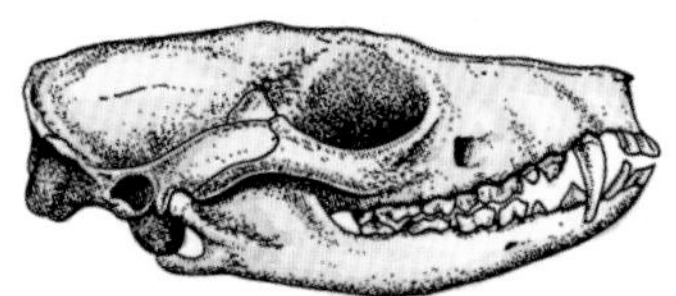

Eastern quoll
7 cm

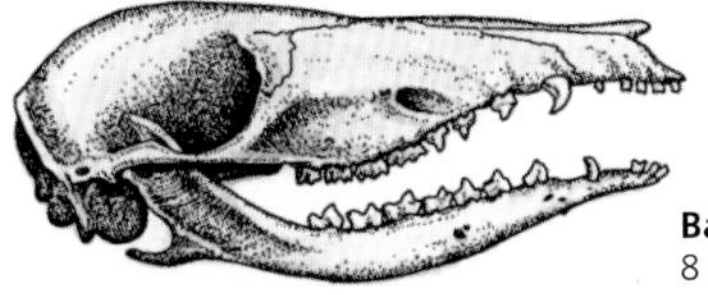

Bandicoot
8 cm

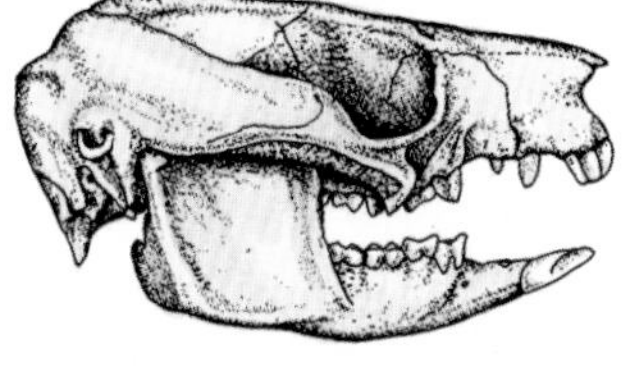

Brushtail possum
8 cm

Common wombat
18 cm

Above *A tiny, hairless, infant Common brushtail possum attached to the mother's nipple in the pouch. It will be weaned at about six months.*

uterus, the marsupial egg is like that of reptiles and birds and quite unlike the egg of placental mammals (eutherians). Whereas placental young undergo most of their development and considerable growth inside the female, marsupial young are born very early in development. For example, a female Eastern gray kangaroo of about 30kg (66lb) gives birth after 36 days' gestation to an offspring that weighs about 0.8g (under 0.03oz). This young is then carried in a pouch on the abdomen of its mother where it suckles her milk, develops and grows until after about 300 days it weighs 5kg (11lb) and is no longer carried in the pouch. After it leaves the pouch the young follows its mother closely and continues to suckle until about 18 months old.

Female young are ready to breed just after weaning, but males do not mature until aged two years or more. An extraordinary adaptation in kangaroos and all other marsupials studied is that the amount and quality of the milk changes during suckling, matching the needs of the growing young. Carbohydrates typically make up over half the solid fraction of milk for the first 6 months of lactation, and protein and fat the remainder. By 8–9 months carbohydrates have almost disappeared, and lipids constitute up to two-thirds of the solid bulk of the milk.

Immediately after birth, the newborn young makes an amazing journey from the opening of the birth canal to the area of the nipples. Forelimbs and head develop far in advance of the rest of the body, and the young is able to move with swimming movements of its forelimbs. Although it is quite blind, it moves against gravity, locates (how is not yet known) a nipple and sucks it into its circular mouth. The end of the nipple enlarges to fit depressions and ridges in the mouth, and the young remains firmly attached to the nipple for 1–2 months until, with further development of its jaws, it is able to open its mouth and let go. In many marsupials the young are protected by a fold of skin that covers the nipple area, forming the pouch (see diagram).

As the main emphasis in the nourishment of the young in marsupials is on lactation, most development and growth occurs outside the uterus. For the short time that the embryo is in the uterus, it is nourished by transfer of nutrients from inside the uterus across the wall of the yolksac that makes only loose contact with the uterine wall. In eutherians, nourishment of the young during its prolonged internal gestation occurs by way of the placenta, in which the membranes surrounding the embryo make close contact with the uterine wall, become very vascular and act as the means of transport of material between maternal circulation and embryo. Although it is commonly believed that marsupials do not have a placentation system at all, the yolksac has a placental function; in bandicoots and the Koala there is also development of a functional, albeit short-lived, placenta.

A further peculiarity of reproduction, similar to the delayed implantation found in some other mammals, occurs in all kangaroos (except the Western gray) and a few species in other marsupial families. Pregnancy in these marsupials occupies more or less the full length of the estrous cycle but does not affect the cycle, so that at about the time a female gives birth, she also becomes receptive and mates. Embryos produced at this mating develop only as far as a hollow ball of cells (the blastocyst) and then become quiescent, entering a state of suspended animation or "embryonic diapause." The hormonal signal (prolactin) that blocks further development of the blastocyst is produced in response to the sucking stimulus from the young in the pouch. When sucking decreases as the young begins to eat other food and to leave the pouch, or if the young is lost from the pouch, the quiescent blastocyst resumes development, the embryo is born, and the cycle begins again. In some species that do not breed all year round, such as the Tammar wallaby, the period of quiescence of the blastocyst is extended by seasonal variables such as changes in day length. The origin of embryonic diapause may have been to prevent a second young being born while the pouch was already occupied, but it has other advantages, allowing rapid replacement of young which are lost, even in the absence of a male.

Four Strategies

Social Organization

While large marsupials such as kangaroos and wombats usually produce single young, smaller species are not so constrained. Litter sizes in arboreal browsers, such as the Common ringtail possum range from 1–3, while litters of 3–4 can be produced twice a year by the nectar-feeding Honey possum, pygmy possums, and Feathertail glider. Similar productivity occurs in omnivores such as bandicoots and some didelphid species. Small insectivores such as antechinuses produce 8–12 young in a single bout of reproduction each year. Hensel's short-tailed opossum of southern Brazil has up to 25 nipples and probably rears the largest litters of any marsupial.

In species that produce litters of several young, individual young weigh less than 0.01g, by far the smallest of any mammalian species. At weaning, between 50 days in some didelphids to over 100 days in antechinuses, the combined weight of the young may be two to three times that of the mother. This represents an extraordinary investment of energy by females, and is often accompanied by high mortality of mothers. Not surprisingly, small marsupials tend to be shorter-lived than larger species and achieve reproductive maturity earlier at 5–11 months. Larger litter sizes or more frequent bouts of reproduction compensate for their shorter life spans, with some species being capable of breeding year round. The shortest-lived marsupials are some male dasyurids that die after mating aged 12 months. In contrast, the Mountain pygmy possum is the longest-lived of any small mammal; wild females may live over 11 years. Kangaroos live up to 25 years in the wild.

In some dasyurid marsupials, males disperse upon weaning up to several hundred meters from their mother's home range and then associate with unrelated females. Daughters remain at home, with one usually inheriting the maternal range after the death or dispersal of the mother. This pattern of dispersal reduces the chance of breeding among kin. Intriguingly, in species where females breed in two or more seasons, the sex ratio of the first litter is often skewed toward sons by a ratio of about 6:4, but returns to parity or less thereafter. The over-production of sons by young mothers probably reduces the chance of future

Below *Red kangaroos watering. This species forms small social groups, known as mobs, which may contain between 2–10 members. These mobs are not temporary aggregations, but are quite organized.*

MARSUPIAL MOLES

The two species of Marsupial moles are the only Australian mammals that have become specialized for a burrowing (fossorial) life. Others, including small native rodents, have failed to exploit this niche. except for a few species that nest in burrows.

Because of their extensive and distinct modifications, Marsupial moles (*Notoryctes typhlops* and *N. caurinus*) are placed in their own order, the Notoryctemorphia. Their limbs are short stubs. The hands are modified for digging, with rudimentary digits and greatly enlarged flat claws on the third and fourth digits. Excavated soil is pushed back behind the animal with the hind limbs, which also give forward thrust to the body and, like the hands, are flattened with reduced digits and three small flat claws on the second, third, and fourth digits. The naked skin (rhinarium) on the tip of the snout has been extended into a horny shield over the front of the head, apparently to help push through the soil. The coat is pale yellow and silky. The nostrils are small slits, there are no functional eyes or external ears, and the ear openings are concealed by fur. The neck vertebrae are fused together, presumably to provide rigidity for thrusting motions. Females have a rear-opening pouch with two teats. The tail, reduced to a stub, is said to be used sometimes as a prop when burrowing. Head–body length is approximately 13–14.5cm (5.1–5.7in), tail length 2–2.5cm (1in), and weight 40g (1.4oz). Dentition is I4/3, C1/1, P2/3, M4/4 = 44.

Little is known of these moles in the wild. They occur in the central deserts, using sandy soils in river-flat country and sandy spinifex grasslands. For food, they favor small reptiles and insects, particularly burrowing larvae of beetles of the family Scarabaeidae. In captivity Marsupial moles will seek out insect larvae buried in the soil and consume them underground. They also feed on the surface. They are not known to make permanent burrows, the soil caving in behind them as they move forward, and in this respect they are most unusual among fossorial mammals. Captive animals have been seen to sleep in a small cavity which collapses after they leave.

Compared to other burrowing animals, Marsupial moles show differences of detail in the adaptive route they have followed. The head shield is much more extensive than in many others, the eyes are more rudimentary than in most, and the rigid head/neck region with fused vertebrae appears to be specific to the Marsupial moles. GG

conflict for resources with stay-at-home daughters. By contrast, in species where females usually breed just once, litter sex ratios are variable. Well-fed mothers produce more sons than daughters, perhaps providing the sons with an edge in growth that will allow them to compete successfully with other males and father more young themselves. Mothers in poor condition produce more daughters. Experimental provision of food allows female Agile antechinuses, Black-eared and American opossums to bias their litters in favor of sons, indicating the importance of body condition. The mechanism producing bias remains elusive, but appears to operate prior to fertilization.

Communication between marsupials is primarily through hearing and smell. Arboreal species in particular use sound to communicate over distances up to several hundred meters. Vocalizations range from chirps and squeaks in small possums to full-blooded bellows in the koala. Olfactory communication occurs by passive deposition of urine and feces, but all species mark actively using secretions from glands in the skin. The secretions may be used to self-anoint, to mark other animals, or to lay claim to nests or other key sites. The Sugar glider recognizes strangers on the basis of scent alone; it is likely that many other species share this ability. Most marsupials are nocturnal, so vision is relatively unimportant.

Four broad types of marsupial social organization can be identified. In the first, the social unit is an individual whose range overlaps with that of several others. Males have large ranges that take in those of several females, and mating is promiscuous. Marsupials with this social system often exploit dispersed food resources, and include small didelphids, dasyurids, and the Honey possum. In a second type of social system, the unit is an individual with limited range overlap. Typically a male's home range overlaps that of one or two females who share exclusive mating rights. Arboreal folivores such as koalas and Brushtail possums exemplify this type of system. A third type of social system is founded on cohesive family units that share a common, and often defended, home range. Groups may contain monogamous pairs and their offspring, or dominant males with several adult females and young. Group-living marsupials include sap- and exudate-feeding gliders and possums that may need force of numbers to defend focal food sources and shared dens. Finally, larger members of the kangaroo family exemplify the fourth type of social organization, in which the social unit is a flexible "mob" of gregarious individuals. Mobs have a promiscuous mating system, in which access to females is based on size and dominance.

Growing Human Encroachment

CONSERVATION ISSUES

Pressures on marsupial habitats have intensified in the last 200 years, with European colonization. Forests and woodland have been cleared for agriculture, while exotic herbivores and predators are widespread. Overhunting occurs in New Guinea. No marsupials have become extinct recently in the Americas or New Guinea, but 10 species and 6 subspecies have disappeared from Australia. A further 55 species in the Australasian region and 22 species from Central and South America are considered Vulnerable or Endangered.

Protection of habitat continues to be an important conservation measure. In New Guinea, where most of the land is owned by indigenous peoples, community support is crucial for conservation, but is sometimes subverted by the interests of rapacious multinationals. In southwestern Australia, a program of poisoning the Red fox has aided the recovery of at least six marsupial species. Habitat protection and better ecological understanding will be the key to effective future conservation of marsupials. CRD/EMR

American Opossums

WHEN MARSUPIALS WERE INTRODUCED TO Europeans for the first time in 1500AD, it was in the shape of a female Southern opossum from Brazil, presented by the explorer Vicente Pinzón to Spain's rulers, Ferdinand and Isabella. The monarchs examined the female with young in her pouch and dubbed her an "incredible mother."

Despite this royal introduction, the popular image of the opossum has never been a lofty one; the animals are often portrayed as foul-smelling and rather slow-witted. Although not as diverse as Australia's marsupials, the American opossums are in fact a successful group incorporating a variety of different species, ranging from the highly specialized tree-dwelling woolly opossums to generalists like the Southern and Virginia opossums.

Above *A Gray-bellied slender mouse opossum foraging on the forest floor in Venezuela. Animals of this species are mainly nocturnal and, in common with most other mouse opossums, feed primarily on insects and fruit.*

Generalists and Specialists

FORM AND FUNCTION

American opossums range from cat- to mouse-sized. The nose is long and pointed, and has long, tactile hairs (vibrissae). Eyesight is generally well-developed; in many species, the eyes are round and somewhat protruding. When an opossum is aroused it will often threaten the intruder with mouth open and lips curled back, revealing its 50 sharp teeth. Hearing is acute, and the naked ears are often in constant motion as an animal tracks different sounds. Most opossums are proficient climbers, with hands and feet well adapted for grasping. Each foot has five digits, and the big toe on the hind foot is opposable. The round tail is generally furred at the base, with the remainder either naked or sparsely haired. Most opossums have prehensile tails used as grasping organs when animals climb or feed in trees. Not all female opossums have a well-developed pouch; in some species the pouch is absent altogether, while in others there are simply two lateral folds of skin on the abdomen. In males the penis is forked and the pendant scrotum often distinctly colored.

The Virginia or Common opossum of North and Central America, the Southern opossum of Central and South America, and the White-eared opossum of higher elevations in South America are generalized species, occurring in a variety of habitats from grasslands to forests. They have cat-sized bodies, but are heavier than cats and have shorter legs. Although primarily terrestrial, these opossums are capable climbers. In tropical grasslands, the Southern opossum becomes highly arboreal during the rainy season when the ground is flooded. Opportunistic feeders, they eat fruit, insects, small vertebrates, carrion, and garbage, varying their diets with seasonal availability. In the tropical forests of southeastern Peru, the Southern opossum climbs to heights of 25m (80ft) to feed on flowers and nectar during the dry season.

FACTFILE

AMERICAN OPOSSUMS

Order: Didelphimorphia

Family: Didelphidae

63 species in 15 genera

HABITAT Wide-ranging, including temperate deciduous forests, tropical forests, grasslands, mountains, and human settlements. Terrestrial, arboreal, and semi-aquatic.

SIZE **Head–body length** ranges from 6.8cm (2.7in) in the Formosan mouse opossum to 33–55cm (13–19.7in) in the Virginia opossum; **tail length** from 4.2cm (1.7in) in the Pygmy short-tailed opossum to 25–54cm (9.8–21.3in) also in the Virginia opossum, whose **weight** is 2–5.5kg (4.4–12.1lb).

COAT Either short, dense, and fine, or woolly, or a combination of short underfur with longer guard hairs. Color varies from dark to light grays and browns or golden; some species have facial masks or stripes.

DISTRIBUTION Throughout most of S and C America, N through E North America to Ontario, Canada; Virginia opossum introduced to the Pacific coast.

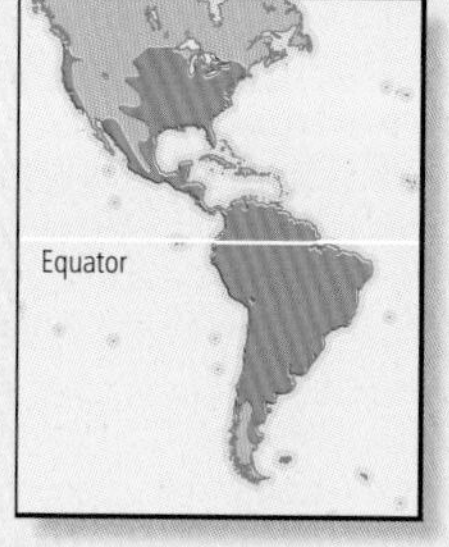

DIET Insectivorous, carnivorous, or (most often) omnivorous.

BREEDING Gestation 12–14 days

LONGEVITY 1–3 years (to about 8 in captivity)

CONSERVATION STATUS 44 of the 63 Didelphidae species are currently listed by the IUCN. Of these, 3 are Critically Endangered, 3 are Endangered, and 15 are Vulnerable; most of the others are ranked as Lower Risk: Near Threatened.

See subfamilies box ▷

The four-eyed opossums from the forests of Central and northern South America are also mostly generalist species. They are smaller than the Virginia opossum, with more slender bodies and distinct white spots above each eye, from which their common name is derived. These opossums are adept climbers, but the degree to which they climb seems to vary between habitats. The four-eyed opossums are also opportunistic feeders; earthworms, fruit, insects, and small vertebrates are all eaten.

The yapok, or Water opossum, is the only marsupial highly adapted to an aquatic lifestyle. The hind feet of this striking species are webbed, making the big toe less opposable than in other didelphids. When swimming, the hind feet alternate strokes, while the forefeet are extended in front, allowing the animals to either feel for prey or carry food items. Yapoks are primarily carnivorous, feeding on crustaceans, fish, and frogs as well as on insects. Although they can climb, they rarely do so, and the long, round tail is not very prehensile. Both male and female yapoks possess a pouch, which opens to the rear. During a dive, the female's pouch becomes a watertight chamber; fatty secretions and long hairs lining its lips form a seal, and strong sphincter muscles close it. In males, the scrotum can be pulled into the pouch when the animal is swimming or moving swiftly.

The Lutrine or Little water opossum is also a good swimmer, although it lacks the specializations of the yapok. Unlike the yapok, which is found primarily in forests, Lutrine opossums often inhabit open grasslands. Known as the *comadreja* ("weasel") in South America, this opossum has a long, low body with short, stout legs. The tail is densely furred and very thick at the base. Lutrine opossums are able predators, being excellent swimmers and climbers and also agile on the ground. They feed on a variety of prey including small mammals, birds, reptiles, frogs, and insects.

The mouse, or murine, opossums are a diverse group, with individual species varying greatly in size, climbing ability, and habitat. All are rather opportunistic feeders. The largest species, the Ashy mouse opossum, is one of the most arboreal, whereas others such as *Marmosa fuscata* are more terrestrial. The tail in most species is long, slender, and very prehensile, but in some species including the Elegant mouse opossum it can become swollen at the base for fat storage. The large, thin ears may become crinkled when the animal is aroused. The females lack a pouch, and the number and arrangement of mammae vary between species. Mouse opossums inhabit most habitats from Mexico through South America; they are absent only from the high Andean *paramo* and *puna* zones, the Chilean desert, and Patagonia, where they are replaced by another small species, the Patagonian opossum, which has the most southerly distribution of any didelphid.

This opossum broadly resembles the mouse opossums, though the muzzle is shorter, which allows for greater biting power; in the light of this adaptation, and because insects and fruit are rare in their habitat, Patagonian opossums are believed to be more carnivorous than mouse opossums. The feet are stronger than in mouse opossums and possess longer claws, suggesting fossorial (burrowing) habits. As in some of the mouse opossums, the tail of the Patagonian opossum can become swollen with fat.

The short-tailed opossums are small didelphids inhabiting forests and grasslands from eastern Panama through most of northern South America east of the Andes. The tail of these shrew-like animals is short and naked; their eyes are smaller than

THE MONITO DEL MONTE

The monito del monte or colocolo lives in the forests of south-central Chile. Once thought to belong to the same family as the American opossums, this small marsupial is now considered the only living member of an otherwise extinct order, the Microbiotheria.

Monitos ("little monkeys") have small bodies with short muzzles, round ears, and thick tails. Head–body length is 8–13cm (3–5in), and they weigh just 16–31g (0.6–1.1oz). They are found in cool, humid forests, especially in bamboo thickets. Conditions are often harsh in these environments, and monitos exhibit various adaptations to the cold. The dense body fur and small, well-furred ears both help prevent heat loss. During winter months when food (mostly insects and other small invertebrates) is scarce, they hibernate. Before hibernation, the base of the tail becomes swollen with fat deposits.

There are various local superstitions about these harmless animals. One is that their bite is venomous and produces convulsions. Another maintains that it is bad luck to see a monito; some people have even reportedly burned their houses to the ground after spotting one in their homes.

Right A large American opossum (Didelphis *sp.*) in Minnesota, near the northerly limit of its range. Since the 19th century these opossums have spread rapidly northward through the USA. However, they are poorly adapted to cold weather conditions. During severe spells they may remain inactive in their nests for days on end, although they do not hibernate.

in most didelphids and not as protruding. As these anatomical features suggest, short-tailed opossums are primarily terrestrial, but they can climb. As in mouse opossums, the females lack a pouch, and the number of mammae varies between species. Short-tailed opossums are omnivorous, feeding on insects, earthworms, carrion, and fruit, among other foods. Often they will inhabit human dwellings, where they are a welcome predator on insects and small rodents.

The three species of woolly opossum, along with the Black-shouldered and Bushy-tailed opossums, are placed in a separate subfamily – the Caluromyinae – from other didelphids on the basis of differences in blood proteins, the anatomy of the females' urogenital system, and the males' spermatozoa. The woolly opossums and the Black-shouldered opossum are among the most specialized of all didelphids. Highly arboreal, they have large, protruding eyes that are directed somewhat forward, making their faces reminiscent of those of primates. Inhabitants of humid tropical forests, these opossums climb through the upper tree canopy in search of fruit. During the dry season, they also feed on the nectar of flowering trees, and serve as pollinators for the trees they visit. While feeding, they can hang by their long prehensile tails to reach fruit or flowers.

Although the Bushy-tailed opossum resembles mouse opossums in its general appearance and proportions, dental characteristics, such as the size and shape of the molars, indicate that it is actually more closely related to the woolly and Black-shouldered opossums. This species is known only from a few museum specimens, all of them taken from humid tropical forests.

Back to North America

DISTRIBUTION PATTERNS

North American fossil deposits from 70–80 million years ago are rich in didelphid remains, and it was probably from North America that didelphids entered South America and Europe. Yet by 10–20 million years ago they had become extinct in both North America and Europe. When South America again became joined to Central America, about 2–5 million years ago, many South American marsupials became extinct in the face of competition from the northern placental mammals that took the opportunity to spread into their territory. Didelphids persisted, however, and even moved north into Central and North America.

During historical times, the early European settlers of North America found no marsupials north of the modern states of Virginia and Ohio. Since then, in the eastern USA, the Virginia opossum has steadily extended its range as far as the Great Lakes. Moreover, following introductions on the Pacific coast in 1890, this species has also spread from southern California to southern Canada. These expansions are most probably related to human impact on the environment.

Left *A Virginia opossum feigning death to deter a potential aggressor. The condition, which brings on symptoms akin to fainting, can last for less than a minute or as long as six hours.*

Playing Possum

SOCIAL BEHAVIOR

Reproduction in didelphids is typical of marsupials: gestation is short and does not interrupt the estrous cycle. The young are poorly developed at birth, and most development takes place during lactation. In the past there was a popular misconception that opossums copulated through the nose and that the young were later blown out through the nostrils into the pouch! The male's bifurcated penis, the tendency for females to lick the pouch area before birth, and the small size of the young at birth (they are just 1cm/0.4in long, and weigh 0.13g/0.005oz) all probably contributed to this notion.

Most opossums appear to have seasonal reproduction. Breeding is timed so that the first young leave the pouch when resources are most abundant; for example, the Virginia opossum breeds during the winter in North America, and the young leave the pouch in the spring. Opossums in the seasonal tropics breed during the dry season, and the first young leave the pouch at the start of the rainy season. Up to three litters can be produced in one season, but the last litter often overlaps the beginning of the period of food scarcity, and these young frequently die in the pouch. Opossums in aseasonal tropical forests may reproduce throughout the year, as may the White-eared opossum in the arid region of northeast Brazil.

There are no elaborate courtship displays nor long-term pair-bonds. The male typically initiates contact, approaching the female while making a clicking vocalization. A non-receptive female will avoid contact or be aggressive, but a female in estrus will allow the male to mount. In some species courtship behavior involves active pursuit of the female. Copulation can be very prolonged – for up to six hours in Robinson's mouse opossums (*Marmosa robinsoni*).

Many of the newborn young die, as many never attach to a teat. A female will often produce more

American Opossum Subfamilies

Subfamily Didelphinae

58 species in 12 genera. S and C America, E USA to Ontario. Virginia opossum introduced to the Pacific coast.

Large American opossums (*Didelphis*, 4 species), including the Virginia opossum (*Didelphis virginiana*), Southern opossum (*D. marsupialis*), and White-eared opossum (*D. albiventris*)

Mouse opossums (*Marmosa*, 9 species), including the Murine mouse opossum (*M. murina*) and Robinson's mouse opossum (*M. robinsoni*). 1 species is Critically Endangered, another Endangered.

Gracile mouse opossums (*Gracilinanus*, 6 species), including the Wood spirit gracile mouse opossum (*G. dryas*). 1 species is Critically Endangered, 2 are Vulnerable.

Slender mouse opossums (*Marmosops*, 9 species), including the Gray-bellied slender mouse opossum (*M. fuscatus*). 1 species is Critically Endangered, 1 Endangered, 1 Vulnerable.

Woolly mouse opossums (*Micoureus*, 4 species), including the Pale-bellied woolly mouse opossum (*M. constantiae*).

Short-tailed opossums (*Monodelphis*, 15 species), including the Gray short-tailed opossum (*M. domestica*) and the Pygmy short-tailed opossum (*M. kunsi*). 1 species is Endangered, 8 are Vulnerable.

Gray and Black four-eyed opossums (*Philander*, 2 species), comprising the Gray four-eyed opossum (*P. opossum*) and Black four-eyed opossum (*P. andersoni*).

Fat-tailed opossums (*Thylamys*, 5 species), including the Elegant fat-tailed opossum (*T. elegans*)

Brown four-eyed opossum (*Metachirus nudicaudatus*)

Water opossum (*Chironectes minimus*)

Lutrine opossum (*Lutreolina crassicaudata*)

Patagonian opossum (*Lestodelphys halli*). Vulnerable.

Subfamily Caluromyinae

5 species in 3 genera. S Mexico through C America and most of northern S America.

Woolly opossums (*Caluromys*, 3 species). 1 species Vulnerable.

Black-shouldered opossum (*Caluromysiops irrupta*). Vulnerable.

Bushy-tailed opossum (*Glironia venusta*).Vulnerable.

For full species list see Appendix ▷

young than she has mammae; for example, most female Virginia opossums have 13 mammae, some of which may not even be functional, but usually give birth to around 21 young (there is anecdotal evidence of 56 having once been produced). The number of young in an opossum litter that do attach ranges from one to 15, but varies both within and between species. Older females tend to have fewer young, and litters born late in the season are often smaller. Litter sizes in Virginia and Southern opossums seem to increase with increasing latitude. The number of mammae provides an indication of maximum possible litter size. In general, some species (e.g. Virginia or Common opossums, short-tailed opossums, and the Robinson's mouse opossum) have comparatively large litters of about seven young, whereas others (for instance the Gray four-eyed and woolly opossums) have 3–5 young. Females of some species including the Virginia opossum usually cannot raise a single offspring because there is insufficient stimulus to maintain lactation.

The rearing cycle in those species that have been studied ranges from about 70 to 125 days. For example, the Gray four-eyed opossum and

Above *Some representative American opossum species:* ***1*** *Central American woolly opossum* (Caluromys derbianus) *resting in a tree;* ***2*** *Black-shouldered opossum* (Caluromysiops irrupta) *climbing down a branch using its prehensile tail;* ***3*** *Mexican mouse opossum* (Marmosa mexicana – *not shown to scale) foraging for fruit;* ***4*** *Gray four-eyed opossum* (Philander opossum) *eating an insect grub;* ***5*** *Water opossum* (Chironectes minimus)*; note the webbed hind feet.*

woolly opossums are similar in size (usually about 400g/14oz), but the time from birth to weaning is 68–75 days in the former and 110–125 days in the latter. Initially the young remain attached to the mother's teats, but later they begin to crawl about her body. Toward the end of lactation, they begin to follow her when she leaves the nest to forage. Female Robinson's mouse opossums will retrieve detached young within a few days of birth; in contrast, Virginia opossum mothers do not respond to their distress calls until after they have left the pouch, at about 70 days.

Although individual vocalizations and odors allow for some mother–infant recognition, maternal care in opossums does not appear to be restricted solely to a female's own offspring. Female Robinson's mouse opossums will retrieve young other than their own, and Virginia and woolly opossums have been observed carrying other females' young in their pouches. Toward the end of lactation, females cease any maternal care, and dispersal is rapid. Sexual maturity is attained within 6–10 months. Age at sexual maturity is not related directly to body size.

In general, opossums are not long-lived. Few Virginia opossums survive beyond 2 years in the wild, and the smaller mouse opossums may not live much beyond one reproductive season. Although animals kept in captivity may survive longer, females are generally not able to reproduce after 2 years. Thus, among many of these didelphids, there is a trend towards the production of a few large litters during a limited reproductive life; indeed, a female Robinson's mouse opossum may typically reproduce only once in a lifetime.

American opossums appear to be locally nomadic, and seemingly do not defend territories. Radio-tracking studies reveal that individual animals occupy home ranges, but do not exclude others of the same species (conspecifics). The length of time for which a home range is occupied varies both between and within species. In the forests of French Guiana, for example, some woolly opossums have been observed to remain for up to a year in the same home range, whereas others shifted home range repeatedly; Gray four-eyed opossums were more likely to shift home range.

In contrast to some other mammals, didelphids do not appear to explore their entire home range on a regular basis. Movements primarily involve feeding and travel to and from a nest site, and are highly variable depending upon food resources and/or reproductive condition. Thus home range estimates for Virginia opossums in the central United States vary from 12.5–38.8 hectares (31–96 acres). An individual woolly opossum's home range may vary from 0.3–1ha (0.75–2.5 acres) from one day to the next. In general, the more carnivorous species have greater movements than similar-sized species that feed more on fruit. Male didelphids become more active during the breeding season, whereas reproductive females generally become more sedentary.

Most opossums use several to many nest sites within their range. Nests are often used alternately with conspecifics in the area. Virginia and Southern opossums use a variety of nest sites, both terrestrial and arboreal, but hollow trees are a common location. Four-eyed opossums also nest in holes and open limbs of trees, and additionally on the ground, in rock crevices, or under tree roots or fallen palm fronds. Mouse opossums nest either on the ground under logs and tree roots or in trees, using holes or abandoned birds' nests.

Shrew Opossums of the High Andes

Five small, shrew-like marsupial species are found in the Andean region of western South America from southern Venezuela to southern Chile. Known sometimes as shrew (or rat) opossums, they are unique among American marsupials in having a reduced number of incisors, the lower middle two of which are large and project forward. The South American group represents a distinct line of evolution that diverged from ancestral stock before the Australian forms did, and its members are now placed not just in their own family, the Caenolestidae, but are also assigned an order, the Paucituberculata, of which they are the only representatives.

Fossil evidence indicates that about 20 million years ago seven genera of shrew opossums occurred in South America. Today the family is represented by only three genera and five species. There are three species of *Caenolestes*: the Gray-bellied (*C. caniventer*), Blackish (*C. convelatus*), and Silky (*C. fuliginosus*); the Incan (*Lestoros inca*) and Chilean (*Rhyncholestes raphanurus*) shrew opossums are placed in separate genera. Known head–body lengths of these small marsupials are in the range of 9–14cm (3.5–5.5in), tail lengths mostly 10–14cm (3.9–5.5in), and weights from 14–41g (0.5–1.4oz).

The animals have elongated snouts equipped with numerous tactile whiskers. The eyes are small and vision is poor. Well-developed ears project above the fur. The ratlike tails are about the same length as the body (rather less in the Chilean shrew opossum) and are covered with stiff, short hairs. The fur on the body is soft and thick and is uniformly dark brown in most species. Females lack a pouch, and most species have four teats (five in the Chilean shrew opossum). Shrew opossums are active during the early evening and/or night, when they forage for insects, earthworms, and other small invertebrates, and also small vertebrates. They are able predators, using their large incisors to kill prey.

Shrew opossums travel about on well-marked ground trails or runways. More than one individual will use a particular trail or runway. When moving slowly, they have a typically symmetrical gait, but when moving faster Incan shrew opossums, and possibly other species, will bound, allowing them to clear obstacles.

The Blackish and Silky shrew opossums are distributed at high elevations in the Andes of western Venezuela, Colombia, and Ecuador. The Gray-bellied shrew opossums of southern Ecuador occur at lower elevations. The Incan shrew opossum is found high in the Peruvian Andes, but in drier habitats than that of the other species; it has been trapped in areas with low trees, bushes, and grasses. The Chilean shrew opossum inhabits the forests of southern Chile. As winter approaches, the tail of this species becomes swollen with fat deposits.

Very little is known about the biology of these elusive marsupials. They inhabit inaccessible and (for humans) rather inhospitable areas, which makes them difficult to study. They have always been considered rare, but recent collecting trips have suggested that some species may be more common than was previously thought.

Left *A Bare-tailed woolly opossum perches on a branch in French Guiana. These opossums, which take their name from their long, thick fur, are agile climbers, using the five digits of all four limbs to help them clamber through the forests in which they live.*

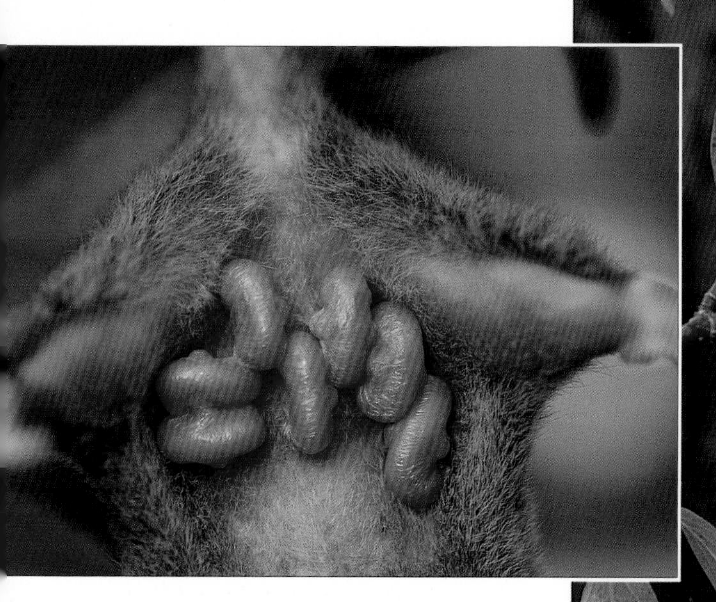

Above *Hanging from a branch, a short-tailed opossum mother in Brazil shows off her seven newborn young, each attached to a separate teat. Pouches are not developed in these species.*

Right *An infant Virginia opossum hitches a ride on its mother's back. For a month or two between leaving the pouch and achieving independence, this is the usual mode of transport for the young.*

Occasionally mouse opossums make nests in banana stalks, and more than once animals have been shipped to grocery stores in the United States and Europe! In the open grasslands, the Lutrine opossum constructs globular nests of leaves or uses abandoned armadillo burrows. In more forested areas, these opossums may use tree holes. Unlike other didelphids, yapoks construct more permanent nests; their underground nesting chambers are located near the waterline and are reached through holes dug into stream banks.

Opossums are solitary animals. Although many may congregate at common food sources during periods of food scarcity, there is no interaction unless individuals get too close. Typically, when two animals do meet, they threaten each other with open-mouth threats and hissing and then continue on their way. If aggression does persist (usually between males), the hissing changes into a growl and then to a screech. Communication by smell is very important; many species have well-developed scent glands on the chest. In addition, male Virginia opossums, Gray four-eyed opossums, and Gray short-tailed opossums have all been observed marking objects with saliva. Marking behavior is carried out primarily by males, and is thought to advertise their presence in an area.

In tropical forests up to seven species of didelphids may be found at the same locality. Competition between these species is avoided through differences in body size and varying tendencies to climb. For example, woolly opossums and the Ashy mouse opossum will generally inhabit the tree canopy, the Common mouse opossum mostly haunts the lower branches, Southern and Gray four-eyed opossums are found either on the ground or in the lower branches, while short-tailed opossums live solely on the ground. Some species appear to vary their tendency to climb depending upon the presence of similar-sized opossums. For example, in a Brazilian forest where both Gray and Brown four-eyed opossums were found together, the former was more arboreal than the latter, yet in a forest in French Guiana where only the Gray was present, it was primarily terrestrial, and elsewhere the Brown four-eyed opossum is mostly arboreal.

Despite being hunted for food and pelts, the Virginia opossum thrives both on farms and in towns and even cities. Elsewhere in the Americas, man's impact on the environment has been detrimental to didelphids. Destruction of humid tropical forests results in loss of habitat for the more specialized species. MAO'C

Large Marsupial Carnivores

THE LARGE MARSUPIAL CARNIVORES CONSIST of six species of quolls, sometimes referred to as marsupial cats, and the Tasmanian devil, a single species assigned to its own genus. Tasmanian devils are perhaps best known to the general public in the form of "Taz," the Warner Brothers cartoon character. But the comic image of a tail-spinning terror devouring everything in its path belies the true nature of the devil, as does its reputation in Tasmania itself as an odious scavenger. While belligerent towards other devils, these predators and specialized scavengers responsive, intelligent, and full of character.

Vertebrate prey is a major part of the diet of large marsupial carnivores. Current diversity is low, but fossil evidence suggests many more species existed in the past. At least nine thylacinids have roamed Australia; their heyday was during the Miocene era (24–5 million years ago), while during the Pleistocene (1.8 million–10,000 years ago), several species of giant dasyurids (quolls) existed. The last thylacine, also known as the Tasmanian wolf because of its dog-like appearance, became extinct only in the 1930s.

Marsupial carnivores are not exclusively Australasian. Three species of South American marsupials are highly carnivorous, and thylacine-like borhyaenids and sabretooth-cat-like marsupial thylacosmilids roamed there in prehistoric times.

A Classic Case of Convergence

FORM AND FUNCTION

At least superficially, quolls look like mongooses, thylacines like dogs, while devils resemble small hyenas, even down to the sloping hindquarters and rolling gait. The remarkable similarities between marsupial and placental carnivores that have evolved on different continents can give the impression of parallel universes.

The observed similarities between the two groups are in fact related to these species leading similar lives. Devils, like hyenas, have highly carnivorous dentition and adaptations for bone consumption, including robust premolar or molar teeth used for cracking bones and a relatively short snout with massive jaw-closing muscles, giving the animals a strong, crushing bite.They are able to consume all parts of a carcass, including thick skin and all but the largest bones. With teeth that are adapted for crushing invertebrates as well as for slicing meat, quolls group with the mongoose and stoat families to fill the role of predator of small to medium-sized mammals and invertebrates. The thylacine, on the other hand, was probably ecologically closer to smaller canids like the coyote than it ever was to the wolf. The animal's extremely long snout, very low rates of canine tooth wear and fracture, and limb ratios typical of slow runners, suggest that it hunted prey such as wallabies that were smaller than itself, and did not use long, fast pursuits.

Below *The Tasmanian devil will take living prey, including lambs and poultry, but has a preference for carrion. It can even chew and swallow sheep bones.*

FACTFILE

LARGE MARSUPIAL CARNIVORES

Order: Dasyuromorphia

Family: Dasyuridae

7 extant species in 2 genera; 1 species (*Thylacinus cynocephalus*) in the related Thylacinidae family recently extinct

DISTRIBUTION Australia and New Guinea

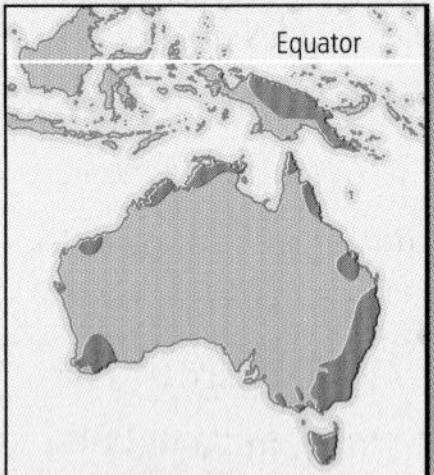

HABITAT Mostly in rain forest or woodland

SIZE **Head–body length** ranges from 12.3–31cm (5–12in) in the male Northern quoll to 50.5–62.5cm (20–25in) in the Tasmanian devil; **weight** ranges from 0.3–0.9kg (0.7–2lb) to 4.4–13kg (10–30lb) in the same two species.

COAT Short-furred; upper parts mostly gray or brown, with white spots or blotches. The Tasmanian devil has thicker fur, and usually only one or two white patches.

DIET Smaller species eat mainly insects, but the Spotted-tailed quoll and the Tasmanian devil will take mammals as large as wallabies.

BREEDING Mostly 4–8 young, carried in pouch for 8–10 weeks in smaller species but for 4–5 months in Tasmanian devil.

LONGEVITY Ranges from 12 months in the smaller species to 6 years in the Tasmanian devil.

CONSERVATION STATUS Four of the 7 extant species are currently listed as Vulnerable, two as Lower Risk: Near Threatened.

See species table ▷

Marsupial carnivore species exhibit variation in the strength of their canine teeth and temporal (jaw) muscles and take prey of different sizes, which consequently minimizes the competition for food. The shape of the canines is oval, being intermediate between the narrow canine teeth of the dog family and the more rounded canines of the cats. Marsupial carnivores kill their prey by use of a generalized crushing bite, which is applied to the skull or nape.

Two morphological features suggest that Dasyuromorphs and Carnivorans may simply have evolved different solutions to the same problems. Marsupials have a longer snout than the placental carnivores, suggesting that they may possess a weaker bite, but this comparative deficiency appears to be compensated for by extra space for larger jaw muscles, which is derived from their smaller brain cases. Limb–bone ratios suggest that devils, Spotted-tailed quolls, and thylacines, but not the smaller quolls, are slow runners compared with their placental counterparts. The granular foot pads, which are limited to the digits in placental carnivores, extend to the ankle and wrist joints in the marsupial carnivores, which sometimes walk and rest on their heels, suggesting differences in their locomotory function.

Above Four-month old Eastern quolls resting in a grass-lined den. Young are usually deposited in a den by the mother about ten weeks after birth, having spent their time up until then in their mother's pouch.

There is a quoll adapted to every environment in Australia and New Guinea: tropical rain forest, monsoonal savanna, woodlands, deserts, grasslands, and temperate forests. The degree of carnivory increases with body size, from the quite insectivorous smaller quolls to the completely carnivorous Spotted-tailed quoll, devil, and thylacine. The largest remaining guild, in Tasmania, had four species until the recent extinction of the thylacine: the Eastern quoll, a small (1kg/2.2lb) ground-dwelling insectivore/carnivore; the Spotted-tailed quoll, a middle-sized (2–4kg/4.5–9lb) tree-climbing predator; the devil, a larger (4.4–13 kg/10–30lb) ground-dwelling carnivore and specialist scavenger; and the predatory thylacine (15–35kg/33–77lb). Spotted-tailed quolls are naturally rare, perhaps because they are specialists on forest habitat and vertebrate food, and because they may compete for food with Eastern quolls, devils, and introduced cats. Their tree-climbing abilities may allow them to exploit the tree-dwelling possum prey resource, however, which is less available to other quolls and devils. Devils are the most common species; their larger size gives them an advantage in stealing carcasses from quolls and monopolizing them.

Solitary but Social

SOCIAL BEHAVIOR

Early settlers can be excused for giving the devil its alarming name. The sight of a jet-black animal with large white teeth and bright red ears (the ears of devils blush red when they are stirred up) creating mayhem in a poultry coop, combined with spine-chilling screeches in the dark, must have been more than enough to convince them that they had indeed "raised the Devil." Devils make a wide range of sounds, including growls, whines, soft barks, snorts, sniffs, and whimpers. Devils are solitary creatures but highly social, feeding together at carcasses and developing quite affectionate relationships for several days while mating. Females and males have very different agendas, however. A female loves and leaves several males in succession over a period of a week, perhaps in an attempt to ensure that her young are sired by the best males available. Intent on protecting his paternity, the male devil indulges in "cave-man" tactics, charging the escaping female and then using a neck-bite to drag or lead her back to the den, where he will copulate with her for prolonged periods. During the mating season female devils develop a swelling on the back of their neck that may serve to protect them from injury. Males fight for females, sustaining deep bites and gouges to the head and rump that may sometimes be life-threatening.

Quolls, like devils, are solitary and rest underground or in hollow log dens during the day. Neither group is territorial, although females sometimes maintain an exclusive part of their home range, especially when they have young in a den. Male young are more likely than females to disperse away from the home range of their mother. Young devils disperse at 12–18 months of age, immediately after weaning, moving some 10–30 km (6–19mi) from their birth site. Scent is important in communication, with latrines possibly assuming the role of community noticeboards in some species. Devils frequently scentmark by dragging their cloacae on the ground. Quolls, unlike devils, call infrequently, making a variety of coughing and hissing sounds or else abrupt, piercing screams; in the case of the Spotted-tailed quoll, these cries have been likened to the sound made by a circular saw.

The Threat from Placentals

CONSERVATION AND ENVIRONMENT

All Australian species have declined in range and abundance as a result of human presence. Concern has also been expressed for the quolls in New Guinea, although their conservation status is poorly known.

Devils and quolls, like many placental carnivores, are persecuted for attacking livestock. Both groups take insecurely-penned poultry, and newly-born lambs and sick sheep are also vulnerable. As a result, devils and quolls are trapped, shot, and poisoned in the tens and occasionally in the hundreds. Similar persecution, combined with loss of habitat and prey as a result of more sheep farming, was a main cause of the thylacine's decline, leading ultimately to its extinction.

The greatest threats to marsupial carnivores, however, are loss of habitat and killings by introduced placental carnivores. These often go hand in hand. Like many carnivores, devils and quolls live at low density (one individual to 1–10sq km/ 0.4–4sq mi, depending on habitat, in Spotted-tailed quolls) and require lots of space (home ranges of male devils average 30sq km/12sq mi). Extensive areas of habitat have been lost through

THE TASMANIAN WOLF

Up to the time of its extinction, the thylacine was the largest of recent marsupial carnivores. Fossil thylacines are widely scattered in Australia and New Guinea, but the living animal was confined in historical times to Tasmania.

Superficially, the thylacine resembled a dog. It stood about 60cm (24in) high at the shoulders, head–body length averaged 80cm (31.5in), and weight 15–35kg (33–77lb). The head was dog-like with a short neck, and the body sloped away from the shoulders. The legs were also short, as in large dasyurids. The features that clearly distinguished the thylacine from dogs were a long (50cm/20in), stiff tail, which was thick at the base, and a coat pattern of black or brown stripes on a sandy yellow ground across the back.

Most of the information available on the behavior of the thylacine is either anecdotal or has been obtained from old film. It ran with diagonally opposing limbs moving alternately, could sit upright on its hindlimbs and tail rather like a kangaroo, and could leap 2–3m (6.5–10ft) with great agility. Thylacines appear to have hunted alone or in pairs, and before Europeans settled in Tasmania they probably fed upon wallabies, possums, bandicoots, rodents, and birds. It is suggested that they caught prey by stealth rather than by chase.

At the time of European settlement, the thylacine appears to have been widespread in Tasmania, and was particularly common where settled areas adjoined dense forest. It was thought to rest during the day on hilly terrain in dense forest, emerging at night to feed in grassland and woodland.

From the early days of European settlement, the thylacine developed a reputation for killing sheep. As early as 1830, bounties were offered for killing thylacines, and the consequent destruction led to fears for the species' survival as early as 1850. Even so, the Tasmanian government introduced its own bounty scheme in 1888, and over the next 21 years, before the last bounty was paid, 2,268 animals were officially killed. The number of bounties paid had declined sharply by the end of this period, and it is thought that epidemic disease combined with hunting to bring about the thylacine' s final disappearance.

The last thylacine to be captured was taken in western Tasmania in 1933; it died in Hobart zoo in 1936. Since then the island has been searched thoroughly on a number of occasions, and even though occasional sightings continue to be reported to this day, the most recent survey concluded that there has been no positive evidence of thylacines since that time. In 1999, the Australian Museum in Sydney decided to explore the possibility of cloning a thylacine, using DNA from a pup preserved in alcohol in 1866, although it admitted that to do so successfully would require substantial advances in biogenetic techniques. AKL

Left *Rare, if not extinct, in some regions that it traditionally occupied, the Spotted-tailed quoll is vulnerable to predation by placental carnivores in many areas.*

Right *The Spotted-tailed quoll is an active hunter, killing its prey – which includes gliders, small wallabies, reptiles, and birds – with a bite to the back of the head.*

degradation, in addition to direct losses to agriculture and intensive forestry, which in turn can limit the availability of prey, especially for the forest-dependent Spotted-tailed quoll, which disappears if more than 50 percent of the canopy is removed. The decline in the number of old-growth, hollow-bearing trees is a cause of particular concern; they support populations of hollow-nesting possums, which are major prey species for Spotted-tailed quolls. The smaller quolls become increasingly vulnerable to predation by introduced predators if vegetative cover is removed by livestock grazing or frequent fires. Northern, Western, and Eastern quolls have lost large tracts of habitat in this way.

Dingoes, cats, and foxes were all introduced to Australia by humans, respectively 3,500–4,000 years ago, as early as the 17th century, and in 1871. Introduced carnivores kill marsupial carnivores for food or to reduce competition. Thylacines and devils declined and went extinct on mainland Australia at the same time as the dingo arrived. Now foxes and cats seem to be major causes of death for the smaller species of quolls; certainly, Northern quoll death rates from predation rise after fires in savanna habitats, but not in rocky habitats where shelter from predators is available; similarly, populations increase when foxes are controlled. On a local scale, quolls tend to become extinct wherever Red foxes live.

Fortunately, there is also some good news to report. The Western quoll – once considered endangered – will shortly be removed from threatened-species lists, following the success of a recovery program that has translocated 200 captive-bred animals to four new sites since the early 1990s, although their continued survival will remain dependent on ongoing fox and cat control.

The Spotted-tailed and Northern quolls are currently focuses for concern. The populations of both species are fragmented and declining, and their survival and population recovery will require a nationally-coordinated approach, with deleterious processes, habitat loss, and predator control all needing to be addressed. MJ

Northern quoll
Dasyurus hallucatus

N Australia. Formerly found in broad band across wet–dry tropics; now only in lowland savanna woodland and rocky terrain.
HBL male: 12.3–31cm (5–12in), female: 12.5–30cm (5–12in); TL male: 12.7–30.8cm (5–12in), female: 20–30cm (8–12in); WT male: 0.4–0.9kg (0.8–2lb), female: 0.3–0.5kg (0.7–1.1lb).
COAT: white spots on brown body, striated foot pads, clawless hallux (1st toe) on 5-toed hind foot, tail long-haired.
BREEDING: mates in June at 12 months old, usually up to 8 young (variation 5–10) carried in pouch for 8–10 weeks, weaned at 6 months.
LONGEVITY: male 12–17 months, female 12–37 months.
CONSERVATION STATUS: Lower Risk, Near Threatened; in extensive decline, with just six fragmented populations remaining.

New Guinea quoll
Dasyurus albopunctatus

New Guinea. Widespread in rainforest habitats above 1,000m (3,300ft).
HBL male: 22.8–35cm (9–14in), female: 24.1–27.5cm (9.5–10.5in); TL male: 21.2–29cm (8–11in), female: 22.1–28cm (9–11in); WT male: 0.6–0.7kg (1.5lb), female: 0.5kg (1.1lb).
COAT: white spots on reddish-brown body, well-developed hallux, tail short-haired.
BREEDING: not seasonal, 4–6 young.
CONSERVATION STATUS: Vulnerable.

Bronze quoll
Dasyurus spartacus

SW New Guinea. Lowland savanna woodlands. Known from only a few specimens; first reported 1979, recognized as a separate species from *D. geoffroii* in 1988.
HBL male: 34.5–38cm (14–15in), female: 30.5cm (12in); TL male: 28.5cm (11in), female: 25cm (10in); WT male: 1.0kg (2.2lb), female: 0.7kg (1.5lb).
COAT: white spots on brown body, small hallux, tail long-haired.
BREEDING: may be seasonal.
CONSERVATION STATUS: Vulnerable.

Western quoll
Dasyurus geoffroii
Western quoll or chuditch

SW Australia. Formerly over two-thirds of the county, from desert to forest, but now restricted to SW alone.
HBL male: 31–40cm (12–16in), female: 26–36cm (10–14in); TL male: 25–35cm (10–14in), female: 21–31cm (8–12in); WT male: 0.7–2.2kg (1.5–4.9lb), female: 0.6–1.1kg (1.3–2.4lb).
COAT: white spots on brown body, white belly, hallux, tail long-haired.
BREEDING: mates in May–June at 12 months old, up to 6 young carried in pouch for 9 weeks, weaned at 6 months.
LONGEVITY: 3 years.
CONSERVATION STATUS: Vulnerable; currently occupies only 2 percent of its former range.

Eastern quoll
Dasyurus viverrinus

Tasmania; formerly also SE mainland. Grasslands and open forests.
HBL male: 32–45cm (13–18in), female: 28–40cm(11–16in); TL male: 20–28cm (8–11in), female: 17–24cm (7–9.5in); WT male: 0.9–2.0kg (2–4.4lb), female: 0.7–1.1kg (1.5–2.4lb).
COAT: white spots on brown body, white belly, no hallux on 4-toed hind foot, tail long-haired.
BREEDING: mates in May–June at 12 months old, as many as 30 young born in June, up to 6 carried in pouch for 8–9 weeks and weaned at 5.5 months.
LONGEVITY: 3–4 years.
CONSERVATION STATUS: Lower Risk, Near Threatened.

Spotted-tailed quoll
Dasyurus maculatus

Tasmania (separate genetic unit); SE mainland and N Queensland (smaller phenotypic subspecies). Forest-dependent in areas of high rainfall or predictably seasonal rainfall.
HBL male: 45–51cm (18–20in), female: 40.5–43cm (16–17in); TL male: 39–49cm (15–19in), female: 34–44cm (13–17in); WT male: 3.0–7.0kg (6.6–15.4lb), female: 1.6–4.0kg (3.5–8.8lb); all data are for southern subspecies.
COAT: white spots on reddish-brown body and on short-haired tail, cream belly, striated foot pads, well-developed hallux.
BREEDING: mating April–July at 12 months old, up to 6 young carried in pouch for 8 weeks, weaned at 5 months.
LONGEVITY: 3–5 years.
CONSERVATION STATUS: Vulnerable; N Queensland subspecies is Endangered.

Tasmanian devil
Sarcophilus laniarius (harrisii)

Tasmania. Open forest and woodland.
HBL male: 50.5–62.5cm (20–25in), female: 53.5–57cm (21–22.5in); TL male: 23.5–28.5cm (9–11in), female: 21.5–27cm (8.5–10.5in); WT male: 7.7–13.0kg (17–28.7lb), female: 4.5–9.0kg (9.9–19.9lb).
COAT: black with variable white markings on chest, shoulder, and rump, fat store in tail base, no hallux on 4-toed on hind foot.
BREEDING: mates in February–March at 12 months old, up to 4 young carried in pouch for 4–5 months, weaned at 9 months.
LONGEVITY: 6 years.
CONSERVATION STATUS: Not listed.

Abbreviations HBL = head–body length TL = tail length WT = weight.

Small Marsupial Carnivores

THE SMALL MARSUPIAL CARNIVORES INCLUDE some of the smallest mammals on Earth, yet the ferocity they display in hunting belies their size. All show a predilection for live food, preying mainly on insects and other invertebrates, but also taking lizards, fledgling birds, and other small mammals. However, their rapaciousness has sometimes brought them undeserved notoriety – for its attacks on poultry in the Sydney area, the diminutive Brush-tailed phascogale, which weighs just 200g (7oz), was unfairly dubbed a "vampire marsupial" by early European settlers.

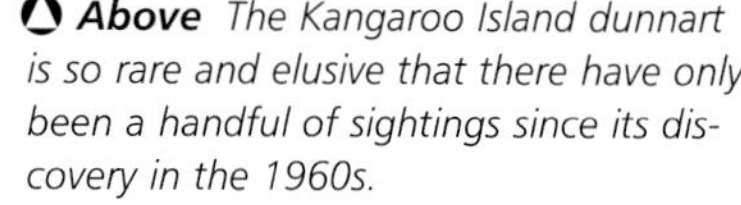

Above *The Kangaroo Island dunnart is so rare and elusive that there have only been a handful of sightings since its discovery in the 1960s.*

Although other marsupials such as American opossums, bandicoots, and the numbat eat animal flesh, most marsupial carnivores are dasyurids. The majority of species in this family weigh less than 250g (8.8oz) and representatives occur in all terrestrial habitats in Australia and New Guinea. Because of their conservative body form and appearance, dasyurids have long been considered as "primitive" marsupials structurally ancestral to the Australasian radiation. However, recent fossil discoveries show the family to be a recent and specialized addition to the region, with the ancestral dasyurid arising in the early to mid-Miocene, perhaps 16 million years ago.

Coping with Extremes

FORM AND FUNCTION

Despite showing three-thousand-fold variation in body mass, all dasyurids have distinctive pointed snouts with three pairs of similar-sized lower incisors, well-developed canines, and 6–7 sharp cheek teeth. This dentition allows prey to be grasped and quickly killed and then comminuted (chewed into small pieces) before swallowing. Dasyurids are united also in having five toes on the forefeet and 4–5 toes on the hind feet, with all except the hallux (big toe) having sharp claws.

Unlike their larger relatives, the small marsupial carnivores mostly have uniform coat colors that range from shades of brown and gray to black. Three New Guinean dasyurids (the Narrow-striped dasyure, Broad-striped dasyure, and Three-striped dasyure) are unusual in having dark dorsal stripes. All are partly diurnal, the coat pattern helping to camouflage them against the dark background of the rainforest floor. Two further diurnal species, the Speckled dasyure of the New Guinea highlands and the dibbler of southwestern Australia, are also unusual in having grizzled, silvery-gray coats that may again serve a camouflage function. In two species of phascogales, as well as in the mulgara, ampurta, and kowari, the terminal half of the tail is a spectacular black brush that contrasts greatly with the light body fur. The bushy tails are thought to have a signaling function, but there are few observations of these species in the wild to confirm this.

The insectivorous diet of small marsupial carnivores has important implications for their physiology. Insects are rich in protein and fat, but have a free water content of more than 60 percent. Water turnover is relatively high in many dasyurids, with species weighing less than 25g (0.9oz) able to turn over their body weight in water each day. In arid areas, marsupial carnivores can obtain all their water from food for periods of months; juicy prey such as insect larvae and centipedes are preferred; water loss is reduced by the production of concentrated urine. If food is limited, several small marsupial carnivores can reduce their metabolic rates and drop their body temperatures by 10°C (18°F) or more to enter torpor. This can last at least 10 hours, reducing energy expenditure and allowing animals to ride out temporary food shortages. If food is not limited, dasyurids have an extraordinary ability to maintain their body temperatures, producing heat by elevating the metabolic rate 8–9 times its normal resting level. The desert-dwelling kowari maintains its body temperature for at least four hours by this method, even at –10°C (14°F). Alternative means of keeping warm include sun-basking and sharing nests with individuals of the same or different species.

Left *The nocturnal Fat-tailed pseudantechinus, which stores fat in the base of its tail, is found mainly on rocky hills.*

Right *Dubbed a "vampire marsupial" by early settlers for its attacks on poultry, the Brush-tailed phascogale can erect the hairs at the end of its tail.*

FACTFILE

SMALL MARSUPIAL CARNIVORES

Order: Dasyuromorphia

Families: Dasyuridae and Myrmecobiidae

64 species in 15 genera

DISTRIBUTION Australia, Papua New Guinea, and Indonesia (Aru Islands).

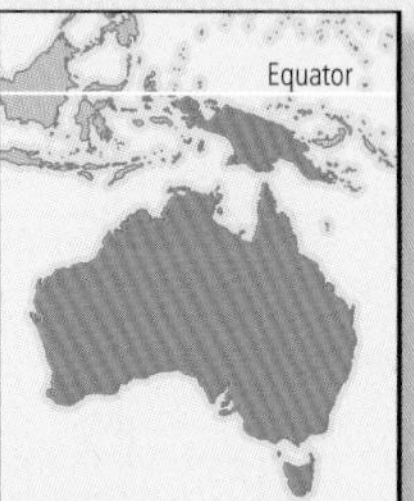

HABITAT Diverse, from stony desert to forest and alpine heath.

SIZE **Head–body length** ranges from 4.6–5.7cm (1.8–2.2in) in the Pilbara ningaui to 24.5cm (9.7in) in the Numbat; **tail length** ranges from 5.9–7.9cm (2.3–3.1in) to 17.7cm (7in), and **weight** from 2–9.4g (0.07–0.33oz) to 0.5kg (1.1lb), both in the same two species. Males are slightly or much heavier than females.

COAT Varied in color, but mostly short and coarse-furred.

DIET Mainly insects and other small invertebrates.(e.g. beetles, cockroaches, arachnids). Also small mammals and birds, including house mice, lizards, and sparrows.

BREEDING Gestation period ranges from 12.5 days in the Fat-tailed dunnart to 55 days in the Fat-tailed pseudantechinus.

LONGEVITY In the Brown antechinus, males live for 11.5 months, females for 3 years.

CONSERVATION STATUS One subspecies is classed as Critically Endangered, six as Endangered, four as Vulnerable, and five as Lower Risk: Near Threatened.

See families box ▷

Lone Ranger of the Desert

DISTRIBUTION PATTERNS

Small marsupial carnivores occupy all terrestrial habitats in Australia and New Guinea. Up to nine species occur locally in some arid areas and in structurally complex forests, due to the diversity of foraging microhabitats that these environments provide. In contrast, only one or two species usually co-occur in woodland or savanna environments, due to the paucity of opportunities they provide for different species to segregate.

The spectacular success of small dasyurids in the deserts of Australia is perhaps the most remarkable feature of their modern radiation. Many denizens of the arid zone occupy drifting home ranges that appear to track changes in levels of food. The tiny Lesser hairy-footed dunnart, for example, may move 2–3km (1.2–1.9mi) a night in search of food. Few small marsupial carnivores dig their own burrows, and those that inhabit the arid zone exploit soil cracks or abandoned burrows. Some dunnarts and ningauis will move several kilometers from drought-stricken areas toward rain. Lesser hairy-footed dunnarts have been recorded moving 12km (7.5mi) in two weeks, possibly following the scent of wet desert sand on the wind.

A Frenetic Search for Mates

SOCIAL BEHAVIOR

In the 12 species of forest-dwelling antechinuses and phascogales, as well as the Little red kaluta, sexual maturity is reached when males and females are 11 months old. Matings occur over a short period (2–3 weeks), at the same time each year in any locality, with ovulation in females being stimulated by subtle increases in the rate of change of day length in spring. All males die at about 1 year of age within a month of mating, but females can survive and reproduce in a second or occasionally third season. All or almost all females breed annually, producing 6–12 young per litter. Male death is due to increased levels of free corticosteroid (stress) hormones in the blood (see A Once-in-a-Lifetime Breeding Opportunity).

Other marsupial carnivores have more flexible life histories. In the Sandstone antechinus, matings still occur synchronously in winter, but some 70 percent of males survive their first breeding season; about a quarter of individuals of both sexes breed at 2 years of age. Reproductive effort in this species is relatively small, as only 65–88 percent of females breed each year, and litter sizes seldom exceed 4–5 young.

In other species of marsupial carnivores, such as some dunnarts, sexual maturity is achieved at 6–8 months, and females are able to produce 2–3 litters over extended breeding seasons that can last for up to 8 months. Repeated reproduction is

Small Marsupial Carnivore Families

Family Dasyuridae

Antechinuses or Broad-footed marsupial mice Genus *Antechinus*
10 species in Australia, including the Brown antechinus (*A. stuartii*), and Dusky antechinus (*A. swainsonii*). The Atherton (*A. godmani*), Swamp (*A. minimus*), and Cinnamon antechinuses (*A. leo*) are all Lower Risk: Near Threatened. A further 5 species of "antechinus" occur in New Guinea; both the taxonomic and conservation status of these species is uncertain.

Crest-tailed marsupial mice Genus *Dasycercus*
3 species in Australia: the mulgara (*D. cristicauda*), kowari (*D. byrnei*), and ampurta (*D. hillieri*). The ampurta is Endangered, and the mulgara and kowari are Vulnerable.

Long-tailed dasyures Genus *Murexia*
2 species in Indonesia and New Guinea: Short-furred dasyure (*M. longicaudata*) and Broad-striped dasyure (*M. rothschildi*).

Ningauis Genus *Ningaui*
3 species in Australia: the Pilbara ningaui (*N. timealeyi*), the Southern ningaui (*N. yvonneae*), and the Inland or Wongai ningaui (*N. ridei*).

Dibblers Genus *Parantechinus*
2 species in Australia: the Sandstone antechinus (*P. bilarni*) and the dibbler (*P. aplicalis*). The dibbler is Endangered.

Phascogales or Brush-tailed marsupial mice Genus *Phascogale*
2 species in Australia: the Red-tailed phascogale or wambenger (*P. calura*) and the Brush-tailed phascogale (*P. tapoatafa*). The former is Endangered, while the latter is Lower Risk: Near Threatened.

Marsupial shrews Genus *Phascolosorex*
2 species in New Guinea: the Red-bellied (*P. doriae*) and Narrow-striped dasyures (*P. dorsalis*).

Planigales or Flat-skulled marsupial mice Genus *Planigale*
6 species in Australia and New Guinea, including the Paucident planigale (*P. gilesi*) and the Common or Pygmy planigale (*P. maculata*). The Papuan planigale (*P. novaeguineae*) is Vulnerable.

Pseudantechinuses Genus *Pseudantechinus* 5 species in Australia, including the Fat-tailed pseudantechinus (*P. macdonnellensis*), and Woolley's pseudantechinus (*P. woolleyae*).

Dunnarts or Narrow-footed marsupial mice Genus *Sminthopsis*
19 species in Australia and Papua New Guinea, including the Carpentarian dunnart (*S. butleri*) and the Red-cheeked dunnart (*S. virginiae*). The Julia Creek (*S. douglasi*), Kangaroo Island (*S. aitkeni*), and Sandhill dunnarts (*S. psammophila*) are Endangered; and the Carpentarian dunnart is Vulnerable.

Kultarr (*Antechinomys laniger*). Australia.

Little red kaluta (*Dasykaluta rosamondae*). Australia.

Three-striped marsupial mouse (*Myoictis melas*). Indonesia and New Guinea.

Long-clawed marsupial mouse or Speckled dasyure (*Neophascogale lorentzi*). New Guinea.

Family Myrmecobidae

Numbat (*Myrmecobius fasciatus*) Australia. Vulnerable.

For full species list see Appendix ▷

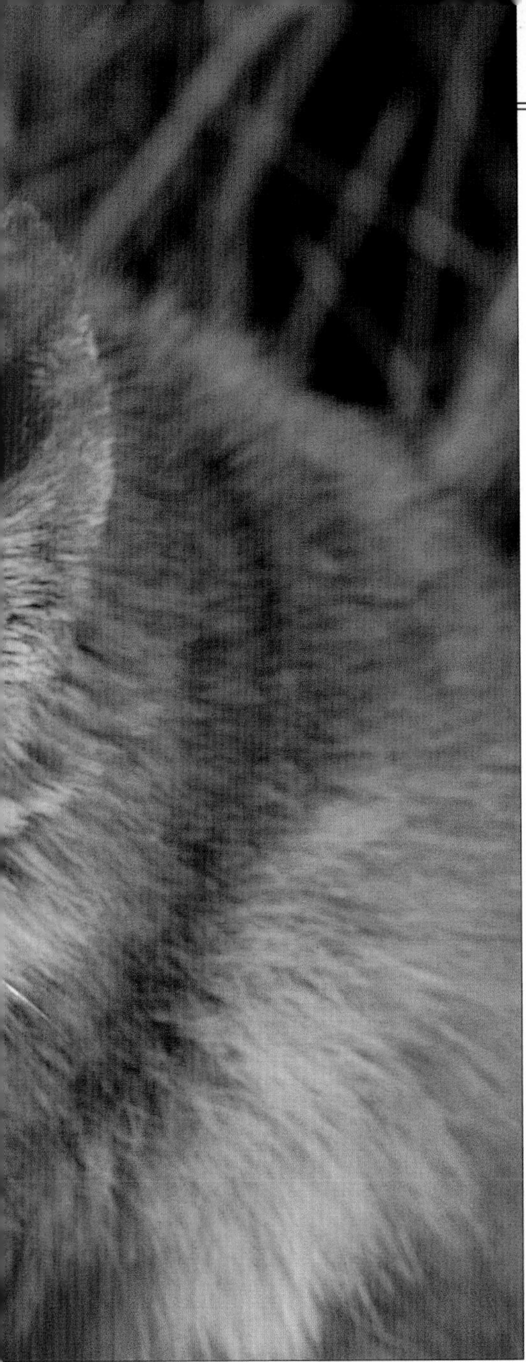

THE NUMBAT – TERMITE-EATER

The numbat (*Myrmecobius fasciatus*), the sole member of the family Myrmecobiidae, is a specialized termite-eater and, perhaps because of the diet, is the only fully day-active Australian marsupial. It sports black-and-white bars across its rump, and a prominent white-bordered dark bar from the base of each ear through the eye to the snout. These distinctive coat markings and its delicate appearance make it one of the most instantly appealing marsupials.

The numbat spends most of its active hours searching for food. It walks, stopping and starting, sniffing at the ground and turning over small pieces of wood in its search for shallow underground termite galleries. On locating a gallery, the numbat squats on its hind feet and digs rapidly with its strong clawed forefeet. Termites are extracted with the extremely long, narrow tongue which darts in and out of the gallery. Some ants are eaten, but it seems that the numbat usually takes these in accidentally while picking up the termites. It does not chew its food, and also swallows grit and soil acquired while feeding.

Numbats are solitary for most of the year, each individual occupying a territory of up to 150ha (370 acres). During the cooler months a male and female may share the same territory, but they are still rarely seen together. Hollow logs are used for shelter and refuge throughout the year, although numbats also dig burrows and often spend the nights in them during the cooler months. The burrows and some logs contain nests of leaves, grass, and sometimes bark. In summer numbats sunbathe on logs.

Four young are born between January and May, and attach themselves to the nipples of the female, which lacks a pouch. In July or August the mother deposits them in a burrow, suckling them at night. By October, the young are half grown and are feeding on termites while remaining in their parents' area. They disperse in early summer (December).

Numbats once occurred across the southern and central parts of Australia, from the west coast to the semi-arid areas of western New South Wales. They are now found only in a few areas of eucalypt forest and woodland in the southwest of Western Australia. Habitat destruction for agriculture and predation by foxes have probably contributed most to this decline. While most of their habitat is now secure, remaining populations are so small that the species is classed as Vulnerable. Efforts are being made to set up a breeding colony from which natural populations may be reestablished. AKL

Left *The mulgara is not a common sight, however it is reported that observed numbers increase when plagues of house mice – a favored food – occur within its range. It eats a mouse from head to tail, inverting the skin of its victim as it goes.*

possible because the gestation period is short (10–13 days) and weaning occurs at 60–70 days. In antechinuses, pseudantechinuses, and phascogales, by contrast, gestation lasts 30–40 days and weaning occurs at least three months after birth. Four marsupial carnivores appear to have no seasonality in their breeding schedules. Northern Australian populations of the Common planigale produce litters of 4–12 young in all months, while three species of antechinus in New Guinea produce smaller litters of 3–4 without any obvious seasonal break.

Differences in life histories of marsupial carnivores have probably arisen in response to variations in the duration and reliability of invertebrate food resources. In the antechinuses and phascogales, peaks in invertebrate abundance occur reliably in spring and summer, and mating is timed so that lactation and weaning coincide with these peaks. The chances of failing to breed at all due to food shortage is thus reduced. In dunnarts, ningauis, and other species where males survive or where females produce two or more litters in a season, food peaks may be smaller or less predictable. The chance of reproductive failure due to food shortage may be high, but the risk can be spread over more than a single litter.

Communication and social organization remain poorly known for most small dasyurids. Most or all species appear solitary except during the breeding season and when the young are dependent for food on the mother. In species that occur usually at low densities or occupy open habitats, such as ningauis, males continuously utter soft clicks or hisses to attract females, while females call in return during periods of receptivity. Loud hissing sounds are made by many species during aggressive encounters or during nest or food defense.

In the Agile antechinus and some other forest-dwelling dasyurids, males disperse from the maternal nest at weaning and reside for periods of days or weeks with unrelated females. Toward the breeding season, males appear to aggregate in treetop leks where females come to "window shop." Both sexes mate with multiple partners. Females store viable sperm in the reproductive tract for up to two weeks, and produce litters sired by more than one father. For the female, mating with several males causes sperm competition, which may be beneficial in producing genetically diverse offspring. For the male, such competition reduces confidence in paternity and may drive the frenetic search for new mates.

Small Survivors

CONSERVATION AND ENVIRONMENT

In contrast to their larger relatives, the small marsupial carnivores have escaped the worst ravages of European settlement. No species has gone extinct, and only seven have suffered range reductions over 25 percent. Nonetheless, many species have small ranges or sparse populations: 15 Australian species are considered threatened, as is the Papuan planigale. Clearing of vegetation for agriculture and predation by feral cats and foxes are serious threats. Populations of most of the threatened species occur at least partly on protected land. Control of introduced predators has stemmed population declines in the endangered Red-tailed phascogale, and provides hope that it would protect other threatened species if implemented at a broad scale. CRD

A Once-in-a-Lifetime Breeding Opportunity

Sex and Death in the Antechinus

Many mammals go to great lengths for sex, but the prize for personal sacrifice has to go to those mammals that reproduce only once in a lifetime, exhausting their own bodies to fuel their reproductive urges. It is the sensible strategy of most mammals to start their reproductive lives with caution, rarely having their largest litter or fattest babies at the first attempt; at least initially, reproductive ability improves with age. In certain species, however, some individuals put all their eggs in one basket. An Alpine vole that has survived the winter often produces only a single litter before it dies, and it will be the offspring of such voles that continue reproduction throughout the spring and summer. And in two groups of carnivorous marsupials, the Australian dasyurids and the American didelphids (opossums), all individuals of certain species commit themselves totally to reproduction at their first attempt. In these species, all the females come into estrus at the same time, once a year. After that all the males die, sometimes over a period of just three or four days. Indeed, all the males can be dead before the females have even ovulated. While the females live on to give birth and suckle their young, they also usually die after rearing only a single litter.

When organisms reproduce only once in their lifetime they are known as semelparous, in contrast to iteroparous organisms, which reproduce repeatedly. The former strategy is a strange and rarified phenomenon. True semelparity appears to have evolved at least twice in didelphids and five times among dasyurids, yet nowhere else among mammals or birds. The species involved range from the well-studied antechinuses, weighing a mere 20g (0.7oz), through the beautiful phascogales to the cat-sized Northern quoll.

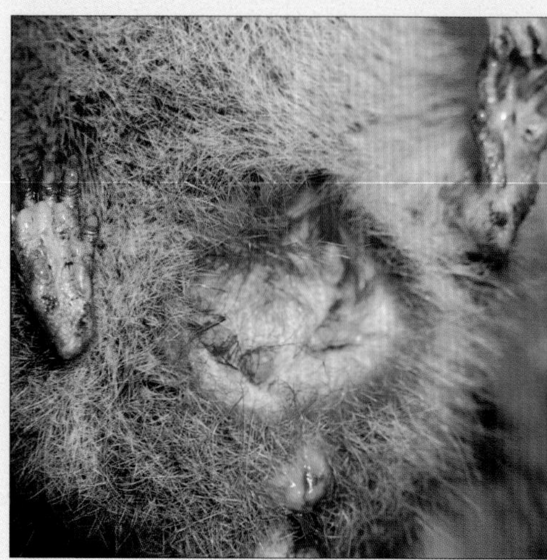

Above *Some species of antechinuses – in this case a Swamp antechinus* (Antechinus minimus) *– lack a pouch as such; instead they have a patch of bare skin from which the mammae or teats protrude.*

Below *Raising litters of as many as ten young places a huge strain on the resources of a female antechinus. To ensure that she can produce enough milk to feed her offspring, the reproductive cycle is timed so that lactation coincides with the period of maximum prey availability, when she is well-fed.*

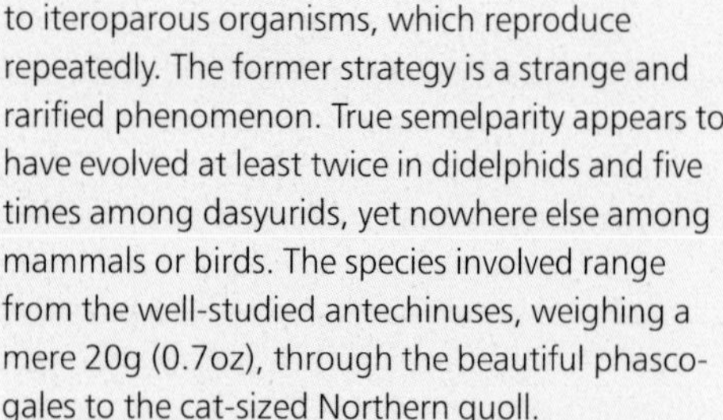

Semelparity only occurs in predictable, highly seasonable environments, and it has its "raison d'être" in the excruciatingly slow reproduction rate of small marsupials. The most famous of the semelparous marsupials, *Antechinus stuartii*, has a four-week pregnancy, at the end of which it gives birth to young weighing only 16mg. The young are deposited in the shallow pouch, where their tiny bodies are unwound by a special swelling on their chest that allows them to attach to a teat, where they continue to develop. After a further 5 weeks of suckling, they have grown to a length of about 1cm (0.4in). They are not weaned until they are 14 weeks of age or more.

Because the mother may be suckling as many as ten young, her metabolic rate in late lactation can be ten to twelve times the basal rate – a mammalian record. Female reproduction is therefore timed to ensure that late lactation coincides with the period of maximum availability of the insect and spider prey on which the species feeds, which falls in late spring or early summer. Females must therefore get pregnant in the winter, when there is little food to eat. But males are put through a further test of endurance by having to congregate in special mating trees where the females come to mate. During the short rut, as many as twenty males may aggregate in the tree cavity, where they are visited by the females.

Males face a threefold dilemma. They have to mate in winter, and at a communal nest as much as 1km (0.6mi) from their own home range; and if they do try to feed at this time, they run the risk of missing the all-important visits by receptive females. It is now that the adaptive advantage of dying becomes apparent. Males resolve the challenge confronting them by exhibiting in an extreme form the stress response mounted by all mammals when presented with an external challenge, or stressor. This response involves the secretion of corticosteroids, of which cortisol is the most potent form in mammals. Cortisol suppresses appetite and promotes gluconeogenesis, the conversion of protein into sugars, which means that reserves other than rapidly-consumed fat can be used to sustain the body during a crisis. Nonetheless, the stress response is a two-edged

Left *A female antechinus returns to her litter of eight-week-old young in the hollow of a tree. Naked and helpless, they will be dependent on their mother's milk until they are weaned at 14 weeks or more.*

weapon. In addition to the benefits it brings, cortisol suppresses the immune and inflammatory responses, exposing stressed animals to a greater risk of disease. In most organisms this eventuality is prevented by corticosteroid-binding globulins that render some of the cortisol inactive, and by negative feedback in the brain that stops cortisol production. Semelparous marsupials, in a suicidal twist, radically reduce the level of binding globulins just as the breeding season starts, and the negative feedback cycle is turned off. As a consequence, males can digest and feed off their own bodies from within, but at the cost of condemning themselves to the most miserable of deaths. The commonest source of mortality is a massive hemorrhage of ulcers in the stomach and intestine, but parasites and other microorganisms that ordinarily have no effect can also often become pathogenic once the immune system fails. Females live on after the males have died, but they need to survive for another 16 months in order to successfully wean a second litter, and they often fail to do so.

This paradoxical solution to the stresses of mating has been arrived at evolutionarily by other organisms that also have to mate in a hostile environment, such as freshwater eels that migrate to the sea to breed or salmon that live in the ocean but spawn in fresh water. They use exactly the same hormonal system to sustain their migration, and they pay a similar price.

The curious life history of these small marsupials is fascinating in its own right, but the extremely simple population structure, producing individuals of identical ages, also provides a unique insight into other intriguing questions affecting mammalian society as a whole. In many mammals, juvenile males disperse, while females remain in the area where they were born. This behavior has been attributed to competition between fathers and sons for mating opportunities. But an alternative explanation, probably relating to incest avoidance, needs to be found for male-biased dispersal in the case of semelparous marsupials. They show extreme male bias in natal dispersal; females continue to live with their mothers after weaning, but all males leave, sometimes traveling many kilometers to a new home-range – and this despite the fact that in these species fathers are dead long before their sons are born. AC

Bandicoots

Bandicoots are ratlike marsupials, agile, with long noses and tails. They share a common name and ancestry with the rabbit-eared bandicoots or bilbies, a smaller group adapted for arid environments, and distinguished not just by their long ears, longer limbs, and silkier hair but also by their burrowing habit. One of the two bilby species is now thought extinct, and the other is threatened.

Bandicoots are notable for having one of the highest reproductive rates among marsupials, exceeded only by that of a single species of dunnart (family Dasyuridae). In this respect, they resemble the rodents in the placental world; like theirs, their life-cycles centre on producing many young with little maternal care. Otherwise, these small insectivores and omnivores fit into an ecological niche similar to that of the shrews and hedgehogs.

Short Necks and Pointed Muzzles

FORM AND FUNCTION

Most bandicoots are rabbit-sized or smaller, have short limbs, a long, pointed muzzle, and a thickset body with a short neck. The ears are normally short, the forefeet have three toes with strong, flattish claws, and the pouch opens backwards. The furthest from this pattern is the recently extinct Pig-footed bandicoot, which had developed longer limbs and hooflike front feet as adaptations to a more cursorial life on open plains. The long-nosed bandicoots of the genus *Perameles* also have longer ears than the other species, but the longest of all are found on the bilbies. Teeth are small and relatively even-sized, and have pointed cusps. Most bandicoots are omnivorous, characteristically obtaining their food from the ground by excavating small, conical pits.

Bandicoots are distinguished from all other marsupials by having fused (syndactylous) toes on the hind feet, forming a comb for grooming, and polyprodont dentition (with more than two well-developed lower incisors). The rear-opening pouch normally has eight teats. It extends forward along the abdomen as the young enlarge, eventually occupying most of the mother's underside, and then contracts again after they have departed. Litter size is normally 2–3.

Bandicoots' sense of smell is well developed. The animals are nocturnal and their eyes are adapted for night vision, although their binocular vision may be limited, perhaps because the elongated nose gets in the way. The Long-nosed bandicoot produces a sharp, squeaky alarm call when disturbed at night, and bandicoots are also sometimes heard to sneeze loudly, probably to clear soil from their noses. They rarely if ever produce loud calls, but a very low, sibilant "huffing" with bared teeth is uttered as a threat by some species.

The dental formula is I5/3, C1/1, P3/3, M4/4 = 48, except in spiny bandicoots, which have four pairs of upper incisors (I4/3). Sexual dimorphism occurs in most species; in some, males may be up to 60 percent heavier and 15 percent longer than females. Males usually have larger canines.

The classification of bandicoots is not fully resolved, although all genera seem to be clearly defined. Currently two families are recognized, one of which (the Peramelidae) contains two distinct subfamilies (see box). Taxonomic relationships within the brown bandicoots and other groups and the taxonomy of most New Guinea forms warrants further study.

Brown bandicoots are stocky, short-eared, plain-colored animals. They inhabit areas of close ground cover, tall grass, or low shrubbery. The Southern brown bandicoot favors heathland, whereas the Northern brown bandicoot occurs in a wide range of habitats from wet forests to open woodland. All have inflated auditory bullae. Dwarfed forms occur, particularly on islands and in more open areas, perhaps as a result of scarcer food resources. Variations in the angle of the ascending rear portion of the lower jaw, and the presence of an extra cusp on the last upper molar, have been used to differentiate between species, but the taxonomy is not satisfactorily understood. The distribution of Southern brown bandicoots does not overlap that of the northern species, except for a single instance. There is, however, overlap between Northern brown bandicoots and the Golden bandicoot.

The long-nosed bandicoots are more lightly built, with a relatively longer skull, small auditory bullae, longer ears, and a preference for areas of open ground cover, although habitat use may be flexible; some species also exhibit barred body markings. The arid-zone species have a wide distribution, from Western Australia to western New South Wales; in contrast, the Long-nosed bandicoot itself is restricted to the eastern coastal areas, and the Eastern barred bandicoot to grasslands and grassy woodlands of the southeast mainland and Tasmania. Important variables between species are ear length and the size of the bullae, which both increase in arid areas, and the positioning of toes on the hind feet. In addition, different species exhibit varying degrees of barring, which is absent in the forest species but conspicuous in grassland species.

Bilbies have lengthened ears, long, narrow rostra, and elongated limbs; other distinctive features include highly developed auditory bullae with twin chambers, long, silky fur, and a long, crested tail. The only burrowing bandicoots, they are an early offshoot from the main bandicoot stock that has become highly specialized for arid areas. Species and populations are differentiated principally by size, coat, and tail coloration, and also by the dimensions of the bullae, which were larger in the Lesser bilby, now thought to be extinct.

The several New Guinea genera (the Peroryctidae) are poorly known. They tend to be little-modified, short-eared, forest bandicoots. The skulls are more cylindrical than in the peramelids, and in the spiny bandicoots and the Seram Island bandicoot the rostrum is long and narrow. The auditory bullae are small. Spiny bandicoots have short tails.

Above The Greater bilby, seen here suckling its young, is a desert species. It now has a much-reduced distribution. Habitat loss and predation have severely reduced its numbers and it is listed as Vulnerable.

Below Behavioral postures of the Northern brown bandicoot. It is nocturnal and frequently sniffs the air **1** to detect any danger. The usual gait is on all fours, but the larger hind limbs are used in an aggressive hop **2** characteristic of males. **3** The Northern brown bandicoot digs out food with its strong fore claws. After the shortest gestation of perhaps any mammal, the newborn young crawl into their mother's rear-opening pouch **4** where they are carried for seven weeks, by which time **5** the pouch is bulging.

FACTFILE

BANDICOOTS

Order: Peramelemorphia

Families: Peramelidae and Peroryctidae

18 extant species in 7 genera

DISTRIBUTION Australia, Papua New Guinea, West Irian

HABITAT All major habitats in Australia and New Guinea from desert to rain forest, including semi-urban areas.

SIZE **Head–body length** ranges from 17–26.5cm (7–10in) in the mouse bandicoots to 50–60cm (20–23in) in the Giant bandicoot; **tail length** from 11–12cm (4.5in) to 15–20cm (6–8in), and **weight** from 140–185g (5–6.5oz) up to 4.8kg (10.5lb), both in the same species. Males of larger species may be up to 50 percent heavier than females.

COAT Mostly short and coarse in bandicoots (stiff and spiny in some New Guinean species); longer and silkier in the Greater bilby.

DIET Insects and other invertebrates, bulbs, roots, tubers.

BREEDING Gestation 12.5 days in the Long-nosed, Eastern Barred, and Northern Brown bandicoots, 14 days in the Greater bilby.

LONGEVITY About 2–3 years in the Eastern barred, and slightly more in the Northern brown bandicoot.

CONSERVATION STATUS Two bandicoot species – the Pig-footed (*Chaeropus ecaudatus*) and the Desert (*Perameles eremiana*) – have recently been declared Extinct, as has the Lesser bilby (*Macrotis leucura*). Several other species are also at risk; the Western barred bandicoot (*Perameles bougainville*) is listed as Endangered, and three other species are Vulnerable, including the Greater bilby (*Macrotis lagotis*). Little is known about the status of many New Guinea bandicoots; some species have only been collected on one or two occasions.

See families box ▷

Above *The Southern brown bandicoot only overlaps with the Northern form in an anomalous population in the Cape York peninsula of northern Australia.*

Bandicoot Families

Family Peramelidae

Subfamily Peramelinae

Long-nosed bandicoots Genus *Perameles*
3 species: Western barred bandicoot (*P. bougainville*); Eastern barred bandicoot (*P. gunnii*); Long-nosed bandicoot (*P. nasuta*). The Desert bandicoot (*P. eremiana*) is now listed as extinct by the IUCN.
Short-nosed or **Brown bandicoots** Genus *Isoodon*
3 species: Golden bandicoot (*I. auratus*); Northern brown bandicoot (*I. macrourus*); Southern brown bandicoot (*I. obesulus*).
Pig-footed bandicoot (*Chaeropus ecaudatus*) is listed in Appendix 1 of CITES, but is now considered extinct by the IUCN.

Subfamily Thylacomyinae

Rabbit-eared bandicoot or **Bilby** Genus *Macrotis*.
Greater bilby (*M. lagotis*). The Lesser bilby (*M. leucura*) is listed in Appendix 1 of CITES, but is now considered extinct by the IUCN.

Family Peroryctidae

New Guinea bandicoots Genus *Peroryctes*
2 species: Giant bandicoot (*P. broadbenti*); Raffray's bandicoot (*P. raffrayana*).
New Guinean mouse bandicoots Genus *Microperoryctes* 3 species: Mouse bandicoot (*M. murina*); Striped bandicoot (*M. longicauda*); Papuan bandicoot (*M. papuensis*).
Spiny bandicoots Genus *Echymipera*
5 species: Rufous spiny bandicoot (*E. rufescens*); Clara's echymipera (*E. clara*); Menzie's echymipera (*E. echinista*); Common echymipera (*E. kalubu*); David's echymipera (*E. davidi*).
Seram Island bandicoot *Rhynchomeles prattorum*

Habitat Specialists

DISTRIBUTION PATTERNS

In recent (Pleistocene) times, bandicoots have to a large extent evolved separately in Australia and New Guinea, as a result both of the intermittent separation of the two land masses and of the marked habitat differences. All but one of the New Guinea genera are endemic; only the Rufous spiny bandicoot extends its range into northern Australia. Conversely, only one Australian species, the Northern brown bandicoot, intrudes into the grassy woodlands of southern New Guinea. This suggests that the main influence of the two land masses on the different bandicoot fauna is habitat, not just the water barrier.

Within New Guinea, different species occur at different altitudes. The Northern brown, Giant, and most species of spiny bandicoots are lowland animals, but some range up to about 2,000m (6,500ft). The Mouse, Striped, and Raffray's bandicoots are all highland species, generally found above 1,000m (3,500ft). The Seram Island bandicoot is only known from high altitudes, at about 1,800m (6,000ft).

Within Australia, there are pronounced climatic influences on the distribution of species, which tend to fall into two groups. Species restricted to semi-arid and arid areas have suffered large population declines since European settlement, and three (the Desert and Pig-footed bandicoots and the Lesser bilby) are now probably extinct. The survivors include the Western Barred and Golden Bandicoots and the Greater bilby.

This pattern is an effect, whether direct or indirect, of rainfall. The Northern brown bandicoot, a coastal species of eastern and northern Australia, is widely distributed as far inland as the 72.5cm (28.5in) isohyet (rainfall line). Beyond this it tends to be largely confined to watercourses, which extend its range much farther inland, almost to the 60cm (23.6in) isohyet. Southern brown bandicoots are more confined to the coast (except in Tasmania), and the Long-nosed bandicoot extends inland beyond the Great Dividing Range only in northeastern Victoria.

Opportunistic and Omnivorous

DIET

Although bandicoots are dentally specialized for feeding on invertebrates, feeding is opportunistic and omnivorous and includes insects, other invertebrates, fruits, seeds of non-woody plants, subterranean fungi, and occasional plant fiber. Diet can also include a high proportion of surface food, and it is likely that bandicoots switch to other food when insects are unavailable. They locate food in the ground by scent and then dig it out with their strong fore claws. The elongated muzzle is presumably used to probe into holes for food.

The Northern brown bandicoot has a characteristic foraging pattern, moving slowly over its whole range. This is an adaptation for finding food that occurs as small, scattered items rather than being concentrated in a few areas. The Eastern barred bandicoot concentrates on areas of increased soil moisture and vegetation diversity, where food species are both more abundant and more readily excavated.

Fast Breeders

SOCIAL BEHAVIOR

Most species are solitary, animals coming together only to mate, and there appears to be no lasting attachment between mother and young. Males are usually larger than females and socially dominant. Dominance between closely-matched males may be established by chases or, rarely, by fights, in which the males approach each other standing on their hind legs.

Male home ranges are larger than females'; for the Northern brown bandicoot 1.7–5.2ha (4.2–12.8 acres) in one study, compared to 0.9–2.1ha (2.2–5.2 acres) for females. Similar values were found for the Eastern barred bandicoot, although these relate to core ranges not entire foraging area. The ranges of both sexes overlap extensively, although core areas may not. Females often dictate local distribution, selecting and perhaps defending high-quality nesting and foraging sites. Males patrol most of the home range each night, perhaps to detect other males or receptive females. In male-biased populations, many males may repeatedly mate with a single female.

Captive Northern brown bandicoots showed intense interest in nests, which consist for them of heaps of raked-up groundlitter with an internal chamber, and dominant males commonly evicted others from them. Nests may therefore be a significant focus of social interactions in the wild in that species. Eastern barred bandicoots make several types of nest, the most complex being a lined, roofed excavation used when females have young. Many species have scent glands present behind the ears; the Northern brown bandicoot uses this gland, which is present in both sexes, to mark the ground or vegetation during aggressive encounters between males. The high reproductive rate of bandicoots means that they are able to recolonize rapidly as habitat recovers from fire or drought.

The reproductive biology of Australian bandicoots has been studied in some detail and is well exemplified by the Northern brown species. The young are gestated for only 12.5 days, less than half the length of time taken by most other marsupials and almost the shortest of any mammal. Development of the embryo is aided by a form of chorioallantoic placentation that is unique to bandicoots among marsupials, in that it resembles the placenta of eutherian mammals. Other marsupials form only a yolksac placenta, whereas bandicoots and eutherians have independently evolved both types of placentation.

At birth the young are about 1cm (0.4in) long and weigh about 0.2g (0.007oz), with well-developed forelimbs. The allantoic stalk anchors the young to the mother whilst the newborn crawls to the pouch, where it attaches to a nipple. The young leave the pouch after 49–50 days and are weaned about 10 days later. In good conditions, sexual maturity may occur at about 90 days, although it is normally attained much later. Females are polyestrous and breed throughout the year in suitable climates; in other conditions they breed seasonally. Mating can occur when the previous litter is near the end of its pouch life. Since the gestation is 12.5 days, the new litter is born at about the time of weaning of the earlier litter. Captive females may have 4–5 litters per year, and may therefore produce about 18 young in a lifetime; in the wild this figure is probably halved. In captivity only about 40 percent of young reach sexual maturity, while in wild populations the survival rate is as low as 11.5 percent, so, despite the high fecundity, recruitment is low.

The reproductive cycle is one of the most distinctive characteristics of bandicoots, setting them apart from all other marsupials. They have become uniquely specialized for a high reproductive rate and reduced parental care. In most bandicoots, this is achieved by accelerated gestation, rapid development of young in the pouch, early sexual maturity, and a rapid succession of litters in the polyestrous females. Female Eastern barred bandicoots may become sexually mature at less than 4 months and, given normal climatic conditions, continue to breed throughout the year for up to 3 years. In one Northern brown bandicoot population with breeding seasons stretching over 6–8-months, females produced an average of 6.4 surviving young in one season, and 9.6 in the next. Litter size, however, while higher than in many marsupial groups, is not exceptional, being smaller than in others, such as dasyurids.

Below *The Eastern barred bandicoot is virtually extinct on mainland Australia, being restricted to a tiny remnant population.*

Above *Young spiny bandicoots* (Echymipera *spp.*) *alone in a nest. Bandicoots expend little effort on parental care, relying instead on a high birth rate.*

Under Threat of Extinction

CONSERVATION AND ENVIRONMENT

Australian bandicoots have suffered one of the greatest declines of all marsupial groups. All species of the semi-arid and arid zones have suffered massive declines or even become extinct; the survivors are reduced now to a few remnant populations that are still endangered. An important feature of most of the extinctions seems to be grazing by cattle, sheep, or rabbits, and the consequent changes in the nature of ground cover. Some authorities blame introduced predators. Removal of sheep and cattle is an important conservation measure in these areas.

Only a few species that occur in higher rainfall zones, including the Long-nosed and the Northern and Southern brown Bandicoots, can be considered secure, although all have been affected by European settlement. Even these "common" species are under threat of habitat alteration or alienation. For example, the Long-nosed bandicoots have become all but extinct in Sydney, and the same is true of Southern brown bandicoots in the Melbourne metropolitan area.

Conservation of the Eastern barred bandicoot depends on an ongoing reintroduction program, in which captive-bred animals have been released to several protected sites in their former range. Success has been variable, with predation by the introduced Red fox and habitat degradation by grazing herbivores, whether native (kangaroos) or introduced (rabbits), being constraining factors. Control management of these issues is required on a continuing basis, but after more than 10 years of effort some of the reintroduced populations have become successfully established. While the species is more common in Tasmania, the population there is also declining. GG/JHS

Cuscuses and Brushtail Possums

DWELLING IN THE REMOTE OUTBACK AS well as in the suburbs of most Australian cities, the Common brushtail possum is perhaps the most frequently encountered of all Australian mammals and is the most studied of the possums. But most of the remaining 19 phalangerid species are relatively unknown to science, either because of their cryptic behavior in dense rain forest or their restricted distributions; for example, the Telefomin cuscus, from the highlands of central New Guinea, is known from only five museum specimens.*

The phalangerids are generally nocturnal, the outstanding exception being the Bear cuscus of Sulawesi (*Ailurops ursinus*), which is the only one with circular pupils, a possible adaptation to diurnal living. The animals are usually arboreal; even the Ground cuscus and Scaly-tailed possum, which habitually rest by day in holes in the ground, spend the night in trees. Cuscuses and possums are careful and deliberate climbers, not given to spectacular leaps; among the adaptations that help them are curved and sharply pointed fore claws, as well as clawless but opposable first hind toes that aid in grasping branches, and prehensile tails with variable amounts of bare skin. Phalangers possess well-developed, forward-opening pouches.

Native Australians

EVOLUTION AND RADIATION

Phalangerids originated in the rain forests of what is now mainland Australia. The earliest fossils of modern genera – *Trichosurus*, *Wyulda*, and *Strigocuscus* – were found in the Miocene rocks of Riversleigh, northern Australia, and date from some 20 million years before the present. *Trichosurus* and *Strigocuscus* were also present in the early Pliocene of southern Australia about 5 million years ago. The genera *Ailurops*, *Phalanger*, and *Spilocuscus* have not appeared in the Australian fossil record and may have originated in New Guinea, possibly from the ancestral phalangerid stock closest to *Ailurops* at a time when New Guinea was connected to Australia during the Miocene or earlier.

Most phalangerid genera, even in the fossil record, are made up of between 1 and 4 species, the only exception being *Phalanger* itself, which numbers 10 species. The stimulus for *Phalanger*'s proliferation was provided by the geographical isolation of its populations, either on islands or on remote mountain ranges in New Guinea, where it is the only genus occurring above 1,200m (4,000ft). *Strigocuscus* is now extinct in Australia, but it has been replaced by two other cuscus genera, the Southern common (*Phalanger intercastellanus*) and Spotted (*Spilocuscus maculatus*) cuscuses. Both are common lowland species in New Guinea that entered Australia less than 2 million years ago over the land bridge that linked the two landmasses during the Pleistocene.

Common and Uncommon

DISTRIBUTION PATTERNS

The Common brushtail possum has the widest distribution of all phalangerids, covering most of Australia in a wide range of habitats from rain forests to semi-arid areas; four subspecies are currently recognized. In temperate Tasmania individuals have thick coats and bushy tails and weigh up to 4.5kg (9.9lb), but there is a general decline in size towards the tropics, with individuals across northern Australia attaining no more than 1.8kg (4lb), having thin coats and little bush to the tail. The predominant color is light gray, but in wetter habitats darker colors are common – black in Tasmania, dark red in northeastern Queensland. The Common brushtail possum's congener, the Mountain brushtail, is geographically much more restricted and not split into subspecies. These possums occupy dense, wet forests in southeastern Australia that are not usually inhabited by the Common brushtail.

Cuscuses are rainforest dwellers, and species often have restricted geographical ranges, either confined to islands or to the highlands of mountain ranges. Most widespread is the Spotted cuscus, found in a wide range of rainforest habitats throughout New Guinea below an elevation of 1,200m (4,000ft), and also on many islands and on Australia's northeastern tip; this species seems able to persist near large centers of human population. Four geographically isolated subspecies are

FACTFILE

CUSCUSES AND BRUSHTAIL POSSUMS

Order: Diprotodontia

Family: Phalangeridae

20 species in 6 genera

DISTRIBUTION Australia, New Guinea, and adjacent islands W to Sulawesi and E to the Solomon Islands. Common brushtail possum introduced to New Zealand; Common and Spotted cuscuses introduced to many of the islands adjacent to New Guinea.

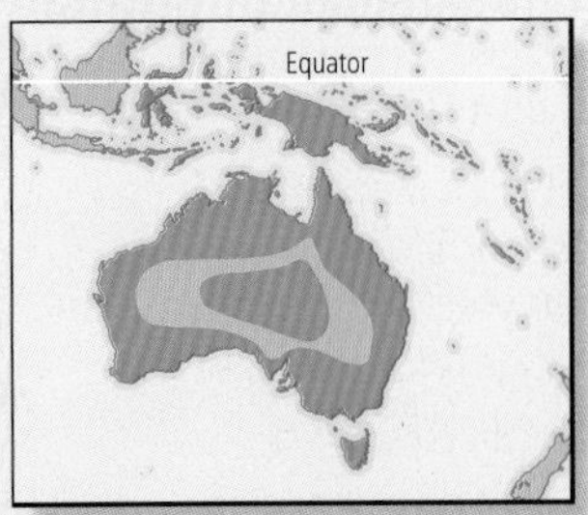

HABITAT All types of forest and woodland: rain forest, moss forest, mangrove, tropical, and temperate eucalypt forest and woodland, arid and alpine woodland.

SIZE Head–body length ranges from 34cm (13.4in) in the Small Sulawesi cuscus to 61cm (24in) in the Bear cuscus; tail length from 34cm (13.4in) to 58cm (22.8in), and weight from about 0.9kg (2lb) to 10kg (22lb), both in the same two species.

COAT Short, dense, gray (Scaly-tailed possum); long, woolly, gray–black (brushtail possums); long, dense, white–black or reddish brown, some species with spots or dorsal stripes (cuscuses).

DIET Leaves, flowers, fruits, seeds, shoots, insects, occasionally small vertebrates and birds' eggs.

BREEDING Gestation lasts 16–17 days in brushtail possums

LONGEVITY Up to 13 years (17 or more in captivity)

CONSERVATION STATUS The Telefomin and Black-spotted cuscuses are currently listed as Endangered, and the Obi and Silky cuscuses as Vulnerable. Three other cuscus and possum species are ranked Lower Risk: Near Threatened.

See species box ▷

Above *Brushtail possum and cuscus species:* ***1*** *the Gray or Northern common cuscus* (Phalanger orientalis) *lives in New Guinea;* ***2*** *Spotted cuscus* (Spilocuscus maculatus)*;* ***3*** *the Scaly-tailed possum* (Wyulda squamicaudata) *– only discovered in 1917;* ***4*** *Common brushtail possum* (Trichosurus vulpecula).

currently recognized, and they exhibit considerable variation in color and size. The Spotted cuscus is remarkable in that there is a distinct color dimorphism between males and females: the males have large, irregular, chocolate-brown spots on a creamy white background, whereas the females lack the spots – indeed, in one subspecies they are pure white. Two other members of the genus, the Admiralty and Black-spotted cuscuses, are the only other phalangers with color dimorphism of the sexes.

The Scaly-tailed possum inhabits very rugged, rocky country, with eucalypt forest and rainforest patches, in the remote Kimberley region of northwestern Australia. The last two-thirds of its tail is naked, prehensile, and rasplike, while the hands and feet have greatly enlarged apical pads as an adaptation to life among the rocks.

Of the nine mainland New Guinea cuscuses, the geographical ranges of some species overlap, whereas others fall within more or less exclusive (allopatric) altitudinal zones. These allopatric species all belong to the genus *Phalanger*, are very similar in body size (2.4–3.5kg/ 5.3–7.7lb) and habits, and are apparently unable to coexist. The restriction of Stein's cuscus, for example, to only a narrow altitudinal band of 1,200–1,500m (about 4,000–5,000ft), has been attributed to competition from the Northern and Southern common cuscuses, which occur abundantly below 1,200m (4,000ft), and the Mountain and Silky cuscuses, which occur at altitudes above 1,400m (4,600ft). In localities where the two highland species are absent, Stein's cuscus has been found up to 2,200m (7,200ft).

Where two species do overlap, they usually differ in size or habits. The Ground cuscus, of the genus *Phalanger*, has the widest altitudinal range of all cuscuses, being found from sea level to 2,700m (8,900ft). It is heavier (at 4.8kg /7.0lb) than its congeners, is less arboreal, and has a more frugivorous diet.

Both species of *Spilocuscus* found on the mainland of New Guinea – the Spotted cuscus (6.0kg/8.2lb) and the Black-spotted cuscus (6.6kg/8.8lb) – are heavier than the members of the genus *Phalanger*. They are confined to low altitudes below 1,200m (4,000ft), and cohabit with

Left A Mountain brushtail possum feeding on eucalyptus leaves. This species is both nocturnal and arboreal and nests in tree hollows; the main elements of its diet are leaves, flowers, and young shoots.

Right A white form of the Spotted cuscus. Mainly inhabiting rain forest, it is active at night and tree-dwelling; the diet of the Spotted cuscus comprises leaves, fruit, and flowers.

Cuscuses and Brushtail Possums

Cuscuses
4 genera, 17 species

Cuscuses Genus *Phalanger* 10 species: Mountain cuscus (*P. carmelitae*), Ground cuscus (*P. gymnotis*, formerly in *Strigocuscus*), Southern common cuscus (*P. intercastellanus*, formerly in *P. orientalis*), Woodlark cuscus (*P. lullulae*), Telefomin cuscus (*P. matanim*), Gray cuscus or Northern common cuscus (*P. orientalis*), Ornate cuscus (*P. ornatus*), Obi cuscus (*P. rothschildi*), Silky cuscus (*P. sericeus*), Stein's cuscus (*P. vestitus*)
Spotted cuscuses Genus *Spilocuscus* 4 species: Admiralty cuscus (*S. kraemeri*, formerly subspecies of *S. maculatus*), Spotted cuscus (*S. maculatus*); Waigeou cuscus (*S. papuensis*, formerly subspecies of *S. maculatus*), Black-spotted cuscus (*S. rufoniger*)
Plain cuscuses Genus *Strigocuscus* 2 species: Small Sulawesi cuscus (*S. celebensis*), Peleng cuscus (*S. pelengensis* formerly in *Phalanger*)
Bear cuscus (*Ailurops ursinus*)

Brushtail possums
2 genera, 3 species

Brushtail possums Genus *Trichosurus* 2 species: Common brushtail possum (*T. vulpecula*), Mountain brushtail possum (*T. caninus*)
Scaly-tailed possum (*Wyulda squamicaudata*)

both the Ground cuscus and one or other of the common cuscuses. The two *Spilocuscus* species may sometimes be found in the same districts; however, the Black-spotted cuscus inhabits primary forest only, whereas the Spotted cuscus lives in a much broader range of habitats, including secondary forest.

Living Off Leaves

DIET

Most species are nonspecialist leaf-eaters, but their relatively generalized dentition allows them to consume a wide range of foods – fruit or blossom, along with the occasional invertebrate, egg, or small vertebrate. The Common brushtail possum's diet reflects its wide geographical distribution; in some areas up to 95 percent consists of eucalypt leaves, but usually a mix of tree species leaves is taken. In tropical woodland up to 53 percent of the diet may be made up of leaves of the Cooktown ironwood, which are extremely toxic to domestic stock such as cattle. In habitat modified for pasture up to 60 percent of its diet is pasture species, while in suburban gardens it has developed an unwelcome taste for rose buds. The brushtail relies on hindgut microbial activity to extract nutrients from its food, and the large cecum and proximal colon enable food to be retained for relatively long periods. Some cuscuses show evidence of particle-sorting in the cecum, which suggests that they have a more specialized leaf diet than the brushtail.

The Ground cuscus is the most frugivorous phalangerid, with up to 90 percent fruit in the diet of captive animals. Its highly expandable stomach, well-developed pyloric sphincter, and long small intestine are all consistent with delaying the passage of food through the foregut to enable the digestion of lipids from the high fruit diet. Female Ground cuscuses have even been reported to carry fruit back to the den in their pouches by local New Guineans.

A Scent-based Bush Telegraph

SOCIAL BEHAVIOR

Phalangerids are generally solitary, but with a well-organized spatial system based primarily on olfactory communication. The Common brushtail possum actively uses four scent glands. Males, and to a lesser extent females, wipe secretions from mouth and chest glands on the branches and twigs of trees, especially den trees, and deposit sinuous urine trails, containing cells from a pair of paracloacal glands, on branches. These advertise both the presence and the status of the marker to other individuals. When a possum is distressed it produces a sticky, pungent secretion from a second pair of paracloacal glands; this is possibly used as an appeasement signal by low-status individuals. Estrous females produce a copious, gelatinous secretion from the cloaca that becomes smeared on branches and may advertise their readiness to mate.

Little is known about scentmarking in cuscuses and the Scaly-tailed possum, but the sternal and paracloacal glands are generally present, and males of the Spotted cuscus smear the sticky secretion from the paracloacal glands on branches. When distressed, the Spotted cuscus secretes a red–brown substance on the bare skin of its face, particularly round the eyes.

Brushtail possums are one of the most vocal of marsupial genera, and many of their calls are audible to humans at up to 300m (1,000ft). They have about seven basic calls: buccal clicks, agonistic grunts, hisses, loud screeches, alarm chatters, very soft appeasement calls given by the male, and juvenile contact calls; a cartilaginous laryngeal resonance chamber, about the size of a pea and unique to the genus, presumably enhances the repertoire. Cuscuses and the Scaly-tailed possum are not noted for their vocal repertoire, although

buccal clicks, hisses, grunts, and screeches are reported, and the female Spotted cuscus has a call, when in estrus, like the bray of a donkey.

Common brushtails are generally solitary, except when they are breeding and rearing young. By the end of their third or fourth year, individuals establish small exclusive areas centered on one or two den trees within their home ranges, which they defend against individuals of the same sex and social status. Individuals of the opposite sex or lower social status are tolerated within the exclusive areas. Even though the home ranges of males (3–8ha/7.5–20 acres) may completely overlap the ranges of females (1–5ha/2.5–12.4 acres), individuals almost always nest alone, and overt interactions are rare. Territoriality appears to break down in some tropical populations, because Aboriginal hunters may extract up to six individuals from the same hollow tree.

Females defend an individual distance of 1m (3.3ft) against the approach of a male. During courtship a consort male overcomes the female's aggression by repeatedly approaching her and giving soft appeasement calls, similar to those of juveniles. In the absence of a consort male, several males may converge on a female at the time of estrus, and mating is accompanied by considerable agonistic behavior. After mating, the male takes no further interest in the female and is not involved in the raising of the young.

Defence of den trees suggests that preferred nest sites are in short supply. Because few offspring (only 15 percent) die before weaning, relatively large numbers of independent young enter the population each year. These young use small, poor-quality dens, and up to 80 percent of males and 50 percent of females die or disperse within their first year.

Females begin to breed at 1 year and produce 1–2 young annually after a gestation period of 16–18 days. In temperate and subtropical Australian populations, 90 percent of females breed in the fall (March–May), but up to 50 percent may also breed in spring (September–November). In the less seasonal tropics, breeding appears to be continuous, with no seasonal peak of births. Only one young is born at a time, and the annual reproductive rate of females averages 1.4. Population density varies with habitat, from 0.4 animals per hectare (1 per acre) in open forest and woodland to 1.4 per ha (3.5/acre) in suburban gardens and 2.1 per ha (5.2/acre) in grazed open forest.

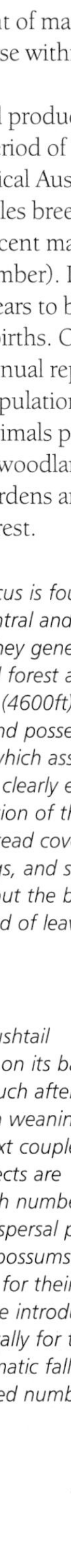

Right *The Silky cuscus is found in the mountains of central and eastern New Guinea; they generally inhabit areas of tropical forest at altitudes above 1400m (4600ft). They are heavily built and possess a strong prehensile tail, which assists them in the trees. As is clearly evident here, the end portion of the tail lacks hair and is instead covered with scales. Insects, eggs, and small vertebrates are eaten, but the bulk of their diet is composed of leaves and fruits.*

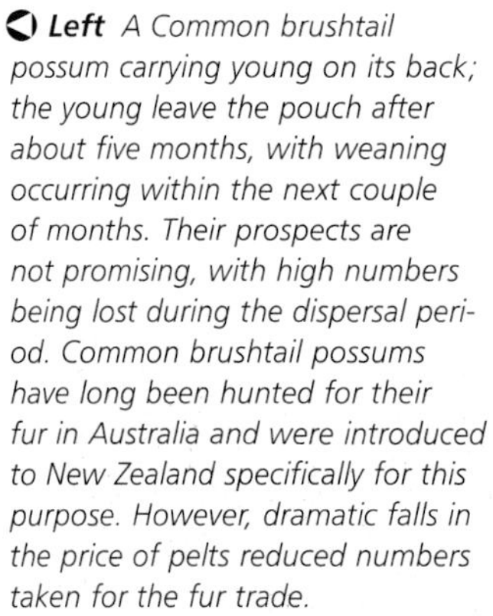

Left *A Common brushtail possum carrying young on its back; the young leave the pouch after about five months, with weaning occurring within the next couple of months. Their prospects are not promising, with high numbers being lost during the dispersal period. Common brushtail possums have long been hunted for their fur in Australia and were introduced to New Zealand specifically for this purpose. However, dramatic falls in the price of pelts reduced numbers taken for the fur trade.*

The Mountain brushtail has a different strategy, associated to a more stable habitat. Far from being solitary, males and females appear to form long-term pair-bonds. In this species, mortality among the young is greatest before weaning (56 percent); about 80 percent survive each year after becoming independent. Females begin to breed at 2–3 years, produce at most only one young in the fall of each year, and reproduce at an annual rate as low as 0.73. The young are weaned at 8 months, as opposed to 6 for the Common Brushtail, and they disperse at 18–36 months (7–18 for the Common brushtail). Population density is 0.4–1.8 per hectare (1–4.5/acre).

The Scaly-tailed possum bears a single young, and its social strategy is closer to that of the Common brushtail possum. Little is known about the pair relationship in cuscuses, but in the Ground cuscus the male follows the female prior to mating and attempts to sniff her head, flanks, and cloaca; he may also utter soft, short clicks. The only

in Victoria and New South Wales, while in Queensland it frequently raids banana and pecan crops. The Common brushtail also damages pines, and in Tasmania is believed to damage regenerating eucalypt forest.

A potentially much more serious problem is that the Common brushtail may become infected with bovine tuberculosis. This discovery, made in New Zealand in 1970, led to fears that brushtails may reinfect cattle. Although a widespread and costly poisoning program was set up, infected brushtails remain firmly established.

More positively from the economic point of view, the Common brushtail has long been valued for its fur. The rich, dense fur of the Tasmanian form has found special favor, and between 1923 and 1959 over 1 million pelts were exported. Exports from New Zealand have also grown rapidly (see box). In eastern Australia, however, the last open season on possums was in 1963, although in Tasmania the Common brushtail is still subject to control measures in agricultural areas. Although the Common brushtail is considered to be secure, there is a worrying trend of populations crashing in eucalypt woodlands over much of northern and inland Australia.

Cuscuses have long been valued by traditional hunters for their coats and meat, which are sold in local markets. Four cuscuses with restricted ranges or restricted habitats are now considered threatened by overhunting or habitat-clearing. The Black-spotted cuscus is particularly susceptible to hunting with firearms as it sleeps exposed on a branch; for the other three – the Telefomin, Stein's, and Obi cuscuses – habitat-clearing is the major threat. The conservation status of many other cuscuses is not known, but without protective measures the continued survival of the susceptible mainland species and the numerous island forms will be gravely threatened. JW/CRD

phalangerid in which the female is known to take a proactive role in courtship is the Spotted cuscus; at 28-day intervals, assumed to coincide with estrus, she calls throughout the night, which excites males.

Most cuscuses also bear a single young, the exceptions being the two common cuscuses, for which twins are the norm. Long-term pair bonding may only occur in the Bear cuscus, the largest and most diurnal of the phalangerids. Male Spotted cuscuses may use sight in determining territoriality, since they are reputed to use daytime sleeping perches that provide clear views of neighboring rivals.

Pelts or Pests?

Conservation and Environment

The brushtail possums are of considerable commercial importance, in both a negative and a positive sense. On the downside, the Mountain brushtail causes damage in exotic pine plantations

A Marsupial Invader: The Common Brushtail in New Zealand

When the first Australian Common brushtail possums were imported to New Zealand around 1840, it was hoped that they would form the basis of a lucrative fur industry. The venture was manifestly successful. Aided by further importations until 1924 and by the freeing of captive-bred animals, populations increased prodigiously, so that sales of pelts became an important source of revenue.

However, the blessings of this marsupial invader are mixed. As well as carrying bovine tuberculosis (see above), the possum has been shown to have subtle but potentially damaging effects on the indigenous vegetation. New Zealand forest trees evolved in the absence of leaf-eating mammals, and, unlike the Australian eucalypts that produce poisonous oils and phenols, the leaves of most species are palatable and lack defenses against predators. When first introduced to particular New Zealand forests, the possums rapidly exploited the new food source, increasing in population density to up to 50 animals per ha (120/acre) – some 25 times more than in Australia. By the time numbers had stabilized at 6–10 per ha (15–25/acre), trees such as ratas and konini had all but disappeared from many areas, and possums were turning their attention to less favored species.

Possums hasten tree death by congregating on individual trees and almost completely defoliating them. These normally solitary creatures evidently abandon their social inhibitions when food is abundant – and, in contrast to their Australian kin, the New Zealand possums occupy small (1–2ha/2.5–5 acre) and extensively overlapping home ranges.

The final verdict on possum damage is unclear. Young individual ratas and other exploited tree species are appearing in many localities, but they now seem to be distasteful to possums. Presumably possums are conferring a selective advantage on unpalatable trees, and so continue, subtly but surely, to alter the structure of the forest. CRD

Ringtails, Pygmy Possums, and Gliders

THE RINGTAIL POSSUMS, GLIDERS, AND PYGMY possums of Australia and New Guinea inhabit a wide range of environments, including forest, shrubby woodland, and even (in the case of the Mountain pygmy possum) alpine upland. Formerly included with the brushtail possums and cuscuses in the family Phalangeridae, they are now divided into four separate families. Although these families may appear superficially similar to one another, the differences between them in external form, internal anatomy, physiology, patterns of genetic variability, and the biochemistry of blood proteins are in fact as great as those between the kangaroos and the koala.

When the Australian continent was invaded some 40–60 million years ago by primitive, possum-like marsupials, it was blanketed in a wet, misty, and humid rain forest. Opening of these forests in the mid to late Tertiary (32–35 million years ago) and their gradual replacement by the marginal eucalypt and acacia forests that now grow there forced this early fauna to seek refuge in the high-altitude regions of northern Queensland and Papua New Guinea, where the ringtail possums radiated to form a diverse family of leaf- and fruit-eating specialists. At the same time, the new nectar-, gum- and insect-rich Australian eucalypt and wattle (*Acacia*) forests provided many niches for the pygmy possums, feeding predominantly on nectar and insects, and the petaurid gliders, which fed on sap and gums. This diversification has led to remarkable convergences of form, function, and behavior with the arboreal lemurs, bush babies, monkeys, and squirrels of other continents.

The Mountain pygmy possum adopted an alternative strategy to the arboreal habits of the other possums and gliders, retreating to a cool, alpine environment, where it became ground-dwelling and inhabited rock deposits formed by periglacial activity. The Mountain pygmy possum is the only Australasian small mammal to undergo deep, seasonal hibernation under snow cover for up to 7 months of the Austral winter.

Fitted for the Forests

FORM AND FUNCTION

The ringtail possums and gliders, and most pygmy possums, are predominantly arboreal, with hand-like feet, an enlarged, opposable big toe on the hind foot, and a range of adaptations suited to moving through wooded environments. In non-gliding species, the tail is prehensile, and may be used for grasping branches and transporting nest material; a naked undersurface effectively increases friction. In gliders (but not the Feathertail glider) the tail is heavily furred and either straight or tapering; it may be used for controlling the direction of flight. Gliding species are specialized for rapid movement in open forest and are thought to have evolved independently in three families during the mid-to-late Tertiary. In the eight species of gliders that survive today, gliding is achieved by use of a thin, furred membrane (patagium) that stretches from fore to hind limbs (wrist to ankle in the Sugar glider, wrist to knee in the Feathertail), increasing surface area in flight to form a large rectangle. It is retracted when not in use and may be seen as a wavy line along the side of the body. The effective surface area has also been increased by a lengthening of the arm and leg bones, and some species cover distances exceeding 100m (330ft) in a single glide, from the top of one tree to the butt or trunk of another. The heavier Greater glider, with a reduced (elbow-to-ankle) gliding membrane, descends steeply with limited control, but the smaller gliders are accomplished acrobats that weave and maneuver gracefully between trees, landing with precision by swooping upwards. What appears to be a gentle landing to the human eye is in fact shown by slow-motion photography to be a high-speed collision. The animals bounce backward after impact and must fasten their long claws into the tree trunk to avoid tumbling to the ground. The fourth and fifth digits of the hand are elongated and have greatly enlarged claws that assist clinging after the landing impact.

Leaves, Insects, Sap, and Nectar

DIET

There are four major dietary groups of possums and gliders – folivores, sapivores and gumivores, insectivores, and nectarivores. All are nocturnal and have large, protruding eyes. Most are also quiet, secretive, and hence rarely seen. The only audible sign of their presence may be the "plop" of gliders landing on tree trunks, the yapping alarm call of the Sugar glider, or the screeching or gurgling call of the Yellow-bellied glider. Ringtail possums are generally quiet but occasionally emit soft twittering calls. The Greater glider is totally silent, emitting only a quiet grumbling sound when being handled. Most possum species (except the Greater glider) make loud screaming and screeching calls when attacked or handled.

Ringtail possums and the Greater glider together form a highly specialized group (Family Pseudocheiridae) of arboreal leaf-eaters (folivores), characterized by an enlargement of the cecum to

Right *A Herbert River ringtail displays the tightly-curled tip of the long, prehensile tail that gives these animals their common group name. Increased logging in Queensland is threatening this species' habitat.*

Inset *Only 8cm (3in) long, a Feathertail glider grooms itself on a branch. Also known as the Pygmy glider, this species is the smallest marsupial capable of gliding, achieving flights of over 50m (165ft).*

FACTFILE

RINGTAILS, PYGMY POSSUMS, & GLIDERS

Order: Diprotodontia

Families: Pseudocheiridae, Burramyidae, Petauridae, Acrobatidae

35 species in 13 genera

DISTRIBUTION SE, E, N, and SW Australia, Tasmania, New Guinea, offshore islands of New Guinea.

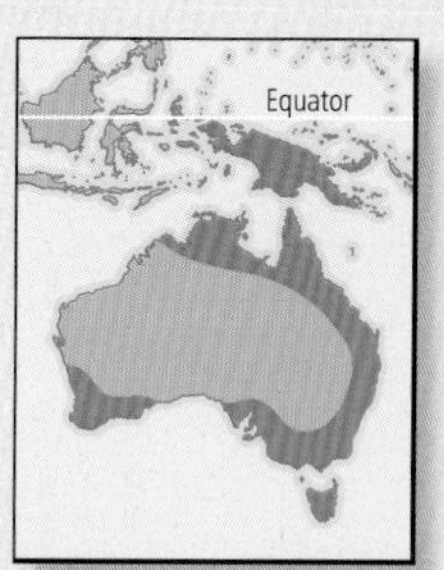

HABITAT Forests, woodland, shrublands, heathland, alpine heathlands

SIZE Head–body length ranges from 6.4cm (2.5in) in the Little pygmy possum to 33–38cm (13–15in) in the Rock ringtail possum; **tail length** from 7.1cm (2.8in) to 20–27cm (7.9–10.6in), and **weight** from 7g (0.2oz) to 1.3–2kg (2.9–4.4lb), both in the same two species.

FORM Coat gray or brown, with paler underside; often darker eye patches or forehead or back stripes (particularly in species feeding on plant gums); tail long, well-furred (in most gliders), prehensile, and part naked, or feather-like.

DIET Ringtails and gliders are primarily folivorous, although they also eat fruit; other species are more omnivorous, also including insects, larvae, spiders, scorpions, and small lizards in their diet.

BREEDING Gestation period 12–50 days; all young weigh less than 1g (0.035oz) at birth.

LONGEVITY 4–15 years (generally shorter in pygmy possums with large litters, and longer in ringtails and large gliders with single young).

CONSERVATION STATUS Four species are classified as Endangered, and four as Vulnerable.

See families box ▷

form a region for microbial fermentation of the cellulose in their highly fibrous diet. Fine grinding of food particles in a battery of well-developed molars with crescent-shaped ridges on the crowns (selenodont molars) enhances digestion. Rates of food intake in these groups are slowed by the time required for cellulose fermentation, and nitrogen and energy is often conserved by slow movement, relatively small litter sizes (averaging 1–1.5 young), coprophagy (reingestion of feces), and adoption of medium to large body size (0.2–2kg/0.4–4.4lb). The preferred diet of the Greater glider of eastern Australia is eucalypt leaves. The quantities of nutrients in these leaves vary substantially between different tree species, and this is a major factor underpinning the patchy patterns of distribution and abundance of the Greater glider through the eastern Australian forests.

The five species of petaurid glider and Leadbeater's possum (all of the Family Petauridae) are specialist plant-exudate (sap and gum) feeders. Arthropods, pollen, and occasionally the green seeds of acacias are also eaten, providing an important source of protein. The petaurid possums and gliders are small to medium in size (70–650g/2.5–21oz). The most primitive member of the group, Leadbeater's possum, is restricted to moist, high-altitude montane eucalypt forests, where it feeds on wattle or acacia gums, insects, and insect exudates. By incising notches in the bark of trees, the possum enhances gum production. Wattle gum is also a principal food of the Sugar glider, and the species may travel hundreds of meters across open pasture to obtain it.

The Sugar glider, which is distributed from Tasmania to northwest Australia and Papua-New Guinea and neighboring islands, also exploits the sap of eucalypts by incising the bark and licking up the sweet, carbohydrate-rich exudates. Such sap-feeding sites are highly prized and may be vigorously defended by chasing and biting intruders. Eucalypt sap also appears in the diet of the rare and highly endangered Mahogany glider in the far northeast of Queensland. Like most other petaurid gliders, this species consumes gum exudates from acacia trees as well as insects. The diet of the Mahogany glider can also include gum tapped from the floral spears of Grass trees. Eucalypt sap feeding has developed to an extreme in the Yellow-bellied glider of eastern Australia, which cuts large notches into the bark of many tree species. The form of these notches varies from deep, V-shaped incisions to long strips of ruffled bark, depending on the eucalypt species that is tapped.

Although a minor component of their diet, pollen and insects are an important protein source for all members of the Petauridae. A high carbohydrate-to-nitrogen ratio in their diet provides additional energy for activity and territorial defense but has limited reproductive potential, and so births are restricted to seasons of insect abundance. The coats of the gum-feeding gliders and possums are characterized by a distinct black dorsal stripe. This is thought to camouflage them when they are feeding – the time when they are most vulnerable to predation by forest owls.

With Leadbeater's possum, the strikingly-colored, black-and-white Striped possum and trioks are the non-gliding members of the Petauridae. In

Ringtail, Pygmy Possum, and Glider Families

Ringtail possums
Family Pseudocheiridae

17 species in 6 genera: 7 species of *Pseudocheirus* (SE, E, N, SW Australia, Tasmania, New Guinea, and West Irian), including Common ringtail possum (*P. peregrinus*) and Western ringtail possum (*P. occidentalis*). The family Pseudocheiridae also includes the Rock ringtail possum (*Petropseudes dahli*) from N Australia; the Greater glider (*Petauroides volans*) from E Australia, and a range of species from the forests of NE Australia such as the Daintree River ringtail possum (*Pseudochirulus cinereus*) and Green ringtail possum (*Pseudochirops archeri*) as well as several poorly-known New Guinea taxa such as the Weyland ringtail possum (*Pseudochirulus caroli*) and Pygmy ringtail possum (*Pseudochirulus mayeri*). The Western ringtail possum, D'Alberti's ringtail possum (*P. albertisii*), and the Plush-coated ringtail possum (*P. corinnae*) are classed as Vulnerable.

Pygmy possums
Family Burramyidae

5 species in 2 genera: pygmy possums (4 species of *Cercartetus*), including the Eastern and Western pygmy possums (*C. nanus* and *C. concinnus*), Tasmania, Kangaroo Island, SE, E, NE, SW Australia, New Guinea; Mountain pygmy possum (*Burramys parvus*), SE Australia. The Mountain pygmy possum is Endangered.

Gliders
Family Petauridae

11 species in 3 genera:. 6 species of *Petaurus* (Tasmania, SE, E, N, NW Australia, New Guinea), including Yellow-bellied or Fluffy glider (*P. australis*), Squirrel glider (*P. norfolcensis*), Mahogany glider (*P. gracilis*), Sugar glider (*P. breviceps*), and two species confined to New Guinea – the Northern glider (*P. abidi*) and *P. biacensis*. The Petauridae also contain the monotypic genus *Gymnobelideus* (Leadbeater's possum, *G. leadbeateri*, Victoria) and four species of *Dactylopsila* (the Striped possum and the trioks). The Striped possum (*Dactylopsila trivirgata*) occurs in both NE coastal Queensland and New Guinea; the remaining three species (*D. megalura*, *D. palpator*, and *D. tatei*) are confined to New Guinea or adjacent offshore islands. The Mahogany glider, Leadbeater's possum, and Tate's triok are classed as Endangered; the Northern glider is Vulnerable.

Feathertail glider and Feathertail possum
Family Acrobatidae

2 species in 2 genera: Feathertail or Pygmy glider or Flying mouse (*Acrobates pygmaeus*), SE to NE Australia; Feathertail possum (*Distoechurus pennatus*), New Guinea.

For full species list see Appendix ▷

a classic case of convergent evolution, the Striped possum and the trioks, like skunks, emit a distinctive, musty odor that is particularly strong in the Long-fingered triok from New Guinea. The four species are medium-sized and are specialized for exploiting social insects, ants, bees, termites, and other wood-boring insects in the tropical lowland rain forests of northern Queensland and New Guinea. A suite of adaptations aids in the noisy extraction of insects from deep within wood crevices – feeding activity may produce a shower of woodchips. These adaptations include an extremely elongated fourth finger (like that of the aye-aye of Madagascar; see Primates: Strepsirhines), an elongated tongue, and enlarged and forward-pointing upper and lower incisors.

Pygmy possums of the genus *Cercartetus* and the Feathertail or Pygmy glider form a fourth group that has diversified in the nectar-rich sclerophyllous Australian heathlands, shrublands, and eucalypt forests. Despite the small size of the Feathertail glider, it is nevertheless highly mobile; the species can glide for distances exceeding 50m (165ft), often spiraling from high in the tree canopy toward the ground like a falling leaf before settling in a flowering shrub. The brush-tipped tongue of the Feathertail glider is used for sipping

Left *Representative species of possums and gliders, exhibiting feeding behavior and movement: **1** Common ringtail possum* (Pseudocheirus peregrinus) *eating an insect. **2** Tasmanian pygmy possum* (Cercartetus lepidus) *foraging. **3** Leadbeater's possum* (Gymnobelideus leadbeateri) *feeding on sap. **4** Striped possum* (Dactylopsila trivirgata) *on branch. **5** Feathertail glider* (Acrobates pygmaeus) *in flight. **6** Mahogany glider* (Petaurus gracilis), *showing the folds on its side where the patagium or flying membrane is stored. **7** Sugar glider* (P. breviceps) *with the patagium extended in flight.*

nectar from flower capsules, and the small size (under 35g/1.2oz) and extreme mobility of all five species increase nectar harvesting rates. In poor seasons, aggregations of many individuals may be found on isolated flowering trees and shrubs. Most species take insects and the abundant pollen available from flowers to provide protein. The Eastern pygmy possum occasionally eats soft fruits and seeds. The combination of small size and abundant dietary nitrogen permit unusually large litter sizes (4–6), and rapid growth and development rates similar to those of the carnivorous marsupials. The other member of the pygmy possum group, the Feathertail possum of Papua New Guinea, has a tail like that of the Feathertail glider but is larger (50–55g/1.8–1.9oz) and has no gliding membrane. Its diet includes insects, fruit, and possibly plant exudates.

For its spring and summer diet, the Mountain pygmy possum depends largely on Bogong moths (*Agrotis infusa*) and other invertebrates. Huge numbers of these moths migrate to the mountains in spring. As Bogong moths become scarce, fleshy fruits and seeds from heathland plants become increasingly important. The remarkable sectorial premolar tooth is adapted for husking and cracking seeds. Excess seeds may be cached for use during periods of winter or early spring shortage.

Smaller Size, Larger Nesting Groups

SOCIAL BEHAVIOR

Mountain pygmy possums have only one litter of four young per year, following snowmelt. This is an adaptation to the short, alpine summer and the need for both adults and young to gain sufficient fat reserves to enable them to survive the long period of winter hibernation.

Most Australian possums and gliders nest or den in cavities in large, old living or dead trees, although sometimes other types of nest sites are occupied, such as bark strips or fallen logs. The Common ringtail possum can build a stick nest or drey, but in cold subalpine or seasonally hot woodland environments hollow trees are used in favor of dreys. Individuals of all hollow-using possums and gliders have den sites in many different trees and will often swap between them on a regular basis. The entrance to the hollow is typically just large enough to permit the entry of the occupant, but small enough to preclude predators and other species that may attempt to usurp the use of the cavity.

Patterns of social organization and mating behavior in possums and gliders are remarkably diverse, but to some extent predictable from species' body size and diet. The larger folivorous ringtail possums and the Greater glider are often solitary; by day they sleep singly or occasionally in pairs in tree hollows or vegetation clumps, emerging to feed on foliage in home ranges of up to 3ha (7.4 acres) at night. Male home ranges of the Greater glider are generally exclusive but may partially overlap those of one or two females. The occupation of exclusive home ranges by males and of overlapping home ranges by females is associated with a greater mortality of sub-adult males and a consequent female-biased sex ratio.

The tendency toward gregariousness increases with decreasing body size, the Yellow-bellied glider forming nesting groups of up to five individuals, the Common ringtail of eastern Australia up to six, the Sugar glider up to 12, and the Feathertail glider up to 25. Most nesting groups consist of mated pairs with offspring, but the Feathertail glider and the petaurids may form truly mixed groups with up to four or more unrelated adults of both sexes (in the Sugar glider), one male and one or several females (the Yellow-bellied glider), or one female and up to three males (Leadbeater's possum). The chief reason for nesting in groups is thought to be improved energy conservation through huddling during winter. In one species, the Sugar glider, large nesting groups disband into smaller units during summer. The aggregation of females during the winter enables dominant males to monopolize access to up to three females in the petaurid gliders, and a harem defense mating system prevails.

An entirely different mating system occurs in Leadbeater's possum. Individual females occupy large nests in hollow trees and actively defend a surrounding territory of 1–1.5ha (2.5–3.7 acres) from other females. Mating is usually monogamous, and male partners assist females in defense of territories. Additional adult males may be tolerated in family groups by the breeding pairs but adult females are not, and an associated higher female mortality results in a male-biased sex ratio. This pattern appears to be associated with the construction of well-insulated nests, avoiding the necessity for females to huddle together during winter, and with the occupation of dense, highly productive habitats in which food resources are readily defensible and surplus energy is available to meet the cost of territorial defense.

The mating patterns of some possum and glider species can be somewhat flexible, varying spatially and temporally depending on the availability and quality of food and other resources like den sites. For example, small, low-density populations of the Greater glider that occupy eucalypt forests with low levels of foliage nutrients appear to be predominately monogamous. In contrast, higher-density populations in more nutrient-rich forest types maintain a polygamous mating system. The patterns of social organization, group size, and mating systems of Leadbeater's possum and the Yellow-bellied glider may also change over time depending on, for example, year-by-year differences in the availability of food.

Selective pressures exerted during competition for mating partners have led to the prolific development of scentmarking glands in the petaurids, for use in marking other members of the social group. Leadbeater's possum, the most primitive member, shows the least development of special scent glands, and scentmarking between partners involves the mutual transfer of saliva to the tail base with its adjacent anal glands. Sugar glider males, in contrast, possess forehead, chest, and anal glands. Males use their head glands to spread scent on the chest of females, and females in turn spread scent on their heads by rubbing the chest gland of dominant males. Male Yellow-bellied gliders have similar glands, but scent transfer is achieved quite differently, by rubbing the head gland against the female's anal gland. Females in turn rub their heads on the anal gland of the dominant male. Such behavior probably facilitates group cohesion by communicating an individual's social status, sex, group membership, and reproductive position.

Above *Dwarfed by their dinner, a pair of Tasmanian pygmy possums* (Cercartetus lepidus) *prepare to feed on nectar from a* Banksia *flower.*

In contrast to the small gliders, pygmy possums of the genus *Cercartetus* appear mainly solitary. Usually only lactating females share nests with their young, although several males may share a nest, sometimes with a non-lactating female. Mountain pygmy possums seem more social, with sedentary females forming kin clusters in high-quality habitats and sometimes sharing nests with non-dependent, apparently related females. Nest sharing among males is common, and home ranges overlap. Although they are not sexually dimorphic, female Eastern and Mountain pygmy possums may be behaviorally dominant. Mountain pygmy possum males leave the habitat of females after breeding and spend the winter in slightly warmer habitats, with more northerly and westerly aspects and lower elevations. It is still not clear whether the resulting sexual segregation during the non-breeding season is a result of female aggression, or is simply a reproductive strategy.

The optimal temperature for hibernation in males is slightly higher than in females, and they arouse more frequently during winter and finish hibernation earlier in spring. This provides them with a reproductive advantage, because they can undergo spermatogenesis and be ready to breed. Because male survival is often lower than for females, sex ratios are frequently female-biased, especially in high-quality habitats. Pygmy

possums generally have relatively short lifespans (less than 3 years), but Eastern pygmy possums have been known to live for more than 6 years. Mountain pygmy possums are remarkably long-lived, with females living for up to 12 years. This is probably a result of their relatively stable environment, single reproductive effort, larger size, and long periods of hibernation.

Back from the Dead

CONSERVATION AND ENVIRONMENT

The story of the discovery, apparent extinction, and subsequent rediscovery of three widely divergent species typifies the plight of the pygmy possums and gliders. In all cases, human pressure for land use is now once more placing their continued survival under threat.

Just after nightfall one evening in 1961, in the wet, misty mountains just 110km (70mi) from Melbourne, the attention of a fauna survey group from the National Museum of Victoria was caught by a small, bright-eyed, alert gray possum leaping nimbly through the forest undergrowth. Its size at first suggested a Sugar glider, but the absence of a gliding membrane and the narrow, bushy, club-shaped tail led to the exciting conclusion that this was the long-lost Leadbeater's possum. This rare little possum is one of the State of Victoria's faunal emblems, and was first discovered in 1867 in the Bass River Valley. Only six specimens were collected, all prior to 1909, and in 1921 it was concluded that the destruction of the scrub and forest in the area had resulted in the complete extermination of the species. Surveys following the rediscovery, however, led to its detection at some 300 separate sites within a 3,600sq km (1,400sq mi) area. Its preferred habitat is Victoria's Central Highland forests, which are dominated by the majestic Mountain ash (*Eucalyptus regnans*), the world's tallest flowering plant and one of Australia's most valued timber-producing trees. Standing beneath such forest giants provides the most reliable method of catching a glimpse of a Leadbeater's possum, as the animals emerge at dusk from their family retreats in hollow tree trunks to feed. Less than 40 years after its rediscovery, however, the possum is once again threatened with extinction through a combination of inappropriate forest management and natural collapse of the large dead trees that provide nest sites in regrowth forests (in 1999 a fire devastated two-thirds of Victoria's Mountain ash forests).

The Mahogany glider was first described in 1883, but was misidentified at the time as a Squirrel glider. Careful examination of specimens from the Queensland Museum subsequently revealed that gliders from a tiny coastal area in the far north of Queensland were, in fact, different in size, tail length, and a number of other particulars from the Squirrel glider. The species has a highly restricted distribution and is confined to open woodlands and adjacent paperbark swamps. Most potentially suitable habitat has been destroyed, and the survival of the species continues to be threatened by land clearance, particularly for the establishment of sugar cane and banana crops.

The Mountain pygmy possum was described from fossil remains in 1896 and was thought to be extinct until 1966, when one turned up in a ski lodge in the Victorian alps. Since it was believed that all pygmy possums were arboreal and nested in tree-hollows, it was reasoned the animal must have been brought to the alps in a load of firewood. Searches were made in the forests at lower elevations, but to no avail. In 1970, however, another animal was trapped in rocky heath under snow gum woodland at the interface of the subalpine and alpine zones on the Kosciuszko plateau of New South Wales. This directed attention back to the ski lodge in Victoria, where trapping in the surrounding rocky heath quickly resulted in the capture of three animals. The following year, 11 animals were trapped well above the tree line on Mt Kosciuszko, the highest mountain on the Australian mainland (2,228m/7,300ft). Since then, intensive research has been conducted on the Mountain pygmy possum. Not coincidentally, because of their requirements for high-elevation sites with good snow cover, the largest local populations all occur within ski-resort concession areas. Here, they are threatened by ski runs and general tourist development. An increasingly apparent and much less easily managed threat is that of increasing temperatures and receding snow cover resulting from global warming.

The survival of Leadbeater's possum, the Mahogany glider, and the Mountain pygmy possum – all of which are nationally endangered – is critically dependent upon effective government action, which is not yet forthcoming. LB/DL

Kangaroos and Wallabies

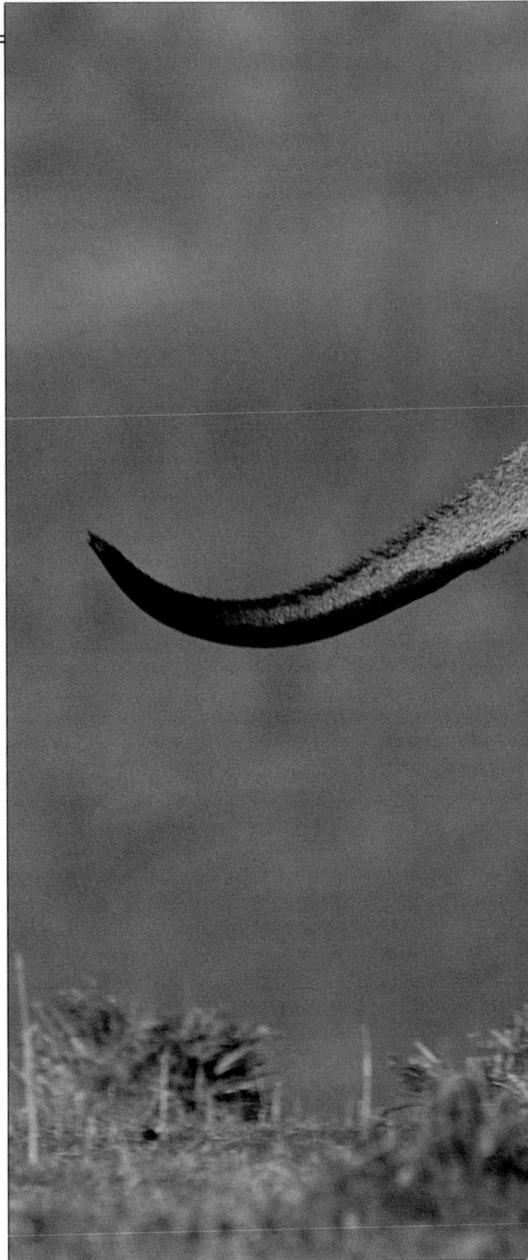

Top left A Swamp wallaby browses on foliage. Despite the name, the species is found in open upland forests as well as in marshy regions and mangroves.

RED KANGAROOS BOUNDING ACROSS THE arid saltbush plains are one of the quintessential images of Australia. Yet the Red is just one among a diverse array of about 68 living species of kangaroos, wallabies, and rat kangaroos that make up the superfamily Macropodoidea. Desert-adapted, grass-eating kangaroos such as the Red have in fact evolved only in the last 5–15 million years. Before then, Australasia was forested, and the ancestors of all macropods were forest-dwelling browsers.

The superfamily Macropodoidea takes its name from *Macropus*, the genus of the Red kangaroo. The word means "big foot" in Latin, and long hind feet do indeed characterize the animals. They are the largest mammals to hop on both feet, a very special gait for a large mammal. Even so, hopping is not the only way that kangaroos get about.

The Mechanics of Hopping

FORM AND FUNCTION

All macropods are furry-coated, long-tailed animals, with thin necks, prominent ears, and strongly developed hindquarters that make the forelimbs and upper body look small. A long, narrow pelvis supports long and muscular thighs; the even more elongate shin bones are not heavily muscled and end in an ankle that is adapted to prevent the foot from rotating sideways (so that the kangaroo cannot twist its ankle while hopping). At rest and in slow motion, the long but narrow sole of the foot bears the animal's weight, making it in effect plantigrade. When hopping, however, macropods rise onto their toes and the "balls" of their hind feet. Only two of the toes, the fourth and fifth, are in fact load-bearing; the second and third are reduced to a single, tiny stump equipped with two claws that are used exclusively for grooming.

The first toe is entirely lost except in the Musky rat kangaroo, the only surviving member of the primitive Hypsiprymnodontidae family. Short-faced kangaroos in the genus *Procoptodon* shed the fifth toe, too. *Procoptodon* went extinct 15–25,000 years ago at the peak of the last ice age, possibly as a result of human-lit fires and hunting, but rock paintings record its distinctive footprints. Limb-lengthening and toe reduction characterize many lineages of mammalian, terrestrial herbivores – they include horses among the perissodactyls and deer, antelopes, and pronghorns among the artiodactyls – that evolved speed to avoid running predators. In these and many other ways, macropods illustrate convergence for lifestyle between eutherian and metatherian mammals.

Macropods do not only hop; they also crawl on all fours when moving slowly, with the pairs of fore- and hind limbs moving together rather than alternately. In medium and large macropodine species, the tail and the forelimbs take the animal's weight while the hind feet are lifted and swung forward. This gait is called "pentapedal" (literally, five-footed). In the larger macropodines the tail is long, thick, and muscular, and the animal sits up by leaning back on it like a sportsman on a shooting stick; it can even briefly be the only means of support during fighting.

In smaller wallabies and rat kangaroos, the tail's major function is for balance and maneuvering, for instance as an aid in abrupt cornering. Most rat kangaroos also use the tail to carry nesting material; grasses or twigs are gathered into a bundle and pushed backward with the hind feet against the underside of the tail, which curls over, holding the bundle against the rat kangaroo's rump as it hops away to the half-built nest.

In contrast to the hind limbs, macropods' forelimbs are relatively small and unspecialized. The forepaws have five equal, strongly-clawed digits set around a short, broad palm. Rat kangaroos dig for their food with elongate second to fourth digits with long claws. Macropods' forepaws can grasp and manipulate food plants; they also serve to grip the skin, hold open the pouch, or scratch the fur while grooming. The larger macropods also use their fore limbs in thermoregulation, licking saliva onto their insides, where it evaporates, cooling blood in a network of vessels that lie just below the skin's surface.

At speeds slower than about 10km/h (6mph), hopping is at best an ungainly way of moving, but above 15–20km/h (9–12mph) it is extremely energy-efficient – more so than four-footed trotting or galloping. At the end of each bound, energy is stored in the tendons of the bent hind legs, contributing to the next driving extension. Like the rider of a spring-loaded pogo-stick, the kangaroo needs only to add a little extra energy in order to keep hopping. Yet hopping probably originated as a way of startling predators by making an explosive burst from cover, a strategy retained by the smaller kangaroos, which conceal themselves in vegetation, and the rat kangaroos, which hide in nests. That explosive burst requires long, strong,

FACTFILE

KANGAROOS AND WALLABIES

Order: Diprotodontia

Families: Macropodidae and Hypsiprymnodontidae

About 68 species in 16 genera

DISTRIBUTION Australia, New Guinea; introduced into Britain, Germany, Hawaii, and New Zealand.

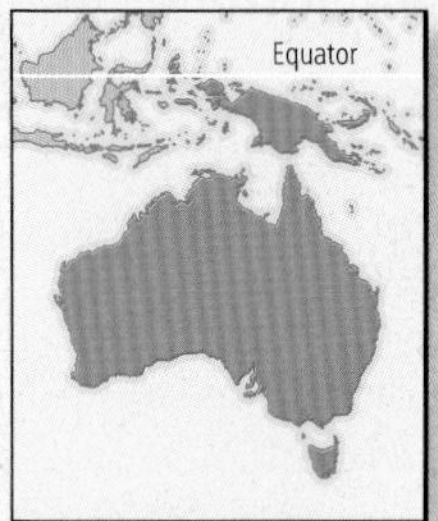

HABITAT Wide-ranging, from deserts to rain forests.

SIZE **Head–body length** ranges from 28.4cm (11.2in) in the Musky rat kangaroo to 165cm (65in) in the male Red kangaroo; **tail length** from 14.2cm(5.6in) to 107cm (42in), and **weight** from 0.5kg (1.2lb) to up to 95kg (200lb), both in the same two species.

COAT Macropod fur, mostly 2–3cm (0.8–1.2in) long, is fine, dense, and not sleek. Colors range from pale gray through various shades of sandy brown to dark brown or black.

DIET Mostly plant foods, including grasses, forbs, leaves, seeds, fruit, tubers, bulbs, and truffles; also some invertebrates, such as insects and beetle larvae.

BREEDING Gestation 30–39 days; newborn attach to a maternal teat within a pouch and remain there for a further 6–11 months.

LONGEVITY Variable according to species and conditions; larger species may attain 12–18 years (28 years in captivity), the smaller rat kangaroos 5–8 years.

CONSERVATION STATUS 2 wallabies and 2 species of hare wallaby (plus 2 subspecies) are now listed as Extinct. A further 7 species of kangaroos and wallabies are Endangered, while 9 more are Vulnerable.

See families box ▷

Above *With a baby, or joey, safely secured in her pouch, a female Eastern gray kangaroo goes foraging in an Australian reserve. At full speed, large kangaroos can travel at over 55km/h (35mph).*

Below *Red kangaroos fighting. Before a fight two males may engage in a "stiff-legged" walk* ***1*** *in the face of the opponent, and in scratching and grooming* ***2***, ***3***, *standing upright on extended rear legs. The fight is initiated by locking forearms* ***4*** *and attempting to push the opponent backward to the ground* ***5***.

synchronized hind limbs, and initiates a bounding gait. Large kangaroos can sustain hopping speeds faster than 55 km/h (35mph), and small species can manage bursts of over 30 km/h (20mph).

Some macropods are adapted to bounding up narrow ledges on near-vertical cliffs and even to climbing trees. Rock wallabies have rather broad hind feet with nonslip soles, and long, bushy tails to help them keep their balance as they escape. Tree kangaroos find refuge high up in the rain forest. They climb by grasping the trunks with huge, heavily-clawed forepaws on the ends of long, strong arms, and pushing upward on short, broad feet that grip the trunk or branches. Their tails are not prehensile. They descend awkwardly, tail first, but are able to jump short distances from tree to tree. When climbing or even moving along branches, their hind limbs move synchronously – a remnant of their long-gone deerlike gait. Nevertheless, they can move them alternately (as all macropods do when forced to swim or while adjusting their stance).

Macropods' limbs, paws, and feet also function as weapons. Rat kangaroos and small wallabies fight by kicking out as they jump at each other, or else by grappling, rolling on the ground biting and scratching. They sometimes kill opponents with their hind feet. The large kangaroos remain more upright, wrestling with the fore limbs around the opponent's head, shoulders, and neck, and kicking with the powerful hind limbs (the tail briefly taking the animal's weight), driving the large toes hard into the opponent's belly. The shoulders and forearms of males of larger kangaroo species are longer and more muscular than those of the females, and male forepaws are more heavily clawed. Males also grow a shield of thickened skin over the belly – more than twice as thick as on the flanks or shoulders – that helps absorb the impact of kicks to the gut.

Macropods have heads that superficially resemble those of deer or antelopes, with moderately long muzzles, wide-set eyes with some binocular vision, and upright ears that can be rotated to catch sounds from all directions. The upper lip is "split" like that of a hare or a squirrel.

The muzzles, teeth, and tongues of macropods are suited to taking small food items rather than large mouthfuls of food. Most macropods pluck single items, even blades of grass, one at a time. Behind the split upper lip lies an arc of incisor teeth surrounding a fleshy pad at the front of the palate. In macropodine kangaroos and wallabies, the two procumbent (horizontally-set) lower incisors hold leaves against the fleshy pad while they are ripped off along the edge of the upper incisor arc. In potoroine rat kangaroos and the Banded hare wallaby, the only living sthenurine, the lower incisors occlude with the second and third upper incisors, while the central (first) upper incisors protrude and are used for gnawing.

Potoroine rat kangaroos' distinctive premolars form serrated blades to cut the tough and fleshy food that constitutes their diet (mainly plant storage organs or fungal fruiting bodies). Small macropodines have similarly sectorial, persistent premolars; but larger kangaroos shed their unspecialized premolars, opening the way for the molar teeth, which erupt sequentially at the back of the jaw, to migrate forward, being shed as they wear out. This adaptation to an abrasive diet (mainly of grasses) parallels that of elephants. Macropods with persistent premolars do not show molar progression, and all four erupted molars in each half jaw are in wear simultaneously.

Macropods can use their forepaws to handle or dig up food. This ability is most advanced in the potoroines, most of which depend to a large

Right *One of two remaining hare wallaby species, the Rufous hare wallaby is itself listed as Vulnerable, surviving on two islands off Western Australia.*

Below *Representative species of the larger kangaroos and wallabies:* **1** *Red kangaroo* (Macropus rufus)*;* **2** *Hill wallaroo* (Macropus robustus) *with young in pouch;* **3** *Bridled nail-tailed wallaby* (Onychogalea fraenata)*;* **4** *Red-legged pademelon* (Thylogale stigmatica) *in pentapedal (literally, five-footed) posture, with tail and all four limbs providing support;* **5** *Whiptail or Prettyface wallaby* (Macropus parryi) *in motion;* **6** *Goodfellow's tree kangaroo* (Dendrolagus goodfellowi) *resting on a branch.*

extent on digging up underground food items. However, even the largest kangaroos pull plants toward them with their paws, and use their "hands" to remove unwanted plant parts from their mouths.

Macropod digestion is aided by a forestomach enlarged to form a fermentation chamber. Longitudinal and transverse bands of muscles (haustrations) in the stomach wall contract to stir the stomach contents. A moderate-sized small intestine opens into an enlarged cecum and proximal colon, presumably a site for secondary fermentation, beyond which digested food flows through a long, water-resorbing distal colon.

The gut resembles that of some eutherian foregut fermenters, although the macropod stomach has not developed the compartmentalization of form and function to the same extent. The suite of bacteria, ciliate protozoa, and anaerobic fungi found in the stomachs of macropods performs the same functions as in ruminants, but the component species are quite different. Macropods may be less limited by poor-quality food than, for example, sheep. Some macropods recycle urea to help cope with low protein availability.

Macropod fur ranges in color from pale gray to dark brown or black. Many macropods have indistinct dark or pale stripes that visually break their outline: down the spine, across the upper thigh, behind the shoulders, or (most commonly) below or through the eye. The paws, feet, and tail are often darker than the body, and the belly is usually paler, making the animals appear "flat" in the dusk or by moonlight. In a few rock wallabies and tree kangaroos, the tail is longitudinally or transversely striped.

Males of some larger species are more boldly colored than the females; for example, the russet neck and shoulder coloring may be stronger in male Red-necked wallabies. Male Red kangaroos are mostly sandy-red, while the females are blue-gray or sandy gray. But the dimorphism is imperfect; some males may be blue-gray and some females red. The sexes' colors are fixed from the time they first show hair, rather than being acquired under a hormonal surge at or after puberty as in many dimorphic ungulates.

Many macropod males spread scented secretions from the skin of the throat and chest onto trees (especially the tree kangaroos), rocks (rock wallabies), or bushes and tussocks of grass (large kangaroos). They may also rub the scent on females during courtship, indicating to other males their association. Other glands within the cloaca add their scent to the urine or feces.

All over Australia

DISTRIBUTION PATTERNS

The single extant Hypsiprymnodontidae species, the Musky rat kangaroo, is confined to rain forests on the eastern side of Australia's Cape York peninsula. In contrast, the Macropodidae are represented by species of the Macropodinae subfamily all over Australia, in New Guinea, and on offshore islands; but the Potoroinae rat kangaroos (10 recent species) are confined to Australia (including Tasmania and other southern islands), and are rare in the tropical north. Two macropodine genera, *Dorcopsis* and *Dorcopsulus*, are confined to New Guinea; 8 of the 10 *Dendrolagus* tree kangaroos, and one of the four *Thylogale* pademelon species, also occur only there. Just two species, the Red-legged pademelon and the Agile wallaby, occur in both Australia and New Guinea. Feral macropod populations occur in a few countries outside Australasia: Brush-tailed rock wallabies in Hawaii; Red-necked wallabies in England's Pennine hills and in Germany; and both those species plus Tammar and Parma wallabies in New Zealand.

Genera of macropodines that are restricted to the rain forest include *Dorcopsis* and *Dorcopsulus*, and the *Dendrolagus* tree kangaroos. Pademelons

are also associated with wet, dense forests, including eucalypt forests; they occur from New Guinea down the east of Australia to Tasmania. Except for the weakly social tree kangaroos, these forest-dwelling macropodines are solitary.

Hare and nail-tailed wallabies occur in arid and semi-arid habitats including spinifex grassland, shrubland, savanna, and light woodland, and are confined to Australia. So are rock wallabies, which are found in habitats ranging from the arid zone of central, western, and southern Australia to rainforest habitats in the tropics. Yet their habitat always contains boulder piles, rocky hillsides, or clifflines to provide secure diurnal refuges.

The rich *Macropus* genus is almost confined to Australia. Its species occur in habitats ranging from desert to the edges of wet eucalypt forest, all characterized by grasses in the understory. The potoroines are confined to Australia, where they occur in rain forest, wet sclerophyll forest, and scrub, always with dense understory. The bettongs are creatures of the open forest, woodland, and savanna, often with a grassy understory. The Desert rat kangaroo used to occur in lightly-vegetated desert.

Macropod communities in Australia used to contain 5–6 sympatric species in the arid and semi-arid regions, but as many as a dozen in broken woodland and forested country along the Dividing Range. Rainforest communities rarely exceed 4 species.

From Grass to Truffles

DIET

The Musky rat kangaroo eats fleshy fruits and fungi and also regularly takes insects; in addition, it sometimes scatter-hoards seeds, although we do not know how efficient it is at finding them again. Macropodids depend on plants, although some of the smaller species (especially potoroines) will also eat invertebrates such as beetle larvae. Potoroos and bettongs feed largely on the underground storage organs of plants – swollen roots, rhizomes, tubers, and bulbs – and in addition eat the underground fruiting bodies (truffles) of some fungi, playing an important role in dispersing their spores (see A Mutually Beneficial Relationship).

Small macropodine wallabies that occupy dry habitats, including the hare and nail-tailed species, feed selectively on growing leaves of grasses and forbs, augmented with seeds and fruits. In mesic, forested habitats, macropodine diets include more fruits and dicot leaves, and these dominate the diets of tree kangaroos, swamp wallabies, and pademelons. Many macropodines feed opportunistically and seasonally from a large range of plant species and parts. *Macropus* species tend to have diets dominated by grass leaf, and also select seedheads of grasses and other monocots; and the largest kangaroos may rely entirely on grasses.

The smallest macropods tend to be highly selective in their feeding habits, seeking out scattered, high-quality food items, many of which have to be carefully sought and processed. In contrast, the largest species generally tolerate a lower-quality diet taken from a wide range of plant species, selecting mainly leaves but also some higher-value seeds and fruits.

Mobs and Loners

SOCIAL BEHAVIOR

At birth juvenile macropods are tiny, measuring just 5–15mm (0.2–0.6in); they look embryonic, with undeveloped eyes, hind limbs, and tail. Using its strong forelimbs, the newly-born infant will climb unaided up the mother's fur and into her forward-opening pouch. There it clamps its mouth onto one of four teats, remaining attached for many weeks of development – from 150–320 days, depending on species. The pouch provides a warm, humid environment for the juvenile, which cannot yet regulate its own temperature and can lose moisture rapidly through its hairless skin.

Once the juvenile has detached from the teat, the mother in many larger species will allow it out of the pouch for short walkabouts, retrieving it when she moves. She will prevent it from returning to the pouch just before the birth of her next young, but it will continue to follow her about as a dependent young-at-foot, and can put its head into the maternal pouch to suck the teat. The quality of milk provided changes as the joey matures, and a mother suckling a juvenile in the pouch at the same time as a young-at-foot will

Kangaroo and Wallaby Families

Family Hypsiprymnodontidae

Musky rat kangaroo *Hypsiprymnodon moschatus*.

Family Macropodidae

Subfamily Sthenurinae (Sthenurines)

Banded hare wallaby *Lagostrophus fasciatus*. Listed as Vulnerable by the IUCN.

Bettongs and Potoroos
Subfamily Potoroinae

Bettongs and Potoroos are sometimes considered a separate family, the Potoroidae.
Bettongs Genus *Bettongia*, 4 species: Brush-tailed bettong or woylie (*B. penicillata*); Burrowing bettong or boodie *B. lesueur*; Northern bettong (*B. tropica*); and Tasmanian bettong (*B. gaimardi*). All 4 species are listed by the IUCN: the Northern bettong is Endangered, and the Burrowing bettong Vulnerable.
Potoroos Genus *Potorous*, 3 species: Long-nosed potoroo (*P. tridactylus*); Long-footed potoroo (*P. longipes*); and Gilbert's potoroo (*P. gilbertii*). Gilbert's potoroo is Critically Endangered, the Long-footed potoroo Endangered.
Desert rat kangaroo *Caloprymnus campestris* Listed as Extinct by the IUCN.
Rufous rat kangaroo *Aepyprymnus rufescens*.

Kangaroos and Wallabies
Subfamily Macropodinae

Kangaroos, Wallaroos, and Wallabies Genus *Macropus*, 14 species: Red kangaroo (*M. rufus*); Eastern gray kangaroo (*M. giganteus*); Western gray kangaroo (*M. fuliginosus*); Common or Hill wallaroo (*M. robustus*); Black wallaroo (*M. bernardus*); Agile wallaby (*M. agilis*); Antilopine wallaroo (*M. antilopinus*); Red-necked wallaby (*M. rufogriseus*); Black-striped wallaby (*M. dorsalis*); Tammar wallaby (*M. eugenii*); Whiptail or Prettyface wallaby (*M. parryi*); Toolache wallaby (*M. greyi*); Western brush wallaby (*M. irma*); and Parma wallaby (*M. parma*). The Toolache wallaby is now listed as Extinct by the IUCN; the Black wallaroo and the Parma and Western brush wallabies are Lower Risk: Near Threatened.
Tree kangaroos Genus *Dendrolagus*, 10 species: Grizzled tree kangaroo (*D. inustus*); Bennett's tree kangaroo (*D. bennettianus*); Lumholtz's tree kangaroo (*D. lumholtzi*); Matschie's or Huon tree kangaroo (*D.matschiei*); Lowland tree kangaroo (*D. spadix*); Doria's tree kangaroo (*D. dorianus*); Dingiso (*D. mbaiso*); tenkile (*D. scottae*); White-throated tree kangaroo (*D. ursinus*); and Goodfellow's tree kangaroo (*D. goodfellowi*). All 10 *Dendrolagus* species are listed by the IUCN; Goodfellow's, Matschie's, and the Tenkile tree kangaroos are Endangered.
Rock wallabies Genus *Petrogale*, about 15 species including: Yellow-footed rock wallaby (*P. xanthopus*); Brush-tailed rock wallaby (*P. penicillata*); Proserpine rock wallaby (*P. persephone*); Black-footed rock wallaby (*P. lateralis*); Cape York rock wallaby (*P. coenensis*); monjon (*P. burbidgei*); nabarlek (*P. concinna*); and Mount Claro rock wallaby (*P. sharmani*). Seven species are listed, including the Prosperine rock wallaby as Endangered, and the Brush-tailed rock wallaby, which is Vulnerable.
Hare wallabies Genus *Lagorchestes*, 4 species: Spectacled hare wallaby (*L. conspicillatus*); Central hare wallaby (*L. asomatus*); Eastern hare wallaby (*L. leporides*); and Rufous hare wallaby or mala (*L. hirsutus*). The Eastern and Central hare wallabies are now listed as Extinct by the IUCN; the Rufous hare wallaby is Vulnerable , while the Spectacled hare wallaby is Lower Risk: Near Threatened.
Pademelons Genus *Thylogale*, 4 species: Red-necked pademelon (*T. thetis*); Red-legged pademelon (*T. stigmatica*); Tasmanian pademelon (*T. billardierii*); and Dusky pademelon (*T. brunii*). The Dusky pademelon is Vulnerable.
Nail-tailed wallabies Genus *Onychogalea*, 3 species: Bridled nail-tailed wallaby (*O. fraenata*); Northern nail-tailed wallaby (*O. unguifera*); and Crescent nail-tailed wallaby (*O. lunata*). The Crescent nail-tailed wallaby is now listed as Extinct by the IUCN; the Bridled nail-tailed wallaby is Endangered.
Dorcopsises Genus *Dorcopsis*, 3 species: White-striped dorcopsis (*D. hageni*); Gray dorcopsis (*D. luctuosa*); Brown dorcopsis (*D. veterum*).
Forest wallabies Genus *Dorcopsulus*, 2 species: Papuan forest wallaby (*D. macleayi*), and Lesser forest wallaby (*D. vanheurni*). The Papuan forest wallaby is Vulnerable.
Quokka *Setonix brachyurus*. Vulnerable.
Swamp or Black wallaby *Wallabia bicolor*.

Below *A Red-necked wallaby and her young relax in the Tasmanian sun. Mothers bear a single young, but the short interval between births means that they often end up rearing an infant in the pouch while still continuing to feed an older offspring that has reached the "young-at-foot" phase.*

produce different qualities of milk from the two teats – a feat achieved by having the mammary glands under separate hormonal control.

The Musky rat kangaroo may give birth to litters of two or even three young, but all macropodids produce only one young at a birth. Few are strictly seasonal breeders; most can conceive and give birth at any time of year. In almost all species gestation lasts a few days short of the length of the estrus cycle – generally 4–5 weeks in macropodines and 3–4 weeks in potoroines.

Giving birth to such small babies is relatively effortless; the female sits with her tail forward between her legs and licks the fur between her cloaca and pouch, producing a path that will keep the climbing neonate moist until it enters the pouch. A few days after giving birth many macropods enter estrus once more. If they are mated and conceive, the new embryo's development halts at an unimplanted blastocyst stage. That "embryonic diapause" lasts until about a month before the current pouch-young is sufficiently developed to quit the pouch. Then the blastocyst implants in the uterus and resumes development. A day or two before birth is due, the mother will exclude the previous young from the pouch, a rebuff that is difficult for it to accept as it has earlier been taught to come when called and to climb back into the pouch. The mother then cleans and prepares the pouch for the next juvenile. Thus many macropod females can simultaneously support a suckling young-at-foot, a suckling pouch-young, and a dormant or developing embryo.

The short interval between births allows females to quickly replace young-at-foot that are killed by predators. It also permits them to easily replace "aborted" pouch-young. A female that is hard-pressed by a dingo may relax the sphincter muscles closing the pouch, dropping her young to get eaten while she escapes. Under the nutritional stress of drought a pouch-young will also die, but will quickly be replaced by the dormant blastocyst, which is stimulated to implant and resume development as soon as the previous pouch-young's suckling stops. At relatively low metabolic cost, a female in drought can maintain a succession of embryos ready to develop as soon as rains break and conditions turn favorable.

The young-at-foot phase comes to an end when the juvenile is weaned; it lasts many months in the large kangaroos, but may be almost absent in small rat kangaroos such as the Rufous bettong. Similarly, large kangaroos grow through a prolonged subadult phase before breeding. Females of the large kangaroos begin breeding at 2–3 years, when they have reached half their full size, and may breed for 8–12 years. Some small rat kangaroos can conceive within a month of weaning, at 4–5 months, but may delay until 10–11 months.

Macropod males may mature physiologically soon after the females, but in larger kangaroos their participation in reproduction is socially inhibited. Female growth decelerates after they begin breeding, but male growth continues strongly, resulting in old males being very much bigger than younger males and females. Indeed, a female Eastern gray or Red kangaroo, in estrus for the first time and weighing as little as 15–20kg (33–44lb), may be courted and mated by a male five or six times her own weight. The large macropods exhibit some of the most exaggerated sexual size dimorphism known for terrestrial mammals, largely because the biggest male in the population gets the majority of the matings. In contrast, males and females of the smaller wallabies and rat kangaroos reach the same adult sizes.

With the exception of females accompanied by dependent young, most macropods are solitary or are found occasionally with one or two others. Potoroines shelter alone during the day in a self-made nest, which a female may share with her unweaned young-at-foot. At night, when she emerges to forage, the female may be found and escorted by a male. In the nights before estrus, several males may attempt to associate with her.

Burrowing bettongs nest in self-dug burrows that form loose colonies, but they too are not truly social. The solitary macropodines that do not use permanent refuges (mostly smaller species living in dense habitat) behave much like potoroines, but association between a female and her most recent offspring may last many weeks beyond weaning. On the day of estrus, a female may be escorted by a chain of ardent males.

Left *The Musky rat kangaroo* (Hypsiprymnodon moschatus) *is a taxonomic oddity. Unlike all other kangaroos, which belong to the Macropodidae family, it is the sole representative of the Hypsiprymnodontidae. Its most distinctive anatomical feature is the presence of a first toe, lost in all the other species.*

Below *Representative small- and medium-sized kangaroos and wallabies:* ***1*** *Proserpine rock wallaby* (Petrogale persephone)*;* ***2*** *Yellow-footed rock wallaby* (P. xanthopus)*;* ***3*** *Burrowing bettong or boodie* (Bettongia lesueur)*;* ***4*** *quokka* (Setonix brachyurus)*;* ***5*** *Banded hare wallaby* (Lagostrophus fasciatus)*;* ***6*** *Rufous rat kangaroo* (Aepyprymnus rufescens)*. Several of these species are now listed by the IUCN as being at risk: the Proserpine rock wallaby is considered Endangered, and the quokka, Burrowing bettong, and Banded hare wallaby are all Vulnerable.*

Rock wallabies shelter during the day in caves and boulder piles, features that are clustered in the landscape, with the result that colonies of the animals inhabit clusters of daytime refuges. Individuals persistently use the same refuges, and males compete to keep other males away from the refuges of one or more females. In some rock wallaby species, males may consort closely with one or more females during the day, although they will not always forage together. A male tree kangaroo may similarly guard access to the trees used by one or a few females with which he associates.

Some of the largest *Macropus* species form groups (often called "mobs") of 50 or more animals. Membership of these groups is extremely flexible, however, with individuals joining and leaving several times a day. Some sex- and age-classes tend to associate with their peers or with specific other classes. Individual females may also associate with their female kin or with particular unrelated females; this association is frequent and persistent but not permanent. However, the stage of development of a female's young determines her association patterns; females with young about to be excluded from the pouch avoid others at the same stage by retreating to a part of their range generally not much used by other kangaroos, in order to stop the young from becoming confused during this period of rejection.

Males in these species move between groups more frequently than do females, and also move over larger ranges. No males are territorial, nor do any attempt to keep others out of a group of females. Males range widely, inspecting as many females as possible by sniffing the cloaca and urine-tasting. If a male detects a female approaching estrus, he will attempt to consort with her, following her about and mating her when she enters estrus. However, he can be displaced by any larger and more dominant male.

In the medium and large macropods, hierarchical position, based largely on size and thus upon age in these persistently growing animals, is the principal factor in male reproductive success. In the Eastern gray kangaroo, a locally dominant male may obtain up to a half of all matings within his home range. He will usually be able to hold top rank for one year only, however, and may have waited 8–10 years to reach that position. Most males never mate, and very few reach the top of the hierarchy. But those that do may father 20–30 offspring, or even more in dense populations.

In contrast, all females are likely to give birth to about one young a year throughout their adult lives. Among Eastern gray kangaroos, the chances of the young surviving to adulthood are strongly

Above *A kangaroo relaxes with her young in a refreshing pool of water. Large kangaroos mostly keep cool by resting in the heat of the day, coming out to feed at twilight or by night.*

affected by the number of female relatives a mother has. Those with many female kin are much more likely to rear their own young, and especially their first, successfully through the young-at-foot period, the time of major mortality. In Eastern gray kangaroos, the survival rate is 35 percent for the offspring of mothers whose own mother was still alive at the time of the birth, but only 8 percent if the mother had died. The chances of the first two joeys – baby kangaroos – surviving without a "grandmother" or "aunt" to assist in parenting is just 12 percent, rising to 25 percent when there is a grandmother but no aunts and to 42 percent when there are also one or more aunts.

Extraordinarily, these benefits seem to have translated into a maternal strategy of giving birth to females early in life, while sons are born correspondingly late in a female's breeding career. In Eastern grays the ratio is about 1 daughter to 0.8 sons for the first two offspring, rising to 1 daughter to 1.3 sons in mid career and to 1 daughter to 2.9 sons in the final offspring.

The larger, social macropods all live in open country (grasslands, shrublands, or savanna), and were formerly preyed upon by cursorial and aerial predators such as dingos, Wedge-tailed eagles, and the now-extinct thylacine. Social grouping has conferred the same anti-predator benefits on large kangaroos as on so many other animals, in that dingoes are less able to get close to large groups, which can thus spend more time feeding. Group size of kangaroos relates to their density, the kind of habitat – especially its lateral cover – the time of day, and the weather.

Pests and Prey

CONSERVATION AND ENVIRONMENT

Between 2 and 4 million Red, Eastern, and Western gray kangaroos and Common wallaroos are shot every year in Australia because they are considered pests of pasture and crops. The cull is licensed, regulated, and for the most part humane. These large species were less numerous when Australia was first settled by Europeans, and from 1850–1900 several scientists feared that they might go extinct. Provision of pasture and of well-distributed water for sheep and cattle, together with (particularly) the reduction in numbers of dingoes, their main natural predators, as well as of hunting by Aboriginal peoples, all allowed the kangaroos to flourish.

Kangaroos used to be the main prey for Aboriginal spear-hunters. Smaller wallabies were flushed by fire or driven into nets or else toward lines of hunters armed with spears and throwing-sticks. In New Guinea, they were once pursued with bows and arrows, but are now killed with firearms instead. In some areas commercial hunting is rapidly depleting densities and endangering tree kangaroos and other restricted species.

In most of Australia outside the rain forest and wet sclerophyll forest, densities of macropod species with an adult weight of less than 5–6kg (11–13lb) have fallen in the past century or less. On the mainland, several such species are now extinct or very severely limited in range outside the tropics, although some have survived on offshore islands. The extinctions have been caused by a combination of habitat clearing for (or modification by) introduced livestock and, most especially, the impact of foxes. Introduced for sport in Victoria from 1860–80, foxes spread rapidly through sheep country, living primarily on rabbits, but taking as secondary prey bettongs and wallabies, which plummeted in numbers. On fox-free islands these species survived.

Where foxes have been suppressed, such species (if still present) have recovered their former densities. However, foxes, rabbits, and land-clearing are still widespread, and the battle to save small and medium-sized macropods in Australia is not yet won. PJ

A MUTUALLY BENEFICIAL RELATIONSHIP

How rat kangaroos help to cultivate the fungi they feed on

ON THE ROOTS OF MOST VASCULAR PLANTS LIVE fungi. The two symbiotically provide for each other; the plant supplies carbohydrate food, while the fungi enhance the uptake by the plant of nutrients (especially phosphorus) and of moisture from the soil. Associations of this sort between plants and fungi are known as mycorrhizal symbiosis, and they represent a very ancient liaison found in practically all terrestrial ecosystems.

Eucalyptuses typically have very high levels of mycorrhizal association, as Australian soils tend to be poor and deficient in phosphorus. So crucial is this relationship that foresters attempting to recreate natural forest must inoculate the trees with mycorrhizal fungi to ensure success. The fungi that associate with eucalypts are of two kinds. Some are mushrooms that produce fruiting bodies above ground and have spores dispersed by the wind; many others, however, fruit below ground. These hypogeous (subterranean) fungi are similar in many respects to European truffles; like them, they release delicious smells that attract mammals to dig them up and eat the fruiting bodies. The spores survive their passage through the mammals' digestive tracts, and germinate after being deposited on the ground in feces. They may, however, first be carried for quite long distances in the mammals' gut, so this is an effective means of dispersing spores throughout the forest.

For some species of fungus, passage through the digestive tract actually seems to stimulate the germination of spores. The "spore rain" produced by mammals is presumably important in maintaining the mycorrhizal association on mature root systems at a high level, as well as in rapidly establishing mycorrhizal fungi on the root systems of seedlings. Living on trees and dispersed by mammals, the fungi are a central link in the forest ecological web.

There are many willing takers for the proffered fungal delights. In Australia, the rat kangaroos (bettongs and potoroos) that live in eucalypt forests feed almost exclusively on these fungi. These animals will dig as deep as 20cm (8in) into the soil to find truffles, and in captivity they prefer freshly-collected truffles over any other food. There are other species of mammals in eucalypt forests – bandicoots and many rodents – that feed on hypogeous fungi, but the fact that rat kangaroos eat fungi year-round and harvest fruiting bodies in large numbers must make them especially efficient spore-dispersers.

In addition to promoting the reproduction of mycorrhizal fungi, rat kangaroos may also be responsible for protecting their diversity. It is common to find 20 or more different species of fungi living in stands of a single species of eucalypt, many of them on the root system of a single tree. Typically, a small number of these species are very abundant, while most are rare. Rat kangaroos are extremely adept at finding fungi of many different species; for example, a study of the Long-footed potoroo showed that it was eating more than 40 species of hypogeous fungi over an area of only a few hectares, far more than even very experienced human mycologists were able to collect. In the absence of spore dispersal, the fungi would spread by growth of their hyphae – the fungal equivalent of root systems – through the soil, and those with the most vigorous growth would probably eventually displace others from the community. The fact that rat kangaroos are so effective at finding uncommon fungi and broadcasting their spores may be an important factor in keeping them healthy.

The rat kangaroos' role does not end there. Into the already complex but precisely choreographed web of life in an Australian forest comes the element of fire. Eucalypt forests are generally very fire-prone; many eucalypt species have features that encourage its spread as well as adaptations (such as stimulation of seed fall by heat and of seed germination by smoke) that link reproduction to the conflagrations. But if fires kill adult trees, this must lead to the death of their fungal associates soon after, so a mechanism is needed to ensure spore dispersal before the fungi die.

Rat kangaroos are very skilled at surviving fire. One study using radio-tracking to follow Brush-tailed bettongs during a hot fire showed that the animals managed to move around the flames while still remaining within their home ranges. After a fire, the rate of digging for hypogeous fungi by rat kangaroos increases dramatically, as animals in the area increase their feeding on the fungi and others move in from neighboring, unburned areas to feed over the burned ground. The result is that after a fire more fungi get dispersed, both within burned patches and from unburned to burned patches, ensuring that spores are introduced to new seedlings growing in the ashes. Thus the continuity of life is ensured.

There is a beautiful postscript to the story that brings an insect into the equation. Several dung beetle species have evolved specialized relationships with particular species of rat kangaroos. The beetles lay their eggs in dung, which their developing young subsequently eat. Unlike most such beetles, which search for fresh dung on the wing, these species cling to the fur at the base of a rat kangaroo's tail, waiting until feces are passed, when they drop off and bury them. This strategy gives the beetles first access to the feces, and the species that practice it tend to be poor competitors for dung. But the association also aids spore dispersal, providing a mechanism by which fungal spores are immediately transported close to the roots of trees, and so facilitating their germination and the reestablishment of the symbiosis. CJ

Below *Tasmanian bettongs are among the species that eat fungi and disperse their spores. Others include the Northern and Brush-tailed bettongs and all three species of potoroos.*

Life in the Pouch

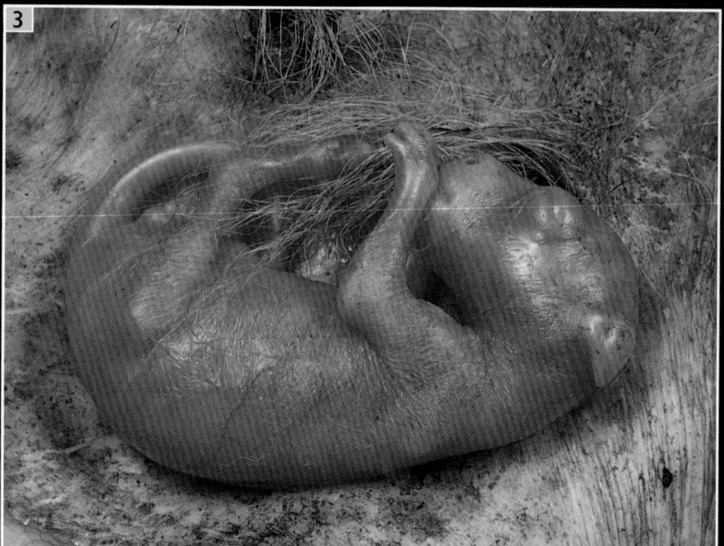

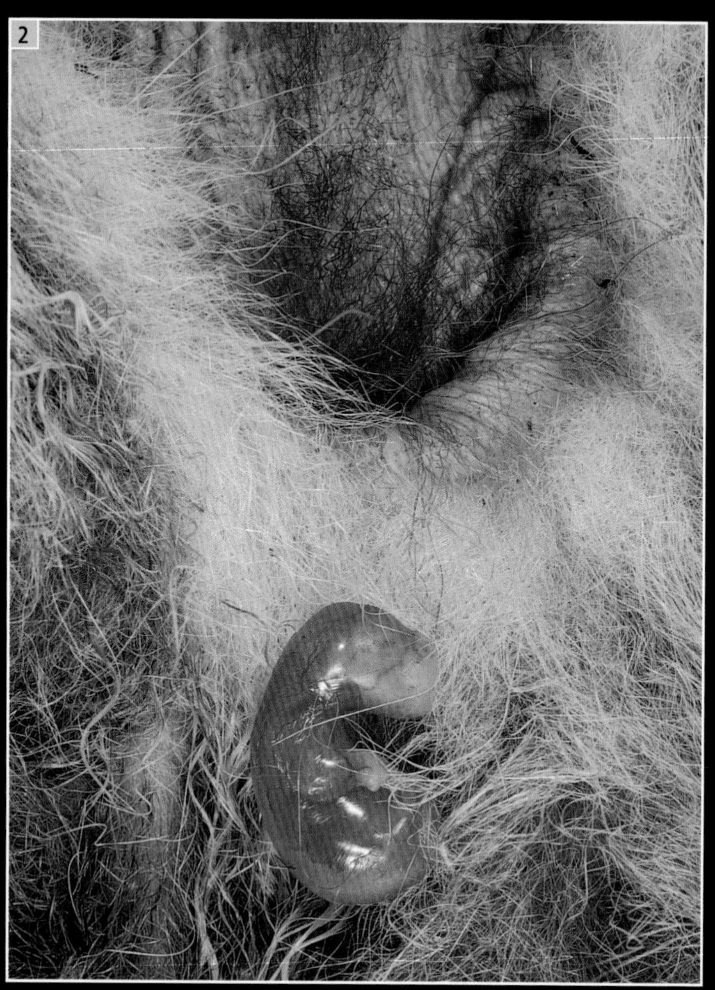

❶❷ *What characterizes all macropods is their highly undeveloped state at birth. In comparison with the newborn of placental mammals, those of marsupials are in an almost embryonic state, with rudimentary hind limbs and tail, ears and eyes closed, and no fur. Yet once the umbilical cord (seen left, below) breaks, the tiny infant is able to propel itself on its relatively strong fore limbs through its mother's fur to reach the safety of her pouch. The climb from birth canal to pouch will take about 2 minutes.*

❸ *The teat (there are four in the pouch) fills the infant's mouth and holds it securely in place; this kangaroo is 4 weeks old. Kangaroos and wallabies suckle for 6–11 months.*

❹ *By 12–14 weeks of age, a kangaroo has grown fast and acquired recognizable features. If a young kangaroo dies or is killed by predators, the mother does not need to mate again to conceive – a second, fertilized egg is immediately implanted in the uterus, and a new embryo begins development.*

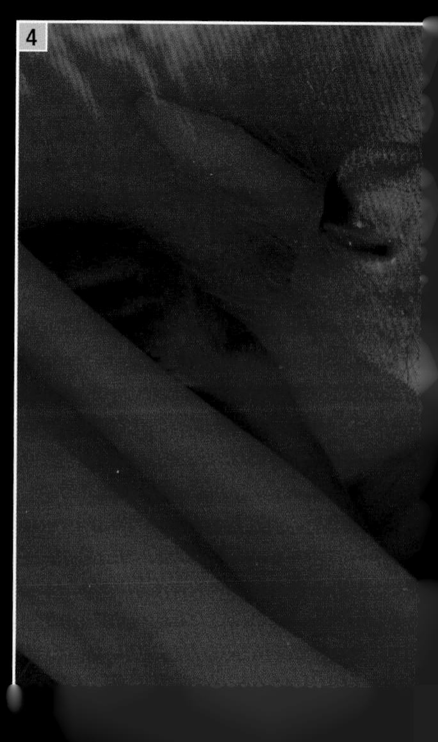

❻ *An Eastern gray kangaroo at the "young at foot" phase. Though it is now denied access to the pouch, it is still not weaned and will suckle for several months to come. To promote rapid growth, the walking young receives fatty milk, while the new infant inside the pouch is provided with fat-free milk. Nurturing two live young simultaneously, with an egg always ready for implantation, has proved an effective reproductive strategy for Australia's large marsupials.*

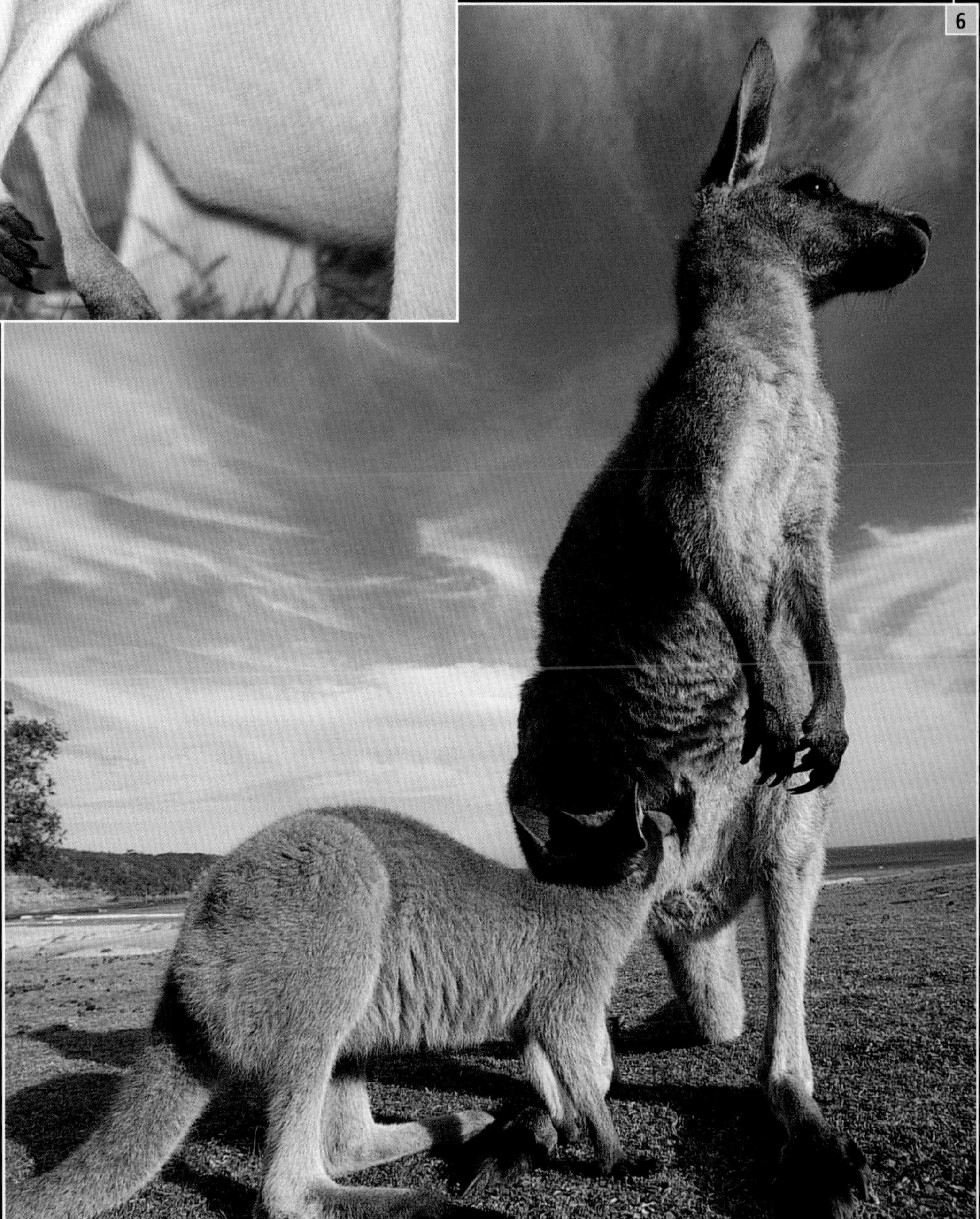

❺ *Almost too large for its accommodation, a well-developed red kangaroo peers from its mother's pouch. This individual is at the stage of semi-independence, where it makes excursions outside but comes back to the pouch to sleep and suckle. It will soon be excluded for good, to make way for a newborn sibling.*

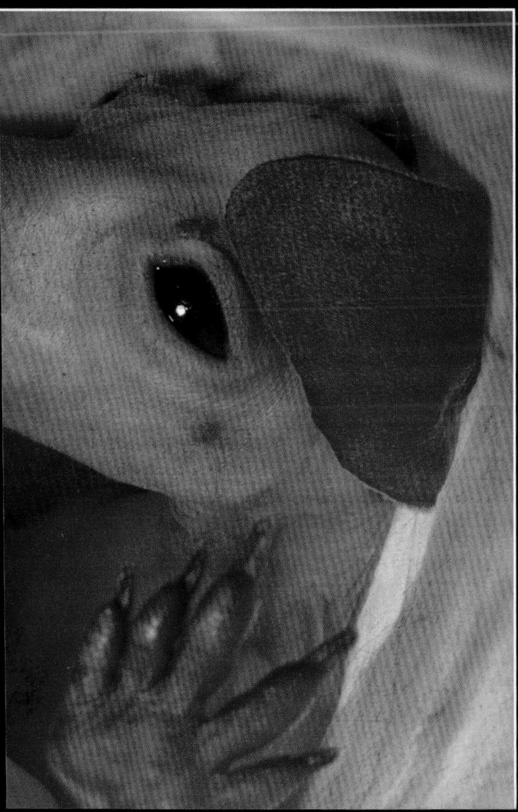

Koala

THE KOALA IS NOW AUSTRALIA'S ANIMAL ICON and one of the world's most charismatic mammals, but this has not always been the case. The first European settlers considered koalas stupid and killed millions for their pelts. Even more serious threats to the animals' survival came from the impact of forest clearance, large-scale forest fires, and the introduction of zoonotic disease, particularly domestic animal strains of chlamydia.

The threat to koalas reached a peak in 1924, when more than 2 million skins were exported. By that time, the species had been exterminated in South Australia, and had largely disappeared from Victoria and New South Wales. As a result of public outcry, bans on hunting were introduced, and intensive management, particularly in the southern populations from 1944 on, has subsequently reversed this decline. Koalas are now once more relatively common in their favored habitat.

Below *A koala rides on its mother's back. At birth the single young are minuscule, weighing less than 0.5g (0.02oz). After 5 months they start to feed on eucalypt leaves partly predigested by their mothers. At 7 months they leave the pouch, but continue to travel with their mothers for another 4 or 5 months.*

Large Bellies, Small Brains

FORM AND FUNCTION

Trees from the genus *Eucalyptus* are widespread in Australia, and koalas are wedded to them. They spend almost their entire lives in eucalypts. Much of the day is taken up in sleeping (which occupies more than 80 percent of their time); less than 10 percent is required for feeding, and the rest is mainly spent just sitting.

Koalas display numerous adaptations for this relatively inactive, arboreal lifestyle. As they use neither dens nor shelters, their tailless, bearlike bodies are well-insulated with a dense covering of fur. Their large paws are equipped with strongly recurved, needle-sharp claws on most digits, and these make the koala a most accomplished climber, able to ascend the largest smooth-barked eucalypts with ease. To climb, they grip onto the trunk with their claws and use their powerful forearms to heave upwards, while simultaneously bringing the hind limbs up in a bounding motion. The forcipate structure of the forepaws (the first and second digits are opposable to the other three) enables them to grip smaller branches and climb into the outer canopy. They are less agile on the ground, but move frequently between trees, using a slow, quadrupedal walk.

The teeth of the koala are adapted to cope with eucalypt leaves, which are extremely fibrous. Using their cheek teeth, which are reduced to a single premolar and four broad, high-cusped molars on each jaw, they chew the leaves into a very fine paste. This digesta then undergoes microbial fermentation in the cecum, which, at 1.8–2.5m (5.9–8.2ft), is the largest of any mammal in proportion to body size, stretching three times the koala's body length or more.

The small brain of the koala may also be an adaptation for a low-energy diet. Energetically, brains are expensive organs to run as they consume a disproportionate amount of the body's total energy budget. Relative to its body size, the koala's brain is one of the smallest found in marsupials. The brain of a southern koala of average size (9.6kg/21lb)) weighs only about 17g/0.6oz (0.2 percent of body weight).

Male koalas are 50 percent heavier than females, and have a broader face, comparatively smaller ears, and a large, odoriferous sternal (chest) gland. The principal secondary sex characteristic of the females is the pouch, which contains two teats and opens to the rear.

Koalas have a broadly polygynous mating system in which some males do most of the mating, but precise details on the distribution of matings

FACTFILE

KOALA

Phascolarctos cinereus

Order: Diprotodontia

Family: Phascolarctidae

Sole memb\er of genus

DISTRIBUTION Disjunct in E Australia S of latitude 17°

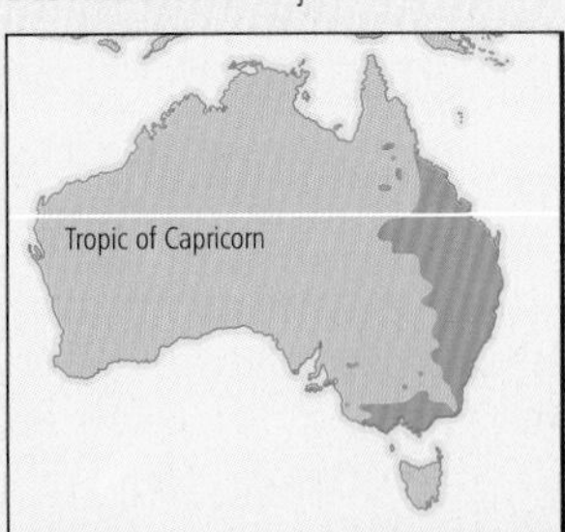

HABITAT Eucalypt forests and woodlands

SIZE **Head–body length** male 78cm (30.7in), female 72cm (28.3in); **weight** male 11.8kg (26lb), female 7.9kg (17.4lb). Animals from N of the range are significantly smaller, averaging only 6.5kg (14.3lb) for males and 5.1kg (11.2lb) for females.

COAT Gray to tawny; white on chin, chest, and inner side of forelimbs; ears fringed with long white hairs; rump dappled with white patches; coat shorter and lighter in N of range.

DIET Foliage, mainly from a limited range of eucalypt species, although leaves from some non-eucalypts including *Acacia*, *Leptospermum*, and *Melaleuca* are also browsed.

BREEDING Females sexually mature at 21–24 months; single young born in summer months (Nov–March) after gestation of about 35 days. Young become independent after 12 months. Females are capable of breeding in successive years.

LONGEVITY Up to 18 years

CONSERVATION STATUS Lower Risk: Near Threatened. Common where habitat is intact, particularly in the S of its range, rarer in the N. Large-scale clearing of woodlands is threatening the northern populations.

Above *Traveling between trees, a koala moves cautiously across the forest floor. The animals usually walk sedately, but can bound forward in emergencies.*

between dominant and subdominant animals have not been comprehensively researched and await elucidation. Female koalas are sexually mature and commence breeding at 2 years of age. Males are fertile at the same age, but their mating success is usually poor until they are older, at about 4–5 years, when they are large enough to compete successfully for females.

Following the Forest

DISTRIBUTION PATTERNS

The koala is often thought of as a fragile and rare species, but in reality it tolerates a wide range of environmental conditions. The eucalypt forests on which koalas depend are widespread but fragmented, and the distribution of the animals now reflects the state of the forest.

Koala populations are often widely separated from each other, usually by extensive tracts of cleared land. Even so, they still occur across several hundred thousands of square kilometers, stretching in a broad swathe across eastern Australia from the edge of the Atherton Tablelands in North Queensland to Cape Otway at the southernmost tip of Victoria.

Koalas occupy a surprisingly diverse range of habitats across this range. These encompass wet montane forests in the south, vine thickets in the tropical north, and woodlands in the semi-arid west of their range. Their abundance varies markedly with the productivity of the habitat. In fertile, high-rainfall country in the south, abundances as high as 8 animals per hectare (more than 3 to an acre) are not uncommon, while in the semi-arid zone 100 hectares (250 acres) may be required to support a single animal.

An Unpromising Food

DIET

As evergreen plants, eucalypts are a constantly available resource for leaf-eating animals. An adult koala eats about 500g (1.1lb) of fresh leaf daily, yet while there are more than 600 species of eucalypts to choose from, koalas feed from only 30 or so of these. Preferences differ between populations, with animals usually focusing on species growing in the wetter, more productive habitats. In the south *Eucalyptus viminalis* and *E. ovata* are preferred, while the northern populations feed predominantly on *E. camaldulensis*, *E. microcorys*, *E. propinqua*, *E. punctata*, and *E. tereticornis*.

Such a diet at first sight might seem unpromising. Eucalypt leaf is inedible, if not downright toxic, to most herbivores. It is low in essential nutrients, including nitrogen and phosphorus; it contains high concentrations of indigestible structural materials such as cellulose and lignin; and it is laced with poisonous phenolics and terpenes (essential oils). Recent research has shown that these last compounds may hold the key to koalas' preferences, as the acceptability of browse species has been found to correlate inversely with the concentration of certain highly toxic phenol–terpene hybrids.

The koala shows a number of adaptations that enable it to cope with such inauspicious food. Some leaves they obviously avoid altogether. Toxic components in others are detoxified in the liver and excreted. Coping with the low available energy provided by such a diet, however, requires behavioral adjustments, and koalas sleep a lot, for up to 20 hours a day. This has given rise to the popular myth that they are drugged by the eucalypt compounds they ingest. Koalas also exhibit very tight water economy and, except in the hottest weather, obtain all of their water requirements from the leaves.

Left Firmly wedged in a fork in a tree, a koala indulges in the species' favorite pastime: sleeping. The animals spend as much as 80 percent of their time asleep, and a substantial proportion of their waking hours is passed in resting. Their inactive lifestyle is linked to a low-energy diet made up almost entirely of eucalypt leaves, which are short of essential nutrients, including nitrogen and phosphorus.

Right Foraging in the branches, a koala strikes an unlikely King Kong pose as it stretches for a eucalypt sprig. Eucalypts are poisonous to most herbivores, but koalas' livers have adapted to be able to cope with at least some of the toxins they contain. Evolution thereby opened up for the animals a relatively uncontested food resource available all the year round.

Solitary and Sedentary

SOCIAL BEHAVIOR

Koalas are solitary animals. They are also sedentary, with adults occupying fixed home ranges. The size of these ranges is related to the productivity of the environment. In the more prolific forests of the south the ranges are comparatively small, with males occupying only 1.5–3ha (3.7–7.4 acres) and females 0.5–1ha (1.2–2.5 acres). In semi-arid areas, however, they are much larger, and males occupy 100ha (250 acres) or more. The home range of socially dominant males overlap the ranges of up to nine females, as well as those of subadult and subordinate males.

Koalas are principally nocturnal, and in the breeding season adult males move around a great deal in the summer nights. Fights usually occur if they meet up with other adult males and matings if they encounter a receptive (estrous) female. Copulation is brief, usually lasting less than 2 minutes, and occurs in a tree. The male mounts the female from behind, usually holding her between himself and the branch while mating.

Females give birth to a single young, with the majority of births occurring in midsummer (December–February). The newborn animal weighs less than 0.5g (0.02oz) and climbs unaided from the urogenital opening to the pouch, where it firmly attaches to one of the two teats there. Over the next 6 months of pouch life, the young grows and develops while suckling this same teat. Weaning commences after 5 months, and is initiated by the young feeding on partially digested leaf material produced from the female's anus. The mother is able to clear the normally hard fecal pellets from the lower bowel before producing this soft material, and may be stimulated into doing so by the young nuzzling the region. The high concentration of microorganisms in this pap is thought to inoculate the gut of the young with the microbes it needs to digest eucalypt leaf. Growth is rapid from this time onward. The young leaves the pouch after 7 months to travel around clinging to the mother's back. It becomes independent at around 11 months of age, but usually continues to live close to the mother for several months afterward.

Males bellow incessantly through the early months of the breeding season, and these calls, which consist of a series of harsh inhalations each followed by a resonant growling expiration, appear to serve both as an advertisement to potential mates as well as a warning threat to competing males. The call of one male usually elicits a response from all the adult males in the area. The only loud vocalization heard from females is a wailing distress call, usually given when they are being harassed by an adult male. At this time of the year males are often seen scentmarking by rubbing their sternal gland against the trunk of trees, but the precise role of this behavior has yet to be elucidated.

When Clusters Become Crowds

CONSERVATION AND ENVIRONMENT

So far there has been no official attempt to enumerate the total population of wild koalas, but unofficial estimates range from 40,000 to more than 1 million. Genetic studies indicate strong differentiation between northern and southern populations, and suggest that there might be a number of distinct subpopulations in the north. No such pattern has been detected among the southern populations, a fact that is thought to reflect the homogenizing effect of the extensive translocation program that has occurred there.

Habitat loss is threatening the viability of many koala populations, particularly in the northern part of their range. Urban and tourist developments are claiming important areas of habitat in coastal regions, but the situation is especially serious in the semi-arid woodlands of central Queensland, where around 400,000 hectares (1 million acres) are being cleared annually for pastoral and other agricultural purposes. While environmentalists are attempting to stop this clearance, it is a politically difficult issue in the conservative farming areas of central Queensland.

Management problems in the south make koala conservation there an even more complex issue. Historically the koala has been a rare species on the mainland, but overpopulation has been a persistent problem in a few koala colonies established on offshore islands in the late 19th century. This issue has been addressed via translocations, and over the last 75 years more than 10,000 koalas have been relocated back to the mainland.

While the translocation program has reestablished the koala throughout most of its southern range, it has also transferred the problems of overpopulation and habitat degradation to many forest remnants on the mainland. Culling to control overpopulation is widely unpopular, and contraceptive methods are now being tried as a method of capping the growth of these populations. RM

Wombats

THERE ARE ONLY THREE LIVING SPECIES OF wombats, but they represent, together with the koala, one of the two great lineages of marsupial herbivores. The suborder Vombatiformes – which comprises the koala and wombats – diverged from the other marsupial herbivores at least 40 million years ago, and since then wombats have evolved a way of life that is unique among mammals.

The wombats are large-bodied, burrowing herbivores. This combination of traits is extraordinary: the few other large mammals that burrow are either carnivores or specialized insectivores, while the numerous other burrowing herbivores are all small. Much of the interest in the biology of wombats comes from the fact that they defy the general rule which dictates that burrowing and large body size among herbivores are mutually exclusive. The time and effort required to dig a burrow are usually precluded by the need to feed constantly, in order to gain sufficient nutrition from low-energy grass or browse.

Equipment for Burrowing and Grazing

FORM AND FUNCTION

Wombats are stocky, with short tails and limbs. The pectoral girdle is heavy and strong, and the humerus is very broad relative to its length, making the shoulders and forelimbs exceptionally powerful. The forepaws are massive, and bear long, heavy claws. Wombats burrow by scratch-digging with the forepaws, throwing soil behind them with the hind feet and using their ample rumps to bulldoze it clear of the burrow entrance. The wombat skeleton has many detailed features that increase the power of the limbs. For example, the posterior angle of the scapula (shoulder blade) is extended to increase the lever arm for the *teres major* muscle. The male and female are similar in all species, but male Northern hairy-nosed wombats have shorter bodies than females, along with thicker necks and heavier shoulders. The significance of this is unknown – perhaps their thick necks equip males for head-to-head confrontations down burrows.

Wombats feed primarily on grasses that are high in fiber and (especially on sandy soils) high in abrasive silica. The skull, teeth, and digestive tract are specially adapted to this diet. The skull is massive, broad, and flattened, allowing the jaws to exert great compressive force that is used to grind their coarse food. This compensates for the lack of a deeply furrowed rasping surface on the teeth, and enables wombats to grind their food to a very small particle size (about half that achieved by kangaroos). The teeth grow throughout life to compensate for tooth wear. The stomach and small intestine are small and simple and there is almost no cecum, but the colon is expanded and elongated, forming about 80 percent of total gut volume. Microbial fermentation takes place primarily in the colon, contributing about one-third of the total energy assimilated by the animal. Food passes slowly through the gut: particles remain there for an average of 70 hours and solutes for about 50 hours, far longer than in other similarly-sized herbivores.

The Low-Maintenance Marsupial

SOCIAL BEHAVIOR

A common feature of all of the three species of wombats is their ability to maintain high population densities even in very unproductive habitats. Common wombats occur in alpine environments up to and above the snowline, as well as in sandy coastal environments where they may reach very high densities. Hairy-nosed wombats occur in dry habitats, where soil fertility may be too low to support grazing by domestic livestock.

Wombats thrive in such environments because they have extremely reduced energy requirements. The basal metabolic rates of wombats are very low – the Southern hairy-nosed wombat has a rate only 44 percent of that predicted for eutherian mammals of similar mass – and their maintenance energy requirements are the lowest known for marsupials. The combination of low maintenance needs and efficient digestion of high-fiber diets means that the daily food intake of wombats is also very low – only about half that of similarly-sized kangaroos. A wombat spends much less time foraging than might be expected for a herbivore of its size. Total feeding times of as little as two hours per day have been recorded for Northern hairy-nosed wombats in good seasons, and feeding ranges are only about 10 percent of those used by kangaroos in similar habitat. This extreme conservatism allows wombats to spend most of their time underground, and this behavior in turn contributes further to energy conservation by protecting them from unfavorable weather conditions. Although they do not enter torpor, wombats may spend several days at a stretch in their burrows, during which time their energy expenditure must be very low indeed.

Because wombats are nocturnal, secretive, and spend so much time underground, little is known of their behavior. Burrows may be 30m (98ft) or more long, and often have several entrances, side tunnels, and resting chambers. The Southern

Above *A Common wombat mother and her offspring use a fallen tree trunk as a table for a meal of foliage. After leaving the pouch at the age of 6 months, the young may continue to follow their mothers about for as much as a year.*

Above left *A Southern hairy-nosed wombat displays the furry muzzle that distinguishes the two* Lasiorhinus *species from the Common wombat.*

hairy-nosed wombat inhabits large warrens that remain in constant use for decades. Groups of up to ten animals may live there, but interactions are rare and they feed solitarily. The family structure of these groups is unknown.

Among Northern hairy-nosed wombats, burrows are arranged in loose clusters, with entrances about 10m (33ft) apart; different clusters are typically several hundred meters distant. Genetic relatedness is higher for animals in the same cluster than between neighboring clusters. There may be up to ten animals in a group, with equal numbers of males and females. This species displays an unusual pattern of dispersal, in which both young males and females remain in their home burrow cluster, but adult females may disperse to a different cluster after rearing an offspring. Dispersal distances of up to 3km (1.8mi) have been recorded. Common wombats appear to be more solitary than Hairy-nosed wombats.

Cause for Concern

CONSERVATION AND ENVIRONMENT

Over the past 200 years both the Common wombat and the Southern hairy-nosed wombat have suffered range reductions of 10–50 percent as a result of habitat clearance and competition with rabbits, but they remain secure across much of their original range. *Vombatus ursinus ursinus* has gone extinct from all the Bass Strait islands except Flinders Island. In parts of Victoria, Common wombats are considered pests because of the damage they do to rabbit-proof fences, and some local control is carried out.

The Northern hairy-nosed wombat is now one of the rarest mammals in the world. This species has only ever been confirmed in three localities, and it went extinct from two of these early last century as a result of competition with cattle and sheep, habitat change, and poisoning campaigns directed at rabbits. The last population was not finally protected until the 3,000-ha (7,400-acre) Epping Forest National Park was declared over its entire range in 1974 and cattle were excluded in 1980. At that time the population probably consisted of just 35 individuals. By 1995, capture–mark–recapture studies estimated a population of around 70 animals.

To date, the management of this population has focussed on protection of its habitat, especially the control of fire and exclusion of cattle, while minimizing direct interference with the animals. This appears to have allowed the species to begin its recovery, but its fate remains precariously balanced, and plans are afoot to begin captive breeding and to establish other wild populations. CJ

FACTFILE

WOMBATS

Order: Diprotodontia

Family: Vombatidae

3 species in 2 genera

DISTRIBUTION SE Australia

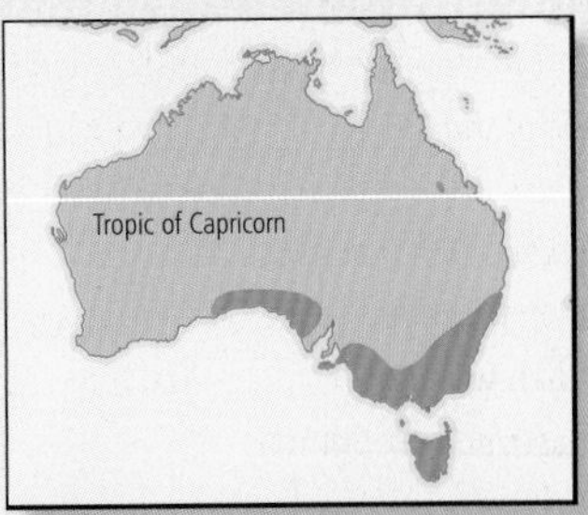

COMMON WOMBAT *Vombatus ursinus*

Three subspecies: *Vombatus ursinus ursinus* (Flinders Island); *V. u. tasmaniensis* (Tasmania); *V. u. hirsutus* (mainland Australia). Temperate forests and woodlands, heaths, and alpine habitats throughout SE Australia, including Flinders Island and Tasmania. HBL 90–115cm (35–45in); TL c.2.5cm (1 in); HT c.36cm (14in); WT 22–39kg (48.5–86lb). Form: coat coarse, black or brown to gray; bare muzzle; short, rounded ears. Diet: primarily grasses, but also sedges, rushes, and the roots of shrubs and trees. Breeding: one offspring, may be born at any time of the year. Pouch life is about 6 months, and the young remains at heel for about another year; sexual maturity is at 2 years of age. Longevity: unknown in the wild, up to 26 years in captivity. Conservation status: Vulnerable.

SOUTHERN HAIRY-NOSED WOMBAT
Lasiorhinus latifrons

Central southern Australia; semi-arid and arid woodlands, grasslands, and shrub steppes. HBL 77–94cm (30–37in); TL c.2.5cm (1 in); HT c.36cm (14in); WT 19–32kg (42–70lb). Form: coat fine, gray to brown, with lighter patches; hairy muzzle; long, pointed ears. Diet: grasses, including forbs and foliage of woody shrubs during drought. Breeding: single young, born in spring or early summer, remains in the pouch for 6–9 months; weaning occurs at approximately 1 year, and sexual maturity at 3 years. Longevity: unknown in the wild, more than 20 years in captivity.

NORTHERN HAIRY-NOSED WOMBAT
Lasiorhinus krefftii

Sole population in Epping Forest National Park, near Clermont in central Queensland; semi-arid woodland. HBL male 102cm (40in), female 107cm (42in); HT c.40cm (16in); WT male 30kg (66lb), female 32.5kg (72lb). Coat: silver gray, dark rings around the eyes. Diet: grasses, plus some sedges and forbs. Breeding: one young born in spring or summer; pouch life c.10 months; weaning age unknown; females breed on average twice every 3 years. Longevity: unknown in the wild; one captive animal lived at least 30 years. Conservation status: Critically Endangered.

Abbreviations HBL = head–body length TL = tail length HT = height WT = weight

Honey Possum

Left Restricted to the south-western corner of Australia, the Honey possum has a tail that is longer than its head and body combined, and a tongue that can be extended 2.5cm (1in) beyond its nose. Bristles on the tongue's tip brush pollen from flowers.

Right Nectar and pollen make up the entire diet of the Honey possum, shown here feeding on Banksia. The pointed snout is a specialization for this food, used to probe deep into individual flowers in search of nectar. With its grasping hands, feet, and tail, the animal can feed even on small terminal flowers on all but the most slender branches.

THE HONEY POSSUM IS THE SOLE MEMBER of a line of marsupials that diverged very early from possum–kangaroo stock. Although its entire fossil history is contained within the last 35,000 years, it probably evolved about 20 million years ago, when heathlands were widespread.

Today, Honey possums are most abundant in heathlands on coastal sandplains in southwestern Australia, one of 25 biodiversity hotspots worldwide, where about 2,000 species of plants ensure a yearlong supply of the flowers upon which the animals depend for their food.

Foragers among the Flowers

FORM AND FUNCTION

The Honey possum's teeth are reduced in number and size, with a dental formula of I2/1, C1/0, P1/0, M3/3 = 22, but the molars are merely tiny cones. They use a long, protrusive tongue with a brush surface to lick nectar from flowers. Combs on the roof of the mouth remove pollen grains from the brush tongue. The contents of these pollen grains are digested during a rapid, six-hour transit through a simple intestine to provide the Honey possum's sole source of nutrients; nectar (20 percent sugar solution) provides only energy and water. Unusual kidneys allow the animals to excrete up to their own weight in water daily. They feed mainly on *Banksias* and dryandras, plants with large blossoms containing from 250 to 2,500 flowers. The food plants they favor have drably-colored flowers that are concealed either inside bushes or else close to the ground.

These tiny, shrewlike mammals use their long, pointed snouts to probe the flowers. The first digit of the hind foot is opposable to the others for gripping branches, and all digits have rough pads on the tips, not claws. Honey possums run fast on the ground and clamber with great agility over dense heathland vegetation. A long, partially prehensile tail provides balance and support for climbing, and frees the grasping hands to grip branches and manipulate flowers while feeding.

Nonstop Motherhood

SOCIAL BEHAVIOR

Honey possums communicate through a small repertoire of visual postures and high-pitched squeaks, a reflection of their mainly nocturnal activity. Smell appears very important in their social behavior and also helps them locate the flowers of their food plants.

The short lifespan of Honey possums is balanced by their continuous reproduction. A female carries young in her pouch for almost all of her adult life. Both sexes mature at around the age of 6 months. Many females breed for the first time while not yet fully grown, just 3 or 4 months after leaving the pouch in which they have spent the first 2 months of their lives. Births occur throughout the year, but reach very low levels when food is scarce. Population sizes are larger, body condition better, and births more common when nectar is most abundant. The timing of these cycles varies seasonally and between years in relation to rainfall, as well as geographically with differences in plant assemblages. Females appear to breed opportunistically whenever food is abundant, irrespective of the later consequences for their young.

A second litter is often born very soon after the first leaves the pouch or is weaned, since the Honey possum exhibits embryonic diapause (the temporary cessation of development in an embryo). In good times, some females can give

FACTFILE

HONEY POSSUM

Tarsipes rostratus

Order: Diprotodontia

Sole member of the family Tarsipedidae

DISTRIBUTION SW Australia

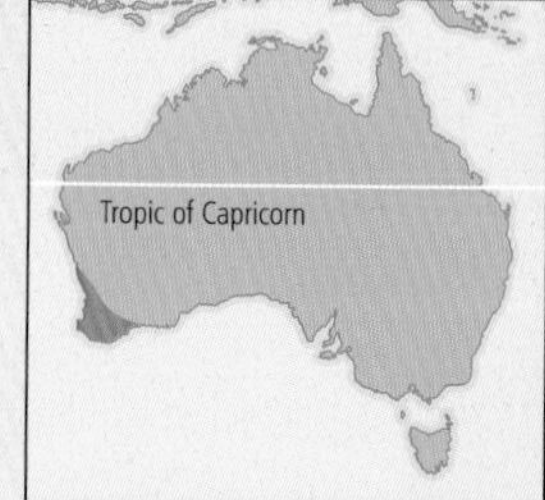

HABITAT Heathland, shrubland, and low open woodland with heath understory.

SIZE **Head–body length** male 6.5–8.5cm (2.6–3.3in), female 7–9cm (2.8–3.5in); **tail length** male 7–10cm (2.8–3.9in), female 7.5–10.5cm (3–4.1in); **weight** male 7–11g (0.3oz), female 8–16g (0.3–0.6oz), averaging 12g (0.4oz). Females are one-third heavier than males, and are larger in the southern part of their distribution than in the northern.

COAT Grizzled grayish-brown above, with orange tinge on flanks and shoulder, next to cream undersurface. Three back stripes: a distinct dark brown stripe from the back of the head to the base of the tail, with a less distinct, lighter brown stripe on each side.

DIET Nectar and pollen

BREEDING Gestation uncertain, but about 28 days

LONGEVITY Typically 1 year, never more than 2

CONSERVATION STATUS Not listed by the IUCN, but dependent on a continued supply of *Eucalyptus*, *Banksia*, and *Callistemon* blossoms.

birth to four litters in a year. At birth, the young are the smallest mammals known, weighing only about 0.0005g (0.00002oz). Their subsequent development is typical of young marsupials. The deep pouch has four teats and, although litters of four occur, two or three are normal. No nest is constructed; instead, mothers carry their young in the pouch as they forage. The small litter size and slow growth of the young, which spend about 60 days in the pouch, indicate the difficulties mothers experience in harvesting enough pollen grains to supply the sucklings with milk.

The young leave the pouch weighing about 2.5g (0.09oz), covered in fur and with eyes open. They follow their mother around as she forages, suckling occasionally, and may even ride on her back. At this time a litter of four young weigh as much as their mother. They disperse to live independently within a week or two of leaving the pouch. Honey possums, especially juveniles, sometimes huddle together to save energy. Their unusually high body temperature and metabolic rate is offset by short-term periods of deep torpor in cold weather when food is short. At such times the body temperature may remain as low as 5°C (41°F) for 10 hours before reviving spontaneously.

Both sexes are solitary and sedentary, living in overlapping home ranges that average 700sq meters (0.17 acres) for females and 1,280sq meters (0.32 acres) for males. In captivity, females are dominant to males as well as to juveniles. In the wild, females that have large young appear to monopolize areas rich in food.

The larger home ranges of males reflect not just their wider search for food, but also their quest for females approaching estrus. Honey possum testes weigh 4.2 percent of the animal's total body weight, the largest proportion for any mammal. Their sperm is also the longest known among mammals (0.36mm). These features imply intense competition between males to father offspring. Courtship is brief; males follow a female nearing estrus, but are only able to mount her when the larger female allows this. DNA microsatellite profiling has shown that two or more males are responsible for fathering each litter.

The Honey possum is still locally abundant in some areas, although its already restricted distribution continues to shrink. Clearance of habitat for agriculture has largely ceased, but within reserves plant diseases and introduced predators (cats and foxes) still pose threats. In addition, management burning can kill the food plants on which the Honey possum depends. RDW/EMR

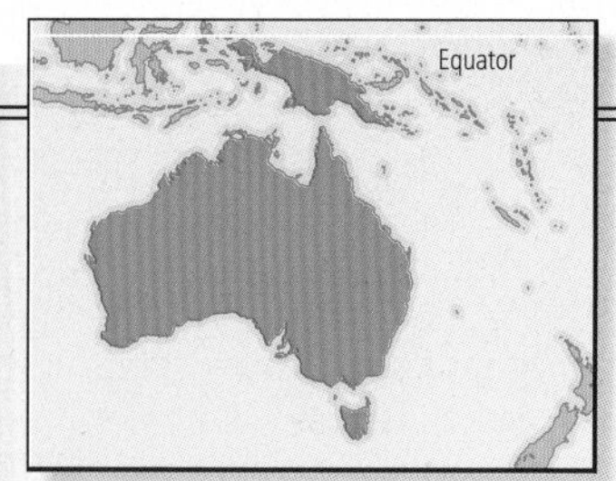

MONOTREMES

WHILE THE DESCRIPTION OF MONOTREMES as "the egg-laying mammals" distinguishes them from other living animals, it exaggerates the significance of egg-laying in this group. The overall pattern of reproduction is mammalian, with only a brief, vestigial period of development of the young within the egg. The soft-shelled eggs hatch after about 10 days, whereupon the young remain (in a pouch in echidnas) dependent on the mother's milk for up to six months in echidnas.

The platypus is confined to eastern Australia and Tasmania, the Long-beaked echidna occurs only in New Guinea, while the Short-beaked echidna is found in all of these regions, in almost all habitats. However, these distributions are relatively recent. There are Pleistocene fossils of Long-beaked echidnas at numerous sites in mainland Australia and Tasmania. Fossil monotremes from the Pleistocene epoch (which began 1.8 million years ago) are much the same as the living types. A platypus fossil from the mid-Miocene (10 million years ago) has been found, which appears very similar to living platypus except that it had fully developed, functional teeth as an adult. In 1991 paleontologists found isolated teeth in early Paleocene (60 million years ago) beds in Patagonia which are almost a perfect match for those of the mid-Miocene platypus. This, however, is not the oldest monotreme fossil; that distinction goes to a partially opalized jaw from the early Cretaceous (120 million years ago). These findings show that monotremes have undergone very conservative evolution, with little change over 100 million years. However, the fossils do not provide any evidence of the origins of monotremes and their ancestral relationships and how they relate to marsupial and placental mammals remains an enigma.

Strange Specialists

PHYSIOLOGY AND DISTRIBUTION

The term "egg-laying mammal" has long been synonymous with "reptile-like" or "primitive mammal," despite the fact that monotremes possess all the major mammalian features: a well-developed fur coat, mammary glands, a single bone in the lower jaw, and three bones (incus, stapes, and malleus) in the middle ear. Monotremes are also endothermic: their body temperature, although variable in echidnas, remains constant regardless of environmental temperatures.

Monotremes have separate uteri entering a common urino-genital passage joined to a cloaca, into which the gut and excretory systems also enter. The one common opening to the outside of the body gave the name to the group that includes the platypus and echidnas – the order Monotremata ("one-holed creatures").

Monotremes are highly specialized feeders. The semiaquatic, carnivorous platypus feeds on invertebrates living on the bottom of freshwater streams. Echidnas are terrestrial carnivores, specializing in ants and termites (Short-beaked or Common echidna) or noncolonial insects and earthworms (Long-beaked echidna). Such diets require grinding rather than cutting or tearing, and, as adults, monotremes lack teeth. In the platypus, teeth actually start to develop and may even serve as grinding surfaces in the very young, but the teeth never fully develop. Rather, they regress and are replaced by horny grinding plates at the back of the jaws. Reduction of teeth is common among ant-eating mammals, and echidnas never develop teeth, nor are their grinding surfaces part of the jaw. In the Long-beaked echidna, a pad of horny spines is located in a groove on the back of the tongue, running from the tip about one-third of the way back. Earthworms are hooked by these spines when the long tongue is extended. The food is broken up as the tongue spines grind against similar spines on the palate. The Long-beaked echidna takes worms into its

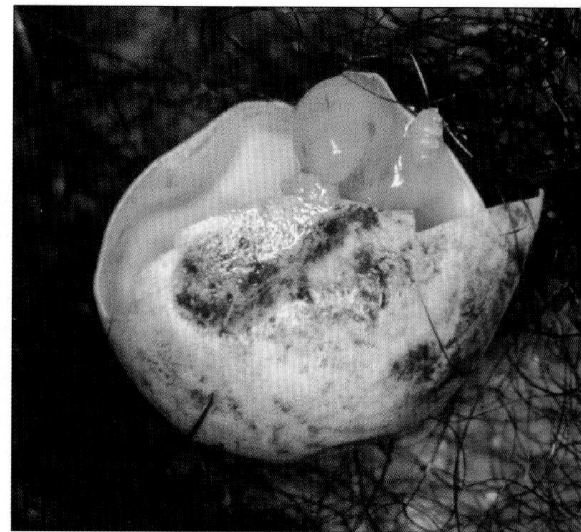

long snout by either the head or tail, and if necessary the forepaws are used to hold the worm while the beak is positioned. In the platypus. the elongation of the front of the skull and the lower jaw to form a bill-like structure is also a foraging specialization. The bill is covered with shiny black skin. Echidnas have a snout that is based on exactly the same modifications of the skull and jaws but is relatively smaller and cylindrical. The mouth is at the tip of this snout and can only be opened enough to allow passage of the cylindrical tongue. MLA

THE POISONOUS SPUR

Monotremes are one of only two groups of venomous mammals (the other includes certain shrews). In the two species of echidnas, the structures that produce and deliver the venom are present but not functional. It is only the male platypus that actually secretes and can deliver the venom. The venom-producing gland is located behind the knee and is connected by a duct to a horny spur on the back of the ankle. This spur is completely lost in the female platypus, but in the male it is hollow and full of venom, which is injected with forceful jabs of the hind limbs. The poison causes agonizing pain in humans and can kill a dog. Because the venom gland enlarges at the beginning of the breeding season, it has been assumed to have a connection with mating behavior. The marked increase in aggressive use of the spurs observed between males in the breeding season may serve to decide spatial relationships in the limited river habitat. Yet this does not explain why, in echidnas, the system is present but non-functional. The spur in male echidnas makes it possible to distinguish them from females, which is otherwise difficult in monotremes since the testes never descend from the abdomen. However, the echidnas' venom duct and gland are degenerate, and the male cannot erect the spur. If it is pushed from under its protective sheath of skin, few echidnas can even retract the spur. It may be that the venom system in monotremes originated as a defense against a predator that has long since gone extinct. Today adult monotremes have few, if any, predators. Dingos occasionally prey on echidnas, but dingos are themselves a relatively recent arrival in Australia.

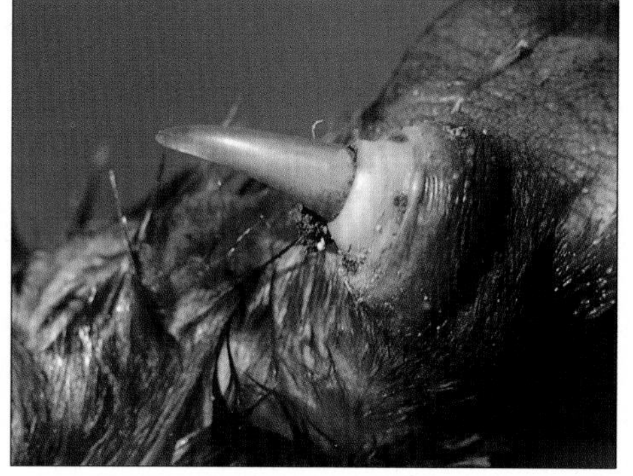

Left *The platypus's spur, which is curved and hollow, is connected by ducts to the venom glands.*

ORDER: MONOTREMATA
2 families; 3 genera; 3 species

PLATYPUS Family Ornithorhynchidae p804

Platypus *Ornithorhynchus anatinus*

ECHIDNAS Family Tachyglossidae p806

Short-beaked echidna *Tachyglossus aculeatus*
Long-beaked echidna *Zaglossus bruijni*

Left A Short-beaked echidna hatches from its soft-shelled egg. Following hatching the tiny newborn will increase in weight at an astonishing rate, perhaps 100–200 times in just a few weeks

Below The mouth of the echidna is positioned at the end of its snout, from which a long tongue is extended to catch termites and ants. The Short-beaked echidna is the most widely dispersed monotreme.

Platypus

Ever since the first platypus specimen (a dried skin) was sent to Britain from the Australian colonies in around 1798, this animal has been surrounded by controversy. At first it was thought to be a fake, stitched together by a taxidermist from the beak of a duck and body parts of a mammal!

Even when the specimen was found to be real, the species was not accepted as a mammal. Although it had fur, it also had a reproductive tract similar to that of birds and reptiles. This led researchers to conclude (correctly) that the platypus laid eggs, and (incorrectly) that it could therefore not be a mammal; all mammals known at the time were viviparous (i.e. gave birth to live young). Ultimately, however, the platypus was recognized as a mammal when it was found to possess the essential characteristic from which the class Mammalia takes its name – mammary glands.

The Sleek Swimmer

FORM AND FUNCTION

At just under 1.7kg (3.7lb), the platypus is smaller than most people imagine. Females are smaller than males and the young are about 85 percent of adult size when they first become independent. The animal is streamlined, with a covering of dense, waterproof fur over its entire body except the feet and the bill. The bill looks superficially like that of a duck, with the nostrils on top, set immediately behind the tip, but it is soft and pliable. Its surface is covered with an array of sensory receptors, which have been found to respond to both electrical and tactile stimuli, and is used by the animal to locate food and find its way around underwater. The eyes, ears, and nostrils are closed when diving. Behind the bill are two internal cheek pouches opening from the mouth. These contain horny ridges that functionally replace the teeth lost by the young soon after they emerge from the burrows. The pouches are used to store food while it is being chewed and sorted.

The limbs are very short and held close to the body. The hind feet are only partially webbed, being used in water only as rudders while the fore feet have large webs and are the main mode of propulsion. The webs of the front feet are turned back to expose large, broad nails when the animal is walking or burrowing. The rear ankles of the males bear a horny spur that is hollow and connected by a duct to a venom gland in the thigh. The venom causes extreme pain in humans; at least one component of the venom has recently been found to act directly on pain receptors, while other components produce inflammation and swelling. The tail is broad and flat and is employed as a fat-storage area.

Below *The prominent bill of the platypus is pliable and touch-sensitive. Underwater, it is the animal's main sensory organ for navigation and locating food.*

FACTFILE

PLATYPUS

Ornithorhynchus anatinus

Duckbill

Order: Monotremata

Family: Ornithorhynchidae

Sole species of the genus

DISTRIBUTION E Australia from Cooktown in Queensland to Tasmania. Introduced in Kangaroo Island, S Australia.

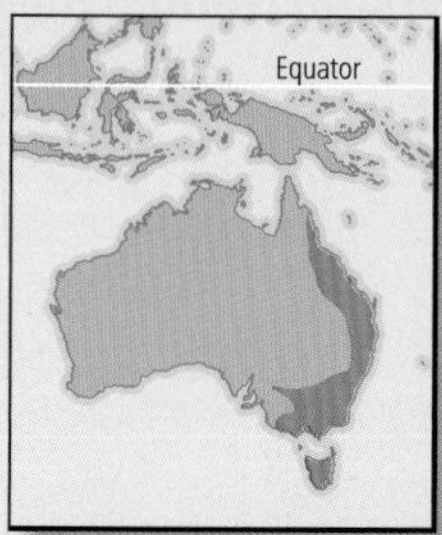

HABITAT Inhabits most streams, rivers, and some lakes that have permanent water and banks suitable for burrows.

SIZE Lengths and weights vary from area to area, and weights change with season. **Head–body length** male 45–60cm (17.7–23.6in) female 39–55cm (15.4–21.7in); **bill length** average male 5.8cm (2.3in) female 5.2cm (2in); **tail length** male 10.5–15.2cm (4.1–6in) female 8.5–13cm (3.3–5.1in); **weight** male 1–2.4kg (2.2–5.3lb) female 0.7–1.6kg (1.5–3.5lb).

COAT Dark brown back, silver to light brown underside with rust-brown midline, especially in young animals, which have the lightest fur. Short, dense fur (about 1cm/0.4in depth). Light patch below eye/ear groove.

BREEDING Gestation period not known (probably 2–3 weeks). Incubation not known (probably about 10 days).

LONGEVITY 10 or more years (17 or more in captivity).

CONSERVATION STATUS Not under threat.

Effective Care of the Young

SOCIAL BEHAVIOR

The platypus is mainly nocturnal in its foraging for prey items, which are almost entirely made up of bottom-dwelling invertebrates, particularly the young stages (larvae) of insects. Normal home ranges of platypuses vary with river systems, ranging from less than 1km (0.6 miles) to over 7km (4.3 miles), with many individuals foraging over 3–4km (1.8–2.5 miles) of stream within a 24-hour period. Two non-native species of trout feed on the same sort of food and are possible competitors of the platypus. Despite this dietary overlap, the platypus is common in many rivers into which these species have been introduced. A study in

one river system showed that the trout ate more of the swimming species of invertebrates, while the platypus fed almost exclusively on those inhabiting the bottom of the river. Waterfowl may also overlap in their diets with platypuses, but most also consume plant material which does not appear to be eaten by the platypus.

Certain areas occupied by platypuses experience water temperatures close to, and air temperatures well below, freezing in winter. When the platypus is exposed to such cold conditions it can increase its metabolic rate to produce sufficient heat to maintain its body temperature around its normal level of 32°C (89.6°F). Good fur and tissue insulation, including well-developed countercurrent blood flow, help the animal to conserve body heat, and its burrows also provide a microclimate that moderates the extremes of outside temperature in both winter and summer.

Although mating is reputed to occur earlier in northern Australia than in the south, it occurs sometime during late winter to spring (between July and October). Mating takes place in water and involves chasing and grasping of the tail of the female by the male. Two (occasionally one or three) eggs measuring 1.7 by 1.5cm (0.7 by 0.5in) are laid. When hatched the young are fed on milk, which they suck from the fur of the mother around the ventral openings of the mammary glands (there is no pouch) for 3–4 months while they are confined to a special breeding burrow. This burrow is normally longer and more complex than the burrows inhabited for resting. Such nesting burrows are reported to be up to 30m (100ft) long and be branched with one or more nesting chambers. The young emerge from these burrows in summer (late January–early March). It is not known how long they continue to take milk from their mothers after leaving the burrow, although they do feed on benthic organisms from the time they enter the water. Individual animals will use a number of resting burrows in an area but it is thought that there is attachment by breeding females to nesting burrows.

Although normally two eggs are laid, it is not known how many young are successfully weaned each year. Not all females breed each year, and new recruits to the population do not breed until they are at least two years of age. In spite of this low reproductive rate, the platypus has returned from near extinction in certain areas since its protection and the cessation of hunting around 1900. This indicates that the reproductive strategy of having only a few young, but looking after them well, is effective in this long-lived species.

The platypus owes its success to its occupation of an ecological niche which has been a perennial one, even in the driest continent in the world. By the same token, because the platypus is such a highly specialized mammal it is extremely susceptible to the effects of changes in its habitat. Changes wrought by humans in Australia, particularly since European settlement began in the late 18th century, have brought about localized reductions and fragmentation of platypus populations. Care and consideration for the environment will have to be rigorously maintained if this unique species is to survive. TRG

Above *The streamlined surface presented by the long guard hairs conceals the thick, dry underfur that insulates the platypus's body in cold water.*

Echidnas

*E*CHIDNAS ARE READILY RECOGNIZED BY *their covering of long spines, which are shorter in the Long-beaked species. There is fur present between the spines as well as on the head, legs and ventral surfaces where there is an absence of spines. In both the Long-beaked echidna and the Tasmanian form of the Short-beaked echidna the fur may be longer than the spines.*

Both genera are further distinguished by their elongated, tubular snout, which in the case of the Long-beaked echidna curves somewhat downward and accounts for two-thirds the length of the head. Echidnas are generally solitary creatures that are seen relatively infrequently, despite the fact that the Short-beaked echidna is in fact quite common across its geographic range; the Long-Beaked echidna, however, is only found in the mountainous areas of New Guinea.

Spiny Anteaters

FORM AND FUNCTION

The echidna's coat of spines (it is sometimes called the "spiny anteater") provides an excellent defense. If surprised on hard ground, an echidna curls up into a ball; on soft soil it may rapidly dig straight down, rather like a sinking ship, until all that can be seen of it are the spines of its well-protected back. By using its powerful limbs and erecting all its spines, an echidna can wedge itself securely in a rock crevice or hollow log.

Echidna spines are individual hairs that are anchored in a thick layer of muscle (*panniculus carnosus*) in the skin. The spines obscure the short, blunt tail and the rather large ear openings, which are vertical slits just behind the eyes. The snout is naked and the small mouth and relatively large nostrils are located at the tip. Echidnas walk with a distinctive rolling gait, although the body is held well above the ground.

Males can be distinguished from females by the presence of a horny spur on the ankle of the hind limb. Males are larger than females within a given population. Yearling Short-beaked echidnas usually weigh less than 1kg (2.2lb), but beyond that there is no way of determining age.

Echidnas have small, bulging eyes. Although they appear to be competent at telling objects apart in laboratory studies, in most natural habitats vision is probably not important in detecting food or danger; their hearing, however is very good. In locating prey, usually by rooting through the forest litter or undergrowth, they use their well-developed sense of smell. When food items are detected, they are rapidly taken in by the long, thin, highly flexible tongue, which Short-beaked echidnas can extend up to 18cm (7in) from the tip of the snout. The tongue is lubricated by a sticky secretion produced by the very large salivary glands. Ants and termites form the bulk of

Below *Echidnas' sense of smell is particularly acute. They use their long snout to probe the undergrowth or leaf litter, and have even been seen to use it as a snorkel when crossing water.*

Above *The Long-beaked echidna feeds principally on earthworms. Echidnas can survive several weeks with no nourishment at all.*

FACTFILE

ECHIDNAS

Order: Monotremata

Family: Tachyglossidae

2 species in 2 genera

DISTRIBUTION Mainland Australia, Tasmania, New Guinea (Short-beaked Echidna); mountains of New Guinea (Long-beaked Echidna).

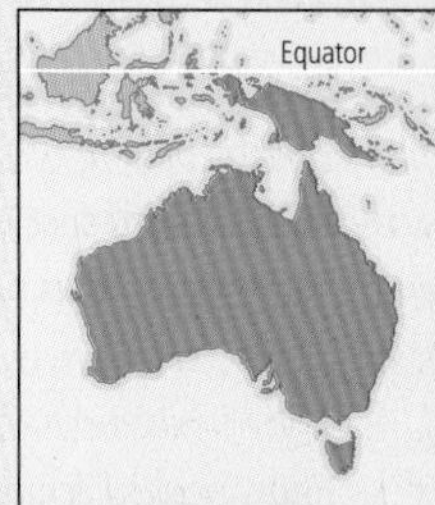

SHORT-BEAKED ECHIDNA *Tachyglossus aculeatus*
Short-beaked or Common echidna (or spiny anteater)
Australia, Tasmania, New Guinea. In almost all types of habitat, from semi-arid to alpine. HBL 30–45cm (12–18in); WT 2.5–8kg (5.5–17.6lb). Males 25 percent larger than females. Coat: black to light brown, with spines on back and sides; long narrow snout without hair. Breeding: gestation about 14 days. Longevity: not known in wild (extremely long-lived in captivity – up to 49 years). Conservation status: generally not threatened, though the Kangaroo Island subspecies (*T. a. multiaculeatus*) is classed as Lower Risk: Near Threatened.

LONG-BEAKED ECHIDNA *Zaglossus bruijni*
Long-beaked or Long-nosed echidna (or spiny anteater)
New Guinea, in mountainous terrain. HBL 45–90cm (18–35in); WT 5–10kg (11–22lb). Coat: brown or black; spines present but usually hidden by fur except on sides; spines shorter and fewer than Short-beaked echidna; very long snout, curved downward. Breeding: gestation period unknown. Longevity: not known in wild (up to 30 years in captivity). Conservation status: Conservation status: Endangered.

Abbreviations HBL = head–body length; WT = weight

the Short-beaked echidna's diet. Around August and September Short-beaked echidnas attack the mounds of the Meat ant (*Iridomyrmex detectus*) to feed on the fat-laden females; this is done in the face of spirited defense by the stinging worker ants, although the mounds are prudently avoided for the rest of the year.

Males in Tow

SOCIAL BEHAVIOR

Short-beaked echidnas are essentially solitary animals, inhabiting a home range the size of which varies according to the environment. In wet areas with abundant food it covers some 50ha (124 acres). The home range appears to change little, and within it there is no fixed shelter site. When inactive, echidnas take shelter in hollow logs, under piles of rubble and brush, or in thick clumps of vegetation. Occasionally they dig shallow burrows up to 1.2m (4ft) in length, which may be reused. A female incubating an egg or suckling young has a fixed burrow. The home ranges of several individuals overlap.

During the mating season the female leaves a scent track by everting the cloaca, the wall of which contains numerous glands. This presumably attracts males in overlapping ranges. At this time echidnas break their normally solitary habits to form "trains," in which a female is followed by as many as six males in a line. In captivity, echidnas that are kept in spacious accommodation do not form any sort of groups but are mutually tolerant. By contrast, if they are kept in confined, overcrowded quarters they may form a size-related dominance order, but this does not seem to be a natural behavior.

The chief periods of activity are related to environmental temperature. Short-beaked echidnas are usually active at dusk and dawn, but in the hot summer are nocturnal. During cold spells they may be active in the middle of the day. They avoid rain and will remain inactive for days if it persists. In cold parts of their range, such as the Snowy Mountains of eastern Australia, echidnas hibernate during winter, with body temperatures as low as 5°C (41°F). Inactive echidnas may enter torpor, with body temperatures as low as 18°C (64.4°F), under less rigorous environmental temperatures.

The female pouch is barely detectable for most of the year. Before the start of the breeding season, folds of skin and muscle on each side of the abdomen enlarge to form an incomplete pouch with milk patches at the front end. There are no teats. The single egg is laid into the pouch by extension of the cloaca while the female lies on her back. After about 10 days the young hatches, using an egg tooth and a horny carbuncle at the tip of the snout. The young remains in the pouch until about the time spines begin to erupt. There are rare reports of females found moving about freely with an egg or young in the pouch. However, for most of the suckling period (up to six months), the offspring is left behind in the nursery burrow while the mother forages, often for days at a time. The young become independent and move out to occupy their own home ranges at about 1year old.

The Short-beaked echidna is widespread and common on mainland Australia and Tasmania. However, its status in New Guinea is uncertain. The Long-beaked echidna and several other similar genera were once distributed throughout Australia but disappeared by the late Pleistocene. Today there is only one species, which is restricted to the New Guinea highlands. It is likely that the disappearance of Long-beaked echidnas from Australia is related to climatic changes that have taken place there. Both the Short-beaked and the Long-beaked echidna are hunted for food; most zoologists now consider the latter species to be under severe threat of extinction. MLA

Appendix: Species list

Including all families, genera, and species of Rodents, Lagomorphs, Elephant Shrews, Insectivores, Bats, Edentates, and Marsupials.

ORDER RODENTIA

RODENTS

SUBORDER SCIUROGNATHI

FAMILY APLODONTIDAE

Aplodontia

A. rufa **Mountain beaver or Sewellel** SW British Columbia (Canada) to C California (USA)

FAMILY SCIURIDAE

Squirrels, Chipmunks, Marmots, and Prairie dogs

SUBFAMILY SCIURINAE

Ammospermophilus **Antelope Squirrels**

A. harrisii **Harris' antelope squirrel** Arizona to SW New Mexico (SW USA) and adj. Sonora (Mexico)

A. insularis **Espirito Santo Island antelope squirrel** Espirito Santo Is, Gulf of California (S Baja California, Mexico)

A. interpres **Texas antelope squirrel** New Mexico and W Texas (SW USA) to Durango (Mexico)

A. leucurus **White-tailed antelope squirrel** SW USA to S Baja California (Mexico)

A. nelsoni **Nelson's antelope squirrel** San Joaquin Valley, S California (USA)

Atlantoxerus

A. getulus **Barbary ground squirrel** Morocco, NW Algeria

Callosciurus **Oriental Tree Squirrels**

C. adamsi **Ear-spot squirrel** Sabah and Sarawak (N Borneo)

C. albescens **Kloss squirrel** Sumatra (Indonesia)

C. baluensis **Kinabalu squirrel** Sabah and Sarawak (N Borneo)

C. caniceps **Gray-bellied squirrel** Burma Pen., Thailand, Malyasia Pen.

C. erythraeus **Pallas' squirrel** India, Burma, SE and S China, Taiwan, Thailand, Malay Pen., Indochina

C. finlaysonii **Finlayson's or Variable squirrel** SC Burma, Thailand, Laos, Cambodia, Vietnam

C. inornatus **Inornate squirrel** S Yunnan (China), N Vietnam, Laos

C. melanogaster **Mentawai squirrel** Mantawi Is (Indonesia)

C. nigrovittatus **Black-striped squirrel** Thailand, S Vietnam, Malaysia, Sumatra and Java (Indonesia), Borneo

C. notatus **Plantain squirrel** Thailand and Malay Pen. to Java, Bali, Lombok and Salayar (Indonesia), Borneo

C. orestes **Borneo black-banded squirrel** Malaysia, Sabah and Sarawak (N Borneo)

C. phayrei **Phayre's squirrel** S Burma

C. prevostii **Prevost's squirrel** Parts of Indo-Malayan region (excl. Java)

C. pygerythrus **Irrawaddy squirrel** NE India and Nepal to Burma, Yunnan (China), and N Vietnam

C. quinquestriatus **Anderson's squirrel** NE Burma, Yunnan (China)

Cynomys **Prairie Dogs**

C. gunnisoni **Gunnison's prairie dog** SE Utah, SW Colorado, NW New Mexico, NE Arizona (USA)

C. leucurus **White-tailed prairie dog** SC Montana, W and C Wyoming, NW Colorado, NE Utah (USA)

C. ludovicianus **Black-tailed prairie dog** Saskatchewan (Canada), Montana through C and SC USA to Sonora and Chihuahua (Mexico)

C. mexicanus **Mexican prairie dog** Coahuila and San Luis Potosi (NC Mexico)

C. parvidens **Utah prairie dog** SC Utah (USA)

Dremomys **Red-cheeked Squirrels**

D. everetti **Bornean mountain ground squirrel** N and W Borneo

D. lokriah **Orange-bellied Himalayan squirrel** E India, C Nepal, Xizang (China) and Bhutan east to Salween R (Burma)

D. pernyi **Perny's long-nosed squirrel** NE India, N Burma, China, Taiwan, N Vietnam

D. pyrrhomerus **Red-hipped squirrel** C and S China, N Vietnam

D. rufigenis **Asian red-cheeked squirrel** NE India, N and C Burma, Yunnan (China), Laos, Vietnam, Thailand, Malay Pen.

Epixerus **African Palm Squirrels**

E. ebii **Western palm squirrel** Sierra Leone, Liberia, Ivory Coast, Ghana

E. wilsoni **Biafran palm squirrel** Cameroon, Rio Muni (Equatorial Guinea), Gabon

Exilisciurus **Pygmy Squirrels**

E. concinnus **Philippine pygmy squirrel** Mindanao, Basilan, Biliran, Bohol, Dinagat, Leyte, and Samar Is (Philippines)

E. exilis **Least pygmy squirrel** Borneo, Banggi Is (Malaysia)

E. whiteheadi **Tufted or Whitehead's pygmy squirrel** Sabah, Sarawak, W Kalimantan (Borneo)

Funambulus **Asiatic Palm Squirrels**

F. layardi **Layard's palm squirrel** S India, S and C Sri Lanka

F. palmarum **Indian palm squirrel** C and S India, Sri Lanka

F. pennantii **Northern palm squirrel** SE Iran to Pakistan, Nepal and N and C India

F. sublineatus **Dusky palm squirrel** SW India, C Sri Lanka

F. tristriatus **Jungle palm squirrel** Coastal W India

Funisciurus **Rope Squirrels**

F. anerythrus **Thomas' rope squirrel** SW Nigeria, Cameroon, CAR, DRC, Uganda

F. bayonii **Lunda or Bayon's tree squirrel** SW DRC, NE Angola

F. carruthersi **Carruther's mountain squirrel** Ruwenzori Mts (S Uganda), Rwanda, Burundi

F. congicus **Congo rope squirrel** DRC, Angola, Namibia

F. isabella **Lady Burton's rope squirrel** Cameroon, CAR, Congo

F. lemniscatus **Ribboned rope squirrel** Cameroon, CAR, DRC

F. leucogenys **Red-cheeked rope squirrel** Ghana, Togo, Benin, Nigeria, Cameroon, CAR, Equatorial Guinea

F. pyrropus **Fire-footed rope squirrel** W and C Africa to Angola

F. substriatus **Kintampo rope squirrel** Ivory Coast, Ghana, Togo, benin, SE Nigeria

Glyphotes

G. simus **Sculptor squirrel** N Borneo

Heliosciurus **Sun Squirrels**

H. gambianus **Gambian sun squirrel** Senegal and Gambia to Sudan and Ethiopia south to Angola, Zambia and Zimbabwe

H. mutabilis **Mutable sun squirrel** SE Zimbabwe, N Mozambique, Malawi, Tanzania

H. punctatus **Small sun squirrel** E Liberia, S Ivory Coast, S Ghana

H. rufobrachium **Red-legged sun squirrel** Senegal and W Gambia to SE Sudan and Kenya south to Malawi, Mozambique and E Zimbabwe

H. ruwenzorii **Ruwenzori sun squirrel** Ruwenzori Mts of E DRC, Rwanda, Burundi, SW Uganda

H. undulatus **Zanj sun squirrel** SE Kenya, NE Tanzania (incl. Mafia and Zanzibar Is)

Hyosciurus **Sulawesi Long-nosed Squirrels**

H. heinrichi **Montane long-nosed squirrel** C Sulawesi (Indonesia)

H. ileile **Lowland long-nosed squirrel** N Sulawesi (Indonesia)

Lariscus **Striped Ground Squirrels**

L. hosei **Four-striped ground squirrel** Sarawak and Sabah (N Borneo)

L. insignis **Three-striped ground squirrel** Thailand, Malay Pen., Sumatra and Java (Indonesia), Borneo

L. niobe **Niobe ground squirrel** Sumatra, Java and Mentawi Is (Indonesia)

L. obscurus **Mentawai three-striped squirrel** Sumatra (Indonesia)

Marmota **Marmots**

M. baibacina **Gray marmot** Altai Mts and SW Siberia (Russia), SE Kazakhstan, Kyrgyzstan, Mongolia, Xinjiang (China)

M. bobak **Bobak marmot** E Europe to Ukraine and Russia to N and C Kazakhstan

M. broweri **Alaska marmot** N Alaska (USA)

M. caligata **Hoary marmot** C Alaska (USA), Yukon and Northwest Territories (Canada) south to NW USA

M. camtschatica **Black-capped marmot** E Siberia (Russia)

M. caudata **Long-tailed marmot** W Tien Shan Mts to the Pamirs (Tajikistan and Kyrgyzstan) to Hindu Kush (Afghanistan), Pakistan, Kashmir, and W Xinjiang and Xizang (China)

M. flaviventris **Yellow-bellied marmot** SC British Columbia and S Alberta (SW Canada) south to SW USA

M. himalayana **Himalayan marmot** N India, Nepal, W China

M. marmota **Alpine marmot** French, Swiss, and Italian Alps, S Germany, W Austria, Carpathians (Romania), and Tatra Mts (Czech Rep. and Poland); introd. to Pyrenees, E Austria, and Yugoslavia

M. menzbieri **Menzbier's or Tien Shan marmot** W Tien Shan Mts (S Kazakhstan and Kyrgyzstan)

M. monax **Woodchuck** Alaska (USA) through S Canada to NE and SC USA and south in Rocky Mts

M. olympus **Olympic marmot** Olympics Mts (W Washington, NW USA)

M. sibirica **Tarbagan marmot** SW Siberia (Russia) to N and W Mongolia, Heilongjiang and Inner Mongolia (China)

M. vancouverensis **Vancouver marmot** Vancouver Is (British Columbia, Canada)

Menetes

M. berdmorei **Indochinese ground squirrel** C Burma to S Yunnan (China), Thailand, S Laos, S Vietnam, Cambodia

Microsciurus **Dwarf Squirrels**

M. alfari **Central American dwarf squirrel** Nicaragua, Costa Rica, Panama, Colombia

M. flaviventer **Amazon dwarf squirrel** Amazon Basin of Colombia, Ecuador, Peru, and W Brazil

M. mimulus **Western dwarf squirrel** Panama, N Colombia, NW Ecuador

M. santanderensis **Santander dwarf squirrel** Colombia

Myosciurus

M. pumilio **African pygmy squirrel** SE Nigeria, Cameroon, Gabon, Bioko (Equatorial Guinea)

Nannosciurus

N. melanotis **Black-eared squirrel** Sumatra and Java (Indonesia), Borneo

Paraxerus **Bush Squirrels**

P. alexandri **Alexander's bush squirrel** NE DRC, Uganda

P. boehmi **Boehm's bush squirrel** S Sudan, DRC, Uganda, W Kenya, NW Tanzania, N Zambia

P. cepapi **Smith's bush squirrel** SW Tanzania to N South Africa

P. cooperi **Cooper's mountain squirrel** Cameroon

P. flavovittis **Striped bush squirrel** S Kenya, Tanzania, Mozambique

P. lucifer **Black and red bush squirrel** SW Tanzania, N Malawi, E Zambia

P. ochraceus **Ochre bush squirrel** S Sudan, Kenya, Tanzania

P. palliatus **Red bush squirrel** S Somalia to E South Africa

P. poensis **Green bush squirrel** Sierra Leone to S Nigeria and Cameroon, Bioko (Equatorial Guinea), Congo, W DRC

P. vexillarius **Swynnerton's bush squirrel** C and E Tanzania

P. vincenti **Vincent's bush squirrel** N Mozambique

Prosciurillus **Sulawesi Dwarf Squirrels**

P. abstrusus **Secretive dwarf squirrel** SE Sulawesi (Indonesia)

P. leucomus **Whitish dwarf squirrel** Sulawesi, Buton, and Sangihe Is (Indonesia)

P. murinus **Sulawesi dwarf squirrel** NE and C Sulawesi (Indonesia)

P. weberi **Weber's dwarf squirrel** C Sulawesi (Indonesia)

Protoxerus **African Giant Squirrels**

P. aubinnii **Slender-tailed squirrel** Liberia, Ivory Coast, Ghana

P. stangeri **Forest giant or Stanger's squirrel** Sierra Leone to S Sudan and W Kenya south to N Tanzania, DRC and N Angola

Ratufa **Oriental Giant Squirrels**

R. affinis **Pale giant squirrel** S Vietnam, Malaysia, Indonesia (excl. Java), Philippines (excl. SW)

R. bicolor **Black giant squirrel** Assam (India), E Nepal, SE Xizang to S Yunnan and Hainan (China), Burma, Thailand, Laos, Vietnam, Cambodia, Malay Pen. to Java and Bali (Indonesia)

R. indica **Indian giant squirrel** C and S India

R. macroura **Sri Lankan giant squirrel** S India, Sri Lanka

Rheithrosciurus

R. macrotis **Tufted ground squirrel** Borneo

Rhinosciurus

R. laticaudatus **Shrew-faced squirrel** Malaysia, Indonesia (excl. Java), Philippines (excl. SW)

Rubrisciurus

R. rubriventer **Sulawesi giant squirrel** N, C, and SE Sulawesi (Indonesia)

Sciurillus

S. pusillus **Neotropical pygmy squirrel** Surinam, Fr. Guiana, Peru, Brazil

Sciurotamias **Asian Rock Squirrels**

S. davidianus **Pere David's rock squirrel** Hebei to Sichuan and Hubei, Guizhou (China)

S. forresti **Forrest's rock squirrel** Yunnan and Sichuan (China)

Sciurus **Tree Squirrels**

S. aberti **Abert's squirrel** Wyoming, Utah, Colorado, New Mexico, Arizona (USA) to Durango (Mexico)

S. aestuans **Guianan squirrel** Venezuela, Guyana, Surinam, Fr. Guiana, Brazil

S. alleni **Allen's squirrel** Mexico

S. anomalus **Caucasian squirrel** Turkey and Caucasus, N and W Iran, Syria, Lebanon, Israel

S. arizonensis **Arizona gray squirrel** SE and C Arizona, WC New Mexico (USA), Sonora (Mexico)

S. aureogaster **Red-bellied squirrel** Mexico, Guatemala

S. carolinensis **Eastern gray squirrel** E Texas (USA) to Saskatchewan (Canada) east to Atl. Oc.; introd. to Britain and South Africa

S. colliaei **Collie's squirrel** W and WC Mexico

S. deppei **Deppe's squirrel** Tamaulipas (Mexico) to Costa Rica

S. flammifer **Fiery squirrel** Venezuela

S. gilvigularis **Yellow-throated squirrel** Venezuela, Guyana, N Brazil

S. granatensis **Red-tailed squirrel** Costa Rica, Panama, Colombia, Venezuela (incl. Margarita Is), Ecuador, Trinidad and Tobago

S. griseus **Western gray squirrel** W USA to Baja California (Mexico)

S. ignitus **Bolivian squirrel** Peru, Brazil, Bolivia, Argentina

S. igniventris **Northern Amazon red squirrel** Colombia, Venezuela, Ecuador, Peru, Brazil

S. lis **Japanese squirrel** Honshu, Shikoku, and Kyushu (Japan)

S. nayaritensis **Mexican fox squirrel** Jalisco (Mexico) north to SE Arizona (USA)

S. niger **Eastern fox squirrel** Texas (USA) and adj. Mexico north to Manitoba (SC Canada) east to Atl. Oc.

S. oculatus **Peters' squirrel** Mexico

S. pucheranii **Andean squirrel** Andes of Colombia

S. pyrrhinus **Junin red squirrel** E slopes of Andes of Peru

S. richmondi **Richmond's squirrel** Nicaragua

S. sanborni **Sanborn's squirrel** Madre de Dios Dept. (Peru)

S. spadiceus **Southern Amazon red squirrel** Colombia, Ecuador, Peru, Brazil, Bolivia

S. stramineus **Guayaquil squirrel** SE Ecuador, NE Peru

S. variegatoides **Variegated squirrel** S Chiapas (Mexico) to Panama

S. vulgaris **Eurasian red squirrel** Forested regions of Palearctic from Iberian Pen. and Britain east to Kamchatka Pen. and Sakhalin Is (Russia) south to Mediterranean and Black Seas, N Mongolia, NE China, Korea

S. yucatanensis **Yucatan squirrel** Yucatan Pen. (Mexico), N and SW Belize, N Guatemala
Spermophilopsis
S. leptodactylus **Long-clawed ground squirrel** SE Kazakhstan, Uzbekistan, Turkmenistan, NE Iran, NW Afghanistan, Tajikistan
Spermophilus **Ground Squirrels**
S. adocetus **Tropical ground squirrel** Jalisco, Michoacan, Guerrero (Mexico)
S. alashanicus **Alashan ground squirrel** SC Mongolia, N China
S. annulatus **Ring-tailed ground squirrel** Nayarit to N Guerrero (Mexico)
S. armatus **Uinta ground squirrel** Utah, Wyoming, Idaho, Montana (NW USA)
S. atricapillus **Baja California rock squirrel** Baja California (Mexico)
S. beecheyi **California ground squirrel** Washington (USA) to Baja California (Mexico)
S. beldingi **Belding's ground squirrel** W USA
S. brunneus **Idaho ground squirrel** WC Idaho (USA)
S. canus **Merriam's ground squirrel** E Oregon, NW Nevada, WC Idaho (USA)
S. citellus **European ground squirrel** SE Germany, SW Poland, Czech Rep. to W Ukraine, Moldova, and W Turkey
S. columbianus **Columbian ground squirrel** SE British Columbia and W Alberta (SW Canada) to NE Oregon, C Idaho, and C Montana (NW USA)
S. dauricus **Daurian ground squirrel** Russia, Mongolia, N China
S. elegans **Wyoming ground squirrel** NE Nevada, SE Oregon, S Idaho and SW Montana to C Colorado and W Nebraska
S. erythrogenys **Red-cheeked ground squirrel** E Kazakhstan, SW Siberia (Russia), and Xinjiang (China); also Mongolia and Inner Mongolia (China)
S. franklinii **Franklin's ground squirrel** Great Plains of Canada to Alberta, Saskatchewan and Manitoba (Canada) south to Kansas, Illinois and Indiana
S. fulvus **Yellow ground squirrel** Kazakhstan, Uzbekistan, W Tajikistan, Turkmenistan, NE Iran, Afghanistan, W Xinjiang (China)
S. lateralis **Golden-mantled ground squirrel** Montana, W North America, from C British Columbia (Canada) south to S New Mexico, Nevada and California (USA)
S. madrensis **Sierra Madre ground squirrel** SW Chihuahua (Mexico)
S. major **Russet ground squirrel** Steppe between Volga and Irtysh R (Russia, N Kazakhstan)
S. mexicanus **Mexican ground squirrel** S New Mexico and W Texas (USA) to Jalisco and S Puebla (Mexico)
S. mohavensis **Mohave ground squirrel** S California (USA)
S. mollis **Piute ground squirrel** SE Oregon and Snake River Valley (Idaho) south to Nevada, W Utah and EC California (USA); also NW Washington
S. musicus **Caucasian Mountain ground squirrel** N Caucasus Mts (Georgia)
S. parryii **Arctic ground squirrel** Alaska (USA), NW Canada, NE Russia
S. perotensis **Perote ground squirrel** Veracruz and Puebla (Mexico)
S. pygmaeus **Little ground squirrel** SW Ukraine, S Ural Mts to Crimea (Ukraine), Kazakhstan, Uzbekistan, Dagestan (Georgia)
S. relictus **Tien Shan ground squirrel** Tien Shan Mts in SE Kazakhstan and Kyrgyzstan
S. richardsonii **Richardson's ground squirrel** Great Plains of Canada from S Alberta, S Saskatchewan, and S Manitoba (Canada) south to Montana, Dakotas, W Minnesota, and NW Iowa (USA)
S. saturatus **Cascade golden-mantled ground squirrel** Cascade Mts of SW British Columbia (SW Canada) and Washington (NW USA)
S. spilosoma **Spotted ground squirrel** C Mexico to S and SC USA
S. suslicus **Spectacled ground squirrel** Steppes of E and S Europe, incl. Poland, E Romania, Ukraine north to Oka R and east to Volga R (Russia)
S. tereticaudus **Round-tailed ground squirrel** SE California, S Nevada, W Arizona (SW USA), NE Baja California and Sonora (Mexico)
S. townsendii **Townsend's ground squirrel** SE Washington (NW USA)
S. tridecemlineatus **Thirteen-lined ground squirrel** Great Plains from C Texas to E Utah and Ohio (USA) and SC Canada
S. undulatus **Long-tailed ground squirrel** E Kazakhstan, S Siberia and SE Russia, N Mongolia, Heilongjiang and Xinjiang (China)
S. variegatus **Rock squirrel** S Nevada and Utah to SW Texas (USA) to Puebla (Mexico)
S. washingtoni **Washington ground squirrel** SE Washington, NE Oregon (USA)
S. xanthoprymnus **Asia Minor ground squirrel** Caucasus, Turkey, Syria, Israel
Sundasciurus **Sunda Squirrels**
S. brookei **Brooke's squirrel** Borneo
S. davensis **Davao squirrel** Mindanao (Philippines)
S. fraterculus **Fraternal squirrel** Sipora, Siberut, and N Pagi Is (Sumatra, Indonesia)
S. hippurus **Horse-tailed squirrel** S Vietnam, Malaysia, Indonesia (excl. Java), Philippines (excl. SW)
S. hoogstraali **Busuanga squirrel** Busuanga Is (Philippines)
S. jentinki **Jentink's squirrel** N Borneo
S. juvencus **Northern Palawan tree squirrel** N Palawan (Philippines)
S. lowii **Low's squirrel** Malaysia, Indonesia (excl. Java), Philippines (excl. SW)
S. mindanensis **Mindanao squirrel** Mindanao (Philippines)
S. moellendorffi **Culion tree squirrel** Calamien Is (Philippines)
S. philippinensis **Philippine tree squirrel** S and W Mindanao and Basilan (Philippines)
S. rabori **Palawan montane squirrel** Palawan (Philippines)
S. samarensis **Samar squirrel** Samar and Leyte (Philippines)
S. steerii **Southern Palawan tree squirrel** S Palawan and Balabac Is (Philippines)
S. tenuis **Slender squirrel** Malaysia, Indonesia (excl. Java), Philippines (excl. SW)
Syntheosciurus
S. brochus **Bangs' mountain squirrel** Costa Rica to N Panama
Tamias **Chipmunks**
T. alpinus **Alpine chipmunk** Sierra Nevada Mts (EC California, USA)
T. amoenus **Yellow-pine chipmunk** C British Columbia (SW Canada) south to California east to C Montana and W Wyoming (USA)
T. bulleri **Buller's chipmunk** Sierra Madre in S Durango, W Zacetecas and N Jalisco (Mexico)
T. canipes **Gray-footed chipmunk** SE New Mexico and W Texas (SW USA)
T. cinereicollis **Gray-collared chipmunk** C and E Arizona and C and SW New Mexico (SW USA)
T. dorsalis **Cliff chipmunk** WC and SW USA to Mexico
T. durangae **Durango chipmunk** Mexico
T. merriami **Merriam's chipmunk** California (USA) to N Baja California (Mexico)
T. minimus **Least chipmunk** Canada, USA
T. obscurus **California chipmunk** S California (USA) to C Baja California (Mexico)
T. ochrogenys **Yellow-cheeked chipmunk** Coastal N California (USA)
T. palmeri **Palmer's chipmunk** Charleston Mts (S Nevada, USA)
T. panamintinus **Panamint chipmunk** SE California and SW Nevada (USA)
T. quadrimaculatus **Long-eared chipmunk** Sierra Nevada Mts of EC California, C and WC Nevada (USA)
T. quadrivittatus **Colorado chipmunk** Colorado and E Utah south to NE Arizona and S New Mexico (USA)
T. ruficaudus **Red-tailed chipmunk** NE Washington to W Montana (USA), SE British Columbia (Canada)
T. rufus **Hopi chipmunk** E and S Utah, W Colorado, NE Arizona (USA)
T. senex **Allen's chipmunk** California, WC Nevada, Oregon (USA)
T. sibiricus **Siberian chipmunk** N Europe and Siberia to Sakhalin and S Kurile Is (Russia), E Kazakhstan to N Mongolia, China, Korea and Hokkaido (Japan)
T. siskiyou **Siskiyou chipmunk** Siskiyou Mts and coastal N California to C Oregon (USA)
T. sonomae **Sonoma chipmunk** NW California (USA)
T. speciosus **Lodgepole chipmunk** California, W Nevada (USA)
T. striatus **Eastern chipmunk** S Manitoba and Nova Scotia (Canada) to SE USA
T. townsendii **Townsend's chipmunk** SW British Columbia (Canada), Washington and Oregon (USA)
T. umbrinus **Uinta chipmunk** California and N Arizona to Colorado, Wyoming and SW Montana (USA)
Tamiasciurus **Red Squirrels**
T. douglasii **Douglas' squirrel** SW British Columbia (Canada) to S California (USA)
T. hudsonicus **American red squirrel** Alaska (USA), Canada, south of tundra (incl. Vancouver Is), W USA and NE USA south to South Carolina
T. mearnsi **Mearns' squirrel** Sierra San Pedro Martir Mts (Baja California, Mexico)
Tamiops **Asiatic Striped Squirrels**
T. macclellandi **Himalayan striped squirrel** Assam (India) to E Nepal, N and C Burma, Yunnan (China), Thailand, Vietnam, Laos, Cambodia, Malay Pen.
T. maritimus **Maritime striped squirrel** China to S Vietnam and Laos, Taiwan
T. rodolphei **Cambodian striped squirrel** E Thailand, S Vietnam, S Laos, Cambodia
T. swinhoei **Swinhoe's striped squirrel** SW Gansu through Xizang, Sichuan and Yunnan (China) to N Burma and N Vietnam
Xerus **African Ground Squirrels**
X. erythropus **Striped ground squirrel** Morocco, Mauritania, Senegal and Gambia east to Sudan, W Ethiopia, W Kenya and N Tanzania
X. inauris **South African ground squirrel** South Africa, W Zimbabwe, Botswana, Namibia, S Angola
X. princeps **Damara ground squirrel** W Namibia, S Angola
X. rutilus **Unstriped ground squirrel** NE and E Africa

SUBFAMILY PETAURISTINAE
Aeretes
A. melanopterus **North Chinese flying squirrel** Hebei and Sichuan (China)
Aeromys **Large Black Flying Squirrels**
A. tephromelas **Black flying squirrel** Malaysia, Indonesia (excl. Java), Philippines (excl. SW)
A. thomasi **Thomas' flying squirrel** Borneo (excl. SE)
Belomys
B. pearsonii **Hairy-footed flying squirrel** Sikkim and Assam (India) to Hunnan, Sichuan, Yunnan, Guizhou, Hainan (China), Taiwan, Bhutan, N Burma, Indochina
Biswamoyopterus
B. biswasi **Namdapha flying squirrel** Arunachal Pradesh (India)
Eupetaurus
E. cinereus **Woolly flying squirrel** N Pakistan and Kashmir to Sikkim (India) to Xizang (China)
Glaucomys **New World Flying Squirrels**
G. sabrinus **Northern flying squirrel** Alaska (USA), Canada, NW USA to S California and South Dakota and NE USA to S Appalachian Mts
G. volans **Southern flying squirrel** Nova Scotia (Canada) to E and C USA, NW Mexico to Honduras
Hylopetes **Arrow-tailed Flying Squirrels**
H. alboniger **Particolored flying squirrel** Nepal and Assam (India) to Sichuan, Yunnan, and Hainan (China), Indochina
H. baberi **Afghan flying squirrel** EC and NW Afghanistan, Kashmir
H. bartelsi **Bartel's flying squirrel** Java (Indonesia)
H. fimbriatus **Kashmir flying squirrel** Punjab (India), Kashmir
H. lepidus **Gray-cheeked flying squirrel** S Vietnam, Thailand to Java (Indonesia), Borneo
H. nigripes **Palawan flying squirrel** Palawan and Bancalan Is (Philippines)
H. phayrei **Indochinese or Phayre's flying squirrel** Fujian and Hainan (China), Burma, Thailand, Laos, S Vietnam
H. sipora **Sipora flying squirrel** Sipora Is (Indonesia)
H. spadiceus **Red-cheeked flying squirrel** Burma, Malaysia, Thailand, S Vietnam, Sumatra (Indonesia)
H. winstoni **Sumatran flying squirrel** N Sumatra (Indonesia)
Iomys **Horsfield's Flying Squirrels**
I. horsfieldi **Javanese flying squirrel** Malay Pen. to Java (Indonesia), Borneo
I. sipora **Mentawi flying squirrel** Mentawi Is (Indonesia)
Petaurillus **Pygmy Flying Squirrels**
P. emiliae **Lesser pygmy flying squirrel** Sarawak (N Borneo)
P. hosei **Hose's pygmy flying squirrel** Sarawak (N Borneo)
P. kinlochii **Selangor pygmy flying squirrel** Selangor (Malay Pen.)
Petaurista **Giant Flying Squirrels**
P. alborufus **Red and white giant flying squirrel** S and C China, Taiwan
P. elegans **Spotted giant flying squirrel** Nepal, Sikkim (India), Sichuan and Yunnan (China), N and W Burma, Laos, Vietnam, Malay Pen., Sumatra and Java (Indonesia), Borneo
P. leucogenys **Japanese giant flying squirrel** Gansu, Sichuan, Yunnan (China), Japan (excl. Hokkaido)
P. magnificus **Hodgson's giant flying squirrel** Sikkim (India), Nepal, Xizang (China), Bhutan
P. nobilis **Bhutan giant flying squirrel** Sikkim (India), C Nepal, Bhutan
P. petaurista **Red giant flying squirrel** E Afghanistan, Kashmir, Punjab to Assam (India), Yunnan and Sichuan (China), Burma, Thailand, Indochina, Malaysia, Sumatra and Java (Indonesia), Borneo
P. philippensis **Indian giant flying squirrel** India, Sri lanka, S China, Taiwan, Burma, Thailand, Indonesia
P. xanthotis **Chinese giant flying squirrel** Mountains of W China
Petinomys **Dwarf Flying Squirrels**
P. crinitus **Mindanao flying squirrel** Basilan, Dinagat, Siargao, and Mindanao (Philippines)
P. fuscocapillus **Travancore flying squirrel** S India, Sri Lanka
P. genibarbis **Whiskered flying squirrel** Malaysia to Sumatra and Java (Indonesia), Borneo
P. hageni **Hagen's flying squirrel** Sumatra (Indonesia), Borneo
P. lugens **Siberut flying squirrel** Siberut and Sipora Is (Sumatra, Indonesia)
P. sagitta **Arrow-tailed flying squirrel** Java (Indonesia)
P. setosus **Temminck's flying squirrel** Burma, Malaysia, Sumatra (Indonesia), S Borneo
P. vordermanni **Vordermann's flying squirrel** S Burma, Malaysia, Borneo
Pteromys **Eurasian Flying Squirrels**
P. momonga **Japanese flying squirrel** Kyushu and Honshu (Japan)
P. volans **Siberian flying squirrel** N Finland to Chukotskoye Pen. (Russia) south in Ural and Altai Mts, Mongolia, N China, Korea, Hokkaido (Japan)
Pteromyscus
P. pulverulentus **Smoky flying squirrel** S Thailand to Sumatra (Indonesia), Borneo
Trogopterus
T. xanthipes **Complex-toothed flying squirrel** Yunnan to C and E China in montane forests

FAMILY CASTORIDAE **Beavers**
Castor
C. canadensis **American or Canadian beaver** Alaska (USA) to Labrador (Canada) south to N Florida (USA) and Tamaulipas (Mexico); introd. to Europe and Asia
C. fiber **Eurasian beaver** NW and NC Eurasia, from France to L. Baikal and Mongolia

FAMILY GEOMYIDAE **Pocket Gophers**
Geomys **Eastern Pocket Gophers**
G. arenarius **Desert pocket gopher** W Texas, New Mexico (USA), Chihuahua (Mexico)
G. bursarius **Plains pocket gopher** SC Manitoba (Canada) to Indiana, Louisiana, SC Texas, and New Mexico (USA)
G. personatus **Texas pocket gopher** S Texas, incl. Padre and Mustang Is (USA), NE Tamaulipas (Mexico)
G. pinetis **Southeastern pocket gopher** C Florida to S Georgia and S Alabama (USA)
G. tropicalis **Tropical pocket gopher** SE Tamaulipas (Mexico)
Orthogeomys **Giant Pocket Gophers**
O. cavator **Chiriqui pocket gopher** C Costa Rica to NW Panama
O. cherriei **Cherrie's pocket gopher** NC Costa Rica
O. cuniculus **Oaxacan pocket gopher** Oaxaca (Mexico)
O. dariensis **Darien pocket gopher** E Panama
O. grandis **Giant pocket gopher** Jalisco (Mexico) to Honduras
O. heterodus **Variable pocket gopher** C Costa Rica
O. hispidus **Hispid pocket gopher** S Tamaulipas and Yucatan Pen. (Mexico), Belize, Guatemala, NW Honduras
O. lanius **Big pocket gopher** Veracruz (Mexico)
O. matagalpae **Nicaraguan pocket gopher** SC Honduras to NC Nicaragua
O. thaeleri **Thaeler's pocket gopher** NW Colombia
O. underwoodi **Underwood's pocket gopher** Pac. Oc. coast of Costa Rica
Pappogeomys **Mexican Pocket Gophers**
P. alcorni **Alcorn's pocket gopher** S Jalisco (Mexico)
P. bulleri **Buller's pocket gopher** Nayarit, Jalisco, and Colima (Mexico)

P. castanops **Yellow-faced pocket gopher** SE Colorado and SW Kansas (USA) to San Luis Potosi (Mexico)
P. fumosus **Smoky pocket gopher** E Colima (Mexico)
P. gymnurus **Llano pocket gopher** S and C Jalisco and NE Michoacan (Mexico)
P. merriami **Merriam's pocket gopher** S Mexico
P. neglectus **Queretaro pocket gopher** Queretaro (Mexico)
P. tylorhinus **Naked-nosed pocket gopher** Distrito Federal and Hidalgo to C Jalisco (Mexico)
P. zinseri **Zinser's pocket gopher** NE Jalisco (Mexico)
Thomomys Western Pocket Gophers
T. bottae **Botta's pocket gopher** W and SW USA south to Sinaloa and Nuevo Leon (Mexico)
T. bulbivorus **Camas pocket gopher** Willamette valley (NW Oregon, USA)
T. clusius **Wyoming pocket gopher** SC Wyoming (USA)
T. idahoensis **Idaho pocket gopher** EC Idaho, adj. Montana, W Wyoming, N Utah (USA)
T. mazama **Western or Mazama pocket gopher** NW Washington to C Oregon to N California (USA)
T. monticola **Mountain pocket gopher** Sierra Nevada Mts of C and N California and WC Nevada (USA)
T. talpoides **Northern pocket gopher** S British Columbia to SW Manitoba (Canada) south to C South Dakota and to N New Mexico, N Arizona, N Nevada and NE California (USA)
T. townsendii **Townsend's pocket gopher** S Idaho to Oregon, NE California, and N Nevada (NW USA)
T. umbrinus **Southern pocket gopher** SC Arizona and SW New Mexico (USA) to Puebla and Veracruz (Mexico)
Zygogeomys
Z. trichopus **Michoacan pocket gopher or Tuza** NC Michoacan (Mexico)

FAMILY HETEROMYIDAE Pocket Mice, Kangaroo Rats, and Kangaroo Mice

SUBFAMILY DIPODOMYINAE

Dipodomys Kangaroo Rats
D. agilis **Agile kangaroo rat** SW and SC California (USA), Baja California (Mexico)
D. californicus **California kangaroo rat** SC Oregon and N California (USA)
D. compactus **Gulf Coast kangaroo rat** S Texas, incl. Padre and Mustang Is (USA) and N Tamaulipas (Mexico)
D. deserti **Desert kangaroo rat** Deserts of E California, W and S Nevada, SW Utah, W and SC Arizona (USA), Sonora and NE Baja California (Mexico)
D. elator **Texas kangaroo rat** SW Oklahoma and NC Texas (USA)
D. elephantinus **Big-eared kangaroo rat** WC California (USA)
D. gravipes **San Quintin kangaroo rat** NW Baja California (USA)
D. heermanni **Heerman's kangaroo rat** C California (USA)
D. ingens **Giant kangaroo rat** WC California (USA)
D. insularis **San Jose Island kangaroo rat** Gulf of California (Baja California, Mexico)
D. margaritae **Margarita Island kangaroo rat** Santa Margarita Is (Baja California, Mexico)
D. merriami **Merriam's kangaroo rat** NE California and NW Nevada to Texas (USA) south to C Mexico (incl. Baja California)
D. microps **Chisel-toothed kangaroo rat** SW USA
D. nelsoni **Nelson's kangaroo rat** NC Mexico
D. nitratoides **Fresno kangaroo rat** WC California (USA)
D. ordii **Ord's kangaroo rat** SW Saskatchewan and SE Alberta (Canada) and SE Washington (USA) south through the Great Plains and W USA to C Mexico
D. panamintinus **Panamint kangaroo rat** E California and W Nevada (USA)
D. phillipsii **Phillips' kangaroo rat** C Durango to N Oaxaca (Mexico)
D. spectabilis **Banner-tailed kangaroo rat** SC Arizona, New Mexico, W Texas (USA) south to N Mexico
D. stephensi **Stephens' kangaroo rat** S California (USA)
D. venustus **Narrow-faced kangaroo rat** WC California (USA)
Microdipodops Kangaroo Mice
M. megacephalus **Dark kangaroo mouse** SE Oregon, S Idaho, W Utah, N and C Nevada, and NE California (USA)
M. pallidus **Pale kangaroo mouse** EC California, W and SC Nevada (USA)

SUBFAMILY HETEROMYINAE

Heteromys Forest Spiny Pocket Mice
H. anomalus **Trinidad spiny pocket mouse** W and N Colombia to N Venezuela (incl. Margarita Is), Trinidad and Tobago
H. australis **Southern spiny pocket mouse** E Panama to SW Colombia and NW Ecuador
H. desmarestianus **Desmarest's spiny pocket mouse** SE Tabasco (Mexico) south to NW Colombia
H. gaumeri **Gaumer's spiny pocket mouse** Yucatan Pen. (Mexico) and N Guatemala
H. goldmani **Goldman's spiny pocket mouse** S Chiapas (Mexico), W Guatemala
H. nelsoni **Nelson's spiny pocket mouse** Chiapas (Mexico)
H. oresterus **Mountain spiny pocket mouse** Cord. Talamanca (Costa Rica)
Liomys Spiny Pocket Mice
L. adspersus **Panamanian spiny pocket mouse** C Panama
L. irroratus **Mexican spiny pocket mouse** S Texas (USA), Mexico
L. pictus **Painted spiny pocket mouse** Mexico, NW Guatemala
L. salvini **Salvin's spiny pocket mouse** E Oaxaca (S Mexico) south to C Costa Rica
L. spectabilis **Jaliscan spiny pocket mouse** SE Jalisco (Mexico)

SUBFAMILY PEROGNATHINAE

Chaetodipus Coarse-haired Pocket Mice
C. arenarius **Little desert pocket mouse** Baja California (Mexico)
C. artus **Narrow-skulled pocket mouse** Mexico
C. baileyi **Bailey's pocket mouse** S California, S Arizona, SW New Mexico (USA) to Sinaloa and Baja California (Mexico)
C. californicus **California pocket mouse** C California (USA) to N Baja California (Mexico)
C. fallax **San Diego pocket mouse** SW California (USA) to W Baja California (Mexico)
C. formosus **Long-tailed pocket mouse** SW USA, Baja California (Mexico)
C. goldmani **Goldman's pocket mouse** Mexico
C. hispidus **Hispid pocket mouse** Great Plains from North Dakota to SE Arizona and W Louisiana (USA) south to Tamaulipas and Hidalgo (Mexico)
C. intermedius **Rock pocket mouse** SC Utah and Arizona to W Texas (USA) south to Sonora and Chihuahua (Mexico)
C. lineatus **Lined pocket mouse** San Luis Potosi (Mexico)
C. nelsoni **Nelson's pocket mouse** SE New Mexico and W Texas (USA) to Jalisco and San Luis Patosi (Mexico)
C. penicillatus **Desert pocket mouse** SW USA to C Mexico (incl. NE Baja California)
C. pernix **Sinaloan pocket mouse** S Sonora to N Nayarit (Mexico)
C. spinatus **Spiny pocket mouse** S Nevada and SE California (USA) to Baja California (Mexico)
Perognathus Silky Pocket Mice
P. alticola **White-eared pocket mouse** SC California (USA)
P. amplus **Arizona pocket mouse** W and C Arizona (USA) to Sonora (Mexico)
P. fasciatus **Olive-backed pocket mouse** Great Plains from SE Alberta, Saskatchewan and SW Manitoba (Canada) to North Dakota, S Colorado and NE Utah (USA)
P. flavescens **Plains pocket mouse** Great Plains from Minnesota and Utah (USA) to Chihuahua (Mexico)
P. flavus **Silky pocket mouse** SW Great Plains from South Dakota, Wyoming and Utah (USA) to Sonora and Puebla (Mexico)
P. inornatus **San Joaquin pocket mouse** California (USA)
P. longimembris **Little pocket mouse** SE Oregon and W Utah (USA) south to Sonora and Baja California (Mexico)
P. merriami **Merriam's pocket mouse** New Mexico to S Texas (USA) to Chihuahua and Tamaulipas (Mexico)
P. parvus **Great Basin pocket mouse** Great Basin from S British Columbia (Canada) south to E California and east to Wyoming and NW Arizona (USA)
P. xanthanotus **Yellow-eared pocket mouse** Freeman Canyon (California, USA)

FAMILY DIPODIDAE Jerboas

SUBFAMILY ALLACTAGINAE

Allactaga Four- and Five-toed Jerboas
A. balikunica **Balikun jerboa** Mongolia, NE Xinjiang (China)
A. bullata **Gobi jerboa** S and W Mongolia, Nei Monggol, E Xinjiang, Ningxia, Gansu, N Shaanxi (China)
A. elater **Small five-toed jerboa** Iran, W Pakistan, Afghanistan, NE Turkey, Armenia, Georgia, Azerbaijan, N Caucasus along Caspian Sea to Lower Volga R south to Turkmenistan, east to Kazakhstan, NE Xinjiang, Nei Monggol, N Gansu (China)
A. euphratica **Euphrates jerboa** Turkey, Caucasus, Syria, Jordan, Iraq, N Iran, Afghanistan, N Saudi Arabia, Kuwait
A. firouzi **Iranian jerboa** Isfahan Prov. (Iran)
A. hotsoni **Hotson's jerboa** Persian Baluchistan (SE Iran), W Pakistan, S Afghanistan
A. major **Great jerboa** Caucasus to Moscow (Russia) and Kyyiv (Ukraine) east to Ob R (W Siberia), Kazakhstan, Uzbekistan, Turkmenistan
A. severtzovi **Severtzov's jerboa** Kazakhstan, Uzbekistan, NE Turkmenistan, SW Tajikistan
A. sibirica **Mongolian five-toed jerboa** Lower Ural R (Kazakhstan) and Caspian Sea east through N Turkmenistan to Mongolia, China
A. tetradactyla **Four-toed jerboa** Egypt, E Libya
A. vinogradovi **Vinogradov's jerboa** S Kazakhstan, E Uzbekistan, Kyrgyzstan, Tajikistan
Allactodipus
A. bobrinskii **Bobrinski's jerboa** W and N Turkmenistan, C and W Uzbekistan
Pygeretmus Fat-tailed Jerboas
P. platyurus **Lesser fat-tailed jerboa** W, C, and E Kazakhstan
P. pumilio **Dwarf fat-tailed jerboa** Don R (Russia) through Kazakhstan to Irtysh R (Russia) south to NE Iran east to S Mongolia, N Xinjiang, W Nei Monggol, Ningxia (China)
P. shitkovi **Greater fat-tailed jerboa** E Kazakhstan

SUBFAMILY CARDIOCRANIINAE

Cardiocranius
C. paradoxus **Five-toed pygmy jerboa** E Kazakhstan, Mongolia, N Xinjiang, W Nei Monggol, N Ningxia, Gansu (China)
Salpingotus Three-toed Pygmy Jerboas
S. crassicauda **Thick-tailed pygmy jerboa** E Kazakhstan, S and SW Mongolia, NW China
S. heptneri **Heptner's pygmy jerboa** Kyzyl Kum Desert (Uzbekistan, S Kazakhstan)
S. kozlovi **Kozlov's pygmy jerboa** S and SE Mongolia, Nei Monggol, Xinjiang, Gansu, Shaanxi, Ningxia (China)
S. michaelis **Baluchistan pygmy jerboa** NW Baluchistan (Pakistan)
S. pallidus **Pallid pygmy jerboa** Deserts of N Aral and S Balqash (Kazakhstan)
S. thomasi **Thomas' pygmy jerboa** Afghanistan

SUBFAMILY DIPODINAE

Dipus
D. sagitta **Northern three-toed jerboa** Don R (Russia), NW coast of Caspian Sea and NE Iran through Turkmenistan, Uzbekistan, Kazakhstan to S Tuva (Russia), Mongolia, China
Eremodipus
E. lichtensteini **Lichtenstein's jerboa** Caspian Sea to L. Balqash (Kazakhstan, Uzbekistan, Turkmenistan)
Jaculus Desert Jerboas
J. blanfordi **Blanford's jerboa** E and S Iran, S and W Afghanistan, W Pakistan
J. jaculus **Lesser Egyptian jerboa** NE Nigeria and Niger, SW Mauritania to Morocco to Egypt, Sudan and Somalia, Arabia to SW Iran
J. orientalis **Greater Egyptian jerboa** Deserts of N Africa and Arabia
J. turcmenicus **Turkmen jerboa** SE Coast of Caspian Sea through Turkmenistan to the Kyzyl Kum Desert (C Uzbekistan)
Stylodipus Three-toed Jerboas
S. andrewsi **Andrews' three-toed jerboa** NW, S, and C Mongolia, Nei Monggol, Xinjiang, Gansu, Ningxia (China)
S. sungorus **Mongolian three-toed jerboa** SW Mongolia, Xinjiang (China)
S. telum **Thick-tailed three-toed jerboa** E Ukraine, N Caucasus, Kazakhstan, W Uzbekistan, N and W Turkmenistan east to N Xinjiang, N Gansu, Nei Monggol (China)

SUBFAMILY EUCHOREUTINAE

Euchoreutes
E. naso **Long-eared jerboa** S Mongolia, Nei Monggol, Xinjiang, Qinghai, Gansu, Ningxia (China)

SUBFAMILY PARADIPODINAE

Paradipus
P. ctenodactylus **Comb-toed jerboa** Turkmenistan, Uzbekistan, E Aral region (Kazakhstan)

SUBFAMILY SICISTINAE

Sicista Birch Mice
S. armenica **Armenian birch mouse** NW Armenia
S. betulina **Northern birch mouse** N and C Europe to SE Siberia (Russia)
S. caucasica **Caucasian birch mouse** NW Caucasus
S. caudata **Long-tailed birch mouse** Ussuri region of NE China, Sakhalin Is (Russia)
S. concolor **Chinese birch mouse** Pakistan, India, Kashmir, Xinjiang, Qinghai, Gansu, Shaanxi, Sichuan (China)
S. kazbegica **Kazbeg birch mouse** Kazbegi (Georgia)
S. kluchorica **Kluchor birch mouse** NW Caucasus
S. napaea **Altai birch mouse** NW Altai Mts (Russia), Kazakhstan
S. pseudonapaea **Gray birch mouse** S Altai Mts (E Kazakhstan)
S. severtzovi **Severtzov's birch mouse** S Russia
S. strandi **Strand's birch mouse** N Caucasus north to Kursk (S Russia)
S. subtilis **Southern birch mouse** E Austria, Hungary, Yugoslavia, Romania east to S Russia, N Kazakhstan, SW Siberia, L. Balqash, Altai Mts, L. Baikal, and NW Xinjiang (China)
S. tianshanica **Tien Shan birch mouse** Tien Shan Mts of Kazakhstan and Xinjiang (China)

SUBFAMILY ZAPODINAE

Eozapus
E. setchuanus **Chinese jumping mouse** Qinghai, Gansu, Ningxia, Shaanxi, Sichuan, Yunnan (China)
Napaeozapus
N. insignis **Woodland jumping mouse** SC and SE Canada, NE and E USA
Zapus Jumping Mice
Z. hudsonius **Meadow jumping mouse** Canada, USA
Z. princeps **Western jumping mouse** W North America
Z. trinotatus **Pacific jumping mouse** SW British Columbia (Canada) south along W coast of USA to California

FAMILY MURIDAE Rats, Mice, Voles, Lemmings, Hamsters, and Gerbils

SUBFAMILY ARVICOLINAE

Alticola Mountain Voles
A. albicauda **White-tailed mountain vole** Himalayas of NW India
A. argentatus **Silver mountain vole** Xinjiang (China) through the Tien Shan Mts and Pamirs to N Afghanistan, Pakistan and N India
A. barakshin **Gobi Altai mountain vole** Tuva (S Russia) east to W and S Mongolia
A. lemminus **Lemming vole** NE Siberia (Russia)
A. macrotis **Large-eared vole** Altai and Sayan Mts to N Mongolia, L. Baikal, and Yakutsk (NE Russia)
A. montosa **Central Kashmir vole** Kashmir
A. roylei **Royle's mountain vole** W Himalayas of N India
A. semicanus **Mongolian silver vole** Tuva (S Russia) to N Mongolia
A. stoliczkanus **Stoliczka's mountain vole** N Ladakh (India) and Nepal to W and N Xizang to Gansu (China)
A. stracheyi **Strachey's mountain vole** Himalayas from E Kashmir to S Xizang (China) and N Nepal to Sikkim (India)
A. strelzowi **Flat-headed vole** Quaraghandy (Kazakhstan) east to Altai Mts of NW Mongolia, Siberia (Russia), and Xinjiang (NW China)
A. tuvinicus **Tuva silver vole** Tuva (S Russia) and Altai Mts to L. Baikal and NW Mongolia
Arborimus Tree Voles
A. albipes **White-footed vole** Coastal W USA, from Oregon to NW Calfiornia
A. longicaudus **Red-tree vole** Coastal Oregon (USA)
A. pomo **Sonoma tree vole** Coastal NW California
Arvicola Water Voles
A. sapidus **Southwestern water vole** Portugal, Spain, W France
A. terrestris **European water vole** Europe east

through Siberia (Russia) south to Israel, Iran, Tien Shan Mts of NW China and L. Baikal
Blanfordimys **Afghan Voles**
B. afghanus **Afghan vole** S Turkmenistan, Uzbekistan, Tajikistan, Afghanistan
B. bucharicus **Bucharian vole** Mountains of SW Tajikistan
Chionomys **Snow Voles**
C. gud **Caucasian snow vole** Caucasus, NE Turkey
C. nivalis **European snow vole** Mountains of Europe (incl. Alps, Carpathians, Balkans, Pindus) east to W Caucasus, Turkey, Israel, Lebanon, Syria, and Zagros and Kopet Dagh Mts (Iran)
C. roberti **Robert's snow vole** W Caucasus Mts, NE Turkey
Clethrionomys **Red-backed Voles**
C. californicus **Western red-backed vole** Coastal W USA from Columbia R south to NW California (USA)
C. centralis **Tien Shan red-backed vole** Tien Shan Mts (Kazakhstan and Kyrgyzstan), Xinjiang (China)
C. gapperi **Southern red-backed vole** Canada (excl. Newfoundland), N USA, Rocky Mts and Appalachians
C. glareolus **Bank vole** W Palearctic from France and Scandinavia to L. Baikal south to N Spain, Italy, the Balkans, W Turkey, N Kazakhstan, Altai and Sayan Mts, Britain, SW Ireland
C. rufocanus **Gray red-backed vole** N Palearctic from Scandinavia through Siberia to Kamchatka Pen. (Russia) south to Ural and Altai Mts, Mongolia, N China, Korea, N Japan
C. rutilus **Northern red-backed vole** N Scandinavia east to Chukotskoye Pen. south to N Kazakhstan, Mongolia, NE China, Korea, Sakhalin Is, Hokkaido (Japan), and St Lawrence Is (Bering Sea, USA); also Alaska (USA) east to Hudson Bay south to N British Columbia and NE Manitoba (Canada)
C. sikotanensis **Sikotan red-backed vole** Sikotan, Daikoku and Rishiri Is (Kurilskiye Is, Russia)
Dicrostonyx **Collared Lemmings**
D. exsul **St. Lawrence Island collared lemming** St Lawrence Is (Bering Sea, USA)
D. groenlandicus **Northern collared lemming** N Greenland, Queen Eilzabeth Is south to Baffin and Southampton Is (Canada)
D. hudsonius **Ungava collared lemming** Labrador, N Quebec (Canada)
D. kilangmiutak **Victoria collared lemming** Victoria and Banks Is, adj. mainland (Canada)
D. nelsoni **Nelson's collared lemming** Alaska (USA)
D. nunatakensis **Ogilvie mountain collared lemming** Ogilvie Mts, NC Yukon Territory (Canada)
D. richardsoni **Richardson's collared lemming** W Coast of Hudson Bay west to Mackenzie District (Canada)
D. rubricatus **Bering collared lemming** N Alaska (USA)
D. torquatus **Arctic lemming** Palearctic from White Sea (W Russia) to Chukotskoye Pen. and Kamchatka Pen. (NE Russia), Novosibirskiye Is and Novaya Zemlya Is
D. unalascensis **Unalaska collared lemming** Aleutian Arch. (Alaska, USA)
D. vinogradovi **Wrangel lemming** Vrangelya Is (NE Siberia, Russia)
Dinaromys
D. bogdanovi **Martino's snow vole** Mountains of Yugoslavia
Ellobius **Mole Voles**
E. alaicus **Alai mole vole** Altai Mts (S Kyrgyzstan)
E. fuscocapillus **Southern or Afghan mole vole** E Iran, Afghanistan, W Pakistan, and Kopet Dagh Mts (S Turkmenistan)
E. lutescens **Transcaucasian mole vole** S Caucasus Mts south to E Turkey and NW Iran
E. talpinus **Northern mole-vole** S Ukraine east through Kazakhstan to N L. Balqash, also Turkmenistan
E. tancrei **Zaisan mole vole** NE Turkmenistan and Uzbekistan east through E Kazakhstan to Xinjiang and Nei Monggol (E China) and Mongolia
Eolagurus **Yellow Steppe Lemmings**
E. luteus **Yellow steppe lemming** N Xinjiang (China), W Mongolia
E. przewalskii **Przewalski's steppe lemming** China, S Mongolia
Eothenomys **South Asian Voles**
E. chinensis **Pratt's vole** Sichuan and Yunnan (China)
E. custos **Southwest China vole** Sichuan and Yunnan (China)
E. eva **Gansu vole** S Gansu, adj. Shaanxi, Sichuan, Hubei (China)
E. inez **Kolan vole** Shaanxi and Shanxi (China)
E. melanogaster **Pere David's vole** W and S China south to N Thailand and N Burma, Taiwan
E. olitor **Chaotung vole** Yunnan (China)
E. proditor **Yulungshan vole** Sichuan and Yunnan (China)
E. regulus **Royal vole** Korea
E. shanseius **Shansei vole** Shanxi and Hebei (China)
Hyperacrius **Kashmir Voles**
H. fertilis **True's vole** Kashmir, N Pakistan
H. wynnei **Murree or Punjab vole** N Pakistan
Lagurus
L. lagurus **Steppe lemming** Ukraine through N Kazakhstan to W Mongolia and NW China
Lasiopodomys **Brandt's Voles**
L. brandtii **Brandt's vole** Mongolia, adj. Russia, Nei Monggol, Heilongjiang, Hebei (China)
L. fuscus **Plateau vole** Qinghai (China)
L. mandarinus **Mandarin vole** N Mongolia, adj. Russia and SE Siberia, C and NE China, Korea
Lemmiscus
L. curtatus **Sagebrush vole** S Alberta and SE Sakatchewan (Canada) south to NW Colorado and EC California
Lemmus **Brown Lemmings**
L. amurensis **Amur lemming** E Siberia from L. Baikal north to Verkhoyansk, Khrebet Cherskogo, and Kolymskoye Nagorye Mts to Omolon R (NE Russia)
L. lemmus **Norway lemming** Scandinavia
L. sibiricus **Brown lemming** Palearctic from White Sea (W Russia) to Chukotskoye Pen. and Kamchatka Pen., Nunivak and St George Is (Bering Sea); Nearctic from W Alaska (USA) to Hudson Bay south in Rocky Mts to C British Columbia (Canada)
Microtus **Meadow Voles**
M. abbreviatus **Insular vole** Hall and St Matthew Is (Bering Sea, USA)
M. agrestis **Field vole** Britain, Scandinavia, France east through Europe and Siberia to Lena R (NE Russia) south to Pyrenees (France, Spain), N Yugoslavia, Ural and Altai Mts, Xinjiang (NW China) and L. Baikal
M. arvalis **Common vole** C and N Spain throughout Europe to west coast of Black Sea northeast to Kirov region (W Russia); also Orkney Is (UK), Guernsey (Channel Is, UK), Yeu (France)
M. bavaricus **Bavarian pine vole** Bavarian Alps (Germany)
M. breweri **Beach vole** Muskeget Is (Massachusets, USA)
M. cabrerae **Cabrera's vole** Spain, Portugal, N Pyrenees (S France)
M. californicus **California vole** Coastal W USA, from SW Oregon to California, to N Baja California (Mexico)
M. canicaudus **Gray-tailed vole** Willamette Valley (NW Oregon), adj. Washington (USA)
M. chrotorrhinus **Rock vole** SE Canada to NE Minnesota (USA) and south in Appalachian Mts to E Tennessee and W North Carolina (USA)
M. daghestanicus **Daghestan pine vole** Caucasus Mts (Dagestan, Russia)
M. duodecimcostatus **Mediterranean pine vole** SE France, E and S Spain, Portugal
M. evoronensis **Evorsk vole** Khabarovsk Krai (Russia)
M. felteni **Felten's vole** S Yugoslavia, Greece
M. fortis **Reed vole** SE Russia south through E China to Lower Yangtze Valley
M. gerbei **Gerbe's vole** SW France, Pyrenees (France, Spain)
M. gregalis **Narrow-headed vole** Palearctic from White Sea (W Russia) to NE, and from Urals east to Amur R and NE China, south to Aral Sea, Pamirs, Tien Shan and Altai Mts, N Mongolia, and NW China
M. guatemalensis **Guatemalan vole** C Chiapas (Mexico), Guatemala
M. guentheri **Gunther's vole** S Bulgaria, S Yugoslavia, E Greece, W Turkey
M. hyperboreus **North Siberian vole** NE Siberia (Russia)
M. irani **Persian vole** NE Libya, E Turkey, N Syria, Lebanon, Israel, Jordan, N Iraq, W and N Iran, Kopet Dagh Mts (Turkmenistan)
M. irene **Chinese scrub vole** N Burma, Xizang, Yunnan, Sichuan, Gansu (China)
M. juldaschi **Juniper vole** Tien Shan Mts, Pamirs (Kyrgyzstan, Tajikistan) west to Samarqand (Uzbekistan) south to NE Afghanistan and N Pakistan then east to Xizang (China)
M. kermanensis **Baluchistan vole** Kerman (SE Iran)
M. kirgisorum **Tien Shan vole** S Kazakhstan, Kyrgyzstan, Tajikistan, SE Turkmenistan
M. leucurus **Blyth's vole** S Qinghai, Xizang (China), and west in the Himalayas to Kashmir
M. limnophilus **Lacustrine vole** Qinghai (China) to W Mongolia
M. longicaudus **Long-tailed vole** E Alaska (USA) and Yukon Territory (Canada) south through SE Canada in Rocky Mts to W Colorado and E California; also S California, Arizona and New Mexico (USA)
M. lusitanicus **Lusitanian pine vole** Portugal, NW Spain, SW France
M. majori **Major's pine vole** S Yugoslavia, Mt Olympus (Greece), N and W Turkey, W and N Caucasus
M. maximowiczii **Maximowicz's vole** E shore of L. Baikal to Upper Amur region (SE Russia), E Mongolia, and Heilongjiang (NE China)
M. mexicanus **Mexican vole** S Utah and SW Colorado (USA) south in Sierra Madres to C Oaxaca (Mexico)
M. middendorffi **Middendorff's vole** NC Siberia (Russia)
M. miurus **Singing vole** N and SE Alaska (USA), NW Canada
M. mongolicus **Mongolian vole** Mongolia, NE China, and adj. Russia
M. montanus **Montane vole** SC British Colombia (Canada) to SW USA in Cascade, Sierra Nevada and Rocky Mts
M. montebelli **Japanese grass vole** Honshu, Sado, Kyushu (Japan)
M. mujanensis **Muisk vole** Vitim River Basin (E Russia)
M. multiplex **Alpine pine vole** S Alps and N Apennines (France, Switzerland, Italy, Austria), NW and C Yugoslavia
M. nasarovi **Nasarov's vole** NE Caucasus
M. oaxacensis **Tarabundi vole** NC Oaxaca (Mexico)
M. obscurus **Altai vole** Russia from E Ukraine through Siberia to Upper Yenesei R (Russia) south to Caucasus, N Iran, Altai Mts, L. Balqash, NW Mongolia, Xinjiang (NW China)
M. ochrogaster **Prairie vole** Northern and Central Great Plains of North America
M. oeconomus **Tundra vole** Palearctic from Scandinavia and Netherlands east to Bering Sea, south to E Germany, Ukraine, S Kazakhstan, Mongolia and the Ussuri region, Sakhalin Is (Russia), St Lawrence Is (Bering Sea, USA); Neartic from Alaska (USA) to Yukon Territory, W Northwest Territories and NW British Columbia (Canada)
M. oregoni **Creeping vole** SW British Columbia (Canada) south to NW California (USA)
M. pennsylvanicus **Meadow vole** Canada, USA (incl. Alaska), Chihuahua (Mexico)
M. pinetorum **Woodland vole** E USA, from S Maine to N Florida west to C Wisconsin and E Texas
M. quasiater **Jalapan pine vole** SE San Luis Potosi to N Oaxaca (Mexico)
M. richardsoni **Water vole** Rocky and Cascade Mts from SW Canada to Wyoming, C Utah and Oregon (USA)
M. rossiaemeridionalis **Southern vole** Finland east to Urals south to N Caucasus west to Ukraine, Romania, Bulgaria, Yugoslavia, N Greece, NW Turkey
M. sachalinensis **Sakhalin vole** Sakhalin Is (Russia)
M. savii **Savi's pine vole** SE France, Italy (incl. Sicily and Elba)
M. schelkovnikovi **Schelkovnikov's pine vole** Talysk and Alborz Mts (S Azerbaijan)
M. sikimensis **Sikkim vole** Himalayas from W Nepal through Sikkim (India) to S and E Xizang (China)
M. socialis **Social vole** Palearctic from Dnipro R (Ukraine) east to L. Balqash and NW Xinjiang (China) south through E Turkey to Syria and NE Iran
M. subterraneus **European pine vole** N and C France through C Europe to Ukraine and Don R, south through Yugoslavia to N Greece; also NE Russia
M. tatricus **Tatra pine vole** W and E Carpathian Mts, Tatra Mts, W Ukraine
M. thomasi **Thomas' pine vole** S coastal Yugoslavia to Greece
M. townsendii **Townsend's vole** SW British Columbia (Canada) to NW California (USA), Vancouver Is (Canada)
M. transcaspicus **Transcaspian vole** S Turkmenistan, N Afghanistan, N Iran
M. umbrosus **Zempoaltepec vole** Mt Zempoaltepec (Oaxaca, Mexico)
M. xanthognathus **Taiga vole** EC Alaska (USA) to W Northwest Territories to C Alberta and W coast of Hudson Bay (Canada)
Myopus
M. schisticolor **Wood lemming** Norway and Sweden through Siberia to Kolyma R and Kamchatka Pen. (NE Russia), south to Altai Mts, N Mongolia, Heilongjiang (NE China), and Sikhote Alin Mts; also in Ural Mts
Neofiber
N. alleni **Round-tailed muskrat** Florida to SE Georgia (USA)
Ondatra
O. zibethicus **Muskrat** North America (south of tree-line); introd. to C and N Europe, Ukraine, Russia, adj. China and Mongolia, Honshu Is (Japan), S Argentina
Phaulomys **Japanese Voles**
P. andersoni **Japanese red-backed vole** Honshu (Japan)
P. smithii **Smith's vole** Dogo, Honshu, Shikoku, Kyushu (Japan)
Phenacomys **Heather Voles**
P. intermedius **Western heather vole** SW British Columbia, adj. Alberta (SW Canada) south to SW USA
P. ungava **Eastern heather vole** S Yukon to Labrador south to S Alberta and along N Great Lakes and St Lawrence R (Canada)
Proedromys
P. bedfordi **Duke of Bedford's vole** Gansu and Sichuan (China)
Prometheomys
P. schaposchnikowi **Long-clawed mole vole** Caucasus Mts, NE Turkey
Synaptomys **Bog Lemmings**
S. borealis **Northern bog lemming** Alaska (USA) to N Washington (USA) east to Labrador (Canada); also from Gaspe Pen. (Quebec, Canada) to New Hampshire (USA)
S. cooperi **Southern bog lemming** Midwestern and E USA through SE Canada (incl. Cape Breton Is)
Volemys **Musser's Voles**
V. clarkei **Clarke's vole** NW Yunnan (China), N Burma
V. kikuchii **Taiwan vole** Highlands of Taiwan
V. millicens **Sichuan vole** E Xizang and Sichuan (China)
V. musseri **Marie's vole** W Sichuan (China)

SUBFAMILY CALOMYSCINAE
Calomyscus **Mouse-like Hamsters**
C. bailwardi **Mouse-like hamster** Iran
C. baluchi **Baluchi mouse-like hamster** W Pakistan, NC and E Afghanistan
C. hotsoni **Hotson's mouse-like hamster** Baluchistan (Pakistan)
C. mystax **Afghan mouse-like hamster** S Turkmenistan, NC and NE Iran, NW Afghanistan
C. tsolovi **Tsolov's mouse-like hamster** SW Syria
C. urartensis **Urartsk mouse-like hamster** Azerbaijan, NW Iran

SUBFAMILY CRICETINAE
Allocricetulus **Mongolian Hamsters**
A. curtatus **Mongolian hamster** North of Altai Mts east to Inner Mongolia, Xinjiang, Ningxia, Anhui (China)
A. eversmanni **Eversmann's hamster** N Kazakhstan, steppes from Volga R to Upper Irtysh R
Cansumys
C. canus **Gansu hamster** S Gansu and Shaanxi (China)
Cricetulus **Dwarf Hamsters**
C. alticola **Tibetan dwarf hamster** W Nepal, Ladak (N India), Kashmir, W Xizang (China)
C. barabensis **Striped dwarf hamster** S Siberia from Irtysh R to Ussuri region (Russia), south to Mongolia, Xinjiang to Nei Monggol (China), and Korea
C. kamensis **Kam dwarf hamster** Xizang (China)
C. longicaudatus **Long-tailed dwarf hamster** Tuva and Altai regions of Russia and Kazakhstan, Xinjiang (NW China), Mongolia, adj. China south to Xizang
C. migratorius **Gray dwarf hamster** SE Europe through Ukraine to Kazakhstan to S Mongolia and N China south to Turkey, Israel, Jordan, Lebanon, Iraq, Iran, Pakistan, and Afghanistan
C. sokolovi **Sokolov's dwarf hamster** W and S Mongolia, C Nei Monggol (China)
Cricetus
C. cricetus **Black-bellied hamster** From Belgium through C Europe, W Siberia and N Kazakhstan to Upper Yenesei R and Altai Mts, and Xinjiang (NW China)

Mesocricetus Golden Hamsters
M. auratus **Golden hamster** Aleppo (Syria)
M. brandti **Brandt's hamster** Turkey and Caucasus south to Israel, Lebanon, Syria, N Iraq, NW Iran
M. newtoni **Romanian hamster** E Romania, Bulgaria
M. raddei **Ciscaucasian hamster** Russia, from N Caucasus to Don R and Sea of Azov
Phodopus Small Desert Hamsters
P. campbelli **Campbell's hamster** Heilongjiang through Nei Monggol to Xinjiang (China), Mongolia, adj. Russia
P. roborovskii **Desert hamster** Tuva (S Russia) and E Kazakhstan, W and S Mongolia, Heilongjiang to N Xinjiang (China)
P. sungorus **Dzungarian hamster** E Kazakhstan, SW Siberia (Russia)
Tscherskia
T. triton **Greater long-tailed hamster** Shaanxi to Dongbei south to Anhui (China), Korea, north to Ussuri region (Russia)

SUBFAMILY CRICETOMYINAE
Beamys Long-tailed Pouched Rats
B. hindei **Long-tailed pouched rat** S Kenya, NE Tanzania
B. major **Greater Long-tailed pouched rat** S Tanzania, Malawi, NE Zambia
Cricetomys African Giant Pouched Rats
C. emini **Giant rat** Sierra Leone to S Nigeria, Cameroon and Gabon through Congo and DRC to S Uganda, Bioko (Equatorial Guinea)
C. gambianus **Gambian rat** Senegal and Sierra Leone to S Sudan south to S Angola, S Zambia, and E South Africa
Saccostomus Pouched Mice
S. campestris **Pouched mouse** SW Tanzania to C Angola south to S South Africa
S. mearnsi **Mearns' pouched mouse** S Ethiopia, S Somalia, Kenya, E Uganda, NE Tanzania

SUBFAMILY DENDROMURINAE
Dendromus African Climbing Mice
D. insignis **Remarkable climbing mouse** Ethiopian highlands, E Kenya, W Uganda south to Rwanda, Mt Kilimanjaro (NE Tanzania)
D. kahuziensis **Mount Kahuzi climbing mouse** Kivu region (E DRC)
D. kivu **Kivu climbing mouse** West and East of the Ruwenzori Mts in W Uganda and E DRC, also Kivu region (DRC)
D. lovati **Lovat's or Ethiopian climbing mouse** Ethiopian plateau
D. melanotis **Gray climbing mouse** South Africa north to Uganda, west to Mt Nimba (Guinea), also Ethiopia
D. mesomelas **Brant's climbing mouse** S, SE, and E South Africa, C Mozambique, N Botswana, NE Zambia, N and S Malawi, SE, NE, and NW DRC, SW and EC Tanzania
D. messorius **Banana climbing mouse** Benin and Nigeria east to DRC, Uganda, Kenya and Sudan
D. mystacalis **Chestnut climbing mouse** South Africa to Ethiopia and S Sudan
D. nyikae **Nyika climbing mouse** E South Africa, E Zimbabwe, Mozambique, Malawi, Zambia, N and C Angola, SC DRC, SW Tanzania
D. oreas **Cameroon climbing mouse** Mt Cameroun, Mt Kupe, and Mt Manenguba (E Cameroon)
D. vernayi **Vernay's climbing mouse** Chitau (EC Angola)
Dendroprionomys
D. rousseloti **Velvet climbing mouse** Brazzaville (Congo)
Deomys
D. ferrugineus **Congo forest mouse or Link rat** Central Africa, from Uganda, Rwanda to S Cameroon, Bioko (Equatorial Guinea)
Leimacomys
L. buettneri **Groove-toothed forest mouse** Bismarckburg (Togo)
Malacothrix
M. typica **Gerbil mouse or Large-eared mouse** South Africa, S Botswana, Namibia, SW Angola
Megadendromus
M. nikolausi **Nikolaus's mouse** Bale Mts (Ethiopia)
Prionomys
P. batesi **Dollman's tree mouse** W and S Cameroon, S CAR
Steatomys Fat Mice
S. caurinus **Northwestern fat mouse** W Africa, from Senegal to C Nigeria
S. cuppedius **Dainty fat mouse** W Africa, from Senegal to NC Nigeria and SC Niger
S. jacksoni **Jackson's fat mouse** Ashanti (Ghana), SW Nigeria
S. krebsii **Kreb's fat mouse** South Africa, NE and SE Botswana, Caprivi Strip (NE Namibia), S Angola, W Zambia
S. parvus **Tiny fat mouse** E South Africa, NW Zimbabwe, N Botswana, N Namibia, Angola, Zambia, Tanzania, Uganda, Kenya, Ethiopia, Somalia, S Sudan
S. pratensis **Common fat mouse** South Africa, Swaziland, Zimbabwe, N Botswana, NE and N Namibia, Angola, Zambia, N Malawi, Mozambique, DRC, SW Sudan west to Cameroon

SUBFAMILY GERBILLINAE
Ammodillus
A. imbellis **Ammodile** Somalia, E Ethiopia
Brachiones
B. przewalskii **Przewalski's gerbil** Xinjiang to Gansu (China)
Desmodilliscus
D. braueri **Pouched gerbil** N and C Sudan, N Cameroon, W Niger, N Nigeria, C Mali, Burkina Faso, Senegal, W Mauritania
Desmodillus
D. auricularis **Cape short-eared gerbil** South Africa, S Botswana, Namibia
Gerbillurus Hairy-footed Gerbils
G. paeba **South African hairy-footed gerbil** South Africa, Namibia, Botswana, Zimbabwe, Mozambique, SW Angola
G. setzeri **Setzer's hairy-footed gerbil** NW Namibia to SW Angola
G. tytonis **Dune hairy-footed gerbil** Namibia
G. vallinus **Bushy-tailed hairy-footed gerbil** W South Africa through Namibia
Gerbillus Gerbils
G. acticola **Berbera gerbil** Somalia
G. agag **Agag gerbil** Mali, Niger and N Nigeria to Chad, Sudan, and Kenya
G. allenbyi **Allenby's gerbil** N of Gaza to Haifa (Israel)
G. amoenus **Pleasant gerbil** Egypt, Libya
G. andersoni **Anderson's gerbil** Nile Delta south to El Faiyum (Egypt)
G. aquilus **Swarthy's gerbil** SE Iran, W Pakistan, S Afghanistan
G. bilensis **Bilen gerbil** Bilen (Ethiopia)
G. bonhotei **Bonhote's gerbil** NE Sinai Pen. (Egypt)
G. bottai **Botta's gerbil** Sudan, Kenya
G. brockmani **Brockman's gerbil** Somalia
G. burtoni **Burton's gerbil** Dharfur (Sudan)
G. campestris **North African gerbil** N Africa, from Morocco to Egypt and Sudan
G. cheesmani **Cheesman's gerbil** SW Iran, Iraq, Kuwait, Saudi Arabia, Oman, Yemen
G. cosensis **Cosens' gerbil** Ngamatak, Kozibiri R (Kenya)
G. dalloni **Dallon's gerbil** Tibesti (Chad)
G. dasyurus **Wagner's gerbil** Arabian Pen., Iraq, Syria, Lebanon, Israel, Sinai (Egypt)
G. diminutus **Diminutive gerbil** Kenya
G. dongolanus **Dongola gerbil** Dongola (Sudan)
G. dunni **Somalia gerbil** Ethiopia, Somalia, Djibouti
G. famulus **Black-tufted gerbil** Yemen
G. floweri **Flower's gerbil** Sinai (Egypt)
G. garamantis **Algerian gerbil** Algeria
G. gerbillus **Lesser Egyptian gerbil** Israel to Egypt and N Sudan to Morocco, also N Chad, N Niger and N Mali
G. gleadowi **Indian hairy-footed gerbil** NW India, Pakistan
G. grobbeni **Grobben's gerbil** Cyrenaica (Libya)
G. harwoodi **Harwood's gerbil** Kenya
G. henleyi **Pygmy gerbil** Algeria to Israel and Jordan, W Saudia Arabia, N Yemen, and Oman, also Burkina Faso, and N Senegal
G. hesperinus **Western gerbil** Coastal Morocco
G. hoogstraali **Hoogstraal's gerbil** Taroudannt (Morocco)
G. jamesi **James' gerbil** Tunisia
G. juliani **Julian's gerbil** Somalia
G. latastei **Lataste's gerbil** Tunisia, Libya
G. lowei **Lowe's gerbil** Jebel Marra (Sudan)
G. mackillingini **Mackillingin's gerbil** S Egypt, adj. Sudan
G. maghrebi **Greater short-eared gerbil** Fes (Morocco)
G. mauritaniae **Mauritanian gerbil** Aouker region (Mauritania)
G. mesopotamiae **Mesopotamian gerbil** SW Iran, Iraq
G. muriculus **Barfur gerbil** Sudan
G. nancillus **Sudan gerbil** El Fasher (Sudan)
G. nanus **Baluchistan gerbil** Morocco through N Africa to Arabian Pen., Jordan, Israel, Iraq, Iran, Pakistan, S Afghanistan to NW India
G. nigeriae **Nigerian gerbil** N Nigeria, Burkina Faso
G. occiduus **Occidental gerbil** Aoreora (Morocco)
G. percivali **Percival's gerbil** Kenya
G. perpallidus **Pale gerbil** N Egypt, west of Nile R
G. poecilops **Large Aden gerbil** Saudi Arabia, Yemen
G. principulus **Principal gerbil** Jebel Meidob (Sudan)
G. pulvinatus **Cushioned gerbil** Ethiopia
G. pusillus **Least gerbil** Kenya, Ethiopia, S Sudan
G. pyramidum **Greater Egyptian gerbil** Nile Delta (Egypt) south to N Sudan
G. quadrimaculatus **Four-spotted gerbil** Nubia (NE Sudan)
G. riggenbachi **Riggenbach's gerbil** Rio de Oro (Western Sahara), N Senegal
G. rosalinda **Rosalinda's gerbil** Sudan
G. ruberrimus **Little red gerbil** Kenya, E Ethiopia, Somalia
G. simoni **Lesser short-tailed gerbil** Egypt, W of Nile Delta, Libya, Tunisia, Algeria
G. somalicus **Somalian gerbil** Somalia
G. stigmonyx **Khartoum gerbil** Sudan
G. syrticus **Sand gerbil** Nofilia (Libya)
G. tarabuli **Tarabul's gerbil** Libya
G. vivax **Vivacious gerbil** Libya
G. watersi **Waters' gerbil** Somalia, Sudan
Meriones Jirds
M. arimalius **Arabian jird** Saudia Arabia, Oman
M. chengi **Cheng's jird** N Xinjiang (China)
M. crassus **Sundevall's jird** N Africa, from Morocco through Niger and Sudan to Egypt then to Saudi Arabia, Jordan, Israel, Syria, Iraq, Iran, Aghanistan
M. dahli **Dahl's jird** Armenia
M. hurrianae **Indian desert jird** SE Iran, Pakistan, NW India
M. libycus **Libyan jird** N Africa, from Western Sahara to Egypt, Saudi Arabia, Jordan, Iraq, Syria, Iran, Afghanistan to S Kazakhstan and Xinjiang (W China)
M. meridianus **Midday jird** N Caucasus and Lower Don R to Mongolia and Xinjiang, Qinghai, Shanxi and Hebei (China) south to E Iran and Afghanistan
M. persicus **Persian jird** Iran, adj. regions of Iraq, Turkey, Caucasus, Turkmenistan, Afghanistan, and Pakistan
M. rex **King jird** Mecca to Aden (SW Saudi Arabia)
M. sacramenti **Buxton's jird** S Israel
M. shawi **Shaw's jird** Morocco to N Sinai (Egypt)
M. tamariscinus **Tamarisk jird** N Caucasus and Kazakhstan to Altai Mts and through N Xinjiang and W Gansu (China)
M. tristrami **Tristram's jird** Jordan, Lebanon and Israel to E Turkey, Caucasus, Syria, Iraq, and NW Iran
M. unguiculatus **Mongolian or Clawed jird** Mongolia, adj. regions of Siberia (Russia), N Gansu through Nei Monggol to Heilongjiang (China)
M. vinogradovi **Vinogradov's jird** N Syria, SE Turkey, Armenia, Azerbaijan, N Iran
M. zarudnyi **Zarudny's jird** NE Iran, S Turkmenistan, N Afghanistan
Microdillus
M. peeli **Somali pygmy gerbil** Somalia
Pachyuromys
P. duprasi **Fat-tailed gerbil** N Sahara, from W Morocco to N Egypt
Psammomys Sand Rats
P. obesus **Fat sand rat** N Africa, from Algeria to coastal Egypt, Syria, Jordan, Israel, Arabia; also coastal Sudan
P. vexillaris **Thin sand rat or Pale fat sand rat** Algeria, Tunisia, Libya
Rhombomys
R. opimus **Great gerbil** S Mongola through Ningxia, Gansu and Xinjiang (China) to Kazakhstan, Afghanistan, Pakistan, and Iran
Sekeetamys
S. calurus **Bushy-tailed jird** E Egypt to Sinai, S Israel, Jordan, C Saudi Arabia
Tatera Large Naked-soled Gerbils
T. afra **Cape gerbil** SW South Africa
T. boehmi **Boehm's gerbil** Angola, Zambia, Malawi, S DRC, Tanzania, Uganda, Kenya
T. brantsii **Highveld gerbil** South Africa, W Zimbabwe, Botswana, C and E Namibia, S Angola, SW Zambia
T. guineae **Guinea gerbil** Senegal and Gambia to Ghana and Burkina Faso
T. inclusa **Gorongoza gerbil** E Zimbabwe, Mozambique, Tanzania
T. indica **Indian gerbil** Syria, Iraq and Kuwait through Iran, Afghanistan and Pakistan to India and north to S Nepal, also Sri Lanka
T. kempi **Kemp's gerbil** Senegal and Guinea to Cameroon
T. leucogaster **Bushveld gerbil** South Africa to S Angola, S DRC, and SW Tanzania
T. nigricauda **Black-tailed gerbil** Tanzania, Kenya, Somalia
T. phillipsi **Phillip's gerbil** Somalia, Rift Valley (Ethiopia, Kenya)
T. robusta **Fringe-tailed gerbil** Chad, Sudan, Ethiopia, Somalia, Kenya, Uganda, Tanzania, also Burkina Faso
T. valida **Savanna gerbil** CAR, Chad east to Sudan and Ethiopia south to SW Tanzania, Zambia, and Angola
Taterillus Small Naked-soled Gerbils
T. arenarius **Sahel gerbil** Mauritania to Niger
T. congicus **Congo gerbil** Cameroon, Chad, CAR, DRC, Sudan, Uganda
T. emini **Emin's gerbil** Sudan, W Ethiopia, NW Kenya, Uganda, NE DRC
T. gracilis **Slender gerbil** Senegal and Gambia to Burkina Faso, Niger, and N Nigeria
T. harringtoni **Harrington's gerbil** CAR, Sudan, Ethiopia, Somalia, Kenya, Uganda, Tanzania
T. lacustris **Lake Chad gerbil** NE Nigeria, Cameroon
T. petteri **Petter's gerbil** Burkina Faso, W Niger
T. pygargus **Senegal gerbil** Senegal, Gambia, S Mauritania, W Mali

SUBFAMILY LOPHIOMYINAE
Lophiomys
L. imhausi **Crested or Maned rat** E Sudan, Ethiopia, Somalia, Kenya, Uganda, Tanzania, poss. Arabia

SUBFAMILY MURINAE
Abditomys
A. latidens **Luzon broad-toothed rat** Luzon (Philippines)
Acomys African Spiny Mice
A. cahirinus **Cairo spiny mouse** W Sahara to Egypt, N Sudan, N Ethiopia, Jordan, Israel, Lebanon, Syria, Saudi Arabia, Yemen, Oman, S Iraq, Iran, Pakistan
A. cilicicus **Asia Minor spiny mouse** Silifke (W Turkey)
A. cinerasceus **Gray spiny mouse** N Ghana and Burkina Faso to C and S Sudan, N Uganda, and C and S Ethiopia
A. ignitus **Fiery spiny mouse** Usambara Mts (Tanzania), Kenya
A. kempi **Kemp's spiny mouse** S Somalia, Kenya, NE Tanzania
A. louisae **Louise's spiny mouse** Somalia
A. minous **Crete spiny mouse** Crete
A. mullah **Mullah spiny mouse** Ethiopia, Somalia
A. nesiotes **Cyprus spiny mouse** Cyprus
A. percivali **Percival's spiny mouse** S Sudan, Ethiopia, Somalia, Kenya, Uganda
A. russatus **Golden spiny mouse** E Egypt (incl. Sinai), Jordan, Israel, Saudi Arabia
A. spinosissimus **Spiny mouse** NE and EC Tanzania, SE DRC, Zambia, Malawi, C Mozambique, Zimbabwe, E and SE Botswana, N and NW South Africa
A. subspinosus **Cape spiny mouse** SW South Africa
A. wilsoni **Wilson's spiny mouse** S Sudan, S Ethiopia, S Somalia, Kenya to EC Tanzania
Aethomys African Rock Rats
A. bocagei **Bocage's rock rat** C and W Angola
A. chrysophilus **Red rock rat** SE Kenya and Tanzania to S Angola, E Botswana, Zimbabwe, Mozambique, and South Africa
A. granti **Grant's rock rat** S South Africa
A. hindei **Hinde's rock rat** N Cameroon, N and NE DRC, S Sudan, SW Ethiopia, Kenya, Uganda, and Tanzania
A. kaiseri **Kaiser's rock rat** S Kenya, Tanzania, SW Uganda, Rwanda, S and E DRC, Malawi, Zambia, and E Angola
A. namaquensis **Namaqua rock rat** South Africa, Botswana, Zimbabwe, S and C Mozambique, S Malawi, SE Zambia, and S Angola
A. nyikae **Nyika rock rat** N Angola, N Zambia, Malawi, S DRC
A. silindensis **Selinda rock rat** Mt Silinda (E Zimbabwe)
A. stannarius **Tinfield's rock rat** N Nigeria to W Cameroon
A. thomasi **Thomas' rock rat** W and C Angola
Anisomys
A. imitator **Squirrel-toothed or Powerful-toothed rat** New Guinea
Anonymomys
A. mindorensis **Mindoro rat** Mindoro (Philippines)
Apodemus Field Mice
A. agrarius **Striped field mouse** C Europe to L. Baikal south to Caucasus and Tien Shan Mts, then

from Amur R through Korea to E Xizang, E Yunnan, Sichuan, and Fujiau (China), Taiwan, Cheju do (S. Korea)

A. alpicola **Alpine field mouse** NW Alps (S Germany, Austria, Liechtenstein, Switzerland, N Italy)

A. argenteus **Small Japanese field mouse** Japan

A. arianus **Persian field mouse** N Iran to Lebanon and N Israel

A. chevrieri **Chevrier's field mouse** W China, from Hubei and S Gansu to N and C Yunnan

A. draco **South China field mouse** China, Burma, Assam (India)

A. flavicollis **Yellow-necked mouse** England and Wales, S Scandinavia, France, and N Spain east through Europe to Ural Mts, S Italy, the Balkans, and Syria, Lebanon and Israel

A. fulvipectus **Yellow-breasted field mouse** E Ukraine through S Russia to the Caucasus, N Turkey, N Iran, east to Kopet Dagh Mts

A. gurkha **Himalayan field mouse** Nepal

A. hermonensis **Mount Hermon field mouse** Mt Hermon (Israel)

A. hyrcanicus **Caucasus field mouse** E Caucasus

A. latronum **Sichuan field mouse** Xizang, Sichuan, Yunnan (China), N Burma

A. mystacinus **Broad-toothed field mouse** SE Europe, S Georgia, NW Iran, Iraq, Jordan, Lebanon, Syria, Saudi Arabia, Rodhos and Crete

A. peninsulae **Korean field mouse** Altai Mts and Ussuri region to Korea, E Mongolia, NE China to SW China, Sakhalin Is, Hokkaido (Japan)

A. ponticus **Black Sea field mice** Sea of Azov south through Caucasus to Armenia, E Turkey, Iraq

A. rusiges **Kashmir field mice** Kashmir, N India

A. semotus **Taiwan field mouse** Taiwan

A. speciosus **Large Japanese field mouse** Japan

A. sylvaticus **Long-tailed field mouse or Wood mouse** Europe, north to Scandinavia and east to Ukraine and Belarus, Iceland, Britain, Ireland, most mediterranean islands; also N Africa, from Atlas Mts (Morocco) to Tunisia

A. uralensis **Ural field mouse** E Europe and Turkey, south into the Caucasus, to the Altai Mts and Xinjiang (NW China)

A. wardi **Ward's field mouse** NC Nepal through Kashmir, N Pakistan and Afghanistan to NW Iran

Apomys **Philippine Forest Mice**

A. abrae **Luzon Cordillera forest mouse** Luzon (Philippines)

A. datae **Luzon montane forest mouse** N Luzon (Philippines)

A. hylocoetes **Mount Apo forest mouse** Mindanao (Philippines)

A. insignis **Mindanao montane forest mouse** Mindanao (Philippines)

A. littoralis **Mindanao lowland forest mouse** Mindanao, Bohol, Biliran, Dinagat, and Leyte (Philippines)

A. microdon **Small Luzon forest mouse** S Luzon (Philippines)

A. musculus **Least forest mouse** Luzon and Mindoro (Philippines)

A. sacobianus **Long-nosed Luzon forest mouse** Luzon (Philippines)

Archboldomys

A. luzonensis **Mount Isarog shrew mouse** Mt Isarog (SE Luzon, Philippines)

Arvicanthis **African or Unstriped Grass Rats**

A. abyssinicus **Abyssinian grass rat** Ethiopia

A. blicki **Blick's grass rat** Ethiopia

A. nairobae **Nairobi grass rat** Rift Valley and east, from C Kenya south to Dodoma region (EC Tanzania)

A. niloticus **African grass rat** S Mauritania, Senegal and Gambia east to Sudan, Egypt, and W Ethiopia, south through NE DRC and Tanzania (west of Rift valley), into E Zambia and N Malawi; also SW Arabia

A. newmanni **Newmann's grass rat** N and E Rift Valleys of Ethiopia, Somalia, SE Sudan, south through E Kenya to C and EC Tanzania

Bandicota **Bandicoot Rats**

B. bengalensis **Lesser bandicoot rat** India (incl. Assam), Sri lanka, Pakistan, Kashmir, Nepal, Bangladesh, Burma, Penang Is (Malaysia), Sumatra and Java (Indonesia), Saudi Arabia

B. indica **Greater bandicoot rat** India (incl. Assam), Sri lanka, Nepal, Burma, Yunnan and Hong Kong (China), Taiwan, Thailand, Laos, Vietnam; introd. to Kedah and Perlis regions (Malay Pen.), Sumatra and Java (Indonesia)

B. savilei **Savile's bandicoot rat** E Burma, Thailand, S Laos, Vietnam, Cambodia

Batomys **Hairy-tailed Rats**

B. dentatus **Large-toothed hairy-tailed rat** N Luzon (Philippines)

B. granti **Luzon hairy-tailed rat** Mt Data and Mt Isarog (Luzon, Philippines)

B. salomonseni **Mindanao hairy-tailed rat** Mindanao, Biliran, and Leyte (Philippines)

Berylmys **White-toothed Rats**

B. berdmorei **Small white-toothed rat** S Burma, N and SE Thailand, N Laos, Cambodia, S Vietnam

B. bowersi **Bower's white-toothed rat** NE India, N and C Burma, Yunnan, Guangxi, Fujiau, S Anhui (S China), Thailand, N Laos, N Vietnam, Malay Pen., NW Sumatra (Indonesia)

B. mackenziei **Kenneth's white-toothed rat** Assam (NE India), C and S Burma, Sichuan (China), S Vietnam

B. manipulus **Manipur white-toothed rat** Assam (NE India), N and C Burma

Bullimus **Philippine rats**

B. bagobus **Bagobo rat** Philippines

B. luzonicus **Luzon forest rat** Luzon (Philippines)

Bunomys **Hill Rats**

B. andrewsi **Andrew's hill rat** Sulawesi (Indonesia)

B. chrysocomus **Yellow-haired hill rat** Sulawesi (Indonesia)

B. coelestis **Heavenly hill rat** Mt Lampobatang (SW Sulawesi, Indonesia)

B. fratrorum **Fraternal hill rat** NE Sulawesi (Indonesia)

B. heinrichi **Heinrich's hill rat** Mt Lampobatang (SW Sulawesi, Indonesia)

B. penitus **Inland hill rat** C and SE Sulawesi (Indonesia)

B. prolatus **Long-headed hill rat** Mt Tambusisi (C Sulawesi, Indonesia)

Canariomys

C. tamarani **Canary mouse** Extinct: formerly Canarias Is

Carpomys **Luzon Tree Rats**

C. melanurus **Short-faced Luzon tree rat** Mt Data (N Luzon, Philippines)

C. phaeurus **White-bellied Luzon tree rat** Mt Data and Mt Kapilingan (N Luzon, Philippines)

Celaenomys

C. silaceus **Blazed Luzon shrew rat** N Luzon (Philippines)

Chiromyscus

C. chiropus **Fea's tree rat** E Burma, N Thailand, C Laos, Vietnam

Chiropodomys **Pencil-tailed Tree Mice**

C. calamianensis **Palawan pencil-tailed tree mouse** Busuanga, Palawan, and Balabac Is (Philippines)

C. gliroides **Pencil-tailed tree mouse** Guangxi and Yunnan (China), Assam (NE India), Burma, Thailand, Laos, Vietnam, Malay Pen., Indonesia

C. karlkoopmani **Koopman's pencil-tailed tree mouse** Pagai and Siberut (Mentawai Is, Indonesia)

C. major **Large pencil-tailed tree mouse** Sarawak and Sabah (N Borneo)

C. muroides **Gray-bellied pencil-tailed tree mouse** Mt Kinabulu (Sabah, Borneo), N Kalimantan (Borneo)

C. pusillus **Small pencil-tailed tree mouse** Sabah, Sarawak, S Kalimantan (Borneo)

Chiruromys **Tree Mice**

C. forbesi **Greater tree mouse** SE Papua New Guinea (incl. D'Entrecasteaux Is)

C. lamia **Broad-headed tree mouse** SE Papua New Guinea

C. vates **Lesser tree mouse** Papua New Guinea

Chrotomys **Philippine Striped Rats**

C. gonzalesi **Isarog striped shrew-rat** Mt Isarog (SE Luzon, Philippines)

C. mindorensis **Mindoro striped rat** Luzon and Mindoro (Philippines)

C. whiteheadi **Luzon striped rat** Luzon (Philippines)

Coccymys **Brush Mice**

C. albidens **White-toothed brush mouse** Irian Jaya (New Guinea)

C. ruemmleri **Rummler's brush mouse** New Guinea

Colomys

C. goslingi **African water rat** Liberia, Cameroon, DRC, NE Angola, Uganda, Rwanda, NW Zambia, E Kenya, W Ethiopia, S Sudan

Conilurus **Rabbit Rats**

C. albipes **White-footed rabbit rat** SE Australia

C. penicillatus **Bushy-tailed rabbit rat** Coastal Northern Territory, NE Western Australia (Australia), adj. islands, SC Papua New Guinea

Coryphomys

C. buhleri **Buhler's rat** Timor (Indonesia)

Crateromys **Bushy-tailed Cloud-rats**

C. australis **Dinagat bushy-tailed cloud-rat** Dinagat Is (Philippines)

C. paulus **Ilin bushy-tailed cloud-rat** Mindoro (Philippines)

C. schadenbergi **Luzon bushy-tailed cloud-rat** N Luzon (Philippines)

Cremnomys **Indian Rats**

C. blanfordi **Blanford's rat** India, Sri Lanka

C. cutchicus **Cutch rat** India

C. elvira **Elvira rat** SE India

Crossomys

C. moncktoni **Earless water rat** Papua New Guinea

Crunomys **Philippines Shrew Rats**

C. celebensis **Celebes or Sulawesi shrew rat** C Sulawesi (Indonesia)

C. fallax **Northern Luzon shrew rat** NC Luzon (Philippines)

C. melanius **Mindanao shrew rat** Mindanao (Philippines)

C. rabori **Leyte shrew rat** Leyte (Philippines)

Dacnomys

D. millardi **Millard's rat** NE India, E Nepal, S Yunnan (S China), N Laos

Dasymys **Shaggy African Marsh Rats**

D. foxi **Fox's shaggy rat** Jos plateau (Nigeria)

D. incomtus **African marsh rat** S Africa, Zimbabwe, Angola, Zambia, Malawi, DRC, Tanzania, Uganda, Kenya, Ethiopia, S Sudan

D. montanus **Montane shaggy rat** Ruwenzori Mts (Uganda)

D. nudipes **Angolan marsh rat** N Botswana, NE Namibia, S Angola, SW Zambia

D. rufulus **West African shaggy rat** Sierra Leone, Liberia, Ivory Coast, Ghana, Togo, Benin, E Nigeria, Cameroon

Dephomys **Defua Rats**

D. defua **Defua rat** Sierra Leone, Guinea, Liberia, Ivory Coast, Ghana

D. eburnea **Ivory Coast rat** Ivory Coast, Liberia

Desmomys

D. harringtoni **Harrington's rat** Ethiopian plateau

Diomys

D. crumpi **Crump's or Manipur mouse** NE India, W Nepal

Diplothrix

D. legatus **Ryukyu rat** Japan

Echiothrix

E. leucura **Sulawesi spiny rat** N and C Sulawesi (Indonesia)

Eropeplus

E. canus **Sulawesi soft-furred rat** C Sulawesi (Indonesia)

Golunda

G. ellioti **Indian Bush Rat** SE Iran, Pakistan, N and NE India south to Sri Lanka, Nepal

Grammomys **African Thicket Rats**

G. aridulus **Arid thicket rat** WC Sudan

G. buntingi **Bunting's thicket rat** W Africa, from Sierra Leone and Guinea to Ivory Coast and Liberia

G. caniceps **Gray-headed thicket rat** S Somalia, N Kenya

G. cometes **Mozambique thicket rat** SE and E South Africa, E Zimbabwe, S Mozambique

G. dolichurus **Woodland thicket rat** Nigeria east to SW Ethiopia, south to Kenya, Uganda, Tanzania, N DRC, Angola, Zambia, Malawi, Zimbabwe, South Africa

G. dryas **Forest thicket rat** Ruwenzoris and Kivu region (Uganda, E DRC), NW Burundi

G. gigas **Giant thicket rat** Mt Kenya (Kenya)

G. ibeanus **Ruwenzori thicket rat** NE Zambia, Malawi, to SC Tanzania and Kenya to S Sudan

G. macmillani **Macmillan's thicket rat** Sierra Leone, Liberia, CAR, S Sudan, Ethiopia, Kenya, Uganda, N DRC, Tanzania, Malawi, Mozambique, Zimbabwe

G. minnae **Ethiopian thicket rat** S Ethiopia

G. rutilans **Shining thicket rat** Guinea

Hadromys

H. humei **Manipur bush rat** NE India, W Yunnan (S China)

Haeromys **Ranne Mice**

H. margarettae **Ranee mouse** Sarawak and Sabah (N Borneo)

H. minahassae **Minahassa Ranee mouse** NE and C Sulawesi (Indonesia)

H. pusillus **Lesser Ranee mouse** Borneo, Palawan (Philippines)

Hapalomys **Marmoset Rats**

H. delacouri **Delacour's marmoset rat** S China, N Laos, S Vietnam

H. longicaudatus **Marmoset rat** SE Burma, Thailand, Malay Pen.

Heimyscus

H. fumosus **African smoky mouse** Gabon, S Cameroon, CAR

Hybomys **Striped Mice**

H. basilii **Father Basilio's striped mouse** Bioko (Equatorial Guinea)

H. eisentrauti **Eisentraut's striped mouse** Mt Lefo and Mt Oku (W Cameroon)

H. lunaris **Moon striped mouse** NE and E DRC, W Uganda, Rwanda

H. planifrons **Miller's striped mouse** NE Sierra Leone, Liberia, SE Guinea, W Ivory Coast

H. trivirgatus **Temminck's striped mouse** E Sierra Leone to S Nigeria

H. univittatus **Peter's striped mouse** SE Nigeria, Cameroon, CAR, Equatorial Guinea, Gabon, Congo, DRC, S Uganda and W Rwanda, NW Zambia

Hydromys **Water Rats**

H. chrysogaster **Golden-bellied water rat** Australia (incl. Tasmania), New Guinea, Kei and Aru Is (Indonesia), Obi Is (Maluku, Indonesia)

H. habbema **Mountain water rat** Irian Jaya (New Guinea)

H. hussoni **Western water rat** New Guinea

H. neobrittanicus **New Britain water rat** New Britain Is (Bismarck Arch., Papua New Guinea)

H. shawmayeri **Shaw Mayer's water rat** Papua New Guinea

Hylomyscus **African Wood Mice**

H. aeta **Beaded wood mouse** Equatorial Guinea, Gabon, Cameroon to W Uganda and Burundi

H. alleni **Allen's wood mouse** W Africa, from Guinea to Cameroon, Gabon, and Equatorial Guinea

H. baeri **Baer's wood mouse** Ivory Coast, Ghana

H. carillus **Angolan wood mouse** N Angola

H. denniae **Montane wood mouse** Kenya, Uganda, Rwanda, Tanzania, Tanzania, NE Zambia, E DRC, also WC Angola

H. parvus **Little wood mouse** S Cameroon, S CAR, N and E DRC, N Gabon

H. stella **Stella wood mouse** S Nigeria, Cameroon, CAR, Gabon, N Angola, DRC, S Sudan, W Kenya, Uganda, Rwanda, Burundi, Tanzania

Hyomys **New Guinean Giant Rats**

H. dammermani **Western white-eared giant rat** New Guinea

H. goliath **Eastern white-eared giant rat** Papua New Guinea

Kadarsanomys

K. sodyi **Sody's tree rat** Java (Indonesia)

Komodomys

K. rintjanus **Komodo rat** Nusa Tenggara (Lesser Sunda Is, Indonesia)

Lamottemys

L. okuensis **Mount Oku rat** Mt Oku (W Cameroon)

Leggadina **Australian Native Mice**

L. forresti **Forrest's mouse** Inland Australia

L. lakedownensis **Lakeland Downs mouse** N Queensland, Western Australia (Australia)

Lemniscomys **Striped Grass Mice**

L. barbarus **Barbary striped grass mouse** Tunisia to Western Sahara, Senegal and Gambia to Cameroon, Sudan, Ethiopia, Kenya, N Uganda, Tanzania, E DRC

L. bellieri **Bellier's striped grass mouse** Ivory Coast

L. griselda **Griselda's striped grass mouse** Angola

L. hoogstraali **Hoogstraal's striped grass mouse** N Sudan

L. linulus **Senegal one-striped grass mouse** Sudan, Senegal, Ivory Coast

L. macculus **Buffoon striped grass mouse** S Sudan, Ethiopia, Kenya, Uganda, NE DRC

L. mittendorfi **Mittendorf's striped grass mouse** L. Oku (Cameroon)

L. rosalia **Single-striped grass mouse** South Africa, Swaziland, Zimbabwe, C and N Botswana, N Namibia, Zambia, Malawi, Mozambique to S Kenya

L. roseveari **Rosevear's striped grass mouse** Zambia

L. striatus **Typical striped grass mouse** Burkina Faso and Sierra Leone east to Ethiopia, south to NW Angola, NE Zambia and N Malawi

Lenomys

L. meyeri **Trefoil-toothed giant rat** N, C, and SW Sulawesi (Indonesia)

Lenothrix

L. canus **Gray tree rat** Malay Pen., Penang and Tuangku Is (Malaysia), Sarawak and Sabah (N Borneo)

Leopoldamys **Long-tailed Giant Rats**

L. edwardsi **Edwards long-tailed giant rat** W Bengal, Assam, Sikkim (India), N Burma, S and C China, N Thailand, Laos, Vietnam, Malay Pen., W Sumatra (Indonesia)

L. neilli **Neill's long-tailed giant rat** C and W Thailand

L. sabanus **Long-tailed giant rat** Bangladesh, Thailand, Laos, Vietnam, Cambodia, Malay Pen.,

Sumatra and Java (Indonesia), Borneo

L. siporanus **Mentawai long-tailed giant rat** Mentawai Is (Indonesia)

Leporillus **Australian Stick-nest Rats**

L. apicalis **Lesser stick-nest rat** S Australia

L. conditor **Greater stick-nest rat** Franklin Is, Nuyt's Arch. (W South Australia)

Leptomys **New Guinean Water Rats**

L. elegans **Long-footed water rat** Papua New Guinea

L. ernstmayri **Ernst Mayr's water rat** Papua New Guinea, Arfak Mts (Irian Jaya, New Guinea)

L. signatus **Fly River water rat** W Papua New Guinea

Limnomys

L. sibuanus **Mindanao mountain rat** Mt Apo and Mt Malindang (Mindanao, Philippines)

Lophuromys **Brush-furred Rats**

L. cinereus **Gray brush-furred rat** Parc National du Kauzi-Biege (DRC)

L. flavopunctatus **Yellow-spotted brush-furred rat** NE Angola, N Zambia, Malawi and N Mozambique to DRC, Uganda, and Kenya; also Ethiopia

L. luteogaster **Yellow-bellied brush-furred rat** NE and E DRC

L. medicaudatus **Medium-tailed brush-furred rat** E DRC, Rwanda

L. melanonyx **Black-clawed brush-furred rat** S and C Ethiopia

L. nudicaudus **Fire-bellied brush-furred rat** W Cameroon, Equatorial Guinea (incl. Bioko), Gabon

L. rahmi **Rahm's brush-furred rat** E DRC, Rwanda

L. sikapusi **Rusty-bellied brush-furred rat** Sierra Leone to DRC, Uganda, and W Kenya; also N Angola

L. woosnami **Woosnam's brush-furred rat** E DRC, W Uganda, Rwanda, Burundi

Lorentzimys

L. nouhuysi **New Guinea jumping mouse** New Guinea

Macruromys **New Guinea Rats**

M. elegans **Western small-toothed rat** Mt Kunupi (Irian Jaya, New Guinea)

M. major **Eastern small-toothed rat** New Guinea

Malacomys **African Swamp Rats**

M. cansdalei **Cansdale's swamp rat** E Liberia, S Ivory Coast, S Ghana

M. edwardsi **Edward's swamp rat** Sierra Leone, Guinea, Liberia, S Ivory Coast, S Ghana, S Nigeria

M. longipes **Big-eared swamp rat** Guinea to S Sudan, Uganda, Rwanda south to NW Zambia and NE Angola

M. lukolelae **Lukolela swamp rat** Lukolela (DRC)

M. verschureni **Verschuren's swamp rat** NE DRC

Mallomys **Woolly Rats**

M. aroaensis **De Vis' woolly rat** New Guinea

M. gunung **Alpine woolly rat** Irian Jaya (New Guinea)

M. istapantap **Subalpine woolly rat** New Guinea

M. rothschildi **Rothschild's woolly rat** New Guinea

Malpaisomys

M. insularis **Lava mouse** Extinct: formerly Canarias Is

Margaretamys **Margareta's Rats**

M. beccarii **Beccari's margareta rat** NE and C Sulawesi (Indonesia)

M. elegans **Elegant margareta rat** Mt Nokilalaki (C Sulawesi, Indonesia)

M. parvus **Little margareta rat** Mt Nokilalaki (C Sulawesi, Indonesia)

Mastomys **Multimammate Mice**

M. angolensis **Angolan multimammate mouse** Angola, S DRC

M. coucha **Southern multimammate mouse** South Africa, Zimbabwe, Namibia

M. erythroleucus **Guinea multimammate mouse** Morocco, then from Senegal and Gambia to S Ethiopia and Somalia, south through E Africa to E DRC

M. hildebrandtii **Hildebrandt's multimammate mouse** Senegal and Gambia to CAR and N DRC to Somalia and Djibouti, south to to Kenya and Burundi

M. natalensis **Natal multimammate mouse** South Africa, Zimbabwe, Namibia, Tanzania, Senegal

M. pernanus **Dwarf multimammate mouse** SW Kenya, NW Tanzania, Rwanda

M. shortridgei **Shortridge's multimammate mouse** NW Botswana, NE Namibia

M. verheyeni **Verheyen's multimammate mouse** Nigeria, Cameroon

Maxomys **Oriental Spiny Rats**

M. alticola **Mountain spiny rat** Mt Kinabulu and Mt Trus Madi (Sabah, N Borneo)

M. baeodon **Small spiny rat** Sabah and Sarawak (N Borneo)

M. bartelsii **Bartel's spiny rat** W and C Java (Indonesia)

M. dollmani **Dollman's spiny rat** C and SE Sulawesi (Indonesia)

M. hellwaldii **Hellwald's spiny rat** Sulawesi (Indonesia)

M. hylomyoides **Sumatran spiny rat** W Sumatra (Indonesia)

M. inas **Malayan mountain spiny rat** Malay Pen.

M. inflatus **Fat-nosed spiny rat** W Sumatra (Indonesia)

M. moi **Mo's spiny rat** S Vietnam, S Laos

M. musschenbroekii **Musschenbroek's spiny rat** Sulawesi (Indonesia)

M. ochraceiventer **Chestnut-bellied spiny rat** Sabah, Sarawak, E Kalimantan (Borneo)

M. pagensis **Pagai spiny rat** Mentawai Is (Indonesia)

M. panglima **Palawan spiny rat** Culion, Palawan, Basuanga, and Balabac Is (Philippines)

M. rajah **Rajah spiny rat** S Thailand, Malay Pen., Riau Arch. and Sumatra (Indonesia), Borneo

M. surifer **Red spiny rat** S Burma, Thailand, Laos, Vietnam, Cambodia, S Thailand, Malay Pen., Sumatra and Java (Indonesia), Borneo

M. wattsi **Watts' spiny rat** Mt Tambusisi (C Sulawesi, Indonesia)

M. whiteheadi **Whitehead's spiny rat** S Thailand, Malay Pen., Sumatra (Indonesia), Borneo

Mayermys

M. ellermani **One-toothed shrew mouse** Papua New Guinea

Melasmothrix

M. naso **Sulawesian shrew-rat** Sulawesi (Indonesia)

Melomys **Mosaic-tailed Rats**

M. aerosus **Dusky mosaic-tailed rat** Seram Is (Indonesia)

M. bougainville **Bougainville mosaic-tailed rat** Bougainville Is (Papua New Guinea) and Buka Is (Solomon Is)

M. burtoni **Grassland mosaic-tailed rat** New Guinea, Louisiade Arch. (Papua New Guinea), Australia

M. capensis **Cape York mosaic-tailed rat** Cape York Pen. (Queensland, Australia)

M. cervinipes **Fawn-footed mosaic-tailed rat** E Australian Coast from Cape York Pen. (Queensland) south to Gosford region (New South Wales)

M. fellowsi **Red-bellied mosaic-tailed rat** Papua New Guinea

M. fraterculus **Manusela mosaic-tailed rat** Seram Is (Indonesia)

M. gracilis **Slender mosaic-tailed rat** Papua New Guinea

M. lanosus **Large-scaled mosaic-tailed rat** N New Guinea

M. leucogaster **White-bellied mosaic-tailed rat** New Guinea, islands off coast of Papua New Guinea, Maluku, Seram and Talaud Is (Indonesia)

M. levipes **Long-nosed mosaic-tailed rat** Papua New Guinea

M. lorentzii **Lorentz's mosaic-tailed rat** New Guinea

M. mollis **Thomas' mosaic-tailed rat** New Guinea

M. moncktoni **Monkton's mosaic-tailed rat** Papua New Guinea

M. obiensis **Obi mosaic-tailed rat** Obi Is (Maluku, Indonesia)

M. platyops **Lowland mosaic-tailed rat** Yapen and Biak Is (Indonesia), New Guinea, New Britian (Bismarck Arch., Papua New Guinea), D'Entrecasteaux Is (Papua NG)

M. rattoides **Large mosaic-tailed rat** Yapen Is (Indonesia), New Guinea

M. rubex **Mountain mosaic-tailed rat** New Guinea

M. rubicola **Bramble Cay mosaic-tailed rat** Bramble Cay (Queensland, Australia)

M. rufescens **Black-tailed mosaic-tailed rat** New Guinea (Bismarck Arch., Papua New Guinea)

M. spechti **Specht's mosaic-tailed rat** Buka Is (Solomon Is)

Mesembriomys **Tree Rats**

M. gouldii **Black-footed tree rat** N Western Australia, N Northern Territory, N Queensland, Melville and Bathurst Is (Australia)

M. macrurus **Golden-backed tree rat** N Western Australia, N Northern Territory (Australia)

Microhydromys **Lesser Shrew Mice**

M. musseri **Musser's shrew mouse** Mt Somoro (Papua New Guinea)

M. richardsoni **Groove-toothed shrew mouse** New Guinea

Micromys

M. minutus **Eurasian harvest mouse** Spain through Europe and Siberia to Ussuri region (Russia) and Korea (incl. Quelpart Is) south to N Caucasus and N Mongolia, then from S China west to Assam (NE India); also Britain, Japan, and Taiwan

Millardia **Asian Soft-furred Rats**

M. gleadowi **Sand-colored soft-furred rat** Afghanistan, Pakistan, adj. India

M. kathleenae **Miss Ryley's soft-furred rat** C Burma

M. kondana **Kondana soft-furred rat** S India

M. meltada **Soft-furred rat** India, Sri lanka, E Pakistan, Nepal

Muriculus

M. imberbis **Striped-backed mouse** Ethiopian highlands

Mus **Old World Mice**

M. baoulei **Baoule's mouse** E Guinea, Ivory Coast

M. booduga **Little Indian field mouse** India, Sri Lanka, S Nepal, C Burma

M. bufo **Toad mouse** E DRC, Uganda, Rwanda, Burundi

M. callewaerti **Callewaert's mouse** N and C Angola, S and W DRC

M. caroli **Ryukyu mouse** Ryukyu Is (Japan) to Taiwan, S China, Thailand, Vietnam, Laos, and Cambodia; introd. to Malay Pen., Sumatra, Java, Madura, and Flores (Indonesia)

M. cervicolor **Fawn-colored mouse** Sikkim, Assam (India) to Nepal, Burma, Thailand, Laos, Vietnam, and Cambodia; introd. to Sumatra and Java (Indonesia)

M. cookii **Cook's mouse** India, Nepal, Burma, SW Yunnan (S China), N and C Thailand, Laos, N Vietnam

M. crociduroides **Sumatran shrewlike mouse** W Sumatra (Indonesia)

M. famulus **Servant mouse** Nilgiri Hills (S India)

M. fernandoni **Sri Lankan spiny mouse** Sri Lanka

M. goundae **Gounda mouse** Gounda R (Cameroon)

M. haussa **Hausa mouse** Senegal and S Mauritania to N Nigeria

M. indutus **Desert pygmy mouse** South Africa, W Zimbabwe, Botswana, C and N Namibia

M. kasaicus **Kasai mouse** Kasai (DRC)

M. macedonicus **Macedonian mouse** Yugoslavia, Bulgaria, Turkey, Syria, Jordan, Israel, Iran

M. mahomet **Mahomet mouse** Ethiopian highlands, SW Kenya, SW Uganda

M. mattheyi **Matthey's mouse** Accra (Ghana)

M. mayori **Mayor's mouse** Sri Lanka

M. minutoides **Pygmy mouse** South Africa, northern limits unknown

M. musculoides **Temminck's mouse** SubSaharan Africa south to contact with previous species

M. musculus **House mouse** Cosmopolitan

M. neavei **Neave's mouse** S Tanzania, S DRC, E Zambia, W Mozambique, S Zimbabwe, NE South Africa

M. orangiae **Orange mouse** South Africa

M. oubanguii **Oubangui mouse** CAR

M. pahari **Gairdner's shrew-mouse** Sikkim, Assam (NE India) to Burma, Yunnan (S China), Thailand, Laos, and Vietnam

M. phillipsi **Phillips' mouse** S India

M. platythrix **Flat-haired mouse** S India

M. saxicola **Rock-loving mouse** S India, S Pakistan, S Nepal

M. setulosus **Peter's mouse** Guinea and Sierra Leone to CAR, N DRC, S Sudan, Ethiopia, W Kenya, N Uganda

M. setzeri **Setzer's pygmy mouse** NE Namibia, NW and S Botswana, W Zambia

M. shortridgei **Shortridge's mouse** Burma, Thailand, NW Vietnam, Cambodia

M. sorella **Thomas' pygmy mouse** E Cameroon, NE and SE DRC, Kenya, Uganda, N Tanzania, EC Angola

M. spicilegus **Mound-building mouse** Hungary, Romania, Yugoslavia, Bulgaria, Ukraine

M. spretus **Algerian mouse** S France, Spain, Portugal, N Africa (Morocco to Libya)

M. tenellus **Delicate mouse** Sudan, S Ethiopia, S Somalia, Kenya to C Tanzania

M. terricolor **Earth-colored mouse** India, Nepal, Pakistan; introd. to N Sumatra (Indonesia)

M. triton **Gray-bellied pygmy mouse** Kenya, Uganda, Tanzania, N and E DRC, Angola, Zambia, Malawi, C Mozambique

M. vulcani **Volcano mouse** W Java (Indonesia)

Mylomys

M. dybowskii **African groove-toothed rat** Guinea, Ivory Coast, Ghana, S Cameroon, CAR, Congo, DRC, S Sudan, Kenya, Uganda, Rwanda, Tanzania

Myomys **African Mice**

M. albipes **Ethiopian white-footed mouse** Ethiopian plateau

M. daltoni **Dalton's mouse** Senegal and Gambia to S Chad and CAR to SW Sudan

M. derooi **Deroo's mouse** Ghana, Togo, Benin, W Nigeria

M. fumatus **African rock mouse** EC Tanzania to Somalia, Ethiopia and S Sudan

M. ruppi **Rupp's mouse** SW Ethiopia

M. verreauxii **Verreaux's mouse** SW South Africa

M. yemeni **Yemeni mouse** N Yemen, SW Saudi Arabia

Neohydromys

N. fuscus **Mottled-tailed shrew mouse** Papua New Guinea

Nesokia **Short-tailed Bandicoot Rats**

N. bunnii **Bunn's short-tailed bandicoot rat** SE Iraq

N. indica **Short-tailed bandicoot rat** N India, Bangladesh, Xinjiang (NW China), Tajikistan, Uzbekistan, Turkmenistan, Afghanistan, Pakistan, Iran, Iraq, Syria, Israel, Saudi Arabia, NE Egypt

Niviventer **White-bellied Rats**

N. andersoni **Anderson's white-bellied rat** SE Xizang, Yunnan, Sichuan, Shaanxi (China)

N. brahma **Brahma white-bellied rat** Assam (India), N Burma

N. confucianus **Chinese white-bellied rat** N Burma, China, N Thailand

N. coxingi **Coxing's white-bellied rat** Taiwan

N. cremoriventer **Dark-tailed tree rat** Thailand, Malay Pen., Myeik Kyunzu (Burma), Sumatra, Java, Bali, Anambas, Nias, and Belitung Is (Indonesia), Borneo

N. culturatus **Oldfield white-bellied rat** Taiwan

N. eha **Smoke-bellied rat** Nepal, Sikkim, Assam (NE India), N Burma, N Yunnan (China)

N. excelsior **Large white-bellied rat** Sichuan (China)

N. fulvescens **Chestnut white-bellied rat** Nepal and N India through Bangladesh and S China to S Thailand, Malaysia Pen., Sumatra, Java, and Bali (Indonesia)

N. hinpoon **Limestone rat** Korat plateau (Thailand)

N. langbianis **Lang Bian white-bellied rat** Assam (NE India), Burma, N Thailand, Laos, Vietnam

N. lepturus **Narrow-tailed white-bellied rat** W and C Java (Indonesia)

N. niviventer **White-bellied rat** NE Pakistan, N India, Nepal

N. rapit **Long-tailed mountain rat** Malay Pen., Sumatra (Indonesia), N Borneo

N. tenaster **Tenasserim white-bellied rat** Assam (NE India), Burma, Vietnam

Notomys **Australian Hopping Mice**

N. alexis **Spinifex hopping mouse** Western Australia, Northern Territory, South Australia, W Queensland (Australia)

N. amplus **Short-tailed hopping mouse** Extinct: formerly S Northern Territory, N South Australia (Australia)

N. aquilo **Northern hopping mouse** N Queensland, N Northern Territory (Australia)

N. cervinus **Fawn-colored hopping mouse** SW Queensland, South Australia, S Northern Territory (Australia)

N. fuscus **Dusky hopping mouse** SE Western Australia, S Northern Territory, South Australia, SW Queensland, W New South Wales (Australia)

N. longicaudatus **Long-tailed hopping mouse** Extinct: formerly Western Australia, Northern Territory (Australia)

N. macrotis **Big-eared hopping mouse** Extinct: formerly Moore R (Western Australia, Australia)

N. mitchellii **Mitchell's hopping mouse** S Western Australia, S South Australia, W Victoria (Australia)

N. mordax **Darling Downs hopping mouse** Extinct: formerly Darling Downs (Queensland, Australia)

Oenomys **Rufous-nosed Rats**

O. hypoxanthus **Rufous-nosed rat** S Nigeria south to N Angola east through DRC to Uganda, Rwanda, Burundi, also in S Sudan, SW Ethiopia, Kenya, and W Tanzania

O. ornatus **Ghana rufous-nosed rat** SE Guinea to Ghana

Otomys **African Vlei Rats**

O. anchietae **Angolan vlei rat** W Kenya, SW Tanzania, N Malawi, C Angola

O. angoniensis **Angoni vlei rat** S Kenya to C South Africa

O. denti **Dent's vlei rat** EC Africa, from Ruwenzori Mts (Uganda) to Zambia and the Nyika Pateau (N Malawi) and to the Usambara and Uluguru Mts (EC Tanzania)

O. irroratus **Vlei rat** South Africa, E Zimbabwe, W Mozambique

O. laminatus **Laminate vlei rat** South Africa

O. maximus **Large vlei rat** S Angola, SW Zambia, NW Botswana, Caprivi (NE Namibia)

O. occidentalis **Western vlei rat** Gotel Mts (SE Nigeria), Mt Oku (W Cameroon)

O. saundersiae **Saunders' vlei rat** SW, S, and C South Africa

O. sloggetti **Sloggett's vlei rat or Ice rat** SE and E South Africa

O. tropicalis **Tropical vlei rat** W Kenya, Uganda, Rwanda, Burundi, DRC, Mt Cameroun (Cameroon)

O. typus **Typical vlei rat** E Africa, from Ethiopia south to the Uzungwe Mts (C Tanzania), Nyika plateau (N Malawi), and adj. Zambia

O. unisulcatus **Bush vlei rat** South Africa

Palawanomys

P. furvus **Palawan soft-furred mountain rat** Palawan (Philippines)

Papagomys Flores Island Giant Tree Rats

P. armandvillei **Flores giant tree rat** Flores (Indonesia)

P. theodorverhoeveni **Verhoeven's giant tree rat** Flores (Indonesia)

Parahydromys

P. asper **Coarse-haired water rat** New Guinea

Paraleptomys Montane Water Rats

P. rufilatus **Northern water rat** NC New Guinea

P. wilhelmina **Short-haired water rat** C New Guinea

Parotomys Whistling Rats

P. brantsii **Brants' whistling rat** W South Africa, SW Botswana, SE Namibia

P. littledalei **Littledale's whistling rat** W South Africa, S and W Namibia

Paruromys Sulawesian Giant Rats

P. dominator **Sulawesi giant rat** Sulawesi (Indonesia)

P. ursinus **Sulawesi bear rat** Mt Lampobatang (SE Sulawesi, Indonesia)

Paulamys

P. naso **Flores long-nosed rat** Flores (Indonesia)

Pelomys Groove-toothed Swamp Rats

P. campanae **Bell groove-toothed swamp rat** WC and N Angola, W DRC

P. fallax **Creek groove-toothed swamp rat** S Kenya, Uganda, Tanzania, DRC south to N Botswana, E and NW Zimbabwe, and Mozambique

P. hopkinsi **Hopkins' groove-toothed swamp rat** SW Kenya, Uganda, Rwanda

P. isseli **Issel's groove-toothed swamp rat** Kome, Bugala, and Bunyama Is (L. Victoria, Uganda)

P. minor **Least groove-toothed swamp rat** W Tanzania, S and E DRC, N Angola, NW Zambia

Phloeomys Giant Cloud Rats

P. cumingi **Southern Luzon giant cloud rat** S Luzon, Marinduque, and Catanduanes Is (Philippines)

P. pallidus **Northern Luzon giant cloud rat** N Luzon (Philippines)

Pithecheir Sunda Tree Rats

P. melanurus **Red tree rat** Java (Indonesia)

P. parvus **Malayan tree rat** Malay Pen.

Pogonomelomys New Guinean Brush Mice

P. bruijni **Lowland brush mouse** New Guinea

P. mayeri **Shaw Mayer's brush mouse** New Guinea

P. sevia **Highland brush mouse** New Guinea

Pogonomys Prehensile-tailed Tree Mice

P. championi **Champion's tree mouse** Papua New Guinea

P. loriae **Large tree mouse** New Guinea, D'Entrecasteaux Is (Papua New Guinea)

P. macrourus **Chestnut tree mouse** New Guinea, Yapen Is (Indonesia), New Britain Is (Bismarck Arch., Papua New Guinea)

P. sylvestris **Gray-bellied tree mouse** Papua New Guinea

Praomys African Soft-furred Mice

P. delectorum **Delectable soft-furred mouse** NE Zambia, Malawi

P. hartwigi **Hartweg's soft-furred mouse** L. Oku (Cameroon), Gotel Mts (Nigeria)

P. jacksoni **Jackson's soft-furred mouse** C Nigeria to S Sudan, DRC, Uganda, Kenya south to N Angola, N and E Zambia, and E Tanzania

P. minor **Least soft-furred mouse** Lukolela (C DRC)

P. misonnei **Misonne's soft-furred mouse** N and E DRC

P. morio **Cameroon soft-furred mouse** Mt Cameroun (Cameroon)

P. mutoni **Muton's soft-furred mouse** Masako Forest Reserve (N DRC)

P. rostratus **Forest soft-furred mouse** Liberia, Guinea, Ivory Coast

P. tullbergi **Tullberg's soft-furred mouse** Gambia to N and E DRC, also NW Angola, Bioko (Equatorial Guinea)

Pseudohydromys New Guinea Shrew Mice

P. murinus **Eastern shrew mouse** Papua New Guinea

P. occidentalis **Western shrew mouse** New Guinea

Pseudomys Australian Mice

P. albocinereus **Ash-gray mouse** SW Western Australia, Bernier, Dorre, Shark Bay, and Woody Is (Australia)

P. apodemoides **Silky mouse** SE South Australia, W Victoria (Australia)

P. australis **Plains mouse** S Northern Territory, South Australia, S Queensland, New South Wales (Australia)

P. bolami **Bolam's mouse** S South Australia, S Western Australia (Australia)

P. chapmani **Western pebble-mound mouse** NW Western Australia (Australia)

P. delicatulus **Little native mouse** SC Papua New Guinea, Coastal N Australia

P. desertor **Brown desert mouse** Arid regions of Australia

P. fieldi **Alice Springs mouse** Alice Springs (S Northern Territory, Australia)

P. fumeus **Smoky mouse** Victoria (Australia)

P. fuscus **Broad-toothed mouse** E New South Wales, S Victoria, Tasmania (Australia)

P. glaucus **Blue-gray mouse** S Queensland, New South Wales (Australia)

P. gouldii **Gould's mouse** Extinct: formerly W Western Australia, E South Australia, New South Wales, N Victoria (Australia)

P. gracilicaudatus **Eastern chestnut mouse** Coast of E Australia, from Townsville (N Queensland) to Sydney region (New South Wales)

P. hermannsburgensis **Sandy Inland mouse** Australia

P. higginsi **Long-tailed mouse** Tasmania (Australia)

P. johnsoni **Central pebble-mound mouse** C Northern Territory (Australia)

P. laborifex **Kimberly mouse** N Western Australia, N Northern Territory (Australia)

P. nanus **Western chestnut mouse** W Western Australia, N Northern Territory, NW Queensland (Australia)

P. novaehollandiae **New Holland mouse** E New South Wales, S Victoria, N Tasmania (Australia)

P. occidentalis **Western mouse** SW Western Australia (Australia)

P. oralis **Hastings River mouse** NE New South Wales, SE Queensland (Australia)

P. patrius **Country mouse** Mt Inkerman (Queensland, Australia)

P. pilligaensis **Pilliga mouse** N New South Wales (Australia)

P. praeconis **Shark Bay mouse** Western Australia, Bernier Is (Australia)

P. shortridgei **Heath rat** SW Western Australia, SW Victoria (Australia)

Rattus Old World Rats

R. adustus **Sunburned rat** Enggano Is (Indonesia)

R. annandalei **Annandale's rat** Malay Pen., Singapore, E Sumatra, Padang and Rupat Is (Indonesia)

R. argentiventer **Rice-field rat** Thailand, S Vietnam, Cambodia, Malay Pen., Sumatra, Java, Bali, Sulawesi, Kangean Is, Lesser Sunda Is (Indonesia), Mindoro and Mindanao (Philippines), New Guinea

R. baluensis **Summit rat** Mt Kinabulu (Sabah, N Borneo)

R. bontanus **Bonthain rat** Mt Lampobatang (SW Sulawesi, Indonesia)

R. burrus **Nonsense rat** Nicobar Is (Ind. Oc.)

R. colletti **Dusky rat** Coastal Northern Territory (Australia)

R. elaphinus **Sula rat** Sula (Indonesia)

R. enganus **Enggano rat** Enggano Is (Indonesia)

R. everetti **Philippine forest rat** Philippines

R. exulans **Polynesian rat** Bangladesh, Burma, Thailand, Laos, Vietnam, Cambodia, Indonesia, Philippines, New Guinea, New Zealand, Micronesia, Polynesia

R. feliceus **Spiny Seram rat** Seram Is (Indonesia)

R. foramineus **Hole rat** SW Sulawesi (Indonesia)

R. fuscipes **Bush rat** SW Western Australia, South Australia, Victoria, Queensland (Australia)

R. giluwensis **Giluwe rat** Mt Giluwe (Papua New Guinea)

R. hainaldi **Hainald's rat** Flores (Philippines)

R. hoffmanni **Hoffmann's rat** Sulawesi (Indonesia)

R. hoogerwerfi **Hoogerwerf's rat** Mt Leuser (Sumatra, Indonesia)

R. jobiensis **Japen rat** Yapen, Owi, and Biak Is (Indonesia)

R. koopmani **Koopman's rat** Peleng Is (Indonesia)

R. korinchi **Korinch's rat** Mt Kerinci and Mt Talakmau (W Sumatra, Indonesia)

R. leucopus **Cape York rat** New Guinea, Queensland (Australia)

R. losea **Lesser rice-field rat** S China, Taiwan, Thailand (excl. S), Laos, Vietnam, Pescadores Is

R. lugens **Mentawai rat** Mentawai Is (Indonesia)

R. lutreolus **Australian swamp rat** SE South Australia, Victoria, New South Wales, SE and N Queensland, Tasmania (Australia)

R. macleari **MacLear's rat** Extinct: formerly Christmas Is (Australia)

R. marmosurus **Opossum rat** NE Sulawesi (Indonesia)

R. mindorensis **Mindoro black rat** Mindoro (Philippines)

R. mollicomulus **Little soft-furred rat** Mt Lampobatang (Sulawesi, Indonesia)

R. montanus **Nillu rat** Sri Lanka

R. mordax **Eastern rat** Papua new Guinea (incl. D'Entrecasteaux Is and Louisiade Arch.)

R. morotaiensis **Molaccan prehensile-tailed rat** Morotai Is (Maluku Is, Indonesia)

R. nativitatis **Bulldog rat** Extinct: formerly Christmas Is (Australia)

R. nitidus **Himalayan field rat** S China, Vietnam, Laos, N Thailand, Burma, Assam, Bhutan, Sikkim, Kumaun (India), Bangladesh, Nepal; also Sulawesi and Seram (Indonesia), Luzon (Philippines), Irian Jaya (New Guinea), Palau Is

R. norvegicus **Brown or Norway rat** Cosmopolitan

R. novaeguineae **New Guinean rat** Papua New Guinea

R. osgoodi **Osgood's rat** S Vietnam

R. palmarum **Palm rat** Nicobar Is (India)

R. pelurus **Peleng rat** Peleng Is (Indonesia)

R. praetor **Spiny rat** New Guinea, Admirality Is, Bismarck Arch. (Papua New Guinea), Solomon Is

R. ranjiniae **Kerala rat** Kerala (SW India)

R. rattus **House rat** S India; introd. widely and now cosmopolitan

R. sanila **New Ireland rat** New Ireland (Bismarck Arch., Papua New Guinea)

R. sikkimensis **Sikkim rat** NE India, E Nepal, C and N Burma, S China (incl. Hong Kong and Hainan Is), Vietnam, Laos, Cambodia, N Thailand

R. simalurensis **Simalur rat** Simalur, Siumat, Lasia, Babi Is (Indonesia)

R. sordidus **Dusky field rat** New Guinea, Queensland, NE New South Wales (Australia)

R. steini **Stein's rat** New Guinea

R. stoicus **Andaman rat** Andaman Is (India)

R. tanezumi **Tanezumi rat** E Afghanistan through Nepal and N India to S and C China, Korea and Indochina, also SW India (and Andaman and Nicobar Is), Myeik Kyunza (Burma), Taiwan, Japan; prob. introd. to Malay Pen., Indonesia, Philippines, W New Guinea east through Micronesia to Fiji

R. tawitawiensis **Tawi-tawi forest rat** Tawitawi Is (Sulu Arch., Philippines)

R. timorensis **Timor rat** Mt Muti (Timor, Indonesia)

R. tiomanicus **Malayan field rat** S Thailand, Malay Pen., Sumatra, Java, Bali, Enggano Is (Indonesia), Borneo, Palawan (Philippines)

R. tunneyi **Pale field rat** NE and SW Western Australia, Northern Territory, E Queensland, NE New South Wales (Australia)

R. turkestanicus **Turkestan rat** Kyrgyzstan, N and E Afghanistan, N Pakistan, NE Iran, N India, Kashmir, Nepal, Yunnan and Guangdong (S China)

R. villosissimus **Long-haired rat** Australia

R. xanthurus **Yellow-tailed rat** Sulawesi, excl. SW (Indonesia)

Rhabdomys

R. pumilio **Four-striped grass mouse** South Africa to Angola, SE DRC, Uganda, and Kenya

Rhynchomys Shrew Rats

R. isarogensis **Isarog shrew rat** Mt Isarog (SE Luzon, Philippines)

R. soricoides **Mount Data shrew rat** N Luzon (Philippines)

Solomys Naked-tailed Rats

S. ponceleti **Poncelet's naked-tailed rat** Bougainville Is (Papua New Guinea), Buka and Choiseul Is (Solomon Is)

S. salamonis **Florida naked-tailed rat** Florida Is (Solomon Is)

S. salebrosus **Bougainville naked-tailed rat** Bougainville Is (Papua New Guinea), Buka and Choiseul Is (Solomon Is)

S. sapientis **Isabel naked-tailed rat** Santa Isabel Is (Solomon Is)

S. spriggsarum **Buka naked-tailed rat** Buka Is (Solomon Is)

Spelaeomys

S. florensis **Flores cave rat** Flores (Indonesia)

Srilankamys

S. ohiensis **Ohiya rat** Sri Lanka

Stenocephalemys Ethiopian Narrow-headed Rats

S. albocaudata **Ethiopian narrow-headed rat** Ethiopia plateau

S. griseicauda **Gray-tailed narrow-headed rat** Ethiopia highlands

Stenomys Slender Rats

S. ceramicus **Seram rat** Seram Is (Indonesia)

S. niobe **Moss-forest rat** New Guinea

S. richardsoni **Glacier rat** Irian Jaya (New Guinea)

S. vandeuseni **Van Deusen's rat** Mt Dayman (Papua New Guinea)

S. verecundus **Slender rat** New Guinea

Stochomys

S. longicaudatus **Target rat** Togo, S Nigeria, CAR, Cameroon, Gabon, DRC, Uganda

Sundamys Giant Sunda Rats

S. infraluteus **Mountain giant rat** Mt Kinabulu and Mt Trus Madi (Sabah, N Borneo), W Sumatra (Indonesia)

S. maxi **Bartels' rat** W Java (Indonesia)

S. muelleri **Muller's giant Sunda rat** SW Burma, S Thailand, Malay Pen., Sumatra (Indonesia), Borneo, Palawan (Philippines)

Taeromys Sulawesi Rats

T. arcuatus **Salokko rat** SE Sulawesi (Indonesia)

T. callitrichus **Lovely-haired rat** NE, C, and SE Sulawesi (Indonesia)

T. celebensis **Celebes rat** Sulawesi (Indonesia)

T. hamatus **Sulawesi montane rat** C Sulawesi (Indonesia)

T. punicans **Sulawesi forest rat** C and SW Sulawesi (Indonesia)

T. taerae **Tondano rat** NE Sulawesi (Indonesia)

Tarsomys Long-footed Rats

T. apoensis **Long-footed rat** Mindanao (Philippines)

T. echinatus **Spiny long-footed rat** Mindanao (Philippines)

Tateomys Greater Sulawesian Shrew Rats

T. macrocercus **Long-tailed shrew rat** Mt Nokilalaki (C Sulawesi, Indonesia)

T. rhinogradoides **Tate's shrew rat** Mt Latimodjong, Mt Tokala, Mt Nokilalaki (Sulawesi, Indonesia)

Thallomys Acacia Rats

T. loringi **Loring's rat** E Kenya, N and E Tanzania

T. nigricauda **Black-tailed tree rat** South Africa, Namibia, Botswana, Angola, Zambia

T. paedulcus **Acacia rat** South Africa to S Ethiopia and Somalia

T. shortridgei **Shortridge's rat** W South Africa

Thamnomys Thicket Rats

T. kempi **Kemp's thicket rat** E DRC, W Uganda, Burundi

T. venustus **Charming thicket rat** E DRC, Uganda, Rwanda

Tokudaia Ryukyu Spiny Rats

T. muenninki **Muennink's spiny rat** Okinawa (Ryukyu Is, Japan)

T. osimensis **Ryukyu spiny rat** Amami-oshima Is (Ryukyu Is, japan)

Tryphomys

T. adustus **Luzon short-nosed rat** Luzon (Philippines)

Uranomys

U. ruddi **Rudd's mouse** Senegal, Guinea, Ivory Coast, Togo, N Nigeria, N Cameroon, NE DRC, Uganda, Kenya, C Mozambique, Malawi, SE Zimbabwe

Uromys Giant Naked-tailed Rats

U. anak **Giant naked-tailed rat** New Guinea

U. caudimaculatus **Giant white-tailed rat** Aru, Kei, and Waigeo Is (Indonesia), New Guinea, D'Entrecasteaux Is (Papua New Guinea), Queensland (Australia)

U. hadrourus **Masked white-tailed rat** Thornton Peak (NE Queensland, Australia)

U. imperator **Emperor rat** Guadalcanal (Solomon Is)

U. neobritanicus **Bismarck giant rat** New Britain Is (Bismarck Arch., Papua New Guinea)

U. porculus **Guadalcanal rat** Guadalcanal (Solomon Is)

U. rex **King rat** Guadalcanal (Solomon Is)

Vandeleuria Long-tailed Climbing Mice

V. nolthenii **Nolthenius' long-tailed climbing mouse** Sri Lanka

V. oleracea **Asiatic long-tailed climbing mouse** India, Sri Lanka, Nepal to Burma, Yunnan (S China), N Thailand, Vietnam

Vernaya

V. fulva **Red climbing mouse** Sichuan and Yunnan (S China), N Burma

Xenuromys

X. barbatus **Rock-dwelling giant rat** New Guinea

Xeromys

X. myoides **False water rat** C and S Queensland, Northern Territory, Melville Is (Australia)

Zelotomys Broad-heaed Mice

Z. hildegardeae **Hildegarde's broad-headed mouse**

CAR, DRC, S Sudan, Kenya, W Uganda, Rwanda, Burundi, Tanzania, Malawi, Zambia, Angola
Z. woosnami **Woosnam's broad-headed mouse** S Africa, Botswana, Namibia
Zyzomys **Australian Rock Rats**
Z. argurus **Silver-tailed rock rat** Western Australia to N coastal Queensland (Australia)
Z. maini **Arnhem Land rock rat** Northern Territory (Australia)
Z. palatilis **Carpentarian rock rat** Echo Gorge (Northern Territory, Australia)
Z. pedunculatus **Central rock rat** Northern Territory (Australia)
Z. woodwardi **Kimberly rock rat** Western Australia, Northern Territory (Australia)

SUBFAMILY MYOSPALACINAE
Myospalax **Zokors**
M. aspalax **False zokor** Upper Amur region (Russia), Nei Monggol (China)
M. epsilanus **Manchurian zokor** NE China, Amur region to Ussuri region (Russia)
M. fontanierii **Common Chinese zokor** China
M. myospalax **Siberian zokor** Russia, Kazakhstan
M. psilurus **Transbaikal zokor** SE Russia (incl. Ussuri region) to E Mongolia and NE and C China
M. rothschildi **Rothschild's zokor** Gansu and Hubei (China)
M. smithii **Smith's zokor** Gansu and Ningxia (China)

SUBFAMILY MYSTROMYINAE
Mystromys
M. albicaudatus **White-tailed mouse** South Africa, Swaziland

SUBFAMILY NESOMYINAE
Brachytarsomys
B. albicauda **White-tailed rat** E Madagascar
Brachyuromys **Short-tailed Rats**
B. betsileoensis **Betsileo short-tailed rat** Madagascar
B. ramirohitra **Gregarious short-tailed rat or Ramirohitra** Madagascar
Eliurus **Tufted-tailed Rats**
E. majori **Major's tufted-tailed rat** Madagascar
E. minor **Lesser tufted-tailed rat** E Madagascar
E. myoxinus **Dormouse tufted-tailed rat** SW and S Madagascar
E. penicillatus **White-tipped tufted-tailed rat** Fianarantsoa (Madagascar)
E. tanala **Tanala tufted-tailed rat** E Madagascar
E. webbi **Webb's tufted-tailed rat** E Madagascar
Gymnuromys
G. roberti **Voalavoanala** E Madagascar
Hypogeomys
H. antimena **Malagasy giant rat or Votsotsa** WC Madagascar
Macrotarsomys **Big-footed Mice**
M. bastardi **Bastard big-footed mouse** W and S Madagascar
M. ingens **Greater big-footed mouse** Mahajanga (Madagascar)
Nesomys
N. rufus **Island mouse** N, E, and WC Madagascar

SUBFAMILY PETROMYSCINAE
Delanymys
D. brooksi **Delany's swamp mouse** SW Uganda, Kivu region (DRC), Rwanda
Petromyscus **Rock Mice**
P. barbouri **Barbour's rock mouse** Little Namaqualand (W South Africa)
P. collinus **Pygmy rock mouse** W South Africa through Namibia to SW Angola
P. monticularis **Brukkaros pygmy rock mouse** S Namibia, adj. South Africa
P. shortridgei **Shortridge's rock mouse** W and S Angola, N Namibia

SUBFAMILY PLATACANTHOMYINAE
Platacanthomys
P. lasiurus **Malabar spiny dormouse** S India
Typhlomys **Chinese Pygmy Dormouse**
T. chapensis **Chapa pygmy dormouse** Chapa (N Vietnam)
T. cinereus **Chinese pygmy dormouse** Yunnan, Fujian, Guangxi, Anhui (S China)

SUBFAMILY RHIZOMYINAE
Cannomys
C. badius **Lesser bamboo rat** N and NE India, E Nepal, Bengladesh, Burma, Yunnan (S China), Thailand, Cambodia
Rhizomys **Bamboo Rats**
R. pruinosus **Hoary bamboo rat** Assam (NE India), Yunnan, Guangxi, Guangdong (S China), E Burma, Thailand, Laos, Vietnam, Cambodia, Malay Pen.
R. sinensis **Chinese bamboo rat** S and C China, N Burma, Vietnam
R. sumatrensis **Large bamboo rat** Yunnan (S China), Burma, Thailand, Laos, Vietnam, Cambodia, Malay Pen., Sumatra (Indonesia)
Tachyoryctes **Root Rats or African Mole-rats**
T. ankoliae **Ankole mole-rat** S Uganda
T. annectens **Mianzini mole-rat** E of L. Naivasha (Kenya)
T. audax **Audacious mole-rat** Aberdare Mts (Kenya)
T. daemon **Demon mole-rat** N Tanzania
T. macrocephalus **Big-headed mole-rat** S Ethiopian plateau
T. naivashae **Naivasha mole-rat** W and S of L. Naivasha (Kenya)
T. rex **King mole-rat** Mt Kenya (Kenya)
T. ruandae **Ruanda mole-rat** Kivu (E DRC), Rwanda, Burundi
T. ruddi **Rudd's mole-rat** SW Kenya, SE Uganda
T. spalacinus **Embi mole-rat** Plains near Mt Kenya (Kenya)
T. splendens **East African mole-rat** Ethiopia, Somalia, NW Kenya

SUBFAMILY SIGMODONTINAE
Abrawayaomys
A. ruschii **Ruschi's rat** Espirito Santo and Minas Gerais (Brazil), Misiones (Argentina)
Aepeomys **Montane Mice**
A. fuscatus **Dusky montane mouse** W and C Andes of Colombia
A. lugens **Olive montane mouse** Cord. Meridae of Venezuela to Andes of Ecuador
Akodon **Grass Mice**
A. aerosus **Highland grass mouse** SE Ecuador, E Peru, NW Bolivia
A. affinis **Colombian grass mouse** Cord. Occid. of Colombia
A. albiventer **White-bellied grass mouse** SE Peru, WC Bolivia to N Argentina and Chile
A. azarae **Azara's grass mouse** S Brazil, Bolivia, Paraguay, NE Argentina, Uruguay
A. bogotensis **Bogota grass mouse** Andes of E and C Colombia and W Venezuela
A. boliviensis **Bolivian grass mouse** Altiplano of SE Peru and NC Bolivia
A. budini **Budin's grass mouse** Mountains of NW Argentina
A. cursor **Cursor grass mouse** C and SE Brazil, E Paraguay, NE Argentina, Uruguay
A. dayi **Day's grass mouse** C to SC Bolivia
A. dolores **Dolorous grass mouse** Sierra de Cordoba (C Argentina)
A. fumeus **Smoky grass mouse** E Andean slopes of SE Peru and W Bolivia
A. hershkovitzi **Hershkovitz's grass mouse** Outer islands of Chilean Arch.
A. illuteus **Gray grass mouse** NW Argentina
A. iniscatus **Intelligent grass mouse** WC to S Argentina
A. juninensis **Junin grass mouse** E and W Andean slopes of C Peru
A. kempi **Kemp's grass mouse** EC Argentina, adj. Uruguay
A. kofordi **Koford's grass mouse** Cusco and Puno (SE Peru)
A. lanosus **Woolly grass mouse** S Chile, S Argentina
A. latebricola **Ecuadorian grass mouse** Andes of Ecuador
A. lindberghi **Lindbergh's grass mouse** Parque Nacional de Brasilia (Distrito Federal, Brazil)
A. longipilis **Long-haired grass mouse** C to S Chile, Argentina
A. mansoensis **Manso grass mouse** Andes of Rio Negro Prov. (Argentina)
A. markhami **Markham's grass mouse** Wellington Is (Chile)
A. mimus **Thespian grass mouse** E Andean slopes of SE Peru to WC Bolivia
A. molinae **Molina's grass mouse** EC Argentina
A. mollis **Soft grass mouse** Andes of Ecuador to NC Peru
A. neocenus **Neuquen grass mouse** C and S Argentina
A. nigrita **Blackish grass mouse** SE Brazil, E Paraguay, NE Argentina
A. olivaceus **Olive grass mouse** Chile, adj. W Argentina
A. orophilus **El Dorado grass mouse** Mountains of N Peru
A. puer **Altiplano grass mouse** Altiplano of C Peru, through W Bolivia to NW Argentina
A. sanborni **Sanborn's grass mouse** S Chile, adj. Argentina
A. sanctipaulensis **Sao Paulo grass mouse** SE Brazil
A. serrensis **Serrado Mar grass mouse** SE Brazil
A. siberiae **Cochabamba grass mouse** Cochabamba (Bolivia)
A. simulator **Gray-bellied grass mouse** E Andean slopes of SC Bolivia to NW Argentina
A. spegazzinii **Spegazzini's grass mouse** E Andean slopes of NW Argentina
A. subfuscus **Puno grass mouse** W and E Andean slopes of SC Peru to La Paz (NW Bolivia)
A. surdus **Silent grass mouse** Andes of SE Peru
A. sylvanus **Forest grass mouse** NW Argentina
A. toba **Chaco grass mouse** E Bolivia, W Paraguay, and N Argentina
A. torques **Cloud Forest grass mouse** E Andean forest of SE Peru
A. urichi **Northern grass mouse** E Colombia, Venezuela, N Brazil, Trinidad and Tobago
A. varius **Variable grass mouse** E Andean slopes of W Bolivia
A. xanthorhinus **Yellow-nosed grass mouse** S Chile, S Argentina (incl. Tierra del Fuego)
Andalgalomys **Chaco Mice**
A. olrogi **Olrog's Chaco mouse** Catamarca (NW Argentina)
A. pearsoni **Pearson's Chaco mouse** Chaco (W Paraguay), SE Bolivia
Andinomys
A. edax **Andean mouse** Altiplano of Puno (S Peru) and N Chile through W Bolivia to Jujuy and Catamarca (NW Argentina)
Anotomys
A. leander **Ecuador fish-eating rat** N Ecuador
Auliscomys **Big-eared Mice**
A. boliviensis **Bolivian big-eared mouse** Altiplano from Arequipa (S Peru) to N Chile and Potosi (W Bolivia)
A. micropus **Southern big-eared mouse** S Andes of Chile and Argentina
A. pictus **Painted big-eared mouse** Andes from Ancash (C Peru) to La Paz (NW Bolivia)
A. sublimis **Andean big-eared mouse** Altiplano from Ayacucho (S Peru) through SW Bolivia and adj. Chile to NW Argentina
Baiomys **American Pygmy Mice**
B. musculus **Southern pygmy mouse** Nayarit and Veracruz (Mexico) to NW Nicaragua
B. taylori **Northern pygmy mouse** SE Arizona, SW New Mexico, and E Texas (USA) south to Michoacan, Hidalgo, and C Veracruz (Mexico)
Bibimys **Crimson-nosed Rats**
B. chacoensis **Chaco crimson-nosed rat** NE Argentina
B. labiosus **Large-lipped crimson-nosed rat** Minas Gerais (SE Brazil)
B. torresi **Torres' crimson-nosed rat** EC Argentina
Blarinomys
B. breviceps **Brazilian shrew-mouse** Bahia to Minas Gerais and Rio de Janeiro (Brazil)
Bolomys **Bolo Mice**
B. amoenus **Pleasant bolo mouse** SE Peru, WC Bolivia
B. lactens **Rufous-bellied bolo mouse** SC Bolivia, NW Argentina
B. lasiurus **Hairy-tailed bolo mouse** Brazil (south of Amazon R), E Bolivia, Paraguay, N Argentina
B. obscurus **Dark bolo mouse** EC Argentina, S Uruguay
B. punctulatus **Spotted bolo mouse** Ecuador
B. temchuki **Temchuk's bolo mouse** Misiones (NE Argentina)
Calomys **Vesper Mice**
C. boliviae **Bolivian vesper mouse** W Bolivia
C. callidus **Crafty vesper mouse** E Paraguay, EC Argentina
C. callosus **Large vesper mouse** WC to EC Brazil, E Bolivia, W Paraguay, N Argentina
C. hummelincki **Hummelinck's vesper mouse** Llanos of NE Colombia, N Venezuela, Curacao and Aruba (Neth. Antilles)
C. laucha **Small vesper mouse** WC Brazil, SE Bolivia, W Paraguay, N Argentina, Uruguay
C. lepidus **Andean vesper mouse** Altiplano of C Peru through W Bolivia to NE Chile and NW Argentina
C. musculinus **Drylands vesper mouse** E Paraguay, N Argentina
C. sorellus **Peruvian vesper mouse** Andes of Peru
C. tener **Delicate vesper mouse** EC Brazil
Chelemys **Greater Long-clawed Mice**
C. macronyx **Andean long-clawed mouse** S Andes, along Chile-Argentina border
C. megalonyx **Large long-clawed mouse** C and S Chile
Chibchanomys
C. trichotis **Chibchan water mouse** Colombia, W Venezuela, Peru
Chilomys
C. instans **Colombian forest mouse** N Andes, from W Venezuela through N and C Colombia to N Ecuador
Chinchillula
C. sahamae **Altiplano chinchilla mouse** Altiplano of S Peru, W Bolivia, N Chile, NW Argentina
Chroeomys **Altiplano Mice**
C. andinus **Andean Altiplano mouse** Peru, Bolivia, N Chile, N Argentina
C. jelskii **Jelski's Altiplano mouse** Altiplano of S Peru to WC Bolivia and NW Argentina
Delomys **Atlantic forest rats**
D. dorsalis **Striped Atlantic forest rat** Coastal SE Brazil and NE Argentina
D. sublineatus **Pallid Atlantic forest rat** Coastal Espirito Santo to Parana (SE Brazil)
Eligmodontia **Gerbil Mice**
E. moreni **Monte gerbil mouse** E Andean slopes of Argentina, from Salta to Neuquen
E. morgani **Morgan's gerbil mouse** S Argentina, adj. Chile
E. puerulus **Andean gerbil mouse** Altiplano of S Peru through W Bolivia to NE Chile and NW Argentina
E. typus **Highland gerbil mouse** C Argentina, adj. Chile
Euneomys **Chinchilla Mice**
E. chinchilloides **Patagonian chinchilla mouse** S Chile (incl. Tierra del Fuego), nearby islands
E. fossor **Burrowing chinchilla mouse** Salta (Argentina)
E. mordax **Biting chinchilla mouse** WC Argentina, adj. Chile
E. petersoni **Peterson's chinchilla mouse** S Argentina, adj. Chile (excl. Tierra del Fuego)
Galenomys
G. garleppi **Garlepp's mouse** Altiplano of S Peru, Bolivia, N Chile
Geoxus
G. valdivianus **Long-clawed mole mouse** C and S Chile (incl. Chiloe Is), S Argentina
Graomys **Leaf-eared Mice**
G. domorum **Pale leaf-eared mouse** E Andean slopes of SC Bolivia and NW Argentina
G. edithae **Edith's leaf-eared mouse** La Rioja (NW Argentina)
G. griseoflavus **Gray leaf-eared mouse** Brazil, S Bolivia, Paraguay south to Chubut (S Argentina)
Habromys **Crested-tailed Deer Mice**
H. chinanteco **Chinanteco deer mouse** NC Oaxaca (Mexico)
H. lepturus **Slender-tailed deer mouse** NC Oaxaca (Mexico)
H. lophurus **Crested-tailed deer mouse** Chiapas (Mexico), C Guatemala, NW El Salvador
H. simulatus **Jico deer mouse** E slopes of Sierra Madre Orient. (C Veracruz, Mexico)
Hodomys
H. alleni **Allen's woodrat** Mexico
Holochilus **Marsh Rats**
H. brasiliensis **Web-footed marsh rat** SE Brazil, EC Argentina, Uruguay
H. chacarius **Chaco marsh rat** Paraguay, NE Argentina
H. magnus **Greater marsh rat** S Brazil, Uruguay
H. sciureus **Marsh rat** Colombia, E and S Venezuela, Guianas, Ecuador, Peru, N and C Brazil, Bolivia
Ichthyomys **Crab-eating Rats**
I. hydrobates **Crab-eating rat** Colombia, W Venezuela, Ecuador
I. pittieri **Pittier's crab-eating rat** N Venezuela
I. stolzmanni **Stolzmann's crab-eating rat** Ecuador, Peru
I. tweedii **Tweedy's crab-eating rat** C Panama, W Ecuador
Irenomys
I. tarsalis **Chilean climbing mouse** C and S Chile (incl. Chiloe Is), adj. Argentina
Isthmomys **Isthmus Rats**
I. flavidus **Yellow isthmus rat** W Panama
I. pirrensis **Mount Pirri isthmus rat** E Panama, adj. Colombia
Juscelinomys **Juscelin's Mice**
J. candango **Candango mouse** C Brazil
J. vulpinus **Molelike mouse** Minas Gerais (Brazil)
Kunsia **South American Giant Rats**
K. fronto **Fossorial giant rat** EC Brazil, NE Argentina
K. tomentosus **Woolly giant rat** Mato Grosso (WC Brazil), Beni (NE Bolivia)

Lenoxus
L. apicalis **Andean rat** E Andean slopes of SE Peru and W Bolivia
Megadontomys **Giant Deer Mice**
M. cryophilus **Oaxaca giant deer mouse** NC Oaxaca (Mexico)
M. nelsoni **Nelson's giant deer mouse** E slopes of Sierra Madre Orient., from SE Hidalgo to C Veracruz (Mexico)
M. thomasi **Thomas' giant deer mouse** Sierra Madre del Sur of Guerrero (Mexico)
Megalomys **Extinct West Indian Giant Rice Rats**
M. desmarestii **Antillean giant rice rat** Extinct: formerly Martinique Is (Lesser Antilles)
M. luciae **Santa Lucia giant rice rat** Extinct: formerly St Lucia (Lesser Antilles)
Melanomys **Dusky Rice Rats**
M. caliginosus **Dusky Rice Rat** E Honduras through Panama to N and W Colombia to NW Venezuela and to SW Ecuador
M. robustulus **Robust dark rice rat** SE Ecuador
M. zunigae **Zuniga's dark rice rat** WC Peru
Microryzomys **Small Rice Rats**
M. altissimus **Highland small rice rat** Andes of Colombia, Ecuador, and Peru
M. minutus **Forest small rice rat** N Venezuela through Colombia, Ecuador, Peru to WC Bolivia
Neacomys **Bristly Mice**
N. guianae **Guiana bristly mouse** Guianas, S Venezuela, N Brazil
N. pictus **Painted bristly mouse** E Panama
N. spinosus **Bristly mouse** C and W Brazil to Andean foothills of E Colombia, Ecuador, Peru, and E Bolivia
N. tenuipes **Narrow-footed bristly mouse** W and NC Colombia, N Venezuela, E Ecuador, N Brazil
Nectomys **Neotropical Water Rats**
N. palmipes **Trinidad water rat** NE Venezuela, Trinidad
N. parvipes **Small-footed water rat** Comte R (Fr. Guiana)
N. squamipes **South American water rat** NC and E Colombia, Venezuela, Guianas south to SE Brazil, NE Argentina, and Uruguay
Nelsonia **Diminutive Wood Rats**
N. goldmani **Nelson and Goldman's wood rat** Colima and S Jalisco east to N Mexico (Mexico)
N. neotomodon **Diminutive wood rat** Sierra Madre Orient., from S Durango to N Jalisco (Mexico)
Neotoma **Wood Rats**
N. albigula **White-throated wood rat** SW USA south to NE Michoacan and W Hidalgo (Mexico)
N. angustapalata **Tamaulipan wood rat** SW Tamaulipas and adj. San Luis Potosi (Mexico)
N. anthonyi **Anthony's wood rat** Todos Santos Is (Baja California, Mexico)
N. bryanti **Bryant's wood rat** Cedros Is (Baja California, Mexico)
N. bunkeri **Bunker's wood rat** Coronados Is (Baja California, Mexico)
N. chrysomelas **Nicaraguan wood rat** Honduras, NW Nicaragua
N. cinerea **Bushy-tailed wood rat** SE Yukon and W Northwest Territories (NW Canada) to NW USA and south to N New Mexico and Arizona and east to W Dakotas
N. devia **Arizona wood rat** EC and S Utah, W Arizona (SW USA), NW Sonora (Mexico)
N. floridana **Eastern wood rat** SC and E USA, from Colorado to E Texas east to Florida north to Connecticut
N. fuscipes **Dusky-footed wood rat** W Oregon through W and C California (W USA) to N Baja California (Mexico)
N. goldmani **Goldman's wood rat** SE Chihuahua to WC San Luis Potosi (Mexico)
N. lepida **Desert wood rat** SE Oregon and SW Idaho (USA) south to S Baja California (Mexico)
N. martinensis **San Martin Island wood rat** San Martin Is (Baja Califonia, Mexico)
N. mexicana **Mexican wood rat** SE Utah and C Colorado (USA) south through Mexico to Guatemala, El Salvador, and W Honduras
N. micropus **Southern Plains wood rat** SC USA south to N Chihuahua, San Luis Potosi and S Tamaulipas (Mexico)
N. nelsoni **Nelson's wood rat** Perote (Veracruz, Mexico)
N. palatina **Bolanos wood rat** EC Jalisco (Mexico)
N. phenax **Sonoran wood rat** SW Sonora and NW Sinaloa (Mexico)
N. stephensi **Stephens' wood rat** SC Utah, N Arizona, NW New Mexico (USA)
N. varia **Turner Island wood rat** Turner Is (Sonora, Mexico)
Neotomodon
N. alstoni **Mexican volcano mouse** WC Michoacan east to C Veracruz (Mexico)
Neotomys
N. ebriosus **Andean swamp rat** Altiplano of C Peru south through W Bolivia to N Chile and and NW Argentina
Nesoryzomys **Galapagos Mice**
N. darwini **Darwin's Galapagos mouse** Santa Cruz Is (Galapagos Is, Ecuador)
N. fernandinae **Fernandina Galapagos mouse** Fernandina Is (Galapagos Is, Ecuador)
N. indefessus **Indefatigable Galapagos mouse** Santa Cruz, Baltra, and Fernandina Is (Galapagos Is, Ecuador)
N. swarthi **Santiago Galapagos mouse** San Salvador Is (Galapagos Is, Ecuador)
Neusticomys **Fish-eating Rats**
N. monticolus **Montane fish-eating rat** Colombia, Ecuador
N. mussoi **Musso's fish-eating rat** Venezuela
N. oyapocki **Oyapock's fish-eating rat** Oyapock R (Fr. Guiana)
N. peruviensis **Peruvian fish-eating rat** Peru
N. venezuelae **Venezuelan fish-eating rat** S Venezuela, Guyana
Notiomys
N. edwardsii **Edwards' long-clawed mouse** S Argentina
Nyctomys
N. sumichrasti **Vesper rat** S Jalisco and S Veracruz (Mexico) south (excl. Yucatan Pen.) to C Panama
Ochrotomys
O. nuttalli **Golden mouse** SE Missouri east to S Virginia south to E Texas, Gulf of Mexico, and Florida
Oecomys **Arboreal Rice Rats**
O. bicolor **Bicolored arboreal rice rat** E Panama to Colombia, Venezuela, Guianas, Ecuador, Peru, N and C Brazil, E Bolivia
O. cleberi **Cleber's arboreal rice rat** Distrito Federal (Brazil)
O. concolor **Unicolored arboreal rice rat** E Colombia, S Venezuela, NW Brazil, N Bolivia
O. flavicans **Yellow arboreal rice rat** N and W Venezuela west to Sierra Nevada de Santa Marta of NE Colombia
O. mamorae **Mamore arboreal rice rat** WC Brazil, E Bolivia, N Paraguay
O. paricola **Brazilian arboreal rice rat** SE Venezuela, Guianas, N and C Brazil
O. phaeotis **Dusky arboreal rice rat** E Andean slopes of Peru
O. rex **King arboreal rice rat** E Venezuela, Guianas, NE Brazil
O. roberti **Robert's arboreal rice rat** S Venezuela, Guianas, E Peru, N Brazil, N Bolivia
O. rutilus **Red arboreal rice rat** Guyana, Surinam, Fr. Guiana
O. speciosus **Arboreal rice rat** NE Colombia, C and N Venezuela, Trinidad
O. superans **Foothill arboreal rice rat** Andean slopes of E Colombia, Ecuador, Peru
O. trinitatis **Trinidad arboreal rice rat** SW Costa Rica to SE Brazil, incl. Guianas, Trinidad and Tobago; also E Andean slopes of WE Colombia to SC Peru
Oligoryzomys **Pygmy Rice Rats**
O. andinus **Andean pygmy rice rat** W Peru, WC Bolivia
O. arenalis **Sandy pygmy rice rat** Peru
O. chacoensis **Chacoan pygmy rice rat** WC Brazil, SE Bolivia, W Paraguay, N Argentina
O. delticola **Delta pygmy rice rat** S Brazil, EC Argentina, Uruguay
O. destructor **Destructive pygmy rice rat** Andes of S Colombia through Ecuador and Peru to WC Bolivia
O. eliurus **Brazilian pygmy rice rat** C and SE Brazil
O. flavescens **Yellow pygmy rice rat** SE Brazil, Argentina, Uruguay
O. fulvescens **Fulvous pygmy rice rat** S Mexico through Central America to Ecuador, Guianas, and N Brazil
O. griseolus **Grayish pygmy rice rat** W Venezuela, Cord. Orient. of E Colombia
O. longicaudatus **Long-tailed pygmy rice rat** NC to S Andes, of Chile and Argentina
O. magellanicus **Magellanic pygmy rice rat** S Chile, S Argentina (incl. Tierra del Fuego)
O. microtis **Small-eared pygmy rice rat** C Brazil, adj. Peru, Bolivia, and Paraguay, and Argentina
O. nigripes **Black-footed pygmy rice rat** E Paraguay, N Argentina
O. vegetus **Sprightly pygmy rice rat** W Panama
O. victus **St. Vincent pygmy rice rat** St Vincent (Lesser Antilles)
Onychomys **Grasshopper Mice**
O. arenicola **Mearns' grasshopper mouse** SE Arizona, SC New Mexico, and W Texas (SC USA) south to San Luis Potosi and W Tamaulipas (C Mexico)
O. leucogaster **Northern grasshopper mouse** SW Canada south through W USA (Great Plains and Great Basin) to N Tamaulipas (Mexico)
O. torridus **Southern grasshopper mouse** C California, S Nevada, and SW Utah (SW USA) south to N Baja California, W Sonora and N Sinaloa (Mexico)
Oryzomys **Rice Rats**
O. albigularis **Tomes' rice rat** E Panama, Andes of Colombia, N and W Venezuela, Andes of Ecuador to N Peru
O. alfaroi **Alfaro's rice rat** S Tamaulipas and Oaxaca (Mexico) through Central America to W Colombia and Ecuador
O. auriventer **Ecuadorean rice rat** E Ecuador, N Peru
O. balneator **Peruvian rice rat** E and S Ecuador, N Peru
O. bolivaris **Bolivar rice rat** E Honduras through E Nicaragua, Costa Rica, and Panama to W Colombia and W Ecuador
O. buccinatus **Paraguayan rice rat** NE Argentina, E Paraguay
O. capito **Large-headed rice rat** Colombia, S Venezuela, Guianas, Ecuador, Peru, Brazil, and Bolivia
O. chapmani **Chapman's rice rat** Oaxaca, Guerrero, Veracruz to Tamaulipas (Mexico)
O. couesi **Coues' rice rat** S Texas (USA), Mexico (incl. Isla Cozumel) south through Central America to NW Colombia, Jamaica
O. devius **Boquete rice rat** Costa Rica, W Panama
O. dimidiatus **Thomas' rice rat** SE Nicaragua
O. galapagoensis **Galapagos rice rat** San Cristobal and Sante Fe Is (Galapagos Is, Ecuador)
O. gorgasi **Gorgas' rice rat** Antioquia (Colombia)
O. hammondi **Hammond's rice rat** NW Ecuador
O. intectus **Colombian rice rat** NC Colombia
O. intermedius **Intermediate rice rat** SE Brazil, E Paraguay, NE Argentina
O. keaysi **Keays' rice rat** E Andes of Peru
O. kelloggi **Kellogg's rice rat** SE Brazil
O. lamia **Monster rice rat** SE Brazil
O. legatus **Big-headed rice rat** E Andean slopes of SC Bolivia and NW Argentina
O. levipes **Light-footed rice rat** SE Peru to WC Bolivia
O. macconnelli **MacConnell's rice rat** SC Colombia, E Ecuador, Peru east to Venezuela, Guianas and N Brazil
O. melanotis **Black-eared rice rat** S Sinaloa to SW Oaxaca (W Mexico)
O. nelsoni **Nelson's rice rat** Extinct: formerly Maria Madre Is (Nayarit, Mexico)
O. nitidus **Elegant rice rat** E Ecuador, Peru, Mato Grosso (WC Brazil), Bolivia
O. oniscus **Sowbug rice rat** E Brazil
O. palustris **Marsh rice rat** SE USA, from SE Kansas to E Texas east to S New Jersey and Florida
O. polius **Gray rice rat** NC Peru
O. ratticeps **Rat-headed rice rat** E Brazil, Paraguay, NE Argentina
O. rhabdops **Striped rice rat** S Chiapas (Mexico), C Guatemala
O. rostratus **Long-nosed rice rat** C Tamaulipas to Oaxaca (Mexico, incl. Yucatan Pen.) through Guatemala, El Salvador, and Honduras to S Nicaragua
O. saturatior **Cloud Forest rice rat** S Oaxaca and Chiapas (Mexico) through Guatemala, El Salvador, and Honduras to NC Nicaragua
O. subflavus **Terraced rice rat** E Brazil
O. talamancae **Talamancan rice rat** E Costa Rica, Panama, W and NC Colombia, N Venezuela, W Ecuador
O. xantheolus **Yellowish rice rat** SW Ecuador to W Peru
O. yunganus **Yungas rice rat** S Venezuela, Guianas and E Andean foothills from C Colombia to WC Bolivia
Osgoodomys
O. banderanus **Michoacan deer mouse** S Mexico
Otonyctomys
O. hatti **Hatt's vesper rat** Yucatan Pen. (Mexico) south to N Belize and NE Guatemala
Ototylomys
O. phyllotis **Big-eared climbing rat** N Chiapas, S Tabasco, and Yucatan Pen. (Mexico) south to C Costa Rica, also NC Guerrero (Mexico)
Oxymycterus **Hocicudos**
O. akodontius **Argentine hocicudo** NW Argentina
O. angularis **Angular hocicudo** E Brazil
O. delator **Spy hocicudo** E Paraguay
O. hiska **Small hocicudo** Puno (Peru)
O. hispidus **Hispid hocicudo** Misiones (NE Argentina) to Bahia (E Brazil)
O. hucucha **Quechuan hocicudo** Cochabamba (Bolivia)
O. iheringi **Ihering's hocicudo** Misiones (NE Argentina) and SE Brazil
O. inca SC **Incan hocicudo** Peru to WC Bolivia
O. nasutus **Long-nosed hocicudo** SE Brazil, Uruguay
O. paramensis **Paramo hocicudo** E Andes of SE Peru, WC Bolivia, and NW Argentina
O. roberti **Robert's hocicudo** Minas Gerais (Brazil)
O. rufus **Red hocicudo** SE Brazil, EC Argentina, Uruguay
Peromyscus **Deer Mice**
P. attwateri **Texas mouse** NC Texas through E Oklahoma to SE Kansas, SW Missouri, and NW Arkansas (USA)
P. aztecus **Aztec mouse** S Jalisco and C Veracruz (Mexico) to Guatemala, N El Salvador, and Honduras
P. boylii **Brush mouse** California to W Oklahoma (USA) south to Queretaro and W Hidalgo (Mexico)
P. bullatus **Perote mouse** Perote (Veracruz, Mexico)
P. californicus **California mouse** C and S California (USA) to NW Baja California (Mexico)
P. caniceps **Burt's deer mouse** Monserrate Is (Baja California, Mexico)
P. crinitus **Canyon mouse** E Oregon and SW Idaho south through Nevada, Utah, and W Colorado (USA) to Baja California and NW Sonora (Mexico)
P. dickeyi **Dickey's deer mouse** Tortuga Is (Baja California, Mexico)
P. difficilis **Zacatecan deer mouse** W Chihuahua and SE Caohuila south to C Oaxaca (Mexico)
P. eremicus **Cactus mouse** S California east to Texas (USA) south to Baja California, C Sinaloa and N San Luis Potosi (Mexico)
P. eva **Eva's desert mouse** S Baja California and Carmen Is (Mexico)
P. furvus **Blackish deer mouse** E Sierra Madre Orient., from S San Luis Potosi to NW Oaxaca (Mexico)
P. gossypinus **Cotton mouse** SE USA, from SE Oklahoma, S Illinois, and SE Virginia south to Gulf of Mexico and Florida
P. grandis **Big deer mouse** Guatemala
P. gratus **Osgood's mouse** SW New Mexico (USA), W Chihuahua and SE Coahuila to C Oaxaca (Mexico)
P. guardia **Angel Island mouse** Angel dela Guarda, Granito and Mehia Is (Gulf of California, Mexico)
P. guatemalensis **Guatemalan deer mouse** S Chiapas (Mexico), SW Guatemala
P. gymnotis **Naked-eared deer mouse** S Chiapas (Mexico) to S Nicaragua
P. hooperi **Hooper's mouse** C Coahuila to NE Zacatecas (Mexico)
P. interparietalis **San Lorenzo mouse** San Lorenzo and Salsipuedes Is (Gulf of California, Mexico)
P. leucopus **White-footed mouse** S Alberta and S Ontario, Quebec and Nova Scotia (Canada) south through C and E USA (excl. Florida) to N Durango and along Caribbean coast to NW Yucatan Pen. (Mexico)
P. levipes **Nimble-footed mouse** Mexico to Guatemala, El Salvador, and Honduras
P. madrensis **Tres Marias Island mouse** Tres Marias Is (Mexico)
P. maniculatus **Deer mouse** Alaska (USA) and N Canada south through North America (excl. SE and E seaboard) to S Baja California and NC Oaxaca (Mexico)
P. mayensis **Maya mouse** Huehuetenango (Guatemala)
P. megalops **Brown deer mouse** Sierra Madre del Sur of Guerrero and Oaxaca (Mexico)
P. mekisturus **Puebla deer mouse** SE Puebla (Mexico)
P. melanocarpus **Zempoaltepec deer mouse** NC Oaxaca (Mexico)
P. melanophrys **Plateau mouse** S Durango and Coahuila south to Chiapas (Mexico)
P. melanotis **Black-eared mouse** SE Arizona (USA), Mexico
P. melanurus **Black-tailed mouse** W Sierra Madre del Sur of Oaxaca (Mexico)
P. merriami **Mesquite mouse** SC Arizona (USA) south through Sonora to C Sinaloa (Mexico)
P. mexicanus **Mexican deer mouse** S San Luis Potosi

to Isthmus of Tehuantepec and Guerrero/Oaxaca border to Chiapas (Mexico), Guatemala, El Salvador, Honduras, Nicaragua, Costa Rica, W Panama
P. nasutus **Northern rock mouse** C Colorado, SE Utah, New Mexico, and W Texas (USA) to NW Coahuila (Mexico)
P. ochraventer **El Carrizo deer mouse** S Tamaulipas and adj. San Luis Potosi (Mexico)
P. oreas **Columbian mouse** SW British Columbia (SW Canada), W Washington (NW USA)
P. pectoralis **White-ankled mouse** SE New Mexico and C Texas (USA) south to N Jalisco and Hidalgo (Mexico)
P. pembertoni **Pemberton's deer mouse** Extinct: formerly San Pedro Nolasco Is (Sonora, Mexico)
P. perfulvus **Marsh mouse** C Mexico
P. polionotus **Oldfield mouse** SE USA
P. polius **Chihuahuan mouse** WC Chihuahua (Mexico)
P. pseudocrinitus **False canyon mouse** Coronados Is (Baja California, Mexico)
P. sejugis **Santa Cruz mouse** Santa Cruz and San Diego Is (Gulf of California, Mexico)
P. simulus **Nayarit mouse** Nayarit and S Sinaloa (Mexico)
P. sitkensis **Sitka mouse** Alexander Arch. (Alaska, USA)
P. slevini **Slevin's mouse** Santa Catalina Is (Baja California, Mexico)
P. spicilegus **Gleaning mouse** Sierra Madre Occid., from S Sinaloa and SW Durango to WC Michoacan (Mexico)
P. stephani **San Esteban Island mouse** San Esteban Is (Sonora, Mexico)
P. stirtoni **Stirton's deer mouse** SE Guatemala, El Salvador, Honduras, to NC Nicaragua
P. truei **Pinyon mouse** SW Oregon to W and SE Colorado and NC Texas (USA) south to Baja California (Mexico)
P. winkelmanni **Winkelmann's mouse** Michoacan and Guerrero (Mexico)
P. yucatanicus **Yucatan deer mouse** N Yucatan Pen. (Mexico)
P. zarhynchus **Chiapan deer mouse** NC Chiapas (Mexico)
Phaenomys
P. ferrugineus **Rio de Janeiro arboreal rat** Rio de Janeiro (Brazil)
Phyllotis **Leaf-eared Mice**
P. amicus **Friendly leaf-eared mouse** W Peru
P. andium **Andean leaf-eared mouse** E and W Andean slopes from Tungurahua (C Ecuador) to Lima (C Peru)
P. bonaeriensis **Buenos Aires leaf-eared mouse** Buenos Aires (Argentina)
P. caprinus **Capricorn leaf-eared mouse** E Andes from S Bolivia to N Argentina
P. darwini **Darwin's leaf-eared mouse** Junin (C Peru) south through W Bolivia to C Chile and WC Argentina
P. definitus **Definitive leaf-eared mouse** Andes of Ancash (Peru)
P. gerbillus **Gerbil leaf-eared mouse** Sechura Desert (NW Peru)
P. haggardi **Haggard's leaf-eared mouse** Andes of C Ecuador
P. magister **Master leaf-eared mouse** Andes from C Peru to N Chile
P. osgoodi **Osgood's leaf-eared mouse** Altiplano of NE Chile
P. osilae **Bunchgrass leaf-eared mouse** E Andes from Cuzco (SC Peru) through WC Bolivia to Catamarca (N Argentina)
P. wolffsohni **Wolffsohn's leaf-eared mouse** E Andes of C Bolivia
P. xanthopygus **Yellow-rumped leaf-eared mouse** Catamarca (NW Argentina) and Atacama (C Chile) south to Santa Cruz (Argentina) and adj. Magallanes (Chile)
Podomys
P. floridanus **Florida mouse** Florida Pen. (USA)
Podoxymys
P. roraimae **Roraima mouse** Guyana, poss. adj. Venezuela and Brazil
Pseudoryzomys
P. simplex **Brazilian false rice rat or Ratos-do-Mato** E Brazil to SW Bolivia, W Paraguay, NE Argentina
Punomys
P. lemminus **Puna mouse** Altiplano of S Peru
Reithrodon
R. auritus **Bunny rat** Argentina, Chile, Uruguay
Reithrodontomys **American Harvest Mice**
R. brevirostris **Short-nosed harvest mouse** NC Nicaragua, C Costa Rica
R. burti **Sonoran or Burt's harvest mouse** WC Sonora to C Sinaloa (Mexico)
R. chrysopsis **Volcano harvest mouse** SE Jalisco to WC Veracruz (Mexico)
R. creper **Chiriqui harvest mouse** Costa Rica to Chiriqui region (Panama)
R. darienensis **Darien harvest mouse** E Panama (incl. Azuero Pen.)
R. fulvescens **Fulvous harvest mouse** SC Arizona to SW Missouri to WC Mississippi (USA) south through Mexico (excl. Yucatan Pen.) to W Nicaragua
R. gracilis **Slender harvest mouse** Yucatan Pen. and coastal Chiapas (Mexico) south to NW Costa Rica
R. hirsutus **Hairy harvest mouse** SC Nayarit and NW Jalisco (Mexico)
R. humulis **Eastern harvest mouse** SE USA, from SE Oklahoma and E Texas east to E Coast, from S Maryland to Florida
R. megalotis **Western harvest mouse** SC British Columbia and SE Alberta (SW Canada), W and NC USA south to N Baja California and to C Oaxaca (Mexico)
R. mexicanus **Mexican harvest mouse** S Tamaulipas and WC Michoacan (Mexico) south through Central America to W Panama, and Andes of W Colombia and N Ecuador
R. microdon **Small-toothed harvest mouse** N Michoacan, Distrito Federal, N Oaxaca, and C Chiapas (Mexico), WC Guatemala
R. montanus **Plains harvest mouse** C USA, from W South Dakota and E Wyoming to EC Texas and SE Arizona, NE Sonora and Chihuahua top N Durango (Mexico)
R. paradoxus **Nicaraguan harvest mouse** SW Nicaragua, WC Costa Rica
R. raviventris **Salt marsh harvest mouse** San Francisco Bay (California, USA)
R. rodriguezi **Rodriguez's harvest mouse** Volcan de Irazu (Cartago, Costa Rica)
R. spectabilis **Cozumel harvest mouse** Cozumel Is (Quintano Roo, Mexico)
R. sumichrasti **Sumichrast's harvest mouse** SW Jalisco and S San Luis Potosi to C Guerrero and EC Oaxaca (Mexico); C Chiapas (Mexico) to NC Nicaragua; C Costa Rica to W Panama
R. tenuirostris **Narrow-nosed harvest mouse** S Chiapas (Mexico), C Guatemala
R. zacatecae **Zacatecas harvest mouse** W Chihuahua to WC Michoacan (Mexico)
Rhagomys
R. rufescens **Brazilian arboreal mouse** Rio de Janeiro (Brazil)
Rheomys **Central American Water Mice**
R. mexicanus **Mexican water mouse** Oaxaca (Mexico)
R. raptor **Goldman's water mouse** Costa Rica, Panama
R. thomasi **Thomas' water mouse** S Mexico, Guatemala, El Salvador
R. underwoodi **Underwood's water mouse** C Costa Rica, W Panama
Rhipidomys **American Climbing Mice**
R. austrinus **Southern climbing mouse** E Andean slopes of SC Bolivia and NW Argentina
R. caucensis **Cauca climbing mouse** W Andes of Colombia
R. couesi **Coues' climbing mouse** Colombia, Venezuela, Ecuador, Peru, Trinidad
R. fulviventer **Buff-bellied climbing mouse** Andes of Colombia and W Venezuela
R. latimanus **Broad-footed climbing mouse** C and W Colombia, Ecuador
R. leucodactylus **White-footed climbing mouse** S Venezuela, Guianas, Ecuador, Peru, N Brazil
R. macconnelli **MacConnell's climbing mouse** S Venezuela, poss. N Brazil and adj. Guyana
R. mastacalis **Long-tailed climbing mouse** C and E Brazil
R. nitela **Splendid climbing mouse** S Venezuela, Guianas, NC Brazil
R. ochrogaster **Yellow-bellied climbing mouse** SE Peru
R. scandens **Mount Pirri climbing mouse** E Panama
R. venezuelae **Venezuelan climbing mouse** N and W Venezuela, E Colombia
R. venustus **Charming climbing mouse** N Venezuela
R. wetzeli **Wetzel's climbing mouse** S Venezuela
Scapteromys
S. tumidus **Swamp rat** S Brazil, E Paraguay, NE Argentina, Uruguay
Scolomys **Spiny Mice**
S. melanops **South American spiny mouse** Pastaza (Ecuador)
S. ucayalensis **Ucayali spiny mouse** Loreto (Peru)
Scotinomys **Brown Mice**
S. teguina **Alston's brown mouse** E Oaxaca (Mexico) to W Panama
S. xerampelinus **Chiriqui brown mouse** Costa Rica to Chiriqui region (W Panama)
Sigmodon **Cotton Rats**
S. alleni **Allen's cotton rat** S Sinaloa to S Oaxaca (W Mexico)
S. alstoni **Alston's cotton rat** NE Colombia, N and E Venezuela, Guyana, Surinam, N Brazil
S. arizonae **Arizona cotton rat** SE California and SC Arizona (SW USA) south to Nayarit (W Mexico)
S. fulviventer **Tawny-bellied cotton rat** SE Arizona and WC New Mexico (USA) south to Guanajuato and NW Michoacan (Mexico)
S. hispidus **Hispid cotton rat** SE USA, from S Nebraska to C Virginia south to SE Arizona and Florida, then E Mexico through Central America to N Colombia and N Venezuela
S. inopinatus **Unexpected cotton rat** Andes of Azuay and Chimborazo (Ecuador)
S. leucotis **White-eared cotton rat** SW Chihuahua and S Nuevo Leon to C Oaxaca (Mexico)
S. mascotensis **Jaliscan cotton rat** S Nayarit to E Oaxaca (W Mexico)
S. ochrognathus **Yellow-nosed cotton rat** SE Arizona, SW New Mexico, and W Texas (USA) south to C Durango (Mexico)
S. peruanus **Peruvian cotton rat** W Andean foothills of W Ecuador and NW Peru
Sigmodontomys **Rice Water Rats**
S. alfari **Alfaro's rice water rat** E Honduras to Panama, C and W Colombia to NW Venezuela and NW Ecuador
S. aphrastus **Harris' rice water rat** San Jose (Costa Rica), Chiriqui (W Panama)
Thalpomys **Cerrado Mice**
T. cerradensis **Cerrado mouse** C Brazil
T. lasiotis **Hairy-eared cerrado mouse** C Brazil
Thomasomys **Thomas' Oldfield Mice**
T. aureus **Golden oldfield mouse** C and W Colombia, NC Venezuela, Ecuador, N Peru
T. baeops **Beady-eyed mouse** W Andes of Ecuador
T. bombycinus **Silky oldfield mouse** Cord. Occid. of Colombia
T. cinereiventer **Ashy-bellied oldfield mouse** Andes of Colombia and Ecuador
T. cinereus **Ash-colored oldfield mouse** SW Ecuador, N Peru
T. daphne **Daphne's oldfield mouse** S Peru to C Bolivia
T. eleusis **Peruvian oldfield mouse** NC Peru
T. gracilis **Slender oldfield mouse** Andes of Ecuador to SE Peru
T. hylophilus **Woodland oldfield mouse** Cord. Orient. of Colombia, Cord. Merida of W Venezuela
T. incanus **Inca oldfield mouse** Andes of C Peru
T. ischyurus **Strong-tailed oldfield mouse** N to C Peru
T. kalinowskii **Kalinowski's oldfield mouse** Andes of C Peru
T. ladewi **Ladew's oldfield mouse** Andes of NW Bolivia
T. laniger **Butcher oldfield mouse** Andes of C Colombia and adj. W Venezuela
T. monochromos **Unicolored oldfield mouse** NE Colombia
T. niveipes **Snow-footed oldfield mouse** C Colombia
T. notatus **Distinguished oldfield mouse** SE Peru
T. oreas **Montane oldfield mouse** WC Bolivia
T. paramorum **Paramo oldfield mouse** Andes of Ecuador
T. pyrrhonotus **Thomas' oldfield mouse** Andes of S Ecuador and NW Peru
T. rhoadsi **Rhoads' oldfield mouse** Andes of Ecuador
T. rosalinda **Rosalinda's oldfield mouse** NC Peru
T. silvestris **Forest oldfield mouse** W Andes of Ecuador
T. taczanowskii **Taczanowski's oldfield mouse** NW Peru
T. vestitus **Dressy oldfield mouse** Cord. Merida of W Venezuela
Tylomys **Naked-tailed Climbing Rats**
T. bullaris **Chiapan climbing rat** Tuxtla Gutierrez (Chiapas, Mexico)
T. fulviventer **Fulvous-bellied climbing rat** E Panama
T. mirae **Mira climbing rat** W Colombia, NW Ecuador
T. nudicaudus **Peters' climbing rat** C Guerrero and C Veracruz (Mexico) south (excl. Yucatan Pen.) to S Nicaragua
T. panamensis **Panamanian climbing rat** E Panama
T. tumbalensis **Tumbala climbing rat** Tumbala (Chiapas, Mexico)
T. watsoni **Watson's climbing rat** Costa Rica, W Panama
Wiedomys
W. pyrrhorhinos **Red-nosed mouse** Ceara to Rio Grane do Sul (SE Brazil)
Wilfredomys **Wilfred's Mice**
W. oenax **Greater Wilfred's mouse** SE Brazil to C Uruguay
W. pictipes **Lesser Wilfred's mouse** NE Argentina and SE Brazil
Xenomys
X. nelsoni **Magdalena rat** Colima and W Jalisco (Mexico)
Zygodontomys **Cane Mice**
Z. brevicauda **Short-tailed cane mouse** SE Costa Rica through Panama, Colombia, Venezuela, Guianas, to N Brazil, Trinidad and Tobago
Z. brunneus **Brown cane mouse** N Colombia

SUBFAMILY SPALACINAE

Nannospalax **Lesser Blind Mole-rats**
N. ehrenbergi **Palestine or Ehrenberg's mole-rat** Syria, Lebanon, Jordan, Israel, N Egypt to N Libya
N. leucodon **Lesser mole-rat** Yugoslavia, Hungary, Bulgaria, Greece, and NW Turkey to SW Ukraine
N. nehringi **Nehring's blind mole-rat** Turkey, Armenia, Georgia
Spalax **Greater Blind Mole-rats**
S. arenarius **Sandy mole-rat** S Ukraine
S. giganteus **Giant mole-rat** NW of Caspian Sea, and Kazakhstan betw. Volga, Dnipro, and Ural R and the Caspian Sea
S. graecus **Bukovin mole-rat** Romania, SW Ukraine
S. microphthalmus **Greater mole-rat** Ukraine and S Russia, betw. Dnipro and Volga R
S. zemni **Podolsk mole-rat** SE Poland east to Ukraine betw. Dnetr and Dnipro R and south to Black Sea

FAMILY ANOMALURIDAE
Scaly-tailed Squirrels

SUBFAMILY ANOMALURINAE

Anomalurus **Scaly-tailed Flying Squirrels**
A. beecrofti **Beecroft's scaly-tailed squirrel** Senegal to Uganda and DRC, Bioko (Equatorial Guinea)
A. derbianus **Lord Derby's scaly-tailed squirrel** Sierra Leone to Angola, east to Kenya south to Zambia and Mozambique
A. pelii **Pel's scaly-tailed squirrel** Sierra Leone to Ghana
A. pusillus **Dwarf scaly-tailed squirrel** S Cameroon, Gabon, DRC

SUBFAMILY ZENKERELLINAE

Idiurus **Pygmy Scaly-tailed Flying Squirrels**
I. macrotis **Long-eared scaly-tailed flying squirrel** Sierra Leone to E DRC
I. zenkeri **Pygmy scaly-tailed flying squirrel** S Cameroon to Uganda
Zenkerella
Z. insignis **Cameroon scaly-tail** SW Cameroon, CAR, Gabon, Rio Muni (Equatorial Guinea)

FAMILY PEDETIDAE

Pedetes
P. capensis **Springhare or Springhaas** South Africa to Tanzania, Kenya

FAMILY CTENODACTYLIDAE Gundis

Ctenodactylus **Common Gundis**
C. gundi **Gundi** N Morocco to NW Libya
C. vali **Val's or Sahara gundi** S Morocco, W Algeria, NW Libya
Felovia
F. vae **Felou gundi** Senegal, Mauritania, Mali
Massoutiera
M. mzabi **Mzab gundi** SE Algeria, SW Libya, NE Mali, N Niger, N Chad
Pectinator
P. spekei **Pectinator or East African gundi** Ethiopia, Somalia, Djibouti

FAMILY MYOXIDAE Dormice

SUBFAMILY GRAPHIURINAE

Graphiurus **African Dormice**
G. christyi **Christy's dormouse** N DRC, S Cameroon
G. crassicaudatus **Jentink's dormouse** Liberia, Ivory Coast, Ghana, Togo, Nigeria, Cameroon
G. hueti **Huet's dormouse** Senegal to Sierra Leone, Liberia, Ivory Coast, Ghana, Nigeria, Cameroon, CAR, Gabon

G. kelleni **Kellen's dormouse** Angola, Zambia, Malawi, Zimbabwe
G. lorraineus **Lorrain dormouse** Sierra Leone, Ivory Coast to Cameroon, Gabon, N Angola, DRC, Uganda, SW Tanzania
G. microtis **Small-eared dormouse** Zambia, Malawi, Tanzania
G. monardi **Monard's dormouse** E Angola, NW Zambia, S DRC
G. murinus **Woodland dormouse** Sudan, Ethiopia, Kenya, Uganda, Tanzania, E DRC, Mozambique, Malawi, Zambia, S Angola, E and N Namibia, Botswana, Zimbabwe, South Africa
G. ocularis **Spectacled dormouse** South Africa
G. olga **Olga's dormouse** N Niger, N Nigeria, NE Cameroon
G. parvus **Savanna dormouse** Sierra Leone, Ivory Coast, Mali, Ghana, Nigeria, Sudan, Ethiopia, Somalia, Kenya, Uganda, Tanzania
G. platyops **Rock dormouse** South Africa to S DRC
G. rupicola **Stone dormouse** Karibib and Mt Brukaros (Namibia) south to Port Nolloth (W coastal South Africa)
G. surdus **Silent dormouse** Rio Muni (Equatorial Guinea), S Cameroon

SUBFAMILY LEITHIINAE
Dryomys **Forest Dormice**
D. laniger **Woolly dormouse** Toros Doglan (Turkey)
D. nitedula **Forest dormouse** C Europe from Germany, Switzerland, Austria, and Italy east to W Russia south to Turkey, Arabia, Iraq, Iran, Afghanistan, N Pakistan, Tajikistan, Turkmenistan, Uzbekistan, Kyrygstan, C Kazakhstan north to S Altai Mts and E Tien Shan Mts
D. sichuanensis **Chinese dormouse** N Sichuan (China)
Eliomys **Garden Dormice**
E. melanurus **Asiatic garden dormouse** S Turkey, Syria, Iraq, Jordan, Lebanon, Israel, Saudi Arabia, Egypt to Morocco
E. quercinus **Garden or Orchard dormouse** Most of Europe from Portugal, S Spain, France, Belgium, Netherlands east to W Russia
Myomimus **Mouse-tailed Dormice**
M. personatus **Masked mouse-tailed dormouse** NE Iran, Kopet Dagh and Malyy Balkhan Mts (Turkmenistan), Uzbekistan
M. roachi **Roach's mouse-tailed dormouse** SE Bulgaria, W Turkey
M. setzeri **Setzer's mouse-tailed dormouse** W Iran

FAMILY SELEVINIA
S. betpakdalaensis **Desert dormouse** SE and E Kazakhstan

FAMILY MYOXINAE
Glirulus
G. japonicus **Japanese dormouse** Honshu, Shikoku, Kyushu Is (Japan)
Muscardinus
M. avellanarius **Hazel dormouse** Europe from S England to W Russia south to N Turkey
Myoxus
M. glis **Edible or Fat dormouse** Most of Europe from N Spain, France, Netherlands, Germany east to W Russia south to N Turkey and through Caucasus to N Iran and SW Turkmenistan

SUBORDER HYSTRICOGNATHI

FAMILY BATHYERGIDAE **Blesmols**
Bathyergus **Dune Mole-rats**
B. janetta **Namaqua dune mole-rat** SW South Africa, S Namibia
B. suillus **Cape dune mole-rat** S South Africa
Cryptomys **Common Mole-rats**
C. bocagei **Bocage's mole-rat** NW Namibia, C Angola, S DRC
C. damarensis **Damara mole-rat** E Namibia, Botswana, W Zimbabwe, S Zambia, S Angola
C. foxi **Nigerian mole-rat** C Nigeria
C. hottentotus **African or Common mole-rat** South Africa to Namibia, S Zambia, and Tanzania
C. mechowi **Mechow's or Giant Angolan mole-rat** Angola, Zambia, Malawi, S DRC, Tanzania
C. ochraceocinereus **Ochre mole-rat** E Nigeria, CAR, N DRC, S Sudan, NW Uganda
C. zechi **Togo mole-rat** EC Ghana, WC Togo
Georychus
G. capensis **Cape mole-rat** South Africa
Heliophobius
H. argenteocinereus **Silvery mole-rat** E Zambia, N Mozambique to DRC, Tanzania, and Kenya
Heterocephalus
H. glaber **Naked mole-rat** C Somalia, C and E Ethiopia, C and S Kenya

FAMILY HYSTRICIDAE **Old World Porcupines**
Atherurus **Brush-tailed Porcupines**
A. africanus **African brush-tailed porcupine** Gambia, Sierra Leone, Liberia, Ghana, DRC, S Sudan, Kenya, Uganda
A. macrourus **Asiatic brush-tailed porcupine** E Assam (India), Sichuan, Yunnan, Hupei, and Hainan (China), Burma to Thailand, Laos, Vietnam, Malaysia, Sumatra (Indonesia)
Hystrix **Short-tailed Porcupines**
H. africaeaustralis **Cape porcupine** South Africa to N Angola, DRC, Uganda, and Kenya
H. brachyura **Malayan porcupine** Nepal, Sikkim and Assam (NE India), C and S China, Burma, Thailand, Indochina, Malaysia, Singapore, Sumatra (Indonesia), Borneo
H. crassispinis **Thick-spined porcupine** N Borneo
H. cristata **Crested porcupine** Morocco to Egypt, Senegal to Ethiopia and N Tanzania, also Italy, Albania, N Greece
H. indica **Indian crested porcupine** Turkey and Caucasus, Israel, Arabia to S Kazakhstan and India, Sri Lanka, Xizang (China)
H. javanica **Sunda porcupine** Indonesia
H. pumila **Philippine porcupine** Palawan and Busuanga (Philippines)
H. Sumatrae **Sumatran porcupine** Sumatra (Indonesia)
Trichys
T. fasciculata **Long-tailed porcupine** Malaysia, Sumatra (Indonesia), Borneo

FAMILY PETROMURIDAE
Petromus
P. typicus **Dassie rat** W South Africa, Namibia to SW Angola

FAMILY THRYONOMYIDAE **Cane Rats**
Thryonomys
T. gregorianus **Lesser canerat** Cameroon, CAR, DRC, S Sudan, Ethiopia, Kenya, Uganda, Tanzania, Mozambique, Malawi, Zambia, Zimbabwe
T. swinderianus **Greater canerat** SubSaharan Africa

FAMILY ERETHIZONTIDAE **New World Porcupines**
Coendou **Prehensile-tailed Porcupines**
C. bicolor **Bicolor-spined porcupine** Colombia, Ecuador, Peru, Bolivia
C. koopmani **Koopman's porcupine** Brazil
C. prehensilis **Brazilian porcupine** E Venezuela, Guianas, C and E Brazil, Bolivia, Trinidad
C. rothschildi **Rothschild's porcupine** Panama
Echinoprocta
E. rufescens **Stump-tailed porcupine** Cord. Orient. of W Colombia
Erethizon
E. dorsatum **North American porcupine** C Alaska (USA) to Labrador and S of Hudson Bay (Canada) south to E Tennessee, C Iowa, and C Texas (USA) to N Mexico and then north to S California (USA)
Sphiggurus **Hairy Dwarf Porcupines**
S. insidiosus **Bahia hairy dwarf porcupine** Surinam, E and Amazonian Brazil
S. mexicanus **Mexican hairy dwarf porcupine** San Luis Potosi and Yucatan Pen. (Mexico) to W Panama
S. pallidus **Pallid or West Indian hairy dwarf porcupine** Extinct: formerly W. Indies
S. spinosus **Paraguay hairy dwarf porcupine** S and E Brazil, Paraguay, NE Argentina, Uruguay
S. vestitus **Brown hairy dwarf porcupine** Colombia, W Venezuela
S. villosus **Orange-spined hairy dwarf porcupine** Minas Gerais to Rio Grande do Sul (SE Brazil)

FAMILY CHINCHILLIDAE **Viscachas and Chinchillas**
Chinchilla **Chinchillas**
C. brevicaudata **Short-tailed chinchilla** Andes of S Peru, S Bolivia, Chile, and NW Argentina
C. lanigera **Chinchilla** N Chile south to Coquimbo
Lagidium **Mountain Viscachas**
L. peruanum **Northern viscacha** C and S Peru
L. viscacia **Southern viscacha** S Peru, S and W Bolivia, W Argentina, N Chile
L. wolffsohni **Wolffsohn's viscacha** SW Argentina, adj. Chile
Lagostomus
L. maximus **Plains viscacha** SE Bolivia, S and W Paraguay, N, C, and E Argentina

FAMILY DINOMYIDAE
Dinomys
D. branickii **Pacarana** Colombia, Venezuela, Ecuador, Peru, Brazil, Bolivia

FAMILY CAVIIDAE

SUBFAMILY CAVIINAE
Cavia **Guinea-pigs**
C. aperea **Brazilian guinea-pig** Colombia, Venezuela, Guianas, Ecuador, Brazil, Paraguay, N Argentina, Uruguay
C. fulgida **Shiny guinea-pig** Minas Gerais to Santa Catarina (E Brazil)
C. magna **Greater guinea-pig** Rocha (Uruguay) to Rio Grande do Sul and Santa Catarina (S Brazil)
C. porcellus **Guinea pig** Domesticated worldwide but poss. feral in South America
C. tschudii **Montane guinea-pig** Peru, S Bolivia, N Chile, NW Argentina
Galea **Yellow-toothed Cavies**
G. flavidens **Yellow-toothed cavy** E Brazil
G. musteloides **Common yellow-toothed cavy** S Peru, Bolivia, N Chile, Argentina
G. spixii **Spix's yellow-toothed cavy** Brazil, E Bolivia
Kerodon
K. rupestris **Rock cavy** E Brazil
Microcavia **Mountain Cavies**
M. australis **Southern mountain cavy** S Bolivia, Jujuy to Santa Cruz (Argentina), Aisen (Chile)
M. niata **Andean mountain cavy** Andes of SW Bolivia
M. shiptoni **Shipton's mountain cavy** Tucuman, Catamarca, and Salta (NW Argentina)

SUBFAMILY DOLICHOTINAE
Dolichotis **Maras**
D. patagonum **Patagonian mara** Argentina
D. salinicola **Chacoan mara** S Bolivia, Chaco (W Paraguay), NW Argentina south to Cordoba

FAMILY HYDROCHAERIDAE
Hydrochaeris
H. hydrochaeris **Capybara** Panama, Colombia, Venezuela, Guianas, Peru, Brazil, Paraguay, NE Argentina, Uruguay

FAMILY DASYPROCTIDAE **Agoutis**
Dasyprocta **Agoutis**
D. azarae **Azara's agouti** E, C, and S Brazil, Paraguay, NE Argentina
D. coibae **Coiban agouti** Coiba Is (Panama)
D. cristata **Crested agouti** Guianas
D. fuliginosa **Black agouti** Colombia, S Venezuela, Surinam, Peru, N Brazil
D. guamara **Orinoco agouti** Orinoco Delta (Venezuela)
D. kalinowskii **Kalinowski's agouti** SE Peru
D. leporina **Brazilian agouti** Venezuela, Guianas, E and Amazonian Brazil, Lesser Antilles; introd. to Virgin Is
D. mexicana **Mexican agouti** C Veracruz and E Oaxaca (Mexico); introd. to W and E Cuba
D. prymnolopha **Black-rumped agouti** NE Brazil
D. punctata **Central American agouti** Chiapas and Yucatan Pen. (S Mexico) to S Bolivia, SW Brazil, and N Argentina; introd. to W and W Cuba, Cayman Is
D. ruatanica **Ruatan Island agouti** Roatan Is (Honduras)
Myoprocta **Acouchis**
M. acouchy **Green acouchi** S Colombia, S Venezuela, Guianas, Ecuador, N Peru, Amazonian Brazil
M. exilis **Red acouchi** Colombia, S Venezuela, Guianas, E Ecuador, N Peru, Amazon Basin of Brazil

FAMILY AGOUTIDAE **Pacas**
Agouti
A. paca **Paca** SE San Luis Potosi (Mexico) to Guianas, S Brazil, and Paraguay; introd. to Cuba
A. taczanowskii **Mountain paca** Colombia, NW Venezuela, Ecuador, Peru

FAMILY CTENOMYIDAE **Tuco-tucos**
Ctenomys
C. argentinus **Argentine tuco-tuco** NC Chaco (NE Argentina)
C. australis **Southern tuco-tuco** Buenos Aires (E Argentina)
C. azarae **Azara's tuco-tuco** La Pampa (S Argentina)
C. boliviensis **Bolivian tuco-tuco** C Bolivia, W Paraguay, Formosa (NE Argentina)
C. bonettoi **Bonetto's tuco-tuco** Chaco (NE Argentina)
C. brasiliensis **Brazilian tuco-tuco** E Brazil
C. colburni **Colburn's tuco-tuco** W Santa Cruz (SW Argentina)
C. conoveri **Conover's tuco-tuco** Chaco (W Paraguay), adj. Argentina
C. dorsalis **Chacoan tuco-tuco** N Chaco (W Paraguay)
C. emilianus **Emily's tuco-tuco** Neuquen (S Argentina)
C. frater **Forest tuco-tuco** Jujuy and Salta (NW Argentina), SW Bolivia
C. fulvus **Tawny tuco-tuco** N Chile, NW Argentina
C. haigi **Haig's tuco-tuco** Chubut and Rio Negro (SW Argentina)
C. knighti **Catamarca tuco-tuco** Tucuman and La Rioja to Salta (W Argentina)
C. latro **Mottled tuco-tuco** Tucuman and Salta (NW Argentina)
C. leucodon **White-toothed tuco-tuco** E Peru, W Bolivia
C. lewisi **Lewis' tuco-tuco** S Bolivia
C. magellanicus **Magellanic tuco-tuco** S Chile, S Argentina
C. maulinus **Maule tuco-tuco** Talca to Cautin (SC Chile), Neuquen (S Argentina)
C. mendocinus **Mendoza tuco-tuco** Salta to Chubut (Argentina)
C. minutus **Tiny tuco-tuco** Rio Grande do Sul and Mato Grosso (SW Brazil), NW Argentina, Uruguay
C. nattereri **Natterer's tuco-tuco** Mato Grosso (SW Brazil)
C. occultus **Furtive tuco-tuco** Tucuman and surrounds (NW Argentina)
C. opimus **Highland tuco-tuco** S Peru, SW Bolivia, N Chile, NW Argentina
C. pearsoni **Pearson's tuco-tuco** Soriana, San Jose, and Colonia (Uruguay)
C. perrensis **Goya tuco-tuco** Corrientes, Entre Rios, and Misiones (NE Argentina)
C. peruanus **Peruvian tuco-tuco** Altiplano of S Peru
C. pontifex **San Luis tuco-tuco** San Luis and Mendoza (W Argentina)
C. porteousi **Porteous' tuco-tuco** Buenos Aires and La Pampa (E Argentina)
C. saltarius **Salta tuco-tuco** Salta and Jujuy (NW Argentina)
C. sericeus **Silky tuco-tuco** Santa Cruz, Chubut, and Rio Negro (SW Argentina)
C. sociabilis **Social tuco-tuco** Neuquen (S Argentina)
C. steinbachi **Steinbach's tuco-tuco** E Bolivia
C. talarum **Talas tuco-tuco** Coastal Buenos Aires (E Argentina)
C. torquatus **Collared tuco-tuco** S Brazil, NE Argentina, Uruguay
C. tuconax **Robust tuco-tuco** Tucuman (NW Argentina)
C. tucumanus **Tucuman tuco-tuco** NW Argentina
C. validus **Strong tuco-tuco** Mendoza (W Argentina)

FAMILY OCTODONTIDAE **Octodonts**
Aconaemys **Rock Rats**
A. fuscus **Chilean rock rat** Andes of Chile, Argentina
A. sagei **Sage's rock rat** Lago Quillen and Lago Hui Hui (Neuquen, S Argentina)
Octodon **Degus**
O. bridgesi **Bridges' degu** Andes of Chile
O. degus **Degu** W Andes from Vallenar to Curico (Chile)
O. lunatus **Moon-toothed degu** Valparaiso, Aconcagua, and Coquimbo (Chile)
Octodontomys
O. gliroides **Mountain degu** Andes of SW Bolivia, N Chile, and NW Argentina
Octomys
O. mimax **Viscacha rat** W Argentina
Spalacopus
S. cyanus **Coruro** Chile, W of Andes
Tympanoctomys
T. barrerae **Plains viscacha rat** Mendoza (W Argentina)

FAMILY ABROCOMIDAE **Chinchilla Rats**
Abrocoma
A. bennetti **Bennett's chinchilla rat** Copiapo to Rio Biobio (Chile)
A. boliviensis **Bolivian chinchilla rat** Santa Cruz (Bolivia)
A. cinerea **Ashy chinchilla rat** SE Peru, W Bolivia, N Chile, NW Argentina

FAMILY ECHIMYIDAE
American Spiny Rats

SUBFAMILY CHAETOMYINAE
Chaetomys
C. subspinosus **Bristle-spined rat** S Bahia and N Espirito Santo (E Brazil)

SUBFAMILY DACTYLOMYINAE
Dactylomys Neotropical Bamboo Rats
D. boliviensis **Bolivian bamboo rat** SE Peru, C Bolivia
D. dactylinus **Amazon bamboo rat** Ecuador, Peru, N Brazil
D. peruanus **Peruvian bamboo rat** SE Peru, Bolivia
Kannabateomys
K. amblyonyx **Atlantic bamboo rat** E Brazil, Paraguay, NE Argentina
Olallamys Olalla Rats
O. albicauda **White-tailed olalla rat** NW and C Colombia
O. edax **Greedy olalla rat** W Venezuela, adj. Colombia

SUBFAMILY ECHIMYINAE
Diplomys Arboreal Soft-furred Spiny Rats
D. caniceps **Arboreal soft-furred spiny rat** W Colombia, N Ecuador
D. labilis **Rufous tree rat** Panama (incl. San Miguel Is), W Colombia, N Ecuador
D. rufodorsalis **Red-crested tree rat** NE Colombia
Echimys Spiny Tree Rats
E. blainvillei **Golden Atlantic tree rat** SE Brazil
E. braziliensis **Red-nosed tree rat** S Brazil
E. chrysurus **White-faced tree rat** Guianas to NE Brazil
E. dasythrix **Drab Atlantic tree rat** SE and E Brazil
E. grandis **Giant tree rat** Rio Negro to Ilha Caviana (Amazonian Brazil)
E. lamarum **Pallid Atlantic tree rat** E Brazil
E. macrurus **Long-tailed tree rat** Brazil, S of Amazon R
E. nigrispinus **Black-spined Atlantic tree rat** E Brazil
E. pictus **Painted tree rat** S Bahia (E Brazil)
E. rhipidurus **Peruvian tree rat** C and N Amazonian Peru
E. saturnus **Dark tree rat** Ecuador, N Peru
E. semivillosus **Speckled tree rat** N Colombia, Venezuela (incl. Margarita Is)
E. thomasi **Giant Atlantic tree rat** San Sebastiao Is (Bahia, E Brazil)
E. unicolor **Unicolored tree rat** Brazil
Isothrix Brush-tailed Rats
I. bistriata **Yellow-crowned brush-tailed rat** W Colombia, S Venezuela, SW to NC Brazil, Bolivia
I. pagurus **Plain brush-tailed rat** Amazon Basin (C Brazil)
Makalata
M. armata **Armored spiny rat** Andes of N Ecuador and Colombia, Venezuela, Guianas, Amzaon Basin (C Brazil), Trinidad and Tobago

SUBFAMILY EUMYSOPINAE
Carterodon
C. sulcidens **Owl's spiny rat** E Brazil
Clyomys Lund's Spiny Rats
C. bishopi **Bishop's fossorial spiny rat** Itapetininga (Sao Paulo, Brazil)
C. laticeps **Broad-headed spiny rat** Minas Gerais to Santa Catarina (E Brazil)
Euryzygomatomys
E. spinosus **Guiara** S and E Brazil, NE Argentina, Paraguay
Hoplomys
H. gymnurus **Armoured rat** EC Honduras to NW Ecuador
Lonchothrix
L. emiliae **Tuft-tailed spiny tree rat** C Brazil, south of Amazon R
Mesomys Spiny Tree Rats
M. didelphoides **Brazilian spiny tree rat** Brazil
M. hispidus **Spiny tree rat** E Ecuador, N and E Peru, N Brazil
M. leniceps **Woolly-headed spiny tree rat** Peru
M. obscurus **Dusky spiny tree rat** Brazil
M. stimulax **Surinam spiny tree rat** Surinam, N Brazil
Proechimys Terrestrial Spiny Rats
P. albispinus **White-spined spiny rat** Bahia, adj. islands (Brazil)
P. amphichoricus **Venezuelan spiny rat** S Venezuela, adj. Brazil
P. bolivianus **Bolivian spiny rat** Upper Amazon
P. brevicauda **Huallaga spiny rat** S Colombia, E Peru, NW Brazil
P. canicollis **Colombian spiny rat** NC Colombia, Venezuela
P. cayennensis **Cayenne spiny rat** E Colombia, Guianas south to C Brazil
P. chrysaeolus **Boyaca spiny rat** E Colombia
P. cuvieri **Cuvier's spiny rat** Fr. Guiana, Surinam, Guyana
P. decumanus **Pacific spiny rat** SW Ecuador, NW Peru
P. dimidiatus **Atlantic spiny rat** E Brazil
P. goeldii **Goeldi's spiny rat** Amazonian Brazil, betw. Jamunda and Tapajoz R
P. gorgonae **Gorgona spiny rat** Gorgona Is (Colombia)
P. guairae **Guaira spiny rat** NC Venezuela
P. gularis **Ecuadoran spiny rat** E Ecuador
P. hendeei **Hendee's spiny rat** S Colombia to NE Peru
P. hoplomyoides **Guyanan spiny rat** SE Venezuela, adj. Guyana and Brazil
P. iheringi **Ihering's spiny rat** E Brazil
P. longicaudatus **Long-tailed spiny rat** C and E Peru, S Brazil, W Bolivia, Paraguay
P. magdalenae **Magdalena spiny rat** Colombia, W of Rio Magdalena
P. mincae **Minca spiny rat** Sierra Nevada Santa Marta (N Colombia)
P. myosuros **Mouse-tailed spiny rat** Bahia (E Brazil)
P. oconnelli **O'Connell's spiny rat** C Colombia, east of Cord. Orient.
P. oris **Para spiny rat** C Brazil
P. poliopus **Gray-footed spiny rat** NW Venezuela, adj. Colombia
P. quadruplicatus **Napo spiny rat** Amazonian E Ecuador and N Peru
P. semispinosus **Tome's spiny rat** SE Honduras to NE Peru and Amazonian Brazil
P. setosus **Hairy spiny rat** Minas Gerais (E Brazil)
P. simonsi **Simon's spiny rat** S Colombia, E Ecuador, NE Peru
P. steerei **Steere's spiny rat** W Peru, E Brazil
P. trinitatis **Trinidad spiny rat** Trinidad
P. urichi **Sucre spiny rat** N Venezuela
P. warreni **Warren's spiny rat** Surinam, Guiana
Thrichomys
T. apereoides **Punare** E Brazil, Paraguay

SUBFAMILY HETEROPSOMYINAE
Boromys Cuban Cave Rats
B. offella **Oriente cave rat** Extinct: formerly Cuba (incl. Juventud Is)
B. torrei **Torre's cave rat** Extinct: formerly Cuba (incl. Juventud Is)
Brotomys Edible rats
B. contractus **Haitian edible rat** Extinct: formerly Hispaniola
B. voratus **Hispaniolan edible rat** Extinct: formerly Haiti (incl. Gonave Is), Dominican Rep.
Heteropsomys Hispaniolan cave rats
H. antillensis **Antillean cave rat** Extinct: formerly Puerto Rico
H. insulans **Insular cave rat** Extinct: formerly Puerto Rico
Puertoricomys
P. corozalus **Corozal rat** Extinct: formerly Puerto Rico

FAMILY CAPROMYIDAE Hutias

SUBFAMILY CAPROMYINAE
Capromys
C. pilorides **Desmarest's hutia** Cuba, many islands and cays in Cuban Arch.
Geocapromys Bahaman and Jamaican Hutias
G. brownii **Brown's hutia** Jamaica
G. ingrahami **Bahamian hutia** Plana Cays (Bahamas); introd. to Little Wax Cay and Warderick Well Cay
G. thoracatus **Swan Island hutia** Extinct: formerly Little Swan Is (Gulf of Honduras)
Mesocapromys Sticknest Hutias
M. angelcabrerai **Cabrera's hutia** Ciego de Avila (Cuba)
M. auritus **Eared hutia** Las Villas (Cuba)
M. nanus **Dwarf hutia** Matanzas (Cuba)
M. sanfelipensis **San Felipe hutia** Extinct: formerly Pinar del Rio (Cuba)
Mysateles Long-tailed Cuban Hutias
M. garridoi **Garrido's hutia** Canarreos Arch. (Cuba)
M. gundlachi **Gundlach's hutia** N Juventud Is (Cuba)
M. melanurus **Black-tailed hutia** E Cuba
M. meridionalis **Southern hutia** Juventud Is (Cuba)
M. prehensilis **Prehensile-tailed hutia** Cuba

SUBFAMILY HEXOLOBODONTINAE
Hexolobodon
H. phenax **Imposter hutia** Extinct: formerly Hispaniola (incl. Gonave Is)

SUBFAMILY ISOLOBOLONTINAE
Isolobodon Laminar-toothed Hutias
I. montanus **Montane hutia** Extinct: formerly Hispaniola (incl. Gonave Is)
I. portoricensis **Puerto Rican hutia** Extinct: formerly Haiti and Dominican Rep. (Hispaniola) and offshore islands (incl. La Tortue Is); introd. to Puerto Rico and elsewhere

SUBFAMILY PLAGIODONTINAE
Plagiodontia Hispaniolan Hutias
P. aedium **Hispaniolan hutia** Hispaniola (incl. Gonave Is)
P. araeum **San Rafael hutia** Extinct: formerly Hispaniola
P. ipnaeum **Samana hutia** Extinct: formerly Hispaniola
Rhizoplagiodontia
R. lemkei **Lemke's hutia** Extinct: formerly Massif de la Hotte (SW Haiti)

FAMILY HEPTAXODONTIDAE Key Mice

SUBFAMILY CLIDOMYINAE
Clidomys Key Mice
C. osborni **Osborn's key mouse** Extinct: formerly Jamaica
C. parvus **Small key mouse** Extinct: formerly Jamaica

SUBFAMILY HEPTAXODONTINAE
Amblyrhiza
A. inundata **Blunt-toothed mouse** Extinct: formerly Anguilla (W. Indies)
Elasmodontomys
E. obliquus **Plate-toothed mouse** Extinct: formerly Puerto Rico
Quemisia
Q. gravis **Twisted-toothed mouse** Extinct: formerly Hispaniola

FAMILY MYOCASTORIDAE
Myocastor
M. coypus **Nutria or Coypu** S Brazil, Bolivia, Paraguay, Chile, Argentina, Uruguay

ORDER LAGOMORPHA
RABBITS, HARES, AND PIKAS

FAMILY LEPORIDAE Hares and Rabbits
see full species list pp 702–705

FAMILY OCHOTONIDAE Pikas
Ochotona
O. alpina **Alpine pika** Altai and Sayan Mts, NW Kazakhstan, S Russia, NW Mongolia, N Gansu-Ningxia border
O. cansus **Gansu pika** Qinghai, Gansu, Sichuan; also Shanxi and Shaanxi (China)
O. collaris **Collared pika** SE Alaska (USA), NW Canada
O. curzoniae **Black-lipped pika** Sikkim (India), E Nepal, Xizang, adj. Gansu, Qinghai, and Sichuan (China)
O. dauurica **Daurian pika** Altai Mts and Tuva south through Mongolia and N China to Qinghai (China)
O. erythrotis **Chinese red pika** E Qinghai, W Gansu, N Sichuan, S Xinjiang, Xizang (China)
O. forresti **Forrest's pika** Assam and Sikkim (India), Bhutan, N Burma, NW Yunnan and SE Xizang (China)
O. gaoligongensis **Gaoligong pika** Mt Gaoligong (NW Yunnan, China)
O. gloveri **Glover's pika** W Sichuan, NW Yunnan, NE Xizang, and SW Qinghai (China)
O. himalayana **Himalayan pika** Mt Jolmolunga (S Xizang, China); poss. adj. Nepal
O. hyperborea **Northern pika** Ural and Sayan Mts east to Chukotskoye and Koryakskoye ranges and Kamchatka Pen., SE Russia (incl. Sakhalin Is), NC Mongolia, NE China, N Korea, Hokkaido (Japan)
O. iliensis **Ili pika** Tien Shan Mts (Xinjiang, China)
O. koslowi **Kozlov's pika** Kunlun Shan Mts (W China)
O. ladacensis **Ladak pika** N Pakistan, Kashmir, SW Xinjiang, Qinghai, E Xizang (China)
O. macrotis **Large-eared pika** W Tien Shan, Pamirs, Hindu Kush and Karakorum Mts in SE Kazakhstan, Kyrgyzstan, Tajikistan, NE Afghanistan, and N Pakistan, the Himalayas from Kashmir and N India through Nepal and Xizang (China) to Bhutan, and mountains of Sichuan and Yunnan (China)
O. muliensis **Muli pika** SE Muli (W Sichuan, China)
O. nubrica **Nubra pika** Ladakh (Kashmir) through E Nepal to E Xizang (China)
O. pallasi **Pallas' pika** E Kazakhstan, Tuva (Russia), Altai Mts, W Mongolia to N Xinjiang and Inner Mongolia (China)
O. princeps **North American pika** C British Columbia (SW Canada) in Rocky, Cascade and Sierra Nevada Mts of W North America to EC California, Utah, and N New Mexico
O. pusilla **Steppe or Small pika** Middle Volga R (Russia), east and south through N Kazakhstan to upper Irtysh R and Chinese border
O. roylei **Royle's pika** Himalayas of NW Pakistan and N India and Kashmir through S Xizang (China) to Nepal
O. rufescens **Afghan pika** Armenia, Iran, Afghanistan, Baluchistan (Pakistan), and SW Turkmenistan
O. rutila **Turkestan Red pika** Pamirs (Tajikistan) to Tien Shan Mts (SE Uzbekistan, Kyrgyzstan, SE Kazakhstan), poss. E Xinjiang (China) and N Afghanistan
O. thibetana **Moupin pika** Sikkim (India), Bhutan, N Burma, SE Qinghai, S Gansu, Shanxi, Shaanxi, W Hubei, W Yunnan, W Sichuan, S Xizang (China)
O. thomasi **Thomas' pika** NE Qinghai, Gansu, and Sichuan (China)
Prolagus
P. sardus **Sardinian pika** Extinct: formerly Corsica (France), Sardinia (Italy), adj. small islands

ORDER MACROSCELIDEA
ELEPHANT SHREWS

FAMILY MACROSCELIDIDAE
Elephantulus Long-eared Elephant Shrews
E. brachyrhynchus **Short-snouted elephant shrew** N South Africa, NE Namibia, Angola, Mozambique and DRC to Uganda and Kenya
E. edwardii **Cape elephant shrew** SW South Africa
E. fuscipes **Dusky-footed elephant shrew** NE DRC, Uganda, S Sudan
E. fuscus **Dusky elephant shrew or Peters' short-snouted elephant shrew** C Mozambique, SE Zambia, S Malawi
E. intufi **Bushveld elephant shrew** W South Africa, Botswana, Namibia, SW Angola
E. myurus **Eastern rock elephant shrew** E and N South Africa, S Zimbabwe, E Botswana, W Mozambique
E. revoili **Somali elephant shrew** N Somalia
E. rozeti **North African elephant shrew** SW Morocco to W Libya
E. rufescens **Rufous elephant shrew** S Sudan, S and E Ethiopia, N and S Somalia, N and SE Kenya, NE Uganda, NC and W Tanzania,
E. rupestris **Western rock elephant shrew** W South Africa, Namibia
Macroscelides
M. proboscideus **Short-eared or Round-eared elephant-shrew** W South Africa, SW Botswana, S and E Namibia
Petrodromus
P. tetradactylus **Four-toed elephant-shrew** South Africa, Zimbabwe, Botswana, NE Angola, Zambia, Malawi, Mozambique, DRC, Congo, S Uganda, Tanzania (incl. Zanzibar and Mafia Is), SE Kenya
Rhynchocyon Checkered Elephant shrews
R. chrysopygus **Golden-rumped elephant-shrew** E Kenya
R. cirnei **Checkered elephant-shrew** Mozambique, NE Zambia, Malawi, E DRC, Uganda, S Tanzania
R. petersi **Black and rufous elephant-shrew** E Tanzania (incl. Zanzibar and Mafia Is), SE Kenya

ORDER INSECTIVORA
INSECTIVORES

Note According to a new account of systematics, the tenrecs and golden moles should be assigned to a new order, the Afrosoricida, part of the superorder Afrotheria. For a full explanation of this restructuring see the introductory essay What is a Mammal? and Insectivores p.722. Correspondingly, in this new scheme, the shrews, moles, and hedgehogs become an order in their own right, the Eulipotyphla.

FAMILY TENRECIDAE Tenrecs

SUBFAMILY GEOGALINAE
Geogale
G. aurita **Large-eared tenrec** NE and SW Madagascar

SUBFAMILY ORYZORICTINAE
Limnogale
L. mergulus **Aquatic tenrec** E Madagascar
Microgale **Shrew Tenrecs**
M. brevicaudata **Short-tailed shrew tenrec** Madagascar
M. cowani **Cowan's shrew tenrec** N, E, and EC Madagascar
M. dobsoni **Dobson's shrew tenrec** E and EC Madagascar
M. dryas **Tree shrew tenrec** NE Madagascar
M. gracilis **Gracile shrew tenrec** E Madagascar
M. longicaudata **Lesser long-tailed shrew tenrec** E and N Madagascar
M. parvula **Pygmy shrew tenrec** N Madagascar
M. principula **Greater long-tailed shrew tenrec** E and SE Madagascar
M. pulla **Dark shrew tenrec** NE Madagascar
M. pusilla **Least shrew tenrec** E and S Madagascar
M. talazaci **Talazac's shrew tenrec** N, E, and EC Madagascar
M. thomasi **Thomas' shrew tenrec** E Madagascar
Oryzorictes **Rice Tenrecs**
O. hova **Hova rice tenrec** C Madagascar
O. talpoides **Molelike rice tenrec** NW Madagascar
O. tetradactylus **Four-toed rice tenrec** C Madagascar

SUBFAMILY POTAMOGALINAE
Micropotamogale **Dwarf Otter Shrews**
M. lamottei **Mount Nimba otter shrew** Guinea, Liberia, Ivory Coast
M. ruwenzorii **Ruwenzori otter shrew** Ruwenzori region (Uganda, DRC), NE DRC
Potamogale
P. velox **Giant otter shrew** Tropical Africa, from Nigeria to W Kenya to Angola

SUBFAMILY TENRECINAE
Echinops
E. telfairi **Lesser hedgehog tenrec** S Madagascar
Hemicentetes
H. semispinosus **Streaked tenrec** E Madagascar
Setifer
S. setosus **Greater hedgehog tenrec** C Madagascar
Tenrec
T. ecaudatus **Tailless or Common tenrec** Madagascar, Comoros; introd. to Reunion, Mauritius, and Seychelles

FAMILY SOLENODONTIDAE Solenodons

Solenodon
S. cubanus **Cuban solenodon** Oriente (Cuba)
S. marcanoi **Marcano's solenodon** Extinct: formerly San Rafael (Dominican Rep.)
S. paradoxus **Hispaniola solenodon** Haiti, Dominican Rep.

FAMILY ERINACEIDAE Hedgehogs and Moonrats

SUBFAMILY ERINACEINAE
Atelerix **African Hedgehogs**
A. albiventris **Four-toed hedgehog** Senegal to Ethiopia south to Zambezi R
A. algirus **North African hedgehog** Western Sahara to Algeria, Tunisia, N Libya; introd. to Canarias and Balearic Is, Malta, S France and Spain
A. frontalis **Southern African hedgehog** South Africa, E Botswana, W Zimbabwe; also Namibia to SW Angola
A. sclateri **Somali hedgehog** N Somalia
Erinaceus **Eurasian Hedgehogs**
E. amurensis **Amur hedgehog** Russia south through E China to Hunan, Korea
E. concolor **Eastern European hedgehog** E Europe, S Russia and W Siberia to Ob R, Turkey to Israel and Iran, Greek and Adriatic Is
E. europaeus **Western European hedgehog** Spain to Italy and Istra Pen. north to Scandinavia and NW Russia; also Ireland and Britain, Corsica (France), Sardinia and Sicily (Italy) and other islands
Hemiechinus **Desert Hedgehogs**
H. aethiopicus **Desert hedgehog** Mauritania to Egypt and Ethiopia, Arabia, Djerba Is (Tunisia), Bahrain
H. auritus **Long-eared hedgehog** E Ukraine to Mongolia in north and Libya to W Pakistan in south
H. collaris **Indian long-eared hedgehog** Pakistan, NW India
H. hypomelas **Brandt's hedgehog** Iran and Turkmenistan east to Uzbekistan and Indus R (Pakistan), Oman, Tanb and Kharg Is (Persian Gulf)
H. micropus **Indian hedgehog** Pakistan, NW India
H. nudiventris **Bare-bellied hedgehog** Tamil Nadu and Kerala (S India)
Mesechinus **Steppe Hedgehogs**
M. dauuricus **Daurian hedgehog** NE Mongolia east to upper Amur basin in Russia, adj. Inner Mongolia and W Manchuria (China)
M. hughi **Hugh's hedgehog** Shaanxi and Shanxi (China)

SUBFAMILY HYLOMYINAE
Echinosorex
E. gymnura **Moonrat** Malay Pen., Sumatra (Indonesia), Borneo
Hylomys **Asian Gymnures**
H. hainanensis **Hainan gymnure** Hainan (China)
H. sinensis **Shrew or Chinese gymnure** Sichuan and Yunnan (S China), adj. Burma and N Vietnam
H. suillus **Short-tailed gymnure** Malay Pen. to Indochina to Yunnan border (China), Java, Sumatra, and Tioman Is (Indonesia), Borneo
Podogymnura **Philippine Gymnures**
P. aureospinula **Dinagat gymnure** Dinagat (Philippines)
P. truei **Mindanao gymnure** Mindanao (Philippines)

FAMILY NESOPHONTIDAE

Nesophontes or Extinct West Indian shrews
Nesophontes
N. edithae **Puerto Rican nesophontes** Extinct: formerly Puerto Rico
N. hypomicrus **Atalyae nesophontes** Extinct: formerly Haiti (incl. Gonave Is)
N. longirostris **Slender Cuban nesophontes** Extinct: formerly Cuba
N. major **Greater Cuban nesophontes** Extinct: formerly Cuba
N. micrus **Western Cuban nesophontes** Extinct: formerly Cuba, Haiti, and Pinos Is
N. paramicrus **St. Michael nesophontes** Extinct: formerly Haiti
N. submicrus **Lesser Cuban nesophontes** Extinct: formerly Cuba
N. zamicrus **Haitian nesophontes** Extinct: formerly Haiti

FAMILY SORICIDAE Shrews

SUBFAMILY CROCIDURINAE
Congosorex
C. polli **Poll's shrew** S DRC
Crocidura **White-toothed Shrews**
C. aleksandrisi **Alexandrian shrew** Cyrenaica (Libya)
C. allex **Highland shrew** SW Kenya, Mt Kilimanjaro, Meru, and Ngorongoro (N Tanzania)
C. andamanensis **Andaman shrew** Andaman Is (India)
C. ansellorum **Ansell's shrew** N Zambia
C. arabica **Arabian shrew** Coastal plains of S Arabian Pen.
C. armenica **Armenian shrew** Armenia
C. attenuata **Indochinese shrew** India, Nepal, Bhutan, Burma, China, Taiwan, Thailand, Vietnam, Malay Pen., Sumatra and Java (Indonesia)
C. attila **Hun shrew** Mt Cameroun (Cameroon) to E DRC
C. baileyi **Bailey's shrew** Ethiopian highlands west of Rift valley
C. batesi **Bates' shrew** S Cameroon, Gabon
C. beatus **Mindanao shrew** Mindanao, Leyte, and Maripipi (Philippines)
C. beccarii **Beccari's shrew** Sumatra (Indonesia)
C. bottegi **Bottego's shrew** Guinea to Ethiopia and N Kenya
C. bottegoides **Bale shrew** Bale Mts and Mt Albasso (Ethiopia)
C. buettikoferi **Buettikofer's shrew** West Africa, from Guinea-Biassau to Liberia, Nigeria
C. caliginea **African foggy shrew** NE DRC
C. canariensis **Canary shrew** E Canarias Is
C. cinderella **Cinderella shrew** Senegal, Gambia, Mali, Niger
C. congobelgica **Congo shrew** NE DRC
C. cossyrensis **Pantellerian shrew** Pantelleria (Italy)
C. crenata **Long-footed shrew** S Cameroon, N Gabon, E DRC
C. crossei **Crosse's shrew** Sierra Leone to W Cameroon
C. cyanea **Reddish-gray musk shrew** South Africa, Namibia, Botswana, Angola, Mozambique
C. denti **Dent's shrew** Cameroon, Gabon, NE DRC
C. desperata **Desperate shrew** Rungwe and Uzungwe Mts (S Tanzania)
C. dhofarensis **Dhofarian shrew** Dhofar (Oman)
C. dolichura **Long-tailed musk shrew** Nigeria, S Cameroon, Gabon, Bioko (Equatorial Guinea), Congo, CAR, DRC, adj. Uganda and Burundi
C. douceti **Doucet's musk shrew** Guinea, Ivory Coast, Nigeria
C. dsinezumi **Dsinezumi shrew** Japan, Quelpart Is (Korea), poss. Taiwan
C. eisentrauti **Eisentraut's shrew** Mt Cameroun (Cameroon)
C. elgonius **Elgon shrew** Mt Elgon (W Kenya), NE Tanzania
C. elongata **Elongated shrew** N and C Sulawesi (Indonesia)
C. erica **Heather shrew** W Angola
C. fischeri **Fischer's shrew** Nguruman (Kenya), Himo (Tanzania)
C. flavescens **Greater red musk shrew** South Africa
C. floweri **Flower's shrew** Egypt
C. foxi **Fox's shrew** Jos plateau (Nigeria)
C. fuliginosa **Southeast Asian shrew** N India, Burma, adj. China, Malay Pen. and adj. islands, poss. Sumatra and Java (Indonesia) and Borneo
C. fulvastra **Savanna shrew** Kenya to Mali
C. fumosa **Smoky white-toothed shrew** Mt Kenya and Aberdares (Kenya)
C. fuscomurina **Tiny musk shrew** Senegal to Ethiopia south to South Africa
C. glassi **Glass' shrew** Ethiopian highlands east of Rift valley
C. goliath **Goliath shrew** S Cameroon, Gabon, DRC
C. gracilipes **Peter's musk shrew** Mt Kilimanjaro (Tanzania)
C. grandiceps **Large-headed shrew** Guinea, Ivory Coast, Ghana, Nigeria
C. grandis **Mount Malindang shrew** Mt Malindang (Mindanao, Philippines)
C. grassei **Grasse's shrew** Belinga (Gabon), Boukoko (CAR), Yaounde (Cameroon)
C. grayi **Luzon shrew** Luzon and Mindoro (Philippines)
C. greenwoodi **Greenwood's shrew** S Somalia
C. gueldenstaedtii **Gueldenstaedt's shrew** Caucasus
C. harenna **Harenna shrew** Bale Mts (Ethiopia)
C. hildegardeae **Hildegarde's shrew** Nigeria, Cameroon, C and E Africa
C. hirta **Lesser red musk shrew** Somalia to DRC to South Africa
C. hispida **Andaman spiny shrew** Andaman Is (India)
C. horsfieldii **Horsfield's shrew** Mysore and Ladak (India), Sri Lanka, Nepal, Yunnan, Fujian, and Hainan (China), Taiwan, Ryukyu Is (Japan), N Thailand to Vietnam
C. jacksoni **Jackson's shrew** E DRC, Uganda, Kenya, N Tanzania
C. jenkinsi **Jenkin's shrew** Andaman Is (india)
C. kivuana **Kivu shrew** Kahuzi-Biega NP (DRC)
C. lamottei **Lamotte's shrew** Senegal to W Cameroon
C. lanosa **Lemara shrew** E DRC, Rwanda
C. lasiura **Ussuri white-toothed shrew** Ussuri region (Russia) and NE China to Korea, also Jiangsu (China)
C. latona **Latona shrew** NE DRC
C. lea **Sulawesi shrew** N and C Sulawesi (Indonesia)
C. leucodon **Bicolored shrew** France to the Volga R and Caucasus, Turkey, south through the Alborz Mts to Israel and Lebanon, Lesvos Is (Greece)
C. levicula **Celebes shrew** C and SE Sulawesi (Indonesia)
C. littoralis **Butiaba naked-tailed shrew** DRC, Uganda, Kenya
C. longipes **Savanna swamp shrew** W Nigeria
C. lucina **Moorland shrew** E Ethiopia
C. ludia **Dramatic shrew** Medje and Tandala (N DRC)
C. luna **Greater gray-brown musk shrew** Zimbabwe, E Angola, Zambia, Malawi, Mozambique, DRC, Uganda, Rwanda, Tanzania, Kenya
C. lusitania **Mauritanian shrew** S Morocco to Senegal, east in Nigeria, Sudan, Ethiopia
C. macarthuri **MacArthur's shrew** Kenya, Somalia
C. macmillani **MacMillan's shrew** Ethiopia
C. macowi **Macow's shrew** N Kenya
C. malayana **Malayan shrew** Malay Pen. and offshore islands
C. manengubae **Manenguba shrew** Cameroon
C. maquassiensis **Maquassie musk shrew** N South Africa, Zimbabwe
C. mariquensis **Swamp musk shrew** South Africa to Mozambique, W Zimbabwe, and Zambia; also NE Namibia and NW Botswana
C. maurisca **Dark shrew** Uganda, Kenya
C. maxi **Max's shrew** Java, Lesser Sunda Is, Maluku (Indonesia)
C. mindorus **Mindoro shrew** Mt Halcon (Mindoro, Philippines)
C. minuta **Minute shrew** Java (Indonesia)
C. miya **Sri Lankan long-tailed shrew** C Sri Lanka
C. monax **Rombo shrew** W Kenya, N Tanzania
C. monticola **Sunda shrew** Malay Pen., Java (Indonesia), Borneo
C. montis **Montane white-toothed shrew** Mt Ruwenzori (Uganda), Mt Meru (Tanzania), Imatong Mts (Sudan), poss. Kenya
C. muricauda **Mouse-tailed shrew** Guinea to Ghana
C. mutesae **Uganda large-toothed shrew** Uganda
C. nana **Dwarf white-toothed shrew** Somalia, Ethiopia
C. nanilla **Tiny white-toothed shrew** Mauritania to Kenya and Uganda
C. neglecta **Neglected shrew** Sumatra (Indonesia)
C. negrina **Negros shrew** S Negros Is (Philippines)
C. nicobarica **Nicobar shrew** Great Nicobar Is (Nicobar Is, India)
C. nigeriae **Nigerian shrew** Nigeria, Cameroon, Bioko (Equatorial Guinea)
C. nigricans **Black white-toothed shrew** Angola
C. nigripes **Black-footed shrew** N and C Sulawesi (Indonesia)
C. nigrofusca **Tenebrous shrew** S Ethiopia and Sudan through E Africa to DRC, Zambia, Angola
C. nimbae **Nimba shrew** Mt Nimba (Guinea, Liberia), Sierra Leone
C. niobe **Stony shrew** Uganda, DRC
C. obscurior **Obscure white-toothed shrew** Sierra Leone to Ivory Coast
C. olivieri **Olivier's shrew** Egypt, Senegal to Ethiopia, south to N South Africa
C. orii **Amami shrew** Ryukyu Is (Japan)
C. osorio **Osorio shrew** Gran Canaria Is (Canarias Is)
C. palawanensis **Palawan shrew** Palawan (Philippines)
C. paradoxura **Paradox shrew** Sumatra (Indonesia)
C. parvipes **Small-footed shrew** Cameroon to S Sudan, Ethiopia, Kenya, Tanzania, DRC, Zambia, Angola
C. pasha **Pasha shrew** Sudan, Ethiopia
C. pergrisea **Pale gray shrew** Kashmir
C. phaeura **Guramba shrew** Mt Guramba (Ethiopia)
C. picea **Pitch shrew** Cameroon
C. pitmani **Pitman's shrew** C and N Zambia
C. planiceps **Flat-headed shrew** Ethiopia, Sudan, Uganda, DRC, Nigeria
C. poensis **Fraser's musk shrew** Cameroon to Liberia, Bioko (Equatorial Guinea), Principe (Sao Tome & Principe)
C. polia **Fuscous shrew** Medje (DRC)
C. pullata **Dusky shrew** Afghanistan, Pakistan, India, Kashmir, Yunnan (China), Thailand
C. raineyi **Rainey shrew** Mt Garguez (Kenya)
C. religiosa **Egyptian pygmy shrew** Nile valley (Egypt)
C. rhoditis **Temboan shrew** N, C, and SW Sulawesi (Indonesia)
C. roosevelti **Roosevelt's shrew** Angola, Cameroon, CAR, DRC, Uganda, Rwanda, Tanzania
C. russula **White-toothed shrew** S and W Europe, Mediterranean Is (Ibiza, Sardinia), N Africa, from Morocco to Tunisia
C. selina **Moon shrew** Uganda
C. serezkyensis **Serezkaya shrew** Turkey, Azerbaijan, Turkmenistan, Tajikistan, Kazakhstan
C. sibirica **Siberian shrew** L. Ysyk-Kol (Kyrgyzstan) to upper Ob R, L. Baikal, poss. Mongolia and Xinjiang (China)
C. sicula **Sicilian shrew** Sicily, Egadi Is (Italy), Gozo (Malta)
C. silacea **Lesser gray-brown musk shrew** South Africa, Botswana, Zimbabwe, Mozambique
C. smithii **Desert musk shrew** Senegal, Ethiopia, poss. Somalia
C. somalica **Somali shrew** Ethiopia, Sudan, Somalia, Mali
C. stenocephala **Narrow-headed shrew** Mt Kahuzi (E DRC)
C. suaveolens **Lesser shrew** Palearctic from Spain to Korea, many Atlantic Is, Mediterranean Is incl. Corsica (France), Crete (Greece), Menorca (Spain), and Cyprus

C. susiana **Iranian shrew** Dezful (SW Iran)
C. tansaniana **Tanzanian shrew** Usambara Mts (Tanzania)
C. tarella **Ugandan shrew** Uganda
C. tarfayensis **Tarfaya shrew** Atlantic coast from Morocco to Mauritania
C. telfordi **Telford's shrew** Uluguru Mts (Tanzania)
C. tenuis **Thin shrew** Timor
C. thalia **Thalia shrew** Ethiopian highlands
C. theresae **Therese's shrew** Ghana to Guinea
C. thomensis **São Tomé shrew** São Tomé Is (São Tomé & Principe)
C. turba **Tumultuous shrew** Angola, Zambia, Malawi, DRC, Cameroon, Uganda, Tanzania, Kenya
C. ultima **Ultimate shrew** Jombeni Mts (Nyeri, Kenya)
C. usambarae **Usambara shrew** Usambara Mts (Tanzania)
C. viaria **Savanna path shrew** S Morocco to Senegal and east to Sudan, Ethiopia, Kenya
C. voi **Voi shrew** Kenya and Somalia to Ethiopia and Sudan; also Nigeria and Mali
C. whitakeri **Whitaker's shrew** Morocco to Tunisia, coastal Egypt
C. wimmeri **Wimmer's shrew** S Ivory Coast
C. xantippe **Vermiculate shrew** SE Kenya, Usambara Mts (Tanzania)
C. yankariensis **Yankari shrew** Cameroon, Nigeria, Sudan, Ethiopia, Kenya, Somalia
C. zaphiri **Zaphir's shrew** Kaffa (S Ethiopia), Kaimosi and Kisumu (Kenya)
C. zarudnyi **Zarudny's shrew** SE Iran, SE Afghanistan, SW Pakistan
C. zimmeri **Zimmer's shrew** Upemba NP (DRC)
C. zimmermanni **Zimmermann's shrew** Crete (Greece)
Diplomesodon
D. pulchellum **Piebald shrew** W and S Kazakhstan, Uzbekistan, Turkmenistan
Feroculus
F. feroculus **Kelaart's long-clawed shrew** C Sri Lanka
Myosorex **Mouse Shrews**
M. babaulti **Babault's mouse shrew** E DRC, W Rwanda, W Burundi
M. blarina **Montane mouse shrew** Mt Ruwenzori (Uganda, DRC)
M. cafer **Dark-footed forest shrew** E and NE South Africa, E Zimbabwe, W Mozambique
M. eisentrauti **Eisentraut's mouse shrew** Bioko (Equatorial Guinea)
M. geata **Geata mouse shrew** SW Tanzania
M. longicaudatus **Long-tailed forest shrew** S and SE South Africa
M. okuensis **Oku mouse shrew** Bamenda plateau (Cameroon)
M. rumpii **Rumpi mouse shrew** Rumpi-Hills (Cameroon)
M. schalleri **Schaller's mouse shrew** Itombwe Mts (E DRC)
M. sclateri **Sclater's tiny mouse shrew** KwaZulu-Natal (South Africa)
M. tenuis **Thin mouse shrew** NE South Africa
M. varius **Forest shrew** South Africa, Lesotho
Paracrocidura **African Shrews**
P. graueri **Grauer's shrew** Itombwe Mts (E DRC)
P. maxima **Greater shrew** DRC, Rwanda, Uganda
P. schoutedeni **Schouteden's shrew** S Cameroon, Gabon, Congo, CAR, DRC
Ruwenzorisorex
R. suncoides **Ruwenzori shrew** W DRC, Uganda, Rwanda, Burundi
Scutisorex
S. somereni **Armored or Hero shrew** DRC, adj. Uganda, Rwanda, Burundi
Solisorex
S. pearsoni **Pearson's long-clawed shrew** C Sri Lanka
Suncus **Pygmy and Dwarf Shrews**
S. ater **Black shrew** Mt Kinabalu (Sabah, N Borneo)
S. dayi **Day's shrew** S India
S. etruscus **White-toothed pygmy shrew or Etruscan shrew** S Europe, N Africa, from Morocco to Egypt, Arabian Pen. and Turkey to Iraq, Turkmenistan, Afghanistan, Pakistan, India, Sri Lanka, Nepal, Bhutan, Burma, Yunnan (China), and Thailand
S. fellowesgordoni **Sri Lankan shrew** C Sri Lanka
S. hosei **Hose's shrew** Borneo
S. infinitesimus **Least dwarf shrew** Cameroon, CAR, Kenya to South Africa
S. lixus **Greater dwarf shrew** Kenya, Tanzania, DRC, Malawi, Zambia, Angola, Botswana, N South Africa
S. madagascariensis **Madagascan shrew** Madagscar, Comoros
S. malayanus **Malayan pygmy shrew** Malay Pen.
S. mertensi **Flores shrew** Flores (Indonesia)
S. montanus **Sri Lanka highveld shrew** S India, Sri Lanka
S. murinus **Asian house shrew** Afghanistan, Pakistan, India, Sri Lanka, Nepal, Bhutan, Burma, China, Taiwan, Japan, south to Malay Pen.; introd. to coastal NE Africa (Egypt to Tanzania), coastal Arabia, Madagascar, Comoros, Mauritius, other Indian Ocean islands, Philippines, Guam and prob. many other islands
S. remyi **Remy's shrew** Belinga and Makokou (NE Gabon)
S. stoliczkanus **Anderson's shrew** Pakistan, India, Nepal, Bangladesh
S. varilla **Lesser dwarf shrew** South Africa, Zimbabwe, Zambia, Malawi, DRC, Tanzania; also Nigeria
S. zeylanicus **Jungle shrew** Sri Lanka
Surdisorex **Kenyan Shrews**
S. norae **Aberdare shrew** Aberdares (Kenya)
S. polulus **Mount Kenya shrew** Mt Kenya (Kenya)
Sylvisorex **Forest Musk Shrews**
S. granti **Grant's shrew** DRC, Uganda, Rwanda, Kenya, Tanzania; also Cameroon
S. howelli **Howell's shrew** Usambara and Uluguru Mts (Tanzania)
S. isabellae **Isabella shrew** Bioko (Equatorial Guinea), Bamenda plateau (Cameroon)
S. johnstoni **Johnston's shrew** Congo, SW Cameroon, Gabon, Bioko (Equatorial Guinea), DRC, Uganda, Burundi, Tanzania
S. lunaris **Crescent shrew** Ruwenzori Mts (Uganda, DRC), Virunga Volcanos (Rwanda), L. Kivu region (Burundi, DRC)
S. megalura **Climbing shrew** Guinea to Ethiopia south to Mozambique and Zimbabwe
S. morio **Arrogant shrew** Mt Cameroun (Cameroon)
S. ollula **Forest musk shrew** S Cameroon, adj. Nigeria, Gabon, S DRC
S. oriundus **Mountain shrew** NE DRC
S. vulcanorum **Volcano shrew** E DRC, Uganda, Rwanda, Burundi

SUBFAMILY SORICINAE
Anourosorex
A. squamipes **Mole-shrew or Sichuan burrowing shrew** Assam (India), Bhutan, N and W Burma, Shaanxi, Hubei to Yunnan (China), Taiwan, Thailand, N Vietnam
Blarina **American Short-tailed Shrews**
B. brevicauda **Northern short-tailed shrew** Saskatchewan (Canada) east in S and SE Canada to Nebraska and N Virginia (USA)
B. carolinensis **Southern short-tailed shrew** S Illinois east to N Virginia south to E Texas and N Florida
B. hylophaga **Elliot's short-tailed shrew** S Nebraska and Iowa south to S Texas and east to Missouri and NW Arkansas, Oklahoma into Louisiana (USA)
Blarinella **Asiatic Short-tailed Shrews**
B. quadraticauda **Sichuan short-tailed shrew** Gansu, Shaanxi, Sichuan, and Yunnan (China)
B. wardi **Ward's short-tailed shrew** Burma, Yunnan (China)
Chimarrogale **Oriental Water Shrews**
C. hantu **Hantu water shrew** Malay Pen.
C. himalayica **Himalayan water shrew** Kashmir through SE Asia to Indochina, C and S China, Taiwan
C. phaeura **Sunda water shrew** Borneo
C. platycephala **Flat-headed water shrew** Japan
C. styani **Styan's water shrew** Shaanxi, Sichuan (China), N Burma
C. Sumatrana **Sumatra water shrew** Sumatra (Indonesia)
Cryptotis **Small-eared Shrews**
C. avia **Andean small-eared shrew** Cord. Orient. of Colombia
C. endersi **Enders' small-eared shrew** Bocas del Toro (Panama)
C. goldmani **Goldman's small-eared shrew** S Mexico, WC Guatemala
C. goodwini **Goodwin's small-eared shrew** S Mexico, S Guatemala, W El Salvador
C. gracilis **Talamancan small-eared shrew** SE Costa Rica, W Panama
C. hondurensis **Honduran small-eared shrew** Tegucigalpa (Honduras), poss. adj. Guatemala, El Salvador, and Nicaragua
C. magna **Big small-eared shrew** NC Oaxaca (Mexico)
C. meridensis **Merida small-eared shrew** Cord. Merida and Mts near Caracas (W Venezuela)
C. mexicana **Mexican small-eared shrew** Tamaulipas to Chiapas (Mexico)
C. montivaga **Ecuadorean small-eared shrew** Andes of S Ecuador
C. nigrescens **Blackish small-eared shrew** S Mexico (incl. Yucatan Pen.), Guatemala, El Salvador, Honduras, Costa Rica, Panama
C. parva **Least shrew** SE Canada through EC and SW USA, Mexico, Central America to Panama
C. squamipes **Scaly-footed small-eared shrew** Cord. Occid. of W Colombia and Ecuador
C. thomasi **Thomas' small-eared shrew** Cord. Orient. of W Colombia, Ecuador, and N Peru
Megasorex
M. gigas **Mexican shrew** Nayarit to Oaxaca (Mexico)
Nectogale
N. elegans **Elegant water shrew** Nepal and Sikkim (India), Bhutan, N Burma, Shaanxi, Sichuan, Yunnan, and Xizang (China)
Neomys **Old World Water Shrews**
N. anomalus **Southern water shrew** Portugal to Poland east to Russia
N. fodiens **Eurasian water shrew** Most of Europe (incl. British Is) east to L. Baikal, Yenisei R (Russia), Tien Shan Mts (China), NW Mongolia; also Sakhalin Is (Russia), Jilin (China), and N Korea
N. schelkovnikovi **Transcaucasian water shrew** Caucasus (Armenia, Azerbaijan, Georgia)
Notiosorex
N. crawfordi **Desert shrew** SW and SC USA to Baja California and N and C Mexico
Sorex **Holarctic Shrews**
S. alaskanus **Glacier Bay water shrew** Glacier Bay (Alaska, USA)
S. alpinus **Alpine shrew** Pyrenees, Jura, Harz, Sudetan, Carpathians, Tatra and other mountains of C Europe
S. araneus **Eurasian shrew** C, E, and N Europe (incl. British Is) east to Siberia (Russia); also in France, Italy, Spain
S. arcticus **Arctic shrew** NW to SE Canada, Dakotas, Minnesota, and Wisconsin (USA)
S. arizonae **Arizona shrew** SE Arizona, SW New Mexico (USA), Chihuahua (N Mexico)
S. asper **Tien Shan shrew** Tien Shan Mts (Kazakhstan, China)
S. bairdii **Baird's shrew** NW Oregon (USA)
S. bedfordiae **Lesser striped shrew** S Gansu and W Shaanxi to Yunnan (China), adj. Burma, Nepal
S. bendirii **Marsh shrew** NW California to Washington (USA), SE British Columbia (Canada)
S. buchariensis **Pamir shrew** Pamirs (Tajikistan)
S. caecutiens **Laxmann's shrew** E Europe to E Siberia and Sakhalin Is (Russia), south to C Ukraine, N Kazakhstan, Altai Mts, Mongolia, Gansu and NE China, Korea
S. camtschatica **Kamchatka shrew** S Kamchatka Pen. (Russia)
S. cansulus **Gansu shrew** Gansu (China)
S. cinereus **Cinereus or Masked shrew** Alaska (USA) and Canada along the Rocky and Appalachian Mts
S. coronatus **Crowned shrew** W Europe, from The Netherlands and NW Germany to France, Switzerland south to N Spain; also in Jersey (Channel Is)
S. cylindricauda **Stripe-backed shrew** N Sichuan (China)
S. daphaenodon **Large-toothed Siberian shrew** Urals to Kolyma R, Kamchatka Pen., Sakhalin Is (Russia), Jilin and Nei Monggol (China)
S. dispar **Long-tailed shrew** S New Brunswick, Nova Scotia (Canada), North Carolina to Maine in Appalachian Mts (USA)
S. emarginatus **Zacatecas shrew** Durango, Zacatecas, and Jalisco (Mexico)
S. excelsus **Lofty shrew** Yunnan, Sichuan (China), poss. Nepal
S. fumeus **Smoky shrew** SE Canada south through Appalachian Mts to NE Georgia (USA)
S. gaspensis **Gaspe shrew** Gaspe Pen., Nova Scotia, N New Brunswick, Cape Breton Is (Canada)
S. gracillimus **Slender shrew** SE Siberia from Sea of Okhotsk to N Korea, Sakhalin Is (Russia), Hokkaido (Japan)
S. granaries **Lagranja shrew** NW Iberian Pen. (Portugal, Spain)
S. haydeni **Prairie shrew** SC Canada, NC USA
S. hosonoi **Azumi shrew** C Honshu (Japan)
S. hoyi **Pygmy shrew** Alaska (USA), Canada, USA south in Appalachian and Rocky Mts
S. hydrodromus **Pribilof Island shrew** Pribilof Is (Bering Sea, USA)
S. isodon **Even-toothed shrew** SE Norway and Finland through Siberia to Pacific coast and Kamchatka Pen, Sakhalin Is, and Kurilskiye Is (Russia), prob. NE China and Korea
S. jacksoni **St. Lawrence Island shrew** St Lawrence Is (Bering Sea, USA)
S. kozlovi **Kozlov's shrew** E Xizang (China)
S. leucogaster **Paramushir shrew** Paramushir Is (Russia)
S. longirostris **Southeastern shrew** SE USA (excl. Florida) west to Louisiana, Arkansas, Missouri, Illinois, Indiana
S. lyelli **Mount Lyell shrew** Sierra Nevada Mts (California, USA)
S. macrodon **Large-toothed shrew** Veracruz and Puebla (Mexico)
S. merriami **Merriam's shrew** EC Washington to N and E California, Arizona to Nebraska and Montana (USA)
S. milleri **Carmen Mountain shrew** Sierra Madre Orient. of Coahuila and Nuevo Leon (NE Mexico)
S. minutissimus **Miniscule shrew** Norway, Sweden, and Estonia to E Siberia, Sakhalin Is (Russia), Hokkaido (Japan), Mongolia, China, S Korea
S. minutus **Eurasian pygmy shrew** Europe to Yenesei R and L. Baikal south to Altai and Tien Shan Mts
S. mirabilis **Ussuri shrew** Ussuri region (Russia), NE China, N Korea
S. monticolus **Montane shrew** Alaska (USA) south through W Canada to California and New Mexico east to Montana, Wyoming, and Colorado (USA), Chihuahua and Durango (Mexico)
S. nanus **Dwarf shrew** Montana to New Mexico in Rocky Mts, South Dakota, Arizona (USA)
S. oreopolus **Mexican long-tailed shrew** Jalisco (Mexico)
S. ornatus **Ornate shrew** California (USA) to Baja California (Mexico), Santa Catalina Is (USA)
S. pacificus **Pacific shrew** Coastal Oregon (USA)
S. palustris **Water shrew** North America, from Alaska (USA) to Sierra Nevada, Rocky and Appalachian Mts
S. planiceps **Kashmir shrew** N Pakistan, Kashmir
S. portenkoi **Portenko's shrew** NE Siberia (Russia)
S. preblei **Preble's shrew** W USA
S. raddei **Radde's shrew** Caucasus, N Turkey
S. roboratus **Flat-skulled shrew** Russia, betw. Ob and Ussuri R, south to Altai Mts and N Mongolia
S. sadonis **Sado shrew** Sado Is (Japan)
S. samniticus **Apennine shrew** Italy
S. satunini **Caucasian shrew** Caucasus, N Turkey
S. saussurei **Saussure's shrew** Coahuila and Durango to Chiapas (Mexico), Guatemala
S. sclateri **Sclater's shrew** Chiapas (Mexico)
S. shinto **Shinto shrew** Honshu, Shikoku, and Hokkaido (Japan)
S. sinalis **Chinese shrew** C and W China
S. sonomae **Fog shrew** Coastal W USA, from Oregon to N California
S. stizodon **San Cristobal shrew** Chiapas (Mexico)
S. tenellus **Inyo shrew** WC Nevada, EC California (USA)
S. thibetanus **Tibetan shrew** Himalayas, NE Xizang (China)
S. trowbridgii **Trowbridge's shrew** Coastal W USA, from Washington to California, SW British Columbia (Canada)
S. tundrensis **Tundra shrew** Siberia, from Pechora R to Chukotskoye Pen. (Russia) south to Altai Mts, Mongolia, and NE China; also Alaska (USA), Yukon and Northwest Territories (NW Canada)
S. ugyunak **Barrend ground shrew** N Alaska (USA), NW Canada
S. unguiculatus **Long-clawed shrew** E Siberian Coast, from Vladivostok to the Amur, Sakhalin Is (Russia), Hokkaido (Japan)
S. vagrans **Vagrant shrew** SW Canada, W USA
S. ventralis **Chestnut-bellied shrew** NW Puebla to Oaxaca (Mexico)
S. veraepacis **Verapaz shrew** Mexico to SW Guatemala
S. volnuchini **Caucasian pygmy shrew** S Ukraine, Caucasus
Soriculus **Asiatic Shrews**
S. caudatus **Hodgson's brown-toothed shrew** Kashmir to N Burma and SW China
S. fumidus **Taiwan brown-toothed shrew** Taiwan
S. hypsibius **De Winton's shrew** SW and C China
S. lamula **Lamulate shrew** Yunnan, Sichuan, Gansu to Fujian (C China)
S. leucops **Long-tailed brown-toothed shrew** Sikkim and Assam (India), C Nepal, to S China, N Burma, and N Vietnam
S. macrurus **Long-tailed mountain shrew** C Nepal to W and S China, N Burma, and Vietnam

S. nigrescens **Himalayan shrew** Himalayas from Assam (India) and SW China to Xizang (China) and Nepal
S. parca **Lowe's shrew** SW China, N Burma, Thailand, N Vietnam
S. salenskii **Salenski's shrew** N Sichuan (China)
S. smithii **Smith's shrew** C Sichuan to W Shaanxi (China)

FAMILY CHRYSOCHLORIDAE
Golden Moles
Amblysomus South African Golden Moles
A. gunningi **Gunning's golden mole** NE South Africa
A. hottentotus **Hottentot golden mole** South Africa
A. iris **Zulu golden mole** S, SE, and E South Africa
A. julianae **Juliana's golden mole** NC and NE South Africa
Calcochloris
C. obtusirostris **Yellow golden mole** E South Africa, S Zimbabwe, S Mozambique
Chlorotalpa African Golden Moles
C. arendsi **Arend's golden mole** E Zimbabwe, adj. Mozambique
C. duthieae **Duthie's golden mole** S South Africa
C. leucorhina **Congo golden mole** N Angola, DRC, Cameroon, CAR
C. sclateri **Sclater's golden mole** S and C South Africa
C. tytonis **Somali golden mole** Giohar (Somalia)
Chrysochloris Cape Golden Moles
C. asiatica **Cape golden mole** SW South Africa, poss. Namibia
C. stuhlmanni **Stuhlmann's golden mole** Cameroon, N DRC, Uganda, Kenya, Tanzania
C. visagiei **Visagie's golden mole** Gouna (Calvinia, South Africa)
Chrysospalax Large Golden Moles
C. trevelyani **Giant golden mole** King Williams' Town region (SE South Africa)
C. villosus **Rough-haired golden mole** E South Africa
Cryptochloris Secretive Golden Moles
C. wintoni **De Winton's golden mole** Little Namaqualand (South Africa)
C. zyli **Van Zyl's golden mole** Lamberts Bay region (SW South Africa)
Eremitalpa
E. granti **Grant's desert golden mole** SW and W South Africa, W Namibia

FAMILY TALPIDAE
Desmans, Moles, and Shrew Moles

SUBFAMILY DESMANINAE
Desmana
D. moschata **Russian desman** Don, Volga, and Ural R drainages in SW Russia; introd. to Dnipro R (Ukraine) and Ob basin
Galemys
G. pyrenaicus **Pyrenean desman** Pyrenees (S France) and N Iberian Pen. (N Spain, N Portugal)

SUBFAMILY TALPINAE
Condylura
C. cristata **Star-nosed mole** Georgia and NW South Carolina (SE USA) to Nova Scotia and Labrador (SE Canada) and Great Lakes region to S Manitoba
Euroscaptor Oriental Moles
E. grandis **Greater Chinese mole** S China, Vietnam
E. klossi **Kloss' mole** Thailand, Laos, Malay Pen.
E. longirostris **Long-nosed mole** S China
E. micrura **Himalayan mole** Sikkim and Assam (India), Nepal, N Burma, S China
E. mizura **Japanese mountain mole** Honshu (Japan)
E. parvidens **Small-toothed mole** Di Linh and Rakho (Vietnam)
Mogera East Asian Moles
M. etigo **Echigo mole** Echigo Plain (Honshu, Japan)
M. insularis **Insular mole** SE China (incl. Hainan), Taiwan
M. kobeae **Kobe mole** Kyushu, Shikoku, and S Honshu (Japan)
M. minor **Small Japanese mole** Honshu (Japan)
M. robusta **Large mole** Korea to NE China, adj. Siberia (Russia)
M. tokudae **Tokuda's mole** Sado Is (Japan)
M. wogura **Japanese mole** Japan
Nesoscaptor
N. uchidai **Ryukyu or Senkaku mole** Senkaku Is (Ryukyu Is, Japan)
Neurotrichus
N. gibbsii **American shrew mole** SW British Columbia (Canada) south to WC California (USA)
Parascalops
P. breweri **Hairy-tailed mole** SE Canada, NE USA
Parascaptor
P. leucura **White-tailed mole** Assam (India), Burma, Yunnan (China)
Scalopus
S. aquaticus **Eastern mole** Minnesota and Massachusetts through E USA to N Coahuila and N Tamaulipas (NE Mexico)
Scapanulus
S. oweni **Gansu mole** Gansu, Shaanxi, Sichuan (C China)
Scapanus Western American Moles
S. latimanus **Broad-footed mole** SC Oregon (USA) to N Baja California (Mexico)
S. orarius **Coast mole** SW British Columbia (Canada) to WC Idaho, N Oregon, and NW California (USA)
S. townsendii **Townsend's mole** SW British Columbia (Canada) to NW California (USA)
Scaptochirus
S. moschatus **Short-faced mole** Hebei, Shandong, Shaanxi, Shanxi (NE China)
Scaptonyx
S. fusicaudus **Long-tailed mole** Qinghai, Shaanxi, Sichuan, and Yunnan (S China), N Burma
Talpa Old World Moles
T. altaica **Siberian mole** C Siberia betw. Ob and Lena R (Russia), south to N Mongolia
T. caeca **Mediterranean mole** S Europe and Turkey
T. caucasica **Caucasian mole** NW Caucasus
T. europaea **European mole** Temperate Europe (incl. Britain) east to Ob and Irtysh R (Russia)
T. levantis **Levantine mole** Bulgaria, Thrace, N Turkey, adj. Caucasus
T. occidentalis **Iberian mole** W and C Iberian Pen. (Portugal, Spain)
T. romana **Roman mole** Apennines (Italy), SE France
T. stankovici **Stankovic's mole** Stara Planina (Romania, Bulgaria, S Yugoslavia), Greece (incl. Kerkira Is)
T. streeti **Persian mole** N Iran
Urotrichus Japanese Shrew Moles
U. pilirostris **True's shrew-mole** Honshu, Shikoku, and Kyushu (Japan)
U. talpoides **Japanese shrew mole** Honshu, Shikoku, Kyushu, Dogo, and Tsushima Is (Japan)

SUBFAMILY UROPSILINAE
Uropsilus Asiatic Shrew Moles
U. andersoni **Anderson's shrew mole** C Sichuan (China)
U. gracilis **Gracile shrew mole** Sichuan and Yunnan (China), N Burma
U. investigator **Inquisitive shrew mole** Yunnan (China)
U. soricipes **Chinese shrew mole** C Sichuan (China)

ORDER CHIROPTERA
BATS

SUBORDER MEGACHIROPTERA
Fruit-eating bats

FAMILY PTEROPODIDAE
Old World Fruit Bats and Flying Foxes

SUBFAMILY PTEROPODINAE
Acerodon Island Fruit Bats
A. celebensis **Sulawesi fruit bat** Sulawesi, Salayar, and Mangole (Indonesia)
A. humilis **Talaud fruit bat** Talaud Is (Indonesia)
A. jubatus **Golden-capped fruit bat** Philippines
A. leucotis **Palawan fruit bat** Palawan, Busuanga, and Balabac Is (Philippines)
A. lucifer **Panay golden-capped fruit bat** Panay (Philippines)
A. mackloti **Sunda fruit bat** Indonesia
Aethalops
A. alecto **Pygmy fruit bat** Malay Pen., Sumatra, W Java, and Lombok (Indonesia), Borneo
Alionycteris
A. paucidentata **Mindanao pygmy fruit bat** Mindanao (Philippines)
Aproteles
A. bulmerae **Bulmer's fruit bat** New Guinea
Balionycteris
B. maculata **Spotted-winged fruit bat** Thailand, Malay Pen., Riau Arch. (Indonesia), Borneo
Boneia
B. bidens **Manada fruit bat** N Sulawesi (Indonesia)
Casinycteris
C. argynnis **Short-palated fruit bat** Cameroon to E DRC
Chironax
C. melanocephalus **Black-capped fruit bat** Thailand, Malay Pen., Sumatra, Java, and Sulawesi (Indonesia), Borneo
Cynopterus Short-nosed Fruit Bats
C. brachyotis **Lesser short-nosed fruit bat** India (incl. Andaman and Nicobar Is), Sri Lanka, SE Asia, Malaysia, Sumatra and Sulawesi (Indonesia), Borneo, Philippines
C. horsfieldi **Horsfield's fruit bat** Thailand, Malay Pen., Java, Sumatra, and Lesser Sunda Is (Indonesia), Borneo
C. nusatenggara **Nusatenggara short-nosed fruit bat** Lesser Sunda Is (Indonesia)
C. sphinx **Greater short-nosed fruit bat** India, Sri Lanka, S China, SE Asia, Malay Pen., Sumatra (Indonesia), poss. Borneo
C. titthaecheileus **Indonesian short-nosed fruit bat** Sumatra, Java, Lombok, and Timor (Indonesia)
Dobsonia Naked-backed Fruit Bats
D. beauforti **Beaufort's naked-backed fruit bat** Waigeo Is (Indonesia)
D. chapmani **Negros naked-backed fruit bat** Extinct: formerly Philippines
D. emersa **Biak naked-backed fruit bat** Biak and Owii Is (Indonesia)
D. exoleta **Sulawesi naked-backed fruit bat** Sulawesi, adj. islands (Indonesia)
D. inermis **Solomons naked-backed fruit bat** Solomon Is
D. minor **Lesser naked-backed fruit bat** Sulawesi (Indonesia), C and W New Guinea
D. moluccensis **Moluccan naked-backed fruit bat** Aru, Batanta, Mysol, and Maluku (Indonesia), New Guinea, Bismarck Arch. (Papua New Guinea), N Queensland (Australia)
D. pannietensis **Panniet naked-backed fruit bat** Louisiade Arch., D'Entrecasteaux, and Trobriand Is (Papua New Guinea)
D. peroni **Western naked-backed fruit bat** Indonesia
D. praedatrix **New Britain naked-backed fruit bat** Bismarck Arch. (Papua New Guinea)
D. viridis **Greenish naked-backed fruit bat** Sulawesi and Maluku (Indonesia)
Dyacopterus
D. spadiceus **Dyak fruit bat** Malay Pen., Sumatra (Indonesia), Borneo, Luzon and Mindanao (Philippines)
Eidolon Eidolon Fruit Bats
E. dupreanum **Madagascan fruit bat** Madagascar
E. helvum **Straw-colored fruit bat** Senegal to Ethiopia to South Africa, SW Arabia, islands off East Africa
Epomophorus Epauletted Fruit Bats
E. angolensis **Angolan epauletted fruit bat** W Angola, NW Namibia
E. gambianus **Gambian epauletted fruit bat** Senegal to W Ethiopia, S Tanzania to Angola and South Africa
E. grandis **Lesser Angolan epauletted fruit bat** N Angola, S Congo
E. labiatus **Ethiopian epauletted fruit bat** Nigeria to Ethiopia south to Congo and Malawi
E. minimus **East African epauletted fruit bat** Ethiopia to Uganda, Tanzania
E. wahlbergi **Wahlberg's epauletted fruit bat** Cameroon to Somalia south to Angola and South Africa, Pemba and Zanzibar Is (Tanzania)
Epomops African Epauletted Bats
E. buettikoferi **Buettikofer's epauletted bat** Guinea to Nigeria
E. dobsoni **Dobson's fruit bat** N Botswana, Angola to Rwanda, Tanzania, and Malawi
E. franqueti **Franquet's epauletted bat or Singing fruit bat** Ivory Coast to Sudan, Uganda, NW Tanzania, N Zambia, Angola
Haplonycteris
H. fischeri **Philippine or Fischer's pygmy fruit bat** Philippines
Harpyionycteris Harpy Fruit Bats
H. celebensis **Sulawesi Harpy Fruit Bat** Sulawesi (Indonesia)
H. whiteheadi **Harpy fruit bat** Philippines
Hypsignathus
H. monstrosus **Hammer-headed fruit bat** Sierra Leone to W Kenya, south to Zambia and Angola, Bioko (Equatorial Guinea)
Latidens
L. salimalii **Salim Ali's fruit bat** S India
Megaerops Tailless Fruit Bats
M. ecaudatus **Temminck's tailless fruit bat** Thailand, Malay Pen., Sumatra (Indonesia), Borneo
M. kusnotoi **Javan tailless fruit bat** Java (Indonesia)
M. niphanae **Ratanaworabhan's fruit bat** India, Thailand, Vietnam
M. wetmorei **White-collared fruit bat** Malay Pen., Borneo, Philippines
Micropteropus Dwarf Epauletted Fruit Bats
M. intermedius **Hayman's dwarf epauletted fruit bat** N Angola, SE DRC
M. pusillus **Peter's dwarf epauletted fruit bat** Gambia to Ethiopia, south to Tanzania, Burundi, Zambia, Angola
Myonycteris Little Collared Fruit Bats
M. brachycephala **São Tomé collared fruit bat** São Tomé Is (São Tomé & Principe)
M. relicta **East African little collared fruit bat** Shimba Hills (Kenya), Nguru and Usambara Mts (Tanzania)
M. torquata **Little collared fruit bat** Sierra Leone to Uganda, south to Angola and Zambia, Bioko (Equatorial Guinea)
Nanonycteris
N. veldkampi **Veldkamp's bat or Little flying cow** Guinea to CAR
Neopteryx
N. frosti **Small-toothed fruit bat** W and N Sulawesi (Indonesia)
Nyctimene Tube-nosed Fruit Bats
N. aello **Broad-striped tube-nosed fruit bat** New Guinea
N. albiventer **Common tube-nosed fruit bat** Maluku and Kei Is (Indonesia), New Guinea, Bismarck Arch. (Papua New Guinea), Solomon Is, N Queensland (Australia)
N. celaeno **Dark tube-nosed fruit bat** Geelvink Bay (Irian Jaya, New Guinea)
N. cephalotes **Pallas' tube-nosed fruit bat** Sulawesi, Timor, Maluku, and Numfoor (Indonesia), S New Guinea
N. certans **Mountain tube-nosed fruit bat** New Guinea
N. cyclotis **Round-eared tube-nosed fruit bat** New Guinea, New Britain (Bismarck Arch., Papua New Guinea)
N. draconilla **Dragon tube-nosed fruit bat** New Guinea
N. major **Island tube-nosed fruit bat** Bismarck and Louisiade Archs., D'Entrecasteaux and Trobriand Is (Papua New Guinea), Solomon Is, islands off N New Guinea coast
N. malaitensis **Malaita Island tube-nosed fruit bat** Malaita Is (Solomon Is)
N. masalai **Demonic tube-nosed fruit bat** New Ireland (Bismarck Arch., Papua New Guinea)
N. minutus **Lesser tube-nosed fruit bat** Sulawesi, C Maluku (Indonesia)
N. rabori **Philippine tube-nosed fruit bat** Negros Is (Philippines)
N. robinsoni **Queensland tube-nosed fruit bat** E Queensland (Australia)
N. sanctacrucis **Nendo tube-nosed fruit bat** Santa Cruz Is (Solomon Is)
N. vizcaccia **Umboi tube-nosed fruit bat** Umboi Is, Bismarck Arch. (Papua New Guinea), Solomon Is
Otopteropus
O. cartilagonodus **Luzon fruit bat** Luzon (Philippines)
Paranyctimene
P. raptor **Unstriped tube-nosed bat** New Guinea
Penthetor
P. lucasi **Lucas' short-nosed fruit bat** Malay Pen., Riau Arch. (Indonesia), Borneo
Plerotes
P. anchietai **Anchieta's fruit bat** Angola, Zambia, S DRC
Ptenochirus Musky Fruit Bats
P. jagori **Greater musky fruit bat** Philippines
P. minor **Lesser musky fruit bat** Philippines
Pteralopex Monkey-faced Bats
P. acrodonta **Fijian monkey-faced bat** Fiji Is
P. anceps **Bougainville monkey-faced bat** Bougainville Is (Papua New Guinea), Choiseul Is (Solomon Is)
P. atrata **Guadalcanal monkey-faced bat** Santa Isabel Is, Guadalcanal (Solomon Is)
P. pulchra **Montane monkey-faced bat** Guadalcanal (Solomon Is)
Pteropus Flying Foxes
P. admiralitatum **Admiralty flying fox** Bismarck Arch. (Papua New Guinea), Solomon Is
P. aldabrensis **Aldabra flying fox** Aldabra Is (Seychelles)
P. alecto **Black flying fox** Indonesia, S New Guinea, N and E Australia

P. anetianus **Vanuatu flying fox** Vanuatu
P. argentatus **Ambon flying fox** Amboina Is (Maluku, Indonesia)
P. brunneus **Dusky flying fox** Percy Is (Queensland, Australia)
P. caniceps **North Moluccan flying fox** Sulawesi, Halmahera and Sula Is (Indonesia)
P. chrysoproctus **Moluccan flying fox** Indonesia
P. conspicillatus **Spectacled flying fox** Halmahera Is (Indonesia), New Guinea, NE Queensland (Australia)
P. dasymallus **Ryukyu flying fox** Taiwan, Ryukyu, Daito, and S Kyushu (Japan)
P. faunulus **Nicobar flying fox** Nicobar Is (India)
P. fundatus **Banks flying fox** N Vanuatu
P. giganteus **Indian flying fox** Maldives, Pakistan, India (incl. Andaman Is), Sri Lanka, Burma, Qinghai (China)
P. gilliardi **Gilliard's flying fox** New Britain (Bismarck Arch., Papua New Guinea)
P. griseus **Gray flying fox** Indonesia, poss. S Luzon (Philippines)
P. howensis **Ontong Java flying fox** Ontong Java Is (Solomon Is)
P. hypomelanus **Variable flying fox** Maldives, Thailand and Vietnam to Indonesia, New Guinea, Philippines, Solomon Is
P. insularis **Ruck flying fox** Truk Is (C Caroline Is)
P. leucopterus **White-winged flying fox** Luzon and Dinagat (Philippines)
P. livingstonei **Comoro black flying fox** Comoros
P. lombocensis **Lombok flying fox** Lombok, Flores, and Alor (Indonesia)
P. lylei **Lyle's flying fox** Thailand, Vietnam
P. macrotis **Big-eared flying fox** Aru Is (Indonesia), New Guinea
P. mahaganus **Sanborn's flying fox** Bougainville (Papua New Guinea), Santa Isabel Is (Solomon Is)
P. mariannus **Mariana flying fox** Mariana Is (Guam), Caroline Is, Ryukyu Is (Japan)
P. mearnsi **Mearns' flying fox** Mindanao and Basilan (Philippines)
P. melanopogon **Black-bearded flying fox** Indonesia
P. melanotus **Black-eared flying fox** Nicobar and Andaman Is (India), Engano and Nias Is (Indonesia), Christmas Is
P. molossinus **Caroline flying fox** Mortlock and Ponape Is (Caroline Is)
P. neohibernicus **Great or Bismarck flying fox** New Guinea, Bismarck Arch. and Admiralty Is (Papua New Guinea)
P. niger **Greater Mascarene flying fox** Reunion, Mauritius
P. nitendiensis **Temotu flying fox** Ndeni Is (Santa Cruz Is, Solomon Is)
P. ocularis **Seram flying fox** Seram, Buru (Indonesia)
P. ornatus **Ornate flying fox** New Caledonia Is, incl. Loyaute Is (France)
P. personatus **Masked flying fox** Halmahera Is (Indonesia)
P. phaeocephalus **Mortlock flying fox** Mortlock Is (C Caroline Is)
P. pilosus **Large Palau flying fox** Palau Is (Caroline Is)
P. pohlei **Geelvink Bay flying fox** Yapen Is (Indonesia)
P. poliocephalus **Gray-headed flying fox** S Queensland to Victoria (E Australia)
P. pselaphon **Bonin flying fox** Bonin and Volcano Is (Japan)
P. pumilus **Little golden-mantled flying fox** Philippines
P. rayneri **Solomons flying fox** Solomon Is
P. rodricensis **Rodriguez flying fox** Rodrigues and Round Is (Ind. Oc.)
P. rufus **Madagascan flying fox** Madagascar
P. samoensis **Somoan flying fox** Fiji, Western Samoa and American Samoa (Samoa Is)
P. sanctacrucis **Santa Cruz flying fox** Santa Cruz Is (Solomon Is)
P. scapulatus **Little Red flying fox** S New Guinea, Australia; introd. to New Zealand
P. seychellensis **Seychelles flying fox** Seychelles (incl. Aldabra Is), Comoros, and Mafia Is
P. speciosus **Philippine flying fox** Sulu Arch, Basilan and Mindanao (Philippines), islands in Java Sea
P. subniger **Dark flying fox** Reunion, Mauritius
P. temmincki **Temminck's flying fox** Buru, Amboina, and Seram (Indonesia), Bismarck Arch. (Papua New Guinea), adj. small islands
P. tokudae **Guam flying fox** Guam
P. tonganus **Pacific flying fox** Karkar Is (Papua New Guinea), Rennell Is (Solomon Is) to New Caledonia Is (France) and to Cook Is
P. tuberculatus **Vanikoro flying fox** Vanikoro Is (Santa Cruz Is, Solomon Is)
P. vampyrus **Large flying fox** Indochina, Malay Pen., Sumatra, Java, and Lesser Sunda Is (Indonesia), Borneo, Philippines
P. vetulus **New Caledonia flying fox** New Caledonia (France)
P. voeltzkowi **Pemba flying fox** Pemba Is (Tanzania)
P. woodfordi **Dwarf flying fox** Fauro Is to Guadalcanal (Solomon Is)
Rousettus **Rousette Fruit Bats**
R. aegyptiacus **Egyptian rousette** Senegal to Egypt south to South Africa, Cyprus, Turkey, Yemen to Pakistan,
R. amplexicaudatus **Geoffroy's rousette** Cambodia, Thailand, Malay Pen. through Indonesia to New Guinea, Bismarck Arch. (Papua New Guinea), Philippines, Solomon Is
R. angolensis **Angolan rousette** Senegal to Ethiopia south to Angola and Mozambique, Bioko (Equatorial Guinea)
R. celebensis **Sulawesi rousette** Sulawesi and Sangihe Is (Indonesia)
R. lanosus **Ruwenzori long-haired rousette** S Sudan, S Ethiopia, Kenya, Uganda, Tanzania, E DRC
R. leschenaulti **Leschenault's rousette** Sri Lanka, Pakistan to S China and Vietnam, Sumatra, Java, Bali, and Mentawai Is (Indonesia)
R. madagascariensis **Madagascan rousette** Madagascar
R. obliviosus **Comoros rousette** Comoros
R. spinalatus **Bare-backed rousette** Sumatra (Indonesia), Borneo
Scotonycteris **West African Fruit Bats**
S. ophiodon **Pohle's fruit bat** Liberia to Congo
S. zenkeri **Zenker's fruit bat** Liberia to Congo and E DRC, Bioko (Equatorial Guinea)
Sphaerias
S. blanfordi **Blanford's fruit bat** N India, Bhutan, Burma, SW China (incl. Xizang), N Thailand
Styloctenium
S. wallacei **Stripe-faced fruit bat** Sulawesi (Indonesia)
Thoopterus
T. nigrescens **Swift fruit bat** Sulawesi, Maluku, and Sangihe Is (Indonesia)

SUBFAMILY MACROGLOSSINAE

Eonycteris **Dawn Bats**
E. major **Greater dawn bat** Borneo, Philippines
E. spelaea **Lesser dawn bat** N India (also Andaman Is), S China, Burma, Thailand, Malay Pen., Sumatra, Java, Sumba, Sulawesi, and Timor (Indonesia), Borneo, Philippines
Macroglossus **Long-tongued Fruit Bats**
M. minimus **Lesser long-tongued fruit bat** Thailand to Philippines, New Guinea, Bismarck Arch. (Papua New Guinea), Solomon Is, N Australia
M. sobrinus **Greater long-tongued fruit bat** SE Asia, Sumatra and Java (Indonesia)
Megaloglossus
M. woermanni **Woermann's bat or African long-tongued fruit bat** Liberia to Uganda, S DRC, and N Angola, Bioko (Equatorial Guinea)
Melonycteris **Black-bellied Fruit Bats**
M. aurantius **Orange fruit bat** Florida and Choiseul Is (Solomon Is)
M. melanops **Black-bellied fruit bat** Bismarck Arch. (Papua New Guinea)
M. woodfordi **Woodford's fruit bat** Solomon Is
Notopteris
N. macdonaldi **Long-tailed fruit bat** Vanuatu, New Caledonia (France), Fiji Is, Caroline Is
Syconycteris **Blossom Bats**
S. australis **Southern blossom bat** Maluku (Indonesia), New Guinea, Louisiade and Bismarck Archs., D'Entrecasteaux and Trobriand Is (Papua New Guinea), E Queensland and New South Wales (Australia)
S. carolinae **Halmahera blossom bat** Halmahera Is (Maluku, Indonesia)
S. hobbit **Moss-forest blossom bat** C New Guinea

SUBORDER MICROCHIROPTERA
Insect-eating bats

FAMILY RHINOPOMATIDAE
Mouse-tailed Bats
Rhinopoma
R. hardwickei **Lesser mouse-tailed bat** Burma to Morocco, south to Mauritania, Nigeria, and Kenya; also Socotra Is (Yemen)
R. microphyllum **Greater mouse-tailed bat** Morocco and Senegal to Thailand and Sumatra (Indonesia)
R. muscatellum **Small mouse-tailed bat** Oman, W Iran, S Afghanistan

FAMILY CRASEONYCTERIDAE
Craseonycteris
C. thonglongyai **Kitti's hog-nosed bat** Kanchanaburi (Thailand)

FAMILY EMBALLONURIDAE
Sheath-tailed Bats
Balantiopteryx **Least Sac-winged Bats**
B. infusca **Ecuadorian sac-winged bat** W Ecuador
B. io **Thomas' sac-winged bat** S Veracruz and Oaxaca (S Mexico) to EC Guatemala and Belize
B. plicata **Gray sac-winged bat** S Baja California and C Sonora (Mexico) to Costa Rica and N Colombia
Centronycteris
C. maximiliani **Shaggy bat** S Veracruz (Mexico) to Guianas, Peru, and Brazil
Coleura **Peters' Sheath-tailed Bats**
C. afra **African sheath-tailed bat** Guinea-Bissau to Somalia, south to Angola, DRC, and Mozambique; also Yemen
C. seychellensis **Seychelles sheath-tailed bat** Seychelles
Cormura
C. brevirostris **Chestnut sac-winged bat** Nicaragua to Peru, Brazil
Cyttarops
C. alecto **Short-eared bat** Nicaragua, Costa Rica, Guyana, Amazonian Brazil
Diclidurus **Ghost or White Bats**
D. albus **Northern ghost bat** Nayarit (S Mexico) to E Brazil and Trinidad
D. ingens **Greater ghost bat** SE Colombia, Venezuela, Guyana, NW Brazil
D. isabellus **Isabelle's ghost bat** Venezuela, NW Brazil
D. scutatus **Lesser ghost bat** Venezuela, Guyana, Surinam, Peru, Amazonian Brazil
Emballonura **Old World Sheath-tailed Bats**
E. alecto **Small Asian sheath-tailed bat** Sulawesi and Tanimbar (Indonesia), Borneo, Philippines
E. atrata **Peter's sheath-tailed bat** E and C Madagascar
E. beccarii **Beccari's sheath-tailed bat** Kei Is (Indonesia), New Guinea, Trobriand Is (Papua New Guinea)
E. dianae **Large-eared sheath-tailed bat** New Guinea, New Ireland (Bismarck Arch., Papua New Guinea), Rennell and Malaita Is (Solomon Is)
E. furax **New Guinea sheath-tailed bat** New Guinea, Bismarck Arch. (Papua New Guinea)
E. monticola **Lesser sheath-tailed bat** Thailand to Malay Pen., Indonesia, Borneo
E. raffrayana **Raffray's sheath-tailed bat** Seram, Kei Is, and Sulawesi (Indonesia), New Guinea, Bismarck Arch. (Papua New Guinea), Choiseul, Santa Isabel, and Malaita Is (Solomon Is)
E. semicaudata **Polynesian sheath-tailed bat** Mariana and Caroline Is, Vanuatu, Fiji Is, Samoa Is
Mosia
M. nigrescens **Dark sheath-tailed bat** Indonesia, New Guinea, Bismarck Arch. (Papua New Guinea), Solomon Is
Peropteryx **Dog-like Bats**
P. kappleri **Greater dog-like bat** S Veracruz (S Mexico) to Peru and E Brazil
P. leucoptera **White-winged dog-like bat** Colombia, Venezuela, Guyana, Surinam, Fr. Guiana, Peru, N and E Brazil
P. macrotis **Lesser dog-like bat** Guerrero and Yucatan (Mexico) to Peru, S and E Brazil, Paraguay, Aruba Is (Neth. Antilles), Margarita Is (Venezuela), Trinidad and Tobago, Grenada
Rhynchonycteris
R. naso **Proboscis or Sharp-nosed bat** E Oaxaca and C Veracruz (S Mexico) to Guyana, Surinam, Fr. Guiana, Peru, C and E Brazil, Bolivia, Trinidad
Saccolaimus **Pouched Bats**
S. flaviventris **Yellow-bellied pouched bat** SE New Guinea, Australia (excl. Tasmania)
S. mixtus **Troughton's pouched bat** SE New Guinea, NE Queensland (Australia)
S. peli **Pel's pouched bat** Liberia to W Kenya to Angola
S. pluto **Philippine pouched bat** Philippines
S. saccolaimus **Naked-rumped pouched bat** India, Sri Lanka through SE Asia to Sumatra, Java, and Timor (Indonesia), Borneo, New Guinea, Guadalcanal (Solomon Is), NE Queensland (Australia)
Saccopteryx **Sac-winged Bats**
S. bilineata **Greater sac-winged bat** Jalisco and Veracruz (Mexico) to Guianas, E Brazil, Bolivia, Trinidad and Tobago
S. canescens **Frosted sac-winged bat** Colombia, Venezuela, Guianas, Peru, N Brazil
S. gymnura **Amazonian sac-winged bat** Amazonian Brazil, poss. Venezuela
S. leptura **Lesser sac-winged bat** Chiapas and Tabasco (S Mexico) to Guianas, Peru, and E Brazil, Margarita Is (Venezuela), Trinidad and Tobago
Taphozous **Tomb Bats**
T. australis **Coastal tomb bat** SE New Guinea, Torres Str. Is, N Queensland (Australia)
T. georgianus **Sharp-nosed tomb bat** Australia
T. hamiltoni **Hamilton's tomb bat** S Sudan, Chad, Kenya
T. hildegardeae **Hildegarde's tomb bat** Kenya, NE Tanzania (incl. Zanzibar Is)
T. hilli **Hill's tomb bat** Western Australia, South Australia, Northern Territory (Australia)
T. kapalgensis **Arnhem tomb bat** Northern Territory (Australia)
T. longimanus **Long-winged tomb bat** Sri Lanka, India to Cambodia, Malay Pen., Sumatra, Java, Bali, and Flores (Indonesia), Borneo
T. mauritianus **Mauritian tomb bat** Senegal to Sudan, Somalia to South Africa, Madagascar, Mauritius, Reunion, Aldabra Is (Seychelles)
T. melanopogon **Black-bearded tomb bat** Sri Lanka, India, S China, Burma, Thailand, Laos, Vietnam, Malay Pen., Indonesia, Borneo
T. nudiventris **Naked-rumped tomb bat** Mauritania, Senegal, Guinea-Bissau east to Egypt south to Tanzania, Arabian Pen. east to Burma
T. perforatus **Egyptian tomb bat** Senegal to Egypt, Somalia south to Botswana, Mozambique, S Arabia, S Iran, Pakistan, NW India
T. philippinensis **Philippine tomb bat** Philippines
T. theobaldi **Theobald's tomb bat** C India to Vietnam, Java and Sulawesi (Indonesia), Borneo

FAMILY NYCTERIDAE **Slit-faced Bats**
Nycteris
N. arge **Bate's slit-faced bat** Sierra Leone to NE Angola, S and E DRC, W Kenya, SW Sudan, Bioko (Equatorial Guinea)
N. gambiensis **Gambian slit-faced bat** W Africa, from Senegal and Gambia to Benin and Burkina Faso
N. grandis **Large slit-faced bat** Senegal to Kenya, Mozambique, and Zimbabwe, Zanzibar and Pemba Is (Tanzania)
N. hispida **Hairy slit-faced bat** Senegal to Somalia south to Angola and South Africa, Zanzibar (Tanzania), Bioko (Equatorial Guinea)
N. intermedia **Intermediate slit-faced bat** Liberia to W Tanzania south to Angola
N. javanica **Javan slit-faced bat** Java, Bali, and Kagean Is (Indonesia)
N. macrotis **Large-eared slit-faced bat** Senegal to Ethiopia south to Malawi, Mozambique, and Zimbabwe, Madagascar, Zanzibar (Tanzania)
N. major **Ja slit-faced bat** Liberia to Zambia
N. nana **Dwarf slit-faced bat** Ivory Coast to SW Sudan, W Kenya, W Tanzania, southwest to NE Angola
N. thebaica **Egyptian slit-faced bat** Central Arabia, Israel, Sinai, Egypt to Morocco and most of SubSaharan Africa (incl. Zanzibar and Pemba Is)
N. tragata **Malayan slit-faced bat** Burma, Thailand, Malay Pen., Sumatra (Indonesia), Borneo
N. woodi **Wood's slit-faced bat** Ethiopia, Somalia, SW Tanzania south to Zambia and South Africa; also Cameroon

FAMILY MEGADERMATIDAE
False Vampire Bats
Cardioderma
C. cor **Heart-nosed bat** E Africa
Lavia
L. frons **African yellow-winged bat** Senegal to Somalia, south to Zambia and Malawi, Zanzibar (Tanzania)
Macroderma
M. gigas **Australian false vampire bat** N and C Australia
Megaderma
M. lyra **Greater false vampire bat** Afghanistan to S China, south to Sri Lanka and Malay Pen.
M. spasma **Lesser false vampire bat** India, Sri Lanka through SE Asia to Lesser Sunda Is and Maluku (Indonesia) and Philippines

FAMILY RHINOLOPHIDAE
Horseshoe Bats

SUBFAMILY RHINOLOPHINAE
***Rhinolophus* Horseshoe Bats**

R. acuminatus **Acuminate horseshoe bat** Thailand, Laos, Cambodia, Sumatra, Java, Lombok, Bali, Nias and Engano Is (Indonesia), Borneo, Palawan (Philippines)
R. adami **Adam's horseshoe bat** Congo
R. affinis **Intermediate horseshoe bat** India (incl. Andaman Is) to S China through Malaysia to Lesser Sunda Is (Indonesia), Borneo
R. alcyone **Halcyon horseshoe bat** Senegal to SW Sudan, N DRC, Uganda; also Gabon and Bioko (Equatorial Guinea)
R. anderseni **Andersen's horseshoe bat** Palawan and Luzon (Philippines)
R. arcuatus **Arcuate horseshoe bat** Indonesia, New Guinea, Philippines
R. blasii **Blasius' horseshoe bat** N South Africa to Ethiopia and Somalia, Morocco to Algeria, Yemen, Israel, Jordan, Syria, Turkey, Yugoslavia, Albania, Bulgaria, Rumania, Italy, Greece, Caucasus, Iran, Turkmenistan, Afghanistan, Pakistan
R. borneensis **Bornean horseshoe bat** Cambodia, Vietnam, Malaysia, Java, Karimata, and South Natuna Is (Indonesia), Borneo
R. canuti **Canut's horseshoe bat** Java, Timor (Indonesia)
R. capensis **Cape horseshoe bat** SW South Africa, Zimbabwe, Mozambique
R. celebensis **Sulawesi horseshoe bat** Indonesia
R. clivosus **Geoffroy's horseshoe bat** SubSaharan Africa, Algeria to Arabia, Turkmenistan to Afghanistan
R. coelophyllus **Croslet horseshoe bat** Burma, Thailand, Malay Pen.
R. cognatus **Andaman horseshoe bat** Andaman Is (India)
R. cornutus **Little Japanese horseshoe bat** Japan
R. creaghi **Creagh's horseshoe bat** Madura, Java, and Timor (Indonesia), Borneo
R. darlingi **Darling's horseshoe bat** N South Africa, Namibia, Botswana, Zimbabwe, S Angola, Malawi, Mozambique, Tanzania
R. deckenii **Decken's horseshoe bat** Kenya, Tanzania (incl. Zanzibar and Pemba Is), Uganda
R. denti **Dent's horseshoe bat** W South Africa, Namibia, Botswana, Zimbabwe, Mozambique; also Ghana, Ivory Coast, Guinea
R. eloquens **Eloquent horseshoe bat** NE DRC, S Sudan, Uganda, Rwanda, Tanzania (incl. Zanzibar and Pemba Is), Kenya, S Somalia
R. euryale **Mediterranean horseshoe bat** Algeria to Morocco, S Europe and Mediterranean islands, Israel to Caucasus, Iran, Turkmenistan
R. euryotis **Broad-eared horseshoe bat** Indonesia, New Guinea, Bismarck Arch. (Papua New Guinea)
R. ferrumequinum **Greater horseshoe bat** S England to Caucasus south to Morocco and Tunisia east through Iran and Himalayas to China and Japan
R. fumigatus **Rüppell's horseshoe bat** SubSaharan Africa
R. guineensis **Guinean horseshoe bat** Guinea, Sierra Leone, Liberia
R. hildebrandti **Hildebrandt's horseshoe bat** South Africa and Mozambique to Ethiopia, S Sudan, and NE DRC
R. hipposideros **Lesser horseshoe bat** S Europe and N Africa (also Sudan and Ethiopia) through Arabia to Kyrgyzstan and Kashmir; also Ireland
R. imaizumii **Imaizumi's horsehose bat** Ryukyu Is (Japan)
R. inops **Philippine Forest horseshoe bat** Mindanao (Philippines)
R. keyensis **Insular horseshoe bat** Halmahera, Seram, Goram, Kei, and Wetter Is (Indonesia)
R. landeri **Lander's horseshoe bat** Senegal to Ethiopia, Somalia south to South Africa, Bioko (Equatorial Guinea), Zanzibar (Tanzania)
R. lepidus **Blyth's horseshoe bat** Afghanistan, N India, Burma, Sichuan and Yunnan (China), Thailand, Malay Pen., Sumatra (Indonesia)
R. luctus **Woolly horseshoe bat** India (incl. Sikkim), Sri Lanka, Nepal, Burma, S China, Taiwan, Vietnam, Laos, Thailand, Malay Pen., Sumatra, Java, and Bali (Indonesia), Borneo
R. maclaudi **Maclaud's horseshoe bat** Guinea, Liberia, E DRC, W Uganda, Rwanda
R. macrotis **Big-eared horseshoe bat** N India to S China, Vietnam, Malay Pen., Sumatra (Indonesia), Philippines
R. malayanus **Malayan horseshoe bat** Vietnam, Laos, Thailand, Malay Pen.
R. marshalli **Marshall's horseshoe bat** Thailand
R. megaphyllus **Smaller horseshoe bat** E New Guinea, Louisiade and Bismarck Archs., D'Entrecasteaux Is (Papua New Guinea), E Queensland, E New South Wales, and E Victoria (Australia)
R. mehelyi **Mehely's horseshoe bat** S Europe (Portgual and Spain to Greece) and N Africa (Morocco to Egypt) to Israel, Turkey, Caucasus, Iran, Afghanistan
R. mitratus **Mitred horseshoe bat** N India
R. monoceros **Formosan horseshoe bat** Taiwan
R. nereis **Neriad horseshoe bat** Anamba and North Natuna Is (Indonesia)
R. osgoodi **Osgood's horseshoe bat** Yunnan (China)
R. paradoxolophus **Bourret's horseshoe bat** Vietnam, Thailand
R. pearsoni **Pearson's horseshoe bat** N India, Burma, Sichuan, Anhui, and Fujian (China), Vietnam, Thailand, Malay Pen.
R. philippinensis **Large-eared horseshoe bat** Sulawesi, Timor, and Kei Is (Indonesia), Borneo, Mindoro, Luzon, Mindanao, and Negros (Philippines), New Guinea, NE Queensland (Australia)
R. pusillus **Least horseshoe bat** India, Thailand, Malay Pen., Java, Mentawai and Lesser Sunda Is (Indonesia)
R. rex **King horseshoe bat** SW China
R. robinsoni **Peninsular or Robinson's horseshoe bat** Thailand, Malay Pen.
R. rouxi **Rufous horseshoe bat** Sri Lanka, India to S China, Vietnam
R. rufus **Large rufus horseshoe bat** Philippines
R. sedulus **Lesser woolly horseshoe bat** Malay Pen., Borneo
R. shameli **Shamel's horseshoe bat** Burma, Cambodia, Thailand, Malay Pen.
R. silvestris **Forest horseshoe bat** Gabon, Congo
R. simplex **Lombok horseshoe bat** Lesser Sunda Is (Indonesia)
R. simulator **Bushveld horseshoe bat** South Africa to S Sudan and Ethiopia; also Cameroon, Nigeria, Guinea
R. stheno **Lesser brown horseshoe bat** Thailand, Malay Pen., Sumatra and Java (Indonesia)
R. subbadius **Little Nepalese horseshoe bat** Assam (India), Nepal, Burma, Vietnam
R. subrufus **Small rufous horseshoe bat** Philippines
R. swinnyi **Swinny's horseshoe bat** South Africa to S DRC and E Africa
R. thomasi **Thomas' horseshoe bat** Yunnan (China), Burma, Vietnam, Thailand
R. trifoliatus **Trefoil horseshoe bat** NE India, Burma, SW Thailand, Malay Pen., Indonesia, Borneo
R. virgo **Yellow-faced horseshoe bat** Philippines
R. yunanensis **Dobson's horseshoe bat** NE India, Yunnan (China), Thailand

SUBFAMILY HIPPOSIDERINAE
Anthops

A. ornatus **Flower-faced bat** Solomon Is
***Asellia* Trident Leaf-nosed Bats**
A. patrizii **Patrizi's trident leaf-nosed bat** N Ethiopia, Red Sea islands
A. tridens **Trident leaf-nosed bat** Senegal, Morocco to Sudan, Egypt, Israel, Arabia to Pakistan
***Asselliscus* Tate's Trident-nosed Bats**
A. stoliczkanus **Stoliczka's trident bat** S China, Burma, Thailand, Laos, Vietnam, Malay Pen.
A. tricuspidatus **Temminck's trident bat** Maluku (Indonesia), New Guinea, Bismarck Arch. (Papua New Guinea), Solomon Is, Vanuatu
Cloeotis
C. percivali **Percival's trident bat** South Africa, Botswana, Zimbabwe, Mozambique to S DRC, Kenya
***Coelops* Tailless Leaf-nosed Bats**
C. frithi **East Asian tailless leaf-nosed bat** NE India to S China, Taiwan, Vietnam, Malay Pen., Java and Bali (Indonesia)
C. hirsutus **Philippine tailless leaf-nosed bat** Mindoro (Philippines)
C. robinsoni **Malayan tailless leaf-nosed bat** Malay Pen., Borneo
***Hipposideros* Roundleaf Bats**
H. abae **Aba roundleaf bat** Guinea-Bissau to SW Sudan, Uganda
H. armiger **Great roundleaf bat bat** N India, Nepal, Burma, S China, Taiwan, Vietnam, Laos, Thailand, Malay Pen.
H. ater **Dusky roundleaf bat** Sri Lanka, India to Malay Pen., Indonesia, Philippines, New Guinea to N Queensland, N Northern Territory, N Western Australia (Australia)
H. beatus **Benito roundleaf bat** Guinea-Bissau, Sierra Leone, Liberia, Ghana, Nigeria, Ivory Coast, Cameroon, Rio Muni (Equatorial Guinea), Gabon, N DRC
H. bicolor **Bicolored roundleaf bat** Malaysia to Philippines, Timor (Indonesia)
H. breviceps **Short-headed roundleaf bat** Mentawai Is (Indonesia)
H. caffer **Sundevall's roundleaf bat** SubSaharan Africa, Morocco, SW Arabian Pen.
H. calcaratus **Spurred roundleaf bat** New Guinea, Bismarck Arch. (Papua New Guinea), Solomon Is
H. camerunensis **Greater roundleaf bat** Cameroon, E DRC, W Kenya
H. cervinus **Fawn roundleaf bat** Malay Pen., Sumatra (Indonesia), Philippines to Vanuatu and NE Australia
H. cineraceus **Ashy roundleaf bat** Pakistan to Vietnam and Borneo
H. commersoni **Commerson's roundleaf bat** Gambia to Somalia south to South Africa, Madascar, São Tomé Is (São Tomé & Principe)
H. coronatus **Large Mindanao roundleaf bat** NE Mindanao (Philippines)
H. corynophyllus **Telefomin roundleaf bat** C New Guinea
H. coxi **Cox's roundleaf bat** Sarawak (N Borneo)
H. crumeniferus **Timor roundleaf bat** Timor (Indonesia)
H. curtus **Short-tailed roundleaf bat** Cameroon, Bioko (Equatorial Guinea)
H. cyclops **Cyclops roundleaf bat** S Sudan, Kenya to Senegal and Guinea-Bissau, Bioko (Equatorial Guinea)
H. diadema **Diadem roundleaf bat** Nicobar Is (India), Burma and Vietnam through Thailand, Malay Pen., Indonesia to New Guinea, Bismarck Arch. (Papua New Guina), Solomon Is, Philippines, NE and NC Australia
H. dinops **Fierce roundleaf bat** Peleng and Sulawesi (Indonesia), Bougainville Is (Papua New Guinea), Solomon Is
H. doriae **Borneo roundleaf bat** Borneo
H. dyacorum **Dayak roundleaf bat** Thailand Pen., Borneo
H. fuliginosus **Sooty roundleaf bat** Liberia to Cameroon, DRC and Ethiopia
H. fulvus **Fulvous roundleaf bat** Pakistan to Vietnam south to Sri Lanka
H. galeritus **Cantor's roundleaf bat** Sri Lanka, India through SE Asia to Java (Indonesia), Borneo
H. halophyllus **Thailand roundleaf bat** Thailand
H. inexpectatus **Crested roundleaf bat** N Sulawesi (Indonesia)
H. jonesi **Jones' roundleaf bat** Sierra Leone, Guinea to Mali, Burkina Faso, Nigeria
H. lamottei **Lamotte's roundleaf bat** Mt Nimba (Guinea, Liberia)
H. lankadiva **Indian roundleaf bat** S and C India, Sri Lanka
H. larvatus **Intermediate roundleaf bat** Bangladesh to Vietnam, Yunnan, Guangxi, Hainan (China), Malay Pen. to Sumatra, Java, and Sumba Is (Indonesia), Borneo
H. lekaguli **Large Asian roundleaf bat** Thailand
H. lylei **Shield-faced roundleaf bat** Burma, Thailand, Malay Pen.
H. macrobullatus **Big-eared roundleaf bat** Sulawesi, Seram, and Kangean Is (Indonesia)
H. maggietaylorae **Maggie Taylor's roundleaf bat** New Guinea, Bismarck Arch. (Papua New Guinea)
H. marisae **Aellen's roundleaf bat** Ivory Coast, Liberia, Guinea
H. megalotis **Ethiopian large-eared roundleaf bat** Saudi Arabia, NE Africa, Kenya
H. muscinus **Fly River roundleaf bat** New Guinea
H. nequam **Malayan roundleaf bat** Selangor (Malaysia)
H. obscurus **Philippine Forest roundleaf bat** Philippines
H. papua **Biak roundleaf bat** Maluku and Biak Is (Indonesia), Irian Jaya (New Guinea)
H. pomona **Pomona roundleaf bat** India to S China and Malay Pen.
H. pratti **Pratt's roundleaf bat** S China, Burma, Thailand, Vietnam, Malay Pen.
H. pygmaeus **Philippine pygmy roundleaf bat** Philippines
H. ridleyi **Ridley's roundleaf bat** Malay Pen., Borneo
H. ruber **Noack's roundleaf bat** Senegal to Ethiopia south to Angola, Zambia, Malawi, and Mozambique, Bioko (Equatorial Guinea), São Tomé and Principe
H. sabanus **Least roundleaf bat** Malay Pen., Sumatra (Indonesia), Borneo
H. schistaceus **Split roundleaf bat** S India
H. semoni **Semon's roundleaf bat** E New Guinea, N Queensland (Australia)
H. speoris **Schneider's roundleaf bat** S India, Sri Lanka
H. stenotis **Narrow-eared roundleaf bat** N Western Australia, Northern Territory, N Queensland (Australia)
H. turpis **Lesser roundleaf bat** Thailand, S Ryukyu Is (Japan)
H. wollastoni **Wollaston's roundleaf bat** W and C New Guinea
Paracoelops
P. megalotis **Vietnam leaf-nosed bat** C Vietnam
Rhinonicteris
R. aurantia **Orange leaf-nosed bat** N Western Australia, Northern Territory, NW Queensland (Australia)
***Triaenops* Triple Nose-leaf Bats**
T. furculus **Trouessart's trident bat** N and W Madagascar, Aldabra Is (Seychelles)
T. persicus **Persian trident bat** Somalia, Ethiopia south to Mozambique, Congo, Yemen, Oman, SW Iran

FAMILY NOCTILIONIDAE **Bulldog Bats**
Noctilio

N. albiventris **Lesser bulldog bat** S Mexico to Guianas, Peru, E Brazil, N Argentina
N. leporinus **Greater bulldog bat** Sinaloa (S Mexico) to Guianas, Peru, S Brazil, N Argentina, Trinidad, Greater and Lesser Antilles, S Bahamas

FAMILY MORMOOPIDAE
Leaf-chinned Bats

***Mormoops* Ghost-faced Bats**
M. blainvillii **Antillean ghost-faced bat or Blainville's leaf-chinned bat** Greater Antilles
M. megalophylla **Ghost-faced bat** S Texas and S Arizona (USA) south to Baja California (Mexico) to N Venezuela (incl. Margarita Is) and NW Peru, Aruba, Curacao, and Bonaire (Neth. Antilles), Trinidad
***Pteronotus* Moustached Bats**
P. davyi **Davy's naked-backed bat** S Baja California, S Sonora, and Nuevo Leon (Mexico) to N Venezuela and NW Peru, Trinidad, S Lesser Antilles
P. gymnonotus **Big naked-backed bat** S Veracruz (S Mexico) to Guyana, Peru, and NE Brazil
P. macleayii **MacLeay's moustached bat** Cuba, Jamaica
P. parnellii **Parnell's moustached bat** S Sonora and S Tamaulipas (Mexico) to Venezuela (incl. Margarita Is), Guianas, Peru, Brazil, Cuba, Jamaica, Hispaniola, Puerto Rico, Trinidad and Tobago
P. personatus **Wagner's moustached bat** S Sonora and S Tamaulipas (Mexico) to Colombia, Surinam, Peru, and Brazil
P. quadridens **Sooty moustached bat** Cuba, Jamaica, Hispaniola, Puerto Rico

FAMILY PHYLLOSTOMIDAE
American Leaf-nosed Bats

SUBFAMILY PHYLLOSTOMINAE
Chrotopterus

C. auritus **Big-eared woolly bat** Veracruz (S Mexico) to Guianas, S Brazil, N Argentina
***Lonchorhina* Sword-nosed Bats**
L. aurita **Tomes' sword-nosed bat** Oaxaca (Mexico) to Euador, Peru, and SE Brazil, Trinidad
L. fernandezi **Fernandez's sword-nosed bat** S Venezuela
L. marinkellei **Marinkelle's sword-nosed bat** E Colombia to Fr. Guiana
L. orinocensis **Orinoco sword-nosed bat** Colombia, Venezuela
Macrophyllum
M. macrophyllum **Long-legged bat** Tabasco (Mexico) to Peru, SE Brazil, Bolivia, NE Argentina
***Macrotus* Leaf-nosed Bats**
M. californicus **California leaf-nosed bat** S California and S Nevada (USA) south to N Mexico (incl. Baja California)
M. waterhousii **Waterhouse's leaf-nosed bat** Sonora and Hidalgo (Mexico) to Guatemala, Cuba, Jamaica, Hispaniola (incl. Beata Is, Dominican Rep.), Bahamas, Cayman Is
***Micronycteris* Little Big-eared Bats**
M. behnii **Behni's big-eared bat** S Peru, C Brazil
M. brachyotis **Yellow-throated big-eared bat** Oaxaca

(Mexico) to Fr. Guiana and Brazil, Trinidad
M. daviesi **Davies' big-eared bat** Costa Rica to Fr. Guiana and Peru
M. hirsuta **Hairy big-eared bat** Honduras to Fr. Guiana, Ecuador, Peru, Amazonian Brazil, Trinidad
M. megalotis **Little big-eared bat** Tamaulipas and Jalisco (Mexico) to Peru, Brazil, Bolivia, Margarita Is (Venezuela), Trinidad and Tobago, Grenada
M. minuta **White-bellied big-eared bat** Nicaragua to Guianas, Peru, S Brazil, Bolivia, Trinidad
M. nicefori **Niceforo's big-eared bat** Belize to N Colombia, Venezuela, Guianas, Peru, and Amazonian Brazil
M. pusilla **Least big-eared bat** E Colombia, NW Brazil
M. schmidtorum **Schmidts's big-eared bat** S Mexico to Venezuela, NE Peru, NE Brazil
M. sylvestris **Tri-colored big-eared bat** Nayarit and Veracruz (Mexico) to Peru and SE Brazil, Trinidad
Mimon **Hairy-nosed Bats**
M. bennettii **Golden bat** S Mexico to Colombia, Guianas, SE Brazil
M. crenulatum **Striped hairy-nosed bat** Chiapas and Campeche (Mexico) to Guianas, Ecuador, E Peru, E Brazil, Bolivia, Trinidad
Phylloderma
P. stenops **Pale-faced bat** S Mexico to Peru, SE Brazil, Bolivia
Phyllostomus **Spear-nosed Bats**
P. discolor **Pale spear-nosed bat** Oaxaca and Veracruz (S Mexico) to Guianas, Peru, SE Brazil, Paraguay, N Argentina, Margarita Is (Venezuela), Trinidad
P. elongatus **Lesser spear-nosed bat** Colombia to Guianas, Ecuador, E Peru, E Brazil, Bolivia
P. hastatus **Greater spear-nosed bat** Honduras to Guianas, Peru, E Brazil, Bolivia, Paraguay, N Argentina, Margarita is (Venezuela), Trinidad and Tobago
P. latifolius **Guianan spear-nosed bat** SE Colombia, Guianas
Tonatia **Round-eared Bats**
T. bidens **Greater round-eared bat** Chiapas (Mexico) and Belize to Brazil, Paraguay, and N Argentina, Trinidad
T. brasiliense **Pygmy round-eared bat** Veracruz (Mexico) to NE Brazil and Bolivia, Trinidad
T. carrikeri **Carriker's round-eared bat** Colombia, Venezuela, Surinam, Peru, N Brazil, Bolivia
T. evotis **Davis' round-eared bat** S Mexico, Belize, Guatemala, Honduras
T. schulzi **Schultz's round-eared bat** Guianas, N Brazil
T. silvicola **White-throated round-eared bat** Honduras to Guianas, E Brazil, Bolivia, and NE Argentina
Trachops
T. cirrhosus **Fringe-lipped bat** Oaxaca (Mexico) to Guianas, Ecuador, SE Brazil, Bolivia, Trinidad
Vampyrum
V. spectrum **Spectral bat or Linnaeus's false vampire bat** Veracruz (S Mexico) to Guianas, Ecuador, Peru, and N and SW Brazil, Trinidad

SUBFAMILY LONCHOPHYLLINAE
Lionycteris
L. spurrelli **Chestnut long-tongued bat** E Panama, Colombia, Venezuela, Guianas, Amazonian Peru and Brazil
Lonchophylla **Nectar Bats**
L. bokermanni **Bokermann's nectar bat** SE Brazil
L. dekeyseri **Dekeyser's nectar bat** E Brazil
L. handleyi **Handley's nectar bat** S Colombia, Ecuador, Peru
L. hesperia **Western nectar bat** Ecuador, N Peru
L. mordax **Goldman's nectar bat** Costa Rica to Ecuador, E Brazil
L. robusta **Orange nectar bat** Nicaragua to Venezuela and Ecuador
L. thomasi **Thomas' nectar bat** E Panama, Colombia, Venezuela, Guianas, Peru, Amazonian Brazil, Bolivia
Platalina
P. genovensium **Long-snouted bat** Peru

SUBFAMILY BRACHYPHYLLINAE
Brachyphylla **West Indian Fruit-eating Bats**
B. cavernarum **Antillean fruit-eating bat** Puerto Rico, Virgin Is, Lesser Antilles south to Barbados
B. nana **Cuban fruit-eating bat** Cuba, Hispaniola, Cayman Is, Caicos Is (W. Indies)

SUBFAMILY PHYLLONYCTERINAE
Erophylla
E. sezekorni **Buffy flower bat** Cuba, Jamaica, Hispaniola, Puerto Rico, Bahamas, Cayman Is
Phyllonycteris **Smooth-toothed Flower Bats**
P. aphylla **Jamaican flower bat** Jamaica
P. poeyi **Cuban flower bat** Cuba (Juventud Is), Hispaniola

SUBFAMILY GLOSSOPHAGINAE
Anoura **Tailless Bats**
A. caudifer **Tailed tailless bat** Colombia, Venezuela, Guianas, Ecuador, Peru, Brazil, Bolivia, NW Argentina
A. cultrata **Handley's tailless bat** Costa Rica, Panama, Colombia, Venezuela, Ecuador, Peru, Bolivia
A. geoffroyi **Geoffroy's tailless bat** Sinaloa and Tamaulipas (Mexico) south to Ecuador and Fr. Guiana, Peru, SE Brazil, Bolivia, Trinidad, Grenada
A. latidens **Broad-toothed tailless bat** Colombia, Venezuela, Peru
Choeroniscus **Long-tailed Bats**
C. godmani **Godman's long-tailed bat** Sinaloa (Mexico) to Colombia, Venezuela, Guyana, Surinam
C. intermedius **Intermediate long-tailed bat** Guianas, Peru, Amazonian Brazil, Trinidad
C. minor **Lesser long-tailed bat** C Colombia, Venezuela, Guianas, Ecuador, Peru, N Brazil, Bolivia
C. periosus **Greater long-tailed bat** W Colombia, W Ecuador
Choeronycteris
C. mexicana **Mexican long-tongued bat** SW USA to Honduras and El Salvador
Glossophaga **Long-tongued Bats**
G. commissarisi **Commissaris' long-tongued bat** Sinaloa (Mexico) to Panama, SE Colombia, E Ecuador, E Peru, NW Brazil
G. leachii **Gray long-tongued bat** Costa Rica to S Mexico
G. longirostris **Miller's long-tongued bat** Colombia, Venezuela (incl. Margarita Is), Guyana, N Ecuador, N Brazil, Aruba, Curacao, Bonaire (Neth. Antilles), Trinidad and Tobago, Grenada, St Vincent (Lesser Antilles)
G. morenoi **Western long-tongued bat** Chiapas to Tlaxala (S Mexico)
G. soricina **Pallas' long-tongued bat** S Mexico (incl. Tres Marias Is) to Guianas, Peru, SE Brazil, N Argentina, Margarita Is (Venezuela), Trinidad, Grenada
Hylonycteris
H. underwoodi **Underwood's long-tongued bat** Nayarit and Veracruz (S Mexico) to W Panama
Leptonycteris **Long-nosed Bats**
L. curasoae **Southern long-nosed bat** Aruba, Curacao, and Bonaire (Neth. Antilles)
L. nivalis **Mexican long-nosed bat** SE Arizona, W Texas (SW USA) to S Mexico
Lichonycteris
L. obscura **Dark long-tongued bat** Guatemala, Belize to Amazonian Brazil, Bolivia
Monophyllus **Single Leaf Bats**
M. plethodon **Insular single leaf bat** Anguila to St Vincent to Barbados (Lesser Antilles)
M. redmani **Leach's single leaf bat** Cuba, Jamaica, Hispaniola, Puerto Rico, S Bahamas
Musonycteris
M. harrisoni **Banana bat or Colima long-nosed bat** Jalisco to Guerrero (S Mexico)
Scleronycteris
S. ega **Ega long-tongued bat** S Venezuela, Amazonian Brazil

SUBFAMILY CAROLLIINAE
Carollia **Short-tailed Bats**
C. brevicauda **Silky short-tailed bat** San Luis Potosi (Mexico) to Peru, E Brazil, Bolivia
C. castanea **Chestnut short-tailed bat** Honduras to Venezuela, Peru, W Brazil, Bolivia
C. perspicillata **Seba's short-tailed bat** S Mexico to Guianas, Peru, SE Brazil, Bolivia, Paraguay, Trinidad and Tobago, Grenada
C. subrufa **Gray short-tailed bat** Jalisco (SW Mexico) to NW Nicaragua, Guyana
Rhinophylla **Little Fruit Bats**
R. alethina **Hairy little fruit bat** W Colombia, W Ecuador
R. fischerae **Fischer's little fruit bat** SE Colombia, Ecuador, Peru, Amazonian Brazil
R. pumilio **Dwarf little fruit bat** Colombia, Guianas, Ecuador, Peru, Brazil, Bolivia

SUBFAMILY STENODERMATINAE
Ametrida
A. centurio **Little white-shouldered bat** Panama, Venezuela, Guianas, Amazonian Brazil, Bonaire (Neth. Antilles), Trinidad
Ardops
A. nichollsi **Tree bat** St Eustatius to St Vincent (Lesser Antilles)
Ariteus
A. flavescens **Jamaican fig-eating bat** Jamaica
Artibeus **Fruit-eating Bats**
A. amplus **Large fruit-eating bat** N Colombia, Venezuela
A. anderseni **Andersen's fruit-eating bat** Ecuador, Peru, W Brazil, Bolivia
A. aztecus **Aztec fruit-eating bat** S Mexico, Guatemala, Honduras, Costa Rica, W Panama
A. cinereus **Gervais' fruit-eating bat** Venezuela, Guianas, N Brazil
A. concolor **Brown fruit-eating bat** Colombia, Venezuela, Guianas, Peru, N Brazil
A. fimbriatus **Fringed fruit-eating bat** S Brazil, Paraguay
A. fraterculus **Fraternal fruit-eating bat** Ecuador, Peru
A. glaucus **Silver fruit-eating bat** S Mexico to S Brazil, Bolivia, Trinidad and Tobago, Grenada
A. hartii **Velvety fruit-eating bat** Arizona (SW USA), Jalisco and Tamaulipas (Mexico) to Venezuela and Bolivia, Trinidad
A. hirsutus **Hairy fruit-eating bat** Sonora to Guerrero (Mexico)
A. inopinatus **Honduran fruit-eating bat** El Salvador, Honduras, Nicaragua
A. jamaicensis **Jamaican fruit-eating bat** Sinaloa and Tamaulipas (Mexico) to Venezuela and Ecuador, Trinidad and Tobago, Greater and Lesser Antilles
A. lituratus **Great fruit-eating bat** Sinaloa and Tamaulipas (Mexico) to S Brazil, Bolivia, N Argentina, Trinidad and Tobago, S Lesser Antilles, Tres Marias Is (Mexico)
A. obscurus **Dark fruit-eating bat** Colombia, Venezuela, Guianas, Ecuador, Peru, Brazil, Bolivia
A. phaeotis **Pygmy fruit-eating bat** Sinaloa and Veracruz (S Mexico) to Guyana and Ecuador
A. planirostris **Flat-faced fruit-eating bat** Colombia, Venezuela to N Argentina and E Brazil
A. toltecus **Toltec fruit-eating bat** S Mexico to Panama
Centurio
C. senex **Wrinkle-faced bat** Tamaulipas and Sinaloa (Mexico) to Venezuela, Trinidad and Tobago
Chiroderma **Big-eyed Bats**
C. doriae **Brazilian big-eyed bat** SE Brazil
C. improvisum **Guadeloupe big-eyed bat** Guadelope and Montserrat (Lesser Antilles)
C. salvini **Salvin's big-eyed bat** N Mexico to Venezuela and Bolivia
C. trinitatum **Little big-eyed bat** Panama to Peru, Amazonian Brazil, Bolivia, Trinidad
C. villosum **Hairy big-eyed bat** Hidalgo (Mexico) to Peru, S Brazil, Bolivia, Trinidad and Tobago
Ectophylla
E. alba **White bat** Honduras to W Panama, W Colombia
Mesophylla
M. macconnelli **MacConnell's bat** Costa Rica to Peru, Amazonian Brazil, Bolivia, Trinidad
Phyllops
P. falcatus **Cuban fig-eating bat** Cuba, Hispaniola
Platyrrhinus **Broad-nosed Bats**
P. aurarius **Eldorado broad-nosed bat** Colombia, S Venezuela, Surinam
P. brachycephalus **Short-headed broad-nosed bat** Colombia to Guianas, Ecuador, Peru, N Brazil, Bolivia
P. chocoensis **Choco broad-nosed bat** W Colombia
P. dorsalis **Thomas' broad-nosed bat** Panama to Peru and Bolivia
P. helleri **Heller's broad-nosed bat** Oaxaca and Veracruz (S Mexico) to Peru, Amazonian Brazil, Bolivia, Trinidad
P. infuscus **Buffy broad-nosed bat** Colombia to Peru, NW Brazil, Bolivia
P. lineatus **White-lined broad-nosed bat** Fr. Guiana, Surinam, Colombia to Peru, S and E Brazil, Bolivia, N Argentina, Uruguay
P. recifinus **Recife broad-nosed bat** E Brazil
P. umbratus **Shadowy broad-nosed bat** Panama, N and W Colombia, N Venezuela
P. vittatus **Greater broad-nosed bat** Costa Rica to Venezuela, Peru, Bolivia
Pygoderma
P. bilabiatum **Ipanema bat** Surinam, S Brazil, Bolivia, Paraguay, N Argentina

Sphaeronycteris
S. toxophyllum **Visored bat** Colombia to Venezuela, Peru, Amazonian Brazil, Bolivia
Stenoderma
S. rufum **Red fruit bat** Puerto Rico, Virgin Is (USA)
Sturnira **Yellow-shouldered Bats**
S. aratathomasi **Aratathomas' yellow-shouldered bat** Colombia, NW Venezuela, Ecuador, Peru
S. bidens **Bidentate yellow-shouldered bat** Colombia, Venezuela, Ecuador, Peru, poss. Amazonian Brazil
S. bogotensis **Bogota yellow-shouldered bat** Colombia, W Venezuela, Ecuador, Peru, Bolivia, NW Argentina
S. erythromos **Hairy yellow-shouldered bat** Venezuela to Bolivia
S. lilium **Little yellow-shouldered bat** Sonora and Tamaulipas (Mexico) to E Brazil, N Argentina, Uruguay, Trinidad and Tobago, Lesser Antilles
S. ludovici **Highland yellow-shouldered bat** Sonora and Tamaulipas (Mexico) to Guyana and Ecuador
S. luisi **Luis' yellow-shouldered bat** Costa Rica to Ecuador, NW Peru
S. magna **Greater yellow-shouldered bat** Colombia, Ecuador, Peru, Bolivia
S. mordax **Talamancan yellow-shouldered bat** Costa Rica, Panama
S. nana **Lesser yellow-shouldered bat** S Peru
S. thomasi **Thomas' yellow-shouldered bat** Guadeloupe (Lesser Antilles)
S. tildae **Tilda yellow-shouldered bat** Colombia, Venezuela, Guianas, Ecuador, Peru, Brazil, Bolivia, Trinidad
Uroderma **Tent-making Bats**
U. bilobatum **Tent-making bat** Veracruz and Oaxaca (Mexico) to Peru, Brazil, Bolivia, Trinidad
U. magnirostrum **Brown tent-making bat** Michoacan (Mexico) to Venezuela, Peru, Brazil, Bolivia
Vampyressa **Yellow-eared Bats**
V. bidens **Bidentate yellow-eared bat** Colombia and Guianas to Peru, Amazonian Brazil, N Bolivia
V. brocki **Brock's yellow-eared bat** Colombia, Guyana, Surinam, Amazonian Brazil
V. melissa **Melissa's yellow-eared bat** S Colombia, Fr. Guiana, Peru
V. nymphaea **Striped yellow-eared bat** Nicaragua to W Ecuador
V. pusilla **Little yellow-eared bat** Oaxaca and Veracruz (Mexico) to Guianas, Brazil, Bolivia, Paraguay
Vampyrodes
V. caraccioli **Great stripe-faced bat** Oaxaca (Mexico) to Peru, N Brazil, Bolivia, Trinidad and Tobago

SUBFAMILY DESMODONTINAE
Desmodus
D. rotundus **Common vampire bat** Mexico to N Chile, N Argentina, Uruguay, Margarita Is (Venezuela), Trinidad
Diaemus
D. youngi **White-winged vampire bat** Tamaulipas (Mexico) to E Brazil and N Argentina, Margarita Is (Venezuela), Trinidad
Diphylla
D. ecaudata **Hairy-legged vampire bat** S Texas (USA) to Venezuela, Peru, E Brazil, Bolivia

FAMILY NATALIDAE
Funnel-eared Bats
Natalus
N. lepidus **Gervais' funnel-eared bat** Cuba, Bahamas
N. micropus **Cuban funnel-eared bat** Cuba, Jamaica, Hispaniola, Providencia Is (Colombia)
N. stramineus **Mexican funnel-eared bat** Mexico (incl. S Baja California) to Brazil, Lesser Antilles, Jamaica, Hispaniola
N. tumidifrons **Bahaman funnel-eared bat** Bahamas
N. tumidirostris **Trinidadian funnel-eared bat** Colombia, Venezuela, Surinam, Curacao and Bonaire (Neth. Antilles), Trinidad and Tobago

FAMILY FURIPTERIDAE **Thumbless Bats**
Amorphochilus
A. schnablii **Smoky bat** W Ecuador (incl. Puna Is), W Peru, N Chile
Furipterus
F. horrens **Thumbless bat** Costa Rica to Peru and E Brazil, Trinidad

FAMILY THYROPTERIDAE
Disk-winged Bats
Thyroptera
T. discifera **Peter's disk-winged bat** Nicaragua, Panama, Colombia to Guianas, Peru, Brazil, Bolivia

T. tricolor **Spix's disk-winged bat** Veracruz (Mexico) to Guianas, Peru, E Brazil, Bolivia, Trinidad

FAMILY MYZOPODIDAE

Myzopoda
M. aurita **Sucker-footed bat** Madagascar

FAMILY VESPERTILIONIDAE **Vesper Bats**

SUBFAMILY KERIVOULINAE

Kerivoula **Woolly Bats**
K. aerosa **Dubious trumpet-eared bat** Poss. South Africa
K. africana **Tanzanian woolly bat** Tanzania
K. agnella **St. Aignan's trumpet-eared bat** Papua New Guinea
K. argentata **Damara woolly bat** S Kenya, Uganda to Angola, Namibia, E South Africa
K. atrox **Groove-toothed bat** S Thailand, Malay Pen., Sumatra (Indonesia), Borneo
K. cuprosa **Copper woolly bat** Kenya, N DRC, S Cameroon
K. eriophora **Ethiopian woolly bat** Ethiopia
K. flora **Flores woolly bat** Lesser Sunda Is (Indonesia), Borneo
K. hardwickei **Hardwicke's woolly bat** India, Sri Lanka, Burma, China, Thailand, Malay Pen., Indonesia, Philippines
K. intermedia **Small woolly bat** Malay Pen., Borneo
K. jagori **Peters' trumpet-eared bat** Indonesia, Borneo, Philippines
K. lanosa **Lesser woolly bat** Liberia to Ethiopia to South Africa
K. minuta **Least woolly bat** S Thailand, Malay Pen., Borneo
K. muscina **Fly River trumpet-eared bat** C New Guinea
K. myrella **Bismarck trumpet-eared bat** Lesser Sunda Is (Indonesia), Bismarck Arch. (Papua New Guinea)
K. papillosa **Papillose woolly bat** NE India, Vietnam, Malay Pen., Sumatra, Java, and Sulawesi (Indonesia), Borneo
K. papuensis **Golden-tipped bat** SE New Guinea, Queensland, New South Wales (Australia)
K. pellucida **Clear-winged woolly bat** Malay Pen., Sumatra and Java (Indonesia), Borneo, Philippines
K. phalaena **Spurrell's woolly bat** Liberia, Ghana, Cameroon, Congo, DRC
K. picta **Painted bat** India, Sri Lanka to S China, Vietnam, Malay Pen., Indonesia, Borneo
K. smithi **Smith's woolly bat** Liberia, Ivory Coast, Nigeria, Cameroon, N and E DRC, Kenya
K. whiteheadi **Whitehead's woolly bat** S Thailand, Malay Pen., Borneo, Philippines

SUBFAMILY VESPERTILIONINAE

Antrozous **Pallid Bats**
A. dubiaquercus **Van Gelder's bat** Mexico (incl. Tres Marias Is), Belize, Honduras, Costa Rica
A. pallidus **Pallid bat** Mexico to Kansas (USA) and British Columbia (SW Canada), Cuba

Barbastella **Barbastelle's**
B. barbastellus **Western barbastelle** England and W Europe to Caucasus, Ukraine, Turkey, Morocco, Mediterranean islands, Canarias Is
B. leucomelas **Eastern barbastelle** Caucasus to Pamir (Tajikistan), N Iran, Afghanistan, India, W China, Honshu and Hokkaido (Japan), Egypt, N Ethiopia

Chalinolobus **Wattled Bats**
C. alboguttatus **Allen's striped bat** DRC, Cameroon
C. argentatus **Silvered bat** Cameroon to Kenya, Tanzania south to Angola
C. beatrix **Beatrix's bat** Ivory Coast, Congo, Kenya
C. dwyeri **Large-eared pied bat** New South Wales, adj. Queensland (Australia)
C. egeria **Bibundi bat** Cameroon, Uganda
C. gleni **Glen's wattled bat** Cameroon, Uganda
C. gouldii **Gould's wattled bat** Australia, Tasmania, New Caledonia, Norfolk Is (Australia)
C. kenyacola **Kenyan wattled bat** Kenya
C. morio **Chocolate wattled bat** S Australia, Tasmania
C. nigrogriseus **Hoary wattled bat** SE New Guinea, N and E Australia
C. picatus **Little pied bat** C and S Queensland, NW New South Wales, South Australia (Australia)
C. poensis **Abo bat** Senegal to Uganda, Bioko (Equatorial Guinea)
C. superbus **Pied bat** Ivory Coast, Ghana, NE DRC
C. tuberculatus **Long-tailed wattled bat** New Zealand
C. variegatus **Butterfly bat** Senegal to Somalia to South Africa

Eptesicus **Serotines**
E. baverstocki **Inland Forest bat** C and S Australia
E. bobrinskii **Bobrinski's serotine** N Caucasus, Turkmenistan, Uzbekistan, Kazakhstan
E. bottae **Botta's serotine** Egypt, Turkey and Yemen east to Pakistan and Mongolia
E. brasiliensis **Brazilian brown bat** Veracruz (S Mexico) to N Argentina, Uruguay, Trinidad and Tobago
E. brunneus **Dark-brown serotine** Liberia to DRC
E. capensis **Cape serotine** Guinea to Ethiopia to South Africa, Madagascar
E. demissus **Surat serotine** Thailand Pen.
E. diminutus **Diminutive serotine** Venezuela, E Brazil, Paraguay, N Argentina, Uruguay
E. douglasorum **Yellow-lipped bat** Kimberley (N Western Australia)
E. flavescens **Yellow serotine** Angola, Burundi
E. floweri **Horn-skinned bat** Sudan, Mali
E. furinalis **Argentine brown-bat** Jalisco and Tamaulipas (Mexico) to Guianas, Brazil, N Argentina
E. fuscus **Big brown bat** S Canada to Colombia, N Brazil, Greater and Lesser Antilles, Bahamas
E. guadeloupensis **Guadeloupe big brown bat** Guadeloupe (Lesser Antilles)
E. guineensis **Tiny serotine** Senegal, Guinea to Ethiopia and NE DRC
E. hottentotus **Long-tailed house bat** South Africa to Angola and Kenya
E. innoxius **Harmless serotine** W Ecuador, NW Peru, Puna Is (Ecuador)
E. kobayashii **Kobayashi's serotine** Korea
E. melckorum **Melck's house bat** S South Africa, Zambia, Mozambique, Tanzania
E. nasutus **Sind bat** Arabia, Iraq, Iran, Afghanistan, Pakistan
E. nilssoni **Northern bat** W and E Europe to E Siberia and Sakhalin Is (Russia) and NW China, Scandinavia south to Bulgaria, Iraq, N Iran, Pamirs (Tajikistan), W China (excl. Xizang), Nepal, Honshu and Hokkaido (Japan)
E. pachyotis **Thick-eared bat** Assam (India), Burma, N Thailand
E. platyops **Lagos serotine** Nigeria, Senegal, Bioko (Equatorial Guinea)
E. pumilus **Eastern Forest bat** N Western Australia, Northern Territory, Queensland, New South Wales, South Australia (Australia)
E. regulus **Southern Forest bat** SW and SE Australia, Tasmania
E. rendalli **Rendall's serotine** Gambia to Somalia to Botswana and Mozambique
E. sagittula **Large Forest bat** SE Australia, Tasmania, Lord Howe Is (Australia)
E. serotinus **Serotine** N and SubSaharan Africa, W Europe to S Russia to Himalayas, China and Thailand to N Korea, Taiwan
E. somalicus **Somali serotine** Guinea-Bissau to Somalia to Namibia and South Africa, Madagascar
E. tatei **Sombre bat** NE India
E. tenuipinnis **White-winged serotine** Senegal to Kenya to DRC and Angola
E. vulturnusi **Little Forest bat** SE Australia, Tasmania

Euderma
E. maculatum **Spotted or Pinto bat** SW Canada, Montana (NW USA) south to Queretaro (Mexico)

Eudiscopus
E. denticulus **Disc-footed bat** C Burma, Laos

Glischropus **Thick-thumbed Bats**
G. javanus **Javan thick-thumbed bat** Java (Indonesia)
G. tylopus **Common thick-thumbed bat** Burma, Thailand, Malay Pen., Sumatra and Maluku Is (Indonesia), Borneo, SW Philippines

Hesperoptenus **False Serotines**
H. blanfordi **Blanford's bat** Burma, Thailand, Malay Pen., Borneo
H. doriae **False serotine bat** Malay Pen., Borneo
H. gaskelli **Gaskell's false serotine** Sulawesi (Indonesia)
H. tickelli **Tickell's bat** India (incl. Andaman Is), Sri Lanka, Nepal, Bhutan, Burma, Thailand
H. tomesi **Large false serotine** Malay Pen., Borneo

Histiotus **Big-eared Brown Bats**
H. alienus **Strange big-eared brown bat** SE Brazil, Uruguay
H. macrotus **Big-eared brown bat** S Peru, S Bolivia, Chile, NW Argentina
H. montanus **Small big-eared brown bat** Colombia, Venezuela, Ecuador, Peru, W Bolivia, Chile, Argentina, Uruguay
H. velatus **Tropical big-eared brown bat** E Brazil, Paraguay

Ia
I. io **Great evening bat** NE India, S China, Vietnam, Laos, Thailand

Idionycteris
I. phyllotis **Allen's big-eared bat** Distrito Federal (Mexico) to S Utah and S Nevada (SW USA)

Laephotis **African Long-eared Bats**
L. angolensis **Angolan long-eared bat** Angola, DRC
L. botswanae **Botswanan long-eared bat** N South Africa, Zimbabwe, Botswana, Zambia, Malawi, DRC
L. namibensis **Namib long-eared bat** Namibia
L. wintoni **De Winton's long-eared bat** Ethiopia, Kenya, SW South Africa

Lasionycteris
L. noctivagans **Silver-haired bat** S Canada, USA (incl. S Alaska), NE Mexico, Bermuda

Lasiurus **Hairy-tailed Bats**
L. borealis **Red bat** C Canada to Brazil, Uruguay, Chile, Argentina, Cuba, Jamaica, Hispaniola, Puerto Rico, Bermuda, Bahamas, Trinidad and Tobago, Galapagos (Ecuador)
L. castaneus **Tacarcuna bat** Costa Rica, Panama
L. cinereus **Hoary bat** Canada, USA, Mexico, Guatemala, Colombia, Venezuela to C Chile, C Argentina, Uruguay, Hawaii (USA), Bermuda, Galapagos (Ecuador)
L. ega **Southern yellow bat** SW USA to Brazil, Argentina, Uruguay, Trinidad
L. egregius **Big red bat** Panama, Fr. Guiana, Brazil
L. intermedius **Northern yellow bat** E and S USA to Sinaloa (Mexico) to Honduras, Cuba
L. seminolus **Seminole bat** S and E USA, Cuba

Mimetillus
M. moloneyi **Moloney's flat-headed bat** Sierra Leone to Ethiopia south to Tanzania, Zambia, Angola, Bioko (Equatorial Guinea)

Myotis **Little Brown Bats**
M. abei **Sakhalin myotis** Sakhalin (Russia)
M. adversus **Large-footed bat** Taiwan and Malay Pen. south to New Guinea, Bismarck Arch. (Papua New Guinea), Solomon Is, Vanuatu, N and E coastal Australia
M. aelleni **Southern myotis** SW Argentina
M. albescens **Silver-tipped myotis** Veracruz (Mexico) to N Argentina, Uruguay
M. altarium **Sichuan myotis** Sichuan (China), Thailand
M. annectans **Hairy-faced bat** NE India to Thailand
M. atacamensis **Atacama myotis** S Peru, N Chile
M. auriculus **Southwestern myotis** Arizona and New Mexico (SW USA) to Jalisco and Veracruz (Mexico)
M. australis **Australian myotis** New South Wales (Australia)
M. austroriparius **Southeastern myotis** SE USA north to Indiana
M. bechsteini **Bechstein's bat** Europe to Caucasus, Iran
M. blythii **Lesser mouse-eared bat** Mediterranean Europe and NW Africa, Israel, Crimea (Ukraine), Turkey and Caucasus to Kyrgyzstan, Afghanistan, and Himalayas, Inner Mongolia and Shaanxi (China)
M. bocagei **Rufous mouse-eared bat** Senegal to S Yemen south to Angola, Zambia, N South Africa
M. bombinus **Far eastern myotis** NE China, SE Siberia (Russia), Korea, Japan
M. brandti **Brandt's bat** Britain, Spain, Greece to Kazakhstan, Mongolia, Korea, Japan, Ussuri region and E Siberia (incl. Sakhalin Is, Kamchatka Pen., Kurile Is)
M. californicus **California myotis** S Alaska (USA) to Baja California (Mexico) and Guatemala
M. capaccinii **Long-fingered myotis** Mediterranean Europe and NW Africa, Israel, Iraq, Iran, Turkey, Uzbekistan
M. chiloensis **Chilean myotis** C and S Chile
M. chinensis **Large myotis** Sichuan and Yunnan to Jiangsu (China), Hong Kong (China), Thailand
M. cobanensis **Guatemalan myotis** C Guatemala
M. dasycneme **Pond bat** France and Sweden east to Yenisei R (Russia) south to Ukraine and Kazakhstan, Manchuria (China)
M. daubentoni **Daubenton's bat** Britain, Scandinavia and Europe east to Kamchatka Pen., Vladivostok, Sakhalin and Kurile Is (Russia), Assam (India), Manchuria, E and S China, Korea, Japan
M. dominicensis **Dominican myotis** N Lesser Antilles
M. elegans **Elegant myotis** San Luis Potosi (N Mexico) to Costa Rica
M. emarginatus **Geoffroy's bat** N Africa (Morocco to Tunisia), Israel, Lebanon, S Europe to Netherlands and Poland east to Caucasus, Iran, Afghanistan, Uzbekistan
M. evotis **Long-eared myotis** SW Canada to New Mexico (USA) and Baja California (Mexico)
M. findleyi **Findley's myotis** Tres Marias Is (Mexico)
M. formosus **Hodgson's bat** Afghanistan to Guizhou, Giangsu, Fujian (China), Taiwan, Korea, Tsushima Is (Japan), Sumatra, Java, Sulawesi, Bali (Indonesia), Philippines
M. fortidens **Cinnamon myotis** Sonora and Veracruz (Mexico) to Guatemala
M. frater **Fraternal myotis** Afghanistan, Uzbekistan and S Sbieria to SE Russia, Heilongjiang (NE China), SE China, Korea, Japan
M. goudoti **Malagasy mouse-eared bat** Madagascar, Comoros
M. grisescens **Gray myotis** C and SE USA
M. hasseltii **Lesser large-footed bat** Sri Lanka, Burma, Thailand, Cambodia, Vietnam, Malay Pen., Sumatra, Java, Mentawai Is, and Riau Arch. (Indonesia), Borneo
M. horsfieldii **Horsfield's bat** India, Sri lanka, SE China, Thailand, Malay Pen., Java, Bali, and Sulawesi (Indonesia), Borneo, Philippines
M. hosonoi **Hosono's bat** Honshu (Japan)
M. ikonnikovi **Ikonnikov's bat** Mongolia, NE China, Ussuris (Russia) and N Korea to L. Baikal (Russia), Sakhalin Is (Russia), Hokkaido Is (Japan)
M. insularum **Insular myotis** Samoa
M. keaysi **Hairy-legged myotis** Tamaulipas (Mexico) to Venezuela and N Argentina, Trinidad
M. keenii **Keen's myotis** Alaska (USA) to W Washington (USA), Mackenzie to Prince Edward Is (Canada) south to Florida (USA)
M. leibii **Eastern small-footed myotis** S British Columbia (Canada) south to Mexico (incl. Baja California) east to Maine (USA) and S Quebec (Canada)
M. lesueuri **Lesueur's hairy bat** SW South Africa
M. levis **Yellowish myotis** SE Brazil, Bolivia, Argentina, Uruguay
M. longipes **Kashmir cave bat** Afghanistan, Kashmir
M. lucifugus **Little brown myotis or bat** Alaska (USA) to Labrador and Newfoundland (Canada) south to Distrito Federal (Mexico)
M. macrodactylus **Big-footed myotis** SE Russia, S China, Japan, Kurile Is (Russia)
M. macrotarsus **Pallid large-footed myotis** N Borneo, Philippines
M. martiniquensis **Schwartz's myotis** Lesser Antilles
M. milleri **Miller's myotis** N Baja California (Mexico)
M. montivagus **Burmese whiskered bat** India, Burma, Yunnan to Fujian (China), Malay Pen., Borneo
M. morrisi **Morris' bat** Ethiopia, Nigeria
M. muricola **Whiskered myotis** Afghanistan to Taiwan and New Guinea
M. myotis **Mouse-eared bat** S England, C and S Europe east to Ukraine, Turkey, Lebanon, Israel, Mediterranean islands
M. mystacinus **Whiskered bat** Ireland and Scandinavia to N China south to Morocco, Iran, NW Himalayas, S China
M. nattereri **Natterer's bat** NW Africa, Europe (excl. Scandinavia), Crimea (Ukraine) and Caucasus to Turkmenistan, Turkey, Israel, Iraq
M. nesopolus **Curacao myotis** NE Venezuela, Curacao and Bonaire (Neth. Antilles)
M. nigricans **Black myotis** Nayarit and Tamaulipas (Mexico) to Peru, S Brazil, N Argentina, Trinidad and Tobago, Grenada
M. oreias **Singapore whiskered bat** Singapore
M. oxyotus **Montane myotis** Costa Rica, Panama, Venezuela to Bolivia
M. ozensis **Honshu myotis** Honshu (Japan)
M. peninsularis **Peninsular myotis** S Baja California (Mexico)
M. pequinius **Peking myotis** Hopeh, Shandong, Henan, Jiangsu (China)
M. planiceps **Flat-headed myotis** Mexico
M. pruinosus **Frosted myotis** Honshu and Shikoku (Japan)
M. ricketti **Rickett's big-footed bat** Fujian, Anhui, Jiangsu, Shandong, Yunnan, Hong Kong (China)
M. ridleyi **Ridley's bat** Malay Pen., Sumatra (Indonesia), Borneo
M. riparius **Riparian myotis** Honduras to E Brazil and Uruguay, Trinidad
M. rosseti **Thick-thumbed myotis** Cambodia, Thailand
M. ruber **Red myotis** SE Brazil, Paraguay, NE Argentina
M. schaubi **Schaub's myotis** Extinct: formerly Caucasus, W Iran
M. scotti **Scott's mouse-eared bat** Ethiopia

M. seabrai **Angola hairy bat** NW South Africa, Namibia, Angola
M. sicarius **Mandelli's mouse-eared bat** Sikkim (NE India)
M. siligorensis **Himalayan whiskered bat** N India to S China and Vietnam to Malay Pen., Borneo
M. simus **Velvety myotis** Colombia, Ecuador, Peru, N Brazil, Bolivia, Paraguay, NE Argentina
M. sodalis **Indiana bat** E USA west to Wisconsin and Oklahoma
M. stalkeri **Kei myotis** Maluku (Indonesia)
M. thysanodes **Fringed myotis** Chiapas (Mexico) to SW South Dakota (USA) and S British Columbia (Canada)
M. tricolor **Cape hairy bat** Ethiopia and DRC south to South Africa
M. velifer **Cave myotis** C and SW USA to Honduras
M. vivesi **Fish-eating bat** Coastal Sonora and Baja California (Mexico)
M. volans **Long-legged myotis** Alaska (USA) to Mexico (incl. Baja California) east to South Dakota (USA) and C Alberta (Canada)
M. welwitschii **Welwitch's bat** Ethiopia to South Africa
M. yesoensis **Yoshiyuki's myotis** Hokkaido (Japan)
M. yumanensis **Yuma myotis** Mexico (incl. Baja California) north to British Columbia (Canada) east to Montana and W Texas (USA)
Nyctalus Noctule Bats
N. aviator **Birdlike noctule** E China, Korea, Japan
N. azoreum **Azores noctule** Azores (Portugal)
N. lasiopterus **Giant noctule** W Europe to Urals and Caucasus, Turkey, Kazakhstan, Iran, Morocco, Libya
N. leisleri **Lesser or Leisler's noctule** Britain, Ireland, W Europe to Urals and Caucasus, E Afghanistan, W Himalayas, NW Africa, Madeira Is (Morocco), Azores (Portugal)
N. montanus **Mountain noctule** Afghanistan, Pakistan, N India, Nepal
N. noctula **Noctule** Europe to Urals and Caucasus, Morocco, Algeria, Israel to SE Turkey, W Turkmenistan to SW Siberia (Russia), Himalayas, China, Taiwan, Honshu (Japan), Malay Pen.
Nycticeius Broad-nosed Bats
N. balstoni **Western broad-nosed bat** Australia
N. greyii **Little broad-nosed bat** Australia
N. humeralis **Evening or Twilight bat** N Veracruz (Mexico) to C, E and SE USA
N. rueppellii **Rüppell's broad-nosed bat** E Queensland and E New South Wales (Australia)
N. sanborni **Northern broad-nosed bat** SE New Guinea, NE Queensland, Northern Territory, N Western Australia (Australia)
N. schlieffeni **Schlieffen's bat** SW Arabia, Mauritania and Ghana to NE Africa and Tanzania, Mozambique, Namibia, Botswana, South Africa
Nyctophilus Long-eared Bats
N. arnhemensis **Northern long-eared bat** N Australia
N. geoffroyi **Lesser long-eared bat** Australia (excl. NE), Tasmania
N. gouldi **Gould's long-eared bat** New Guinea, N and E Queensland, Victoria, E New South Wales, N Northern Territory, N and W Western Australia (Australia)
N. heran **Sunda long-eared bat** Lesser Sunda Is (Indonesia)
N. microdon **Small-toothed long-eared bat** EC New Guinea
N. microtis **New Guinea long-eared bat** E New Guinea
N. timoriensis **Greater long-eared bat** E New Guinea, Timor (Indonesia), Australia (incl. Tasmania)
N. walkeri **Pygmy long-eared bat** Northern Territory and N Western Australia (Australia)
Otonycteris
O. hemprichi **Desert or Hemprich's long-eared bat** Morocco and Niger to Egypt and Arabia to Tajikistan, Afghanistan, and Kashmir
Pharotis
P. imogene **New Guinea big-eared bat** SE New Guinea
Philetor
P. brachypterus **Rohu's bat** Nepal, Malay Pen., Sumatra, Java, Sulawesi (Indonesia), Borneo, Philippines, New Guinea, New Britain Is (Bismarck Arch., Papua New Guinea)
Pipistrellus Pipistrelles
P. aegyptius **Egyptian pipistrelle** Egypt, N Sudan, Libya, Algeria, Burkina Faso
P. aero **Mt. Gargyes pipistrelle** NW Kenya
P. affinis **Chocolate pipistrelle** N India, NE Burma, Yunnan (China)
P. anchietai **Anchieta's pipistrelle** S DRC, Angola, Zambia
P. anthonyi **Anthony's pipistrelle** Changyinku (Burma)
P. arabicus **Arabian pipistrelle** Oman
P. ariel **Desert pipistrelle** Egypt, N Sudan
P. babu **Himalayan pipistrelle** Afghanistan, Pakistan, N India, Nepal, Bhutan, Burma, SW China
P. bodenheimeri **Bodenheimer's pipistrelle** Israel, S Yemen, Oman
P. cadornae **Cadorna's pipistrelle** NE India, Burma, Thailand
P. ceylonicus **Kelaart's pipistrelle** Pakistan, India, Sri Lanka, Burma, Guangxi and Hainan (China), Vietnam, Borneo
P. circumdatus **Black gilded pipistrelle** NE India, Burma, SW China, Malay Pen., Java (Indonesia)
P. coromandra **Indian pipistrelle** Afghanistan, Pakistan, India, Sri Lanka, Nepal, Bhutan, Burma, S China, Vietnam, Thailand, Nicobar Is (India)
P. crassulus **Broad-headed pipistrelle** S Sudan, Cameroon, DRC, Angola
P. cuprosus **Coppery pipistrelle** Borneo
P. dormeri **Dormer's pipistrelle** Pakistan, NW, S and E India
P. eisentrauti **Eisentraut's pipistrelle** Liberia to Kenya and Somalia
P. endoi **Endo's pipistrelle** Honshu (Japan)
P. hesperus **Western pipistrelle** Washington to SW Oklahoma (USA), Mexico (incl. Baja California)
P. imbricatus **Brown pipistrelle** Java, Bali, Lesser Sunda Is, Kangean Is (Indonesia), Borneo
P. inexspectatus **Aellen's pipistrelle** Kenya, Uganda, DRC, Cameroon, Benin
P. javanicus **Javan pipistrelle** Ussuris, China, Korea and SE Asia to Lesser Sunda Is (Indonesia), Philippines, Japan
P. joffrei **Joffre's pipistrelle** N Burma
P. kitcheneri **Red-brown pipistrelle** Borneo
P. kuhlii **Kuhl's pipistrelle** S Europe to the Caucasus to Kazakhstan and Pakistan, SW Asia, Africa, Canarias Is
P. lophurus **Burma pipistrelle** Burma Pen.
P. macrotis **Big-eared pipistrelle** Malay Pen., Sumatra and Bali (Indonesia), Borneo
P. maderensis **Madeira pipistrelle** Madeira (Portugal), Canarias Is
P. mimus **Indian pygmy pipistrelle** Afghanistan, Pakistan, India, Sri Lanka, Nepal, Bhutan, Burma, Vietnam, Thailand
P. minahassae **Minahassa pipistrelle** Sulawesi (Indonesia)
P. mordax **Pungent pipistrelle** Java (Indonesia)
P. musciculus **Mouselike pipistrelle** Cameroon, Gabon, DRC
P. nanulus **Tiny pipistrelle** Sierra Leone to Kenya, Bioko (Equatorial Guinea)
P. nanus **Banana pipistrelle** South Africa to Ethiopia and Sudan, Niger, Mali, Senegal, Madagascar
P. nathusii **Nathusius' pipistrelle** W Europe to Urals and Caucasus and W Turkey; also S England
P. paterculus **Mount Popa pipistrelle** N India, Burma, SW China, Thailand
P. peguensis **Pegu pipistrelle** Burma
P. permixtus **Dar-es-Salaam pipistrelle** Tanzania
P. petersi **Peters' pipistrelle** Sulawesi and Maluku (Indonesia), Borneo, Philippines
P. pipistrellus **Common pipistrelle** S Scandinavia and W Europe to Volga R and Caucasus, Morocco, Israel and Turkey to Kazakhstan, Kashmir and Xinjiang (China); also British Isles
P. pulveratus **Chinese pipistrelle** Sichuan, Yunnan, Hunan, Giangsu, Fujian, Hong Kong (China), Thailand
P. rueppelli **Rüppell's pipistrelle** Senegal and Algeria and Egypt and Iraq south to Botswana and N South Africa
P. rusticus **Rusty pipistrelle** Liberia and Ethiopia south to South Africa
P. savii **Savi's pipistrelle** Iberian Pen., Morocco and Canarias Is through the Caucasus to NE China, Korea, and Japan and through Iran and Afghanistan to N India and Burma
P. societatis **Social pipistrelle** Malay Pen.
P. stenopterus **Narrow-winged pipistrelle** Malay Pen., Sumatra and Riau Arch. (Indonesia), N Borneo, Mindanao (Philippines)
P. sturdeei **Sturdee's pipistrelle** Bonin Is (Japan)
P. subflavus **Eastern pipistrelle** SE Canada, E USA, Honduras
P. tasmaniensis **Eastern false or Tasmanian pipistrelle** S Australia (excl. South Australia), Tasmania
P. tenuis **Least pipistrelle** Thailand to New Guinea, Bismarck Arch. (Papua New Guinea), Solomon Is, Vanuatu, N Australia, Cocos Keeling and Christmas Is (Ind. Oc.)
Plecotus Big-eared Bats
P. auritus **Brown big-eared bat** Spain, Ireland, and Norway to Sakhalin Is (Russia), N China, Nepal, Japan
P. austriacus **Gray big-eared bat** Senegal, Spain, and England to Mongolia and W China, Canarias Is, Cape Verde Is (Atl. Oc.)
P. mexicanus **Mexican big-eared bat** Mexico (incl. Cozumel Is)
P. rafinesquii **Rafinesque's big-eared bat** SE USA
P. taivanus **Taiwan big-eared bat** Taiwan
P. teneriffae **Canary big-eared bat** Canarias Is
P. townsendii **Townsend's big-eared bat** S British Columbia (Canada) to W USA to Oaxaca (Mexico) east to Virginia (E USA)
Rhogeessa Little Yellow Bats
R. alleni **Allen's yellow bat** Oaxaca to Zacatecas (Mexico)
R. genowaysi **Genoways' yellow bat** S Chiapas (S Mexico)
R. gracilis **Slender yellow bat** Mexico
R. minutilla **Tiny yellow bat** Colombia, Venezuela (incl. Margarita Is)
R. mira **Least yellow bat** S Michoacan (S Mexico)
R. parvula **Little yellow bat** Oaxaca to Sonoro (Mexico), Tres Marias Is (Mexico)
R. tumida **Black-winged little yellow bat** Tamaulipas (Mexico) to Ecuador, NE Brazil, Bolivia, Trinidad and Tobago
Scotoecus House Bats
S. albofuscus **Light-winged lesser house bat** Gambia to Kenya and Mozambique
S. hirundo **Dark-winged lesser house bat** Senegal to Ethiopia south to Angola, Zambia, Malawi
S. pallidus **Desert yellow bat** Pakistan, N India
Scotomanes Harlequin Bats
S. emarginatus **Emarginate harlequin bat** India
S. ornatus **Harlequin bat** NE India, Burma, S China, Vietnam, Thailand
Scotophilus Yellow Bats
S. borbonicus **Lesser yellow bat** Madagascar, Reunion
S. celebensis **Sulawesi yellow bat** Sulawesi (Indonesia)
S. dinganii **African yellow bat** Senegal and Sierra Leone to Somalia and S Yemen south to Namibia and South Africa
S. heathi **Greater Asiatic yellow bat** Afghanistan to S China south to Sri Lanka and Vietnam
S. kuhlii **Lesser Asiatic yellow bat** Pakistan to Taiwan, south to Sri Lanka and Malay Pen., to Philippines and Aru Is (Indonesia)
S. leucogaster **White-bellied yellow bat** Mauritania and Senegal to Ethiopia and N Kenya
S. nigrita **Schreber's yellow bat** Senegal to Sudan and Kenya to Mozambique
S. nux **Nut-colored yellow bat** Sierra Leone to Kenya
S. robustus **Robust yellow bat** Madagascar
S. viridis **Greenish yellow bat** Senegal to Ethiopia south to Namibia and South Africa
Tylonycteris Bamboo Bats
T. pachypus **Lesser bamboo bat** India (incl. Andaman Is) and S China to Lesser Sunda Is (Indonesia) and Philippines
T. robustula **Greater bamboo bat** S China to Sulawesi and Lesser Sunda Is (Indonesia) and Philippines
Vespertilio Particolored Bats
V. murinus **Particolored bat** Norway and Britain to Ussuris, Korea, Taiwan, Japan
V. superans **Asian particolored bat** China, Ussuris, Korea, Taiwan, Japan

SUBFAMILY MURININAE
Harpiocephalus
H. harpia **Hairy-winged bat** India to Taiwan and Vietnam, south to Indonesia
Murina Tube-nosed Insectivorous Bats
M. aenea **Bronze tube-nosed bat** Malay Pen., Borneo
M. aurata **Little tube-nosed bat** Nepal to SW China and Burma
M. cyclotis **Round-eared tube-nosed bat** India, Sri Lanka to Guangdong and Hainan (China), Vietnam, south to Malay Pen., Lesser Sunda Is (Indonesia), Borneo, Philippines
M. florium **Flores tube-nosed bat** Leser Sunda Is and Sulawesi (Indonesia), New Guinea, NE Australia
M. fusca **Dusky tube-nosed bat** Manchuria (China)
M. grisea **Peters' tube-nosed bat** NW Himalayas
M. huttoni **Hutton's tube-nosed bat** NW India to Vietnam, Fujian (China), Thailand, Malay Pen.
M. leucogaster **Greater tube-nosed bat** E Himalayas, China, Upper Yenisei R (Russia), Altai Mts, Korea, Ussuris, Sakhalin Is (Russia), Japan
M. puta **Taiwan tube-nosed bat** Taiwan
M. rozendaali **Gilded tube-nosed bat** Borneo
M. silvatica **Forest tube-nosed bat** Japan (incl. Tsushima Is)
M. suilla **Brown tube-nosed bat** Malay Pen., Sumatra and Java (Indonesia), Borneo
M. tenebrosa **Gloomy tube-nosed bat** Tsushima Is (Japan)
M. tubinaris **Scully's tube-nosed bat** Pakistan, N India, Burma, Vietnam, Laos, Thailand
M. ussuriensis **Ussuri tube-nosed bat** Ussuris, Kurile Is and Sakhalin (Russia), Korea

SUBFAMILY MINIOPTERINAE
Miniopterus Bent-winged Bats
M. australis **Little long-fingered bat** Java (Indonesia), Borneo, Philippines, Vanuatu, E Australia
M. fraterculus **Lesser long-fingered bat** South Africa, Mozambique, Malawi, Zambia, Angola
M. fuscus **Southeast Asian long-fingered bat** SE China, Ryukyu Is (Japan), Thailand, Malay Pen., Java and Sulawesi (Indonesia), Borneo, Philippines, New Guinea
M. inflatus **Greater long-fingered bat** W to E Africa
M. magnater **Western bent-winged bat** NE India and SE China to Timor (Indonesia) and New Guinea
M. minor **Least long-fingered bat** Kenya, Tanzania, DRC, Congo, Madagascar, São Tomé and Comoros
M. pusillus **Small bent-winged bat** India to Maluku (Indonesia) and Philippines, Solomon Is to New Caledonia
M. robustior **Loyalty bent-winged bat** Loyaute Is (E of New Caledonia)
M. schreibersi **Schreiber's long-fingered bat** SubSaharan Africa (also Madagascar), Morocco and S Europe to Iran and Caucasus to China and Japan, much of Indo-Malayan region, New Guinea, Bismarck Arch. (Papua New Guinea), Solomon Is, Australia
M. tristis **Great bent-winged bat** Sulawesi (Indonesia), Philippines, New Guinea, Bismarck Arch. (Papua New Guinea), Solomon Is, Vanuatu

SUBFAMILY TOMOPEATINAE
Tomopeas
T. ravus **Blunt-eared bat** W Peru

FAMILY MYSTACINIDAE
New Zealand Short-tailed Bats
Mystacina
M. robusta **New Zealand greater short-tailed bat** Extinct: formerly Big South Cape Is (New Zealand)
M. tuberculata **New Zealand lesser short-tailed bat** New Zealand

FAMILY MOLOSSIDAE
Free-tailed Bats
Chaerephon Lesser Free-tailed Bats
C. aloysiisabaudiae **Duke of Abruzzi's free-tailed bat** Ghana, Gabon, DRC, Uganda
C. ansorgei **Ansorge's free-tailed bat** Cameroon to Ethiopia south to Angola and E South Africa
C. bemmeleni **Gland-tailed free-tailed bat** Liberia, Cameroon, DRC, Uganda, Tanzania, Kenya, Sudan
C. bivittata **Spotted free-tailed bat** Sudan, Ethiopia, Kenya, Tanzania, Uganda, Zambia, Mozambique, Zimbabwe
C. chapini **Chapin's free-tailed bat** Ethiopia, Uganda, DRC, Zambia, Angola, Namibia, Botswana, Zimbabwe
C. gallagheri **Gallagher's free-tailed bat** DRC
C. jobensis **Northern mastiff bat** New Guinea, Solomon Is, Vanuatu, Fiji, N and C Australia
C. johorensis **Northern free-tailed bat** W Malaysia, Sumatra (Indonesia)
C. major **Lappet-eared free-tailed bat** Liberia, Mali, Burkina Faso, Ghana, Togo, Niger, Nigeria, NE DRC, Uganda, Sudan, Tanzania
C. nigeriae **Nigerian free-tailed bat** Ghana and Niger to Ethiopia and Saudi Arabia south to Namibia, Botswana and Zimbabwe
C. plicata **Wrinkle-lipped free-tailed bat** India and Sri Lanka to S China and Vietnam, to Lesser Sunda Is (Indonesia), Borneo, Philippines, Cocos Keeling Is (Ind. Oc.)
C. pumila **Little free-tailed bat** Senegal to Yemen south to South Africa, Bioko (Equatorial Guinea), Pemba and Zanzibar Is (Tanzania), Madagascar, Comoros, Seychelles

C. russata **Russet free-tailed bat** Ghana, Cameroon, DRC, Kenya
Cheiromeles
C. torquatus **Hairless bat** Malay Pen., Sumatra, Java and Sulawesi (Indonesia), Borneo, SW Philippines
Eumops Bonneted Bats
E. auripendulus **Black bonneted bat** Oaxaca and Yucatan (Mexico) to Peru, E Brazil, N Argentina, Trinidad
E. bonariensis **Dwarf bonneted bat** Veracruz (Mexico) to NW Peru, Brazil, N Argentina, and Uruguay
E. dabbenei **Big bonneted bat** Colombia, Venezuela, Paraguay, N Argentina
E. glaucinus **Wagner's bonneted bat** Jalisco (Mexico) to Peru, Brazil, and N Argentina, Cuba, Jamaica, Florida (USA)
E. hansae **Sanborn's bonneted bat** Costa Rica, Panama, Venezuela, Guyana, Fr. Guiana, Peru, Brazil, Bolivia
E. maurus **Guianan bonneted bat** Guyana, Surinam
E. perotis **Western bonneted bat** California and Texas (SW USA) to Zacatecas and Hidalgo (Mexico), Colombia to E Brazil and N Argentina, Cuba
E. underwoodi **Underwood's bonneted bat** Arizona (SW USA) to Nicaragua
Molossops Dog-faced Bats
M. abrasus **Cinnamon dog-faced bat** Venezuela, Guyana, Surinam, Peru, Brazil, Bolivia, Paraguay, N Argentina
M. aequatorianus **Equatorial dog-faced bat** Ecuador
M. greenhalli **Greenhall's dog-faced bat** Nayarit (Mexico) to Ecuador and NE Brazil, Trinidad
M. mattogrossensis **Mato Grosso dog-faced bat** Venezuela, Guyana, C and NE Brazil
M. neglectus **Rufous dog-faced bat** Surinam, Peru, Amazonian Brazil
M. planirostris **Southern dog-faced bat** Panama to Surinam, Peru, Brazil, Paraguay, N Argentina
M. temminckii **Dwarf dog-faced bat** Colombia, Venezuela, Peru, S Brazil, Bolivia, Paraguay, N Argentina, Uruguay
Molossus Mastiff Bats
M. ater **Black mastiff bat** Tamaulipas and Sinaloa (Mexico) to Guianas, Peru, Brazil and N Argentina, Trinidad
M. bondae **Bonda mastiff bat** Honduras to Venezuela and Ecuador, Cozumel Is (Mexico)
M. molossus **Pallas' mastiff bat** Sinaloa and Coahuila (Mexico) to Guianas, Peru, Brazil, N Argentina, Uruguay, Margarita Is (Venezuela), Greater and Lesser Antilles (incl. Neth. Antilles), Trinidad and Tobago
M. pretiosus **Miller's mastiff bat** Guerrero and Oaxaca (Mexico), Nicaragua to Colombia, Venezuela and Guyana
M. sinaloae **Sinaloan mastiff bat** Sinaloa (Mexico) to Colombia and Surinam, Trinidad
Mops Greater Free-tailed Bats
M. brachypterus **Sierra Leone free-tailed bat** Gambia to Kenya, Tanzania, Mozambique
M. condylurus **Angolan free-tailed bat** Senegal to Somalia south to Angola, Botswana, and E South Africa
M. congicus **Medje free-tailed bat** Ghana, Nigeria, Cameroon, DRC, Uganda
M. demonstrator **Mongalla free-tailed bat** Sudan, DRC, Uganda, Burkina Faso
M. midas **Midas free-tailed bat** Senegal to Saudi Arabia south to Botswana and N South Africa, Madagascar
M. mops **Malayan free-tailed bat** Malay Pen., Sumatra (Indonesia), Borneo
M. nanulus **Dwarf free-tailed bat** Sierra Leone to Ethiopia and Kenya
M. niangarae **Niangara free-tailed bat** Niangara (DRC)
M. niveiventer **White-bellied free-tailed bat** DRC, Rwanda, Burundi, Tanzania, Mozambique, Zambia, Angola
M. petersoni **Peterson's free-tailed bat** Cameroon and Ghana
M. sarasinorum **Sulawesi free-tailed bat** Sulawesi (Indonesia), Philippines
M. spurrelli **Spurrell's free-tailed bat** Liberia, Ivory Coast, Ghana, Togo, Benin, Equatorial Guinea, DRC
M. thersites **Railer bat** Sierra Leone to Rwanda, Bioko (Equatorial Guinea)
M. trevori **Trevor's free-tailed bat** NW DRC, Uganda
Mormopterus Little Mastiff Bats
M. acetabulosus **Natal free-tailed bat** Madagascar, Réunion, Mauritius; Ethiopia, South Africa
M. beccarii **Beccari's mastiff bat** Maluku (Indonesia), New Guinea, N Australia
M. doriae **Sumatran mastiff bat** Sumatra (Indonesia)
M. jugularis **Peters' wrinkle-lipped bat** Madagascar
M. kalinowskii **Kalinowski's mastiff bat** Peru, N Chile
M. minutus **Little goblin bat** Cuba
M. norfolkensis **Eastern little mastiff bat** SE Queensland, E New South Wales (Australia), Norfolk Is (S Pac. Oc.)
M. petrophilus **Roberts' flat-headed bat** Southern African Subregion
M. phrudus **Incan little mastiff bat** Peru
M. planiceps **Southern free-tailed bat** New Guinea, Australia
M. setiger **Peters' flat-headed bat** S Sudan, Ethiopia, Kenya
Myopterus African Free-tailed Bats
M. daubentonii **Daubenton's free-tailed bat** Senegal, Ivory Coast, NE DRC
M. whitleyi **Bini free-tailed bat** Ghana, Nigeria, Cameroon, DRC, Uganda
Nyctinomops New World Free-tailed Bats
N. aurispinosus **Peale's free-tailed bat** Sonora and Tamaulipas (Mexico) to Peru, Brazil, and Bolivia
N. femorosaccus **Pocketed free-tailed bat** SW USA, Mexico (Incl. Baja California)
N. laticaudatus **Broad-eared bat** Tamaulipas and Jalisco (Mexico) to NW Peru, Brazil and N Argentina, Trinidad, Cuba
N. macrotis **Big free-tailed bat** SW British Columbia (Canada) and Iowa (USA) to Peru, N Argentina and Uruguay, Cuba, Jamaica, Hispaniola
Otomops Big-eared Free-tailed Bats
O. formosus **Java mastiff bat** Java (Indonesia)
O. martiensseni **Large-eared free-tailed bat** Djibouti and CAR to Angola and E South Africa, Madagascar
O. papuensis **Big-eared mastiff bat** SE New Guinea
O. secundus **Mantled mastiff bat** NE New Guinea
O. wroughtoni **Wroughton's free-tailed bat** S India
Promops Crested Mastiff Bats
P. centralis **Big crested mastiff bat** Jalisco and Yucatan (Mexico) to Surinam, Peru, and N Argentina, Trinidad
P. nasutus **Brown mastiff bat** Venezuela, Surinam, Ecuador, Peru, Brazil, Bolivia, Paraguay, N Argentina, Trinidad
Tadarida Free-tailed Bats
T. aegyptiaca **Egyptian free-tailed bat** South Africa to Algeria, Egypt to Yemen and Oman east to India, Sri Lanka
T. australis **White-striped free-tailed bat** New Guinea, S and C Australia
T. brasiliensis **Brazilian free-tailed bat** USA to Chile, Argentina and S Brazil, Greater and Lesser Antilles
T. espiritosantensis **Espirito Santo free-tailed bat** Brazil
T. fulminans **Madagascan large free-tailed bat** N South Africa, Zimbabwe, Zambia, Malawi, Tanzania, Rwanda, DRC, Kenya, Madagascar
T. lobata **Kenyan big-eared free-tailed bat** Kenya, Zimbabwe
T. teniotis **European free-tailed bat** France, Portugal, and Morocco to S China, Taiwan, and Japan, Madeira Is (Portugal), Canarias Is
T. ventralis **African giant free-tailed bat** Ethiopia to South Africa

ORDER XENARTHRA

EDENTATES

FAMILY MYRMECOPHAGIDAE
American Anteaters

Cyclopes
C. didactylus **Silky anteater** Veracruz and Oaxaca (S Mexico) to Colombia then west of Andes to S Ecuador and east of Andes to Venezuela, Guyana, Surinam, Fr. Guiana, Trinidad, and S Colombia and Venezuela south to Santa Cruz (Bolivia) and Brazil
Myrmecophaga
M. tridactyla **Giant anteater** Belize and Guatemala through South America to the Gran Chaco of Bolivia, Paraguay, and Argentina, and Uruguay
Tamandua Tamanduas
T. mexicana **Northern tamandua** Tamaulipas (E Mexico), Central America south to NW Venezuela and NW Peru
T. tetradactyla **Southern tamandua** South America (east of the Andes) from Colombia, Venezuela, Guianas, south to Argentina and Uruguay, Trinidad

FAMILY BRADYPODIDAE
Three-toed Sloths

Bradypus
B. torquatus **Maned three-toed sloth** SE Brazil in coastal forests
B. tridactylus **Pale-throated three-toed sloth** Venezuela, Guyana, Surinam, Fr. Guiana, N Brazil
B. variegatus **Brown-throated three-toed sloth** Honduras to Colombia, W Venezuela, Ecuador, E Peru, Brazil, Bolivia, Paraguay, Argentina

FAMILY MEGALONYCHIDAE
Two-toed Tree Sloths

SUBFAMILY CHOLOEPINAE
Choloepus
C. didactylus **Southern two-toed sloth** Venezuela and Guianas south to Brazil west into upper Amazon Basin of Ecuador and Peru
C. hoffmanni **Hoffmann's two-toed sloth** Nicaragua into South America east to Venezuela and south to Brazil and E Bolivia

FAMILY DASYPODIDAE Armadillos

SUBFAMILY CHLAMYPHORINAE
Chlamyphorus Fairy Armadillos
C. retusus **Chacoan fairy armadillo** Gran Chaco of SE Bolivia, W Paraguay, and N Argentina
C. truncatus **Pink fairy armadillo** Argentina

SUBFAMILY DASYPODINAE
Cabassous Naked-tailed Armadillos
C. centralis **Northern naked-tailed armadillo** Chiapas (Mexico) to N Colombia
C. chacoensis **Chacoan naked-tailed armadillo** Gran Chaco of W Paraguay and NW Argentina; also Mato Grasso (Brazil)
C. tatouay **Greater naked-tailed armadillo** S Brazil, SE Paraguay, NE Argentina, Uruguay
C. unicinctus **Southern naked-tailed armadillo** South America (east of the Andes) from Colombia to Mato Grasso (Brazil)
Chaetophractus Hairy Armadillos
C. nationi **Andean hairy armadillo** Cochabamba, Oruro, and La Paz (Bolivia)
C. vellerosus **Screaming hairy armadillo** Chaco Boreal of Bolivia and Paraguay south to C Argentina and west to Tarapaca (Chile)
C. villosus **Large hairy armadillo** Gran Chaco of Bolivia, Paraguay and N Argentina south to Santa Cruz (S Argentina) and Magallanes (S Chile)
Dasypus Long-nosed Armadillos
D. hybridus **Southern long-nosed armadillo** S Brazil, Paraguay, Argentina
D. kappleri **Great long-nosed armadillo** E Colombia, Venezuela (south of Orinoco R), Guyana, Surinam, south through Ecuador, Peru, and the Amazon Basin of Brazil
D. novemcinctus **Nine-banded armadillo** S USA, Mexico, Central and South America to N Argentina, Trinidad and Tobago, Grenada
D. pilosus **Hairy long-nosed armadillo** Andes of Peru
D. sabanicola **Llanos long-nosed armadillo** Llanos of Colombia and Venezuela
D. septemcinctus **Seven-banded armadillo** Lower Amazon Basin of Brazil to the Gran Chaco of Bolivia, Paraguay, and N Argentina
Euphractus
E. sexcinctus **Six-banded armadillo** S Surinam and adj. Brazil; also E Brazil to Bolivia, Paraguay, N Argentina, Uruguay
Priodontes
P. maximus **Giant armadillo** South America (east of the Andes), from N Venezuela and Guianas to Paraguay and N Argentina
Tolypeutes Three-banded Armadillos
T. matacus **Southern three-banded armadillo** SW Brazil and E Bolivia south through Gran Chaco of Paraguay to Buenos Aires (Argentina)
T. tricinctus **Brazilian three-banded armadillo** Bahia, Ceara, and Pernambuco (Brazil)
Zaedyus
Z. pichiy **Pichi** C and S Argentina and E Chile south to the Magellan Str.

ORDER DIDELPHIMORPHIA

AMERICAN OPOSSUMS

FAMILY DIDELPHIDAE

SUBFAMILY CALUROMYINAE
Caluromys Woolly Opossums
C. derbianus **Central American or Derby's woolly opossum** Mexico, Central America, Colombia, Ecuador
C. lanatus **Western or Ecuadorian woolly opossum** N and C Colombia, NW and S Venezuela, E Ecuador, E Peru, W and S Brazil, E Bolivia, E and S Paraguay, Misiones (N Argentina)
C. philander **Bare-tailed woolly opossum** Venezuela (incl. Margarita Is), Guyana, Surinam, Fr. Guiana, Brazil, Trinidad and Tobago
Caluromysiops
C. irrupta **Black-shouldered opossum** SE Peru, W Brazil
Glironia
G. venusta **Bushy-tailed opossum** Ecuador, Peru, Amazonian Brazil, Bolivia

SUBFAMILY DIDELPHINAE
Chironectes
C. minimus **Water opossum or Yapok** Oaxaca and Tabasco (S Mexico) south through Central America to Colombia, Venezuela, Guianas, Ecuador, Peru, Brazil, Paraguay, Argentina
Didelphis Large American Opossums
D. albiventris **White-eared opossum** Colombia, Ecuador, Peru, Brazil, Bolivia, Paraguay, N Argentina, Uruguay; also S Venezuela, SW Surinam, and N Brazil
D. aurita **Big-eared opossum** E Brazil, SE Paraguay, NE Argentina
D. marsupialis **Southern opossum** Tamaulipas (E Mexico) south throughout Central and South America to Peru, Brazil, Bolivia
D. virginiana **Virginia or Common opossum** S Canada, E and C USA, Mexico, Central America south to N Costa Rica
Gracilinanus Gracile Mouse Opossums
G. aceramarcae **Aceramarca gracile mouse opossum** Bolivia
G. agilis **Agile gracile mouse opossum** E Peru, Brazil, E Bolivia, Paraguay, NE Argentina, Uruguay
G. dryas **Wood sprite gracile mouse opossum** Andes of W Venezuela
G. emiliae **Emilia's gracile mouse opossum** NE Brazil
G. marica **Northern or Venezuelan gracile mouse opossum** N Colombia, Venezuela
G. microtarsus **Brazilian or Small-footed gracile mouse opossum** SE Brazil
Lestodelphys
L. halli **Patagonian opossum** Mendoza south to Santa Cruz (Argentina)
Lutreolina
L. crassicaudata **Lutrine opossum or Thick-tailed water opossum** E Colombia, Venezuela, W Guyana; also SE Brazil, E Bolivia, Paraguay, N Argentina, and Uruguay
Marmosa Mouse Opossums
M. andersoni **Anderson's mouse opossum** Cuzco (S Peru)
M. canescens **Grayish mouse opossum** S Sonora to Oaxaca and Yucatan, Tres Marias Is (Mexico)
M. lepida **Little rufous mouse opossum** E Colombia, Surinam, Ecuador, Peru, Bolivia, poss. Brazil
M. mexicana **Mexican mouse opossum** Tamaulipas (Mexico) to W Panama
M. murina **Murine or Common mouse opossum** Colombia, Venezuela, Guianas, Surinam, E Ecuador, E Peru, Brazil, E Bolivia, Trinidad and Tobago
M. robinsoni **Robinson's or Pale-bellied mouse opossum** Belize, Honduras, Panama, Colombia, Venezuela, W Ecuador, NW Peru, Trinidad and Tobago, Grenada
M. rubra **Red mouse opossum** E Ecuador, Peru
M. tyleriana **Tyler's mouse opossum** S Venezuela
M. xerophila **Dryland mouse opossum** NE Colombia, NW Venezuela
Marmosops Slender Mouse Opossums
M. cracens **Slim-faced slender mouse opossum** Falcon (Venezuela)
M. dorothea **Dorothy's slender mouse opossum** Yungas, Beni, and Chaco (Bolivia)
M. fuscatus **Gray-bellied slender mouse opossum** E Andes of Colombia, N Venezuela, Trinidad and Tobago
M. handleyi **Handley's slender mouse opossum** Antioquia (C Colombia)

M. impavidus **Andean slender mouse opossum** W Panama to Colombia, W Venezuela, Ecuador, and Peru; also S Venezuela
M. incanus **Gray slender mouse opossum** Bahia south to Parana (E Brazil)
M. invictus **Slaty slender mouse opossum** Panama
M. noctivagus **White-bellied slender mouse opossum** Ecuador, Peru, Amazonian Brazil, Bolivia
M. parvidens **Delicate slender mouse opossum** Colombia, Venezuela, Guyana, Surinam, Peru, Brazil
Metachirus
M. nudicaudatus **Brown "four-eyed" opossum** Nicaragua to Paraguay and NE Argentina
Micoureus Woolly Mouse Opossums
M. alstoni **Alston's woolly mouse opossum** Belize to Panama
M. constantiae **Pale-bellied woolly mouse opossum** E Bolivia and adj. Brazil south to N Argentina
M. demerarae **Long-furred woolly mouse opossum** Colombia, Venezuela, Guyana, Surinam, Fr. Guiana, Brazil, E Paraguay
M. regina **Short-furred woolly mouse opossum** Colombia, Ecuador, Peru, Bolivia
Monodelphis Short-tailed Opossums
M. adusta **Sepia or Cloudy short-tailed opossum** E Panama, Colombia, Ecuador, N Peru
M. americana **Three-striped short-tailed opossum** Para south to Santa Catarina (E Brazil)
M. brevicaudata **Red-legged short-tailed opossum** Venezuela, Surinam, Fr. Guiana, Amazon Basin of Brazil, Bolivia
M. dimidiata **Southern short-tailed opossum** SE Brazil, NE Argentina, Uruguay
M. domestica **Gray short-tailed opossum** Brazil, Bolivia, Paraguay
M. emiliae **Emilia's short-tailed opossum** Amazon Basin of Peru and Brazil
M. iheringi **Ihering's short-tailed opossum** SE Brazil
M. kunsi **Pygmy or Kuns' short-tailed opossum** Brazil, Bolivia
M. maraxina **Marajo short-tailed opossum** Marajo Is (Para, NE Brazil)
M. osgoodi **Osgood's short-tailed opossum** SE Peru, C Bolivia
M. rubida **Chestnut-striped short-tailed opossum** Goias south to Sao Paulo (E Brazil)
M. scalops **Long-nosed short-tailed opossum** Espirito Santo south to Santa Catarina (SE Brazil)
M. sorex **Shrewish short-tailed opossum** SE Brazil, S Paraguay, NE Argentina
M. theresa **Theresa's short-tailed opossum** Andes of Peru, E Brazil
M. unistriata **One-striped short-tailed opossum** Sao Paulo (Brazil)
Philander Gray and Black "Four-eyed" Opossums
P. andersoni **Black "four-eyed"opossum** E Colombia, S Venezuela, Ecuador, Peru, W Brazil
P. opossum **Gray "four-eyed"opossum** Tamaulipas (Mexico) through Central and South America to Paraguay and NE Argentina
Thylamys Fat-tailed Opossums
T. elegans **Elegant fat-tailed opossum** S Peru and Cochabamba (Bolivia) south to Valdivia (Chile) and Neuquen (Argentina)
T. macrura **Long-tailed fat-tailed opossum** S Brazil, Paraguay
T. pallidior **Pallid fat-tailed opossum** E and S Bolivia, Argentina
T. pusilla **Small fat-tailed opossum** C and S Brazil, SE Bolivia, Paraguay, N Argentina
T. velutinus **Velvety fat-tailed opossum** SE Brazil

ORDER PAUCITUBERCULATA

SHREW OPOSSUMS

FAMILY CAENOLESTIDAE
Caenolestes Northern Shrew Opossums
C. caniventer **Gray-bellied shrew opossum** Andes of SW Ecuador and NW Peru
C. convelatus **Blackish shrew opossum** Andes of W Colombia and NW Ecuador
C. fuliginosus **Silky shrew opossum** Andes of Colombia, NW Venezuela, and Ecuador
Lestoros
L. inca **Incan or Peruvian shrew opossum** Andes of S Peru
Rhyncholestes
R. raphanurus **Chilean shrew opossum** SC Chile (incl. Chiloe Is)

ORDER MICROBIOTHERIA

FAMILY MICROBIOTHERIIDAE
Dromiciops
D. gliroides **Monito del Monte or Colocolos** Chile, adj. WC Argentina

ORDER DASYUROMORPHIA

AUSTRALASIAN CARNIVOROUS MARSUPIALS

FAMILY THYLACINIDAE
Thylacinus
T. cynocephalus **Thylacine or Tasmanian wolf or tiger** Extinct: formerly Tasmania (Australia)

FAMILY MYRMECOBIIDAE
Myrmecobius
M. fasciatus **Numbat or Banded anteater** SW Western Australia (Australia)

FAMILY DASYURIDAE Dasyurids
Antechinus Antechinuses
A. bellus **Fawn antechinus** N Northern Territory (Australia)
A. flavipes **Yellow-footed antechinus** Cape York Pen. (Queensland) to Victoria, SE South Australia, and SW Western Australia (Australia)
A. godmani **Atherton antechinus** NE Queensland (Australia)
A. leo **Cinnamon antechinus** Cape York Pen. (Queensland, Australia)
A. melanurus **Black-tailed antechinus** New Guinea
A. minimus **Swamp antechinus** Coastal SE South Australia to Tasmania (Australia)
A. naso **Long-nosed antechinus** C New Guinea
A. stuartii **Brown antechinus** E Queensland, E New South Wales, Victoria (Australia)
A. swainsonii **Dusky antechinus** SE Queensland, E New South Wales, E and SE Victoria, Tasmania (Australia)
A. wilhelmina **Lesser antechinus** C New Guinea
Dasycercus Crested-tailed Marsupial Mice
D. byrnei **Kowari** Junction of Northern Territory, South Australia, and Queensland (C Australia)
D. cristicauda **Mulgara** NW Western Australia to SW Queensland and N South Australia (Australia)
Dasykaluta
D. rosamondae **Little red kaluta** NW Western Australia (Australia)
Dasyurus Quolls
D. albopunctatus **New Guinean quoll** New Guinea
D. geoffroii **Western quoll** Western Australia (Australia)
D. hallucatus **Northern quoll** N Western Australia, N Northern Territory, N and NE Queensland (Australia)
D. maculatus **Spotted-tailed or Tiger quoll** E Queensland, E New South Wales, E and S Victoria, SE South Australia, Tasmania (Australia)
D. spartacus **Bronze quoll** Papua New Guinea
D. viverrinus **Eastern quoll** Tasmania (Australia), poss. SE Australia
Murexia Long-tailed Dasyures
M. longicaudata **Short-furred dasyure** Aru Is (Indonesia), New Guinea
M. rothschildi **Broad-striped dasyure** SE New Guinea
Myoictis
M. melas **Three-striped dasyure** Salawati and Aru Is (Indonesia), New Guinea
Neophascogale
N. lorentzi **Speckled dasyure** C New Guinea
Ningaui Ningauis
N. ridei **Wongai or Inland ningaui** Western Australia, Northern Territory, South Australia (Australia)
N. timealeyi **Pilbara ningaui** NW Western Australia (Australia)
N. yvonnae **Southern ningaui** Western Australia to New South Wales and Victoria (Australia)
Parantechinus Dibblers
P. apicalis **Southern dibbler** SW Western Australia (Australia)
P. bilarni **Sandstone dibbler** Northern Territory (Australia)
Phascogale Phascogales
P. calura **Red-tailed phascogale or Wambenger** SW Western Australia (Australia)
P. tapoatafa **Brush-tailed phascogale** SW Western Australia, SE South Australia, S Victoria, E New South Wales, Queensland, Northern Territory (Australia)
Phascolosorex Marsupial Shrews
P. doriae **Red-bellied marsupial shrew** W New Guinea
P. dorsalis **Narrow-striped marsupial shrew** W and E New Guinea
Planigale Planigales
P. gilesi **Paucident planigale** NE South Australia, NW New South Wales, SW Queensland (Australia)
P. ingrami **Long-tailed planigale** NE Western Australia, NE Northern Territory, N and E Queensland (Australia)
P. maculata **Pygmy or Common planigale** E Queensland, NE New South Wales, N Northern Territory (Australia)
P. novaeguineae **New Guinean planigale** S New Guinea
P. tenuirostris **Narrow-nosed planigale** NW New South Wales, SC Queensland (Australia)
Pseudantechinus Pseudantechinuses
P. macdonnellensis **Fat-tailed pseudantechinus** N Western Australia, Northern Territory, central deserts (Australia)
P. ningbing **Ningbing pseudantechinus** Kimberley (N Western Australia, Australia)
P. woolleyae **Woolley's pseudantechinus** Western Australia (Australia)
Sarcophilus
S. laniarius **Tasmanian devil** Tasmania, poss. S Victoria (Australia)
Sminthopsis Dunnarts
S. aitkeni **Kangaroo Island dunnart** Kangaroo Is (South Australia, Australia)
S. archeri **Chestnut dunnart** S Papua New Guinea, Queensland (Australia)
S. butleri **Carpentarian dunnart** Kalumburu (Western Australia, Australia), Papua New Guinea
S. crassicaudata **Fat-tailed dunnart** S Western Australia, South Australia, W Victoria, W New South Wales, SW Queensland, SE Northern Territory (Australia)
S. dolichura **Little long-tailed dunnart** Western Australia, South Australia (Australia)
S. douglasi **Julia creek dunnart** NW Queensland (Australia)
S. fuliginosus **Sooty dunnart** SW Western Australia (Australia)
S. gilberti **Gilbert's dunnart** SW Western Australia (Australia)
S. granulipes **White-tailed dunnart** SW Western Australia (Australia)
S. griseoventer **Gray-bellied dunnart** SW Western Australia (Australia)
S. hirtipes **Hairy-footed dunnart** S Northern Territory, WC Western Australia (Australia)
S. laniger **Kultarr** Western Australia, S Northern Territory, N South Australia, N Victoria, W New South Wales, SW Queensland (Australia)
S. leucopus **White-footed dunnart** Tasmania, S and SE Victoria, New South Wales, Queensland (Australia)
S. longicaudata **Long-tailed dunnart** Western Australia (Australia)
S. macroura **Stripe-faced dunnart** NW New South Wales, W Queensland, S Northern Territory, N South Australia, N Western Australia (Australia)
S. murina **Slender-tailed dunnart** SW Western Australia, SE South Australia, Victoria, New South Wales, E Queensland (Australia)
S. ooldea **Ooldea dunnart** SE Western Australia, S South Australia, S Northern Territory (Australia)
S. psammophila **Sandhill dunnart** SW Northern Territory, S South Australia (Australia)
S. virginiae **Red-cheeked dunnart** N Queensland, N Northern Territory (Australia), Aru Is (Indonesia), S New Guinea
S. youngsoni **Lesser hairy-footed dunnart** Western Australia, Northern Territory (Australia)

ORDER PERAMELEMORPHIA

BANDICOOTS AND BILBIES

FAMILY PERAMELIDAE
Australian Bandicoots and Bilbies
Chaeropus
C. ecaudatus **Pig-footed bandicoot** Western Australia, S Northern Territory, N South Australia, SW New South Wales, Victoria (Australia)
Isoodon Short-nosed Bandicoots
I. auratus **Golden bandicoot** NW Western Australia, Barrow Is (Australia)
I. macrourus **Northern brown bandicoot** NE Western Australia, N Northern Territory, E Queensland, NE New South Wales (Australia), S and E New Guinea
I. obesulus **Southern brown bandicoot or Quenda** N Queensland, SE New South Wales, S Victoria, SE South Australia, SW Western Australia, Tasmania (Australia)
Macrotis Bilbies
M. lagotis **Greater bilby** SW Queensland, Northern Territory/Western Australia border and Kimberley (N Western Australia, Australia)
M. leucura **Lesser bilby** C Australia
Perameles Long-nosed Bandicoots
P. bougainville **Western barred bandicoot** Bernier and Dorre Is (off Western Australia, Australia)
P. eremiana **Desert bandicoot** Great Victoria Desert (Western Australia), N South Australia, S Northern Territory (Australia)
P. gunnii **Eastern barred bandicoot** S Victoria, Tasmania (Australia)
P. nasuta **Long-nosed bandicoot** E Queensland, E New South Wales, E Victoria (Australia)

FAMILY PERORYCTIDAE
Rainforest Bandicoots
Echymipera Echymiperas
E. clara **Clara's echymipera** NC New Guinea
E. davidi **David's echymipera** Kiriwina Is (Papua New Guinea)
E. echinista **Menzie's echymipera** Papua New Guinea
E. kalubu **Kalubu echymipera** New Guinea, adj. small islands incl. Bismarck Arch. (Papua New Guinea) and Salawati Is (Indonesia)
E. rufescens **Long-nosed echymipera** Cape York Pen. (Queensland, Australia), New Guinea (incl. small islands off SE coast), Kei and Aru Is (Indonesia)
Microperoryctes Mouse Bandicoots
M. longicauda **Striped bandicoot** New Guinea
M. murina **Mouse bandicoot** W New Guinea
M. papuensis **Papuan bandicoot** SE New Guinea
Peroryctes New Guinean Bandicoots
P. broadbenti **Giant bandicoot** SE New Guinea
P. raffrayana **Raffray's bandicoot** New Guinea
Rhynchomeles
R. prattorum **Seram bandicoot** Seram Is (Indonesia)

ORDER NOTORYCTEMORPHIA

MARSUPIAL MOLES

FAMILY NOTORYCTIDAE
Notoryctes
N. caurinus **Northwestern marsupial mole** NW Western Australia (Australia)
N. typhlops **Marsupial mole** Western Australia, South Australia, S Northern Territory (Australia)

ORDER DIPROTODONTIA

KOALA, WOMBATS, POSSUMS, KANGAROOS, AND RELATIVES

FAMILY PHASCOLARCTIDAE
Phascolarctos
P. cinereus **Koala** SE Queensland, E New South Wales, Victoria, SE South Australia (Australia); introd. elsewhere

FAMILY VOMBATIDAE Wombats
Lasiorhinus Hairy-nosed Wombats
L. krefftii **Northern or Queensland hairy-nosed wombat** SE and E Queensland, Deniliquin (New South Wales, Australia)
L. latifrons **Southern hairy-nosed or Plains wombat** S South Australia, SE Western Australia (Australia)
Vombatus
V. ursinus **Coarse-haired, Common, Forest, or Naked-nosed wombat** SE Queensland, E New South Wales, S Victoria, Tasmania (and islands in Bass Str.), SE South Australia (Australia)

FAMILY PHALANGERIDAE
Cuscuses and Brushtail Possums
Ailurops
A. ursinus **Bear cuscus** Sulawesi, Peleng, Talaud, Togian, Muna, Buton, and Lembeh Is (Indonesia)
Phalanger Cuscuses
P. carmelitae **Mountain cuscus** C New Guinea
P. lullulae **Woodlark Island cuscus** Woodlark Is (Papua New Guinea)
P. matanim **Telefomin cuscus** Telefomin (W Papua New Guinea)
P. orientalis **Gray cuscus** Timor and Seram Is (Indonesia) to N New Guinea and adj. small islands, Bismarck Arch. (Papua New Guinea), Solomon Is, E Cape York Pen. (Queensland, Australia)

P. ornatus **Moluccan cuscus** Halmahera, Ternate, Tidore, Bacan, and Morotai Is (Indonesia)
P. pelengensis **Peleng Island cuscus** Peleng and Sulu Is (Indonesia)
P. rothschildi **Obi Island cuscus** Pulau Is (Maluku, Indonesia)
P. sericeus **Silky cuscus** C and E New Guinea
P. vestitus **Stein's cuscus** C New Guinea
Spilocuscus **Spotted Cuscuses**
S. maculatus **Short-tailed spotted cuscus** Aru, Kei, Seram, Amboina, and Selayar Is (Indonesia), New Guinea and adj. small islands, Cape York Pen. (Queensland, Australia)
S. rufoniger **Black-spotted cuscus** N New Guinea
Strigocuscus **Plain Cuscuses**
S. celebensis **Little Celebes cuscus** Sulawesi, Peleng, Sanghir, Sula, and Obi Is (Indonesia)
S. gymnotis **Ground cuscus** Aru, Wetar, Timor and other Indonesian islands, New Guinea
Trichosurus **Brushtail Possums**
T. arnhemensis **Northern brushtail possum** N Northern Territory, NE Western Australia, Barrow Is (Australia)
T. caninus **Mountain brushtail possum** SE Queensland, E New South Wales, E Victoria (Australia)
T. vulpecula **Silver gray brushtail possum** E Queensland, E New South Wales, Victoria, Tasmania, SE and N South Australia, SW Western Australia (Australia); introd. to New Zealand
Wyulda
W. squamicaudata **Scaly-tailed possum** Kimberley (NE Western Australia, Australia)

FAMILY POTOROIDAE
Bettongs, "Rat" kangaroos, and Potoroos
Aepyprymnus
A. rufescens **Rufous bettong** NE Victoria, E New South Wales, E Queensland (Australia)
Bettongia **Bettongs**
B. gaimardi **Tasmanian or Gaimard's bettong** Tasmania (Australia)
B. lesueur **Burrowing or Lesueur's bettong or Boodie** W Australian Is
B. penicillata **Brush-tailed bettong or Woylie** SW Western Australia, S South Australia (incl. St Francis Is), NW Victoria, C New South Wales, E Queensland (Australia)
Caloprymnus
C. campestris **Desert "rat" kangaroo** South Australia/Queensland border (Australia)
Hypsiprymnodon
H. moschatus **Musky "rat" kangaroo** NE Queensland (Australia)
Potorous **Potoroos**
P. longipes **Long-footed potoroo** NE Victoria (Australia)
P. platyops **Broad-faced potoroo** Extinct: formerly SW Western Australia, Kangaroo Is (Australia)
P. tridactylus **Long-nosed potoroo** SE Queensland, coastal New South Wales, NE Victoria, SE South Australia, SW Western Australia, Tasmania, King Is (Australia)

FAMILY MACROPODIDAE
Kangaroos and Wallabies
Dendrolagus **Tree Kangaroos**
D. bennettianus **Bennett's tree kangaroo** NE Queenland (Australia)
D. dorianus **Doria's, Dusky or Unicolored tree kangaroo** New Guinea
D. goodfellowi **Goodfellow's or Ornate tree kangaroo** E New Guinea
D. inustus **Grizzled tree kangaroo** Yapen Is (Indonesia), N and W New Guinea
D. lumholtzi **Lumholtz's tree kangaroo** NE Queensland (Australia)
D. matschiei **Huon or Matschie's tree kangaroo** NE New Guinea; introd. to Umboi Is
D. scottae **Tenkile tree kangaroo** Torricelli Mts (Papua New Guinea)
D. spadix **Lowland tree kangaroo** S New Guinea
D. ursinus **White-throated tree kangaroo** NW New Guinea
Dorcopsis **Dorcopsises**
D. atrata **Black dorcopsis** Goodenough Is (Papua New Guinea)
D. hageni **White-striped dorcopsis** NC New Guinea
D. luctuosa **Gray dorcopsis** S New Guinea
D. muelleri **Brown dorcopsis** Misool, Salawati, Aru, and Yapen Is (Indonesia), W New Guinea
Dorcopsulus **Forest Wallabies**
D. macleayi **Papuan or Macleay's forest wallaby** SE New Guinea
D. vanheurni **Lesser forest wallaby** New Guinea
Lagorchestes **Hare Wallabies**
L. asomatus **Central hare wallaby** Extinct: formerly L. Mackay (Northern Territory, Australia)
L. conspicillatus **Spectacled hare wallaby** N Western Australia and adj. islands, N Northern Territory, N and W Queensland (Australia)
L. hirsutus **Western or Rufous hare wallaby** Bernier and Dorre Is (Western Australia) and near Alice Springs (Northern Territory, Australia)
L. leporides **Eastern hare wallaby** Extinct: formerly W New South Wales, NW Victoria, E South Australia (Australia)
Lagostrophus
L. fasciatus **Banded hare wallaby or Munning** Bernier and Dorre Is (Western Australia, Australia)
Macropus **Wallabies, Wallaroos, and Kangaroos**
M. agilis **Agile wallaby** NE Western Australia, Northern Territory, Queensland (Australia), S New Guinea, Kiriwina Is and other islands off SE coast of New Guinea
M. antilopinus **Antilopine wallaroo** N Queensland, Northern Territory, NE Western Australia (Australia)
M. bernardus **Black wallaroo** N Northern Territory (Australia)
M. dorsalis **Black-striped wallaby** E Queensland, E New South Wales (Australia)
M. eugenii **Tammar or Scrub wallaby** SW Western Australia, South Australia, Kangaroo and Wallaby Is and others (Australia)
M. fuliginosus **Western gray or Black-faced kangaroo** SW New South Wales, NW Victoria, South Australia, SW Western Australia, Tasmania, King and Kangaroo Is (Australia)
M. giganteus **Eastern gray or Great gray kangaroo** E and C Queensland, New South Wales, Victoria, SE South Australia, Tasmania (Australia)
M. greyi **Toolache wallaby** Extinct: formerly SE South Australia, adj. Victoria (Australia)
M. irma **Western brush wallaby** SW Western Australia (Australia)
M. parma **Parma or White-fronted wallaby** E New South Wales (Australia); introd. to Kawau Is (New Zealand)
M. parryi **Whiptail or Parry's wallaby** E Queensland, NE New South Wales (Australia)
M. robustus **Hill wallaroo or Euro** Western Australia, South Australia, S Northern Territory, Queensland, New South Wales, Barrow Is (Australia)
M. rufogriseus **Red-necked wallaby** SE South Australia, Victoria, E New South Wales, SE Queensland, Tasmania, King Is and adj. islands (Australia); introd. into England
M. rufus **Red kangaroo** Mainland Australia
Onychogalea **Nail-tailed Wallabies**
O. fraenata **Bridled nail-tailed wallaby** Taunton (Queensland, Australia)
O. lunata **Crescent nail-tailed wallaby** SC and SW Western Australia, S Northern Territory (Australia)
O. unguifera **Northern nail-tailed wallaby** Western Australia, Northern Territory, Queensland (Australia)
Petrogale **Rock Wallabies**
P. assimilis **Allied rock wallaby** Queensland (Australia)
P. brachyotis **Short-eared rock wallaby** Coastal NW Australia, N Northern Territory (Australia)
P. burbidgei **Burbidge's rock wallaby or Monjon** Kimberley (NE Western Australia), Bonaparte Arch. and adj. Islands (Australia)
P. concinna **Pygmy rock wallaby or Nabarlek** NE and NW Northern Territory, NE Western Australia (Australia)
P. godmani **Godman's rock wallaby** Cape York Pen. (Queensland, Australia)
P. inornata **Unadorned rock wallaby** N Queensland (Australia)
P. lateralis **Black-footed rock wallaby** Western Australia, South Australia, Northern Territory, W Queensland (Australia)
P. penicillata **Brush-tailed rock wallaby** E Australia
P. persephone **Proserpine rock wallaby** Proserpine (Queensland, Australia)
P. rothschildi **Rothschild's rock wallaby** NW Western Australia (Australia)
P. xanthopus **Yellow-footed rock wallaby** SW Queensland, NW New South Wales, South Australia (Australia)
Setonix
S. brachyurus **Quokka** SW Western Australia, Rottnest and Bald Is (Australia)
Thylogale **Pademelons**
T. billardierii **Tasmanian pademelon** Tasmania (Australia)
T. brunii **Dusky pademelon** C and E New Guinea and adj. small islands, Bismarck Arch. (Papua New Guinea), Aru Is (Indonesia)
T. stigmatica **Red-legged pademelon** E Queensland, E New South Wales (Australia), SC New Guinea
T. thetis **Red-necked pademelon** E Queensland, E New South Wales (Australia)
Wallabia
W. bicolor **Swamp wallaby** E Queensland, E New South Wales, Victoria, SE South Australia, Stradbroke and Fraser Is (Australia)

FAMILY BURRAMYIDAE
Pygmy Possums
Burramys
B. parvus **Mountain pygmy possum** NE Victoria, S New South Wales (Australia)
Cercartetus **Pygmy possums**
C. caudatus **Long-tailed pygmy possum** New Guinea, Fergusson Is (Papua New Guinea), NE Queensland (Australia)
C. concinnus **Western pygmy possum** SW Western Australia, S and SE South Australia, W Victoria, SW New South Wales (Australia)
C. lepidus **Tasmanian pygmy possum** Tasmania, NW Victoria/South Australia border, Kangaroo Is (Australia)
C. nanus **Eastern pygmy possum** SE South Australia, E New South Wales, Victoria, Tasmania (Australia)

FAMILY PSEUDOCHEIRIDAE
Ringtail Possums
Hemibelideus
H. lemuroides **Lemuroid ringtail possum** NE Queensland (Australia)
Petauroides
P. volans **Greater glider** E Australia
Petropseudes
P. dahli **Rock ringtail possum** N Northern Territory, NW Western Australia (Australia)
Pseudocheirus **Ringtails**
P. canescens **Daintree River ringtail** New Guinea, Salawati Is (Indonesia)
P. caroli **Weyland ringtail** WC New Guinea
P. forbesi **Moss-forest ringtail** New Guinea
P. herbertensis **Herbert River ringtail** NE Queensland (Australia)
P. mayeri **Pygmy ringtail** C New Guinea
P. peregrinus **Queensland ringtail** Cape York Pen. (Queensland) to SE South Australia and SW Western Australia, Tasmania, and islands of the Bass Str. (Australia)
P. schlegeli **Arfak ringtail** NW New Guinea
Pseudochirops **Ringtail Possums**
P. albertisii **D'Albertis' ringtail possum** N and W New Guinea, Yapen Is (Indonesia)
P. archeri **Green ringtail possum** NE Queensland (Australia)
P. corinnae **Golden ringtail possum** New Guinea
P. cupreus **Coppery ringtail possum** New Guinea

FAMILY PETAURIDAE
Gliding and Striped Possums
Dactylopsila **Striped Possums**
D. megalura **Great-tailed triok** New Guinea
D. palpator **Long-fingered triok** New Guinea
D. tatei **Tate's triok** Fergusson Is (Papua New Guinea)
D. trivirgata **Striped possum** New Guinea and adj. small islands, Aru Is (Indonesia), NE Queensland (Australia)
Gymnobelideus
G. leadbeateri **Leadbeater's possum** NE Victoria (Australia)
Petaurus **Lesser Gliding Possums**
P. abidi **Northern glider** NC New Guinea
P. australis **Fluffy or Yellow-bellied glider** Coastal Queensland, New South Wales, Victoria (Australia)
P. breviceps **Sugar glider** SE South Australia to Cape York Pen. (Queensland), N Northern Territory, NE Western Australia (Australia), New Guinea and adj. small islands, Aru Is and Maluku (Indonesia); introd. to Tasmania (Australia)
P. gracilis **Mahogany glider** Barrett's lagoon (Queensland, Australia)
P. norfolcensis **Squirrel glider** E Queensland, E New South Wales, E Victoria (Australia)

FAMILY TARSIPEDIDAE
Tarsipes
T. rostratus **Honey possum** SW Western Australia (Australia)

FAMILY ACROBATIDAE
Feathertail Gliders and Possums
Acrobates
A. pygmaeus **Feathertail glider** E Queensland to SE South Australia, inland to Deniliquin (New South Wales, Australia)
Distoechurus
D. pennatus **Feathertail possum** New Guinea

Glossary

Abiotic non-living.
Abomasum the final chamber of the four sections of the ruminant artiodactyl stomach (following the RUMEN, RETICULUM and OMASUM). The abomasum alone corresponds to the stomach "proper" of other mammals and the other three are elaborations of its proximal part.
Adaptation features of an animal which adjust it to its environment. Adaptations may be genetic, produced by evolution and hence not alterable within the animal's lifetime, or they may be phenotypic, produced by adjustment on the behalf of the individual and may be reversible within its lifetime. NATURAL SELECTION favors the survival of individuals whose adaptations adjust them better to their surroundings than other individuals with less successful adaptations.
Adaptive radiation the pattern in which different species develop from a common ancestor (as distinct from CONVERGENT EVOLUTION, a process whereby species from different origins became similar in response to the same selective pressures).
Adult a fully developed and mature individual, capable of breeding, but not necessarily doing so until social and/or ecological conditions allow.
Aerobic deriving energy from processes that require free atmospheric oxygen. (cf **Anaerobic**)
Afrotheria a strongly supported interordinal group of African mammals that includes the golden moles, tenrecs, elephant shrews, aardvark, and the PAENUNGULATA (hyraxes, elephants, sirenians).
Afrotropical see **Ethiopian**
Age structure the proportion of individuals in a population in different age classes.
Aggression behavior in an animal that serves to injure or threaten another animal, but that is not connected with predation.
Agonistic behavior behavior patterns used during conflict with a CONSPECIFIC, including overt aggression, threats, appeasement, or avoidance.
Agouti a grizzled coloration resulting from alternate light and dark barring of each hair. This banding is well exemplified in the eponymous agouti (Family Dasyproctidae: Order Rodentia).
Air sac a side-pouch of the larynx (the upper part of the windpipe), used in some primates and male walruses as resonating chambers in producing calls.
Albinism the heritable condition in which all hairs are white due to the inability to form MELANIN in the hair, skin, or vascular coating of the eyes.
Allantoic stalk a sac-like outgrowth of the hinder part of the gut of the mammalian fetus, containing a rich network of blood vessels. It connects fetal circulation with the placenta, facilitating nutrition of the young, respiration and excretion. (see **Chorioallantoic placentation**)
Alleles one of several alternative forms of a GENE.
Allogrooming grooming performed by one animal upon another animal of the same species. (cf **Autogrooming**)
Alloparent an animal behaving parentally towards infants that are not its own offspring; the shorthand jargon "helper" is most commonly applied to alloparents without any offspring of their own. The term can be misleading if it is used to describe any non-breeding adults associated with infants, but which may or may not be "helping" by promoting their survival. Alloparents may help suckle young (allosuckling).
Allopatry condition in which populations of different species are geographically separated (cf **Sympatry**).
Allosuckling see **Alloparent**.
Allozyme a form of protein that is produced by a given ALLELE at a single gene LOCUS.
Alpine of the Alps or any lofty mountains; usually pertaining to altitudes above 1,500m (4,900ft).
Altricial young that are born at a rudimentary stage of development and require an extended period of nursing by parent(s). (cf **Precocial**)
Altruistic behavior that reduces personal fitness for the benefit of others.
Alveolus a microscopic sac within the lungs providing the surface for gaseous exchange during respiration. Also used to define the socket of the jaw bone into which the tooth fits.
Ambergris a form of excrement of sperm whales.
Amniote a higher vertebrate whose embryo is enclosed in a fluid-filled embryo, the so-called "amnion".
Amphibious able to live on both land and in water.
Amphilestid a family of TRICONODONT mammals that survived for about 50 million years between the mid-Jurassic and the early Cretaceous.
Amphipod a crustacean of the invertebrate order Amphipoda. Includes many freshwater and marine shrimps.
Ampullary glands paired accessory reproductive glands in some male mammals that contribute their products to the semen.
Amynodont a member of the family Amynodontidae, large rhinoceros-like mammals (order Perissodactyla), which became extinct in the Tertiary.
Anaerobic deriving energy from processes that do not require free oxygen. (cf **Aerobic**)
Anal gland (anal sac) a gland opening by a short duct either just inside the anus or on either side of it.
Ancestral stock a group of animals, usually showing primitive characteristics, which is believed to have given rise to later, more specialized forms.
Androgens hormones, secreted by the testes, that regulate the development of male secondary sexual characteristics.
Angle of attack the angle of the wings of a bat relative to the ground.
Anestrus the non-breeding condition of the reproductive cycle of a mammal when sexual organs are quiescent.
Anomodontia a suborder of the THERAPSIDA, which were extinct by the late Triassic.
Antarctic Convergence the region between 50°–55°S where the Antarctic surface water slides beneath the less-dense southward-flowing subantarctic water.
Anthracothere a member of the family Anthracotheriidae (order Artiodactyla), which became extinct in the late Tertiary.
Anthropoid literally "man-like"; a member of the primate suborder Anthropoidea – monkeys, apes and man. In modern classification systems the Anthropoidea (or Simiiformes) comprises the Catarrhini and Platyrrhini and are included with the tarsiers in the suborder Haplorrhini (**Haplorhines**).
Antigen a substance, whether organic or inorganic, that stimulates the production of antibodies when introduced into the body.
Antitragus the lower posterior part of the outer ear, which lies opposite the TRAGUS.
Antlers paired, branched processes found only on the skull of cervids, made of bone, and shed annually. (cf **Horns**)
Antrum a cavity in the body, especially one in the upper jaw hone.
Apomorphic characters that are derived or of more recent origin. The long neck of the giraffe is apomorphic, the short neck of its ancestor is plesiomorphic (primitive). Apomorphic features possessed by a group of biological organisms distinguish these organisms from others descended from the same ancestor.
Aquatic living chiefly in water.
Arboreal living in trees.
Archaeoceti an extinct order of whales that had features intermediate between terrestrial mammals and fully marine species.
Arteriole a small artery (i.e. muscular blood vessel carrying blood from the heart), eventually subdividing into minute capillaries.
Arterio-venous anastomosis (AVA) a connection between the arterioles carrying blood from the heart and the venules back to the heart.
Arthropod the largest phylum in the animal kingdom in number of species, including insects, spiders, crabs etc. Arthropods have hard, jointed exoskeletons and paired, jointed legs.
Artiodactyl a member of the order Artiodactyla, the even-toed ungulates.
Aspect ratio the ratio of the length of a wing to its width; short, wide wings have a low aspect ratio.
Association a mixed-species group (polyspecific association) involving two or more species; relatively common among both Old and New World monkeys, but the most stable associations are found in forest-living guenons.
Astragalus a bone in the ungulate tarsus (ankle) which (due to reorganization of ankle bones following reduction in the number of digits) bears most of the body weight, a task shared by the CALCANEUM bone in most other mammals).
Asymptote a line (usually straight) that is approached progressively by a given curve, but which is never met within a finite distance. An asymptotic population is the maximum sustainable population size for a given habitat or area, i.e. the growth rate of the population tends asymptotically to zero as the population approaches CARRYING CAPACITY (which is the upper asymptote on a graph).
Atlas one of the top two cervical vertebrae that articulate the skull and vertebral column. (see also **Axis**)
Atrophied of a structure or tissue that is diminished or reduced in size.

Auditory bullae see **Bullae**
Australian a geographic region comprising Australia and New Guinea. (see also **Wallace's line**)
Autogrooming grooming of an animal by itself. (cf **Allogrooming**)
Awns the most common guard hairs on mammals. They usually lie in one direction giving PELAGE a distinctive nap.
Axilla the angle between a forelimb and the body (in humans, the armpit).
Axis one of the top two cervical vertebrae that articulate the skull and vertebral column. (see also **Atlas**)

Baculum (**os penis**, **os baculum** or **penis bone**) an elongate bone present in the penis of certain mammals.
Baleen a horny substance, commonly known as whalebone, growing as plates from the upper jaws of whales of the suborder Mysticeti, and forming a fringelike sieve for extraction of plankton from seawater.
Basal metabolic rate the minimum METABOLIC RATE of an animal needed to sustain the life of an organism that is in an environment at a temperature equal to its own.
Bends the colloquial name for caisson disease, a condition produced by pressure changes in the blood as a diving mammal surfaces. Too rapid an ascent results in nitrogen dissolved in the blood forming bubbles which cause excruciating pain.
Benthic the bottom layer of the marine environment.
Bergmann's rule biogeographic rule that races of species from cold climates tend to be composed of individuals physically larger than those from warmer climates.
Bicornuate type of uterus in eutherian mammals characterized by a single cervix and the two uterine horns fused for part of their length. Found in insectivores, most bats, pangolins, primitive primates, most ungulates, elephants, sirenians, and some carnivores.
Bifid of the penis, with the head divided into two parts by a deep cleft.
Bifurcated paired, having two corresponding halves.
Bilophodont cheek teeth having an OCCLUSAL pattern with paired transverse ridges or LOPHS. (see also **Lophodont**)
Binocular form of vision typical of mammals in which the same object is viewed simultaneously by both eyes; the coordination of the two images in the brain permits precise perception of distance.
Binomial nomenclature (binomial classification) a system, introduced by Carolus Linnaeus, for naming all organisms by means of two Latin names, one for the GENUS (first letter capitalized) and one for the SPECIES (and both names written in italics; e.g. lion, *Panthera leo*)
Biodiversity the living plants, animals and other organisms that characterize a particular region, area, country, or even planet.
Biogeography the study of the patterns of distribution of organisms, either living or extinct, their habitats, and the historical and ecological factors that produced the distributions.
Biological control using one species to reduce the population density of another species in an area through parasitism or predation.
Biomass a measure of the abundance of a life-form in terms of its mass, either absolute or per unit area (the population densities of two species may be identical in terms of the number of individuals of each, but due to their different sizes their biomasses may be quite different).
Biome a broad ecosystem characterized by particular plant life, soil type and climatic conditions. They are the largest geographical BIOTIC COMMUNITIES that it is convenient to recognize.
Biotic community a naturally occurring group of plants and animals in the same environment.
Bipartite a type of uterus in eutherian mammals that is almost completely divided along the median line, with a single cervical opening into the vagina. Found in whales and many carnivores.
Bipedal walking on two legs. Only human beings exhibit habitual striding bipedalism. Some primate species may travel bipedally for short distances, and some (e.g. indri, bushbabies, tarsiers) hop bipedally on the ground.
Blastocyst see **Implantation**
Blowhole the opening of the nostril(s) of a whale, situated on the animal's head, from which the "spout" or "blow" is produced.
Blubber a layer of fat beneath the skin, well developed in whales and seals.
Boreal region a zone geographically situated south of the Arctic and north of latitude 50°N; dominated by coniferous forest.
Bovid a member of the cow-like artiodactyl family, Bovidae.
Brachiate to move around in the trees by arm-swinging beneath branches. In a broad sense all apes are brachiators, but only gibbons and siamangs exhibit a freeflight phase between hand-holds.
Brachydont a type of short-crowned teeth whose growth ceases when full-grown, whereupon the pulp cavity in the root closes. Typical of most mammals, but unlike the HYPSODONT teeth of many herbivores.
Bradycardia a condition in which the heart rate is reduced substantially.
Breaching leaping clear of the water.
Brindled having inconspicuous dark streaks or flecks on a gray or tawny background.
Brontothere a member of the family Brontotheriidae (order Perissodactyla), which became extinct in the early Tertiary.
Browser a herbivore which feeds on shoots and leaves of trees, shrubs etc, as distinct from grasses. (cf **Grazer**)
Bruce effect an effect demonstrated in mice where the presence of a strange male or his odor causes a female to abort her pregnancy and become receptive.
Buccal cavity mouth cavity.
Bullae (auditory) globular, bony capsules housing the middle and inner ear structures, situated on the underside of the skull.
Bunodont molar teeth whose cusps form separate, rounded hillocks which crush and grind.
Bursa (pl. **bursae**) a sac-like cavity (e.g. in ear of civets and Madagascan mongooses).

Cache a hidden store of food; also (verb) to hide food for future use.
Calcaneum one of the tarsal (ankle) bones which forms the heel and in many mammalian orders bears the body weight together with the ASTRAGALUS.
Calcar a process that extends medially from the ankle of bats and helps support the UROPATAGIUM.
Callosities hardened, thickened areas on the skin (e.g. the ISCHIAL callosities in some primates).
Camelid a member of the family Camelidae (the camels), of the Artiodactyla.
Cameloid one of the South American camels.
Caniform dog-like.
Canine a unicuspid tooth posterior to the incisors and anterior to the premolars that is usually elongated and single-rooted.
Caniniform canine-shaped.
Cannon bone a bone formed by the fusion of metatarsal bones in the feet of some families.
Canopy a fairly continuous layer in forests produced by the intermingling of branches of trees; may be fully continuous (closed) or broken by gaps (open). The crowns of some trees project above the canopy layer and are known as emergents.
Caprid a member of the bovid tribe Caprini, of the Artiodactyla.
Carnassial (teeth) opposing pair of teeth especially adapted to shear with a cutting (scissor-like) edge; in extant mammals the arrangement is unique to Carnivora and the teeth involved are the fourth upper premolar and first lower molar.
Carnivore any meat-eating organism (alternatively, a member of the order Carnivora, many of whose members are carnivores).
Carotid rete an interwoven network of bloodvessels formed from the carotid artery.
Carpals wrist bones which articulate between the forelimb bones (radius and ulna) and the metacarpals.
Carrion dead animal matter used as a food source by scavengers
Carrying capacity the maximum number of animals that can be supported in a given area or habitat. In a logistic equation, it is represented by the upper ASYMPTOTE.
Catarrhine a "drooping-nosed" monkey, with nostrils relatively close together and open downward; term used for Old World monkeys, gibbons, apes, and man in contrast to PLATYRRHINE monkeys of the New World. The Catarrhini and Platyrrhini (collectively sometimes referred to as the Anthropoidea or Simiiformes) are usually included along with tarsiers in the HAPLORHINES.
Cathemeral applied to an animal that is irregularly active at any time of day or night, according to the prevailing circumstances.
Caudal gland an enlarged skin gland associated with the root of the tail. Subcaudal, placed below the root; supracaudal, above the root.
Cecum a blind sac in the digestive tract, opening out from the junction between the small and large intestines. In herbivorous mammals it is often very large; it is the site of bacterial action on cellulose. The end of the cecum is the appendix; in species with reduced ceca the appendix may retain an antibacterial function.
Cellulose the fundamental constituent of the cell walls of all green plants, and some algae and fungi. It is very tough and fibrous, and can be digested only by the intestinal flora in mammalian guts.
Cementum hard material which coats the roots of mammalian teeth. In some species, cementum is laid down in annual layers which, under a microscope, can be counted to estimate the age of individuals.
Cephalopod a member of an order of molluscs including such marine invertebrates as squid, octopus, and cuttlefish.
Cerebral cortex the surface layer of cells (gray matter) covering the main part of the brain, consisting of the cerebral hemispheres.
Cerrado (central Brazil) a dry savanna region punctuated by patches of sparsely wooded vegetation.
Cetacea mammalian order comprising whales, dolphins and porpoises.
Cervical of, or pertaining to, the neck; of, or pertaining to, the cervix of the uterus.

Cervid a member of the family Cervidae (the deer), of the Artiodactyla.
Cervix the neck of the womb.
Chaco (Bolivia and Paraguay) a lowland plains area containing soils carried down from the Andes; characterized by dry deciduous forest and scrub, transitional between rain forest and pampas grasslands.
Chalicothere a member of the family Chalicotheriidae (order Perissodactyla), which became extinct in the Pleistocene.
Character displacement divergence in the characteristics of two otherwise similar species where their ranges overlap, caused by competition in the area of overlap
Cheek pouch a pouch used for the temporary storage of food, found only in the typical monkeys of the Old World.
Cheek teeth teeth lying behind the canines in mammals, comprising premolars and molars.
Chiropatagium the portion of the wing membrane of a bat that extends between the digits.
Chorioallantoic placentation a system whereby fetal mammals are nourished by the blood supply of the mother. The CHORION is a superficial layer enclosing all the embryonic structures of the fetus, and is in close contact with the maternal blood supply at the PLACENTA. The union of the chorion (with its vascularized ALLANTOIC STALK and yolk sac) with the placenta facilitates the exchange of food substances and gases, and hence the nutrition of the growing fetus.
Chorion the outer cellular layer of the embryonic sac of mammals, birds, and reptiles. In mammals, the outer layer of the chorion forms the PLACENTA that maintains close contact with the maternal tissues.
Chorionic villi finger-like projections from the CHORION that invade the maternal tissues and form the PLACENTA.
Choriovitelline placentation a type of PLACENTA found in all metatherians (except bandicoots) in which there are no CHORIONIC VILLI and there is only a weak connection to the uterus.
Chromatin materials in the CHROMOSOMES of living cells containing the GENES and proteins.
Chromosome a DNA protein thread occurring in the nucleus of the cell. (see also **DNA**)
Circadian rhythms activity patterns with a period of about 24 hours.
Clade a set of species derived from a single common ancestor.
Cladistics a method by which organisms are organized into TAXA on the basis of joint descent from a common ancestor and their shared derived character states.
Cladogram a branching diagram that illustrates hypothetical relationships between TAXA and shows the evolution of lineages of organisms that have diverged from a common ancestor; it does not however represent rates of evolutionary divergence.
Class in taxonomy, a category subordinate to a phylum and superior to an order. (e.g. Class Mammalia)
Clavicle the collar bone.
Cline a gradual change of character states, such as size, within a species across its geographic range.
Clitoris the small erectile body at the anterior angle of the female vulva; HOMOLOGOUS to the penis in the male.
Cloaca terminal part of the gut into which the reproductive and urinary ducts open. There is one opening to the body, the cloacal aperture, instead of a separate anus and UROGENITAL opening.
Closed-rooted teeth teeth that do not grow throughout the life of an individual. (cf **Open-rooted teeth**)
Cloud forest moist, high-altitude forest characterized by dense undergrowth, and abundance of ferns, mosses, orchids and other plants on the trunks and branches of the trees.
Clupeid a bony fish of the family Clupeidae, including herrings and similar fish, with soft fin-rays, a scaly body and four pairs of gills.
Cochlea the portion of the bony labyrinth of the inner ear. In mammals, except monotremes, it is spirally coiled.
Co-evolution complementary evolution of closely related species. (e.g. the related adaptations of flowering plants and their pollinating insects)
Cohort a group of individuals of the same age.
Colon the large intestine of vertebrates, excluding the terminal rectum. It is concerned with the absorption of water from feces.
Colonial living together in colonies. In bats, more usually applied to the communal sleeping habit, in which tens of thousands of individuals may participate.
Colostrum a special type of protein-rich mammalian milk secreted during the first few days before and after parturition. It contains antibodies that confer the mother's immunity to various diseases to the young.
Commensalism a symbiotic relationship in which one organism benefits from the association and the other organism/s is neither helped nor harmed by the relationship. (cf **Mutualism**, **Parasitism**) (see also **Symbiosis**)
Communal pertaining to the co-operation between members of the same generation in nest building but not care for the young.
Concentrate selector a herbivore which feeds on those plant parts (such as shoots and fruits) which are rich in nutrients.
Condylarthra a diverse lineage of Palaeocene herbivores, a generalized ancestral order, from which arose several orders including proboscideans, sirenians, cetaceans, perissodactyls, and artiodactyls.
Condyle a rounded process at the end of a bone, that fits into the socket of an adjacent bone to form an articulating joint. (e.g. occipital condyles provide articulation between the skull and vertebral column)
Congener a member of the same species (or genus).
Coniferous forest forest comprising largely evergreen conifers (firs, pines, spruces etc). typically in climates either too dry or too cold to support deciduous forest. Most frequent in northern latitudes or in mountain ranges.
Consort (consortship) in certain primates (e.g. Rhesus monkey, Savanna baboon, chimpanzees, orang-utan) males form temporary associations (consortships) with the females, ensuring priority of mating at the appropriate time.
Conspecific member of the same species.
Convergent evolution the independent acquisition of similar characters in evolution, as opposed to possession of similarities by virtue of descent from a common ancestor.
Copepod a small marine crustacean of the invertebrate order Copepoda.
Coprophagy the eating of feces or fecal pellets. (see also **Refection**)
Copulatory plug a plug of coagulated semen formed in the vagina after copulation; found only in certain species of mammals (e.g. springhare).
Coracoid a bone in the pectoral girdle of vertebrates between the scapula and the sternum. In mammals, other than monotremes, it is reduced to a small process on the scapula.
Corpus callosum a broad band of nerve fibres that interlinks the right and left cerebral hemispheres in eutherian mammals.
Corpus luteum the progesterone-secreting mass of follicle cells that develops in the ovary after the egg has been released at ovulation.
Coteries small groups of some mammals (e.g. prairie dogs and some squirrels), which occupy communal burrows.
Cotyledonary placenta a type of CHORIOALLANTOIC PLACENTA in which the CHORIONIC VILLI are grouped into tufts or balls separated by regions of smooth CHORION.
Countercurrent heat exchange mechanism an arrangement of blood vessels that allows peripheral cooling, particularly of appendages, and at the same time maintains an adequate blood supply without excessive heat loss.
Cranium the upper portion of the skull including the bones that surround the brain.
Crenulated finely notched.
Crepuscular active in twilight.
Cretaceous geological time period 144–65 million years ago.
Cricetine adjective and noun used to refer to (a) the primitive rodents from which the New World rats and mice, voles and lemmings, hamsters and gerbils are descended, (b) these modern rodents. In some taxonomic classification systems these subfamilies of the family Muridae are classified as members of a separate family called Cricetidae, with members of the Old World rats and mice alone constituting the Muridae.
Crown the portion of a tooth that projects above the gum, composed of enamel and dentine.
Crustaceans members of a class within the phylum Arthropoda typified by five pairs of legs, two pairs of antennae, head and thorax joined, and calcareous deposits in the exoskeleton (eg crayfish, crabs, shrimps).
Crypsis an aspect of the appearance of an organism which camouflages it from the view of others, such as predators or competitors.
Cryptic (coloration or locomotion) protecting through concealment.
Cue a signal, or stimulus (e.g. olfactory) produced by an individual which elicits a response in other individuals.
Cursorial being adapted for running.
Cusp a prominence on a cheek tooth (premolars or molar).
Cuticle the thin, transparent, outer layer of hair. It forms a distinct, scale-like pattern on the surface.
Cyamids amphipod crustaceans of the family Cyamidae that parasitize the skin of the whales (hence the popular name "whale lice").
Cynodontia a diverse group of THERIODONT THERAPSID reptiles from which mammals supposedly evolved.

Deciduous forest temperate and tropical forest with moderate rainfall and marked seasons. Typically, trees shed leaves during either cold or dry periods.
Deciduous placenta a type of PLACENTA in which a portion of the uterine wall is lost at birth.
Deciduous teeth teeth that are replaced usually early in a mammal's life.
Delayed development a type of embryonic development in which the growth rate of the embryo slows following implantation in the uterine lining. Found in some bats.

Delayed fertilization see **Fertilization**
Delayed implantation see **Implantation**
Deme a local population within which breeding occurs more or less at random.
Den a shelter, natural or constructed, used for sleeping, for giving birth and raising young, and/or in winter; also the act of retiring to a den to give birth and raise young, or for winter shelter.
Dendrogram a treelike diagram of the relationships in a PHYLOGENY.
Dental formula a convention for summarizing the dental arrangement whereby the numbers of each type of tooth in each half of the upper and lower jaw are given. The numbers are always presented in the order: incisor (I), canine (C), premolar (P), molar (M). The final figure is the total number of teeth to be found in the skull. A typical example for Carnivora would be I3/3, C1/1, P4/4, M3/3 = 44.
Dentition the arrangement of teeth characteristic of a particular species.
Dentary bone the single bone of the lower jaw or mandible in mammals.
Dentine a bone-like material (containing calcium phosphate) that forms the body of the tooth.
Dermis the layer of skin lying beneath the outer epidermis.
Derived character refers to a character state that is a modified version of that in the ancestral stock. (see also **Apomorphy**)
Desert areas of low rainfall, typically with sparse scrub or grassland vegetation or lacking vegetation altogether.
Diapause temporary cessation in the growth and development of an insect or mammal. (see also **Embryonic diapause**)
Diaphragm the transverse, muscular partition separating the thoracic and abdominal cavities.
Diastema a space between the teeth, usually the incisors and cheek teeth. It is typical of rodents and lagomorphs, though also found in artiodactyls and perissodactyls, and may be used in grooming.
Dicerathere a member of the family Diceratheriidae (order Perissodactyla), which became extinct in the Miocene.
Dichromatic in dichromatic species, males and females exhibit quite different color patterns (e.g. certain day-active lemurs, some New World monkeys, some Old World monkeys, and certain gibbons).
Dicotyledon one of the two classes of flowering plants (the other class comprises monocotyledons), characterized by the presence of two seed leaves in the young plant, and by net-veined, often broad leaves, in mature plants. Includes deciduous trees, roses etc.
Didactylous the condition in metatherians in which the digits are unfused.
Didelphous pertaining to the female reproductive tract of metatherians in which the uterus, oviduct, and vagina are paired.
Digesta digested food or material.
Digit a finger or toe.
Digital glands glands occurring between or on the toes.
Digitigrade method of walking on the toes without the heel touching the ground. (cf **Plantigrade**)
Dilambodont arrangement of the tooth cusps and associated ridges to form a W-shaped pattern.
Dimorphism the existence of two distinct forms (polymorphism several distinct forms); the term "sexual dimorphism" is applied to cases where the male and female of a species differ consistently in, for example, shape, size, coloration and armament.
Dioecious male and female reproductive organs in separate, unisexual individuals.
Diestrus the period between two estrous cycles in a female mammal.
Diphyletic a group whose members are descended from two distinct lineages.
Diphyodont having two sets of teeth during a lifetime, typically a set of deciduous ("milk") teeth and a set of permanent teeth.
Diploid number the total number of paired CHROMOSOME sets in the cell nucleus. The diploid state is expressed as 2n= (cf haploid state of n=). Almost all animal cells are diploid (e.g. human beings have 2n=46).
Diprotodont having the incisors of the lower jaw reduced to one functional pair, as in possums and kangaroos (small, non-functional incisors may also be present). (cf **Polyprotodont**)
distribution geographical distribution of a species that is marked by gaps. Commonly brought about by fragmentation of suitable habitat, especially as a result of human intervention.
Dispersal the movements of animals, often as they reach maturity, away from their previous HOME RANGE (equivalent to EMIGRATION). Distinct from dispersion, however, the pattern in which things (perhaps animals, food supplies, nest sites) are distributed or scattered.
Display any relatively conspicuous pattern of behavior that conveys specific information to others, usually to members of the same species; can involve visual and or vocal elements, as in threat, courtship or "greeting" displays.
Distal far from the point of attachment or origin (e.g. tip of tail).
Diurnal active in daytime.
DNA (Deoxyribonucleic acid) the genetic material of organisms, its sequence of paired bases constituting the genetic code. It is characterized by the presence of a sugar (deoxyribose) and four bases: cytosine, thymine, adenine, and guanine.
Docodonta an extinct order of late Jurassic mammals known only from the remains of complex tooth and jaw fragments.
Domestication selective breeding of animal species by humans in controlled environments in order to accommodate human needs (e.g. cattle).
Dominant see **Hierarchy**
Doppler shift change in sound frequency caused by movement of the source or the receiver.
Dormancy a period of inactivity; many bears, for example, are dormant for a period in winter; this is not true hibernation, as pulse rate and body temperature do not drop markedly.
Dorsal on the upper or top side or surface (e.g. dorsal stripe).
Dryolestidae a family of early omnivorous mammals in the order EUPANTOTHERIA that were extinct by the mid-Cretaceous.
Ductus deferens (or **Vas deferens**) the duct or tube that carries sperm from the epididymus to the urethra or the cloaca in male mammals.
Duplex a type of uterus in which the right and left parts are completely unfused and each has a distinct cervix. Found in lagomorphs, rodents, hyraxes, and aardvark.
Durophagy the eating of hard or chitinous materials, such as shells and hulls.

Echolocation the process of perception, often direction finding, based upon reaction to the pattern of reflected sound waves (echoes).
Ecological succession replacement of populations in a community through a more or less regular progression culminating in a stable climax community.
Ecological zoogeography the study of the relationships between living organisms in relation to their physical and biotic environment.
Ecology the study of plants and animals in relation to their natural environmental setting. Each species may be said to occupy a distinctive ecological niche.
Ecosystem a unit of the environment within which living and nonliving elements interact.
Ecotone an intermediary habitat created by the juxtaposition of distinctly different habitats (e.g. the zone of transition between grassland and woodland).
Ecotype a genetic variety within a single species, adapted for local ecological conditions.
Ectoparasites parasites that occur on or embedded in the surface of their host organism.
Ectothermy maintenance of body temperature by behavioral means (e.g. basking in the sun).
Edentate a term, literally meaning "without teeth," formerly applied to the clade including the Xenarthra (sloths, armadillos, anteaters) and the Pholidota (pangolins).
Eimer's organ a specialized touch receptor located on the snouts of moles and desmans.
Elongate relatively long (e.g. of canine teeth, longer than those of an ancestor, a related animal, or than adjacent teeth).
Emarginate having a notch or notches at the end.
Embryonic diapause the temporary cessation of development of an embryo leg in some bats and kangaroos.
Emigration departure of animal(s), usually at or about the time of reaching adulthood, from the group or place of birth. (see also **Dispersal**)
Enamel a hard crystalline material, similar in composition to bone, which occurs on the outside portion on the crown of a tooth. It is the hardest and heaviest tissue in vertebrates.
Endemic (endemism) a taxon restricted to a limited geographic area and not found anywhere else.
Endogenous originating from within an organism.
Endometrium the inner lining of the uterus in which blastocysts implant during gestation.
Endoparasites parasites that occur inside the body of their host organism.
Endotheliochorial placenta an arrangement of the CHORIOALLANTOIC PLACENTA in which the CHORION of the embryo is in direct contact with the maternal capillaries.
Endothermy maintenance of constant body temperature by means of heat produced by ENDOGENOUS means (e.g. sweating, panting, shivering)
Entelodont a member of the family Entelodontidae, Oligocene artiodactyls which represent an early branch of the pig family, Suidae.
Entoconid a major cusp found in the lingual portion of the TALONID of the lower molars.
Enzootic concerning disease regularly found within an animal population (endemic applies specifically to people) as distinct from EPIZOOTIC.
Eocene geological epoch 55–34 million years ago.
Epidemic a severe outbreak of a particular disease, usually over a widespread area.
Epidermis the outer layer of mammalian skin (and in plants the outer tissue of young stem, leaf, or root).

Epididymus a coiled duct that receives the sperm from the SEMINIFEROUS TUBULES of the testes and then transmits the sperm to the DUCTUS DEFERENS.
Epipubic bones a pair of bones that extend anteriorly from the pubic bones of the pelvis in monotremes, most metatherians, and also reptiles.
Epiphysis the head of a bone, usually bearing a surface for articulation with another bone.
Epitheliochorial placenta an arrangement of the CHORIOALLANTOIC PLACENTA characterized by having six tissue layers separating the fetal and maternal blood supply, and with the CHORIONIC VILLI resting in pockets in the ENDOMETRIUM. This is the least modified placental arrangement.
Epizootic a disease outbreak in an animal population at a specific time (but not persistently, as in ENZOOTIC); if an epizootic wave of infection eventually stabilizes in an area, it becomes enzootic.
Erectile capable of being raised to an erect position (erectile mane).
Esophagus the gullet connecting the mouth with the stomach.
Estivate (noun: estivation) to enter a state of dormancy or TORPOR in seasonal hot, dry weather, when food is scarce.
Estrus (adj.: estrous) the period in the estrous cycle of female mammals at which they are often attractive to males and receptive to mating. The period coincides with the maturation of eggs and ovulation (the release of mature eggs from the ovaries). Animals in estrus are often said to be "on heat" or "in heat." In primates, if the egg is not fertilized the subsequent degeneration of uterine walls (ENDOMETRIUM) leads to menstrual bleeding. In some species ovulation is triggered by copulation and this is called induced ovulation, as distinct from spontaneous ovulation.
Ethiopian a geographical region comprising Africa, south of the Sahara. Sometimes referred to as Afrotropical.
Eucalypt forest Australian forest, dominated by trees of the genus *Eucalyptus*.
Eupantotheria an order of extinct mammals, known from the Jurassic of North America and Europe.
Euphausiids see **Krill**
Eusocial a social system whereby only one female produces offspring and there is reproductive division of labor (castes) and the cooperative rearing of young by members of previous generations (who also help defend and maintain the colony). It is best typified by honey bees, but in mammals is recorded only in two species of mole-rat.
Eutherian a mammal of the subclass Eutheria, the dominant group of mammals. The embryonic young are nourished by an allantoic placenta.
Evaporative cooling loss of heat through the evaporation of sweat or saliva from the skin, or otherwise of water vapour from the nasal mucosa or lungs.
Exogenous originating from outside the organism.
Exotic a species introduced to an area in which it does not occur naturally.
Extant not extinct; still surviving.
External auditory meatus a passageway leading from the base of the pinna or surface of the head to the TYMPANIC MEMBRANE.
Extinction loss of a taxon.
Extirpation the extermination of a population or taxon from a given area.
Exudate natural plant exudates include gums and resins; damage to plants (e.g. by marmosets) can lead to loss of sap as well. Certain primates (e.g. Bush babies) rely heavily on exudates as a food source.

Facultative optional. (cf **Obligate**)
Facultative delayed implantation a form of delayed IMPLANTATION in which a delay results because the female is nursing a large litter or faces harsh environmental conditions.
Falcate curved or hooked.
Family in taxonomy, a division subordinate to an order and superior to a genus (e.g. family Felidae).
Fast ice sea ice which forms in polar regions along the coast, and remains fast, being attached to the shore, to an ice wall, an ice front, or over shoals, generally in the position where it originally formed.
Feces excrement from the bowels; colloquially known as droppings or scats.
Fecundity the number of offspring produced during a certain amount of time.
Female defense polygyny a mating system whereby males control access to females by directly competing or interfering with other males.
Feral living in the wild (of domesticated animals, e.g. cat, dog, pig).
Fermentation the decomposition of organic substances by microorganisms. In some mammals, parts of the digestive tract (e.g. the cecum) may be inhabited by bacteria that break down cellulose and release nutrients.
Fertilization the penetration of an egg by a sperm resulting in the combination of maternal and paternal DNA and formation of a ZYGOTE. Most aquatic mammals achieve fertilization externally. Delayed fertilization occurs following mating when sperm are deposited in the uterine tract of the female but ovulation and fertilization are delayed for several months. The sperm remain viable in the female's reproductive tract during this time.
Fetal development rate the rate of development, or growth, of unborn young.
Fetlock joint above the hooves.
Fetus the mammalian embryo
Filiform thin and threadlike.
Fimbriation a stiff fringe of hairs between the toes that aid some species in locomotion (e.g. shrews).
Fin an organ projecting from the body of aquatic animals and generally used in steering and propulsion.
Fission splitting or parting.
Fissipedia (suborder) name given by some taxonomists to modern terrestrial carnivores to distinguish them from the suborder Pinnipedia which describes the marine carnivores. Here we treat both as full orders, the Carnivora and the Pinnipedia.
Fitness a measure of the ability of an animal (with one genotype or genetic make-up) to leave viable offspring in comparison to other individuals (with different genotypes). The process of natural selection, often called survival of the fittest, determines which characteristics have the greatest fitness, i.e. are most likely to enable their bearers to survive and rear young which will in turn bear those characteristics. (see **Inclusive fitness**, **Natural selection**)
Flehmen German word describing a facial expression in which the lips are pulled back, head often lifted, teeth sometimes clapped rapidly together and nose wrinkled. Often associated with animals (especially males) sniffing scent marks or socially important odors (e.g. scent of estrous female). Possibly involved in transmission of odor to JACOBSON'S ORGAN.
Flense to strip blubber from a whale or seal.
Flipper a limb adapted for swimming.
Floe a sheet of floating ice.
Fluke one of the lobes of a whale's tail; the name refers to their broad, triangular shape.
Folivory consuming mainly leaves.
Follicle a small sac, therefore (a) a mass of ovarian cells that produces an ovum, (b) an indentation in the skin from which hair grows.
Foramen an opening or passage through bone.
Forbs a general term applied to ephemeral or weedy plant species (not grasses). In arid and semi-arid regions they grow abundantly and profusely after rains.
Foregut fermentation see **Ruminant**
Forestomach a specialized part of the stomach consisting of two compartments (presaccus and saccus).
Fossorial burrowing (of life-style or behavior); adapted to a subterranean lifestyle. Animals that are only partially adapted to such a lifestyle are semi-fossorial.
Frequency the number of wave lengths per second, expressed in Hertz (Hz).
Frugivory consuming mainly fruits.
Furbearer term applied to mammals whose pelts have commercial value and form part of the fur harvest.
Fusiform elongated with tapering ends.
Fusion opposite of FISSION; often applied to a fission–fusion social system in some species whereby some group members leave the group and then rejoin it later.

Gadoid cod-like fish of the suborder Gadoidei.
Gait manner of walking.
Gallery forest luxuriant forest lining the banks of watercourses.
Gamete a male or female reproductive cell (ovum or spermatozoon).
Gape the extent to which the mouth can be opened.
Gene the basic unit of heredity; a portion of DNA molecule coding for a given trait and passed, through replication at reproduction, from generation to generation. Genes are expressed as adaptations and consequently are the most fundamental units (more so than individuals) on which natural selection acts.
Generalist an animal whose lifestyle does not involve highly specialized strategems (cf **Specialist**); for example, feeding on a variety of foods which may require different foraging techniques.
Genotype the genetic constitution of an organism, determining all aspects of its appearance, structure and function. (cf **Phenotype**)
Genus (pl. **genera**) in taxonomy, a division superior to species and subordinate to family (e.g. genus *Panthera*).
Gestation the period of development within the uterus; the process of delayed IMPLANTATION can result in the period of pregnancy being longer than the period during which the embryo is actually developing.
Glanils (marking) glandular areas of the skin, used in depositing scent marks.
Glans penis the head or distal portion of the penis.
Gliding aerial locomotion (not powered as in bats) involving the use of a membrane (the PATAGIUM) to provide lift.
Glissant gliding locomotion. Found in flying lemurs, colugos, flying squirrels and some other mammals.
Granivory consuming a diet of seeds or nuts.
Graviportal animals in which the weight is carried by the limbs acting as rigid, extensible struts, powered by extrinsic muscles (e.g. elephants and rhinos).

Grazer a herbivore which feeds upon grasses. (cf **Browser**)
Great call a protracted series of notes, rising to a climax, produced by the female as part of the group song in lesser apes.
Gregarious living in groups or herds.
Grizzled sprinkled or streaked with gray.
Guano bat fecal droppings. They may accumulate in large quantities where colonies roost.
Guard hair an element of the coat of seals consisting of a longer, stiffer, more bristle-like hair which lies outside and supports the warmer, softer underfur.
Guild a group of species that exploits a common resource base in a similar fashion (e.g. the carnivore guild).
Gumivory consuming a diet of gum (plant EXUDATE).

Hallux the first digit of the hind foot.
Haplorhine a member of the primate suborder Haplorrhini that comprises the anthropoids (suborder Simiiformes) and the infraorder Tarsiiformes (tarsiers). In all members the upper lip is whole and the placenta is hemochorial. (cf **Strepsirhine**)
Haplotype a set of genetic determinants located on a single chromosome; also the single species included in a genus at the time of its designation, thereby becoming the type species of the genus.
Harem group a social group consisting of a single adult male, at least two adult females and immature animals; a common pattern of social organization among mammals.
Haulout behavior of sea mammals pulling themselves ashore.
Heath low-growing shrubs with woody stems and narrow leaves (e.g. heather), which often predominate on acidic or upland soils.
Helper jargon for an individual, generally without young of its own, which contributes to the survival of the offspring of another by behaving parentally towards them. (see also **Alloparent**)
Hemochorial placenta the arrangement of the CHORIOALLANTOIC PLACENTA whereby the CHORIONIC VILLI are in direct contact with the maternal blood supply.
Hemoendothelial placenta the arrangement of the CHORIOALLANTOIC PLACENTA in which the fetal capillaries are surrounded by maternal blood. This arrangement shows the last separation between fetal and maternal bloodstreams.
Hemoglobin an iron-containing protein in the red corpuscles which plays a crucial role in oxygen exchange between blood and tissues in mammals.
Herbivore an animal eating mainly plants or parts of plants.
Hermaphrodite an individual that has both male and female reproductive organs.
Heterodont teeth that vary in form and function in different parts of the jaws (e.g. incisors, canines, premolars, and molars in mammals). (cf **Homodont**)
Heterothermy (Poikilothermy) a condition in which the internal temperature of the body follows the temperature of the outside environment. (cf **Homeotherm**)
Hibernaculum the place in which an animal hibernates.
Hibernation a period of winter inactivity during which the normal physiological process is greatly reduced and thus during which the energy requirements of the animal are lowered.
Hierarchy (social or dominance) the existence of divisions within society, based on the outcome of interactions which show some individuals to be consistently dominant to others. Higher-ranking individuals thus have control of aspects (e.g. access to food or mates) of the life and behavior of low-ranking ones. Hierarchies may be branching, but simple linear ones are often called pecking orders (after the behavior of farmyard chickens).
Higher primate one of the more advanced primates (e.g. Chimpanzee).
Hindgut fermenter herbivores among which the bacterial breakdown of plant tissue occurs in the cecum, rather than in the rumen or foregut.
Historical zoogeography the study of the distribution of animal species in terms of their origin, dispersal and extinction.
Holarctic realm a region of the world including North America, Greenland, Europe, and Asia apart from the southwest, southeast and India.
Holotype (type specimen) in taxonomy, the individual specimen chosen as the future representative during the naming and descriptive process of a specific animal. This specimen is housed within a museum collection and marked accordingly.
Home range the area in which an animal normally lives (generally excluding rare excursions or migrations), irrespective of whether or not the area is defended from other animals. (cf **Territory**)
Homodont teeth that do not vary in form or function; they are often peg-like in structure (e.g. in toothed whales). (cf **Heterodont**)
Homoeothermy (homoiothermy) regulation of constant body temperature by physiological means regardless of the external temperature. (cf **Heterothermy**)
Homologous applied to an organ of one animal that is thought to have the same evolutionary origin as the organ of another animal, even though they differ in function (e.g. penis in males and clitoris in females).
Homoplasy the appearance of similar structures in different lineages in the course of evolution (i.e. not inherited from a common ancestor)
Hormones chemical substances, regulatory in function, released into the bloodstream or into bodily fluids from endocrine glands.
Horns cranial processes, found in bovids, formed from an inner core of bone and covered by a sheath of keratinized material and derived from the epidermis. (cf **Antlers**)
Hybrid the offspring of parents of different species.
Hydrophone a waterproof microphone held in position under the sea surface and used to detect the sounds emitted by sea mammals.
Hyoid bones skeletal elements in the throat region, supporting the trachea, larynx and base of the tongue (derived in evolutionary history from the gill arches of ancestral fish).
Hyperthermy a condition in which internal body temperature is above normal. (cf **Hypothermy**)
Hypocone a cusp posterior to the PROTOCONE and lingual (toward the tongue) in upper molars but labial (toward the cheeks) in lower molars (then referred to as a hypoconid).
Hypoconid see **Hypocone**
Hypoconulid a prominent accessory cusp found in the posterior portion of the TALONID of lower molars.
Hypodermis the innermost layer of the integument, consisting of fatty tissue.
Hypothermy a condition in which internal body temperature is below normal. (cf **Hyperthermy**)
Hypsodont high-crowned teeth, which continue to grow when full-sized and whose pulp cavity remains open; typical of herbivorous mammals. (cf **Brachydont**)
Hyracodont a member of the family Hyracodontidae (order Perissodactyla) which became extinct in the Oligocene.
Hystricognathous in rodents, having the angular process of the mandible lateral to the plane of the alveolus of the lower incisor. (cf **Sciurognathous**)
Hystricomorphous in rodents, having a greatly enlarged infraorbital foramen. (cf **Sciuromorphous**)

Ilium the largest and most dorsal of the three pelvic bones.
Imbricate overlapping.
Immigration movement of individuals into a population or given area.
Implantation the process whereby the free-floating BLASTOCYST (early embryo) becomes attached to the uterine wall in mammals. At the point of implantation a complex network of blood vessels develops to link mother and embryo (the placenta). In delayed implantation, the blastocyst remains dormant in the uterus for periods varying, between species, from 12 days to 11 months. Delayed implantation may be obligatory or facultative and is known for some members of the Carnivora and Pinnipedia and others.
Inbreeding mating among related individuals.
Inbreeding depression reduced reproductive success and survival of offspring as a result of INBREEDING.
Incisor a unicuspid tooth in mammals located anterior to the canines.
Inclusive fitness a measure of the animal's fitness which is based on the number of its genes, rather than the number of its offspring, present in subsequent generations. This is a more complete measure of fitness, since it incorporates the effect of, for example, alloparenthood, wherein individuals may help to rear the offspring of their relatives. (see also **Kin selection**, **Alloparent**)
Incus the second of three bones of the middle ear in mammals.
Induced ovulation see **Estrus**
Infanticide the killing of infants. Infanticide has been recorded notably in species in which a bachelor male may take over a harem from its resident male(s) (e.g. lions).
Infraorbital foramen a canal in the maxilla, below and slightly in front of the orbit, through which bloodvessels and nerve fibres pass.
Infrasound sound frequencies below 20 Hz.
Infundibulum a funnel-shaped opening of the oviduct situated near the ovary that receives the oocytes at ovulation.
Inguinal pertaining to the groin.
Innervated having a supply of nerves to and from an organ.
Insectivore an animal eating mainly arthropods (insects, spiders).
Integument the skin.
Interdigital between the digits.
Interfemoral a membrane stretching between the femora, or thigh bones in bats.
Interordinal between different orders.
Interspecific between different species.
Intestinal flora simple plants (e.g. bacteria) which live in the intestines, especially the cecum, of mammals. They produce enzymes which break down the cellulose in the leaves and stems of green plants and convert it to digestible sugars.
Intraspecific between individuals of the same species.
Introduced of a species which has been brought, by man, from lands where it

occurs naturally to lands where it has not previously occurred. Some introductions are accidental (e.g. rats which have travelled unseen on ships), but some are made on purpose for biological control, farming or other economic reasons (e.g. the common brush-tail possum, which was introduced to New Zealand from Australia to establish a fur industry).
Introgression the mixing of gene pools.
Invertebrate an animal which lacks a backbone (e.g. insects, spiders, crustaceans).
Ischial pertaining to the hip.
Ischial callosities specialized, hardened pads of tissue present on the buttocks of some monkeys and apes. Each overlies a flattened projection of the ischium bone of the pelvis. Known also as "sitting pads," they are found in Old World _monkeys and lesser apes. (see also **Callosities**)
Ischium one of the three bones of the pelvis.
Iteroparous the production of offspring on a regular basis by an organism. (cf **Semelparous**)

Jacobson's organ (vomeronasal organ) a structure in a foramen (small opening) in the palate of many vertebrates which appears to be involved in olfactory communication. Molecules of scent may be sampled in these organs.
Joey a young kangaroo that is still nursing but not restricted to the pouch.
Jurassic geological time period 213–144 million years ago.
Juvenile no longer having the characteristics of an infant, but not yet fully adult.

Karyotype the characteristic number and shape of the chromosomes of a cell, individual or species.
Keratin a tough, fibrous material found in epidermal tissues, such as hair and hooves.
Keratinized made of KERATIN
Kin related individuals.
Kin selection a facet of natural selection whereby an animal's fitness is affected by the survival of its relatives or KIN. Kin selection may be the process whereby some alloparental behavior evolved; an individual behaving in a way which promotes the survival of its kin increases its own INCLUSIVE FITNESS, despite the apparent selflessness of its behavior.
Kleptoparasite an animal that steals food from other animals.
Knuckle-walk to walk on all fours with the weight of the front part of the body carried on the knuckles. Found only in gorillas and chimpanzees.
Kopje (koppie) a rocky outcrop, typically on otherwise flat plains of African grasslands.
Krill shrimp-like crustaceans of the genera *Euphausia*, *Meganyctiphanes* etc., occurring in huge numbers in polar seas, particularly of Antarctica, where they form the principal prey of baleen whales.
K-selection selection favouring slow rates of reproduction and growth for maximizing competitive ability as a response to a stable environment. (cf **R-selection**)

Labial of, or pertaining to, the cheek.
Labile (body temperature) an internal body temperature which may be lowered or raised from an average body temperature.
Lactation (verb: lactate) the secretion of milk, from mammary glands.
Lactose a disaccharide sugar that is the principal sugar of milk.
Lambdoidal crest a bony ridge at the rear of the cranium.
Laminae ridges on teeth sometimes with distinct cusps.
Laminar flow streamline flow in a viscous fluid near a solid boundary; the flow of water over the surface of whales is laminar.
Lamoid Llama-like; one of the South American cameloids.
Lanugo the birth-coat of mammals which is shed to be replaced by the adult coat.
Larynx dilated region of upper part of windpipe, containing vocal chords. Vibration of cords produces vocal sounds.
Latrine a place where feces are regularly left (often together with other scent marks); associated with olfactory communication.
Lead a channel of open water between ice floes.
Lek a display ground at which individuals of one sex maintain miniature territories into which they seek to attract potential mates.
Lesser apes the gibbons and siamang.
Liana a climbing plant. In rain forests large numbers of often woody, twisted lianas hang down like ropes from the crowns of trees.
Lingual of, or pertaining to, the tongue.
Lipotyphlan an early insectivore classification; menotyphlan insectivores possess a cecum, lipotyphlans do not. Only lipotyphlans are now classified as Insectivora. Recent phylogenetic reclassification (cf **Afrotheria**) has seen a subdivision of the Lipotyphlans into the orders Afrosoricida and Eulipotyphla.
Llano South American semi-arid savanna country (e.g. of Venezuela).
Lobtailing a whale beating the water with its tail flukes, perhaps to communicate with other whales.
Locus the specific location of a GENE on a CHROMOSOME.
Loph a transverse ridge on the crown of molar teeth.
Lophiodont a member of the family Lophiodontidae (order Perissodactyla) which became extinct in the early Tertiary.
Lophodont molar teeth whose cusps form ridges or lophs.
Lordosis a behavior, performed by females signaling their willingness to mate, in which the lumbar curvature is exaggerated.
Lower critical temperature the temperature at which an animal must increase its METABOLIC RATE in order to balance heat loss. (cf **Upper critical temperature**)
Lower primate one of the more primitive primates (e.g. lorises).
Lumbar a term locating anatomical features in the loin region (e.g. lumbar vertebrae are at the base of the spine).
Luteinizing hormone (LH) a hormone that stimulates development of corpora lutea and progesterone production in females.

m.y.a. abbreviation for million years ago.
Male dominance polygyny a mating system whereby the males maintain a dominance hierarchy thereby influencing their access to females; higher-ranking males obtain more mates.
Mallee a grassy, open woodland habitat characteristic of many semi-arid parts of Australia. "Mallee" also describes the multi-stemmed habit of eucalypt trees which dominate this habitat.
Malleus the first of the three bones of the middle ear in mammals.
Mamma (pl. **mammae**) (mammary glands) the milk-secreting organ of female mammals, probably evolved from sweat glands.
Mammal a member of the class of vertebrate animals (the Mammalia) having mammary glands which produce milk with which they nurse their young.
Mammalogy the study of mammals.
Mammalogist someone who studies mammals.
Mammilla (pl. **mammillae**) nipple, or teat, on the mamma of female mammals; the conduit through which milk is passed from the mother to the young.
Mandible the lower jaw
Mandibular fossa part of the cranium with which the mandible (lower jaw) interacts.
Mandibular ramus one of the major portions of the dentary bone of the lower jaw. The horizontal part holds the teeth while the ascending part articulates with the skull.
Mangrove forest tropical forest developed on sheltered muddy shores of deltas and estuaries exposed to tide. Vegetation is almost entirely woody.
Manus the hindfoot.
Marine living in the sea.
Marsupium the pouch found in many marsupials and in echidnas that encloses the mammary glands and serves as an incubation chamber for the young (see also **pouch**).
Mask colloquial term for the face of a mammal, especially a dog, fox or cat.
Masseter a powerful muscle, subdivided into parts, joining the mandible to the upper jaw. Used to bring jaws together when chewing.
Mastication the act of chewing.
Maternity the state of being the maternal parent (mother) to an offspring.
Matriarchal of a society in which most activity and behavior is centred around the dominant female.
Matriline a related group of animals linked by descent through females alone.
Maxilla one of the paired bones making up the upper jaw and carrying the teeth. Sometimes applied to the whole upper jaw.
Melanin a dark pigment found in the skin.
Melanism darkness of color due to the presence of MELANIN. (cf **Albinism**)
Menstrual cycle an approximately monthly cycle involving alternation of ovulation and menstruation (loss of blood from the vulva at monthly intervals) until pregnancy intervenes; found in humans, great apes, Old World monkeys and, to varying degrees, in New World monkeys.
Menotyphlan see **Lipotyphlan**
Mesic pertaining to conditions of moderate moisture or water-supply; used of animals occupying moist habitats (i.e. mesic-adapted). (cf **Xeric**)
Metabolic rate the rate at which the chemical processes of the body occur.
Metabolism the chemical processes occurring within an organism, including the production of protein from amino acids, the exchange of gasses in respiration, the liberation of energy from foods and innumerable other chemical reactions.
Metacarpal bones of the hand, between the carpals of the wrist and the phalanges of the digits.
Metacone a cusp posterior to the PROTOCONE and labial in upper molars and lingual in lower molars (then called a metaconid).
Metaconid see **Metacone**
Metapodial the proximal element of a digit (contained within the palm or sole). The metapodial bones are metacarpals in the manus and metatarsals in the pes.
Metapopulation a set of semi-isolated populations linked together via dispersal and having some regular gene flow.

Metatarsal bones of the foot articulating between the tarsals of the ankle and the phalanges of the digits.
Metatheria the group of mammals that comprises the marsupials and all extinct relatives.
Metestrus third stage in the estrous cycle, in which the corpora lutea are formed and progesterone levels are high.
Microhabitat the particular parts of the habitat that are encountered by an individual in the course of its activities.
Microsatellite DNA tandem repeats of short sequences of DNA, most often multiples of two to four bases.
Midden a dunghill, or site for the regular deposition of feces by mammals.
Migration movement, usually seasonal, from one region or climate to another for purposes of feeding or breeding.
Miocene geological epoch 24–5 million years ago.
Molar a non-deciduous cheek tooth posterior to the premolar.
Molariform having the shape and appearance of a molar.
Molecular phylogeny a hypothetical representation of the evolutionary history of a group of organisms based on characters defined at the molecular level.
Molting seasonal replacement of hair.
Monestrus having a single estrous period per year or breeding season. (cf **Polyestrus**)
Monogamy a mating system in which individuals have only one mate per breeding season. (cf **Polygamy**)
Monophyletic a group whose members are descended from a common ancestor. (cf **Paraphyletic**)
Monotreme a mammal of the subclass Monotremata (platypus and echidnas). The only egg-laying mammals.
Monotypic a genus comprising a single species.
Monozygotic polyembryony a reproductive process, characteristic of some armadillos, in which a single zygote splits into individual zygotes and forms several identical, same-sex embryos.
Montane pertaining to mountainous country.
Montane forest forest occurring at middle altitudes on the slopes of mountains, below the alpine zone but above the lowland forests.
Morphology (morphological) the structure and shape of an organism.
Moss forest moist forest occurring on higher mountain slopes, e.g. 1,500–3,200m (4,900–10,500ft) in New Guinea. It is characterized by rich growth of mosses and other plants on tree trunks and branches.
Mucosa mucous membrane; a membrane rich in mucous glands such as the lining of the mouth.
Multiparous a female that has had several litters or young.
Murine adjective and noun used to refer to members of the subfamily (of the family Muridae) Murinae, which consists of the Old World rats and mice. In some taxonomic classification systems this subfamily is given the status of a family, Muridae, and the members then are sometimes referred to as murids. (see also **Cricetine**)
Musk scent secreted from scent glands (musk gland) in mustelids and other mammal species.
Musth the period of heightened reproductive activity in male elephants; aggression increases during this period, usually lasting two to three months.
Mutualism a symbiotic relationship that involves a mutually beneficial association between members of two species. (cf. **Commensalism**, **Parasitism**; see also **Symbiosis**)
Mutation a structural change in a gene which can thus give rise to a new heritable characteristic.
Mycophagy consuming a diet of fungi.
Myoglobin a protein related to HEMOGLOBIN in the muscles of vertebrates; like hemoglobin, it is involved in the oxygen exchange processes of respiration.
Myomorphous in rodents, having a slip of the medial masseter muscle pass through an oval or V-shaped infraorbital foramen.
Myopia short-sightedness.
Myrmecophagy consuming a diet of ants and termites.
Mystacial pad the region on the snout from which most facial vibrissae originate.
Mysticete a member of the suborder Mysticeti, whales with baleen plates rather than teeth as their feeding apparatus.

Nares external nostrils.
Nasolacrimal duct a duct or canal between the nostrils and the eye.
Natal (natality) of, or pertaining to, birth.
Natal range the home range into which an individual was born.
Natural selection the process whereby individuals with the most appropriate adaptations are more successful than other individuals, and hence survive to produce more offspring. To the extent that the successful traits are heritable (genetic) they will therefore spread in the population.
Nearctic the geographical region comprising North America south to Mexico.
Nectivory consuming mainly nectar.
Neonate newborn animal.
Neotropical a geographical area comprising Central and South America, as well as the West Indies and the Galapagos.
New World a geographical term for the region including the Nearctic and Neotropical regions. (cf **Old World**)
Niche the role of a species within the community, defined in terms of all aspects of its life-style (e.g. food, competitors, predators, and other resource requirements).
Nicker a vocalization of horses, also called neighing.
Nictitating (nictating) membrane a thin, transparent membrane beneath the eyelid of some vertebrates that can cover and protect the eye.
Nocturnal active at nighttime.
Nomadic among mammals, species that have no clearly defined residence most of the time. Distinct from migratory species, which may be resident except when migrating.
Nonshivering thermogenesis means of heat production in mammals that does not involve muscle contraction. (see also **Thermogenesis**)
Noseleaf characteristically shaped flaps of skin surrounding the nasal passages of horseshoe, or nose-leaf bats (family Rhinolophidae). Ultrasonic cries are uttered through the nostrils, with the nose leaves serving to direct the echolocating pulses forwards.
Nulliparous a female that has never given birth.
Nunatak refugia within ice sheets during periods of glaciation.

Obligate required, binding. (cf **Facultative**)
Obligate delayed implantation a form of delayed IMPLANTATION in which the delay occurs as a normal part of the reproductive cycle (e.g. in armadillos).
Occipital pertaining to the posterior part of the head.
Occlusal the grinding or biting surfaces of a tooth.
Odontocete a member of the suborder Odontoceti, the toothed whales.
Old World a geographical term for the region including the Palearctic, Oriental, Ethiopian, and Australian regions. (cf **New World**)
Olfaction (olfactory) the olfactory sense is the sense of smell, depending on receptors located in the epithelium (surface membrane) lining the nasal cavity.
Oligocene geological epoch 34–24 million years ago.
Omasum third of the four chambers in the ruminant artiodactyl stomach.
Omnivore an animal eating a varied diet including both animal and plant tissue.
Ontogeny the development of an individual from fertilization of the egg to adulthood.
Open-rooted teeth teeth that grow throughout the life of the individual. (cf **Closed-rooted teeth**)
Opposable (of first digit) of the thumb and forefinger in some mammals, which may be brought together in a grasping action, thus enabling objects to be picked up and held.
Opportunist (of feeding) flexible behavior of exploiting circumstances to take a wide range of food items; characteristic of many species. (see **Generalist**, **Specialist**)
Order in taxonomy, a division subordinate to class and superior to family (e.g. order Carnivora).
Oreodont a member of the family Oreodontidae (order Artiodactyla), which became extinct in the late Tertiary.
Oriental the geographical region comprising India and Asia south of the Himalayan-Tibetan barrier, and the Australasian archipelago (excluding New Guinea and Sulawesi).
Os baculum see **Baculum**
Os clitoris a small bone present in the clitoris of some female mammal species. HOMOLOGOUS to the baculum in males.
Os penis see **Baculum**
Os sacrum fused SACRAL vertebrae in mammals.
Ossicles one of the three middle ear bones.
Ossicones short, permanent, unbranched processes of bone forming the horns in giraffes.
Ovaries the site of egg production and maturation in females.
Oviducts (Fallopian tubes) the ducts that carry the eggs from the ovary to the uterus.
Oviparous a method of reproduction involving the laying of eggs.
Ovoviviparous a method of reproduction whereby young hatch from eggs retained within the mother's uterus.
Ovulation (verb: ovulate) the shedding of mature ova (eggs) from the ovaries where they are produced. (see **Estrus**)

Pack ice large blocks of ice formed on the surface of the sea when an ice field has been broken up by wind and waves, and drifted from its original position.
Paenungulata a strongly supported interordinal group of herbivorous African mammals, which includes the hyraxes (Hyracoidea), elephants (Proboscidea), and manatees and dugongs (Sirenia). The Paenungulata are included within the AFROTHERIA.
Pair-bond an association between a male and female, lasting from courtship at least until mating is completed, and in some species, until the death of one partner.
Paleocene geological epoch 65–55 million years ago.
Palearctic a geographical region encompassing Europe and Asia north of the

Himalayas, and Africa north of the Sahara.
Paleothere a member of the family Paleotheriidae (order Perissodactyla), which became extinct in the early Tertiary.
Palmate palm-shaped.
Pampas Argentinian steppe grasslands.
Pandemic a large-scale outbreak of disease over a very wide geographic area.
Panting a thermoregulatory behavior that involves very rapid, shallow breathing in order to increase evaporation of water from the upper respiratory tract.
Papilla (pl. **papillae**) a small, nipple-like projection.
Paracone a cusp that is anterior to the PROTOCONE and labial in upper molars and lingual in lower molars (then called a paraconid).
Paraconid see **Paracone**
Páramo alpine meadow of northern and western South American uplands.
Paraphyletic a taxonomic group in which some, but not all, members are descended from a single common ancestor. (cf **Monophyletic**)
Parasitism a symbiotic relationship whereby one organism benefits from the association and the other is usually harmed. (cf **Commensalism**, **Mutualism**) (see also **Symbiosis**)
Paratype in taxonomy, a specimen (other than the HOLOTYPE) used by the author at the time of the description. It is housed in a museum and labelled accordingly.
Parous a female mammal that is pregnant or shows evidence of previous pregnancies.
Parturition the process of giving birth (hence post-partum – after birth).
Patagium a gliding membrane typically stretching down the sides of the body between the fore- and hindlimbs and perhaps including part of the tail. Found in colugos, flying squirrels, bats etc.
Paternity the state of being the paternal parent (father) to an offspring.
Pecoran a ruminant of the infra-order Pecora, which is characterized by the presence of horns on the forehead.
Pectinate resembling a comb in shape.
Pectoral girdle the bones of the shoulder region providing support for the forelimbs.
Pedicel a bony supporting structure for an antler.
Pelage all the hairs on an individual mammal.
Pelagic the upper part of the open sea, above the BENTHIC zone.
Pelvis a girdle of bones that supports the hindlimbs of vertebrates.
Penis the male copulatory organ.
Pentadactyl having five digits.
Peramuridae a family of Jurassic mammals that probably gave rise to the advanced therians.
Perineal glands glandular tissue occurring between the anus and genitalia.
Perineal swelling a swelling of the naked area of skin around the anus and vulva of a female primate, as in chimpanzees and some Old World monkeys.
Perissodactyl a member of the Perissodactyla (the odd-toed ungulates).
Pes the forefoot.
Phalanges the bones of the digits.
Phenetic similarity based on observable external characteristics.
Phenotype (phenotypic) the sum total of the observable structural and functional properties of an organism. (cf **Genotype**)
Pheromone secretions whose odors act as chemical messengers in animal communication, and which prompt a specific response on behalf of the animal receiving the message. (see also **Scent marking**)
Philopatry living and breeding in the natal area.
Phylogenetic pertaining to evolutionary relationships between groups.
Phylogeny a classification or relationship based on the closeness of evolutionary descent.
Phylogram a tree diagram (not unlike a CLADOGRAM) which shows the degree of genetic divergence among the represented taxa by means of the lengths of the branches and the angles between them.
Phylum in taxonomy, a division comprising a number of classes (e.g. Phylum Chordata)
Physiology study of the processes which go on in living organisms.
Phytoplankton minute plants floating near the surface of aquatic environments. (cf **Zooplankton**)
Piloerection fluffing or erection of the fur or hair.
Pinna (pl. **pinnae**) the projecting cartilaginous portion of the external ear.
Pinnipedia a member of the order of aquatic carnivorous mammals with all four limbs modified into flippers; the true seals, eared seals and walrus. Sometimes classified as a suborder of Carnivora.
Piscivory consuming a diet of fish.
Pituitary gland the main gland of the endocrine system that secretes a range of hormones.
Placenta, placental mammals a structure that connects the fetus and the mother's womb to ensure a supply of nutrients to the fetus and removal of its waste products. Only placental mammals have a well-developed placenta; marsupials have a rudimentary placenta or none and monotremes lay eggs.
Placental scar a pigmented area on the wall of the uterus formed from prior attachment of a fetus. It is therefore indicative of previous pregnancies.
Plankton floating plant and animal life in lakes and oceans.
Plantigrade way of walking on the soles of the feet, including the heels. (cf **Digitigrade**)
Platyrrhine a "flat-nosed" monkey with widely separated nostrils. Term commonly used for all New World monkeys in contrast to CATARRHINE monkeys of the Old World.
Pleistocene geological epoch 1.8 million – 10,000 years ago.
Pliocene geological epoch 5–1.8 million years ago.
Plesiomorphic see **Apomorphic**
Pod a group of individuals, usually applied to whales or dolphins, with some, at least temporary, cohesive social structure.
Pollex the first digit of the forefoot.
Polyandrous see **Polygynous**
Polyestrus having two or more estrous cycles in one breeding season. (cf **Monestrus**)
Polygamous a mating system wherein an individual has more than one mate per breeding season. (cf **Monogamous**)
Polygynous a mating system in which a male mates with several females during one breeding season (as opposed to polyandrous, where one female mates with several males).
Polymorphism occurrence of more than one morphological form of individual in a population. (see also **Sexual dimorphism**)
Polyprotodont having more than three well-developed lower incisor teeth (as in bandicoots and carnivorous marsupials). (cf **Diprodont**)
Population a more or less separate (discrete) group of animals of the same species within a given biotic community.
Postorbital bar a bony strut behind the eye-socket (orbit) in the skull.
Post-partum estrus ovulation and an increase in the sexual receptivity of female mammals, hours or days after the birth of a litter. (see also **Estrus**, **Parturition**)
Pouch a flap of skin on the underbelly of female marsupials which covers the mammillae. The pouch may be a simple open structure as in most carnivorous marsupials, or a more enclosed pocket-like structure as in phalangers and kangaroos. (see also **Marsupium**)
Prairie North American steppe grassland between 30°N and 55°N.
Predator an animal that forages for live prey; hence "anti-predator behavior" describes the evasive actions of the prey.
Precocial of young born at a relatively advanced stage of development, requiring a short period of nursing by parents. (cf **Altricial**)
Prehensile capable of grasping.
Premolar cheek teeth that are anterior to the molars and posterior to the canines. They may be either deciduous or non-deciduous.
Pre-orbital in front of the eye socket.
Preputial pertaining to the prepuce or loose skin covering the penis.
Primary forest forest that has remained undisturbed for a long time and has reached a mature (climax) condition; primary rain forest may take centuries to become established.
Primate a member of the order Primates comprising the apes, monkeys and related forms, including man, tarsiers, as well as the lorises, bushbabies, lemurs, and potto.
Proboscidean a member of the order of primitive ungulates, Proboscidea.
Proboscis a long flexible snout.
Process (anatomical) an outgrowth or protuberance.
Procumbent (incisors) projecting forward more or less horizontally.
Proestrus the first stage of the estrous cycle when estrogen, progesterone and LH levels are at their peak.
Progesterone a steroid hormone, secreted mainly by the CORPUS LUTEUM, which promotes growth of the uterine lining and enables the implantation of the fertilized egg.
Promiscuous a mating system wherein an individual mates more or less indiscriminately.
Pronking (stotting) movement where an animal leaps vertically, on the spot, with all four feet off the ground. Typical of antelopes (e.g. springbok), especially when alarmed.
Propatagium the anterior portion of the PATAGIUM.
Prosimian literally "before the monkeys"; a member of the relatively primitive primate suborder Prosimii (lemurs, lorises, potto, and tarsiers). Modern classification systems include the tarsiers with the anthropoids in the suborder Haplorrhini (**Haplorhines**). The remaining members comprise the suborder Strepsirrhini.
Protein a complex organic compound made of amino acids. Many different kinds of proteins are present in the muscles and tissues of all mammals.
Protein electrophoresis (allozyme analysis) a method that compares the characteristic migration distance of various proteins acting in an electric field to identify and compare individuals.
Protoceratid a member of the family Protoceratidae (order Artiodactyla), which became extinct in the late Tertiary.
Protocone the primary cusp in a molar, lingual in upper molars and labial in lower molars (then called the protoconid).
Protoconid see **Protocone**

Proximal near to the point of attachment or origin (e.g. the base of the tail).
Pseudoallantoic placentation a kind of placenta shown only by the marsupial bandicoots. Compared with the true eutherian kind of plancentation, transfer of food and gas across the chorioallantoic placental interface is inefficient, as contact between the fetal and maternal membranes is never close.
Pseudopregnancy any period characterized by a functional CORPUS LUTEUM and buildup of the uterine layer in the absence of a pregnancy.
Puberty the attainment of sexual maturity. In addition to maturation of the primary sex organs (ovaries, testes), primates may exhibit "secondary sexual characteristics" at puberty. Among higher primates it is usual to find a growth spurt at the time of puberty in males and females.
Pubis one of the three bones of the pelvis.
Puna a treeless tableland or basin of the high Andes.
Purse seine a fishing net, the bottom of which can be closed by cords, operated usually from boats. (cf **Seine**)
Pylorus the region of the stomach at its intestinal end, which is closed by the pyloric sphincter.

Quadrate bone at rear of skull which serves as a point of articulation for lower jaw.
Quadrumanous using both hands and feet for grasping.
Quadrupedal walking on all fours, as opposed to walking on two legs (BIPEDAL) or moving suspended beneath branches in trees (suspensory movements).
Quaternary geological sub-era covering the last two million years and comprising the Pleistocene and Holocene.

Race a taxonomic division subordinate to subspecies but linking populations with similar distinct characteristics.
Radiation see **Adaptive radiation**
Radiotracking a technique used for monitoring an individual's movements remotely; it involves affixing a radio transmitter to the animal and thereafter receiving a signal through directional antennas which enables the subject's position to be plotted. The transmitter is often attached to a collar, hence "radiocollar."
Rain forest tropical and subtropical forest with abundant and year-round rainfall. Typically species rich and diverse.
Range (geographical) area over which an organism is distributed.
Receptive state of a female mammal ready to mate or in ESTRUS.
Reciprocal altruism a situation whereby the short term costs for providing other individuals with some resource are offset when the recipient returns the favour at a later stage.
Reduced (anatomical) of relatively small dimension (e.g. of certain bones, by comparison with those of an ancestor or related animals).
Refection process in which food is excreted and then reingested a second time from the anus to ensure complete digestion (e.g. in some shrews).
Refugium a delimited geographical region that provides temporary shelter or protection.
Regurgitation the reverse movement of food from the stomach to the mouth.
Reingestion process in which food is digested twice, to ensure that the maximum amount of energy is extracted from it. Food may be brought up from the stomach to the mouth for further chewing before reingestion, or an individual may eat its own feces. (see also **Refection**)
Relict a persistent remnant population.
Reproductive rate the rate of production of offspring; the net productive rate may be defined as the average number of female offspring produced by each female during her entire lifetime.
Resident a mammal which normally inhabits a defined area, whether this is a HOME RANGE or a TERRITORY.
Resource defense polygyny a mating system whereby males control access to females indirectly by monopolizing the resources needed by females.
Rete mirabile a complex mass of capillaries which functions mainly as a COUNTERCURRENT HEAT EXCHANGE MECHANISM.
Reticulum second chamber of the ruminant artiodactyl four-chambered stomach. The criss-crossed (reticulated) walls give rise to honeycomb tripe. (see also **Rumen**, **Omasum**, **Abomasum**)
Retractile (of claws) able to be withdrawn into protective sheaths.
Rhinarium a naked area of moist skin surrounding the nostrils in many mammals.
Riparian vegetation or habitat along the banks of a watercourse.
Rodent a member of the order Rodentia, the largest mammalian order, which includes rats and mice, squirrels, porcupines, capybara etc.
Rookery a colony of pinnipeds.
Rorqual one of the eight species of baleen whales of the family *Balaenopteridae*.
Root the portion of tooth below the gum.
Rostrum a forward-directed process at the front of the skull of some whales and dolphins, forming a beak.
Rumen first chamber of the ruminant artiodactyl four-chambered stomach. In the rumen the food is liquefied, kneaded by muscular walls and subjected to fermentation by bacteria. The product, cud, is regurgitated for further chewing; when it is swallowed again it bypasses the rumen and RETICULUM and enters the OMASUM.
Ruminant a mammal with a specialized digestive system typified by the behavior of chewing the cud. Their stomach is modified so that vegetation is stored, regurgitated for further maceration, then broken down by symbiotic bacteria. The process of rumination is an adaptation to digesting the cellulose walls of plant cells.
Rupicaprid a member of the tribe Rupicaprini (the chamois etc.) of the Artiodactyla.
Rut a period of sexual excitement; the mating season.
R-selection selection favoring rapid reproductive rates and growth rates and typical of species found in unstable environments. When favorable conditions occur, the species can rapidly colonize the given area. (cf **K-Selection**)

Sacculated a stomach, characteristic of certain herbivores, whales, and marsupials, having more than one chamber and with microorganisms present in the first chamber for cellulose digestion.
Sacral of, or pertaining to, the vertebrae that are fused to form the sacrum to which the pelvic girdle is attached.
Sagittal crest the bony ridge on the top of the cranium (formed by the temporal ridges).
Saltatorial locomotion that involves jumping or leaping.
Sanguininvory consuming a diet of blood (e.g. vampire bats).
Satellite male an animal excluded from the core of the social system but loosely associated on the periphery, in the sense of being a "hanger-on" or part of the retinue of more dominant individuals.
Savanna (savannah) tropical grasslands of Africa, Central and South America and Australia. Typically on flat plains and plateaux with seasonal pattern of rainfall. Three categories – savanna woodland, savanna parkland and savanna grassland – represent a gradual transition from closed woodland to open grassland.
Scapula the shoulder-blade. Primates typically have a mobile scapula in association with their versatile movements in the trees
Scatterhoarding the storage of food items at various scattered localities within the confines of an animal's territory or home range.
Scent gland an organ secreting odorous material with communicative properties. (see **Scent mark**)
Scent mark a site where the secretions of scent glands, or urine or feces, are deposited and which has communicative significance. Often left regularly at traditional sites which are also visually conspicuous. Also the "chemical message" left by this means; and (verb) to leave such a deposit.
Sciurognathous in rodents, having the angular process of the mandible in line with the alveolus of the incisor. (cf **Hystricognathous**)
Sciuromorphous in rodents, having a relatively small infraorbital foramen. (cf **Hystricomorphous**)
Sclerophyll forest a general term for the hard-leafed eucalypt forest that covers much of Australia.
Scombroid a bony marine fish of the family Scombridae, with two small dorsal fins, small scales and smooth skin (e.g. mackerel and tunny).
Scrotum the bag or pouch containing the testicles in many male mammals.
Scrub a vegetation dominated by shrubs woody plants usually with more than one stem. Naturally occurs most often on the arid side of forest or grassland types, but often artificially created by man as a result of forest destruction.
Scute a bony plate, overlaid by horn, which is derived from the outer layers of the skin. In armadillos, bony scute plates provide armor for all the upper, outer surfaces of the body.
Seasonality (of births) the restriction of births to a particular time of the year.
Sebaceous gland secretory tissue producing oily substances, for example lubricating and waterproofing hair, or specialized to produce odorous secretions.
Secondary forest (or growth) regenerating forest that has not yet reached the climax condition of primary forest.
Secondary sexual character a characteristic of animals which differs between the two sexes, but excluding the sexual organs and associated structures.
Sectorial premolar one of the front lower premolars of Old World monkeys and apes, specially adapted for shearing against the rear edge of the upper canine.
Sedentary pertaining to mammals which occupy relatively small home ranges, and exhibiting weak dispersal or migratory tendencies.
Seine a fishing net with floats at the top and weights at the bottom, used for encircling fish.
Seismic signal a communication signal comprising a series of low frequency vibrations that travel through the ground.
Selective pressure a factor affecting the reproductive success of individuals (whose success will depend on their fitness, i.e. the extent to which they are adapted to thrive under that selective pressure).

Selenodont molar teeth with crescent shaped cusps.
Sella one of the nasal processes of leafnose bats; an upstanding central projection which may form a fluted ridge running backwards from between the nostrils.
Semantic of, or relating to, the meaning of signals.
Semelparous the production of offspring only once in an organisms life. (cf **Iteroparous**)
Semen (seminal fluid) the ejaculatory fluid of the male reproductive system, produced by the testes, and containing spermatazoa and secretions of various glands.
Semi-fossorial see **Fossorial**
Seminal vessicles the portion of the male reproductive tract in which sperm are stored.
Seminiferous tubules the long, convoluted tubules of the testes in which sperm are produced and mature.
Senescence the process of deterioration of an organism with age, eventually culminating in the death of the organism.
Serrate toothed or notched.
Septum a partition separating two parts of an organism. The nasal septum consists of a fleshy part separating the nostrils and a vertical, bony plate dividing the nasal cavity.
Serum blood from which corpuscles and clotting agents have been removed; a clear, almost colorless fluid.
Sexual dimorphism a condition in which males and females of a species differ consistently in form (e.g. size, shape). (see **Dimorphism**, **Polymorphism**)
Serology the study of blood sera; investigates antigen-antibody reactions to elucidate responses to disease organisms and also phylogenetic relationships between species.
Seta a stiff, bristle-like structure.
Sex ratio the ratio of males to females in a population.
Sexual selection the selection of animals in relation to mating. Males may compete for access to females; females may permit particular males mating rights.
Siblicide the killing of siblings by littermates (e.g. in spotted hyenas).
Siblings individuals who share one or both parents. An individual's siblings are its brothers and sisters, regardless of their sex.
Simian (literally "ape-like") a monkey or ape. Often used as a synonym of anthropoid or higher primate (the Simiiformes)
Sinus a cavity in bone or tissue.
Sirenia an order of herbivorous aquatic mammals, comprising the manatees and dugong.
Sister group in phylogenetics, the MONOPHYLETIC group most closely related to another monophyletic group (the two taxa are connected by a single internal node).
Sivathere a member of a giraffe family which became extinct during the last Ice Age.
Social behavior the interactive behavior of two or more individuals all of the same species.
Sociality the tendency to form social groups.
Society a group of individuals of the same species organized in a co-operative manner.
Solitary living on its own, as opposed to social or group-living life-style. (cf **Gregarious**)
Sonar sound used in connection with navigation (sound navigation ranging).
Sounder the collective term for a group of pigs.
Spatulate broad and flattened with a narrow base.
Specialist an animal whose life-style involves highly specialized stratagems (e.g. feeding with one technique on a particular food). (cf **Generalist**)
Speciation the process by which new species arise in evolution. It is widely accepted that it occurs when a single species population is divided by some geographical barrier.
Species a taxonomic division subordinate to genus and superior to subspecies. In general a species is a group of animals similar in structure and which are able to breed and produce viable offspring. (see **Taxonomy**)
Species richness the number of species in an area.
Spermaceti organ an organ found in the head of whales of some toothed whales. The organ contains a waxy fluid which may help heat loss, provide neutral buoyancy, and contribute to the production of sounds.
Spermatogenesis the formation of sperm resulting from a series of cell divisions.
Sperm competition competition between sperm to fertilize female eggs, particularly after a female has copulated with more than one male.
Sphincter a ring of smooth muscle around a pouch, rectum or other hollow organ, which can be contracted to narrow or close the entrance to the organ.
Spinifex a grass which grows in large, distinctive clumps or hummocks in the driest areas of central and Western Australia.
Spontaneous ovulation OVULATION that occurs without copulation. (see also **Estrus**)
Spoor footprints.
Stapes the last of the three middle ear bones found in mammals.
Steppe open grassy plains of the central temperate zone of Eurasia or North America (prairies), characterized by low and sporadic rainfall and a wide annual temperature variation. In cold steppe, temperatures drop well below freezing point in winter, with rainfall concentrated in the summer or evenly distributed throughout year, while in hot steppe, winter temperatures are higher and rainfall concentrated in winter months.
Stotting see **Pronking**
Strepsirhine a member of the primate suborder Strepsirrhini that comprises the lemurs, bushbabies, lorises and potto. All members have a moist RHINARIUM and a cleft upper lip bound to the gum. (cf **Haplorhine**)
Stridulation production of sound by rubbing together modified surfaces of the body. Found in tenrecs.
Subadult no longer an infant or juvenile but not yet fully adult physically and/or socially.
Subfamily in taxonomy, a division of a family.
Subfossil an incompletely fossilized specimen from a recent species.
Sublingua (subtongue) a flap of tissue beneath the tongue in mammals, retained in most primates though vestigial in New World monkeys; particularly in lemurs and lorises.
Suborder in taxonomy, a subdivision of an order.
Subordinate see **Hierarchy**
Subspecies a recognizable subpopulation of a single species, typically with a distinct geographical distribution.
Subunguis the lower or ventral portion of the claw.
Successional habitat a stage in the progressive change in composition of a community of plants, from the original colonization of a bare area towards a largely stable climax.
Suckling taking nourishment or milk from the nipple or teat in mammals.
Suid a member of the family of pigs, Suidae, of the Artiodactyla.
Supernumerary additional teeth in a position where they do not normally occur.
Superordinal above the rank of order.
Supraorbital pertaining to above the eye (eye-socket or orbit).
Surplus killing a phenomenon where more (sometimes very many more) prey are killed than can immediately be consumed by the killer or its companions.
Suspensory movement movement through the trees by hanging and swinging beneath, rather than running along the tops of branches. (see also **Brachiate**)
Suture the contact line between two bones, such as those of the skull.
Sweat gland (eccrine gland) a gland located in the skin that opens on the surface and excretes sweat, the evaporation of which cools the surface.
Symbiosis an interaction between two species in which one benefits, and the other either benefits, is harmed, or is unaffected. (see also **Commensalism**, **Parasitism**, **Mutualism**)
Symmetrodonta an early order of mammals that includes small carnivores and insectivores from the late Triassic.
Sympatry a condition in which the geographical ranges of two or more different species overlap. (cf **Allopatry**)
Symplesiomorphy in pylogenetics, an ancestral (primitive) character shared by two or more taxa. (see also **Plesiomorphic**)
Synapomorphy in phylogenetics, a derived, HOMOLOGOUS character shared by two or more taxa. (see also **Apomorphic**)
Synapsida a subclass of the Reptilia, from which mammals supposedly evolved.
Syndactylous pertaining to the second and third toes of some mammals, which are joined together so that they appear to be a single toe with a split nail. In kangaroos, these syndactyl toes are used as a fur comb. (cf **Didactylous**)
Synonym in taxonomy, a different name for the same species; the earlier name has priority of use.
Synterritorial sharing a territory.
Syntopic present at the same time and place.
Systematics the study of patterns and processes of evolution used to construct phylogenies or classify organisms. It includes TAXONOMY.
Systematist someone who practises SYSTEMATICS.

Taiga northernmost coniferous forest, with open boggy, rocky areas in between.
Talonid the "heel" or posterior part of a lower molar that occludes with the PROTOCONE of an upper molar.
Tandem-marking communal scent-marking, characterized by repeated sniffing and marking (with urine and faeces) of the same (similar) spot or object by several members of a social carnivore. Often along home range boundaries, indicating a territorial function.
Tapetum lucidum a reflecting layer located behind the retina of the eye, commonly found in nocturnal mammals.
Tarsal pertaining to the tarsus bones in the ankle, articulating between the tibia and fibia of the leg and the metatarsals of the foot (pes).
Taxon (pl. **taxa**) a group of organisms of any taxonomic rank.
Taxonomy the science of classifying organisms, grouping together animals

which share common features and are thought to have common descent. Each individual is thus a member of a series of ever-broader categories (individual-species-genus-family-order-class-phylum) and each of these can be further divided where it is convenient (e.g. subspecies, superfamily, or infraorder).
Temporal of, or pertaining to, the side of the skull.
Terrestrial living on land.
Territoriality behavior related to the defence of a TERRITORY against predators.
Territory an area defended from intruders by an individual or group. Originally the term was used where ranges were exclusive and obviously defended at their borders. A more general definition of territoriality allows some overlap between neighbors by defining territoriality as a system of spacing wherein home ranges do not overlap randomly, i.e., the location of one individual's, or group's, home range influences those of others. (see also **Home range**)
Tertiary geological sub-era between 65–1.7 million years ago and comprising the Palaeocene, Eocene, Oligocene, Miocene, and Pliocene.
Testosterone a male hormone synthesized in the testes and responsible for the expression of many male characteristics (contrast the female hormone ESTROGEN produced in the ovaries).
Therapsida an order within the subclass SYNAPSIDA, which supposedly gave rise to the mammals.
Theria a subclass of the Class Mammalia, which includes the marsupials (Metatheria), the placental mammals (Eutheria), and the ancestral mammals (Pantotheria), but not the monotremes (Prototheria).
Theriodontia a suborder within the order THERAPSIDA that were primarily carnivorous.
Thermal conductance heat loss from the skin to the environment.
Thermogenesis generation of heat.
Thermoneutral range (or **Thermal neutral zone**) the range in outside environmental temperature in which a mammal uses the minimum amount of energy to maintain a constant internal body temperature. The limits to the thermoneutral range are the lower and upper critical temperatures, at which points the mammals must use increasing amounts of energy to maintain a constant body temperature. (cf **Heterothermy**) (see also **Lower** and **Upper critical temperature**)
Thermoregulation the regulation and maintenance of a constant internal body temperature in mammals.
Thoracic pertaining to the thorax or chest.
Tine a point or projection on an antler.
Tooth-comb a dental modification in which the incisor teeth form a comb-like structure.
Torpor a temporary physiological state in some mammals, akin to short-term hibernation, in which the body temperature drops and the rate of metabolism is reduced. Torpor is an adaptation for reducing energy expenditure in periods of extreme cold or food shortage.
Tragus a flap, sometimes moveable, situated in front of the opening of the outer ear in bats.
Triassic geological time period 248–213 million years ago.
Tribosphenic molars with three main cusps (the TRIGON) arranged in a triangular pattern.
Triconodont a member of the order that includes the earliest of all mammals, living from the Triassic until the early Cretaceous.
Trigon the three cusps (PROTOCONE, PARACONE, METACONE) of a TRIBOSPHENIC molar.
Trophic of, or pertaining to, food or nutrition.
Trophoblast the superficial layer of the BLASTOCYST in mammals.
Trypanosome a group of protozoa causing sleeping sickness.
Tubercle a small rounded projection or nodule (e.g. of bone).
Tundra barren treeless lands of the far north of Eurasia and North America, on mountain tops and Arctic islands. Vegetation is dominated by low shrubs, herbaceous perennials, mosses, and lichens.
Turbinate (turbinal) bones bones found within the nasal area that provide increased surface area for moisturizing, warming, and filtering inhaled air.
Tylopod a member of the suborder Tylopoda (order Artiodactyla), which includes camels and llamas.
Tympanic membrane (tympanum) the ear drum.

Ultrasound sound frequencies greater than 20 Hz.
Umbilicus navel.
Underfur the thick, soft undercoat fur lying beneath the longer and coarser hair (guard hairs).
Understory the layer of shrubs, herbs and small trees beneath the forest canopy.
Unguiculate having nails or claws instead of hooves.
Unguis the upper or dorsal portion of the claw.
Ungulate a member of the orders Artiodactyla (even-toed ungulates), Perissodactyla (odd-toed ungulates), Proboscidea (elephants), Hyracoidea (hyraxes) and Tubulidentata (aardvark), all of which have their feet modified as hooves of various types (hence the alternative name, hoofed mammals). Most are large and totally herbivorous. Also considered by some to include members of the orders Cetacea (whales and dolphins) and Sirenia (manatees and dugong).
Unguligrade locomotion on the tips of the "fingers" and "toes," the most distal phalanges. A condition associated with reduction in the number of digits to one or two in the perissodactyls and artiodactyls. (cf **Digitigrade**, **Plantigrade**)
Unicuspid teeth having a single cusp.
Upper critical temperature the maximum temperature at which an animal must lose heat in order to maintain a stable internal temperature. (cf **Lower critical temperature**)
Upwelling an upward movement of ocean currents, resulting from convection, causing an upward movement of nutrients and hence an increase in plankton populations.
Urethra the tube through which urine is expelled from the bladder.
Urogenital sinus a common opening from the reproductive and urinary system. In mammals, found in monotremes and marsupials.
Uropatagium the part of the PATAGIUM in some bats that extends between the hindlimbs and the tail.
Uterus the organ in which the embryo develops in female mammals (except monotremes).

Vagina the part of the female reproductive tract that receives the penis during copulation.
Vascular of, or with vessels which conduct blood and other body fluids.
Vector an individual or species which transmits a disease.
Velvet furry skin covering a growing antler.
Ventral on the lower or bottom side or surface; thus ventral or abdominal glands occur on the underside of the abdomen.
Venule a small tributary conveying blood from the capillary bed to a vein. (cf **Arteriole**)
Vertebrate an animal with a backbone; a division of the phylum Chordata which includes animals with notochords (as distinct from invertebrates).
Vestigial a characteristic with little or no contemporary use, but derived from one which was useful and well developed in an ancestral form.
Vibrissae stiff, coarse hairs richly supplied with nerves, found especially around the snout, and with a sensory (tactile) function.
Viviparous giving birth to live young.
Vocalization calls or sounds produced by the vocal cords of a mammal, and uttered through the mouth. Vocalizations differ with the age and sex of mammals but are usually similar within a species.
Volant having powered flight.

Wallace's line an imaginary line passing between the Philippines and the Moluccas in the north and between Sulawesi and Borneo and between Lombok and Bali in the south. It separates the Oriental and Australian zoogeographical regions.
Warren a communal series of burrows used by rabbits or squirrels.
Wavelength the distance from one peak to the next in a sound wave.
Wing loading in bats, the body mass divided by the total surface area of the wings.
Withers ridge between shoulder blades, especially of horses.

Xenarthrales bony elements between the lumbar vertebrae of xenarthran mammals, which provide extra support to the pelvic region for digging, climbing etc.
Xenarthran a member of the order Xenarthra, which comprises the living armadillos, sloths and anteaters.
Xeric having very little moisture; used of animals inhabiting dry regions (i.e. xeric-adapted). (cf **Mesic**)
Xerophytic forest a forest found in areas with relatively low rainfall. Xerophytic plants are adapted to protect themselves against browsing (e.g. well-developed spines) and to limit water loss (e.g. small, leathery leaves, often with a waxy coating).

Yolk sac a sac, usually containing yolk, which hangs from the ventral surface of the vertebrate fetus. In mammals, the yolk sac contains no yolk, but helps to nourish the embryonic young via a network of blood vessels.

Zalambdodont tooth cusps forming a V-shape.
Zoonoses diseases transmitted from vertebrate, non-human mammals to people.
Zooplankton minute animals living near the surface of the sea. (cf. **Phytoplankton**)
Zygomatic arch the bony arch on the side of a mammal skull that surrounds and protects the eye.
Zygote a fertilized egg.

Bibliography

The following list of titles indicates key reference works used in the preparation of this volume and those recommended for further reading. The list is divided into a number of categories: general mammalogy and particular areas of interest related to specific mammal groups.

A full technical bibliography can be found on: http://www.wildcru.org

General

Allen, G. (1939–1940). *The Mammals of China and Mongolia. Vols I & II.* American Museum of Natural History, New York.

Anderson, S. & Knox Jones, J. Jr., (eds) (1984). *Orders and Families of Recent Mammals of the World.* John Wiley and Sons, New York.

Birney, E.C. & Choate, J.R. (eds) (1994). *Seventy-five Years of Mammalogy (1919–1994).* Special Publ. No. 11, American Society of Mammalogists.

Bjarvall, A. & Ullstrom, S. (1986). *The Mammals of Britain and Europe.* Croom Helm, London.

Bourliere, F. (1970). *The Natural History of Mammals.* Alfred A. Knopf, New York.

Boyle, C. L. (ed) (1981). *The RSPCA Book of British Mammals.* Collins, London.

Chapman, J.A. & Feldhamer, G.A. (eds) (1982). *Wild Mammals of North America: Biology, Management and Economics.* Johns Hopkins University Press, Baltimore.

Corbet, G.B. & Harris, S. (eds). (1991). *The Handbook of British Mammals.* 3rd edn. Blackwell Scientific Publications, Oxford.

Corbet, G.B. & Hill, J.E. (1991). *A World List of Mammalian Species.* 3rd edn. Oxford University Press, Oxford.

Corbet, G.B. & Hill, J.E. (1992). *The Mammals of the Indomalayan Region: a Systematic Review.* Oxford University Press, Oxford.

Cranbrook, G. (1991). *Mammals of South-East Asia.* 2nd edn. Oxford University Press, New York.

Delany, M. J. & Happold, D.C.D. (1979). *Ecology of African Mammals.* Longman, London and New York.

Dorst, J. & Dandelot, P. (1972). *Larger Mammals of Africa.* Collins, London.

Dunstone, N. & Gorman, M.L. (eds) (1993). *Mammals as Predators. Symp. Zool. Soc. Lond.* No. 65. Clarendon Press, Oxford.

Dunstone, N. & Gorman, M.L. (eds) (1998). *Behaviour and Ecology of Riparian Mammals. Symp. Zool. Soc. Lond.* No. 71. Cambridge University Press, Cambridge.

Eisenberg, J.F. (1981). *The Mammalian Radiations: An Analysis of Trends in Evolution, Adaptation and Behavior.* University of Chicago Press, Chicago.

Eisenberg, J.F. (1989). *Mammals of the Neotropics. The Northern Neotropics, Vol. I, Panama, Colombia, Venezuela, Guyana, Suriname, French Guiana.* University of Chicago Press, Chicago.

Eisenberg, J.F. & Redford, K.H. (1999). *The Mammals of the Neotropics. Vol. III. The Central Neotropics: Ecuador, Peru, Bolivia, Brazil.* University of Chicago Press, Chicago

Ellerman, J.R. (1961). *The Fauna of India: Mammalia, Vol III.* Delhi.

Ellerman, J.R. & Morrison Scott, T.C.S. (1951). *Checklist of Palearctic and Indian Mammals, 1758–1946.* British Museum (Natural History), London.

Emmons, L.H. (1997). *Neotropical Rainforest Mammals: a Field Guide.* University of Chicago Press, Chicago.

Estes, R.D. (1991). *The Behavior Guide to African Mammals: Including Hoofed Mammals, Carnivores, Primates.* University of California Press, Berkeley.

Feldhamer, G.A., Drickhamer, L.C., Vessey, S.H. & Merritt, J.F. (1999). *Mammalogy: Adaptation, Diversity, and Ecology.* McGraw-Hill, New York.

Flannery, T.F. (1990). *Mammals of New Guinea.* Robert Brown & Associates, New South Wales.

Forsyth, A. (1999). *Mammals of North America: Temperate and Arctic Regions.* Firefly Books, Willowdale, Ontario.

Garbutt, N. (1999). *The Mammals of Madagascar.* Pica Press, East Sussex.

Hall, E.R. (1981). *The Mammals of North America.* John Wiley and Sons, New York.

Harrison, D.L. & Bates, P.J.J. (1991). *The Mammals of Arabia.* Harrison Zoological Museum, Sevenoaks, Kent.

Harrison Matthews, L. (1969). *The Life of Mammals. Vols I & II.* Weidenfeld & Nicolson, London.

Heptner, V.G., Nasimovich, A.A. & Bannikov, A. (1988). *Mammals of the Soviet Union. Vol. I. Artiodactyla and Perissodactyla* [A Translation of Heptner et al., 1961, Mlekopitayuschie Sovetskovo Soyuza: Parnokopytyne i neparnokopytyne]. Smithsonian Institution Libraries, Washington.

Heptner, V.G. & Sludskii, A.A. (1992). *Mammals of the Soviet Union. Vol. II. Carnivora (Hyaenas and cats).* [A Translation of Heptner et al., 1972, Mlekopitayushchie Sovetskovo Soyuza. Khishchye (gienyi i koshki)]. Smithsonian Institution Libraries, Washington.

Hilton-Taylor, C. (compiler) (2000). *2000 IUCN Red List of Threatened Species.* IUCN, Gland, Switzerland and Cambridge.

Jewell, P.A. & Maloiy, G. (1989). *The Biology of Large African Mammals in their Environment. Symp. Zool. Soc. Lond.* No. 61, Oxford University Press, Oxford.

King, C.M. (ed). (1995). *The Handbook of New Zealand Mammals.* Oxford University Press, Oxford.

Kingdon, J. (1971–1982). *East African Mammals. Vols I–III.* Academic Press, New York.

Kingdon, J. (1997). *The Kingdon Field Guide to African Mammals.* Academic Press, London.

Lekagul, B. & McNeely, J.A. (1988). *Mammals of Thailand.* Darnsutha Press, Bangkok.

Macdonald, D. & Barrett, P. (1995). *Collins European Mammals: Evolution and Behaviour.* HarperCollins, London.

Macdonald, D.W. & Barrett, P. (1995). *Collins Field Guide to Mammals of Britain and Europe.* HarperCollins, London.

Mares, M.A. & Schmidly, D.J. (eds) (1991). *Latin American Mammalogy, History, Biodiversity, and Conservation.* Univ Oklahoma Press, Norman.

McKenna, M.C. & Bell, S.K. (1997). *Classification of Mammals Above the Species Level.* Columbia University Press, New York.

Meester, J. & Setzer, H. W. (1971–1977) *The Mammals of Africa: an Identification Manual.* Smithsonian Institution, Washington DC.

Mitchell-Jones, A.J., Amori, G., Bogdanowicz, W., Krystufek, B., Reijnders, P.J.H., Spitzenberger, F., Stubbe, M., Thissen, J.B.M., Vohralik, V. & Zima, J. (1999). *The Atlas of European Mammals.* T&AD Poyser Natural History, London.

Morris, D. (1965). *The Mammals.* Hodder & Stoughton, London.

Niethammer, J. & Krapp, F. (1978–1992). *Handbuch der Säugetiere Europas [Handbook of European Mammals].* Aula-Verlag, Wiesbaden.

Nowak, R.M. (1999). *Walker's Mammals of the World.* Sixth Edition. Johns Hopkins University Press, Baltimore.

Ognev, S.I. (1962–1966). *Mammals of Eastern Europe and Northern Asia* [A Translation of S.I. Ognev, 1928–1950, Zveri vostochnoi Evropy i severnoi Azii]. Israel Program for Scientific Translations, Jerusalem.

Owen-Smith, R.N. (1988). *Megaherbivores: the Influence of Very Large Body Size on Ecology.* Cambridge University Press, New York.

Parker, S.P. (ed) (1990). *Grzimek's Encyclopedia of Mammals.* McGraw-Hill, New York.

Qumsiyeh, M.B. (1996). *Mammals of the Holy Land.* University of Texas Press, Austin.

Redford, K.H. & Eisenberg, J.F. (1992). *Mammals of the Neotropics. Volume II. The Southern Cone: Chile, Argentina, Uruguay and Paraguay.* University of Chicago Press, Chicago

Reid, F.A. (1997). *A Field Guide to the Mammals of Central America and Southeast Mexico.* Oxford University Press, New York.

Roberts, A. (1951). *The Mammals of South Africa.* Trustees of "The mammals of South Africa" book fund.

Roberts, T.J. (1997). *Mammals of Pakistan.* Oxford University Press, Pakistan.

Simpson, G.G. (1945). *The Principles of Classification and a Classification of Mammals. Bul. Amer. Mus. Nat. Hist.* 85: 1–350

Skinner, J.D. & Smithers, R.H.N. (1990). *The Mammals of the Southern African Subregion.* University of Pretoria, Pretoria.

Sokolov, V.E. (1973–1979). *Sistematika mlekopitayushchikh [Systematics of Mammals].* Vysshaya Shkola, Moscow. (in Russian).

Sokolov, V.E. & Orlov, V.N. (1980). *Guide to the Mammals of the Mongolian People's Republic.* Nauka, Moscow. (in Russian).

Strahan, R. (1998). *The Mammals of Australia.* Reed New Holland, Australia.

Szalay, F.S., Novacek, M.J. & McKenna, M.C. (eds) (1993). *Mammal Phylogeny: Placentals.* Springer-Verlag, New York.

Vaughan, T.A., Ryan, J.M. & Czaplewski, N.J. (2000). *Mammalogy.* Saunders College Publishing, Philadelphia.

Whitaker, J.O. (1996). *National Audubon Society Field Guide to North American Mammals.* Knopf, Canada.

Wilson, D.E. & Cole, F.R. (2000). *Common Names of Mammals of the World.* Smithsonian Institution Press, Washington.

Wilson, D.E. & Reeder, D.M. (eds) (1993). *Mammal Species of the World: a Taxonomic and Geographic Reference.* 2nd edn. Smithsonian Institution Press, Washington.

Wilson, D.E. & Ruff, S. (eds) (1999). *The Smithsonian Book of North American Mammals.* Smithsonian Institution Press, Washington.

Yalden, D. (2000). *The History of British Mammals.* T&AD Poyser Natural History, London.

Young, J.Z. (1975). *The Life of Mammals: their Anatomy and Physiology.* Oxford University Press, Oxford.

Carnivores

Bailey, T.N. (1993). *The African Leopard: Ecology and Behavior of a Solitary Felid.* Columbia University Press, New York.

Bauer, E.A. & Bauer, P. (1998). *Bears: Behaviour, Ecology, Conservation.* Voyageur Press, Stillwater, MN.

Bekoff, M. (1978). *Coyotes: Biology, Behavior and Management.* Academic Press, New York.

Bertram, B. C. (1978). *Pride of Lions.* Charles Scribner, New York.

Busch, R.H. (1996). *The Cougar Almanac: A Complete Natural History of the Mountain Lion.* The Lyons Press, New York, NY.

Busch, R.H. (2000). *The Grizzly Almanac.* The Lyons Press, New York, NY.

Buskirk, S.W., Harestad, A.S., Raphael, M.G. and Powell, R.A. (1994). *Martens, Sables and Fishers: Biology and Conservation.* Cornell University Press, Ithaca, NY.

Caro, T.M. (1994). *Cheetahs of the Serengeti Plains.* University of Chicago Press, Chicago.

Corbett, L. (1995). *The Dingo: in Australia and Asia.* Cornell University Press, Ithaca, NY.

de la Rosa, C.L. & Nocke, C.C. (2000). *A Guide to the Carnivores of Central America:*

Natural History, Ecology, and Conservation. University of Texas Press, Austin.
Dominis, I. & Edey. M. (1968). *The Cats of Africa*. Time-Life, New York.
Eaton, R.L. (1974). *The Cheetah: the Biology, Ecology, and Behavior of an Endangered Species*. Van Nostrand Reinhold, New York.
Ewer, R.F. (1973). *The Carnivores*. Weidenfeld & Nicolson, London.
Fox, M. W. (ed) (1975). *The Wild Canids: their Systematics, Behavioral Ecology, Evolution*. Van Nostrand Reinhold, London and New York.
Frame, G. & Frame, L. (1981). *Swift and Enduring: Cheetahs and Wild Dogs of the Serengeti*. Dutton, New York.
Gittleman, J.L. (ed) (1989, 1996). *Carnivore Behavior, Ecology and Evolution. Vols I & II*. Cornell University Press, Ithaca, NY.
Gittleman, J., Funk, S., Macdonald, D.W & Wayne R (eds) (2001). *Carnivore Conservation*. Cambridge University Press, Cambridge.
Gould, E. & McKay, G. (1998). *Encyclopedia of Mammals. A Comprehensive Illustrated Guide by International Experts*. Academic Press, London.
Griffiths, H.I. (ed) (2000). *Mustelids in a Modern World: Management and Conservation Aspects of Small Carnivore and Human Interactions*. Backhuys, Netherlands.
Gromov, I.M. & Baranova, G.I. (eds) (1981). *Catalog of Mammals of the USSR*. Nauka, Leningrad. (in Russian).
Guggisberg, C.A.W. (1961). *Simba: the Life of the Lion*. Howard Timmins, Cape Town.
Gurung, K.K. & Singh, R. (1998). *Field Guide to the Mammals of the Indian Subcontinent: Where to Watch Mammals in India, Nepal, Bhutan, Bangladesh, Sri Lanka and Pakistan*. Academic Press, London.
Hampton, B. (1997). *The Great American Wolf*. Henry Holt, New York.
Herrero, S. (ed) (1972). *Bears: their Biology and Management*. IUCN Publ. New Series no.23, Morges, Switzerland.
Hinton, H.E. & Dunn, A.M.S. (1967). *Mongooses: their Natural History and Behaviour*. Oliver & Boyd, Edinburgh and London.
Kanchanasakha, B., Simcharoen, S. & Than, U.T. (1998). *Carnivores of Mainland South East Asia*. WWF, Thailand.
King, C. (1989). *The Natural History of Weasels and Stoats*. Christopher Helm, London.
Kitchener, A. (1991). *The Natural History of the Wild Cats*. Christopher Helm, London.
Kruuk, H. (1972). *The Spotted Hyena: a Study of Predation and Social Behavior*. University of Chicago Press, Chicago.
Kruuk, H. (1989). *The Social Badger*. Oxford University Press, Oxford.
Kruuk, H. (1995). *Wild Otters: Predation and Populations*. Oxford University Press, Oxford.
Long, C. & Killingley, C.A. (1983). *The Badgers of the World*. Charles C. Thomas, Springfield, IL.
Macdonald, D.W. (1987). *Running with the Fox*. Unwin Hyman, London.
Macdonald, D.W. (1992). *The Velvet Claw*. BBC Books, London.
Maehr, D.S. (1997). *The Florida Panther: Life and Death of a Vanishing Carnivore*. Island Press, Washington.
Mason, C.F. & MacDonald, S.M. (1986). *Otters: Ecology and Conservation*. Cambridge University Press, Cambridge.
Mech, L.D. (1970). *The Wolf: the Ecology and Behavior of an Endangered Species*. Natural History Press, Garden City, New York.
Mech, L.D. (1995). *The Way of the Wolf*. Voyageur Press, Stillwater, MN.
Mech, L.D. (2000). *The Wolves of Minnesota: Howl in the Heartland*. Voyageur Press, Stillwater, MN.
Meinzer, W. (1996). *Coyote*. University of Texas Press, Austin.
Mills, M.G. (1990). *Kalahari Hyaenas: The Comparative Behavioural Ecology of Two Species*. Chapman & Hall, London.
Mountfort, G. (1981). *Saving the Tiger*. Michael Joseph, London.
Neal, E.G. (1977). *Badgers*. Blandford, Poole, Dorset.
Neal, E. (1986). *The Natural History of Badgers*. Croom Helm, London.
Neal, E. & Cheeseman, C. (1996). *Badgers*. T&AD Poyser Natural History Ltd, London.
Ovsyanikov, N. (1999). *Polar Bears: Living with the White Bear*. Voyageur Press, Stillwater, MN.
Pelton, M. R., Lentfer, I. W & Stokes, G.E. (eds) (1976). *Bears: their Biology and Management*. IUCN Publ. New Series no. 40, Morges, Switzerland.
Powell, R.A. (1993). *The Fisher: Life History, Ecology and Behavior*. University of Minnesota Press, Minneapolis, MN.
Rosevear, D.R. (1974). *The Carnivores of West Africa*. British Museum (Natural History), London.
Schaller, G.B. (1967). *The Deer and the Tiger: a Study of Wildlife in India*. Chicago University Press, Chicago.
Schaller, G.B. (1972). *The Serengeti Lion: a Study of Predator–Prey Relations*. University of Chicago Press, Chicago.
Schaller, G.B. (1993). *The Last Panda*. University of Chicago Press, Chicago.
Seidensticker, J., Christie, S. & Jackson, P. (eds) (1999). *Riding the Tiger: Tiger Conservation in Human-dominated Landscapes*. Cambridge University Press, Cambridge.
Turner, A. & Anton, M. (1997). *The Big Cats and their Fossil Relatives: an Illustrated Guide to their Evolution and Natural History*. Columbia University Press, New York.
van Lawick, H. & van Lawick-Goodall, J. (1970). *The Innocent Killers*. Collins, London.
Verts, B.J. (1967). *The Biology of the Striped Skunk*. University of Illinois Press, Urbana.
Wrogemann, N. (1975). *Cheetah Under the Sun*. McGraw-Hill, Johannesburg.

MARINE MAMMALS

Allen, K. R. (1980). *Conservation and Management of Whales*. Butterworths, London.
Andersen, H.T. (ed). (1969). *The Biology of Marine Mammals*. Academic Press, New York.
Baker, M.L. (1987). *Whales, Dolphins, and Porpoises of the World*. Garden City, New York.
Berta, A. & Sumich, J.L. (1999). *Marine Mammals: Evolutionary Biology*. Academic Press, London.
Bonner, N. (1989). *The Natural History of Seals*. Academic Press, London.
Bonner, N. (1994). *Seals and Sea Lions of the World*. Facts on File Publ., New York.
Bonner, W.N. (1980). *Whales*. Blandford, Poole.
Bonner, W.N. & Berry. R.J. (eds) (1981). *Ecology in the Antarctic*. Academic Press, London.
Boyd, I.L. (ed) (1993). *Marine Mammals: Advances in Behavioural and Population Biology*. Oxford University Press, Oxford.
Bryden, M.M., Marsh, H. & Shaughnessy, P. (1999). *Dugongs, Whales, Dolphins and Seals: A Guide to the Sea Mammals of Australasia*. Allen & Unwin, Sydney.
Carwardine, M. (1998). *Whales and Dolphins*. HarperCollins, New York.
Carwardine, M., Harrison, P. & Bryden, M (eds) (1999). *Whales, Dolphins and Porpoises*. 2nd edn. Checkmark Books, New York.
Carwardine, M., Hoyt, E., Ewan Fordyce, R. & Gill, P. (1998). *Whales, Dolphins and Porpoises*. Time Life Books, New York.
Ellis, R. (1983). *Dolphins and Porpoises*. R. Hale, London.
Evans, P.G.H. (1987). *The Natural History of Whales and Dolphins*. Christopher Helm, London.
Fontaine, P.-H. (1998). *Whales of the North Atlantic: Biology and Ecology*. Editions MultiMondes, Sainte-Foy, Québec.
Gaskin, D.E. (1972). *Whales, Dolphins and Seals*. Heinemann Educational Books, London.
Gaskin, D.E. (1982). *The Ecology of Whales and Dolphins*. Heinemann, London.
Gentry, R.L. (1998). *Behavior and Ecology of the Northern Fur Seal*. Princeton University Press, Princeton, NJ.
Harrison Matthews, L. (1978). *The Natural History of the Whale*. Weidenfeld & Nicolson, London.
Harrison Matthews, L. (1979). *Seals and the Scientists*. P. Owen, London.
Herman, L.M. (1980). *Cetacean Behavior: Mechanisms and Functions*. John Wiley & Sons, Chichester.
King, J.E. (1983). *Seals of the World*. Oxford University Press, Oxford.
Laws, R.M. (ed) (1993). *Antarctic Seals: Research Methods and Techniques*. Cambridge University Press, Cambridge.
Leatherwood, S. & Reeves, R. (1983). *The Sierra Club Handbook of Seals and Sirenians*. Sierra Club, San Francisco, CA.
Le Boeuf, B.J. & Laws, R.M. (1994). *Elephant Seals: Population Ecology, Behavior, and Physiology*. University of California Press, Berkeley.
Mann, J., Connor, R.C., Tyack, P.L. & Whitehead, H. (1999). *Cetacean Societies: Field Studies of Dolphins and Whales*. Chicago University Press, Chicago.
Martin, R.M. (1977). *Mammals of the Seas*. Batsford, London.
Norris, K.S., Würsig, B., Wells, R.S. & Würsig, M. (1994). *The Hawaiian Spinner Dolphin*. California University Press, Berkeley.
Owen, W. (1999). *Whales, Dolphins and Porpoises*. Checkmark Books, New York.
Perrin, W.F., Würsig, B. & Thewissen, J.G.M. (2001). *Encyclopedia of Marine Mammals*. Academic Press, London.
Pryor, K. & Norris, K.S. (1998). *Dolphin Societies: Discoveries and Puzzles*. University of California Press, Berkeley.
Read, A.J., Wiepkema, P.R. & Nachtigall, P.E. (1997). *The Biology of the Harbour Porpoise*. De Spil Publishers, Woerden, Netherlands.
Reeves, R.R., Stewart, B. & Leatherwood, S. (1992). *The Sierra Club Handbook of Seals and Sirenians*. Sierra Club, San Francisco, California.
Renouf, D. (1990). *The Behaviour of Pinnipeds*. Chapman & Hall, London.
Reynolds, J.E. (2000). *The Bottlenose Dolphin: Biology and Conservation*. University of Florida Press, Gainesville.
Reynolds, J.E. & Rommel, S.A. (1999). *Biology of Marine Mammals*. Smithsonian Institution Press, Washington.
Rice, D.W. (1998). *Marine Mammals of the World: Systematics and Distribution*. Allen Press, Lawrence, KS.
Ridgeway, S.H. & Harrison, R.J. (eds) (1981–1998). *The Handbook of Marine Mammals. Vols I – VI*. Academic Press, London.
Riedman, M. (1991). *The Pinnipeds: Seals, Sea Lions, and Walruses*. University of California Press, Berkeley.
Ripple, J. & Perrine, D. (1999). *Manatees and Dugongs of the World*. Voyageur Press, Stillwater, MN.
Slijper, E.J. (1979). *Whales*. Hutchinson, London.
Watson, L. (1981). *Sea Guide to Whales of the World*. Hutchinson, London.
Winn, H.E. & Olla, B.L. (1979). *The Behavior of Marine Mammals. Vol 3. Cetaceans*. Plenum Press, New York.
Würsig, B., Jefferson, T.A. & Schmidly, D.J. (2000). *The Marine Mammals of the Gulf of Mexico*. Texas A & M University Press, College Station.

PRIMATES

Alterman, L., Doyle, G.A. & Izard, M.K. (eds) (1995). *Creatures of the Dark: the Nocturnal Primates*. Plenum Press, New York.
Altmann, J. (1980). *Baboon Mothers and Infants*. Harvard University Press, Cambridge.
Altmann, S.A. & Altmann, J. (1970). *Baboon Ecology*. University of Chicago Press, Chicago.
Barrett, L. (2000). *Baboons: Survivors of the African Continent*. BBC Books, Bristol.
Bramblett, C.A. (1976). *Patterns of Primate Behaviour*. Mayfield Publishing Co., Palo Alto.
Chalmers, N. (1979). *Social Behaviour in Primates*. Edward Arnold, London.
Charles-Dominique, P. (1977). *Ecology and Behaviour of Nocturnal Primates: Prosimians of Equatorial West Africa*. Duckworth, London.
Chivers, D.J. (ed) (1980). *Malayan Forest Primates*. Plenum Press, New York.
Clutton-Brock, T.H. (ed) (1977). *Primate Ecology*. Academic Press, London.

Clutton-Brock, T.H. & Harvey, P.H. (eds) (1978). *Readings in Sociobiology*. W. H. Freeman, Reading.

Coimbra-Filho, A. F. & Mittermeier, R.A. (1981). *Ecology and Behavior of Neotropical Primates*. Academia Brasileira de Ciencias, Rio de Janeiro.

Cowlishaw, G. & Dunbar, R. (2000). *Primate Conservation Biology*. Chicago University Press, Chicago.

Davies, G. & Oates, J. (1994). *Colobine Monkeys: Their Ecology, Behaviour and Evolution*. Cambridge University Press, Cambridge.

Devore, I. (ed) (1965). *Primate Behavior: Field Studies of Monkeys and Apes*. Holt, Rinehart and Winston, New York.

Doyle, G. A. & Martin, R.D. (eds) (1979). *The Study of Prosimian Behavior*. Academic Press, New York.

Fa, J.E. & Lindburg, J.G. (eds) (1996). *Evolution and Ecology of Macaque Societies*. Cambridge University Press, New York.

Fleagle, J.G. (1988). *Primate Adaptation and Evolution*. Academic Press, New York.

Fleagle, J.G. (1999). *Primate Communities*. Cambridge University Press, Cambridge.

Hill, W.C.O. (1953–1974). *Primates: Comparative Anatomy and Taxonomy*. Edinburgh University Press, Edinburgh, and Wiley-Interscience, New York.

Hrdy, S.B. (1977). *The Langurs of Abu: Female and Male Strategies of Reproduction*. Harvard University Press, Cambridge.

Jay, P.C. (1968). *Primates: Studies in Adaptation and Variability*. Holt, Rinehart and Winston, New York.

Jolly, A. (1972). *The Evolution of Primate Behavior*. Macmillan, New York.

Jolly, A. (1966). *Lemur Behavior: A Malagasy Field Study*. University of Chicago Press, Chicago.

Kinzey, W.G. (1997). *New World Primates: Ecology, Evolution and Behaviour*. Aldine de Gruyter, Hawthorne, NY.

Kleiman, D.G. (ed) (1977). *The Biology and Conservation of the Callitrichidae*. Smithsonian Institution Press, Washington.

Kummer, H. (1971). *Primate Societies: Group Techniques of Ecological Adaptation*. Aldine Atherton, Chicago.

Lee, P.C. (1999). *Comparative Primate Socioecology*. Cambridge University Press, New York.

Lindburg, D.G. (ed) (1980). *The Macaques: Studies in Ecology, Behavior and Evolution*. Van Nostrand Reinhold, New York.

Martin, R.D. (1990). *Primate Origins and Evolution*. Princeton University Press, Princeton, NJ.

Martin, R.D., Doyle, G.A. & Walker, A.C. (eds) (1974). *Prosimian Biology*. Duckworth, London.

Michael, R.P. & Crook, J.H. (eds) (1973). *Comparative Ecology and Behaviour of Primates*. Academic Press, London.

Milton, K. (1980). *The Foraging Strategy of Howler Monkeys*. Columbia University Press, New York.

Moynihan, M. (1976). *The New World Primates*. Princeton University Press, Princeton.

Napier, J.R. & Napier, P.H. (1967). *A Handbook of Living Primates*. Academic Press, New York and London.

Napier, J.R. & Napier, P.H. (1970). *Old World Monkeys*. Academic Press, New York.

Rainier III, H.S.H. & Bourne, G.H. (1977). *Primate Conservation*. Academic Press, New York.

Rijksen, H.D. & Meijaard, E. (1999). *Our Vanishing Relative: The Status of Wild Orang-Utans at the Close of the Twentieth Century*. Kluwer Academic Publishers, Boston.

Rylands, A.B. (1993). *Marmosets and Tamarins: Systematics, Behavior, and Ecology*. Oxford University Press, Oxford.

Schaller, G.B. (1963). *The Mountain Gorilla: Ecology and Behaviour*. University of Chicago Press, Chicago and London.

Schwartz, J.H. (1988). *Orang-utan Biology*. Oxford University Press, Oxford.

Short, R.V. & Weir, B.J. (eds) (1980). *The Great Apes of Africa*. Journals of Reproduction and Fertility, Colchester.

Simons, F.L. (1972). *Primate Evolution*. Collier Macmillan, London.

Smuts, B.B., Cheney, D.L., Seyfarth, R.M., Wrangham, R.W. & Struhsaker, T.T. (1986). *Primate Societies*. Chicago University Press, Chicago.

Struhsaker, T.T. (1975). *The Red Colobus Monkey*. University of Chicago Press, Chicago.

Sussman, R.W. (ed) (1979). *Primate Ecology: Problem-orientated Field Studies*. John Wiley, New York.

Szalay, F.S. & Delson, F. (1979). *Evolutionary History of the Primates*. Academic Press, New York.

van Lawick-Goodall, J. (1971). *In the Shadow of Man*. Collins, London.

Whitehead, P.F. & Jolly, C.J. (2000). *Old World Monkeys*. Cambridge University Press, Cambridge.

Wolfheim, J.H. (1983). *Primates of the World: Distribution, Abundance and Conservation*. University of Washington Press, Seattle.

SCANDENTIA

Emmons, L.H. (2000). *A Field Study of Bornean Treeshrews*. University of California Press, Berkeley.

Luckett, W. P. (ed) (1980). *Comparative Biology and Evolutionary Relationships of Tree Shrews*. Plenum Press, New York.

PROBOSCIDEA

Haynes, G. (1993). *Mammoths, Mastodons, and Elephants: Biology, Behaviour and the Fossil Record*. Cambridge University Press, New York.

Moss, C. (2000). *Elephant Memories*. University of Chicago Press, Chicago.

Shoshani, J. (ed) (1992). *Elephants: Majestic Creatures of the Wild*. Rodale Press, Emmaus, PA.

Shoshani, J. & Tassy, P. (eds) (1996). *The Proboscidea: Evolution and Palaeoecology of Elephants and their Relatives*. Oxford University Press, New York.

Spinage, C. (1994). *Elephants*. T&AD Poyser Natural History, London.

Sukumar, R. & Swaminathan, M.S. (1992). *The Asian Elephant: Ecology and Management*. Cambridge University Press, Cambridge.

HOOFED MAMMALS

Andersen, R., Duncan, P. & Linnel, J.D.C. (1998). *The European Roe Deer: The Biology of Success*. Scandinavian University Press, Norway.

Bauer, E.A. & Bauer, P. (1996). *Mule Deer: Behaviour, Ecology, Conservation*. Voyageur Press, Stillwater, MN.

Bauer, E.A. & Bauer, P. (1999). *Elk: Behaviour, Ecology, Conservation*. Voyageur Press, Stillwater, MN.

Boyd, L. & Houpt, K.L. (1994). *Przewalski's Horse: The History and Biology of an Endangered Species*. SUNY Press, Albany, NY.

Bubenik, G.A. & Bubenik, A.B. (eds) (1990). *Horns, Pronghorns and Antlers*. Springer-Verlag, New York.

Byers, J.A. (1998). *American Pronghorn: Social Adaptation and the Ghosts of Predators Past*. University of Chicago Press, Chicago.

Chaplin, R.E. (1977). *Deer*. Blandford, Poole, Dorset, England.

Chapman, D. & Chapman, N. (1975). *Fallow Deer: Their History, Distribution and Biology*. Terrence Dalton, Lavenham, Suffolk, England.

Clutton-Brock, T.H., Guinness, F.E. & Albon, S.D. (1982). *Red Deer: Behaviour and Ecology of Two Sexes*. Edinburgh University Press, Edinburgh.

Dagg, A.I. & Foster, J.B. (1976). *The Giraffe: its Biology, Behavior and Ecology*. Van Nostrand Reinhold, New York.

Danilkin, A. & Hewison, A.J.M. (1996). *Behavioural Ecology of Siberian and European Roe Deer*. Chapman & Hall, London.

Eltringham, S.K. (1982). *Elephants*. Blandford, Poole, Dorset, England.

Eltringham, S.K. (1999). *The Hippos*. T&AD Poyser Natural History Ltd, London.

Franzmann, A.W. (ed) (1998). *Ecology and Management of the North American Moose*. Smithsonian Institution Press, Washington.

Gauthier-Pilters, H. & Dagg. A.I. (1981). *The Camel: its Evolution, Ecology, Behavior and Relationship to Man*. University of Chicago Press, Chicago.

Geist, V. (1971). *Mountain Sheep: a Study in Behavior and Evolution*. University of Chicago Press, Chicago.

Geist, V. (1999). *Deer of the World: Their Evolution, Behavior and Ecology*. Stackpole Books, Mechanicsburg, PA.

Geist, V. & Francis, M.H. (1999). *Moose*. Voyageur Press, Stillwater, MN.

Groves, C.P. (1974). *Horses, Asses and Zebras in the Wild*. David and Charles, Newton Abbot, England.

Habibi, K. (1994). *The Desert Ibex: Life History, Ecology and Behaviour of the Nubian Ibex in Saudi Arabia*. Immel, Saudi Arabia.

Haltenorth, T. & Diller, H. (1980). *A Field Guide to the Mammals of Africa: Including Madagascar*. Collins, London.

Laws, R.M., Parker, I.S.C. & Johnstone, R.C.B. (1975). *Elephants and Their Habitats: the Ecology of Elephants in North Bunyoro, Uganda*. Clarendon Press, Oxford.

Leuthold, W. (1977). *African Ungulates: a Comparative Review of their Ecology and Behavioral Ecology*. Springer-Verlag, Berlin.

Mloszewski, M.J. (1983). *The Behaviour and Ecology of the African Buffalo*. Cambridge University Press, Cambridge.

Moss, C. (1976). *Portraits in the Wild: Animal Behaviour in East Africa*. Hamish Hamilton, London.

Nievergelt, B. (1981). *Ibexes in an African Environrnent: Ecology and Social System of the Walia Ibex in the Simien Mountains, Ethiopia*. Springer-Verlag, Berlin.

Prins, H.H.T. (1996). *Ecology and Behaviour of the African Buffalo: Social Inequality and Decision Making*. Chapman & Hall, London.

Putman, R. (1988). *The Natural History of Deer*. Cornell University Press, Ithaca, NY.

Schaller, G.B. (1967). *The Deer and the Tiger: a Study of Wildlife in India*. University of Chicago Press, Chicago.

Schaller, G.B. (1977). *Mountain Monarchs: Wild Sheep and Goats of the Himalaya*. University of Chicago Press, Chicago.

Sinclair, A.R.E. (1977). *The African Buffalo*. University of Chicago Press, Chicago.

Spinage, C.A. (1982). *A Territorial Antelope: The Uganda Waterbuck*. Academic Press, London.

Spinage, C.A. (1986). *The Natural History of Antelopes*. Croom Helm, London.

Vrba, E.S. & Schaller, G.B. (eds) (2000). *Antelopes, Deer, and Relatives: Fossil Record, Behavioral Ecology, Systematics, and Conservation*. Yale University Press, New Haven, CT.

Walther, F.R., Mungall. F.C. & Grau, G.A. (1983). *Gazelles and their Relatives: A Study in Territorial Behavior*. Noyes Publications, Park Ridge, New Jersey.

Wemmer, C.M. (1987). *Biology and Management of the Cervidae*. Smithsonian Institution Press, Washington.

Whitehead, G.K. (1972). *Deer of the World*. Constable, London.

Wilson, R.T. (1998). *Camels*. Palgrave, New York.

RODENTS AND LAGOMORPHS

Barash, D. (1989). *Marmots: Social Behaviour and Ecology*. Stanford University Press, Stanford, CA.

Barnett, S.A. (1975). *The Rat: A Study in Behavior*. University of Chicago Press, Chicago and London.

Bennett, N.C. & Faulkes, C.G. (2000). *African Mole-rats: Ecology and Eusociality*. Cambridge University Press, Cambridge.

Berry, R.J. (ed) (1981). *Biology of the House Mouse*. Academic Press, London.

Calhoun, J.B. (1962). *The Ecology and Welfare of the Norway Rat*. US Public Health Service, Baltimore.

Curry-Lindahl, K. (1980). *Der Berglemming*. A. Ziemsen Verlag, Wittenberg.

Delany, M. J. (1975). *The Rodents of Uganda*. British Museum (Natural History), London.

Eisenberg, J.F. (1963). *The Behavior of Heteromyid Rodents*. University of California Publications in Zoology, vol 69, pp 1–100.

Ellerman, J.R. (1940). *The Families and Genera of Living Rodents*. British Museum (Natural History), London.

Elton, C. (1942). *Voles, Mice and Lemmings*. Oxford University Press, Oxford.

Errington, P.L. (1963). *Muskrat Populations*. University of Iowa Press, Iowa City.

Genoways, H.H. & Brown, J.H. (1993). *Biology of the Heteromyidae*. American Society of Mammalogists Spec. Publ. 10, American Society of Mammalogists, USA.

de Graaff, G. (1981). *The Rodents of Southern Africa*. Butterworth, Durban.

Gurnell, J. (1987). *The Natural History of Squirrels*. Croom Helm, London.

Hilfiker, E.L. (1991). *Beavers: Water, Wildlife and History*. Windswept Press, New York.

Hoogland, J.L. (1994). *The Black-tailed Prairie Dog: Social Life of a Burrowing Mammal*. Chicago University Press, Chicago.

King, J. (ed) (1968). *The Biology of Peromyscus*. Special Publication no.2., American Society of Mammalogists, Oswego, N.Y.

Lacey, E.A., Patton, J.L. & Cameron, G.N. (2001). *Life Underground: the Biology of Subterranean Rodents*. Chicago University Press, Chicago.

Laidler, K. (1980). *Squirrels in Britain*. David and Charles, Newton Abbot and North Pomfret, Vermont.

Linsdale, J.M. (1946). *The California Ground Squirrel*. University of California Press, Berkeley.

Linsdale, J.M. & Tevis, L.P. (1951). *The Dusky-footed Woodrat*. University of California Press, Berkeley.

Lockley, R.M. (1976). *The Private Life of the Rabbit*. 2nd edn. Andre Deutsch, London.

Luckett, W.P. & Hartenberger, J-L. (eds) (1985). *Evolutionary Relationships Among Rodents: A Multidisciplinary Analysis*. Plenum Press, New York.

Menzies, J.I. & Dennis, E. (1979). *Handbook of New Guinea Rodents*. Handbook no. 6. Wau Ecology Institute, Wau, New Guinea.

Morgan, L.H. (1868). *The American Beaver and his Works*. Burt Franklin, New York.

Orr, R.T. (1977). *The Little-known Pika*. Collier Macmillan, New York.

Pavlinov, I.J., Dubrovsky, Y.A., Rossolimo, O.L. & Potapova, E.G. (1990). *Gerbils of the World*. Nauka, Moscow.

Prakash, I. & Ghosh, P.K. (eds) (1975). *Rodents in Desert Environments*. Monographae Biologicae, W. Junk, The Hague.

Rosevear, D.R. (1969). *The Rodents of West Africa*. British Museum (Natural History), London.

Rowlands, I. W. & Weir, B. (eds) (1974) *The Biology of Hystricomorph Rodents. Zool. Soc. Symp*. No. 34. Academic Press, London and New York.

Shenbrot, G.Y., Krasnov, B.R. & Rogovin, K.A. (1999). *Spatial Ecology of Desert Rodent Communities: Adaptations of Desert Organisms*. Springer, Heidelberg.

Sherman, P.W., Jarvis, J.U.M. & Alexander, R.D. (eds) (1991). *The Biology of the Naked Mole-rat*. Princeton University Press, Princeton, NJ.

Stenseth, N.C. & Ims, R.A. (eds) (1993). *The Biology of Lemmings*. Academic Press, London.

Strong, P.I.V. (1997). *Beavers: Where Waters Run*. NorthWord Press, Minocqua, WI.

Thompson, H.V. & King, C.M. (1994). *The European Rabbit: History and Biology of a Successful Colonizer*. Oxford University Press, Oxford.

Watts, C.H.S. & Aslin, H.J. (1981). *The Rodents of Australia*. Angus and Robertson, Sydney and London.

INSECTIVORES, EDENTATES AND ALLIES

Churchfield, S. (1990). *The Natural History of Shrews*. Christopher Helm, London.

Crowcroft, P. (1957). *The Life of the Shrew*. Max Reinhart, London.

Dolgov, V.A. (1985). *Burozubki Starovo Sveta [Shrews of the Old World]*. Moscow University Press, Moscow.

Eisenberg, J. F. (1970). *The Tenrecs: a Study in Mammalian Behavior and Evolution*. Smithsonian Institution Press, Washington.

Godfrey, G.K. & Crowcroft, P. (1960). *The Life of the Mole*. Museum Press, London.

Gorman, M.L. & Stone, R.D. (1990). *The Natural History of Moles*. Christopher Helm, London.

Mellanby, K. (1976). *Talpa: Story of a Mole*. Collins, London.

Merritt, J.F., Kirkland, G.L. Jr & Rose, R.K. (1994). *Advances in the Biology of Shrews*. Carnegie Museum Natural History, Pittsburgh.

Montgomery, G.G. (ed) (1978). *The Ecology of Arboreal Folivores*. Smithsonian Institution Press, Washington.

Montgomery, G.G. (ed) (1985). *The Evolution and Ecology of Armadillos, Sloths, and Vermilinguas*. Smithsonian Institution Press, Washington.

Morris, P. (1983). *Hedgehogs*. Whittet Books, London.

Reeve, N. (1994). *The Natural History of Hedgehogs*. T&AD Poyser Natural History, London.

van Zyll de Jong, C.G. (1983). *Handbook of Canadian Mammals. Part I. Marsupials and Insectivores*. National Museum of Natural Sciences, Ottawa.

Wolsan, M. & Wojcik, J.M. (eds) (1998). *Evolution of Shrews*. Polish Academy of Sciences, Bialowieza.

BATS

Allen, G.M. (1939). *Bats*. Harvard University Press, Cambridge.

Altringham, J.D. (1996). *Bats: Biology and Behaviour*. Oxford University Press, New York.

Adams, R.A. & Pederson, S.C. (eds) (2000). *Ontogeny, Functional Ecology and Evolution of Bats*. Cambridge University Press, Cambridge.

Barbour. R.W. & Davis, W.H. (1969). *Bats of America*. University of Kentucky Press, Lexington, Kentucky.

Bates, P.J.J. & Harrison, D.L. (1997). *Bats of the Indian Subcontinent*. Harrison Zoological Museum, Sevenoaks, Kent.

Churchill, S. (1999). *Australian Bats*. New Holland/Struik.

Crichton, E.G. & Kutzsch, P.H. (2000). *Reproductive Biology of Bats*. Academic Press, London.

Fenton, M.B. (1983). *Just Bats*. University of Toronto Press, Toronto.

Fenton, M.B. (1998). *The Bat: Wings in the Night Sky*. Firefly Books, Willowdale, Ontario.

Findley, J.S. (1993). *Bats: a Community Perspective*. Cambridge University Press, Cambridge.

Griffin, D.R. (1958). *Listening in the Dark*. Yale University Press, New Haven.

Hill, J.E. & Smith, J.D. (1984). *Bats: A Natural History*. British Museum (Natural History), London.

Koopman, K.F. (1994). *Chiroptera: Systematics*. De Gruyter, Berlin.

Kunz, T.H. (ed) (1982). *Ecology of Bats*. Plenum Press, New York.

Kunz, T.H. & Racey, P.A. (1998). *Bat Biology and Conservation*. Smithsonian Institution Press, Washington.

Leen, N. & Norvic, A. (1969). *The World of Bats*. Holt, Rinehart and Winston, New York.

Neuweiler, N. (2000). *The Biology of Bats*. Oxford University Press, Oxford.

Racey, P.A. & Swift, S.M. (2001). *Ecology, Evolution and Behaviour of Bats. Symp. Zool. Soc. Lond*. No. 67, Oxford University Press, Oxford.

Ransome, R.D. (1990). *The Natural History of Hibernating Bats*. Christopher Helm, London.

Rosevear, J. R. (1965). *The Bats of West Africa*. British Museum (Natural History), London.

Schober, W. & Grimmberger, E. (1989). *A Guide to Bats of Britain and Europe*. Hamlyn, London.

Stebbings, R.E. (1988). *Conservation of European Bats*. Christopher Helm, London.

Stebbings, R.E. & Griffith, F. (1986). *The Distribution and Status of Bats in Europe*. Institute of Terrestrial Ecology, Abbots Ripton.

Swift, S.M. (1998). *Long-eared Bats*. T&AD Poyser Natural History, London.

Turner, D.E. (1975). *The Vampire Bat: a Field Study in Behaviour and Ecology*. Johns Hopkins University Press, Baltimore.

Tuttle, M.D. (1997). *America's Neighborhood Bats*. University of Texas Press, Austin.

van Zyll de Jong, C.G. (1985). *Handbook of Canadian Mammals. Part II. Bats*. National Museum of Natural Sciences, Ottawa.

Wilson, D.E. & Tuttle, M.D. (1997). *Bats in Question: the Smithsonian Answer Book*. Smithsonian Institution Press, Washington.

Wimsatt, W. A. (ed) (1970, 1977). *Biology of Bats*. Vols I, II & III. Academic Press, New York.

Yalden, D.W. & Morris, P.A. (1975). *The Lives of Bats*. David and Charles, Newton Abbot.

MARSUPIALS AND MONOTREMES

Archer, M. (ed) (1987). *Possums and Opossums: Studies in Evolution. Vols I & II*. Surrey Beatty and Sons, Chipping Norton, New South Wales.

Archer, M. (ed) (1982). *Carnivorous Marsupials*. Royal Zoological Society of New South Wales, Sydney.

Augee, M.L. (ed) (1978). *Monotreme Biology*. Royal Zoological Society of New South Wales, Sydney.

Augee, M.L. (ed) (1992). *Platypus and Echidnas*. Royal Zoological Society, New South Wales.

Dawson, T.J. (1995). *Kangaroos: Biology of the Largest Marsupials*. Cornell University Press, Ithaca, NY.

Flannery, T.F. (1994). *Possums of the World: A Monograph of the Phalangeroidea*. Chatswood, New South Wales.

Flannery, T.F., Martin, R. & Szalay, A. (1996). *Tree Kangaroos: A Curious Natural History*. Reed New Holland, Melbourne.

Fleay, D.M. (1980). *The Paradoxical Platypus*. Jacaranda Press, Brisbane.

Frith, H.J. & Calaby, J.H. (1969). *Kangaroos*. F. W. Cheshire, Melbourne.

Grant, T.R. (1983). *The Platypus*. University of New South Wales Press, Kensington.

Griffiths, M.F. (1978). *The Biology of Monotremes*. Academic Press, New York.

Grigg, G., Jarman, P. & Hume, I. (eds) (1989). *Kangaroos, Wallabies, and Rat-Kangaroos. Vols I & II*. Surrey Beatty and Sons, Chipping Norton, New South Wales.

Hume, I. D. (1999). *Marsupial Nutrition*. Cambridge and New York, Cambridge.

Hunsaker II, D. (ed) (1977). *The Biology of Marsupials*. Academic Press, New York.

Lee, A.K. & Cockburn, A. (1985). *Evolutionary Ecology of Marsupials*. Cambridge University Press, Cambridge.

Mares, M.A. & Genoways, H.H. (eds) (1982). *Mammalian Biology in South America*. University of Pittsburgh, Pennsylvania.

Marlow, B.J. (1965). *Marsupials of Australia*. Jacaranda Press, Brisbane.

Martin, R. & Handasyde, K. (1999). *The Koala: Natural History, Conservation and Management*. 2nd edn. Krieger, Florida.

Mustrangi, M.A. & Patton, J.L. (1997). *Phylogeography and Systematics of the Slender Mouse Opossum* Marmosops *(Marsupialia, Didelphidae)*. University of California Press, Berkeley.

Ride, W.D.L. (1970). *The Native Mammals of Australia*. Oxford University Press, Melbourne.

Rismiller, P. (1999). *The Echidna: Australia's Enigma*. Hugh Lauter Levin Associates, Southport, CT.

Saunders, N.R. & Hinds, L.A. (1997). *Marsupial Biology: Recent Research, New Perspectives*. University of New South Wales Press, Sydney.

Seebeck, J.H., Brown, P.R., Wallis, R.W. & Kemper, C.M. (eds) (1990). *Bandicoots and Bilbies*. Surrey Beatty and Sons, Chipping Norton, New South Wales.

Smith, A. & Hume, I. (1984). *Possums and Gliders*. Royal Zoological Society of New South Wales, Sydney.

Stonehouse, B. (ed) (1977). *The Biology of Marsupials*. Macmillan, London.

Troughton, E. le G. (1941). *Furred Mammals of Australia*. Angus and Robertson, Sydney.

Tyndale-Biscoe, C.H. (1973). *Life of Marsupials*. Edward Arnold, London.

Wood-Jones, F. (1923–1925). *The Mammals of South Australia. Vols I–III*. Government Printer, Adelaide.

The IUCN (World Conservation Union) produces a number of outstanding Species Action Plans, many of which have become authoritative sources of information. For further details visit the IUCN website http://www.iucn.org

Index

Page numbers in *italic* type refer to picture captions. Page numbers in **bold** indicate extensive coverage or feature treatment of a subject.

A

B

C

D

E

I

J

K

N

T

U

V

W

X

Y

Z

Picture Credits

Key: **t** top; **b** bottom; **c** center; **l** left; **r** right
Abbreviations: **AL** Ardea London; **BBC** BBC Natural History Unit; **BCC** Bruce Coleman Collection; **C** Corbis; **FLPA** Frank Lane Picture Agency; **NHPA** Natural History Photographic Agency; **OSF** Oxford Scientific Films; **PEP** Planet Earth Pictures

xvi-xvii Stephen J. Krasemann/BCC; xx Peter Davey/FLPA; xxiv-xxv K.G. Preston-Mafham/Premaphotos Wildlife; xxvi-xxvii Doug Allan/OSF; xxviii Andy Purcell/ICCE; xxix Terry Andrewartha/FLPA; xxx Fritz Polking/FLPA; 2-3 Peter Blackwell/BBC; 3 Manfred Danegger/NHPA; 5 Andy Rouse/NHPA; 7 Daryl Balfour/NHPA; 9 Animals Animals/Fabio Colombini/OSF; 10 Mike Hill/OSF; 10-11t Kevin Schafer/NHPA; 10-11b Mark Deeble & Victoria Stone/OSF; 12 Nobuyuki Yamaguchi; 13t &13b M. & C. Denis-Huot/PEP; 14-15 Jonathan Scott/PEP; 16 Anup Shah/BBC; 16-17 Stefan Meyers/AL; 17 Bernard Castelein/BBC; 18 Kevin Schafer/NHPA; 19 Images Colour Library; 20 Frank Schneidermeyer/OSF; 20-21 & 22 Martin Harvey/NHPA; 23 Ferrero-Labat/AL; 24-25 Peter Davey/BCC; 25 Jonathan Scott/PEP; 26t Anup Shah/BBC; 26b John Downer/OSF; 26-27 Anup Shah/BBC; 27t Jonathan Scott/PEP; 27b Fritz Polking/FLPA; 28 Pete Oxford/BBC; 28-29 Pete Oxford; 30 Tom Brakefield/PEP; 30-31 Gerard Lacz/NHPA; 31 Alan & Sandy Carey/OSF; 33 Daniel J. Cox/OSF; 34t Jean-Paul Ferrero/AL; 34b Pete Oxford; 35 Pete Oxford/BBC; 38-39 John Robinson/ICCE; 39 Philip Perry/FLPA; 40 Pete Oxford; 42 Daniel J. Cox/OSF; 42-43 Mike Potts/PEP; 44 M. Watson/AL; 45 Gerard Lacz/FLPA; 46 Joel Sartore/ NGS Image Collection; 47 Allan G. Potts/BCC; 48-49 Jeff Foott/BBC; 50 Ronald Rogoff/PEP; 51 Yossi Eshbol/FLPA; 52-53 Michel Gunther/Still Pictures; 53 Charlie Hamilton-James/BBC; 55 Eric Dragesco/AL; 56-57 Alan & Sandy Carey/OSF; 58t Eyal Bartov/OSF; 58b Nigel J. Dennis/NHPA; 59 Erwin & Peggy Bauer/BCC; 61 W. Wisniewski/FLPA; 62-63 Bruce Davidson/BBC; 64 W. Wisniewski/FLPA; 65 Dave Hamman; 66 Glen & Rebecca Grambo; 66-67 A.J.T. Johnsingh; 68t Silvestris/FLPA; 68b Simon King/BBC; 69t Vadim Sidorovich/BBC; 69c Gerard Lacz/FLPA; 70 Rich Kirchner/NHPA; 71 Jeff Foott/BBC; 72 Daniel J. Cox/OSF; 73 John Shaw/NHPA; 74-75 Animals Animals/David C. Fritts/OSF; 76 Robert Harding Picture Library; 77 Thomas D. Mangelsen/Still Pictures; 78t Thomas D. Mangelsen/BBC; 78b John Shaw/NHPA; 78-79 Fred Bruemmer; 79t Konrad Wothe/OSF; 79r Jeff Foott/BBC; 80 T. Kitchen & V. Hurst/NHPA; 80-81 Daniel J. Cox/OSF; 81 Mark Hamblin/OSF; 82 Keren Su/OSF; 83 Irvine Cushing/OSF; 84 Mark Newman/FLPA; 85 E.A. Kuttapan/BBC; 87 Jurgen & Christine Sohns/FLPA; 88 Stefan Meyers/AL; 89 Daniel J. Cox/OSF; 90 Rod Williams/BCC; 92 Alan & Sandy Carey/OSF; 92-93 M.P. L. Fogden/BCC; 93 Joaquin Gutierrez/OSF; 94 Mark Newman/FLPA; 94-95 Tom Vezo/BBC; 95 Rod Williams/BCC; 97 Brian Kenney/PEP; 98 Richard Day/OSF; 98-99 Silvestris/FLPA; 100 S. Maslowski/FLPA; 101 Robin Redfern/Ecoscene; 102t Chris Knights/AL; 102b Roger Tidman/NHPA; 105 T. Leeson/Sunset/FLPA; 106 Dietmar Nill/BBC; 107 Manfred Danegger/NHPA; 108 Erwin & Peggy Bauer/BCC; 108-109 M. Watson/AL; 110 Mark Newman/FLPA; 111 Stephen Dalton/NHPA; 112 Brake/Sunset/FLPA; 114 Mark Deeble & Victoria Stone/OSF; 115 Daniel J. Cox/OSF; 116 Jurgen & Christine Sohns/FLPA; 116-117 Joe Blossom/ICCE; 118t Anthony Bannister/NHPA; 118c Martin B. Withers/FLPA; 121 L. Lee Rue/FLPA; 122-123 Nigel J. Dennis/NHPA; 123 Ann & Steve Toon/NHPA; 124 Gerard Lacz/FLPA; 125 Anup Shah/BBC; 126 Kenneth W. Fink/AL; 128 Roger de la Harpe/PEP; 129 Pete Oxford; 134 Mark Deeble & Victoria Stone/OSF; 134-135 Johan le Roux/PEP; 135 Eliot Lyons/BBC; 136-137 Daniel Heuclin/NHPA; 138 Dr. A. Rosa; 138-139 Nigel J. Dennis/NHPA; 141 Peter Davey/BCC; 142-143 Clem Haagner/AL; 143 Terry Whittaker/FLPA; 144 Eliot Lyons/BBC; 144-145 Jurgen & Christine Sohns/FLPA; 145 Terry Whittaker/FLPA; 147 Norbert Wu/NHPA; 148 Ben Osborne/OSF; 150 Doc White/BBC; 151 David Hosking/FLPA; 152-153 Sophie de Wilde/Jacana; 154 Fred Bruemmer/BCC; 154-155 David Hosking/FLPA; 155 Doug Allan/OSF; 155 inset Smithsonian Museum/Museum of the American Indian; 156c x4 NERC, Sea Mammal Research Unit; 156-157 Andy Rouse/NHPA; 158t Norbert Wu/NHPA; 158b Dieter & Mary Plage/OSF; 158-159 Howard Hall/OSF; 160 Tom Ulrich/OSF; 161 & 162-163 Martin Harvey/NHPA; 164 Fritz Polking/FLPA; 164-165 D. Parer & E. Parer-Cook/AL; 166t Jeff Foott/BCC; 166b HPH Photography/BCC; 167 Richard Herrmann/OSF; 168-169 & 172 Jurgen & Christine Sohns/FLPA; 173t Norbert Wu/NHPA; 173b Pete Oxford/BBC; 174-175 Stephen J. Krasemann/NHPA; 176 Lon E. Lauber/OSF; 177 Ingrid N. Visser/PEP; 178 Norbert Rosing/OSF; 179 Lon E. Lauber/OSF; 180c Fred Bruemmer/BCC; 180b Doug Allan/OSF; 184-185 Martyn Colbeck/OSF; 185c Lloyd Lowry; 185b Doug Allan/BBC; 186t François Gohier/AL; 186b Dr. Robert Franz/PEP; 187 Hamish Laird/ICCE; 188 A.W. Erikson; 188-189 Andy Rouse/NHPA; 189 Dr. Eckart Pott/BCC; 193 Martyn Colbeck/OSF; 194t BCC; 194b Fred Bruemmer; 195 Doug Allan/OSF; 196 Tom Brakefield/PEP; 196-197 Alberto Nardi/NHPA; 198 Frans Lanting/BCC; 198-199 F. Di Domenico/Panda/FLPA; 199 Pacific Stock/BCC; 200t Ingo Arndt/BCC; 200b Fred Bruemmer/BCC; 200-201 Ingo Arndt/BCC; 201 Pete Oxford; 202 Doug Perrine/PEP; 203t Jeff Rotman/BBC; 203b François Gohier/AL; 205 James Hudnall/PEP; 206 & 208-209 François Gohier/AL; 209t Andrew Syred/SPL; 209b Norbert Wu/NHPA; 210t D. Parer & E. Parer-Cook/AL; 210b Brake/Sunset/FLPA; 211 Norbert Wu/NHPA; 212tl AKG London; 212tr National Maritime Museum, San Franciso; 212b Bodleian Library; 213 Adam Woolfitt/Robert Harding Picture Library; 214 Mark Cawardine/Still Pictures; 215t François Gohier/AL; 215b Doug Allan/OSF; 217 Kenneth W. Fink/AL; 220 Dr. Eckart Pott/NHPA; 220-221 Armin Maywald/BBC; 221 Doug Perrine/PEP; 224t François Gohier/AL; 224b Dave Watts/NHPA; 225 Bernd Würsig/Sea Watch Foundation; 227 Pete Oxford/BBC; 229t, 229b & 230-231 Robert Harding Picture Library; 232-233 Ingrid N. Visser/PEP; 234t, 234c, 234b, 235t, 235c & 235b A.L. Stanzani/Fondazione Cetacea; 236 Tony Bomford/OSF; 237 François Gohier/AL; 240 Gunter Ziesler/BCC; 241 Doc White/BBC; 242-243 Jeff Foott/BCC; 243 Doc White/BBC; 246-247 Ron & Valerie Taylor/AL; 248 Pieter Folkens/PEP; 248-249 Sea Mammal Research Unit; 253 Fabian Ritter/Sea Watch Foundation; 254 Dan Gotshall/PEP; 256 François Gohier/AL; 258t François Gohier; 258c & 259 François Gohier/AL; 260 Pieter Folkens/PEP; 260-261 François Gohier/AL; 262 Douglas David Seifert/PEP; 262-263 Jeff Foott/BCC; 264 Kim Taylor/BCC; 266-267 Daniel J. Cox/OSF; 268 J. Gordon/Sea Watch Foundation; 268-269 Pacific Stock/BCC; 270 François Gohier/AL; 271 Jeff Foott/BCC; 273 Howard Hall/OSF; 274t Doug Perrine/PEP; 274-275 Survival Anglia/Rick Price/OSF; 275 Galen Rowell/C; 276 David Currey/NHPA; 276-277 Rich Kirchner/NHPA; 280-281 Bruce Coleman Inc./BCC; 281t Haroldo Palo Jr./NHPA; 281b & 282 Doug Perrine/PEP; 283l Norbert Wu/NHPA; 283r Pete Oxford; 284 François Gohier/AL; 284-285 Doug Perrine/PEP; 286 Historical Picture Archive/C; 287t Trevor McDonald/NHPA; 287b Georgette Douwma/BBC; 288 Foto Natura Stock/FLPA; 288-289 Roger Garwood & Trish Ainslie/C; 290-291 Martin Harvey/NHPA; 293 Anup Shah/BBC; 294 Pete Oxford; 295 Nigel J. Dennis/NHPA; 296 Martin Rügner/PEP; 297 John Daniels/AL; 298-299 Konrad Wothe/OSF; 303 Anup Shah/BBC; 304 Rod Williams/PEP; 305 François Gohier/AL; 306 Stephen Dalton/NHPA; 306-307 Jean-Paul Ferrero/AL; 309 Mike Hill/PEP; 310 Nigel J. Dennis/NHPA; 312t Werner Layer/BCC; 312b Erwin & Peggy Bauer/BCC; 314 Roine Magnusson/BCC; 315 Pete Oxford; 316 David Haring/OSF; 317 Daniel Heuclin/NHPA; 319t Manfred Eberle; 319c David Haring/OSF; 320 Pete Oxford/BBC; 321 Nigel J. Dennis/NHPA; 322 A. & E. Bomford/AL; 323 Nigel J. Dennis/NHPA; 326t C. & R. Aveling/ICCE; 326c Stephen Dalton/NHPA; 327 Bruce Davidson/BBC; 329 Anthony Bannister/NHPA; 331 Gary Bell/PEP; 336 M. Watson/AL; 337 Babs & Bert Wells/OSF; 338 Claus Meyer/PEP; 340 M. Watson/AL; 342 John Downer/BBC; 343 Michael Sewell/OSF; 344 Anup Shah/BBC; 344-345 Martin Rügner/PEP; 347 C. Janson; 348 Staffan Widstrand/BBC; 349 Roine Magnusson/BCC; 351 & 354 Kevin Schafer/NHPA; 355 & 356 Anup Shah/BBC; 357t Kevin Schafer/NHPA; 357b Stephen Mills/OSF; 360-361t Dr. Eckart Pott/BCC; 360-361b Richard du Toit/BBC; 362 Jean-Michel Labat/AL; 364-365 Anup Shah/BBC; 366 Kevin Schafer/NHPA; 366-367 Jeff Foott/BBC; 369 Cameron Read/PEP; 370 Richard du Toit/BBC; 371t Zig Leszczynski/OSF; 371b J.J. Brooks/Aquila; 373 Rod Williams/BCC; 375 Dave Watts; 376-377 P. & J. Wegner/Foto Natura/FLPA; 378tl Konrad Wothe/OSF; 378tr, 378bl & 378br Fritz Polking/Still Pictures; 378-379 Jean-Paul Ferrero/AL; 379 Fritz Polking/Still Pictures; 380 Anup Shah/BBC; 381 Martin Harvey/NHPA; 382-383 Anup Shah/BBC; 383 Art Wolfe; 384-385 Anup Shah/BBC; 386 Bernard Castelein/BBC; 386-387 Stan Osolinski/OSF; 387t Florian Möllers; 387b Xi Zhinong/BBC; 389 Art Wolfe; 392 Rafi Ben-Shahar/OSF; 392-393 J. Moore/Anthro-Photo; 394 Anup Shah/BBC; 394-395 Cameron Read/PEP; 395 Florian Möllers; 397 Timothy Laman/ NGS Image Collection; 398 Animals Animals/Howie Garber/OSF; 398-399 Anup Shah/BBC; 400 Joe Blossom/OSF; 402 Dave Watts; 403l Anup Shah/BBC; 403r M. Watson/AL; 406 Martin Harvey/NHPA; 407 & 408 Steve Robinson/NHPA; 409t Kenneth W. Fink/AL; 409b Jorg & Petra Wegner/BCC; 410 Anup Shah/BBC; 412t Steve Robinson/NHPA; 412b Christophe Ratier/NHPA; 413 Karl Ammann/Ecoscene; 414 Martin Harvey/NHPA; 415 C. & R. Aveling/ICCE; 417 Martin Rügner/PEP; 418 Adrian Warren/AL; 419 Martin Harvey/NHPA; 420 & 421 Anup Shah/BBC; 422-423 Mike Hill/OSF; 423 C. & R. Aveling/ICCE; 424t Hoppe-UNEP/Still Pictures; 424b Nick Nichols/NGS Image Collection; 424-425 Konrad Wothe/Minden Pictures; 425t Anup Shah/BBC; 425bl C. & R. Aveling/ICCE; 425br James P. Blair/NGS Image Collection; 428-429 Rod Williams/BCC; 430t T. Kitchen & V. Hurst/NHPA; 430b Geoff du Feu/PEP; 432 BCC; 435 Steven Kaufman/BCC; 437 Art Wolfe/Getty Images Stone; 438 G.I. Bernard/OSF; 439t & 439b Martin Harvey/NHPA; 440, 440-441 & 442-443 Martyn Colbeck/OSF; 444t Richard Packwood/OSF; 444b Mark Boulton/ICCE; 445t B. Francais/Hoa-Qui/Jacana; 445b David Shale/BBC; 446t Martyn Colbeck/OSF; 446b M. Denis-Huot/Hoa-Qui/Jacana; 446-447t & 446-447b Martyn Colbeck/OSF; 447t Anup Shah/BBC; 447b M. Denis-Huot/Hoa-Qui/Jacana; 448 John Cancalosi/AL; 449 H.N. Hoeck; 450 Peter Blackwell/BBC; 450-451 Kenneth W. Fink/AL; 453 Rudi van Aarde; 454-455 Tony Heald/BBC; 461 M. & C. Denis-Huot/PEP; 462 Lon E. Lauber/OSF; 463t Pete Oxford/BBC; 463b Robert Maier/BCC; 464-465 Anup Shah/BBC; 467 Jean-Paul Ferrero/Auscape; 468 Terry Whittaker/FLPA; 468-469 Masahiro Iijima/AL; 472 Konrad Wothe/OSF; 473 Martyn Colbeck/OSF; 476 Nigel J. Dennis/NHPA; 477 Martin Harvey/NHPA; 478 Stan Osolinski/OSF; 480 & 480-481 Martin Harvey/NHPA; 484 François Gohier/AL; 485 A. Warburton & S. Toon/NHPA; 486 Anup Shah/BBC; 486-487 Florian Möllers; 488 M. Gunther/Bios/Foto Natura/FLPA; 489 Carol Farneti/PEP; 490 Fritz Polking/Still Pictures; 491 Mark Newman/FLPA; 492-493 Anup Shah/BBC; 494 Mike Hill/OSF; 494-495 Mark Boulton/BCC; 495 Gerard Lacz/FLPA; 498t François Gohier/AL; 498b G. & H. Denzau/BBC; 498-499 Laurie Campbell/NHPA; 500 F.W. Lane/FLPA; 501 Ken Lucas/PEP; 505 Stan Osolinski/OSF; 506 Chris Brunskill/AL; 507 Stephen J. Krasemann/NHPA; 508 Manfred Danegger/NHPA; 509 Niall Benvie/OSF; 510-511 Images Colour Library; 511 Stefan Meyers/AL; 514 John Cancalosi/BBC; 515t Yann Arthus-Bertrand/AL; 515b Paul Hobson/BBC; 516-517 & 517 John

Cancalosi/BBC; 518t, 518b, 518-519, 519t & 519b B. & C. Alexander; 520 Gerard Lacz/FLPA; 521 Ronald Rogoff/PEP; 522-523 Steve Turner/OSF; 524 W. Wisniewski/FLPA; 525 Koos Delport/FLPA; 526 J. Zimmermann/FLPA; 527 Richard Kirby/BBC; 528-529 R. Planck/Dembinsky/FLPA; 529 David Hosking/FLPA; 530-531 Anup Shah/BBC; 534 Eliot Lyons/BBC; 535 Mary Heys/Sylvia Cordaiy Photo Library; 537 David Samuel Robbins/C; 540 Thomas D. Mangelsen/BBC; 540-541 David Hosking/FLPA; 541 Kennan Ward/C; 542 Roger de la Harpe/PEP; 544t F.W. Lane/FLPA; 544b Nigel J. Dennis/NHPA; 545 N. Dennis/Sunset/FLPA; 546 Anup Shah/PEP; 546-547 Richard du Toit/BBC; 550-551 Jonathan Scott/Telegraph Colour Library; 552 Chris Harvey/AL; 552-553 Ferrero-Labat/AL; 553 Nigel J. Dennis/NHPA; 556-557 Jonathan Scott/PEP; 558 George Lepp/C; 558-559 & 559 Steven Kaufman/C; 560 Jonathan Scott/PEP; 560-561 Richard du Toit/BBC; 561 Rudi van Aarde; 564 Anthony Bannister/NHPA; 565 Daryl Balfour/NHPA; 566 Kenneth W. Fink/AL; 567 John Shaw/BCC; 572 Rich Kirchner/NHPA; 572-573 Stefan Meyers/AL; 573 Anup Shah/BBC; 576 William S. Paton/BCC; 576-577 David Tipling/OSF; 578 Mike Wilkes/BBC; 579 François Gohier/AL; 580 Anthony Bannister/NHPA; 582-583 Daniel J. Cox/OSF; 584 Stephen Dalton/NHPA; 585tl ICI Plant Protection Division; 585tr Bettmann/C; 585b Andy Purcell/ICCE; 586 John Hawkins/FLPA; 586-587 Michael Freeman/C; 587 inset Nicole Duplaix/C; 588 Manfred Danegger/NHPA; 589t Joe McDonald/C; 589 inset François Gohier/AL; 590 Jim Brandenburg/Minden Pictures; 591 Alan & Sandy Carey/OSF; 592t Jeff Foott/BBC; 592b Mark Hamblin/OSF; 593 François Gohier/AL; 594t Stephen J. Krasemann/NHPA; 594b Janos Jurka/BCC; 594-595t John Shaw/BCC; 594-595b David Kjaer/BBC; 595 Norbert Rosing/OSF; 596-597 Tom & Pat Leeson; 598 Rob Jordan/BCC; 598-599 John Brown/OSF; 602t Wendy Shattil & Bob Rozinski/OSF; 602b Bernard Castelein/BBC; 603 John Cancalosi/AL; 604-605 Paul van Gaalen/BCC; 606 Gunter Ziesler/BCC; 606-607 Clem Haagner/AL; 607 Andrew Cooper/BBC; 609t Pete Oxford/BBC; 609b Krupaker Senani/OSF; 610 & 610-611 George Lepp/Leppstock; 611 T. & P. Gardner/FLPA; 612-613 George Lepp/C; 614-615 Carol Farneti/Partridge Films Ltd/OSF; 618 B. "Moose" Peterson/AL; 619 Joe McDonald/C; 621 Claude Steelman/Survival Anglia/OSF; 622 David M. Dennis/OSF; 622-623 Michael Fogden/OSF; 624 Ken Preston-Mafham/Premaphotos Wildlife; 626-627 Wardene Weisser/AL; 628t Colin Varndell/BCC; 628b Tom Ulrich/OSF; 629 Stephen Dalton/NHPA; 630 Paal Hermansen/NHPA; 634-635 Robin Redfern/Ecoscene; 636 Press-Tige Pictures/OSF; 640t Yann Arthus-Bertrand/C; 640c Kathie Atkinson/OSF; 641 Jean-Paul Ferrero/AL; 642t Andrew Purcell/BCC; 642b G. I. Bernard/OSF; 643 Ken Preston-Mafham/Premaphotos Wildlife; 644-645 Ian Beames/AL; 648-649 Nick Garbutt/BBC; 650 Rod Williams/BCC; 651 Dennis Avon/AL; 654 Mike Brown/OSF; 655t Ken Preston-Mafham/Premaphotos Wildlife; 655b Rodger Jackman/OSF; 656t P. Kaya/BCC; 656b Ian Beames/AL; 657 Michael Powles/OSF; 658-659 Gerard Lacz/FLPA; 660 K. Maslowski/FLPA; 661 Daniel Heuclin/NHPA; 662 & 662-663 Jeff Foott/BBC; 666 John Cancalosi/Okapia/OSF; 666-667 Wendy Shattil & Bob Rozinski/OSF; 669 Ric Ergenbright/C; 670 Rod Williams/BCC; 671 T. Kitchen & V. Hurst/NHPA; 672-673 W. Meinderts/Foto Natura/FLPA; 674 Ian Beames/AL; 674-675 Jen & Des Bartlett/Survival Anglia/OSF; 676b Pete Oxford/BBC; 676t Terry Whittaker/FLPA; 677 Frank Schneidermeyer/OSF; 678-679 Michael Gore/FLPA; 679 Luiz Claudio Marigo/BCC; 680 Eric Soder/NHPA; 681t Roland Seitre/Still Pictures; 681b François Gohier/AL; 685t Nick Gordon/AL; 685b Robert Maier/BCC; 686-687 Barrie Wilkins/Getty Images Stone; 689 W. George; 690 N. Eden; 690-691 J. Jarvis; 692b Neil Bromhall/BBC; 692c Neil Bromhall/OSF; 694 Terry Andrewartha/Survival Anglia/OSF; 695 W. Wisniewski/FLPA; 696 Mike Wilkes/BBC; 697 Kenneth W. Fink/AL; 700-701 Jorg & Petra Wegner/BCC; 701 K. Maslowski/FLPA; 703 Agence Nature; 705 Steven Kaufman/BCC; 706-707 G.I. Bernard/OSF; 707 William Osborn/BBC; 708 Leeson/Sunset/FLPA; 708-709 Lynn Stone/BBC; 710tl Jorg & Petra Wegner/BCC; 710tr, 710b & 710-711 Manfred Danegger/NHPA; 711 D.A. Robinson/FLPA; 712 & 713t George Lepp/C; 713b G. & H. Denzau/BBC; 714 D. Robert Franz/C; 714-715 BCC; 718 P. Morris/AL; 719 Bruce Davidson/BBC; 720-721 P. Morris/AL; 722 G. Marcoaldi/Panda Photo/FLPA; 722-723 Owen Newman/OSF; 724 Tony & Liz Bomford/AL; 726 Stephen Dalton/NHPA; 726-727 Mark Hamblin/OSF; 730-731 Pete Oxford/BBC; 733 P. Morris/AL; 734t G.R. Aveling/ICCE; 734b Dietmar Nill/BBC; 735 Foto Natura Stock/FLPA; 738-739 B. Borrell/FLPA; 740t Derek Middleton/FLPA; 740b & 741t Daniel Heuclin/NHPA; 741b Robert Maier/BCC; 742 Daniel Heuclin/NHPA; 742-743 Robert Maier/BCC; 743 Stephen Dalton/NHPA; 744 Daniel Heuclin/NHPA; 745 P. Morris/AL; 746 Barrie Watts/OSF; 746-747 OSF; 747 D. Kuhn; 749t Peter Steyn/AL; 749b Michael Fogden/OSF; 750 Dembinsky Photo Ass./FLPA; 752 Manfred Danegger/NHPA; 753 Duncan McEwan/BBC; 754 Jim Clare/BBC; 755 Dietmar Nill/BBC; 756 Jean-Paul Ferrero/AL; 760t Dennis Avon/AL; 760b C. Andrew Henley/LARUS; 761 Dietmar Nill/BBC; 762 Stephen Dalton/NHPA; 766 Adrian Warren/AL; 766-767 Jens Rydell/BCC; 767 J.W. Wilkinson; 768 Jacana; 768-769 Jens Rydell/BCC; 769 Dietmar Nill/BBC; 770 J. Mason/AL; 771 Jean-Paul Ferrero/AL; 772l Pete Oxford/BBC; 772r David Thompson/OSF; 772-773 J.A.L. Cooke/OSF; 774 Merlin D. Tuttle/Bat Conservation International; 777 Alain Compost/BCC; 779 M. Watson/AL; 780 J.A.L. Cooke/OSF; 780-781 Merlin D. Tuttle/Bat Conservation International; 782 Kenneth W. Fink/AL; 782-783 Jacana; 784t, 784b, 784-785 & 785 Stephen Dalton/NHPA; 788-789 Kevin Schafer/NHPA; 790t Pete Oxford/BBC; 790b Kevin Schafer/NHPA; 791 Tom Brakefield/C; 792t Jurgen & Christine Sohns/FLPA; 792b Luiz Claudio Marigo/BCC; 793 Michael & Patricia Fogden; 794-795 Staffan Widstrand/BCC; 796 Mark Payne-Gill/BBC; 798t Foto Natura Stock/FLPA; 798b Jeff Foott/BBC; 799 Pete Oxford/BBC; 800 Dr. Ivan Polunin/NHPA; 800-801 N. Dennis/Sunset/FLPA; 802 Dave Watts/NHPA; 803 A.N.T./NHPA; 805 John Cancalosi/BCC; 806 Jean-Paul Ferrero/AL; 807 M.W. Gillam/AL; 808 G.I. Bernard/NHPA; 809 D. Robert Franz/C; 810 Lynda Richardson/C; 812 J. Sauvanet/Okapia/OSF; 813l Alan & Sandy Carey/OSF; 813r T. Kitchen & V. Hurst/NHPA; 814 John Cancalosi/BBC; 814-815 C. Andrew Henley/LARUS; 816 Dave Watts/NHPA; 817 Jean-Paul Ferrero/AL; 818 A.N.T./NHPA; 819 & 820-821 Jean-Paul Ferrero/AL; 822t Dave Watts; 822b & 823 C. Andrew Henley/LARUS; 824-825 A.N.T./NHPA; 826 John Cancalosi/BBC; 827t Jean-Paul Ferrero/AL; 827b Dave Watts/NHPA; 830 Hans & Judy Beste/AL; 831 Jean-Paul Ferrero/AL; 832 Papilio Photographic; 832-833 Daniel Heuclin/NHPA; 835 Jean-Paul Ferrero/AL; 835 inset C. Andrew Henley/LARUS; 838-839 Dave Watts/NHPA; 840 Martin Harvey/NHPA; 840-841 C. Andrew Henley/LARUS; 843 Kathie Atkinson/OSF; 845 & 846 Dave Watts; 848 Bruce Burkhardt/C; 849 Pete Oxford/BBC; 850tl & 850tr Jean-Paul Ferrero/Auscape; 850b D. Parer & E. Parer-Cook/Auscape; 850-851 Jean-Paul Ferrero/Auscape; 851t Roland Seitre/Still Pictures; 851b Martin Harvey/NHPA; 852 C. Andrew Henley/LARUS; 853 Tom Ulrich/OSF; 854 Martin Harvey/NHPA; 855 & 856 John Cancalosi/BBC; 856-857 Dave Watts/NHPA; 858-859 A. Smith; 860t M. McKelvey & P. Rismiller; 860b Jean-Paul Ferrero/Auscape; 861, 862 & 862-863 Dave Watts; 864-865 M. McKelvey & P. Rismiller; 865 Jean-Paul Ferrero/AL

Artwork

Key: **t** top; **b** bottom; **c** center; **l** left; **r** right
Abbreviations: **PB** Priscilla Barrett. **DO** Denys Ovenden. **MM** Malcolm McGregor. **ML** Michael Long. **GA** Graham Allen.

xviii-xix DO; xxi GA; xxi, xxii, xxvi, 6, 8, 18 PB; 22 DO; 32, 38, 41 PB; 41b DO; 43, 44, 51, 54, 56, 64, 70, 84, 86 PB; 89 DO; 96, 99, 101, 103 PB; 106 DO; 113, 119, 120, 123, 127, 128, 133, 140, 146, 163, 181 PB; 183c, 186 DO; 216, 218, 222, 238, 240 MM; 241 DO; 242, 244, 250, 255, 256 MM; 257 DO; 264, 272 MM; 278, 301, 309 PB; 309b DO; 311, 325, 331, 333, 334, 346, 349, 354, 358, 362, 368, 396, 401, 404, 426 PB; 433 DO; 434 ML; 436 MM; 452, 458, 460 DO; 466, 470, 474, 478, 482l, 482l PB; 482r, 483l DO; 483c,483r PB; 496 DO; 502, 504, 506, 525, 532, 536, 542, 548, 562, 570 PB; 588 DO; 600 PB; 607, 616l, 617l DO; 616-7, 620, 624, 630 PB; 637 DO; 638, 646, 652, 656, 664 PB; 667, 668-9(1,3,5) DO; 668bl(2) Sean Milne; 668-9(4,6), 684 PB; 686, 688, 698l DO; 698, 716 PB; 728, 732 DO; 736l PB; 736, 750 DO; 758, 746 GA; 775(1) DO; 775(2) PB; 775(3) GA; 786 ML; 788, 797, 800 DO; 811 PB; 816, 818, 821, 828, 836, 842, 846, 858 DO.

Illustrators:
Martin Anderson
Julian Baker
Lizzie Harper
Graham Rosewarne
Roger Courthold
John Fuller
Simon Driver